LAND LAW

Text, Cases, and Materials

Ben McFarlane, Nicholas Hopkins, and Sarah Nield

OXFORD
UNIVERSITY PRESS

OXFORD
UNIVERSITY PRESS

Great Clarendon Street, Oxford OX2 6DP

Oxford University Press is a department of the University of Oxford.
It furthers the University's objective of excellence in research, scholarship,
and education by publishing worldwide in

Oxford New York

Auckland Cape Town Dar es Salaam Hong Kong Karachi
Kuala Lumpur Madrid Melbourne Mexico City Nairobi
New Delhi Shanghai Taipei Toronto

With offices in

Argentina Austria Brazil Chile Czech Republic France Greece
Guatemala Hungary Italy Japan Poland Portugal Singapore
South Korea Switzerland Thailand Turkey Ukraine Vietnam

Oxford is a registered trade mark of Oxford University Press
in the UK and in certain other countries

Published in the United States
by Oxford University Press Inc., New York

© B. McFarlane, N. P. Hopkins, and S. A. Nield 2009

The moral rights of the authors have been asserted

Crown copyright material is reproduced under Class Licence
Number C01P0000148 with the permission of OPSI
and the Queen's Printer for Scotland

Database right Oxford University Press (maker)

First published 2009

British Library Cataloguing in Publication Data

Data available

Library of Congress Cataloging in Publication Data
McFarlane, Ben.
Land law : text, cases, and materials / Ben McFarlane, Nick Hopkins,
and Sarah Nield.
p. cm.
Includes index.
ISBN 978–0–19–920821–0
1. Real property—England—Cases. 2. Estates (Law)—England—Cases.
3. Leases—England—Cases. 4. Real property—Wales—Cases. 5. Estates
(Law)—Wales—Cases. 6. Leases—Wales—Cases. I. Hopkins, Nicholas S.
II. Nield, Sarah. III. Title.
KD841.M38 2009
346.4204′3—dc22   2009012762

Typeset by Newgen Imaging Systems Pvt Ltd., Chennai, India
Printed in Great Britain
on acid-free paper by
Ashford Colour Press, Gosport, Hampshire

ISBN 978–0–19–920821–0

1 3 5 7 9 10 8 6 4 2

PREFACE

The task of writing a book for a series with such well-regarded works as Craig & de Burca's *EU Law* and McKendrick's *Contract Law* is somewhat daunting. Taking inspiration (rather than fear) from joining such company, our view has always been that the Text, Cases and Materials format is ideally suited to land law. As all teachers of land law know, it has a well-earned reputation as a difficult subject. When grappling with the leading cases and key statutory provisions, students often find that technical language obscures the core principles. As a result, they may also find it hard to engage with the academic criticism, reform proposals and empirical analysis.

For us, the real attraction of the Text, Cases and Materials format is that we can use it to place both the primary and secondary materials in context. Very early in the writing process, we agreed to devote just over 50% of the book to author commentary. This has allowed us to guide readers, helping them carefully to pick their way through the complexities of the primary material. It also meant we had more space to explain just why many of the current rules are controversial, and why secondary material has a crucial role to play in addressing those controversies. In doing so, we hope to have shown that land law's apparently arcane appearance belies a subject that inspires vibrant debate and confronts pressing social issues with sophistication.

Each of us has brought our own signature to our contributions. Sarah has presented the social, commercial and regulatory context in which mortgages operate; Nick has examined co-ownership and trusts through the particular perspective of the shared home; Ben has provided a three-step approach, which breaks down the analysis of interests in land into the content question, the acquisition question, and the defences question. Our individual perspectives have helped fulfil one of the aims of a Text, Cases, and Materials title in setting out and balancing different views. We have sought to present these within a clear structure and consistent approach. The frequent adoption of Ben's three-step approach has assisted in this regard.

While there are some areas in which we can all claim a level of expertise, our individual interests meant that the division of labour was perhaps more readily determined than might have been the case. Ben is responsible for chapters 1–4, 6–8, 11, 13, 17 and 23–24; Nick for chapters 9–10, 12, 14–16, 18–19 and 21–22; Sarah for chapters 5 and 25–31. Nick and Sarah jointly wrote chapter 20. Each of us has read and commented on chapters written by the others.

Our thanks are wholeheartedly extended to colleagues, friends and to staff at OUP who have helped us in writing this book. Professor John Mee and a number of anonymous referees took on the unenviable task of reading and commenting on the manuscript. Their generosity both in giving of their time and their own insights into the subject is gratefully acknowledged and has undoubtedly improved the finished text. Likewise, a number of people have commented on individual chapters: we are particularly indebted to Amy Goymour (chapter 5) and to Professor David Clarke and Peter Smith (chapters 25 and 28). The enthusiasm and commitment of OUP have helped make the process of writing an enjoyable one. Our initial contacts were with Jasmin Naim and Ruth Ballantyne. Particular thanks are due to Rebecca Gleave, our commissioning editor throughout the period that the manuscript was written, Gareth Malna who has steered the book through its production, Clare Weaver for her management of the marketing, and Lucy Hyde for her management of the development of the Online Resource Centre that accompanies this book. Rupert Seal and Ruth Hudson have played a significant role in writing materials for that resource. Ben is grateful to Siobhan Wills and Dervla Simm, who provided research assistance at the very early stages of the project, and to the Oxford University Law Faculty for funding that assistance.

The end result of everyone's efforts is a big book; but one which we hope will be a comprehensive, accessible resource. It is, we hope, something that will make the lives of students and teachers easier; even if it makes their bags slightly heavier.

Ben McFarlane
Nicholas Hopkins
Sarah Nield
March 2009

ACKNOWLEDGMENTS

Grateful acknowledgement is made to all the authors and publishers of copyright material which appears in this book, and in particular to the following for permission to reprint material from the sources indicated:

Crown copyright material is reproduced under Class Licence Number C2006010631 with the permission of the Controller of OPSI and the Queen's Printer for Scotland. Parliamentary copyright material is reproduced with the permission of the Controller of Her Majesty's Stationery Office on behalf of Parliament.

Cambridge Law Review Association and the authors for extracts from *Cambridge Law Journal*: Susan Bright: 'Avoiding Tenancy Legislation: Sham and Contracting Out Revisited', CLJ 146 (2002); J Hill: 'The Termination of Bare Licences' CLJ 87 (2001); S Bright and B McFarlane: 'Proprietary Estoppel and Property Rights', CLJ 449 (2005); A Goymour: 'Proprietary Claims and Human Rights—"A Reservoir of Entitlement"', 65 CLJ 696 (2006); and C Harpum: 'Overreaching, Trustees' Powers and the Reform of the 1925 Legislation' 49 CLJ 277 (1990).

Jeffrey Hackney for extracts from Jeffrey Hackney: *Understanding Equity and Trusts* (Fontana, 1987).

Hart Publishing for extracts from Susan Bright: *Landlord and Tenant Law in Context* (Hart, 2007); E Cooke: *The New Law of Land Registration* (Hart, 2003); L Fox: *Conceptualising Home: Theories, Laws and Policies* (Hart, 2007); S Gardner: *An Introduction to Land Law* (Hart, 2007): and McFarlane: *The Structure of Property Law* (Hart, 2008); and from M Davey: 'The Regulation of Long Leases in Modern Studies in Property Law'; M Dixon: 'Proprietary Estoppel and Formalities in Land Law and the Land Registration Act 2002: A Theory of Unconscionability'; S A Nield: 'Charges, Possessions and Human Rights: A reappraisal of Section 87(1) Law of Property Act 1926'; and P O'Connor: 'Registration of Title in England and Australia: A Theoretical and Comparative Analysis' in E Cooke (ed.): *Modern Studies in Property Law*, Volume 2 (Hart, 2003).

Incorporated Council of Law Reporting: extracts from the *Law Reports: Appeal Cases* (AC), *Chancery Division* (Ch), *Family Division* (Fam), *King's Bench Division* (KB), *Queen's Bench Division* (QB), and *Weekly Law Reports* (WLR).

Informa Law for extracts from *Lloyd's Maritime and Commercial Quarterly*: B McFarlane and A Robertson: 'The Death of Proprietary Estoppel', LMCQ 449 (2008).

Jordan Publishing Ltd for extract from the *Family Law Reports*.

Oxford University Press for extracts from J H Baker: *An Introduction to English Legal History* (4th edn, OUP, 2002); P Birks: 'Five Keys to Land Law' and D Clarke: 'Occupying "Cheek by Jowl"' in S Bright and J Dewar (eds.): *Land Law: Themes and Perspectives* (OUP, 1998); K Gray and S F Gray: *Elements of Land Law* (5th edn, OUP, 2009); J W Harris: *Property and Justice* (Clarendon Press, 1996); J W Harris: 'Legal Doctrine and Interests in Land' in J Eekelaar and J Bell (eds.) *Oxford Essays in Jurisprudence* (3rd series, Clarendon Press, 1987); R J Smith: *Plural Ownership* (OUP, 2005); and W Swadling: 'The Law of Property' in A Burrows (ed.): *English Private Law* (2nd edn, OUP, 2007).

Reed Business Information for extracts from case reports published in *Estates Gazette*: *Botham and others v TSB Bank plc* (1996) and *Michael v Miller* (2004) copyright © Reed Business Information.

Reed Elsevier (UK) Ltd trading as LexisNexis: extracts from *All England Law Reports* (All ER) and *Family Court Reports* (FCR); and for extracts from C Harpum: 'Registered Land: A Law unto Itself?; and B McFarlane and E Simpson: 'Tackling Avoidance' in J Getzler (ed.): *Rationalizing Property, Equity, and Trusts: Essays in Honour of Edward Burn* (Butterworths, 2002).

Springer and the authors for extract from L Flynn and A Lawson: 'Gender, Sexuality and the Doctrine of Detrimental Reliance', *Feminist Legal Studies* 105 (1995).

Sweet & Maxwell Ltd for extracts from N Hopkins: *The Informal Acquisition of Rights in Land* (Sweet & Maxwell, 2000) and R Smith: 'How Proprietary is Proprietary Estoppel' in F D Rose (Ed.): *Consensus ad Idem: Essays on the Law of Contract in Honour of Guenther Treitel* (Sweet & Maxwell, 1996); extracts from *Law Quarterly Review*: S Bright: 'Leases, Exclusive Possession and Estates', 116 LQR 7 (2000); E Cooke and P O'Connor: 'Purchaser Liability to Third Parties in the English Land Registration System: A Comparative Perspective', 120 LQR 640 (2004); B C Crown: 'Severance of a Joint Tenancy of Land by Partial Alienation', 117 LQR 477 (2001); S Gardner: 'The Remedial Discretion in Proprietary Estoppel', 122 LQR 492 (2006); J Howell: 'The Human Rights Act 1998: Land, Private Citizens, and the Common Law', 123 LQR 618 (2007); N Jackson: 'Title by Registration and Concealed Overriding Interests: The Cause and Effect of Antipathy to Documentary Proof', 119 LQR 669 (2003); B McFarlane: 'Constructive Trusts Arising on a Receipt of Property *Sub Conditione*', 118 LQR 667 (2004); P J Millett: '*Crabb v Arun District Council*: A Riposte', 92 LQR 342 (1976); R J Smith: 'Mortgages and Trust Beneficiaries', 109 LQR 545 (1990); and M Sturley: 'Easements in Gross', 96 LQR 557 (1980); extracts from *The Conveyancer*: S Bright: 'The Third Party's Conscience in Land Law', Conv 398 (2000); S Brown: 'The Consumer Credit Act 2006: Real Additional Mortgagor Protection', Conv 325 (2007); M Dixon: 'The Reform of Property Law and the Land Registration Act 2002: A Risk Assessment', Conv 136 (2002); B McFarlane: 'Identifying Property Rights: A Reply to Mr Watt', Conv 473 (2003); E Paton and G Seabourne: 'Can't get there from here? Permissible use of easements after *Das*', Conv 127 (2003); R Street: 'Coach and Horses Trip Cancelled? Rent Act Avoidance after *Street v Mountford*', Conv 328 (1985); L Tee: 'Severance Revisited', Conv 105 (1995); and S Wong: 'Potential Pitfalls in the Commonhold Community Statement and the Corporate Mechanisms of the Commonhold Association', Conv 14 (2006); A Robertson: 'The Reliance Basis of Proprietary Estoppel Remedies', Conv 295 (2008); and extracts from *European Human Rights Reports* (EHRR) and *Property, Planning and Compensation Reports* (P&CR).

*Thomson Reuters for extract from L Smith: 'Fusion and Tradition' in Simone Degeling and James Edelman (eds.): *Equity in Commercial Law* (Lawbook Co, 2005).

*Vathek Publishing for extracts from *Anglo American Law Review*: P Sparkes: 'Co-Tenants, Joint Tenants and Tenants in Common' 18 *AALR* 151 (1989).

Wiley-Blackwell Publishing Ltd: extracts from *Modern Law Review*: M Routley: 'Tenancies and Estoppel—After *Bruton v London & Quadrant Housing Trust*', 63 MLR 424 (2000); and from *Legal Studies*: J Hill: 'Intention and the Creation of Proprietary Rights: Are Leases Different?', LS 200 (1996)

Willan Publishing for extracts from S Bridge: 'Leases—Contract, Property and Status' and R Smith: 'The Role of Registration in Modern Land Law' in L Tee (Ed): *Land Law: Issues, Debates, Policy* (Willan, 2002).

Every effort has been made to trace and contact copyright holders prior to going to press but this has not been possible in every case. If notified, the publisher will undertake to rectify any errors or omissions at the earliest opportunity.

OUTLINE CONTENTS

PART A   INTRODUCTION   1

  1   What's special about land?   3

  2   Land, property, and equity   29

  3   Legal estates and legal interests   61

  4   Equitable interests   81

  5   Human rights and land   109

PART B   THE PRIORITY TRIANGLE   165

  6   The priority triangle   167

  7   Direct rights   192

  8   The priority triangle in action: Licences   212

**PART B1   THE ACQUISITION OF A LEGAL ESTATE
             OR INTEREST IN LAND**   263

  9   Formal methods of acquisition: Contracts, deeds,
      and registration   265

  10   Informal methods of acquisition: Adverse possession   319

**PART B2   THE ACQUISITION OF AN EQUITABLE
             INTEREST IN LAND**   357

  11   Introduction   359

  12   The doctrine of anticipation: *Walsh v Lonsdale*   371

  13   Proprietary estoppel   383

  14   Trusts of land   433

PART B3   PRIORITY   463

  15   Unregistered land and priorities   465

  16   Registered land and priorities   492

  17   Evaluating the Land Registration Act 2002   522

PART C   THE SHARED HOME   553

  18   Interests in the home   555

  19   Regulating co-ownership   593

  20   Co-ownership and third parties: Priorities   636

  21   Co-ownership and third parties: Applications for sale   676

  22   Successive ownership   699

PART D   LEASES   713

  23   The lease   715

  24   Regulating leases and protecting occupiers   775

  25   Leasehold covenants   797

PART E   NEIGHBOURS AND NEIGHBOURHOODS   851

  26   Easements   853

  27   Freehold covenants   917

  28   Flat ownership: Long leases and commonhold   965

PART F   SECURITY RIGHTS   989

  29   Security interests in land   991

  30   Protection of the borrower   1023

  31   Lender's rights and remedies   1077

CONTENTS

Table of Cases   xxix
Table of Statutes   xliii
List of Abbreviations   li

PART A   INTRODUCTION   1

1   WHAT'S SPECIAL ABOUT LAND?   3

1 The importance of land   4

2 The scope of this book   4

3 Three underlying questions   7

4 The special features of land   8

5 Land law in practice: Occupiers v banks   12

   5.1 The cases and the dilemma   12

   5.2 Two possible approaches   14

   5.3 The approach in *Ainsworth*   15

   5.4 The approach in *Boland*   17

   5.5 Comparing the approaches in *Ainsworth* and *Boland*   22

   5.6 Lessons from *Ainsworth* and *Boland*?   23

   5.7 *Ainsworth*: Later developments and further lessons   24

6 Conclusion   26

2   LAND, PROPERTY, AND EQUITY   29

1 Land as a form of private property   30

2 The meaning of 'property' in land law   31

3 The meaning of 'land'   34

   3.1 The physical reach of land   34

   3.2 What objects does the land include?   38

4 Equity and land law   55

5 Conclusion   59

3 LEGAL ESTATES AND LEGAL INTERESTS   61

1 The concept of a property right   62

2 The concept of a legal estate in land   66

3 Legal estates in land: The *content* question   69
    3.1 The content of a legal freehold   70
    3.2 The content of a legal lease   72
    3.3 Why only two legal estates in land?   72

4 Legal estates in land: The *acquisition* question   73

5 The concept of a legal interest in land   74

6 Legal interests in land: The *content* question   75

7 Legal interests in land: The *acquisition* question   79

8 Conclusion   79

4 EQUITABLE INTERESTS   81

1 The concept of an equitable property right   82

2 The concept of an equitable interest in land   84
    2.1 Equitable estates in land?   85
    2.2 Rights under trusts and other forms of equitable interest   86

3 Rights under trusts: The *content* question   86

4 Rights under trusts: The *acquisition* question   88

5 Other equitable interests: The *content* question   92
    5.1 A longer list of property rights   92
    5.2 The list of equitable interests   93
    5.3 Limiting the content of equitable interests   93
    5.4 Equitable interests and the *numerus clausus* principle   95

6 Other equitable interests: The *acquisition* question   98

7 The relationship between common law and equity   101

5 HUMAN RIGHTS AND LAND   109

1 Introduction   110

2 The mechanics of the Human Rights Act 1998   111
    2.1 Vertical effect   111
    2.2 Horizontal effect   114
    2.3 Absolute and qualified rights   121
    2.4 The justification formula   121

2.5 Retrospective application   129

3 Article 1 of the first protocol to the ECHR   131
   3.1 When is Art 1 engaged?   132
   3.2 When is an interference justified?   137

4 Article 8: The right to respect for private and family life   140
   4.1 When is Article 8(1) engaged?   142
   4.2 When is an interference justified under Art 8(2)?   145

5 Article 14: Freedom from discrimination   154

6 Article 6(1): The right to a fair trial   155
   6.1 Civil rights and obligations   156
   6.2 A fair hearing   158

7 The impact of human rights   159

PART B   THE PRIORITY TRIANGLE   165

6   THE PRIORITY TRIANGLE   167

1 Introduction: The priority triangle in practice   167

2 The basic rule and the *timing* question   169
   2.1 The basic rule   169
   2.2 The *timing* question   169

3 Exceptions to the basic rule: The *defences* question   173
   3.1 The possibility of a defence   173
   3.2 Registered land and the lack of registration defence   175
   3.3 Overreaching under s 2 of the Law of Property Act 1925   179
   3.4 Defences based on B's consent   182
   3.5 Defences based on the lapse of time   185
   3.6 Defences and the distinction between legal and equitable
        property rights   187

4 Conclusion   189

7   DIRECT RIGHTS   192

1 Introduction: The concept of a direct right   193

2 When will B have a direct right against C?   194
   2.1 Where C gives B a direct right by means of a deed   194
   2.2 Where C gives B a direct right by means of a contractual promise   195
   2.3 Where C gives B a direct right by means of a non-contractual promise   196
   2.4 Where C commits a tort against B   203

2.5 The 'benefit and burden' principle   204

2.6 Where C knows about a pre-existing right of B   204

3 Is B's direct right a property right or a personal right?   208

4 Direct rights and registered land   209

5 Conclusion   210

8   THE PRIORITY TRIANGLE IN ACTION: LICENCES   212

1 The nature of a licence   213

2 Bare licences   215

2.1 B's rights against A   215

2.2 B's rights against X   218

2.3 B's rights against C   218

3 Contractual licences   220

3.1 B's rights against A   221

3.2 B's rights against X   227

3.3 B's rights against C   231

4 Estoppel licences   251

4.1 B's rights against A   252

4.2 B's rights against X   254

4.3 B's rights against C   254

5 Statutory licences   256

5.1 B's rights against A   257

5.2 B's rights against X   257

5.3 B's rights against C   258

6 Licences coupled with an interest   259

6.1 B's rights against A   259

6.2 B's rights against X   261

6.3 B's rights against C   261

PART B1   THE ACQUISITION OF A LEGAL ESTATE OR INTEREST IN LAND   263

9   FORMAL METHODS OF ACQUISITION: CONTRACTS, DEEDS, AND REGISTRATION   265

1 Introduction   266

2 Formality requirements for the creation or transfer of legal rights   268

3 Contract   269

   3.1 When does s 2 apply?   271

   3.2 The concept of an exchange   272

   3.3 The requirement of a signature   274

   3.4 The effect of non-compliance   275

   3.5 Collateral contracts   277

   3.6 Rectification   280

   3.7 Estoppel   283

4 Creation and transfer   293

5 Registration of title   297

   5.1 Why registration of title?   297

   5.2 The principles of registration of title   299

   5.3 The scope of registration   300

   5.4 The registration gap   304

   5.5 Outline of a registered title   307

   5.6 Indefeasability   307

6 The future: E-conveyancing   312

   6.1 Electronic dispositions: The legal impact   313

   6.2 Electronic dispositions: Formalities   315

   6.3 Electronic signatures   316

10   INFORMAL METHODS OF ACQUISITION: ADVERSE POSSESSION   319

1 Introduction   319

2 Is adverse possession justified?   321

3 An outline of the operation of adverse possession   323

4 The inception of adverse possession   324

   4.1 'Adverse' possession defined   326

   4.2 'Possession' defined   329

5 The effect of adverse possession   335

   5.1 Unregistered Land   335

   5.2 Registered land: Land Registration Act 1925   337

   5.3 Registered land: Land Registration Act 2002   339

   5.4 Human rights and adverse possession   346

6 Adverse possession and leasehold titles   350

7 Conclusion   354

PART B2   THE ACQUISITION OF AN EQUITABLE INTEREST IN LAND   357

11   INTRODUCTION   359

1 The acquisition of equitable interests: A reminder   360

2 Informality   361

  2.1 The three formality rules   361

  2.2 Room for informality?   364

  2.3 Justifying informality?   365

3 Diversity   366

  3.1 Diversity and unconscionability   366

  3.2 Diversity and duties   368

  3.3 Diversity, duties, and informality   369

12   THE DOCTRINE OF ANTICIPATION: *WALSH V LONSDALE*   371

1 Introduction   371

2 *Walsh v Lonsdale* in context   372

3 The significance of specific performance   374

4 The nature of the rights acquired   377

  4.1 Enforceability of rights against third parties   377

  4.2 The nature of the trust   379

5 Conclusion   381

13   PROPRIETARY ESTOPPEL   383

1 Introduction: Proprietary estoppel in practice   384

2 The nature of proprietary estoppel   387

  2.1 A contractual explanation?   387

  2.2 Proprietary estoppel as an independent means of acquiring a right?   389

  2.3 Proprietary estoppel as a standard form of estoppel?   392

3 The Test: The requirements of proprietary estoppel   399

  3.1 Introduction   399

  3.2 Case 1: *Taylor Fashions*   401

  3.3 Case 2: *Gillett v Holt*   404

3.4 Case 3: *Wayling v Jones*   413

4 The extent of A's duty to B: Responding to a proprietary estoppel   416
   4.1 Introduction   416
   4.2 *Jennings v Rice*   417

5 The effect of proprietary estoppel on a third party:
   The priority question   426
   5.1 Introduction   426
   5.2 B's position *after* a court order in his or her favour   427
   5.3 B's position *before* a court order in his or her favour   427
   5.4 The effect of *Yeoman's Row*   431

14 TRUSTS OF LAND   433

1 Introduction   434

2 Express trusts   435

3 Resulting trusts   436
   3.1 The purchase money resulting trust   438
   3.2 The scope of the purchase money resulting trust   442

4 Constructive Trusts   443
   4.1 Institutional and remedial constructive trusts   443
   4.2 The doctrine in *Rochefoucauld v Boustead*   446
   4.3 The two-party case   447
   4.4 The three-party case   452

5 The *Pallant v Morgan* constructive trust   455
   5.1 The elements of the *Pallant v Morgan* constructive trust   455
   5.2 The nature of the unconscionability   458

6 Towards a rationalization of constructive trusts   460

PART B3 PRIORITY   463

15 UNREGISTERED LAND AND PRIORITIES   465

1 Introduction   466

2 Investigation of title   467

3 The two basic priority rules   467

4 The defence of bona fide purchaser   468
   4.1 'Bona fide'   469
   4.2 'Purchase for value'   470

	4.3 'Of a legal estate'	470
	4.4 'Without notice'	470
5	The Land Charges Act 1972	477
	5.1 The scope of the Land Charges Act 1972	478
	5.2 The effect of registration and non-registration	480
	5.3 The mechanics of registration	481
	5.4 Searching the land charges register	482
	5.5 Problems with a names-based register	483
	5.6 Land charges registration and the doctrine of notice	486
	5.7 Fraudulent transactions	488
	5.8 Claims to alternative property rights	489
6	Conclusion	490

16 REGISTERED LAND AND PRIORITIES   492

1	Introduction	493
2	An overview: Priorities and principles of registration of title	493
	2.1 Owner's powers	495
	2.2 The effect of a registered disposition	496
3	Restrictions on owner's powers	497
4	Entry of a notice	499
	4.1 Nature and effect	500
	4.2 Scope	500
	4.3 Application for entry of a notice	501
5	Overriding interest	502
	5.1 Property rights held by persons in occupation	503
	5.2 Short leases	512
	5.3 Easements and profits à Prendre	512
6	Investigation of registered title and search of the register	513
7	Registration, fraud, and liability	514
	7.1 The Land Registration Act 1925 and the decision in Peffer v Rigg	515
	7.2 The Land Registration Act 2002: A focus on new direct rights	518
8	Conclusion	520

17 EVALUATING THE LAND REGISTRATION ACT 2002   522

1	Introduction: The aims of the Land Registration Act 2002	523
	1.1 The general aims of registration	523

1.2 The prominence of registration in land law 524

1.3 The aims of a particular land registration system 526

1.4 The aims of the Land Registration Act 2002 528

2 The impact of the Land Registration Act 2002: A summary 531

2.1 The immediate impact of the Land Registration Act 2002 531

2.2 The future impact of the Land Registration Act 2002: The effect of
e-conveyancing 535

3 Evaluating the Land Registration Act 2002 537

3.1 A complete and accurate register? 537

3.2 Evaluating the law commission's aim 544

PART C   THE SHARED HOME

PART C   THE SHARED HOME 553

18   INTERESTS IN THE HOME

18 INTERESTS IN THE HOME 555

1 Introduction 556

2 Trusts and the home 558

2.1 Sole legal owner 559

2.2 Joint legal owners 576

2.3 Quantification of beneficial interests under a constructive trust 577

2.4 A critique of the common intention 580

2.5 Can *Stack v Dowden* be used to rationalize trusts of the home? 583

3 Occupation rights 585

4 Recommendations for reform 586

19   REGULATING CO-OWNERSHIP

19 REGULATING CO-OWNERSHIP 593

1 Introduction 593

2 Joint tenants and tenants in common 594

2.1 Identifying joint tenants and tenants in common 596

2.2 Survivorship 598

2.3 Severance 598

3 Termination of co-ownership 616

4 Is the beneficial joint tenancy desirable? 617

5 Trusts and co-ownership 619

5.1 Scope of the trust of land 621

5.2 Trustees' powers 621

5.3 Beneficiaries' rights 623

5.4 Occupation, the Trusts of Land and Appointment of Trustees
Act 1996, and the Family Law Act 1996   628

5.5 Applications to court   629

5.6 Regulation of co-ownership outside of the Trusts of Land and
Appointment of Trustees Act 1996   634

20 CO-OWNERSHIP AND THIRD PARTIES: PRIORITIES   636

1 Introduction   636

2 Overreaching   637

  2.1 The scope of overreaching   638

  2.2 Interests capable of being overreached   640

  2.3 Transactions with overreaching effect   648

3 Co-ownership, overreaching, and occupying beneficiaries   653

4 Overreaching and breach of trust   658

  4.1 Trustees' ability, authority, and duties   659

  4.2 Protection of purchasers   661

  4.3 Summary   663

5 Is overreaching justified?   664

6 The future of overreaching   666

  6.1 Qualifying and restricting the scope of overreaching   667

  6.2 Human rights and overreaching   668

  6.3 Alternative causes of action   670

7 Priority rules where overreaching does not take place   672

21 CO-OWNERSHIP AND THIRD PARTIES: APPLICATIONS FOR SALE   676

1 Introduction   676

2 Policy considerations   678

3 Applications by creditors   680

  3.1 Applications for sale by creditors post-*shaire*   684

  3.2 Has s 15 of the Trusts of Land and Appointment of Trustees
Act 1996 changed the law?   688

4 Applications by trustees in bankruptcy   689

  4.1 The courts' general approach to defining 'exceptional circumstances'   692

  4.2 Exceptional circumstances: The human rights dimension   694

5 Applications for sale by creditors and trustees in bankruptcy:
A summary   697

22 SUCCESSIVE OWNERSHIP   699

1 Introduction   699

2 The significance of successive ownership   700

3 Forms of successive ownership   701
    3.1 The rule against perpetuities   702
    3.2 Entailed interests   704

4 The nature of the life estate   704

5 The creation of successive interests   706

6 Regulation of successive ownership   709

PART D   LEASES   713

23 THE LEASE   715

1 Introduction: The importance of the lease   716
    1.1 The effect of a lease   716
    1.2 The practical importance and diversity of leases   727
    1.3 The landlord–tenant relationship   730

2 The *content* question   730
    2.1 Where A does not intend to grant a lease   730
    2.2 Intention to create legal relations   734
    2.3 A right to exclusive possession: General position   735
    2.4 A right to exclusive possession: Shams and pretences   739
    2.5 A right to exclusive possession: Multiple occupancy   750
    2.6 A proprietary right to exclusive possession   755
    2.7 A right to exclusive possession for a limited period   755
    2.8 Exceptions?   760
    2.9 Summary   762

3 The *acquisition* question   763
    3.1 Legal leases   763
    3.2 Equitable leases   768

4 The *defences* question   770
    4.1 B has a legal lease   770
    4.2 B has an equitable lease   770

5 The contractual aspect of a lease   771

24 REGULATING LEASES AND PROTECTING OCCUPIERS 775

1	Introduction	776
2	The *status-conferring* aspect of a lease: Background	777
3	The *status-conferring* aspect of a lease: Practice	783
4	The *status-conferring* aspect of a lease: Reform?	792

25 LEASEHOLD COVENANTS 797

1	Introduction	798
	1.1 Leasehold covenant terminology	799
	1.2 Contract and estate-based liability	799
2	The original parties (LO and TO) and contractual enforceability	801
	2.1 Pre-1996 law	801
	2.2 Post-1995 law	804
3	Assignees (LA and TA) and estate-based liability	808
	3.1 Pre-1996 law	808
	3.2 Post-1995 leases	813
4	The continuing liability for breaches of covenant	816
	4.1 continuing rights to enforce breaches of covenant	817
5	Sub-lessees	819
6	Remedies for breach of leasehold covenants	822
	6.1 Damages	822
	6.2 Specific performance	823
	6.3 Distress and taking control of the tenant's goods	823
	6.4 Forfeiture	823

PART E NEIGHBOURS AND NEIGHBOURHOODS 851

26 EASEMENTS 853

1	Introduction	854
	1.1 What are easements?	854
	1.2 The utility balance	855
2	The *content* question	856
	2.1 'There must be a dominant tenement and a servient tenement'	856

2.2 The dominant and servient tenements must be in separate
ownership and occupation 864

2.3 An easement must accommodate the dominant land 865

2.4 The right must be capable of being the subject matter of a grant 869

3 The *acquisition* question 877

3.1 Express grant 877

3.2 Implied grant 877

3.3 Presumed grant: Prescription 899

4 Easements: The *defences* question 911

4.1 Registered land 911

4.2 Unregistered land 913

5 Excessive user 913

6 Extinguishment of easements 914

27 FREEHOLD COVENANTS 917

1 Introduction 917

1.1 The role of land covenants 918

1.2 The structure and terminology of land covenants 919

2 The burden: Who can sue? 921

2.1 The covenant must relate to land 922

2.2 Benefit to dominant land 923

2.3 Negativity 928

2.4 Indirect enforcement of positive covenants 932

2.5 The acquisition and priority of restrictive covenants 935

3 The benefit: Who can sue? 936

3.1 Assignment 937

3.2 Annexation 938

3.3 Building scheme 948

4 Enforcement, discharge, and modification of covenants 954

4.1 Enforcement 954

4.2 Extinction and modification of covenants 958

5 Reform 962

28 FLAT OWNERSHIP: LONG LEASES AND COMMONHOLD 965

1 Introduction 966

2 Long leases of flats 968

2.1 Who is the landlord? 968

2.2 The leasehold term, and rights to enfranchisement and extension 969

2.3 Maintenance and repair 970

2.4 Communal living 972

2.5 Variation 973

2.6 Forfeiture 973

3 Commonhold 974

3.1 The structure of commonhold 974

3.2 Creation of commonhold 975

3.3 Commonhold land ownership 976

3.4 The commonhold association 978

3.5 Commonhold community statement 980

3.6 The management of commonhold 982

3.7 Dispute resolution 985

4 Conclusion 985

PART F   SECURITY RIGHTS
989

29 SECURITY INTERESTS IN LAND
991

1 Introduction 991

2 The role and importance of security 992

3 General forms of security 997

3.1 The pledge 997

3.2 The lien 998

3.3 The mortgage 998

3.4 The charge 999

4 Forms of security over land: Mortgages and charges 1001

4.1 Development of mortgages of land 1001

4.2 The legal charge by way of mortgage 1002

4.3 Equitable mortgages and equitable charges of land 1006

4.4 Charging orders 1010

5 Equity of redemption 1013

5.1 Development of the equity of redemption 1014

5.2 Equity of redemption and the legal charge 1015

6 Modern developments in mortgage forms 1018

6.1 Islamic mortgages or home purchase plans 1018

6.2 Shared ownership 1019

6.3 Equity release or home reversion plans 1019

6.4 The eurohypothec 1020

30 PROTECTION OF THE BORROWER · 1023

1 Introduction · 1023

2 Market regulation · 1024
  2.1 Financial Services and Markets Act 2000, and regulated
      mortgage contracts · 1027
  2.2 Consumer Credit Act 1974 (as amended) · 1032

3 Creation of the mortgage · 1037
  3.1 Factors governing procedural fairness · 1038
  3.2 The conceptual underpinnings · 1043
  3.3 Undue influence and mortgages · 1044

4 Control of mortgage terms · 1055
  4.1 Sources of control · 1056
  4.2 Redemption · 1063
  4.3 Collateral advantages · 1067
  4.4 Interest rates and other payment terms · 1070

31 LENDER'S RIGHTS AND REMEDIES · 1077

1 Introduction · 1077
  1.1 Source of the lender's rights and remedies · 1078
  1.2 Regulation of the lender's rights and remedies · 1080

2 Possession · 1082
  2.1 The starting point: An immediate right to possession · 1082
  2.2 The equitable duty to account · 1084
  2.3 The purpose of taking possession · 1085
  2.4 Procedural safeguards · 1086
  2.5 Dwelling houses and s 36 of the Administration of Justice
      Act 1970 (as amended) · 1086
  2.6 Possession and human rights · 1102

3 Sale · 1105
  3.1 Mechanics of sale · 1105
  3.2 Duties of the mortgagee in the conduct of the sale · 1108

4 Appointment of a receiver · 1120
  4.1 Functions and powers of a receiver · 1120
  4.2 Receiver as agent for the borrower · 1121
  4.3 Duties of a receiver · 1122

5 A final word about the covenant to repay · 1124

Index · 1127

TABLE OF CASES

Case names and page references in **bold** indicate extracts from the judgment

8 Berkeley Road, Re [1971] 1 All ER 254 . . . 602, 605

A Ketley Ltd v Scott [1980] CCLR 37 . . . 1036

AG Securities v Vaughan and ors; Antoniades v Villiers and anor [1990] 1 AC 417 . . . **740–745**, 746–755, 774, 790, 791

AGOSI v UK (1987) 9 EHRR 1 . . . 140

Abbey National Bank plc v Stringer [2006] EWCA Civ 338 . . . 1050

Abbey National Building Society v Maybeech [1985] Ch 190 . . . 845

Abbey National v Cann [1991] 1 AC 56 . . . **170–171**, 172, **183–184**, 185, 503, 509

Abbott v Abbott [2007] UKPC 53 . . . 584

Ackroyd v Smith (1850) 10 CB 164 . . . 859

Adealon International Corp Pty Ltd v Merton LBC [2007] EWCA Civ 362; [2007] 1 WLR 1898 . . . 881

Adekunle v Ritchie [2007] BPIR 1177 . . . 559, 577, 597

Ahmed v Kendrick [1988] 2 FLR 22 . . . 1008

Air Canada v UK (1995) 20 EHRR 150 . . . 140

Akici v LR Butlin Ltd [2005] EWCA Civ 1296 . . . **831–832, 835–837**

Albany Home Loans Ltd v Massey (1997) 37 P & CR 509 . . . 1086

Alec Lobb Garages Ltd v Total Oil (GB) [1985] 1 WLR 173 . . . **1041–1042**, 1069

Allan v Liverpool Overseers (1874) LR 9 QB 180 . . . 719, 724

Allcard v Skinner (1887) 36 Ch D 145 . . . 1039, 1051

Alliance and Leicester plc v Slayford (2001) 33 HLR 66 . . . 689

Alliance Perpetual Building Society v Belrum Investments Ltd [1957] 1 WLR 720 . . . 1083

Amalgamated Investment & Property Co Ltd v Texas Commerce International Bank Ltd [1982] QB 84 . . . 415

Amsprop Trading Ltd v Harris Distribution Ltd [1997] 1 WLR 1025 . . . 195, 820

Amstrong v Shappard & Shroff [1959] 2 QB 384 . . . 915

Angus v Dalton (1877) LR 3 QBD 85 . . . 903

Anneveld v Robinson [2005] WL 3142400 . . . 631

Antoniades v Villiers and anor: see AG Securities v Vaughan and ors

Antoniades v UK (App No 15434/89) . . . 133

Argyle Building Society v Hammond (1984) 49 P & CR 148 . . . 540

Armory v Delamirie (1722) 5 Stra 505 . . . 46–48, 50, 74

Arrondelle v UK (1982) 5 EHRR 123 . . . 143

Ashburn and Anstalt v Arnold [1989] Ch 1 . . . 201, 202, 207, **235–236**, 237, 241, **242–243, 244**, 249, **726–727**, 755, 858

Asher v Whitlock (1865) LR 1 QB 1 . . . 724

Ashley Guarantee v Zacaria [1993] 1 WLR 62 . . . 1084

Aslan v Murphy (Nos 1 & 2): Duke v Wynne [1990] 1 WLR 766 . . . 747

Astley v Reynolds (1731) 2 Str 915 . . . 1039

Aston Cantlow and Wilmcote with Billesley Parochial Church Council v Wallbank [2003] UKHL 37, [2004] 1 AC 546 . . . 112, 113, 131, **133**, 349

Attorney-General v Antrobus [1905] 2 Ch 188 . . . 869

Attorney-General v Blake [2001] 1 AC 268 . . . 36, 221, 957

Attorney-General of Hong Kong v Fairfax Ltd [1997] 1 WLR 149 . . . 958

Attorney-General of Hong Kong v Humphrey's Estate (Queen's Gardens) Ltd [1987] 2 All ER 387 . . . 397

Attorney-General of Hong Kong v Reid [1994] 1 AC 324, PC . . . 88, 100, 360, 364, 367, 368

Attorney-General of Scotland v Taylor [2003] SLT 1340 . . . 140

Attorney-General of Southern Nigeria v John Holt & Co (Liverpool) Ltd [1915] AC 599 . . . 873

Austerberry v Oldham Corp (1885) 29 Ch D 750 . . . 921

Azfar's Application, Re (2002) 1 P & CR 215 . . . 960, 961

B Johnson & Co (Builders) Ltd, Re [1955] Ch 634 . . . 1122

BCCI v Aboody [1991] 1 QB 923 . . . 1048

BHP Great Britain Petroleum Ltd v Chesterfield Properties Ltd [2001] EWCA Civ 1797; [2002] Ch 194 . . . 804, **815**

BP Properties Ltd v Buckler (1988) 55 P & CR 337 . . . **326–327**

Baker v Baker (1993) 25 HLR 408 . . . 426

Bakewell Management Ltd v Brandwood [2004] UKHL 14 . . . **907–908**

Ballards Conveyance, Re [1937] Ch 473 . . . 941

Banco Exterior Internacional SA v Thomas [1997] 1 WLR 221 . . . 1046

Baner v Sweden (App No 11763/85) (1989) 60 D & R 128 . . . 135, 139

Banfield v Leeds Building Society [2007] EWCA Civ 1369 . . . 1094

Bank of Credit & Commerce International (Overseas) Ltd v Akindele [2001] Ch 437 . . . 410

Bank of Ireland Home Mortgages Ltd v Bell [2001] 2 FLR 908 . . . 677, 684, **685–686**

Bank of Scotland v Grimes [1986] QB1179 . . . 1091

Bank of Scotland v Miller [2002] EWCA Civ 344; [2002] QB 255 . . . 1088

Banner Homes Group plc v Luff Developments Ltd [2000] Ch 372 . . . **455–457, 459**

Bannister v Bannister [1948] 2 All ER 133 . . . **197–199**, 200, 234, 238, 244, **449**, 451

Barca v Mears [2004] EWHC 2170 . . . **694–696**, 697

Barclays Bank v Coleman [2002] 2 AC 773 . . . 1050

Barclays Bank v O'Brien [1994] 1 AC 180 . . . 1040, 1041, 1043, **1044–1045**, 1052, 1053

Barkshire v Grubb (1881) 18 Ch D 816 . . . 881

Barnhart v Greenshields (1853) 9 Moo PCC 18 . . . 471, 472

Barrett v Hilton Developments (1975) 29 P & CR 300 . . . 481

Barton v Armstrong [1976] AC 104 . . . 1039

Basham, Re [1986] 1 WLR 1498 . . . **409**

Basset v Nosworthy (1673) 23 ER 55 . . . 470

Batt v Adams [2001] 32 EG 90 . . . 332

Battersea Property Co v London Borough of Wandsworth [2001] 19 EG 148 . . . 332

Baxter v Four Oaks Properties Ltd [1965] Ch 816 . . . 949, 952

Beaulane Properties Ltd v Palmer [2006] Ch 79; [2006] EWHC 817 . . . 115, 329

Belfast City Council v Miss Behavin' Ltd [2007] 1 WLR 1420 . . . 153

Benn v Hardinge (1993) 66 P & CR 246 . . . 915

Bernstein of Leigh (Baron) v Skyviews & General Ltd [1978] QB 479 . . . **36–38**

Berwick & co v Price [1905] 1 Ch 632 . . . 469

Beswick v Beswick [1968] AC 58 . . . 194, 195

Beyeler v Italy (2001) 33 EHRR 52 (2003) 36 EHRR 5 . . . 134

Bhojwani v Kingsley Investment Trust Ltd [1992] EGLR 70 . . . 837

Biggs v Hodinott [1898] 2 Ch 307 . . . 1067

Billson v Residential Apartments Ltd [1992] 1 AC 494; [1991] 3 WLR 264 . . . **825–826**, 839, **841–843, 845–846**

Billson v Residential Apartments Ltd (No 2) [1993] EGCS 155 . . . 841

Binions v Evans [1972] Ch 359 . . . **199–200**, 208, 231, **234**, 237, 238, 244, 447

Bird v Syme-Thomson [1979] 1 WLR 440 . . . 21, 505, **510**

Birmingham & Dudley District Banking Company v Ross (1889) 38 Ch D 295 . . . 892

Birmingham Citizens Permanent Building Society v Caunt [1962] Ch 883 . . . **1083**, 1086

Birmingham City Council v Doherty [2008] UKHL 57; [2008] 3 WLR 636 . . . **116–121**, 146, 147, **151–153**, 159

Birmingham Midshires Mortgage Services Ltd v Sabherwal (2000) 80 P & CR 256 . . . 640, **645–647**, 648, **657–658**, 664, 668

Birmingham, Dudley and District Banking Co v Ross (1887) 38 Ch D 295 . . . 878

Bishop v Bonham 1988] 1 WLR 742 . . . 1114

Bland v Ingrams Estates Ltd (No 2) [2001] EWCA Civ 1088; [2002] Ch 177 . . . 840, 843, 845

Blecic v Croatia (2005) 41 EHRR 13 . . . 114, 145

Booker v Palmer [1942] 2 All ER 674 . . . 761

Borman v Griffith [1930] 1 Ch 493 . . . 889–891

Botham and ors v TSB Bank plc [1996] EWCA Civ 549 . . . **42–45**

Boyer v Warbey [1953] 1 QB 234 . . . **812**

Bradford & Bingley plc v Ross [2005] EWCA Civ 394 . . . 1117

Bradley v Carritt [1903] AC 25 . . . 1067

Bremner, Re [1999] 1 FLR 912 . . . **693**

Bridges v Hawkesworth (1821) 21 LJ (QB) 75 . . . 47–49

Bright v Walker (1834) 1 CM&R 211 . . . 906

Brikom Investments Ltd v Carr [1979] 2 All ER 753 . . . 414

Bristol & West Building Society v Ellis (1997) 73 P & CR 158 . . . **1094–1095**, 1125

Bristol & West Building Society v Henning [1985] 1 WLR 778 . . . 184, 185

Bristol Airport v Powdrill [1990] Ch 744 . . . 241, **992**

Britannia Building Society v Earl [1990] 1 WLR 422 . . . 1090

British Anzani (Felixstowe) Ltd v International Marine Management (UK) Ltd [1980] QB 137 . . . 822

British Petroleum Pension Trust Ltd v Behrendt (1985) 52 P & CR 117 . . . 834

British Railways Board v Glass [1965] Ch 538 . . . 913

Brown & Root Technology Ltd v Sun Alliance and London Assurance Co Ltd [2001] Ch 733 . . . **304–305**

Brown v Raindle (1796) 3 Ves 296; (1796) 30 ER 998 . . . 606

Browne v Pritchard [1975] 1 WLR 1366 . . . 634

Brunner v Greenslade [1971] Ch 993 . . . 821, 953

Bruton v London & Quadrant Housing Trust [2000] 1 AC 406 . . . 147, 755, **761**, 763, **783–786**, 787–789, 791

Bryan v UK (1995) 21 EHRR 342 . . . 157–159

Buck v Howarth [1947] 1 All ER 342 . . . 198

Buckingham County Council v Moran [1990] Ch 623 . . . 320, 333, 335, 354, 320

Buckley v United Kingdom (1997) 23 EHRR 101 . . . 123, 142, 143, 145

Burgess v Rawnsley [1975] Ch 429 . . . 600, 602, 606, **611–612**, 613

Burke v Burke [1974] 1 WLR 1063 . . . 634

Burrows v Brent London Borough Council [1996] 1 WLR 1448 . . . 763

CIBC v Pitt [1994] 1 AC 200 . . . 1040

Cable v Bryant [1908] 1 Ch 259 . . . 878

Cadogan v Dimovic [1984] 1 WLR 609 . . . 844

Caern Motor Services Ltd v Texaco Ltd [1994] 1 WLR 1249 . . . 811, 812

Camden London Borough v Shortlife Community Housing (1992) 25 HLR 330 . . . 761

Campbell v Holyland (1877) 7 Ch D 166 . . . 1078

Canas Property Co Ltd v KL Television Services Ltd [1970] 2 QB 433 . . . 826

Cardwell v Walker [2003] EWHC 3117 . . . 811, 812

Carlton v Goodman [2002] 2 FLR 259 . . . **558**

Casborne v Scarfe (1738) 1 Atk 603, 26 ER 377 . . . 1014

Catt v Tourle (1869) LR 4 Ch 654 . . . 923

Caunce v Caunce [1969] 1 WLR 286 . . . 19, 21, **472–473**, 505

Cave v Cave (1880) 15 Ch D 639 . . . 671

Celsteel Ltd v Alton House Holdings Ltd [1985] 1 WLR 204 . . . 513, 911

Central Estates (Belgravia) Ltd v Woolgar (No 2) [1972] 1 WLR 1048 . . . 828, 834, 843

Central London Commercial Estates Ltd v Kato Kagaku Co Ltd [1998] EWHC 314 . . . 339, **353**

Central London Property Trust Ltd v High Trees House Ltd [1947] KB 130 . . . 385, **391**

Central Midlands Estates Ltd v Leicester Dyers Ltd [2003] 2 P & CR D1 . . . 873

Centrax Trustees v Ross [1979] 2 All ER 952 . . . 1091

Centrovincial Estates plc v Bulk Storage Ltd (1983) 46 P & CR 393 . . . 802

Chaffe v Kingsley (2000) 79 P & CR 404 . . . 885

Chan v Cresdon Proprietary Ltd (1989) 168 CLR 350 . . . 377

Chan v Leung [2003] 1 FLR 23 . . . **628–629**

Chapman v UK (2001) 33 EHRR 399 . . . 141

Charles Rickards Ltd v Oppenhaim [1950] 1 KB 616 . . . 385

Chartered Trust plc v Davies [1997] 2 EGLR 83 . . . 773

Chase Manhattan Bank NA v Israel-British Bank (London) Ltd [1981] Ch 105 . . . 437

Chassagnou v France (App Nos 25088/94, 28331/95&28443/95) (2000) 29 EHRR 615 . . . 135, 139, 155

Chatham Empire Theatres (1955) Ltd v Ultrans Ltd [1961] 1 WLR 817 . . . 845

Chatsworth Estates Co v Fewell [1931] 1 Ch 224 . . . 958

Chattey v Farndale Holdings Inc [1997] 1 EGLR 153 . . . 238

Cheltenham & Gloucester Building Society v Booker (1997) 73 P & CR 412 . . . **1096–1097**

Cheltenham & Gloucester Building Society v Krausz [1997] 1 WLR 1558 . . . **1098–1099**

Cheltenham & Gloucester Building Society v Norgan [1996] 1 WLR 343 . . . **1092–1094**, 1125

Chester v Buckingham Travel Ltd [1981] 1 WLR 96 . . . 823

Chesterfid and Midland Silkstone Colliery Co Ltd v Hawkins (1865) 3 H & C 677 . . . 194

Chhokar v Chhokar [1984] FLR 313 . . . 509

China and South Seas Bank v Tan [1990] 1 AC 536 . . . **1113**

Christine Goodwin v United Kingdom (2002) 35 EHRR 18 . . . 123

Citibank Trust Ltd v Ayivor [1987] 1 WLR 1157 . . . 1084

Citro, Re [1991] Ch 142 . . . 680, 688, 689, **692**, 693

City and Metropolitan Properties Ltd v Greycroft Ltd [1987] 1 WLR 1085 . . . **818–819**

City of London Building Society v Flegg [1988] AC 54 . . . **180–181**, 182, 624, **638**, 643, 652, **654–657**

City of London Corp v Fell [1994] 1 AC 458 . . . **800–801**, 802

City Permanent Building Society v Miller [1952] Ch 840 . . . **187–188**, 189, 770

Cityland and Property Holdings Ltd v Dabrah [1968] Ch 166 . . . 1067

Claughton v Charalamabous [1999] 1 FLR 740 . . . 693

Cleveland Petroleum Ltd v Dartstone Ltd [1969] 1 WLR 116 . . . 1069

Clore v Theatrical Properties Ltd [1936] 3 All ER 483 . . . 240, 250, 251

Cobb v Lane [1952] 1 All ER 1199; [1952] 1 TLR 1037 . . . 247, 734

Collier v Wright [2008] 1 WLR 643 . . . 391

Collins Application, Re (1974) 30 P & CR 527 . . . 961

Combe v Combe [1915] 2 KB 215 . . . 392

Commission for the New Towns v Cooper [1995] Ch 259 . . . **273–274**, 280, 1046

Commission for the New Towns v Gallagher [2002] EWHC 2668, (2003) 2 P & CR 24 . . . 893

Commonwealth Bank of Australia Ltd v Amadio (1983) 151 CLR 447 . . . 1042

Commonwealth v Verwayen (1990) 117 CLR 394 . . . 425

Connaught Restaurants Ltd v Indoor Leisure Ltd [1994] 1 WLR 501 . . . 822

Connolly Brothers Ltd (No. 2), Re [1912] 2 Ch 25 . . . 171

Connors v UK (2005) 40 EHRR 9 . . . 114, **123**, **125**, 126, 143, 145, 146, 154, 246

Cooke v Chilcott (1876) 3 Ch D 694 . . . 928

Copeland v Greenhalf [1952] Ch 488 . . . **872–873**, 876

Corbett v Halifax plc [2004] 1 WLR 997 . . . 1114, 1117, **1118–1119**

Cornillie v Saha (1996) 72 P & CR 147 . . . 828

Coronation Street Industrial Properties Ltd v Ignall Industries Ltd [1989] 1 WLR 304 . . . 811

Corporation of London v Riggs (1880) 13 Ch D 798 . . . 881

Cosslett Contractors, Re [1998] Ch 495 . . . **997**, **999–1000**

County Leasing v East [2007] EWHC 2907 . . . 1075

Coventry Permanent Economic Building Society v Jones [1951] 1 All ER 901 . . . 171

Cowcher v Cowcher [1972] 1 WLR 425, Ch D . . . **367–368**, 596

Cox v Bishop (1857) 8 De GM&G 815 . . . 812

Cox v Jones [2004] EWHC 1486 . . . 457

Crabb v Arun District Council [1976] Ch 179 . . . 100, **384–387**, 388–389, 392, 396, 398, 400, 406, 420, 427, 430, 432, 448, 877

Crago v Julian [1992] 1 WLR 372 . . . 768

Credit Lyonnais v Burch [1997] 1 All ER 144 . . . 1050

Crest Nicholson Residential South Ltd v McAllister [2004] EWCA Civ 410 . . . **944–947**

Crofter Hand Woven Harris Tweed Co Ltd v Veitch [1942] AC 435 . . . 203

Cryer v Scott Brothers (Sudbury) Ltd (1988) 55 P & CR 183 . . . 927

Cuckmere Brick Co Ltd v Mutual Finance Ltd [1971] Ch 494 . . . **1108–1110**, 1111–1114, 1123

Cumberland Court (Brighton) Ltd v Taylor [1964] Ch 29 . . . 1004

DHN Food Distributors Ltd v London Borough of Tower Hamlets [1976] 3 All ER 462 . . . **243–244**, 247

DSDN Subsea Ltd v Petroleum Geo-services ASA [2000] BLR 1 . . . 1039

D v East Berkshire Community NHS Trust [2004] QB 558 . . . 114

Dalton v Angus (1881) 6 App Cas 740 . . . 871, **902–903**, **908–909**

Das v Linden Mews [2002] EWCA Civ 590; [2003] 2 P & CR 4 . . . 859, 861

Davies v Bramwell [2007 EWCA Civ 821 . . . 883

Davies v Direct Loans [1986] 1 WLR 823 . . . 1036

Dempster v Cleghorn (1813) 2 Dow 40 . . . 868

Dennis v McDonald [1982] Fam 63 . . . 625

Dennis, Re [1996] Ch 80 . . . 610

Diligent Finance Co Ltd v Alleyne (1972) 23 P & CR 346 . . . 483, 485

Dillwyn v Llewellyn (1862) 4 De G F & J 517 . . . 252

Director General of Fair Trading v First National Bank plc [2001] UKHL 52 . . . **1060–1062**, 1072

Doherty v Allman (1878) 3 App Cas 709 . . . 956

Dolphin's Conveyance, Re [1970] Ch 654 . . . 948, **950–953**

Domb v Isoz [1980] Ch 548 . . . 274

Donaldson v Smith [2006] All ER (D) 293 . . . 881, 887

Donohoe v Ingram [2006] EWHC 282 . . . 693

Downsview Nominees Ltd v First City Corporation Ltd [1993] AC 295 . . . 1086, 1110, 1122, 1123

Drake v Whipp [1996] 1 FLR 826 . . . 577

Draper's Conveyance, Re [1969] 1 Ch 486 . . . **600–601**, 602

Driscoll v Church Commissioners [1957] Ch 70 . . . 827

Duffy v Lamb (1998) 75 P & CR 364 . . . 870

Duke of Beaufort v Patrick (1853) 17 Beav 60 . . . 428

Duke of Bedford v British Museum Trustees (1822) 2 My & K 552 . . . 958

Duke of Westminster v Guild [1985] QB 688 . . . 870

Duke v Robson [1973] 1 WLR 267 . . . 1090

Dunbar v Plant [1998] Ch 412 . . . 614

Duncan v Louch (1845) 6 QB 904 . . . 870

Dunlop Pneumatic Tyre Ltd v New Garage and Motor Co Ltd [1915] AC 79 . . . 1058

Dunraven Securities Ltd v Hollaway [1982] 2 EGLR 47 . . . 834

Dyce v Lady James Hay (1852) 1 Macq 305 . . . 868, 871

Dyer v Dyer (1788) 2 Cox 92 . . . **438**

ER Ives Investments Ltd v High [1967] 2 QB 379 . . . 93, 255, 428, 429, 479, 489, 490, 646

Earl of Leicester v Wells-next-the-Sea UDC [1973] Ch 110 . . . 927

Eccles v Bryant and Pollock [1948] Ch 93 . . . 274

Ecclesiastical Commissioners for England v Kino (1880) 14 Ch D 213 . . . 915

Edwardes v Barrington (1901) 85 LT 650 . . . 242

Edwards v Lee's Administrator 96 SW 2d 1028 (1936) . . . **34–36**, 59

Edwards v Lloyds TSB [2004] EWHC 1745 . . . 684, **686– 687**, 689

Egerton v Esplanade Hotels, London Ltd [1947] 2 All ER 88 . . . 834

Elitestone Ltd v Morris [1997] 1 WLR 687 . . . **39–41**, 59

Ellenborough Park, Re [1956] 1 Ch 181 . . . **856, 865–867, 868**, 869, **870**, 871, 876

Ellis v Rowbotham [1900] 1 QB 740 . . . 829

Elliston v Reacher [1908] 2 Ch 374 . . . **949**, 952, 953

Embassy Court Residents Association v Lipman (1984) 271 EG 545 . . . 972

Emile Elias & Co Ltd v Pine Groves Ltd [1993] 1 WLR 305 . . . 952

Emmanuel College v Evans (1625) 1 Ch Rep 18 . . . 1014

Entick v Carrington (1765) 2 Wils KB 274 . . . **30–31**, 33, 59

Equity & Law Home Loans Ltd v Prestidge [1992] 1 WLR 137 . . . 184, 185

Errington v Errington & Woods [1952] 1 KB 290 . . . **240–241**, 244, 247–251

Escalus Properties Ltd v Robinson [1996] QB 231 . . . 839, 844

Esso Petroleum Co Ltd v Harpers Garage (Stourport) Ltd [1968] AC 269 . . . 1070

Esso Petroleum Co Ltd v Kingswood Motors Ltd and ors [1974] QB 142 . . . 232

Ettl v Austria (1987) 10 EHRR 255 . . . 158

Evans v Cherry Tree Finance Ltd [2008] EWCA Civ 331 . . . 1067

Evans v Hoare [1892] 1 QB 593 . . . 275

Evers' Trust, Re [1980] 1 WLR 1327 . . . 634

Eves v Eves [1975] 1 WLR 1338 . . . 444, 568, 572

Ewart v Fryer [1901] 1 Ch 499 . . . 844

Expert Clothing Service & Sales Ltd v Hillgate House Ltd [1986] Ch 340 . . . **833–834**, 835–837, **838**

Fairclough v Swan Brewery Co [1912] AC 565 . . . 1064

Fairweather v St Marylebone Property Co Ltd [1963] AC 510 . . . **336**, 339, **350–351**, **352–353**

Falco Finance Ltd v Gough [1999] CCLR 16 . . . 1067, 1072, 1075

Family Housing Association v Jones [1990] 1 WLR 779 . . . 784

Farah Constructions Pty Ltd v Say-Dee Pty Ltd [2007] HCA 22 . . . 671

Farrer v Farrers Ltd (1888) 40 Ch D 395 . . . 1116

Federated Homes Ltd v Mill Lodge Properties Ltd [1980] 1 WLR 594 . . . **941**, **942–943**

Ferris v Weaven [1952] 2 All ER 233 . . . 70–72

Ferrishurst Ltd v Wallcite Ltd [1999] Ch 353 . . . 504

Ffrench's Estate (1887) 21 LR (Ir) 283 . . . 671

Figgins Holdings Pty Ltd v SEAA Enterpises Ltd (1999) 196 CLR 245 . . . 1004, **1016**

Finchbourne Ltd v Rodrigues [1976] 3 All ER 581 . . . 972

First National Bank plc v Achampong [2003] EWCA 487 . . . 677, **684–685**

First National Security v Hegerty [1965] 1 QB 850 . . . 607, 1008, 1013

Firstpost Homes Ltd v Johnson [1995] 1 WLR 1567 . . . 269, **274–275**

Flight v Bentley (1835) 7 Sim 149 . . . 818

Foenander v Allan [2006] BPIR 1392 . . . 693, 694

Former King of Greece v Greece (App No 25701/94) (2001) 33 EHRR 21 . . . 138

Forster v Hale (1783) 3 Ves Jr 696 . . . 88, 362

Foskett v McKeown [2001] AC 102 . . . 671

Foster v Warblington Urban District Council [1906] 1 KB 648 . . . 723–725

Four Maids Ltd v Dudley Marshall Properties Ltd [1957] Ch 317 . . . **1083**

Fowler v Barron 2008] EWCA 377 . . . 577, 580

Fox v Jolly [1916] 1 AC 1 . . . 832

Frazer v Walker [1967] 1 AC 569 . . . 210

French v Barcham [2008] EWHC 1505 . . . 625

Frencher Ltd (In liq) v Bank of East Asia [1995] 2 HKC 263 . . . 1078

Friends Provident Life Office, Re [1999] 1 All ER (Comm) 437 . . . 787

Friends Provident Life Office v British Railways Board (1997) 73 P & CR 9 . . . 802

G&K Kreglinger v New Patagonia Meat and Cold Storage Co Ltd [1914] AC 25 . . . **1057–1058**, **1067–1069**

GS Fashions Ltd v B&Q plc [1995] 1 WLR 1088 . . . 827

Gadds Land Transfer, Re [1966] Ch 56 . . . 926

Gafford v Graham (1999) 77 P & CR 73 . . . 956, **957–958**

Gardner v Hodgson's Kingston Brewery Co [1903] AC 229 . . . 903

Gardner v Rowe (1825) 2 S & S 346; (1827–28) 5 Russ 258 . . . 88, **362–363**

Gaskell v Gosling [1896] 1 QB 669 . . . 1121

George Inglefield Ltd, Re [1933] Ch 1 . . . 747

Ghaidan v Godin-Mendoza [2004] UKHL 30; [2004] 2 AC 557 . . . 114, 115, **154–155**

Gill v Lewis [1956] 2 QB 1 . . . **840**

Gillett v Holt [2001] Ch 210 . . . 403, **404–406**, 407, **408**, 409, 412, 417, 421, 432, 460

Gillow v UK (1989) 11 EHRR 335 . . . 123, 135, 142, 143, 154

Gissing v Gissing [1971] AC 886 . . . 18, 291, 440, 561, 564, **565**

Glass v Kencakes [1966] 1 QB 611 . . . 834

Godden v Merthyr Tydfil Housing Association [1997] NPC 1 . . . 286

Goldberg v Edwards [1950] Ch 247 . . . 889, 897, **898–899**

Gomba Holdings UK Ltd v Homan [1986] 1 WLR 1301 . . . 1122

Goodman v Gallant [1986] 2 WLR 236 . . . 436, 558, 576, 596, 598

Goodman v J. Eban Ltd [1954] 1 QB 550 . . . 275

Grand Junction Co Ltd v Bates [1954] 2 QB 160 . . . 843, 1004

Grant v Edwards [1986] 2 All ER 426 . . . 563, 566, 568, **568–571**, 572, 584, 591, 646, 647

Gray v Taylor [1998] 4 All ER 17 . . . 761, 762

Greasley v Cooke [1980] 3 All ER 710 . . . **406, 414–415**

Green v Ashco Horticulturist Ltd [1966] 1 WLR 889 . . . 893, 897–899

Gregory v Mighell (1811) 18 Ves328 . . . 285

Greig v Watson (1881) 7 VR 79 . . . 1017

Grigsby v Melville [1972] 1 WLR 1355 . . . 873

Grindal v Hooper, unreported, judgment 6 December 1999 . . . 470, **673–674**

Grossman v Hooper [2001] EWCA Civ 615 . . . **278–279**, 280–281

Grundt v Great Boulder Pty Gold Mines Ltd (1938) 59 CLR 641 . . . 406

Guardian Ocean Cargors Ltd v Banco Brasil SA (No 3) [1992] 2 Lloyds Rep 193 . . . 1072

Guerra v Italy (1998) 26 EHRR 357 . . . 143

H v France (1989) 12 EHRR 74 . . . 157

HSBC v Kloeckner [1990] 2 QB 514 . . . 822

Habib Bank Ltd v Tailor [1982] 1 WLR 1218 . . . 1091

Hair v Gillman (2000) 80 P & CR 108 . . . 873, 893

Halifax Building Society v Clark [1973] Ch 307 . . . 1091

Hall v Ewin (1887) 37 Ch D 74 . . . 820, 923

Hammersmith and Fulham LBC v Monk [1992] 1 AC 478 . . . 146

Hammond v Mitchell [1991] 1 WLR 1127 . . . **567**, 573, 574, 589

Hang Seng Bank v Mee Ching Development Ltd [1970] HKLR 94 . . . 1078

Hannah v Peel [1945] 1 KB 509 . . . **46–48**, 50, 52, 54

Hansford v Jargo [1921] 1 Ch 322 . . . 890

Harman v Glencross [1986] Fam 81 . . . **1012–1013**

Harris v De Pinna (1886) 33 Ch D 238 . . . 869

Harris v Flower (1904) 74 LJ Ch 127 . . . 859, 860, 862, 863

Harris v Goddard [1983] 3 All ER 242 . . . **601–602**

Harrow LBC v Qazi [2003] UKHL 43 . . . **142–143, 144–145**, 146

Hart v O'Connor [1985] AC 1000 . . . 104

Harwood v Harwood [1991] 2 FLR 274 . . . 597

Hastings and Thanet Building Society v Goddard [1970] 1 WLR 1544 . . . 1090

Hatton v UK (App No 36022/97) (2002) 34 EHRR 1; (2003) 37 EHRR 28 . . . 123, 143, **144**, 145

Hayward v Brunswick Permanent Benefit Building Society (1881) 8 QBD 403 . . . 928

Helby v Matthews [1895] AC 471 . . . 747

Hemingway Securities Ltd v Dunraven Ltd (1994) 71 P & CR 30 . . . **821**

Hentrich v France (1994) 18 EHRR 440 . . . 137, 140

Herbert v Doyle [2008] EWHC 1950 . . . 399

Hill v Griffin [1987] 1 EGLR 81 . . . 844

Hill v Tupper (1863) 2 H & C 122 . . . **64–65**, 75, 79, 80

Hindcastle Ltd v Barbara Attenborough & Associates Ltd [1997] AC 70 . . . **802**

Hitch v Stone [2001] STC 214 . . . 745

Hodgson v Marks [1971] Ch 892 . . . 19, 21, **89–92**, 104, 106, 107, 169, **177–179**, 190, 360, 364, 367, 368, 505, 511

Hoffmann v Fineberg [1949] Ch 245 . . . 834

Holland v Hodgson (1872) LR 7 CP 328 . . . 40, 41

Holliday, Re [1981] Ch 405 . . . 689

Holman v Howes [2007] EWCA 877 . . . 585

Holmes v Goring (1824) 2 Bing 76 . . . 881

Holwell Securities Ltd v Hughes [1973] 2 All ER 476 . . . 604

Holy Monasteries v Greece (1994) 20 EHRR 91 . . . 138, 157

Hooper v Sherman [1994] NPC 153 . . . 273

Horrocks v Forray [1976] 1 WLR 230 . . . 221

Horsefall v Mather (1815) Holt NP 7 . . . 717

Horsey Estate Ltd v Steiger [1899] 2 QB 79 . . . **830**, 838

Horsham Properties Group Ltd v Clark [2008] EWHC 2327 . . . 641, 1015, 1079, 1090, **1104**, 1106, 1107

Hosking v Michaelides [2004] All ER (D) 147 . . . 692

Hounslow LBC v Twickenham GD Ltd [1971] Ch 233 . . . 225, **227**

Housden v Conservators of Wimbledon and Putney Commons [2007] EWHC 1171 . . . 902

Howard E Perry v British Railway Board [1980] 1 WLR 1375 . . . 261

Howard v Fanshawe [1895] 2 Ch 581 . . . 839, 840

Howard v UK (1987) 9 EHRR 91 . . . 134, 143

Hua Chiao Commercial Bank Ltd v Chiap Hua Industries Ltd [1987] AC 99 . . . 812

Huckvale v Aegean Hotels Ltd (1989) 58 P & CR 163 . . . 881

Hughes v Waite [1957] 1 WLR 713 . . . 1083

Hughes v Metropolitan Railway Co (1877) 2 App Cas 439 . . . 385

Hunt v Luck [1902] 1 Ch 428 . . . 472, **476**

Hunter v Babbage (1995) 69 P & CR 548 . . . 612, 613

Hunter v Canary Wharf [1997] AC 655 . . . 10, 722–724, 725, 869, **905**

Huntingford v Hobbs [1993] 1 FLR 736 . . . 577, 597

Hunts Refuse Disposals Ltd v Norfolk Environmental Waste Services Ltd [1997] 1 EGLR 16 . . . **736–737**

Hurst v Picture Theatres Ltd [1915] 1 KB 1 . . . **225–226**, 260

Hussein v Mehlman [1992] 2 EGLR 87 . . . 773, 778

Hussey v Palmer [1972] 1 WLR 1286 . . . 367, **444–445**

Huyton SA v Peter Cremer & Co [1998] All ER 494 . . . 1039

Hydeshire Ltd's Application, Re (1994) 67 P & CR 93 . . . 960

Hypo Mortgage Services Ltd v Robinson [1997] 2 FLR 71 . . . 511

IDC Group v Clark (1992) 65 P & CR 179 . . . 733

IKSCON v UK (App No 20490/92) . . . 158

Ingram v IRC [2001] 1 AC 293 . . . 172, 700

International Tea Stores v Hobbs [1903] 2 Ch 165 . . . 869, **891**, 892

Inwards v Baker [1965] 2 QB 29 . . . **251–252**, 254, 392

Ivory Gate Ltd v Spetale (1999) 77 P & CR 141 . . . 827

J Sainsbury plc v Enfield LBC [1989] 1 WLR 590 . . . 941

J Willis & Sons v Willis 1986] 1 EGLR 62 . . . 420

JA Pye (Oxford) Ltd v Graham [2001] EWCA Civ 117; [2002] UKHL 30; [2003] 1 AC 419 . . . 115, 124, 129, 134, 320, **325–326**, **330**, 331–334, **335**, 346, 354, 320

JA Pye (Oxford) Ltd v UK (App No 44302/02) [2008] 1 EHRLR 132; (2008) 46 EHRR 45, Grand Chamber . . . **135–136**, **139**, 320, **346–348**, 669

Jaggard v Sawyer [1995] 1 WLR 269 . . . **955–956**, 957, 961

Jamaica Mutual Life Assurance Society v Hillsborough Ltd [1989] 1 WLR 1101 . . . 952

James Jones & Sons Ltd v Earl of Tankerville [1909] 2 Ch 440 . . . **259–260**

James v Thomas [2007] EWCA 1212; [2008] 1 FLR 1598 . . . 563, 584

James v UK (1986) 8 EHRR 123 . . . **122**, **132**, 135, **137–139**, 155, 157, 778

Javins v First National Realty (1970) 428 F 2d 1071, District of Columbia Court of Appeals . . . 717

Jennings v Rice [2003] 1 P & CR 100 . . . 252, **417–421**, 422, 425, 431, 432, 571

Jervis v Harris [1996] 1 ALL ER 303 . . . 822

Jeune v Queen's Cross Properties Ltd [1974] Ch 97 . . . 823

Jobson v Record [1998] 1 EGLR 113 . . . 862

Jones v Challenger [1960] 2 WLR 695 . . . 632

Jones v Morgan [2001] EWCA Civ 995 . . . 1039, 1058

Jones v Price [1965] 2 QB 618 . . . 870

Jordan v Money (1854) 5 HL Cas 185 . . . 391

Josceleyne v Nissen [1970] 2 QB 86 . . . 280

K, Re [1985] Ch 85 . . . 614

Karl Construction Ltd v Palisade Properties Ltd [2002] SLT 312 . . . 140

Kaur v Gill [1988] Fam 110 . . . 25

Kay v Lambeth LBC; Leeds CC v Price [2006] UKHL 10; [2006] 2 AC 465 . . . 112, **113**, 114, 117, 128, 142, 145–146, **147–151**, 153, **160**, 246, 669, 788, 1102

Keegan v UK [2007] 44 EHRR 33 . . . 143

Kelsen v Imperial Tobacco Co [1957] 2 QB 334 . . . 36

Kennedy v de Trafford [1896] 1 Ch 762 . . . 1108

Kennet Properties Ltd's Application, Re (1996) 72 P & CR 353 . . . 959–961

Kent v Kavanagh [2006] EWCA Civ 162 . . . 894, **895–897**

Keppell v Bailey (1834) 2 My & K 517 . . . **76–77**, **206**, 248, 935

Khatun v Newham LBC [2005] QB 37 . . . 778

Khatun v UK (1998) 26 EHRR CD 212 . . . 143, 145

Khorasandijan v Bush [1993] QB 727 . . . 723

Kilcarne Holdings Ltd v Targetfellow (Birmingham) Ltd [2005] EWCA 1355 . . . 457

Kilgour v Gaddes [1904] 1 KB 457 . . . 864, 909

Kinane v Mackie-Conteh [2005] EWCA Civ 45 . . . **289–291**, 292, 1006, 1008

Kinch v Bullard [1999] 1 WLR 423 . . . **603–605**

King, Re [1963] Ch 459 . . . **817–818**, 819

King v David Allan & Sons, Billposting Ltd [1916] 2 AC 54 . . . 233, **239**, 245, 250

Kingsnorth Finance v Tizard [1986] 1 WLR 783 . . . 468, **473–474**, 475–477, 510, 672

Knightsbridge Estates Trust Ltd v Byrne [1939] Ch 441 . . . **1065–1066**

Kok Hoong v Leong Cheong Kweng Mines Ltd [1964] AC 993 . . . 284

König v Federal Republic of Germany (1978) 2 EHRR 170 . . . 157

Kumar v Dunning [1989] QB 193 . . . 812, 948

Kuwaiti Airways v Iraqi Airways (Nos 4 & 5) [2002] 2 AC 883 . . . 261

L'Office Cherifien des Phosphates v Yamashita-Shinnihon Steamship Co Ltd [1994] 1 AC 486 . . . 130

Lace v Chantler [1944] KB 368 . . . 758

Ladup Ltd v William & Glynns Bank plc [1985] 1 WLR 851 . . . 839

Larkos v Cyprus: (2000) 30 EHRR 597 . . . 125

Laskar v Laskar [2008] EWCA 347; [2008] 2 P & CR 14 . . . 439, 559

Lawntown Ltd v Kamenzuli [2007] EWCA Civ 949 . . . 961

Lawrence v South County Freeholds Ltd [1939] Ch 656 . . . 948

Lee Parker v Izzet [1971] 1 WLR 1688 . . . 822

Lee's Application, Re (1996) 72 P & CR 439 . . . 960

Leigh and Sillivan Ltd v Aliakmon Shipping Co Ltd (The Aliakmon) [1986] AC 785 . . . 104

Leigh v Jack (1879) 5 Ex D 264 . . . 328, 334

Lemmon v Webb [1894] 3 Ch 1 . . . 37

Lewis v Frank Love [1961] 1 WLR 261 . . . 1063

Lithgow v UK (1986) 8 EHRR 329 . . . 123, 134

Littledale v Liverpool College [1990] 1 Ch 19 . . . 332

Liverpool City Council v Irwin [1977] AC 239 . . . 773, 871

Lloyd v Banks (1868) LR 3 Ch App 488 . . . **471**

Lloyd v Dugdale [2001] EWCA Civ 1754 . . . **200–202**, 209, **236**, 510, 769

Lloyds and Lloyds Application, Re (1993) 66 P & CR 112 . . . 961

Lloyds Bank plc v Carrick (1997) 73 P & CR 314 . . . 377, **378–379**, 489, 490, 647

Lloyds Bank Plc v Rosset [1991] 1 AC 107 . . . 285, **507**, 509, 510, **562**, 564, 647

Lloyds Bank v Byrne [1993] 1 FLR 369 . . . 680

London & Blenheim Estates Ltd v Ladbroke Retail Parks Ltd [1994] 1 WLR 31 . . . **858–859**, 873, **874**, 875–875

London & County (A&D) Ltd v Wilfred Sportsman Ltd [1971] Ch 764 . . . 818, 819

London & Regional Investments Ltd v TBI plc [2002] EWCA 355 . . . 458

London & SW Railway Co v Gomm (1882) 20 Ch D 562 . . . 207, 928

London CC v Allen [1914] 3 KB 642 . . . **924–925**

London Diocesan Fund v Phithwa [2005] UKHL 70 . . . **806–808**, 816

Long v Gowlett [1923] 2 Ch 177 . . . **894–895**

Long v Tower Hamlets LBC [1998] Ch 197 . . . 294, **765–766**

Longman v Viscount Chelsea (1989) 58 P & CR 189 . . . **296**–297

Lopez Ostra v Spain (1994) 20 EHRR 277 . . . 143

Lord Southampton v Brown (1827) 6 B & C 718 . . . 194

Lord Waring v London and Manchester Assurance Co Ltd [1935] Ch 310 . . . 1118

Lordsvale Finance Ltd v Bank of Zambia [1996] QB 752 . . . 1075

Louth v Diprose (1992) 175 CLR 621 . . . 1041

Lovelock v Margo [1963] 2 QB 786 . . . 840

Lovett v Fairclough (1991) 61 P&CR 385 . . . 320

Luker v Dennis (1877) 7 Ch D 227 . . . 923

Lumley v Gye (1853) 2 E & B 215 . . . 203, 231

Lund v Taylor (1975) 31 P & CR 16 . . . 952

Lysaght v Edwards (1876) 2 Ch D 499 . . . 373

Lyus v Prowsa Development Ltd [1982] 1 WLR 1044 . . . 201, 202, 235, 447

MCC Proceeds v Shearson Lehmann [1998] 4 All ER 675 . . . 104

MRA Engineering Ltd v Trimster (1988) 50 P & CR 1 . . . 881

Mabey v United Kingdom (1996) 22 EHRR CD 123 . . . 143

McAdams Homes Ltd v Robinson [2004] EWCA Civ 214 . . . **913–914**

McCann v UK (2008) 47 EHRR 40 . . . **126–127**

McCausland v Duncan Lawrie Ltd [1997] 1 WLR 38 . . . 271

Mcleod v UK (1990) 27 EHRR 493 . . . 143

McMorris v Brown [1999] 1 AC 142 . . . 959, 961

Macedo v Stroud [1922] 2 AC 330 . . . 194

Macepark (Whittlebury) Ltd v Sargeant (No 2) [2003] EWHC 427 . . . **861–863**

Maguire v Ito [2004] SLT (Sheri- Ct) 120 . . . 140

Maira, The [1990] 1 AC 637 . . . 1072

Malayan Credit v Chia-Mph (Jack) [1986] AC 549, PC . . . 442, 597

Malory Enterprises Ltd v Cheshire Homes (UK) Ltd [2002] Ch 216 . . . **538–539**, 540–541

Manchester Airport plc v Dutton [2000] QB 133 . . . 218, **228–229**, 230

Manjang v Drammeh (1991) 61 P & CR 194 . . . **880**, 881

Mann v Stephens (1846) 15 Sim 377 . . . 921

Mannai Investment Co Ltd v Eagle Star Life Assurance Co Ltd [1997] AC 749 . . . 831, 832

Marchant v Charters [1977] 1 WLR 1181 . . . 248, 734

Marchx v Belgium (1979) 2 EHRR 330 . . . 133, 143

Marcroft Wagons v Smith [1951] 2 KB 496 . . . 247, 734

Marquess of Zetland v Driver [1938] 1 Ch 1 . . . 927, **939–940**, 941, 946

Marsden v Edward Heyes [1927] 2 KB 1 . . . 717

Marten v Flight Refuelling Ltd [1962] 1 Ch 115 . . . 925, 927, 940, 950

Martin-Sklan v White [2006] EWHC 3313 . . . 694

Maryland Estate v Joseph [1991] 1 WLR 83 . . . 827

Massey v Boulden [2003] 1 WLR 1792 . . . 862

Matos E Silva Lda v Portugal (1996) 24 EHRR 573 . . . 132

Matthew v TH Sutton [1949] 4 All ER 793 . . . 997

Matthews v Smallwood [1910] 1 Ch 777 . . . 828, 829

Mayo, Re [1943] 1 Ch 302 . . . 632

Meadows v Clerical Medical & General Life Assurance Society [1981] Ch 70 . . . **827**

Medforth v Blake [2000] Ch 86; [1999] 3 All ER 97 . . . 1084, 1121, **1123–1124**

Melbury Road Properties 1995 Ltd v Kreidi [1999] 44 EG 157 . . . 207

Mellacher v Austria (A/169) (1990) 12 EHRR 391 . . . 123

Melville v Grapelodge Developments Ltd (1978) 39 P & CR 179 . . . 822

Meretz Investment NV v ACP Ltd [2006] EWHC 74, [2007] Ch 197 . . . 1117

Metropolitan Railway Co v Fowler [1892] 1 QB 165 . . . 864

Michael v Miller [2002] EWCA Civ 282 . . . 1114, **1115–1116**

Midland Bank plc v Cooke [1995] 4 All ER 562 . . . 577, 583

Midland Bank Trust Co Ltd v Green [1981] AC 513 . . . **174**, 175–176, 190, 203, 208, **469**, 470, **486–487**, 490, 516, 524, 675, 771

Midland Bank Trust Co Ltd v Green (No 3) [1982] 2 WLR 1; [1982] Ch 529 . . . 487

Midland Bank Trust Co Ltd v Hett, Stubbs and Kemp [1978] Ch 384 . . . 487

Midland Railway Co's Agreement, Re [1971] Ch 725 . . . 755

Mikeover v Brady [1989] 3 All ER 618 . . . **751–753**

Miles v Bull [1969] 1 QB 258 . . . **70–72**

Miles v Easter [1933] Ch 611 . . . **938**

Miller v Emcer [1956] 1 Ch 304 . . . 873

Millman v Ellis (1995) 71 P & CR 158 . . . 889

Mills v Silver [1991] Ch 271 . . . 902, **909**

Mills v Colchester Corporation (1867) LR 2 CP 476 . . . 901

Milmo v Carreras [1946] KB 306 . . . 787

Ministry of Housing and Local Government v Sharp [1970] 2 QB 223 . . . 483

Mobil Oil Co Ltd v Rawlinson (1982) 43 P & CR 221 . . . 1084

Moncrieff v Jamieson [2007] UKHL 42, [2007] 1 WLR 2620 . . . 873, **874–876**

Montrose Court Holdings Ltd v Shamash [2006] All ER D 272 . . . 873

Moody v Steggles (1879) 12 Ch D 261 . . . **865**, 867

Morland v Cook (1868) LR 6 Eq 252 . . . 928

Morrells of Oxford Ltd v Oxford United Football Club Ltd [2001] Ch 459 . . . 922, **923**

Morris v Morris [2008] EWCA 257 . . . 563

Mortgage Corporation v Shaire [2001] Ch 743 . . . 633, 677, **680–683**, 688

Mortgage Express v Mardner [2004] EWCA Civ 1859 . . . 1117

Moule v Garrett (1872) LR 7 Ex 101 . . . 802

Mounsey v Ismay (1865) 3 H & C 486 . . . 868

Mountney v Treharne [2003] Ch 135 . . . 100, 374

Multiservice Bookbinding Ltd v Marden (1979) Ch 84 . . . 1042, **1072–1074**

Murphy v Gooch [2007] EWCA 603 . . . 625

Murray Bull & Co v Murray [1953] 1 QB 211 . . . 247

Mutliservice Bookbinding Ltd v Marden [1978] Ch 84 . . . 1070, 1072

Nash v Eads (1880) 25 SJ 95 . . . 1108

National Carriers Ltd v Panalpina (Northern) Ltd [1981] AC 675 . . . 773

National Provincial Bank v Ainsworth [1965] AC 1175 . . . 12, 14, **15–18**, 22–27, **96–98**, 101, 107, 168, 169, 179, 190, 193, **206–207**, 218, **219**, 230, **242**, 243, 245, 257, 258, 537

National Provincial Building Society v Ahmed [1995] 2 EGLR 127 . . . 1090

National Trust v White [1987] 1 WLR 907 . . . 861

National Westminster Bank Ltd v Skelton [1993] 1 WLR 72 . . . 1084

National Westminster Bank Plc v Malhan [2004] EWHC 847 . . . 668–670

National Westminster Bank v Morgan [1985] AC 686 . . . 1050, 1051

Neale v Willis (1968) 19 P & CR 836 . . . **452–453**

New Pinehurst Residents Association (Cambridge) v Silow [1988] 1 EGLR 227 . . . 972

Newham LBC v Khatun [2004 EWCA Civ 55 . . . 1059

Newton Abbott Co-operative Society v Williamson & Treadgold Ltd [1952] 1 Ch 286 . . . 922, **925–927**

Nicholls v Lan [2006] EWHC 1255 . . . 694, 696

Nickerson v Barraclough [1981] Ch 426 . . . **881**

Nielson-Jones v Fedden 1975] Ch 222 . . . 600, 602, 606

Nisbet & Potts Contract, Re [1906] 1 Ch 386 . . . 336, **936**

Noakes v Rice [1902] AC 24 . . . 1067

Nocton v Lord Ashburton [1914] AC 932 . . . 448

North Sydney Printing Pty. Ltd v Sabemo Investment Corporation Pty Ltd [1971] 2 NSWLR 150 . . . 881

OBG Ltd v Allan [2008] 1 AC 1 . . . 203, 231

O'Rourke v United Kingdom (Application No 39022/97) . . . 143

Oak Co-operative Building Society v Blackburn [1968] Ch 730 . . . **484**, 485

Oceanic Village Ltd v United Attractions Ltd [2000] Ch 234 . . . 821

Odell, Re [1906] 2 Ch 47 . . . 309

Odessa, The [1916] 1 AC 145 . . . 997

Office of Fair Trading v Abbey National plc [2008] EWHC 875 . . . 1062

Official Custodian for Charities v Parway Estates Development Ltd [1984] 3 WLR 525 . . . 845

Ofulue v Bossert [2008] EWCA Civ 7 . . . 115, **124–125**, 147, **349–350**

Old Grovebury Manor Farm Ltd v W Seymour Plant Sales and Hire Ltd (No 2) [1979] 1 WLR 1397 . . . 768

Oliver v Hinton [1899] 2 Ch 264 . . . 469

Onslow v Corriw (1817) 2 Madd 330 . . . 816

Ottey v Grundy [2003] EWCA Civ 1176 . . . 424

Oughtred v IRC [1960] AC 206 . . . 374

Oun v Ahmad [2008] EWHC 545 . . . **281–282**

Oxley v Hiscock [2004] EWCA Civ 546 . . . 566, 577, **578**, 579–580, 584

P&A Swift Investments v Combined English Stores Group plc [1989] AC 632 . . . **811**, 812

P&S Platt Ltd v Crouch [2003] EWCA Civ 1110 . . . 873, 890, 895

Paddington BC v Mendelsohn (1985) 50 P & CR 244 . . . 184, 185

Page's Application, Re (1996) 71 P & CR 440 . . . 960

Palk v Mortgage Service Funding Ltd [1993] Ch 330 . . . **1080**, 1097

Pallant v Morgan [1953] 1 Ch 43 . . . 433, 446, 455–461

Palmer, Re [1994] Ch 316 . . . 610

Pao On v Lau Yiu Long [1980] AC 614 . . . 1039

Paragon Finance plc v DB Thakerar & Co [1999] 1 All ER 400 . . . **443**

Paragon Finance plc v Nash [2002] 1 WLR 685 . . . 1036, **1070–1071**

Paragon Finance v Pender [2005] EWCA Civ 760 . . . 1070

Paragon Finance v Staunton [2001] EWCA Civ 1466 . . . 1070

Parker v British Airways Board [1982] QB 1004 . . . **49–52**, 53–55, 59, 762

Parker v Taswell (1858) 2 De G & J 559 . . . 373, 769, 771

Parker-Tweedale v Dunbar Bank (No 2) [1991] Ch 12 . . . **1111–1112**

Pascoe v Turner [1979] 1 WLR 431 . . . 420

Payne v Cardi, RDC [1932] 1 KB 241 . . . 1105

Peacock v Custins [2002] 1 WLR 1815 . . . **860**, **861**, 863

Peckham v Ellison (2000) 79 P & CR 276 . . . 885

Peffer v Rigg [1977] 1 WLR 285 . . . **515–516**, 517–519, 541

Pennine Raceways Ltd v Kirklees MBC [1983] QB 382 . . . 244

Pennington v Waine [2002] 1 WLR 2075 . . . 367

Penton v Barnett [1898] 1 QB 276 . . . 828, 829

Perry v Rolfe [1848] VLR 297 . . . 1017

Pettitt v Pettitt [1970] AC 777 . . . **439**, 561, 567, 572

Pettkus v Becker (1980) 117 DLR (3d) 257 . . . 581

Philips Hong Kong Ltd v Attorney-General of Hong Kong (1993) 63 BLR 41 . . . 1058

Phillips v Mobil Oil Co Ltd [1989] 1 WLR 888 . . . 812

Phipps v Pears [1965] 1 QB 77 . . . **871–872**, **898**

Pickard v Sears (1837) 6 Ad & El 469 . . . **390**

Pickering v Rudd (1815) 4 Camp 219 . . . 37

Pilcher v Rawlins (1872) LR 7 Ch App 259 . . . 469

Pine Valley Developments Ltd v Ireland (1991) 14 EHRR 319 . . . 133, 135

Pinewood Estates, Re [1958] Ch 280 . . . 948

Piskor's Case [1954] Ch 553 . . . 170

Plimmer v Wellington Corpn (1884) 9 App Cas 699 . . . 252

Polly Peck International (No 2), Re [1998] 3 All ER 812 . . . **445**

Poplar Housing and Regeneration Community Association v Donoghue [2001] EWCA Civ 595, [2002] QB 48 . . . 112

Port Line Ltd v Ben Line Steamers Ltd [1958] 2 QB 146 . . . 207

Powell and Rayner v UK (1990) 12 EHRR 355 . . . 143, 145, 156

Powell v McFarlane (1979) 38 P&CR 452 . . . 325, 330, **331**, **332**, 333

Pretty v UK (2002) 35 ECHR 1 . . . 123

Pritchard v Briggs [1980] Ch 338 . . . 532

Proctor v Hodgson (1855) 10 Exch 824 . . . 881

Property and Bloodstock Ltd v Emerton [1968] Ch 94 . . . 1118

Prudential Assurance Ltd v London Residuary Body [1992] 2 AC 386 . . . 727, **756–758**, 767, 774, 788

Pugh v Savage [1970] 2 QB 373 . . . 910

Purbrick v London Borough of Hackney [2003] EWHC 1871 . . . 334

Purchase v Lichfield Brewery Co [1915] 1 KB 184 . . . 812

Pwllbach Colliery v Woodman [1915] AC 634 . . . **883**

Qazi v Harrow LBC [2003] UKHL 43, [2004] 1 AC 983 . . . 112, 114, 116

Quaffers Ltd, Re (1988) 56 P & CR 142 . . . 959

Quennell v Maltby [1979] 1 WLR 318 . . . **1085**, 1117

RHP Ltd v Mirror Group Newspapers and Mirror Group Holdings (1992) 65 P & CR 252 . . . 802

R v Benjafield [2002] UKHL 2 . . . 131

R v Kansal (No 2) [2001] UKHL 62 . . . 131

R v Lyons (No 3) [2002] UKHL 44 . . . 131

R v Rezvi [2002] UKHL 1 . . . 131

R (Alconbury Developments Ltd) v Secretary of State for the Environment, Transport and the Regions [2003] 2 AC 295 . . . **157**, **158–159**

R (Association of British Civilian Internees: Far East Region) v Secretary of State for Defence [2003] QB 1397 . . . 153

R (Begbie) v Secretary of State for Education and Employment [2000] 1 WLR 1115 . . . 153

R (Bugdaycay) v Secretary of State for the Home Department [1987] AC 514 . . . 153

R (Daly) v Secretary of State for the Home Department [2001] 2 AC 532 . . . 153

R (Hooper) v Secretary of State for Work and Pensions [2005] UKHL 2931 . . . **119–120**

R (RJM) v Secretary of State for Work and Pensions [2008] UKHL 63 . . . 114

R (SB) v Governors of Denbigh High School [2007] 1 AC 100 . . . 153

R (Smith) v Ministry of Defence [1996] QB 517 . . . 153

R (Sunningwell Parish Council) v Oxfordshire City Council [2000] 1 AC 335 . . . **900–901**, 910

R (Wilkinson) v Inland Revenue Commissioners [2005] 1 WLR 1718 . . . 119, 120

Radaich v Smith (1959) 101 CLR 209 . . . 720, 727

Rainbow Estates Ltd v Tokenhold Ltd 1999] Ch 64 . . . 823

Rains v Buxton (1880) 14 Ch D 537 . . . 326

Raja v Austin Gray [2003] 1 EGLR 91 . . . 1121

Ramsden v Dyson (1866) LR 1 HL 129 . . . 396

Rance v Elvin (1985) 50 P & CR 9 . . . 870

Record v Bell [1991] 1 WLR 853 . . . 278, 280

Rees Investment Ltd v Groves [2002] 1 P & CR DG 9 . . . 1091

Rees v Sherrett [2001] EWCA Civ 760 . . . 871

Reeve v Lisle [1902] AC 461 . . . 1063

Regent Oil Co Ltd v JA Gregory (Hatch End) Ltd [1966] Ch 402 . . . 1004

Reid v Bickerstaff [1909] 2 Ch 305 . . . **949–950**

Renals v Colishaw (1878) 9 Ch D 125 . . . 939, 949

Rexhaven Ltd v Nurse (1995) 28 HLR 241 . . . 846

Rhone v Stephens [1994] 2 AC 310 . . . **94–95**, 98, 193, 921, 922, **929–931**, 933

Richard Clarke & Co Ltd v Widnall [1976] 1 WLR 845 . . . 824

Rimmer v Rimmer [1953] 1 QB 63 . . . 561

Ringeisen v Austria (No 1) (1971) 1 EHRR 455 . . . 157

Roake v Chadha [1984] 1 WLR 40 . . . **943–944**, 948

Robert Leonard Developments v Wright [1994] NPC 49 . . . 277, 281

Roberts Petroleum Ltd v Bernard Kenny Ltd [1983] 2 AC 192 . . . 1012

Robertson v Fraser (1870–71) LR 6 Ch App 696 . . . 597

Rochefoucauld v Boustead [1897] 1 Ch 196 . . . 433, 436, 446, **447–448**, 449–454, 461, 519

Rodway v Landy [2001] Ch 703 . . . **625–626**, 630, 631

Roe v Siddons (1889) 22 QBD 224 . . . 864

Rogers v Hosegood [1900] 2 Ch 388 . . . 939, 940

Ropaigealach v Barclays Bank [2000] QB 263 . . . **1088–1089**, 1106

Ropemaker Properties Ltd v Noonhaven Ltd [1989] 2 EGLR 50 . . . 843

Rose v Hyman [1912] AC 623 . . . 843

Rose, Re [1949] Ch 78 . . . 305

Rowland v Environment Agency [2003] EWCA Civ 1885 . . . 133

Royal Bank of Scotland v Etridge (No 2) [2001] UKHL 44; [2002] 2 AC 773 . . . 312, 677, 1039, **1040**, 1041, 1044, 1045, **1046–1055**

Royal Brunei Airlines v Tan [1995] 2 AC 378 . . . 671

Royal Trust Co of Canada v Markham [1975] 1 WLR 1416 . . . 1087

Royal Victoria Pavilion, Ramsgate, Re [1961] Ch 58 . . . 922

Rugby School (Governors) v Tannahill [1935] 1 KB 87 . . . 832, 834, 836

SEDAC Investments Ltd v Tanner [1982] 1 WLR 1342 . . . 822

Saeed v Plustrade Ltd [2001] EWCA Civ 2011, [2002] 2 P & CR 19 . . . 873

Samuel Keller Holdings Ltd v Martins Bank Ltd [1971] 1 WLR 43 . . . 1084

Samuel v Jarrah Timber & Wood Paving Corporation Ltd [1904] AC 323 . . . **1063**

Saunders v Anglia Building Society, sub nom Gallie v Lee [1971] AC 1004 . . . 1038

Saunders v Vautier (1845) 4 Beav 115; (1845) Cr & Ph 240 . . . 540, 617

Savva v Hussein (1996) 73 P & CR 150 . . . **833**, 836

Sayers v Collyer (1885) 28 Ch D 103 . . . 958

Scala House & District Property Co Ltd v Forbes . . . 835, 837, 838

Schwann v Cotton [1916] 2 Ch 120, [1916] 2 Ch 459 . . . 870, 887

Scott v UK (App No 10741/84) . . . 133, 961

Seddon v Smith (1877) 36 LT 168 . . . 333

Segal Securities Ltd v Thoseby [1963] 1 QB 887 . . . **828–830**

Selby DC v Samuel Smith Old Brewery (Tadcaster) Ltd (2000) 80 P & CR 466 . . . 890

Selous Street Properties Ltd v Oronel Fabrics Ltd (1984) 270 EG 643, . . . 802

Semiahmoo Indian Band v Canada (1997) 148 DLR (4th) 523 . . . 448

Shah v Shah [2002] QB 35 . . . 295

Sharpe, Re [1980] 1 WLR 219 . . . 244

Shaw v Applegate [1977] 1 WLR 970 . . . 957

Shelfer v City of London Electric Lighting Co [1895] 1 Ch 287 . . . 957

Shepherd Homes Ltd v Sandham [1971] Ch 340 . . . 956

Sheppard v Turner [2006] 2 P & CR 28 . . . 960

Shiloh Spinners Ltd v Harding [1973] AC 691 . . . 468, 479, 646, 647, 845

Shropshire CC v Edwards (1982) 46 P & CR 270 . . . 948

Sidnell v Wilson [1966] 2 QB 67 . . . 974

Siew Soon Wah alias Siew Pooi Tong v Yong Tong Hong [1973] AC 836 . . . 244

Silven Properties Ltd v Royal Bank of Scotland [2003] EWCA Civ 1409 . . . **1110–1111, 1113–1114, 1121–1123**

Simmons v Dobson [1991] 1 WLR 720 . . . 909

Singh v Beggs (1996) 71 P & CR 120 . . . 271

Site Developments (Ferndown) Ltd v Barrett Homes Ltd [2007] EWHC 415 . . . 961

Skilleter v Charles [1992] 13 EG 113 . . . 972

Smith and Snipes Hall Farm Ltd v River Douglas Catchment Board [1949] 2 KB 500 . . . 938

Smith v Brudenell [2002] 2 P & CR 51 . . . **907**

Smith v United Kingdom (1999) 29 EHRR 493 . . . 153

Snaith and Dolding's Application, Re (1995) 67 P & CR 93 . . . 960

Snook v London and West Ridings Investments Ltd [1967] 2 QB 786 . . . **745**, 748

Sobey v Sainsbury [1913] 2 Ch 513 . . . 958

Sovmots Investment Ltd v Secretary of State for the Environment [1979] AC 144 . . . 888, 890

Spectrum Investment Co v Holmes [1981] 1 WLR 221 . . . **352**, 353

Spectrum Plus, Re [2005] 2 AC 580 . . . **1000–1001**

Spencer's Case (1583) 5 Co Rep 16a . . . **811**, 812, 819

Spicer v Martin (1888) 14 App Cas 12 . . . 949

Spiro v Glencrown Properties Ltd [1991] Ch 537 . . . **272**

Sporrong and Lonnroth v Sweden (1982) 5 EHRR 35 . . . **131**, 132, 136, 157, 669

Springette v Defoe (1993) 65 P & CR 1 . . . 557, 577

Stack v Dowden [2007] 2 AC 432 . . . 440, 442, 555, 558–559, **560–561, 563–564**, 566, **576**, 577, **579–580**, 581–583, **587–588**, 591, 597

Stafford v Lee (1993) 63 P & CR 172 . . . **884**

Standard Chartered Bank Ltd v Walker [1982] 1 WLR 1410 . . . 1111

Standard Property Investment plc v British Plastics Federation (1987) 53 P & CR 25 . . . 481

Stanhope v Haworth (1886) 3 TLR 34 . . . 840

Stannard v Issa [1987] AC 175 . . . 960

State Bank of India v Sood [1997] Ch 276 . . . **649–652**, 653, 669, 670

Steadman v Steadman [1976] AC 536 . . . 270, 1007

Stockholm Finance Ltd v Garden Holdings Inc [1995] NPC 162 . . . 509

Stocks v Whitgift Homes Ltd [2001] EWCA Civ 1732 . . . 947, 950

Stokes v Anderson [1991] 1 FLR 391 . . . 577

Strand Securities v Caswell [1965] Ch 958 . . . **504**, 510

Street v Mountford [1985] AC 809 . . . 214, **717–720**, 721, 725, 727, 730–734, **735**, 736–740, 750, 760, 762, 780, 782, 789, 791

Sturges v Bridgman (1879) 11 Ch D 852 . . . **906**

Sugarman v Porter [2006] EWHC 331 . . . 948

Surrey County Council v Bredero Homes Ltd [1993] 1 WLR 1361 . . . 957

Swallow Securities Ltd v Brand (1981) 45 P & CR 328 . . . 822

Swiss Bank Corp v Lloyds Bank Ltd [1979] 1 Ch 548 . . . 207, 249

Swiss Banking Corp v Lloyds Banking Ltd [1982] AC 584 . . . **998–999**

TSB plc v Marshall [1998] 2 FLR 769 . . . 682

Tanner v Tanner [1975] 1 WLR 1346 . . . **220–221**, 223

Taylor Fashions v Liverpool Victoria Trustees; Old & Campbell v Liverpool Victoria Friendly Society [1982] QB 133 . . . **401–402**, 403, 409, 432

Taylor v Dickens [1988] 1 FLR 806 . . . 407

Taylor v London and County Bankingco [1901] 2 Ch 231 . . . 469

Tecbild Ltd v Chamberlain (1969) 20 P & CR 633 . . . 328

Tehidy Minerals Ltd v Norman [1971] 2 QB 518 . . . 902, 903, 905, 915

Texaco Antilles v Kernochan [1973] AC 609 . . . 953

Texaco v Mulberry Filling Station [1972] 1 WLR 814 . . . 1070

Thames Guaranty Ltd v Campbell [1985] QB 210 . . . 1008

Thamesmead Town Ltd v Allotey (2000) 79 P & CR 557 . . . 932, **933–934**

Thomas v Hayward (1869) LR 4 Ex 311 . . . 812

Thomas v Sorrell (1673) Vaugh 330 . . . **213**

Thompson v Park [1944] KB 408 . . . **224**, 227, 717

Thorner v Curtis [2008] EWCA Civ 732; Thorner v Majors and ors [2009] UKHL 18 . . . 383, 399, 408, 432

Tichborne v Weir (1892) 67 LTR 735 . . . 336

Tinsley v Milligan [1994] 1 AC 340 . . . **441**

Titchmarsh v Royston Water Co Ltd (1899) 81 LT 673 . . . 881

Tito v Wadell (No 2) [1977] 1 Ch 106 . . . 932

Tomlin v Luce (1889) 43 Ch D 191 . . . 1108

Tool Metal Manufacturing Co Ltd v Tungsten Electric Co Ltd [1955] 1 WLR 761 . . . 392

Tootal Clothing Ltd v Guinea Property Management Ltd (1992) 64 P & CR 452 . . . **276–277**

Tophams Ltd v Earl of Sefton [1967] 1 AC 50 . . . 922

Topplan Estates v Townley [2004] EWCA 1369 . . . 334, 337

Tribe v Tribe [1996] Ch 107 . . . 442

Truman Hanbury Buxton & Co Ltd's Application, Re [1956] 1 QB 261 . . . 959

Tse Kwong Lam v Wong Chit Sen [1983] 1 WLR 1349 . . . 1114, 1117

Tulk v Moxhay (1848) 2 Ph 774 . . . 95, **205**, 250, 798, 820, 821, **921**, 922, 928, 929, 935, 973

Twentieth Century Banking Corp v Wilkinson [1977] Ch 99 . . . 1105

Twinsectra Ltd v Hynes [(1995) 71 P & CR 145 . . . 827

Twinsectra v Yardley [2002] UKHL 12 . . . 671

UBC Corporate Services Ltd v Williams [2002] EWCA Civ 555 . . . 1051

Ulrich v Ulrich and Felton [1968] 1 WLR 180 . . . 561

Ungurian v Lesnoff [1990] Ch 206 . . . **706–707**

Union Lighterage Co v London Graving Dock Co [1902] 2 Ch 577 . . . 881, **908**

United Bank of Kuwait plc v Sahib [1996] 3 WLR 472; [1997] Ch 107 . . . 381, **1007–1008**

United Bank of Kuwait v Sahib [1997] Ch 107 . . . 271

United Dominions Trust Ltd v Shellpoint Trustees Ltd [1993] 4 All ER 310 . . . 840

Universe Sentinel, The [1983] 1 AC 366 . . . **1039**

Van Haarlam v Kasner (1992) 64 P & CR 214 . . . 834, 843

Vandervell's Trusts (No 2), Re [1974] Ch 269 . . . 436

Vernon v Bethell (1761) 2 Eden 113 . . . 1055

Verrall v Great Yarmouth Borough Council [1981] QB 202 . . . **223–224**, 225, 717

Vincent v Premo Enterprises (Voucher Sales) Ltd [1969] 2 QB 609 . . . **295**

Voyce v Voyce (1991) 62 P & CR 290 . . . 431

Wainwright v Home Office [2002] QB 1334 . . . 130, 131

Wakeham v Wood (1982) 43 P & CR 40 . . . 956

Walker v Hall [1984] 1 FLR 126 . . . 577

Wall v Collins [2007] EWCA Civ 644 . . . 914

Wallingford v Mutual Society (1880) 5 App Cas 685 . . . 1075

Wallis & Simmonds (Builders) Ltd [1974] 1 All ER 561, [1974] 1 WLR 391 . . . 1007

Wallis's Cayton Bay Holiday Camp Ltd v Shell-Mex and BP Ltd [1975] 1 QB 94 . . . **328**

Walsh v Lonsdale (1882) LR 21 Ch D 9 . . . 98–100, 193, 364, 371, **372**, 373–382, 768

Waltons Stores (Interstate Ltd) v Maher (1988) 164 CLR 387 . . . 398

Wandsworth Board of Works v United Telephoneco Ltd (1884) 13 QBD 904 . . . 37, 38

Wandsworth LBC v Winder [1985] AC 461 . . . 150, 152

Ward v Kirkland [1967] 1 Ch 194 . . . **888–889**, 890, 897

Warnborough Ltd v Garmite [2003] EWCA Civ 1544 . . . **1064**

Waverley Borough Council v Fletcher [1996] QB 334 . . . **52–54**, 59

Wayling v Jones (1993) 69 P & CR 170 . . . **413–414**, 573, **575**, 576

Webb v Frank Bevis Ltd [1940] 1 All ER 247 . . . 41

Webb v Pollmount [1966] Ch 584 . . . 503

Webb's Lease, Re [1951] 1 Ch 808 . . . **885, 886**

Weg Motors Ltd v Hales [1962] Ch 49 . . . 1004

West London Commercial Bank v Reliance Permanent Building Society (1885) 29 Ch D 954 . . . 1107

Westdeutsche Landesbank Girozentrale v Islington LBC [1996] AC 669 . . . 367, 380, 436, 437, 443, **444**, 1072

Western Bank Ltd v Schindler [1977] Ch 1 . . . **1099**–1100

Westminster City Council v Clarke [1992] 2 AC 288 . . . **737–739**, 782

Whatman v Gibson (1839) 2 My & K 517 . . . 921

Wheeldon v Burrows (1878) 12 Ch D 31 . . . 853, 864, 878, 886, **887, 888**, 889–890, 894, 896

Wheeler v Saunders [1996] Ch 19 . . . 889, 890

White v Betalli [2007] NSWCA 243 . . . 876

White v Bijou Mansions Ltd [1938] Ch 351 . . . 194, 195

White v City of London Brewery (1889) 42 Ch D 237 . . . 1084

White v White [2003] EWCA 924 . . . **630–631**, 632, 634, 680

Whittingham v Whittingham [1979] Fam 21 . . . 1013

Wilkes v Spooner [1911] 2 KB 473 . . . 468

Wilkinson v West Bromwich Building Society [2005] UKHL 44 . . . 1124

Williams & Glyn's Bank v Boland [1981] AC 487 . . . 12, 14, **17–22**, 23–27, 84, 89, 179, 360, 364, 367, 368, 472, 480, **505–506**, 508, 510, 557, 624, 654, 673

Williams v Hensman (!861) J&H 546; (1861) 70 ER 862 . . . **598–599**, 605, 606, 611

Williams v Kiley (t/a CK Supermarkets Ltd) (No 1) [2003] L & TR 20 . . . 821

Williams v Staite [1979] Ch 291 . . . 252, **253**, 255

Williams v Williams [1976] 3 WLR 494 . . . 634

Wilson v First County Trust Ltd (No 2) [2003] UKHL 40 . . . **127, 129–130**, 131, 134, **156**, 160

Wilson v Secretary of State for Trade & Industry [2003] UKHL 40 . . . 668

Winter Garden Theatre (London) Ltd v Millennium Productions Ltd [1948] AC 173 . . . **215–216, 222–223, 225**

Winter v Traditional & Contemporary Contracts [2007] EWCA Civ 1088 . . . 957

Wong v Beaumont Property Trust Ltd [1965] 1 QB 173 . . . 883

Wood v Leadbitter (1845) 13 M & W 838 . . . 215, 226, 260

Wood v United Kingdom (23414/02) [2004] Po LR 326 . . . 1104

Woodall v Clifton [1905] 2 Ch 257 . . . 812

Woolwich Building Society v Brown [1996] CLC 625 . . . 1094

Wright v Macadam [1949] 2 KB 744 . . . 873, **891–893**, 899

Wroth v Tyler [1974] Ch 30 . . . 480

Wrotham Park Estate Co Ltd v Parkside Homes Ltd [1974] 1 WLR 798 . . . **927–928**, 956

X (Minors) v Bedfordshire County Council [1995] 2 AC 633 . . . 114

X and Y v Netherlands (1985) 8 ECRR 235 . . . 144

YL v Birmingham CC [2007] UKHL 27, [2008] 1 AC 95 . . . 113

Yanner v Eaton (1999) 201 CLR 351 . . . 32

Yaxley v Gotts [2000] 1 Ch 162 . . . **284–287**, 288–292, 449

Yeoman's Row Management Ltd v Cobbe [2008] 1 WLR 1752 . . . 283, **291**, 383, **392–397**, 398–400, 403, 406, **407**, 408, **409**, 416, 421, 431, 432, **443**, 458, 537, 769, 1008

Yorkshire Bank Plc v Hall [1999] 1 WLR 1713 . . . 1123

Yorkshire Railway Co v Maclure (1882) 21 Ch D 309 . . . 747

Zumtobel v Austria (1993) 17 EHRR 116 . . . 158

TABLE OF STATUTES

Page references in **bold** indicate that the text is reproduced in full
Articles of the European Convention on Human Rights are tabled under Sch 1, Human Rights Act 1998

Statutes

Access to Neighbouring Land Act 1992 . . . 877
Administration of Estates Act 1925
  s 9(1)(ii) . . . 641
Administration of Justice Act 1970 . . . 1025
  s 36 . . . 1080, **1086**, 1088, 1090, 1091, 1097, 1101, 1104, 1125
  s 39(1) . . . 1090
Administration of Justice Act 1973
  s 8 . . . **1091**, 1092

Banking Act 1987 . . . 1033
Banking (Special Provisions) Act 2008 . . . 13
Bankruptcy Act 1914 . . . 610
Building Societies Act 1986 . . . 1033

Capital Transfer Tax Act 1984 . . . 481
Charging Orders Act 1979 . . . 1010
  s 1(1) . . . **1010**
  s 1(5) . . . **1011**
  s 2(1)(a) . . . 1011
  s 3(4) . . . 1011
  s 3(5) . . . 1011, 1013
Children Act 1989 . . . 635
  s 15 . . . 221
  Sch 1 . . . 221, 634
Civil Aviation Act 1949
  s 40 . . . 38
  s 76(1) . . . 156
Civil Partnership Act 2004
  s 82 . . . 25, 256
  Sch 5 . . . 587
  Sch 5, para 2 . . . 557, 634
  Sch 5, para 3 . . . 634
  Sch 9, para 1 . . . 25, 256
Common Law Procedure Act 1852
  s 210 . . . 830
  s 212 . . . 839
Commonhold and Leasehold Reform Act 2002 . . . 965, 966, 971
  s 3(1)(b) . . . 976
  s 7(3) . . . 976

s 8 . . . 976
s 9 . . . 976
s 9(3)(f) . . . 976
s 10 . . . 976
s 14 . . . **982**
s 15(2) . . . **977**
s 16(1) . . . **981**
s 16(2) . . . **981**
s 16(3) . . . **982**
s 17(1) . . . 977
s 17(5) . . . 977
s 20(1) . . . 977
s 20(2) . . . 977
s 21 . . . 971, 977
s 21(1) . . . **978**
s 21(2) . . . **978**
s 22 . . . 977
s 22(1) . . . **978**
s 23 . . . 976
s 24 . . . 976
s 25 . . . 976
s 25(3) . . . 976
s 26 . . . **982**
ss 27–29 . . . 978
s 30 . . . 976
s 31 . . . **980**
s 35 . . . **984**
s 35(3)(b) . . . 985
s 38(1) . . . **983**
s 39 . . . **983**
s 39(4) . . . 983
s 42 . . . 985
s 51 . . . 980
s 119 . . . 969
s 120 . . . 969
s 156 . . . 972
s 162 . . . 972
s 167 . . . 973
Sch 1 . . . 975, 979
Sch 2 . . . 975, 979
Sch 3 . . . 981, 985
Criminal Law Act 1977
  s 6 . . . 4, 246, 838, 1086

Commons Registration Act 1965 . . . 304, 512
Consumer Credit Act 1974 (CCA 1974) . . . 134,
    1023, 1024, 1026, 1081
    s 8 . . . 1032
    s 16(6C) . . . 1033
    s 16A . . . 1033
    s 16B . . . 1032
    s 32 . . . 1035
    s 33A-33E . . . 1035
    s 36 . . . 1034
    s 36B-36F . . . 1035
    s 40(1) . . . 1034
    s 55 . . . 1035
    s 58 . . . 1035
    s 60 . . . 1035
    s 61 . . . 1035
    s 62 . . . 1035
    s 64 . . . 1035
    s 65 . . . 1036
    s 67 . . . 1035
    s 68 . . . 1035
    s 76 . . . 1035, 1086
    s 77 . . . 1035
    s 77A . . . 1035
    s 78 . . . 1035
    s 86B-86E . . . 1035, 1086
    s 87 . . . 1035, 1036, 1086
    s 88 . . . 1035, 1086
    s 88B . . . 1036, 1106
    s 88C . . . 1036, 1106
    s 88D(3) . . . 1036
    s 88D(4) . . . 1036
    s 92 . . . 1036
    s 105 . . . 1035, 1036
    s 126 . . . 1036, 1086
    s 127 . . . 1036
    s 127(3) . . . 129
    s 129 . . . 1088
    s 130 . . . 1088
    s 135 . . . 1036
    s 136 . . . 1036
    ss 137–140 . . . 1036
    s 140A . . . **1036**, 1037, 1059, 1067, 1072, 1075
    s 140A(5) . . . 1033
    s 140A-140C . . . 1033, 1058
    s 140B(1) . . . 1037
    Sch 1 . . . 1062
Consumer Credit Act 2006 (CCA 2006) . . . 1027
    s 15 . . . 129
    ss 59–61 . . . 1036
Contract (Rights of Third Parties) Act 1999 . . .
    236, 820, 954
    s 1 . . . **195**, 232, **954**

    s 2(1) . . . 233
Conveyancing Act 1882 . . . 808
Conveyancing Act 1911 . . . 808
    s 3 . . . 469
Conveyancing and Law of Property Act 1881
    s 6 . . . 891
    s 58 . . . 941, 945
Countryside and Rights of Way Act 2000 . . . 854
County Court Act 1984
    s 138(2) . . . 839
    s 138(3) . . . 839
    s 138(9A) . . . 840
    s 139(2) . . . 840

Defective Premises Act 1972 . . . 822

Electricity Act 1989 . . . 854
Electronic Communications Act 2000
    s 7(2) . . . 316
    s 7(3) . . . 316
Enterprise Act 2002 . . . 691, 996
    s 8 . . . 1035
Environmental Protection Act 1990
    ss 79–82 . . . 778
European Communities Act 1972
    s 3(1) . . . 113

Family Law Act 1996 . . . 501, 634, 723, 1013
    s 30 . . . 256, **257**, 259, 585
    s 30(1) . . . **586**
    s 30(9) . . . **586**
    s 31 . . . **258**
    s 33 . . . 25, 257, 628
    s 33(5) . . . 586
    s 35 . . . 586
    s 36 . . . 586
    s 55(2) . . . 1090
    s 56(1) . . . 1090
    s 56(2) . . . 1090
    s 62(3) . . . 628
Financial Services and Markets Act 2000 (FSMA
    2000) . . . 1023, 1024, 1026, 1067, 1081
    s 2(21)(c) . . . 1028
    s 5(2) . . . 1028
    ss 8–10 . . . 1029
    s 19 . . . 1028
    s 20(1) . . . 1028
    s 22 . . . 270
    s 23 . . . 1028
    s 26 . . . 1028
    s 28 . . . 1028
    s 56 . . . 1028
    s 64 . . . 1028

s 64(8) ... 1029
s 66 ... 1029
s 71 ... 1028
s 138 ... 1028
s 150 ... 1029
s 229 ... 1031
s 232 ... 1031

Gas Act 1986 ... 854
Grantee of Reversions Act 1540 ... 808

Housing Act 1974 ... 971
Housing Act 1980 ... 6, 971
Housing Act 1985 ... 6, 721, 764
 Pt IV ... 737
 s 79(1) ... 782
 s 79(3) ... 782
 s 80 ... 782
 s 81 ... 782
 s 84 ... 146
 s 609 ... 925
Housing Act 1988 ... 780
Housing Act 1996 ... 971
 s 81 ... 973
Housing Act 2004 ... 1019
Housing Finance Act 1971 ... 971
Housing and Regeneration Act 2008 ... 795
Human Rights Act 1998 ... 110, 638, 676, 823
 s 2 ... 109, 124
 s 3 ... 109, 114–116, 129, 149, 152, 329, 668, 694
 s 3(1) ... **114**, 130
 s 3(2) ... **115**, 130
 s 4 ... 118, 152, 668
 s 6 ... 109, **111**, 114–116, 130, 131, 152
 s 6(1) ... 118
 s 6(2) ... **118**, 119, 120
 s 6(3) ... 112, 113
 s 7(1) ... 112, 120, 149
 s 7(7) ... 112
 s 8 ... 112
 s 22(4) ... 130
 Sch 1 ECHR ... 110
 Art 1 ... 129, 133
 Art 3 ... 121
 Art 4 ... 121
 Art 6 ... 109, 129
 Art 6(1) ... **155**, 157–158
 Art 8 ... 10, 109–111, 115, 117, 121, 122, 125,
  126, 128, 129, **140**, 141, 144, 147, 150, 153,
  156, 161, 162, **245**, 668, 669, 694, 696, 1102,
  1103
 Art 8(1) ... 142, 143

 Art 8(2) ... 143–146, 154
 Art 10 ... 111
 Art 11 ... 111
 Art 14 ... 109–111, 115, **154**, 155, 162, 668–670,
  1105
 Art 34 ... 112
 Protocol 1, Art 1 ... 109, 110, 121, 122, **131**, 153,
  156, 161, 162, 246, 346, 668, 669, 778, 880,
  1102, 1104
 Protocol 12 ... 154

Inheritance Tax Act 1984
 s 49 ... 701
Inheritance (Provision for Family and
 Dependants) Act 1975 ... 26, 414
Insolvency Act 1986 ... 676
 s 122 ... 979
 s 124 ... 979
 s 283A ... 691
 s 306 ... 610
 s 313A ... 691
 s 335A ... 678, 680, 689–697
 s 335A ... **689**
 s 336 ... 693
 s 421A ... 610
 Sch BI ... 996
Insolvency Act 2000 ... 610
Insolvency Act 2006
 s 72A ... 1120
Interpretation Act 1978
 s 6 ... 645
 s 6(3) ... 653

Land Charges Act 1925 ... 175
 s 10(1) ... 946
 s 13(2) ... 174
 s 17 ... 484
 s 20(8) ... 174
 s 101 ... 936
Land Charges Act 1972 ... 167, 465, 477, 516, 524,
 709, 770
 s 2(1) ... **478**
 s 2(4) ... **478**, 771
 s 2(5) ... **478**, 936, 946
 s 2(4)(iv) ... 378, 479
 s 2(7) ... **479**
 s 3(1) ... **481**, 482
 s 4 ... 486
 s 4(5) ... **480**, 490
 s 4(6) ... 490
 s 6(1)(a) ... 1011
 s 9 ... 482
 s 10 ... 482, 484

s 10(4) . . . **482**
s 11(5) . . . **483**
s 11(6) . . . **483**
s 17 . . . 479, 481

Land Registration Act 1925 (LRA 1925)
s 3 . . . 515
s 5 . . . 539
s 18 . . . 644
s 20 . . . 515, 539
s 50 . . . 946
s 59 . . . 515
s 69 . . . 538, 539, 541
s 69(1) . . . 540
s 70 . . . 181, 655
s 70(1) . . . 544
s 70(1)(a) . . . 513
s 70(1)(g) . . . 177, 179, 181, 504, 506, 507, 656
s 70(1)(k) . . . 188
s 74 . . . 515
s 75 . . . 135, **337**, 339, 351, 353
s 75(1) . . . 338
s 75(2) . . . 338

Land Registration Act 2002 (LRA 2002) . . . 139,
    167, 856
s 2 . . . **301**, 302
s 3 . . . 301, 302
s 4 . . . 302, 467, 708, 764, 913
s 4(1) . . . **302**, 532
s 4(1)(g) . . . 1003
s 4(2 . . . **302**
s 11 . . . 303, 946
s 12 . . . 303
s 23 . . . 533, 658, 663
s 23(1) . . . **495, 662, 1003**
s 23(2) . . . **495, 662**
s 23(3) . . . **663**
s 24 . . . 495, 533
s 26 . . . 495, 658, **663**, 664, 670
s 27 . . . **536**, 764, 877
s 27(1) . . . **303**, 304, 313
s 27(2) . . . **303**, 502, 513, 532
s 27(7) . . . 891
s 28 . . . 175, 493
s 28(1) . . . **169**, 493
s 28(2) . . . **169**, 494
s 29 . . . 494, 514, 515, 518, 936
s 29(1) . . . **175**, 177, **496**
s 29(2) . . . **176**, 177, **496**, 911
s 29(3) . . . **176**, **496**
s 29(4) . . . **176**, **496**, 769
s 30 . . . 176, 494, 514, 518
s 32 . . . **500**, 708

ss 32–34 . . . 936, 1011
ss 32–39 . . . 378
s 33 . . . **500**, 672
s 34 . . . 501
s 35 . . . 501
s 35(3) . . . 502
s 36 . . . 501
s 37 . . . 501
s 40 . . . **497**
ss 40–47 . . . 495
s 41 . . . **498**
s 42 . . . 497
s 42(1)(c) . . . 1011
s 43 . . . **497**
s 44 . . . 1011
s 44(1) . . . **498**
s 51 . . . **1003**
s 52 . . . 662, **1119**
s 58 . . . **533**, 538, 541, 764
s 70 . . . 514
s 72 . . . 514
s 73 . . . 502
s 74 . . . 304
s 91 . . . **315**
s 93(1) . . . **313**
s 93(2) . . . **313**, 314, 536
s 93(4) . . . 313
s 96 . . . **186**, 245
s 115 . . . 93
s 116 . . . 93, 133, 245, 255, **428**, 429–432
s 131 . . . 308
s 132(1) . . . 494
Sch 1, para 3 . . . 913
Sch 3 . . . 378, 503
Sch 3, para 1 . . . **187**, 503, 535, 708
Sch 3, para 2 . . . 177, **503**, 508, 672, 708, 770
Sch 3, para 3 . . . **189, 512, 912**
Sch 4 . . . 533
Sch 4, para 1 . . . **309**, 538
Sch 4, para 2 . . . 308, **309**
Sch 4, para 3 . . . 310
Sch 5, para 9 . . . 549
Sch 6 . . . 339, 343, 348, 354
Sch 6, paras 1–4 . . . **341**
Sch 6, para 5 . . . **342**
Sch 6, para 9 . . . 346, 494
Sch 6, para 11 . . . 324
Sch 6, para 13 . . . 342
Sch 8 . . . 300
Sch 8, para 1 . . . **309**
Sch 8, para 3 . . . **310**
Sch 8, para 5 . . . **310**

Sch 12, para 18 . . . **339**
Sch 12, para 20 . . . 802
Land Registry Act 1862 . . . 298, 525
Land Transfer Act 1875 . . . 298
Land Transfer Act 1897 . . . 300
Landlord and Tenant Act 1927
   s 18 . . . 822
Landlord and Tenant Act 1985 . . . 971
   s 11 . . . 721, **781**, 783–786, 789, 791, 794
   s 18(1) . . . **971**
   s 19(1) . . . **972**
   s 19(2) . . . **972**
   s 20 . . . 972
   s 20ZA . . . 972
   s 21 . . . 972
   s 21A . . . 972
   s 21B . . . 972
   s 22 . . . 972
   s 27A . . . 972
   s 30A . . . 972
   Sch 1, para 9 . . . 972
Landlord and Tenant Act 1987 . . . 971
   s 35 . . . 973
   s 42 . . . 972
   s 42A . . . 972
   s 42B . . . 972
Landlord and Tenant (Covenants) Act 1995 . . .
501, 849
   s 2(1) . . . **814**
   s 3 . . . 797, **813**
   s 3(5) . . . 820, **821**
   s 4 . . . 814
   s 5 . . . 797, **804**, 817
   s 6 . . . 797, **805**, 817
   s 8 . . . 797, **805**, 808
   s 16 . . . 804
   s 17 . . . 803, 804
   s 18 . . . 803
   s 19 . . . 804
   s 23 . . . **817**
   s 25 . . . 805, 806
   s 27 . . . 804
   s 28(1) . . . **814**
Law of Property Act 1922
   s 96(3) . . . 945
Law of Property Act 1925 (LPA 1925) . . . 79, 81
   s 1 . . . 69, 72, 87, 219, 239, 730, 736, 755
   s 1(1) . . . 70, **78**, 85, 704, 823
   s 1(2) . . . **78**, 85, 93, 95
   s 1(2)(b) . . . 304
   s 1(3) . . . 704, 974
   s 1(5) . . . 974

s 1(6) . . . **595**
s 2 . . . 87, 179, 182, 638, **639**, 645, 659, 664
s 2(1) . . . 640
s 2(3) . . . 640
s 4 . . . 219, 249
s 4(1) . . . **95**, 240
s 4(5)-(6) . . . **481**
s 14 . . . 654, 655
s 27 . . . 181, 182, 639, 645, 655, 656
s 27(1) . . . 641, **642**, 671
s 27(2) . . . **648**, 652, 653
s 28 . . . 180, 655, 660, 661
s 28(1) . . . 181, 656, 709
s 30 . . . 620, 632, 680, 681, 684, 688, 692, 1012
s 34(2) . . . **596**, 750, 751
s 36(2) . . . **595, 599**, 602, 605, 606, 613
s 40 . . . 270, 273–275, 388, 612
s 52 . . . 188, **293**, 399, 708, 764, 788, 1016
s 52(2) . . . 320
s 53 . . . 91, 188, 197, 449
s 53(1) . . . 91, **361**
s 53(1)(a) . . . 99, 100, 361, 364, 365, 769, 935,
   1009
s 53(1)(b) . . . 88, 92, 361, 362, 365, 435, 436, 449,
   454, 558, 706
s 53(2) . . . **89, 100, 362, 436**, 449, 558
s 54 . . . 188, 197, 198, **293**, 708, 764, 788
s 54(2) . . . 294, 366, 375, 377, 467, 536, **765**,
   766–768
s 56 . . . 194–196, 820, 954
s 56(1) . . . **195, 953**, 954
s 62 . . . 853, 878, 879, 890-899, 912, 948
s 62(1) . . . **890**
s 63 . . . 948
s 77(1)(c) . . . 802
s 78 . . . 937, **941**, 942–942, 946, 947, 962, 964
s 78(1) . . . 945
s 79 . . . 923, 942–944, 964
s 79(1) . . . **922,** 945
s 84 . . . 857, 915, 917, 958, 963
s 84(1) . . . 958, **959**, 961
s 84(1A) . . . **960**
s 84(1B) . . . **960**
s 84(3) . . . 959
s 84(7) . . . 959
s 85(1) . . . **1002**
s 85(2) . . . **1003**
s 86 . . . 1002
s 87(1) . . . **1004**, 1015, 1078, 1083, 1102
s 88(1) . . . **1106**
s 88(2) . . . 1078
s 88(6) . . . 1006

s 89(2) . . . 1078
s 91 . . . 1098, 1125
s 91(1) . . . **1097**
s 91(2) . . . **1097**
s 93 . . . 1017
s 101 . . . 1079
s 101(1) . . . **1079**
s 101(1)(i) . . . 1077, 1119
s 101(1)(iii) . . . 1077, 1120
s 101(3) . . . 1079
s 101(4) . . . 1079
s 103 . . . **1105**
s 104 . . . 1107, 1117, **1118**
s 105 . . . **1107**
s 107(1) . . . 1107
s 109 . . . **1120**
s 115 . . . 1016
s 141 . . . 797, 808, **809**, 810–812
s 142 . . . 797, 808, 811, 812
s 142(1) . . . **808**
s 146 . . . 822, 842, 843, 849, 944
s 146(1) . . . **831**, 832–837, 841, 973
s 146(2) . . . 838, **840**, 845
s 146(4) . . . **844**, 845
s 146(5) . . . **844**
s 149(6) . . . **758**, 759
s 146(7) . . . 824
s 146(9) . . . 831
s 146(10) . . . 831
s 184 . . . **598**
s 193 . . . 854
s 193(4) . . . 907, 908
s 196 . . . 602
s 196(3) . . . **603**
s 196(4) . . . **603**
s 198 . . . 485
s 198(1) . . . **480**
s 199 . . . **471**, 474, 476, **477**
s 205(1)(xxi) . . . 653
s 205(1)(xxvii) . . . 718, 766
Law of Property Act 1969
  s 23 . . . 467
  s 24 . . . 482
  s 25 . . . 485
Law of Property (Amendment) Act 1924 . . . 945
Law of Property (Joint Tenants) Act 1964 . . . 673, 675
  s 1 . . . **672**
Law of Property (Miscellaneous Provisions) Act 1989 (LP(MP)A 1989) . . . 233
  s 1 . . . **294**
  s 2 . . . 99, **269,** 270, 271–295, 317, 361, 363–365, 381, 388, 393, 398, 399, 419, 421, 449, 536, 612, 708, 764, 768, 788

s 2(1) . . . 134, 1006
Leasehold Property (Repairs) Act 1938 . . . 822
  s 1 . . . **973**
Leasehold Reform Act 1967 . . . 122, 135, 137, 778, 969
  s 8 . . . **894**
  s 10 . . . 894
Leasehold Reform Housing and Urban Development Act 1993 . . . 969
  s 87 . . . **971**
Limitation Act 1623 . . . 900
Limitation Act 1939 . . . 328
  s 10 . . . 327
Limitation Act 1980 . . . 353
  s 8(4) . . . 334, 335
  s 15 . . . 135, 336, 340
  s 15(1) . . . **185**, 186, 324
  s 17 . . . 135, 185, **186**, 324, 336, 340
  s 18 . . . 186
  s 20(1) . . . 1124
  s 20(5) . . . 1124
  s 28 . . . **336**
  s 29 . . . 337
  s 32 . . . 337
  Sch 1, para 1 . . . **325**
  Sch 1, para 5 . . . 765
  Sch 1, para 8(1) . . . **325**
  Sch 1, para 8(4) . . . **328**
  Sch 1, para 9 . . . 337
  Sch 1, para 10 . . . 337
Lord Cairns Act 1858 (Chancery Amendment Act 1858) . . . 957

Married Women's Property Act 1882 . . . 601
Matrimonial Causes Act 1973 . . . 26, 582
  s 23 . . . 557, 601
  s 24 . . . 601, 634
Matrimonial Homes Act 1967 . . . 25
Moneylenders Act 1900 . . . 1072

Occupiers Liability Act 1984 . . . 871

Party Walls Act 1996 . . . 877
Perpetuities and Accumulations Act 1964 . . . 703
Postal Services Act 2000 . . . 603
Prescription Act 1832 . . . 901, 902, 905
  s 2 . . . 908
Protection from Eviction Act 1977 . . . 778, 792, 838
  s 1 . . . 4, 10
  s 1(2) . . . 246
  s 1(3) . . . 1086
  s 3A . . . 246
  s 5(1A) . . . 246

Protection from Harassment Act 1997 . . . 723

Real Property Limitation Act 1833 . . . 328
Rent Act 1977 . . . 39, 155, 721, 740, 779
  s 2(1) . . . 115
  s 2(2) . . . 115
Rentcharges Act 1977 . . . 78
  s 2(1) . . . 935
  s 2(2) . . . 935
  s 2(3)(c) . . . 935
  s 2(4)(b) . . . 935
  s 2(5) . . . 935

Settled Land Act 1925 . . . 181, 501, 707
  s 1(1) . . . 709
  s 1(7) . . . 621, 709
  s 4 . . . 709
  s 19(1) . . . 709
  s 26 . . . 709
  s 72 . . . 641, 651
Statute Law Revision (No 2) Act 1888 . . . 901
Statute Law Revision Act 1890 . . . 901
Statute of Frauds 1677 . . . 267, 274, 275, 449
  s 3 . . . 91
  s 7 . . . 91, 362
  s 8 . . . 91
  s 9 . . . 91
Statute of Gloucester 1278 . . . 718
Statute of Merton 1235 . . . 900
Statute of Westminster 1275 . . . 900
Supreme Court of Judicature Acts 1873–75 . . . 58

Telecommunications Act 1984 . . . 854
Torts (Interference with Goods) Act 1977
  s 3 . . . 261
Town and Country Planning Act 1990
  s 106 . . . 925
Tribunals, Courts and Enforcement Act 2007
  ss 71–80 . . . 823
Trustee Act 1925
  s 17 . . . 659
  s 34(2) . . . **595**, 596, 702
Trustee Act 2000
  s 1 . . . 659
Trusts of Land and Appointment of Trustees Act
  1996 (TOLATA 1996) . . . 85, 619, 709, 753, 1105
  s 1 . . . **621**
  s 1(2)(a) . . . 435, 710
  s 1(2)(b) . . . 710
  s 1(3) . . . 710
  s 3 . . . 620, 642
  s 4 . . . 623
  s 5 . . . 657

  s 6 . . . **622**, 643, 658
  s 6(1) . . . **85**
  s 6(5) . . . 659, 710
  s 6(6) . . . **85**, 659, 710, 711
  s 7 . . . 617
  s 7(1)-(5) . . . **617**
  s 8 . . . 622, 623, **660**, 710
  s 11 . . . 623
  s 12 . . . 585, **624**, 628, 657
  s 12(1) . . . 627
  s 13 . . . 624, 626, 657
  s 13(3) . . . 625
  s 13(6) . . . 625
  s 14 . . . 585, 620, 629, 630, 633, 676, 677, 685,
    689, 1090
  s 15 . . . 585, 620, **629**, 631–632, 676–696, 1090
  s 15(1)(c) . . . 631
  s 15(3) . . . 711
  s 16 . . . 658, **661**, 670
  Sch 1, para 5 . . . 704

Unfair Contract Terms Act 1977 . . . 750, 779
Usury Laws Repeal Act 1854 . . . 1001

Water Industry Act 1991 . . . 854

Statutory Instruments

Consumer Credit (Exempt Agreements) Order
  2007 (SI 2007/1168) . . . 1033

Financial Services and Markets Act 2000
  (Regulated Activities) Order 2001
  (SI 2001/544) . . . 1027
  art 61 . . . **1027**

Land Registration Fee Order 2006 (SI 2006/1332)
  . . . art 2(6) . . . 301
Land Registration Rules 2003 (SI 2003/1417)
  r 74 . . . 912
  r 86(3) . . . 501
  rr 147–154 . . . 514
  r 189 . . . 342

Registration of Title Order 1989 (SI 1989/1347)
  . . . 301

Unfair Terms in Consumer Contracts
  Regulations 1999 (SI 1999/2083) . . . 778, 779,
  794, 1037, 1058
  reg 3 . . . 795
  reg 5 . . . **1059**
  reg 5(1) . . . 1061
  reg 5(2) . . . 1060

reg 6 . . . **1060**
reg 6(2) . . . 1060
reg 7 . . . **1062**
reg 8 . . . 1059
regs 10–15 . . . 1059
Sch 2 . . . 1061
Sch 2, para 1 . . . 1075

Sch 2, para 2 . . . 1070
Unfair Practices Regulations 2008 (SI 2008/1277)
. . . 1058, 1059
reg 3 . . . 1063
reg 5 . . . 1063
reg 6 . . . 1063
reg 7 . . . 1063

LIST OF ABBREVIATIONS

AALR	Anglo-American Law Review
APR	annual percentage rate
BERR	Department of Business Enterprise and Regulatory Reform
CBLJ	Canadian Business Law Journal
CCA 1974	Consumer Credit Act 1974
CCA 2006	Consumer Credit Act 1006
CLJ	Cambridge Law Journal
ECHR	European Convention on Human Rights
FLA 1996	Family Law Act 1996
FSA	Financial Services Authority
FSMA 2000	Financial Services and Markets Act 2000
FSO	Financial Services Ombudsman
HRA 1998	Human Rights Act 1998
LCA 1925	Land Charges Act 1925
LCA 1972	Land Charges Act 1972
LPA 1925	Law of Property Act 1925
LPA 1969	Law of Property Act 1969
LP(MP)A 1989	Law of Property (Miscellaneous Provisions) Act 1989
LQR	Law Quarterly Review
LRA 1925	Land Registration Act 1925
LRA 2002	Land Registration Act 2002
LS	Legal Studies
MCOB	Mortgage Conduct of Business Sourcebook
MLR	Modern Law Review
OFT	Office of Fair Trading
TOLATA 1996	Trusts of Land and Appointment of Trustees Act 1996

LIST OF ABBREVIATIONS

AALR	Anglo-American Law Review
APR	annual percentage rate
DCLR	Department of Constitutional Affairs and Regulatory Reform
CBLJ	Canadian Business Law Journal
CCA 1974	Consumer Credit Act 1974
CCA 2006	Consumer Credit Act 2006
CLP	Current Legal Problems
ECHR	European Convention on Human Rights
FLA 1996	Family Law Act 1996
FSA	Financial Services Authority
FSMA 2000	Financial Services and Markets Act 2000
FOS	Financial Services Ombudsman
HRA 1998	Human Rights Act 1998
LCA 1925	Land Charges Act 1925
LCA 1972	Land Charges Act 1972
LPA 1925	Law of Property Act 1925
LPA 1969	Law of Property Act 1969
LP(MP)A 1989	Law of Property (Miscellaneous Provisions) Act 1989
LQR	Law Quarterly Review
LRA 1925	Land Registration Act 1925
LRA 2002	Land Registration Act 2002
LS	Legal Studies
MCOB	Mortgage Conduct of Business Sourcebook
MLR	Modern Law Review
OFT	Office of Fair Trading
TOLATA 1996	Trusts of Land and Appointment of Trustees Act 1996

PART A

INTRODUCTION

1

WHAT'S SPECIAL
ABOUT LAND?

CENTRAL ISSUES

1. This introductory chapter aims to show the importance of land, and hence of land law. It focuses on the features that make land special and the distinctive legal rules produced by those features. By considering some specific examples, it also shows how and why land law can give rise to very difficult questions of both doctrine and policy.

2. This chapter thus helps to answer an important question: why is it worth studying land law? Firstly, the special features of land mean that rules regulating the use of land are very important *in practice*. Secondly, those special features mean that the rules are *analytically* interesting: they try to perform the very difficult job of balancing the interests of a number of deserving parties. Thirdly, although many land law rules are rooted in tradition, the practical importance of land law means that the rules must change in response to new social and economic conditions. This means that land law can be a *topical* and *lively* subject.

3. In this chapter, our focus is on what makes land (and thus land law) special. In Chapter 2, we will focus on those key aspects of land law that apply more widely and so also arise when considering other forms of property. This gives us a further important reason for studying land law: it is a very useful way in which to learn about core concepts that apply not only where land is concerned, but in many other situations as well.

4. In this chapter, we will look at particular situations that show the sharp debates and difficult questions that can arise in land law. In later chapters, we will return to each of those situations in more detail and closely examine the relevant legal rules. Our purpose here, however, is to look at those situations more generally and to see what they can tell us about the special concerns of land law.

1 THE IMPORTANCE OF LAND

No one needs to be told that land is important. In fact, in the United Kingdom, land is something of a national obsession. We would not necessarily think it odd if a friend were to spend the morning on some do-it-yourself jobs in her house, stop to look in the windows of a local estate agency whilst out for lunch, come back to do some gardening in the afternoon, and then spend the evening watching a television programme about the property market, and playing a board game based on buying land and renting out houses in London. And that is only at the weekend, when she is not out at work earning money to make her mortgage payments. And, of course, land can be even more important for those who are not fortunate enough to own a home: a tenant may worry that his landlord will fail to make the necessary repairs to his roof or is about to raise his rent, while someone with nowhere at all to live will face the more urgent task of finding shelter for the night.

So, whilst we may sometimes take it for granted, land is always there: under our noses, beneath our feet, and perhaps even in our souls. As a result, land looms large in much of the law. For example, in the law of torts, occupiers' liability forms a discrete area due to the special responsibilities placed on those with control of land. Conversely, the criminal law gives special protection to a residential occupier of land: if another party uses force or the threat of force to come onto land despite the objections of the occupier, that party can be guilty of a special criminal offence.[1] In the law of contract, special rules regulate agreements relating to land: the importance of land is recognized by the requirement that contracts to sell land must be made in writing, signed by both vendor and purchaser. In administrative and public law, special responsibilities are placed on local authorities, in certain circumstances, to provide accommodation to those with nowhere to live.

2 THE SCOPE OF THIS BOOK

This book cannot focus on all of the varied areas of law in which land is important. Its focus instead is on the special rules that govern *private rights to use land*. By 'private' rights, we mean the rights that, in theory, *any* of us might acquire. For example, the government or a local authority may have a statutory power to acquire land for particular purposes: for example, the London Development Agency, by means of compulsory purchase orders approved by the Secretary of State for Trade and Industry in 2005, is permitted to buy land needed for use in connection with the 2012 Olympics, even if the current owners of that land do not agree to sell. Such special powers to use land are *not* considered in this book.

Similarly, we will not examine the various tort claims that may arise against an occupier of land: if you are injured at a friend's house and claim damages from her, you claim a right to be paid money, not a right to use her land. Nor will we look at the special crimes that may apply where land is concerned: to be seen as criminal, a party's conduct must be deserving of public sanction; it is not enough for that conduct simply to interfere with another party's rights. And we will not look directly at the special statutory responsibilities placed on local authorities: those duties do not necessarily respond to any individual's private right.

---

[1] See Criminal Law Act 1977, s 6. To commit the crime, the party must know of the occupier's presence on the land and of his objection to that party's entry. The crime is not committed if the party entering is a 'displaced residential occupier'—i.e. someone who was himself earlier removed from the land. See also the Protection from Eviction Act 1977, s 1, for a further example of a crime protecting the use of land.

Equally, we will not examine the special public limits that may be placed on private rights. For example, if you own a house, you may wish to convert it into a block of flats: to do so, you will need planning permission, because your private rights, as an owner of the land, are limited by the need for the approval of a public body.

This is not to suggest that the areas not covered by this book are unimportant, or lacking in interest. In fact, to have a full picture of how the law regulates the use of land, it is vital to be aware of the relevant parts of the law of torts or of public law. But no book can sensibly examine *all* of the legal rules that can regulate the use of land; rather, this book focuses on a set of rules that are joined together not only by the *context* in which they apply, but also by the *concepts* that underlie them. In this way, the book fits with the meaning of 'land law', as set out in the following extract.[2]

Birks, 'Before We Begin: Five Keys to Land Law' in Land Law: Themes and Perspectives (eds Bright and Dewar, 1998, pp 457–60)

The name 'land law' suggests a simple contextual category: all the law about land. The law does use many such categories, ordered only by the alphabet: all the law about aviation, banks, commerce, dogs, education and so on. They take as their subject some aspect of life, just as a non-lawyer would identify it. But in this case things are not quite so straightforward. By the end of this section we will have formulated a more complex proposition: land law, as generally understood, is a contextual subset of a legal-conceptual category.

The socio-historical context

It will help to start with some background. The role of land, and hence of land law, has changed dramatically since the Industrial Revolution and the rise of the limited liability company. The paragraphs which follow sketch in that change and two others.

The managed fund

For institutions and individuals with serious wealth, land has lost its central role. The managed fund has displaced the rolling acres. Land used to be the pre-eminent form of wealth. Landed property was the focus of dynastic ambition. Land opened the door to high social status and political power. A landed family had by that fact alone a stake in governmental power. Keeping land in the family mattered. That has changed. Land, important as it is, has lost its pride of place. For the mega-wealthy, land has become just one species of investment, just as agriculture has become just one more industry. Pension funds and wealthy institutions hold mixed portfolios. They hold some land, some works of art, and many shares in many companies. Rich individuals do the same. The dynastic urge has been translated, with one eye constantly on the tax man, into trust funds and private companies [...]

The fragility of the environment

The notion of land as scarce and fragile is relatively new. The Industrial Revolution created a few black spots. Blake's dark, satanic mills were terrible to behold, but local. It is only relatively recently that we have realized that our transport systems, our power stations, our

---

[2] As is the case with all such extracts in this book, footnotes, numbering, and cross-references have been omitted unless essential to understanding the extract.

industrial processes, and our intensive agricultural methods have the potential utterly to destroy this green and pleasant land. The private law of nuisance, the historic role of which was to control annoying activities as between one neighbour and another, cannot sufficiently express the social interest in the safety of this scarce resource. Protection of the environment means more social control of land use. There will have to be more planning control, more conservation legislation, more anti-pollution legislation [...]

Public-sector housing

Local government is nowadays a powerful force in the provision of housing, adding a public law dimension new to land law as it been historically determined. During the Thatcher era the public sector experienced an upheaval, partly from shortage of money, partly from being opened to the private market through the right-to-buy legislation[3] [...] The public sector ultimately rests on concepts identical to those of the private sector, overlaid by principles of public law and a mass of highly technical legislation. It is in every way a part of land law, but, because of the mass of detail, it has become a specialism. As a lawyer you have at some stage to decide whether to make yourself an expert in that field. The same is largely true of the statutory regime controlling the relations of landlord and tenant in the private sector.

The core of land law

A target has a centre. Taking land law as a simple contextual category, we can identify at least five topics, all of which have already figured in the discussion. Four of these must on reflection be located in the second or third circles, just outside the bull's-eye at which we are aiming. They matter, but they do not relieve us of the intellectual necessity of mastering the core. Two belong largely in public law. One of these comprises the social control essential if the environment is to be protected. The other is the housing law which applies to local government tenancies. Within private law, a third until lies in the law of civil wrongs and deals with the duties imposed by the law for regulating the behaviours of neighbours towards each other, especially through the torts of nuisance and trespass to land. Fourthly, there is the structuring of mega-wealth, the mission of the old Lincoln's Inn conveyancers. That is breaking away, not specifically land law any longer but wealth management. Its principal vehicle is the trust, often enough off-shore, in which land becomes just one kind of asset in a rolling fund. Fifthly and last of all, there is the unit at the very centre of the target. When lawyers speak of land law, it is usually to this core that they refer.

Every business needs premises, every factory needs a site. For most of us as private individuals our home is the centre of our lives. Functionally, this core of land law has the task of providing the structure within which people and business can safely acquire and exploit land for daily use, to live and to work. To discharge that function, it has to have its own conceptual apparatus. The proper content of this fifth unit thus becomes the nature, creation and protection of interests in land. Those interests and their implications are the conceptual apparatus of our land law.

The word 'interests' is slightly evasive. The law recognizes different kinds of rights, among them property rights. By 'interest' we mean 'property right'. The category of all property rights (or, in other words and more simply, 'the law of property') is a legal-conceptual category. It differs from, say, the law of dogs in that its subject is a legal concept, the concept of a proprietary right. The core of land law is the subset formed when the conceptual category of 'property right' is confined to one context: the law relating to property rights in land. To

---

[3] Housing Act 1980, followed by the Housing Act 1985.

focus on that core is neither to downgrade the importance of the units in the next circles nor to forget that in real life all the units which we have identified, and others, cohere together.

3 THREE UNDERLYING QUESTIONS

As Birks suggests, the focus of land law, and hence of this book, is on private *property rights to use land*. We will examine the concept of a property right in Chapters 3 and 4. Birks suggests that land law examines the '*nature, creation and protection*' of property rights relating to land. Certainly, at a very general level, the questions that we will examine in this book can be organized into three broad groups: firstly, there are questions about the *content* of rights to use land; secondly, there are questions about the *acquisition* of rights to use land; thirdly, there are questions about the *defences* available to one party where another party has a right to use land.

For example, imagine that you are interested in buying a house advertised in the window of a local estate agency. It is important to know whether the house is advertised as 'freehold' or 'leasehold'. The point is that the vendor is not simply selling a house: she is selling her *right to use the land*. If you go ahead and buy her house, you will acquire a particular private right to use land. As Birks suggests, land law deals with the nature of her right. In particular, it is vital for you to know the *content* of that right: if you acquire the right, how will you be able to use the land? As we will see in Chapter 3, a freehold will give you ownership of the land for an unlimited period; a leasehold also gives you ownership, but only for a limited period.

Let us say that you have established that the vendor is selling a freehold, and that you have decided to go ahead and make an offer. Your focus will then shift to the *acquisition* question: what has to be done in order for you to acquire the vendor's freehold? In Birks' terms, land law deals with the creation of your right to use the land. There will generally be two stages to the process, often known as 'contract' and 'conveyance'. At the first stage, you need to know (or, at least, your solicitor or conveyancer needs to know) what has to be done in order to reach a legally binding agreement with the vendor. As noted above, there are special rules that regulate contracts to transfer a right such as a freehold. We will examine those rules in this book (see Chapter 9), because they are crucial in defining how a party can acquire a private right to use land.

At the second stage, you need to know (or, at least, your solicitor or conveyancer needs to know) what has to be done in order for you actually to acquire the vendor's freehold: we will also examine those rules in Chapter 9. As we will see, *registration* forms a crucial part of the process: even if you pay the vendor and even if you move into her house, you do not actually acquire her freehold unless and until you are recorded on the central register as holding that right.

If all goes well and you are now registered as holding a freehold, it might seem that you are home and dry. But let us say that one of your new neighbours, when walking to his house from the road, regularly takes a short cut across your new front garden. You (very politely) object to this and he (equally politely) claims that a former owner of your land granted him a right of way over your land. This is the first that you have heard of such a right: in fact, when acquiring your freehold, you checked on the central register and there was no mention of the land being subject to a right of way. In such a case, as we will see in Chapter 6, the *defences* question is crucial. Even if your neighbour can show that he was given a right of way over your land, it may well be that you have a defence to his right and so do not need to let him walk across your land. In our example, that defence may come from the facts that: (i) you paid for, and registered, your freehold; and (ii) your neighbour failed to have his right of way noted on the register. This is just one example of how land law, to use Birks' words, deals with the protection of rights: it may be that your neighbour should have protected his right by having it noted on the register.

What if your neighbour instead claims that there is a *public* right of way, such as a public footpath, running over your land? If that is the case, then any member of the public will be able to walk over your front garden. We will not examine such public rights in this book, because our focus is on *private* rights: rights that can be held by an individual as an individual, not as a member of the public.

4 THE SPECIAL FEATURES OF LAND

Birks suggests that land law is a 'contextual subset' of property law. This raises the question of why we should gather together the legal rules relating to private rights to use land. We could equally, for example, study private rights to use chairs. Yet, whilst there are lots of books and courses dealing with 'land law', very few deal with 'chair law'. One reason, of course, is the practical importance of land—but then chairs are pretty useful too. A linked, but better, reason is that land has certain features that make it a unique resource, fundamentally different from other types of physical thing. The legal rules relating to rights to use chairs are essentially identical to those relating to rights to use tables, bikes, or cauliflowers. So, these rules can be found in books or courses dealing with 'personal property law'. In fact, personal property law deals with private rights to use just about any physical thing *other* than land. Land is separated out for special treatment because, due to its fundamentally different physical characteristics, rights to use land are regulated by fundamentally different legal rules.

The following extract discusses those special features and the special legal rules to which they give rise.

McFarlane, *The Structure of Property Law* (2008, pp 7–11)

Permanence

Subject to the rarest of exceptions, land is permanent. Whereas other objects that can be physically located (e.g. bikes) wear out, the usefulness of land endures. This special feature of land is reflected by a special feature of the land law system: ownership of land can be split up over time. For example, A, an owner of land, can give B a Lease: B then has ownership of that land for a limited period. In contrast, if A is an owner of a bike, A *cannot* give B ownership of that bike for a limited period.

Uniqueness

"Location, location, location": a crucial feature of any piece of land is its physical location. That physical location can never be shared by another piece of land. In this significant sense, all pieces of land are unique. This special feature of land explains two special rules of land law.

Recovery of the thing itself from X or C?

First, let us say that: (i) B owns a thing, such as a bike; and (ii) X takes physical control of that thing without B's consent or other lawful authority. B can assert his right, as an owner of the thing, against X: by interfering with B's right, X commits a wrong against B. However, there is no guarantee that a court will order X to return the bike to B: rather than getting his thing back, B may well have to settle for receiving money from X [...]

In contrast, if: (i) B has ownership of some land; and (ii) X takes physical control of that land without B's consent or other lawful authority; then (iii) a court *will* make an order (a "possession order") allowing B to remove X and to take physical control of the land. This difference between land and other things thus relates to the **remedies question**: the question of how a court will protect B's right. It explains why land is sometimes known as "real property". "Real" comes from the Latin for "thing" (*res*); when used in the phrase "real property" it indicates that B can recover the *thing itself* if wrongfully deprived of it by X or C.

Forcing A to transfer the thing itself to B?

Second, let's say A owns a bike and makes a contractual promise to transfer his ownership to B. A then changes his mind and refuses to go ahead with the transfer. B can assert his right against A: by breaching his contractual duty to B, A commits a wrong against B. However, it is unlikely that the court will order A to transfer the bike itself to B; B will, almost always, have to settle for receiving money from A. The aim of remedies for breach of contract is to put B in the position he would have been in had A kept his promise: B's right is adequately protected if A gives B any money necessary to allow B to buy a similar bike elsewhere.

However, where A promises to transfer a *unique thing* to B, the position is different. To put B in the position he would have been had A kept his promise, A must give B the *thing itself*. So, in the rare case where A promises to transfer a unique bike to B, A may be ordered to keep his promise. In contrast, if A promises to transfer land to B, the standard position is that a court will order A to keep his promise and to transfer his right to the land to B: after all, each piece of land is unique. Again, this difference between land and other things relates to the **remedies question**: the question of how a court will protect B's right. Where B's contractual right is to acquire a right to land, it is, in general, specifically protected; where B's contractual right is to acquire a right to a thing other than land, B usually has to settle for receiving money.

Capacity for multiple simultaneous use

The same piece of land can be used in many different ways, by many different people, at the same time. For example, let's say:

1. A buys No.32 Acacia Gardens from A0.

2. A0 owns a local shop and makes A promise, when buying No.32, that neither A nor future owners of No.32 will use it as a shop.

3. A acquires No.32 with a "mortgage" loan: in return for a loan from C Bank, A gives C Bank a security right. C Bank thus has a right, if A fails to pay back the loan, to: (i) remove A and other occupiers from the land; (ii) sell the land; and (iii) use the proceeds to pay off A's debt.

4. In return for payment from E, a neighbour, A gives E a right to reach E's house by using a path crossing the garden of No.32.

5. A then moves away. He decides to keep the land and use it as an investment by renting it to B. So, in return for paying money to A, B is permitted to occupy the land. B uses the land as his home and allows his lover, D, to live with him.

Each of A0, A, B, C, D and E has a right to make some use (or at least to prevent a particular use) of the land. Things other than land are also capable of multiple, simultaneous use. If A owns a bike, A can: (i) give B permission to ride the bike; and (ii) offer his bike as security for a loan from C. The difference between land and other things is therefore one of *degree*. However, the difference remains important as it poses a significant question for the land law system: can it reconcile the competing desires of all those who simultaneously want to use the same piece of land? It certainly helps to explain another special feature of the land law system: the longer list of property rights in land.

Social importance

Land is uniquely capable of meeting important social needs. B can only acquire the sense of security and identity that comes with establishing a home *if* he has some sort of right in relation to land. Similarly, it is very difficult to establish business premises without a right to use land. As a result, an interference with B's use of land can have dramatic consequences. For example, eviction from a settled home can cause great stress and disruption; eviction from business premises can cause grave commercial harm.

This special feature of land is reflected in a number of special rules. For example, if: (i) B occupies land as his home; and (ii) C unlawfully prevents B occupying that land *or* with the intention of causing B to leave the land, interferes with the "peace or comfort" of B or members of B's household, then (iii) C commits a criminal offence.[4] Further, if B has ownership of some land, the rest of the world is under a *prima facie* duty not to unreasonably interfere with B's use and enjoyment of that land. So, if C's pig farm, next to B's land, produces nauseating smells, C breaches that duty and thus commits the wrong of nuisance against B. However, C commits no such wrong if he interferes, in a similar way, with B's enjoyment of a thing other than land.[5] Further, in some circumstances, A and B's private agreement can be regulated by mandatory rules protecting B's use of land. So, if A gives B a Lease of land for one year, B may have a statutory right to remain even after the year has expired.

This special feature of land also means that certain human rights may be of particular relevance in land law. For example, Article 8 of the European Convention of Human Rights states that: "Everyone has the right to respect for his private and family life, his home and his correspondence." [. . .] [T]his right is of course subject to qualifications; but the social importance of land means that the right *may* have a role in shaping the rules of the land law system.

Limited availability

It is impossible to make more land. This special feature of land has a number of consequences. First, coupled with the many valuable uses to which land can be put, it ensures that land is an *expensive commodity*. For most, acquiring ownership of land is impossible unless a lender, such as C Bank, is willing to provide a substantial loan. In return, C Bank will demand a security right over the land. Second, the limited availability of land intensifies the need for

---

[4] [Under the Protection from Eviction Act 1977, s 1.]

[5] [To bring a claim in nuisance, B must have a property right in land: see *Hunter v Canary Wharf* [1997] AC 655.]

the stock of land to be *freely marketable*. As a result, it is particularly undesirable for an owner to remove land from the market by placing permanent restrictions on its use.

The limited availability of land, coupled with its importance and uniqueness, can lead to special limits being placed on an owner of land. For example, the need to promote the marketability of land has led the land law system to give protection to certain parties [e.g. C] who acquire rights relating to land. As we will see, registration rules, particularly prominent in land law, are one means of giving C such protection. Equally, the rules of the land law system have long tried to promote marketability by preventing an owner from limiting the use of land after his death. Further, legislation commonly allows public bodies compulsory purchase powers: powers to acquire land from an owner in order to use it for a specific purpose, such as the building of a motorway.

More startling is the doctrine of *adverse possession*: a means by which an owner of land can lose his right without receiving any compensation. Due to changes in the registered land system, the doctrine of adverse possession now has much less of an impact. However, where it applies, its effect is dramatic. If: (i) X occupies B's land without B's consent; and (ii) B fails, over a long period, to take steps to remove X; then (iii) B's right to the land can be extinguished. The doctrine only applies if X has been acting as an owner of the land: it protects X's claimed ownership, exercised over the long period, by extinguishing B's prior ownership. It can protect X even if X is fully aware that the land initially belongs to B. In this way, the doctrine recognises X's claim (established by his long use) and removes the right of B, who has failed to make use of his land.

The doctrine of adverse possession applies only to land. If: (i) X takes physical control of B's bike without B's consent or other authority; and (ii) B fails, over a long period, to assert his ownership against X; then (iii) there is *no* general rule that the passage of time, by itself, can lead to B losing his ownership of the bike. The limited availability of land supports the idea that land is too scarce a commodity to remain under the ownership of a party who fails, over a long period, to assert his right. As seen above, it also heightens the need for land to be freely marketable. The doctrine of adverse possession certainly promotes that goal: the extinction of B's right not only protects X, but also anyone later acquiring a right from X.

As demonstrated by the extract, the special *physical* features of land lead to special *legal* rules that regulate private rights to use land. Those rules can be organized into three general groups by looking at: the *content* of those rights; the means by which they can be *acquired*; and the *defences* that may be used against them.

One of the most distinctive features of land law is that certain types of right to use land (known as 'property rights') can exist *only* in relation to land. This means that, where land is concerned, the *content* of property rights can be more varied than the content of property rights relating to, say, chairs. Many of the property rights that we will examine in later chapters can exist *only* in relation to land: this is the case, for example, with the lease (see Chapters 23 and 24), easement (see Chapter 26), and restrictive covenant (see Chapter 27). Due to the social importance of land, there may be special means by which a party can *acquire* a right to use land. For example, if you set up home with your partner, then, even if your partner is registered as the sole owner of the home, you may nonetheless be able to rely on special rules, developed by the courts, to show that you have acquired a property right: we will examine those rules in detail in Chapter 18. In contrast, the limited availability of land may make it easier for you to lose a property right relating to land: there may be special *defences* that someone can use against your right to use the land. For example, the extract above refers to the doctrine of adverse possession: if you own land, but fail, over a long period, to assert your right to that land, a squatter may then gain a defence to your property right. We will examine adverse possession in detail in Chapter 10.

5 LAND LAW IN PRACTICE: OCCUPIERS V BANKS

There is no doubt that land law is a difficult subject. In defining and regulating private rights to use land, land law has some very tough choices to make. The best way to see this is by considering some examples. In this section, we will consider the facts and results of two important land law cases, each of which involved a dispute between an occupier of land and a bank. We will return to these cases in later chapters, when we will examine the relevant principles in greater detail. Our purpose here is simply to use these two cases, focusing on one specific aspect of land law, to highlight some of the difficult questions faced by land law and the different ways in which those questions can be approached.

When examining these two cases, as well as the other cases included in this book, we will necessarily look at how the rules of land law are used to solve disputes about the use of land. It is important, however, to bear in mind that those rules, as well as solving disputes, affect parties' future conduct. In particular, the rules form the background against which an owner of land can arrange his affairs. It is therefore important to remember that land law is not only about resolving disputes; it is also aims to create a settled legal background against which parties can plan their future use of land.

5.1 THE CASES AND THE DILEMMA

In *National Provincial Bank v Ainsworth*,[6] Mr and Mrs Ainsworth lived together in Milward Road, Hastings, Sussex. Mr Ainsworth was registered as owner of the home. In 1957, Mr Ainsworth moved out. In 1958, he borrowed £1,000 from the National Provincial Bank. The money was borrowed as part of a mortgage deal: to secure his duty to repay that sum, plus interest, Mr Ainsworth gave the bank a particular right (a charge) over his home. This meant that, if Mr Ainsworth were to fall behind in his repayments, the bank would have a power to sell the land and use the proceeds to meet his debt. By 1962, Mr Ainsworth had fallen behind on his repayments to the bank. The bank wished to sell the land. To get a good price, the bank knew that it had to sell the home with vacant possession. Because Mrs Ainsworth refused to leave, the bank applied for an order for possession of the home.

The Court of Appeal found that Mrs Ainsworth had a right to occupy the land that bound the bank. On that basis, the bank's claim for possession would fail. But the House of Lords reversed the finding of the Court of Appeal: Mrs Ainsworth had to leave the land. As we will see in Chapter 4, section 5.4, the House of Lords' decision depended on the *content* question: in contrast to the Court of Appeal, it found that Mrs Ainsworth's right did *not* count as a property right and so was not capable of binding the bank.

In *Williams & Glyn's Bank v Boland*,[7] Mr and Mrs Boland lived together in Ridge Park, Beddington, Surrey. Mr Boland was registered as owner of the home; Mrs Boland also made a substantial financial contribution to the costs of acquiring the home. Mr Boland and his brother were directors of Epsom Contractors Ltd, a building company. To support

6 [1965] AC 1175, HL.
7 [1981] AC 487, HL.

the business, Mr Boland borrowed money from the Williams & Glyn's Bank. The money was borrowed as part of a mortgage deal: to secure his duty to repay that sum, plus interest, Mr Boland gave the bank a particular right (a charge) over his home. This meant that, if Mr Boland were to fall behind in his repayments, the bank would have a power to sell the land and use the proceeds to meet his debt. Mr Boland had fallen behind on his repayments to the bank. The bank wished to sell the land. To get a good price, the bank knew that it had to sell the home with vacant possession. Because Mrs Boland refused to leave, the bank applied for an order for possession of the home.

The Court of Appeal found that Mrs Boland had a right to occupy the land that bound the bank. On that basis, the bank's claim for possession would fail. The House of Lords upheld the finding of the Court of Appeal: the bank's action for possession therefore failed. The crucial questions were the *content* and *defences* questions: the House of Lords, rejecting the bank's arguments, found that Mrs Boland's right counted as a property right *and* that the bank had no defence to that right. (We will examine the aspect of the *defences* question discussed in *Boland* in Chapter 6, section 3.2.2.)

In both cases, the court had a tough choice to make. As the following extract shows, the special features of land sharpen the court's dilemma. To translate the passage to these two cases, Mr Ainsworth and Mr Boland equate to the party referred to in the passage as 'A'; Mrs Ainsworth and Mrs Boland to 'B'; and the banks take the role of 'C Bank'.

McFarlane, *The Structure of Property Law* (2008, pp 11–12)

On the one hand, B can point to the social importance of land: [she] is currently using the land as a home and uprooting that home will cause severe disruption. B can also point to the uniqueness of land: even if B is able to find a home elsewhere, it will be in a different location and so B may be forced to change many aspects of [her] life. So it might seem that the social importance and uniqueness of land should cause the rules of the land law system to lean in favour of someone, such as B, who is currently occupying or otherwise making use of land.

However, C Bank can make a powerful counter-argument. It may well have made a substantial loan to A: the limited availability of land, along with its social importance, ensures that land has a high value. So, if C Bank is unable to sell the land, it is likely to be left substantially out of pocket. It is also important to think about the wider consequences of finding in favour of B. First, whilst it is easy to have sympathy with B rather than with a faceless bank, it should be remembered that if banks have systematic problems in recovering loans, this can have repercussions not just for the bank's customers but for the wider economy.[8] Second, if C Bank is unable to sell the land, we need to consider the effect of such a decision on lenders' future practice. Will lenders have to carry out extensive and expensive checks to ensure that there are no other users of the home who may later thwart a lender's attempt to sell the land? After all, as land is capable of multiple, simultaneous use, there may be many potential rights that a lender will need to watch out for. The costs incurred by lenders would then be passed on to borrowers. As land is already very expensive, this will make it harder still for would-be homeowners to enter the market. And, given its limited availability, it would be unfortunate

---

[8] The importance to the wider economy of such banks has been dramatically emphasized by the UK government's [nationalization of] Northern Rock plc using powers under the Banking (Special Provisions) Act 2008. The problems faced by that bank, a major 'mortgage' lender, were *not* caused by difficulties faced by the bank in recovering loans, but the highly unusual steps taken by the government nonetheless demonstrate the importance of such banks to the wider economy.

if land became very difficult to trade in. Given we can't produce new land, we should be particularly careful to make sure the land we do have does not become permanently burdened and thus difficult to buy or sell.

[...T]he dispute between B and C Bank could be characterised as part of a wider clash between commerce and market forces on the one hand and the need for social protection and the maintenance of a home on the other. The fact that the dispute involves land, a special kind of thing, does *not* help us resolve this conflict; instead, it *heightens the tension*. The dispute between market forces and social protection thus draws out the ambivalent nature of land itself. On the one hand, it is of limited availability and constitutes an important financial investment: we therefore do not want the process of buying land to be unduly difficult. Yet on the other hand, it is unique and socially important: we therefore do not want to give insufficient protection to those who use and, in particular, occupy land.

5.2 TWO POSSIBLE APPROACHES

On the face of it, the facts of *Ainsworth* and *Boland* seem to be very similar—yet the results of the cases differ. Before we examine the specific reasons for that difference, it is worth asking how a court should approach the dispute between the occupier and the bank. In the following extract, Harris contrasts two broad types of possible approach. He opens with a quotation from Max Weber, the influential political economist and sociologist.

Harris, 'Legal Doctrine and Interests in Land' in *Oxford Essays in Jurisprudence* (3rd series, eds Eekelaar and Bell, 1987, pp 168–9)

'The expectations of the parties are oriented towards the economic and utilitarian meaning of a legal proposition. However, from the point of view of legal logic, this meaning is an 'irrational one' [...] a 'lawyers' law' has never been and never will be brought into conformity with lay expectation unless it totally renounce that formal character which is immanent in it. This is just as true of the English law which we glorify so much to-day, as it has been of the ancient Roman jurists or of the methods of modern continental legal thought.'[9]

So wrote Max Weber some seventy years ago. It constitutes one of his leading conclusions about the nature of lawyers' law. It points to a contrast between formal-doctrinal (and hence circumscribed) reasoning which, he claimed, was intrinsic to professional legal thinking, and open-ended consequentialist controversy over the interpretation of legal propositions. If there are rival views as to the meaning of a legal rule, the layman expects the choice to be made according to which version will have the best outcome, all things considered. The professional lawyer, however, will settle the issue by reference to doctrinal arguments based upon existing legal materials.

I propose to examine this alleged contrast in the context of current issues concerning interests in land in English law. I shall argue that the dichotomy exists, but not in the stark Weberian form. Consequentialist interpretation is not, from the point of view of legal logic, 'irrational'. On the contrary, it constitutes the basis of one professionally accepted style of reasoning— what I call the 'utility model of rationality'. However, the 'doctrine model of rationality'—along with two other models—also plays a crucial role in the development of the law. To the extent

---

9 Weber, *Law in Economy and Society* (ed Rheinstein, 1954, pp 307–8).

that 'policy' can never totally displace doctrine, so long as our legal institutions retain anything like their present character, Weber was correct [...] if we want to ditch doctrine, we need to invent new institutions, new lawyers, and a new conception of 'law' itself.

Harris thus identifies two prominent, but contrasting, models that may inform a court's approach when dealing with cases such as *Ainsworth* and *Boland*. The 'utility model of rationality' is based on what Weber sees as a non-specialist's expectation of how the dispute should be decided: it essentially consists of weighing up, on one side, the practical advantages of favouring the occupier and, on the other, the practical advantages of finding for the bank. The 'doctrinal model of rationality' is based on what Weber calls 'lawyers' law': the dispute is resolved by the application of specific legal rules, not by a general weighing of the consequences of finding in favour of the occupier or the bank.

Was either of those models important in the House of Lords' decisions in either *Ainsworth* or *Boland*? To test this, we can examine an extract from each decision.

5.3 THE APPROACH IN *AINSWORTH*

In the following passage, Lord Wilberforce considers the nature of Mrs Ainsworth's right to occupy her home; that right, arising when her husband left her, was known as a 'deserted wife's equity'. The Court of Appeal, led by Lord Denning MR, had held that the 'deserted wife's equity' was capable of binding a third party, such as a bank later acquiring a charge over the land. The House of Lords, however, rejected that analysis.

National Provincial Bank v Ainsworth [1965] AC 1175, HL

Lord Wilberforce

At 1241–3

My Lords, the doctrine of the 'deserted wife's equity' has been evolved by the courts during the past 13 years in an attempt to mitigate some effects of the housing shortage which has persisted since the 1939–45 war. To a woman, whose husband has left her, especially if she has children, it is of little use to receive periodical payments for her maintenance (even if these are in fact punctually made) if she is left without a home. Once possession of a house has been lost, the process of acquiring another place to live in may be painful and prolonged. So, even though, as is normally the case, the home is in law the property of the husband, the courts have intervened to prevent him from using his right of property to remove his deserted wife from it and they have correspondingly recognised that she has a right, or "equity" as it has come to be called, which the law will protect, to remain there.

This case relates to one aspect, and one aspect only, of that right. No question arises here as to any claim which a deserted wife may have against her husband: all that we are concerned with is the right of a deserted wife to remain in possession as against a third party, claiming, in good faith, under the husband. And the issue is even narrower than that: it relates only to the position of a third party whose title arises subsequently to the desertion [...]

The issue is thus a narrow one, affecting a small proportion only of those deserted wives who are left in occupation of their husband's house. Nevertheless as to them, as to [Mrs Ainsworth], issues of importance, and probably of hardship, are involved. The ultimate question must be whether such persons can be given the protection which social considerations of humanity evidently indicate without injustice to third parties and a radical departure from sound principles of real property law [...]

The appeal raises two questions, one of general, the other of more limited scope.[10] The general question is whether the respondent Mrs. Ainsworth as the deserted wife of her husband, the owner of the house, has any interest in or right over it which is capable of binding the bank as the proprietor of a legal interest in the land. This is a general question of real property law [...]

I turn to the first and more general question: what is the nature of the deserted wife's interest, or right? In the cases which have evolved from 1952 onwards it is variously described: it is called an "equity," a "clog," a "licence," a "status of irremovability." The description is shifting and evolutionary as different situations appear. I shall have to refer to some of these cases in some detail. But before doing so I think it useful to look at the wife's situation more generally, as it stands under well-established principles of law. After all, married women and deserted wives are familiar enough in our legal system and there cannot be much doubt what their rights are [...]

At 1247–8

[Having analysed the duties imposed on Mr Ainsworth by the deserted wife's equity, Lord Wilberforce continued thus:]

The position then, at the present time, is this. The wife has no specific right against her husband to be provided with any particular house, nor to remain in any particular house. She has a right to cohabitation and support. But, in considering whether the husband should be given possession of property of his, the court will have regard to the duty of the spouses to each other, and the decision it reaches will be based on a consideration of what may be called the matrimonial circumstances. These include such matters as whether the husband can provide alternative accommodation and if so whether such accommodation is suitable having regard to the estate and condition of the spouses; whether the husband's conduct amounts to desertion, whether the conduct of the wife has been such as to deprive her of any of her rights against the husband. And the order to be made must be fashioned accordingly: it may be that the wife should leave immediately or after a certain period: it may be subject to revision on a change of circumstances.

The conclusion emerges to my mind very clearly from this that the wife's rights, as regards the occupation of her husband's property, are essentially of a personal kind: personal in the sense that a decision can only be reached on the basis of considerations essentially dependent on the mutual claims of husband and wife as spouses and as the result of a broad weighing of circumstances and merit. Moreover, these rights are at no time definitive, they are provisional and subject to review at any time according as changes take place in the material circumstances and conduct of the parties.

On any division, then, which is to be made between property rights on the one hand, and personal rights on the other hand, however broad or penumbral the separating band between these two kinds of rights may be, there can be little doubt where the wife's rights fall. Before a right or an interest can be admitted into the category of property, or of a right affecting property, it must be definable, identifiable by third parties, capable in its nature of assumption by

---

[10] [The second question was whether, even if Mrs Ainsworth's right counted as a property right, the bank had a defence to that right. We will consider the particular defence raised by the bank in Chapter 6, section 3.2.2. In the end, because the House of Lords decided that Mrs Ainsworth did not have a property right, there was no need for the bank to rely on that defence.]

> third parties, and have some degree of permanence or stability. The wife's right has none of these qualities, it is characterised by the reverse of them.

A key passage from that extract may help to reveal Lord Wilberforce's approach to the case:

> The ultimate question must be whether [Mrs Ainsworth] can be given the protection which social considerations of humanity evidently indicate without injustice to third parties and a radical departure from sound principles of real property law.

The sentence contains two suggestions. Firstly, whilst there may be good reasons for allowing Mrs Ainsworth the chance to remain in her home, there may also be good reasons for protecting a lender, such as the National Provincial Bank. That point alone is consistent with the 'utility model'—that is, of weighing up the practical advantages and disadvantages of favouring either the occupier or the bank. Secondly, and much more important, is the need to avoid a '*radical departure from sound principles of real property law*'. As noted by Harris,[11] that part of the statement gives prominence to the 'doctrinal model'—that is, a decision in favour of Mrs Ainsworth can be made only if it can be reconciled with the doctrinal, technical rules of land law. And, according to Lord Wilberforce, those rules meant that Mrs Ainsworth's right could count as a property right (a right capable of binding the bank) only if it was '*definable, identifiable by third parties, capable in its nature of assumption by third parties, and have some degree of permanence or stability*'. Because Mrs Ainsworth's right did not have those features, the *content* question was decided against her and the bank was therefore free to remove her from her home.

5.4 THE APPROACH IN *BOLAND*

Before looking at an extract from the House of Lords' decision in *Boland*, it is useful to look at the Court of Appeal's decision in that case and, in particular, parts of Lord Denning MR's judgment.

Williams & Glyn's Bank v Boland [1979] 2 WLR 550, CA

Facts: There was a clear difference between the facts of *Ainsworth* and those of *Boland*. Unlike Mrs Ainsworth, Mrs Boland had made a significant financial contribution to the cost of the land owned by her husband. As a result, Mrs Boland's right differed from the 'deserted wife's equity' of Mrs Ainsworth. Instead, Mrs Boland had a right under a trust of the land (see further Chapters 4, 18. and 19). Nonetheless, the bank argued that, like the 'deserted wife's equity', that right failed the *content* test: it did not count as a property right that could bind a third party, such as the bank, later acquiring a right in the land. This argument was based on a land law technicality: the doctrine of 'conversion', which we will examine in Chapter 19, section 5.3. According to the bank, it meant that Mrs Boland's right under the trust did not give her a right enabling her to use the land: it only gave her a right to a share of any money made by her husband from the land.

---

[11] See Harris, 'Legal Doctrine and Interests in Land' in *Oxford Essays in Jurisprudence* (3rd series, eds Eekelaar and Bell, 1987, n 60), in which that part of Lord Wilberforce's statement is highlighted.

The bank also made a second argument: even if Mrs Boland did have a property right that was capable of binding the bank, the bank had a *defence* to that right. The particular defence relied on by the bank was provided by a land registration statute and was based on the fact that, when the bank acquired its charge, Mrs Boland's right was not noted on the entry in the register relating to her home. As we will see in Chapter 6, that 'lack of registration defence' does *not* apply if the party with the unregistered property right is in 'actual occupation' of the land. In such a case, the property right held by the party in occupation is known as an 'overriding interest'—that is, a right that is immune from the lack of registration defence (see further Chapter 6, section 3.2.2, and Chapter 16). Because Mrs Boland had lived in the home throughout, it seemed clear that she was in actual occupation and therefore that the bank could *not* use the lack of registration defence. But the bank had another technical argument: it contended that, where a wife occupies alongside her husband, the wife does not count as a person in 'actual occupation'. This argument is based on the idea that, if the bank were to investigate the land before making its loan to the husband, the presence of the wife there would *not* alert the bank to the risk that she had a property right in the land. After all, even if the wife were to have no property right, it would be no surprise to see her sharing occupation with her husband.

Each of the bank's two technical arguments was rejected by the Court of Appeal and the House of Lords. The *content* and *defences* questions were thus decided in Mrs Boland's favour: her right under the trust counted as a property right in land and, due to her actual occupation, the lack of registration of that right did not give the bank a defence to it.

Lord Denning MR

At 556–7

To clear the air, I would put on one side the cases from 1949 onwards about deserted wives. In those cases the wife had no share whatever in the matrimonial home. She was a "bare" wife [...] In this court we gave her the protection which she rightly deserved. But the House of Lords stripped her of it. They held that she had no protection against a lender who took security on the matrimonial home: see *National Provincial Bank Ltd. v. Ainsworth*[12] [...]

Alongside the deserted wife's equity, there was another development of even greater significance. It was the concept of the 'wife's share' in the matrimonial home. In former times the house was usually conveyed into the name of the husband alone. He was the one who went out to work, earned the money, paid the deposit and the mortgage instalments. But when the wife went out to work, things changed. Her earnings came in very useful. They went into the family pool. Out of it the outgoings were paid including the deposit and the mortgage instalments. The conveyancers in the old days would have held that the wife gained no interest whatever in the house by reason of her contributions. She got no share in the house itself. Nor, if it was sold, did she have any share in the proceeds of sale. For the simple reason that she could show no contract, no legal right whatever to support any claim [...] But by a remarkable series of decisions—I do not hesitate, looking back, to call them remarkable—it was held that when a wife contributed in money or money's worth to the purchase of the house, she acquired a share in it [...]

But the decisions were justified in the next year by the House of Lords on a very new—and very acceptable—ground. It was in *Gissing v. Gissing*[13] when the House held that, in these

---

[12] [Lord Denning MR referred to the House of Lords' decision as *National Provincial Bank Ltd v Hastings Car Mart Ltd*: that is an alternative name for the same case.]
[13] [1971] AC 886.

cases of the matrimonial home, a wife, who contributes in money or money's worth, does obtain a proprietary interest. It is done by way of a trust imposed on the husband [...]

What is the nature of this trust? It was suggested to us that it was not a trust of the house itself, but only a trust in the proceeds of sale. That cannot be right. When a married man and his wife buy a house, they do it so as to live in it—so that it should be home for them both and their children—for the foreseeable future. They do not intend to sell it—at any rate not for many years hence. In determining what the nature of the trust is, the court must give effect to the intention of the parties—to be inferred from their words and conduct... In nearly all these cases the inexorable inference is that the husband is to hold the legal estate in the house in trust for them both—for both to live in for the foreseeable future. The couple do not have in mind a sale—nor a division of the proceeds of sale—except in the far distance.

The wife clearly has rights. The only question is whether she is herself a person "in actual occupation of the land". [...] In *Caunce v. Caunce*[14] Stamp J. seems to have held that, when a wife was living in the matrimonial home with her husband, it was the husband alone who was in actual occupation of it. The wife was not. Stamp J. said that she:

"[...] was not in apparent occupation or possession. She was there, ostensibly, because she was the wife, and her presence there was wholly consistent with the title offered by the husband to the bank"[15] [...]

[At first instance in *Boland*, Templeman J accepted that Mrs Boland was not in actual occupation] when he said:

"actual occupation for the purposes of [the relevant registration statute] does not include the position of the wife of the legal owner who is in occupation."

Any other view, he said, would lead to chaos.

I profoundly disagree. Such statements would have been true a hundred years ago when the law regarded husband and wife as one: and the husband as that one. But they are not true today.

I do not think those statements can stand with the decision of this court in *Hodgson v. Marks*:[16] nor with the standing of women in our society today. Most wives now are joint owners of the matrimonial home—in law or in equity—with their husbands. They go out to work just as their husbands do. Their earnings go to build up the home just as much as their husband's earnings. Visit the home and you will find that she is in personal occupation of it just as much as he is. She eats there and sleeps there just as he does. She is in control of all that goes on there—just as much as he. In no respect whatever does the nature of her occupation differ from his. If he is a sailor away for months at a time, she is in actual occupation. If he deserts her, she is in actual occupation. These instances all show that "actual occupation" is matter of fact, not matter of law. It need not be single. Two partners in a business can be in actual occupation. It does not depend on title. A squatter is often in actual occupation. Taking it simply as matter of fact, I would conclude that in the cases before us the wife is in actual occupation [...]

Once it is found that a wife is in actual occupation, then it is clear that in the case of registered land, a purchaser or lender would be well advised to make inquiry of the wife. If she then discloses her rights, he takes subject to them. If she does not disclose them, he takes

[14] [1969] 1 WLR 286.
[15] [1986] 1 WLR 286, 293.
[16] [1971] Ch 892. [We will examine that decision in Chapter 4, section 4, and Chapter 6, section 3.2.2. As we will see, it did not involve the actual occupation of a wife and so, technically, is not incompatible with the views expressed by Stamp J and Templeman J.]

free of them. I see no reason why this should cause any difficulty to conveyancers. Nor should it impair the proper conduct of businesses. Anyone who lends money on the security of a matrimonial home nowadays ought to realise that the wife may have a share in it. He ought to make sure that the wife agrees to it, or to go to the house and make inquiries of her. It seems to me utterly wrong that a lender should turn a blind eye to the wife's interest or the possibility of it—and afterwards seek to turn her and the family out—on the plea that he did not know she was in actual occupation. If a bank is to do its duty, in the society in which we live, it should recognise the integrity of the matrimonial home. It should not destroy it by disregarding the wife's interest in it—simply to ensure that it is paid the husband's debt in full—with the high interest rate now prevailing. We should not give monied might priority over social justice. We should protect the position of a wife who has a share—just as years ago we protected the deserted wife. In the hope that the House of Lords will not reverse us now as it did then [...]

In my opinion [Mrs Boland] is entitled to be protected in her occupation of the matrimonial home. The bank is not entitled to throw [her] out into the street—simply to get the last penny of the husband's debt.

Williams & Glyn's Bank v Boland [1981] AC 487, HL

Lord Denning MR was clearly concerned that, as had occurred in *Ainsworth* over fifteen years earlier, the House of Lords would reverse the decision of the Court of Appeal and favour the bank rather than the occupier. His Lordship's fears were, however, unjustified.

Lord Wilberforce

At 502–9

My Lords, these appeals [...] raise for decision the same question: whether a husband or a wife, (in each actual case a wife) who has a beneficial interest in the matrimonial home, by virtue of having contributed to its purchase price, but whose spouse is the legal and registered owner, has an 'overriding interest' binding on a mortgagee who claims possession of the matrimonial home under a mortgage granted by that spouse alone. Although this statement of the issue uses the words 'spouse,' 'husband and wife,' 'matrimonial home,' the appeals do not, in my understanding, involve any question of matrimonial law, or of the rights of married women or of women as such. Exactly the same issue could arise if the roles of husband and wife were reversed, or if the persons interested in the house were not married to each other. The solution must be derived from a consideration in the light of current social conditions of the Land Registration Act 1925 and other property statutes [...]

I now deal with the first question. Were the wives here in 'actual occupation'? These words are ordinary words of plain English, and should, in my opinion, be interpreted as such [...] Given occupation, i.e., presence on the land, I do not think that the word 'actual' was intended to introduce any additional qualification, certainly not to suggest that possession must be 'adverse': it merely emphasises that what is required is physical presence, not some entitlement in law. So even if it were necessary to look behind these plain words into history, I would find no reason for denying them their plain meaning.

Then, were the wives in actual occupation? I ask: why not? There was physical presence, with all the rights that occupiers have, including the right to exclude all others except those having similar rights. The house was a matrimonial home, intended to be occupied, and in fact occupied by both spouses, both of whom have an interest in it: it would require some special doctrine of law to avoid the result that each is in occupation. Three arguments were used for a contrary conclusion. First, it was said that if the vendor (I use this word to include a mortgagor) is in occupation, that is enough to prevent the application of the paragraph. This seems to be a proposition of general application, not limited to the case of husbands, and no doubt, if correct, would be very convenient for purchasers and intending mortgagees. But the presence of the vendor, with occupation, does not exclude the possibility of occupation of others. There are observations which suggest the contrary in the unregistered land case of *Caunce v. Caunce*, but I agree with the disapproval of these, and with the assertion of the proposition I have just stated by Russell L.J. in *Hodgson v. Marks*.[17] Then it was suggested that the wife's occupation was nothing but the shadow of the husband's—a version I suppose of the doctrine of unity of husband and wife. This expression and the argument flowing from it was used by Templeman J. in *Bird v. Syme-Thomson*,[18] a decision preceding and which he followed in the present case. The argument was also inherent in the judgment in *Caunce v. Caunce* which influenced the decisions of Templeman J. It somewhat faded from the arguments in the present case and appears to me to be heavily obsolete. The [bank's] main and final position became in the end this: that, to come within the paragraph, the occupation in question must be apparently inconsistent with the title of the vendor. This, it was suggested, would exclude the wife of a husband-vendor because her apparent occupation would be satisfactorily accounted for by his. But, apart from the rewriting of the paragraph which this would involve, the suggestion is unacceptable. Consistency, or inconsistency, involves the absence, or presence, of an independent right to occupy, though I must observe that 'inconsistency' in this context is an inappropriate word. But how can either quality be predicated of a wife, simply qua wife? A wife may, and everyone knows this, have rights of her own, particularly, many wives have a share in a matrimonial home. How can it be said that the presence of a wife in the house, as occupier, is consistent or inconsistent with the husband's rights until one knows what rights she has? And if she has rights, why, just because she is a wife (or in the converse case, just because an occupier is the husband), should these rights be denied protection under the paragraph? If one looks beyond the case or husband and wife, the difficulty of all these arguments stands out if one considers the case of a man living with a mistress, or of a man and a woman—or for that matter two persons of the same sex—living in a house in separate or partially shared rooms. Are these cases of apparently consistent occupation, so that the rights of the other person (other than the vendor) can be disregarded? The only solution which is consistent with the Act [i.e. the land registration statute] and with common sense is to read the paragraph for what it says. Occupation, existing as a fact, may protect rights if the person in occupation has rights. On this part of the case I have no difficulty in concluding that a spouse, living in a house, has an actual occupation capable of conferring protection, as an overriding interest, upon rights of that spouse [...]

This brings me to the second question, which is whether such rights as a spouse has under a trust for sale are capable of recognition as overriding interests—a question to my mind of some difficulty [...]

As Lord Denning M.R. points out, to describe the interests of spouses in a house jointly bought to be lived in as a matrimonial home as merely an interest in proceeds of sale, or rents and profits until sale, is just a little unreal [...]

I would only add, in conclusion, on the appeal as it concerns the wives a brief observation on the conveyancing consequences of dismissing the appeal. These were alarming to Templeman J., and I can agree with him to the extent that whereas the object of a land registration system is to reduce the risks to purchasers from anything not on the register, to

[17] [1971] Ch 892, 934.
[18] [1979] 1 WLR 440, 444.

extend (if it be an extension) the area of risk so as to include possible interests of spouses, and indeed, in theory, of other members of the family or even outside it, may add to the burdens of purchasers, and involve them in enquiries which in some cases may be troublesome.

But conceded, as it must be, that the Act, following established practice, gives protection to occupation, the extension of the risk area follows necessarily from the extension, beyond the paterfamilias, of rights of ownership, itself following from the diffusion of property and earning capacity. What is involved is a departure from an easy-going practice of dispensing with enquiries as to occupation beyond that of the vendor and accepting the risks of doing so. To substitute for this a practice of more careful enquiry as to the fact of occupation, and if necessary, as to the rights of occupiers can not, in my view of the matter, be considered as unacceptable except at the price of overlooking the widespread development of shared interests of ownership.

5.5 COMPARING THE APPROACHES IN *AINSWORTH* AND *BOLAND*

Clearly, the House of Lords reached different results in *Ainsworth* and *Boland*. In the former case, the bank's claim for possession was successful; in the latter, that claim was denied and the occupying wife won out. From a doctrinal point of view, that difference can be simply explained: it depends on the different *content* of the right held by each occupier. Mrs Ainsworth's right, a 'deserted wife's equity', was not seen as capable of binding the bank; Mrs Boland's right, arising under a trust of the land, was capable of doing so. Harris argues, however, that there is also a difference in the underlying approach adopted by the House of Lords in each case.

Harris, 'Legal Doctrine and Interests in Land' in *Oxford Essays in Jurisprudence* (3rd series, eds Eekelaar and Bell, 1987, pp 183–4)

In the *Ainsworth* case, the principal substantive objections to admitting that a deserted wife's right could bind her husband's successors [including the bank] were these: first, such successors, not being acquainted with the details of intramarital relations, could not be expected to know whether the right had arisen; and, second, the right had an evanescent quality, since it could always be terminated by the court in the exercise of its discretion. If these objections had been fed into a consequentialist calculation, they might have been outweighed by the injustice-consequences to wives of not recognizing the right's proprietary status. In *Boland*, precisely comparable objections were so outweighed. An equitable co-owner's interest [i.e. a right such as that held by Mrs Boland] may arise through an implied trust whose existence depends on private dealings beyond the ken of purchasers and mortgagees [such as the bank] . . . The two considerations acquired special force in *Ainsworth* because, in contrast with *Boland*, the doctrine model, rather the utility model, structured the reasoning. Their Lordships asked themselves, not whether a ruling one way or the other would have best consequences, but whether the right under review had the characteristics we expect to find in an interest in land. It did not. It was obviously not transmissible by the wife; and it was lacking in clarity and permanence.

Harris's analysis emphasizes the fact that, *at a general level*, each of *Ainsworth* and *Boland* raised the same question: should the pre-existing right of an occupier, even if it was not created by the bank nor was necessarily easy for the bank to discover, bind the bank? In *Ainsworth*, the facts that the occupier's right was uncertain and hard to discover led the court, adopting a technical, doctrinal approach, to find that her right could not bind the bank, because it did not count as a property right. In *Boland*, those same facts did not stand in the occupier's way. Harris suggests this is because, in *Boland*, the House of Lords: (i) prioritized the need to reach what it regarded as a just result; and (ii) decided that it was just to require banks, before lending money to an owner of land, to check whether any other occupier of that land claimed a right in relation to that land, and, if so, to get the consent of that occupier to any right that the owner might give the bank.

Nonetheless, it would be oversimplistic to say that, in *Ainsworth*, the court preferred doctrine and ignored the practical effects of its decision, whilst, in *Boland*, the opposite was true. Indeed, Harris goes on to point out that, in land law as in other areas, judges never entirely jettison doctrinal reasoning.[19] For example, Harris notes that, in *Boland*, the House of Lords did not state, and *could not* have said, that: "'*Wives, but only wives, ought to be protected against banks, but only banks.*' [...] *Parliament may enact such distinctions, but it is unthinkable that an English court would.*"[20] The point is that, in *Boland*, the House of Lords' decision depended on its assessment of the nature of Mrs Boland's right: a right under a trust. As a result, its decision must necessarily apply to anyone who has such a right and is in occupation of land; doctrinally, it cannot be limited to wives.

Further, Conaglen has persuasively argued that, despite the emotive rhetoric of Lord Denning MR in the Court of Appeal ('W[e] *should not give monied might priority over social justice*'), the House of Lords in *Boland* simply adopted a 'commonsense application' of the land registration statute and '*the result was driven by the statutory regime far more than it was by social justice concerns to protect wives over money lenders*'.[21] Certainly, any reader of either the Court of Appeal or House of Lords decisions in *Boland* will be struck by the careful, technical analysis carried out by each court.

5.6 LESSONS FROM *AINSWORTH* AND *BOLAND*?

Although *Ainsworth* and *Boland* each focus on one particular corner of land law, they can provide us with a number of general lessons. Firstly, as we noted in section 1 above, land law is clearly very important in practice: the decisions in each case had significant practical consequences not only for Mrs Ainsworth, Mrs Boland, and the respective banks, but also for thousands of other occupiers and mortgage lenders sharing their positions.

Secondly, the cases focused on whether the occupier had a *private right* to use land that she could assert against the bank: the key question was whether the occupier had an interest in land (i.e. a property right) that could bind the bank. As we noted in section 2, other cases at the core of land law also focus on that key question.

Thirdly, in analysing the decisions in *Ainsworth* and *Boland*, it is useful to focus on the *content*, *acquisition*, and *defences* questions. As suggested in section 3 above, those questions

---

[19] At pp 196–7, Harris notes that '*even where consequentialism dominates the elucidation of some interest made dispositive by a legal rule, as in the* Boland *case, the range of possible interpretations is limited by the immanent necessity to give the concept some definite meaning*'.

[20] Harris, at p 177.

[21] Conaglen, 'Mortgagee Powers Rhetoric' (2006) 69 MLR 583, 587.

are a useful way in which to break down the key question of whether one party can assert a property right against another.

Further, as Harris's analysis shows, cases such as *Ainsworth* and *Boland* also raise a broader question about the approach that a court should adopt when deciding a dispute about private rights to use land. The 'utility model' focuses on finding an outcome with the best practical consequences. As suggested in section 5.1 above, however, *Ainsworth* and *Boland* also demonstrate that the special features of land, discussed in section 4 above, can make that model particularly difficult to apply. Indeed, McFarlane's analysis, quoted in section 5.1 above, suggests that it may be impossible to resolve such disputes simply by weighing up the factors favouring each party. As a result, the 'doctrinal model', which aims for a result consistent with the existing, technical rules, is pervasive in land law. Certainly, according to Harris, the doctrinal approach is dominant in *Ainsworth* and is also present, even if outweighed by the 'utility model', in *Boland*.

This leads us to perhaps the most important lesson of *Ainsworth* and *Boland*. Imagine that you are employed to act as a lawyer for one of the participants in those cases. If acting for the occupier, you may want to emphasize the social importance of land and the need to allow the occupier to continue living in her home. If you are acting for the bank, you may instead want to focus on the limited availability of land and the need to keep the cost of mortgages down by eliminating the need for a bank to undertake time-consuming enquiries before making a mortgage loan. Either way, however, it will not be enough simply to go to court and make those general points. If you want to do the best job for your client, it is vital to understand, and to be confident in using, the doctrinal rules that make up land law.

This should not be taken to mean that the 'utility model' is irrelevant or that there is no need to consider the practical merits or wider justice of the doctrinal rules of land law. On the contrary, the social importance of land law means that it is vital not only to understand land law rules, but also to evaluate them. After all, land law, like other areas of law, necessarily changes over time; those changes must be based on a view that the previous legal rules were, in some way, deficient. We can see this by briefly considering developments occurring after *Ainsworth*.

5.7 *AINSWORTH*: LATER DEVELOPMENTS AND FURTHER LESSONS

We have seen that Harris viewed the approach of the House of Lords in *Ainsworth* as based on the 'doctrinal model'. Harris also considered some of the benefits of that approach.

Harris, 'Legal Doctrine and Interests in Land' in *Oxford Essays in Jurisprudence* (3rd series, eds Eekelaar and Bell, 1987, pp 170–1)

[In many instances] to be found in land-law books, courts invoke doctrine to settle disputed questions about the present law. Should they do so? Weber purports to offer explanations, not justifications, of different kinds of professional legal reasoning. Yet he accepts uncritically one of the common rationales for doctrine as against policy, namely, that it augments the certainty and predictability of the law:

'Juridical formalism enables the legal system to operate like a technically rational machine. Thus it guarantees to individuals and groups within the system a relative maximum of freedom and greatly increases for them the possibility of predicting the legal consequences of their actions.'[22]

Two other justifications for doctrinal reasoning (not mentioned by Weber) lie close to the surface of the present-day legal culture. They concern 'separation of powers' and the 'rule of law'. If judges resolve an uncertain question about the present law by an assessment and balancing of social consequences, are they not trespassing on the functions of the legislature?

This analysis suggests that, in developing and reforming land law, there are some options open to Parliament that are not available to judges. For example, as noted above, Harris argued that it would be 'unthinkable' for a judge to come up with a rule that, in a dispute between an occupier and a party later acquiring a right in land, the former will win whenever she is a wife and the later party is a bank. In contrast, Parliament has the sovereign authority needed to make such doctrinally unjustified distinctions, and it can do so if it believes such a rule will have beneficial consequences.

We can see this by considering the Matrimonial Homes Act 1967—that is, Parliament's response to the House of Lords' decision in *Ainsworth*. That Act established: (i) that a spouse has a (qualified) statutory right to occupy a home owned by his or her partner; and (ii) that the statutory right to occupy, if protected by registration, was capable of binding a third party, such as a bank, later acquiring a right in relation to the matrimonial home. Parliament thus reformed the law by coming up with a specific, tailored solution that it believed formed the best compromise between the need to protect an occupying spouse and the need to protect a third party such as a bank.[23] That compromise, now found in the Family Law Act 1996 (FLA 1996), ss 30–33, avoids the doctrinal question of whether the right to occupy counts as a property right; instead, the right is allowed to bind a third party, such as a bank, *only* if it is registered. Actual occupation cannot protect the statutory right to occupy: if it is not registered, it cannot bind a third party. And, even if the right is registered, a court still has the discretion to allow a third party to remove the occupying spouse.[24]

The contrast between the approach adopted in *Ainsworth* and the solution implemented by the Matrimonial Homes Act 1967 reflects a wider tension in land law—that is, between judicial and legislative reform. At a number of points in this book, we will come across land law rules that are subject to disapproval. At such points, it is important to consider not only *if* the rules should be changed, but also *how* they should be changed. As we will see in Chapter 18, a topical example of this problem concerns the acquisition of rights under a trust of a family home. For example, we have seen that the key difference between *Ainsworth* and *Boland* is that, in the latter case, Mrs Boland had a right capable of binding a third party: a right under a trust. Mrs Boland acquired such a right as a result of making a financial contribution to Mr Boland's purchase of the home. According to Lord Denning MR in the Court of Appeal in *Boland*, the courts' willingness to recognize such rights stems from a 'remarkable series of decisions'[25] confirmed by the House of Lords in 1970 in *Gissing v Gissing*.[26]

[22] Weber, *Law in Economy and Society* (ed Rheinstein, 1954, pp 226–7).
[23] That solution has been extended so that it now applies to parties in a civil partnership as well as to spouses: see Civil Partnership Act 2004, s 82 and Sch 9, para 1, amending Pt 4 of the Family Law Act 1996.
[24] See Family Law Act 1996, s 33: *Kaur v Gill* [1988] Fam 110 provides an example of the court exercising that discretion in favour of a third party.
[25] [1979] 2 WLR 550, 557.
[26] [1971] AC 886.

It has often been said, however, that the courts have not gone far enough in recognizing such rights: for example, it has been argued that it ought to be easier for a partner to acquire a right even where he or she has *not* made a financial contribution to the purchase of his or her partner's land. If those arguments are correct, the question then is *how* the law should be changed: by Parliament or by the courts? In particular, is it legitimate for judges to change the law in order to reflect changes in society—or is that exclusively the province of an elected legislature?

The topical debate around when a partner can acquire a right under a trust of a family home also raises a further general issue that underlies Parliament's response to the House of Lords' decision in *Ainsworth*. The question here is not whether the land law rules should be reformed by Parliament or by the courts; it is the logically prior question of whether the necessary changes can be made *without reforming land law at all*. A good example of this is provided by the Law Commission's recent work on the family home, which we will examine in detail in Chapter 18, section 4. Initially, that work attempted to respond directly to the criticism that the land law rules make it too difficult for a partner to acquire a right under a trust of a family home.[27] The Commission concluded, however, that it was impossible to come up with a satisfactory legislative scheme setting out precisely when a partner should acquire such a property right.[28] Its focus therefore shifted away from a core land law question (when a party can acquire a property right in relation to land) to a different question: if the relationship of cohabiting, but unmarried,[29] partners ends (whether due to the parties splitting up or to death), are there circumstances in which one of the parties should be under a duty to provide some financial support to the other partner? The Commission concluded that Parliament should enact such a scheme.[30]

One way of analysing the Law Commission's approach is to say that it has moved from a 'land law' solution to a 'family law' solution. Certainly, its focus is no longer on private rights to use land; rather, it has shifted to the question of whether a partner should be able to receive financial support. In Chapter 18, section 4, we will consider the specific advantages and disadvantages of such a shift. For present purposes, the key point is that, whilst our focus in this book will remain on private rights to use land and, in particular, on property rights relating to land, it is also important to bear in mind that the best solution to particular problems may lie not in reforming land law, but in developing other areas of the law.

6 CONCLUSION

As a result of the special physical features of land, special legal rules apply to land. The subject of land law does not consider all of those legal rules; instead, it focuses on private rights to use land and, at its core, considers property rights to use land. In very general terms, the

---

[27] See Law Commission Report No 23, *Sixth Programme of Law Reform* (1995, item 8).

[28] See Law Commission Report No 278, *Sharing Homes: A Discussion Paper* (2005, esp Pt VI and [15] of the Executive Summary).

[29] Married partners, like those in a civil partnership, are already covered by legislation permitting a court to adjust the parties' property rights and/or to impose payment obligations if the parties' relationship breaks down: see Matrimonial Causes Act 1973. Such partners are also in a stronger position if the relationship ends by death: see Inheritance (Provision for Family and Dependants) Act 1975.

[30] See Law Commission Report No 307, *Cohabitation: The Financial Consequences of Relationship Breakdown* (2007).

core of land law deals with three key questions. The *content* question considers the nature of a party's right and, in particular, asks if that right counts as a property right. The *acquisition* question concerns the means by which a party can acquire a private right to use land and, in particular, how a property right can be acquired. The *defences* question asks whether a party later acquiring a private right to use land may have a defence to a pre-existing property right held by another party.

By organizing land law in this way, we can begin to understand the legal rules that make up the subject. But no ordering of the rules can disguise the various tensions that run throughout land law. At a simple factual level, there is often a tension between two parties who each claim competing rights to use the land. For example, in each of *National Provincial Bank v Ainsworth* and *Williams & Glyn's Bank v Boland*, there is a tension between protecting an occupier who wishes to stay in her home and protecting the bank that has lent money on the security of that home.

At a more abstract level, there may be a tension between the different approaches that a court can take to such a dispute. For example, as noted in section 5.2 above, Harris has contrasted a 'utility model' (in which a court should make the decision with what it regards as the best practical consequences) with a 'doctrinal model' (in which a court should make the decision that best accords with the existing legal rules).

Further, if it is felt that the existing land law rules need to be changed, there is a tension between judicial and legislative reform: can judges develop the law in the appropriate direction, or should they hold back and wait for parliamentary intervention?

Finally, there is the wider question of whether the best response to a particular problem necessarily consists in changing the land law rules: it may be, as the Law Commission has suggested in the context of disputes over the family home, that we have to look beyond land law for a solution.

Of course, not all of these tensions are unique to land law. For example, Harris's 'utility model' and 'doctrinal model' are developed from Weber's general analysis of the law, and the tension between judicial and legislative reform runs throughout the law. But the special physical features of land mean that the way in which land law responds to these tensions is of great practical importance, as Mrs Ainsworth and Mrs Boland might testify.

QUESTIONS

1. In what ways does land differ from other physical things? What consequences do those differences have for land law?

2. What is 'land law'? Does it involve all legal rules related to the use of land?

3. Harris suggests that the 'utility model' and the 'doctrinal model' may be useful in understanding particular approaches to land law. What are the differences between the two models?

4. Why did the House of Lords reach differing results in *National Provincial Bank v Ainsworth* and *Williams & Glyn's Bank v Boland*? Do you agree with the results in each of these cases?

5. Land law has a reputation as a subject that is full of technical rules. Even if that reputation is true, is it necessarily a bad thing?

FURTHER READING

Birks, 'Five Keys to Land Law' in *Land Law: Themes and Perspectives* (eds Bright and Dewar, Oxford: OUP, 1998)

Conaglen, 'Mortgages Powers Rhetoric' (2006) 69 MLR 583

Harris, 'Legal Doctrine and Interests in Land' in *Oxford Essays in Jurisprudence* (3rd series, eds Eekelaar and Bell, Oxford: OUP, 1987)

Law Commission Report No 307, *Cohabitation: The Financial Consequences of Relationship Breakdown* (2007, Pts I and II)

McFarlane, *The Structure of Property Law* (Oxford: Hart, 2008, Pt A)

2

LAND, PROPERTY, AND EQUITY

CENTRAL ISSUES

1. In Chapter 1, we looked at the special features of land and saw that land law is a special part of property law. In this chapter, we will look at certain key features that land law shares with other parts of property law.

2. Firstly, we will see how land is regarded by the law as a form of (private) property: it is a resource that can come under the exclusive control of a particular individual, who can be called an 'owner' of land. In establishing this, we will consider some of the different meanings that can be given to the term 'property'.

3. We will also examine what it means to say that a party has a right to exclusive control of 'land'. We will see that such a party's rights are not limited to the physical surface of the land: they extend both downwards and upwards from that surface. We will also consider the extent to which a party's right to exclusive control of land entails a right to exclusive control of objects attached to that land, or found in or on that land.

4. Secondly, we will see that in land law, as in all of property law, doctrines developed by courts of equity play a vital role. In Chapter 4, we will look at the impact of equity in more detail; here, we will briefly set out the nature of equity and point out the important fact that equitable rules, as well as common law rules, play a vital role in land law.

5. In particular, it is necessary to bear in mind that, even if B cannot show he has a legal estate or legal interest in land, it may still be possible for B to show he has an equitable interest. The important point is that the *content* question and *acquisition* question may be answered differently where equitable property rights are concerned. We will examine the nature of equitable interests in Chapter 4.

1 LAND AS A FORM OF PRIVATE PROPERTY

In Chapter 1, section 1, we noted that rules relating to land can be seen throughout the law, not only in land law. The following extract, taken from a seminal constitutional law case, provides an example of this. It is important to note that the case does not only concern the protection of land; the claimant also complained of the theft of some of his papers. Those two aspects of the case are not separated out by the court: as we will see, the case depends not on the special features of land, but rather on the protection given to *any* property right.

Entick v Carrington (1765) 2 Wils KB 274, Common Pleas

Facts: Carrington and three others (messengers to the King) entered the house of Entick without his consent, searched it, and removed various papers. They were acting under a warrant issued by the Earl of Halifax, one of the King's Secretaries of State. The warrant authorized them to search for papers at the house of Entick, because he was '*the author of, or one concerned in the writing of several weekly very seditious papers, entitled* The Monitor *or* British Freeholder *containing gross and scandalous reflections and invectives upon His Majesty's Government, and upon both Houses of Parliament*'.

Lord Camden, Lord Chief Justice, considered whether the warrant could authorize the actions of Carrington and the other messengers.

Lord Camden, LCJ

At 291–2

The warrant in our case was an execution in the first instance, without any previous summons, examination, hearing, or proof that he [Entick] was author of the supposed libels; a power claimed by no other magistrate whatsoever; [...] it was left to the discretion of these defendants to execute the warrant in the absence or presence of [Entick], when he might have no witness present to see what they did; for they were to seize all papers, bank bills, or any other valuable papers they might take away if they were so disposed; there might be nobody to detect them.

[W]e were told by one of these messengers that he was obliged by his oath to sweep away all papers whatsoever; if this is law it would be found in our books, but no such law ever existed in this country; our law holds the property of every man so sacred, that no man can set his foot upon his neighbour's close without leave; if he does he is a trespasser, though he does no damage at all; if he will tread upon his neighbour's ground he must justify it by law.

The defendants have no right to avail themselves of the usage of these warrants since the Revolution [...] we can safely say there is no law in this country to justify the defendants in what they have done; if there was, it would destroy all the comforts of society; for papers are often the dearest property a man can have [...]

We shall now consider the usage of these warrants since the Revolution; if it began then, it is too modern to be law; the common law did not begin with the Revolution; the ancient constitution which had almost been overthrown and destroyed was then repaired and revived; the Revolution added a new buttress to the ancient venerable edifice: the Kings Bench lately said that no objection had ever been taken to general warrants, they have passed *sub silentio:*[1] this

---

[1] [Under silence; without comment.]

is the first instance of an attempt to prove a modern practice of a private office to make and execute warrants to enter a man's house, search for and take way all his books and papers in the first instance, to be law, which is not to be found in our books. It must have been the guilt or poverty of those upon whom such warrants have been executed, that deterred or hindered them from contending against the power of the Secretary of State, or such warrants could never have passed for lawful till this time [. . .]

Our law is wise and merciful, and supposes every man accused to be innocent before he is tried by his peers: upon the whole, we are all of opinion that this warrant is wholly illegal and void. One word more for ourselves; we are no advocates for libels, all Governments must set their faces against them, and whenever they come before us and a jury we shall set our faces against them; and if juries do not prevent them they may prove fatal to liberty, destroy Government and introduce anarchy; but tyranny is better than anarchy, and the worst Government better than none at all.

When analysing *Entick v Carrington*, it is useful to bear in mind the Fourth Amendment to the Constitution of the United States:

The right of the people to be secure in their persons, houses, papers, and effects, against unreasonable searches and seizures, shall not be violated, and no warrants shall issue, but upon probable cause, supported by oath or affirmation, and particularly describing the place to be searched, and the persons or things to be seized.

That constitutional guarantee was passed, in large part, to prevent an abuse of governmental power that had occurred in the 1760s, when tax collectors had been given a very wide power to enter and search private homes. It is worth noting that, in *Entick*, the reasoning of Lord Camden was not based on a *special* limit on governmental power, such as that later established by the Fourth Amendment, but rather on the *general* rules of property law. More precisely, because Entick had a property right in relation to both his house and papers, *no one* could interfere with those things without showing some lawful authority to do so. So, even without an explicit constitutional guarantee, Entick's land, like his papers, could be seen as private property, safe from unjustified interference.

2 THE MEANING OF 'PROPERTY' IN LAND LAW

In a case such as *Entick*, it is tempting to say that the land and papers were each 'Entick's property'. As the following extract shows, however, that general description may not, in fact, be an accurate picture of the legal position.

Gray and Gray, *Elements of Land Law* (5th edn, 2009, pp 86–8)

Few concepts are quite so fragile, so elusive and so frequently misused as the notion of property. There is a pervasive element of shared deception in our normal property talk: property is not theft, but *fraud*. We commonly speak of property as if its meaning were entirely clear and logical, but property is a conceptual mirage which slips tantalisingly from view just when it seems most solidly attainable. Amongst the misperceptions which dominate the conventional analysis of both lay persons and lawyers is the lazy myth that property is a 'monolithic notion of standard content and invariable intensity'.[2] Our daily references to property there-fore tend to comprise a mutual conspiracy of unsophisticated sematic allusions and confu-sions, which we tolerate—frequently, indeed, do not notice—largely because our linguistic shorthand commands a certain low-level communicative efficiency [. . .]

It remains painfully true that most of our everyday references to property are unreflective, naïve and relatively meaningless. In our crude way we are seldom concerned to look behind the immediately practical or functional sense in which we employ the term 'property' in rela-tion to land. What does it really mean to say that Julian Bishop 'owns' 25 Mountfield Gardens or that these premises are his 'property'? [. . .]

The mistaken reification of property[3]

As the High Court of Australia acknowledged in *Yanner v Eaton*,[4] much of our false think-ing about property 'stems from the residual perception that "property" is itself a thing or resource rather than a legally endorsed concentration of power over things and resources.' The root of the difficulty lies in the fact that non-lawyers (and often lawyers) tend to speak rather loosely of 'property' as the *thing* which is owned (eg 'that book/car/house is my prop-erty'). Whilst this reification of property is harmless enough in casual conversation, it has the effect of obscuring important features of property as a legal and social institution.

Property is not a thing but a power relationship

Deep at the heart of the phenomenon of property is the semantic reality that 'property' is not a thing, but rather the condition of being 'proper' to a particular person (eg 'That book/car/house is *proper* to me'). For serious students of property, the beginning of truth is the recognition that property is not a thing but a *power relationship*—a relationship of social and legal legitimacy existing between a person and a valued resource (whether tangible or intan-gible). To claim 'property' in a resource is, in effect, to assert a significant degree of control over that resource. Moreover, as Karl Renner once said, '[p]ower over matter begets personal power'.[5] 'Property' ultimately articulates a political relationship between persons. Land—the physical substratum of all human interaction—becomes a vital component of all social and economic engineering.

All property talk is value-laden

All property references are, at some level, a statement about the social legitimacy attaching to the claim in question. The etymological links between terms such as 'property', 'proper', 'appropriate', and 'propriety' underscore the value-laden complexity of inter-relating nuances of property talk. Genuine property discourse thinly conceals a subtext of social propriety. The law of property incorporates a series of critical value judgments, reflecting the cultural norms, the social ethics and the political economy prevalent in any given community. It is inevitable that property law should serve in this way as a vehicle for ideology, for 'property' has commonly been the epithet used to identify that which people most greatly value. The

  [2] See *Yanner v Eaton* (1999) 201 CLR 351 (High Court of Australia), [19], *per* Gleeson CJ, and Gaudron, Kirby, and Hayne JJ.

  [3] [Reification means 'turning into a thing'—the argument here is that it is a mistake to equate 'property' as a concept or organizing idea with physical things, such as land or cars.]

  [4] [(1999) 201 CLR 351, [18], *per* Gleeson CJ, and Gaudron, Kirby and Hayne JJ.]

  [5] *The Institutions of Private Law and Their Social Functions* (ed O Kahn-Freund, 1949, p 107).

terminology of 'property' also points more subtly to relationships of dependence, for dependence is the inescapable outcome of unequal distributions of that which is valued. The terms 'property' and 'dependence' are merely positive and negative descriptions of existing distributions of control over socially valued resources.

Gray and Gray make a number of important points: some of them can assist us to understand, internally, how land law works; others can help us to stand outside land law and evaluate the system. The first crucial point is that, to understand property as it is used in legal contexts, we cannot equate it with physical things: so, in *Entick v Carrington*, it is not enough simply to say that the land or papers were Mr Entick's property; instead, we need to make clear that there is something *in between* Mr Entick and those physical things. Gray and Gray develop this point by focusing on property as a 'power relationship' between, say, Mr Entick and his land or papers. A different way of developing the point (linking it into our discussion of the scope of land law in Chapter 1, section 2) is to say that what stands between Mr Entick and his land or papers is a *right*. In defining the *content* of that right, we can build on Gray and Gray's definition of the content of the 'power relationship': it is a right to a '*significant degree of control over that resource*'.

So, the first vital lesson to take from Gray and Gray's analysis is that we cannot always equate 'property' with 'things'. If we say that the house broken into by Mr Carrington was Mr Entick's property, what we really mean is that Mr Entick had a particular type of *right* in relation to that land—a right that gave him a significant degree of control over that land. We can describe Mr Entick's right as a *property right* in relation to that land. As suggested by Birks in the extract set out in Chapter 1, section 2, the core of land law is concerned with the '*nature, creation and protection*' of such rights. We can therefore say that land (like papers) counts as a form of private property in the sense that land is a resource in relation to which a private individual (such as Mr Entick) can have a property right. This means that, in thinking about the notion of property in land law, we really need to focus on the concept of a *property right*. We will examine the nature of a property right in land in more detail in Chapter 3. A key feature of such a right is that imposes a prima facie duty on the rest of the world. In *Entick*, the King's messengers, along with everyone else in the world, were thus under a duty to Mr Entick, and that duty arose because Mr Entick had a property right in relation to both the land and papers.

In the extract above, Gray and Gray also point out the assumptions that we may make when saying, for example, that the land and papers are Mr Entick's property. That formulation implies that the land and papers are *proper to* Mr Entick—that is, they are due to, or appropriate to, him. That point is made clearer if, instead of describing the land and papers as his property, we say that Mr Entick has a property right in relation to them. The terminology of 'rights' is also, to use Gray and Gray's term, 'value-laden' because it implies something about the legitimacy of Mr Entick's claim.

At this point, it is very useful to distinguish between two different kinds of legitimacy. In *Entick* itself, Mr Entick was not concerned to show that, for moral, social, or economic reasons, it was appropriate for him to have a significant degree of control over the land or papers; his only concern was to show that his claim to that control was *legally* legitimate—that is, to show that he had a right that the courts were prepared to protect and enforce. His focus was therefore on showing that the rules of property law gave him a property right in relation to both the land and the papers. When considering his claim from that internal perspective, we can therefore limit ourselves to looking at the land law rules and seeing if they do, indeed, give him a property right in relation to the land in question. We can, however, say that Mr Entick does have such a property right and still consider whether, for moral, social, or economic (or other) reasons, Mr Entick *should* have that degree of control over the land or papers. It is at this point that the *'critical value judgements'* referred to by Gray and Gray play a very important role.

Of course, it would be naive to think that these two kinds of legitimacy can, or should, be kept firmly separate. After all, as judges or legislators develop the law, they have to keep in mind the wider (moral, social, economic, etc.) effects of the legal rules. In fact, the contrast between two kinds of legitimacy links in to the contrast between the two approaches that we examined in Chapter 1, section 5.2—that is, what Harris called the 'doctrinal model' and the 'utility model'. The first question in *Entick* is whether Mr Entick's claim to a property right in the land and papers is legally legitimate: does it accord with the doctrinal rules of property law? The second question, is whether, taking into account a broad range of considerations (e.g. moral, social, economic, etc.), it would be better or worse to recognize that Mr Entick has such a right: does recognizing such a right have better consequences than not recognizing it? And, as we saw in the previous chapter, the 'utility model' can play a role not only when Parliament decides how to reform the law for the future, but also when judges decide on the current state of the law.

3 THE MEANING OF 'LAND'

3.1 THE PHYSICAL REACH OF LAND

In the extract set out above, Gray and Gray raise a fundamental question: *'What does it really mean to say that Julian Bishop "owns" 25 Mountfield Gardens or that these premises are his "property"?'* As we have seen, the first step is to understand that statement as simply a shorthand for the more accurate analysis: Julian Bishop has a property right in relation to that land. After all, as we noted in Chapter 1, section 3, if Julian Bishop puts 25 Mountfield Gardens up for sale and you decide to put a bid in, then you are not bidding for the land as such; instead, you are bidding for his property right in that land—either a freehold or a lease. Gray and Gray's question therefore boils down to a question about the *content* of a freehold or a lease: if you acquire such a right, what rights to use the land will you get? We will examine that question in Chapter 3, section 3, when we focus on the nature of the freehold and the lease.

There is also a more practical side to the content of your freehold or lease. It will give you rights to use the land—but what do we mean by 'the land'? You might think of yourself as buying 'a house', but, clearly, if you get Julian Bishop's freehold or lease, you get more than the house. After all, if the house were to burn down, you would still have your freehold or lease. Indeed, as the following extract shows, your freehold or lease gives you more than just a right in relation to the house and the surface on which it stands.

Edwards v Lee's Administrator 96 SW 2d 1028 (1936, Court of Appeals of Kentucky)

Facts: Mr and Mrs Edwards owned land in Kentucky, located close to the famous Mammoth Cave. They discovered a spectacular cave under their land. They dubbed it the 'Great Onyx Cave', built a hotel on the land, and attracted tourists by offering them a chance to visit the cave. The tourists entered the cave through the Edwards' land, but a third of the cave lay underneath land owned by Lee, one of the Edwards' neighbours. Lee had not given permission for the visitors to enter that part of the cave. He therefore claimed that, by encouraging the tourists to enter that part of the cave, the Edwards had committed the tort of trespass to Lee's land. Lee also claimed that, as a result, the Edwards should be made to pay Lee a share of the profits that they had made from allowing visitors to enter the cave. The lower court found in favour of Lee on both points, ordering the Edwards to pay a third of the net profits that they had made from offering visitors access to the cave. The Edwards appealed, but the Court of Appeals confirmed the approach of the lower court.

Stites J

At 1029–32

At the inception of this litigation, Lee undertook to procure a survey of the cave in order that it might be determined what portion of it was on his land. The chancellor ordered that a survey be made [...] Edwards sought a writ of prohibition in this court against the circuit judge to prevent the carrying out of the order of survey. The writ was denied [...] In this last case the maxim, "Cujus est solum, ejus est usque ad cœlum et ad infernos" (to whomsoever the soil belongs, he owns also to the sky and to the depths) was considered and applied, and an analogy drawn between trespassing through mining beneath another's land and passing under it through a cave.

[Mr and Mrs Edwards], in their attack here on the measure of damages and its application to the facts adduced, urge: (1) That [Lee] had simply a hole in the ground, about 360 feet below the surface, which they could not use and which they could not even enter except by going through the mouth of the cave on Edwards' property; (2) the cave was of no practical use to [Lee] without an entrance, and there was no one except [the Edwards] on whom they might confer a right of beneficial use; (3) Lee's portion of the cave had no rental value; (4) [Lee was] not ousted of the physical occupation or use of the property because [he] did not and could not occupy it; (5) the property has not in any way been injured by the use to which it has been put by [the Edwards], and since this is fundamentally an action for damages arising from trespass, the recovery must be limited to the damages suffered by [Lee] (in other words, nominal damages) and cannot properly be measured by the benefits accruing to the trespasser from his wrongful use of the property; (6) as a result of the injunction, [Lee has his] cave in exactly the condition it has always been, handicapped by no greater degree of uselessness than it was before [the Edwards] trespassed upon it.

[Lee], on the other hand, argues that this was admittedly a case of willful trespass; that it is not analogous to a situation where a trespasser simply walks across the land of another, for here the trespasser actually used the property of Lee to make a profit for himself; that even if nothing tangible was taken or disturbed in the various trips through Lee's portion of the cave, nevertheless there was a taking of esthetic enjoyment which, under ordinary circumstances, would justify a recovery of the reasonable rental value for the use of the cave; that there being no basis for arriving at reasonable rental values, the [lower court] took the only course open to it under the circumstances and properly assessed the damages on the basis of the profits realized from the use of Lee's portion of the cave.

We may begin our consideration of the proper measure of damages to be applied with the postulate that [Lee] held legal title to a definite segment of the cave and that [he was] possessed, therefore, of a right which it is the policy of the law to protect. We may assume that

> the [Edwards] were guilty of repeated trespasses upon the property of [Lee...] The proof likewise clearly indicates that the trespasses were willful, and not innocent [...]
>
> [W]e are led inevitably to the conclusion that the measure of recovery in this case must be the benefits, or net profits, received by [the Edwards] from the use of the property of [Lee]. The philosophy of all these decisions is that a wrongdoer shall not be permitted to make a profit from his own wrong.

There are two key points in the *Great Onyx Cave Case*, as it sometimes known. Firstly, and most importantly for our present purposes, it shows that Lee's property right in his land was not simply limited to his house and the surface of his land; rather, Lee's property right imposed a duty on the rest of the world (including the Edwards) not to go into that part of the cave which lay underneath Lee's land. It made no difference that Lee himself could not, in practice, get into that part of the cave without using an entrance on the Edwards' land.

The second point concerns the measure of damages available to Lee for the trespass to his land. The orthodox position is that, if the defendant commits a tort, he is under a duty to compensate the claimant for loss caused by that tort. In the *Great Onyx Cave Case*, however, the Kentucky courts accepted that, in some cases at least, a different approach can be applied: Lee received a substantial payment from the Edwards even though their conduct had caused no loss to Lee. And one possible method of defending that different approach, which has also been relied on by English courts,[6] is to say that property rights need special protection.

In deciding that the Edwards had interfered with Lee's property right in his land, the Kentucky courts referred to the maxim *Cujus est solum, ejus est usque ad cœlum et ad infernos* ('to whomsoever the soil belongs, he owns also to the sky and to the depths'). Certainly, whilst *Edwards v Lee's Administrator* relates to the depths, the decision of McNair J in *Kelsen v Imperial Tobacco Co*[7] shows that a party with a property right in land also has rights in relation to the sky.

Mr Kelsen had a lease of a tobacconist's shop in City Road, Islington. The Imperial Tobacco Co maintained a large advertising sign that projected into the air above that shop. Initially, Mr Kelsen made no complaint, but he later demanded that the sign be removed. The company refused, arguing that, because its sign did not substantially interfere with Mr Kelsen's enjoyment of his land, it was not committing the tort of nuisance. McNair J ordered the sign to be removed, however: Mr Kelsen's lease gave him a right to exclusive control not only of the shop itself, but also of the air above. As a result, the tobacco company, like the rest of the world, had a prima facie duty not to encroach on that space without Mr Kelsen's consent. An injunction could therefore be granted to prevent the company's ongoing act of trespass.

Like most maxims, however—particularly those in Latin—the expression *Cujus est solum, ejus est usque ad cœlum et ad infernos* can be very misleading, as the next extract shows.

Bernstein of Leigh (Baron) v Skyviews & General Ltd [1978] QB 479

Facts: Skyviews took aerial photographs of houses and then offered to sell copies of the photographs to residents of the houses. On receiving an offer to buy such a photograph

---

[6] See, e.g., *Attorney-General v Blake* [2001] 1 AC 268, 278–80, *per* Lord Nicholls. This method can, however, be questioned: why should a party's property right be protected more jealously than, for example, his rights not to be punched or not to be deceived?
[7] [1957] 2 QB 334.

of his country house in Leigh, Kent, Lord Bernstein took exception, not only turning down the offer, but also complaining of an invasion of his privacy and requesting the destruction of any negatives or prints of his house. Unfortunately, his letter of complaint was answered by an 18-year-old who had just joined the Skyviews. She replied by offering to sell Lord Bernstein the negative of his house. This led to another letter of complaint, in the absence of an answer to which, Lord Bernstein began legal proceedings. The chief part of his claim was that Skyviews had committed the wrong of trespass by flying over his land without permission. Griffiths J, however, dismissed the claim, finding that Skyviews had not interfered with Lord Bernstein's property right.

Griffiths J

At 485–8

I therefore find that on August 3, 1974, [Skyviews] flew over [Lord Bernstein's] land for the purpose of photographing his house and did so without his permission.

I turn now to the law. [Lord Bernstein] claims that as owner of the land he is also owner of the air space above the land, or at least has the right to exclude any entry into the air space above his land. He relies upon the old Latin maxim, *cujus est solum ejus est usque ad coelum et ad inferos*, a colourful phrase often upon the lips of lawyers since it was first coined by Accursius in Bologna in the 13th century.[8] There are a number of cases in which the maxim has been used by English judges, but an examination of those cases shows that they have all been concerned with structures attached to the adjoining land, such as overhanging buildings, signs or telegraph wires, and for their solution it has not been necessary for the judge to cast his eyes towards the heavens; he has been concerned with the rights of the owner in the air space immediately adjacent to the surface of the land.

That an owner has certain rights in the air space above his land is well established by authority. He has the right to lop the branches of trees that may overhang his boundary, although this right seems to be founded in nuisance rather than trespass: see *Lemmon v. Webb*.[9] In *Wandsworth Board of Works v. United Telephone Co. Ltd.*,[10] the Court of Appeal did not doubt that the owner of land would have the right to cut a wire placed over his land [...]

It may be a sound and practical rule to regard any incursion into the air space at a height which may interfere with the ordinary user of the land as a trespass rather than a nuisance. Adjoining owners then know where they stand; they have no right to erect structures overhanging or passing over their neighbours' land and there is no room for argument whether they are thereby causing damage or annoyance to their neighbours about which there may be much room for argument and uncertainty. But wholly different considerations arise when considering the passage of aircraft at a height which in no way affects the user of the land.

There is no direct authority on this question, but as long ago as 1815 Lord Ellenborough in *Pickering v. Rudd*[11] expressed the view that it would not be a trespass to pass over a man's land in a balloon [...]

I can find no support in authority for the view that a landowner's rights in the air space above his property extend to an unlimited height. In *Wandsworth Board of Works v. United*

---

[8] [Franciscus Accursius was a professor of law at the University of Bologna. By compiling the 'Great Gloss' of the Roman law under Justinian, he played a pivotal role in the spread of Roman law thinking in the European medieval world and beyond.]

[9] [1894] 3 Ch 1.

[10] (1884) 13 QBD 904.

[11] (1815) 4 Camp 219.

Telephone Co. Ltd.,[12] Bowen L.J. described the maxim, *usque ad coelum*, as a fanciful phrase, to which I would add that if applied literally it is a fanciful notion leading to the absurdity of a trespass at common law being committed by a satellite every time it passes over a suburban garden. The academic writers speak with one voice in rejecting the uncritical and literal application of the maxim [. . .]

The problem is to balance the rights of an owner to enjoy the use of his land against the rights of the general public to take advantage of all that science now offers in the use of air space. This balance is in my judgment best struck in our present society by restricting the rights of an owner in the air space above his land to such height as is necessary for the ordinary use and enjoyment of his land and the structures upon it, and declaring that above that height he has no greater rights in the air space than any other member of the public.

Applying this test to the facts of this case, I find that [Skyviews'] aircraft did not infringe any rights in [Lord Bernstein's] air space, and thus no trespass was committed. It was on any view of the evidence flying many hundreds of feet above the ground and it is not suggested that by its mere presence in the air space it caused any interference with any use to which [Lord Bernstein] put or might wish to put his land. [Lord Bernstein's] complaint is not that the aircraft interfered with the use of his land but that a photograph was taken from it. There is, however, no law against taking a photograph, and the mere taking of a photograph cannot turn an act which is not a trespass into the plaintiff's air space into one that is a trespass.

Section 40 of the Civil Aviation Act 1949 makes clear that simply flying at a reasonable height above another's land does not constitute a wrong against that landowner. Griffiths J decided that, in any case, there is an inherent limit on a landowner's property right. So, whilst a property right unquestionably allows its holder to assert a significant degree of control over a resource, that control must be limited—in some circumstances, at least—in order to take account of the needs of others. After all, as we noted in Chapter 1, section 2, a public body may have a statutory power, in certain circumstances, to buy a party's property right in land whether that party agrees to the sale or not. Such compulsory purchase rules are simply a more dramatic example of the point underlying the decision in *Bernstein v Skyviews*—that is, that a property right in land, whilst it may give its holder valuable protection, is never absolute.

3.2 WHAT OBJECTS DOES THE LAND INCLUDE?

3.2.1 Things attached to, or part and parcel of, the land

On 23 May 2002, the BBC News website reported on a decision from the Colchester county court. Mr Bennis had a property right in a large detached house. He sold that right to Mr and Mrs McMahon. When the McMahons moved in, they were disappointed to find that Mr Bennis had removed a number of items from the house (including a towel rail attached to the central heating system, and signs with the name and number of the house), as well as taking paving stones from the garden. Mr Bennis believed that he was entitled to remove those things: it seems that the contract between him and the McMahons did not specifically list those items as part of the sale. Nonetheless, the county court found in favour of the McMahons and Mr Bennis was ordered to pay them £1,166. The point is that Mr Bennis had clearly agreed to transfer his property right in the land—and that property

---

12 (1884) 13 QBD 904.

right includes not only the house and the surface of the land, but also any items that are viewed as part of that land.

How, then, can we tell if a particular object is included within the scope of a property right in land? The relevant principles are considered in the following extract.

Elitestone Ltd v Morris [1997] 1 WLR 687, HL

Facts: Elitestone Ltd had a property right in land in Murton, Swansea. Mr Morris (along with Ms Sked) lived in a wooden bungalow on that land and paid an annual fee to Elitestone Ltd. Elitestone Ltd wished to redevelop the land and brought proceedings to remove Mr Morris from the land. Mr Morris claimed that, under the provisions of the Rent Act 1977, he had a protected tenancy. If that claim were correct, the grounds on which Elitestone Ltd could apply for possession of the land were limited by statute and none of those grounds was available to them. Both sides accepted that, to have a protected tenancy, Mr Morris had to show that he had a property right in land (a lease). Elitestone Ltd argued that Mr Morris could not have a property right in land because, instead, he simply owned a wooden bungalow—that is, a separate object not forming part of any land. The Court of Appeal accepted that argument and Mr Morris appealed to the House of Lords, which allowed his appeal.

Lord Lloyd
At 689–93

The assistant recorder held, correctly, at the end of what was necessarily a very lengthy judgment that the question in Mr. Morris's case turned on whether or not the bungalow formed part of the realty.[13] [...]

Having visited the site, the assistant recorder had this to say:

'While the house rested on the concrete pillars which were themselves attached to the ground, it seems to me clear that at least by 1985 and probably before, it would have been clear to anybody that this was a structure that was not meant to be enjoyed as a chattel to be picked up and moved in due course but that it should be a long-term feature of the realty albeit that, because of its construction, it would plainly need more regular maintenance.'

The Court of Appeal disagreed[14] [...] Aldous L.J., who gave the leading judgment, was much influenced by the fact that the bungalow was resting by its own weight on concrete pillars, without any attachment. He was also influenced by the uncertainty of Mr. Morris's tenure. Although Mr. Morris had been in occupation since 1971, he was required to obtain an annual "licence." At first the licence fee was £3 a year. It rose to £10 in 1984, then to £52 in 1985, and finally to £85 in 1989. In 1990 the plaintiffs required a licence fee of £1,000: but Mr. Morris, and the other occupiers declined to pay.

On these facts Aldous L.J. inferred that it was the common intention of the parties that the occupiers should acquire the ownership of their bungalows, but the ownership of the sites should remain in [Elitestone Ltd]. On that footing Mr. Morris's bungalow was to be regarded as a chattel. It was never annexed to the soil, so it never became part of the realty. It followed that the tenancy did not include the bungalow, and Mr. Morris was not a protected tenant.

---

[13] ['[T]he realty' here refers to the land in relation to which Elitestone Ltd had a property right.]
[14] Court of Appeal (Civil Division) Transcript No. 1025 of 1995 (unreported, 28 July 1995).

Unlike the judge, the Court of Appeal did not have the advantage of having seen the bungalow. Nor were they shown any of the photographs, some of which were put before your Lordships. These photographs were taken only very recently. Like all photographs they can be deceptive. But if the Court of Appeal had seen the photographs, it is at least possible that they would have taken a different view. For the photographs show very clearly what the bungalow is, and especially what it is not. It is *not* like a Portakabin, or mobile home. The nature of the structure is such that it could not be taken down and re-erected elsewhere. It could only be removed by a process of demolition. This, as will appear later, is a factor of great importance in the present case. If a structure can only be enjoyed *in situ*, and is such that it cannot be removed in whole or in sections to another site, there is at least a strong inference that the purpose of placing the structure on the original site was that it should form part of the realty at that site, and therefore cease to be a chattel [...]

It will be noticed that in framing the issue for decision I have avoided the use of the word 'fixture.' There are two reasons for this. The first is that 'fixture,' though a hallowed term in this branch of the law, does not always bear the same meaning in law as it does in everyday life. In ordinary language one thinks of a fixture as being something fixed to a building. One would not ordinarily think of the building itself as a fixture [...] There is another reason. The term fixture is apt to be a source of misunderstanding owing to the existence of the category of so called 'tenants' fixtures' (a term used to cover both trade fixtures and ornamental fixtures), which are fixtures in the full sense of the word (and therefore part of the realty) but which may nevertheless be removed by the tenant in the course of or at the end of his tenancy. Such fixtures are sometimes confused with chattels which have never become fixtures at all. Indeed the confusion arose in this very case [...]

For my part I find it better in the present case to avoid the traditional twofold distinction between chattels and fixtures, and to adopt the three-fold classification set out in *Woodfall, Landlord and Tenant*:

> "An object which is brought onto land may be classified under one of three broad heads. It may be (a) a chattel; (b) a fixture; or (c) part and parcel of the land itself. Objects in categories (b) and (c) are treated as being part of the land."

So the question in the present appeal is whether, when the bungalow was built, it became part and parcel of the land itself. The materials out of which the bungalow was constructed, that is to say, the timber frame walls, the feather boarding, the suspended timber floors, the chipboard ceilings, and so on, were all, of course, chattels when they were brought onto the site. Did they cease to be chattels when they were built into the composite structure? The answer to the question, as Blackburn J. pointed out in *Holland v. Hodgson*,[15] depends on the circumstances of each case, but mainly on two factors, the degree of annexation to the land, and the object of the annexation.

Degree of annexation

The importance of the degree of annexation will vary from object to object. In the case of a large object, such as a house, the question does not often arise. Annexation goes without saying [...]

Purpose of annexation

Many different tests have been suggested, such as whether the object which has been fixed to the property has been so fixed for the better enjoyment of the object as a chattel, or

---

15 (1872) LR 7 CP 328.

whether it has been fixed with a view to effecting a permanent improvement of the freehold. This and similar tests are useful when one is considering an object such as a tapestry, which may or may not be fixed to a house so as to become part of the freehold: see *Leigh v. Taylor*.[16] These tests are less useful when one is considering the house itself. In the case of the house the answer is as much a matter of common sense as precise analysis. A house which is constructed in such a way so as to be removable, whether as a unit, or in sections, may well remain a chattel, even though it is connected temporarily to mains services such as water and electricity. But a house which is constructed in such a way that it cannot be removed at all, save by destruction, cannot have been intended to remain as a chattel. It must have been intended to form part of the realty. I know of no better analogy than the example given by Blackburn J. in *Holland v. Hodgson*:[17]

> "Thus blocks of stone placed one on the top of another without any mortar or cement for the purpose of forming a dry stone wall would become part of the land, though the same stones, if deposited in a builder's yard and for convenience sake stacked on the top of each other in the form of a wall, would remain chattels."

Applying that analogy to the present case, I do not doubt that when Mr. Morris's bungalow was built, and as each of the timber frame walls were placed in position, they all became part of the structure, which was itself part and parcel of the land. The object of bringing the individual bits of wood onto the site seems to be so clear that the absence of any attachment to the soil (save by gravity) becomes an irrelevance.

Lord Clyde also gave a reasoned speech, and the other members of the House of Lords agreed with both Lord Clyde and Lord Lloyd. Mr Morris's bungalow was therefore regarded as part of the land in relation to which Elitestone Ltd had a property right. As a result, Mr Morris had a lease (another property right in relation to that same land) and the resulting statutory protection that allowed him to resist Elitestone Ltd's claim for possession.

Lord Lloyd's reasoning is important because it shows the potentially confusing nature of the term 'fixture'. For example, it used to be said that an object (such as the towel rail and paving stones in the McMahon's case, or the bungalow in Mr Morris's case) had to be *either* a chattel (something independent of the land and so not covered by a property right in that land) *or* a fixture (something attached to the land and so covered by a property right in that land). As Lord Lloyd points out, however, it would be odd to think of a building, such as a house, as merely attached to land: it is covered by a property right in the land not because of its attachment, but rather because it is part and parcel of the land itself.

Lord Lloyd's second reason for treating the word 'fixture' with care is that it has a special meaning when used to refer to 'tenant's fixtures' or 'landlord's fixtures'. Those terms are used to solve a related, but different problem. Imagine that an owner of land gives you a lease of business premises. When the lease ends, you can clearly take your office furniture with you; equally clearly, you cannot rip out the toilets and take those with you. But what if you have installed a special shed in which to store your stock? That shed may have become attached to, or part and parcel of the land, because you may have attached it with iron straps to a concrete floor. But, as the Court of Appeal confirmed in *Webb v Frank Bevis Ltd*,[18] you may nonetheless be allowed to remove the shed at the end of the lease. The term

[16] [1902] AC 157.
[17] (1872) LR 7 CP 328, 335.
[18] [1940] 1 All ER 247.

'tenant's fixtures' is used to refer to objects attached to the land or forming part and parcel of the land that the tenant is allowed to remove at the end of the lease (such as the shed); the term 'landlord's fixtures' is used to refer to such objects (such as the toilets) that the tenant cannot remove.

Once any confusion over the concept of 'fixtures' is dealt with, we are left with the position that a property right in land covers: (i) the surface of the land itself; (ii) anything that is part and parcel of that land (e.g. a house built on the land); and (iii) anything that is sufficiently attached to that land (e.g. a towel rail connected to the central heating system). Of course, in practice, it may not be obvious whether a particular object falls into either of (ii) or (iii); in such cases, as shown by Lord Lloyd's approach in *Elitestone Ltd v Morris*, a court has to look at both the degree of attachment to the land and the purpose of such attachment.

The following extract provides a useful practical example of the results that a court may reach.

Botham and ors v TSB Bank plc [1996] EWCA Civ 549, CA

Facts: Mr Botham owned a luxury flat at 90 Cheyne Walk, Chelsea, London. He borrowed money from TSB Bank and, in return, granted TSB a mortgage over his flat. TSB thus acquired a property right (technically, a charge by way of legal mortgage—see Chapter 29, section 4.2) in the land. Mr Botham failed to repay TSB as agreed; TSB therefore acquired a power to sell the flat and use the proceeds towards meeting Mr Botham's debt. A dispute arose as to the scope of TSB's property right in the land: did it give TSB a power to sell (and use the proceeds) of particular objects within the flat, such as the fitted carpets, light fittings, the dishwasher in the fitted kitchen, etc.? Mr Botham claimed that such items were *not* covered by TSB's property right, because they were not fixtures and therefore not part of the land.

The first instance judge split the various objects in dispute into nine groups. Table 1 sets out the groups, along with the related decision of the first instance judge and then of the Court of Appeal.

The first instance judge, by examining the degree and purpose of annexation, thus found that almost all of the disputed objects (including the kitchen sink) were fixtures, and therefore that TSB did have the power to sell those objects and use the proceeds of sale towards meeting Mr Botham's debt.

The Court of Appeal applied the same basic test, but reached different conclusions.

Lord Justice Roch

The tests, in the case of an item which has been attached to the building in some way other than simply by its own weight, seem to be the purpose of the item and the purpose of the link between the item and the building. If the item viewed objectively is intended to be permanent and to afford a lasting improvement to the building, the thing will have become a fixture. If the attachment is temporary and is no more than is necessary for the item to be used and enjoyed, then it will remain a chattel. Some indicators can be identified. For example, if the item is ornamental and the attachment is simply to enable the item to be displayed and enjoyed as an adornment that will often indicate that this item is a chattel. Obvious examples are pictures. But this will not be the result in every case; for example ornamental tiles on the walls of kitchens and bathrooms. The ability to remove an item or its attachment from the

Table 1 Items considered in *Botham and ors v TSB Bank plc*

	First instance judge	Court of Appeal
1. Fitted carpets	Fixtures: part of the land	*Not fixtures*
2. Light fittings fixed to a wall or ceiling	Fixtures: part of the land	*Not fixtures*[1]
3. Four decorative gas flame-effect fires of the mock coal type	Fixtures: part of the land	*Not fixtures*
4. Curtains and blinds	Fixtures: part of the land	*Not fixtures*
5. Bathroom fittings A (towel rails, soap dishes, and lavatory roll holders)	Fixtures: part of the land	Fixtures: part of the land
6. Bathroom fittings B (fittings on baths and basins—namely, the taps, plugs, and shower heads)	Fixtures: part of the land	Fixtures: part of the land
7. Bathroom fittings C (mirrors and marble panels on the walls)	Conceded by Mr Botham as fixtures: part of the land	Conceded by Mr Botham as fixtures: part of the land
8. Kitchen units and work surfaces (including a fitted sink)	Fixtures: part of the land	Fixtures: part of the land
9. White goods in the kitchen (the oven, the dishwasher, the extractor, the hob, the fridge, and the freezer)	Fixtures: part of the land	*Not fixtures*

[1] Subject to two exceptions, conceded by Mr Botham to be fixtures.

building without damaging the fabric of the building is another indicator. The same item may in some areas be a chattel and in others a fixture. For example a cooker will, if free standing and connected to the building only by an electric flex, be a chattel. But it may be otherwise if the cooker is a split level cooker with the hob set into a work surface and the oven forming part of one of the cabinets in the kitchen. It must be remembered that in many cases the item being considered may be one that has been bought by the mortgagor on hire purchase, where the ownership of the item remains in the supplier until the instalments have been paid. Holding such items to be fixtures simply because they are housed in a fitted cupboard and linked to the building by an electric cable, and, in cases of washing machines, by the necessary plumbing would cause difficulties and such findings should only be made where the intent to effect a permanent improvement in the building is incontrovertible. The type of person who instals or attaches the item to the land can be a further indicator. Thus items installed by a builder, eg the wall tiles will probably be fixtures, whereas items installed by eg a carpet contractor or curtain supplier or by the occupier of the building himself or herself may well not be [...]

I have no hesitation in agreeing with the judge that Groups 5 and 6, the bathroom fittings namely the taps, plugs and showerhead together with the towel rails, soap dishes and lavatory roll holders which are all the items listed under the heading "Ironmongery" in the schedule of disputed items helpfully prepared by Mr Chapman, the Bank's counsel for the purpose of this appeal, are fixtures.

Those items are attached to the building in such a way as to demonstrate a significant connection with the building, and are of a type consistent with the bathroom fittings such as the basins, baths, bidets and lavatories, as to demonstrate an intention to effect a permanent improvement to the flat. They are items necessary for a room which is used as a bathroom. They are not there, on the evidence which was before the judge and which is before us, to be enjoyed for themselves, but they are there as accessories which enable the room to be used and enjoyed as a bathroom. Viewed objectively, they were intended to be permanent and to afford a lasting improvement to the property.

The third group about which I have no doubt is Group 8, the kitchen units, including the sink [...]. Again in my judgment the degree of annexation, the fact that between the working surfaces and the underside of the wall cupboards of the wall units there is tiling, demonstrates both a degree of annexation and an intention to effect a permanent improvement to the kitchen of the flat so as to make those units fixtures. Further, as a matter of common sense, those units could not be removed without damaging the fabric of the flat, even if the damage is no more that the leaving of a pattern of tiling which is unlikely to be of use if different units had to be installed.

The seventh group of items, the marble panels and mirrors in the principal bathroom were conceded by Mr Botham's counsel before the judge to be fixtures and [counsel for Mr Botham] in this appeal, accepts that that concession was rightly made [...]

I would allow the appeal with regard to the fitted carpets and the curtains and blinds i.e., Groups 1 and 4. These items, although made or cut to fit the particular floor or window concerned, are attached to the building in an insubstantial manner. Carpets can easily be lifted off gripper rods and removed and can be used again elsewhere. In my judgment neither the degree of annexation nor the surrounding circumstances indicate an intention to effect a permanent improvement in the building. Although many people take with them their curtains and carpets when they move, it is true that others leave curtains and carpets for the incoming occupier, but normally only where the incoming occupier has bought those items separately from the purchase of the property itself. Curtains are attached merely by being hung from curtain rails. The removal of carpets and curtains has no effect damaging or otherwise on the fabric of the building. In my opinion, the method of keeping fitted carpets in place and keeping curtains hung are no more than is required for enjoyment of those items as curtains and carpets. Such items are not considered to be or to have become part of the building. They are not installed, in the case of new buildings, by the builders when the building is constructed, but by the occupier himself or herself or by specialist contractors who supply and install such items. The same is true of curtains. Both will be changed from time to time as the occupier decides to change the decoration of one or more rooms in his or her house or flat. There may be cases where carpeting or carpet squares are stuck to a concrete screed in such a way as to make them part of the floor and thus fixtures. In this case, there was no evidence, in my opinion, to justify the judge's finding that the carpets in this flat were fixtures.

With regard to Group 2, the light fittings, [counsel for Mr Botham] conceded that two of the light fittings recessed into the ceilings shown in photographs 129 and 138 were fixtures. I would hold that [TSB Bank] on the admissible evidence have failed to show that the other lighting items were fixtures. There is no admissible evidence as to the method of attachment of these items to the walls and ceilings other than that the photographs show that they must be attached in some manner. [Counsel for Mr Botham] submitted that their removal cannot be too difficult because in many cases the fitting would have to be removed in order to replace a bulb or connection that had failed. In my judgment, these light fittings, in the absence of evidence other than the photographs of them, remain chattels as would lamp shades or ornamental light fittings or chandeliers suspended from a ceiling rose.

Group 3 were the gas fires. In their case the only connection between them and the building was a gas pipe. In the gas pipes, shortly before the pipes enter these gas fires, gas taps are to be seen in the photographs. Apart from that link, which essential if they are to be used as gas fires, nothing secures the gas fires, on the evidence, other than their own weight.

[Counsel for Mr Botham] argues that their function was purely ornamental, the flat actually being heated by water filled radiators. I would not accept that submission. These fires have two purposes: one decorative, the mock coal fire aspect, and one functional, the gas fire aspect. Nevertheless I am of the view that electric fires and heaters which are simply plugged into the electricity supply of a house are not fixtures and I do not see any sensible distinction between such electric fires and these four gas fires on the evidence which was available to the judge and is available to us. [. . .]

Many of [the items in Groups 8 & 9] were made by a single manufacturer, Neff. The judge said that whilst the kitchen units and sink were manifestly fixtures, the white goods he had found to be the most difficult items he had had to decide. He found that they were manufactured to standard sizes, they were fitted into standard sized holes and that they were removable. They were very probably expensive items, although he had no direct evidence of their value. He held them to be fixtures because:

'They were there as part of the overall kitchen. If one were taking a flat on a lease one would expect them to be there. They were put in to be part of the kitchen as it stood. They were all physically fixed in, not only resting on their own weight, but being plumbed in, wired in and in most cases aligned with and perhaps to some extent abutted to, so that they could not be too easily removed, the remaining parts of the fitted kitchen. A fitted kitchen is a whole.'

I differ from the judge on this group of items on the slender facts in this case. What one might expect to be in a flat if one were taking a flat, would depend on the type of letting one was seeking. That is not, in my view, a test of whether an item is or is not a fixture. Clearly all of these items are items one would not be surprised to find in a kitchen, but then so is an electric kettle, a food mixer and a microwave oven, which are all normally 'plugged in'. No one, I venture to suggest would look on these as fixtures. Here the judge should have reminded himself that the degree of annexation was slight: no more than that which was need for these items to be used for their normal purposes. In fact these items remain in position by their own weight and not by virtue of the links between them and the building. All these items can be bought separately, and are often acquired on an instalment payment basis, when ownership does not pass to the householder immediately. Many of these items are designed to last for a limited period of time and will require replacing after a relatively short number of years. The degree of annexation is therefore slight. Disconnection can be done without damage to the fabric of the building and normally without difficulty. The purpose of such links as there were to the building was to enable these machines to be used to wash clothes or dishes or preserve or cook food. Absent any evidence other than the photographs, it was not open to the judge, in my opinion, to infer that these items were installed with the intention that they were to be a permanent or lasting improvement to the building. This is not a case where the intent to effect a permanent improvement in the building by installing these machines so that they became part of the realty was incontrovertible, as the judge's doubts illustrated.

The Court of Appeal's decision in *Botham v TSB Bank* is useful not only because it shows how the fixtures test can be applied in practice, but also because it underlines that the test is *not* based on reasonable expectations or common practice as to what B, a party buying or renting land from A, would expect to find when moving in. It might be unusual, as noted by the first instance judge, for A to remove gas fires previously connected to pipes, or an oven fitted and installed into a particular slot in the kitchen. Nonetheless, this does not mean that such items necessarily count as part of the land. If B wants to ensure that, as well as acquiring a property right in the land, she also acquires the right to have or use those items, she needs to ensure that A makes a contractual promise to give B such rights.

3.2.2 Things found on, or in, the land

We have seen that if a party (B) has a property right in land, he also has a right to control of: (i) (within limits) the area above and below the surface of the land; (ii) anything that is part and parcel of the land (such as a house); and (iii) anything that is sufficiently attached to the land (such as a towel rail attached to the central heating system). Of course, this does not mean that B's property right in the land gives him a right to control of *everything* that may be in or on his land. That point is clear from the following extract.

Hannah v Peel [1945] 1 KB 509

Facts: In 1938, Major Peel bought Gwernhaylod House, Overton-on-Dee, Shropshire, and thereby acquired a property right in that land: a freehold. He did not move in immediately and the house remained empty, apart from periods during which it was requisitioned by the government and used by the armed forces. In August 1940, during one of those periods of requisition, Mr Hannah, a lance corporal stationed at the house, dislodged a brooch that had been in a crevice by a window frame. He later handed it to the police. No one came forward to claim the brooch and it was given by the police to Major Peel. He offered Mr Hannah a reward for having found the brooch, but Mr Hannah refused to accept the reward: he claimed that, because he found the brooch, he had a property right to it and that Major Peel was under a duty not to interfere with that property right. Major Peel, however, kept and then sold the brooch. Mr Hannah claimed that Major Peel thereby committed a tort: he had interfered with Mr Hannah's property right and so should pay damages as a result. Major Peel claimed that he was, in fact, entitled to the brooch because it had been found on his land. Birkett J found in favour of Mr Hannah.

Birkett J

At 513–15

As to the issue in law, the rival claims of the parties can be stated in this way: [Mr Hannah] says: "I claim the brooch as its finder and I have a good title against all the world, save only the true owner." [Major Peel] says: "My claim is superior to yours inasmuch as I am the free-holder. The brooch was found on my property, although I was never in occupation, and my title, therefore, ousts yours and in the absence of the true owner I am entitled to the brooch or its value." Unhappily the law on this issue is in a very uncertain state and there is need of an authoritative decision of a higher court [...].

In the famous case of *Armory v. Delamirie*,[19] the plaintiff, who was a chimney sweeper's boy, found a jewel and carried it to the defendant's shop, who was a goldsmith, in order to know what it was, and he delivered it into the hands of the apprentice in the goldsmith's shop, who made a pretence of weighing it and took out the stones and called to the master to let him know that it came to three-halfpence. The master offered the boy the money who refused to take it and insisted on having the jewel again. Whereupon the apprentice handed him back the socket of the jewel without the stones, and an action was brought in trover against the master [i.e. the boy claimed that the master committed a tort by interfering with the boy's property right in the jewel], and it was ruled "that the finder of a jewel, though

---

[19] (1722) 5 Stra 505.

he does not by such finding acquire an absolute property or ownership, yet he has such a property as will enable him to keep it against all but the rightful owner, and consequently may maintain trover [i.e. sue in tort]." The case of *Bridges v. Hawkesworth*[20] is in process of becoming almost equally as famous because of the disputation which has raged around it. The headnote in the Jurist is as follows: "The place in which a lost article is found does not constitute any exception to the general rule of law, that the finder is entitled to it as against all persons except the owner."

The case was in fact an appeal against a decision of the county court judge at Westminster. The facts appear to have been that in the year 1847 the plaintiff, who was a commercial traveller, called on a firm named Byfield & Hawkesworth on business, as he was in the habit of doing, and as he was leaving the shop he picked up a small parcel which was lying on the floor. He immediately showed it to the shopman, and opened it in his presence, when it was found to consist of a quantity of Bank of England notes, to the amount of £65. The defendant, who was a partner in the firm of Byfield & Hawkesworth, was then called, and the plaintiff told him he had found the notes, and asked the defendant to keep them until the owner appeared to claim them. Then various advertisements were put in the papers asking for the owner, but the true owner was never found. No person having appeared to claim them, and three years having elapsed since they were found, the plaintiff applied to the defendant to have the notes returned to him, and offered to pay the expenses of the advertisements, and to give an indemnity. The defendant refused to deliver them up to the plaintiff, and an action was brought in the county court of Westminster in consequence of that refusal. The county court judge decided that the defendant, the shopkeeper, was entitled to the custody of the notes as against the plaintiff, and gave judgment for the defendant. Thereupon the appeal was brought which came before the court composed of Patteson J. and Wightman J. Patteson J. said:

"The notes which are the subject of this action were incidentally dropped, by mere accident, in the shop of the defendant, by the owner of them. The facts do not warrant the supposition that they had been deposited there intentionally, nor has the case been put at all upon that ground. The plaintiff found them on the floor, they being manifestly lost by someone. The general right of the finder to any article which has been lost, as against all the world, except the true owner, was established in the case of *Armory v. Delamirie* which has never been disputed. This right would clearly have accrued to the plaintiff had the notes been picked up by him outside the shop of the defendant and if he once had the right, the case finds that he did not intend, by delivering the notes to the defendant, to waive the title (if any) which he had to them, but they were handed to the defendant merely for the purpose of delivering them to the owner should he appear."

Then a little later:

"The case, therefore, resolves itself into the single point on which it appears that the learned judge decided it, namely, whether the circumstance of the notes being found inside the defendant's shop gives him, the defendant, the right to have them as against the plaintiff, who found them."

After discussing the cases, and the argument, the learned judge said:

"If the discovery had never been communicated to the defendant, could the real owner have had any cause of action against him because they were found in his house? Certainly not. The notes never were in the custody of the defendant, nor within the protection of his house, before they were found, as they would have been had they been intentionally deposited there; and the defendant has come under no responsibility, except from the communication made

---

[20] (1821) 21 LJ (QB) 75.

to him by the plaintiff, the finder, and the steps taken by way of advertisement. [...] We find, therefore, no circumstances in this case to take it out of the general rule of law, that the finder of a lost article is entitled to it as against all persons except the real owner, and we think that that rule must prevail, and that the learned judge was mistaken in holding that the place in which they were found makes any legal difference. Our judgment, therefore, is that the plaintiff is entitled to these notes as against the defendant."

It is to be observed that in *Bridges v. Hawkesworth* which has been the subject of immense disputation, neither counsel put forward any argument on the fact that the notes were found in a shop. Counsel for the appellant assumed throughout that the position was the same as if the parcel had been found in a private house, and the learned judge spoke of "the protection of his (the shopkeeper's) house." The case for the appellant was that the shopkeeper never knew of the notes. Again, what is curious is that there was no suggestion that the place where the notes were found was in any way material; indeed, the judge in giving the judgment of the court expressly repudiates this and said in terms "The learned judge was mistaken in holding that the place in which they were found makes any legal difference." [...]

At 521

There is no doubt that in this case the brooch was lost in the ordinary meaning of that term, and I should imagine it had been lost for a very considerable time. Indeed, from this correspondence it appears that at one time the predecessors in title of the defendant were considering making some claim. But the moment the plaintiff discovered that the brooch might be of some value, he took the advice of his commanding officer and handed it to the police. His conduct was commendable and meritorious. The defendant was never physically in possession of these premises at any time. It is clear that the brooch was never his, in the ordinary acceptation of the term, in that he had the prior possession. He had no knowledge of it, until it was brought to his notice by the finder. A discussion of the merits does not seem to help, but it is clear on the facts that the brooch was "lost" in the ordinary meaning of that word; that it was "found" by the plaintiff in the ordinary meaning of that word, that its true owner has never been found, that the defendant was the owner of the premises and had his notice drawn to this matter by the plaintiff, who found the brooch. In those circumstances I propose to follow the decision in *Bridges v. Hawkesworth*, and to give judgment in this case for [Mr Hannah] for £66.

The first point to take from this decision is the important general principle that if a party takes physical control of an object (e.g. by finding it), he acquires a property right in that object. This is a fundamental principle of property law. Indeed, even a thief can use it: even though he has dishonestly taken physical control of an object, he still acquires a property right in it. Of course, this does not mean that the finder or thief has the *best* property right: the party who lost the thing, or from whom it was stolen, also has a property right. And the general rule is that he or she can assert that property right against the finder or thief, because his or her property right arose *before* that of the finder or thief. As we will see in Chapter 6, section 2, timing is absolutely crucial when considering conflicting property rights: the general rule is that the party with the *earliest* property right will win.

So, in *Hannah v Peel*, Mr Hannah clearly had a property right in the brooch: he acquired that right simply by taking physical control of the brooch, just as the chimney sweep's boy in *Armory v Delamrie* acquired a property right by taking physical control of the jewel. Equally clearly, the party who lost the brooch had an earlier property right in the brooch: so, *if* that party were to have come forward, she would have been able to bring a claim against

Mr Hannah. But that party did *not* come forward: the dispute was between Mr Hannah (who clearly had a property right in the brooch) and Major Peel. So, Major Peel had to show that: (i) he, too, had a property right in the brooch; *and* (ii) he acquired that property right *before* Mr Hannah found the brooch.

How could Major Peel show that he had such a property right? In theory, he could try to claim that his property right in the land also covered the brooch. But, as we saw in section 3.2.1 above, he could only make that argument if the brooch, when lost, had become part and parcel of his land, or was sufficiently attached to his land. Given that the brooch was easily dislodged from the crevice, it clearly was not part and parcel of, or sufficiently attached to, Major Peel's land. Further, if that argument were accepted, then the party who lost the brooch, even were she to come forward, would not be able to claim the brooch: her property right would have disappeared when the brooch became part of Major Peel's land.

So, Major Peel tried a different argument, proposing that he automatically acquired a property right in *anything* found on his land. Birkett J rejected that argument. As shown by the earlier decision in *Bridges v Hawkesworth*, the mere fact that something was lost or found on a party's land does not give that party a property right in the thing. After all, as was the case in *Hannah v Peel*, the party with the property right in the land may not even know that the thing is on his land.

It may therefore seem that the position is fairly simple: a party with a property right in land has no special rights in relation to anything lost or found on his land. The following extract, however, is from a case that (perhaps unnecessarily) introduced some complications.

Parker v British Airways Board [1982] QB 1004, CA

Facts: In November 1978, Mr Parker was waiting for a flight in an executive lounge at Heathrow Terminal One. He spotted a gold bracelet on the floor that had been dropped by an unknown passenger. He handed the bracelet to British Airways staff in case that unknown passenger should come forward to claim it; he also gave the staff his contact details and said that the bracelet should be returned to him if no one came forward to claim it. By June 1979, no one had come forward. Although Mr Parker had requested that it be sent to him, British Airways sold the bracelet for £850. Mr Parker claimed that, by finding and taking control of the bracelet, he had a property right in the bracelet and that, by refusing to give it to him, British Airways had committed the tort of conversion. The first instance judge accepted Mr Parker's arguments and ordered British Airways to pay him £850 plus interest. The Court of Appeal dismissed British Airways' appeal.

Donaldson LJ

On November 15, 1978, the plaintiff, Alan George Parker, had a date with fate—and perhaps with legal immortality. He found himself in the international executive lounge at terminal one, Heathrow Airport. And that was not all that he found. He also found a gold bracelet lying on the floor.

We know very little about the plaintiff, and it would be nice to know more. He was lawfully in the lounge and, as events showed, he was an honest man. Clearly he had not forgotten the schoolboy maxim 'Finders keepers.' But, equally clearly, he was well aware of the adult qualification 'unless the true owner claims the article.' He had had to clear customs and security to reach the lounge. He was almost certainly an outgoing passenger because the defendants, British Airways Board, as lessees of the lounge from the British Airports Authority and its occupiers, limit its use to passengers who hold first class tickets or boarding passes or who are members of their Executive Club which is a passengers' 'club.' Perhaps the plaintiff's flight had just been called and he was pressed for time. Perhaps the only officials in sight were employees of the defendants. Whatever the reason, he gave the bracelet to an anonymous official of the defendants instead of to the police. He also gave the official a note of his name and address and asked for the bracelet to be returned to him if it was not claimed by the owner. The official handed the bracelet to the lost property department of the defendants. Although the owner never claimed the bracelet, the defendants did not return it to the plaintiff. Instead they sold it and kept the proceeds which amounted to £850. The plaintiff discovered what had happened and was more than a little annoyed. I can understand his annoyance. He sued the defendants in the Brentford County Court and was awarded £850 as damages and £50 as interest. The defendants now appeal.

It is astonishing that there should be any doubt as to who is right. But there is. Indeed, it seems that the academics have been debating this problem for years. In 1971 the Law Reform Committee reported that it was by no means clear who had the better claim to lost property when the protagonists were the finder and the occupier of the premises where the property was found. Whatever else may be in doubt, the committee was abundantly right in this conclusion. The committee recommended legislative action but, as is not uncommon, nothing has been done. The rights of the parties thus depend upon the common law.

As a matter of legal theory, the common law has a ready made solution for every problem and it is only for the judges, as legal technicians, to find it. The reality is somewhat different. Take the present case. The conflicting rights of finder and occupier have indeed been considered by various courts in the past. But under the rules of English jurisprudence, none of their decisions binds this court. We therefore have both the right and the duty to extend and adapt the common law in the light of established principles and the current needs of the community. This is not to say that we start with a clean sheet. In doing so, we should draw from the experience of the past as revealed by the previous decisions of the courts.

Neither the plaintiff nor the defendants lay any claim to the bracelet either as owner of it or as one who derives title from that owner. The plaintiff's claim is founded upon the ancient common law rule that the act of finding a chattel which has been lost and taking control of it gives the finder rights with respect to that chattel. The defendants' claim has a different basis. They cannot and do not claim to have found the bracelet when it was handed to them by the plaintiff. At that stage it was no longer lost and they received and accepted the bracelet from the plaintiff on terms that it would be returned to him if the owner could not be found. They must and do claim on the basis that they had rights in relation to the bracelet immediately *before* the plaintiff found it and that these rights are superior to the plaintiff's. The defendants' claim is based upon the proposition that at common law an occupier of land has such rights over all lost chattels which are on that land, whether or not the occupier knows of their existence.

The common law right asserted by the plaintiff has been recognised for centuries. [Donaldson LJ here referred to *Armory v Delamrie*,[21] which is considered in the extract above from *Hannah v Peel*...] Some qualification has also to be made in the case of the trespassing finder. The person vis à vis whom he is a trespasser has a better title. The fundamental basis of this is clearly public policy. Wrongdoers should not benefit from their wrongdoing. This

[21] (1722) 2 Stra 505.

requirement would be met if the trespassing finder acquired no rights. That would, however, produce [a] free-for-all situation [...], in that anyone could take the article from the trespassing finder. Accordingly, the common law has been obliged to give rights to someone else, the owner *ex hypothesi* being unknown. The obvious candidate is the occupier of the property upon which the finder was trespassing.

Curiously enough, it is difficult to find any case in which the rule is stated in this simple form, but I have no doubt that this is the law [...] One might have expected there to be decisions clearly qualifying the general rule where the circumstances are that someone finds a chattel and thereupon forms the dishonest intention of keeping it regardless of the rights of the true owner or of anyone else. But that is not the case [...]

[Donaldson LJ then surveyed previous cases and set out the following five propositions as to the rights and duties of a finder:]

1. The finder of a chattel acquires no rights over it unless (a) it has been abandoned or lost and (b) he takes it into his care and control.

2. The finder of a chattel acquires very limited rights over it if he takes it into his care and control with dishonest intent or in the course of trespassing.

3. Subject to the foregoing and to point 4 below, a finder of a chattel, whilst not acquiring any absolute property or ownership in the chattel, acquires a right to keep it against all but the true owner or those in a position to claim through the true owner or one who can assert a prior right to keep the chattel which was subsisting at the time when the finder took the chattel into his care and control.

4. Unless otherwise agreed, any servant or agent who finds a chattel in the course of his employment or agency and not wholly incidentally or collaterally thereto and who takes it into his care and control does so on behalf of his employer or principal who acquires a finder's rights to the exclusion of those of the actual finder.

5. A person having a finder's rights has an obligation to take such measures as in all the circumstances are reasonable to acquaint the true owner of the finding and present whereabouts of the chattel and to care for it meanwhile.

[Donaldson LJ also set out the following four propositions as to the rights and duties of an occupier of land on which a thing is found:]

1. An occupier of land has rights superior to those of a finder over chattels in or attached to that land and an occupier of a building has similar rights in respect of chattels attached to that building, whether in either case the occupier is aware of the presence of the chattel.

2. An occupier of a building has rights superior to those of a finder over chattels upon or in, but not attached to, that building if, but only if, before the chattel is found, he has manifested an intention to exercise control over the building and the things which may be upon it or in it.

3. An occupier who manifests an intention to exercise control over a building and the things which may be upon or in it so as to acquire rights superior to those of a finder is under an obligation to take such measures as in all the circumstances are reasonable to ensure that lost chattels are found and, upon their being found, whether by him or by a third party, to acquaint the true owner of the finding and to care for the chattels meanwhile. The manifestation of intention may be express or implied from the circumstances including, in particular, the circumstance that the occupier manifestly accepts or is obliged by law to accept liability for chattels lost upon his "premises," e.g. an innkeeper or carrier's liability.

4. An 'occupier' of a chattel, e.g. a ship, motor car, caravan or aircraft, is to be treated as if he were the occupier of a building for the purposes of the foregoing rules [...]

The plaintiff was not a trespasser in the executive lounge and, in taking the bracelet into his care and control, he was acting with obvious honesty. Prima facie, therefore, he had a full finder's rights and obligations. He in fact discharged those obligations by handing the bracelet to an official of the defendants' although he could equally have done so by handing the bracelet to the police or in other ways such as informing the police of the find and himself caring for the bracelet.

The plaintiff's prima facie entitlement to a finder's rights was not displaced in favour of an employer or principal. There is no evidence that he was in the executive lounge in the course of any employment or agency and, if he was, the finding of the bracelet was quite clearly collateral thereto. The position would have been otherwise in the case of most or perhaps all the defendants' employees.

The defendants, for their part, cannot assert any title to the bracelet based upon the rights of an occupier over chattels attached to a building. The bracelet was lying loose on the floor. Their claim must, on my view of the law, be based upon a manifest intention to exercise control over the lounge and all things which might be in it. The evidence is that they claimed the right to decide who should and who should not be permitted to enter and use the lounge, but their control was in general exercised upon the basis of classes or categories of user and the availability of the lounge in the light of the need to clean and maintain it. I do not doubt that they also claimed the right to exclude individual undesirables, such as drunks, and specific types of chattels such as guns and bombs. But this control has no real relevance to a manifest intention to assert custody and control over lost articles. There was no evidence that they searched for such articles regularly or at all.

On the evidence available, there was no sufficient manifestation of any intention to exercise control over lost property before it was found such as would give the defendants a right superior to that of the plaintiff or indeed any right over the bracelet. As the true owner has never come forward, it is a case of 'finders keepers.'

On the one hand, the *result* in *Parker v British Airways Board* is thus consistent with the simple position adopted in *Hannah v Peel*: British Airways did not acquire a property right in the bracelet simply because it was lost and found on its land. On the other, the *reasoning* of Donaldson LJ introduces a complication: it means that a party with a property right in land can acquire a property right in a thing lost and found on its land *if* it can show a *'manifest intention to exercise control over the* [land] *and all things which might be in it'*. It is not immediately obvious why a landowner's *intention* to control such things should give it a property right: why change the general rule that, to acquire a property right in relation to a lost or found thing, a party needs to take actual physical control of the thing?

Despite this problem, the reasoning of Donaldson LJ was relied on by the Court of Appeal in the following case.

Waverley Borough Council v Fletcher [1996] QB 334, CA

Facts: Waverley Borough Council had a property right (a freehold) in Farnham Park, Farnham, Surrey. The park was open to the public for recreational use. In August 1992, Mr Fletcher visited the park with a metal detector and, after some digging, uncovered a medieval gold brooch about nine inches below the surface of the ground. Mr Fletcher thus took physical control of the brooch. Under the terms of the Treasure Act 1996, the Crown acquires a property right to any 'treasure' as soon as it is found. It was determined, however, that the brooch did not count as treasure and that the Crown consequently had no claim to it. The Council, however, claimed that, because it had been lost and found on its land, it had a prior property right in the brooch. The first instance judge found in favour of Mr Fletcher; the Court of Appeal allowed the Council's appeal.

Auld LJ

At 341–2

[Auld LJ, adding his own emphasis, referred to the following passage from Pollock and Wright, *Possession in the Common Law* (1888) at p 41, dealing with objects attached to or in land]:

'The possession of land carries with it in general, by our law, possession of everything which is *attached to or under* that land, and, in the absence of a better title elsewhere, the right to possess it also. And it makes no difference that the possessor is not aware of the thing's existence. So it was lately held concerning a prehistoric boat imbedded in the soil. It is free to any one who requires a specific intention as part of de facto possession to treat this as a positive rule of law. But it seems preferable to say that the legal possession rests on a real de facto possession, constituted by the occupier's general power and intent to exclude unauthorized interference.'

[...] The test of possession, in its most abstract form, may have a constant meaning whether applied to objects in or unattached and on land. But it is clear from Pollock and Wright's statement [...] that they regarded its application to objects in land to be free from the uncertainties inherent in disputes about entitlement to unattached objects found on land. Their proposition was that in practice possession of land should generally be taken as carrying with it an intent to possession of objects in or attached to it [...]

At 345–6

[Counsel for Mr Fletcher] argued that it is against commonsense that it should make all the difference whether an object is just under or on the surface. That was also the view of the [first instance] judge. He said that he could see no reason in common sense why the better possessory claim should depend upon whether an object was found on or in ground. [Counsel for Mr Fletcher] gave as one of a number of examples in support of his argument, a lost watch on a muddy path which might within a day or two become covered by a thin coating of mud. Why, he asked, should the landowner's claim be different and stronger when the watch finally, but only just, disappears from sight?

In my view, the authorities reveal a number of sound and practical reasons for the distinction.

First, as Donaldson L.J. said in *Parker v. British Airways Board*,[22] an object in land "is to be treated as an integral part of the realty as against all but the true owner" or that the finder in detaching the object would, in the absence of licence to do so, become a trespasser. [Counsel for Mr Fletcher] suggested that this is wrong because if an object is treated as part of the realty the true owner cannot have priority. However, the English law of ownership and possession, unlike that of Roman Law, is not a system of identifying absolute entitlement but of priority of entitlement, and Donaldson L.J.'s rationale is consistent with that [...]

[22] [1982] QB 1004, 1010.

Second, removal of an object in or attached to land would normally involve interference with the land and may damage it [...]

Third, putting aside the borderline case of a recently lost article which has worked its way just under the surface, in the case of an object in the ground its original owner is unlikely in most cases to be there to claim it. The law, therefore, looks for a substitute owner, the owner or possessor of the land in which it is lodged. Whereas in the case of an unattached object on the surface, it is likely in most cases to have been recently lost, and the true owner may well claim it. In the meantime, there is no compelling reason why it should pass into the possession of the landowner as against a finder unless he, the landowner, has manifested an intention to possess it. As to borderline cases of the sort mentioned by [counsel for Mr Fletcher], potential absurdities can always be found at the margins in the application of any sound principle. It is for the trial judge to determine as a matter of fact and degree on which side of the line, on or in the land, an object is found [...]

In my view, the two main principles established by the authorities, and for good practical reasons, are as stated by Donaldson L.J. in *Parker v. British Airways Board*. I venture to restate them with particular reference to objects found on or in land, for he was concerned primarily with an object found in a building. (1) Where an article is found in or attached to land, as between the owner or lawful possessor of the land and the finder of the article, the owner or lawful possessor of the land has the better title. (2) Where an article is found unattached on land, as between the two, the owner or lawful possessor of the land has a better title only if he exercised such manifest control over the land as to indicate an intention to control the land and anything that might be found on it [...] ·

At 350

Accordingly, I can see no basis for not applying the general rule that an owner or lawful possessor of land has a better title to an object found in or attached to his land than the finder, or for modifying it in some way to produce a different result in the circumstances of this case. Mr. Fletcher did not derive a superior right to the brooch simply because he was entitled as a member of the public to engage in recreational pursuits in the park. Metal detecting was not a recreation of the sort permitted under the terms under which the council held the land on behalf of the general public. In any event, digging and removal of property in the land were not such a permitted use, and were acts of trespass. And the council was entitled to exercise its civil remedy for protection of its property regardless of the absence of any applicable byelaw.

According to the reasoning of Auld LJ, the crucial point in *Waverley BC v Fletcher*, which distinguishes that case from *Hannah v Peel*, is that the brooch was found *in* the land rather than *on* the land. As the following extract suggests, however, there are some problems with that reasoning.

McFarlane, *The Structure of Property Law* (2008, pp 157–8)

The Court of Appeal's reasoning in *Waverley BC* is flawed. First, it was said that once the brooch was submerged, it became part and parcel of [the Council's] land, so that [the Council], as an owner of the land, also had Ownership of the brooch. It is true that if one thing loses its physical identity and becomes subsumed into another thing, the first thing ceases to have an independent existence [...] However, if this had occurred in *Waverley BC* then *all* pre-existing property rights in the brooch would have ceased to exist. On that view, the person who originally lost the brooch (A) would lose his Ownership of the brooch and so would be unable to assert a right against either [Mr Fletcher] or [the Council]. However, the Court of Appeal's view was that A *retained* Ownership and so, if he came forward, could assert his right against each of [Mr Fletcher] and [the Council].[23] But a court cannot have it both ways: *either* (i) the brooch lost its identity and became part of the land, so that A's pre-existing property right is destroyed; *or* (ii) the brooch did not lose its identity and A still has a property right he can assert against each of of [Mr Fletcher] and [the Council]. On that second view, the brooch does not count as part of [the Council's] land: so [the Council's] position as an owner of the land does *not* give [it] Ownership of the brooch.

The puzzling statement of Donaldson LJ in *Parker v British Airways Board*,[24] relied on in *Waverley BC*, that a thing can become an "integral part of the realty [i.e. the land] as against all but the true owner" must be rejected. Either the brooch lost its identity and became part of the land or it did not. The better view must be that it did not. The brooch did not become part of [the Council's] land simply by being submerged by the top soil. The brooch remained a distinct physical object: after all, once he found the brooch, [Mr Fletcher] was easily able to remove it from [the Council's] land.

4 EQUITY AND LAND LAW

In Chapter 1, section 2, it was explained that land law (and hence this book) is focused on private rights to use land. When examining such rights, we need to be aware of the distinction between *common law* rules and *equitable* rules. That distinction is important throughout the law. For example, in contract law, there is a question as to what effect, if any, a defect in one party's consent should have on the existence or enforceability of an apparent contract. So, A may complain that he should not have to perform an apparent contract with B because he only signed the contract due to improper pressure exerted by B. In such cases, we have to be aware of *both* the common law rules *and* the equitable rules: each set of rules provides a different answer to the question of when B's improper pressure can have an effect on the existence or enforceability of the apparent contract.

As the following extract makes clear, the presence of the different sets of rules (common law rules and equitable rules) comes from the fact that, in England and Wales, there were formerly different sets of courts (common law courts and equitable courts).

Hackney, *Understanding Equity and Trusts* (1987, pp 15–20)

At the beginning of the nineteenth century, the court structure in England and Wales was in a mess. The population was subject to the jurisdiction of a dual system of superior courts. On the one side were the three 'common law' courts—the Common Pleas, the Queen's Bench and the Exchequer of Pleas—and on the other was the Court of Chancery.

From any managerial viewpoint, this arrangement was ludicrous. The three common law courts had grown up under the authority of the English kings during the Middle Ages. They were known as courts of 'common' law because, according to royal propaganda, that law

---

[23] See *per* Auld LJ at 345.
[24] [1984] QB 1004, 1010.

applied to all subjects and the whole realm, in contrast to the welter of local and specialised jurisdictions which previously prevailed. Only an 'historical' explanation can be offered for why there were three such common law courts with substantially overlapping jurisdictions, and it sets the tone for the rest of this strange story to say that, 'common' or not, they could, and often did, give different answers to the same questions, and that even as late as the nineteenth century there was no reliable method of ironing out those differences. But, and much stranger still, rules based on judgments given in these common law courts, and even the judgments themselves, were in some cases, being denied or added to in the Chancery. This was not by way of appeal. The common law judgment was not formally set aside or reversed; the Chancery, while leaving it intact, simply issued an order which was incon-sistent with that of the common law judges, and the constitutional position was that this second order prevailed, leaving the common law answer as an overshadowed solution to the problem. These Chancery orders had come to be made by applying a body of doctrine and principles invented initially by the Chancellor, and later by his subordinate the Master of the Rolls (and later still, the Vice-Chancellors). These rules, principles and doctrines of the court of Chancery, bearing this complex relationship with the doctrines of the common law were to be known as Equity. This body of law did not however cover the entire area of business which the common law courts had taken as their jurisdiction. It was essentially a 'private law' juris-diction, dealing with matters raised by private individuals, protecting their private interests. There was no involvement with the common law of crime. The principal focuses of attention were the laws of property and contract and only incidentally to these was it to develop a law of private wrongs. Equity was not the only jurisdiction exercised in the Chancery, and there were others which their successors exercise today, but it was the one which was to leave the greatest impression on the development of the legal system.

'Conscience'

Chancery has had a reputation as a court administering an individual discretionary justice in contrast to the inflexible monoliths of the common law. Whether this was perceived by all litigants in Chancery (or even at common law) may be doubted, and certainly much of the jurisprudence of the court has been concerned with working out the detailed implications of having taken an earlier moral stance, and many of its decisions, like much administration, had little reference to individuated notions of right and wrong. But the tradition is fundamentally well-based and it is impossible to read Equity cases of any period without being aware of it. The explanation for the flavour is, of course, also historical. The early history of the jurisdiction is obscure and in any case quite irrelevant for a modern lawyer. The history which leaves rele-vant traces begins at the end of the middle ages in the early sixteenth century. By that date it can be said that the common law courts had in some areas become inadequate... Reform of these defects by statute was not seen to be an answer, and disappointed parties petitioned the king to get them out of the mess into which his common law courts had put them, and to receive the ordinary justice, the fair and commonsense solution, the equity, which they were otherwise denied.

These petitions had come to be heard by the king's greatest officer of state, the Chancellor. By the early sixteenth century, he was giving decisions in his own name and had established a jurisdiction over freehold land. It soon became a trade mark of Chancery thinking to empha-sise 'good faith' and to appeal to notions of 'conscience', though there is justification for the view that the intervention was not so much to enforce the good faith solution as to prevent the accrual of benefits arising from bad faith. The avoidance of unconscionability may be the central informing idea [...] Step by step [the Chancellors] set about plugging the loopholes left by the common law's shortcomings [...]

Difference and conflict

The Chancellor's decisions had begun, it seems, as individual decisions solving individual grievances or sometimes simply dilemmas posed by conscientious [applicants] wanting to know what to do. They were what Benjamin Cardozo called a sequence of 'isolated dooms' There were 'suits' in the Chancery, not actions, and the Chancellor issued 'decrees', not judgments. The contrast with the regular court system was enhanced by the absence of a jury (which accounted for much of the hostility to Equity in the American colonies [...]), and by the Chancellor's practice of not taking oral evidence. But a combination of repeated circumstance and a desire to treat like cases alike was ultimately to drive the Chancellor into developing a system of rules: equity was to become Equity. The early days of this development were not marked by hostility from the common lawyers, but in the sixteenth century trouble began to brew [...] Matters came to a head in the early seventeenth century when Coke, then Chief Justice of the King's Bench, challenged the right of the Chancellor, Ellesmere, to override common law results. Coke's appeal to the King in 1616 failed however, and from that date it has not been questioned that 'when the rules of Equity and common law conflict, it is the rules of Equity which will prevail'.

Equity and common law in the narrow sense

There are now two usages of 'common law': the wider usage, meaning the whole of the royal law, includes Equity; the narrower usage, focussing on the contrast, excludes it. If there was continuing resentment about the divergence after 1616, it did not surface, and relations between the two systems were on the surface amicable, much aided by the diplomatic formulations of equitable rules which hid the substance of what was going on: 'we are not overturning the common law rules; all we are saying is that while Y may own at common law, X owns in Equity', so disguising the fact that X may be happy—Y may not. Equally effectively, decisions were often attributed to the demands of Equity as if it were some creature with a will of its own, some personified virtue, some Marianne, pulling the strings of the judicial marionettes. This mode of speech—'Equity will not allow...' seems less aggressive than 'I will not allow...' to which it must often have been substantially identical. The mode is still occasionally used, and serves to divert the attention of a potentially critical audience from perceiving what might, if otherwise phrased, look like an expression of the individual preference of an individual judge. It can give Chancery law an unnecessary but highly characteristic air of mysticism [...]

The systematisation of Equity by the Chancellors

In the course of the mid seventeenth to early nineteenth centuries, Equity was turned into a systematic body of principles as refined, rigorous and ultimately as unyielding as anything produced by the common law. This was however a slow process, and it was not complete in the 18th century. The letters of Junius, around 1770, could still attack Lord Mansfield, then Chief Justice of the King's Bench, on the ground that he had turned it into a 'court of equity and the judge, instead of consulting strictly the law of the land, refers only to the wisdom of the court and the purity of his conscience'. The final product was the result of the work of a series of professional, legally trained Chancellors. Sir Thomas More (1529-32) might count as the first, but the names of Lords Nottingham (1673-82), Hardwicke (1737-56) and Eldon (1801-6, 1807-27, but hearing cases to 1835) justly figure as amongst the greatest in all stories of this development.

To Lord Hardwicke we owe a pair of opposed thoughts of great importance in our understanding of the limits of the Equity jurisdiction. On the one hand he pointed out the self evident truth that the common law courts were also enforcing obligations which had a moral foundation, especially for our purposes, in their laws of agency and bailments (deliveries of chattels which were often, like their land law equivalent, leases, based on contract). What Equity was doing, was conferring rights to enforce conscience-based obligations in situations where the common law would not do so. Equity did not have a monopoly of conscience, and the differences between some of its institutions and those of the common law can be very small, and sometimes seem to be no more than matters of presentation. On the other hand, not every breach of confidence attracted the trust solution, or received sanction in the Chancery. Some such breaches were to be left to the (withering) ecclesiastical jurisdiction or enforced via the forum of the moral disapproval of one's friends and neighbours.

Reform

But to say that the period 1530-1830 was one of much development is not the same as saying that the system underwent a process of continuous improvement so far as litigants were concerned. In particular the court's attention to detail became obsessive, and its proceedings much delayed. A late eighteenth-century letter-writer complained that it was not easy to escape from the 'amicable gripe of the court of Chancery'. In Lord Eldon's time, Chancery proceedings became a by-word for delay, and his fastidiousness caused much perceived and real injustice. Charles Dickens' 'Bleak House' suggests that his immediate successor was no improvement. The reformist mood of the nineteenth century did, however, make its mark on the Chancery. Apart from substantial statutory reform of the court, there were some important innovations from within.

As Hackney later points out, the most dramatic stage in the relationship between common law and equity came with the *cataclysmic events of 1873–75 which scrapped the dual system in England and Wales and set up a unified judicature'*. The reference is to Parliament's passing of the Supreme Court of Judicature Acts 1873–75. These Acts abolished the distinction between courts of common law and courts of equity; but we are left with the legacy of that distinction: the difference between *rules* of common law and *rules* of equity. As Hackney notes in the extract above, equitable rules are particularly prominent in the law of property and thus in land law, which, as we saw in Chapter 1, section 2, is a subset of property law. For example, we saw in section 2 above that if B describes 25 Mountfield Gardens as 'her land', she means that she has a property right in that land. The distinction between common law and equity opens up the possibility that there may be *two sets of rules* about property rights in land: common law rules and equitable rules. So, common law may provide one set of answers to the *content*, *acquisition*, and *defences* questions (see Chapter 1, section 3), whilst equity may give us a different set of answers to those questions. (We will examine this point in Chapter 4, when examining equitable property rights in land.) For present purposes, the key point is simply that, in trying to understand land law rules, we have to keep in mind the possibility of there being different approaches at common law and equity. In Chapter 4, we will also begin to consider whether any differences between the two sets of rules can be *justified*.

5 CONCLUSION

In Chapter 1, we saw that land law is a subset of property law and focused on the *special* features of land. In this chapter, we have also looked at aspects that land shares with other parts of property law. Firstly, we examined the fundamental question of what it means to say that land is a form of property. We saw that, as Gray and Gray argue, we need to focus not on the land itself, but rather on the *relationship* between a person and the land. That relationship can take the form of a *right*: so, if we say that 25 Mountfield Gardens is 'B's property', what we mean is that B has a *property right* in relation to that land. We will examine property rights in more detail in the next chapter; a key feature of such a right is that it gives its holder a degree of control over a thing and also imposes a prima facie duty on the rest of the world. So, in a case such as *Entick v Carrington*, Mr Entick had a property right in relation to his land and papers; no one acting without lawful authority could enter that land or take those papers—not even a messenger of the King.

Secondly, we began to see how the concept of a property right can apply to land. In particular, we examined what it means to say that a party has a freehold or lease of land: (i) B's right relates not only to the surface of the land, but also (within certain limits) to the vertical space both above and below the surface of the land;[25] (ii) B's right also relates to any object that is part and parcel of the land, *or* which is sufficiently attached to the land;[26] (iii) by virtue of her property right in the land, it seems that B also has a property right to anything that is lost or found *in* the land,[27] and, if she has shown an intention to exercise control over the land and anything that may be on the land, B will also acquire a property right in anything lost or found *on* the land.[28] As we have seen, however, it is not easy to explain *why* B's property right in the land should give her such property rights in relation to things that are *not* part and parcel of the land, *nor* sufficiently attached to the land.

Thirdly, we noted that, in land law, as in property law as a whole, equitable rules have a key part to play. We saw that history can explain the presence of two different sets of rules within the same legal system. This means, for example, that if we ask a fundamental question such as 'Does B have a property right in relation to the land?', we need to bear in mind that common law rules might give us one answer, whilst equitable rules give us a different one. We will develop this point further in Chapter 4, when considering equitable interests in land.

QUESTIONS

1. In *Entick v Carrington*, what rights did Mr Entick assert against the King's messengers?

2. What does it mean if we say that 25 Mountfield Gardens is 'B's property'?

---

[25] See, e.g., *Edwards v Lee's Administrator* 96 SW 2d 1028 (1936, Court of Appeals of Kentucky).
[26] See, e.g., *Elitestone Ltd v Morris* [1997] 1 WLR 687.
[27] See *Waverley Borough Council v Fletcher* [1996] QB 334.
[28] See *Parker v British Airways Board* [1982] QB 1004, CA.

3. '*To whomsoever the soil belongs, he owns also to the sky and to the depths.*' Is that an accurate statement of English law?

4. Why might it matter whether or not a particular thing counts as part of a plot of land?

5. Whilst on B's land, A finds a gold ring. What factors are relevant to deciding which of A or B has a better claim to the ring?

6. Would it make sense for common law and equity to have two different sets of answers to the question of whether B has a property right in land?

FURTHER READING

Goodhart, 'Three Cases on Possession' [1929] CLJ 195

Gray, 'Property in Thin Air' [1991] CLJ 252

Gray and Gray, *Elements of Land Law* (5th edn, Oxford: OUP, 2009, Part 1.5)

Hackney, *Understanding Equity and Trusts* (London: Fontana, 1987, chs 1 and 2)

McFarlane, *The Structure of Property Law* (Oxford: Hart, 2008, pp 154–60)

Meagher, Heydon, and Leeming (eds), *Meagher, Gummow and Lehane's Equity: Doctrines and Remedies* (4th edn, Sydney: LexisNexis, 2002, esp chs 1 and 2)

3

LEGAL ESTATES AND
LEGAL INTERESTS

CENTRAL ISSUES

1. In Chapter 1, we looked at the special features of land. In Chapter 2, we saw that land is a form of private property. In this chapter, we will look at one of the key building blocks of land law: the concept of a legal property right in land. When asking if B has a legal property right, it is useful to ask two questions: the *content* question and the *acquisition* question.

2. As we saw in Chapter 1, section 3, the *content* question looks to the nature of B's right. It asks whether the type of right claimed by B can count as a property right in land. When considering this question, it is useful to split legal property rights into two general kinds: legal estates and legal interests.

3. When considering the *content* question, the *numerus clausus* (or 'closed list principle') is of crucial importance. It ensures that there are a limited number of legal property rights in land. There are only two forms of legal estate in land: the freehold and the lease. So, when applied to legal *estates* in land, the *content* question consists of asking if B's right counts as either a freehold or a lease. A freehold gives B ownership rights over a piece of land for an

unlimited period; a lease consists of ownership for a limited period.

4. The *acquisition* question, in contrast, asks if B has, on the facts of the case, acquired the particular right that he claims. To establish whether B has a legal estate, we also have to ask if B has, in fact, acquired that right. For example, if B claims to have a legal freehold, it will generally be necessary for B to show that he is registered as holding that right. Even if registration is not necessary, other formality rules—for example, requiring the use of a deed—may need to be satisfied before B can acquire a legal estate in land.

5. The *numerus clausus* principle also ensures that there are a limited number of legal *interests* in land. So, when applied to legal interests in land, the *content* question consists of asking if B's right counts as one of the permitted legal interests in land—that is, as an easement, charge, rentcharge, or profit. Unlike legal estates in land, none of these rights involves B having ownership of land.

6. To establish whether B has a legal *interest*, we also have to ask if B has, in fact, acquired that right. For example, if B

claims to have a legal easement, it will often be necessary for B to show that he is registered as holding that right. Even if registration is not necessary, other formality rules—for example, requiring the use of a deed—may need to be satisfied before B can acquire a legal interest in land.

7. It is important to bear in mind that even if B cannot show he has a legal estate or legal interest in land, it may still be possible for B to show that he has an *equitable* property right. This is because, as we noted in Chapter 2, section 4, the equitable rules applying to the *content* and *acquisition* questions may differ from the common law rules. We will examine the content and acquisition of these equitable property rights in Chapter 4. One important point to bear in mind is that certain equitable property rights may be related to certain legal property rights. For example, a lease can count as a legal property right in land, but it is also possible for B to have an *equitable* lease. In Chapter 4, we will consider how the effect of such an equitable property right may differ from the effect of a legal property right.

1 THE CONCEPT OF A PROPERTY RIGHT

In Chapter 2, we saw that land is a form of private property. To understand the law relating to private property, it is crucial to understand the concept of a 'property right'. A number of different terms can be used to describe such a right: for example, a property right can also be referred to as a 'right *in rem*' (from the Latin, this literally means a right against a thing), or, on the same basis, as 'a real right'. As we saw in Chapter 2, land is sometimes referred to as 'real property', but, as the following extract notes, it is important to realize that property rights can exist not only in relation to land, but also in relation to other things, such as books.

Lawson and Rudden, *The Law of Property* (3rd edn, 2002, p 14)

Real, or property rights. At this juncture, however, a further complication of terminology needs to be explained. '*Real property*' means land. But the expression '*real right*' can be used with regard to *any* type of property (movable or immovable). It is used to describe those interests which, broadly speaking, (a) can be alienated; (b) die when their object perishes or is lost without trace; (c) until then can be asserted against an indefinite number of people; (d) if the holder of the thing itself is bankrupt, enable the holder of the real right to take out of the bankruptcy the interest protected by the real right.

This apparently complicated statement can be illustrated quite simply. If you own this book you have a real right. As to point (a), you can give away or sell both the book and ownership of the book. As to point (b) if the book is destroyed in a fire, it is no longer yours and you bear the loss. As to (c) if you lend the book to a friend, of course you can claim it (or its value) back from him or her. But if your friend lends it to someone else you can claim it from them; indeed, in English law, you can claim it from someone to whom your friend sells it—your right is enforceable against an indefinite number of persons. Finally, as to (d), if your friend goes bankrupt while reading the book, you do not have to prove as a creditor in the bankruptcy proceedings. The book does not vest in the trustee in bankruptcy, since your friend cannot pay off his or her creditors with your book.

Other ways of referring to these features of a 'real right' are to speak of 'a *property* right' or '*proprietary* right'.

The term 'property right' is often used to distinguish a particular right from a 'personal right'. Again, the term 'personal right' is often referred to using Latin, as a 'right *in personam*' (i.e. a right against a person). To understand the concept of a property right, it can therefore be useful to see how it differs from a personal right. And because the distinction flows from Roman law, it is helpful to consider the following extract.

Nicholas, *An Introduction to Roman Law* (1962, pp 99–100)

Property and obligations—actions and rights in rem and in personam. A man's assets are either property or obligations. The difference between the two is the difference between owning and being owed something. Thus a man's assets may be his house and his furniture, which he owns, his bank balance which, however much one may speak of 'having money in the bank', is a debt owed by the bank, and his right to his unpaid salary, which is likewise a debt. His assets will often, of course, be more complicated than this, but they will still fall into one of the two categories. For example, if he is a shopkeeper he will own, we may suppose, his shop and his stock-in-trade; he may have ordered, but not received, further supplies from a wholesaler, and these will, from the Roman point of view, be still owned by the wholesalers but will be owed to him (and if he has not yet paid for them he will correspondingly owe the price); he will have supplied goods on credit to his customers, and here again there is obviously a debt. He may have acquired the goodwill of the business of a former competitor, and this constitutes once more a debt—the debtor's duty being not, as in the previous cases, to pay a sum of money or to supply goods, but to refrain from soliciting his former customers.

This difference between owning and being owed is expressed by the Roman lawyer in the distinction between actions *in rem* and actions *in personam*. Any claim is either *in rem* or *in personam*, and there is an unbridgeable division between them. An action *in rem* asserts a relationship between a person and a thing, an action *in personam* a relationship between persons [. . .] The Romans think in terms of actions not of rights, but in substance one action asserts a right over a thing, the other a right against a person, and hence comes the modern dichotomy between rights *in rem* and rights *in personam*. Obviously there cannot be a dispute between a person and a thing, and therefore even in an action *in rem* there must be a defendant, but he is there not because he is alleged to be under a duty to the plaintiff but because by some act he is denying the alleged right of the plaintiff.

Of course, it may be thought that, in the modern world, this distinction between 'owning' (property rights) and 'owing' (personal rights) is too simplistic. Certainly, there is no obvious reason why a distinction derived from Roman law should help us to classify concepts such as intellectual property rights. Indeed, as we will see in Chapter 4, it is not obvious that the Roman distinction can be applied to equitable property rights. But modern-day land law still retains the key distinction between a personal right (which can be asserted only against a specific person) and a legal property right (a right relating to land that is capable of binding the whole world). That distinction was particularly important in the following case.

Hill v Tupper (1863) 2 H & C 122, Exchequer Chamber

Facts: The Company of Proprietors of the Basingstoke Canal Navigation owned the Basingstoke Canal. It made a contractual promise to Mr Hill that he would have the exclusive right to put pleasure boats on the canal and to hire out those boats to paying customers. Mr Tupper was the landlord of an inn at Aldershot, which adjoined the canal. He also started to hire out pleasure boats on the canal. Mr Hill objected, claiming that Mr Tupper was interfering with Mr Hill's exclusive right and was thus committing a tort against Mr Hill. The Exchequer Chamber rejected Mr Hill's claim.

Pollock CB

At 127–8

After the very full argument which has taken place, I do not think it necessary to assign any other reason for our decision, than that the case of *Ackroyd v Smith*[1] expressly decided that it is not competent to create rights unconnected with the use and enjoyment of land, and annex them to it so as to constitute a property in the grantee.[2] This grant merely operates as a licence or covenant on the part of the grantors, and is binding on them as between themselves and [Mr Hill], but gives [Mr Hill] no right of action in his own name for any infringement of the supposed exclusive right. It is argued that, as the owner of an estate may grant a right to cut turves, or to fish or hunt,[3] there is no reason why he may not grant such a right as is now claimed by [Mr Hill]. The answer is, that the law will not allow it. So the law will not permit the owner of an estate to grant it alternately to his heirs male and heirs female. A new species of incorporeal hereditament[4] cannot be created at the will and pleasure of the owner of property, but he must be content to accept the estate and the right to dispose of it subject to the law as settled by decisions or controlled by acts of parliament. A grantor may bind himself by covenant to allow any right he pleases over his property, but he cannot annex it to a new incident, so as to enable the grantee to sue in his own name for an infringement of such a limited right as that now claimed.

Martin B

At 128

I am of the same opinion. This grant is perfectly valid as between [Mr Hill] and the canal Company, but in order to support this action, [Mr Hill] must establish that such an estate or interest vested in him that the act of [Mr Tupper] amounted to an eviction. None of the cases

---

[1] (1850) 10 CB 164.

[2] [On the fact of *Hill v Tupper*, the canal company is the *grantor* (because it gave Mr Hill a right) and Mr Hill is the *grantee* (because he was given a right by the canal company).]

[3] [Such rights are example of profits, a recognized legal property right in land: see section 6 below. A right to cut turves is a right to remove turf or peat from another's land to use as fuel: it is more commonly called a 'right of turbary'.]

[4] [As used in this particular context, that term is synonymous with 'a legal property right'. Technically, a 'hereditament' is a right that can count as 'real property' and so, for example, will be included in the scope of a term in a will 'leaving all my real property to X'. Land (including fixtures) can be seen as a 'corporeal hereditament', because it has a physical form; an easement (a right capable of counting as a legal property right in land, e.g. a right of way over another's land) is an 'incorporeal hereditament', because it has no physical form.]

cited are at all analogous to this, and some authority must be produced before we can hold that such a right can be created. To admit the right would lead to the creation of an infinite variety of interests in land, and an indefinite increase of possible estates. The only consequence is that, as between [Mr Hill] and the canal Company, he has a perfect right to enjoy the advantage of the covenant or contract; and, if he has been disturbed in the enjoyment of it, he must obtain the permission of the canal Company to sue in their name.

Hill v Tupper is an important case for a number of reasons. One reason, which we will examine in section 6 below, concerns the approach of the Exchequer Chamber in deciding whether Mr Hill's right counted as a legal property right in land. For our present purposes, the case is significant because it is a very good example of a key difference between a property right in land (i.e. an estate or interest in land) and a personal right. The Exchequer Chamber found that the canal company's contractual promise to Mr Hill gave him only a personal right against the company. So, if a third party, such as Mr Tupper, also puts out boats on the canal, Mr Hill's only option is to assert his right against the company. He can ask for an injunction, forcing the company, as owner of the canal, to take action against Mr Tupper; he can also ask for damages, to compensate him for any loss that he has suffered as a result of Mr Tupper's action. Mr Hill's only recourse is against the canal company: he has no claim against Mr Tupper. If his contract with the company had instead given Mr Hill a *legal property right*, things would be very different. Mr Hill's exclusive right to put boats on the canal would then be capable of binding not only the party who granted that right (in this case, the canal company), but also *any other party* who interferes with that right (such as Mr Tupper).

In the following extract, Birks explains both this fundamental difference between a personal right and a property right, and also its importance to land law.[5]

Birks, 'Five Keys to Land Law' in *Land Law: Themes and Perspectives* (eds Bright and Dewar, 1998, pp 472–3)

Real rights and personal rights

We move now to the kind of 'reality' or 'thing-relatedness' which matters in the modern law. The key proposition is that land law is, centrally, the law of real rights in land [...] 'Real' and 'personal' here anglicize the Latin labels *in rem* and *in personam*. Many people prefer to use the Latin labels. The Latin tells us that a right *in rem* is a right in or against a thing, while a right *in personam* is a right in or against a person.

One can change to different language. A right *in personam* can be called an obligation. A right *in personam* and an obligation are one and the same thing, but looked at from different ends. I have an overdraft. I owe my bank £1,000. The bank has a right *in personam*, the person here being me. I have an obligation to pay. The relationship can be named from either end, and in practice we usually name it from the liability end. Here we very frequently speak, not of the law of personal rights or of rights *in personam*, but of obligations. As for rights *in*

---

[5] The usefulness of the distinction between personal rights and property rights has been challenged (see, e.g., Worthington, 'The Disappearing Divide between Property and Obligation: The Impact of Aligning Legal Analysis and Commercial Expectation' in *Equity in Commercial Law* (eds Degeling and Edelman, 2005)). Such challenges have, however, tended to focus on the application of the distinction to commercial dealings with intangible wealth, rather than on its usefulness in land law.

rem, if we drop both the Latin and the latinate English, they usually become 'property rights' or 'proprietary rights'.

We sometimes use 'property' loosely to mean 'wealth'. In that loose sense 'property' wobbles. Sometimes 'my property' evokes and is intended to evoke more specific things, such as cars and clothes and cottages. Sometimes, and rather more technically, 'my property' denoted mere rights vested in me, such as a fee simple, a lease, ownership, or the obligations of my debtors. Whichever the focus, the loose notion of property as wealth is too broad to be useful in analysis. To think clearly the law has to draw a bright line between two classes of right, both of which can fall within the loose notion of wealth.

The bright line distinguishes between property and obligations. When that line is drawn, property clearly has a narrower and much more technical sense. Within wealth, taken as including all assets, the law of obligations is the law of rights *in personam* and the law of property is the law of rights *in rem*. Hence a 'property right' or 'proprietary right' is a real right, is a right *in rem*. The law of property is the law of all known real rights, and land law is the law of real rights in land.

What is the difference? The practical difference bears on this question. Against whom can the right be demanded? 'Demandability' is intelligible but not really English. But another word for 'to demand' is 'to exact', which gives us 'exigible' and 'exigibility'. A right *in rem* is a right the exigibility of which is defined by the location of a thing. The exigibility of a right *in personam* is defined by the location of the person. Where I have a right *in personam* the notional chain in my hand is tied round that person's neck. Where I have a right *in rem*, the notional chain in my hand is tied around a thing. Between me and the car which I own there is such a chain.

So, if B has a personal right against A, it is only possible for him to assert that right against A. If B has a property right in a piece of land, then B's right is *capable* of binding the rest of the world. The word 'capable' is important: as we will see in Chapter 6, it is possible for a particular third party to have a *defence* to B's property right. But this does not undermine the usefulness to B of a property right. Unlike a personal right, such a right is prima facie binding on anyone who later interferes with B's use of the land: it will bind that party as long as he cannot show that he has a defence to B's property right.

2 THE CONCEPT OF A LEGAL ESTATE IN LAND

The extracts in section 1 all use ownership as the core example of a property right; indeed, Nicholas portrays the distinction between a property right and a personal right as the difference between owning and being owed. In Chapter 2, we saw how it is possible to identify a particular person (B) as an owner of land. Technically speaking, however, it is true to say that, in English law, no one owns land. Even if you buy a house and think of yourself as owning that land, you technically have an estate in that land: either a freehold or a lease. This raises an important question: is the concept of ownership irrelevant to English land law?

In the following extract, Harris: (i) outlines the historical reasons why English law has a doctrine of estates in land; (ii) notes the argument that, as a result, ownership is irrelevant to English land law; but (iii) argues that ownership *is* nonetheless crucial to understanding English land law, because it enables us to understand the very concept of an estate in land.

Harris, *Property and Justice* (1996, pp 68–9)

The significance of ownership interests as an every-day organizing idea is commonly obscured for lawyers in common law systems, and for theorists who seek to build upon the insights of the common law, by the doctrine of estates in land. Land-transfer transactions in common law systems convey or create estates, freehold or leasehold, never *dominium* or ownership. This is a consequence of the feudal origins of English real property law.

In Early English feudal law, that interest which was to develop into the fee simple estate was a grant of seisin by a superior lord to be held by the grantee and his heirs subject to one or other variant of free tenure. It seems that the consent of both the lord and the heir were necessary before the grantee could alienate his land. Free alienability *inter vivos* of this estate evolved at common law, and free testamentary disposition of it was conferred by statute in the sixteenth century. There were as well lesser estates of freehold: estates for life; estates *pur autre vie*;[6] and the estate tail which emerged as the result of judicial interpretation of the Statute *de donis conditionalibus* of 1285.[7] There were also a variety of copyhold estates, the outcome of the progressive emancipation of land held on non-free tenure.

The leasehold estate was unknown to feudal law, but evolved from the end of the Middle Ages as common law actions were adapted to confer trespassory protection on a leaseholder, eventually, against all-comers to the land. Like the fee simple, the leasehold estate became freely transmissible *inter vivos* or on death. A covenant in a lease may prohibit assignment of the estate. Its effect is not, technically, to make the estate inalienable but to give rise to a ground for forfeiture should the estate be assigned in breach of covenant.

The terminology and conceptual structures elaborated in works on English real property law have reflected the technical concerns of conveyancers. Since what is conveyed is always an estate in the land, it has been widely assumed that 'ownership' of land, as such, is not a conception internal to English land law. A. D. Hargreaves gave robust expression to this view:

'English land law has made no contribution to the legal theory of ownership more striking, more brilliant and of more permanent value than the separation of the land from the estate in the land [...]. By distinguishing the land from the estate, English land law has shown conclusively that even within a society as individualistic and as legalistic as England in the nineteenth century, ownership is not a necessary legal concept. The problem of ownership remains, but it is not a legal problem; it is the concern of the politician, the economist, the sociologist, the moralist, the psychologist—of any and every specialist who can contribute his grain to the common heap. Ultimately the philosopher will try to unify this shifting mass into a coherent whole.'[8]

The story of the evolution of the doctrine of estates is one of complex elaboration based on the writ system, ancient statutes, and the conveyancing cunning of legal practitioners. If asked what was the content of the interests which came thus to be freely disposable by their holders, the traditional real property lawyer will answer that it consisted of a right to seisin or possession of the land. But if a man was the beneficiary of seisin or possession, what use-privileges over the land did that entail, and what powers to control uses by others? No general answer to that question is usually to be found in land law textbooks, although the case law on nuisance summarized in works on tort is replete with partial answers to it.

---

[6] [For the life of another: e.g. A could give B a right to land for the duration of X's life.]

[7] [*De donis conditionalibus* means 'relating to conditional gifts'. So, if A leaves land in his will to B1 for B1's life, then to B2 provided that B2 is married, B2's right to the land is conditional on both his marriage and the death of B1.]

[8] Hargreaves, 'Modern Real Property' (1956) 19 MLR 14, 17.

The answer to the general question about the normative content of a right to seisin or a right to possession is glaringly obvious. Perhaps it is so manifest as to be trite, and so beneath the notice of a technical lawyer who seeks to expound only that which is obscure and arcane. The truth is that ownership interests in land, of varying magnitudes, are and always have been incidents of legal estates in land. The jurist of the early medieval period took it for granted that the tenant who holds land in demesne is as much *dominus rei* as is the owner of a chattel.[9] As Pollock and Maitland point out, Bracton and contemporaries (rightly in their view) 'ascribed to the tenant in demesne ownership and nothing less than ownership'.[10] [...]

This truth, however trite, makes claims such as those contained in the above citation from Hargreaves patently absurd. Ownership of land is not a conveyancer's problem, but it is a conception—or rather a battery of conceptions—internal to the law. An indefinitely large set of use-privileges and control-powers over the land follow from the fact that, as an incident to the estate, a person has an ownership interest over the land itself.

Harris' argument may seem complicated, but it can be summed up quite shortly. Although it is *technically* true to say that B can never own land itself, it is also true to say that, if B has an estate in land, he has ownership rights over that land. So, if we want to know what, in practice, the holder of a freehold can do with his land, we need to consider, as we did in Chapter 2, what 'ownership' means. If this is right, we may well wonder why English law developed the doctrine of estates: it seems strange to have a system in which, whilst B cannot own the land itself, he can hold an estate that gives him ownership rights.

The following extract tackles this point.

Birks, 'Five Keys to Land Law' in *Land Law: Themes and Perspectives* (eds Bright and Dewar, 1998, pp 462–3)

Although bits do occasionally wash away or slip into the sea, land is in general permanent. For most human purposes we have to regard it as lasting for ever. There is a powerful urge to deal in slices of time. It is not confined to land. The institution of the trust makes it relatively easy to turn all kinds of wealth into an enduring fund, and that facility in turn excites and to a degree gratifies the urge to deal in slices of time. However, it is the natural permanence of land which makes slices of time a dominant feature of land law.

Two motivations

Why do people want to deal in slices of time? It is an urge which has been fed from at least two sources. One is essentially commercial, the other not.

The commercial motivation

Commercial motivation means, in plain words, the desire to get money out of land. There are all sorts of ways of getting money out of land. For instance, one can farm the land and

9 [Demesne is pronounced 'demean'. A tenant holding in demesne acquired rights in relation to the land under a grant from a feudal lord.]
10 Pollock and Maitland, *History of English Law* (1911, pp ii, 2–6).

sell the produce. The most extreme method of all is to sell one's whole interest in the land. This means selling the whole slice of time over which one has control. The largest interest in land—the greatest slice of time—is "for ever". In everyday conversation I tend to say 'my house' or 'the house I own'. In all probability, what I actually have is my house 'for ever', a slice of time measured by the length of time the land will last. There is no harm in calling that ownership. That is in effect what it is. But in the technical language of the law that huge slice of time measured by the life of the land itself is called a fee simple. The fee simple in the land on which my house stands is worth about £200,000. I could mortgage it or sell it. But there is another possibility. I could keep 'for ever' and deal instead in a shorter slice of time.

The commercial motivation for dealing in lesser slices of time is to realize in money some of the value of the land without giving up one's whole interest. The lease is the proprietary interest which most obviously facilitates this. I might let my land for a fixed number of years, say for ten years. If I go for that option, I have further choices. I could take a single capital sum, or I might prefer a flow of income in the form of an annual rent, or a mixture of both, say £20,000 now and £5,000 per annum by way of rent. Whichever I choose, the fee simple remains mine, though occluded by the lease. When the ten years have passed, the shadow occluding my interest will vanish, and my fee simple will once again be unencumbered. The reversion has value even during the ten years during which I am out of possession. If I choose to, I can sell it even while the ten years are running.

The family motivation

The primary non-commercial motivation for dealing in slices of time is concern for one's family. In obsolescent aristocratic terms this might be restated as a dynastic motivation. The idea of benefiting the different generations of one's family is perfectly natural. The desire to keep land permanently in the family or part of the family has been a routine temptation.

As Birks notes, it is useful to see an estate in land as a 'slice of time'. We noted in Chapter 1, section 4 that permanence is one of the distinctive features of land. This means that, where land is concerned, it is very useful for an owner of land to be able to divide up his ownership over time. The doctrine of estates allows this to happen. As Birks notes, an owner of a thing other than land (e.g. a painting) can divide up the benefit of that thing by setting up a trust: for example, if A owns a painting, he can transfer it to T to hold on trust for B1 for ten years, then for B2. B2 can thus acquire an equitable property right. It is impossible, however, for A to give B1 a *legal* property right amounting to ownership of the painting for ten years. A special feature of land, then, is that, by creating a lease, an owner of land can give B ownership rights over that land *for a limited period*.

3 LEGAL ESTATES IN LAND: THE *CONTENT* QUESTION

When examining if B has a legal estate in land, the first question to ask is the *content* question: does the right claimed by B count as a legal estate in land? As a result of s 1 of the Law of Property Act 1925 (LPA 1925), that question is relatively easy: there are now only two permissible legal estates in land.

Law of Property Act 1925, s 1

> (1) The only estates in land which are capable of subsisting or of being conveyed or created at law are—
>
> (a) An estate in fee simple absolute in possession;
>
> (b) A term of years absolute.

'*An estate in fee simple absolute in possession*' is more commonly referred to as a 'fee simple'[11] or, as we will call it in this book, a *freehold*. And '*a term of years absolute*' is more commonly referred to as a 'leasehold' or, as we will call it in this book, a *lease*. So, for example, if you are buying a house, you are, in fact, buying either a freehold or a lease. In this section, we will examine the content of a freehold and of a lease, before asking the important question of *why* the LPA 1925 imposed this limit on the types of permissible legal estate in land.

3.1 THE CONTENT OF A LEGAL FREEHOLD

A freehold can be described as 'ownership of land for an unlimited period'. In practice, there is usually very little doubt as to whether B's right counts as a freehold: in particular, if A has a freehold of land and simply transfers that right to B, it is clear that B now has a freehold. There are, however, some contexts in which we do have to test to see if B really does have a freehold. The following extract provides an example.

Miles v Bull [1969] 1 QB 258

Facts: Mr Bull and his brother had a freehold of a farmhouse and adjacent land. Mr Bull occupied the land with his wife until 1965, when he left the home. Under the Matrimonial Homes Act 1967, Mrs Bull had a statutory right to remain in occupation of the home. As a result, Mr Bull and his brother could not remove her from the land. In 1968, Mr Bull and his brother sold their freehold to Mr Miles for £10,000. Mr Miles wished to remove Mrs Bull from the land. Mrs Bull could not assert her statutory right to remain in occupation against Mr Miles, because she had not properly registered that right. Mr Miles therefore applied for summary judgment in his favour. Mrs Bull claimed, however, that she deserved to have the chance to argue her case at a full trial because: (i) the supposed transfer of the freehold to Mr Miles was, in fact, a sham; so (ii) the freehold was still held by Mr Bull and his brother; and therefore (iii) Mr Miles had no right to remove her from the land. In considering that argument, Megarry J had to consider the decision of Jones J in *Ferris v Weaven*,[12] in which it had been held that a purported transfer of a freehold was, in fact, a sham.

Megarry J

At 262–5

Accordingly, it seems to me that there is a strong preponderance of high authority for the view that the decision in *Ferris v. Weaven* can be supported on the basis that the transaction

---

[11] As in the extract by Birks given in section 2 above.
[12] [1952] 2 All ER 233.

there was a sham, and that although a genuine purchaser will take free from the rights of a deserted wife, a sham purchaser will not. It is therefore necessary to examine the facts of *Ferris v. Weaven* with some care [...]

In that case the husband deserted his wife in 1941, leaving her in occupation of his house; he continued to pay the building society instalments and the rates on it. He wrote to her telling her that he would "carry on paying on the house providing you do not annoy me." This state of affairs continued for some 10 years. Then:

> 'In June, 1951, wishing to obtain possession of the house so that he could dispose of it, the husband sold it for £30 to his brother-in-law, Herbert James Ferris, the plaintiff. The £30 was not, in fact, paid to the husband, the plaintiff entering into the transaction only to oblige the husband and enable him to obtain possession of the house from the wife. He did not exercise any act of ownership in respect of it, and the husband continued to pay the rates and the mortgage instalments, the amount of which due at the time of the sale was £1,600.'[13]

[...] In his judgment, dismissing the plaintiff's claim for possession against the wife, Jones J. said of the plaintiff:

> 'I find that he bought the house by agreement with the husband, not because he wanted to buy it, but simply to enable the husband to defeat a right which the husband believed the wife possessed as a result of the arrangement which the husband had made with her in 1941.'[14]

[...] The essential features of the so-called sale in that case were thus that the price was £30; that the purchaser neither paid it nor exercised any act of ownership over the house, even though it was conveyed to him; that the husband continued paying the rates and mortgage instalments as he had done before entering into the transaction; and that the object of both the husband and the purchaser was to obtain possession of the house for the husband so that he could dispose of it. The purchaser (who was the husband's brother-in-law) entered into the transaction with the object of obliging the husband. I can readily see how such a transaction could properly be described as a 'sham' for; although in outward show the ownership was vested in the purchaser, in substance and reality it was still vested in the husband. The documents lied; they made false representations, concealing what was and asserting what was not. The purchaser could not evict the wife, for the ownership of the property upon which he based his claim to possession was a mere pretence.

On the other hand, a transaction is no sham merely because it is carried out with a particular purpose or object. If what is done is genuinely done, it does not remain undone merely because there was an ulterior purpose in doing it. If in *Ferris v. Weaven* the purchaser had sought to exercise acts of ownership, and the husband had ceased to do them, and there had been no common objective of enabling the husband (as distinct from the purchaser) to dispose of the property, it would, in my judgment, be very difficult to contend that the low price and the failure to pay it made the transaction a sham. After all, some genuine transactions within the family are carried out at low prices; and some genuine purchasers fail to discharge their obligation to pay the full purchase price, if the vendor is incautious enough to make this possible. Mere circumstances of suspicion do not by themselves establish a transaction as a sham; it must be shown that the outward and visible form does not coincide with the inward and substantial truth.

---

[13] [1952] 2 All ER 233, 234.
[14] Ibid, at 237.

In the end, Megarry J decided that summary judgment in Mr Miles' favour should *not* be given: Mrs Bull's argument that there had, in fact, been no transfer of the freehold deserved to be evaluated at a full trial.

For our purposes, the important point about Megarry J's analysis is his use of the concept of ownership. On his Lordship's analysis, the simple fact that it was carried out with the motive of removing Mrs Weaven did not make the supposed transfer in *Ferris v Weaven* a sham. Instead, it was a sham because the documents lied. They said that Mr Ferris had a free-hold, but *'although in outward show the ownership was vested in the purchaser, in substance and reality it was still vested in the husband'*. This confirms the analysis given by Harris (see the extract in section 2 above): the concept of ownership is vital to understanding the con-cept of a freehold. It is therefore no surprise that, in *Property and Justice*, Harris refers to *Miles v Bull* in order to support his analysis.[15]

3.2 THE CONTENT OF A LEGAL LEASE

We will examine the content of a lease in detail in Chapter 23. Three general points are, how-ever, worth noting here. Firstly, as Harris has argued, the content of a lease, like the content of a freehold, can be understood by using the concept of ownership. In fact, in a seminal case on the content of a lease, *Street v Mountford*,[16] Lord Templeman referred to a tenant (a party holding a lease) as someone *'able to exercise the rights of an owner of land which is in the real sense his land, albeit temporarily and subject to certain restrictions'*.

Secondly, as Lord Templeman's statement makes clear, the difference between a freehold and a lease is that the latter consists of ownership *for a limited period*. This is why s 1 of the LPA 1925 describes the lease as a *'term of years absolute'*. 'Term', here, comes from the same root as 'terminal' or 'terminus', and means that a lease must come to an end—that is, that it must be for a limited period (see Chapter 23, section 2.7).

Thirdly, as we will see in Chapter 4, it is possible for B to have an *equitable lease*. In such a case, B does not have a legal property right in land, nor, according to the terminology of the LPA 1925, does he have an estate in land; instead, B has an equitable interest in land. In Chapter 4, we will consider how the effect of an equitable interest may differ from that of a legal estate or interest; in Chapter 23, section 3.2, we will specifically see why it may be better for B to show that he has a legal lease rather than an equitable lease.

3.3 WHY ONLY TWO LEGAL ESTATES IN LAND?

It may seem puzzling that the LPA 1925 imposes a limit on the types of legal estate. After all, in the final extract given in section 2 above, Birks set out some of the advantages, to an owner of land, of being able to divide his ownership into slices of time and then distribute those slices to others. An owner may well want to give another a legal estate that is neither a freehold nor a lease: for example, he may want to give his eldest child ownership of the land for her life, then give ownership for the future, taking effect on the eldest child's death, to his eldest grandchild, and so on. So why has English law limited an owner's ability to create those different sorts of legal estate in land?

---

[15] See *Property and Justice*, p 71.
[16] [1985] AC 809, 816.

Birks, 'Five Keys to Land Law' in *Land Law: Themes and Perspectives*
(eds Bright and Dewar, 1998, p 464)

Carried to extremes, the dynastic temptation might have led to an infinite series of life estates: to A, my eldest son, for life, then to A's eldest son for life, then to the eldest son of A's eldest son, and so on. The effect would have been to give each successive son only the slice of time measured by the thread of his life. He could deal in that slice, but no buyer would ever get, or pay for, more than an estate *pur autre vie* [i.e. an estate ending with the death of another person . . .] Some of the bad effects of such an arrangement are instantly appreciable. Nobody would ever have a marketable slice of time. No money could be raised to invest in the land. It is in nobody's interest to produce an impoverished class of landowners. If such arrangements prevailed, the value of land would be locked up and sterilized.

At p 463

[. . .] The law now does everything it can to ensure that land is freely alienable and that any future interests granted to descendants are detached from the land and transferred to the fund represented by the money for which it is sold. Since the great reforms of 1925, anyone wanting to deal in slices of time other than leases, and less than for ever, has had to do it in equity, behind the curtain of a trust. In other words, in front of the curtain there are now only two slices of time known to the law, 'for ever' and the lease for whatever time is agreed. All other slices of time once recognized directly by the common law have been abolished.

As Birks notes, it is no longer possible for A to give B1 a *legal* property right consisting of ownership of land for his life, or to give B2 a *legal* property right consisting of ownership from the time of B1's death. The closest that A can come to dividing up his ownership in that way is to set up a trust, under which B1 and B2 each acquire an *equitable* property right. We will consider those types of trust in Chapter 20, but two basic points can be noted now. Firstly, A's ability to set up such a trust is not limited to land and so does not depend on the doctrine of estates: for example, A can set up an identical trust in relation to his ownership of a painting. Secondly, under such a trust, it is very important that B1 and B2 each have an *equitable*, and not a *legal*, property right. In particular, as we will see in Chapters 6 and 21, it means that there may well be situations in which B1 and B2 cannot assert that right against a later purchaser of the land. This may be bad news for B1 and B2, but, by protecting the purchaser, it promotes the goal of allowing land to be 'freely alienable'—that is, to be transferred free from pre-existing rights of parties such as B1 and B2.

4 LEGAL ESTATES IN LAND: THE *ACQUISITION* QUESTION

To show that he has a legal estate in land, B needs to show not only that his claimed right counts as a freehold or lease, but also that he has, in fact, acquired that right. The obvious way for B to acquire a freehold or lease is through a *dependent acquisition*—that is, by showing that A, an owner of the land, has given B that legal estate. So, if B claims that A has transferred his freehold to B, or that A has granted him a lease, B relies on a dependent acquisition. We will examine the rules applying to a dependent acquisition of a legal estate in Chapter 9. One basic point worth noting here is that, to rely on a dependent acquisition, B will generally need to show that: (i) he has *registered* his legal estate, by ensuring that he is recorded on the Land Register as holding that right; and (ii) A has used a deed to give B that legal estate. As we will see in Chapter 9, there are some exceptions where leases are concerned: the general rule is that legal leases of seven years or less do not have to be registered; and some legal leases of three years or less can even be created orally, without the use of a deed or any writing.

We noted in the previous section that, if B's right does not count as a legal estate in land, it may nonetheless count as an *equitable* property right. Similarly, if B cannot show that he has acquired a legal estate in land (for example, because he is not registered as holding that right), it may still be possible for B to show that he has acquired an *equitable* property right. For example, if A attempts to give B a legal lease, but fails to do so (the failure may result, for example, from a failure to comply with the need for registration or the need for a deed), it may still be possible for B to show that he has an equitable lease. We will examine this general point in Chapter 4, sections 4 and 6, as well as in Chapter 11; we will consider the specific question of the acquisition of an equitable lease in Chapter 23, section 3.2.

It is also possible for B to acquire a legal freehold by means of an *independent acquisition*.[17] In such a case, B does not claim that A has given him a legal estate; instead, B acquires that right through his own, unilateral conduct. For example, if B simply goes onto A's land and takes physical control of it, B acquires a legal freehold of that land, even if he acts without A's permission.[18] We will examine this point in detail in Chapter 10.

It may seem surprising that B can acquire a legal estate in this way, but it is the consequence of a general rule of English property law: B can acquire ownership simply by taking physical control of a thing. For example, in *Armory v Delamirie*,[19] a chimney sweep's boy found a jewel. He took to a jeweller to have it valued. The jeweller then removed the precious stones from the jewel and refused to return them. The boy sued the jeweller, claiming that the jeweller had interfered with his legal property right in the jewel. The court found in favour of the boy: he acquired his legal property right simply by taking physical control of the jewel and it made no difference that another party (e.g. the person who lost the jewel) might have a better right to it. So, it is sometimes true to say that 'possession is nine-tenths of the law'.

5 THE CONCEPT OF A LEGAL INTEREST IN LAND

A legal interest in land is a legal property right in land that does not give its holder ownership of that land. In the following extract, Lawson and Rudden discuss one example of a legal interest in land: a legal easement.

Lawson and Rudden, *The Law of Property* (3rd edn, 2002, pp 14–15)

We have used the simple example of ownership, but as we shall see later there is a limited number of other interests which can be described as 'real' or 'proprietary'. This can

---

[17] As to whether a legal lease can be acquired independently, see Chapter 23, section 3.1.

[18] It has been suggested that, in such a case, B acquires only an *equitable* freehold. That view is, however, difficult to support: see Chapter 10, section 3.

[19] (1722) 5 Stra 505. See also Chapter 2, section 3.2.2 at pp 46–8.

> be illustrated by considering your right to leave your car in next door's yard. Probably at the moment you have no such right. If your neighbour lets you, you can park but you have no right to stay. If you pay for parking, say by the month, you have a contractual right to leave your car, enforceable by an action for damages and possibly an injunction, but enforceable against your neighbour only.[20] If, however, you have an easement—a recognized real right—your claim to park will prevail against whoever owns next door. But before the common law will recognize it as a property interest, the right to park must comply with certain requirements both of substance and form; you must own the freehold or leasehold of your house; the parking must not be a claim to possession of your neighbour's entire yard; it must be intended to add to the value of the house and not just to confer a personal benefit on you; and it must be created by deed and entered on the Land Register, or else have been acquired by over twenty years open user.

The key *positive* feature of a legal interest in land, such as an easement, is thus that it counts as a legal property right in land. As a result, it is capable of binding not only A (the party giving B the right), but also the rest of the world (including, for example, any later owners of A's land). For example, in *Hill v Tupper*,[21] which we examined in section 1 above, Mr Hill was unable to show that the right he acquired from the canal company counted as an easement, or as any other form of legal interest in land. As a result, Mr Hill could not assert that right against Mr Tupper. In contrast, if Mr Hill *had* been able to show that he had a legal interest in land, that right would have been prima facie binding not only on the canal company, but also on the rest of the world—including, of course, Mr Tupper.

The key *negative* feature of a legal interest in land, such as an easement, is that it does *not* give its holder any ownership rights. As we will see in Chapter 26, that point can be important when considering B's claim to an easement. The 'ouster principle' means that B's right cannot count as an easement if it amounts to a claim of ownership of a particular piece of land. If B wants to claim such a right, he must show that he has an estate in land—that is, a freehold or a lease.

It is worth noting that the concept of a property right that does not involve ownership may well be unique to land law. Certainly, it is impossible, for example, to have an easement over property other than land. It seems that the special features of land that we examined in Chapter 1 (in particular, its capacity for multiple, simultaneous use) may justify the recognition of special forms of property right that can exist only in relation to land.

6 LEGAL INTERESTS IN LAND: THE *CONTENT* QUESTION

In *Hill v Tupper*,[22] which we examined in section 1 above, Mr Hill tried to argue that his exclusive right to put boats on the canal should be regarded by the court as a new form of legal interest in land. The Exchequer Chamber made very clear, however, that individuals, such as Mr Hill and the canal company, cannot simply choose to create new forms of legal interest in land. That important point is confirmed by the following extract.

---

[20] [Such a right is an example of a *contractual licence*, which is a type of right that we will examine in Chapter 8, section 3.]

[21] (1863) 2 H & C 122.

[22] Ibid.

Keppell v Bailey (1834) 2 My & K 517

Facts: Edward and John Kendall were the proprietors of an ironworks in Monmouthshire. They set up a joint stock company, along with a number of other parties, to build the Trevill railroad. The Kendalls made a binding promise to the other stockholders that the limestone used in their ironworks would come only from the Trevill quarry (and so would be carried on the Trevill railroad, thus earning money for the joint stock company). Following the deaths of the Kendalls, the ironworks was passed on, and was eventually bought by Joseph and Crayshaw Bailey. The Baileys planned to use limestone from a different quarry and to build a new railroad to carry that limestone to the ironworks. Stockholders in the joint stock company (including Mr Keppell) applied for an injunction preventing the Baileys from using any limestone not taken from the Trevill quarry. They argued: (i) that the promise made by the Kendalls bound not only themselves, but also any later owners of the ironworks, such as the Baileys; and, alternatively, that (ii) even if the promise made by the Kendalls did not create a property right, it should bind the Baileys, because they acquired the ironworks knowing of that earlier promise. The High Court of Chancery rejected both of those arguments.

We will examine that second argument in Chapter 7, section 2.6; our focus here is on the first argument.

Lord Brougham LC

At 535

There are certain known incidents to property and its enjoyment; among others, certain burdens wherewith it may be affected, or rights which may be created and may be enjoyed over it by parties other than the owner; all which incidents are recognised by the law [. . .] All these kinds of property, however, all these holdings, are well known to the law and familiarly dealt with by its principles. But it must not therefore be supposed that incidents of a novel kind can be devised and attached to property at the fancy or caprice of any owner. It is clearly inconvenient both to the science of the law and to the public weal that such a latitude should be given. There can be no harm in allowing the fullest latitude to men in binding themselves and their representatives, that is, their assets real and personal, to answer in damages for breach of their obligations. This tends to no mischief, and is a reasonable liberty to bestow; but great detriment would arise and much confusion of rights if parties were allowed to invent new modes of holding and enjoying real property, and to impress upon their lands and tenements a peculiar character, which should follow them into all hands, however remote. Every close, every messuage,[23] might thus be held in a several fashion; and it would hardly be possible to know what rights the acquisition of any parcel conferred, or what obligations it imposed. The right of way or of common is of a public as well as of a simple nature, and no one who sees the premises can be ignorant of what the vicinage[24] knows. But if one man may bind his messuage and land to take lime from a particular kiln, another may bind his to take coals from a certain pit, while a third may load his property with further obligations to employ one blacksmith's forge, or the members of one corporate body, in various operations upon the premises, besides many other restraints as infinite in variety as the imagination can make

---

[23] [That is, every piece of land; 'messuage' means a piece of land on which a house stands.]

[24] ['Vicinage' here means the neighbourhood or, more specifically, other neighbours who are entitled to exercise rights of common over a piece of land.]

> them; for there can be no reason whatever to support the covenant in question, which would not extend to every covenant that can be devised.

Lord Brougham LC thus set out some of the dangers that would come from allowing individuals to create new legal interests in land. The central point is that a third party, such as someone later acquiring a right in that land, would then find it very difficult to know what burdens he may have to bear. We can also make the separate point that if new types of burden are imposed on land, the value of that land may be severely reduced. These fears have resulted in the adoption of the *numerus clausus* ('closed list') principle: there is a set list of legal property rights in relation to land and if B's right is not on that list, it simply cannot count as a legal property right in land.

Doubts have been expressed about the true usefulness of the principle. For example, whilst noting that the principle seems to exist in all non-feudal legal systems, Rudden[25] also argues that it may not be efficient: if A and B are unable to create a desired property right, they may well resort to complicated legal mechanisms in an effort to achieve, as far as possible, the same effect. As Rudden puts it:

> all that the law of many countries does is to prevent an owner from simply and cheaply creating fancy property interests; he can almost always achieve his aims at some cost by the use of devices [. . .] which, when one stands back and contemplates them calmly, appear largely mumbo-jumbo.

As we will see in Chapter 27, section 2.4, when examining the law relating to positive covenants, there is some truth in that observation.

It can also be argued that the *numerus clausus* principle allows judges to evade their responsibility to explain precisely why particular rights count as legal interests in land, whilst others do not. Gray and Gray have made this criticism forcefully.[26]

Gray and Gray, *Elements of Land Law* (5th edn, 2009, pp 96–7)

Nowhere, perhaps, is the imperfect logic of English land law more clearly apparent than in its attempt to demarcate proprietary rights from merely personal rights in land. The outcome is a philosophical shambles, but English law has never been overly concerned with philosophical propriety. Although the way in which the law identifies the categories of proprietary right is deeply unsatisfactory, the difficulties (albeit irksome) should not be over-estimated. Somehow English law blunders its way towards roughly the correct conclusions and there is usually little doubt, except perhaps at the perimeters of the field, as to whether a particular entitlement is or is not proprietary in the relevant conveyancing sense [. . .]

The difficulty with this orthodox understanding of proprietary quality is, of course, that it is riddled with circularity: the definition of proprietary character becomes entirely self-fulfilling. If naively we ask which entitlements are 'proprietary', we are told that they are those rights

---

[25] 'Economic Theory v Property Law' in *Oxford Essays in Jurisprudence* (3rd series, eds Eekelaar and Bell, 1987).

[26] See, also, Gray and Gray, 'The Rhetoric of Realty' in *Rationalizing Property, Equity and Trusts: Essays in Honour of Edward Burn* (ed Getzler, 2003).

which are assignable to and enforceable against third parties. When we then ask which rights these may be, we are told that they comprise, of course, the entitlements which are traditionally identified as 'proprietary'. It is radical and obscurantist nonsense to formulate a test of proprietary quality in this way.

Nonetheless, as the following extract shows, the *numerus clausus* principle, as far as legal interests in land is concerned, has been given statutory confirmation.

Law of Property Act 1925, s 1

(1) The only interests or charges in or over land which are capable of subsisting or of being conveyed or created at law are—

    (a) An easement, right or privilege in or over land for an interest equivalent to an estate in fee simple absolute in possession or a term of years absolute;

    (b) A rentcharge in possession issuing out of or charged on land being either perpetual or for a term of years absolute;

    (c) A charge by way of legal mortgage;

    (d) Any other similar charge on land which is not created by an instrument;

    (e) Rights of entry exercisable over or in respect of a legal term of years absolute, or annexed, for any purpose, to a legal rentcharge.

(2) All other estates, interests, and charges in or over land take effect as equitable interests.

So, just as s 1(1) of the LPA 1925 limits the number of possible legal estates in land, s 1(2) of the same Act limits the numbers of possible legal interests in land. Essentially, there are five types of permissible legal interest: an easement; a profit; a charge; a rentcharge; and a right of entry. If B's right does not match the content of one of those five rights, it cannot count as a legal interest in land.

In Chapter 26, we will examine the content of the easement in detail; we will do the same for the charge in Chapter 29. Profits, rentcharges, and rights of entry are of less practical importance, and will not be examined in detail. A profit is a right to take something from A's land (e.g. turf, timber, fish, or wild animals);[27] a rentcharge is a right to receive money from a freehold owner of land.[28] A right of entry may arise as part of a lease, where a landlord reserves a right to enter the land if, for example, the tenant fails to pay rent as agreed; it may also arise as part of a rentcharge to allow the party holding the rentcharge to enter the freeholder's land if that charge is not paid.

The list imposed by s 1(2) of the 1925 Act is not necessarily fixed forever. For example, as we will see in Chapter 27, the Law Commission has recently suggested an addition: the 'land obligation'. It does mean, however, that any change to the list can be made only by Parliament, and by amending s 1(2).

---

[27] For more detail, see, e.g., Law Commission Consultation Paper No 186 (2008, Pt 6).
[28] For more detail, see, e.g., Rentcharges Act 1977; Gray and Gray, *Elements of Land Law* (5th edn, 2009, Part 6.6).

7 LEGAL INTERESTS IN LAND: THE *ACQUISITION* QUESTION

The obvious way for B to acquire a legal interest in land is through a *dependent acquisition*—that is, by showing that A has given B that right. In Chapters 26 and 29, we will examine the rules applying to a dependent acquisition of, respectively, a legal easement and a legal charge. One basic point worth noting here is that, where B claims that A has given him a legal charge or legal easement over registered land, B will generally need to show that: (i) he has *registered* his legal interest, by ensuring that he is recorded on the Land Register as holding that right; and (ii) A has used a deed to give B that legal interest. There is, however, an exception where B claims to have an *implied easement*: as we will see in Chapter 26, section 3.2, this type of legal easement can be acquired without registration, although it does require the use of a deed. If A attempts to give B a legal interest in land, but fails to do so (the failure may result, for example, from a failure to comply with the need for registration or the need for a deed), it may still be possible for B to show that he has an equitable interest. We will examine this general point in Chapter 4, sections 4 and 6, as well as in Chapter 11.

It is also possible for B to acquire an easement simply by exercising a right over a long period. In such a case, B's easement is said to arise 'through prescription' and there is no need for B to show that he has registered that right, or that A used a deed (or even any writing) to give B that right. Where B relies on prescription to acquire an easement, it may well seem that he is relying on an *independent acquisition*—that is, he is claiming a right as a result of his own, unilateral conduct, just as occurs where B acquires a freehold by taking physical control of land. As we will see in Chapter 26, section 3.3, however, the courts have not adopted this view.

8 CONCLUSION

The facts of *Hill v Tupper*[29] (see section 1 above) and *Keppell v Bailey*[30] (see section 6 above) provide particular examples of a more general question that land law has to tackle: if A owns land and B then acquires a right that relates to A's land, can B also assert that right against C, a third party? To answer that question, we need to be aware of the crucial distinction between: (i) a legal property right in land; and (ii) a personal right. If, as in both *Hill* and *Keppell*, B's right is simply a personal right against A, then it is impossible for B to assert that right against C. But if B can instead show that his right is a legal property right in land, that right is capable of binding the rest of the world, including C.

Legal property rights in land can be divided into two types: legal estates and legal interests. The difference is that the former category, unlike the latter, give their holder ownership rights over a piece of land. The LPA 1925 carefully restricts the number of legal estates and legal interests in land: there are only two permissible legal estates (freehold and lease), and, for our purposes, there are only two significant legal interests (easement and charge). If B claims to have a legal estate or legal interest, he must pass both the *content* test and the *acquisition* test. To pass the *content* test, B needs to show that the right he claims counts as a legal estate or legal interest. To pass the *acquisition* test, B needs to show that he has, in fact,

---

[29] (1863) 2 H & C 122.
[30] (1834) 2 My & K 517.

acquired that right: it is generally the case that, to do so, B needs to show that he is registered as holding that right and/or that A has used a particular form (such as a deed) to give him that right.

Clearly, legal estates and interests form a crucial part of land law. But to avoid overstating their importance, we need to bear four points in mind. Firstly, if B fails to show that he has a legal property right in land, this does not necessarily mean that B has only a personal right against A. Instead, as we will see in Chapter 4, it is still possible for B to have an *equitable* property right. And such a right may give B precisely the protection that he needs: not only against A, but also against a third party later acquiring a right in A's land.

Secondly, even if B has no legal or equitable property right in land, there may be some cases in which B can nonetheless rely on a *human right* as protection against both A and C. We will examine the impact of human rights on land law in Chapter 5.

Thirdly, even if B *does* have a legal property right in land, there may, in theory, be circumstances in which he cannot assert that right against a particular third party: as we will see in Chapter 6, it may be possible for C to have a *defence* against B's legal property right.

Finally, if B wants protection simply against a specific third party (rather than any third party later acquiring a right in A's land), it is not always necessary for B to show that he has either a legal or equitable property right. Instead, B may be protected by showing he has a *direct right* against that particular third party. We will examine such direct rights in Chapter 7.

QUESTIONS

1. What is the difference between a 'personal' right and a 'property' right?
2. How might the result in *Hill v Tupper* have been different if Mr Hill's right had counted as a property right?
3. What role, if any, does the concept of ownership play in English land law?
4. Why did the Law of Property Act 1925 limit the number of possible legal estates in land?
5. What is the difference between dependent and independent acquisition?
6. What is the *numerus clausus* principle? Is it an unjustified limit on the ability of an owner of land to create new property rights in that land?

FURTHER READING

Birks, 'Five Keys to *Land Law*' in *Land Law: Themes and Perspectives* (eds Bright and Dewar, Oxford: OUP, 1998)

Bright, 'Of Estates and Interests: A Tale of Ownership and Property Rights' in *Land Law: Themes and Perspectives* (eds Bright and Dewar, Oxford: OUP, 1998)

Harris, 'Legal Doctrine and Interests in Land' in *Oxford Essays in Jurisprudence* (3rd series, eds Eekelaar and Bell, Oxford: OUP, 1987)

Merrill and Smith, 'Optimal Standardization in the Law of Property: The Numerus Clausus Principle' (2000) 110 Yale LJ 1

Rudden, 'Economic Theory v Property Law' in *Oxford Essays in Jurisprudence* (3rd series, eds Eekelaar and Bell, Oxford: OUP, 1987)

4

EQUITABLE INTERESTS

CENTRAL ISSUES

1. It is generally said that there are two sorts of property right in land: legal property rights and equitable property right. We examined legal property rights in Chapter 3; we will examine equitable property rights in this chapter. When asking if B has an equitable property right, it is useful to ask the same two questions we discussed in Chapter 3—that is, the *content* question and the *acquisition* question.

2. We saw in Chapter 3 that legal property rights in land can be split into two groups: legal estates and legal interests. In contrast, under the scheme of the Law of Property Act 1925, there is no such thing as an equitable estate in land. All equitable property rights in land are equitable *interests*. Equitable interests in land can usefully be split into two groups: equitable interests arising under a trust; and other equitable interests.

3. As we also saw in Chapter 3, there is a limited number of legal estates and legal interests in land. The list of possible equitable interests in land is also limited, but is longer than the list of legal interests. In particular, a right under a trust counts as an equitable interest—and rights under a trust can have very varied content. This means

that whilst the content of B's right may prevent it from being a legal interest in land, it may still count as an equitable interest in land.

4. To see if B has an equitable interest, we again have to ask if B has, in fact, acquired that right. The formality rules regulating to the acquisition of an equitable interest differ from those applying to legal interests. As a result, it is often easier for B to show that he has acquired an equitable interest: for example, a failure to register his right can never prevent B from acquiring an equitable interest in land.

5. It is therefore clear that the *content* and *acquisition* questions are answered differently depending on whether B claims a legal or equitable property right. In section 7 of this chapter, we will consider whether these differences can be justified. One important point is that if B has an equitable property right rather than a legal property right, it will generally be easier for a third party to show that he has a defence to B's right. We will focus on the *defences* question in Chapter 6. It may also be the case that equitable interests are conceptually, as well as historically, distinct from legal property rights.

1 THE CONCEPT OF AN EQUITABLE PROPERTY RIGHT

In Chapter 3, section 1, we considered the fundamental distinction between a personal right and a property right: whereas a personal right can be asserted only against a specific person, a property right is capable of binding the whole world. In Chapter 2, section 4, we noted that rules developed by courts of equity have taken their place alongside rules developed by common law courts and play a vital role in land law. One of the key contributions of those equitable rules is the concept of an *equitable property right*. An equitable property right shares a very important feature with a legal property right: it does more than simply bind a specific person. For example, if A has a freehold or lease of land and then gives B an equitable property right, B has a right that is capable of binding not only A, *but also C*, a party who later acquires A's land.

In the following extract, Lionel Smith discusses the development of equitable property rights. He makes the important point that these rights, unlike the legal property rights that we examined in Chapter 3, are based on A's being under a *duty* to B.

Smith, 'Fusion and Tradition' in *Equity in Commercial Law*
(eds Degeling and Edelman, 2005, pp 32–3)

I would argue that there are at least two examples of norms that are enforced routinely by Equity, but only sporadically by the common law, and that it is here that the true distinctiveness of Equity may lie. In other words, leaving aside the mass of detailed doctrine in both traditions, these are examples of situations in which Equity enforces a norm or value which the common law generally does not.

Respect for other people's obligations

This section can be introduced with a simple normative problem. Imagine that John owns a boat. He lends it to Mary, promising her that she can keep it for one month. After one week, Eleanor offers to buy the boat from John. John accepts her offer and Eleanor becomes the owner of the boat. Is she required to allow Mary to retain possession during the rest of the one-month period? Reasonable people could differ. Many people would say that it depends upon whether Eleanor was aware of the arrangements between John and Mary, and some might think it was relevant whether Mary had paid for her one month of use, or whether it was in the nature of a gift.

In the Romanist tradition, the most fundamental distinction in private law is the one between obligations and property rights. A right of ownership binds everyone. Obligations bind only the parties to the obligation: the debtor is bound to the creditor. The common law, in the narrow sense that excludes Equity, basically follows this line. Both modern civil law and the common law in the narrow sense admit the possibility that someone can commit a wrongful act by interfering with the fulfilment of another person's obligation.[1] But short of that fault-based wrong, obligations do not have effects except on the debtor and the creditor. Equity takes a different view. Some obligations systematically have third-party effects,

---

[1] [We will examine those wrongs in Chapter 7, section 2.4.]

without recourse to the law of wrongs. These are obligations that relate to the benefit of particular property, or an interest therein.

This approach is seen in a crucial technique of legal reasoning that underlies much of the original jurisdiction of Equity. At the risk of leaving out much doctrinal detail, it can be stated in this way. If a person is under an obligation, and the obligation relates to the benefit of particular property or an interest therein, then another person who comes into possession or control of that particular property—even though he does so without any personal culpability—is not allowed to get in the way of the fulfilment of the obligation. The defendant can free himself of this constraint only by affirmative proof that he gave value in good faith without notice of the obligation, and that the interest he acquired was a common law interest and not an Equitable one only [...] The representative of creditors is also caught, although he represents persons who are in good faith and who, for the most part, gave value.

This principle is not totally alien to the common law. First, as we have noted, the common law recognises that one person should not deliberately interfere in another person's performance of his obligations. But in this tort context, it looks for a level of cognition on the part of the defendant that allows us to understand the defendant as having committed a genuinely wrongful act. In that setting, of course, it is irrelevant whether the obligation relates to specific property or not. More interestingly, in one crucial context, the common law did exactly what Equity does routinely: it said that if the obligation does relate to specific property, then a recipient of that property must allow the obligation to be performed, even though the recipient does not owe the obligation, and without any finding that the recipient acted wrongfully. That context is the lease of land. The lessee's rights were enforceable against a transferee from the lessor, and later against all the world, first in damages only, but later by specific recovery.

In Equity, however, this principle is ubiquitous, and routinely turns an obligation relating to a particular asset into a kind of property right, held by the beneficiary or creditor of the obligation, in the particular asset. Effectively, people are bound by other people's obligations—not bound to perform them, but bound not to interfere with them.

In the following extract, Hackney also discusses how equitable property rights developed from an initial duty of A to B. In doing so, he uses the trust as an example. As we will see in this chapter, the trust is a classic example of a situation in which B has an equitable property right. A trust arises where A (the trustee) has a right (the trust property) and is under a duty to use that right for the benefit of B (or B and others, known as the 'beneficiaries'), as well as a duty not to use that right for A's own benefit.[2] If another party has specifically set up the trust, that party is often referred to as the 'settlor'.

Hackney, *Understanding Equity and Trusts* (1987, pp 21–2)

One consequence of the 'regularisation' of Equity [see the extract in Chapter 2, section 4] was the creation of a law of property. The Chancellor had originally intervened by imposing personal obligations on particular defendants. So the early trustee of land would be under a personal obligation to administer the property for his beneficiary, but the trustee might still be

---

[2] It is possible for there to be trusts in which A, as well as being a trustee, is also a beneficiary of the trust. In such a case, A is permitted to use the trust property for his own benefit (to the extent that he is a beneficiary).

seen as the owner of the land. The particular novelty of the trust is that the beneficiary need not have been a party to a transaction establishing the trust, yet he is still able to enforce it, and what is more, the person who does set up the transaction finds he has no standing to intervene to see that it is honoured. By the end of this period the beneficiary of the trust is perceived as having an equitable proprietary interest in the asset, not just rights enforceable only against the trustee. He can enforce his rights against total strangers, from whom he can demand the asset. This 'exigibility'—demandability—is one of the characteristics of property. He can also alienate and pass a good equitable title. For some of the beneficiary's protection his trustee will have to use the mechanism of the common law courts, and the beneficiary of the trust may have to invoke the assistance of the Chancellor to drive a reluctant trustee to take the necessary steps. But it is important to see that the trustee is no longer exercising rights. His common law ownership was made up of a set of rights, powers and duties. The Chancellor's intervention has overridden or destroyed the rights, which the trustee can no longer exercise at his own election and for his own benefit, and has converted them into equitable duties, to be performed for the sole benefit of the beneficiary. No principle seems more central to the law of trusts than that the trustee may not derive a profit from the trust. There is today no sensible usage of 'owner' which can apply to the trustee, and every sensible usage which can apply to the beneficiary. The trustee has a legal title and access to common law courts and remedies, but he is a driven vehicle for the superior rights of his beneficiary. He litigates at common law in response to his equitable duties, and not to his common law rights, which have been subordinated. The trustee is now a manager in an institution which is a hybrid between the creation of an agency and the disposition of property.

2 THE CONCEPT OF AN EQUITABLE INTEREST IN LAND

The decision of the House of Lords in *Williams & Glyn's Bank v Boland*[3] provides a practical example of the 'exigibility' of an equitable property right—that is, the ability of such a right, acquired by B as a result of A's conduct, to bind a party other than A. Mr Boland was registered as holding a freehold of a home in Beddington, Surrey. Because that freehold had been acquired with the financial assistance of his wife, Mrs Boland had an equitable property right; Mr Boland held his freehold on trust, and both he and Mrs Boland were the beneficiaries of that trust. We will consider the circumstances in which such trusts arise in Chapter 18. The important point for present purposes is that, when Mr Boland later gave the Williams & Glyn's Bank a charge over the land, the House of Lords held that Mrs Boland's pre-existing right under the trust was binding on the bank. This demonstrates that Mrs Boland's right under the trust was more than a mere personal right against her husband.

It is important to note that, in *Williams & Glyn's Bank v Boland*, the House of Lords considered whether the bank had a defence to Mrs Boland's pre-existing equitable property right. The fact that her equitable property right was *capable* of binding a party other than A did not mean that her right would *always* bind such parties. We noted in Chapter 3, section 1, that it is possible for a third party to have a defence to a pre-existing legal property right; it is also possible for a third party to have a defence to a pre-existing *equitable* property right. We will consider such defences in detail in Chapter 6.

---

[3] [1981] AC 813.

2.1 EQUITABLE ESTATES IN LAND?

In some situations, it may be tempting to describe B's equitable property right as an equitable estate in land. For example, let us say that S, who has a freehold, wants to divide up his ownership of land by making B1 owner of the land for B1's life, with B2 becoming owner on the death of B1. We know that S cannot achieve his aims by giving either of B1 or B2 a *legal* estate in land. As we saw in Chapter 3, section 2, there are only two forms of such right: the freehold and the lease. S can, however, transfer his freehold to A1 and A2 subject to a duty to use that freehold: (i) for the benefit of B1 during B1's life; then (ii) for the benefit of B2 forever. In such a case, A1 and A2 clearly have a legal estate: a freehold. But, as noted in the Hackney extract above, the trust imposed on A1 and A2 means that they cannot use their ownership rights for their own benefit: instead, they must use their freehold for the benefit of B1, then for the benefit of B2. So, whilst A1 and A2 have ownership, they are under equitable duties to B1 and B2; and those duties ensure that it is B1 and B2 who take the benefit of A1 and A2's ownership.

This structure is made clear in the Trusts of Land and Appointment of Trustees Act 1996 (TOLATA 1996).

Trusts of Land and Appointment of Trustees Act 1996, s 6(1) and (6)

(1) For the purpose of exercising their functions as trustee, the trustees of land have in relation to the land subject to the trust all the powers of an absolute owner.

[...]

(6) The powers conferred by this section shall not be exercised in contravention of, or of any order made in pursuance of, any other enactment or any rule of law or equity.

In our example, it could be said that each of B1 and B2 has an *equitable estate*—that is, an equitable property right that allows its holder to benefit from ownership of land. But we do need to be slightly careful when using the term 'equitable estate'. Firstly, the Law of Property Act 1925 (LPA 1925) does not use that term. As we saw in Chapter 3, section 6, s 1(1) of the Act sets out permissible legal estates and s 1(2) sets out permissible legal interests. Section 1(3) then states that: '*All other estates, interests, and charges in or over land take effect as equitable interests.*' So, if we were to follow that terminology strictly, we would have to treat all equitable property rights as equitable interests.

Secondly, and more importantly, in Chapter 3, section 2, we defined an estate as a property right giving its holder ownership rights. In our example in which A1 and A2 hold a freehold on trust for B1 and B2, it is not strictly accurate to say that B1 and B2 have ownership rights; rather, A1 and A2 have ownership, and B1 and B2 have the *benefit* of A1 and A2's ownership. There is thus a subtle distinction between a *legal* estate in land and an *equitable* estate in land: the former gives its holder ownership rights; the latter gives its holder the benefit of ownership rights held by trustees. The term 'equitable estate', where it is used, can thus be understood as a label that distinguishes those equitable property rights that give their holder the benefit of ownership rights from those that do not. But because a holder of an 'equitable estate' does not have true ownership rights, it is better to follow the scheme of the LPA 1925 and to avoid the term 'equitable estate'.

2.2 RIGHTS UNDER TRUSTS AND OTHER FORMS OF EQUITABLE INTEREST

In analysing equitable interests in land, we can make a useful distinction between rights under trusts and other forms of equitable interest in land. The distinction is important in practice for at least two reasons: firstly, as we will see in Chapters 19 and 22, a special statutory regime regulates trusts of land, but does not apply to other equitable interests in land; secondly, as we will see in section 4 below, a special formality rule regulates the acquisition of rights under trusts of land. It differs from the general formality rule applying to other equitable interests in land, which we will examine in section 6 below.

These differences mean that it is important to tell rights under a trust apart from other forms of equitable interest. The following extract may help.

McFarlane, *The Structure of Property Law* (2008, p 551)

B's right counts as a right under a Trust if two conditions are met:

- A is under a duty to B to use a specific right, in a particular way, for B's benefit; *and*
- A is, overall, under a duty in relation to the whole of that right.

In such a case, A is under the core Trust duty: a duty not to use a right for his own benefit, unless and to the extent that A is also a beneficiary of the trust.

---

3 RIGHTS UNDER TRUSTS: THE *CONTENT* QUESTION

In Chapter 3, section 3, we saw that there are only two forms of legal estate in land: the freehold and the lease. So, as we have seen, it is impossible for S to give B1 an immediate right to ownership of land for B1's life and to give B2 an immediate right to ownership of the same land as from the date of B1's death. The nearest thing that S can do is to set up a trust: to transfer his freehold to A1 and A2 to hold on trust for B1 during B1's life, and then on trust for B2.

In Chapter 3, section 6, we saw that there is also a limit on the types of legal interest in land. For example, if S simply makes a contractual promise to B to allow B to share occupation of S's land for the next ten years, that promise does not give B a legal interest in land: it does not count as an easement, charge, profit, rentcharge, or right of entry. It is, however, possible for S to transfer his freehold to A1 and A2 subject to a duty to allow B to share occupation of the land for the next ten years, and a duty otherwise to use the freehold for S's benefit. In such a case, each of B and S will have an equitable property right: a right under a trust.

These examples demonstrate the points made in the following extract: one of the advantages of the trust is that it can be used by a party with a right (S, in our examples) to divide up the benefits of his right in almost any way[4] that he wishes. The extract considers examples

---

[4] One of the limits is imposed by the rule against perpetuities: see Chapter 22, section 3.1.

that do not involve land, but, as shown by our examples above, the flexibility of the trust also applies where the right held on trust is a freehold or lease of land.

Worthington, *Equity* (2nd edn, 2006, pp 73–7)

Now that the idea of a trust is clearer, with its ingenious splitting of the ownership 'bundle of rights' into legal and Equitable ownership, it is possible to explore some of the enormous practical advantages of the trust [...]

[...T]rusts enable proprietary interests to be divided along a time line. A trustee can hold a Rembrandt painting on trust 'for A for life, then B for life, remainder to C' (and death need not be the only marker along the time line). This arrangement gives each party (the trustee, A, B and C) some immediate proprietary interest in the painting, with all the protection this entails, even though B and C have to wait some time before they are entitled to possession of the painting. A contract could achieve a similar result, but again without the important protections that proprietary interests afford [...]

[...T]rusts are enormously flexible in slicing up property rights in ways that would be inconceivable without the trust. Consider company shares. A shareholder who wishes to deal with his shares can only transfer full ownership or a security interest in the entire bundle of rights associated with the share. He cannot sell part of a share; he certainly cannot parcel out the different benefits inherent in shareholding to different transferees, giving one the right to dividends, another the right to vote and yet another the right to capital gains. Under the umbrella of a trust, however, all of this is possible. The owner (as settlor) simply has to specify the beneficiaries' rights under the trust in the appropriate way.

In Chapter 22, we will look at more closely at the ways in which a trust can be used to divide up the benefits of ownership over time (as in our first example). One question is, however, worth asking here: does the possibility of creating diverse equitable interests in land undermine the aim of s 1 of the LPA 1925? After all, as we saw in Chapter 3, section 3.3, part of the purpose of that provision is to protect third parties against the risk of being bound by complicated and unusual property rights. Yet in our first example above, B1 and B2 each have an *equitable* property right, capable of binding a third party who, for example, acquires the freehold of A1 and A2; in our second example, each of B and S also have such a right. So there may seem to be little point limiting the content of legal estates and interests in land if S can evade those limits by simply setting up a trust.

The key point, however, is that where a party has an equitable interest, it is far easier for C (a third party later acquiring a right from A1 and A2) to have a *defence* to that pre-existing right. Indeed, in our examples, if C acquires the freehold of A1 and A2, he may well be able to rely on a special application of the overreaching defence. We will explore this defence, which is regulated by s 2 of the LPA 1925, in Chapter 6, section 3.3, and in Chapter 20: it gives C valuable protection against the risk of being bound by a pre-existing equitable interest arising under a trust. It thus seems that, as far as the protection of third parties is concerned, the LPA 1925 has a clear, logical structure:

- s 1 limits the list of legal estates and interests in land;
- s 2 recognizes that C can use a special defence against a pre-existing *equitable* property right arising under a trust.

4 RIGHTS UNDER TRUSTS: THE *ACQUISITION* QUESTION

As we noted in section 1 above, any equitable property right depends on A being under an initial duty to B. So, the first step for B in showing that he has a right under a trust is to show that A is under a duty to him. In Chapter 3, section 4, we saw that it may be possible for B to acquire a legal estate in land by an *independent acquisition*—that is, through relying simply on his own, unilateral conduct. In contrast, it is *impossible* for B to acquire a right under a trust by relying on an independent acquisition. This is because B can acquire an equitable property right only when A is under a duty to B; and A cannot come under a duty to B simply as a result of B's own, unilateral conduct.

In other ways, however, the need to show that A is under a duty to B can *increase* B's chances of showing that he has acquired a right under a trust. There are many different means by which A can come under a duty to B.[5] For example, in *Attorney-General of Hong Kong v Reid*,[6] A acted as a prosecutor for B, the Hong Kong government. A accepted a bribe to act contrary to his duties to B. The Privy Council found that, as a result, A was under a duty to pay that bribe over to B. This meant that A held the bribe on trust for B; so when A later used the bribe to buy some freeholds, A also held those freeholds on trust for B. Clearly, B's right under the trust did not arise because A decided to give that right to B; rather, it arose by operation of law as soon as A came under a duty to pay the bribe to B.

A further important difference between legal estates and interests in land, on the one hand, and equitable interests, on the other, is that, to acquire an equitable interest, B *never* needs to register that right. For example, we noted above that S may wish to set up a trust by transferring a freehold to A1 and A2 to hold on trust for B1 during B1's life, and then for B2. In such a case, there is no need for B1 and B2 to register in order to acquire their equitable property rights. In fact, S can set up the trust without using a deed and without using *any* writing. As the following statutory provision shows, however, each of B1 and B2 will need to be able to point to some writing used by S (or A1 and A2)[7] in order to *prove* that he has a right under trust.

Law of Property Act 1925, s 53

Instruments required to be in writing

(1) Subject to the provision hereinafter contained with respect to the creation of interests in land by parol—

(a) [. . .]

(b) a declaration of trust respecting any land or any interest therein must be manifested and proved by some writing signed by some person who is able to declare such trust or by his will;

(c) [. . .]

---

[5] This point is noted by Smith, 'Fusion and Tradition' in *Equity and Commercial Law* (eds Degeling and Edelman, 2005, p 34). See, also, Chambers, 'Constructive Trusts in Canada' (1999) 37 Alberta Law Rev 173.

[6] [1994] 1 AC 324, PC.

[7] The point that writing signed by A1 and A2 suffices is confirmed by *Forster v Hale* (1798) 3 Ves Jr 696 and *Gardner v Rowe* (1825) 2 S & S 346. For discussion, see Youdan, 'Formalities for Trusts of Land and the doctrine in *Rochefoucauld v Boustead*' [1984] CLJ 306, 315–20.

> (2) This section does not affect the creation or operation of resulting, implied or constructive trusts.

The following extract makes clear that, in some circumstances at least, B can acquire, and prove that he has, a right under a trust of land even if no writing at all has been used. Like *Williams & Glyn's Bank v Boland*[8] (see section 2 above), it also provides a good example of the ability of a right under a trust to bind a third party.

Hodgson v Marks [1971] Ch 892, CA

Facts: In 1939, Mrs Hodgson bought a freehold of 31 Gibbs Green, Edgware, Middlesex. By 1959, she was a widow and took in lodgers. Mr Evans moved in as a lodger in April 1959. In June 1960, Mrs Hodgson, at Mr Evans' urging, transferred her freehold to him, for free. Mr Evans was then registered as holding that freehold, which he then sold to Mr Marks, who gave a charge over the land to the Cheltenham & Gloucester Building Society. Mrs Hodgson had continued to live in the home throughout. When she learned that Mr Marks now claimed to be an owner of the home, Mrs Hodgson applied to court for a declaration that Mr Marks should transfer his freehold to her, free from the charge in favour of the building society. Her argument was that: (i) although Mr Evans acquired her legal property right (her freehold), he held that right on trust for her; and (ii) her equitable property right, arising under the trust, was capable of binding both Mr Marks and the building society. Ungoed-Thomas J, at first instance, found in favour of Mrs Hodgson. The Court of Appeal upheld that decision.

The first extract is from the judgment of Ungoed-Thomas J. It includes an important finding of fact, not challenged on appeal, that Mrs Hodgson intended Mr Evans, at least during Mrs Hodgson's life, to be under a duty to use the freehold for the benefit of Mrs Hodgson and not for his own benefit. It also includes Ungoed-Thomas J's analysis of why Mrs Hodgson was able to prove that she had a right under a trust, despite the absence of any signed writing. As we will see, his Lordship's analysis differs from that adopted by Russell LJ in the Court of Appeal.

Ungoed-Thomas J (at first instance)

At 901–2

Mr. Evans approached Mrs. Hodgson again about the deeds [to the house]. He told her that her nephew (who was in the foreign service and returned on six months' leave from time to time) would or might turn him out of the house; and he asked her to make the deeds over to him. He was to keep the deeds in safe-keeping for her. So again the deeds were to be held by him in safe-keeping for her; but apparently he now obtained the deeds [. . .]

[Mrs Hodgson also gave Mr Evans various sums of money to invest on her behalf.] This arrangement apparently started soon after he became a lodger and persisted through-out until he left in 1965. The dates of all these payments were subjected to meticulous examination, but, whatever the precise total amount of the payments by Mrs. Hodgson to Mr. Evans at any particular date, it is clear that he had, before the transfer of the house

---

8 [1981] AC 413.

to him, established such a relationship of trust and confidence by her in him that she had handed over the deeds of the house to him for safe-keeping and that she was making to him what were very substantial payments to invest for her. She was before the transfer entrusting management of her money and affairs to him, because of her trust and confidence in him.

At 903–4

But over a period, although it does not appear for how long, Mr. Evans pestered Mrs. Hodgson to transfer the house to him: 'He talked me into things'; 'there was no saying no to him.' She said she made the transfer because of his kindness to her and his 'doing everything' for her as well as 'for the sake of peace.'

But on what footing did she make the transfer? Her evidence about this, given in the context of what happened in June, is unshaken and appears in its significant aspects quite clear. In approaching this evidence, it is important to bear in mind that she thought then and at all relevant times that a person who made a will could not make another will in its place—that a will was irrevocable. [Mrs Hodgson had made a will leaving her house to Mr Evans.] She said time and again that Mr. Evans said that her nephew would turn him out and that the transfer was made to prevent this. She agreed that the house was not the nephew's, but she said it was hers; and she agreed that she did not know how the transfer would prevent the nephew turning Mr. Evans out. She seemed to me to be puzzled by it: and just accepted at that time, for some reason or other, that it would have that effect. Mr. Evans, whom she trusted, certainly led her to believe that it would have that effect. She said that she could not say whether Mr. Evans was afraid of being turned out in her lifetime or when she died; but she said that she thought he was afraid of being turned out in her lifetime. She said that she did not intend to give it to him 'to sell or anything like that'; that she did not intend to make a gift of the house to him. She said that she made it a condition that he would keep it for her as long as she lived and that Mr. Evans said that he would look after her 'until the end of the chapter.' She said that she signed the house over to him to keep until she died, that is, as I understand it, to keep for her. She said that she did not care what happened to the house after she died. She supposed it would go to her executors and pass to Mr. Evans. Later, she said: 'Mr. Evans said this is your house until you die, but if you put it in my name your nephew can't turn me out, that's all.'

At 905–6

Some sentences in Mrs. Hodgson's evidence, taken in isolation, may appear inconsistent with other sentences. But after hearing her and taking her evidence as a whole I am satisfied that she executed the transfer in June, because of her trust and confidence in Mr. Evans—without that she certainly would not have done it—and out of misconceived gratitude to him and to end his pestering her for it; that the sole purpose of the transfer, as known to her and orally stated between her and Mr. Evans, was to prevent her nephew turning Mr. Evans out of the house; and that, as orally agreed between her and Mr. Evans, the house was to remain her house, though in his name. She believed that when she died her will was bound to take effect, at any rate if he survived her; and that Mr. Evans' will would correspondingly be bound to take effect, at any rate if she survived him. The wills looked after the position after death; and the transfer was not intended or directed at all to deal with the beneficial interests after her death. Her will, which she thought irrevocable, governed that.

The undisputed evidence that Mr. Evans held on trust for Mrs. Hodgson all investments of Mrs. Hodgson's moneys handed to him, and [Mrs Hodgson's solicitor's] evidence that Mr. Evans drew no distinction at all between his holding of them and his holding of the house transferred to him, support Mrs. Hodgson's evidence to the effect that the property was to remain beneficially hers [...]

My conclusion, therefore, is that the transfer of the house by Mrs. Hodgson to Mr. Evans was under an oral arrangement between them, under which no beneficial interest was to pass to Mr. Evans, and was on trust for Mrs. Hodgson [...]

At 907–9

The question now arises whether the trust in favour of Mrs. Hodgson, absolutely beneficially, under the oral arrangement in accordance with which the house was transferred to Mr. Evans, is void or ineffective by reason of section 53 of the Law of Property Act, 1925. The provisions of section 53 replace corresponding provisions of sections 3, 7, 8 and 9 of the Statute of Frauds. As argued before me, nothing turns on section 54 or on there being any resulting implied or constructive trust within section 53 (2). So the question as argued became: Did the principle that the Statute of Frauds should not be used as an instrument of fraud dispense with the writing that would otherwise be essential under section 53 to establish the trust in Mrs. Hodgson's favour?

[...] Whoever relies upon the statutory requirement of writing is himself using the statute as an instrument to avoid cognisance being taken of the trust. This might occur in circumstances in which establishment of the trust would establish fraud, for example, where, as here, a transfer on oral trust would be taken free of the trust [...] This is so, whether the defendant be, for example, a volunteer or a purchaser for value without notice. So to the extent to which a person relies on the statutory defence to exclude the establishment of fraud, he uses the statute as an instrument of fraud—to succeed by using the statute to exclude evidence of fraud [...]

My conclusion, therefore, is that the defendants are not entitled to exclude parol [i.e. oral] evidence of the trust.

Russell LJ

At 933

I turn next to the question whether section 53 (1) of the Law of Property Act 1925 prevents the assertion by the plaintiff of her entitlement in equity to the house. Let me first assume that, contrary to the view expressed by the judge, Mr. Marks is not debarred from relying upon the section, and the express oral arrangement or declaration of trust between the plaintiff and Mr. Evans found by the judge was not effective as such. Nevertheless, the evidence is clear that the transfer was not intended to operate as a gift, and, in those circumstances, I do not see why there was not a resulting trust of the beneficial interest to the plaintiff, which would not, of course, be affected by section 53 (1). It was argued that a resulting trust is based upon implied intention, and that where there is an express trust for the transferor intended and declared—albeit ineffectively—there is no room for such an implication. I do not accept that. If an attempted express trust fails, that seems to me just the occasion for implication of a resulting trust, whether the failure be due to uncertainty, or perpetuity, or lack of form. It would be a strange outcome if the plaintiff were to lose her beneficial interest because her evidence had not been confined to negativing a gift but had additionally moved into a field forbidden by section 53 (1) for lack of writing. I remark in this connection that we are not concerned with the debatable question whether on a voluntary transfer of land by A to stranger B there is a presumption of a resulting trust. The accepted evidence is that this was not intended as a gift, notwithstanding the reference to love and affection in the transfer, and section 53 (1) does not exclude that evidence [...]

> On the above footing it matters not whether Mr. Marks was or was not debarred from rely-
> ing upon section 53 (1) by the principle that the section is not to be used as an instrument for
> fraud. Mr. Marks was in fact ignorant of the plaintiff's interest and it is forcefully argued that
> there is nothing fraudulent in his taking advantage of the section.

So Ungoed-Thomas J and Russell LJ agreed, albeit for different reasons, that a trust arose in favour of Mrs Hodgson as soon as she transferred her freehold, for free, to Mr Evans. We will examine their analyses (and, in particular, the notion that a statutory provision such as s 53(1)(b) of the LPA 1925 cannot be used as an instrument of fraud) in more detail in Chapter 14. Ungoed-Thomas J went on to hold that Mr Marks and the building society had a defence to Mrs Hodgson's right under the trust, but, as we will see in Chapter 6, section 3.2.2, the Court of Appeal reversed that finding, and held that Mrs Hodgson's right under the trust did, in fact, bind both Mr Marks and the building society.

For our present purposes, there are two important points to take from *Hodgson v Marks*. Firstly, Mr Evans, by virtue of his registration, clearly acquired a legal estate in the land, but Mrs Hodgson was protected by the fact that Mr Evans was under a duty to use his freehold entirely for her benefit (at least during her life).

Secondly, as soon as Mr Evans came under that duty, Mrs Hodgson acquired a right under a trust—that is, an equitable property right that was capable of binding not only Mr Evans, but also Mr Marks and the building society (third parties later acquiring a right in the land).

5 OTHER EQUITABLE INTERESTS: THE *CONTENT* QUESTION

5.1 A LONGER LIST OF PROPERTY RIGHTS

In the following extract, Swadling considers one of the contributions of equity to property law: the recognition of a longer list of property rights.

Swadling, 'The Law of Property' in *English Private Law*
(ed Burrows, 2nd edn, 2007, [4.26])

A longer list

All rights recognized as property rights at common law are also recognized as such by equity. So, for example, it is possible to have an easement, for example a right of way over land, both at common law and in equity. But there are also some rights recognized in equity as proprietary which at common law either do not exist at all or, if they do, are only recognized as personal rights. An example of the latter is the restrictive covenant over land. Others are contracts and options to purchase certain types of legal property rights. The mortgagor's equity of redemption is an example of equity creating a property right where not even a cor-responding personal right exists at law.

5.2 THE LIST OF EQUITABLE INTERESTS

It is possible to come up with a list of rights that, in addition to rights under a trust, count as equitable interests in land. Building on Swadling's approach in the extract above, that list can be usefully split into two categories. In the first category are those rights that do not correspond to any legal estate or legal interest in land. Examples of such rights are: (i) the restrictive covenant (which we will examine in Chapter 27); and (ii) the mortgagor's equity of redemption (see Chapter 29). Where registered land is concerned, we can also include: (i) an 'equity by estoppel' (see Chapter 13, section 5.3); and (ii) a 'mere equity'. Under s 116 of the Land Registration Act 2002 (LRA 2002), those rights are expressly said to be capable of binding a third party acquiring a right in relation to registered land.

In the second category are equitable interests that do correspond to a legal estate or legal interest in land. Clear examples of such rights are: (i) equitable leases (see Chapter 23, section 3.2); (ii) equitable easements (as noted by Swadling in the extract above, and see further Chapter 26); and (iii) equitable charges (see Chapter 29). In those cases, the content of the equitable property right reflects the content of the legal estate or interest in question.[9] The real distinction between, say, an equitable lease and a legal lease depends not on the *content* question, but on the *acquisition* question, as we will see in section 6 below. In this category, we can also include what Swadling refers to as '*contracts and options to purchase certain types of legal property rights*'. Such equitable property rights can be broken down into: (i) estate contracts (see Chapter 12); and (ii) options to purchase. Where registered land is concerned, we can add a further right: (i) the right of pre-emption. Under s 115(b) of the LRA 2002, that right is expressly said to be capable of binding a third party acquiring a right in relation to registered land.

Again, as we will see in section 6 below, equity's contribution here relates to the *acquisition* question, not the *content* question. To show that he has an estate contract, option to purchase, or right of pre-emption, B always needs to show that A has a legal estate. To show that he has an estate contract, B also needs to show that A is under an existing contractual duty to transfer that estate to B. To show that he has an option to purchase, B need only show that B has the option to impose a contractual duty on A to transfer A's estate to B. And to show that he has a right of pre-emption, B only needs to show that, if A chooses to sell A's estate, B has the option to impose a contractual duty on A to transfer that estate to B.

It is therefore possible to come up with the set of equitable interests in land illustrated in Table 2.

5.3 LIMITING THE CONTENT OF EQUITABLE INTERESTS

The restrictive covenant, mentioned in the extract above, provides a good example of a right that cannot count as a legal interest in land (because it is not on the list of permissible legal interests in land set out by s 1(2) of the LPA 1925), but which can nonetheless count as an equitable interest. We will examine the restrictive covenant in detail in Chapter 27. Here, we need to note that, whilst the list of equitable interests is longer than the list of legal interests

---

[9] There can, however, be a slight difference. To count as a legal interest in land, an easement or charge must last forever (like a freehold) or for a certain, limited period (like a lease). As a result, if A gives B a right of way that is due to last only for B's life, that right, even if passes the content test for an easement (see Chapter 26, section 2), cannot count as a legal easement. Nonetheless, it can count as an equitable easement: see, e.g., *ER Ives Investments Ltd v High* [1967] 2 QB 379, 395, *per* Lord Denning MR.

Table 2 Equitable Interests in Land

Group A	**Rights under trusts**
Group B	**Rights with a content not corresponding to a legal estate or legal interest** *General:* (i) restrictive covenants; (ii) mortgagor's equity of redemption *In relation to registered land:* (i) equity by estoppel; (ii) mere equity
Group C	**Rights with a content corresponding to a legal estate or legal interest** *General:* (i) equitable lease; (ii) equitable easement; (iii) equitable charge; (iv) estate contract; (v) option to purchase *In relation to registered land:* (i) right of pre-emption

in land, there are nonetheless careful restrictions on the content of equitable interests. This can be shown by the following extract, in which Lord Templeman considers the content of the restrictive covenant. As we will see in Chapter 27, it is possible to take issue with Lord Templeman's reasoning, but, for our present purposes, it is important to note one key point. We saw in section 1 above that equitable property rights arose because of equity's willingness to allow an obligation owed by A to B to affect a third party, C; as the following extract demonstrates, it is clear that equity does not allow *all* obligations to have that effect.

Rhone v Stephens [1994] 2 AC 310, HL

Facts: Walford House in Combwich, Somerset, was divided by its owner into a house and a cottage. The roof of the house overhung the cottage. In 1960, the former owner then sold a freehold of the cottage. When doing so, he promised the purchasers of the cottage '*for himself and his successors in title* [...] *to maintain* [...] *such part of the roof of Walford House* [...] *as lies above the property conveyed in wind and watertight condition*'. After that, both the house and the cottage were sold on. By 1991, the freehold of the house was held by Ms Stephens, and the freehold of the cottage was held by Mr and Mrs Rhone. Mr and Mrs Rhone claimed that Ms Stephens was under a duty to repair the roof of the house, as a result of the covenant entered into by the former owner of the house in 1960. As a result, they claimed compensation from Ms Stephens for damage that they had suffered as a result of the state of the roof and also asked for an order forcing Ms Stephens to ensure that the necessary repairs were done. The first instance judge found in favour of Mr and Mrs Rhone; but the Court of Appeal reversed that finding, holding that the promise made in 1960 did not give rise to an equitable property right, because it imposed a *positive* burden (a duty to do repairs) and so did not count as a *restrictive* covenant. The House of Lords upheld that finding.

Lord Templeman

At 317–18

My Lords, equity supplements but does not contradict the common law. When freehold land is conveyed without restriction, the conveyance confers on the purchaser the right to do with the land as he pleases provided that he does not interfere with the rights of others or infringe statutory restrictions. The conveyance may however impose restrictions which, in favour of the covenantee, deprive the purchaser of some of the rights inherent in the ownership of unrestricted land. In *Tulk v. Moxhay* (1848) 2 Ph. 774 [see Chapter 7, section 2.6] a purchaser of land covenanted that no buildings would be erected on Leicester Square. A subsequent purchaser of Leicester Square was restrained from building. The conveyance to the original purchaser deprived him and every subsequent purchaser taking with notice of the covenant of the right, otherwise part and parcel of the freehold, to develop the square by the construction of buildings. Equity does not contradict the common law by enforcing a restrictive covenant against a successor in title of the covenantor but prevents the successor from exercising a right which he never acquired [...]

Equity can thus prevent or punish the breach of a negative covenant which restricts the user of land or the exercise of other rights in connection with land. Restrictive covenants deprive an owner of a right which he could otherwise exercise. Equity cannot compel an owner to comply with a positive covenant entered into by his predecessors in title without flatly contradicting the common law rule that a person cannot be made liable upon a contract unless he was a party to it. Enforcement of a positive covenant lies in contract; a positive covenant compels an owner to exercise his rights. Enforcement of a negative covenant lies in property; a negative covenant deprives the owner of a right over property.

5.4 EQUITABLE INTERESTS AND THE *NUMERUS CLAUSUS* PRINCIPLE

In the extract above, Lord Templeman could have supported his analysis by referring to the following statutory provision (emphasis added), which seems to make clear that there is a limit to the content of equitable interests.

Law of Property Act 1925, s 4(1)

Creation and disposition of equitable interests

(1) Interests in land validly created or arising after the commencement of this Act, which are not capable of subsisting as legal estates, shall take effect as equitable interests, and, save as otherwise expressly provided by statute, interests in land which under the Statute of Uses or otherwise could before the commencement of this Act have been created as legal interests, shall be capable of being created as equitable interests:

Provided that, after the commencement of this Act (and save as hereinafter expressly enacted) an equitable interest in land shall only be capable of being validly created in any case in which an equivalent equitable interest in property real or personal could have been validly created before such commencement.

It thus seems that, whilst s 1(2) of the Act limits the content of legal interests, s 4(1) does the same job for the content of equitable interests. Rather than setting out the permissible equitable interests, s 4(1) instead imposes a freeze on the development of new equitable interests. As noted by Briggs:[10] '[Section 4(1)] *seems clear enough* [...] *If* [particular rights] *are to bind*

---

[10] 'Contractual Licences: A Reply' [1983] Conv 285, 290.

purchasers of land as proprietary interests, then they must be shown to have existed in pre-1926 land law […]'

It is certainly the case that the courts have developed no new equitable interests since 1926. Perhaps surprisingly, however, the courts have not supported that approach by relying on s 4(1); instead, as in the following extract (from a case we first examined in Chapter 1, section 5), there has been a tendency to refer to more general considerations.[11]

National Provincial Bank v Ainsworth [1965] AC 1175, HL

Facts: Mr and Mrs Ainsworth lived together in Milward Rd, Hastings, Sussex. Mr Ainsworth was registered as holding a freehold of their home. In 1957, Mr Ainsworth moved out. In 1958, Mr Ainsworth borrowed £1,000 from the National Provincial Bank. To secure his duty to repay that sum plus interest, Mr Ainsworth gave the bank a charge over the home. The bank duly registered as holder of that charge.

By 1962, Mr Ainsworth had fallen behind on his repayments to the bank. The bank wished to enforce its security by selling Mr Ainsworth's freehold. To ensure a good price for the freehold, the bank wanted to sell the home with vacant possession. Because Mrs Ainsworth refused to leave, the bank applied for an order for possession of the home.

When Mr Ainsworth moved out, Mrs Ainsworth acquired an equitable right known as a 'deserted wife's equity'—that is, Mr Ainsworth came under various duties to Mrs Ainsworth, including a duty to ensure that she had somewhere to live. The 'deserted wife's equity' was created by the courts to ensure that a party who had formerly been relying on his or her spouse had some protection when that spouse left. As we saw in Chapter 1, section 5.7, it has now been replaced by a specific statutory duty. In this case, the crucial question was whether equitable rules could turn Mr Ainsworth's duty to Mrs Ainsworth into a right capable of binding not only Mr Ainsworth, but also third parties later acquiring a right in his land. The Court of Appeal found in favour of Mrs Ainsworth; Lord Denning MR held that Mrs Ainsworth had an 'equity' that she could assert against the bank.[12] The House of Lords, however, decided that her 'deserted wife's equity' gave her only a personal right against Mr Ainsworth.

Lord Wilberforce

At 1241–3

My Lords, the doctrine of the 'deserted wife's equity' has been evolved by the courts during the past 13 years in an attempt to mitigate some effects of the housing shortage which has persisted since the 1939–45 war. To a woman, whose husband has left her, especially if she has children, it is of little use to receive periodical payments for her maintenance (even if these are in fact punctually made) if she is left without a home. Once possession of a house has been lost, the process of acquiring another place to live in may be painful and prolonged. So, even though, as is normally the case, the home is in law the property of the husband, the

---

[11] As a result, some commentators have argued for a different interpretation of s 4(1). For example, Smith, *Property Law* (5th edn, 2005, p 43), argues that the section simply means that the provisions of the Law of Property Act 1925 itself should not be taken to create any new equitable interests. On that view, the courts may still develop new equitable interests.

[12] [1964] Ch 665, 686–8.

courts have intervened to prevent him from using his right of property to remove his deserted wife from it and they have correspondingly recognised that she has a right, or "equity" as it has come to be called, which the law will protect, to remain there.

This case relates to one aspect, and one aspect only, of that right. No question arises here as to any claim which a deserted wife may have against her husband: all that we are concerned with is the right of a deserted wife to remain in possession as against a third party, claiming, in good faith, under the husband. And the issue is even narrower than that: it relates only to the position of a third party whose title arises subsequently to the desertion [...]

The issue is thus a narrow one, affecting a small proportion only of those deserted wives who are left in occupation of their husband's house. Nevertheless as to them, as to the respondent in the present case, issues of importance, and probably of hardship, are involved. The ultimate question must be whether such persons can be given the protection which social considerations of humanity evidently indicate without injustice to third parties and a radical departure from sound principles of real property law [...]

The appeal raises two questions, one of general, the other of more limited scope.[13] The general question is whether the respondent Mrs. Ainsworth as the deserted wife of her husband, the owner of the house, has any interest in or right over it which is capable of binding the bank as the proprietor of a legal interest in the land. This is a general question of real property law [...]

I turn to the first and more general question: what is the nature of the deserted wife's interest, or right? In the cases which have evolved from 1952 onwards it is variously described: it is called an "equity," a "clog," a "licence," a "status of irremovability." The description is shifting and evolutionary as different situations appear. I shall have to refer to some of these cases in some detail. But before doing so I think it useful to look at the wife's situation more generally, as it stands under well-established principles of law. After all, married women and deserted wives are familiar enough in our legal system and there cannot be much doubt what their rights are [...]

At 1247–8

[Having analysed the duties imposed on Mr Ainsworth by the deserted wife's equity, Lord Wilberforce continued thus:]

The position then, at the present time, is this. The wife has no specific right against her husband to be provided with any particular house, nor to remain in any particular house. She has a right to cohabitation and support. But, in considering whether the husband should be given possession of property of his, the court will have regard to the duty of the spouses to each other, and the decision it reaches will be based on a consideration of what may be called the matrimonial circumstances. These include such matters as whether the husband can provide alternative accommodation and if so whether such accommodation is suitable having regard to the estate and condition of the spouses; whether the husband's conduct amounts to desertion, whether the conduct of the wife has been such as to deprive her of any of her rights against the husband. And the order to be made must be fashioned accordingly: it may be that the wife should leave immediately or after a certain period: it may be subject to revision on a change of circumstances.

The conclusion emerges to my mind very clearly from this that the wife's rights, as regards the occupation of her husband's property, are essentially of a personal kind: personal in the

---

[13] [The second question was whether Mrs Ainsworth's right, if it counted as an equitable property right, could also count as an 'overriding interest', due to Mrs Ainsworth's actual occupation of the land. We will examine overriding interests in Chapter 6, section 3.2.2.]

sense that a decision can only be reached on the basis of considerations essentially dependent on the mutual claims of husband and wife as spouses and as the result of a broad weighing of circumstances and merit. Moreover, these rights are at no time definitive, they are provisional and subject to review at any time according as changes take place in the material circumstances and conduct of the parties.

On any division, then, which is to be made between property rights on the one hand, and personal rights on the other hand, however broad or penumbral the separating band between these two kinds of rights may be, there can be little doubt where the wife's rights fall. Before a right or an interest can be admitted into the category of property, or of a right affecting property, it must be definable, identifiable by third parties, capable in its nature of assumption by third parties, and have some degree of permanence or stability. The wife's right has none of these qualities, it is characterised by the reverse of them.

Once it was decided that Mr Ainsworth was not under a duty to allow Mrs Ainsworth to live in *her current house*, but instead simply had a duty to provide her with *some* accommodation, Mrs Ainsworth's claim to an equitable property right was doomed to fail: she could not show that her husband's duty to her related to his freehold. But Lord Wilberforce went further and set out criteria that can be used to analyse a claim that B has an equitable property right. To count as such a right, B's right must be:

- definable;
- identifiable by third parties;
- capable in its nature of assumption by third parties; and
- (to some degree) permanent and stable.

It is important to realise, however, that a right will not count as an equitable property right *simply* because it meets Lord Wilberforce's criteria. For example, a positive covenant, such as that considered in *Rhone v Stephens*[14] (see section 5.3 above), gives its holder a right that has all of the characteristic specified by Lord Wilberforce. So whilst these characteristics may be *necessary* if B's right is to count as an equitable property right, they are clearly not *sufficient*.

6 OTHER EQUITABLE INTERESTS: THE *ACQUISITION* QUESTION

In Chapter 3, sections 4 and 7, we saw that B may have to satisfy certain formality rules in order to acquire a legal estate or legal interest in land. For example, if B claims that A has granted B a legal lease lasting seven years, B does not generally need to register that right; under s 52 of the LPA 1925, B does, however, need to show that A used a deed to grant B that right—but the absence of a deed will not prevent B acquiring an *equitable* lease. In *Walsh v Lonsdale*,[15] which we will examine in detail in Chapter 12, Mr Lonsdale had made a contractual agreement to grant Mr Walsh a seven-year lease. Mr Walsh did not acquire a legal lease

---

[14] [1994] 2 AC 310, HL.
[15] (1882) LR 21 Ch D 9, CA.

because no deed had been used. Nonetheless, the Court of Appeal held that Mr Walsh had an *equitable* lease, arising as a result of Mr Lonsdale's contractual duty to grant Mr Walsh the promised legal lease.

Walsh v Lonsdale provides a good example of the point made by Smith, in the extract set out in section 1 above, that equitable property rights depend on A being under an initial duty to B. Of course, as we saw in section 5 above, not all duties give rise to equitable property rights. But there is a general principle that if A is under a duty to give B a recognized legal estate or legal interest in land (be it a freehold, lease, easement, or charge),[16] then B will acquire an *immediate* equitable property right.[17] In Chapter 12, we will examine that principle, which can be called the 'doctrine of anticipation', in detail. For the moment, we simply need to note its importance in allowing B to acquire an equitable interest without needing to satisfy a formality rule regulating the acquisition of a legal estate or interest. That importance is emphasized in the following extract.

Swadling, 'The Law of Property' in *English Private Law*
(ed Burrows, 2nd edn, 2007, [4.26])

Forgiving absence of formality

An intended property right may fail to be created at law because of some absence of formality, generally the failure to use a deed. The common law does not condone any absence of formality, but in certain circumstances equity will, more particularly where there is present a contract to grant the interest in question [. . .] Indeed, one of the most common reasons why a particular property right is equitable rather than legal is because of equity's more relaxed attitude to the issue of formalities.

At this stage, it is important to bear in mind two further points. Firstly, it is true that the formality rules applying to the acquisition of equitable interests are less strict than those applying to the acquisition of legal property rights in land. For example, it is *never* the case that B needs to register in order to acquire an equitable interest. Nonetheless, this does not mean that formality rules are irrelevant in equity. Indeed, if a case such as *Walsh v Lonsdale* were to arise today, Mr Walsh, in order to show that Mr Lonsdale is under a contractual duty to grant him a lease, would have to satisfy the formality rule imposed by s 2 of the Law of Property (Miscellaneous Provisions) Act 1989 (LP(MP)A 1989). We will examine that rule in detail in Chapter 9, section 3. Its basic effect is that A cannot be under a contractual duty to give B a legal estate or interest in land *unless* the agreement between A and B is made in writing, signed by both A and B. In addition, s 53(1)(a) of the LPA 1925 sets out a general rule that applies to the acquisition of equitable interests, even if B does not claim that A is under a contractual duty to give B a legal estate or interest in land:

---

[16] The principle also applies where A's duty is to give B a profit, rentcharge, or right of entry: as we saw in Chapter 3, section 6, each of those rights can also count as a legal interest in land.

[17] As we will see in Chapter 12, it may be the case that B only acquires an equitable property right where A's duty is specifically enforceable: i.e. where a court will order A to perform that duty.

Law of Property Act 1925, s 53

Instruments required to be in writing

(1) Subject to the provision hereinafter contained with respect to the creation of interests in land by parol—

    (a) no interest in land can be created or disposed of except by writing signed by the person creating or conveying the same, or by his agent thereunto lawfully authorised in writing, or by will, or by operation of law.

    (b) [...];

    (c) [...]

(2) This section does not affect the creation or operation of resulting, implied or constructive trusts.

Secondly, whilst *Walsh v Lonsdale* involved A being under a *contractual* duty to grant B a legal property right in land, the principle that applied in that case can also apply where A is under a *non-contractual* duty to give B such a right. For example, in section 4 above, we considered *Attorney-General of Hong Kong v Reid*.[18] In that case, A's duty to transfer a bribe to B meant that A held the bribe on trust for B. As a result, when A later used the bribe to buy some freeholds, A also held those freeholds on trust for B. Similarly, in *Mountney v Treharne*,[19] a court made an order, in divorce proceedings, that Mr Mountney should transfer his freehold of his home in Hockley, Essex, to Mrs Mountney. That order came into effect on 13 July 2000. The very next day, Mr Mountney went bankrupt: his rights, including his freehold, were thus transferred to his trustee in bankruptcy, Mr Treharne. The question for the court was whether the court order gave Mrs Mountney an equitable property right in relation to Mr Mountney's freehold. The Court of Appeal found in favour of Mrs Mountney: having surveyed both English and Australian authority, it was held that the principle that 'equity looks on as done that which ought to be done' meant that, as soon as the court order came into effect so that Mr Mountney was under a duty to transfer his freehold to his wife, Mrs Mountney acquired an equitable property right. As Jonathan Parker LJ put it at [76]: '*In my judgment [...] the order in the instant case had the effect of conferring on Mrs Mountney an equitable interest in the property at the moment when the order took effect.*'

The decisions in *Attorney-General of Hong Kong v Reid* and *Mountney v Treharne* each involve B acquiring an equitable property right under a trust; the principle applied in those cases ('equity looks on as done that which ought to be done') can, however, also apply to give B a different form of equitable interest. So it seems, for example, that if A is under a non-contractual duty to grant B an easement, B should acquire an immediate equitable easement. This point may be important in Chapter 13, section 5, when we examine the effect of rights arising through proprietary estoppel.[20]

---

[18] [1994] 1 AC 324, PC.

[19] [2003] Ch 135, CA.

[20] For example, in *Crabb v Arun District Council* [1976] Ch 179 (see Chapter 13, section 1), the Court of Appeal seems to have viewed the council as under a duty, arising as a result of proprietary estoppel, to grant Mr Crabb an easement. As a result, it can be argued that Mr Crabb acquired an equitable easement from the moment at which that duty arose.

7 THE RELATIONSHIP BETWEEN COMMON LAW AND EQUITY

Many land law cases share a basic form: A, an owner of land, has some dealings with B; as a result, B acquires a right to make a particular use of A's land. A then gives C a right in relation to the land: for example, by selling his freehold or lease to C. B wishes to carry on using the land, but C wants to prevent B from using the land in that way. For example, in *National Provincial Bank v Ainsworth*[21] (see section 5.4 above), the bank (C) wanted to prevent Mrs Ainsworth (B) from continuing to occupy the home owned by Mr Ainsworth (A).

In such cases, it is important to ask if B's right, acquired from A, counts as a property right. If it does, it is capable of binding C. If it does not, and is simply a personal right against A, B cannot assert that right against C (although, as we will see in Chapter 7, it may still be possible for B to assert a *new*, direct right against C, arising as a result of C's conduct). To see if B's right counts as a property right, we need to look at both the *content* question and the *acquisition* question. But in the past two chapters, we have seen that there are two sets of answers to those questions: one set is provided by the common law rules; another set, by the equitable rules. For example, a restrictive covenant does not count as a legal estate or interest in land, but it can count as an equitable interest (see section 5.3 above). And, to acquire a legal estate or interest in land, B generally needs to register his right, but B never needs to register to acquire an equitable interest.

As pointed out in the following extract, these differences raise an awkward question: does it make sense for common law and equity to give different answers to the same question?

Burrows, 'We Do This at Common Law But That in Equity' (2002) 22 OJLS 1

[T]he fusion of law and equity is a topic that provokes strong reactions. But the question remains of what, exactly, is meant by fusion. One way of answering this is to give a short description of the essence of first, the anti-fusion school of thought; and second, the fusion school of thought.

According to the anti-fusion school of thought, the Supreme Court of Judicature Acts 1873–5 fused the administration of the courts but did not fuse the substantive law. Common law and equity sit alongside one another. Moreover, they can happily sit alongside one another. Clashes or conflicts or inconsistencies between them are very rare. Where they exist, and in so far as they are not resolved by the more specific provisions of the 1873–5 Acts, they are resolved by the general provision in section 11 of the 1873 Act which lays down that 'equity shall prevail'. This is not to say that common law or equity is frozen in the position it was in before 1873. Rather common law and equity can independently develop incrementally. But one should not develop the law by reasoning from common law to equity or vice versa. To do so would cut across the historical underpinnings of the two areas; and a harmonized rule or principle that has features of both common law and equity but cannot be said clearly to be one or the other, would be unacceptable.

In contrast, the fusion school of thought argues that the fusion of the administration of the courts brought about by the 1873–5 Acts, whilst not dictating the fusion of the substantive law, rendered this, for the first time, a realistic possibility. While there are areas where

---

[21] [1965] AC 1175.

common law and equity can happily sit alongside one another, there are many examples of inconsistencies between them. It is important to remove the inconsistencies thereby producing a coherent or harmonized law. In developing the law it is legitimate for the courts to reason from common law to equity and vice versa. A harmonized rule or principle that has features of both common law and equity is at the very least acceptable and, depending on the rule or principle in question, may represent the best way for the law to develop.

It is submitted that the latter view is to be strongly preferred. There are numerous instances of inconsistencies between common law and equity; and to support fusion seems self-evident, resting, as it does, on not being slaves to history and on recognizing the importance of coherence in the law and of 'like cases being treated alike' [...]

[Burrows goes on to suggest that cases in which common law and equitable rules do differ can be placed into one of three categories:]

The first category is where common law and equity co-exist coherently and where the historical labels of common law and equity remain the best or, at least, useful terminology [...]

The second category is where common law and equity co-exist coherently but, in contrast to the first category, there is nothing to be gained by adherence to those historical labels. If we are to take fusion seriously, the labels common law and equity in the areas of the law covered by this category should be abandoned at a stroke [...]

The third category is more complex. It comprises probably most of our civil law. In this category, in contrast to both of the first two categories, common law and equity do not exist co-exist coherently. If we are to take fusion seriously, what is needed is a change in the law, albeit often only a small change, so as to produce a principled product which may combine elements of law and equity.

As Burrows notes, the 'fusion' debate provokes strong reactions. Certainly, his preference for what he calls the 'fusion approach' is not universally shared: for a robustly-expressed alternative view, see, for example, *Meagher, Gummow and Lehane's Equity: Doctrines and Remedies.*[22] Nonetheless, the central point raised by Burrows seems to be a valid one: where there is a difference between common law rules and equitable rules, we need to ask whether that difference can be justified. After all, history can explain why we *have* two different sets of rules, but, by itself, history cannot justify why we should *keep* them. If we apply that same approach to the law of property rights, we need to be able to justify the special rules, applying to equitable, but not legal, property rights, which we have noted in this chapter.

It seems that these differences can be justified if we focus on the different *effects* of legal and equitable property rights. The list of legal property rights is shorter, and such rights are, in general, harder to acquire—but, if B has a legal property right, then he receives better protection. Firstly, as we will see in Chapter 6, it is far harder for C to have a defence to a pre-existing *legal* property right in land; where B has a pre-existing *equitable* interest, a number of additional defences may be available to C.

Secondly, as we saw in Chapter 3, section 1, a key feature of a legal property right is that it imposes a prima facie duty on the rest of the world. As noted in the following extracts, however, that does not seem to be the case with equitable interests.

---

[22] *Meagher Gummow and Lehane's Equity: Doctrine and Remedies* (4th edn, eds Meagher, Heydon, and Leeming, 2002, ch 2).

Swadling, 'The Law of Property' in *English Private Law*
(ed Burrows, 2nd edn, 2007, [4.23])

[E]quitable rights which might be seen as 'proprietary' behave in a slightly different fashion to those at common law. At common law, as we have seen, the right is exigible directly against anyone interfering with it. Thus, the holder of a common law easement can sue for damages and an injunction against any third party, be it a successor in title of the original grantor or even a complete stranger, who interferes with his right. This is not generally true for equitable property rights. Take, for example, the case of an option to purchase a fee simple estate in land [...] such a right will generally bind transferees of the fee simple in question from its grantor, and so is classed as a property right. But it will not bind other third parties, such as squatters. Although a squatter will be bound by easements granted by the person he has dispossessed, he will not be bound by an option to purchase. Indeed, he could not be bound by any such right, for the burden of such a right entails a duty to convey the right contracted to be sold, and the squatter does not have that right. The only exception would seem to be the restrictive covenant, which has been held to bind persons other than a successor in title of the grantor.

Penner, 'Duty and Liability in Respect of Funds' in *Commercial Law: Perspectives and Practice* (eds Lowry and Mistelis, 2006, pp 214–16)

[I]t is necessary to make a distinction between two version of the notion of rights *in rem*, both of which operate in law but which are often not clearly distinguished. The best way to see the distinction is not to focus on the right, but on the corresponding duties or liabilities. Under the first, 'trespassory' version of rights *in rem*, a right is protected by duties *in rem* that everyone owes to the right holder, which bind everyone unconditionally all the time. The best example is the case of the ownership of a chattel: all persons presently have a right not to interfere with your chattels. Of course there may be factual contingency here—I may be in no position to interfere with your Rolls-Royce at the minute because it is in the shop in Guildford, but that doesn't mean I have no duty not to interfere with it in law. This notion of rights/duties *in rem* is the one normally spoken of by philosophers when they speak of rights of property binding all the world.

The second, 'successor' version is distinct but equally often encountered in the law. Such a right *in rem* is one which *in principle, may* bind all others, not because of the fact that each of us all presently owe a duty to the rightholder, but because of the fact that in principle all persons may become a successor in title or possession to property which is bound by the right-holder's right. Here, the right-holder's right is *in rem*, binds all the world, because it binds successors in title or possession to another distinct property, and the right holder's interest runs with that property, and anyone, in principle, might be a successor in title or possession to it [...]

I will now look at the liability of third party recipients of trust property [...i]n doing so I will rely upon the distinction just drawn. It is one of the features of the particular property interest that exists in a trust fund that the trust reveals the distinction between the trespassory and successor versions of the right *in rem* in the following way: in so far as their proprietary rights are concerned, the trust divides the rights of the trustee and the rights of the beneficiary such that the trustee has all the trespassory rights *in rem* to the trust property, while the beneficiaries' rights are purely successor rights *in rem*—rights to enforce the trust against successors in title to the trustee of any property which can be seen to constitute an asset of the [trust] fund.

The distinction made by Penner between 'trespassory' and 'successor' liability is—conceptually, at least—a very important one. It may help us to understand how legal property rights differ from equitable property rights. If B has a legal property right (as when, in Penner's example, B owns a car, or, to take a land law example, as when B has a legal freehold, a legal lease, a legal easement, or a legal charge) then the rest of the world is under a prima facie duty to B: a duty not to interfere with the thing to which B's right relates (the car or the land). This is the 'trespassory' form of liability.

But, if B instead has an *equitable* property right, arising as a result of a particular duty owed by A to B, it seems that the rest of the world is *not* under such a general duty to B. So if X were to come along and steal, or carelessly damage, the car (or trespass on the land), B would have no claim against X.[23] An equitable property right *can* bind a third party, but only if that third party becomes a 'successor' to A, by later acquiring a right from A or (perhaps) by later taking possession of property initially possessed by A.[24]

In practice, that important difference between legal and equitable property rights is often hidden. Certainly, it makes no difference to the cases that we have examined in this chapter. For example, in *Hodgson v Marks*[25] (see section 4 above), Mrs Hodgson did not need a right that was capable of binding the whole world; she simply needed a right that was capable of binding a party (such as Mr Marks) who acquired a right *from* Mr Evans. So the 'successor' liability provided by her equitable property right was all that Mrs Hodgson required.

The distinction between the effect of a legal property right and an equitable property right can, however, make a difference in a case such as *Hill v Tupper*[26] (see Chapter 3, section 1), in which Mr Hill wanted to assert his right against Mr Tupper—that is, a party who had *not* acquired any right from the Basingstoke Canal Company. In such a case, if the analysis set out above is accepted, an *equitable* interest will not assist Mr Hill, because Mr Tupper is simply a stranger who has interfered with B's use of the canal; he is not a 'successor' who acquired any rights from A. So, to make his claim, Mr Hill needs to show that he has a right that is capable of binding the whole world—and only legal property rights have that effect.

There are two ways in which we can react to this difference between legal and equitable property rights. The first is to adapt the definition of property rights given in, for example, the extracts from Nicholas[27] and Birks,[28] set out in Chapter 3, section 1. That approach is adopted in the extract from Penner set out above: legal and equitable property rights are seen as two different subgroups of the wider category of rights *in rem*. It is also adopted in the following extract.

---

[23] As noted by Penner, this seems to be the case: see, e.g., *MCC Proceeds v Shearson Lehmann* [1998] 4 All ER 675; noted by Tettenborn [1996] CLJ 36 and *Leigh and Sillivan Ltd v Aliakmon Shipping Co Ltd (The Aliakmon)* [1986] AC 785.

[24] *Re Nisbet and Potts Contract* [1906] 1 Ch 386 supports the proposition that an equitable interest in land can bind a squatter later taking possession of the land, but the authority of that case can be doubted, because it proceeds by way of an analogy to legal interests in land: see, e.g., Maitland, *Lectures on Equity* (1909, ch 12, pp 169–70); McFarlane, *The Structure of Property Law* (2008, p 894).

[25] [1971] Ch 892.

[26] (1863) 2 H & C 122.

[27] *An Introduction to Roman Law* (1962).

[28] 'Five Keys to Land Law' in *Land Law: Themes and Perspectives* (eds Bright and Dewar, 1998).

Bright, 'Of Estates and Interests' in *Land Law: Themes and Perspectives* (eds Bright and Dewar, 1998, pp 538–9)

When land lawyers describe a non-ownership interest [e.g. an easement] as a 'property right', what is meant is that the right can be enforced not only against the person who granted it (as with a 'personal right') but also against any successor in title to the burdened (servient) land (subject to complying with formalities and registration requirements). The comparison sometimes drawn is between property rights as 'rights in rem' in contrast to 'rights in personam', but this is apt to mislead. Rights in rem are generally taken to refer to rights 'enforceable against the world'. The defining feature of property rights, however, is not that they are enforceable against 'persons generally' but that they are enforceable against the successor in title to the burdened (servient) land. This right of property 'does not actually bind everybody: the only person actually bound is the person in whose hands the property currently is'.[29] Some of these rights might *also* give claims 'against the world'; the holder of an easement of way can prevent the landowner *and all other persons* from interfering with the right of way. But what tells us whether these rights are property is whether the same package of 'rights, privileges, etc.' that the right-holder possesses can continue to be enforced when there is a new owner of the burdened land.

An alternative approach is to keep to the definition of a property right as a right capable of binding the whole world and so to admit that equitable property rights are not, in fact, true property rights. As we saw in section 1 above, it is clear that an equitable property right differs from a personal right, so this approach necessarily entails finding a new name for equitable property rights, to ensure that they are distinguished from both personal rights and true property rights.

That approach is adopted in the following extract. The author's approach is a general one, applying not only to land, but also to other forms of property. (In fact, the examples given in the extract have been changed, with the author's permission, so that they refer exclusively to land law.) The argument in the extract is based on an approach in which there are three forms of right: a right against a thing (a 'property right'); a right against a right (a 'persistent right'); and a right against a person (a 'personal right'). On that view, legal estates and interests in land count as true property rights, but equitable interests count as persistent rights.

McFarlane, *The Structure of Property Law* (2008, pp 70–1)

On the orthodox view, Common Law and Equity give different answers to both: (i) the **content question**; and (ii) the **acquisition question**. On that view: (i) Common Law has one list of property rights and Equity has a different, longer list; and (ii) Common Law recognises a number of means by which B can acquire a property right and Equity recognises further ways. This means we are left with two sets of answers to two fundamental questions. So, if we ask "Does B have a right against that land?" we may well get one answer at Common Law, and a different answer in Equity.

Example 1: A, a freehold owner of land, declares that he holds his freehold on Trust for B.

In such a case, on the orthodox view, the property law system gives two different answers to the fundamental question of "Who owns the land?": (i) at Common Law, A has ownership;

---

[29] Bell, *The Modern Law of Personal Property in England and Ireland* (1989, p 9).

but (ii) in Equity, B has ownership. It seems absurd to think that the property law system could give two different answers to such a fundamental question. On the orthodox view, that absurdity is the product of an historical anomaly: the presence of two competing court systems within one jurisdiction. Whilst that anomaly has now been eliminated, we are left with its legacy. However, that historical analysis can only explain how we have reached the current, paradoxical position; it does not provide us with a reason for maintaining that position.

Despite this, the current position of the property law system *can* be justified. To do so, we need to focus on the *conceptual difference* between a "Common Law property right" and an "Equitable property right". It then becomes clear that Common Law and Equity *do not* give differing answers to the fundamental questions of: (i) what counts as a property right; and (ii) of how property rights are acquired.

The key point is that, contrary to the orthodox view, *there is no such thing as an "Equitable property right"*. So, in Example 1, it is *not* the case that: (i) A has a Common Law property right; and (ii) B has an Equitable property right. After all, the rest of the world is *not* under a prima facie duty to B not to interfere with B's use of the land. The better analysis is that: (i) A has a property right (a legal freehold); and (ii) A is under a duty to B in relation to that right; so (iii) B has a persistent right: a right against A's freehold. On this view, the apparent conflict between Common Law and Equity disappears. The two bodies of law do *not* have differing views as to: (i) what rights count as a property right; or (ii) as to how such rights can be acquired. Instead: (i) Common Law deals with the **content** and **acquisition questions** as they apply to property rights; and (ii) Equity deals with the **content** and **acquisition questions** as they apply to persistent rights.

This point was made by Maitland, in his *Lectures on Equity*,[30] in relation to a case such as Example 1.[31] The extract is worth quoting at length:

"Take the case of a trust. An examiner will sometimes be told that whereas the common law said that [A] was the owner of the [land], equity said that [B] was the owner [...] Think what this would mean if it were really true. There are two courts of co-ordinate jurisdiction—one says that A is the owner, the other says that B is the owner of the land. That means civil war and utter anarchy. Of course the statement is an extremely crude one: it is a misleading and dangerous statement [...] Equity did not say that [B] was the owner of the land, it said that [A] was the owner of the land, but added that he was bound to hold the land for the benefit of [B]. There was no conflict here."

McFarlane's argument certainly reflects an important point: if B has an equitable interest, it seems that he does not have a right in A's land; rather, he has a right against A's freehold or lease of that land. For example, in *Hodgson v Marks*,[32] Mr Evans did not hold the land itself on trust for Mrs Hodgson; instead, he held his freehold on trust for her. Further, the notion of an equitable interest as a right against A's right ties in with the idea that all equitable interests stem from A being under a duty to B: the point is that, if A's duty relates to a particular right held by A, B may then acquire not only a personal right against A, but also a right against A's right.[33]

Another possible advantage of analysing equitable interests in this way is that it can explain why equitable interests can bind a 'successor'. For example, consider a case in which

30 *Lectures on Equity* (1909, Lecture 1).

31 Maitland took the view that, in Example 1, B has only a personal right against A: ibid, Lecture 10. But that view cannot be correct: in Example 1, B has more than only a personal right against A; he also has a power to impose a duty on C if C acquires a right that depends on A's freehold.

32 [1971] Ch 892.

33 See e.g. Chambers *An Introduction to Property Law in Australia* (2nd edn, 2008).

A holds a freehold on trust for B and then transfers that freehold, for free, to C. If B's equitable interest is seen not as an interest *in land,* but instead as a right against A's initial right (A's freehold), it is still to possible explain why B can make a claim against C. The crucial point is that, as B initially had a right against A's right, B can follow that right into C's hands and make a claim against C. In contrast, if X comes along and simply trespasses on the land, B has no claim against X, because: (i) B has no right in relation to the land itself;[34] and (ii) whilst B has a right against A's freehold, X has not acquired a right that depends on A's freehold.

Nonetheless, as acknowledged by McFarlane:[35] *'Judges, statutes and commentators do not use the term "persistent rights". Instead, they refer to persistent rights as "Equitable property rights" or, where land is involved, as "Equitable interests in land".'* So, for consistency with the extracts from cases and materials that we will use in this book, we will continue to use the term 'equitable property right'. It is important, however, to bear in mind that there are conceptual differences between legal estates and legal interests in land, on the one hand, and equitable interests, on the other. And it may be that those conceptual differences can justify the fact that the *content, acquisition,* and *defences* questions are answered differently according to whether B is making a claim to a legal property right or to an equitable property right.

QUESTIONS

1. How did equitable property rights develop?

2. Why might the term 'equitable estate in land' be misleading?

3. Why might a party with a freehold or lease decide to set up a trust of that right?

4. In *Hodgson v Marks,*[36] should the absence of written evidence have prevented Mrs Hodgson from proving that Mr Evans had held his freehold on trust for her?

5. The criteria for proprietary status set out by Lord Wilberforce in *National Provincial Bank v Ainsworth*[37] have been described as 'riddled with circularity'.[38] Do you agree?

6. In what ways do equitable property rights have a different effect from that of legal property rights? Do these differences mean that equitable property rights should not be thought of as property rights at all?

FURTHER READING

Bright, 'Of Estates and Interests: A Tale of Ownership and Property Rights' in *Land Law: Themes and Perspectives* (eds Bright and Dewar, Oxford: OUP, 1998)

Hackney, *Understanding Equity and Trusts* (London: Fontana, 1987, ch 1)

---

[34] Things are different if B is, in fact, in sole occupation of the land when X trespasses thereon. In such a case, B has not only his equitable interest under the trust, but also a *legal* property right (a freehold) independently acquired as a result of his exclusive control of the land: see Chapter 3, section 4, and Chapter 10, section 3.

[35] *The Structure of Property Law* (2008, p 25).

[36] [1971] Ch 892.

[37] [1965] AC 1175.

[38] See Gray and Gray, *Elements of Land Law* (5th edn, 2009, p 97).

Harris, 'Legal Doctrine and Interests in Land' in *Oxford Essays in Jurisprudence* (3rd series, eds Eekelaar and Bell, Oxford: OUP, 1987)

McFarlane, *The Structure of Property Law* (Oxford: Hart, 2008, Pts B & C1)

Smith, 'Fusion and Tradition' in *Equity in Commercial Law* (eds Degeling and Edelman, Sydney: Lawbook Co, 2005)

Swadling, 'A Hard Look at *Hodgson v Marks*' in *Restitution and Equity Vol 1: Resulting Trusts and Equitable Compensation* (eds Birks and Rose, London: Mansfield Press, 2000)

Worthington, *Equity* (2nd edn, Oxford: OUP, 2006, ch 3)

5

HUMAN RIGHTS AND LAND

CENTRAL ISSUES

1. The Human Rights Act 1998 (HRA 1998) prospectively incorporates the European Convention on Human Rights (ECHR) into domestic law. Article 1 of the First Protocol and Art 8 have particular relevance to land law.

2. The HRA 1998 has vertical effect: under s 6, public authorities must act in accordance with the ECHR, while s 2 requires the courts to take account of the decisions of the European Court of Human Rights in Strasbourg (the Strasbourg Court).

3. The HRA 1998 may also have horizontal effect (i.e. between private individuals) as a consequence of s 3, which requires legislation to be interpreted in accordance with the ECHR, and s 6, which requires the courts (as public authorities) to act in accordance with the ECHR.

4. The Articles of the ECHR confer qualified protections. Infringements may be justified in the wider public interest. The government enjoys a wide margin of appreciation in identifying and implementing a legitimate purpose, but nevertheless must act proportionately.

5. Article 1 of the First Protocol guarantees the peaceful enjoyment of possessions. It provides that a person is not to be deprived of, or subject to controls over, their possessions except in the public or general interest.

6. Article 8 guarantees respect for the home, the enjoyment of which may only be infringed in proscribed circumstances: for example, in the national economic interest or to protect the rights of others.

7. Article 6 ensures the right to a fair trial in the determination of property rights, and Art 14 provides that individuals should not be discriminated against in the exercise of their ECHR rights.

8. The effect of the HRA 1998 on property rights is still uncertain, but two views have been advanced. The first is that the Act will have little impact, because English law is already founded on the fundamental principles that it espouses. The second suggests that the HRA 1998 will have a wider effect by providing an alternative measure against which conflicting rights may be balanced, and by the possibility that it founds a free-standing property right.

1 INTRODUCTION

The Human Rights Act 1998 (HRA 1998) incorporates the European Convention on Human Rights (ECHR) into the domestic law of England and Wales. As such, it is said to bring human rights home by permitting an infringement of the ECHR to be raised and considered in the domestic courts.[1] Previously, a claimant had to bring his or her case before the European Court of Human Rights in Strasbourg (the Strasbourg Court) once he or she had exhausted any redress under English law in the domestic courts.[2]

The ECHR is a product of post-war Europe. In the face of the cold war, its object was to set out the freedoms that are considered central to human life in a civilized and democratic society. The majority of these rights were agreed and incorporated into the original form of the ECHR, to which the United Kingdom became a signatory in 1951, but the right to property proved more controversial and was not agreed until 1954. It is thus contained in a separate Protocol.

Although the ECHR was only incorporated into domestic law by the HRA 1998, the rights that it espouses are not a radical departure from the traditional principles upon which property law has been founded for centuries. The principle that no one should be arbitrarily deprived of their property found in Art 1 of the First Protocol has been a hallmark of democratic government, whilst the sanctity of the home that forms the basis of Art 8 reflects the sentiments of the time-honoured phrase that 'an Englishman's home is his castle'.

Gray, 'Land Law and Human Rights' in *Land Law Issues, Debates, Policy* (ed Tee, 2002, p 216)

The safeguards provided by the Convention are, in their way, mirrored across the expanse of European history during the past millennium. The human right to protection from arbitrary dispossession by the state is born of a deep impulse which views lawless seizure of property as a particularly violating kind of molestation—a form of proprietary rape. An instinct against arbitrary dissessin of freehold is at least as old as the Magna Carta and went on to animate the great eighteenth century declarations of social and civil liberties. For Blackstone, writing in 1765, it was inconceivable that 'sacred and inviolable rights to private property' should be postponed to 'public necessity' without 'a full indemnification and equivalent for the injury thereby sustained'. As Blackstone explained in strikingly modern parlance, the state cannot act 'even for the general good of the community [...] by simply stripping the subject of his property in an arbitrary manner'. Blackstone's premise was adopted, quickly and in virtually identical terms, in the French Declaration of the Rights of Man and of the Citizen and has since inspired a vast range of national and international prohibitions on the taking of property by the state except for justifiable purposes and on payment of a fair value.

In this chapter, we will look firstly at the mechanics of how the HRA 1998 brings human rights home; we will then go on to examine the two principle Articles of the ECHR that are of direct importance to property lawyers—namely, Art 1 of the First Protocol (protection of

---

[1] *Rights Brought Home* CM 3782.

[2] In 1966, the UK adopted the optional clauses that enabled an individual claimant to bring a case before the Strasbourg Court. See Harpum, 'Property Law: The Human Rights Dimension—Part 1' [2000] L&T Rev 4, for details of the pre-HRA effect of the ECHR.

possessions) and Art 8 (respect for the home). Article 14 (protection from discrimination) and Art 6 (right to a fair trial) will also be considered, but only in outline.[3] The chapter will conclude with an assessment of the likely impact of the HRA 1998 on property law.

2 THE MECHANICS OF THE HUMAN RIGHTS ACT 1998

We need, firstly, to examine how the HRA 1998 incorporates the ECHR into domestic law, because it is only then that we can begin to appreciate its impact on land law. Unfortunately, the answer to this question is uncertain, because the interpretation of the HRA 1998—and, in particular, its horizontal effect—is not yet fully clear. By 'horizontal effect', we mean whether human rights may also affect the resolution of disputes between private persons.[4] This contrasts with 'vertical effect'—that is, the impact of human rights upon the relationship between public bodies and individuals. The question as to horizontal effect is particularly pertinent to land law, in which we are primarily concerned with the regulation of the relationship between private persons to property.

2.1 VERTICAL EFFECT

Section 6 of the HRA 1998 provides that a public authority must act in manner that is compatible with the EHCR.

Human Rights Act 1998, s 6

Acts of public authorities

(1) It is unlawful for a public authority to act in a way which is incompatible with a Convention right.

(2) [. . . see section 2.2.3 below]

(3) In this section "public authority" includes—

    (a) a court or tribunal, and

    (b) any person certain of whose functions are functions of a public nature,

but does not include either House of Parliament or a person exercising functions in connection with proceedings in Parliament.

(4) In subsection (3) "Parliament" does not include the House of Lords in its judicial capacity.

(5) In relation to a particular act, a person is not a public authority by virtue only of subsection (3)(b) if the nature of the act is private.

---

[3] Gray and Gray question whether Arts 10 and 11—the right to freedom of speech, and to assembly and association—raise the possibility of uncontested access to private land: see Gray and Gray, *Elements of Land Law* (5th edn, 2009, [1.68]).

[4] Legal persons include corporate bodies; thus a company has human rights.

> (6) "An act" includes a failure to act but does not include a failure to—
>
> (a) introduce in, or lay before, Parliament a proposal for legislation; or
>
> (b) make any primary legislation or remedial order.

A victim of an infringement of his or her human rights by a public authority may bring proceedings against, or defend proceedings brought by, that authority.[5] A 'victim' is a person who is directly affected by the act or omission of the public authority.[6] Where the court finds that a public authority has failed to act as required by s 6, the court may grant such remedy as it deems to be 'just and appropriate', including the award of damages.[7]

2.1.1 Public authorities

Central to vertical effect is what we mean by a 'public authority'. A distinction must be drawn between *core* public authorities, the entire functions of which fall to be considered under s 6, and *hybrid* public authorities, which may not appear to be public in nature, but which may nevertheless carry out some public functions. In the performance of these public functions, hybrid bodies are subject to s 6.[8] The House of Lords made this functional distinction in *Aston Cantlow and Wilmcote with Billesley Parochial Church Council v Wallbank*,[9] when rejecting the suggestion that a parochial church council was a public authority.

A core public authority is required to comply with the ECHR in the performance of all of its functions because it is a public authority 'through and through'.[10] The identification of a core public authority should be relatively straightforward: for example, a local authority is a public authority and thus must observe the ECHR when exercising all of its functions, including when acting as a landlord of local authority housing.[11]

A hybrid public authority is only required to comply with the ECHR when exercising those functions that are of a public nature. It is not so constrained when performing a private function.

Whether or not a particular body is subject to s 6 thus requires 'a two-fold assessment':[12] firstly, a consideration of whether some of its functions have a public character, so that it qualifies as a hybrid public authority; and secondly, whether the particular function in question was a public function and thus subject to scrutiny. For example, a housing association, although not a core public authority, may be a hybrid public authority where its functions are so closely aligned with the local housing authority that it is performing a public function in the provision of housing.[13] The tests are not always easy to

---

[5] Section 7(1), HRA 1998.

[6] Section 7(7), HRA 1998, and Art 34 of the ECHR.

[7] Section 8.

[8] See s 6(3).

[9] [2003] UKHL 37, [2004] 1 AC 546.

[10] *Per* Lord Hope at [35].

[11] See, e.g., *Qazi v Harrow LBC* [2003] UKHL 43, [2004] 1 AC 983, and *Kay v Lambeth LBC* [2006] UKHL 10, [2006] 2 AC 465.

[12] *Aston Cantlow and Wilmcote with Billesley Parochial Church Council v Wallbank* [2003] UKHL 37, [2004] 1 AC 546, *per* Lord Hobhouse at [85].

[13] *Poplar Housing and Regeneration Community Association v Donoghue* [2001] EWCA Civ 595, [2002] QB 48.

divine[14] and Howell[15] has complained that *'unfortunately the cases reveal at best a lack of consistency and, at worst an apparent lack of awareness of the importance of the question, or at least a disinclination to deal with it directly'.*

A further distinction between a core and hybrid public authority should also be noted.[16] A core hybrid authority cannot be a victim of a breach of its human rights; by contrast, a hybrid public authority, when acting in a private capacity, may be a victim. This distinction may be relevant in determining whether or not a body is a core or hybrid public authority.

2.1.2 The courts as public authorities

By s 6(3) of the HRA 1998, a court is a public authority and thus is required to act in a manner that is compliant with the ECHR. We will examine the possible implications when examining the horizontal application of the ECHR. Before we do so, we need to consider s 2, which requires the courts to 'take into account' the decisions of the Strasbourg Court, which has built up a considerable body of jurisprudence on the interpretation of the ECHR.

Lord Bingham explained the meaning of 'must take account of' in the conjoined appeals in the following cases.

Kay v Lambeth LBC; Leeds CC v Price [2006] 2 AC 465

Lord Bingham

At [28]

The mandatory duty imposed on domestic courts by section 2 of the 1998 Act is to take account of any judgment of the Strasbourg court and any opinion of the commission. Thus they are not strictly required to follow Strasbourg rulings, as they are bound by section 3(1) of the European Communities Act 1972 and as they are bound by the rulings of superior courts in the domestic curial hierarchy. But by section 6 of the 1998 Act it is unlawful for domestic courts, as public authorities, to act in a way which is incompatible with a Convention right such as a right arising under article 8. There are isolated occasions [. . .] when a domestic court may challenge the application by the Strasbourg Court of the principles it has expounded to the detailed facts of a particular class of case peculiarly within the knowledge of national authorities. The 1998 Act gives it scope to do so. But it is ordinarily the clear duty of our domestic courts, save where and so far as constrained by the primary domestic legislation, to give practical recognition to the principals laid down by the Strasbourg court as governing the Convention rights specified in s 1(1) of the 1998 Act. That court is the highest judicial authority on the interpretation of those rights, and the effectiveness of the Convention as an international instrument depends on the loyal acceptance by member states of the principles it lays down.

---

[14] The House of Lords was divided in *Aston Cantlow*, with Lord Scott deciding that the parochial church council, whilst not a core public authority, was exercising a public function as a hybrid public authority. See, also, *YL v Birmingham CC* [2007] UKHL 27, [2008] 1 AC 95. The restricted scope of the definition has been criticized: see Clayton, 'The Human Rights Act Six Years On: Where Are We Now?' [2007] EHRLR 11.

[15] 'The Human Rights Act 1998: Land, Private Citizens, and the Common Law' (2007) 123 LQR 618.

[16] *Aston Cantlow and Wilmcote with Billesley Parochial Church Council v Wallbank* [2003] UKHL 37, [2004] 1 AC 546, at [9] and [11].

The House of Lords considered the effect on precedent of Strasbourg decisions in *Kay; Price*.[17] The House of Lords is free to depart from its own decisions and will need to do so if that decision is subsequently found not to take adequate account of the views of the Strasbourg Court. But the Lords in *Kay* decided that their decisions would continue to bind the lower courts: it is for their Lordships alone to consider the consistency, or otherwise, of their decisions with the Strasbourg jurisprudence.[18]

The House of Lords, in *R v Secretary of State for Work and Pensions*,[19] also expressed the view that, although the Court of Appeal was bound by House of Lords' decisions, it should be free (but not obliged) to depart from its own decisions that it believed to be inconsistent with a subsequent decision of the Strasbourg Court.

2.2 HORIZONTAL EFFECT

The question of whether or not a body is a public authority becomes less significant if human rights' issues may be raised in a dispute between private individuals. This is a much-debated question.[20]

The ECHR is an international treaty that affects signatory States. Accordingly, it is drafted with State responsibilities in mind. A case for horizontal application of the ECHR can, however, be made based upon ss 3 and 6 of the HRA 1998. It should also be noted at the outset that neither of these sections confers a cause of action between individual litigants: an individual cannot thus directly claim that his or her human rights have been infringed by another individual; he or she can only claim a breach of human rights in the context of other proceedings.[21]

2.2.1 Human Rights Act 1998, s 3: the interpretation of legislation

Human Rights Act 1998, s 3

Interpretation of legislation

(1) So far as it is possible to do so, primary legislation and subordinate legislation must be read and given effect in a way which is compatible with the Convention rights.

---

[17] Ibid. Doubt was cast on the House of Lords' previous decision in *Qazi v Harrow LBC* [2003] UKHL 43, [2004] 1 AC 983, by two subsequent decisions of the Strasbourg Court: see *Connors v UK* (2005) 40 EHRR 9, and *Blecic v Croatia* (2005) 41 EHRR 13. The question thus arose as to whether *Qazi* should be followed.

[18] To this general principle, the Lords accepted one exception, being where the decision was based upon policy considerations that are subsequently found to be contrary to the very terms of the ECHR: see *D v East Berkshire Community NHS Trust* [2004] QB 558, CA; [2005] 2 AC 373, HL, as an example of such exceptional circumstances, in which the Court of Appeal had departed from the House of Lords' decision in *X (Minors) v Bedfordshire County Council* [1995] 2 AC 633.

[19] [2008] UKHL 63, at [65]–[57].

[20] Hunt, 'The Horizontal Effect of the Human Rights Act' [1998] PL 423; Bamforth, 'The Application of the Human Rights Act 1998 to Public Authorities and Private Bodies' [1999] CLJ 159; Phillipson, 'The Human Rights Act, Horizontal Effect and the Common Law: A Bang or a Whimper?' (1999) 62 MLR 824; Buxton, 'The Human Rights Act and Private Law' [2001] 116 LQR 48; Morgan, 'Questioning the True Effect of the Human Rights Act' (2002) 22 LS 259.

[21] For example, as a defence to a claim to possession, as in *Ghaidan v Godin-Medoza* [2004] 2 AC 557.

(2) This section—

(a) applies to primary legislation and subordinate legislation whenever enacted;

(b) does not affect the validity, continuing operation or enforcement of any incompatible primary legislation; and

(c) does not affect the validity, continuing operation or enforcement of any incompatible subordinate legislation if (disregarding any possibility of revocation) primary legislation prevents removal of the incompatibility.

Section 3 requires a court to interpret legislation in a manner that is compatible with the ECHR. Where a court finds that it cannot do so, it may issue a declaration of incompatibility under s 4, whereupon the government may amend the offending legislation using the fast-track procedure set out in s 10.[22] In this manner, parliamentary sovereignty is respected, whilst ensuring that Parliament itself does not infringe the ECHR.

Thus, where we find that the outcome of a property dispute depends upon the interpretation of a piece of legislation, the court must take due account of the ECHR. An example is found in the case of *Ghaidan v Godin-Medoza*,[23] in which the provisions of the Rent Act 1977 affecting a private landlord and tenant were considered. The tenant had died and his landlord was seeking possession against the tenant's homosexual partner, who claimed to be entitled to succeed to the tenancy under the terms of s 2(1) and (2) of the Rent Act 1977, which provided that a spouse or person living with the tenant 'as his or her wife or husband' could take over the tenancy. The House of Lords held that, to be compatible with Arts 8 and 14, these terms must be interpreted to include a homosexual partner.

Likewise, we shall see, in Chapter 10, that courts have been prepared to consider the human rights compatibility of the law on adverse possession, even though the protagonists are private individuals, because the law is statute-based.[24]

2.2.2 Section 6 and the common law

Property law is increasingly regulated by legislation, but much is still reliant upon common law and equitable principles: do these also have to comply with the ECHR? Despite the clear application of HRA 1998, s 3 solely to legislation (whether primary or subordinate), an argument that they do is put forward based upon the operation of s 6. The courts, as public bodies, are required to act, and thus decide cases before them, in a manner that is compliant with the ECHR regardless of whether those cases concern the interpretation of a statute, and/or the application of the common law and equitable principles. Howell has also pointed out that it is arbitrary to draw a distinction.

---

[22] The High Court, Court of Appeal, or House of Lords can issue a declaration of incompatibility, and, thus, where the proceedings are before the county court, those proceedings will have to be adjourned to enable the higher courts to deal with the matter of incompatibility: see s 4(5), HRA, and *Kay v Lambeth LBC* [2006] UKHL 10, [2006] 2 AC 465, *per* Lord Hope at [110].

[23] [2004] 2 AC 557. See section 5 below.

[24] *Beaulane Properties Ltd v Palmer* [2006] EWHC 817; *Ofulue v Bossert* [2008] EWCA Civ 7. In *JA Pye (Oxford) Ltd v Graham* [2001] EWCA Civ 117, the Court of Appeal considered briefly the application of the HRA 1998. The House of Lords ([2002] UKHL 30) decided that the HRA 1998 was not applicable, because it did not have retrospective effect, not because it did not have horizontal application.

Howell, 'The Human Rights Act 1998: Land, Private Citizens, and the Common Law' (2007) 123 LQR 618, 627

It must also follow that if the court is itself a public authority sufficient under s.3, there is a strong argument that the courts must equally interpret the common law in a way compatible with the Convention. Although s.3 refers only to statute law not to common law, under its obligation as a public body under s.6 the court has to act in a way which is compatible with the Convention. The fact that the HRA does not refer to the common law is understandable if it is the actions of public authorities as emanations of the State (as in *Qazi* and *Kay*) which are being scrutinised. Public bodies owe their existence and obtain their legitimacy solely through legislation, although they are, of course, also bound by any relevant common law principles. But once the HRA is applied to actions between private parties, then not only is all legislation potentially open to scrutiny under s.3 but also by the same reasoning all common law. Not to apply the Convention to the common law would itself lead to arbitrary distinctions.

Whether a particular area of property law is covered by legislation is largely a matter of chance. Much of the law relating to landlord and tenant is subject to statutory regulation as various Governments have sought to give protection first to the tenant and then to the landlord as political expediency and social trends dictated. On the other hand much of the law relating to real property is still left to the common law with occasional statutory regulation (which may itself be largely a codification of the common law). For example, at present the rules governing the acquisition of a beneficial interest under a constructive or resulting trust are governed by the common law, but may in the future be put into statutory form.

The House of Lords in the following case (in the context of a local authority's possession proceedings) noted the difficulty of separating common law and statute when legislation is inevitably drawn against the landscape of the common law to produce a framework of rights and duties.[25]

Birmingham City Council v Doherty [2008] 2 WLR 636, HL

Lord Walker

At [100]

At common law, a landlord is entitled to possession of the demised premises if the tenant's lease or tenancy expired or been validly terminated, and similarly a fortiori if there was only a licence. To that extent [. . .] the City Council was, in seeking possession, relying on a common law right. That is part of the picture, but it is far from the whole picture, and in my opinion, it would be unrealistic, and productive of error, not to look at the whole picture. The fact is that the City Council's common law right was surrounded on all sides by statutory infrastructure, like a patch of grass in the middle of a motorway junction [. . .]

At [104]

The paramount consideration, I think, will be whether the composite legal scheme in general, and the offending provision in particular (offending that is against someone's Convention right) clearly represents the considered intention of Parliament [. . .] By contrast the fact that

---

[25] See also Lord Mance at [155].

Parliament has made some limited statutory modification to the common law [his Lordship referred to defamation as an example] could not, I think be treated as a general parliamentary endorsement of those extensive areas which have been left unmodified. Within these two extremes there may be some difficult problems to be determined on a case-by-case basis.

Rather surprisingly, the horizontal application of the ECHR in property disputes has not been the subject of conscious scrutiny by the courts.[26] There have been only occasional references to the issue.[27] We have noted that the House of Lords, in *Ghaidan*, applied human rights principles horizontally, when considering the interpretation of legislation, but equally *Aston Cantlow* suggests that these principles have no application in private disputes. The parochial church council was found to be a private body, or at least a body exercising a private function,[28] when enforcing the common law governing chancel repairs, yet the House of Lords considered only in passing the human rights' compatibility of this ancient law. The Lords' decision turned upon the vertical operation of the ECHR. In *Kay; Price*, Lords Bingham, Nicholls, and Hope did advert to the possibility of Art 8 being engaged by a private landlord's possession proceedings, but only Lord Hope was prepared to admit the likelihood.[29]

The horizontal application of the ECHR to property law, whilst beguiling, is problematic on a number of fronts. Nield has summarized some of these problems as follows.

Nield, 'Charges, Possession and Human Rights: A Reappraisal of s 87(1) Law of Property Act 1925' in *Modern Studies in Property Law: Vol 3* (ed Cooke, 2005, p 166)

The application of Convention rights between individual parties does raise difficulties of interpretation as the Convention is not drafted with the evaluation of the rights of individuals inter se in mind. It is drafted to apply to state authorities and the decisions of the European court are limited to the interpretation of the Convention between states and the individual. For instance the qualifications to the right to respect for property found in Article 1 and to respect for the home in Article 8(2) are drafted with state interference in mind. In deciding whether an interference is justified under these qualifications a "fair balance" must be struck between the interests of the individual and the state and the means used to achieve that balance must be reasonably within the discretion of the state. In human rights speak there must be proportionality between the legitimate aim of the interference and the right itself and the particular means or method of interference must be within the state's margin of appreciation.

Jean Howell has pointed out that these tests are likely to be different when balancing the public interest, as represented by the state, and the individual as opposed to balancing the respective rights and obligations of individuals and she calls upon the courts to formulate a different test to strike a "fair balance" between the rights of individuals. Meanwhile Deborah Rook has observed that the concept of a state's margin of appreciation, developed

---

[26] See Howell, 'The Human Rights Act 1998: Land, Private Citizens, and the Common Law' (2007) 123 LQR 618, 619–26.

[27] The House of Lords, whilst mindful of the question in *Birmingham City Council v Doherty* [2008] UKHL 57, [2008] 3 WLR 636, consciously avoided expressing their opinion: see Lord Walker at [99].

[28] Lord Scott, in the minority, decided that the parochial church council was a hybrid public authority, but was exercising a private function.

[29] [2006] UKHL 10, [2006] 2 AC 465, at [64]. Lords Bingham, at [28], and Nicholls, at [61], declined to express an opinion. See also *Birmingham City Council v Doherty* [2008] 3 WLR 636, at [23].

in international law, does not transport logically to the domestic context. Instead the courts will need to develop an alternative but analogous doctrine to allow the government a "discretionary area of judgement" where policy is in issue.

Inevitably there is also the possibility that both parties may claim an infringement of their rights.

Perhaps the most significant of the problems of applying human rights between private individuals is that the assertion of one party's human rights may lead to the infringement of another's human rights. It is thus a question of where the balance between competing rights should come to rest. In resolving that issue, the established human rights' jurisprudence, which has been developed with state authorities in mind, may be of only limited assistance.

2.2.3 Section 6(2): defences

The duty imposed by s 6(1) upon public authorities to act in a manner that is compliant with the ECHR is subject to the defences set out in s 6(2).

Human Rights Act 1998, s 6(2)

(2) Subsection (1) does not apply to an act if—

(a) as the result of one or more provisions of primary legislation, the authority could not have acted differently; or

(b) in the case of one or more provisions of, or made under, primary legislation which cannot be read or given effect in a way which is compatible with the Convention rights, the authority was acting so as to give effect to or enforce those provisions.

The courts as public authorities cannot change the law so that it complies with the ECHR; they can only try to interpret the law to comply with the ECHR, in pursuance of their duty under s 3, or, if that is not possible, issue a declaration of incompatibility under s 4 to instigate a change in the law by Parliament.[30] Until an incompatible law is brought into line with the ECHR, public authorities must still go about their work, which may involve applying an incompatible law. Section 6(2) provides a defence to public authorities if they find themselves in this unenviable position.

Lord Hope in the following case explains the situation with regard to the courts' role as a public authority.

Birmingham City Council v Doherty [2008] 2 WLR 636, HL

Lord Hope

At [46]

Legislation which cannot be read and given effect in a way which is compatible with the Convention right must nevertheless be enforced, as Parliamentary sovereignty requires this.

---

[30] The county court does not have jurisdiction to issue a declaration of incompatibility. It will therefore have to adjourn proceedings to enable a higher court to do so.

Giving effect to a decision to do what the legislation authorises will not be an unlawful act within the meaning of section 6(1).

Section 6(2)(a) provides a defence where a public authority is under a duty to apply an incompatible provision because it 'could not have acted differently'; s 6(2)(b) provides a defence where a public authority has a power, which it may or may not exercise, conferred by an incompatible, but still current, statute.

The operation of s 6(2)(b) raises several difficult questions. Lord Walker poses the first in the same case.

Birmingham City Council v Doherty [2008] 2 WLR 636, HL

Lord Walker

At [111]

It is generally accepted that section 6(2)(a) applies to statutory duties, and section 6(2)(b) to statutory powers and discretions. But there is need for more analysis. A public authority with a statutory power may exercise it or not as it thinks fit, subject only to the usual public law restraints. Does section 6(2)(b) enable it to exercise the power with impunity in a way that infringes Convention rights, when it could act differently?

The answer appears to be 'yes', as Lords Hoffmann and Hope explained in the following case.[31]

R (Hooper) v Secretary of State for Work and Pensions [2005] 1 WLR 1681, HL

Lord Hoffmann

At [48], [49], and [51]

But section 6(2)(b) says nothing about a decision having to be necessary for any particular purpose. [He observes that if the decision had been necessary, a defence would have fallen with s 6(2)(a).]

Clearly, section 6(2)(b) has a different purpose. It assumes that the public authority could have acted differently but nevertheless excludes liability if it was giving effect to a statutory provision which cannot be read as Convention-compliant in accordance with section 3.

[...]

This reasoning is in my opinion supported by the evident purpose of section 6(2), which was to preserve the sovereignty of Parliament: see Lord Nicholls of Birkenhead in *Aston Cantlow and Wilmcote with Billesley Parochial Church Council v Wallbank* [2004] 1 AC 546, para 19. If legislation cannot be read compatibly with Convention rights, a public authority is not obliged to subvert the intention of Parliament by treating itself as under a duty to neutralise the effect of the legislation.

---

[31] See also *R (Wilkinson) v Inland Revenue Commissioners* [2005] 1 WLR 1718.

Lord Hope

At [73]

The important point to notice about paragraph (b) is that the source of the discretion does not matter. What matters is (a) that the provisions in regard to which the authority has this discretion cannot be read or given effect compatibly with the Convention rights and (b) that the authority has decided to exercise or not to exercise its discretion, whatever its source, so as to give effect to those provisions or to enforce them. If it does this, this paragraph affords it a defence to a claim under section 7(1) that by acting or failing to act in this way it has acted unlawfully. In this way it enables the primary legislation to remain effective in the way Parliament intended. If the defence was not there the authority would have no alternative but to exercise its discretion in a way that was compatible with the Convention rights. This power would become a duty to act compatibly with the Convention, even if to do so was plainly in conflict with the intention of Parliament.

An added difficulty is working out when a public authority is acting in a manner that falls within s 6(2)—that is, under incompatible primary legislation. Lord Hope, in *Doherty*, identified three situations.

Birmingham City Council v Doherty [2008] 2 WLR 636, HL

Lord Hope

At [39]

The cases in which the effect of section 6(2)(b) of the 1998 Act has been considered so far demonstrate that three distinct situations may arise. The first is where a decision to exercise or not to exercise a power that is given by primary legislation would inevitably give rise to an incompatibility [...] The second, which lies at the opposite end of the spectrum, is where the act or omission of the public authority which is incompatible with a Convention right is not touched by one or more provisions of primary legislation in any way at all. As the matter is not to any extent the product of primary legislation, the sovereignty of Parliament is not engaged. The act or omission will be unlawful under section 6(1) because section 6(2)(b) does not apply to it. The third situation lies in the middle. This is where the act or omission takes place within the context of a scheme which primary legislation has laid down that gives general powers, such as powers of management, to a public authority. That is the situation in this case. The answer to the question whether or not section 6(2)(b) applies will depend on the extent to which the act or omission can be said to be giving effect to any of the provisions of the scheme that is to be found in the statutes.

At [40]

Guidance as to how the third situation is to be approached was given in *R (Hooper) v Secretary of State for Work and Pensions* [2005] UKHL 29; [2005] 1 WLR 1681, with which the House's decision in *R (Wilkinson) v Inland Revenue Commissioners* [2005] UKHL 30; [2005] 1 WLR 1718 should also be read [...] The important point, as Lord Hoffmann explained in paras 48 and 49, is that section 6(2)(b) assumes that the public authority could have acted differently but excludes liability if it was giving effect to a statutory provision which could not be read in a way that was compatible with the Convention rights. It protects a decision to exercise or not to exercise a discretion that is available to it under the statute [...] Public authorities which make use of the common law in the exercise of their statutory powers of management are in no less favourable a position under that section 6(2)(b) than they would have been had their powers been derived entirely from statute.

Yet a further difficulty arises in determining the scope of powers arising under incompliant primary legislation. As we have noted, statute and the common law are often entwined, which led the Lords in *Doherty* to accept the possibility that a local authority's statutory scheme of housing management could encompass both statutory and common law rights, powers, and duties. From the above extract from *Doherty*, we can see that Lord Hope was prepared to accept that a s 6(2) defence could apply to common law rules, which operate within a statutory framework, when a local authority is seeking to recover possession. His fellow Lords were not, however, so ready to do so.[32]

2.3 ABSOLUTE AND QUALIFIED RIGHTS

The nature of the Articles contained in the ECHR differs. Some provide an absolute protection: for example, no circumstances can justify a departure from the absolute prohibitions against torture and slavery contained in Arts 3 and 4. The two Articles with which we are primarily concerned are clearly qualified, however, in the sense that an interference with the protections that they enshrine may be justified in prescribed circumstances.

Article 1 of the First Protocol, which protects the peaceful enjoyment of an individual's possessions, is qualified by three conditions, as follows.

1. A person may be deprived of his or her possessions *'in the public interest and subject to the conditions provided for by law and by the general principles of international law'*.

2. A State may enact *'such laws as it deems necessary to control the use of property in accordance with the general interest [...]'*.

3. A State may also enact *'such laws as it deems necessary [...] to secure the payment of taxes or other contributions or penalties'*.

Likewise, Art 8, which provides that every individual is entitled to respect for his or her home, is qualified to allow an interference that *'is in accordance with the law and is necessary in a democratic society in the interests of national security, public safety or the economic well-being of the country, for the prevention of disorder or crime, for the protection of health or morals, or for the protection of the rights and freedoms of others'*.

A human rights challenge is thus frequently focused upon whether or not an infringement is justified by the qualifications outlined.

2.4 THE JUSTIFICATION FORMULA

In considering whether or not an interference is justified, the Strasbourg Court has developed a tried-and-tested formula: the interference must be in pursuit of a *legitimate aim*, and

---

[32] See Lord Walker at [113] and Lord Mance at [153]–[159].

a State has a wide *margin of appreciation* in identifying a legitimate aim and the means to achieve that aim—although there must be *proportionality* between those means and the interference with the individual's human rights.

We need to examine each of these elements.

2.4.1 Legitimate aim

Firstly, the interference must be lawful and made for a legitimate purpose that serves the appropriate qualification. Thus, for example, an interference with Art 1 of the First Protocol must be in the public or general interest; an interference with Art 8 must be necessary in a democratic society, because, for example, it is for the economic well-being of the country, or because it protects the rights and freedoms of others.

2.4.2 Margin of appreciation

A State is afforded a wide margin of appreciation, or discretion, in determining the legitimate aim and the means of achieving that aim, because a State is generally in a better position to assess both society's needs and the best means of achieving those needs within its own country. The Strasbourg Court explained the concept in the context of a challenge to the compatibility with Art 1 of the First Protocol of legislation entitling a tenant to purchase his landlord's reversion.

James v UK (1986) 8 EHRR 123

Facts: The Duke of Westminster, whose estate comprised a significant number of houses in London let on long leases, unsuccessfully questioned the compatibility with Art 1 of the First Protocol of the Leasehold Reform Act 1967. The Act entitled the tenants of the houses to require him to transfer the freehold reversion to them for sums (as defined by the legislation) that were less than their market value.

At [46]

Because of their direct knowledge of their society and its needs, the national authorities are in principle better placed than the international judge to appreciate what is "in the public interest." Under the system of protection established by the Convention, it is thus for the national authorities to make the initial assessment both of the existence of the problem of public concern warranting measures of deprivation of property and of the remedial action to be taken [. . .] Here as in other fields to which the safeguards of the Convention extend, the national authorities accordingly enjoy a certain margin of appreciation.

Furthermore, the notion of "public interest " is necessarily extensive, in particular, as the Commission noted, the decision to enact laws expropriating property will commonly involve consideration of political, economic and social issues on which opinions within a democratic society may reasonably differ widely. The Court finding it natural that the margin of appreciation available to the legislature in implementing social and economic policies should be a wide one, will respect the legislature judgment as to what is "in the public interest" unless that judgement be manifestly without reasonable foundation [. . .]

Thus a State's actions will be respected unless they are 'manifestly without reasonable foundation', in the sense that no reasonable government would have come to a similar decision in the circumstances.[33]

A State's margin of appreciation, however, will depend on, and may vary according to, the context in which it is exercised.

Connors v UK (2005) 40 EHRR 9

Facts: The Connors were gypsies. The family occupied the same local authority site under a licence for over thirteen years, but, after their daughter married and their sons grew up, it was alleged that their pitch was a 'magnet for trouble'. As a result, the local authority terminated their licence to occupy and summarily evicted them from the site, but without citing any reasons. The local authority chose not to rely upon the Connors' alleged 'antisocial' behaviour. The Connor family successfully claimed that their summary eviction breached their rights to respect for their home and way of life as gypsies under Art 8.

At [82]

In this regard, a margin of appreciation must, inevitably, be left to the national authorities, who by reason of their direct and continuous contact with the vital forces of their countries are in principle better placed than an international court to evaluate local needs and conditions. This margin will vary according to the nature of the Convention right in issue, its importance for the individual and the nature of the activities restricted, as well as the nature of the aim pursued by the restrictions. The margin will tend to be narrower where the right at stake is crucial to the individual's effective enjoyment of intimate or key rights. See, e.g. [. . .] *Gillow v United Kingdom* (A/104): (1989) 11 E.H.R.R. 335 at [55]. On the other hand, in spheres involving the application of social or economic policies, there is authority that the margin of appreciation is wide, as in the planning context where the Court has found that: "[i]n so far as the exercise of discretion involving a multitude of local factors is inherent in the choice and implementation of planning policies, the national authorities in principle enjoy a wide margin of appreciation". *Buckley v United Kingdom* (1997) 23 E.H.R.R. 101 at [75].

The Court has also stated that in spheres such as housing, which play a central role in the welfare and economic policies of modern societies, it will respect the legislature's judgment as to what is in the general interest unless that judgment is manifestly without reasonable foundation. See *Mellacher v Austria* (A/169): (1990) 12 E.H.R.R. 391 at [45]; *Immobiliare Saffi v Italy*: (2000) 30 E.H.R.R.756 at [49]. It may be noted however that this was in the context of Art.1 of Protocol No.1, not Art.8 which concerns rights of central importance to the individual's identity, self-determination, physical and moral integrity, maintenance of relationships with others and a settled and secure place in the community. See, *Gillow v United Kingdom* at [55]; *Pretty v United Kingdom*: (2002) 35 E.C.H.R. 1; *Christine Goodwin v United Kingdom*: (2002) 35 E.H.R.R. 18 at [90]. Where general social and economic policy considerations have arisen in the context of Art.8 itself, the scope of the margin of appreciation depends on the context of the case, with particular significance attaching to the extent of the intrusion into the personal sphere of the applicant. *Hatton v United Kingdom*: (2002) 34 E.H.R.R. 1 at [103] and [123].

---

[33] See, also, *Lithgow v UK* (1986) 8 EHRR 329, which concerned the compensation to be paid for nationalization of certain areas of the ship and aircraft-building business.

The idea of the State's margin of appreciation does not sit easily with the potential horizontal effect of the HRA 1998. As Nield summarizes in the extract in section 2.2 above, the ECHR has State actions in mind rather than reconciling the respective rights and duties of individuals in a private dispute. Indeed, its application in our domestic courts has been widely questioned.[34] The Court of Appeal, however, recognized the concept by making clear that the decisions of the Strasbourg Court, in which the margin of appreciation is applied, should be followed, save in exceptional circumstances. Thus, if the Strasbourg Court has found that a particular law is compliant, a case governed by that law cannot be found to breach the ECHR solely on its facts.[35]

Ofulue v Bossert [2009] Ch 1, CA

Facts: Ofulue moved to Nigeria and let his house. The Bosserts were let into possession by the tenant, and claimed that, despite negotiations with Ofulue for a lease, they had been in adverse possession and acquired title as a result. The court found that the Strasbourg Court's decision in *Pye v UK* led to the conclusion that the law governing adverse possession was ECHR-compatible. The width of a State's margin of appreciation did not mean that the domestic courts should consider the facts of each case by reference to the compliance criteria decided at Strasbourg.

Arden LJ

At [37]

The next task is to connect the doctrine of the margin of appreciation to the principle [...], that save in special circumstances our domestic courts should follow the decisions of the Strasbourg Court but not venture further. In my judgment, it must follow from the obligation in s.2 of the Human Rights Act 1998, [...] that, in the absence of special circumstances, (1) if domestic law within an area found by the Strasbourg court to be within the contracting states' margin of appreciation were challenged before an English court, the English court should consider whether the domestic rule serves a legitimate aim and is proportionate (according the appropriate degree of respect to the decision-maker in domestic law) but that it should find that the law is Convention-compliant if those tests are satisfied; and (2) where the Strasbourg court has itself already carried out this exercise, the English court should follow the decision of the Strasbourg Court [...]

At [52]

The written submissions of the Ofulues proceed on the basis that it is open to this court to distinguish the decision in *Pye* on its facts or by reference to the applicability of the policy reasons for adverse possession identified by the Law Commission. In my judgment, this approach fundamentally misunderstands the purpose of the doctrine of the margin of appreciation. The Strasbourg Court accepted that the national authorities could in general

---

[34] See, e.g., Lavender, 'The Problem of the Margin of Appreciation' [1997] EHRLR 380; Howell, 'Land Law and Human Rights' [1999] Conv 287; Howell, 'The Human Rights Act 1998: The Horizontal Effect on Land Law' in *Modern Studies in Property Law: Vol 1* (ed Cooke, 2001, p 149); Rook, *Property Law and Human Rights* (2001, p 38).

[35] A similar approach is evident in the House of Lords' approach to the human rights implications of local authority possession actions examined in section 4.2.2 below.

determine the rules for the extinction of title as a result of the occupation of the land by a person who was not the true owner. That determination applies to all decisions on adverse possession and it is not open to this court not to follow that determination because the case is distinguishable on its facts. For the doctrine of the margin of appreciation to be inapplicable, the results would have to be so anomalous as to render the legislation unacceptable (see [83] of the judgment of the Strasbourg Court set out above), and in my judgment that has not been demonstrated in this case [. . .]

2.4.3 Proportionality

Although States enjoy a wide margin of appreciation, there must nevertheless be a fair balance struck, or proportionality, between the means employed to address the legitimate aim and the interference with an individual's human rights that results. The principle is that no single individual should be expected to bear an excessive burden in meeting the particular community or social object of the legitimate aim. If it is possible to achieve that aim without interfering unduly with an individual's rights, then that route should be adopted in preference to other solutions that do so trespass. Proportionality also calls for a consideration of the process by which the legitimate aim is achieved.

Thus, although there is proportionality between the legitimate aim and the interference, there may still be a breach of the relevant Article where the victim is afforded no, or an inadequate, opportunity to assert their rights. It was the lack of procedural safeguards that contributed to a breach of Art 8 in the following case.

Connors v UK (2005) 40 EHRR 9

Facts: See above.

At [83]

The procedural safeguards available to the individual will be especially material in determining whether the respondent state has, when fixing the regulatory framework, remained within its margin of appreciation. In particular, the Court must examine whether the decision-making process leading to measures of interference was fair and such as to afford due respect to the interests safeguarded to the individual by Art.8 [. . .]

At [94]

The power to evict without the burden of giving reasons liable to be examined as to their merits by an independent tribunal has not been convincingly shown to respond to any specific goal or to provide any specific benefit to members of the gypsy community. The references to "flexibility" or "administrative burden" have not been supported by any concrete indications of the difficulties that the regime is thereby intended to avoid. See, *mutatis mutandis*, *Larkos v Cyprus*: (2000) 30 E.H.R.R. 597 [. . .] It would rather appear that the situation in England as it has developed, for which the authorities must take some responsibility, places considerable obstacles in the way of gypsies pursuing an actively nomadic lifestyle while at the same time excluding from procedural protection those who decide to take up a more settled lifestyle.

The nature of procedural safeguards may differ according to which Article is engaged and the infringement in question. The Strasbourg Court has emphasized the importance of procedural safeguards where Art 8 is engaged by possession proceedings, even though the claimant's case may not seem at all meritorious.

McCann v UK (2008) 47 EHRR 40

Facts: The McCanns were joint tenants of a local authority house under a secure tenancy. Mr McCann was abusive to his wife and their marriage broke down, with Mrs McCann obtaining a non-molestation order against her husband. Mr McCann moved out of the house, as required by the order, but he broke back in using a crowbar and assaulted his wife. Mrs McCann fled with the children and was rehoused by the local authority. Mr McCann moved back into the house. When the local authority discovered that Mr McCann was living in the house, it approached Mrs McCann and asked her to sign a notice terminating the tenancy, which had the effect of bringing the tenancy to an end, not only in respect of her interest, but also her husband's, although the local authority did not explain these consequences fully. The local authority brought possession proceedings to evict Mr McCann as a trespasser. Mr McCann successfully alleged that his right to respect for his home had been infringed under Art 8, because his right to occupy the house had been brought to an end without recourse to court proceedings, but by his wife's notice.

At [48]–[52]

The court considers that this interference was in accordance with the law and pursued a legitimate aim of protecting the right and freedom of others in two respects. First, it protected the local authority's right to regain possession of the property against an individual who had no contractual or other right to be there [...] the interference also pursued the aim of ensuring that the statutory scheme for housing provision was properly applied. The "others" in such a case are the intended beneficiaries of the complex arrangements set up by, amongst others, the Housing Acts. The Court accepts that it is only by limiting the protection of the Acts to the categories to which it applies that the policy underlying the Acts can sensibly be implemented.

The central question in this case is, therefore whether the interference was proportionate to the aim pursued and thus "necessary in a democratic society". It must be recalled that this requirement under para 2 of art 8 raises a question of procedure as well as one of substance [...]

The Court is unable to accept the Government's argument that the reasoning in *Connors v UK* [2004] ECHR 66746/01 was to be largely confined only to cases involving the eviction of gypsies or cases where the applicant sought to challenge the law itself rather than its application in his particular case. The loss of one's home is a most extreme form of interference with the right to respect for the home. Any person at risk of an interference of this magnitude should in principle be able to have the proportionality of the measure determined by an independent tribunal in the light of the relevant principles under art 8 of the Convention, notwithstanding that, under domestic law, his right to occupation has come to an end.

[...] Had the local authority sought to evict the applicant in accordance with this statutory scheme, it would have been open to the applicant to have asked the court to examine, for example, whether his wife had really left the family home because of domestic violence and whether in his personal circumstances, including his need to provide accommodation for his

children during overnight visits several times a week, it was reasonable to grant the possession order.

In the present case, however the local authority chose to bypass the statutory scheme
by requesting Mrs McCann to sign a common law notice to quit, the effect of which was
immediately to terminate the applicant's right to remain in the house. It does not appear that
the authority, in the course of this procedure, gave any consideration to the applicant's right
to respect for his home. Moreover in domestic law [...] in summary proceedings such as
those brought against the applicant it was not open to the county court to consider any issue
concerning proportionality of the possession order, save in exceptional cases [...] No such
exceptional circumstances applied in the present case.

The court's application of the justification formula is explained by Lord Nicholls in the
following case by what he dubs the statutory 'compatibility' exercise.

Wilson v First County Trust Ltd (No 2) [2004] 1 AC 816, HL

Lord Nicholls

At [61]–[63]

The Human Rights Act 1998 requires the court to exercise a new role in respect of primary
legislation. This new role is fundamentally different from interpreting and applying legislation. The courts are now required to evaluate the effect of primary legislation in terms
of Convention rights and, where appropriate, make a formal declaration of incompatibility.
In carrying out this evaluation the court has to compare the effect of the legislation with
the Convention right. If the legislation impinges upon a Convention right the court must then
compare the policy objective of the legislation with the policy objective which under the
Convention may justify a prima facie infringement of the Convention right. When making
these two comparisons the court will look primarily at the legislation, but not exclusively so.
Convention rights are concerned with practicalities. When identifying the practical effect of
an impugned statutory provision the court may need to look outside the statute in order to
see the complete picture [...] As to the objective of the statute, at one level this will be coin-
cident with its effect [...] But that is not the relevant level for Convention purposes. What is
relevant is the underlying social purpose sought to be achieved by the statutory provision.
Frequently that purpose will be self-evident, but this will not always be so.

The legislation must not only have a legitimate policy objective. It must also satisfy a "proportionality" test. The court must decide whether the means employed by the statute to
achieve the policy objective is appropriate and not disproportionate in its adverse effect. This
involves a "value judgment" by the court, made by reference to the circumstances prevailing
when the issue has to be decided. It is the current effect and impact of the legislation which
matter, not the position when the legislation was enacted or came into force [...]

When a court makes this value judgment the facts will often speak for themselves. But
sometimes the court may need additional background information tending to show, for
instance, the likely practical impact of the statutory measure and why the course adopted
by the legislature is or is not appropriate. Moreover, as when interpreting a statute, so when
identifying the policy objective of a statutory provision or assessing the "proportionality" of a
statutory provision, the court may need enlightenment on the nature and extent of the social
problem (the "mischief") at which the legislation is aimed. This may throw light on the rationale underlying the legislation.

This different role will entail the court considering government policy to a greater extent than previously. That consideration may well require an examination of policy documents and statements prepared for government.

Lord Nicholls went on in his judgment in *Wilson* to consider the likely field of the court's enquiry, which he concluded could include a government White Paper and explanatory notes, which may accompany a Bill or which are prepared during the Bill's course through Parliament. He doubted, however, that Hansard or ministerial statements would often assist the court.[36]

Goymour, when examining the Art 8 challenge in *Kay; Price*, has suggested that a proprietary claim can be divided into three elements: the substantive law; the decision to exercise those rights; and the procedure that must be followed in doing so. The first and third elements are the primary candidates for a human rights attack. The second element is susceptible to an administrative law challenge where the rights are being exercised by a public authority. We will return to these elements when considering *Kay; Price* in section 4.2.2 below.

Goymour, 'Proprietary Claims and Human Rights: "A Reservoir of Entitlement"' (2006) 65 CLJ 696, 704

It is possible to take the process of dissecting a proprietary claim further than it was in *Kay; Price*. An alternative framework for analysis might divide the process of bringing a proprietary claim into the following three parts, according to which a claimant must:

(i) identify a proprietary right in an asset which entitled him to seek particular remedies;

(ii) decide to make a claim to enforce that right; and

(iii) identify and follow the correct legal procedure for making the claim.

This framework builds on, but is more precise than, the distinction drawn in *Kay; Price* between the rules and their application. Parts (i) and (iii) of a proprietary claim concern the rules and part (ii) their application

Generally, in terms of domestic law, part (i) concerns substantive property law [...] Part (ii) of a proprietary claim is regulated by domestic public law where the claimant is a public body; where a private party brings a claim, however, the domestic law is silent. Part (iii) of the claims is a matter for procedural law. For example, a landlord evicting a former tenant must follow the relevant procedural rules in order to bring his action.

The three parts are not water tight categories and sometimes overlap [...]

To advance a human rights argument in defence of a proprietary claim, the argument would necessarily target one or more of the three parts. The majority in *Kay; Price* seemed to regard part (ii) of the claim as immune from an Article 8 violation. The decision of the local authority to enforce its proprietary rights against a particular occupier was susceptible to challenge on traditional administrative law grounds, for example on grounds of unreasonableness, either by application for judicial review or by way of defence to possession proceedings. However, it would not be possible to ground a defence solely in Article 8. The reason given was that where a landlord's domestic proprietary and procedural rights are compatible with article 8, the decision to enforce those rights is necessarily compliant also. It should be noted that this conclusion is not inevitable.

---

36 [2003] UKHL 40, [2004] 1 AC 816, at [64]–[67].

However, their Lordships agreed that it would be possible to attack by Article 8 "the law which enables the court to make the possession order" in "seriously arguable" cases. Such language is sufficiently broad to cover both substantive property law (part (i) of the proprietary claim) and the corresponding procedural rules (part (ii) of the claim). But whether the case is authority for such a broad proposition is open to question.

2.5 RETROSPECTIVE APPLICATION

The HRA 1998 came into force on 2 October 2000, but, of course, property disputes may have a much longer history. It is thus important to consider to what extent (if any) the Act has retrospective application. The question is procedural, in the sense that its importance is directed to whether an individual can bring a human rights issue before the domestic courts. An individual will still be able to bring proceedings before the Strasbourg Court where the cause of action arose before 2 October 2000. For example, in *JA Pye (Oxford) Ltd v Graham*,[37] the House of Lords declined to consider the question of whether adverse possession was incompatible with Art 1 of the First Protocol because the relevant events had taken place before 2 October 2000, but Pye then pursued its claim before both the Chamber[38] and, on appeal, the Grand Chamber the Strasbourg Court.[39]

The HRA 1998 follows the general presumption that legislation does not have retrospective effect. Thus the court, in performance of its obligations under s 3, does not have to consider the ECHR where the right of action accrued before the Act came into force, even though the hearing may take place after that date. Such a situation arose in the following case, when the House of Lords decided that s 3 did not have retrospective effect.

Wilson v First County Trust Ltd (No 2) [2004] 1 AC 816, HL

Facts: Mrs Wilson entered into a consumer credit agreement with First County in January 1999. The agreement was unenforceable, because it breached the Consumer Credit Act 1974 by failing to state accurately the total amount of credit.[40] First County argued that the statutory provision was incompatible with Arts 1 and 6, but the House of Lords decline to determine the questions, because the HRA 1998 did not have retrospective effect.

Lord Nicholls

At [17]–[20]

On its face section 3 is of general application. So far as possible legislation must be read and given effect in a way compatible with the Convention rights. Section 3 is retrospective in the sense that, expressly, it applies to legislation whenever enacted. Thus section 3 may have the effect of changing the interpretation and effect of legislation already in force. An interpretation appropriate before the Act came into force may have to be reconsidered and

---

[37] [2002] UKHL 30, [2003] 1 AC 419.
[38] (2006) 42 EHRR 3.
[39] (2008) 46 EHRR 45.
[40] See s 127(3), which has since been amended by the Consumer Credit Act 2006, s 15.

revised in post-Act proceedings. This effect of section 3(1) is implicit in section 3(2)(a). So much is clear.

Considerable difficulties, however, might arise if the new interpretation of legislation, consequent on an application of section 3, were always to apply to pre-Act events. It would mean that parties' rights under existing legislation in respect of a transaction completed before the Act came into force could be changed overnight, to the benefit of one party and the prejudice of the other. This change, moreover, would operate capriciously, with the outcome depending on whether the parties' rights were determined by a court before or after 2 October 2000. The outcome in one case involving pre-Act happenings could differ from the outcome in another comparable case depending solely on when the cases were heard by a court. Parliament cannot have intended section 3(1) should operate in this unfair and arbitrary fashion.

The answer to this difficulty lies in the principle underlying the presumption against retrospective operation and the similar but rather narrower presumption against interference with vested interests. These are established presumptions but they are vague and imprecise. As Lord Mustill pointed out in *L'Office Cherifien des Phosphates v Yamashita-Shinnihon Steamship Co Ltd* [1994] 1 AC 486, 524–525, the subject matter of statutes is so varied that these generalised maxims are not a reliable guide. As always, therefore, the underlying rationale should be sought. This was well identified by Staughton LJ in *Secretary of State for Social Security v Tunnicliffe* [1991] 2 All ER 712, 724:

> "the true principle is that Parliament is presumed not to have intended to alter the law applicable to past events and transactions in a manner which is unfair to those concerned in them, unless a contrary intention appears. It is not simply a question of classifying an enactment as retrospective or not retrospective. Rather it may well be a matter of degree—the greater the unfairness, the more it is to be expected that Parliament will make it clear if that is intended."

Thus the appropriate approach is to identify the intention of Parliament in respect of the relevant statutory provision in accordance with this statement of principle.

Applying this approach to the Human Rights Act 1998, I agree with Mummery LJ in *Wainwright v Home Office* [2002] QB 1334, 1352, para 61, that in general the principle of interpretation set out in section 3(1) does not apply to causes of action accruing before the section came into force. The principle does not apply because to apply it in such cases, and thereby change the interpretation and effect of existing legislation, might well produce an unfair result for one party or the other. The Human Rights Act was not intended to have this effect.

As Lord Nicholls explains, this does not mean that the interpretation of a particular provision may not change as a result of the HRA 1998. It has long been accepted that the parties' respective rights and obligations may be altered as a result of legislation.

Lord Rogers also pointed out that retrospective application differs according to which Articles are being considered. He noted that where procedure is in issue—for example, because of an alleged breach of Art 6—the Act will have immediate effect upon any proceedings conducted after 20 October 2000.[41]

There is one instance in which the HRA 1998 does make express provision for retrospective application and that is contained in s 22(4), which provides that the Act is to have retrospective application in proceedings 'brought by or at the instigation of a public authority whenever the act in question took place'. It may thus be used defensively against public

---

[41] At [209].

authorities that have acted in breach of their obligations under s 6. An argument that this provision may operate retrospectively to effect the decisions of the courts (as public authorities) made prior to 20 October 2000 and in accordance with the law then in force has, however, been rejected.[42]

3 ARTICLE 1 OF THE FIRST PROTOCOL TO THE ECHR

European Convention on Human Rights, First Protocol, Art 1

Protection of property

Every natural or legal person is entitled to the peaceful enjoyment of his possessions. No one shall be deprived of his possessions except in the public interest and subject to the conditions provided for by law and by the general principles of international law.

The preceding provisions shall not, however, in any way impair the right of a State to enforce such laws as it deems necessary to control the use of property in accordance with the general interest or to secure the payment of taxes or other contributions or penalties.

Article 1 provides a right *of* property and not *to* property. Its object is thus to protect existing property that a person holds by both positively guaranteeing that a person is entitled to the peaceful enjoyment of his or her property, and by providing supporting negative prohibitions upon a person being deprived of his or her possession or being subject to controls over his or her enjoyment of those possessions.

The Strasbourg Court, in the following case, analysed Art 1 as comprising three distinct rules.

Sporrong and Lonnroth v Sweden (1982) 5 EHRR 35

At [61]

The first rule, which is of a general nature, announces the principle of peaceful enjoyment of property; it is set out in the first sentence of the first paragraph. The second rule covers deprivation of possessions and subjects it to certain conditions; it appears in the second sentence of the same paragraph. The third rule recognizes that the States are entitled, amongst other things, to control the use of property in accordance with the general interest, by enforcing such laws as they deem necessary for the purpose; it is contained in the second paragraph.

The rules may be distinct, but it is clear that they are also interrelated, as the Strasbourg Court stated in the following case.

---

[42] *R v Kansal (No 2)* [2001] UKHL 62; *R v Rezvi* [2002] UKHL 1; *R v Benjafield* [2002] UKHL 2; *R v Lyons (No 3)* [2002] UKHL 44. See also *Wainwright v Home Office* [2002] QB 1334. Approved in *Wilson v First County Council Trust Ltd* [2003] UKHL 40, [2004] 1 AC 816, and *Aston Cantlow and Wilmcote with Billesley Parochial Church Council v Wallbank* [2003] UKHL 37, [2004] 1 AC 546.

James v UK [1986] 8 EHRR 123

At [37]

The three rules are not however "distinct" in the sense of being unconnected. The second and third rules are concerned with particular instances of interference with the right to peaceful enjoyment of property and should therefore be construed in the light of the general principle enunciated in the first rule.

Thus the second and third rules need to be considered in the light of the overarching nature of the first rule. An interference that is justified under these rules by their limiting conditions will also satisfy the first rule. This point was also made in *James*.

James v UK [1986] 8 EHRR 123

At [71]

The rule (in the second sentence) subjects deprivation of possessions to certain conditions concerns a particular category, indeed of the most radical kind, of interference with the right to peaceful enjoyment of property [...]; the second sentence supplements and qualifies the general principle enunciated in the first sentence. This being so, it is inconceivable that application of the general principle to the present case should lead to any conclusion different from that already arrived at by the court in the application of the second sentence.

The courts will look to see whether the last two rules are applicable before considering whether the first rule has been infringed.[43] This analysis and approach has been adopted in subsequent cases.

3.1 WHEN IS ART 1 ENGAGED?

The first step to consider is whether Art 1 has been engaged, because there has been an interference with possessions under one of the three elements of the Article. This will depend on what we mean by 'possessions' as well as what may constitute an interference.

3.1.1 The meaning of 'possessions'

'Possessions' bears what is known as an autonomous meaning in Strasbourg jurisprudence.[44] This means that the Strasbourg Court develops its own interpretation of a term. In so doing, it will look to, but will not be bound by, the meaning of the term within the appropriate domestic jurisdiction.[45] In fact, the Strasbourg Court has adopted a wide interpretation of 'possessions', and there is no doubt that our established notions of estates and interests in land fall within its meaning. The term also covers other accepted categories of

---

43 See *Sporrong and Lonnroth v Sweden* (1982) 5 EHRR 35, at [61].

44 Allen, 'The Autonomous Meaning of "Possessions" under the European Convention on Human Rights' in *Modern Studies in Property Law: Vol 2* (ed Cooke, 2003, p 58).

45 See, e.g., *Matos E Silva Lda v Portugal* (1996) 24 EHRR 573.

property rights that fall outside the scope of this book, such as personal and intellectual property, as well as rights that may arise from contractual relations or a tortious claim. But an expectation that you may receive property in the future—for example, by inheritance—is not a possession for the purposes of Art 1.[46] This raises the question of whether an inchoate equity—for example, arising by estoppel (see Chapter 13)—constitutes a possession for the purpose of Art 1. Unfortunately, we do not yet have guidance of the courts, although there is some support for the proposition.[47] The Strasbourg Court, in *Stretch v UK*,[48] has accepted that a legitimate expectation of entitlement upon which the claimant had acted constitutes a possession for the purposes of Art 1[49] and we will see that s 116 of the Land Registration Act 2002 (LRA 2002) does categorize an estoppel as a property right for the purposes of the Act (see Chapter 13).

Land may have the benefit of certain rights: for example, an easement (see Chapter 26), or the benefit of a covenant (see Chapter 27), or, in the case of a leasehold reversion, a right to receive rent and to re-enter for breach of the tenant's covenants (see Chapter 25). These benefits do not constitute separate possessions for the purposes of Art 1; rather, they are encompassed within the property to which they are attached.[50] Likewise, land may be subject to an encumbrance in favour of a third person: for example, an easement or restrictive covenant in favour of a neighbouring owner. The possession that is vested in the landowner is the appropriate estate in the land, as burdened by the encumbrance. In other words, if you acquire land that is already subject to a burden, the burden does not engage Art 1.

The House of Lords confirmed this approach in the following case. The encumbrance in question was a liability to pay for chancel repairs to the local church: an unusual liability that can be difficult to discover, but which Lord Hope described as follows.

Aston Cantlow and Wilmcote with Billesley Parochial Church Council v Wallbank [2004] 1 AC 546, HL

Lord Hope

At [71]

[...] just like any other burden which runs with the land which is, and has been at all times within the scope of the property right which [was] acquired and among other factors to be taken into account in determining its value [...] The enforcement of the liability under the general law is an incident of the property right which is now vested jointly in Mr and Mrs Wallbank. It is not [...] an outside intervention by way of a form of tax.

The creation of a new encumbrance or burden may, however, engage Art 1. In most cases, the owner will have created that encumbrance and so can hardly complain that his or her

---

[46] *Marckx v Belgium* (1979) 2 EHRR 330.

[47] Howell is not optimistic: see 'Land and Human Rights' [1999] Conv 287.

[48] (2004) 38 EHRR 12. See also *Pine Valley Developments Ltd v Ireland* (1991) 14 EHRR 319. The principle has been applied by the domestic courts in *Rowland v. Environment Agency* [2003] EWCA Civ 1885. See Elliot, 'Legitimate Expectations and Unlawful Representations' (2004) 63 CLJ 261.

[49] The legitimate expectation arose from an ultra vires representation by a local authority, that the claimant was entitled to an option to renew his lease, which both the claimant and the local authority assumed was valid during the 22-year term of the original lease. In fact, the local authority had no power to grant the option.

[50] *Antoniades v UK* (App No 15434/89) and *Scott v UK* (App No 10741/84).

rights have been infringed. It is where that encumbrance has arisen, or is deemed to have arisen, by operation of external legal rules that Art 1 may be engaged.[51]

A further difficult question is whether or not a contract that is void under the terms of a statute is capable of comprising a possession within the terms of the Article. The House of Lords considered this issue in *Wilson v First County Trust Ltd*,[52] although they did not speak with one voice. In *Wilson*, the credit agreement was void for failing to comply with the statutory requirements of the Consumer Credit Act 1974 (CCA 1974).[53] Lords Hope and Scott decided that no agreement had been created in the first place, and that thus there was no possession of which First County could be deprived.

Lord Nicholls disagreed. He believed that a statutory provision that robbed an agreement of its force should not escape review under the HRA 1998, otherwise '[a] *Convention right guaranteeing a right to property would have nothing to say*'.

Lord Hobhouse was more equivocal. He felt that the question turned upon whether or not an agreement had been created.[54]

A similar, although slightly different, question is whether a possession is also inherently limited by the operation of the legal rules to which it is subject and therefore cannot be infringed by the operation of those rules. Here, the law regulates the possession, rather than dictates its creation. The answer to this question is clear: the operation of such rules may engage Art 1.[55] Goymour explains why.

Goymour, 'Proprietary Claims and Human Rights: A "Reservoir of Entitlement"?' (2006) 65 CLJ 696, 711

However this argument, whilst technically compelling, would largely strip Article 1 of any sensible meaning. Indeed, one type of conduct which Article 1 Protocol 1 typically regulates is arbitrary compulsory acquisition of private property by the State. If one were to say that all property is inherently liable to compulsory acquisition, Article 1 Protocol 1 would rarely, if ever, bite. The Convention is supposed to guard against interference with property rights. To say Article 1, Protocol 1 fails to be engaged because property rights are inherently vulnerable is logical but circular.

3.1.2 Deprivation of possessions: the second limb

The second limb of Art 1 is concerned with the deprivation of possessions. A 'deprivation' is generally defined by a transfer or shift in ownership: examples include the compulsory purchase of land,[56] or the nationalization of a business by the government.[57] The transfer need not be to the government, or other public authority; it may be to another private

---

[51] For example, an easement may arise by prescription: see, further, Chapter 26.

[52] [2003] UKHL 40, [2004] 1 AC 816, although their comments are dicta.

[53] Similar concerns may arise with a contract for the sale of land that is void under s 2(1), Law of Property (Miscellaneous Provisions) Act 1989.

[54] His approach draws some support from *Beyeler v Italy* (2001) 33 EHRR 52, (2003) 36 EHRR 5, in which Art 1 was engaged when the sale of a work of art was void because it was not declared to the relevant authorities within the required time limits. The sale was treated by the Italian government as having some effect prior to the failure to declare rendered it void.

[55] *JA Pye (Oxford) Ltd v UK* (2008) 46 EHRR 45. See also (2006) 43 EHRR 3.

[56] *Howard v UK* (1987) 9 EHRR 91.

[57] *Lithgow v UK* (1986) 8 EHRR 329.

individual, where the State has sanctioned that transfer by legislation. For example, the Leasehold Reform Act 1967 confers a right of enfranchisement upon certain tenants by which they are entitled to acquire their landlord's freehold reversion. The deprivation thus involves the transfer of a possession from landlord to tenant.[58] By contrast, the determination of a lease (whether by the expiry of the term, by a notice to quit, or by a right of forfeiture) does not deprive the tenant of his or her possessions, because the lease is defined by these means of termination from the outset. These modes of termination are part and parcel of the lease itself.

3.1.3 Controls over possessions: the third limb

A government may enact laws that control the use of land, the most obvious examples being the planning controls that prevent development of land without the consent of the local planning authority.[59] More unusual examples include controls over fishing,[60] and hunting rights over land,[61] or controls over who can actually use the land.[62]

3.1.4 Deprivation or control?

Whether or not an interference constitutes a deprivation or control of property is not always as clear-cut as the above examples. The distinction is significant when it comes to considering whether or not the interference is proportionate. As we will see, there is an expectation that a deprivation of property under the second limb will be balanced by the payment of compensation whereas there is not necessarily the same expectation where there is a control over property under the third limb.

It might initially be thought that the extinction of the paper owner's title by the operation of adverse possession is a clear example of a deprivation of property.[63] The Grand Chamber of the Strasbourg Court decided, however, that the effect of the limitation periods for the recovery of possession of land and the consequent effect of their expiry on the paper owner's title was a control of property. In effect, the Court viewed the extinction of the paper owner's title more as an administrative step that brought the legal evidence of ownership into line with the de facto position when the squatter could no longer be evicted from the land.

JA Pye (Oxford) Ltd v UK (2008) 46 EHRR 45, Grand Chamber

Facts: Pye owned land that it intended to develop. In the meantime, it licensed the land to a neighbouring farmer, Mr Graham. When the licence expired, Mr Graham continued in adverse possession of the land for a period in excess of the limitation period of twelve years. When Pye eventually tried to evict Mr Graham, the House of Lords dismissed its claim and held that Mr Graham was entitled to be registered as the owner. Pye unsuccessfully claimed that it had been deprived of its ownership in breach of Art 1 of the First Protocol.

---

[58] *James v UK* (1986) 8 EHRR 123.
[59] *Pine Valley Development Ltd v Ireland* (1991) 14 EHRR 319.
[60] *Baner v Sweden* (App No 11763/85).
[61] *Chassagnou v France* (App Nos 25088/94, 28331/95, and 28443/95).
[62] *Gillow v UK* (1989) 11 EHRR 335.
[63] See Limitation Act 1980, ss 15 and 17, Land Registration Act 1925, s 75, and Chapter 10.

At [65]

The applicant companies did not lose their land because of a legislative provision which permitted the State to transfer ownership in particular circumstances (as in the cases of *AGOSI*, *Air Canada, Gasus*), or because of a social policy of transfer of ownership (as in the case of *James*), but rather as the result of the operation of the generally applicable rules on limitation periods for actions for recovery of land. Those provided that at the end of the limitation period, the paper owner's title to unregistered land was extinguished (section 17 of the 1980 Act). In the case of registered land, the position was amended to take into account of the fact that until the register was rectified, the former owner continued to appear as registered proprietor. Thus in the present case, section 75(1) of the 1925 Act provided that on expiry of the limitation period the title was not extinguished, but the registered proprietor was deemed to hold the land in trust for the adverse possessor.

At [66]

The statutory provisions which resulted in the applicant companies' loss of beneficial ownership were thus not intended to deprive paper owners of their ownership, but rather to regulate questions of title in a system in which, historically, 12 years' adverse possession was sufficient to extinguish the former owner's right to re-enter or to recover possession, and the new title depended on the principle that unchallenged lengthy possession gave a title. The provisions of the 1925 and 1980 Acts which were applied to the applicant companies were part of the general land law, and were concerned to regulate, amongst other things, limitation periods in the context of the use and ownership of land as between individuals. The applicant companies were therefore affected, not by a "deprivation of possessions" within the meaning of the second sentence of the first paragraph of Article 1, but rather by a "control of use" of land within the meaning of the second paragraph of the provision.

There are other areas of uncertainty: for example, does overreaching lead to a deprivation of property, or is it a control of property? The beneficiary or mortgagor loses its interest in the land itself, but its interest shifts instead to the proceeds of sale.[64] One might argue that the effect of this shift is a control, rather than a deprivation of property. One might argue, as Goymour has suggested, that there may be no interference at all, because the beneficiaries' and the mortgagor's interests are inherently limited by the trustees' or mortgagee's powers of sale.[65]

3.1.5 Peaceful enjoyment: the first limb

An interference that does not fall within the second or third limb may nevertheless be an interference with the peaceful enjoyment of possession under the residual category provided by the first limb. *Sporrong and Lonnroth v Sweden*[66] provides an example. The complainants owed land in Stockholm that was earmarked for development and the authorities issued expropriation notices.[67] Although the notices were never implemented, the complainants' ability to deal with their land was blighted. The Court found that there was no deprivation

---

[64] See Chapter 20.
[65] Goymour, 'Proprietary Claims and Human Rights: A Reservoir of Entitlement' (2006) CLJ 696, 714.
[66] (1982) 5 EHRR 35.
[67] Prohibition notices prohibiting building were also issued, but these had lapsed.

or control under the second and third limbs, but did find that there was an infringement of the first rule.

3.2 WHEN IS AN INTERFERENCE JUSTIFIED?

Here, we must apply the justification formula at which we looked in section 2.4 above. Under Art 1 of the First Protocol, a deprivation of possession may be justified if it is '*in the public interest and subject to the conditions provided for by law and by the general principles of international law*', whilst a control of possessions may be justified if it is made pursuant to '*laws as* [the State] *deems necessary* [...] *in accordance with the general interest or to secure the payment of taxes or other contributions or penalties*'.

3.2.1 Subject to the law

The interference must be in accordance with domestic law. Furthermore, that domestic law must satisfy the fundamental requirements of the rule of law. It must not operate arbitrarily, it must be certain and accessible, and it must provide adequate procedural safeguards.[68]

3.2.2 The public and general interest

It is not thought that there is a distinction between the public and general interest, nor that these expressions necessarily call for the deprivation to accrue directly to, or the control be exercised by, the government.[69] The expressions 'general' and 'public' interest define the legitimate interest in respect of which a deprivation or control may be justified, and States enjoy a wide margin of appreciation in both identifying what is in the public interest and in formulating the appropriate measures to address that interest. The width of a State's margin of appreciation is evident from *James v UK*.

James v UK (1986) 8 EHRR 123

At [43]

In the Court's opinion, even if there could be a difference between the concepts of "public interest" and "general interest" in Article 1 (P-1), on the point under consideration no fundamental distinction of the kind contended for by the applicants can be drawn between them [...]

At [47]

The aim of the 1967 Act as spelt out in the 1966 White Paper, was to right the injustice which was felt to be caused to occupying tenants by the operation of the long leasehold system of tenure (see para 18 above). The Act was designed to reform the existing law, said to be

---

[68] In *Lithgow v UK* (1986) 8 EHRR 329, and *James v UK* (1986) 8 EHRR 329, claims that the assessment of compensation was arbitrary were rejected, but in *Hentrich v France* (1994) 18 EHRR 440, the Court found that the domestic law failed to satisfy the rule of law. It operated arbitrarily and did not provide adequate procedural safeguards.

[69] See *James v UK*, ibid.

inequitable to the leaseholder," and to give effect to what was described as the occupying tenant's "moral entitlement" to the ownership of the house.

Eliminating what are judged to be social injustices is an example of the functions of a democratic legislature. More especially, modern societies consider housing of the population to be a prime social need, the regulation of which cannot entirely be left to the play of market forces. The margin of appreciation is wide enough to cover legislation aimed at securing greater social justice in the sphere of people's homes, even where such legislation interferes with the existing contractual relations between private parties and confers no direct benefit on the State or the community at large. In principle therefore the aim pursued by the leasehold reform legislation is a legitimate one.

The real focus of the courts' review is thus on the proportionality of the interference in meeting the public interest. In assessing proportionality, the courts will need to determine whether a fair balance has been struck between the public interest to be addressed and the individual's right to the protection of his or her possessions. A number of factors may need to be considered, depending on the circumstances of the particular case, but two factors are particularly prominent in this enquiry: firstly, the availability of compensation; and secondly, the adequacy of the process to challenge the interference.

3.2.3 Compensation

Many constitutional guarantees of property rights include an express right to compensation upon the compulsory acquisition of property by the State. Article 1 does not expressly do so, but the Strasbourg Court has made clear that where the second limb of the Article is engaged (i.e. where there is a deprivation of property), compensation is to be expected, although that compensation may be less than market value.[70]

James v UK (1986) 8 EHRR 123

At [54]

The taking of property in the public interest without payment of compensation is treated as justifiable only in exceptional circumstances [...] As far as Article 1 (P1–1) is concerned, the protection of the right to property it affords would be largely illusory and ineffective in the absence of any equivalent principle. Clearly compensation terms are material to the assessment whether the contested legislation respects a fair balance between the various interests at stake and, notably, it does not impose a disproportionate burden on the applicants [...]

The Court further accepts the Commission's conclusion as to the standard of compensation: the taking of property without payment of an amount reasonably related to the value would normally constitute a disproportionate interference which could not be considered justifiable under Article 1 (P1–1). Article 1 (P1–1) does not, however guarantee a right to full compensation in all circumstances. Legitimate objectives of "public interest" such as pursued in measures of economic reform or measures designed to achieve greater social justice may call for less than reimbursement of the full market value. Furthermore, the Court's power of

---

[70] See also *Holy Monasteries v Greece* (1994) 20 EHRR 91 and *The Former King of Greece v Greece* (App No 25701/94).

review is limited to ascertaining whether the choice of compensation terms falls outside the State's wide margin of appreciation in this domain.

The requirement for compensation is not so strong where the interference is a control over property under the third limb.[71] For example, the Grand Chamber in *Pye*, having decided that the interference was a control rather than a deprivation of possession, went on to hold that a lack of compensation to the paper owner whose title is extinguished could be justified.

JA Pye *(Oxford) Ltd v UK* (2008) 46 EHRR 45

Facts: See section 3.1.4 above.

At [79]

The Chamber and the applicant companies emphasised the absence of compensation for what they both perceived as a deprivation of the applicant's companies' possessions. The Court has found the interference with the applicant's companies' possession was a control of use, rather than a deprivation of possession, such that the case-law on compensation for deprivations is not directly applicable. Further, in the cases in which a situation was analysed as a control of use even though the application lost possessions (*AGOSI*, and *Air Canada* [...]), no mention was made of a right to compensation. The Court would note, in agreement with the Government, that a requirement of compensation for the situation brought about by a party failing to observe a limitation period would sit uneasily alongside the very concept of limitation periods, whose aim is to further legal certainty by preventing a party from pursuing action after a certain date. The Court would also add that, even under the provisions of the Land Registration Act 2002, which the applicant companies use as confirmation that the provisions of earlier legislation were not compatible with the Convention, no compensation is payable by a person who is ultimately registered as a new owner of registered land on expiry of the limitation period.

The question of whether or not compensation is required is thus likely to call for a closer examination of the legitimate aim, as well as the financial impact of the control or disturbance upon the complainant. The minority in *Pye* also drew a connection between the need for compensation and the procedural safeguards available:[72] '[...] *the fact that the landowner received no compensation made the loss of beneficial ownership the more serious and required, in our view, particularly strong measures of protection of the registered owner's property rights if a fair balance was to be preserved*'.

3.2.4 Procedural safeguards

The process by which a person is deprived of their possessions, or by which controls are imposed upon their possessions, is an important aspect of proportionality. The fair

---

[71] *Baner v Sweden* (1989) 60 DR 128; *Chassagnou v France* (2000) 29 EHRR 615.
[72] At [16].

balance may be upset if the individual has no opportunity to question the interference.[73] The availability of judicial review of a public authority's decision that precipitates the interference may be sufficient in this respect.[74]

The Chamber's decision in *Pye* was largely premised on the lack of procedural safeguards afforded to the paper owner, whose registered title was automatically extinguished (without notification) on the expiration of the twelve-year limitation period.[75] On appeal, the majority of the Grand Chamber, however, was satisfied that adequate procedural safeguards did exist. The paper owners were entitled to take proceedings for possession at any time before expiry of the limitation period and, furthermore, they could challenge proof of the squatter's adverse possession. The LRA 2002 now provides extensive procedural safeguards to protect a registered owner's title against the risk of adverse possession.[76]

4 ARTICLE 8: THE RIGHT TO RESPECT FOR PRIVATE AND FAMILY LIFE

European Convention on Human Rights, Art 8

1. Everyone has the right to respect for his private and family life, his home and his correspondence.

2. There shall be no interference by a public authority with the exercise of this right except such as is in accordance with the law and is necessary in a democratic society in the interests of national security, public safety or the economic well-being of the country, for the prevention of disorder or crime, for the protection of health or morals, or for the protection of the rights and freedoms of others.

The inspiration for Art 8 is drawn from rights to privacy enshrined in other international human rights instruments,[77] although it does not refer explicitly to a right to privacy, but rather to a right to respect. Feldman has noted the implications of this shift in emphasis.

Feldman, *Civil Liberties and Human Rights in England and Wales* (2nd edn, 2002, pp 524–5)

This movement from a right to freedom from interference with privacy to a right to respect for it might seem to weaken the right, as there may be circumstances in which it could be

---

[73] *Hentrich v France* (1994) 18 EHRR 440. See also the Scottish decisions of *Karl Construction Ltd v Palisade Properties Ltd* [2002] SLT 312; *AG for Scotland v Taylor* [2003] SLT 1340; *Maguire v Ito* [2004] SLT (Sheriff Ct) 120.

[74] *AGOSI v UK* (1987) 9 EHRR 1; *Air Canada v UK* (1995) 20 EHRR 150.

[75] See ss 15 and 17, Limitation Act 1980, and s 75 of the Land Registration Act 1925. The same lack of notification also affects unregistered land.

[76] See Chapter 10.

[77] For example, Art 17 of the International Covenant on Civil and Political Rights provides that: 'No one shall be subjected to arbitrary or unlawful interference with his privacy, family and home or correspondence, not to unlawful attacks on his honour and reputation. Everyone has the right to the protection of the law against such interference or attacks.' Article 12 of the Universal Declaration of Human Rights is identical, but is contained in a single paragraph.

argued that interfering with a person's privacy would not indicate a lack of respect. Examples would be interfering with privacy paternalistically, to protect the individual against further loss of autonomy resulting from untreated illness, deficient family management, or poor child rearing practices [...]

This potential limitation on the negative (freedom from interference) aspects of the right to privacy should not blind us to the considerable extension of the right which the notion of respect may entail, and which has been influential in the case law of the Court on Article 8. [...] Furthermore, a right to respect is capable of imposing positive duties on public authorities, because it can be interpreted as requiring them to take active measures to enable people to have a private and family life, going beyond providing remedies for interference.

Our discussion of Art 8 will concentrate on the respect that it affords to the home. At the outset, it should be noted that the Article does not confer a right to a home, nor does it place upon the government an obligation to meet an individual's housing needs.[78] The focus is upon the protection afforded to an individual's existing home. In this context, there are clear interactions between the home, and a person's private and family life. Fox has explored these interactions, in relation to Art 8.

Fox, *Conceptualising Home: Theories, Laws and Policies* (2007, pp 460–1)

It is important to note that the right to respect for the home in Article 8 is clearly embedded in the overall context of Article 8, which is strongly associated with *privacy*. The references in Article 8 to right to respect for family life, for home and for correspondence are often viewed conjunctively, as aspects of the right to private life. [...] Indeed, in *Marchx v Belgium*, Sir Gerald Fitzmaurice stated that; 'the main, if not the sole object and intended sphere of application of Article 8 was that of what I will call the 'domiciliary protection' of the individual'.

[...] While privacy has been recognised as a sub-set of the cluster of values concerned with 'home as territory'—including safety, security, continuity, a sense of belonging, and a sense of 'rootedness' for the occupier—empirical studies have also identified a range of other meanings associated with *home* for occupiers, including home as a financial asset, home as a physical structure, home as identity and home as a socio-cultural unit. Although these other types of 'home' meanings are not *prima facie*, recognised in relation to respect for the *home* in Article 8, it is interesting to bear in mind the importance of 'family' in relation to each of these clusters of value types. The empirical evidence [...] indicated that the desire for security within the home was enhanced by the presence of family, and particularly children; the right to privacy in the home was often linked to views concerning 'family life'; home as identity included not just individual identities but the identity of the family unit; the desire for a good quality house and the impetus to make improvements (especially amongst fathers) were linked to associations with family life; the meaning of home as a financial assets was heightened by the desire to have an asset to pass on to one's children; and family was identified as a significant socio-cultural facet of home.

---

[78] *Chapman v UK* (2001) 33 EHRR 399, at [99].

4.1 WHEN IS ARTICLE 8(1) ENGAGED

4.1.1 Meaning of 'home'

'Home' has an autonomous meaning, being a place of residence with which the individual has *'sufficient and continuing links'*, and is not dependent upon that person having a legal right of occupation. This test was developed by the Strasbourg Court in the case of *Gillow v UK*,[79] and has been consistently applied in subsequent cases by both the Strasbourg Court and the House of Lords.[80]

Harrow LBC v Qazi [2004] 1 AC 983, HL

Facts: Mr Qazi was a tenant, with his wife, of a house owned by the local housing authority. When his wife left him, she terminated their tenancy of the house—a step which she was entitled to take without her husband's knowledge or agreement. Mr Qazi sought a tenancy of the house in his own right, but the housing authority refused, on the grounds that the house was too large for his needs. When Mr Qazi refused to move out, the housing authority successfully took possession proceedings.

Lord Bingham

At [8]–[10]

Not surprisingly, the need for some protection of the home was recognised in the Convention, since few things are more central to the enjoyment of human life than having somewhere to live. On a straightforward reading of the Convention, its use of the expression "home" appears to invite a down-to-earth and pragmatic consideration whether (as Lord Millett put it in *Uratemp Ventures Ltd v Collins* [2002] 1 AC 301, para 31) the place in question is that where a person "lives and to which he returns and which forms the centre of his existence", since "home" is not a legal term of art and article 8 is not directed to the protection of property interests or contractual rights.

[...] Save in one case mentioned below (para 10) this has been the approach of the Strasbourg institutions also. In *Gillow v United Kingdom* (1986) 11 EHRR 335, para 46, the court held that the house in question was the applicants' home because although they had been absent from Guernsey for many years they had not established any other home elsewhere in the United Kingdom and had retained "sufficient continuing links" with the house for it to be considered their home for the purposes of article 8. This test was repeated and elaborated by the commission in *Buckley v United Kingdom* (1996) 23 EHRR 101, 115, para 63:

> "'Home' is an autonomous concept which does not depend on classification under domestic law. Whether or not a particular habitation constitutes a 'home' which attracts the protection of article 8(1) will depend on the factual circumstances, namely, the existence of sufficient and continuous links. The factor of 'unlawfulness' is relevant rather to considerations under paragraph 2 of that provision of 'in accordance with law' and to the balancing exercise undertaken

---

[79] (1986) 11 EHRR 335.
[80] See also *Leeds CC v Price* [2006] UKHL 10, [2006] 2 AC 465, in which gypsies who had moved onto a site for just two days had not established a 'home'.

between the interests of the community and those of the individual in assessing the necessity of any interference."

The commission repeated the substance of this passage in *Mabey v United Kingdom* (1996) 22 EHRR CD 123, 124, and in *O'Rourke v United Kingdom* (Application No 39022/97), 26 June 2001, the court once again insisted on an individual's need to show sufficient and continuing links with a place in order to establish that it is his home for purposes of article 8.

In none of these cases, as Mr Arden for the council correctly submitted, were the facts indistinguishable from those of this case. In some the applicant had a proprietary interest in a house (*Gillow's case*) or land (*Buckley's case*, *Mabey's case*), but could not lawfully live in the house or on the land. In O'Rourke's case the applicant claimed as his home a hotel room which he had occupied for less than a month at the discretion of the proprietors before being evicted: in this case the court had "significant doubts over whether or not the applicant's links with the hotel room were sufficient and continuous enough to make it his 'home' at the time of his eviction". The general approach of the Strasbourg institutions has however been to apply a simple, factual and untechnical test, taking full account of the factual circumstances but very little of legal niceties.

4.1.2 The implications of respect

As Feldman notes, respect has both negative and positive connotations that can encompass a wide variety of actions. Negative protection of the home encompasses protection from government interference, from (for example) police powers of entry and search,[81] or the regulation of land use through compulsory purchase,[82] and planning or residency controls.[83] Positive obligations are also placed upon governments to frame the law in such a way that individuals are at liberty to enjoy their homes and to exercise their chosen way of life.[84]

An example of this positive duty is evident from a series of cases that have challenged environmental pollution.[85] For example, in *Lopez Ostra v Spain*,[86] the siting of a waste treatment plant and its operation without the requisite licence presented a health risk and nuisance to the applicant that breached Art 8. The Spanish government was responsible, because it had authorized and facilitated the construction of the plant close to the applicant's home,[87] and had failed to take steps to ensure that it was operated without causing a nuisance to neighbouring occupiers. Similar challenges to environmental pollution, caused by Heathrow and Gatwick Airports,[88] and road construction in the East End of London,[89] have also constituted an interference with the respect that Art 8(1) affords the home—although, in each case, that interference has been justified under Art 8(2).

---

[81] *Mcleod v UK* (1990) 27 EHRR 493 and *Keegan v UK* [2007] 44 EHRR 33.

[82] *Howard v UK* (1987) 9 EHRR 91.

[83] *Gillow v UK* (1986) 11 EHRR 335 and *Buckley v United Kingdom* (1996) 23 EHRR 101.

[84] *Marckx v Belgium* (1979) 2 EHRR 330. A positive duty may also arise to protect a particularly vulnerable group: see *Connors v UK* (2005) 40 EHRR 9.

[85] *Arrondelle v UK* (1982) 5 EHRR 123; *Hatton v UK* [2003] EHCR 36022/97; *Powell and Ryaner v UK* (1990) 12 EHRR 355; *Khatun v UK* (1998) 26 EHRR CD 212; *Lopez Ostra v Spain* (1994) 20 EHRR 277; *Guerra v Italy* (1998) 26 EHRR 357. A positive duty may also arise to protect a particularly vulnerable group: see *Connors v UK* (2005) 40 EHRR 9.

[86] Ibid.

[87] It was only 12 metres from the applicant's home.

[88] *Hatton v UK* [2003] EHCR 36022/97 and *Powell and Ryaner v UK* (1990) 12 EHRR 355.

[89] *Khatun v UK* (1998) 26 EHRR CD 212.

These cases also demonstrate that governments' responsibilities may extend to the activities of private bodies, where there is a direct and immediate link between a government's duties under Art 8 and the interference.[90] Article 8(2) suggests that the interference must be by a public authority, but a public authority will be taken to have engaged Art 8(1) where it is responsible for the conditions that allow a private body to disturb an individual's enjoyment of his or her home. In the following case, the Grand Chamber made the following observation.

Hatton v UK [2003] EHCR 36022/97

At [98]

Article 8 may apply in environmental cases whether the pollution is directly caused by the State or whether State responsibility arises from the failure properly to regulate private industry. Whether the case is analysed in terms of a positive duty on the State to take reasonable and appropriate measures to secure the applicants' rights under para 1 of art 8 or in terms of an interference by a public authority to be justified in accordance with para 2, the applicable principles are broadly similar.

Although it is clear that the Article is widely framed, the courts have struggled to define the extent to which it protects the sanctity of the home. Their dilemma is evident from a series of decisions raising the question of whether the Article is engaged by possession proceedings brought by a local authority. The tension arises from the interaction between the respect due to the home and the exercise of proprietary rights to possession conferred by the domestic law. We have seen that an occupier need not have a proprietary interest in a property for it to be regarded as his or her home, but that his or her occupation will be precarious if he or she can be dispossessed by the proprietary rights of others. In *Qazi*, the House of Lords was called upon to consider whether or not the exercise of domestic property rights to dispossess an occupier would engage Art 8. The Lords were split on this question. Their initial views are exemplified by the comments of Lord Millett, speaking for the majority, on the one hand, and Lord Steyn, representing the minority, on the other.

Harrow LBC v Qazi [2004] 1 AC 983, HL

Facts: See above. The possession proceedings did not breach Art 8. They were brought in exercise of the local authority's rights as landlord against Mr Qazi, who, as a trespasser, had no right to occupy his home.

Lord Millet

At [100]

It necessarily follows that article 8 was applicable. But it does not follow that it was even arguably infringed. In my opinion article 8 is not ordinarily infringed by enforcing the terms on which the applicant occupies premises as his home. Article 8(1) does not give a right to a home, but

---

[90] *X and Y v Netherlands* (1985) 8 ECRR 235.

only to "respect" for the home. This meaning of "respect" for the home cannot be understood in isolation; it can be understood only if article 8(1) is read together with article 8(2). This forbids interference with the right conferred by article 8(1) except in the circumstances specified. By explaining the circumstances in which there may be lawful interference with the right to "respect", article 8(2) gives meaning to that concept and limits the scope of the article.

Lord Steyn

At [27]

It would be surprising if the views of the majority on the interpretation and application of article 8 of the European Convention of Human Rights, as incorporated into our legal system by the Human Rights Act 1998, withstood European scrutiny. It is contrary to a purposive interpretation of article 8 read against the structure of the Convention. It is inconsistent with the general thrust of the decisions of the European Court of Human Rights, and of the commission. It is contrary to the position adopted by the United Kingdom Government on more than one occasion before the European Court of Human Rights. It does not accord to individuals "the full measure of the [protection] referred to": *Minister of Home Affairs v Fisher* [1980] AC 319, 328. On the contrary, it empties article 8(1) of any or virtually any meaningful content. The basic fallacy in the approach is that it allows domestic notions of title, legal and equitable rights, and interests, to colour the interpretation of article 8(1). The decision of today does not fit into the new landscape created by the Human Rights Act 1998.

As Lord Steyn predicted, the majority was forced to review its approach, as a result of decisions of the Strasbourg Court—in particular, *Connors v UK*[91]—when hearing the conjoined appeals in *Kay; Price*.[92] The House in *Kay; Price* did finally acknowledge that possession proceedings can constitute an interference with the home that engages Art 8(1) even where those proceedings are brought in pursuance of rights conferred by domestic law. The focus of the enquiry is upon whether or not such interference is justified under Art 8(2).

4.2 WHEN IS AN INTERFERENCE JUSTIFIED UNDER ART 8(2)?

Article 8(2) sets out the grounds upon which an interference with the home may be justified. These grounds, in effect, set out the legitimate aims. They are comprehensive and, in many instances, an interference will be justified under one or more grounds. The most common grounds for our purposes are measures that are designed to promote the economic well-being of the country, to protect public safety, or to protect the rights and freedom of others. For example, planning controls and powers of compulsory purchase will often be justified on all three grounds,[93] whilst environmental pollution may be justified to attain national economic goals.[94]

---

[91] (2005) 40 EHRR 9. See also *Blecic v Croatia* (2004) 41 EHRR 185.

[92] [2006] UKHL 10, [2006] 2 AC 465, noted by Bright, 'Article 8 Again in the House of Lords' [2006] Conv 294; Hughes and Davis, 'Human Rights and The Triumph of Property: Marginalisation of the European Convention on Human Rights in Housing Law' [2006] Conv 526.

[93] See,e.g., *Buckley v United Kingdom* (1996) 23 EHRR 101.

[94] See, e.g., *Hatton v UK* [2003] EHCR 36022/97; *Powell and Rayner v UK* (1990) 12 EHRR 355; *Khatun v UK* (1998) 26 EHRR CD 212.

4.2.1 Necessary in a democratic society

The measures taken to achieve one or more of the legitimate aims identified in Art 8(2) must be necessary in a democratic society in order to address a pressing social need. Furthermore, they must be a proportionate response to that need, which strikes a fair balance between the respect due to an individual's home and the necessary social objective. In formulating these needs and the measures to achieve them, the government enjoys a wide margin of appreciation (see section 2.4.2 above).

4.2.2 Justification and local authority possession proceedings

A pressing social need is, without doubt, the provision of adequate housing, in which local housing authorities play a vital and prominent role. It is thus not surprising that local authority possession proceedings have come under scrutiny in recent years on human rights grounds.

These cases fall into two broad groups. The first group is that in which the local authority has recovered possession from a licensee following the termination of his or her licence.[95] Gypsies, evicted by the local authority from their mobile home sites, brought a number of these cases when their status as a vulnerable cultural group called for special consideration.[96]

The second group relates to cases in which one joint tenant has served a notice terminating his or her periodic tenancy without the knowledge or consent of his or her fellow joint tenant.[97]

In both groups, the licensee/tenant had become a trespasser, with no legal right to remain, as a result of the local authority's exercise of its common law, rather than statutory, powers, which nevertheless were exercised in pursuance of its obligation to regulate housing provision, either of rental accommodation or mobile home sites.

It should be noted that reliance on these common law grounds forms only a small portion of a local authority's claims to possession. In most cases, the local authority will be seeking possession of secure tenancies on statutory grounds, when it must satisfy the court that the requisite grounds for possession exist, and, furthermore, that it is reasonable to make a possession order and/or that suitable alternative accommodation is available.[98] These latter cases are not thought to raise human rights difficulties.

When focusing upon the justification formula under Art 8(2), we need to apply Goymour's 'three parts' to a claim—namely, the law upon which the claim is based, the decision to make the claim, and the procedure adopted.[99] The first and third elements are susceptible to a human rights challenge. The second element may form the basis for judicial review of the local authority's decision to evict the tenant/licensee. Both *Connors* and *MacCann* failed the justification formula on procedural grounds—that is, the third element (see section 2.4.3)—and so it is to the first and second elements that we must now turn. Before doing so, it is also

---

[95] *Connors v UK* (2005) 40 EHRR 9; *Kay v Lambeth LBC*; *Leeds CC v Price* [2006] UKHL 10, [2006] 2 AC 465; *Birmingham CC v Doherty* [2008] UKHL 57, [2008] 3 WLR 636.

[96] *Connnors v UK*, ibid; *Leeds CC v Price*, ibid; *Birmingham CC v Doherty*, ibid.

[97] *Qazi v Harrow LBC* [2003] UKHL 43, [2004] 1 AC 983; *McCann v UK* (2008) 47 EHRR 40, considering the incompatibility of *Hammersmith and Fulham LBC v Monk* [1992] 1 AC 478.

[98] See s 84, Housing Act 1985.

[99] See section 2.4.3 above.

important to appreciate that possession proceedings are a common feature of county court work, and it is clear that the Lords were concerned to ensure that such proceedings did not become time-consuming or unworkable.

In *Kay; Price*, the House of Lords was called upon to consider whether the domestic law governing a local authority's rights to recover possession will always constitute a justified interference with the respect due to the occupant's home. Unfortunately, their Lordships did not speak with one voice, although their decision was unanimous that, in exceptional circumstances, the domestic law *could* be challenged as an unjustified interference with the respect due to an individual's home. Their views diverged, however, on what matters could constitute exceptional circumstances. The majority (Lords Hope, Scott, and Brown, and Baroness Hale) maintained that the exceptional circumstances must relate to the law itself,[100] but the minority (Lords Bingham, Nicholls, and Walker) were prepared to accept that the application of that law to an individual's personal circumstances could also be considered. Thus, whilst the definition of 'home' is not dependent on any proprietary right to occupy, any justification for an occupier to remain in his or her home is likely to turn solely upon proprietary rights and the procedure by which they are exercised. The status of an occupier who has no proprietary rights is precarious, unless, perhaps, he or she can claim that, as a member of a vulnerable group, the government has a positive duty to protect his or her home and way of life, which the current law fails adequately to address. Baroness Hale summarized the issues upon which their Lordships agreed and disagreed.[101]

Kay v Lambeth LBC; Leeds CC v Price [2006] 2 AC 465, HL

Facts:

(1) *Kay v Lambeth LBC* The case concerned the last instalment of the *Bruton* litigation (see Chapter 23). In response to the House of Lords' decision in *Bruton v London & Quadrant Housing Trust*,[102] the local authority terminated the licence that it had granted to Quadrant and replaced it with a lease. It then terminated the lease to Quadrant and began possession proceedings against the occupiers. The occupiers, including Kay, claimed that the proceedings breached Art 8, but the Lords were of the view that the possession proceedings were justified under Art 8(2), there being no exceptional circumstances to upset the fair balance achieved by the relevant housing legislation.

(2) *Leeds v Price* The Prices were gypsies who, without permission, had moved onto a recreation ground owned by Leeds CC. The council brought possession proceedings after only a few days. The Prices claimed that the respect for their home was breached under Art 8, but they failed to establish that the recreation ground was their home, because they had only been there a short time.

---

[100] See also *Ofulue v Bossert* [2008] EWCA Civ 7, [2008] HRLR 20, noted at Dixon [2008] Conv 160, in the context of Art 1 of the First Protocol.

[101] See also *Birmingham CC v Doherty* [2006] EWCA Civ 1739, in which the Court of Appeal also summarized their Lordships' differing views.

[102] [2000] 1 AC 406.

Baroness Hale

At [179]–[183]

[...] if the ratio decidendi of the majority's decision [in *Harrow LBC v Qazi*] was that the enforcement of a right to possession in accordance with the domestic law of property can *never* be incompatible with that right, then it must now be modified in the light of the decision of the European Court of Human Rights in *Connors v United Kingdom*. There both the local authority and the court had acted entirely in accordance with the domestic law but the United Kingdom was nevertheless held to have acted in breach of article 8.

Secondly, however, we are all agreed that in the vast majority of cases, the right of a public landowner to enforce a claim to possession of his own land in accordance with the relevant domestic law would automatically supply the justification required by article 8(2) for an interference with the occupier's right to respect for his home. By definition, it would be "in accordance with the law"; it would serve the legitimate aim of protecting the property rights of the landowner and in some cases the rights of neighbouring occupiers; and it would be proportionate to that aim, the proper balance between the competing rights having been struck by Parliament: see Lord Bingham, at paras 35, 36. If that is so, in most cases, granting a possession order in accordance with the domestic law would be the only means available of protecting the right which the landowner wished to assert, and thus could not be disproportionate in the individual case.

Thirdly, we are all agreed that there can be no question of requiring the public landowner to plead and prove individual justification for that interference in every case: see Lord Bingham, at para 29 [...]

[...] This is because the court is entitled to make two assumptions. The first is that the domestic law has struck the right balance between the competing interests involved: those of a person occupying premises as his home and those of the landowner seeking to regain possession of those premises in accordance with the law. The second is that the landowner, if a public authority, has acted compatibly with the Convention rights of the individual occupier in deciding to enforce its proprietary rights.

Hence it is only if the occupier advances grounds for challenging either or both of those assumptions that there need be any modification to present practice [...]

At [185]–[192]

My Lords, we are all agreed that it must be possible for the defendant in a possession action to claim that the balance between respect for his home and the property rights of the owner, struck by the general law in the type of case of which his is an example, does not comply with the Convention. We also agree that the cases in which such a claim will have a real prospect of success are rare. This is an area of the law much trampled over by the legislature as it has tried to respond to shifting and conflicting social and economic pressures. If there were enough suitable and affordable housing to share amongst those who needed it there would be no problem. But there is not, so priorities have to be established, either by Parliament or by the public sector landlord, who has to allocate this scarce resource in accordance with the priorities set by Parliament.

The balance has changed over time in accordance with what were perceived to be the needs of the time. Once upon a time, it was thought necessary to control the freedom of private landlords to let for such terms and on such rents as the market allowed. Public sector landlords, on the other hand, could be left to manage the public housing stock in a responsible manner. Then things changed. Controls over private landlords were progressively relaxed, although never abandoned, with a view to expanding the supply of privately rented homes.

Controls over public sector landlords, on the other hand, were increased and public sector tenants were given the security which previously only private sector tenants had enjoyed. This and other measures reduced the supply of public sector rented homes. These were all intensely political judgments. The extent to which, and the terms on which, public authorities should be engaged in providing housing for those who for whatever reason cannot or will not buy it on the private market was one of the most politically controversial issues of the 20th century.

To the extent that a court insists that a public authority does not rely upon its right to evict an occupier, it is obliging that public authority to continue to supply that person with a home in circumstances where Parliament has not obliged (and may not even have empowered) it to do so. In this politically contentious area of social and economic policy, any court should think long and hard before intervening in the balance currently struck by the elected legislature. There may be more scope for argument in a case not covered by statute, but the most obvious example of that is a trespasser who has never had any right to occupy the premises in question.

We are also agreed as to the procedural route whereby a challenge to the general law may be made. The Human Rights Act 1998, section 7(1), provides that a person who wishes to rely upon his Convention rights may do so either in a freestanding action or by defending an action brought against him by a public authority. In those very rare cases where a person may be evicted from his home without any court order at all, a challenge would have to raised by way of a freestanding action or judicial review. Otherwise, a defence can be raised in the possession action itself. However, the county court will not always be able to supply a remedy. In some cases the statute under which it is operating may be sufficiently flexible to enable the argument to be accommodated. But in many others, it will not. The very source of the complaint of incompatibility will be the inflexibility of the statutory scheme, leaving no discretion to the county court. The court will then have to decide whether the interpretative obligation in section 3 of the 1998 Act will enable it to solve the problem. If not, the matter could only be resolved by a declaration of incompatibility in the High Court, which would have no effect upon the outcome of the individual case.

Thus far I believe that we are all agreed. But, as I understand it, some of your Lordships would go further and accept that there may be highly exceptional cases in which the occupier could argue that his individual personal circumstances made the application of the general law disproportionate in his case. When, if at all, should the court be able to say that, even though there is no obligation to continue to provide housing in these circumstances, it is not "necessary in a democratic society" to permit the landowner to assert its property rights?

My Lords, I myself do not think that the purpose of article 8 was to oblige a social landlord to continue to supply housing to a person who has no right in domestic law to continue to be supplied with that housing, assuming that the general balance struck by domestic law was not amenable to attack and that the authority's decision to invoke that law was not open to judicial review on conventional grounds. It should not be forgotten that in an appropriate case, the range of considerations which any public authority should take into account in deciding whether to invoke its powers can be very wide [...]

There is no doubt that article 8 entails both negative obligations-not to interfere-and positive obligations-to secure the right to respect for a person's private and family life, his home and his correspondence. But it does not confer any right to health or welfare benefits or to housing. The extent to which any member state assumes responsibility for supplying these is very much a matter for that member state. In this country, housing law defines the extent of the obligation and the power to provide housing at public expense. Social services law defines the extent of the obligation to provide services (which sometimes includes assistance with housing) for vulnerable people, such as children, the elderly, the sick and the disabled. If social services law does not provide assistance to an occupier whose personal circumstances are said to make eviction from this particular accommodation disproportionate, then I question whether housing law should be made to do so. In an appropriate case, it is incumbent upon the housing authority to liaise with the social services and education authorities before deciding to take action. There is nothing in the jurisprudence to indicate that article 8 requires more of them than is already required.

The Convention began life as a code of individual civil and political rights, not a code of social and economic rights. The distinction between the two is not clear cut, particularly in the context of article 8. But to refuse to allow a landowner to recover possession of the dwelling to which he is entitled is to impose upon him a positive obligation to continue to make those premises available to the occupier. There might be more scope for argument where the claim lies in common law unregulated by legislation, but in such cases the landowner is likely to be a private person, upon whom no such positive obligation could be laid, or the occupiers are likely to be squatters who have never had a right to occupy the premises.

Given their reluctant acceptance that possession proceedings may be susceptible to a human rights challenge in exceptional circumstances (whatever that may encompass), the Lords went on to consider how possession proceedings should accommodate that possibility. The public authority (as landlord) is not required to plead that its claim to possession is justifiable; it is for the occupier to raise the Art 8 challenge in his or her defence to possession proceedings or, where he or she has already been evicted, by a free-standing action.

Kay v Lambeth LBC; Leeds CC v Price [2006] 2 AC 465, HL

Lord Bingham

At [29]

[. . .] I do not accept, as the appellants argued, that the public authority must from the outset plead and prove that the possession order sought is justified. That would in the overwhelming majority of cases, be burdensome and futile. It is enough for the public authority to assert its claim in accordance with domestic property law. If the occupier wishes to raise an article 8 defence to prevent or defer the making of a possession order it is for him to do so and the public authority must rebut the claim, if and to the extent that, it is called upon to do so. In the overwhelming majority of cases this will be in no way burdensome. In rare and exceptional cases it will not be futile.

If the county court is unable to interpret the law in a manner that is ECHR-compliant, the proceedings will have to be adjourned so that compatibility can be dealt with by the High Court. The occupier might also, by way of defence to possession proceedings, question, by way of judicial review, the local authority's decision to institute possession proceedings as an improper exercise of its administrative powers.[103] Lord Hope, reflecting the majority view of exceptional circumstances, explained these two 'gateways'.

---

[103] For example, because of procedural irregularity, or because it was a decision that no reasonable person would justify: see *Wandsworth LBC v Winder* [1985] AC 461. The Court of Appeal considered the interaction

Kay v Lambeth LBC; Leeds CC v Price [2006] 2 AC 465, HL

Lord Hope

At [110]

[...] if the requirements of the law have been established and the right to recover possession is unqualified, the only situations in which it would be open to the court to refrain from
proceeding to summary judgment and making the possession order are these: (a) if a seriously arguable point is raised that the law which enables the court to make the possession
order is incompatible with article 8, the county court in the exercise of its jurisdiction under
the Human Rights Act 1998 should deal with the argument in one or other of two ways:
(i) by giving effect to the law, so far as it is possible for it do so under section 3, in a way that
is compatible with article 8, or (ii) by adjourning the proceedings to enable the compatibility
issue to be dealt with in the High Court; (b) if the defendant wishes to challenge the decision
of a public authority to recover possession as an improper exercise of its powers at common
law on the ground that it was a decision that no reasonable person would consider justifiable,
he should be permitted to do this provided again that the point is seriously arguable.

The House of Lords was called upon to revisit its decision in *Kay; Price* in the following case,
during the hearing of which the Strasbourg Court handed down its ruling in *McCann v UK*.
Their Lordships did not depart materially from their decision in *Kay; Price*; instead, they
endeavoured to clarify the two gateways outlined by Lord Hope in that case.

Birmingham CC v Doherty [2008] 3 WLR 636, HL

Facts: The Doherty family were gypsies who had lived at the same caravan site for seven-
teen years. The council wished to improve the site and to make it available for use as
temporary accommodation for travellers. It thus needed vacant possession of the site
and served notice upon the Doherty family, terminating their licence to occupy. Statute
afforded the Doherty family no protection, although had they had been in occupation of
a privately owned site, they would have been entitled to a measure of protection. During
the course of the hearing, this anomaly was removed by legislation. The Doherty family
successfully argued that their eviction would be incompatible with their rights under
Art 8, but that did not, in the light of s 6(2)(b) of the HRA 1998 and the amending legislation, overcome the possession order that had been made against them. Instead, it was
possible that the local authority's decision to evict them might be susceptible to judicial
review and that the case would be returned to the county court to that end.

Lord Hope

At [46]

Gateway (a) is divided into two parts. Part (i) envisages that it may be possible for the court
to give effect to the law in a way that is compatible with the Convention right by making use

---

between the human rights and administrative law challenges to a local authority's possession proceedings
in *Birmingham CC v Doherty* [2006] EWCA Civ 1739.

of the interpretative obligation in section 3 of the 1998 Act. But this may not be possible, and the court then comes face to face with the fact that it is a public authority: section 6(3)(a). It is unlawful for it to act in a way which is incompatible with the Convention right: section 6(1). Legislation which cannot be read or given effect in a way which is compatible with the Convention right must nevertheless be enforced, as Parliamentary sovereignty requires this. Giving effect to a decision to do what the legislation authorises will not be an unlawful act within the meaning of section 6(1): see section 6(2)(b). Part (ii) recognises that, if effect must be given to legislation which is incompatible with a Convention right, consideration should be given, in the public interest, to the making of a remedial order under section 10. A county court is not among the courts listed in section 4(5) which may make a declaration of incompatibility under section 4(2). So, unless gateway (b) provides a solution, the proper course for a county court judge in the situation that section 6(2)(b) refers to will be to adjourn the proceedings to enable the issue of incompatibility to be dealt with in the High Court which has that power. If part (ii) applies and no solution is available under gateway (b), the court will be unable to refrain from making a possession order. That is the effect of section 6(2)(b). But a declaration by a High Court judge under section 4 will enable the minister to consider taking remedial action to avoid the incompatibility in future cases.

The court is thus required to order possession even though the law is found to be incompatible. This apparently inconsistent result stems from the operation of the HRA 1998. To preserve the sovereignty of Parliament, the courts can only assess the compatibility of the law; they cannot, unlike constitutional courts in other jurisdictions, amend it. The Lords tried to find a way through the maze of the Act by using gateway (b) and the possibility of judicial review of the local authority's decision to instigate possession proceedings. But what they failed to clarify was whether judicial review should be confined to conventional grounds based upon the *Wednesday* test—namely, was the decision one that no authority acting reasonably could have reached,[104] or could wider grounds be considered (in particular, the proportionality of the decision in human rights terms). For example, Lord Walker observed that a local authority's '*decision-making process leading up to the commencement of proceedings ought to be Convention-compliant*',[105] but it is Lord Mance who identifies this distinction more fully.

Birmingham CC v Doherty [2008] 3 WLR 636, HL

Lord Mance

At [133]–[135]

Gateway (b), as expressed in para 110 in *Kay*, was, as I see it, phrased so as to exclude any direct application of the Convention rights or of the Strasbourg court's test of proportionality, and to confine attention to common law grounds for judicial review, informed though they may increasingly be by ideas of fundamental rights: see also per Baroness Hale of Richmond, at para 190, and Lord Brown of Eaton-under-Heywood, at paras 208–211, and contrast the approach of the minority as set out in para 39 of Lord Bingham of Cornhill's speech in *Kay*.

---

[104] See, e.g., *Wandsworth LBC v Winder* [1985] AC 461.
[105] At [121]. Lord Mance is a particular advocate of wider grounds for judicial review: see [154] and [161]–[164].

The general distinction which thus emerges is recognised and described in *R (Daly) v Secretary of State for the Home Department* [2001] 2 AC 532, per Lord Steyn, at para 27, and Lord Cooke of Thorndon, at para 32, recognising though regretting the distinction, and in *R (Association of British Civilian Internees: Far East Region) v Secretary of State for Defence* [2003] QB 1397, paras 32–37, where Dyson LJ, giving the judgment of the Court of Appeal, said that any abandonment of the common law's Wednesbury unreasonableness test for a proportionality test was a step which could only be taken by this House. Other potential differences between conventional (or "domestic") judicial review were discussed in *R (SB) v Governors of Denbigh High School* [2007] 1 AC 100 (see in particular per Lord Hoffmann, at para 68) and *Belfast City Council v Miss Behavin' Ltd* [2007] 1 WLR 1420.

The difference in approach between the grounds of conventional or domestic judicial review and review for compatibility with Human Rights Convention rights should not however be exaggerated and can be seen to have narrowed, with "the 'Wednesbury' test [...] moving closer to proportionality [so that] in some cases it is not possible to see any daylight between the two tests": *R (Association of British Civilian Internees: Far East Region) v Secretary of State for Defence*, para 34, citing an extra-judicial lecture by Lord Hoffmann. The common law has been increasingly ready to identify certain basic rights in respect of which "the most anxious" scrutiny is appropriate: see *R v Secretary of State for the Home Department, Ex p Bugdaycay* [1987] AC 514, 531, per Lord Bridge of Harwich, quoted in *R v Ministry of Defence, Ex p Smith* [1996] QB 517, 554–555; and see *R v Secretary of State for Education and Employment, Ex p Begbie* [2000] 1 WLR 1115, 1130 B–C, per Laws LJ: "the Wednesbury principle itself constitutes a sliding scale of review, more or less intrusive according to the nature and gravity of what is at stake." My noble and learned friends Lord Hope and Lord Walker draw on this theme in paras 55 and 108 to 109 of their speeches. Even so, as the subsequent history of *Ex p Smith* demonstrates, the result may not always achieve the degree of protection for Convention rights which the Strasbourg court requires: *Smith v United Kingdom* (1999) 29 EHRR 493. So there remains room in another case to reconsider how far conventional or domestic judicial review and Convention review can be further assimilated, and in particular whether proportionality has a role in conventional judicial review. This was not, however, argued on the present appeal, and, in common I understand with the majority of your Lordships, I do not consider that it is appropriate to embark on such a review on this appeal.

It is evident that some of their Lordships in *Doherty* felt in a dilemma.[106] A panel of five Law Lords heard *Doherty*, whereas a panel of seven heard *Kay; Price*. The Lords in the former thus felt unable to overrule the latter.[107] They were left to present a workable solution to the 'exceptional case' in which the law failed to achieve a compliant solution.

It is unlikely that this is an end to the problem of Art 8 and possession proceedings, whether brought a local authority or, perhaps, even a private landlord, or by a creditor enforcing a security interest over the home. In these latter instances, judicial review will have no part to play.

4.2.3 The overlap between Art 1 of the First Protocol and Art 8

It is not uncommon for a victim to allege a breach of both Art 1 of the First Protocol and Art 8 where the possession of which they are deprived is their home. It is clear that the

---

106 See Lord Walker, who had been in the minority in *Kay; Price*, at [107]–[108], and Lord Mance, who did not sit in *Kay; Price*, at [162]–[164]. Lords Hope and Scott, who had been in the majority in *Kay; Price*, did not express similar doubts. Lord Rogers delivered a judgment concurring with Lords Hope and Walker.

107 A panel of nine would have been required to overrule the decision in *Kay; Price*.

protections afford by the two Articles do overlap and an interference may be justified on similar grounds, although it has been observed that general and public interest justifications found in Art 1 may allow the State a wider margin of appreciation than the legitimate aims contained Art 8(2).[108] The difference is unlikely to be material given the flexibility of action that each contemplates.

The application of the justification formula under both Articles is also similar, with the need in each case being to achieve the fair balance demands of proportionality, including procedural fairness. The issue of compensation is perhaps a point of departure. The defining role that compensation plays in the fair balance test under the second limb of Art 1 is not as evident under Art 8; rather, compensation is a factor to be brought into the balance.

5   ARTICLE 14: FREEDOM FROM DISCRIMINATION

European Convention on Human Rights, Art 14

The enjoyment of the rights and freedoms set forth in this Convention shall be secured without discrimination on any ground such as sex, race, colour, language, religion, political or other opinion, national or social origin, association with a national minority, property birth or other status.

The target of Art 14 is discrimination, but the Article does not provide a free-standing protection against discrimination.[109] Its operation is directed against discrimination in the enjoyment of the other rights protected by the ECHR. It is said to be parasitic in nature. It is thus necessary for another Article (the 'host Article') to be engaged before Art 14 can be considered. If the breach of the host Article is proved, the court will often not progress to consider whether or not Art 14 has been infringed.[110] But if there is no breach of the host Article, the court may go on to consider whether or not there has been a breach of Art 14: for example, because the justification for engagement of the host Article operates in a discriminatory fashion. In this sense, Art 14 is said to be autonomous and can provide an effective weapon that belies its parasitic nature.

Baroness Hale, in the following case, outlined the issues to be established under Art 14.

Ghaidan v Godin-Mendoza [2004] 2 AC 557, HL

Facts: Mr Godin-Mendoza lived in a stable, homosexual relationship. When his partner died, the landlord of the flat that they had shared together wished to repossess the flat. In defence to these proceedings, Mr Godin-Mendoza claimed to be entitled to succeed to the tenancy under the Rent Act 1977 as '*a person who was living with the original tenant as his or her wife or husband*'. He successfully established that Art 8 was engaged and, to

---

[108] *Gillow v UK* (1989) 11 EHRR 335.

[109] The Twelfth Protocol of the ECHR includes a free-standing right against discrimination, but the Protocol has not been signed or ratified by the United Kingdom.

[110] See *Connors v UK* (2005) 40 EHRR 9, although the House of Lords in *Kay; Price* noted the discriminatory treatment of occupiers evicted from local authority and privately owned travellers' sites—a distinction that has now been removed from the legislation.

avoid a breach of Art 14, the appropriate provisions of the Rent Act 1977 should be read to include homosexual partners.

Baroness Hale

At [133] and [134]

It is common ground that five questions arise in an article 14 inquiry [. . .] The original four questions were: (i) Do the facts fall within the ambit of one or more of the Convention rights? (ii) Was there a difference in treatment in respect of that right between the complainant and others put forward for comparison? (iii) Were those others in an analogous situation? (iv) Was the difference in treatment objectively justifiable? i.e, did it have a legitimate aim and bear a reasonable relationship of proportionality to that aim?

The additional question is whether the difference in treatment is based on one or more of the grounds proscribed-whether expressly or by inference-in article 14. The appellant argued that that question should be asked after question (iv), the respondent that it should be asked after question (ii). In my view, the [. . .] questions are a useful tool of analysis but there is a considerable overlap between them: in particular between whether the situations to be compared were truly analogous, whether the difference in treatment was based on a pro-scribed ground and whether it had an objective justification. If the situations were not truly analogous it may be easier to conclude that the difference was based on something other than a proscribed ground. The reasons why their situations are analogous but their treatment different will be relevant to whether the treatment is objectively justified. A rigidly formulaic approach is to be avoided.

The victim must thus establish that he or she was treated differently from another person who is in an analogous position. For example, Mr Godin-Mendoza was able to prove that he would be treated differently from a heterosexual partner. The victim must then prove that his or her discriminatory treatment was not reasonably and objectively justifiable: not only must the discrimination be based upon unacceptable grounds, of which the Article provides a non-exhaustive list, but it must also be unjustified, following the process that we have already examined. For example, in *James v UK*,[111] the enfranchisement legislation under review applied only to certain landlords, but was not discriminatory under Art 14 because it met a pressing social need and, in so doing, provided a proportionate response.

6 ARTICLE 6(1): THE RIGHT TO A FAIR TRIAL

European Convention on Human Rights, Art 6(1)

In the determination of his civil rights and obligations or of any criminal charge against him, everyone is entitled to a fair and public hearing within a reasonable time by an independent and impartial tribunal established by law. Judgement shall be pronounced publicly but the press and public may be excluded from all or part of the trial in the interest of morals, public order or national security in a democratic society where the interests of juveniles or the protection of private life of the parties so require, or to the extent strictly necessary in

---

111 See also *Chassagnou v France* (2000) 29 EHRR 615.

the opinion of the court in the special circumstances where publicity would prejudice the interests of justice.

Article 6(1) demands due process in the determination of civil rights and obligations, including proprietary rights and duties. That process requires a timely, fair, and public hearing before an independent and impartial tribunal. We have already seen a concern for proper procedural guarantees inherent in the assessment of whether or not a fair balance has been struck to justify an infringement of either Art 1 of the First Protocol or Art 8. Article 6(1) provides a further procedural guarantee, but, this time, where there is a dispute in which a person's civil rights and obligations are determined.

6.1 CIVIL RIGHTS AND OBLIGATIONS

A 'civil right' is an autonomous concept, which is defined by the Strasbourg jurisprudence rather than domestic law. A civil right equates to a right defined by private, rather than public, law: it thus includes, for example, property rights in land and personal rights to use land.[112] There must, however, be a right recognized by the domestic law in the first place, because Art 6(1) relates to proceedings that determine substantive rights. For example, in the following case, the void credit agreement never conferred a right upon First County in the first place, so Art 6 had no role to play.[113]

Wilson v First County Trust Ltd [2004] 1 AC 816, HL

Lord Nicholls

At [33]

For present purposes it is sufficient to note that the established case law of the European Court of Human Rights is to the effect that article 6(1) does not itself guarantee any particular content for civil rights and obligations. [Article] 6(1) applies only to disputes over what, at least arguably, are recognised under domestic law to be "rights and obligations" see Z v UK [2001] 2 FLR 612, 634 at para 87. Article 6(1) may not be used as a means of creating a substantive civil right having no basis in national law. The content of the substantive national law may call for scrutiny under other articles of the Convention or its Protocols, but that is not a target of article 6(1).

The distinction between public and private rights, although fundamental to Art 6(1), is not always easy to draw. For example, a private individual's interaction with a public authority will not necessarily be regarded as a matter of public law and thus will be outside the scope of Art 6(1). It is necessary to look to the character of the particular right. A measure within the administrative control of a public authority may nevertheless affect the exercise of private rights. For example, planning controls will determine whether or not an owner is able

---

112 The scope of Art 6(1) is, of course, much wider.
113 See also *Powell and Rayner v UK* (1990) 12 EHRR 355, in which the applicants were deprived by statute of any claim in nuisance against the Civil Aviation Authority by s 76(1) of Civil Aviation Act 1982. They thus had no right to be determined.

to exercise his or her private rights of ownership by building on the land. It is thus said to be 'decisive' of private law rights and subject to Art 6(1).[114] The expropriation of land by a public authority, and any compensation payable as a result, are also clearly matters that are decisive of private law rights, and thus fall to be determined in a manner required by Art 6(1).[115]

Lord Clyde, referring to the established Strasbourg jurisprudence, described the distinction in the following case.

Regina (Alconbury Developments Ltd) v Secretary of State for the Environment, Transport and the Regions [2003] 2 AC 295, HL

Facts: The development of Alconbury Airfield, near Huntingdon, ran into planning difficulties when the local planning authority refused permission. Given the national importance of the development, it was called in for decision by the Secretary of State. Local protestors objected on the ground that the decision made by the Secretary of State contravened Art 6(1). They successfully argued that the planning decision by the Secretary of State, although administrative in nature, did affect Alconbury's civil rights and thus engaged Art 6(1). Although an independent and impartial tribunal clearly did not make the decision of the Secretary of State, however, the availability of judicial review to question his or her decision was sufficient to satisfy Art 6(1).

Lord Clyde

At [147]

In considering the scope of article 6(1) it is proper to take a broad approach to the language used and seek to give effect to the purpose of the provision. In *Ringeisen v Austria (No 1)* (1971) 1 EHRR 455, para 94 the phrase was taken to cover "all proceedings the result of which is decisive for private rights and obligations". This included cases where the proceedings concerned a dispute between a private individual and a public authority [...]

The scope of article 6 accordingly extends to administrative determinations as well as judicial determinations [...] the article also requires that the determination should be of a person's civil rights and obligations. The concept of civil rights in article 6(1) is an autonomous one: *König v Federal Republic of Germany* (1978) 2 EHRR 170. In *H v France* (1989) 12 EHRR 74, para 47 the court stated: "It is clear from the court's established case law that the concept of ' civil rights and obligations' is not to be interpreted solely by reference to the respondent state's domestic law and that article 6(1) applies irrespective of the parties' status, be it public or private, and of the nature of the legislation which governs the manner in which the dispute is to be determined; it is sufficient that the outcome of the proceedings should be 'decisive for private rights and obligations'."

It relates to rights and obligations "which can be said, at least on arguable grounds, to be recognised under domestic law": *James v United Kingdom* (1986) 8 EHRR 123, para 81. The rights with which the present appeals are concerned are the rights of property which are affected by development or acquisition. Those clearly fall within the scope of "civil rights".

---

[114] *Bryan v UK* (1995) 21 EHRR 342.
[115] *Sporrong and Lonnroth v Sweden* (1982) 5 EHRR 35 and *Holy Monasteries v Greece* (1994) 20 EHRR 1.

6.2 A FAIR HEARING

Article 6(1) requires proprietary rights to be determined by a hearing before an independent and impartial tribunal at which the parties have an opportunity to state their case, having access to all relevant information. That hearing must be held within a reasonable time and it is anticipated that it will take place, and the judgment be given, in public, unless the exceptions set out in the Article are satisfied. These requirements will be met where the proceedings take place before a court, but a number of self-help remedies will fall short of these requirements. For example, a landlord's exercise of a right of re-entry, or right to seize the tenant's possessions by way of distress for unpaid rent, will not do so where the landlord is able to exercise these rights without seeking the assistance of the court.[116]

The entire course of proceedings, including any right of appeal, will be considered when assessing compliance with the above requirements. Thus, the fact that a body that is neither independent nor impartial initially decides a matter will not necessarily be fatal where there is an adequate right of appeal to a court that is independent and impartial. That right of appeal may be sufficient even though it is limited (for example, to points of law), provided that, taken as a whole, the proceedings satisfy the requirements of fairness.[117] Where the administrative decision of a public authority is the subject of scrutiny, the availability of judicial review may be sufficient even though the court is unable to consider the merits of the case, but is merely able to consider the legality and reasonableness of the administrative decision.

R (Alconbury Developments Ltd) v Secretary of State for the Environment, Transport and the Regions [2003] 2 AC 295, HL

Lord Clyde

At [152]

The first point to be noticed here, however, is that the opening phrase in article 6(1), "in the determination", refers not only to the particular process of the making of the decision but extends more widely to the whole process which leads up to the final resolution. In *Zumtobel v Austria* (1993) 17 EHRR 116, para 64 the Commission under reference to *Ettl v Austria* (1987) 10 EHRR 255, paras 77 et seq, recalled that:

> "article 6(1) of the Convention does not require that the procedure which determines civil rights and obligations is conducted at each of its stages before tribunals meeting the requirements of this provision. An administrative procedure may thus precede the determination of civil rights by the tribunal envisaged in article 6(1) of the Convention."

It is possible that in some circumstances a breach in one respect can be overcome by the existence of a sufficient opportunity for appeal or review. While the failure to give reasons for a decision may in the context of some cases constitute a breach of the article, the existence of a right of appeal may provide a remedy in enabling a reasoned decision eventually to be given and so result in an overall compliance with the article [...] In the civil context the whole process must be considered to see if the article has been breached. Not every stage need comply. If a global view is adopted one may then take into account not only the

---

[116] See Chapter 25.
[117] *IKSCON v UK* (App No 20490/92) and *Bryan v UK* (1995) 21 EHRR 342.

eventual opportunity for appeal or review to a court of law, but also the earlier processes and in particular the process of public inquiry at which essentially the facts can be explored in a quasi-judicial procedure and a determination on factual matters achieved.

At [153]

Next, account has to be taken of the context and circumstances of the decision. [...]

In the first place consideration has to be given to the expression "full jurisdiction". At first sight the expression might seem to require in every case an exhaustive and comprehensive review of the decision including a thorough review of the facts as well as the law. If that were so a remedy by way of a statutory appeal or an application to the supervisory jurisdiction of the courts in judicial review would be inadequate. But it is evident that this is not a correct understanding of the expression. Full jurisdiction means a full jurisdiction in the context of the case. As Mr N Bratza stated in his concurring opinion in the decision of the Commission in *Bryan v United Kingdom* (1995) 21 EHRR 342, 354:

> "It appears to me that the requirement that a court or tribunal should have 'full jurisdiction' cannot be mechanically applied with the result that, in all circumstances and whatever the subject matter of the dispute, the court or tribunal must have full power to substitute its own findings of fact, and its own inferences from those facts, for that of the administrative authority concerned."

The nature and circumstances of the case have accordingly to be considered before one can determine what may comprise a "full jurisdiction".

7 THE IMPACT OF HUMAN RIGHTS

The crucial question is to what extent the HRA 1998 will impact on proprietary rights. The House of Lords has been tussling with these issues for almost a decade and is cautiously inching its way forward. But the Lords have often expressed different opinions and so the way is not yet clear.[118]

Allen suggests two possibilities: either there will be little change, because human rights values are already embedded in our fundamental proprietary principles, or there will be a greater impact through the influence of an alternative process of balancing competing proprietary interests, and, possibly, also a further basis on which to claim rights affecting property.

Allen, *Property and The Human Rights Act 1998* (2005, p 250)

This leaves the central question open: what are the values that may affect the development of substantive principles of the private law of property? In the discussion on the applicability of P1(1) [Art 1 of the First Protocol] and other Convention rights, it was said that human autonomy and dignity are values in both human rights law and private law, Similarly, both human rights and private law often require a balance to be struck between competing interests.

---

[118] This lack of unanimity has drawn criticism from the lower courts: see *Birmingham CC v Doherty* [2006] EWCA Civ 1739, at [62]–[65].

However, if the values only take effect at a very high level of generality, alongside other private law values such as certainty, fairness and the like, the effect of human rights law is unlikely to be significant. It may add a new rhetorical dimension to the reasoning in private law cases, but without changing the outcome. But once values are identified at a high level of generality, it should be possible to move to two more specific aspects relating to the development of private law doctrines where human rights law may prove significant (and is already proving significant). The first relates to the nature of the balancing process, and the second to the interest which private law seeks to protect.

The alternative balancing process to which Allen refers is found in the elements that we have examined in the justification formula and, in particular, the fair balance upon which proportionality depends. Fox has described the human rights framework as offering 'a useful lens',[119] whilst Gray and Gray have offered the analogy of a 'prism'[120] through which compliant legislation must pass. We have seen that the courts have identified that, when assessing the compatibility of legislation, they are engaged in a 'new role',[121] which calls upon them to consider policy to greater extent than has previously been required. Although the ECHR is a product of traditional property values, it does seek to articulate those values in a manner that affords greater clarity and legitimacy to the balancing process.

Nevertheless, we have also seen, in *Kay; Price*, that the House of Lords is unlikely to question the social and economic policy ramifications of housing policy. Baroness Hale's judgment (see section 4.2 above) illustrates this reluctance, which is echoed by Lord Bingham.

Kay v Lambeth LBC; Leeds CC v Price [2006] 2 AC 465, HL

Lord Bingham

At [33]

[...] For the general property law of England and Wales has developed over the centuries reconciling rights and interests sometimes in harmony, sometimes conflicting of owners, landlords and licensors on the one hand and occupiers, tenants and licensees on the other. Over the last century or so, this general property law has been overlaid by a mass of very detailed, very specific housing legislation [...] The demand for housing at a reasonable price is greater than the supply. This of course means that security of tenure for A means a denial of accommodation for B, a recognition of a right for C to succeed to a tenancy means there is no tenancy for D, an extension of time granted to E defers the date when F can find somewhere to live. Our housing legislation strikes a balance between competing claims to which scarcity gives rise, taking account, no doubt imperfectly but as well as may be, of the human, social and economic considerations involved [...]

The implementation of policy through the law reform process is, however, not always logical and seamless. Anomalies and lacunae do occur—particularly in land law, in which, throughout its long history, prospective and piecemeal evolution predominates. It is in these circumstances that the new balancing process may have most to contribute and we will, in

---

119 Fox, *Conceptualising Home: Theories, Law, and Policies* (2007, p 512).
120 Gray and Gray, *Land Law* (5th edn, 2009 at [1.6.17]).
121 *Per* Lord Nicholls in *Wilson v First County Trust (No 2)* [2003] UKHL 40, [2004] 1 AC 816, at [61] (see section 2.4.3 above).

the remainder of this book, try to identify those areas in which we think that a human rights challenge might make a difference.

Allen notes that Art 1 of the First Protocol *'is a very conservative element in the protection of human rights'*.[122] By contrast, Art 8 has attracted attention as a possible foundation for new human rights to property.[123] Article 8 has already provided a platform from which claimants can seek environmental protection; there is also the possibility that claimants, with no recognized proprietary rights or for whom the existing property rules provide no redress, might be able to look to Art 8 for protection. This protection springs instead from their particular status or way of life, which the government, under Art 8, is under a positive duty to protect. Gray and Gray point out that this human property right could operate *'to modify or even override'*[124] the existing proprietary rights of others. This possibility lies at the heart of the recent string of cases that have occupied the House of Lords and the Strasbourg Court, and a divide could be opening up between these two august bodies. The majority of the Lords are reluctant to accept that a claimant's personal circumstances should be brought into the equation, but the Strasbourg Court might demand a change of approach. Uncertainty thus continues to haunt what exactly defines the exceptional circumstances upon which existing proprietary rights may be challenged.

The implication of this more radical agenda could prove particularly potent should the HRA 1998 have horizontal effect, and thus extend to relations between private individuals, as well as those between public authorities and individuals. The danger is that the Act could prove a precipitous rollercoaster ride and commentators have warned against upsetting the traditional balance.[125]

Howell, 'The Human Rights Act 1998: Land, Private Citizens, and the Common Law' (2007) 123 LQR 618

At 632

On one view, the HRA is to be welcomed: land law has never acted in a vacuum. Legislation and judgments are already driven by social, economic and to an extent, moral, considerations, whose weight and content change over time. Land Law is already going through a period of unprecedented but largely unremarked change. The HRA is simply one more factor to be absorbed and given its value [...] But the problem [...] is that what is driving the change is a human rights rather than a property law agenda. Replacing established rules with individual decisions based upon human rights principles may seem attractive but will lead to uncertainty [...]

At 634

But the seductive effects of the HRA should be resisted. Land law must, it is suggested, keep to the narrow and stony path. Land law is essentially pragmatic and practical and, most importantly, has consequences for third parties: certainty is almost always justice. Already

---

[122] Allen, 'The Autonomous Meaning of "Possessions" under the European Convention of Human Rights' in *Modern Studies in Property Law: Vol 2* (ed Cooke, 2003, p 57).

[123] Gray and Gray, *Land Law* (5th edn, 2009, at [1.6.7]).

[124] Ibid.

[125] See also Goymour, 'Proprietary Claims and Human Rights: A "Reservoir of Entitlement"' (2006) 65 CLJ 696, 706.

the uncertainty over the circumstances in which the courts will find that a beneficial interest has arisen under a constructive trust or through estoppel is making life difficult for practitioners. The introduction of human rights values is a wild card which is wholly unpredictable in effect. Parties will not enter into agreements over land if they cannot be sure of their effect, and practitioners will not be able to advise them. The Convention is a "living instrument", but it will be unfortunate indeed if this principle were to be applied to agreements relating to land.

QUESTIONS

1. To what extent does the European Convention on Human Rights affect relations between private landowners?

2. How does Art 1 of the First Protocol operate to protect rights of property?

3. What is the role of compensation in determining whether or not an Act that affects property rights is compliant with the ECHR?

4. Article 8 provides that respect is to be afforded to an individual's home. What does 'respect' mean in this context?

5. Is there such a concept as a human property right?

6. Article 14 has been described as 'parasitic'. How may the Article assist in a challenge based upon the Human Rights Act 1998?

7. To what extent is it appropriate for the courts to consider government policy in determining the compliance of property rules with the ECHR?

8. How useful is the human rights 'prism' through which the law governing property rights must now pass?

FURTHER READING

Allen, *Property and The Human Rights Act 1998* (Oxford: Hart, 2005)

Allen, 'The Autonomous Meaning of "Possessions" under the European Convention of Human Rights' in *Modern Studies in Property Law: Vol 2* (ed Cooke, Oxford: Hart, 2003)

Bright, 'Article 8 Again in the House of Lords' [2006] Conv 294

Fox, *Conceptualising Home: Theories, Law and Policies* (Oxford: Hart, 2007, ch 10)

Goymour, 'Proprietary Claims and Human Rights: A "Reservoir of Entitlement"' (2006) 65 CLJ 696

Gray, 'Land Law and Human Rights' in *Land Law: Issues, Debates, Policy* (ed Tee: Devon: Willan, 2002, ch 7)

Harpum, 'Property Law: The Human Rights Dimension—Part 1' [2000] L&T Rev 4

Harpum, 'Property Law: The Human Rights Dimension—Part 2' [2000] L&T Rev 29

Howell, 'Land and Human Rights' [1999] Conv 287

Howell, 'The Human Rights Act 1998: Land, Private Citizens, and the Common Law' (2007) 123 LQR 618

Howell, 'The Human Rights Act 1998: The Horizontal Effect on Land Law' in *Modern Studies in Property Law: Vol 1* (ed Cooke, Oxford: Hart, 2001)

Hughes and Davis, 'Human Rights and The Triumph of Property: Marginalisation of the European Convention on Human Rights in Housing Law' [2006] Conv 526

Nield, 'Charges, Possession and Human Rights: A Reappraisal of s 87(1) Law of Property Act 1925' in *Modern Studies in Property Law: Vol 3* (ed Cooke, Oxford: Hart, 2005)

Rook, *Property Law and Human Rights* (London: Blackstone, 2001)

PART B

THE PRIORITY TRIANGLE

6

THE PRIORITY TRIANGLE

CENTRAL ISSUES

1. Many land law cases share a basic form: a dispute arises between B and C, each of whom wants to make an inconsistent use of the land. In the abstract, it may be very hard to decide which party should win: after all, both B and C may be completely innocent.

2. The law has adopted a very clear structure to deal with these difficult disputes. Firstly, does B have a pre-existing (legal or equitable) property right that he or she can assert against C? Secondly, if B does have such a property right, does C have a defence to it? Thirdly, does B have a direct right against C?

3. In Chapters 3 and 4, we examined the first question—whether B's right counts as a (legal or equitable) property right.

In Chapter 7, we will look in detail at the question of when B can acquire a direct right against C. In this chapter, our focus is on the question of when C can have a *defence* to B's pre-existing property right. This question can be thought of as the *priority* question: does B's property right have priority over C's right?

4. We will return to the priority question in Chapters 15 and 16. There, our focus will be on the *detail* of the *specific* statutory rules imposed by the Land Charges Act 1972 (in relation to unregistered land) and the Land Registration Act 2002. The aim of this chapter is to set out the *basic principles* that apply when answering the priority question.

---

1 INTRODUCTION: THE PRIORITY TRIANGLE IN PRACTICE

The cases that we will examine in this chapter share a basic set of facts:

1. A is an owner of some land (i.e. A has a freehold or lease of some land); *and*

2. B then acquires a right to make some use of that land; *and*

3. C then acquires a right in relation to A's land (e.g. C buys A's freehold or lease, or A gives C a charge over A's land).

If C is content for B to continue using the land, there will be no problem for B. In practice, however, C may want to prevent B from continuing to use the land. For example, it may be that A, who has a freehold or lease, has allowed B to occupy all or part of A's land. If C then buys A's freehold or lease, it is likely that C will want to remove B. In such a case, we need to ask if B has a right that he or she can assert against C. This question is sometimes put in the following terms: does B's right to use the land *take priority* over C's right? As Figure 1 shows, we can consequently think of there being a *priority triangle* involving A, B, and C.

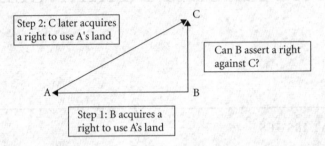

Figure 1 The priority triangle

For example, in Chapter 1, section 5, and Chapter 4, section 5.4, we examined the decision of the House of Lords in *National Provincial Bank v Ainsworth*.[1] The facts of the case provide a good example of the priority triangle in practice. A (Mr Ainsworth) held a freehold. B (Mrs Ainsworth) had a right to use A's land ('a deserted wife's equity').[2] C (National Provincial Bank) then acquired a charge over A's land. That charge gave it the power, if A failed to repay a loan as agreed, to sell A's freehold and use the proceeds towards meeting the debt owed to C. As long as A (or someone acting on A's behalf) continued to repay the debt, there was no problem for B. But when A defaulted on the debt, C wanted to recover the sums due to it by selling A's freehold. And, of course, to get a reasonable price for A's freehold, C needed to sell the land with vacant possession (i.e. without B remaining in occupation). So the question was whether B had a right that she could assert against C—or, in other words, who had priority: B or C?

To determine the *priority* question, we have to do more than simply ask whose right came first in time. For example, in *National Provincial Bank v Ainsworth*, Mrs Ainsworth's 'deserted wife's equity' arose *before* the bank received its charge, and yet, as we saw in Chapter 4, section 5.4, Mrs Ainsworth had *no* right that she could assert against the bank: the bank was free to remove Mrs Ainsworth from the land. The crucial point was that the House of Lords saw the 'deserted wife's equity' as giving Mrs Ainsworth only a *personal right* against Mr Ainsworth. As we saw in Chapter 3, section 1, a personal right, by itself, cannot be asserted against a third party. So, in answering the priority question, we firstly need to ask whether, when C acquired C's right, B already had a (legal or equitable) property right in relation to the land. As demonstrated by Chapters 3 and 4, the question of whether B had a pre-existing property right can, in turn, be split into two questions. Firstly, we need to ask the *content* question: does the type of right claimed by B count as a property right in relation to land? Secondly, if B's claimed

---

[1] [1965] AC 1175.

[2] As we saw in Chapter 1, section 5.3, a 'deserted wife's equity' was the name given to the right held by a wife as a result of a duty imposed on a husband, having moved out of the matrimonial home, to provide her with financial support and, perhaps, accommodation.

right *does* count as a property right, we then need to ask the *acquisition* question: on the facts of the case, had B, in fact, acquired that right before C acquired C's right?

National Provincial Bank v Ainsworth provides a good example of the *content* question in practice. There was no doubt that, when Mr Ainsworth moved out of the matrimonial home, Mrs Ainsworth acquired a right: a 'deserted wife's equity'. And there was no doubt that Mrs Ainsworth had that right *before* the bank acquired its right in the land. But Mrs Ainsworth's right could not bind the bank, because, according to the House of Lords, it did not count as a property right in land: it thus failed the content test. As we saw in Chapters 3 and 4, the *numerus clausus* (or 'closed list') principle is crucial when considering the *content* question: the basic approach of the courts (as seen in *National Provincial Bank v Ainsworth*) is that B's right can only pass the content test if it is on the recognized list of property rights relating to land.

2 THE BASIC RULE AND THE *TIMING* QUESTION

2.1 THE BASIC RULE

When considering the priority triangle, the most difficult cases are those in which *each of* B and C has a property right in relation to the same piece of land. In such a case, the starting point is that *the first in time prevails*. So, if (i) A has a freehold or lease, and (ii) B then acquires a property right in relation to A's land, and (iii) A then transfers his freehold or lease to C, the starting point, in relation to both registered and unregistered land, is that (iv) B's pre-existing property right will take priority over C's later property right. As far as registered land is concerned, that basic rule is now enshrined by statute:

Land Registration Act 2002, s 28

(1) Except as provided by sections 29 and 30, the priority of an interest affecting a registered estate or charge is not affected by a disposition of the estate or charge.

(2) It makes no difference for the purposes of this section whether the interest or disposition is registered.

2.2 THE *TIMING* QUESTION

To apply the basic rule, we must, of course, know whether or not B's property right arose before C's property right. In most cases, it will be very easy to work out the order of the parties' rights. For example, in *Hodgson v Marks*[3] (which we examined in Chapter 4, section 4), Mrs Hodgson transferred her freehold, for free, to Mr Evans. Mr Evans then sold that freehold to Mr Marks, who also gave a charge over the land to the Cheltenham & Gloucester Building Society. It was held that a trust arose in favour of Mrs Hodgson as soon as she transferred her freehold, for free, to Mr Evans. It is thus clear that, in such a case, the basic rule favours Mrs Hodgson, who acquired her equitable property right *before* Mr Marks or the building society acquired any property right in relation to the land.

[3] [1971] Ch 89.

2.2.1 Whose right is first in time? Charges

A particular problem can arise, however, in the very common case in which: (i) A borrows money from C in order to buy a freehold or lease; and (ii) in return, C acquires a charge over the land to secure A's duty to repay the loan. In such a case, when does C acquire its right? The traditional view was a technical one: C acquires its charge from A, and A can only give C a right in relation to the land if A *already* has a freehold or lease. On that view, A must acquire a property right *before* C: logically, there must be a *scintilla temporis*—that is, a tiny spark of time during which A holds his or her right free from C's charge.

But that view may seem unrealistic: after all, if A needs to borrow money from C in order to acquire his or her freehold or lease, why should A's property right take priority to C's charge? In the following case, the House of Lords considered the problem and decided to depart from the traditional view.

Abbey National v Cann [1991] 1 AC 56, HL

Facts: George Cann lived with his mother, Daisy, in Island Road, Mitcham, in a home that was registered in George's sole name. Because Daisy had contributed to the purchase price of that home, George held his estate on trust for both himself and Daisy. George and Daisy decided to move to a smaller home in South Lodge Avenue, also in Mitcham. They paid for that home by means of: (i) the proceeds of sale of their previous home in Island Road; and (ii) a loan from the Abbey National Building Society, secured by a charge over their new South Lodge Avenue home. The new home was registered in George's sole name and Daisy was not a party to the loan from the Abbey National. Daisy had known that a mortgage loan was necessary, because the new South Lodge Avenue home cost £4,000 more than the proceeds of sale of the Island Road home. Acting without Daisy's knowledge, however, George had taken out a loan of £25,000 from the Abbey National. When George failed to repay that loan as agreed, the building society attempted to remove Daisy (along with her new husband) from the home so that it could sell the home with vacant possession and use the proceeds to meet George's outstanding debt.

It was accepted that Daisy had an equitable property right: George held his estate in the South Lodge Avenue home on trust for himself and Daisy, because she had contributed to the purchase price by allowing all of the proceeds of sale of Island Road to be used in buying the new home. It was also clear that the Abbey National had a legal property right: the charge that it had acquired from George and then registered. The Abbey National argued that its property right arose *before* Daisy's property right. The Court of Appeal had rejected that argument, but found in favour of the Abbey National on other grounds. The House of Lords, whilst also supporting those other grounds (see below), also accepted Abbey National's argument that its charge arose before Daisy's equitable property right.

Lord Oliver

At 92–3

Of course, as a matter of legal theory, a person cannot charge a legal estate that he does not have, so that there is an attractive legal logic in the ratio in *Piskor's Case* [a decision of the Court of Appeal applying the traditional *scintilla tempors* view].[4] Nevertheless, I cannot help

---

[4] [1954] Ch 553.

feeling that it flies in the face of reality. The reality is that,in the vast majority of cases, the acquisition of the legal estate and the charge are not only precisely simultaneous but indissolubly bound together. The acquisition of the legal estate is entirely dependent upon the provision of funds which will have been provided before the conveyance can take effect and which are provided only against an agreement that the estate will be charged to secure them. Indeed, in many, if not most, cases of building society mortgages, there will have been, as there was in this case, a formal offer and acceptance of an advance which will ripen into a specifically enforceable agreement immediately the funds are advanced which will normally be a day or more before completion. In many, if not most, cases, the charge itself will have been executed before the execution, let alone the exchange, of the conveyance or transfer of the property. This is given particular point in the case of registered land where the vesting of the estate is made to depend upon registration, for it may well be that the transfer and the charge will be lodged for registration on different days so that the charge, when registered, may actually take effect from a date prior in time to the date from which the registration of the transfer takes effect...The reality is that the purchaser of land who relies upon a building society or bank loan for the completion of his purchase never in fact acquires anything but an equity of redemption [a concept we will examine in Chapter 29, section 5], for the land is, from the very inception, charged with the amount of the loan without which it could never have been transferred at all and it was never intended that it should be otherwise. The "scintilla temporis" is no more than a legal artifice and, for my part, I would adopt the reasoning of the Court of Appeal in *In re Connolly Brothers Ltd. (No. 2)*[5] and of Harman J. in *Coventry Permanent Economic Building Society v. Jones*[6] and hold that *Piskor's Case* was wrongly decided.

Lord Jauncey

At 101–2

It is of course correct as a matter of strict legal analysis that a purchaser of property cannot grant a mortgage over it until the legal estate has vested in him. The question however is whether having borrowed money in order to complete the purchase against an undertaking to grant security for the loan over the property the purchaser is, for a moment of time, in a position to deal with the legal estate as though the mortgagee had no interest therein...In my view a purchaser who can only complete the transaction by borrowing money for the security of which he is contractually bound to grant a mortgage to the lender [simultaneously] with the execution of the conveyance in his favour cannot in reality ever be said to have acquired even for a scintilla temporis the unencumbered fee simple or leasehold interest in land whereby he could grant interests having priority over the mortgage [...]. Since no one can grant what he does not have it follows that such a purchaser could never grant an interest which was not subject to the limitations on his own interest. In so far as *Piskor* decided that such a purchaser could be vested for a moment of time in the unencumbered freehold or leasehold estate with the consequences to which I have just referred, I consider that it was wrongly decided.

The decision in *Cann* certainly has an important effect: it means that, if A takes out a mortgage to assist in acquiring a freehold or lease, then C (the mortgagee: i.e., bank or building society providing the loan) will take priority over B (a party also providing money towards the purchase of the freehold or lease).

5 [1912] 2 Ch 25.
6 [1951] 1 All ER 901.

The approach adopted in *Cann* has since received further support: for example, in *Ingram v IRC*,[7] Lord Hoffmann stated that: '*For my part, I do not think that a theory based upon the notion of the scintilla temporis can have a very powerful grasp on reality.*' But its operation in a case such as *Cann* itself seems somewhat harsh.[8] Firstly, whilst it may be true to say that George could not have acquired his estate in the South Lodge Avenue home without the mortgage loan, it is equally true to say that George could not have acquired that right without Daisy's financial contribution. Secondly, whilst Daisy knew that a mortgage of around £4,000 was necessary to complete the purchase, George went well beyond that in borrowing £25,000. It may therefore be that the courts should take a more nuanced approach, as explored by the following extract.[9]

Smith, 'Mortgagees and Trust Beneficiaries' (1990) 109 LQR 545, 548–9

Let us turn to the economic reality behind these cases. What is objectionable about the old *scintilla temporis* cases is that the mortgagee's finance [i.e., the money provided by the bank or building society] enables the interest of the claimant to arise. How does this apply to the facts of *Cann*? The proceeds of the previous house (after repayment of a mortgage) amounted to £30,000, owned equally by George Cann (the legal owner) and Mrs Cann. The new house (costing £34,000) required extra finance of £4,000. In fact George Cann, without authority from his mother, raised £25,000 on mortgage. It can be appreciated that the house could not have been purchased without mortgage finance of £4,000 and that to this extent the mortgagee should have priority. This may be explained either on the basis of Mrs Cann's authorising the mortgage [see section 3.4.2 below] or on the rejection of *scintilla temporis*. Beyond £4,000, however, George Cann had two overlapping sources of finance: the proceeds from the previous house and the mortgage. What logic or sense is there in saying that the mortgagee must have priority?

If we suppose that the second house had been purchased for £30,000, it is easy to see that no mortgage would have been necessary. In such a case, Lord Jauncey's analysis fails to operate: no longer is there "a purchaser who can only complete the transaction by borrowing money." Yet to the mortgagee the situation looks exactly the same, whatever the financial position of the purchaser is. The problem is most obviously acute if [...] the purchaser obtains loan finance sufficient to purchase the property from each of two sources, promising each of them a legal mortgage.

How can these problems be resolved? We may start by saying that where finance is required to complete a purchase, then the mortgagee should to that extent have priority. Such a proposition represents the very minimum that *Cann* is authority for. If there are overlapping sources of finance then three solutions offer themselves (all subject to the operation of land registration or other priority rules). First, we could simply favour the mortgagee. As has been argued, it is difficult to support this conclusion in terms of legal logic or economic reality. A second solution is to favour the source of finance that is first in time. The difficulty here is partly that establishing a time order may be difficult and partly that it is difficult to reconcile with the *Cann* decision favouring the mortgagee when finance is required. The final solution is to accord the sources of finance equal priority (proportionate to their quantum).

---

[7] [2001] 1 AC 293, 303.

[8] For criticism, see, e.g., Beaumont [1990] Law Society Gazette, 23 May, p 25, and 25 July, p 27. See also Gardner, *An Introduction to Land Law* (2007, p 309).

[9] For further disapproval of this aspect of the decision in *Cann*, see, e.g., Thompson [1992] Conv 206; Dixon [1992] CLJ 223.

A variation on this is to deny that either of the sources has priority over the other (see A. M. Prichard (1964) 80 L.Q.R. 370 at pp. 381–382): this may be appropriate when it is not possible to quantify a contribution in financial terms or the dispute concerns possession. It is worth noting that if a mortgagee fails to obtain possession then he is likely to bankrupt the mortgagor. Almost inevitably, the house will be sold and an equal priority analysis can be applied to the proceeds of sale. The third solution seems most likely to do justice, although it would require considerable elucidation. It has to be recognised, however, that it is at odds with other real property priority rules, which invariably strive to prefer one proprietary claim to another. On the other hand, once the *scintilla temporis* doctrine (designed to provide us with a preference) is dismissed, the law appears to be at a loss as to what to put in its place.

2.2.2 Whose right is first in time? Independently acquired rights

We saw in Chapter 3 that, where A has an estate in land, it is possible for B *independently* to acquire a property right in that land. For example, if B takes physical control of A's land, even without A's consent, B acquires a freehold of that land. But because A's property right arose before B's freehold, the basic rule tells us that A's pre-existing property right takes priority to that of B. So, A is free to remove B from the land, either by using reasonable force or by seeking a possession order from a court. Initially then, B's freehold may give him or her useful protection against X (a party who later tries to move into the home), but it does not protect him or her against A.

Similarly, if A then gives C a property right in the land (for example, by transferring his or her estate to C), C is also free to remove B from the land. From a technical point of view, it may seem that B's pre-existing property right should take priority: after all, B had that right before C acquired his or her right. But the point is that C, by acquiring a property right *from* A, is essentially basing his or her claim on A's property right, which arose before B's property right. In a case in which A gives a property right to B, and then to C, this 'backdating' process cannot assist C because *each of* B and C can backdate his or her right to A's right. Where B acquires his or her right independently, however, he or she does not base the claim on A's right: in such a case, C alone can rely on backdating to take priority to B's right.

It is important to note that if either A or C delays in exercising his or her right to remove B from the land, it may then be possible for B to take priority: the lapse of time may give B a defence to the pre-existing property right of A, or to C's backdated property right. We will examine this point in section 3.5 below.

3 EXCEPTIONS TO THE BASIC RULE: THE *DEFENCES* QUESTION

3.1 THE POSSIBILITY OF A DEFENCE

There are exceptions to the basic rule that B's property right, where it arises before C's property right, will take priority. As we noted in Chapters 3 and 4, we have to bear in mind that, even if B has a pre-existing property right relating to land, it may be possible for C to have a *defence* to that right. In such a case, C can use that defence to take priority to B's property right. The following case, concerning unregistered land, provides a particularly memorable example of this point.

Midland Bank Trust Co Ltd v Green [1981] AC 513, HL

Facts: Walter Green owned Gravel Hill Farm, a 300-acre farm in Lincolnshire. Walter made a contractual promise to his son, Geoffrey, that Geoffrey could, if he wished, purchase the farm at a price of £75 per acre at any time in the next ten years. As a result of this contractual promise, Geoffrey acquired an 'option to purchase': a recognized equitable property right—but Walter and Geoffrey then fell out. Walter was determined to prevent Geoffrey from buying the farm. Walter therefore transferred ownership of the farm to his wife, Evelyne. At the time, the farm was worth about £40,000, but Evelyne paid only £500. Evelyne, of course, was fully aware of Geoffrey's pre-existing option to purchase, but she argued that, because Geoffrey had failed to enter that option to purchase on the Land Charges Register, the Land Charges Act 1925 (LCA 1925) enabled her to take priority over his right. The Court of Appeal found in favour of Geoffrey, but the House of Lords upheld Evelyne's appeal.

Lord Wilberforce

At 526–8

[Geoffrey's] option was, in legal terms, an estate contract and so a legal charge, class C, within the meaning of the Land Charges Act 1925. The correct and statutory method for protection of such an option is by means of entering it in the Register of Land Charges maintained under the Act. If so registered, the option would have been enforceable, not only (contractually) against Walter, but against any purchaser of the farm [...]

My Lords, section 13 (2) of the Land Charges Act 1925 reads as follows:

"A land charge of class B, class C or class D, created or arising after the commencement of this Act, shall (except as hereinafter provided) be void as against a purchaser of the land charged therewith [...] unless the land charge is registered in the appropriate register before the completion of the purchase: Provided that, as respects a land charge of class D and an estate contract created or entered into after the commencement of this Act, this subsection only applies in favour of a purchaser of a legal estate for money or money's worth."

As regards the word "purchaser" section 20 (8) of the same Act reads: " 'Purchaser' means any person [...] who, for valuable consideration, takes any interest in land [...]"

Thus the case appears to be a plain one. The "estate contract," which by definition (section 11) includes an option of purchase, was entered into after January 1, 1926; Evelyne took an interest (in fee simple) in the land "for valuable consideration"—so was a "purchaser"; she was a purchaser for money—namely £500; the option was not registered before the completion of the purchase. It is therefore void as against her.

In my opinion this appearance is also the reality. The case is plain: the Act is clear and definite. Intended as it was to provide a simple and understandable system for the protection of title to land, it should not be read down or glossed: to do so would destroy the usefulness of the Act. Any temptation to remould the Act to meet the facts of the present case, on the supposition that it is a hard one and that justice requires it, is, for me at least, removed by the consideration that the Act itself provides a simple and effective protection for persons in Geoffrey's position—viz.—by registration.

Midland Bank Trust Co Ltd v Green provides a very good example of the priority triangle in practice: Geoffrey (B) acquired a property right in relation to the farm *before* Evelyne (C) acquired her right. So the basic rule is that Geoffrey's property right will take priority. But that basic rule was changed by s 13(2) of the LCA 1925, which can be seen as giving Evelyne a *defence* against Geoffrey's pre-existing equitable property right. To use that defence, Evelyne had to show three things: (i) that Geoffrey's right was one of those property rights that was covered by the registration rules of the Act; (ii) that Geoffrey had not registered that right as a land charge; and (iii) that Evelyne had acquired her property right in land 'for valuable consideration' and so counted as a 'purchaser' for the purposes of the Act. Because Evelyne was able to show all of these three things, she had priority to Geoffrey's right *even though* she knew all about it.

Since the decision in *Green*, the LCA 1925 has been replaced by the Land Charges Act 1972 (LCA 1972). But the relevant provisions of that new Act operate in exactly the same way as the previous Act: so, if the facts of *Green* were to occur again today in relation to unregistered land, the result would be exactly the same. Of course, it is possible to disapprove of that result: for example, Battersby[10] has argued that '*the decision in* Midland Bank v Green, *though correct on the present statutory provisions, is unacceptable and the Land Charges Act needs amendment*'. We will examine that argument, and the wider issues that it raises, when looking in detail at the priority question in Chapters 15–17. The crucial point to note here is that, whether or not we agree with the current provisions of the LCA 1972, the decision in *Green* makes very clear that it may be possible for C, by relying on a defence, to take priority over B's *pre-existing* property right in land.

3.2 REGISTERED LAND AND THE LACK OF REGISTRATION DEFENCE

3.2.1 The basic defence

In *Green*, the specific defence relied on by Evelyne is now provided by the LCA 1972, which applies only to dealings with unregistered land. That defence can, however, be seen as an example of a more general type of defence: the lack of registration defence. A lack of registration defence forms a very important part of the registered land system. As we saw in section 2.1 above, s 28 of the Land Registration Act 2002 (LRA 2002) ensures that, where dealings with registered land are concerned, the basic rule applies: B's pre-existing property right will take priority over a later property right of C. But as s 28(1) makes clear, that basic rule is subject to the exceptions provided by ss 29 and 30 of the same Act. Those sections ensure that, in relation to registered land, it may be possible for C to take priority over a pre-existing property right of B that is not recorded on the register. Section 29 is set out below: it governs the position in which A has a registered freehold or lease (a 'registered estate'), and then gives C a property right in the land by means of a 'registrable disposition' (e.g. by transferring his freehold or lease to C, by granting C a new lease of more than seven years' duration, or by giving C a charge). Section 30 is not set out below: it is very similar in effect, and applies only where A has a registered charge.

Land Registration Act 2002, s 29

(1) If a registrable disposition of a registered estate is made for valuable consideration, completion of the disposition by registration has the effect of postponing to the interest under the disposition any interest affecting the estate immediately before the disposition whose priority is not protected at the time of registration.

---

[10] 'Informal Transactions in Land, Estoppel and Registration' [1995] MLR 637, 655.

(2) For the purposes of subsection (1), the priority of an interest is protected—

    (a) in any case, if the interest—

        (i)   is a registered charge or the subject of a notice in the register;

        (ii) falls within any of the paragraphs of Schedule 3, or

        (iii) appears from the register to be excepted from the effect of registration, and

    (b) in the case of a disposition of a leasehold estate, if the burden of the interest is incident to the estate.

(3) Subsection 2(a)(ii) does not apply to an interest which has been the subject of a notice in the register at any time since the coming into force of this section

(4) Where the grant of a leasehold estate in land out of a registered estate does not involve a registered disposition, this section has effect as if—

    (a) the grant involved such a disposition; and

    (b) the disposition was registered at the time of the grant.

In Chapter 16, we will examine the lack of registration defence provided by the LRA 2002 in more detail. Some general points are, however, worth noting here. When analysing any lack of registration defence, it is useful to ask two questions: firstly, what does C have to do to take advantage of the defence? Secondly, when will B's pre-existing property right be vulnerable to that defence? For example, in *Green*, C was able to take advantage of the lack of registration defence provided by the LCA 1925, because she was a 'purchaser of a legal estate for money or money's worth', and B's right was vulnerable to that defence, because it counted as an estate contract and thus as a Class C land charge.

When applying the first question to s 29 of the LRA 2002, we can see that C must meet certain requirements in order to rely on the lack of registration defence. Firstly, there must be a '*registrable disposition of a registered estate*' in favour of C. In Chapters 9 and 16, we will examine the meaning of 'registrable disposition' in more detail. As noted in Chapter 3, it includes almost all situations in which A, a holder of a registered freehold or lease, might attempt to give C a *legal* property right. An important exception occurs if A gives C a lease of seven years or less: in general, that does not count as a 'registrable disposition'. But in such a case, s 29(4) comes to C's rescue: it means that C may nonetheless qualify for the lack of registration defence because, for the purposes of s 29, he will be regarded as having acquired his property right by means of a 'registrable disposition'.

Secondly, the disposition in C's favour must be made for 'valuable consideration'. This is an important qualification. It means, for example, that if C acquires his property right by means of a gift from A, or on A's death, then C *cannot* use the lack of registration defence against a pre-existing property right of B.

Thirdly, to qualify for the defence, the '*completion of the disposition by registration*' is necessary: so C must register his newly acquired property right. Again, s 29(4) means that C is viewed as having met that requirement if he acquires a lease that, due to its length, cannot be registered.

3.2.2 Exceptions to the basic defence

If C does qualify for the lack of registration defence, we need to ask if B's pre-existing property right is vulnerable to that defence. The starting point, under both ss 29 and 30 of the LRA 2002, is that B's pre-existing property right *will* be vulnerable to the lack of registration defence. The 2002 Act thus works in the opposite way to the LCA 1972. The 1972 Act sets out a list of property rights that need to be registered, the 2002 Act: (i) sets out a general rule, in s 29(1), that *any 'interest affecting* [A's estate] *immediately before the disposition* [to C]' is vulnerable to the lack of registration defence; and (ii) in s 29(2), sets out exceptions to that rule. Section 29(2)(a)(i) and (iii) simply protect a pre-existing property right of B that C can see by examining the register. Section 29(2)(b) applies a special rule ensuring that if B's right arises because A is a tenant of B, C will also be subject to those duties: again, it will be easy for C to discover any such right of B, because he simply needs to examine the terms of A's lease with B. So the really important provision is s 29(2)(a)(ii): it means that, if B's property right is on the list of rights set out by Sch 3 of the Act, it will *not* be vulnerable to the lack of registration defence.

Those pre-existing property rights of B that are not vulnerable to the lack of registration defence are known as *overriding interests*. We will examine the list in detail in Chapter 16, but it is worth noting here one important example of an overriding interest. The Land Registration Act 1925 (LRA 1925), by means of s 70(1)(g), allowed a property right of B to count as an overriding interest if B was in *'actual occupation of the land or in receipt of the rents and profits thereof, save where enquiry is made of such person and the rights are not disclosed'*. The LRA 2002 contains a very similar provision (Sch 3, para 2), which can again be used by B if he is in actual occupation of the registered land. That provision does vary from its predecessor, but not in such a way as to change the result of the following case, which provides a good example of the role of actual occupation.

Hodgson v Marks [1971] Ch 892, CA

Facts: We examined the facts of *Hodgson v Marks* in Chapter 4, section 4. We saw there that: (i) Mrs Hodgson had transferred her freehold of 31 Gibbs Green to her lodger, John Evans; but that (ii) Mr Evans held that freehold on trust for Mrs Hodgson; and so (iii) Mrs Hodgson had a pre-existing equitable property right that was capable of binding both David Marks, to whom Mr Evans had sold the freehold, and also the Cheltenham & Gloucester Building Society, which had acquired a charge from Mr Marks. The Court of Appeal also had to consider the question of *priority*: could Mr Marks or the building society show that he or it had priority to Mrs Hodgson's pre-existing equitable property right?

Mr Marks and the building society tried to rely on the lack of registration defence provided by the LRA 1925. Their argument was that: (i) each had paid for, and registered, a property right in the land; and that (ii) Mrs Hodgson's pre-existing equitable property right had not been noted on the register. Mrs Hodgson argued that she had an *overriding interest*: her property right was *not* vulnerable to the lack of registration defence, because she had been in actual occupation of the land when Mr Marks and the building society acquired their later property rights.

At first instance, Ungoed-Thomas J held that Mrs Hodgson had *not* been in actual occupation of the land at the relevant time: although she had been living there, her presence was not such as to alert Mr Marks or the building society to the risk that she had a pre-existing property right. This reasoning seems to be based on the idea that Mr Marks and the building society could reasonably believe that Mrs Hodgson's presence showed only that Mr Evans permitted her to share occupation of the land with him. The Court of Appeal disagreed with that analysis and held that Mrs Hodgson *was* in actual occupation of the land at the relevant time.

Russell LJ

At 93–3

[Ungoed-Thomas J, having decided that Mrs Hodgson was in physical occupation of the premises at the relevant time,] then proceeded to attach a different and special meaning to the words "in actual occupation" in section 70(1)(g). He took as a starting point to justify departure from the ordinary meaning of the words first the fact that every person in actual occupation could not include the vendor himself; but that only puts a gloss on the words "every person" and, indeed, assumes the ordinary meaning of "actual occupation"; moreover, it is not in the context a special construction of "every person" to exclude the vendor who ex hypothesi has transferred his rights to the purchaser. Secondly, the judge relied upon the correct conclusion that "the land" included part of the land. I cannot see that this can properly be used as a justification for departure from the ordinary meaning of the words "in actual occupation." Having by this means freed himself from the fetters of the golden rule, he then, after considering the circumstances in which in the case of unregistered land a purchaser would be fixed with constructive notice of the rights of persons in occupation of the land sold, concluded that "actual" should be construed in the sense of "actual and apparent." [. . .] But, nevertheless, how can it be said that the plaintiff was not in actual occupation of the house? The judge said that in all fairness a purchaser of this house (if unregistered) should not be fixed with notice of the plaintiff's rights. But why not? It is a principle of law (and of the Land Registration Act 1925) that a person in occupation is protected in his rights by that occupation, unless, of course, the rights are such that they require registration if they are to be protected. A purchaser must pay heed to anyone in occupation if he is to be sure of getting a good title. It was argued, on the basis of a quotation from the judgment of Vaughan Williams L.J. in *Hunt v. Luck*[11] that this does not apply when the vendor is in occupation, and that (as is the fact) there is no reported case of unregistered land where a purchaser was fixed with constructive notice of the rights of any other occupier when the vendor was in occupation, and that any other view would lead to an impossible burden of inquiry on a purchaser and more particularly on a lender of money on mortgage such as the building society. (As to the defendant building society it is plain that it made no inquiries on the spot save as to repairs; it relied on Mr. Marks, who lied to it; and I waste no tears on it.) I do not think this is a real problem. Conveyancing is conducted generally upon a basis of good faith, with something of a long stop in the shape of covenants for title. Moreover, I do not consider that it is correct in law to say that any rights of a person who is in occupation will be overridden whenever the vendor is, or appears to be, also in occupation.

I do not think it desirable to attempt to lay down a code or catalogue of situations in which a person other than the vendor should be held to be in occupation of unregistered land for the purpose of constructive notice of his rights, or in actual occupation of registered land for the purposes of section 70(1)(g). It must depend on the circumstances, and a wise purchaser or lender will take no risks. Indeed, however wise he may be he may have no ready opportunity of finding out; but, nevertheless, the law will protect the occupier. Reliance upon the untrue [statement] of the vendor will not suffice. Take the present case—though the test of occupation must be objective. Mr. Evans was only a lodger, and whether in law he was in occupation at all is at least doubtful. But the plaintiff was there for Mr. Marks to see and he saw her on two occasions. He did not introduce himself to her as an intending purchaser. He made no inquiry of her. He assumed her to be Mr. Evans' wife who knew all about the proposed purchase. This assumption may well have stemmed from a lie told by Mr. Evans, though neither

---

11 [1902] 1 Ch 428, 432.

Mr. Marks nor Mrs. Marks actually said so. Nonetheless, there was the plaintiff de facto living in the house as her house, and, if the judge's gloss were to be accepted, I should say just as much in apparent actual occupation of it as before the transfer to Mr. Evans; and, indeed, if Mr. Evans had stopped lodging there before the registration in Mr. Marks' name she would unquestionably have been in actual occupation. In short, unless it can be established in law that a person is not to be regarded as in actual occupation for the purposes of section 70(1)(g) merely because the vendor appears also to be occupying the property, it seems to me that the judge's decision on this point cannot be supported.

Accordingly, I would hold that the plaintiff was at all material times a person in actual occupation of the property.

As we saw in Chapter 1, section 5.4, this approach to the term 'actual occupation' later won the support of the House of Lords in *Williams & Glyn's Bank v Boland*.[12] Nonetheless, as we will see in Chapter 16, section 5.1, there is an important debate about how the term 'actual occupation' should be interpreted. For our present purposes, however, the crucial point is to understand how the priority triangle was resolved in *Hodgson*.

1. The basic rule is that Mrs Hodgson's pre-existing property right takes priority over the later property rights of Mr Marks and the building society.

2. Mr Marks and the building society then attempted to displace that basic rule by using the lack of registration defence.

3. That attempt failed: because Mrs Hodgson was in actual occupation of the registered land at the relevant time, her pre-existing property right counted as an overriding interest. As a result, it was immune from the lack of registration defence.

It is important to remember that Mrs Hodgson's actual occupation was important only because she had a pre-existing property right. For example, in *National Provincial Bank v Ainsworth* (see Chapter 1, section 5.3 and Chapter 4, section 5.4), Mrs Ainsworth lived in the home throughout—but her actual occupation was irrelevant, because she had no pre-existing property right that she could assert against the bank. So, without the support of a pre-existing property right, actual occupation is irrelevant.

Similarly, as we will see in the next extract, there may also be cases in which C takes priority even though B: (i) has a pre-existing property right; *and* (ii) is in actual occupation of the land at the relevant time.

3.3 OVERREACHING UNDER S 2 OF THE LAW OF PROPERTY ACT 1925

Midland Bank v Green concerns the application of the lack of registration defence in unregistered land; *Hodgson v Marks* deals with its application to registered land. The following extract considers a wholly different defence, which does not depend on B's failure to protect a pre-existing property right through registration. The defence is known as *overreaching* and we will examine it in detail in Chapter 20.

A few points need, however, to be made here to put the following extract in context. Overreaching is a general defence that can be used by C whenever A has a *power* to give C a

---

[12] [1981] AC 487.

right free from B's pre-existing property right.[13] It is particularly important where trusts are concerned: it may be that, if A holds on trust for B, the terms of the trust give A a power to give C a right free from B's pre-existing property right. Under the Law of Property Act 1925 (LPA 1925), a particular form of trust (a 'trust for sale') was deemed to arise in a number of situations: one of these was where A1 and A2 held a freehold or lease on trust for A1, A2, B1, and B2. Under such a trust for sale: (i) s 28 of the LPA 1925 gave A1 and A2 a power to give C a charge over the land; and (ii) s 2 of the 1925 Act regulated when C could rely on the overreaching defence.

In the following case, the particular question was whether, given that the requirements imposed by s 2 had been satisfied, C could rely on the overreaching defence *even though* B1 and B2 were in actual occupation of the land when C acquired its charge.

City of London Building Society v Flegg [1988] AC 54, HL

Facts: Following a request from their daughter and son-in-law, Mrs and Mrs Maxwell-Brown, Mr and Mrs Flegg sold their home of twenty-eight years and contributed the proceeds to the purchase of Bleak House. The plan was that Bleak House was to be a home for the Fleggs and the Maxwell-Browns. Only Mr and Mrs Maxwell-Brown were registered as holding the freehold; they raised the remainder of the purchase price by means of a mortgage loan. As a result of their contributions to the purchase price, Mr and Mrs Flegg had an equitable property right: Mr and Mrs Maxwell-Brown held their freehold on trust for themselves and for Mr and Mrs Flegg. The Maxwell-Browns ran into financial difficulties and, without the knowledge or consent of the Fleggs, remortgaged Bleak House: they took out a loan from the City of London Building Society and, in return, gave the building society a charge. When the Maxwell-Browns were unable to meet the repayments, the building society wished to remove the Fleggs from Bleak House, sell the Maxwell-Brown's freehold, and use the proceeds of sale to meet the debt owed by the Maxwell-Browns. The Fleggs argued that their pre-existing property right under the trust had priority to the later charge of the building society. However, the House of Lords held that the society's charge took priority: it was able to use the overreaching defence against the Fleggs' pre-existing right under the trust.

Lord Templeman

At 73–4

[The Fleggs] claim to be entitled to overriding interests because they were in actual occupation of Bleak House on the date of the legal charge. But the interests of [the Fleggs] cannot at one and the same time be overreached and overridden and at the same time be overriding interests. The [building society] cannot at one and the same time take free from all the interests of [the Fleggs] yet at the same time be subject to some of those interests. The right of [the Fleggs] to be and remain in actual occupation of Bleak House ceased when [the Fleggs'] interests were overreached by the legal charge save in so far as their rights were transferred to the equity of redemption [see Chapter 29, section 5]. As persons interested under the trust for sale [the Fleggs] had no right to possession as against [the building society] and the fact that [the Fleggs] were in actual occupation at the date of the legal charge did not create a new right or transfer an old right so as to make the right enforceable against [the building society].

---

[13] See Harpum, 'Overreaching, Trustees' Powers and the Reform of the 1925 Legislation' [1990] CLJ 277.

One of the main objects of the legislation of 1925 was to effect a compromise between on the one hand the interests of the public in securing that land held in trust is freely marketable and, on the other hand, the interests of the beneficiaries in preserving their rights under the trusts. By the Settled Land Act 1925 a tenant for life may convey the settled land discharged from all the trusts powers and provisions of the settlement. By the Law of Property Act 1925 trustees for sale may convey land held on trust for sale discharged from the trusts affecting the proceeds of sale and rents and profits until sale. Under both forms of trust the protection and the only protection of the beneficiaries is that capital money must be paid to at least two trustees or a trust corporation [...] section 70 of the Land Registration Act 1925 cannot have been intended to frustrate this compromise and to subject the purchaser to some beneficial interests but not others depending on the waywardness of actual occupation [...] There must be a combination of an interest which justifies continuing occupation plus actual occupation to constitute an overriding interest. Actual occupation is not an interest in itself.

Lord Oliver

At 90–1

Considered in the context of a transaction complying with the statutory requirements of the Law of Property Act 1925 the question of the effect of section 70(1)(g) of the Land Registration Act 1925 must, in my judgment, be approached by asking first what are the "rights" of the person in occupation and whether they are, at the material time, subsisting in reference to the land. In the instant case the exercise by the registered proprietors of the powers conferred on trustees for sale by section 28(1) of the Law of Property Act 1925 had the effect of overreaching the interests of the [Fleggs] under the statutory trusts upon which depended their right to continue in occupation of the land. [The building society] took free from those trusts (section 27) and were not, in any event, concerned to see that the [Fleggs]' consent to the transaction was obtained (section 26). If, then, one asks what were the subsisting rights of the [Fleggs] referable to their occupation, the answer must, in my judgment, be that they were rights which, vis-à-vis [the building society], were, [simultaneously] with the creation of the charge, overreached and therefore subsisted only in relation to the equity of redemption [...] Section 70(1)(g) protects only the rights in reference to the land of the occupier whatever they are at the material time—in the instant case the right to enjoy in specie the rents and profits of the land held in trust for him. Once the beneficiary's rights have been shifted from the land to capital moneys in the hands of the trustees, there is no longer an interest in the land to which the occupation can be referred or which it can protect. If the trustees sell in accordance with the statutory provisions and so overreach the beneficial interests in reference to the land, nothing remains to which a right of occupation can attach and the same result must, in my judgment, follow vis-à-vis a chargee by way of legal mortgage so long as the transaction is carried out in the manner prescribed by the Law of Property Act 1925 [...] In the instant case, therefore, I would, for my part, hold that the charge created in favour of [the building society] overreached the beneficial interests of the respondents and that there is nothing in section 70(1)(g) of the Land Registration Act 1925 [...] which has the effect of preserving against [the building society] any rights of [the Fleggs] to occupy the land by virtue of their beneficial interests in the equity of redemption which remains vested in the trustees.

The decision of the House of Lords in *Flegg* provoked a good deal of controversy. Indeed, the Law Commission recommended that the law should be changed so that it is *not*

possible for C to use the overreaching defence where B is an adult and in actual occupation of land.[14]

We will examine some of the specific arguments against the *Flegg* decision in Chapter 20.
Here, our concern is with what *Flegg* can tell us about how, in general, the courts deal with
the priority triangle. The first point concerns the role of actual occupation. It is wrong to
think that if B has a pre-existing property right and is in actual occupation of registered
land, B will *always* take priority over C. B's actual occupation may prevent C from using the
lack of registration defence against B, but it does *not* prevent C from relying on a different
defence, such as overreaching.

The second point demonstrated by *Flegg* is that the defences available to C may depend on
the nature of B's pre-existing property right. In *Flegg*, B's right arose under a 'trust for sale';
as a result, that right was vulnerable to the overreaching defence regulated by s 2 of the LPA
1925. As we will see in Chapter 20, B is now vulnerable to that defence whenever his equitable property right arises under a trust of land. Similarly, C's ability to rely on a defence may
depend on C satisfying certain requirements: for example, as we will see in Chapter 20, s 2 of
the LPA 1925 meant that, in *Flegg*, it was crucial that the building society had paid the loan
money to *two* trustees.[15]

3.4 DEFENCES BASED ON B'S CONSENT

3.4.1 Where B expressly consents to C taking priority

Imagine a case in which A holds a freehold on trust for both A and B, who share occupation of the home. That freehold was acquired without a mortgage loan. A and B then decide
to raise some money by taking out a mortgage loan. A approaches C Bank and informs C
Bank that B has a pre-existing equitable property right. If C Bank deals with A alone, it can
acquire a charge over the land, because A is a sole registered owner of the land. But C Bank is
aware that, due to B's actual occupation of the land, B has an overriding interest. As a result,
C Bank requires B to give his consent to C Bank's later charge taking priority over B's right.
Clearly, if B gives that consent, C Bank's later charge will take priority: B's consent gives C
Bank a defence to B's pre-existing equitable property right.

Problems can, however, arise if B later claims that his consent was not freely given: for
example, it may be that A pressured B into giving the consent, or that A lied to B about the
terms of the loan. In that case, two questions arise: firstly, was there really any flaw in B's
consent—for example, did A use undue influence or make a misrepresentation in order to
convince B to give that consent? Secondly, if so, should that flaw in B's consent affect C Bank:
after all, if it was A who used the undue influence or made the misrepresentation, why should
C Bank lose out?

We will examine the special principles developed to deal with this difficult question in
Chapter 30, section 3.3. For the moment, we simply need to note that, *in some circumstances*,
a flaw in B's consent, even if procured by A, *can* prevent C Bank from taking priority.

---

[14] See Law Commission Report No 188, *Overreaching: Beneficiaries in Occupation* (1989). That reform
was *not* adopted by Parliament when passing the Trusts of Land and Appointment of Trustees Act 1996.

[15] Section 2(1)(ii) limits overreaching in a case such as *Flegg* to situations in which '*the statutory requirements respecting the payment of capital money arising under the settlement are complied with*'. Section 27 of
the Law of Property Act 1925 then imposes such a requirement: *if* C pays money in return for its property
right, that money must be paid to at least two trustees or to a trust corporation (see Chapter 20, section 2.3).

3.4.2 Where B impliedly consents to C taking priority

We saw above that, in *Abbey National v Cann*, Daisy Cann did not give her express consent to the Abbey National taking priority. The Abbey National did not have the chance to ask for such consent, because it was unaware that Daisy had any pre-existing property right: when George Cann applied for the mortgage loan, he lied to the building society and said that he did not plan to share occupation of the home. Daisy did, however, know that a loan would be necessary to provide the extra £4,000 that she and George needed to buy that land. The Court of Appeal therefore decided that Daisy had *impliedly* consented to a mortgage lender (the Abbey National) taking priority. We have seen that the House of Lords held that, in any case, there was no need for such consent: the Abbey National did not need a defence to Daisy's equitable property right, because its charge arose *before* Daisy acquired that right.

Nonetheless, in the following extracts from the House of Lords' decision, Lord Oliver (with whom Lords Bridge, Ackner, and Griffiths agreed)[16] supported the Court of Appeal's reasoning.

Abbey National Building Society v Cann [1991] 1 AC 56, HL

Facts: See section 2.2.1 above.

Lord Oliver

At 94

The view that I have formed renders it strictly unnecessary to consider the ground upon which Mrs. Cann's claim failed in the Court of Appeal. What was said was that, despite her initial evidence (in her affidavit) that she did not know of her son's intention to raise any of the money required for the purchase on mortgage, nevertheless her oral evidence before the judge disclosed that she was well aware that there was a shortfall which would have to be met from somewhere. Her own account of the matter was that his reason for selling was that he was in financial difficulties, so that she must have known that he was not going to be able to meet it out of his own resources. Dillon L.J. (with whom, on this point, the other two members of the court agreed) inferred that "she left it to George Cann to raise the balance"[17] from which he further inferred that George Cann had authority to raise that sum from the society. There was no finding to this effect by the judge, but I think, for my part, that it is a necessary conclusion once it is accepted, as it has to be, that she knew that there was a shortfall of some £4,000 apart from conveyancing costs, that George Cann was going to raise it, and that he was in financial difficulties. It is said that there was no evidence that he was going to raise it on the security of this property. There might, for instance, be other property available to him. He might obtain an unsecured loan. In the circumstances of his known lack of resources, however, this is fanciful and in my judgment the court was entitled to draw the inference that it did draw. If that is right, it follows that George Cann was permitted by her to raise money on the security of the property without any limitation on his authority being communicated to the society. She is not, therefore, in a position to complain, as against the

---

16 Lord Jauncey's reasoning is also consistent with that of Lord Oliver, but at 102–3, Lord Jauncey noted that, in finding that the Abbey National's charge arose before Daisy Cann's equitable property right, '*it is unnecessary to consider whether or not Mrs Cann was aware that George Cann would require to borrow money in order to finance the purchase of* [the new home]'.

17 [1989] 2 FLR 265, 276.

> lender, that too much was raised and even if, contrary to the view which I have formed, she had been able to establish an interest in the property which would otherwise prevail against the society, the circumstances to which I have alluded would preclude her from relying upon it as prevailing over the society's interest for the reasons given in the judgment of Dillon L.J. in the Court of Appeal. For all these reasons, I would accordingly dismiss the appeal.

The idea that B can be taken to have *impliedly* consented to giving priority to C did not originate in *Cann*,[18] and it has been applied since the House of Lords' decision in that case.[19] Nonetheless, it is somewhat controversial.[20] Firstly, there is a practical question: in *Cann* itself, was it really true to say that Daisy 'must have known' that George would take out a mortgage? After all, it may have been possible to raise the £4,000 by other means.[21]

Secondly, even if Daisy did know that a mortgage would be necessary, there is a conceptual problem. As we will see in Chapter 13, section 2.2.2, there is a general doctrine, often referred to as 'promissory estoppel', which can be used to give C a defence against a right of B. For that defence to operate, however, it is usually necessary: (i) for B to make some form of promise to C (e.g. a promise not to enforce his right against C); and (ii) for C to rely on that promise. The difficulty in a case such as *Cann* is that Daisy Cann did not make any promise to the Abbey National; indeed, the cause of the problem was that the Abbey National was entirely unaware of her.

The following extract makes this point, as well as suggesting a way of understanding other cases that adopt the implied consent reasoning. In the extract: (i) 'promissory estoppel' is referred to as 'defensive estoppel'; (ii) 'A' represents George Cann, 'B' represents Daisy Cann, and 'C Bank' represents the Abbey National; and (iii) the term 'persistent right' is used to refer to an equitable property right (see Chapter 4, section 7).

McFarlane, *The Structure of Property Law* (2008, p 823)

> As there have been no direct dealings between B and C Bank, the defensive estoppel defence can apply only if we can say that: (i) A, acting as an agent for B, made an implied commitment to C Bank on behalf of B; *or* (ii) B was under a *duty* to inform C Bank of her right. Yet neither (i) nor (ii) is persuasive. As to (i), in [a case such as *Cann*], it is *at most* tenable to say that B allowed A to give C Bank a Charge in order to raise [£4,000: the extra money necessary to purchase the home]. B certainly did not give A any authority to borrow [£25,000]. And yet, in *Cann*, the House of Lords stated that C Bank has a defence *irrespective* of the fact that A borrowed more than was necessary to achieve A and B's plan. As to (ii), it is very odd to say that B, with a pre-existing persistent right, is under any duty to inform others of that right: such an idea is entirely absent from the property law system. Rather, if anything, the opposite approach is adopted: C's failure to check for a pre-existing persistent right of B may be important in denying C a defence to that right.
>
> So, as a matter of doctrine, the position adopted in *Cann* cannot be defended [...] The *Cann* position thus gives *special* protection to a secured lender. Can that special treatment

---

[18] It was also applied in *Bristol & West BS v Henning* [1985] 1 WLR 778 and *Paddington BC v Mendelsohn* (1985) 50 P & CR 244.

[19] See, e.g., *Equity & Law Home Loans Ltd v Prestidge* [1992] 1 WLR 137.

[20] See, e.g., Smith (1990) 109 LQR 545.

[21] This point is noted by Sawyer, 'A World Safe for Mortgagees? Registering a Scintilla of Doubt' in *Modern Studies in Propety Law: Vol 1* (ed Cooke, 2001, p 209).

be justified by the needs of practical convenience? Probably not. The *Cann* position is *not* a simple rule that C Bank always wins; rather, it is based on B's knowledge of the shortfall in A and B's funds. So to defend the *Cann* position we need to show why that knowledge should affect C Bank's position. And it is hard to find a convincing practical reason why that knowledge should make any difference.

In practice, this particular aspect of the *Cann* decision is not too important: the real impact of that decision is in protecting C Bank whenever it makes a secured loan used by A to *acquire* a Freehold or Lease. In fact, cases before *Cann* adopting the modified "defensive estoppel" defence may well have done so precisely because, at that time, it was *not* possible for C Bank to argue that its Charge arose before B's persistent right.[22] So, when changing the approach to the timing question in *Cann* [see section 2.2.1 above], the House of Lords should also have taken the opportunity to change the approach to "defensive estoppel" by stating that C Bank cannot use that defence if, as in [*Cann*], B has made no commitment to C Bank.

3.5 DEFENCES BASED ON THE LAPSE OF TIME

3.5.1 Unregistered land

As we saw in Chapter 3, B can acquire a legal property right (a freehold) simply by taking physical control of a piece of land. That is the case even if B acts with full knowledge that A has a pre-existing property right in the same land. For example, if A has a freehold of a holiday home, and B moves into that home whilst A is away and starts to use the house as his own, B acquires his own freehold. But because A's freehold arose before B's freehold, the basic rule tells us that A's pre-existing property right takes priority to that of B. So, A is free to remove B from the land, either by using reasonable force or by seeking a possession order from a court. Initially, then, B's freehold may give him useful protection against X (a party who later tries to move into the home), but it does not protect him against A.

If B continues to act as an owner of the home over a long period, however, the lapse of time can give B a defence to A's pre-existing property right. Where unregistered land is concerned, the basic rules are set out by ss 15(1) and 17 of the Limitation Act 1980.

Limitation Act 1980, ss 15(1) and 17

15 Time limit for actions to recover land

(1) No action shall be brought by any person to recover any land after the expiration of twelve years from the date on which the right of action accrued to him or, if it first accrued to some person through whom he claims, to that person [...]

---

[22] [The footnote in the original refers to *Bristol & West BS v Henning* [1985] 1 WLR 778 and *Paddington BC v Mendelsohn* (1985) 50 P & CR 244, noting that the result in those cases need not depend on the 'implied consent' of B: following the decision in *Cann* on the *scintilla temporis* point, the result can instead be seen as depending on the fact that C Bank's charge arises before B's equitable property right. The decision in *Equity & Law Home Loans Ltd v Prestidge* [1992] 1 WLR 137 is explained on the basis that: (i) following the *Cann* decision on the *scintilla temporis* point, the holder of the first charge took priority over B; and (ii) the holder of the second charge, when providing the money used to pay off that first loan, then stepped into the shoes of the holder of the first charge. See further Dixon, 'Consenting Away Proprietary Rights' in *Modern Studies in Property Law: Vol I* (ed Cooke, 2001, pp 193–8).]

17 Extinction of title to land after expiration of time limit

Subject to section 18 of this Act, at the expiration of the period prescribed by this Act for any person to recover land (including a redemption action) the title of that person to the land shall be extinguished.

Section 15(1) allows the lapse of time (twelve years) to give B a defence against A's pre-existing property right. Section 17 goes further: it means that, once twelve years has elapsed, A loses that pre-existing right. This means that not only is B protected from A's previous right, but also that any later users of the land are safe from a claim by A. As a result, B's acquisition of a freehold (which occurs as soon as B takes physical control of the land), coupled with the lapse of time, means that B can acquire the best right to the land. In such a case, B's protection is said to depend on the doctrine of *adverse possession*.

We will examine the detail of that doctrine in Chapter 10; as far as the priority triangle is concerned, two points are worth noting here. Firstly—in relation to unregistered land, at least—the lapse of time can operate to give a later property right priority to an earlier property right, even if the holder of the later property right has deliberately acted inconsistently with that earlier right.

Secondly, the defence provided by s 15(1) of the Limitation Act 1980 is unique: it not only protects an adverse possessor from a pre-existing property right; it also *extinguishes* that right.

3.5.2 Registered land

Land Registration Act 2002, s 96

(1) No period of limitation under section 15 of the Limitation Act 1980 (time limits in relation to recovery of land) shall run against any person, other than a chargee, in relation to an estate in land or rentcharge the title to which is registered.

(2) [. . .]

(3) Accordingly, section 17 of that Act (extinction of title on expiry of time limit) does not operate to extinguish the title of any person where, by virtue of this section, a period of limitation does not run against him.

Section 96 of the LRA 2002 thus makes clear that, if A has a registered freehold or lease, the lapse of time, by itself, can *never* give B a defence against A's pre-existing property right. Instead, the 2002 Act provides a new set of rules to deal with cases in which B takes physical control of land covered by a freehold or lease that is registered in A's name.

We will examine the detail of those rules in Chapter 10. One important point to note here is that the 2002 Act enacted a deliberate policy of giving greater protection to A where he or she has a registered freehold or lease. Indeed, if A has a freehold or lease of unregistered land and has no current plans to sell that land, the extra protection given against an adverse possessor provides perhaps the best incentive for A to register his or her property right.

3.6 DEFENCES AND THE DISTINCTION BETWEEN LEGAL AND EQUITABLE PROPERTY RIGHTS

If B has a pre-existing *legal* property right, it is possible for C's later property right to take priority: C may have a defence to B's legal property right. For example, B's express consent can clearly give C such a defence, and we have seen that—in unregistered land, at least—the lapse of time can also give a party a defence against a legal freehold or lease. It is, however, far easier for C to have a defence against a pre-existing *equitable* property right. Indeed, this is one of the main reasons why it is so important to distinguish between legal and equitable property rights.

This difference between legal and equitable property rights is particularly clear when we look at the lack of registration defence. For example, we saw in *Midland Bank Trust Co Ltd v Green* that Geoffrey's failure to register his equitable property right as a land charge allowed Evelyne to have a defence against that right. Under the LCA 1972, however, it is impossible for that lack of registration defence to be used against a pre-existing *legal* property right.

Similarly, under the LRA 2002, it is almost impossible for C to use the lack of registration defence against a pre-existing *legal* property right. This is for two reasons: firstly, in order to acquire such a legal property right in the first place, B will often need to register it; in such a case, the lack of registration defence is irrelevant. Secondly, if the LRA 2002 does allow B to acquire a legal property right without registering it, that right will almost always count as an overriding interest; as a result, it will be immune to the lack of registration defence (see section 3.2.2 above). We will examine the detail of overriding interests in Chapter 16, but we can see the crucial difference between legal and equitable property rights in the following provisions.

Land Registration Act 2002, Sch 3, para 1

Unregistered interests which override registered dispositions

Leasehold estates in land

A leasehold estate in land granted for a term not exceeding seven years from the date of the grant, except for—

(a) a lease the grant of which falls within section 4(1)(d)(e) or (f);

(b) a lease the grant of which constitutes a registrable disposition.

The exceptions in (a) and (b) simply ensure that, in those exceptional cases in which a lease of seven years or less must be registered, it cannot count as an overriding interest. The crucial word in setting the scope of the main rule is 'granted'. That word is used because, following the decision in the case set out below, it means that only a *legal* lease is covered by the LRA 2002, Sch 3, para 1. In that case, the court considered s 70(1)(k) of the LRA 1925, which allowed '*Leases granted for a term not exceeding twenty-one years*' to count as an overriding interest.

City Permanent Building Society v Miller [1952] Ch 840, CA

Facts: Louie Cumberland had seven children and was in desperate need of somewhere to live. Henry Miller agreed to give Ms Cumberland a lease of the first and second floors of a house in Earl's Court, London. The lease was stated to run for three years, initially, and then to run from week to week. In return, she paid three years' rent in advance. At that point, however, Mr Miller had no rights in relation to the house and Ms Cumberland was not able to move in until three months later, when Mr Miller acquired a long lease of the house. To acquire that lease, Mr Miller borrowed £650 from the City Permanent Building Society: that sum was secured by a charge over the house. When Mr Miller failed to repay the loan as agreed, the building society attempted to remove Ms Cumberland so that it could sell the house with vacant possession and use the proceeds to meet Mr Miller's debt. Ms Cumberland argued that she had an overriding interest under s 70(1)(k) of the LRA 1925, which protected 'Leases granted for a term not exceeding twenty-one years'.

Lord Evershed MR

At 848

[T]he effect of the contract was that [Mr Miller] obliged himself to grant to the tenant a term in these premises of three years plus one week at the least [...] such an agreement is not capable of conferring upon the tenant any estate in the property; in order that a tenant may acquire an estate of over three years, a deed is necessary [see Chapter 9, section 4 and Chapter 23, section 3.1.2].

I therefore proceed to a consideration of the main problem, bearing in mind that all the tenant took at the most was, as I have said, a specifically enforceable contract to grant a lease of at least three years and a week. [Counsel for Ms Cumberland], in his reply, has said that she took an equitable term and that during the moment of time when the mortgagor was registered proprietor unencumbered by the charge that equitable term ripened into a legal interest. I am unable to accept any stage of that argument. I do not think she had an equitable term. Indeed, I do not think that that phrase really can mean anything except that she had the right to get specific performance of this contract; and, assuming in [Ms Cumberland's] favour that there was a [point in time] when the mortgagor was the unencumbered proprietor of the property, I am clear that the effect of it was not to create any legal estate in the tenant, more particularly since she was not, as I have explained, at that time in occupation.

Now having dealt with all those points, I return to give my reasons for the conclusion which I have already anticipated. It seems to me that as a matter of English the use of the word "granted" in paragraph (k), whether it he applied to the word "lease" or the word "term," indicates, on the face of it, that the lease or agreement for lease which is to be an overriding interest must be a lease or agreement which is effective to create a term. An agreement for a tenancy or to grant a tenancy for a year would be so effective if the tenant were in possession, but I have felt compelled, upon a review of the whole of the relevant legislation, to conclude that such a limitation of the expanded word "lease" is inevitably imposed by the use of the word "granted"; and since, as I have already stated, the definitions must be read subject to the requirement of the context, that is my conclusion.

So, in *City Permanent Building Society v Miller*, the crucial point was that Ms Cumberland's agreement with Mr Miller could not give her a legal lease: because the lease was due to last for more than three years, s 52 of the LPA 1925 means that it could only be legal if created by means of a deed. The agreement did give Ms Cumberland an equitable lease (under the doctrine of anticipation)[23] and that equitable lease arose *before* the building society acquired

---

[23] See the discussion of *Walsh v Lonsdale* in Chapter 4, section 6 and also in Chapter 12.

its charge. But the building society was able to use the lack of registration defence: Ms Cumberland had not protected her lease by entering a notice on the register, and that lease, because it was only equitable, could not count, by itself, as an overriding interest.

Of course, in *Miller*, things would have been different if Ms Cumberland had been in actual occupation of the land when the building society acquired its charge. In fact, where B has a pre-existing equitable property right, actual occupation is the *only* means by which that right can count as an overriding interest. This is why actual occupation is so important in practice and why we will consider the concept in detail in Chapter 16, section 5.1.

Land Registration Act 2002, Sch 3, para 3

Unregistered interests which override registered dispositions

Easements and profits a prendre

(1) A legal easement or profit a prendre, except for an easement, or a profit a prendre which is not registered under the Commons Registration Act 1965, which at the time of the disposition—

(a) is not within the actual knowledge of the person to whom the disposition is made, and

(b) would not have been obvious on a reasonably careful inspection of the land over which the easement or profit is exercisable.

(2) The exception in sub-paragraph (1) does not apply if the person entitled to the easement or profit proves that it has been exercised in the period of one year ending with the day of the disposition.

This paragraph is badly drafted (we will unpick its detailed meaning in Chapter 16, section 5.3), but one point is made very clear: the paragraph protects only *legal* easements and profits. Under the LRA 1925, the comparable provision (s 70(1)(a)) had, rather controversially, been interpreted as including at least some equitable easements. Following the recommendation of the Law Commission, however, the new Act makes clear that equitable easements and profits cannot count, by themselves, as overriding interests. So, such a right can only be immune from the lack of registration defence in the unlikely case that B is in actual occupation of the land to which his or her equitable easement or profit relates.

4 CONCLUSION

Many disputes about the use of land have the same basic form: (i) B acquires a right to make some use of land from A, who has an estate in that land; (ii) C then acquires a similar right from A; and (iii) B and C want to use that land in mutually inconsistent ways. In such a case, the first question to ask is whether B acquired a legal or equitable property right: as we saw in Chapters 3 and 4, we can break that question down into the *content* and *acquisition* questions. It may be the case that C also acquired a legal or equitable property right from A. If so, there is a *priority triangle*: we need to ask whether B or C's property right is to take priority.

The basic rule is clear: B's property right will take priority because it is *first in time*—that is, it arose before C's property right. As we saw in section 2.2 above, however, there are some cases in which we need to take care in working out the order in which the property rights arose. And, even if it is clear that B's property right arose before C's property right, it may still be possible for C to take priority: to do so, C needs to show he has a *defence* to B's pre-existing right. In section 3 above, we saw a number of examples of such a defence. In later chapters, we will return to examine some of those defences in more detail: for example, Chapter 15 will look at the lack of registration defence in unregistered land, Chapter 16 will focus on that defence in registered land, and Chapter 20 will explore overreaching. We have, however, already seen a number of important points. Firstly, it is always vital to keep in mind the possibility of C having a defence to B's pre-existing property right. Secondly, the availability of a defence can depend on both: (i) the nature of B's property right; and (ii) the circumstances in which C acquired his property right. In particular, C's chances of having a defence are much greater where B's property right is an equitable, rather than a legal, right.

So, even if B can clear the hurdles discussed in Chapters 3 and 4, and show that he has a legal or equitable property right in relation to land, there is no guarantee that his right will *always* bind a third party. Equally, however, it is important to remember that, even if he cannot assert a pre-existing property right against C, there is another means by which B's claim can prevail: if B can show that he has a *direct right* against C, arising as a result of C's conduct, B can simply rely on that right. We will examine these direct rights in Chapter 7.

QUESTIONS

1. In *National Provincial Bank v Ainsworth*, Mrs Ainsworth acquired her 'deserted wife's equity' before National Provincial Bank acquired its charge. So why was her claim to remain in occupation of the land unsuccessful?

2. Do you agree with the approach to the *scintilla temporis* question adopted by the House of Lords in *Abbey National v Cann*? Should that approach be limited to cases in which a mortgage loan is necessary in order to enable the borrower to buy the land in question?

3. In *Midland Bank Trust Co Ltd v Green*, Geoffrey Green acquired his equitable property right before Evelyne Green acquired her freehold. So why was Evelyne free to ignore Geoffrey's right? Should the fact that Evelyne was fully aware of Geoffrey's right make any difference to the result?

4. What is an 'overriding interest'? Can you explain why Mrs Hodgson had such a right in *Hodgson v Marks*, but Mrs Ainsworth did not in *National Provincial Bank v Ainsworth*?

5. In a case such as *Abbey National Building Society v Cann*, does it make sense to say that Mrs Cann impliedly consented to the building society taking priority?

FURTHER READING

Battersby, 'Informal Transactions in Land, Estoppel and Registration' [1995] MLR 637

Dixon, 'Consenting Away Proprietary Rights' in *Modern Studies in Property Law: Vol 1* (ed Cooke, Oxford: Hart, 2001)

Harpum, 'Overreaching, Trustees' Powers and the Reform of the 1925 Legislation' [1990] CLJ 277

Law Commission Report No 188, *Overreaching: Beneficiaries in Occupation* (1989)

Law Commission Report No 271, *Land Registration for the 21st Century* (2001, Pts I, II, and V)

McFarlane, *The Structure of Property Law* (Oxford: Hart, 2008, Pts B5, E1.3, E2.3, and G4.4)

Sawyer, 'A World Safe for Mortgagees? Registering a Scintilla of Doubt' in *Modern Studies in Property Law: Vol 1* (ed Cooke, Oxford: Hart, 2001, ch 12)

Smith, 'Mortgagees and Trust Beneficiaries' (1990) 109 LQR 545

7

DIRECT RIGHTS

CENTRAL ISSUES

1. Many land law cases share a basic form: a dispute arises between B and C, each of whom wants to make an inconsistent use of the land. We saw in Chapter 6 that the courts will find in favour of B if B has a pre-existing legal or equitable property right, and C has no defence to that right.

2. It is possible, however, for B to prevail even if he or she has no pre-existing property right; and even if he or she has a property right to which C has a defence. B can do so if he or she can assert a direct right against C.

3. A direct right, unlike a pre-existing property right, arises as a result of C's conduct. In this chapter, we will consider some examples of situations in which C's conduct allows a court to recognise that B has a direct right against C.

4. In most cases, it will be very difficult for B to show that he or she has a direct right against C. For example, if C buys some land by acquiring A's freehold or lease, it is very unlikely that C will act in such a way as to give B a direct right. Nonetheless, in some cases, direct rights may provide a court with a useful means to protect B. For example, a direct right can protect B even if he or she has failed to ensure that his or her pre-existing property right is recorded on the register.

5. It is not always clear whether the result of a particular case depends on B asserting a direct right against C or, instead, on B having a pre-existing property right to which C has no defence. When analysing the cases, however, it is very important to distinguish between those two possibilities. We will see the importance of this distinction in Chapter 8, when analysing licences.

1 INTRODUCTION: THE CONCEPT OF A DIRECT RIGHT

We saw in Chapter 6 that, if B and C each wish to make an inconsistent use of the same piece of land, it is important to ask: (i) whether B has a pre-existing legal or equitable property right; and (ii) if so, whether C has a defence to that right. But it is also important to bear in mind the possibility of B having a direct right against C. For example, in *National Provincial Bank v Ainsworth*,[1] a case that we examined in Chapter 1, section 5, and Chapter 4, section 5.4, we saw that, when the bank acquired its charge, Mrs Ainsworth had no pre-existing property right. Imagine, however, that the bank had nonetheless made a contractual promise to Mrs Ainsworth to allow her to remain in occupation of the land. In such a case, the fact that Mrs Ainsworth had no pre-existing property right would be irrelevant: she would simply be able to rely on her direct, contractual right against the bank.

The important point about a direct right, as opposed to a pre-existing property right, is that it arises as a result of C's own conduct. Of course, in *Ainsworth*, the bank did *not* make a contractual promise to Mrs Ainsworth; nor did it do anything else to give her a direct right. After all, the bank wanted to ensure that, if Mr Ainsworth failed to repay the mortgage loan, it would be able to sell the land with vacant possession: it therefore had no reason to act in such a way as to give Mrs Ainsworth a direct right. In some cases, however, there may be an incentive for A, when giving C a right, to ensure that C does, indeed, act in such a way as to give B a direct right.

For example, consider the situation in *Rhone v Stephens*,[2] a case that we examined in Chapter 4, section 5.3. There, A's roof overhung B's land, and A had made a promise to B that he and future owners of his land would keep that roof in good repair. The question then arose of whether A's promise could give B, and later owners of B's land, an equitable interest in A's land: a right that was capable of binding C, who later acquired A's freehold. As we saw, the House of Lords found that A's promise did *not* give B an equitable interest: in general,[3] a promise to act in a certain way, unlike a promise *not* to act in a certain way, cannot give B a legal or equitable interest in land (see Chapter 27, section 2.3, for more detail). The rule applied in *Rhone v Stephens* thus causes B a problem if he or she wants to ensure that later owners of A's land, as well as A, will be under a duty to perform a positive act, such as repairing a roof. As we will see in Chapter 27, section 2.4.2, one possible response to this problem is for B to give A an incentive, when transferring his or her freehold to C, to make C agree to repair the roof. This can be done by a chain of 'indemnity covenants': the initial agreement between A and B makes clear that A not only has a duty to repair the roof, but also to ensure that, if he or she later transfers his or her freehold to C, C will also agree to repair the roof. Of course, B still faces the risk that A, when transferring the land to C, will not extract that promise from C—but the terms of A's initial promise to B do at least give A an incentive to ensure that C makes that promise. The question then arises of whether C's promise, if made to A, can give B a direct right against C.

---

[1] [1965] AC 1175.
[2] [1994] 2 AC 310.
[3] As we saw when examining *Walsh v Lonsdale* in Chapter 4, section 6, there is an exception where A's promise is to give B a property right in relation to A's land: this point will be explored further in Chapter 12.

2 WHEN WILL B HAVE A DIRECT RIGHT AGAINST C?

There are many different means by which B can acquire a direct right against C. We will concentrate here on those that are most likely to be relevant in a dispute relating to the use of land.

2.1 WHERE C GIVES B A DIRECT RIGHT BY MEANS OF A DEED

If C chooses to give B a direct right, C can use a deed to do so. As the following extract shows, it is important to distinguish between cases in which the deed is executed by C alone; and those in which the deed is entered into by both C and another party. In the latter case, it may well be that C makes the deed with A, not with B. After all, C, when acquiring his or her right, must deal with A, and, if C is acquiring a legal estate in the land from A, it will usually be necessary for a deed to be used. The fact that C deals with A, not B, may seem to make it more difficult for B to acquire a direct right against C. As discussed in the following extract, however, that problem is alleviated by s 56 of the Law of Property Act 1925 (LPA 1925) (set out after the extract). We will return to s 56 in Chapter 27, section 3.3.3, when examining promises made between owners of neighbouring land.

McFarlane, *The Structure of Property Law* (2008, pp 268–9)[4]

C can use a deed to give B a direct right [...] If the deed is executed by C alone, it is known as a *deed poll*. C can use such a deed to give B a direct right even if there is no agreement between B and C and even if B is not aware of the deed.[5]

An additional requirement applies to a deed executed not just by C, but by C and another party, such as A. Such a deed is known as an *inter partes* (between parties) deed: the deed itself will record that it is made *between* C and A. Again, C can use such a deed to give B a right. However, the traditional rule is that B can only acquire a right by means of an *inter partes* deed if B is *named* as one of the parties to the deed.[6] So, the deed itself must record that it is made *between* all three parties: A, B and C.

However, where C attempts to give B a right relating to a thing,[7] section 56 of the Law of Property Act 1925 provides an exception. Even if C uses an *inter partes* deed, and fails to name B as a party to the deed, B *can* acquire a right. The section thus means that where C attempts to deal directly with B by means of an *inter partes* deed, C's failure to include B as a party to the deed will *not* prevent B acquiring a direct right against C.

---

[4] The footnotes in the original are included here.

[5] See, e.g., *Macedo v Stroud* [1922] 2 AC 330.

[6] See, e.g., *Lord Southampton v Brown* (1827) 6 B & C 718; *Chesterfield and Midland Silkstone Colliery Co Ltd v Hawkins* (1865) 3 H & C 677, 692; *White v Bijou Mansions Ltd* [1938] Ch 351.

[7] Section 56 allows B to acquire a right relating to '*land or other property*'. The majority of the House of Lords in *Beswick v Beswick* [1968] AC 58 take the strange view that the section can only apply to give B a right relating to land, or to a property right in land. The natural reading of the section, however, is that it can apply whenever C attempts to give B a right relating to the use of a thing.

It is important to note the limits of the section 56 exception: it cannot be used *whenever* C makes a promise in a deed that happens to, or is even intended to, benefit B.[8] Instead, C must *purport to deal directly with B*: C must make a promise to B or otherwise attempt to give B a right.[9] As a result, B must be identifiable at the time the deed is executed.[10]

Law of Property Act 1925, s 56(1)

(1) A person may take an immediate or other interest in land or other property, or the benefit of any condition, right of entry, covenant, or agreement over or respecting land or other property, although he may not be named as a party to the conveyance or other instrument.

2.2 WHERE C GIVES B A DIRECT RIGHT BY MEANS OF A CONTRACTUAL PROMISE

If C chooses to give B a direct right, C may also do so by means of a contractual promise. Again, the fact that C is likely to deal only with A may seem to cause B a problem: if C's promise is made to A, and if only A provides consideration for it, then it seems that B cannot acquire a contractual right against C. The Contract (Rights of Third Parties) Act 1999, however, now allows B, in certain situations, to acquire a right as a result of C's contractual promise to A.

Contract (Rights of Third Parties) Act 1999, s 1

(1) Subject to the provisions of this Act, a person who is not a party to a contract (a "third party") may in his own right enforce a term of the contract if—

  (a) the contract expressly provides that he may, or

  (b) subject to subsection (2), the term purports to confer a benefit on him.

(2) Subsection (1)(b) does not apply if on a proper construction of the contract it appears that the parties did not intend the term to be enforceable by the third party.

(3) The third party must be expressly identified in the contract by name, as a member of a class or as answering a particular description but need not be in existence when the contract is entered into.

---

[8] As was made clear by Neuberger J in *Amsprop Trading Ltd v Harris Distribution Ltd* [1997] 1 WLR 1025.

[9] See also Simonds J in *White v Bijou Mansions Ltd* [1937] Ch 610, 625: B can only rely on s 56 if '*although not named as a party to the instrument*, [B] *is yet a person to whom that conveyance or other instrument purports to grant some thing or with whom some agreement or covenant is purported to be made*'. That view was cited with approval by Lords Upjohn and Pearce in *Beswick v Beswick* [1968] AC 58, 106 (Lord Upjohn) and 92–4 (Lord Pearce), and was also accepted by Neuberger J in *Amsprop Trading Ltd v Harris Distribution Ltd* [1997] 1 WLR 1025.

[10] For example, if C has promised to give a right to 'future owners of A's property', then B, a future owner of that thing, cannot use s 56, because he could not have been specifically identified when C made the promise in the deed.

(4) This section does not confer a right on a third party to enforce a term of a contract otherwise than subject to and in accordance with any other relevant terms of the contract.

(5) For the purpose of exercising his right to enforce a term of the contract, there shall be available to the third party any remedy that would have been available to him in an action for breach of contract if he had been a party to the contract (and the rules relating to damages, injunctions, specific performance and other relief shall apply accordingly).

[...]

Section 1(5) is particularly worth noting: where land is concerned, it is often the case that a court will protect a contractual right by means of specific performance or an injunction: for example, as we will see in Chapter 8, section 3.1.2, if A makes a contractual promise to B to allow B to occupy land for a period, a court will usually intervene, at B's request, to grant an injunction preventing A from breaching that promise. Similarly, then, if C makes a contractual promise to A to allow B to occupy land for a period, it will generally be the case that if B has a right against C, arising under s 1 of the 1999 Act, that right will be protected by means of an injunction.

The effect of the 1999 Act can be compared to that of s 56 of the LPA 1925. It is clear that the 1999 Act has a wider scope: for example, there is no need for C's promise to be made in a deed. Further, B does not need to be in existence and identifiable when C makes his or her promise: a promise by C for the benefit of *'A's current and future neighbours'* can give B a right under the 1999 Act even if B becomes A's neighbour *after* C has made his or her promise. As a result, the 1999 Act can be important in practice: we will return to it in Chapter 8, section 3.3.1 and Chapter 27, section 3.3.3. It is worth noting here, however, that, in some circumstances,[11] it is possible for B to rely on s 56 of the LPA 1925 in order to acquire a *legal* estate or interest in C's land. In contrast, if B relies instead on the 1999 Act, C's promise can, at most, give B an *equitable* interest in C's land (see section 3 below).

2.3 WHERE C GIVES B A DIRECT RIGHT BY MEANS OF A NON-CONTRACTUAL PROMISE

The Contract (Rights of Third Parties) Act 1999 can only assist B where C has made a *contractual* promise to A. If C makes any promise to benefit B, it is likely to be made as part of the contract under which C acquires an estate or interest in land from A. This means that, as we noted in Chapter 4, section 6, the *formality rule* imposed by s 2 of the Law of Property (Miscellaneous Provisions) Act 1989 (LP(MP)A 1989) will apply. We will examine that rule in more detail in Chapter 9, section 3. Its basic effect is that C's promise will be contractually binding on C *only* if it is recorded in writing signed by both A and C. So, if A transfers his or her estate to C and C simply makes an *oral* promise for B's benefit, it seems that: (i) C's promise will not be contractually binding; and so (ii) B will not be able to rely on the 1999 Act to acquire a direct right against C.

In such a case, B may, however, be able to rely on a *different* principle to acquire a direct right against C. Even before the passing of the 1999 Act, the courts recognized that, in certain situations, a promise made by C to A could give B a direct right against C. The following extract provides one example.

---

[11] For example, where C grants B a non-exceptional lease of seven years or less: see Chapter 23, section 3.1.2.

Bannister v Bannister [1948] 2 All ER 133, CA

Facts: Mrs Bannister had a freehold of two cottages: 30 and 31 Maryland Cottages, Mountnessing, Essex. She planned to sell her freehold to Mr Bannister, her brother-in-law. She told him that she was only willing to sell if she could continue to live in No 30. He orally agreed to this, telling her: '*I will let you stay as long as you like, rent free.*' The freehold of the two cottages was then transferred to Mr Bannister by means of a standard conveyance, which made no mention of Mrs Bannister's right to remain in No 30. But Mr Bannister paid only £250 for the land, which was, in fact, worth around £400. Following a dispute between Mrs Bannister and her brother-in-law, Mr Bannister sought an order for possession of No 30. He argued that his oral promise, at most, gave Mrs Bannister a 'tenancy at will'—that is, a permission to occupy that could be revoked by Mr Bannister at any time. The Court of Appeal rejected that argument and found that Mr Bannister, as a result of his promise, held his freehold of No 30 on trust for Mrs Bannister: under that trust, he had a duty to use the freehold for her benefit for the rest of her life, provided that she continued to occupy No 30.

Scott LJ

At 135–6

In view of the learned county court judge's acceptance of [Mrs Bannister's] evidence he necessarily found as a fact that the oral agreement as a result of which [Mrs Bannister] conveyed Nos 30 and 31 to [Mr Bannister] for £250 included an undertaking by [Mr Bannister] to permit [Mrs Bannister] to stay in No 30 for as long as she liked rent free, and that, but for this undertaking, [Mrs Bannister] would not have sold the two cottages to [Mr Bannister] at what, on the uncontradicted evidence of value, he rightly described as "a bargain price." He further found as a fact that there was no fraud in the case. On these findings of fact he held that on well-known equitable principles there was (as he put it) an implied or inferential trust, or, in other words, a constructive trust, of No 30 under which [Mr Bannister] held that property in trust for [Mrs Bannister] for life.

The conclusion thus reached by the learned county court judge was attacked in this court on substantially the following three grounds:—First, it was said that the oral undertaking found by the learned county court judge to have formed part of the agreement—namely, that [Mr Bannister] would let [Mrs Bannister] stay in No 30 as long as she liked rent free—did not, as a matter of construction of the language used, amount to a promise that [Mrs Bannister] should retain a life interest in No 30, but amounted merely to a promise that [Mr Bannister] would allow [Mrs Bannister] to remain in No 30 rent free as his tenant at will. Secondly, it was said that, even if the terms of the oral undertaking were such as to amount to a promise that [Mrs Bannister] should retain a life interest in No 30, a tenancy at will free of rent was, nevertheless, the greatest interest she could claim in view of the absence of writing and the provisions of ss 53 and 54 of the Law of Property Act, 1925. Thirdly, it was said that a constructive trust in favour of [Mrs Bannister] (which the absence of writing admittedly would not defeat) could only be raised by findings to the effect that there was actual fraud on the part of [Mr Bannister] and that the property was sold and conveyed to him on the faith of an express oral declaration of trust which it would be fraudulent in him to deny. It was, accordingly, submitted that the learned county court judge's conclusion that there was a constructive trust could not stand since it was negatived by his finding that there was no fraud in the case and by the absence of any evidence of anything amounting to an express oral declaration of trust.

In support of the first of these three objections reliance was placed on *Buck v Howarth*,[12] in which a King's Bench Divisional Court held that the occupant of a house who had been told by a predecessor in title of the freeholder "that he could live in the house until he died" (an oral and, it would seem, a purely voluntary promise) was given an uncertain interest in the premises and that the law would presume a tenancy at will [...] That was, obviously, a very different case from the present one and we find ourselves unable to derive any assistance from it. The promise was a purely voluntary one, and any court would naturally have been slow to construe it as intended to confer a life interest, even if it was literally capable of that construction. Moreover, whatever the words may have meant, the case clearly fell within s 54 of the Law of Property Act, 1925, under which interests in land created by parol have the force and effect of interests at will only. There was, of course, no question of a resulting trust as there might have been if the occupant of the house had been a former owner who had sold the freehold on the faith of a similar promise. In the present case [Mrs Bannister] did, on the facts found, sell and convey the property on the faith of the oral undertaking and would not otherwise have done so, and the undertaking must be assumed to have been regarded as reserving to her a benefit worth at least £150, or three-eights of the contemporary market value of the property without vacant possession. We, therefore, see no reason why the words of the undertaking should not be given the most favourable construction, from [Mrs Bannister's] point of view, of which they are properly capable. Similar words in deeds and wills have frequently been held to create a life interest determinable (apart from the special considerations introduced by the Settled Land Act, 1925) on the beneficiary ceasing to occupy the premises [...] In our view, that is the meaning which should, in the circumstances of the present case, be placed on the words of the oral undertaking found by the learned county court judge to have been given by the [Mr Bannister]. We are, accordingly, of opinion that the first objection fails, though the interest promised to [Mrs Bannister] by [Mr Bannister] must, we think, be taken to have been a life interest determinable on her ceasing to occupy No 30 and not a life interest *simpliciter* as held by the learned county court judge.

As will be seen from what is said below, the second objection (based on want of writing) in effect stands or falls with the third, and it will, therefore, be convenient to deal with that next. It is, we think, clearly a mistake to suppose that the equitable principle on which a constructive trust is raised against a person who insists on the absolute character of a conveyance to himself for the purpose of defeating a beneficial interest, which, according to the true bargain, was to belong to another, is confined to cases in which the conveyance itself was fraudulently obtained. The fraud which brings the principle into play arises as soon as the absolute character of the conveyance is set up for the purpose of defeating the beneficial interest, and that is the fraud to cover which the Statute of Frauds or the corresponding provisions of the Law of Property Act, 1925, cannot be called in aid in cases in which no written evidence of the real bargain is available. Nor is it, in our opinion, necessary that the bargain on which the absolute conveyance is made should include any express stipulation that the grantee is in so many words to hold as trustee. It is enough that the bargain should have included a stipulation under which some sufficiently defined beneficial interest in the property was to be taken by another [...] We see no distinction in principle between a case in which property is conveyed to a purchaser on terms that the entire beneficial interest in some part of it is to be retained by the vendor [...] and a case, like the present, in which property is conveyed to a purchaser on terms that a limited beneficial interest in some part of it is to be retained by the vendor. We are, accordingly, of the opinion that the third ground of objection to the learned county court judge's conclusion also fails. His finding that there was no fraud in the case cannot be taken as

12 [1947] 1 All ER 342.

meaning that it was not fraudulent in [Mr Bannister] to insist on the absolute character of the conveyance for the purpose of defeating the beneficial interest which he had agreed [Mrs Bannister] should retain. The conclusion that [Mr Bannister] was fraudulent, in this sense, necessarily follows from the facts found, and, as indicated above, the fact that he may have been innocent of any fraudulent intent in taking the conveyance in absolute form is for this purpose immaterial. The failure of the third ground of objection necessarily also destroys the second objection based on want of writing and the provisions of ss 53 and 54 of the Law of Property Act, 1925.

One important point in *Bannister* is that Mrs Bannister's right arose under a *trust*: there is a slight puzzle as to the nature of this trust, and so we will examine it further in Chapter 14, section 4.3.1. For our present purposes, however, the importance of the decision in *Bannister* lies in the recognition that a party acquiring an estate or interest in land can come under a duty as a result of an oral, non-contractual promise made when acquiring that estate or interest. Certainly, Mrs Bannister did not assert her pre-existing freehold against Mr Bannister: after all, she transferred that very right to him. Instead, she relied on a new, direct right, arising as a result of Mr Bannister's promise to her.

Of course, there is a difference between the facts of *Bannister* and the three-party situation in which C, on acquiring an estate or interest from A, makes a promise to give B a direct right. But it seems that the principle set out in *Bannister* can also apply in a three-party case. Certainly, Lord Denning MR took that view in the following extract.

Binions v Evans [1972] Ch 359, CA

Facts: Mrs Evans lived with her husband in a cottage in Cardiff Road, Newport. The cottage was owned by the husband's employers, the trustees of the Tredegar Estate. After her husband died, Mrs Evans entered into an agreement with the trustees, under which she was allowed to remain in the cottage for the rest of her life. The trustees then sold some land, including the cottage, to Mr and Mrs Binions. The trustees warned them that Mrs Evans was entitled to remain in the cottage for the rest of her life and sold the land 'subject to' her right; as a result, Mr and Mrs Binions bought the land for a reduced price. They then brought proceedings to remove Mrs Evans from the cottage. Mrs Evans claimed that: (i) her agreement with the trustees gave her a pre-existing property right that was binding on Mr and Mrs Binions; and, in any case, (ii) the term included in the sale to Mr and Mrs Binions gave her a direct right against them.

Lord Denning MR

At 367

[Lord Denning MR first examined the argument that the agreement between Mrs Evans and the trustees gave her a pre-existing property right. His Lordship then considered the position if the agreement gave her no such right.]

Suppose, however, that [Mrs Evans] did not have an equitable interest at the outset, nevertheless it is quite plain that she obtained one afterwards when the Tredegar Estate sold the cottage. They stipulated with [Mr and Mrs Binions] that they were to take the house 'subject to' [Mrs Evans'] rights under the agreement. They supplied [Mr and Mrs Binions] with a copy of the contract: and [Mr and Mrs Binions] paid less because of her right to stay there. In these circumstances, this court will impose on [Mr and Mrs Binions] a constructive trust for [Mrs Evans'] benefit: for the simple reason that it would be utterly inequitable for Mr and Mrs Binions to turn Mrs Evans out contrary to the stipulation subject to which they took the premises. That seems to me clear from the important decision of *Bannister v Bannister*,[13] which was applied by the judge and which I gladly follow.

Lord Denning MR thus adopted the view that C's oral promise to A could give B a direct right against C, arising under a constructive trust. In Chapter 8, section 3.3.1, we will see that there are a number of significant problems with the view that B's right arose under a trust. For present purposes, however, the important point is the recognition that B can acquire a direct right as a result of C's oral promise to A.

This particular means by which B can acquire a direct right against C is considered further in the following extract. The analysis in that extract also provides a very good example of the fact that, even if C has a defence to a pre-existing property right of B, it may nonetheless be possible for B to have a direct right against C.

Lloyd v Dugdale [2001] EWCA Civ 1754, CA

Facts: Mr Ingham had a long lease (999 years) of Moorcroft Mill in Haywood, Greater Manchester. Mr Dugdale was the major shareholder and managing director of JAD Flooring Ltd. He was looking for new business premises and entered into negotiations with Mr Ingham about acquiring Mr Ingham's rights in a part of the Mill, including an office and warehouse. This part of the Mill was referred to as the 'Unit'. Mr Dugdale reached a preliminary agreement with Mr Ingham, but no formal contract was signed. Because Mr Dugdale had urgent need of the premises, however, Mr Ingham allowed JAD to begin operating from the Unit. Mr Dugdale wanted to spend money on improving the Unit, but was worried that Mr Ingham might pull out of the planned sale. Mr Ingham assured Mr Dugdale that he was a 'man of his word'. After Mr Dugdale had improved the Unit and before any formal contract of sale was signed, Mr Ingham decided to pull out of the proposed sale, and sought to remove Mr Dugdale and JAD from the Unit. Mr Dugdale refused and legal proceedings were commenced. Mr Ingham then died. His executors purchased a freehold of the Mill and then sold the Mill to the trustees of a pension scheme. By virtue of clause 14, the sale agreement was made 'subject to' the legal proceedings between Mr Ingham and Mr Dugdale. Those trustees then sought to remove Mr Dugdale and JAD from the Unit.

Mr Dugdale's first argument was that he had a pre-existing equitable property right that was binding on the pension scheme trustees. The Court of Appeal found that Mr Dugdale did, indeed, have a right, arising as a result of proprietary estoppel, that was capable of binding a third party (see further Chapter 13, section 5). But it also held that the pension scheme trustees could use the lack of registration defence provided by the Land Registration Act 1925 (LRA 1925) against Mr Dugdale's right. Mr Dugdale argued that he had an overriding interest, because he was in actual occupation of the Unit (see Chapter 6, section 3.2.2). The Court of Appeal found, however, that it was JAD, and not Mr Dugdale, who occupied the Unit. Nonetheless, the Court of Appeal, as can be seen

13 [1948] 2 All ER 133.

in the following extract, did consider whether Mr Dugdale had a direct right against the pension scheme trustees, arising under a constructive trust and based on the trustees' purchase 'subject to' the legal proceedings between Mr Dugdale and Mr Ingham.

Sir Christopher Slade LJ

At [50]–[56]

Issue (D): Constructive trust

Even if Mr Dugdale did not enjoy an overriding interest in the Unit, the claimants acquired the Unit with notice of his claim and, by virtue of clause 14 of the 1994 Agreement, expressly subject thereto. There is no general principle which renders it unconscionable for a purchaser of land to rely on a want of registration of a claim against registered land, even though he took with express notice of it. A decision to the contrary would defeat the purpose of the legislature in introducing the system of registration embodied in the 1925 Act. Nevertheless, the authorities show that, in certain special circumstances the court will impose on a purchaser, who has taken a disposition expressed to be subject to specified incumbrances or prior interests, a constructive trust obliging him to give effect to them, if it considers it unconscionable for him to do otherwise, in the particular circumstances of the case.

Counsel have helpfully taken us through a number of authorities in which the court has been invited to find a constructive trust on this basis [. . .] I do not find it necessary to traverse the authorities at any length in this judgment, because I consider the relevant principles and their application to the particular facts of this case fairly clear. The relevant principles to be extracted from the authorities may for present purposes be summarised as follows:

(1) Even in a case where, on a sale of land, the vendor has stipulated that the sale shall be subject to stated possible incumbrances or prior interests, there is no general rule that the court will impose a constructive trust on the purchaser to give effect to them. In *Ashburn and Anstalt v Arnold* Fox LJ,[14] delivering the judgment of the court, expressed agreement with the following observations of Dillon J in *Lyus v Prowsa Development Ltd*:[15]

> "By contrast, there are many cases in which land is expressly conveyed subject to possible incumbrances when there is no thought at all of conferring any fresh rights on third parties who may be entitled to the benefit of the incumbrances. The land is expressed to be sold subject to incumbrances to satisfy the vendor's duty to disclose all possible incumbrances known to him, and to protect the vendor against any possible claim by the purchaser. [. . .] So, for instance, land may be contracted to be sold and may be expressed to be conveyed subject to the restrictive covenants contained in a conveyance some 60 or 90 years old. No one would suggest that by accepting such a form of contract or conveyance a purchaser is assuming a new liability in favour of third parties to observe the covenants if there was for any reason before the contract or conveyance no one who could make out a title as against the purchaser to the benefit of the covenants."

(2) The court will not impose a constructive trust in such circumstances unless it is satisfied that the conscience of the estate owner is affected so that it would be inequitable to allow him to deny the claimant an interest in the property: see *Ashburn Anstalt v Arnold* (supra) at pp 22E-F and 25H.

(3) In deciding whether or not the conscience of the new estate owner is affected in such circumstances, the crucially important question is whether he has undertaken a new

---

[14] [1989] Ch 1, 25E.
[15] [1982] 1 WLR 1044, 1051.

obligation, not otherwise existing, to give effect to the relevant incumbrance or prior interest. If, but only if, he has undertaken such a new obligation will a constructive trust be imposed. The importance of this point was repeatedly stressed in *Ashburn Anstalt v Arnold* (supra): see for example at pp 23G, 25A-26A, and 27B. See also *Lyus v Prowsa Development Ltd* (supra) at p 1051; *IDC Group Ltd v Clark* (1992) 1 EGLR at p 190B-C; *Melbury Road Properties 1995 Ltd v Kreidi* [[1999] 3 EGLR 10] at p 110G [. . .]

(5) Proof that the purchase price by a transferee has been reduced upon the footing that he would give effect to the relevant incumbrance or prior interest may provide some indication that the transferee has undertaken a new obligation to give effect to it: see *Ashburn Anstalt v Arnold* (supra) at p 23F-G. However, since in matters relating to the title to land certainty is of prime importance, it is not desirable that constructive trusts of land should be imposed in reliance on inferences from "slender materials" (ibid at p 26E) [. . .]

The Judge also inferred that the purchase price paid by the claimants for the Unit had been reduced by reason of the potential claims of Mr Dugdale, but there was no evidence whatever to support this inference, which was not in my opinion justified [. . .] In my judgment, however, [the arguments made by counsel for Mr Dugdale] do not suffice to support the Judge's decision that the provisions of the 1994 Agreement gave rise to very special circumstances showing that, when the [pension fund trustees] acquired the Unit, they undertook a new liability to give effect to any rights which Mr Dugdale might have enjoyed in equity immediately prior to that acquisition. That Agreement certainly demonstrated an intention to protect the claimants against any future claims which might be made by Mr Dugdale. But, as [counsel for the pension fund trustees] pointed out, so far from imposing on the [trustees] an obligation to give effect to Mr Dugdale's asserted rights, it plainly contemplated that the [trustees] would be proceeding with the claim for possession of the Unit against him and JAD on the basis that neither he nor JAD had any rights in equity in relation to the Unit. Mr Dugdale's rights, if they existed at all, were at best uncertain and ill defined. To impose a constructive trust on the claimants would be to do so on the basis of very slender materials. There was in my judgment no thought of conferring any fresh rights on Mr Dugdale himself by the 1994 Agreement. In all the circumstances Mr Dugdale's defence based on constructive trust must in my judgment also fail.

The analysis of Sir Christopher Slade LJ is helpful in clarifying the principle applied in *Binions v Evans*. Firstly, B cannot acquire a direct right against C simply because C *knows* that B has some form of pre-existing right in relation to the land. Secondly, even if the contract between A and C states that C acquires his right 'subject to' a right of B, this may not be enough to give B a direct right against C. The question in all cases is whether C has '*undertaken a new obligation*' to B.

Nonetheless, even if C has made a promise to A to give B a right in relation to the land, we are left with the question of precisely *why* B should acquire a direct right against C. This point has attracted a good deal of academic attention; a number of different answers have been suggested.[16] Certainly, the question is a difficult one, and has been complicated by the courts' insistence that B's right arises under a constructive trust. We will return to it in Chapter 14, section 4, when examining such trusts.

---

[16] For a survey of these answers, see McFarlane, 'Constructive Trusts Arising on a Receipt of Property 'Sub Conditione" (2004) 120 LQR 667, 683–90.

2.4 WHERE C COMMITS A TORT AGAINST B

The situations we have examined so far all involve C *choosing* to give B a direct right, whether by means of a deed (section 2.1), a contractual promise (section 2.2), or a non-contractual promise (section 2.3). But it is also possible for B to acquire a direct right against C even if C has *not* chosen to give B such a right. For example, it may be that C's conduct gives B a direct right because it counts as a tort against B. This was the case in *Midland Bank Trust Co Ltd v Green*,[17] which we examined in Chapter 6, section 3.1. We saw there that, although Geoffrey Green (B) had a pre-existing equitable property right, Evelyne Green (C) took priority, because she was able to rely on the lack of registration defence provided by the Land Charges Act 1925 (LCA 1925). This means that Geoffrey could *not* assert his pre-existing property right. And Evelyne had certainly not made a promise to give Geoffrey a direct right: the whole purpose of the sale from Walter to Evelyne was to prevent Geoffrey from having any rights in relation to the land. In later proceedings, however, Geoffrey argued that, by working together with the predominant motive of causing him loss, Walter and Evelyne had committed a tort: the tort of 'lawful act conspiracy'. That argument was accepted by Oliver J[18] and was confirmed by the Court of Appeal in *Midland Bank Trust Co Ltd v Green (No 3)*.[19] As a result, *each of* Walter and Evelyne was liable to pay damages to Geoffrey to compensate him for the loss that he suffered as a result of losing his right to purchase the farm from Walter.[20]

The tort of 'lawful act conspiracy' is a controversial and difficult one, and we cannot examine it in detail here. One important point is that it requires B to show that A and C have acted with the 'predominant purpose' of harming B.[21] That may be possible in a case such as *Green*, in which the *only* point of the transfer of A's estate to C was to prevent B from exercising his option to purchase that estate. In most situations, however, C's principal purpose will simply be to acquire a right to use the land for his own benefit. Nonetheless, *Green* shows us that, if B can complete the difficult task of showing that A and C acted with the predominant purpose of harming B, B will acquire a direct right against C *even if* C has a defence (such as the lack of registration defence) to B's pre-existing property right. We will explore this point further in section 3 below.

There is a further tort that may provide some assistance to B in a case in which his initial right to use A's land comes from a contract with A. In such a case, B may try to argue that C, by acquiring a right from A and then attempting to stop B's use of the land, commits the tort of *procuring a breach by A of A's contract with B*.[22] We will examine this possibility in more detail in Chapter 8, section 3.3.1. As with 'lawful act conspiracy', the exact boundaries of the tort are unclear. Moreover, there is also a problem that, if the tort is applied too readily, it will undermine the basic position that C, when acquiring a right in relation to A's land, cannot be bound by his mere knowledge of a pre-existing *personal* right of B (see section 2.6 below).

---

[17] [1981] AC 413.

[18] See [1980] Ch 590 for Oliver J's decision.

[19] [1982] Ch 529.

[20] Of course, Walter was, in any case, liable to pay damages to Geoffrey, because he had breached his contractual promise to allow Geoffrey to buy the farm.

[21] See, e.g., *per* Viscount Simon LC in *Crofter Hand Woven Harris Tweed Co Ltd v Veitch* [1942] AC 435, 445.

[22] This tort is often associated with the reasoning of the majority of the Court of Queen's Bench in *Lumley v Gye* (1853) 2 E & B 215 (although it was held that, on the facts of the case, the tort had not been committed). For a more recent consideration of the tort at the highest judicial level, see *OBG Ltd v Allan* [2008] 1 AC 1.

2.5 THE 'BENEFIT AND BURDEN' PRINCIPLE

The 'benefit and burden' principle provides another means by which B can acquire a direct right against C even if C has not made a promise to give B a right. It can be particularly important when considering disputes between neighbours and we will examine it in more detail in Chapter 27, section 2.4.1, when looking at freehold covenants.

As noted in the extract below, the basis of the principle is that: (i) if an arrangement between A and B links the enjoyment of a particular right by A (and later owners of A's land, such as C) to the bearing of a particular burden (e.g. if A is permitted to use roads on B's land only if he pays an annual charge to B); and (ii) C, a later owner of A's land, chooses to enjoy the benefit (e.g. if C chooses to use the roads on B's land); then (iii) C will be under a duty to B (or a later owner of B's land) to bear that burden.

Davis, 'The Principle of Benefit and Burden' [1998] CLJ 522

At 544–7

The cases have all involved what may loosely be termed as an 'arrangement'. The arrangement may take various forms: a gift, whether inter vivos or by will; an agreement, whether by deed, writing or oral; or a grant. What is common to the arrangements is that they confer a benefit and also impose a burden. The burden only binds persons who accept or exercise the benefit, have no other right to do so other than by relying on the arrangement, and have a choice whether or not they accept it. Although in a large number of the cases the benefit was a right relating to land, there has been no indication in any of the cases that the principle is limited to real property and there are a number of cases where the benefit was personal property, money or a contractual right [...]

The burden must be linked to the benefit, or made a condition of it, by the original arrangement. This link may be express, implied or even presumed. If it is clear that the burden is personal to the original party or separate from the benefit then the principle will be inapplicable [...]

It is impossible to find adequate discussion of the issue whether a person needs to have knowledge of the burden and the fact that it is linked to the benefit before being bound [...]

The principle seems to operate both at law and in equity and imposes a personal obligation on the person who seeks to use the benefit without affecting the liability of the original party. It can be used as a cause of action, not only by the original party, but also by his successors.

At 552

It is arguable that 'benefit and burden' is a principle, reasonably clear in its application, that promotes fairness and, consequently, far greater use should be made of it. It seems only fair that a right or benefit originally granted subject to a condition or linked with a reciprocal right or obligation should remain conditional or linked.

2.6 WHERE C KNOWS ABOUT A PRE-EXISTING RIGHT OF B

As the following extract shows, it has occasionally been suggested that B will acquire a direct right against C if: (i) B has a pre-existing *personal* right against A; and (ii) C then acquires a right from A with knowledge of B's personal right.

Tulk v Moxhay (1848) 2 Ph 774, High Court of Chancery

Facts: Mr Tulk owned land in Leicester Square, London. He sold part of that land to Mr Elms, and demanded that Elms promise that he would '*at all times thereafter at his own cost keep and maintain the piece of ground in sufficient and proper repair, and in an open state, uncovered with any buildings, in neat and ornamental order*'. Elms' land then passed to Mr Moxhay. When acquiring the land, Moxhay did not make a promise to maintain the garden. Moxhay did, however, know about Elms' promise and paid a lower price for the land as a result. When Moxhay decided to develop the land by building on the garden, Tulk applied for an injunction to prevent Moxhay from acting inconsistently with Elms' promise.

Lord Cottenham LC

At 777

It is said that, the covenant being one which does not run with the land, this Court cannot enforce it; but the question is, not whether the covenant runs with the land, but whether a party shall be permitted to use the land in a manner inconsistent with the contract entered into by his vendor, and with notice of which he purchased. Of course, the price would be affected by the covenant, and nothing could be more inequitable than that the original purchaser should be able to sell the property the next day for a greater price, in consideration of the assignee being allowed to escape from the liability which he had himself undertaken.

That the question does not depend upon whether the covenant runs with the land is evident from this, that if there was a mere agreement and no covenant, this Court would enforce it against a party purchasing with notice of it; for if an equity is attached to the property by the owner, no one purchasing with notice of that equity can stand in a different situation from the party from whom he purchased.

Today, as we will see in Chapter 27, section 2, *Tulk v Moxhay* is generally regarded as a case in which B was able to assert a pre-existing *property* right against C. Certainly, Elms' promise not to build on the garden can nowadays be seen as giving B a restrictive covenant: as we saw in Chapter 4, such a right counts as an equitable property right in relation to land. But Lord Cottenham LC's reasoning in the extract above does *not* depend on B having a pre-existing property right; indeed, his Lordship expressly says that the question is *not* '*whether the covenant runs with the land*'. Instead, Lord Cottenham's reasoning seems to be that because: (i) Moxhay knew about Elms' promise; and (ii) Moxhay paid a lower price for his estate as a result; then (iii) Tulk acquired a direct right against Moxhay. It therefore seems that, as a matter of history, the recognition of such a direct right played an important part in the journey by which the restrictive covenant came to be an equitable property right: this is a point to which we will return in Chapter 8, section 3.3.2.

As noted in the following extract, however, it is now generally accepted that C's knowledge of B's pre-existing personal right, by itself, *cannot* give B a direct right against C. The basic point is a simple one: in Chapters 3 and 4, we saw that the *content* test is used to ensure that only a limited class of rights can count as property rights in relation to land. This provides important protection for third parties later acquiring a right in land: if C knows that B's pre-existing right does *not* count as a property right, and is only a personal right against A, C knows that he or she cannot be bound by B's right. That protection would be fatally undermined if B were able to acquire a direct right against C whenever C knows of B's pre-existing personal right.[23]

Keppell v Bailey (1834) 2 My & K 517

Facts: We examined this case in Chapter 3, section 6, and the facts are set out there. We saw that Mr Keppell, on behalf of the shareholders in a joint stock company, wished to assert a right to stop the Baileys from buying limestone from anywhere other than the Trevill quarry. Mr Keppell made two arguments: (i) that the promise made by the Kendalls bound not only them, but also any later owners of the ironworks, such as the Baileys; and, alternatively, that (ii) even if the promise made by the Kendalls did not create a property right, it should bind the Baileys, because they acquired the ironworks knowing of that earlier promise. As we saw in Chapter 3, section 6, the High Court of Chancery rejected that first argument. The extract set out below shows that the second argument was also rejected.

Lord Brougham LC

At 546–8

[Given that the Kendalls' promise does not give rise to a pre-existing right capable of binding the Baileys], does the notice which the [Baileys] had of its existence alter the case in this Court, upon an application for an injunction; or would it, upon the application of a co-relative and co-extensive nature, for a specific performance? Certainly not [...] The knowledge by an assignee of an estate, that his assignor had assumed to bind other than the law authorises him to affect by his contracts—that he had attempted to create a real burden upon property which is inconsistent with the nature of that property, and unknown to the principles of the law—cannot bind such assignee by affecting his conscience. If it did, then the illegality would be of no consequence; and however wild the attempt might be to create new kinds of holding and new species of estate, and however repugnant such devices might be to the rules of law, they would prove perfectly successful in the result, because equity would enable their authors to prevail; nay, not only to compass their object, but to obtain a great deal more than they could at law, were their contrivances ever so accordant with strict legal principle [...]

So a person who had conveyed land, and subjected it to covenants in the hands of his [purchaser], could at once make sure of those burdens following it into the hands of all holders to whom it might pass, by taking the precaution of notifying the covenants in some effectual though easy manner, as by publication in some place near the premises, where the purchaser needs must observe the announcement. It is clear then that this Court will never interefere, by way of injunction, or in any other more direct manner to enforce such covenants, when satisfied that they could receive no support or countenance at law.

National Provincial Bank v Ainsworth [1965] AC 1175, HL

Facts: We examined this case in Chapter 1, section 5, and Chapter 4, section 5.4; the facts can be found in either of those sections. We saw that the House of Lords viewed

---

[23] As stated by Swadling, 'The Law of Property' in *English Private Law* (2nd edn, ed Burrows, 2007, [4.11]): '*if knowledge of a personal right did transform it into a property right, the* numerus clausus *would be destroyed*.' To support this point, Swadling also quotes part of the extract from *Keppell v Bailey* set out above.

Mrs Ainsworth's 'deserted wife's equity' as a purely personal right against her husband. The following extract makes clear that the bank's notice of that pre-existing personal right, by itself, could not give Mrs Ainsworth a direct right against the bank.

Lord Wilberforce

At 1253

It was said that the wife's right was an equitable claim, binding on the husband's conscience, and that consistently with what has been decided in relation to such matters as restrictive covenants, it should be held to be binding on the conscience of a "purchaser" with notice [...] In my opinion, this line of argument is but a revival of a fallacy that, because an obligation binds a man's conscience, it therefore becomes binding on the consciences of those who take from him with notice of the obligation. But this has been decisively rejected, not only in relation to covenants (enforceable by specific performance) entered into by the predecessor of the purchaser whom it is sought to bind[24] but in the law of restrictive covenants to which an appeal by way of analogy was made.

Equally, if B has a pre-existing property right to which C has a defence (e.g., as in *Midland Bank v Green*, a lack of registration defence), then C's knowledge of B's right will not, by itself, give B a direct right against C. As we saw in Chapter 6, the possibility of having a defence to B's pre-existing property right also gives C important protection. That protection would also be significantly undermined if B were able to acquire a direct right against C whenever C knows of B's pre-existing property right. As Bright argues in the following extract, it therefore seems that C's notice of B's pre-existing right, *by itself*, will not give B a direct right against C.

Bright, 'The Third Party's Conscience in Land Law' [2000] Conv 398, 407–8[25]

Part 3 What good reasons are there for holding C liable?

There are various reasons why we might want to argue that C is liable. One is that C bought with notice of B's rights and it would, therefore, be "unconscionable" to deny these rights. Although it has been suggested at various times that notice is enough, there are many judicial utterances showing that notice alone will not suffice to impose liability.[26] To hold otherwise would undermine land law. If a property statute clearly states that a purchaser shall not be affected with notice, then it cannot be unconscionable to rely on this statute. *Midland Bank v. Green* provides the highest judicial authority for this. The mother bought the farm at

---

[24] Lord Wilberforce here referred to the judgment of Lindley LJ in *London & SW Railway Co v Gomm* (1882) 20 Ch D 562, 587.

[25] In the original, the party potentially subject to a direct right is referred to as 'B' and the party potentially acquiring a direct right is referred to as 'X'. These letters have been changed so as to be consistent with the usage in this chapter: i.e. B becomes 'C' and X becomes 'B'.

[26] [The original here refers to Fox LJ in *Ashburn Anstalt v Arnold* [1989] Ch 1, 25; Sir Browne-Wilkinson V-C in *IDC Group Ltd v Clark* [1992] 1 EGLR 187; Cowell J in *Melbury Road Properties 1995 Ltd v Kreidi* [1999] 44 EG 157. Further support, arising in relation to dealing with property other than land, comes from Diplock J in *Port Line Ltd v Ben Line Steamers Ltd* [1958] 2 QB 146 and Browne-Wilkinson V-C in *Swiss Bank Corp v Lloyds Bank Ltd* [1979] 1 Ch 548.]

considerable undervalue in order to defeat her son's option, which she knew he had not protected by registration. There was seemingly no other reason for the purchase, Lord Denning described her behaviour as fraudulent. The House of Lords held, however, that she took free of the option. C is not liable if that is what the statutes clearly state; old equitable doctrines of notice and so on should not be read into modern Acts of Parliament.[27]

In each case something more than notice is required. What that "something more" is will depend upon the circumstances. In some cases the "something more" stems from wrongful conduct by C in relation to the transfer itself, the fact that C is knowingly interfering with B's rights. In *Midland Bank v. Green* (not a constructive trust case), the mother should be held liable, not as a matter of property law, but in tort because she bought the property for the sole purpose of defeating the son's unprotected interest [...] In other cases, C should be held liable not because he behaved badly at the time of the transfer, but because he assumes some responsibility towards B at the time of the transfer and it would be wrong later to turn his back on this responsibility. In *Binions* [...] the inequity stems from the fact that having clearly promised to honour the agreement with B (and in *Binions* even paid less in recognition of this) C later tries to deny this promise.

3 IS B'S DIRECT RIGHT A PROPERTY RIGHT OR A PERSONAL RIGHT?

A direct right is simply a right that arises as a result of C's conduct. It can be a property right (as, for example, if C chooses to give B a lease), or simply a personal right against C (as, for example, in *Midland Bank Trust Co Ltd v Green*, in which, as a result of C's commission of the tort of conspiracy, B acquired a right to claim damages from C). Where B simply wants to assert his right against C, it makes very little difference whether B's direct right counts as a property right or as a personal right. Things are different, however, if C later transfers his estate to C2, as Figure 2 illustrates.

In such a case, B may wish to argue that: (i) as a result of C's conduct, B acquired a direct right against C; and (ii) that right counts as a legal or equitable property in relation to the land; and so (iii) B can assert that right against C2, provided that C2 has no defence to it. This shows us that the *content* and *acquisition* questions, which we examined in Chapters 3 and 4, may also be important where direct rights are concerned.

Where B's direct right against C arises because of C's commission of a tort, B will simply have a right to claim damages from C and so the *content* question is easy to answer: B has only a personal right against C. In other cases, as when B's direct right arises because of C's use of a deed, or a contractual or non-contractual promise of C, we simply need to look at the right C has given B and see if it matches the content of any of the legal or equitable property rights examined in Chapters 3 and 4. It is important to note that, in cases such as *Bannister v Bannister* and *Binions v Evans*, B's direct right against C is said to arise under a constructive trust. As we saw in Chapter 4, if B has a right under a trust, he has

---

[27] [The original here refers to *Midland Bank Trust Co Ltd v Green* [1981] AC 513, 528B, *per* Lord Wilberforce: '*Any temptation to remould the Act to meet the facts of the present case, on the supposition that it is a hard one and that justice requires it, is, for me at least, removed by the consideration that the Act itself provides a simple and effective protection for persons in Geoffrey's position-viz-by registration.*']

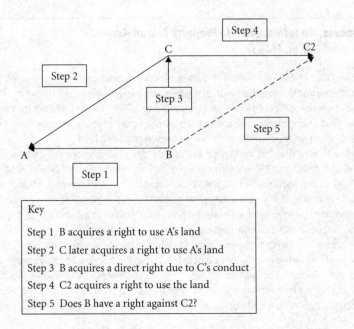

Figure 2 Direct Rights and Later Parties: The Priority Parallelogram

an equitable property right. But it is not clear that, in all of those cases, B's direct right should necessarily be an equitable property right. We will consider this point in detail in Chapter 8, section 3.3.1.

As for the *acquisition* question, any relevant formality rules will, of course, apply if B claims that the direct right that he has acquired against C is a legal or equitable property right. For example, if B claims that C has given B a legal lease of five years' duration, B will need to show that C used a deed to give B that right (see Chapter 9, section 4, and Chapter 23, section 3.1.1).

4 DIRECT RIGHTS AND REGISTERED LAND

If B claims that the direct right that he has acquired against C counts as a legal property right, then B may have to satisfy a formality rule laid down by the Land Registration Act 2002 (LRA 2002) to show that he has acquired that right. For example, if B claims that C has given B a lease of more than seven years' duration, B will need to show that he is registered as holding that lease. There is, however, no general rule, even in relation to registered land, that says that B must be on the register in order to acquire a direct right against C. For example, when examining *Lloyd v Dugdale* in section 2.3 above, we saw that, although B was not on the register, the Court of Appeal was still prepared to *consider* whether C's conduct gave B a direct right. Indeed, as the following extract argues, even Australian jurisdictions using the strict 'Torrens' forms of registration system (under which C, by registering his right, is said to have 'indefeasible title') have accepted that it may still be possible for an unregistered B to acquire a direct right against C.

Chambers, *An Introduction to Property Law in Australia*
(2nd edn, 2008, pp 464–5)

Indefeasibility of title provides a registered proprietor with powerful protection from older unregistered rights. However, with one important exception[28] [. . .] it does not affect the creation of new property rights to land. Registered proprietors are free to create property rights to their land. Property rights can also arise without their consent, in response to events such as detrimental reliance, unjust enrichment and wrongdoing [. . .]

This principle, that the indefeasibility of title does not prevent the creation of rights, is sometimes called the "*in personam* exception" to indefeasibility. This phrase was coined following a comment made by Lord Wilberforce in *Frazer v Walker*.[29] After setting out the principle of immediate indefeasibility, he said that "this principle in no way denies the right of a plaintiff to bring against a registered proprietor a claim *in personam*, founded in law or in equity, for such relief as a court acting *in personam* may grant."[30]

The phrase "*in personam* exception" is unfortunate for two reasons. First, it is not really an exception to indefeasibility of title. It refers not to the survival of older unregistered rights, but to the creation of newer unregistered rights. Indefeasibility of title is about the priority of rights and has (almost) nothing to do with their creation. The *in personam* exception is an "exception" to indefeasibility only because a registered right can be affected by the creation of a new right [. . .]

Secondly, this "exception" is not limited to the creation of personal rights. Registered proprietors often create personal rights to use their land (such as a licence to stay in a guest room for the weekend), but they also create unregistered property rights, through tenancy agreements, contracts of sale, equitable mortgages and the like. Both fall within the *in personam* exception.

In this extract, Chambers draws on the key distinction between: (i) cases in which B attempts to assert a pre-existing property right against C; and (ii) cases in which B claims that he or she has acquired a direct right against C. Whilst a registration system may protect C in the first set of cases, by giving C a defence against a pre-existing property right of B that is not recorded on the register, it does not assist C in the second set of cases. As we will see in Chapter 16, section 7, this is true not only of the Australian registration systems discussed by Chambers, but also of the system applying in England and Wales under the LRA 2002. Indeed, the provisions of the 2002 Act, by making it more difficult for B to assert an unregistered right against C, have increased the importance of direct rights.

5 CONCLUSION

We have seen that many land law cases share a basic form: B has some sort of right to use A's land; A then gives C a right in relation to that land; and B and C each want to use the land in incompatible ways. The first question to ask in such a case is whether B has a pre-existing

---

[28] [The exception given occurs where C acquires a registered right with notice that the registered document was a forgery or obtained by fraud. In that case, provided that C has not been dishonest, a Torrens system will ensure that B does not acquire a direct right against C; B's protection will instead come from making a claim on the assurance fund—i.e. through the Australian equivalent of an English claim for indemnity (see Chapter 16, section 7).]

[29] [1967] 1 AC 569.

[30] [1967] 1 AC 569, 585.

legal or equitable property right (see Chapters 3 and 4). If B *does* have such a right, we then need to consider whether C has a defence to that right (see Chapter 6). But if B has no such property right, or even if C has a defence to B's property right, it may still be possible for B to prevail. To do so, B needs to show that he or she has acquired a direct right, arising as a result of C's conduct.

In most cases, it will be impossible for B to show he or she has a direct right against C. For example, we have seen that C's knowledge of a pre-existing right of B, by itself, will not give B a direct right against C (see section 2.6 above). It is always important, however, to keep in mind the possibility that B may have such a right. A direct right against C can give B crucial protection even where B has failed to register his or her pre-existing property right, and, as we will see in Chapter 8, it may also protect B where his or her initial right to use the land is simply a personal right against A.

QUESTIONS

1. What is the difference between a direct right and a pre-existing property right?

2. When can a promise made by C to A give B a direct right against C?

3. Is the Court of Appeal's decision in *Midland Bank Trust Co Ltd v Green (No 3)* that Evelyne Green was liable to pay damages to Geoffrey Green compatible with the House of Lords' earlier decision that Geoffrey's unregistered equitable property right did not bind Evelyne?

4. When might it be important to know if a direct right acquired by B as a result of C's conduct is a property right as opposed to a personal right against C?

FURTHER READING

Bright, 'The Third Party's Conscience in Land Law' [2000] Conv 398

Cooke and O'Connor, 'Purchaser Liability to Third Parties in the English Land Registration System: A Comparative Perspective' (2004) 120 LQR 640

Law Commission Report No 254, *Land Registration for the 21st Century: A Consultative Document* (1998, [3.48]–[3.49])

McFarlane, 'Identifying Property Rights: A Reply to Mr Watt' [2003] Conv 473

McFarlane, *The Structure of Property Law* (Oxford: Hart, 2008, Part E3)

Smith, 'The Economic Torts: their Impact on Real Property' (1977) 41 Conv 318

8

THE PRIORITY TRIANGLE IN ACTION: LICENCES

CENTRAL ISSUES

1. A licence exists where one party (B) has a liberty to use land belonging to another (A). In considering licences, we need to examine: the rights that B has against A; the rights that B has against X, a stranger who interferes with B's use of A's land; and the rights that B has against C, a party who acquires a right from A and then interferes with B's use of the land.

2. Licences can be grouped into a number of categories. A bare licence exists where B has *only* a liberty to use A's land. The law governing such a licence is straightforward. It can be revoked by A, and B cannot assert it against X or C.

3. A contractual licence exists where B has a liberty to use A's land *and* A is under a contractual duty to B not to revoke that liberty. A's contractual duty is clearly important when considering what rights B has against A. The crucial question is whether the existence of this contract can also affect B's rights against X and C. This has been a controversial question.

4. In considering what rights B, a party with a contractual licence, may have against X or C, we need to keep in mind the two different ways in which it may be possible for B to assert a right against such a party. Firstly, B may be able to assert a new, direct right against X or C, arising as a result of X or C's conduct. Such a right may arise under a 'constructive trust'—but controversy surrounds both the source and nature of this trust.

5. Secondly, if B is unable to assert a direct right against X or C, he or she will have to argue that his or her contractual licence counts as a legal or equitable property right in land. The current position is that a contractual licence does *not* count as such a right—but this is another controversial area. A number of arguments have been made in favour of the view that at least some types of contractual licence should count as an equitable interest in land. One of these arguments involves a comparison with a third type of licence: an estoppel licence.

6. When examining licences to use land, we also need to consider statutory licences and licences coupled with an interest. The latter category, however, is of dubious value.

1 THE NATURE OF A LICENCE

Let us say that A, a freehold owner of land, invites B to his house for dinner. When B is on A's land, he is described as having a licence. The word 'licence' simply means *permission*. Because A has a legal estate in the land, B, like the rest of the world, is under a prima facie duty not to make any use of A's land (see Chapter 3, section 1). If, however, A gives B permission to make a particular use of A's land, B's duty disappears: an act that would otherwise be wrongful (coming onto A's land) becomes permissible.

Thomas v Sorrell (1673) Vaugh 330, Exchequer Chamber

Facts: Mr Thomas, acting on behalf of the Crown, demanded payment from Mr Sorrell on the basis that Mr Sorrell had sold wine in the parish of Stepney without a licence. Mr Sorrell claimed that he had a licence to sell wine in his capacity of a member of the *'Master, Warden, Freemen, and Commonality of the Mystery of Vintners of the City of London'*. Vaughan CJ considered the meaning of the term 'licence'.

Vaughan CJ

At 351

A dispensation or licence properly passeth no interest, nor alters or transfers property in any thing, but only makes an action lawful which, without it, had been unlawful. As a licence to go beyond the seas, to hunt in a man's park, to come into his house, are only actions, which without licence, had been unlawful.

So, even when B is enjoying his dinner at A's home, we need to be careful in saying that B has a 'right' to be on A's land.

The great American jurist Hohfeld noted that we use the word 'right' to cover many different situations.[1] For example, if we say that B has a right that A must not poison B's food, we mean that A is under a *duty to B* not to poison B's food. In such a case, in Hohfeld's terms, B has a particular form of right: a *claim right*. In contrast, if we say that B has a right to be on A's land, we mean something different. In our example, after all, A is not under a duty to allow B to stay on his land. So, if B makes a controversial comment over dinner, A is free to ask B to leave without any dessert. So, when we say that B has a right to be on A's land, what we really mean is that, at least until A revokes his permission, B is *not under a duty to A not to be on A's land*. In such a case, in Hohfeld's terms, B has a particular form of right: a *privilege* or *liberty*.

---

[1] See, e.g., Hohfeld, *Fundamental Legal Conceptions as Applied in Judicial Reasoning* (1920; based on (1913) 23 Yale LJ 16 and (1917) 26 Yale LJ 710).

Hohfeld, 'Faulty Analysis in Easement and License Cases'[2]
(1917) Yale LJ 66, 94

Suppose that A says to B, "I give you permission to walk across my land, Longacre." This language in and of itself purports merely to create in B the privilege, or more strictly, series of privileges, of walking across A's land. In correlative terms, A's right that B stay off the land is extinguished, and no-rights substituted. The important point is that the permission consti-tutes a *grant* to B of privileges alone: B is not granted any accompanying rights (or claims) that A or other persons shall not interfere with B's entering on the land, Longacre, and walking across. If, therefore, B succeeds in entering on the land, no rights (or claims) of A are violated; but if on the other hand, A closes the gate in the high stone wall, or bars the one and only path midway, no rights (or claims) of B are violated; and so also if some third party locks the gate or bars the path halfway across Longacre.

All licences thus involve a *liberty* of B to make some use of A's land.[3] There are, however, situations in which B has a liberty to use A's land and is not treated as having a licence. We can modify Hohfeld's example so that A, instead of simply giving B permission to walk across his land, grants B a legal easement that allows B to walk across A's land. If B has a legal easement, he has a liberty to make some use of A's land, *and* A is under a duty not to interfere with B's liberty, *and* the rest of the world is also under a duty not to interfere with B's liberty. These duties are imposed on A and the rest of the world because, as we saw in Chapter 3, sections 5 and 6, B's easement counts as a legal interest in land. In such a case, we would not say that B has a licence. The term 'licence' is thus reserved for cases in which B has a liberty to make some use of A's land, *and* that liberty is not part of a legal or equitable property right held by B.

So, in *Street v Mountford*,[4] a case that we will examine in Chapter 23, section 1.1.1, the House of Lords considered a situation in which, in return for payment from B, A made a contractual promise to allow B to occupy A's land for a limited period. The contract described B's right as a 'licence'—but the House of Lords held that, because B had a right to exclusive possession of the land for a limited period, A had instead given B a *lease*. This meant that B had more than permission to make some use of A's land: he had a legal property right in A's land. So, during the period fixed by the contract, A and the rest of the world had a duty not to interfere with B's occupation of the land.

Strictly speaking, then, to define a 'licence', we also need to define property rights such as an 'easement' or a 'lease'. We will consider those definitions in Chapters 26 (the easement) and 23 (the lease). In the meantime, we can define a licence as follows.

B has a licence where he has:

• a liberty to make some use of A's land; *and*

• that liberty is *not* part of a property right held by B.

---

[2] 'License' is the American English spelling for the noun. In British English usage, 'licence' is the noun and 'license' the verb (hence 'licensor' for a party granting a licence and 'licensee' for a party with the benefit of a licence).

[3] Hohfeld preferred the term 'privilege' to refer to the right of a party, such as B in the extract above, who has a *special* liberty not held by others. On this view, almost all licences give B a privilege. But the term 'liberty' is used in this chapter, because it can also encompass cases in which B has a licence not because of his special position, or any dealings with A, but because of a general rule permitting a particular use of A's land.

[4] [1985] AC 809.

Within that general definition, we can then identify different forms of licence. There are five main varieties: bare licences; contractual licences; estoppel licences; statutory licences; and licences coupled with an interest.

2 BARE LICENCES

A bare licence is the simplest form of licence. It exists where B has a liberty to make some use of A's land *and* A is free to revoke that liberty—that is, A is not under a duty to B not to revoke B's permission to use A's land. When A invites B to A's house for dinner, B has a bare licence. As we have seen, A is free to revoke B's liberty and may do so either before B arrives or during B's visit. A bare licence may also be implied: for example, although not expressly invited by A, a collector for a charity, unless expressly warned otherwise,[5] has a bare licence to come onto A's land and knock on A's door to pursue his lawful business.

2.1 B'S RIGHTS AGAINST A

The key feature of a bare licence is that A is under no duty to B not to revoke the licence: as Alderson B put it in *Wood v Leadbitter*:[6] '[A] *mere licence is revocable.*' So, if A invites B around for dinner, A can change his mind and revoke the invitation. If B decides to come anyway, B commits the tort of trespass: he breaches his duty to A not to interfere with A's land.[7] If B is *already* on A's land when A revokes his invitation, there is a problem with saying that B immediately becomes a trespasser. If that were the case, A would be able to use reasonable force to remove B from the land. Instead, given A's initial invitation and B's reliance on that invitation by coming onto A's land, the law does not allow A's revocation of the licence to turn B immediately into a trespasser.

Winter Garden Theatre (London) Ltd v Millennium Productions Ltd [1948] AC 173, HL

Facts: Winter Garden Theatre (London) Ltd owned the Winter Garden Theatre, Drury Lane, London. In July 1942, the company made a contractual promise to Millennium Productions Ltd to allow Millennium to use the theatre for six months, with an option to renew the licence for a further six months. The contract stated that, at the end of those two six-month periods, Millennium would have the option to continue the licence at a flat weekly price of £300. The contract stipulated that, in such a case, Millennium would have to give Winter Garden one month's notice if it wished to terminate the licence. The written agreement said nothing, however, about Winter Garden's ability, in such a case, to revoke the licence. The licence did, indeed, continue for more than a year and was still in operation by the start of September 1945. Millennium entered a contract with a production company allowing it to put on performances of a play (*Young*

---

[5] For example, if A puts up a notice expressly denying permission to such callers to enter A's land, no licence can be implied.

[6] (1845) 13 M & W 838, 844.

[7] That is the case even if B is unaware that A has revoked the invitation and so honestly believes that he is entitled to come onto A's land.

Mrs Barrington)[8] from 5 September 1945 until January 1946. On 13 September, however, Winter Garden (A Ltd) decided to revoke the licence of Millennium (B Ltd). A Ltd gave B Ltd one month's notice, but demanded that it leave by 13 October. B Ltd sought a declaration that A Ltd had breached its contractual duty, because either: (i) the licence could be revoked only if B Ltd breached one or more of its terms; or (ii) even if the licence could be revoked, A Ltd had not given it a reasonable period of notice. The House of Lords rejected both of these arguments and found in favour of A Ltd.

Viscount Simon

At 188–9

The effect of a licence by A to permit B to enter upon A's land or to use his premises for some purpose is in effect an authority which prevents B from being regarded as a trespasser when he avails himself of the licence (*Thomas v Sorrell*). Such a licence may fall into one of various classes. It may be a purely gratuitous licence in return for which A gets nothing at all, e.g., a licence to B to walk across A's field. Such a gratuitous licence would plainly be revocable by notice given by A to B. Even in that case, however, notice of revocation conveyed to B when he was in the act of crossing A's field could not turn him into a trespasser until he was off the premises, but his future right of crossing would thereupon cease.

Lord Macdermott

At 204

It is, I think, safe, as well as desirable for the decision of this case, to say that one who remains on the land of another after his licence to use it has terminated will not be considered a trespasser before he has had a reasonable time in which to vacate the premises [...] This period of grace can, of course, be the subject of agreement, but it exists for gratuitous as well as for contractual licensees and, on that account, must, I think, be generally ascribed to a rule of law rather than to an implied stipulation.

The courts have consistently reached the conclusion that A's revocation does not immediately turn B into a trespasser. As Hill notes, this conclusion has been reached in a number of different ways.

Hill, 'The Termination of Bare Licences' [2001] Cambridge LJ 87, 89

The position with regard to bare licences should be more straightforward [...] As the fundamental feature of a bare gratuitous licence is that it is not based on a contract, it might be supposed that a bare licence imposes no obligations on the licensor. If this were the case, once revocation has occurred, the licensee [...] would, on failing to vacate the land, immediately become a trespasser. There are, however, four aspects of the law which indicate that the law relating to bare licences is not quite as simple as this.

---

[8] A play by Warren Chetham Strode. The part of 'Arthur Barrington' was played by Peter Hammond, who went on to direct many of the well-known television adaptations of Sherlock Holmes stories (starting Jeremy Brett in the title role) from 1986–94.

First, through the operation of the doctrine of proprietary estoppel, the licensor may be estopped from revoking the licence. Second, a licence which has been acted upon is not revocable. Third, on revocation of a bare licence, the licensee must be given a reasonable 'period of grace' or 'packing up period' and only at the end of this period does a licensee, who has failed to vacate the land, become a trespasser. Fourth, it is sometimes said that a bare licence may be revoked only 'on reasonable notice'.

Hill goes on to examine these four methods, each of which has been used to ensure that, when A revokes or attempts to revoke B's bare licence, B does not immediately become a trespasser. His conclusion is that only two of those methods should be used: the notion of a 'packing up' period, and the idea that the doctrine of proprietary estoppel may impose a duty on A to B. In doing so, he divides bare licences into two categories. The first is that in which the doctrine of proprietary estoppel does *not* impose a duty on A: he refers to these cases as involving a 'one-sided' licence.

Hill, 'The Termination of Bare Licences' [2001] Cambridge LJ 87, 107

Cases involving this type of "one sided" licence present fewest problems, both doctrinally and practically. If the licensee has not acted to his detriment there is no policy reason why the licensor's freedom of action should be unduly circumscribed. In terms of fairness, the only rationale for the law's intervention is to ensure that the licensee is given a reasonable period in which to make alternative arrangements (where necessary). The packing-up period provides the mechanism whereby the law can achieve an appropriate balance between the licensor's interest in determining the licence and the licensee's interest in not suffering excessive disruption.

Hill's second category consists of cases in which the doctrine of proprietary estoppel does impose a duty on A. Hill includes those cases in his discussion of bare licences, because he defines any non-contractual licence as a bare licence. Given the duty imposed on A, however, we will treat estoppel licences as distinct from bare licences and examine them separately in section 4 below. Nonetheless, it is worth noting Hill's conclusion that the courts' handling of this second class of cases can be explained by using only two ideas: firstly, the concept of a 'packing up' period applied in the first category; secondly, the idea that the doctrine of proprietary estoppel imposes a duty on A.

Hill, 'The Termination of Bare Licences' [2001] Cambridge LJ 87, 107–8

The second category, which might be termed "two-sided" licences, includes cases where, although there is no contractual bargain between the parties, the licensee, as a consequence of the (express or implied) licence, undertakes some activity or incurs some expenditure which otherwise he would not have undertaken or incurred. The courts have dealt with cases falling within this category in one of three ways: the largely forgotten common law doctrine of a licence acted upon, the equitable doctrine of proprietary estoppel; the licensor's obligation to give reasonable notice. In policy terms, it is far from clear that the licensor's obligation to give reasonable notice is required to ensure that a "two-sided" licensee does not suffer hardship as a consequence of the licence's summary termination;

the doctrine of proprietary estoppel and the packing-up period provide the court with sufficient tools to enable the licensee's reasonable expectations to be protected.

All the cases in which the basis of the court's decision has been either the doctrine of a licence acted upon or the licensor's obligation to give reasonable notice could have been decided equally or more satisfactorily by the proper application of the doctrine of proprietary estoppel or the packing-up period. Furthermore, there is no argument of principle in support of the proposition that a licensor should be under an obligation to give the licensee a period of notice before revocation of a bare licence is to take effect [...] When bare licences are located in the broader picture of rights in relation to land, the notion that a bare licensee is entitled to a period of notice is illogical [...]

Whilst we can question his terminology (Hill's second class of bare licences is perhaps better seen as a class of estoppel licences), Hill's analysis is otherwise persuasive. In a simple bare licence case, in which the doctrine of proprietary estoppel does not apply, the concept of a 'packing up' period is the *only* concept that a court needs to explain why A's revocation of a bare licence whilst B is on A's land does not immediately turn B into a wrongdoer.

2.2 B'S RIGHTS AGAINST X

If B has a bare licence, then, as Hohfeld notes in the extract above, that licence does not impose any duty on X, a stranger, not to interfere with B's use of A's land. In some cases, however, B can acquire a property right *in addition* to his bare licence; that property right will then impose a duty on X. For example, let us say that A goes on holiday for a week and asks B to 'house-sit'. A and B's arrangement is that B is under no duty to do so, and that, if he does choose to house-sit, A will not pay him. If B does go onto and occupy A's land for that week, X is under a duty not to interfere with B's occupation of the land. This is confirmed by Lord Upjohn's analysis, in *National Provincial Bank v Ainsworth*,[9] of the position of Mrs Ainsworth *after* Mr Ainsworth moved out of the family home (see Chapter 1, section 5.1, and Chapter 4, section 5.4, for discussion of this case). His Lordship stated that '*in this case in truth and in fact the wife at all material times was and is in exclusive occupation of the home. Until her husband returns she has dominion over the house and she could clearly bring proceedings against trespassers*'.[10]

In such a case, however, X's duty does not arise because of B's licence; instead, it arises because B, as a result of having possession of A's land, has a legal estate in land—that is, a freehold. That right is acquired *independently* of A: B acquires the right simply by taking possession of the land (see Chapter 3, section 4, for discussion of the concept of independent acquisition). This means that B acquires such a right even if he takes possession of the land *without* A's permission and therefore has no licence. We will explore this point further in Chapter 10, when examining how B can independently acquire a legal estate in land.

2.3 B'S RIGHTS AGAINST C

If B has a bare licence and A then gives C an inconsistent right—for example, by transferring his freehold of the land to C—we have an example of the priority triangle.

---

9 [1965] AC 1175, 1232.
10 That view was confirmed by the Court of Appeal in *Manchester Airport plc v Dutton* [2000] QB 133.

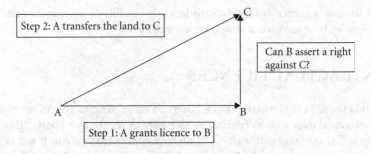

Figure 3 Bare Licences and the Priority Triangle

As we saw in Chapters 6 and 7, there are two ways in which B *may* have a right against C: firstly, it may be that C has acted in such a way as to give B a *new, direct right* against C; secondly, it may be that B has a *pre-existing property right* that he can assert against C.

2.3.1 Direct rights

There are many different ways in which B may acquire a direct right against C. As we saw in Chapter 7, section 2, however, all of these methods depend on C's conduct: there must be something in the way that C behaves that justifies B's acquisition of a new, direct right against C. For example, if C, when acquiring his freehold from A, enters into a contract with B to allow B to continue using the land, B will acquire a direct contractual right against C. In practice, however, that situation will almost never arise. If B simply has a bare licence, there is no reason why A, when transferring the land to C, would insist on C making such a contractual promise to B. And there is no obvious reason why C would, on his or her own initiative, make such a promise to B.

2.3.2 A pre-existing property right?

If B's bare licence counts as a property right, then, as we saw in Chapter 6, it will be prima facie binding on C. It is clear, however, that a bare licence does *not* count as a property right. Firstly, as we saw in Chapter 3, section 6, and Chapter 4, section 5.4, the *numerus clausus* principle, confirmed by ss 1 and 4 of the Law of Property Act 1925 (LPA 1925), means that there is a *closed* list of legal and equitable property rights in land. As confirmed by the House of Lords in *National Provincial Bank v Ainsworth*, licences do not form part of this list. Further, it is very unlikely that a bare licence will ever be admitted into the list of property rights: it cannot meet the criteria laid down by Lord Wilberforce in the following extract.

National Provincial Bank v Ainsworth [1965] AC 1175, HL

Lord Wilberforce

At 1247–8

Before a right or interest can be admitted into the category of property, or of a right affecting property, it must be definable, identifiable by third parties, capable in its nature of assumption by third parties, and have some degree of permanence or stability.

If B simply has a bare licence, his right clearly lacks that quality of 'permanence and stability'; after all, as we have seen, it can simply be revoked by A.

3 CONTRACTUAL LICENCES

A contractual licence exists where B has a liberty to make some use of A's land *and* A is under a contractual duty to B in relation to A's power to revoke that liberty. This means that—in some circumstances, at least—A is under a contractual duty to B not to revoke B's licence. For example, let us say A and B make an agreement that B, in return for paying A £500 up front, can share occupation of A's house for three months. As we will see in Chapter 23, section 1.1.1, such an arrangement will not give B a lease: because he can only share occupation of A's house, B does not have a right to exclusive possession of any land. B does, however, have more than a bare licence: A is also under a contractual duty not to revoke B's permission to occupy during the next three months. Of course, A's duty is not absolute: even if they have not expressly agreed it, A will have an implied power to revoke B's permission in certain circumstances—for example, if he discovers that B is stealing from him.

The distinction between a bare licence and a contractual licence thus turns on the question of whether A is under a contractual duty to B. Contractual duties can be implied as well as expressed and, in some cases, the courts have been very creative in finding such a contract.

Tanner v Tanner [1975] 1 WLR 1346, CA

Facts: Mr Tanner (described by Lord Denning MR as a *'milkman by day and a croupier by night'*) entered into an extramarital relationship with Miss Macdermott. She later gave birth to twins fathered by Mr Tanner and changed her name to 'Mrs Tanner'—but the two never married. Mr Tanner bought a house in which Mrs Tanner and the twins were to live. To move into this house, Mrs Tanner gave up her rent-controlled tenancy on the basis that she and the twins would be allowed to remain in the new house, at least until the twins left school. Mr Tanner and his first wife divorced, but Mr Tanner then married another woman and decided to remove Mrs Tanner from the house. He offered her £4,000 to leave, but she refused. Mr Tanner (A) brought proceedings to remove Mrs Tanner (B). A succeeded at first instance and B (with the children) moved into local authority accommodation. B appealed, arguing that A was under a contractual duty to allow B to remain, at least until the twins left school. B did not, however, ask the Court of Appeal for an order forcing A to let her back into occupation. The Court of Appeal found that, in removing B and the twins, A had breached his contractual duty to B and so should pay B damages of £2,000.

Lord Denning MR

At 1350

It is said that [B and the twins] were only licensees—bare licensees—under a licence revocable at will; and that [A] was entitled in law to turn her and the twins out on a moment's notice. I cannot believe that this is the law [...] I think he had a legal duty towards them. Not only towards the babies but also towards their mother. She was looking after them and bringing them up. In order to fulfil his duty towards the babies, he was under a duty to provide for the mother too. She had given up her flat where she was protected by the Rent Acts [. . .] at his instance so as to be able the better to bring up the children. It is impossible to suppose that in that situation she and the babies were bare licensees whom he could turn out at a moment's notice. He recognised this when he offered to pay her £4,000 to get her out.

What then was their legal position? She herself said in evidence: 'The house was supposed to be ours until the children left school.' It seems to me [. . .] that in all the circumstances it is to be implied that she had a licence—a contractual licence—to have accommodation in the house for herself and the children so long as they were of school age and the accommodation was reasonably required for her and the children. There was, it is true, no express contract to that effect, but the circumstances are such that the court should imply a contract by him [. . .] whereby they were entitled to have the use of the house as their home until the girls had finished school. It may be that if circumstances changed—so that the accommodation was not reasonably required—the licence might be determinable. But it was not determinable in the circumstances in which he sought to determine it, namely to turn her out with the children and to bring in his new wife with her family. It was a contractual licence of the kind which is specifically enforceable on her behalf, and which he can be restrained from breaking; and he could not sell the house over her head so as to get her out in that way.

If therefore the lady had sought an injunction restraining him from determining the licence, it should have been granted [. . .]

It is important to note that a contemporary court is unlikely to adopt the very creative approach to finding a contractual licence taken by Lord Denning MR in *Tanner v Tanner*.[11] In that case, the contractual licence seems to have been imposed as a means to the end of imposing a duty on Mr Tanner to provide some form of financial assistance to Mrs Tanner and the twins (in the case itself, Mrs Tanner's only claim was for damages). Nowadays, because Parliament has recognized that particular policy need, there are statutory means by which a party such as Mr Tanner can come under a duty to make financial provision for his children. As a result, there is no longer a need to bend doctrinal rules, as in *Tanner v Tanner*, in order to find a contractual licence. Indeed, under the Children Act 1989, s 15 and Sch 1, it is possible to impose a duty on a party such as Mr Tanner to allow his children (and their mother) to remain in occupation of a particular home until leaving school. As a result, there is no longer a need to stretch the concept of a contractual licence.

3.1 B'S RIGHTS AGAINST A

The Court of Appeal's decision in *Tanner v Tanner* provides a good example of the protection available to B if he has a contractual licence. Lord Denning MR indicated that, *if* B had applied to court in time, a court would have prevented A from breaching his contractual duty not to revoke B's liberty to occupy A's land. In *Tanner* itself, it was too late for the court to protect B in that way. As a result, A was ordered to pay B damages; those damages had the aim of putting B, as far as possible, in the position in which she would have been had A kept his contractual promise.[12]

---

[11] Indeed, in *Horrocks v Forray* [1976] 1 WLR 230, a differently constituted Court of Appeal, faced with a similar case, distinguished *Tanner v Tanner*.

[12] In very rare cases, as a result of A's breach of contract, B can obtain damages based on the gain that A has made by the breach: see, e.g., *A-G v Blake* [2001] 1 AC 268.

In assessing B's position against A, there are two key questions: firstly, is A's actual or threatened action a breach of his contractual duty to B? Secondly, if it is, or would be, a breach, how will a court respond?

3.1.1 Is A's actual or threatened conduct a breach of contract?

Of course, this will depend on the precise terms of the contract between A and B. It is vital to note that, in most cases, it may be possible, in certain circumstances, for A to revoke B's liberty to use A's land *without* breaching his contract with B.

Winter Garden Theatre (London) Ltd v Millennium Productions Ltd [1948] AC 173, HL

Facts: See section 2.1 above.

Viscount Simon

At 191

[W]hen the clauses of the present licence are carefully studied, the proper inference from the language used is that the licence was not perpetual but that the intention of the parties, to be inferred from the document, though not expressly stated, was that, upon [A Ltd] indicating their decision that the permission given by the licence would be withdrawn, [B Ltd] were to have a reasonable time to withdraw after which they would become trespassers.

Lord Porter

At 194

It is one thing to say that a limited and temporal licence remains in force until the particular object for which it is given is fulfilled or the definite period of time has elapsed, it is quite a different matter to allege that a licence once given in general terms can never be terminated.

Lord Macdermott

At 206

[T]he conclusion I reach is that in this contract there should be implied a stipulation to the effect that, after the expiration of the first year, the licence might be terminated by the licensors on the expiration of a reasonable notice period duly communicated to the licensees. That, to my mind, is what accords best with the express terms of the contract and the nature of the transaction.

The House of Lords further found that the one-month notice given by A Ltd was a reasonable notice period and so A Ltd, although it had revoked B Ltd's licence, had *not* breached its contract in doing so.

3.1.2 If A's conduct is a breach, how will a court respond?

We have already seen that, in *Tanner v Tanner*, Lord Denning MR stated that, if approached in time, a court would have issued an injunction to prevent A's breach of B's contractual licence. Lord Uthwatt also considered this question in *Winter Garden*.

Winter Garden Theatre (London) Ltd v Millennium Productions Ltd [1948] AC 173, HL

Lord Uthwatt

At 202

The settled practice of the courts of equity is to do what they can by an injunction to preserve the sanctity of a bargain. To my mind, as at present advised, a licensee who has refused to accept the wrongful repudiation of the bargain which is involved in an unauthorised revocation of the licence is as much entitled to the protection of an injunction as a licensee who has not received any notice of revocation.

This preference for specifically protecting B's contractual licence (rather than allowing A to breach it and leaving B to claim money from A) can also be seen in cases in which, in contrast to *Tanner* and *Winter Garden*, B has not yet started to make use of A's land.

Verrall v Great Yarmouth Borough Council [1981] QB 202, CA

Facts: Great Yarmouth Borough Council owned a hall (the Wellington Pier Pavilion) in that seaside town. It made a contractual promise in April 1979 to allow the National Front to use the hall for its two-day national conference in October. Following a change in its political control, the council (A) attempted, in May, to revoke the National Front's licence. Mr Verrall (B), suing on his own behalf and representing all members of that organization, applied for an order forcing A to perform its contractual promise. Such an order was granted. The council appealed unsuccessfully to the Court of Appeal.

Lord Denning MR

At 216

Since the *Winter Garden* case, it is clear that once a man has entered under his contract of licence, he cannot be turned out. An injunction can be obtained against the licensor to prevent his being turned out. On principle it is the same if it happens before he enters. If he has a contractual right to enter, and the licensor refuses to let him come in, then he can come to the court and in a proper case get an order for specific performance to allow him to come in. An illustration was taken in the course of the argument. Supposing one of the great political parties—say, the Conservative Party—had booked its hall at Brighton for its conference in September of this year: it had made all its arrangements accordingly: it had all its delegates coming: it had booked its hotels, and so on. Would it be open to the local council to repudiate that agreement, and say that the Conservative Party could not go there? Would the only remedy be damages? Clearly not. The court would order the council in such a case to perform its contract. It would be the same in the case of the Labour Party, or whoever it may be. When arrangements are made for a licence of this kind of such importance and magnitude affecting many people, the licensors cannot be allowed to repudiate it and simply pay damages. It must be open to the court to grant specific performance in such cases.

It should not be assumed, however, that a court will *always* specifically protect B's contractual licence. After all, a court has a discretion as to whether to give B an equitable remedy such as specific performance or an injunction. And, in some circumstances, it may be inappropriate to prevent A from revoking B's contractual licence.

Thompson v Park [1944] KB 408, CA

Facts: Mr Thompson and Mr Park each owned a school. The schools were amalgamated and the new school was set up on the site of Mr Thompson's school, Broughton Hall, near Eccleshall, Staffordshire. Mr Thompson gave Mr Park, and twenty-five of Mr Park's pupils, permission to join the school. The working relationship between Mr Thompson and Mr Park broke down, and Mr Thompson attempted to revoke the licence of Mr Park and his pupils to remain at the school. Having initially left, Mr Park forced his way back onto the premises and refused to leave. Mr Thompson (A) brought proceedings for an injunction ordering Mr Park (B) to leave. A also asked for an interim injunction ordering B to leave before the court determined A's application for an injunction. The Court of Appeal granted the interim injunction.

Goddard LJ

At 409–10

If [B] thought that he had a grievance which could be lawfully asserted the courts were open to him. I am not saying what the result of any application by him would have been, for though this is not the sort of agreement which any court could specifically enforce—for the court cannot specifically enforce an agreement for two people to live peaceably under the same roof—yet, of course, if the contract is broken, [B] has got a common law remedy in damages, which, if he is right, might be heavy. [B], however did not seek the intervention of the court, but took the law into his own hands and remedied the grievances under which he felt he was suffering in a manner which seems to me to have been wholly deplorable, all the more so when one considers that he is in charge of small boys at a preparatory school and ought to be inculcating into them a respect for authority and discipline. It appears to me that on his own showing he has been guilty at least of riot, affray, wilful damage, forcible entry and, perhaps, conspiracy [...]

The strength of the argument which was put forward on [B]'s behalf was that, assuming that there had been a breach of contract on the part of [A], [B] had a right to be where he was. That is an entire misconception of the legal position, which was that the defendant was a licensee on the premises. That licence has been withdrawn. Whether it has been rightly withdrawn or wrongly withdrawn matters nothing for this purpose. The licensee, once his licence is withdrawn, has no right to re-enter on the land. If he does, he is a common trespasser.

It is important to separate out two questions, both discussed by Goddard LJ in *Thompson v Park*. The first is whether, if B had applied to court *after* leaving A's land, a court would order

A to perform his contractual promise to share occupation with B. Goddard LJ's statement is surely correct: 'the court cannot specifically enforce an agreement for two people to live peaceably under the same roof.'[13] It would be unduly onerous on A to force him to live with B, given the breakdown in their relationship. And B would not receive the full value of his promise: sharing occupation with A, after the two have fallen out, is clearly different from sharing occupation when A and B are on good terms. So, whilst A's action in revoking the licence may well be a breach of contract, B may have to settle for receiving money from A.

The second question is whether, if A revokes his licence in breach of contract, B can then insist on re-entering A's land. Goddard LJ thought not—but it is not clear that this is consistent with the decision in *Verall v Great Yarmouth BC*,[14] or with the reasoning of Viscount Simon in the following extract.

Winter Garden Theatre (London) Ltd v Millennium Productions Ltd [1948] AC 173

Viscount Simon

At 189

[Viscount Simon referred to cases involving, for example:] the sale of a ticket to enter premises and witness a particular event, such as a ticket for a seat at a particular performance at a theatre or for entering private ground to witness a day's sport. In this last class of case, the implication of the arrangement, however it may be classified in law, plainly is that the ticket entitles the purchaser to enter and, if he behaves himself, to remain on the premises until the end of the event which he has paid his money to witness.

The point is that, even if a court would not order specific performance of A's contractual promise, once A has made such a promise, B does have a *legal right* to be on A's land for the duration of his contractual licence. In other words, even if the contract is not specifically enforced, A is under a contractual *duty* to B to allow B to use the land as promised.

This has important consequences.

Hurst v Picture Theatres Ltd [1915] 1 KB 1, CA

Facts: On 17 March 1913, a film of Lake Garda[15] was shown at a cinema in High Street Kensington, London, owned by Picture Theatres Ltd. Mr Hurst bought a ticket. He did not misbehave, but was forced to leave by the manager of the cinema, who mistakenly believed that B had not paid for his seat. Mr Hurst (B) claimed that Picture Theatres Ltd (A), through the actions of its employee, had committed the tort of trespass to the person: it had breached its duty not to interfere with B's physical integrity. A argued that, once it had exercised its power to revoke B's licence, B became a trespasser and so A was permitted to use reasonable force to remove B from the land. A argued that even if

---

[13] That statement was also approved by Megarry V-C in *Hounslow LBC v Twickenham GD Ltd* [1971] Ch 233, 250.

[14] [1981] 1 QB 202, 216.

[15] It is likely to have been a Kinemacolor film produced in 1910 (entitled *Lake Garda, Italy*), currently held by the Nederlands Filmmuseum and shown at the British Film Institute's Conservation Centre in February 2008.

its action in revoking the licence was a breach of contract, that did not change the fact that, once the licence was revoked, B was a trespasser on A's land and so reasonable force could be used to remove him. The Court of Appeal rejected that argument, affirming the decision of Channell J that B was entitled to substantial damages.

Buckley LJ

At 7

[B] in the present action paid his money to enjoy the sight of a particular spectacle. He was anxious to go into a picture theatre to see a series of views or pictures during, I suppose, an hour or a couple of hours. That which was granted to him was the right to enjoy looking at a spectacle, to attend a performance from its beginning to its end. That which was called the licence, the right to go upon the premises, was only something granted to him for the purpose of enabling him to have that which had been granted him, namely, the right to see. He could not see the performance unless he went into the building. His right to go into the building was something given to him in order to enable him to have the benefit of that which had been granted to him, namely, the right to hear the opera, or see the theatrical performance, or see the moving pictures as was the case here.

At 11

[A] had, I think, for value contracted that [B] should see a certain spectacle from its commencement to its termination. They broke that contract and it was a tort on their part to remove him. They committed an assault upon him in law. It was not of a violent kind, because, like a wise man, [B] gave way to superior force and left the theatre. They sought to justify the assault by saying that they were entitled to remove him because he had not paid. He had paid, the jury have so found. Failing on that question of fact, they say that they were entitled to remove him because his licence was revocable. In my opinion, it was not. There was, I think, no justification for the assault here committed. Under the circumstances it was for the jury to give him such a sum as was right for the assault which was committed upon him, and for the serious indignity to a gentleman of being seized and treated in this way in a place of public resort. The jury have found that he was originally in the theatre as a spectator, that the assault was committed upon him, and that it was a wrongful act.

An earlier decision, *Wood v Leadbitter*,[16] had held to the contrary on the basis that, because a contractual licence does not count as a property right in land, A remains free to revoke it. That approach is, however, impossible to defend; the decision in *Hurst* is clearly correct. A contractual licence is different from a bare licence: B has a liberty to use A's land *and* A is under a contractual duty to B not to revoke that liberty. So, even if A does attempt to revoke the licence by removing B, B's *right* (in Hohfeld's terms, a 'claim right') to be on the land remains. So A's attempt to revoke the licence does *not* turn B into a trespasser. That means that A is *not* allowed to use reasonable force to remove B from the land.

It is important to note that this analysis applies whether or not a court would grant an order of specific performance to protect B's contractual right. That point was made in the following case.

---

16 (1845) 13 M & W 838.

Hounslow London Borough Council v Twickenham GD Ltd [1971] 1 Ch 233

Megarry V-C

At 254–5

I have said nothing about an ejected licensee's right to claim damages for assault, for such issues do not arise in this case. All that I need say, in order to avoid possible misunderstanding, is that in light of the *Winter Garden* case I find it difficult to see how a contractual licensee can be treated as a trespasser so long as his contract entitles him to be on the land; and this is so whether or not his contract is specifically enforceable. I do not think that the licence can be detached from the contract, as it were, and separately revoked; the licensee is on the land by contractual right and is not as a trespasser. I may add that I say nothing about the rights of licensees against third parties.

It therefore seems clear that even if B's contractual licence would not be protected by an order for specific performance, B nonetheless has a right against A to be on A's land for the duration of his contractual licence. This suggests that the decision in *Hurst v Picture Theatres Ltd* should be the same *whether or not* A's contractual duty to B is specifically enforceable. This means that in a case like *Thompson v Park*, in which B's contractual licence allows him to share occupation of A's land with A, the following position applies if A and B fall out during the period of the contractual licence.

- If A attempts to revoke B's licence in breach of contract and B remains on the land, B does not become a trespasser—so A cannot use reasonable force to remove B from the land. Instead, A needs to apply to court for an order that B must leave. Because A's contractual duty is not specifically enforceable, a court is likely to grant such an order (although A will, of course, have to pay B damages for revoking B's licence in breach of contract).

- If A attempts to revoke B's licence in breach of contract and B is *not* on the land, B cannot force his way back onto the land. Instead, B needs to apply to court for an order that A must allow him back onto the land—but because A's contractual duty is not specifically enforceable, a court is unlikely to grant such an order.

3.2 B'S RIGHTS AGAINST X

In the passage from *Hounslow LBC v Twickenham GD Ltd* set out above, Megarry V-C concludes his survey of B's rights against A by stating that: '*I may add that I say nothing about the rights of licensees against third parties.*' It is indeed very important to draw this distinction. For example, if we say that B has a right to be on A's land for the duration of his contractual licence, this means that B has a right *against A* to be on A's land. A thus has a duty not to interfere with B's use of the land. That does *not* mean that a third party, such as X, has a duty to B: after all, A's duty arises as a result of his contractual promise to B, and X has made no such promise.

We noted in section 2.2 above that, even if B only has a bare licence, X will be under a duty to B *if* B acquires a property right by taking physical control of A's land. Clearly, the same is true if B has a contractual licence; in such a case it is not the licence itself that binds X, but rather the property right that B acquires by taking physical control of A's land. The following decision of the Court of Appeal goes further: it assumes that, if A gives B a contractual licence permitting B to take physical control of A's land, X can be under a duty to B even *before* B goes onto A's land.

Manchester Airport plc v Dutton and ors [2000] QB 133, CA

Facts: The National Trust owned some land adjacent to Manchester Airport. Manchester Airport plc was building a new runway. It needed to ensure that trees on the National Trust's land were cut down to prevent interference with flight paths to and from the new runway. The National Trust (A) gave Manchester Airport plc (B) and its authorized subcontractors permission to go onto the National Trust land to do the necessary work. Before B or its subcontractors entered the land, Mr Dutton (one of a number of environmental protestors) occupied the land with the intention of interfering with the planned work. Manchester Airport plc (B) applied for an order against Mr Dutton (X) for possession of the land, using the special summary procedure provided by Order 113 of the Rules of the Supreme Court.

Laws LJ (with whom Kennedy LJ agreed)

At 147–50

Now, I think it is clear that if [B] had been in actual occupation under the licence and the trespassers had then entered on the site, [B] could have obtained an order for possession; at least if it was in effective control of the land. Clause 1 of the licence confers a right to occupy the whole of the area edged red on the plan. The places where the trespassers have gone lie within that area. [B's] claim for possession would not, were it in occupation, fall in my judgment to be defeated by the circumstance that it enjoys no title or estate in the land, nor any right of exclusive possession as against [A...]

But if [B], were it in actual occupation and control of the site, could obtain an order for possession against the trespassers, why may it not obtain such an order *before* it enters into occupation, so as to evict the trespassers and enjoy the licence granted to it? As I understand it, the principal objection to the grant of such relief is that it would amount to an ejectment, and ejectment is a remedy available only to a party with title to or estate in the land; which as a mere licensee [B] plainly lacks [...]

But I think there is a logical mistake in the notion that because ejectment was only available to estate owners, possession cannot be available to licensees who do not enjoy de facto occupation. The mistake inheres in this: if the action for ejectment was by definition concerned *only* with the rights of estate owners, it is necessarily silent upon the question, what relief might be available to a licensee. The limited and specific nature of ejectment means only that it was not available to a licensee; it does not imply the further proposition that *no* remedy by way of possession can now be granted to a licensee not in occupation. Nowadays there is no distinct remedy of ejectment; a plaintiff sues for an order of possession, whether he is himself in occupation or not. The proposition that a plaintiff not in occupation may only obtain the remedy if he is an estate owner assumes that he must bring himself within the old law of ejectment. I think it is a false assumption.

I would hold that the court today has ample power to grant a remedy to a licensee which will protect but not exceed his legal rights granted by the licence. If, as here, that requires an order for possession, the spectre of history (which, in the true tradition of the common law, ought to be a friendly ghost) does not stand in the way. The law of ejectment has no voice in the question; it cannot speak beyond its own limits.

In my judgment the true principle is that a licensee not in occupation may claim possession against a trespasser if that is a necessary remedy to vindicate and give effect to such rights of occupation as by contract with his licensor he enjoys. This is the same principle as allows a licensee who is in de facto possession to evict a trespasser. There is no respectable distinction, in law or logic, between the two situations. An estate owner may seek an order whether he is in possession or not. So, in my judgment, may a licensee, if other things are equal. In both cases, the plaintiff's remedy is strictly limited to what is required to make good his legal right. The principle applies although the licensee has no right to exclude the licensor himself. Elementarily he cannot exclude any occupier who, by contract or estate, has a claim to possession equal or superior to his own. Obviously, however, that will not avail a bare trespasser.

Chadwick LJ (dissenting)

At 146–7

There was no material, in the present case, on which the judge could reach the conclusion that [B] was in de facto possession of the relevant part of [A's land]; and, for my part, I do not think that she did reach that conclusion. She treated the question as one which turned on the construction of the licence. In my view the judge was in error when she held, in a passage in her judgment to which I have already referred, that:

'The licence gives the right of possession and this is, I am satisfied, a right of possession which does not give absolute title, but it does nevertheless give a power against trespassers.'

She did not make the distinction, essential in cases of this nature, between a plaintiff who is in possession and who seeks protection from those who interfere with that possession, and a plaintiff who has not gone into possession but who seeks to evict those who are already on the land. In the latter case (which is this case) the plaintiff must succeed by the strength of his title, not on the weakness (or lack) of any title in the defendant.

All three members of the Court of Appeal thus agreed that if X interfered with B's use of A's land *after* B had gone into occupation of the land, B would be able to bring a claim for possession against X. That is certainly the case: it is simply an application of the point made in section 2.2 above—that is, whenever B takes possession of land, whether with the consent of an owner or not, he acquires a legal property right in that land and so the rest of the world comes under a prima facie duty to B not to interfere with B's use of the land. We will examine this point further in Chapter 10.

But Chadwick LJ and the majority disagreed about the answer in a situation in which, as in *Manchester Airport* itself, X interfered with B's use of A's land *before* B had gone into occupation. There is a strong argument in favour of Chadwick LJ's analysis. The crucial point is that, once B takes physical control of A's land—whether under a licence or not—B acquires a legal property right in A's land. Before that point, B has only a contractual right against A: there is no reason why A's contract with B should impose a duty on X.

Swadling makes this point in the following extract.

Swadling, 'Opening the *Numerus Clausus*' (2000) 116 LQ Rev 358

[...In *Manchester Airport v Dutton* Laws LJ asserted] that no logical distinction can be drawn between a licensee in and a licensee out of possession, so that if the former can bring

> trespass against third parties, so can the latter. With respect, it would have been appropriate at this point to consider why a licensee in possession is able to bring trespass; the reason is in fact one which cannot apply in the case of a licensee out of possession. The reason why a licensee in possession can bring an action for possession is that he has a right of possession which is completely independent of the licence under which he occupies the land.
>
> Take the deserted wife in *Ainsworth's case* [*National Provincial Bank v Ainsworth*[17]—see the discussion in section 2.2 above]. She is, we are told, entitled to sue those who interfere with her possession of the matrimonial home, from which it follows that she has a right to the possession of that matrimonial home. But from where does her right to possession spring? Not from her licence to be on the premises, for that is a right which the House of Lords held bound the husband alone. It must therefore be some other event which creates this right of possession [...] and this other event is her unilateral act of taking possession of the house. In other words, her right of possession arises from the fact of her possession...
>
> The error into which, with respect, Laws L.J. falls is in failing to notice that a contractual licensee in occupation of land has rights derived from two separate sources, some from the contract, some from the fact of possession. Those derived from the contract prevent the licensor from denying him possession of the land. But those rights, because of the doctrine of privity, and notwithstanding the recent reform of that doctrine, bind the licensor alone. It is the rights derived from the second source, from the fact of possession, which bind third parties [...] There is, therefore, a distinction which does still need to be drawn between a plaintiff whose right to occupy the land in question arises from title and one whose right arises from the contract alone.

It is thus possible to disapprove of the decision of the Court of Appeal in *Manchester Airport plc v Dutton*. Indeed, it is interesting to compare it to the decision of in *Hill v Tupper*,[18] which we examined in Chapter 3, section 1. In that case, the Basingstoke Canal Company (A) gave Mr Hill (B) an 'exclusive' contractual licence to hire boats out on the canal. The Exchequer Chamber made clear that A's contract with B did *not* give B a legal property right and so did not impose a duty to B on Mr Tupper (X), who had also hired out boats on the canal. So, if Mr Hill wanted to stop Mr Tupper from hiring out boats, he had to ask or force the Canal Company, as owner of the canal, to assert its property right against Mr Tupper.

The same analysis should apply in *Manchester Airport plc v Dutton*: the airport should use its contract with the National Trust to ask or force the National Trust to use its property right, as owner of the land, against Mr Dutton and the other protestors. The interesting point, of course, is that at least some members of the National Trust may have refused to support such an action against the protestors.[19]

Alternatively, the decision in *Manchester Airport plc v Dutton* could be seen as part of a deliberate move to increase the protection given to a contractual licensee against third parties. Swadling criticizes the decision for blurring the divide between personal rights and property rights, but others see the decision as taking a welcome step towards allowing (at least some) contractual licences to count as property rights.[20] To that extent, one's view of the *Manchester Airport* decision depends on one's view as to the crucial question, to be examined in section 3.3.2 below, as to whether a contractual licence counts as a property right in land.

---

[17] [1965] AC 1175.
[18] (1863) 2 H & C 122.
[19] See McFarlane, *The Structure of Property Law* (2008, p 345, fn 22).
[20] See, e.g., Gray and Gray, *Elements of Land Law* (5th edn, 2009, [10.5.13]–[10.5.15]).

3.3 B's RIGHTS AGAINST C

If B has a contractual licence and A then gives C an inconsistent right—for example, by transferring his freehold to C—we have an example of the priority triangle.

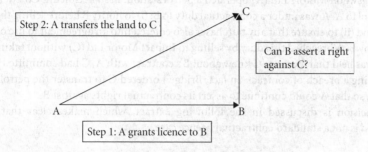

Figure 4 Contractual Licences and the Priority Triangle

As we have seen, there are two ways in which B *may* have a right against C: firstly, it may be that C has acted in such a way as to give B a *new, direct right* against C; secondly, it may be that B has a *pre-existing property right* that he can assert against C.

3.3.1 Direct rights

In Chapter 7, section 2, we considered some of the means by which B can show that he has acquired a new, direct right against C. In this section, we will look at the principles most likely to be relevant where, prior to his dealings with C, A has given B a contractual licence.

The tort of procuring a breach by A of A's contract with B

As we noted in Chapter 7, section 2.4, the existence of a contract between A and B imposes a duty on the rest of the world not to procure a breach by A of A's contractual duty to B.[21] For example, if A has a contract to perform at B's theatre, and C, knowing about that contract, persuades A to breach it and to perform at C's theatre instead, C commits a wrong against B.[22] There is a very difficult question as to whether C commits this tort if he simply knows about A's contractual licence with B, and, despite that, goes ahead and acquires a right from A with the intention of *not* allowing B to continue using A's land. Megaw LJ noted the possibility, in passing, in *Binions v Evans*.[23] But his Lordship went on to note that: '*However, it may be that there are special technical considerations in the law relating to land that would require to be reviewed before one could confidently assert that the ordinary principles as to the protection of known contractual rights would apply.*'

Certainly, as Roger Smith has pointed out,[24] there is a fear that allowing the tort to apply would make it far too easy for B to assert a direct right against C, and would thus undermine the protection due to a party acquiring a right in land. Indeed, Smith suggests that '*where real property principles accord priority to a contract or conveyance over an earlier contract, it should not be open to the earlier contracting party to rely on tort*'.[25]

---

[21] See *OBG Ltd v Allan* [2007] 2 WLR 920.
[22] See, e.g., *Lumley v Gye* (1853) 2 E & B 216.
[23] [1972] Ch 359, 371.
[24] 'The Economic Torts: Their Impact on Real Property' (1977) 41 Conv 318.
[25] Ibid, at 329.

On that view, the tort should *not* be able to provide any protection to B's contractual licence, because such a right does not currently count as a property right in land. There is, however, at least one case in which the tort was applied to a case involving land in relation to which B did not have a property right. In *Esso Petroleum Co Ltd v Kingswood Motors Ltd and ors*,[26] Kingswood Motors Ltd (A) operated a petrol station. Esso Petroleum Co Ltd (B) supplied petrol to A. A was under a contractual duty to B: (i) to notify B before selling the petrol station; and (ii) to ensure that any purchaser also entered into an agreement to use only fuel supplied by B. A breached this duty by selling to Impact Motor Ltd (C) without taking those steps. It was held that, because C knew about B's contract with A, C had committed the tort of procuring a breach of contract. In fact, Bridge J ordered C to transfer the petrol station back to B, so that A could continue to assert its contractual rights against B.

The decision is discussed in the following extract, which makes clear that *Esso v Kingswood* is not a standard contractual licence case.

McFarlane, *The Structure of Property Law* (2008, p 438)

[T]he courts *are* willing to apply the wrong [of procuring a breach of contract] even where land is concerned. This is demonstrated by *Esso Petroleum Co Ltd v Kingswood Motors Ltd* [...] This willingness to apply the wrong even where land is concerned seems correct. The purpose of the wrong is to protect B's contractual right against A: it should therefore apply *whenever* B has a contractual right against A. It seems that the wrong is based on the need for the rest of the world to respect B's contractual relationship with A. There is no obvious reason why contractual rights relating to the use of land should attract less protection. For example, let's say that A, a cinema owner, makes a contractual promise to allow B to run a confectionary stall from part of that land for five years. That promise gives B a contractual licence: a personal right against A. However, if C, a competitor of B, pays A money to persuade A to breach the contract by removing B from the land, C commits the wrong of procuring a breach of the contract.

However, this does *not* mean that C will necessarily commit the wrong if, in [a standard contractual licence case] he goes ahead and buys A's Freehold and then seeks to remove B from the land. There is an important difference between [a standard contractual licence case] and the situation in *Kingswood Motors*. In the latter case, A was under an explicit contractual duty *not to transfer his Freehold to C* unless certain conditions were met. A therefore breached his contractual duty to B *as soon as* he transferred that right to C: that is, as soon as A sold the land to C. C, by participating in a sale that he knew to breach those conditions, was actively facilitating A's breach of contract. In [a standard contractual licence case], however [...] A has *not* made a contractual promise not to transfer his Freehold unless certain conditions are met. As a result, the sale to C, *by itself*, does *not* breach A's contractual duty to B: that duty is breached only at a later stage: when C asserts his right and prevents B from using the land.

This analysis *may* provide a way in which to justify the courts' apparent reluctance to apply the tort of procuring a breach of contract in a standard contractual licence case. After all, as we saw in Chapter 7, section 2.6, the courts have been careful to ensure that the means by which B can acquire a direct right are not expanded to the point at which C can be bound simply as a result of his knowledge of B's pre-existing personal right against A.

[26] [1974] QB 142.

The Contract (Rights of Third Parties) Act 1999

The presence of a contractual licence between A and B may have a different, more significant impact on B's chances of acquiring a direct right against C. We noted in section 2.3.2 above that, if B has a bare licence, it is very unlikely that he will acquire such a right: C simply has no incentive to act in such a way as to give B such a right. But things may be different where B has a contractual licence. For example, let us say that A makes a contractual promise to B to allow B to make a particular use A's land for five years. Two years later, A plans to sell the land to C. A knows that if he sells the land to C and C stops B from using the land, A will be in breach of his contractual promise to B. A will therefore have to pay money to B to put B in the position in which he would have been had A kept his promise to allow B to use the land for the full five years.[27] This gives A a reason to insist that C, when buying the land, makes a promise to allow B to continue using the land until the five years are up.

As we saw in Chapter 7, section 2.2, the Contract (Rights of Third Parties) Act 1999 allows B, in certain circumstances, to acquire a direct right against C as a result of a contractual promise made by C to A. If C makes a contractual promise to A to allow B to continue to use the land for the remainder of the five years, that promise clearly 'purports to confer a benefit' on B. Section 1(1)(b) of the 1999 Act can therefore operate to give B a direct right against C *even though*: (i) C's promise to allow B to use the land is made to A not B; and (ii) consideration for the promise is provided by A not B. Section 1(5) of the 1999 Act means that the remedies available to B as against C can then be determined by applying the principles (examined in section 3.1 above) that govern the remedies available to B against A. It is true that, under s 2 of the 1999 Act, A and C may have a power to vary C's contractual promise and hence to weaken or remove B's right against C.[28] In our example, however, there is no reason for A to wish to do so: A's aim is to give B a right against C that will absolve A from having to pay damages for breach of contract to B.

For the 1999 Act to apply, C must make a *contractual* promise to A. If, as in our example, C's promise is made as part of the contractual deal in which A promises to transfer his land to C, C's promise only counts as a contractual promise if the formality rule set out by the Law of Property (Miscellaneous Provisions) Act 1989 (LP(MP)A 1989) is satisfied. We will examine that rule in detail in Chapter 9, section 3. For present purposes, it suffices to note that if, when acquiring his right from A, C makes an *oral* promise A to allow B to continue using A's land, that promise will *not* be contractually binding on C.[29] If so, B will be unable to rely on the 1999 Act to acquire a direct right against C—but B may be able to rely on a different means of enforcing C's promise.

The 'constructive trust' principle in Binions v Evans

In Chapter 7, section 2.3, we examined cases in which B acquired a direct right against C as a result of C's promise to A *without* needing to rely on the Contract (Rights of Third Parties) Act 1999. One such case was *Binions v Evans*.

---

[27] See, e.g., *King v David Allen & Sons Billposting Ltd* [1916] 2 AC 54.

[28] There are limits to that power—e.g., it is lost if B has 'communicated his assent' to C's promise to C; if C is aware that B has relied on C's promise; or if B has relied on the promise and C could reasonably be expected to have foreseen such reliance: see s 2(1) of the 1999 Act.

[29] C's oral promise may be contractually binding if it seen as separate from the contract dealing with C's acquisition of a right from A and so counts as a 'collateral contract'. As we will see in Chapter 9, section 3.5, however, the courts are generally reluctant to view such promises as collateral to the main contract between A and C.

Binions v Evans [1972] Ch 359, CA

Facts: See Chapter 7, section 2.3, for the facts of the case. We saw that Lord Denning MR took the view that, even if Mrs Evans (B) had no legal or equitable property right that she could assert against Mr and Mrs Binions (C), the Binions could still be prevented from removing Mrs Evans from the cottage. That reasoning was based on the fact that, when acquiring a freehold of the cottage from the trustees of the Tredegar Estate (A), the Binions had made a promise to allow Mrs Evans to remain in the cottage for the rest of her life.

Lord Denning MR

At 367

[A] stipulated with [C] that [C was] to take the house 'subject to' [B's] rights under the agreement. They supplied [C] with a copy of the contract: and [C] paid less because of [B's] right to stay there. In these circumstances, this court will impose on [C] a constructive trust for [B's] benefit: for the simple reason that it would be utterly inequitable for [C] to turn [B] out contrary to the stipulation subject to which [C] took the premises. That seems to me clear from the important decision of *Bannister v Bannister*,[30] which was applied by the judge and which I gladly follow.

It is worth noting that there are a number of other possible explanations for the result in *Binions v Evans*. Firstly, the majority of the Court of Appeal (Megaw and Stephenson LJJ) found that B's initial agreement with A gave B more than a contractual licence: she had an equitable life interest in the land and that property right was capable of binding C. On that analysis, the case has nothing to do with contractual licences.

Secondly, Lord Denning MR also contended that B's contractual licence counted, by itself, as an equitable interest in land. We will examine that argument in the next section. As we will see, it is, to say the least, somewhat controversial: it is therefore no surprise that Lord Denning MR also considered whether B had a new, direct right against C.

It is that suggestion on which we will focus here: the idea that B acquired a direct right against C, because, given that C acquired the land on the basis of allowing B to remain in occupation, it would be 'utterly inequitable' if C were now free to go back on that promise. As we saw in Chapter 7, section 2.3, that suggestion is consistent with a number of cases in which B acquires a direct right against C where:

- C acquires a property right in land from A; *and*
- prior to that, C made a promise to A to give B a right to make some use of that land; *and*
- as a result of that promise, A allowed C to acquire the property right in the land, or allowed C to acquire that right for a lower price.

As we noted in Chapter 7, section 2.3 (and as we will see in Chapter 14, section 4), the precise basis of the principle applied in these cases has been contested. Nonetheless, the following extract is from a Court of Appeal decision confirming that this principle may be used in a case in which B initially has a contractual licence from A.

[30] [1948] 2 All ER 133.

Ashburn Anstalt v Arnold [1989] Ch 1, CA

Facts: Arnold & Co had a lease of business premises. It sold that lease to Matlodge Ltd. As part of the sale, Matlodge made a contractual promise to Arnold & Co that it could remain in occupation of the land until it was needed for redevelopment. Cavendish Land Co Ltd then acquired both a freehold and the lease of the land, and took on Matlodge's contractual duties to Arnold & Co. Cavendish was later taken over by Legal & General Assurance Society Ltd, which also took on the contractual duties to Arnold & Co. Legal & General (A) then sold its freehold to Ashburn Anstalt (C). Under the terms of the sale contract, C took its freehold 'subject to' the contractual rights of Arnold & Co (B) against A, arising as a result of the original agreement with Matlodge. C had no plans to redevelop the land, but sought possession from B. B's first argument was that its initial agreement with A gave B a property right (a lease) that was binding on C. As we will see in Chapter 23, section 1.1.3, the Court of Appeal accepted that argument and found in B's favour. The Court of Appeal also went on to consider B's argument that, even if its agreement with A gave it only a contractual licence, B could assert that contractual licence against C. As we will see in section 3.3.2, the Court of Appeal rejected that argument. It was pointed out, however, that, in some circumstances, a party with a contractual licence can acquire a right against C as a result of a promise made by C to A.

Fox LJ

At 25–6

It is said that when a person sells land and stipulates that the sale should be 'subject to' a contractual licence, the court will impose a constructive trust upon the purchaser to give effect to the licence [...]

We do not feel able to accept that as a general proposition. We agree with the observations of Dillon J. in *Lyus v. Prowsa Developments Ltd* [1982] 1 W.L.R. 1044, 1051:

> 'By contrast, there are many cases in which land is expressly conveyed subject to possible incumbrances when there is no thought at all of conferring any fresh rights on third parties who may be entitled to the benefit of the incumbrances. The land is expressed to be sold subject to incumbrances to satisfy the vendor's duty to disclose all possible incumbrances known to him, and to protect the vendor against any possible claim by the purchaser [...] So, for instance, land may be contracted to be sold and may be expressed to be conveyed subject to the restrictive covenants contained in a conveyance some 60 or 90 years old. No one would suggest that by accepting such a form of contract or conveyance a purchaser is assuming a new liability in favour of third parties to observe the covenants if there was for any reason before the contract or conveyance no one who could make out a title as against the purchaser to the benefit of the covenants.'

The court will not impose a constructive trust unless it is satisfied that the conscience of the estate owner is affected. The mere fact that that land is expressed to be conveyed 'subject to' a contract does not necessarily imply that the grantee is to be under an obligation, not otherwise existing, to give effect to the provisions of the contract. The fact that the conveyance is expressed to be subject to the contract may often, for the reasons indicated by Dillon J., be at least as consistent with an intention merely to protect the grantor against claims by the grantee as an intention to impose an obligation on the grantee. The words 'subject to' will, of course, impose notice. But notice is not enough to impose on somebody an obligation to give effect to a contract into which he did not enter. Thus, mere notice of a restrictive covenant is not enough to impose upon the estate owner an obligation or equity to give effect to it [...]

[...] In matters relating to the title to land, certainty is of prime importance. We do not think it desirable that constructive trusts of land should be imposed in reliance on inferences from slender materials. In our opinion the available evidence in the present case is insufficient. The deputy judge, while he did not have to decide the matter, was not disposed to infer a constructive trust, and we agree with him.

So far as [A and B's initial agreement] is concerned, it created either a lease or some form of licence. If it created a lease, there was no need to impose any obligation upon [C ...] If, on the other hand, the agreement created some form of licence and [A] was insisting that [C] assume an obligation to give effect to [A and B's initial agreement], it seems to us highly unlikely that it would have relied upon such vague words as 'subject to' without the addition of an express obligation. Thus, if [A] was concerned about the possibility of claims against either [A's predecessor] or itself, we would have expected a clearly expressed obligation imposed on [C...but] we see no indication in the 1973 agreement that [A] was concerned with the protection of [B...]

In general, we should emphasise that it is important not to lose sight of the question: 'Whose conscience are we considering?' It is [C's], and the issue is whether [C] has acted in such a way that, as a matter of justice, a trust must be imposed. For the reasons which we have indicated, we are not satisfied that it should be.

This discussion makes the important point that B will not acquire a direct right against C *simply* because C acquires his land 'subject to' any rights that B may have against A. The key point of C's promise must be to protect B from a claim by C, not to protect A from a claim by C.

The provisions of the 1999 Act make the same distinction: under s 1, B acquires a right against C only if C's promise to A 'purports to confer a benefit' on B. So, the crucial question is whether C, when acquiring his land, made an express or implied promise to give B a *new* right.

As we saw in Chapter 7, section 2.3, Sir Christopher Slade summed up the crucial question when giving the judgment of the Court of Appeal in the following case.

Lloyd v Dugdale [2002] 2 P & CR 13

Sir Christopher Slade

At [52]

In deciding whether or not the conscience of the new estate owner is affected in such circumstances, the crucially important question is whether he has undertaken a new obligation, not otherwise existing, to give effect to the relevant incumbrance or prior interest. If, but only if, he has undertaken such a new obligation will a constructive trust be imposed.

There are two key questions about this principle. The first is whether it makes sense for B to acquire a direct right against C in these cases. We examined that question in Chapter 7, section 2.3, and will also consider it in Chapter 14, section 4. Here, it is perhaps enough to note an argument made by Bright.

Bright, 'The Third Party's Conscience in Land Law' [2000] Conv 398, 417

There are situations in which [B] ought, as a minimum, to be able to prevent [C] from suing in breach of the promise made to A. To allow [C] to succeed would effectively mean that the courts are sanctioning [C] to do the very thing that he promised not to do. This does not seem proper, nor does it seem just.

The second key question is whether it makes sense for B to acquire a right against C *under a constructive trust*. It was assumed by Lord Denning MR in *Binions* itself, and by the Court of Appeal in *Ashburn Anstalt v Arnold*, that, if the principle applies, B's right arises under such a trust. We will examine constructive trusts in more detail in Chapter 14, section 4. As we saw in Chapter 4, section 1, to say that C holds 'on trust' for B means that C (the trustee) has a right (the trust property or subject matter of the trust) and is under a duty to use that right for the benefit of B (or for B and others—that is, for the beneficiaries), as well as a duty not to use that right for C's own benefit.[31] In cases such as *Binions*, it is very difficult to see how the facts fit with that basic pattern.

Swadling, 'Property' in *English Private Law* (2nd edn, ed Burrows, 2007, [4.126])

[I]t is not clear what might have been the subject matter of this constructive trust [i.e. the constructive trust in *Binions*]. The subject matter can hardly have been the title to the cottage for, were that to be so, it would have given [B] far more than she was ever intended to have. And it cannot have been the benefit of the licence either, for that was already vested in her, and it was [C] who we are told [is] the trustee. It might be argued that the subject matter of the trust was the benefit of the covenant in the conveyance of the fee simple title under which [C] promised [A] that [it] would respect [B's] rights, and, further, that [C's] liability for breach of this covenant could be enforced by [B] by compelling [A] to sue on it. But this analysis does not work either, for the benefit of the promise was in the hands of [A], not [C].

Why, then, does Lord Denning MR describe B's right in *Binions* as arising under a constructive trust? One explanation is that, as is evident from the passage from *Binions* set out above, his Lordship relied on the decision of the Court of Appeal in *Bannister v Bannister*.[32] In that case, as we saw in Chapter 7, section 2.3, C, when buying a freehold from A, had promised to hold that freehold *on trust* for A (only two parties were involved). So, when forcing C to keep that promise, the Court of Appeal found that C held his land on constructive trust for A. As we will see in Chapter 14, section 4.3.1, it makes sense to say that a trust arose in that case: after all, the court simply enforced C's promise, and C's promise was to hold his freehold on trust. In *Binions*, however, C had *not* promised to hold any rights on trust; he had simply promised to allow B to remain in occupation of the land. So, as confirmed in the following extracts, there should be no trust in a case such as *Binions*.

---

[31] It is possible for there to be trusts in which A, as well as being a trustee, is also a beneficiary of the trust. In such a case, A is permitted to use the trust property for his own benefit (to the extent that he is a beneficiary).

[32] [1948] 2 All ER 133.

Bright, 'The Third Party's Conscience in Land Law' [2000] Conv 398, 402

[T]he *Binions* [...] use of the constructive trust raises conceptual difficulties which do not occur with the true *Bannister* constructive trust. With trusts, the legal and equitable titles are owned by different persons, and the trustee owes fiduciary duties. This is the model found in *Bannister* [...] where [C] holds the legal title subject to a (proprietary) beneficial interest for [A]. But if we look at *Binions*, [C] held the ownership interest, which was not split between legal and equitable title, and what was held on trust was [B's] 'right to remain'.

McFarlane, 'Constructive Trusts Arising on a Receipt of Property Sub Conditione' (2004) 118 LQR 667, 691

[T]he fact that B can acquire a right against C will not always justify the imposition of a constructive trust. In cases where C's undertaking is to recognise that B has a beneficial interest in the property [...] then a constructive trust of the property will be appropriate. [...] Where C's undertaking is to confer a personal right on B, then a constructive trust of the property C has received will not be appropriate, as it will give B a property right. Rather, B's personal right should be enforced directly.

On this analysis, we have to assess the nature of C's promise. If C promises to hold his freehold on trust for B, as in *Bannister*, it is appropriate for C to hold subject to a constructive trust and B thus acquires an equitable interest in C's land. If C instead simply promises to allow B to remain on the land, as in *Binions*, C comes under a duty to honour B's licence. In such a case, there is no need for a trust. After all, when A makes a promise to B to allow B to use A's land, there is no trust; there is simply a licence.

In a case such as *Binions*, the use of the 'constructive trust' label can cause confusion. In particular, it may be very important if C, having promised to honour B's licence, then transfers his land to C2.[33] As we saw in Chapter 7, section 3, it is then very important to know if the direct right that B acquired against C is a personal right or, instead, a legal or equitable property right. *If* C held the land subject to a constructive trust in B's favour, as *Binions* suggests, then B's direct right against C is an equitable property right and is therefore prima facie binding on C2. But the answer suggested by the extracts above is that, if C promised simply to honour B's licence, there should be no constructive trust. On that view, B will only be protected against C2 if he can show that he has a *second* direct right, arising because of C2's conduct.[34]

3.3.2 A pre-existing property right?

The current position

We saw, in section 2.2, that a bare licence does not count as a property right—but does it make a difference if A is under a contractual duty to B not to revoke B's licence?

---

[33] Such a situation was inconclusively considered by the Court of Appeal in *Chattey v Farndale Holdings Inc* [1997] 1 EGLR 153.

[34] For further discussion, see McFarlane, *The Structure of Property Law* (2008, pp 434–5).

King v David Allan & Sons, Billposting Ltd [1916] 2 AC 54, HL

Facts: Mr King owned land in Madras Place, Dublin.[35] He planned to build a cinema on the land and made a contractual promise to the David Allan & Sons billposting company allowing it to display posters on the wall of the cinema, when built. Mr King then gave a forty-year lease of the site to the Phibsboro' Picture House company. The cinema was completed in May 1914. In June 1924, David Allan & Sons (B) attempted to display its posters on its wall, but the Phibsboro' Picture House company (C) prevented B from doing so. B brought a claim for breach of contract against Mr King (A). A claimed that its action had caused B no loss, because B could simply assert its contractual licence against C. A decision in favour of B was affirmed by the Court of Appeal in Ireland. A appealed unsuccessfully to the House of Lords.

Lord Buckmaster LC

At 61

There is a contract between [A] and [B] which creates nothing but a personal obligation. It is a licence given for good and valuable consideration and to endure for a certain time. [. . .] [T]he sole right is to fix bills against a flank wall, and it is unreasonable to attempt to construct the relationship of landlord and tenant or grantor and grantee of an easement out of such a transaction, and I find it difficult to see how it can be reasonably urged that anything beyond personal rights was ever contemplated by the parties. Those rights have undoubtedly been taken away by the action on the part of [C], who has been enabled to prevent [B] from exercising [its] rights owing to the lease granted by [A], and [A] is accordingly liable in damages, although it was certainly not with his will, and indeed against his own express desire, that [C] has declined to honour his agreement.

Earl Loreburn

At 62

But we must look at the [agreement between A and B], and it seems to me that it does not create any interest in land at all; it merely amounts to a promise on the part of [A] that he would allow the other party to the contract to use the wall for advertising purposes, and there was an implied undertaking that he would not disable himself from carrying out his contract. Now [A] has altered his legal position in respect of his control of this land. Those to whom he granted the lease have disregarded his wishes and refused to allow his bargain to be carried out, and they have been practically enabled to do so by reason of the demise that he executed. In these circumstances it seems to me that there has been a breach in law of the contract of July 1, and [A] has disabled himself from giving effect to it as intended by parting with his right to present possession.

In *King*, the House of Lords thus made clear that the contractual licence is *not* on the list of property rights in land. That was certainly the position before the LPA 1925 came into force. As we saw in Chapter 3, section 3, s 1 of that Act sets out the list of legal property rights in land; the

---

[35] Madras Place was the base of Antoni Rabaiotti, whose ice-cream car is mentioned in Joyce's *Ulysses* (1922, ch 10). Joyce himself was a driving force behind *The Volta*, Dublin's first permanent cinema, which opened in 1909 and closed in 1910.

contractual licence is not included; as we saw in Chapter 4, section 5.4, s 4(1) of the Act appears to state that a court cannot add to the list of equitable interests in land recognized at the time of the 1925 Act. So, because the contractual licence was not recognized as an equitable property right in land before the passing of the 1925 Act, it seems clear that it cannot be recognized as such after that Act. This point is forcefully made by Briggs:[36] *'If contractual licences are to bind purchasers as proprietary interests, then they must be shown so to have existed in pre-1926 land law (and* King v David Allen *makes that impossible) or section 4 must be conjured out of existence.'*

This orthodox position continued to operate—it was, for example, confirmed by the Court of Appeal in *Clore v Theatrical Properties Ltd*[37]—until the judgment of Denning LJ in the following case.

Errington v Errington & Woods [1952] 1 KB 290, CA

Facts: Mr Errington bought a house in Milvain Avenue, Newcastle, as a home for his son and daughter-in-law. Mr Errington paid £250 and the remaining £500 of the purchase price was financed by a mortgage loan. The mortgage instalments were paid by the son and daughter-in-law, who occupied the land. Mr Errington (A) promised the son (B1) and daughter-in-law (B2) that they could remain in occupation as long as they paid the mortgage instalments. He also promised them that, when all of the instalments were paid, the land would be theirs. A died and B1 left the home, moving in with A's widow, his mother. B2 remained in occupation. A's widow sought possession of the house from B2. The county court judge dismissed that claim for possession. A's widow unsuccessfully appealed to the Court of Appeal.

Denning LJ

At 295

Ample content is given to the whole arrangement by holding that [A] promised that the house should belong to the couple as soon as they paid off the mortgage. The parties did not discuss what was to happen if the couple failed to pay the instalments to the building society, but I should have thought it clear that, if they did fail to pay the instalments, [A] would not be bound to transfer the house to them. [A's] promise was a unilateral contract—a promise of the house in return for their act of paying the instalments. It could not be revoked by him once the couple entered on performance of the act, but it would cease to bind him if they left it incomplete and unperformed, which they have not done. If that was the position during [A's] lifetime, so it must be after his death. If [B2] continues to pay all the building society instalments, [B1 and B2] will be entitled to have the property transferred to them as soon as the mortgage is paid off; but if [B2] does not do so, then the building society will claim the instalments from [A's] estate and the estate will have to pay them. I cannot think that in those circumstances [A's] estate would be bound to transfer the house to them, any more than the [A] himself would have been.

At 298–9

[I]t seems to me that, although the couple had exclusive possession of the house, there was clearly no relationship of landlord and tenant. They were not tenants at will but licensees. They had a mere personal privilege to remain there, with no right to assign or sub-let. They

---

[36] 'Contractual Licences: A Reply' [1983] Conv 285, 290–1.
[37] [1936] 3 All ER 483, CA.

were, however, not bare licensees. They were licensees with a contractual right to remain. As such they have no right at law to remain, but only in equity, and equitable rights now prevail. I confess, however, that it has taken the courts some time to reach this position. At common law a licence was always revocable at will, notwithstanding a contract to the contrary: *Wood v Leadbitter*.[38] The remedy for a breach of the contract was only in damages. That was the view generally held until a few years ago [...] The rule has, however, been altered owing to the interposition of equity.

Law and equity have been fused for nearly 80 years, and since 1948 it has been clear that, as a result of the fusion, a licensor will not be permitted to eject a licensee in breach of a contract to allow him to remain: see *Winter Garden Theatre v. Millennium Productions Ltd*,[39] *per* Lord Greene, and in the House of Lords *per* Lord Simon [...] This infusion of equity means that contractual licences now have a force and validity of their own and cannot be revoked in breach of the contract. Neither the licensor nor anyone who claims through him can disregard the contract except a purchaser for value without notice [...]

The actual decision in *Errington* can be justified on a number of different grounds.[40] For example, A had made a contractual promise to transfer his land to B1 and B2. As we noted in Chapter 4, section 5.2, such a promise is acknowledged to give rise to an equitable property right, often known as an 'estate contract' (see Chapter 12 for more details). So there was no need for B2 to rely only on her contractual licence. Nonetheless, the reasoning of Denning LJ is important, because it constitutes one attempt to turn the contractual licence into an equitable property right. His Lordship's reasoning is based on the fact that a court will often protect B's contractual licence by ordering A not to revoke that licence in breach of his contract with B. Lord Denning assumes that B therefore has a right to use A's land for the duration of his contract, and so B has a right not only against A, but also in relation to A's land.

Whilst it has found some academic[41] and judicial[42] support, there is, however, a clear flaw in Denning LJ's argument.

McFarlane, 'Identifying Property Rights: A Reply to Mr Watt' [2003] Conv 473, 475

[Denning LJ's argument] misunderstands the true effect of the availability of specific performance on the proprietary status of a right: it treats something which is at most a *necessary* condition of a right to use property's being proprietary as a *sufficient* condition of that consequence. When deciding if specific performance is available against A, a court is simply deciding on the most appropriate remedy to give in response to B's clear contractual right against A. In so doing, the court will have to balance the various interests of A and B and will consider, for example, any practical difficulties which may prevent specific performance of the contract and the adequacy of damages as a means to protect B's interests. If, in general, specific performance is not granted in cases where B has a particular type of right to use property, that right is unlikely to be viewed as proprietary—if B's enjoyment of the property itself does not merit protection as against A, the party who made a contractual promise to B, then there seems to be little reason why B's right to use the property should be capable of

---

[38] (1845) 13 M & W 838.
[39] [1948] AC 173, 191.
[40] As noted by Fox LJ in *Ashburn Anstalt v Arnold* [1989] Ch 1, 17.
[41] See, e.g., Watt, 'The Proprietary Effect of a Chattel Lease' [2003] Conv 61.
[42] See, e.g., *per* Browne-Wilkinson V-C in *Bristol Airport v Powdrill* [1990] Ch 744, 759.

> enduring against C. However, the mere fact that specific performance is available against A does not prove that B's right *must* be proprietary. The question of whether to confer proprietary status on a right involves considerations additional to those addressed when deciding that specific performance is available against A. The needs of B must be balanced not just against those of A but also against those of actual and potential third parties. Most obviously, B must show why he should be protected as against a party who, unlike A, has made no contractual promise to him. Further, B's needs must be strong enough to overcome the disadvantages inherent in allowing the contract between A and B to impose a burden on the property and hence to restrict the ease of its transfer. This is not to say that no initially contractual right can ever gain proprietary status, but rather that the concerns to be addressed before allowing such a shift are additional to, and more serious than, those to be overcome before awarding B specific performance against his contractual partner. Hence, the mere fact that B can gain specific performance against A does not demonstrate that B's right has the proprietary status it needs to be protected from interference by C.

Lord Wilberforce also pointed out this flaw in Denning LJ's argument.

National Provincial Bank v Ainsworth [1965] AC 1175, HL

Lord Wilberforce

At 1253

> [T]he fact that a contractual right can be specifically performed, or its breach prevented by injunction, does not mean that the right is any the less of a personal character or that a purchaser with notice is bound by it: what is relevant is the nature of the right, not the remedy which exists for its enforcement.

As we will see in Chapter 12, there is a principle (it can be called the 'doctrine of anticipation') that allows B to acquire an equitable interest in land if A is under a specifically enforceable contractual duty to give B a legal estate or interest in land. But that principle cannot apply if A's contractual duty is simply not to revoke a licence: in such a case, there is no eventual grant of a legal property right for equity to anticipate.[43] It is therefore no surprise that, in the following case, the Court of Appeal rejected B's attempt to rely on *Errington* in order to show that a contractual licence could bind a third party.

Ashburn Anstalt v Arnold [1989] Ch 1, CA

Fox LJ

At 21–2

> But there must be very real doubts whether *Errington* can be reconciled with the earlier decisions of the House of Lords in *Edwardes v. Barrington*[44] and *King v. David Allen and Sons*

---

[43] This point is also made by Wade (1952) 68 LQR 337, 338–9, and Swadling, 'Property' in *English Private Law* (2nd edn, ed Burrows, 2007, [4.33]).
[44] (1901) 85 LT 650.

(Billposting) Ltd. It would seem that we must follow those cases or choose between the two lines of authority. It is not, however, necessary to consider those alternative courses in detail, since in our judgment the House of Lords cases, whether or not as a matter of strict precedent they conclude this question, state the correct principle which we should follow.

Our reasons for reaching this conclusion are based upon essentially the same reasons as those given by Russell L.J. in the *Hastings Car Mart* case[45] and by Professor Wade in the article, 'Licences and Third Parties'[46] to which Russell L.J. refers. Before *Errington* the law appears to have been clear and well understood. It rested on an important and intelligible distinction between contractual obligations which gave rise to no estate or interest in the land and proprietary rights which, by definition, did. The far-reaching statement of principle in *Errington* was not supported by authority, not necessary for the decision of the case and *per incuriam* in the sense that it was made without reference to authorities which, if they would not have compelled, would surely have persuaded the court to adopt a different ratio. Of course, the law must be free to develop. But as a response to problems which had arisen, the *Errington* rule (without more) was neither practically necessary nor theoretically convincing.

Denning LJ's bold reasoning in *Errington* is thus not an accurate reflection of the current law.

Lord Denning later adopted a different technique for reaching his desired conclusion that a contractual licence can count as a property right. That technique built on the idea in *Binions v Evans*[47] that a constructive trust can be used to protect a party with a contractual licence.

DHN Food Distributors Ltd v London Borough of Tower Hamlets [1976] 3 All ER 462, CA

Facts: Bronze Ltd, a wholly owned subsidiary company of DHN Food Distributors Ltd, owned a warehouse and cash-and-carry in Malmesbury Road, Bow, London. DHN (B) ran its fruit distribution business from the premises; it occupied the land under a contractual agreement with Bronze (A). The Tower Hamlets London Borough Council made a compulsory purchase order relating to the land; it planned to demolish the warehouse and build housing. The council paid A for the land. The council argued that it had no statutory duty to pay A compensation for disturbance of its business, because A was not carrying out any business on the land. B was carrying out a business, but the relevant statute stated that B qualified for compensation for disturbance only if it had an 'interest' in the land. The council argued that B had no such right, because it simply had a contractual licence, and so had no legal or equitable interest in the land. The Lands Tribunal accepted the council's argument. B (along with a third associated company in the same position as B) successfully appealed to the Court of Appeal.

Lord Denning MR

At 466–7

The directors of [A] could not turn out themselves as directors of [B] . . . In the circumstances, I think the licence was virtually an irrevocable licence. [B was] the parent company holding

---

[45] The name given to *NPB v Ainsworth* in the Court of Appeal: [1964] Ch 665, 697.

[46] (1952) 68 LQR 337.

[47] [1972] Ch 359.

all the shares in [A]. In those circumstances, [B was] in a position to carry on their business on these premises unless and until, in their own interests, B no longer wished to continue to stay there. It was equivalent to a contract between the two companies whereby A granted an irrevocable licence to B to carry on [its] business on the premises. In this situation counsel for the claimants cited to us *Binions v Evans*, to which I would add *Bannister v Bannister* and *Siew Soon Wah alias Siew Pooi Tong v Yong Tong Hong* [1973] AC 836. Those cases show that a contractual licence (under which a person has the right to occupy premises indefinitely) gives rise to a constructive trust, under which the legal owner is not allowed to turn out the licensee. So here. This irrevocable licence gave to [B] a sufficient interest in the land to qualify them for compensation for disturbance.

The decision in *DHN*, like that in *Errington*, can be justified on other grounds. For example, both Goff and Shaw LJJ found that, as a result of various transactions between A and B, A held its right to the land on trust for B. B therefore had a recognized equitable interest and could claim compensation on that basis. Further, it can be argued that the term 'interest', when used in a statute setting rules for compensation for disturbance caused by a compulsory purchase order, is not necessarily confined to legal or equitable property rights in land.[48] Moreover, it could even be argued that, when interpreting such a statute, a court can 'pierce the corporate veil' and treat constituent companies within a group, such as Bronze Ltd and DHN Ltd, as one entity.

Lord Denning's specific reasoning in *DHN*, like that in *Errington*, is, however, impossible to defend. His Lordship's argument is that, *as soon as* A comes under a duty to B not to revoke B's licence, a constructive trust arises in B's favour. This means that, if A were later to transfer his freehold to C, C would prima facie be bound by B's licence.[49] *Bannister v Bannister* and *Binions v Evans* are cited in favour of that proposition—but the constructive trusts in those cases did *not* arise as soon as A made a contractual promise to B; rather, the constructive trusts arose as a result of *C's* later promise to A, made when acquiring his right from A.

Certainly, in the following case, the Court or Appeal rejected the *DHN* analysis.

Ashburn Anstalt v Arnold [1989] Ch 1, CA

Fox LJ

At 24

For the reasons which we have already indicated, we prefer the line of authorities which determine that a contractual licence does not create a property interest. We do not think that the argument is assisted by the bare assertion that the interest arises under a constructive trust.

It is clear, then, that Lord Denning MR in *DHN* used the constructive trust not as a means for B to acquire a new, direct right against C, but rather as a vehicle to turn all contractual

---

[48] See, e.g., *Pennine Raceways Ltd v Kirklees MBC* [1983] QB 382.

[49] Of course, *DHN v Tower Hamlets* itself did not involve a third party. In *Re Sharpe* [1980] 1 WLR 219, however, Browne-Wilkinson J (somewhat reluctantly) applied the reasoning in *DHN* to allow a licence between A and B to bind C, A's trustee in bankruptcy.

licences into equitable property rights. That approach, of course, is illegitimate as a matter of precedent: the House of Lords in *King v David Allan* and *National Provincial Bank v Ainsworth* had already made clear that a contractual licence does *not* count as an equitable interest in land. Parliament may be able to change the law and turn a contractual licence into an equitable interest, but Lord Denning MR had no power to do so.

The interesting question is, of course, whether Parliament *should* make such a change. Before looking at that question, we need briefly to consider an argument that Parliament may already (and inadvertently) have allowed a contractual licence to bind a third party.

Land Registration Act 2002, s 116

It is hereby declared for the avoidance of doubt that, in relation to registered land, each of the following:

(a) an equity by estoppel, and

(b) a mere equity

has effect from the time the equity arises as an interest capable of binding successors in title (subject to the rules about the effect of dispositions on priority).

If B has a contractual licence, B may try to argue that he or she has a 'mere equity' and thus that, under s 116(b), that right is capable of binding C. Certainly, B has an 'equity' in the sense that, as we saw in section 3.1.2, a court may well protect B's contract with A through the equitable remedies of specific performance or an injunction. It is clear, however, that, when proposing the clause that became s 116(b), the Law Commission did not intend to change the status of a contractual licence.[50] Instead, the term 'mere equity' is intended to refer to situations in which B has a power to obtain an equitable property right by, for example, having a document rectified or setting aside a transfer of a right to A.[51] Certainly, it would be very odd if a section of the Land Registration Act 2002 (LRA 2002)—an Act, as we will see in Chapter 17, primarily intended to protect a third party acquiring a right in registered land—were to *increase* the burdens on such a third party by allowing a contractual licence to function as an equitable interest.

Future reform?

It is thus clear that, as the law stands, a contractual licence does *not* count as a property right. A number of arguments have, however, been made in favour of changing the law.

European Convention on Human Rights, Art 8

(1) Everyone has the right to respect for his private and family life, his home and his correspondence.

---

[50] See Law Com No 271, [5.32]–[5.37].

[51] For further discussion of mere equities, see, e.g., McFarlane, *The Structure of Property Law* (2008, pp 226–7); *Snell's Equity* (31st edn, eds McGhee et al., 2005, [2–05]).

> (2) There shall be no interference by a public authority with the exercise of this right except such as is in accordance with the law and is necessary in a democratic society in the interests of national security, public safety or the economic well-being of the country, for the prevention of disorder or crime, for the protection of health or morals, or for the protection of the rights and freedoms of others.

In some cases, B's only right to his 'home' may come from a contractual licence with A. B may then argue that if C, a party to whom A has sold his land, is able to remove B from the land, B's right to respect for his home is interfered with.[52]

In Chapter 5, we looked in detail at how such human rights arguments can have an impact in land law. Two points are particularly worth noting here. Firstly, there is more than one way in which B's right to his home can be respected. As we have seen, if C removes B from the land before the end of the period of B's contractual licence with A, B will be able to claim damages for breach of contract from A. This right to receive money provides B with some protection for his Art 8 right.[53] Further, the law also protects B by allowing B, in certain situations, to acquire a new, direct right against C (see section 3.3.1 above). And, even if C is allowed to remove B, the Protection from Eviction Act 1977 may ensure that C has to give B four weeks' notice before insisting that B moves out.[54] Indeed, that Act provides strong protection for B: s 1(2) means that C commits a criminal offence if he attempts to remove B without giving the requisite notice.[55]

Secondly, it is not clear whether, if C removes B from the land, there is any breach of Art 8. Article 8(2) allows for B's right to be compromised in order to protect the 'rights' of others. In our example, C has a right, as an owner of the land; that right must be balanced against B's right to respect for his home. It is true that, if C is a local authority or other public body, the special duty imposed by s 6 of the Human Rights Act 1998 (HRA 1998) can (in theory) mean that it is unlawful for C to exercise its prima facie right to remove B from the land.[56] In *Kay v Lambeth LBC*,[57] however, the House of Lords, when considering the position of a licensee, held that, in all but the most exceptional cases,[58] there will be *no* breach of B's Art 8 right if C removes B in a situation in which the current land law rules allow C to do so. On that view, the introduction of the HRA 1998 does not necessitate allowing B's contractual licence of his home to count as an equitable interest in land.

---

[52] As we saw in Chapter 5, section 4.1.1, particular land can count as B's home even if B has no recognized legal or equitable property right in relation to that land.

[53] A contractual right, such as a contractual licence, can also count as a 'possession' for the purposes of Art 1 of the First Protocol to the ECHR: see Chapter 5, section 3. Clearly, B's right to peaceful enjoyment of that possession does not mean that B must be able to assert his contractual right against a third party such as C; instead, B must rely on his remedies against A, including a claim for damages for A's breach of contract.

[54] Section 5(1A) applies where B has a *'periodic licence to occupy premises as a dwelling'*—e.g. where B pays A £50 a week to occupy A's land. Some contractual licences are excluded from the 1977 Act: see s 3A. The Act does not apply, for example, if the licence involves B sharing accommodation with A or a member of A's family, or if, immediately before giving B the licence, A occupied the land as his only or principal home.

[55] C does not commit the offence if he deprives B of occupation whilst reasonably believing that B had, in any case, moved out: see s 1(2). Under the Criminal Law Act 1977, s 6, it is also a criminal offence to use or threaten violence in an attempt to gain possession of residential premises occupied by B.

[56] This means that B may be able to apply for judicial review of a public body's decision to exercise its power to remove B: see Chapter 5, section 4.2.2.

[57] [2006] 2 AC 465.

[58] A case may be exceptional if, for example, B is a member of a particularly vulnerable group: see, e.g., the decision of the European Court of Human Rights in *Connors v UK* (2004) 40 EHRR 189, discussed in Chapter 5, section 2.4.

In the following article, Maudsley draws a distinction between contractual licences that give B a right to exclusive possession of A's land, and other contractual licences. He argues that the former, but not the latter, should count as equitable property rights in land.

Maudsley, 'Licences to Remain on Land (Other than a Wife's Licence)' (1956) 20 Conv 281

At 285

For, while it is consistent with principle, authority and policy to protect licensees in certain cases where they have exclusive possession of land, the protection of contractual licensees having something less than exclusive possession would cause far more problems than it would solve. For it would mean that every lodger would be entitled to remain in his room after a sale to anyone except a purchaser of the legal estate for value without notice;[59] and this would have a serious effect on land sales.

At 288–9

In most cases, of course, in which one party goes into possession of land in consideration of payment to the owner, he will be a tenant; but that is not invariably the case [...]

The present practice of holding certain persons who are in exclusive possession to be licensees and not tenants is of importance only in the opposite type of case, where the object is to help the landlord; the result of it is that in certain cases where the landlord, who would be unable to evict a tenant because of the tenant's statutory protection (by the Rent Acts[60] or the Limitation Acts)[61] is able to do so if the court can be persuaded that the party in occupation is not a tenant but only a licensee [...] It is submitted therefore that cases in which one party goes into exclusive possession in consideration of making periodic payments to the owners will be held to create tenancies unless the court, in order to deprive an undeserving tenant of the statutory protection, can do justice between the parties by construing the tenancy, according to the intentions of the parties, as a licence.

Maudsley's argument is important, because it reveals the context in which Lord Denning made his attempts (in cases such as *Errington v Errington*[62] and *DHN v Tower Hamlets*)[63] to establish a contractual licence as an equitable property right. As we will see in Chapter 23, section 2, the standard position today is that if the contract between A and B gives B a right, for a limited period, to exclusive possession of A's land, B has a lease. A lease counts as property right and B therefore has a right that is capable of binding C.

But from the 1950s until the mid-1980s, the Court of Appeal, again led by Lord Denning, adopted a much narrower definition of a lease. Under that definition, A could give B a right to exclusive possession of A's land for a fixed period and still deny B a lease: A simply needed

---

59 [Note that the reference here to the 'bona fide purchaser' defence is now outdated. In registered land, a registered purchaser for value is protected against a pre-existing equitable interest unless: (i) that interest is protected by a notice on the register; or (ii) the holder of the interest is in actual occupation of the land at the relevant time—see Chapter 6, section 3.2, and Chapter 16, section 5.]

60 *Marcroft Wagons v Smith* [1951] 2 KB 496; *Murray Bull & Co v Murray* [1953] 1 QB 211.

61 *Cobb v Lane* [1952] 1 All ER 1199.

62 [1952] 1 KB 290.

63 [1976] 3 All ER 462.

to make clear that he did not intend to give B a 'stake in the land'. As Lord Denning MR put it in *Errington v Errington & Woods*:[64] '*The result of all these cases is that, although a person who is let into exclusive possession is, prima facie, to be considered to be a tenant, nevertheless he will not be held to be so if the circumstances negative any intention to create a tenancy.*'

The chief reason for this narrow definition of a lease, it seems, was to allow A to avoid the statutes that gave extra rights to a party with a lease:[65] for example, if he had a lease, B might gain a statutory right to remain in occupation of A's land even after the end of the agreed contractual period (we will consider the question of statutory protection for residential tenants in Chapter 24). But the courts' narrow definition of a lease meant that, in some cases in which B would nowadays be regarded as having a lease—that is, where B had a contractual right to exclusive possession of A's land for a limited period—B was instead regarded as having only a contractual licence. Maudsley's argument recognizes that, in such cases, B should have a property right. The law *has* now adopted that argument—but by recognizing that, in such cases, B has a lease. This means that much of the pressure for allowing contractual licences to count as property rights has now disappeared.

In the following article, Cheshire discusses and defends the reasoning of Denning LJ in *Errington v Errington*.

Cheshire, 'A New Equitable Interest in Land' (1953) 16 MLR 1, 9

[I]s the equity to specific performance enforceable against the successor in title to the licensor? Does the licensee acquire a proprietary, not a merely contractual right? [. . .] At least one learned writer in the Law Quarterly Review, Mr HWR Wade, holds it to be unjustifiable on several counts. 'It is,' he says, 'revolutionary to hold that a contract for a licence, (not being a contract for sale or lease, or a restrictive covenant) can be enforced against a person not a party to it.'[66] Perhaps, however, it may be suggested with respect that the recent decisions illustrate a peaceful penetration, not a revolution. The doctrine of privity was penetrated by the common law courts themselves in *Spencer's Case*[67] and by the Court of Chancery in *Tulk v Moxhay*,[68] and there seems no reason that what was possible and beneficial in an earlier age should become outmoded by the mere passage of time.

Another criticism made by Mr Wade is that the list of equitable proprietary interests in land should be regarded as closed and that this invention of a new type will unsettle the law of real property for many years. Similar warnings have been uttered in the past, but they have failed to impede the living growth of English law. For example, in 1834, Lord Brougham, in holding that a covenant does not run with land at law and cannot be made to run with it in equity, adorned his judgment with the following homily:

'Great detriment would arise and much confusion of rights if parties were allowed to invent new modes of holding and enjoying real property, and to impress upon their lands and tenements a peculiar character which should follow them into all hands, no matter how remote.'[69]

Yet, only fourteen years later, *Tulk v Moxhay* invented the restrictive covenant, a new interest of remarkable virility that nobody then or since has regretted.

---

[64] [1952] KB 290, 298.
[65] See, e.g., *Marchant v Charters* [1977] 1 WLR 1181, 1185.
[66] (1952) 68 LQR 337, 338–9.
[67] (1583) 5 Co Rep 16a.
[68] (1848) 2 Ph 774.
[69] *Keppell v Bailey* (1834) 2 My & K 517, 536.

The Court of Appeal referred with approval to Wade's article, with which Cheshire takes issue, in *Ashburn Anstalt v Arnold*.[70] And, as we saw when considering the decision in *Errington v Errington*, Wade is right to emphasize the difference between cases in which A makes a contractual promise to give B a recognized property right and those in which A simply promises to allow B to make a particular use of A's land. Cheshire's reply therefore focuses on the restrictive covenant: as we will see in Chapter 27, it is a recognized equitable property right that can arise as a result of a contractual promise by A to B, even though A's promise is *not* a promise give B, in the future, a property right.

The restrictive covenant is a very important point of comparison: it is the most recent example of the courts developing a new form of equitable property right in land. As Cheshire notes, it shows that the list of property rights *can* be added to. Two points are, however, worth noting. Firstly, the restrictive covenant was recognized as a property right *before* 1925 (see Chapter 3, section 6). In contrast, as we have seen, s 4 of the LPA 1925 now prevents the courts from developing the contractual licence as a new form of property right; any such change would have to come from Parliament.

Secondly, when the restrictive covenant was recognized as an equitable property right, the courts imposed important restrictions on precisely what type of promise by A to B could give rise to such a property right. Such restrictions would also have to be imposed by Parliament if it were to allow any contractual licences to count as property rights. Certainly, the debate is not as to whether *all* contractual licences should become property rights; rather, it is as to whether *particular sorts* of contractual licence should do so.

Thirdly, it is important to note *how* restrictive covenants came to be regarded as property rights. Cheshire cites *Tulk v Moxhay* as a key decision, but, as we noted in Chapter 7, section 2.6, that case, in fact, involved B acquiring a new, direct right against C.[71] This raises the question of whether a gradual extension of the circumstances in which B can acquire such a right could, over time, prompt Parliament to elevate some forms of contractual licence to the status of an equitable interest in land.

McFarlane, 'Identifying Property Rights: A Reply to Mr Watt' [2003] Conv 473

At 482

[The passage to proprietary status of restrictive covenants] depended on an initial recognition that a covenantee could be protected against a third party by means of a new, direct right. This can be seen from a consideration of *Tulk v Moxhay*. That decision did not in itself establish the proprietary status of a restrictive covenant, as is clear from Lord Cottenham L.C.'s judgment:

> 'the question is, not whether the covenant runs with the land, but whether a party shall be permitted to use the land in a manner inconsistent with the contract entered into by his vendor, and with notice of which he purchased.'

B's protection in *Tulk v Moxhay* therefore seems to depend on a new right which arises as a result of C's conduct in purchasing the property with notice of the covenant. However, from this starting point, the restrictive covenant began a journey which culminated in the acquisition of proprietary status.

---

[70] [1989] Ch 1, 22.
[71] This point was noted by Browne-Wilkinson V-C in *Swiss Bank v Lloyds Bank* [1979] 1 Ch 548, 571.

At 485–6

[The] history [of restrictive covenants] demonstrates that a right is generally only allowed to become proprietary on certain terms. In *Tulk v Moxhay* itself, no distinction is made between positive and negative covenants; nor does it seem necessary for the covenantee to have land for the benefit of which the covenant was taken. As the judgment in that case focuses on the culpability of C's conduct, these requirements, relating to the nature of B's original right, may well seem out of place. However, as the analysis shifts and that original right comes to be regarded as proprietary, it is inevitable that the courts will consider such restrictions. For a recognition that a particular right is proprietary must be based on a decision that the right is, by its nature, sufficiently important to warrant protection even if the property to which it relates changes hands. Therefore it is scarcely surprising that the courts will think carefully about the precise nature of the right in question before allowing it to have proprietary status. For example, given the burdens which will be placed on C's property as a result, it may well make sense to restrict proprietary status to those rights that confer a compensating benefit on another piece of property. Further, the particular disadvantage of allowing a right to be pro-prietary, that it can bind third parties without their consent, may be thought too great when dealing with certain types of right, such as those that impose positive obligations. Hence it may be thought unlikely that English law will ever accept that *all* [. . .] licences of land have proprietary status. As a result, it can be concluded not only that a general category consist-ing of all . . . licences of land is currently absent from the list of property rights recognised by English law, but also that it may well always remain so.

A final argument in favour of the proprietary status of contractual licences is made by Moriarty in the following extract. It rests on an unusual definition of a contractual licence.

Moriarty, 'Licences and Land Law: Legal Principles and Public Policies' (1984) 100 LQR 376

At 376

The device of the licence, it will be argued, is no more than a mechanism by which the law sanctions the informal creation of proprietary rights in land.

At 397

The point, then is that we have to make a distinction between two different kinds of rule in land law. There are, first, the substantive rules of the subject which govern and define what kinds of right the law will accept as having the potential to bind third parties, as property rights, in the first place. And then there are the procedural rules of the subject which, import-ant as they are, merely regulate the method by which they are created. *King* [v *David Allen Ltd*] and *Clore* [v *Theatrical Properties Ltd*], it is suggested, authoritatively rule out the pos-sibility of the contractual licence being used to subvert the former, and more fundamental, rules of the subject. But they leave untouched the use of the contractual licence as a means of supplementing the procedural rules for creation. It is in this latter context that the contrac-tual licence is most commonly found; and it is in this latter context that the device shares so much in common with the estoppel licence. In such a context, therefore, there can be no objection to contractual licences binding third parties, unless it is an objection to all licences binding third parties.

The distinction made by Moriarty between the 'substantive' and 'procedural' rules of land law seems to match the distinction between the *content* question and the *acquisition* question (see Chapter 1, section 3). Moriarty's argument is thus slightly surprising. The issue that we are currently considering relates to the *content* question: should a particular type of right (a contractual licence) be regarded as an equitable interest in land? Yet Moriarty sees the issue as instead related to the *acquisition* question: given our list of equitable interests in land, by what means should B be able to acquire such a right? It is therefore important to note that Moriarty's argument does *not* involve reversing the results in cases such as *King v David Allen*[72] and *Clore v Theatrical Properties Ltd*;[73] rather, his argument is that, in a case such as *Errington v Errington*,[74] B2 had, in fact, acquired, through an informal means, a recognized equitable property right. That analysis seems to be correct: it was noted above that *Errington* could be analysed as a case in which, as a result of A's informal promise to transfer his land to them, B1 and B2 had acquired an estate contract. Crucially, then, Moriarty's analysis does *not* involve promoting the contractual licence to a property right; instead, it can be used to defend the status quo, by re-analysing some (but not all) contractual licence cases as cases in which, in fact, B acquired not only a licence, but also a recognized equitable property right.

In his article, Moriarty also draws a link between the contractual licence and the estoppel licence. He notes, firstly, that the courts have regularly held that an estoppel licence can bind a third party, and, secondly, that estoppel licences and contractual licences are very similar. We will consider estoppel licences, and their effect on third parties, in the next section.

4 ESTOPPEL LICENCES

An estoppel licence exists where B has a liberty to make some use of A's land *and* A is under a duty to B, arising as a result of the doctrine of proprietary estoppel. This means that—in some circumstances, at least—A is under a duty to B not to revoke B's licence. An estoppel licence is thus similar to a contractual licence. The key difference is the *source* of A's duty to B: in this case, the duty arises not because of a contract, but, instead, under the doctrine of proprietary estoppel. We will examine that doctrine in Chapter 13. It seems to allow B to acquire a right against A where B has reasonably relied on a commitment made by A to allow B a right relating to land. As the following extract demonstrates, the doctrine can thus impose a duty on A even if A has made no contractual bargain with B.

Inwards v Baker [1965] 2 QB 29, CA

Facts: Mr Baker owned land at Dunsmore, near Wendover, in Buckinghamshire. In 1931, Mr Baker (A) invited his son, John (B), to build a bungalow on the land. B accepted the invitation. He moved into the bungalow and lived there in the belief that he could remain, if he wished, for the rest of his life. A died in 1951 and, under his will, made in 1922, his land passed to trustees who were to hold the land for the benefit of parties other than B. The trustees attempted to remove B from the land. The judge at the Aylesbury county court found in favour of the trustees, but B successfully appealed to the Court of Appeal.

---

72 [1916] 2 AC 54.
73 [1936] 3 All ER 483.
74 [1952] 1 KB 290.

Lord Denning MR

At 36–7

The trustees say that at the most [B] had a licence to be in the bungalow but that it had been revoked and he had no right to stay. The judge has held in their favour. He was referred to *Errington v. Errington and Woods*, but the judge held that that decision only protected a contractual licensee. He thought that, in order to be protected, the licensee must have a contract or promise by which he is entitled to be there. The judge said:

> 'I can find no promise made by the father to the son that he should remain in the property at all—no contractual arrangement between them. True the father said that the son could live in the property, expressly or impliedly, but there is no evidence that this was arrived at as the result of a contract or promise—merely an arrangement made casually because of the relationship which existed and knowledge that the son wished to erect a bungalow for residence.'

Thereupon, the judge, with much reluctance, thought the case was not within *Errington's* case, and said the son must go.

The son appeals to this court. We have had the advantage of cases which were not cited to the county court judge[75] [...] It is quite plain from those authorities that if the owner of land requests another, or indeed allows another, to expend money on the land under an expectation created or encouraged by the landlord that he will be able to remain there, that raises an equity in the licensee such as to entitle him to stay. He has a licence coupled with an equity.

So in this case, even though there is no binding contract to grant any particular interest to the licensee, nevertheless the court can look at the circumstances and see whether there is an equity arising out of the expenditure of money. All that is necessary is that the licensee should, at the request or with the encouragement of the landlord, have spent the money in the expectation of being allowed to stay there. If so, the court will not allow that expectation to be defeated where it would be inequitable so to do. In this case it is quite plain that the father allowed an expectation to be created in the son's mind that this bungalow was to be his home. It was to be his home for his life or, at all events, his home as long as he wished it to remain his home. It seems to me, in the light of that equity, that the father could not in 1932 have turned to his son and said: 'You are to go. It is my land and my house.' Nor could he at any time thereafter so long as the son wanted it as his home.

4.1 B'S RIGHTS AGAINST A

The nature of B's rights against A depends on the nature of A's duty to B. The key point is that the doctrine of proprietary estoppel, as we will see in Chapter 13, may have a number of different effects. For example, in *Jennings v Rice*,[76] B had been staying for a number of nights each week on A's land, in order to care for A. A had promised B that she would leave her land to B in her will; A did not do so. The Court of Appeal confirmed the finding of the trial judge: the doctrine of proprietary estoppel imposed a duty on A (and now on A's estate) to pay B £200,000. In that case, it seems, A was *not* under a duty not to revoke B's licence: A would have been able to remove B from the land. As a result of failing to honour her promise to leave her land to B, however, A was instead under a duty to pay B a sum of money.

---

[75] [The cases mentioned are classic proprietary estoppel cases: *Dillwyn v Llewellyn* (1862) 4 De G F & J 517; *Plimmer v Wellington Corpn* (1884) 9 App Cas 699 (PC); *Ramsden v Dyson* (1866) LR 1 HL 129.]

[76] [2003] 1 P & CR 100.

In some cases, the doctrine of proprietary estoppel may impose a duty on A not to revoke B's licence. For example, in the passage from *Inwards v Baker* quoted above, Lord Denning MR confirms that, at least once B had built and moved into his bungalow, A was under a duty not to remove B from the land. In such a case, it seems, the discussion set out in section 2.1 above will apply: firstly, in general, a court will specifically enforce A's duty not to revoke B's licence; secondly, for as long as A's duty lasts and B remains on A's land, B will not become a trespasser, even if A attempts to revoke B's licence.

It might be thought that where A's duty not to revoke a licence arises under the equitable doctrine of proprietary estoppel, B's right to remain on the land is dependent on factors such as B's behaviour and is thus more fragile than in a case in which B has a contractual licence. As the following extract shows, however, that does not seem to be the case.

Williams v Staite [1979] Ch 291, CA

Facts: Mrs Moore (A) owned two neighbouring cottages in Llangibby, Gwent. Her daughter married Mr Staite. A then invited the Staites to move into one of the cottages. A promised them that they could remain in that cottage for as long as they wished. Mr Staite lived in a cottage provided with his job, but, following A's promise, he gave up that accommodation to move into A's cottage. After moving in, the Staites spent money improving the cottage; they also cared for A and her husband, who lived next door. A died and her land was eventually sold to C. C then attempted to remove the Staites (B1 and B2) from the cottage. The judge found in favour of B1 and B2, holding that their licence was binding on C. C did not appeal against that finding—but C later claimed that, due to the bad behaviour of B1 and B2, he was entitled to remove them from the cottage. The judge in the Pontypool and Abergavenny county court found in C's favour. B1 and B2 then successfully appealed to the Court of Appeal.

Lord Denning MR

At 297–8

[B1 and B2] had an equitable licence under which they were entitled to live in [the cottage] for their lives or for as long as they wished it to be their home. It may in some circumstances be revoked, but I do not think it can be revoked in such circumstances as are found in the present case. I know that the judge took a poor view of the conduct of [B1 and B2]—and I am not sure he was altogether fair to them—[...] but to my mind their conduct, however reprehensible, was not such as to justify revocation of their licence to occupy the cottage as their home.

Goff LJ

At 300

Excessive user or bad behaviour towards the legal owner cannot bring the equity to an end or forfeit it. It may give rise to an action for damages for trespass or nuisance or to injunctions to restrain such behaviour, but I see no ground on which the equity, once established, can be forfeited. Of course, the court might have held, and might hold in any proper case, that the equity is in its nature for a limited period only or determinable upon a condition certain. In such a case the court must then see whether, in the events which have happened, it has determined or it has expired or been determined by the happening of that condition.

It is important to note that C did not appeal against the initial holding that the estoppel licence of B1 and B2 was capable of binding C. We will consider that question in detail in section 4.3 below.

4.2 B'S RIGHTS AGAINST X

If the doctrine of proprietary estoppel simply imposes a duty on A not to revoke B's licence, B's position against X should be exactly the same as if he had a contractual licence. In such a case, the discussion in section 3.2 above should apply.

4.3 B'S RIGHTS AGAINST C

4.3.1 Direct rights

The discussion of direct rights in section 3.3.1 above applies equally where B has an estoppel licence. Certainly, if the doctrine of proprietary estoppel imposes a duty on A not to revoke B's licence, A will have the same incentive, when transferring his land to C, to ask C to promise to respect B's licence.

4.3.2 A pre-existing property right?

Inwards v Baker [1965] 2 QB 29, CA

Facts: See pp 251–2 above.

> **Lord Denning MR**
>
> At 37
>
> [C's counsel] put the case of a purchaser. He suggested that the father could sell the land to a purchaser who could get the son out. But I think that any purchaser who took with notice would clearly be bound by the equity. So here, too, the present plaintiffs, the successors in title of the father, are clearly themselves bound by this equity. It is an equity well recognised in law. It arises from the expenditure of money by a person in actual occupation of land when he is led to believe that, as the result of that expenditure, he will be allowed to remain there. It is for the court to say in what way the equity can be satisfied. I am quite clear in this case it can be satisfied by holding that the defendant can remain there as long as he desires to as his home.

Lord Denning MR's view is thus that, on the facts of *Inwards v Baker*, B had a right that was capable of binding C. That conclusion seems correct. In a case such as *Inwards*, as Lord Denning noted, it would be inequitable for B's expectation of a home for life to be defeated. It can therefore be argued that the doctrine of proprietary estoppel imposes a duty on A to allow B to exclusive possession of the bungalow for B's life (at least). If that is correct, B has a recognized equitable property right: an equitable life interest arising under a trust (see Chapter 22, section 4). It can be argued that it is B's equitable interest, rather than any licence, that is capable of binding C.

A number of cases in which an estoppel licence is said to be capable of binding C can be explained in this way. For example, in *ER Ives Investment Ltd v High*,[77] A agreed that, in return for A being able to place foundations on part of B's land, B would have a right of way across A's land. The Court of Appeal held that B had a right that was capable of binding C, a later owner of A's land. There are a number of possible explanations for this decision.[78] One explanation is that B had a licence to use A's land *and* the doctrine of proprietary estoppel imposed a duty on A to give B the promised right of way: an easement. On that view, A was under a duty to give B a recognized property right and so B acquired an equitable easement. It is that easement, rather than B's licence, that is capable of binding C.

There are, however, some cases in which the doctrine of proprietary estoppel has simply imposed a duty on A not to revoke B's licence. *Williams v Staite*,[79] discussed above, is one example. In that case, as we have seen, it had earlier been held that a pre-existing estoppel licence was binding on C. That assumption does seem to create an inconsistency with the law relating to contractual licences. A contractual licence, like the estoppel licence in *Williams v Staite*, consists of B having a liberty to use A's land and A being under a duty to B not to revoke that liberty. As a number of commentators have suggested,[80] B's right should not be treated differently only because A's duty arises under proprietary estoppel rather than due to a contract.

On this view, either *both* estoppel licences and contractual licences can count as equitable property rights, or neither can. We saw in section 3.3.2 above that no contractual licences are currently viewed as equitable property rights. This means that no estoppel licences should be viewed as equitable property rights. But this does not mean that the assumption made in *Williams v Staite* was a surprising one: after all, *at the time*, the Court of Appeal, led by Lord Denning MR, regarded the contractual licence as an equitable property right. It is therefore no surprise that the Court also viewed B's estoppel licence as such a right. Now that it is clear that a contractual licence is *not* an equitable property right, however, the same must also be true of an estoppel licence.

Land Registration Act 2002, s 116

It is hereby declared for the avoidance of doubt that, in relation to registered land, each of the following:

(a) an equity by estoppel, and

(b) a mere equity

has effect from the time the equity arises as an interest capable of binding successors in title (subject to the rules about the effect of dispositions on priority).

We looked at the possible effect of s 116(b) of the LRA 2002 on contractual licences in section 3.3.2 above. It seems that s 116(a) may have an important effect on estoppel licences. As we will see in Chapter 13, section 5.3, an 'equity by estoppel' is said to arise *whenever* A is under a duty to B arising as a result of the doctrine of proprietary estoppel. The 'equity' is the right

---

[77] [1967] 2 QB 379.

[78] See, e.g., Battersby [1995] MLR 637; Swadling, 'Property' in *English Private Law* (2nd edn, ed Burrows, 2007, [4.128]).

[79] [1979] Ch 291.

[80] See, e.g., Thompson [1983] Conv 57; Moriarty, 'Informal Transactions in Land: Estoppel and Registration' (1984) 100 LQR 376.

that B has in the period *after* the estoppel has arisen and *before* a court makes an order in B's favour. So, even in a case in which A's only duty is a duty not to revoke B's licence, B initially has an 'equity by estoppel'—and the effect of s 116(a), on its natural reading, is to allow that 'equity by estoppel' to be capable of binding C, and thus to function as an equitable property right. That result does seem to have been intended by the Law Commission, the report of which led to the LRA 2002.[81] As the following extract points out, however, it also seems to lead to an inconsistency in the law.

McFarlane, 'Proprietary Estoppel and Third Parties After the Land Registration Act 2002' [2003] CLJ 661, 690

Although they view s.116(a) as solving one of the most persistent debates relating to estoppel, the Law Commission's interpretation of that section re-awakens another such debate which might have been thought settled. As a result of s.116(a), a licence arising through proprietary estoppel would operate differently to a contractual licence: the former could bind C, provided the land was transferred to him before a court order granting B the licence. It could be argued in such a case that it is not the licence itself which binds C, but rather the independent 'equity' that arose as a result of the estoppel before the licence was awarded by the court. Yet why does no such 'equity' arise in the case of a contractual licence: surely a contractual licensee also has the right to [go to court: see further Chapter 13, section 5.3]? Once again, unconvincing distinctions arise as a result of separating estoppel from other means of acquiring rights. Indeed, it seems that the position under s.116(a) could be even less satisfactory than that favoured by Lord Denning [...] at least his Lordship intended that contractual and estoppel licences should be treated consistently.

As we will see in Chapter 13, section 5.3, it can therefore be argued that s 116(a) should *not* be interpreted so as to mean that B acquires a right that is capable of binding C *whenever* the doctrine of proprietary estoppel imposes a duty on A to B. Under the interpretation intended by the Law Commission, however, the holder of an estoppel licence, at least in the period before a court order is made in his or her favour, has a right that is capable of binding C.[82]

5 STATUTORY LICENCES

We can use the term 'statutory licence' to refer to situations in which B has a liberty to make some use of A's land *and* A is under a statutory duty to B not to revoke B's licence. A statutory licence is thus similar to a contractual licence or an estoppel licence. The key difference again is the *source* of A's duty to B. When considering the effect of a statutory licence on A, X, and C, it is difficult to set out general principles: the statute in question will generally specify the effect of B's right. In this section, we will consider, in outline only, one particularly important form of statutory licence: the licence of one spouse[83] to occupy land owned by another.

---

81 Law Commission Report No 271, *Land Registration for the Twenty-First Century* (2001, [5.29]–[5.32]).

82 It is very unlikely that B will have protected his or her right by entering a notice on the register and so, if B is not in actual occupation of the registered land, C may well have be able to use the lack of registration defence to B's 'equity by estoppel': see Chapter 6, section 3.2, and Chapter 16, section 5.

83 The statutory licence arising under the Family Law Act 1996, s 30, now also applies to parties in a registered civil partnership: see Civil Partnership Act 2004, s 82 and Sch 9, para 1, amending the 1996 Act.

Family Law Act 1996, s 30

(1) This section applies if—

  (a) one spouse is entitled to occupy a dwelling-house by virtue of

    (i) a beneficial estate or interest or contract; or

    (ii) any enactment giving that spouse the right to remain in occupation; and

  (b) the other spouse is not so entitled.

(2) Subject to the provisions of this Part, the spouse not so entitled has the following rights ("matrimonial home rights")—

  (a) if in occupation, a right not to be evicted or excluded from the dwelling-house or any part of it by the other spouse except with the leave of the court given by an order under s.33;

  (b) if not in occupation, a right with the leave of the court so given to enter into and occupy the dwelling-house.

5.1 B'S RIGHTS AGAINST A

The statutory predecessors of s 30 of the Family Law Act 1996 (FLA 1996) were, in part, a reaction to the House of Lords' decision in *National Provincial Bank v Ainsworth*[84] (see Chapter 1, section 5, and Chapter 4, section 5.4). In that case, Mrs Ainsworth's right to occupy the matrimonial home was said to depend on a 'deserted wife's equity'. This right, essentially improvised by the courts, arose only after Mr Ainsworth left the home. And it was of a very uncertain nature: in particular, it would not always be clear if the home-owning spouse (A) was under a duty to allow the non-owning spouse (B) to remain in occupation of the current home. Parliament intervened, first through the Matrimonial Homes Act 1967, in the hope of making B's position clearer and more secure (see Chapter 1, section 5.7).

Whilst B's basic right to occupy A's land is set out in s 30, s 33 gives a court wide powers to exclude or restrict B's right. Section 33(6) directs a court exercising those powers to take into account a number of factors, including: (i) the housing needs and resources of A and B, and of any 'relevant child'; (ii) the financial resources of A and B; (iii) the likely effect of any order on the health, safety, or well-being of A and B, and of any relevant child; and (iv) the conduct of A and B in relation to each other and otherwise. Under s 33(7), special rules apply where there is a likelihood of one of the parties or a relevant child suffering '*significant harm attributable to conduct*' of the other party.

It is thus clear that, in order to balance the various needs of the spouses and any relevant children, the court has a wide discretion to exclude or restrict B's right against A.

5.2 B'S RIGHTS AGAINST X

The provisions of the FLA 1996 are not too important in regulating B's position against X. In *National Provincial Bank v Ainsworth* itself, Lord Upjohn noted that, if B is in sole occupation of A's land, strangers such as X are under a duty not to interfere with B's possession

---

[84] [1965] AC 1175.

of that land.[85] As noted in section 2.2 above, B's right, in such a case, does not arise from any licence, but rather from the fact of B's physical control of the land.

5.3 B'S RIGHTS AGAINST C

5.3.1 Direct rights

Where B has a statutory licence under the FLA 1996, it is, of course, possible for B to acquire a direct right against C. Such a right can only arise, however, if C's conduct falls into one of the means, examined in Chapter 7, section 2, by which B can acquire a direct right against C.

5.3.2 A pre-existing property right?

Family Law Act 1996, s 31

(1) Subsections (2) and (3) apply if, at any time during a marriage, one spouse is entitled to occupy a dwelling-house by virtue of a beneficial estate or interest.

(2) The other spouse's matrimonial home rights are a charge on the estate or interest.

(3) The charge created by subsection (2) has the same priority as if it were an equitable interest created at whichever is the latest of the following dates—

    (a) the date on which the spouse so entitled acquires the estate or interest;

    (b) the date of the marriage; and

    (c) 1st January 1968 (the commencement date of the Matrimonial Homes Act 1967) [...]

(8) Even though a spouse's matrimonial home rights are a charge on an estate or interest in the dwelling-house, those rights are brought to an end by—

    (a) the death of the other spouse, or

    (b) the termination (otherwise than by death) of the marriage,

unless the court directs under s.33(5) [...]

(10) If the title to the legal estate by virtue of which a spouse is entitled to occupy a dwelling-house [...] is registered under the Land Registration Act 2002 or any enactment replaced by that Act—

    (a) registration of a land charge affecting the dwelling-house by virtue of this Part is to be effected by registering a notice under the Act; and

    (b) a spouse's matrimonial home rights are not to be capable of falling within paragraph 2 of Schedule 1 or 3 of that Act.

In *National Provincial Bank v Ainsworth*, the House of Lords held that B's right to occupy A's land, arising under a 'deserted wife's equity', did *not* count as a property right in land and so was not capable of binding C. Section 31(2) of the FLA 1996 clearly adopts a different position: B's statutory right to occupy is capable of binding C.

---

[85] [1965] AC 1175, 1232.

It is important to note, however, that B's statutory right does not operate in quite the same way as a standard interest in land. For example, consider the case in which B has a standard equitable interest in relation to registered land. If B fails to protect that right by entering a notice on the register, then it may be possible for C to use the lack of registration defence against it (see Chapter 6, section 3.2). But if B is in *actual occupation* of the registered land at the relevant time, C cannot use that lack of registration defence against B (see further Chapter 16, section 5). That rule, giving some protection to B's unregistered right, is set out by para 2 of Schs 1 and 3 to the LRA 2002.

In contrast, if B does not have a standard equitable interest, and instead has only a statutory right under s 30 of the FLA 1996, B's failure to protect that right by entering a notice on the register *prevents* B from asserting that right against C. B's actual occupation makes no difference: s 33(10) ensures that B's right remains subject to the lack of registration defence. This means that, in most cases,[86] B can only assert his or her right against C if, before C registers C's right, B protects his or her statutory right by entering a notice on the register.

6 LICENCES COUPLED WITH AN INTEREST

A licence coupled with an interest arises where B has a liberty to make some use of A's land *and* that liberty protects, or arises as part of, a property right held by B. It is very doubtful, however, that 'licences coupled with an interest' are a useful concept. As against A, we would expect B's position to depend on: (i) the terms of the contract between A and B, if any; and (ii) the nature of B's property right. As against X and C, we would expect B's position simply to depend on the nature of B's property right. This does, indeed, seem to be the case; it is therefore of little use to speak of B as *also* having a licence coupled to his property right. In fact, as we will see in section 6.1, the concept of a 'licence coupled with an interest' has chiefly been used by the courts as a way in which to develop the remedies available to B when he has a contractual licence, whilst at the same time *technically* respecting past (and outdated) decisions that limited those remedies.

6.1 B'S RIGHTS AGAINST A

James Jones & Sons Ltd v Earl of Tankerville [1909] 2 Ch 440

Facts: The Earl of Tankerville (A) owned the Chillingham estate in Northumberland.[87] He made a contractual promise to James Jones & Sons Ltd (B) allowing them to come onto A's land, cut down timber on that land, set up a sawmill on A's land, and then remove the timber from A's land. A breached the agreement and forcibly removed B's employees from the land. B applied for an injunction to restrain A from acting in that way. Parker J granted the injunction.

---

[86] If C does not acquire his right for value, C cannot rely on B's failure to register as a defence to B's statutory right to occupy: the protection given to C by ss 29 and 30 of the Land Registration Act 2002 applies only if C acquires his right 'for valuable consideration'.

[87] Lord Grey succeeded to the estate in 1674 and was made Earl of Tankerville. The estate, including Chillingham Castle, remained with the family until the death of the ninth Earl in 1980. The twelfth-century castle (claimed to be one of the most haunted places in Britain) is now open to the public. The estate remains home to a rare breed of white cattle, said to be the only wild cattle in the world.

Parker J

At 442

A contract for the sale of specific timber growing on the vendor's property, on the terms that such timber is cut and carried away by the purchaser, certainly confers on the purchaser a licence to enter and cut the timber sold, and, at any rate as soon as the purchaser has severed the timber, the legal property in the severed trees vests in him. A licence to enter a man's property is prima facie revocable, but is irrevocable even at law if coupled with or granted in aid of a legal interest conferred on the purchaser, and the interest so conferred may be a purely chattel interest or an interest in realty. If A sells to B felled timber lying on A's land on the terms that B may enter and carry it away, the licence conferred is an irrevocable licence coupled with and granted in aid of the legal property in the timber which the contract for sale confers on B: *Wood v. Manley*.[88] [. . .] Even, therefore, if no interest at law passes by a contract for the sale of specific growing timber to be cut by the purchaser, it is difficult to see why on principle equity should not restrain the vendor from revoking the licence conferred by such a contract, though it might be unable to compel the purchaser to cut the timber if he refused to do so. When once the purchaser has cut any part of the timber, the legal property in the timber so cut is certainly in the purchaser, and the licence so far as that timber is concerned is irrevocable even at law, and a Court of Equity in granting an injunction would only be restraining the violation of a legal right. An injunction restraining the revocation of the licence, when it is revocable at law, may in a sense be called relief by way of specific performance, but it is not specific performance in the sense of compelling the vendor to do anything. It merely prevents him from breaking his contract [. . .]

It is important to note the date of this judgment. When it was given, there was some doubt as to whether a court could order specific performance of a standard contractual licence: *Hurst v Picture Theatres Ltd*[89] (see section 3.1.2 above) had not yet been decided. It was therefore helpful for the judge to distinguish past cases[90] in which it had been assumed that a standard contractual licence could not be protected by specific performance, by saying that B had a 'licence coupled with an interest'.[91] Nowadays, as we saw in section 3.1.2 above, there is no such difficulty in ordering A to perform a contractual duty not to revoke B's licence. It seems, then, that, in a case such as *James Jones*, B's rights against A—as far as his liberty to use A's land is concerned—should be governed simply by A's contractual agreement with B and the principles discussed in section 3.1.2 above.

The concept of a 'licence coupled with an interest' may be more important in a case in which A is *not* under a contractual duty to B. For example, let us say that property belonging to B finds its way onto A's land. It may be that B's car is stolen and then parked on A's land. In such a case, A may refuse B permission to come onto A's land and retrieve the car.

There are two ways in which the law could respond. Firstly, it could be said that B has a 'licence coupled with an interest': B's ownership of the car imposes a duty on A *either* to deliver the car to B *or* to allow B to come onto the land to collect it. The question then

---

[88] (1839) 11 Ad & E 34.

[89] [1915] 1 KB 1.

[90] Such as *Wood v Leadbitter* (1845) 13 M & W 838.

[91] Indeed, in *Hurst* itself, the chief argument of Mr Hurst's counsel was that Mr Hurst, on buying the cinema ticket, had a licence coupled with an interest. And Buckley and Kennedy LJJ do both refer to that argument at points in their judgments.

would be whether a court would grant an order forcing A to comply with that duty, or would instead order A to pay damages to B.

Secondly, it could be said that, by refusing to allow B to collect the car, A is interfering with B's ownership of the car and so is committing a wrong: the tort of conversion.[92] If A commits such a tort, B can ask the court to order A to 'deliver up' the car to B,[93] but the court does not have to make such an order. In fact, the usual response of the court is to order A to pay B damages.

6.2 B'S RIGHTS AGAINST X

Where B has a licence coupled with an interest, B also has a property right. If X interferes with that property right, he commits a wrong against B. For example, in *James Jones*, if X were to trespass onto A's land and take away some of B's timber, X would commit the tort of conversion against B. It is also possible for B's licence to be coupled with a property right in A's land. For example, as we will see in Chapter 26, section 1.1, there is a particular form of property right in land, akin to an easement, known as a 'profit' or 'profit *à prendre*'. It is a property right that allows B to come onto A's land and remove something that would other-wise be owned by A—for example, turf or trees growing on A's land. If B has such a right, X is under a duty not to interfere with B's right to come onto A's land and remove the thing in question. But X's duty does not arise because B has a licence; rather, it arises because B has a profit—that is, a property right in A's land. In *James Jones*, it is unclear whether B had such a property right: it seems that, because A had not used a deed to give B his right, B could not claim a *legal* profit *à prendre*—but B may have had an equitable profit *à prendre*.

6.3 B'S RIGHTS AGAINST C

6.3.1 Direct rights

If, as in *James Jones*, A is under a contractual duty to allow B to make a particular use of A's land, the discussion of direct rights in section 3.3.1 above is applicable. Certainly, A will have the same incentive, when transferring his land to C, to ask C to promise to respect B's licence.

6.3.2 A pre-existing property right?

We have seen that, in general, the fact that A is under a duty not to revoke B's licence does *not*, by itself, give B a property right in A's land. But where B has a licence coupled with an interest, the interest is, in itself, a property right. So, if the interest is a property right in A's land, such as a profit *à prendre*, it is capable of binding C. If the interest is instead a property right in a thing on A's land, that property right is also capable of binding C, just as it is cap-able of binding X. So, if, in *James Jones*, A were to sell his land to C, the timber already cut

---

[92] For a discussion of the requirements of the tort, see *Kuwait Airways v Iraqi Airways (Nos 4 & 5)* [2002] 2 AC 883. *Howard E Perry v British Railway Board* [1980] 1 WLR 1375 provides an example in which the defendant committed the tort of conversion simply by refusing to return goods, currently controlled by the defendant, to the claimant.

[93] See Torts (Interference with Goods) Act 1977, s 3.

down by B and stored on A's land would continue to belong to B. C would therefore commit the tort of conversion if he were to refuse to allow B to collect that timber.

QUESTIONS

1. What is the key feature of a licence? Does Hohfeld's distinction between a 'privilege', or 'liberty' on the one hand and a 'claim right' on the other help in understanding the position of a licensee?

2. What are the different forms of licence? Given their variety, is it useful to think of licences as a single category?

3. In what circumstances might a court refuse to order specific performance of A's duty not to revoke B's contractual licence?

4. When can B rely on a 'constructive trust' to assert a right against C? Does such a constructive trust arise as soon as A gives B a contractual licence, or does it only arise at a later point?

5. Do you think that particular forms of contractual licence may one day be recognized as property rights?

6. Are cases in which 'estoppel licences' bind third parties cases in which B has more than a licence, and instead has a recognized equitable interest, arising as a result of proprietary estoppel?

FURTHER READING

Battersby, 'Informally Created Interests' in *Land Law: Themes and Perspectives* (eds Bright and Dewar, Oxford: OUP, 1998)

Bright, 'The Third Party's Conscience in Land Law' [2000] Conv 398

Hohfeld, 'Faulty Analysis in Easement and License Cases' (1917) Yale LJ 66

McFarlane, 'Identifying Property Rights: A Reply to Mr Watt' [2003] Conv 473

Moriarty, 'Licences and Land Law: Legal Principles and Public Policies' (1984) 100 LQR 376

Smith, 'The Economic Torts: Their Impact on Real Property' (1977) 41 Conv 318

Swadling, 'Property' in *English Private Law* (2nd edn, ed Burrows, Oxford: OUP, 2007, [4.114]–[4.128])

Wade, 'Licences and Third Parties' (1952) 68 LQR 337

PART B1

THE ACQUISITION
OF A LEGAL ESTATE OR
INTEREST IN LAND

9

FORMAL METHODS OF ACQUISITION: CONTRACTS, DEEDS, AND REGISTRATION

CENTRAL ISSUES

1. The creation and transfer of legal rights is heavily regulated by statutory formality requirements. Land is more complex to deal with than other property—a position that is considered desirable because of the uniqueness of land.

2. Specific formality requirements must be met to enter a contract for sale or other disposition of an interest in land and to create or transfer legal rights. The creation and transfer of legal estates is generally subject to a further requirement of registration.

3. The requirements for a contract for sale or other disposition of land are provided in the Law of Property (Miscellaneous Provisions) Act 1989. The effect of non-compliance is that no contract exists, although devices of rectification and collateral contracts may be used to save invalid agreements.

4. In the absence of a contract, rights may also arise through the doctrine of proprietary estoppel. This is just one possible application of a much broader doctrine (which is discussed fully in Chapter 13) and its application in the context of a failed contract remains highly controversial.

5. The creation or transfer of legal rights generally requires a deed. In the absence of a deed, legal rights will not be created. Equitable rights may, however, be obtained through the doctrine of anticipation if the parties have entered a valid contract.

6. A system of registration of title has been spreading gradually since its introduction in the nineteenth century. With the exception of short leases, all legal estates are now either registered, or will become subject to compulsory first registration the next time that a specified transaction occurs. Additionally, it is possible to register a title voluntarily.

7. In registered land, title to legal estates does not pass until registration. Registered land is now governed by the Land Registration Act 2002, which repealed and replaced the Land Registration Act 1925. The 2002 Act purports to provide 'a conveyancing revolution'. It introduced significant amendments, with the underlying objective of facilitating the introduction of e-conveyancing. It marks a shift in English law from a system of 'registration of title' to one of 'title by registration'.

1 INTRODUCTION

In Chapter 3, we saw that legal estates and interests in land can be acquired *dependently*, where they are granted by a person with property rights in land, and *independently*, by the unilateral conduct of the person acquiring the right. In most cases, dependent acquisition of a legal right requires compliance with statutory formality requirements.

In this chapter, we consider the formality requirements that must be complied with for the creation or transfer of legal estates and interests in land. These statutory requirements are generally based on the need for the transaction to be in signed writing, usually witnessed, and sometimes require the written document to take the specific form of a deed. For the creation and transfer of legal estates (except for short leases), there is an overarching requirement of registration. In the introduction to this chapter, we will explore two issues: what are formality requirements and why do we have them in relation to land?

Critchley considers a legal definition of 'formality'.[1]

Critchley, 'Taking Formalities Seriously' in *Land Law: Themes and Perspectives* (eds Bright and Dewar, 1998, p 508)

One good starting point might be the common legal distinction between matters of 'substance' and 'form'. This suggests a definition of formality as something which is external or *added* to the transaction, rather than a constituent, substantive part of it. In legal usage, formality is generally also seen as a *requirement*, rather than a mere habit or convention, so it would be helpful for our definition to express the notion that formality is something mandatory. Further, it is typical (though not essential), where a legal formality is imposed, to have some sort of *sanction* for breach of the rule: some legal disbenefit, or some failure to obtain a legal benefit. The sanction is frequently the invalidation of a non-complying transaction, but there are other possibilities: for example, there might be procedural disadvantages (limiting the type of evidence which may be used to prove the transaction in legal proceedings); or the transaction might be valid as regards the original parties to it, but invalid against third parties. Whatever the sanction is, it would clearly also be useful to have a definition which would cover a formality rule with a sanction attached. Putting all of this together, then, we reach the following definition: 'in law, a formality is a requirement that matters of substance must be put into a particular form (in order to have a specified legal effect).'

The effect of formality requirements is undoubtedly that land is more complex to deal with than other forms of property. Why, then, are they considered desirable? Ultimately, it is for all of the reasons relating to the uniqueness of land that we have outlined in Chapter 1. This is reflected, too, in the following extract, in which Birks highlights the particular need for formality requirements in light of the nature of rights in land.

Birks, 'Before We Begin: Five Keys to Land Law' in *Land Law: Themes and Perspectives* (eds Bright and Dewar, 1998, p 483)

There is an extra reason [for formality requirements] too. It derives from the invisibility of real rights. Just as one cannot see a fee simple, so one cannot see an easement or a restrictive

---

[1] See further Fuller, 'Consideration and Form' (1941) 41 CL Rev 799.

covenant. A neighbour's right to pass over a field does not reveal itself in a pink line, nor will even an infra-red camera disclose his right to restrict or forbid building. If one is buying a fee simple from a company, and a firm of solicitors is in daily occupation of the premises doing the business of soliciting, one might reasonably infer that the firm holds a lease. But still a lease is not visible, nor a pyramid of sub-leases. Real rights have to be made apparent through documents. Acquiring land would otherwise be a nightmare unless the law made really massive erosions of the principle of *nemo dat*.

In addition, however, formality requirements serve functional roles. Immediately prior to the comment extracted above, Birks acknowledges, for example, their role in encouraging people to think about the job in hand, and in preventing doubt and argument.

In making recommendations relating to one aspect of formality requirements (those concerning contracts for sale of land), the Law Commission highlighted the practical functions served by the requirements in issue. These can fairly be carried over to all formality requirements.

Law Commission Report No 164, *Transfer of Land Formalities for Contracts for Sale etc of Land* (1987, [2.7]–[2.13])

One principal justification for perpetuating formalities for contracts dealing with land is the need for certainty. The existence and terms of oral contracts are always difficult to establish and the resulting confusion [...] would, we anticipate, lead to increased litigation. To minimise disputes, reliable uncontrovertible evidence of the existence and terms of a transaction needs to be available for later reference. In the light of this, the value of the evidential function of writing cannot be doubted.

The evidential function of writing is also valuable in assisting the prevention of fraud. The requirement goes some way to ensuring that parties are not bound in the absence of actual agreement. In fact, the prevention of fraud was the rationale of the original Act, the Statute of Frauds 1677 [...]

A related argument in favour of formalities for contracts for the sale of land is based upon consumer protection. Whilst it has been suggested that laymen appreciate the significance of entering into a contract for the sale of land, we still consider that some form of protection imposed from outside is necessary. The consumer should be warned about the gravity of the transaction into which he is about to enter. He needs time to reflect and, if necessary, to seek legal advice. This is especially important in the case of contracts dealing with land because they often involve acceptance of a complexity of rights and duties. A formal requirement of writing is, in our view, suited to this cautionary role. At least, it prevents a person from becoming bound without realizing it, since most people nowadays are aware that signature of a written document imports some binding effect. The need for consumer protection is particularly strong in the case of the sale or purchase of a dwelling, house or flat. The majority of people, at some time in their life, will enter into such a transaction, and it will involve them in major financial commitments and general upheaval. In such circumstances, it appears vital that a consumer takes all reasonable precautions and is fully protected. [...]

The cautionary role of formalities is not confined to the consumer protection context. It is equally important for all types of contract dealing with land, whether in domestic or commercial conveyancing, because it prevents the parties from being bound inadvertently or prematurely. Without formalities, it may be difficult to ascertain the exact time when a contract is created, and this would lead to confusion. As a result, pre-contract negotiations would be unnecessarily uncertain and hazardous.

Another recognised function performed by formalities is the "channelling" function. This describes the way in which formalities mark off transactions from one another and create a standardised form of transaction. As a result, the identification and classification of certain types of transaction are facilitated, enabling them to be dealt with routinely. Such a function contributes to certainty by making clear the effect of non-compliance with formalities. [...]

The general uniqueness of land constitutes another argument for requiring formalities for contracts relating to it: each particular piece of land is regarded as unique from which it follows that interests in or rights over it should not be created or disposed of casually. [...] It has also been argued that land is different from other property because there can exist simultaneously several interests, whether corporeal or incorporeal, in or over the same piece of land. Therefore, so the argument goes, writing is desirable to avoid so far as possible confusion about who owns what. As was said in the working paper, this argument may be found persuasive but not totally compelling, because third party interests can also be created in other forms of property.

Finally [...] most other legal jurisdictions require more formality for contracts relating to land.

2 FORMALITY REQUIREMENTS FOR THE CREATION OR TRANSFER OF LEGAL RIGHTS

The process of creating and transferring legal rights can be divided into three stages: contract; creation, or transfer; and registration. These stages are most apparent in a typical conveyance, or sale, of a home.

1. *Contract* The vendor and purchaser enter a contract for sale of the legal estate (whether freehold or leasehold). The purchaser usually pays a deposit.

2. *Creation or transfer* The contract is executed by the vendor transferring title. This stage is commonly referred to as 'completion', and is the stage at which the purchase money is paid (less the deposit) and the purchaser takes possession of the land.

3. *Registration* The purchaser applies to be registered as proprietor of the estate. Legal title does not vest in the purchaser until registration.

Although legal title does not vest in the purchaser until registration, equitable rights arise under the doctrine of anticipation from the moment at which the parties have entered a specifically enforceable contract. Under that doctrine, in the period between transfer and registration, the vendor holds the legal estate as bare trustee in favour of the purchaser. The nature of these rights is discussed fully in Chapter 12.

The same three-stage process may be followed whether the conveyance of land involves the transfer of an existing legal estate (for example, the transfer of a freehold or assignment of the existing term of a lease) or the creation of a new one (such as the grant of a new lease). Not every transaction in which a legal right is created or transferred will follow each stage of this process. For example, a contract is a convenient stage in the sale of land, but is not an essential requirement. A gift of land necessarily does not involve a contract. The requirement of registration only arises in relation to specified legal rights. Further, as we will see in section 4 (and discuss further in Chapter 23, section 3.1.2), it remains possible to create certain short leases without the need to comply with any formality requirements. Where any stage in the process is applicable, however, compliance with the formality requirements is mandatory.

3 CONTRACT

The requirements for a valid contract for the sale or other disposition of an interest in land are provided by s 2 of the Law of Property (Miscellaneous Provisions) Act 1989 (LP(MP)A 1989). That Act is the product of work of the Law Commission[2] and replaced the previous formality requirement contained in s 40 of the Law of Property Act 1925 (LPA 1925). The 1989 Act has been considered to mark a change in philosophy from previous legislation, focusing attention on the written contract. As a result, case law under the previous legislation may no longer be authoritative.[3]

As will be apparent from the following analysis, the 1989 Act has proved controversial in a number of respects. It increased the formality requirements for contracts and made more severe the consequences of non-compliance. Recurring concerns have been that the report and the legislation (which differs from the draft Bill annexed to the Law Commission's report) have failed to consider the consequences of the changes, and to enable parties to escape from what appears to be a clear bargain.

Law of Property (Miscellaneous Provisions) Act 1989, s 2

(1) A contract for the sale or other disposition of an interest in land can only be made in writing and only by incorporating all the terms which the parties have expressly agreed in one document or, where contracts are exchanged, in each.

(2) The terms may be incorporated in a document either by being set out in it or by reference to some other document.

(3) The document incorporating the terms or, where contracts are exchanged, one of the documents incorporating them (but not necessarily the same one) must be signed by or on behalf of each party to the contract.

(4) Where a contract for the sale or other disposition of an interest in land satisfies the conditions of this section by reason only of the rectification of one or more documents in pursuance of an order of a court, the contract shall come into being, or be deemed to have come into being, at such time as may be specified in the order.

(5) This section does not apply in relation to—

   (a) a contract to grant such a lease as is mentioned in section 54(2) of the Law of Property Act 1925 (short leases);

   (b) a contract made in the course of a public auction; or

   (c) a contract regulated under the Financial Services and Markets Act 2000, other than a regulated mortgage contract, a regulated home reversion plan or a regulated home purchase plan;

---

[2] Law Commission Report No 164, *Transfer of Land: Formalities for Contracts for Sale etc of Land* (1987).
[3] These comments were made in *Firstpost Homes Ltd v Johnson* [1995] 1 WLR 1567 in relation to the requirement of a signature under the 1989 Act, but are clearly of more general application.

and nothing in this section affects the creation or operation of resulting, implied or construct-ive trusts.

(6) In this section—

"disposition" has the same meaning as in the Law of Property Act 1925;

"interest in land" means any estate, interest or charge in or over land;

"regulated mortgage contract"[,"regulated home reversion plan" and "regulated home pur-chase plan"] must be read with—

    (a) section 22 of the Financial Services and Markets Act 2000,

    (b) any relevant order under that section, and

    (c) Schedule 2 to that Act.

(7) Nothing in this section shall apply in relation to contracts made before this section comes into force.

(8) Section 40 of the Law of Property Act 1925 (which is superseded by this section) shall cease to have effect.

Section 2 governs all contracts entered into on or after the 27 September 1989. It differs from s 40 of the LPA 1925 both as regards the formality requirements specified and the conse-quences of non-compliance.[4] As regards the formality requirements, under s 40, there was no requirement for a contract to be in writing; it was necessary only for it to be *evidenced* in writing. In contrast, s 2 of the LP(MP)A 1989 requires the contract to be in writing. This difference has a direct effect on the consequence of non-compliance. Under s 40 of the 1925 Act, a contract that was not evidenced in writing remained valid, but was not enforceable by action. Under s 2 of the 1989 Act, no contract exists unless and until formality requirements are fulfilled. There is no concept of a contract being valid, but unenforceable.

The principal significance of this difference is the abolition by s 2 of the doctrine of part performance.[5] That doctrine enabled the court to order specific performance of an oral con-tract if there was a sufficient act of part performance by the claimant.[6] Essential to the appli-cation of the doctrine was the fact that, under s 40 of the LPA 1925, an oral contract was valid. Without a valid contract, there is nothing in relation to which specific performance can be ordered. The uncertainty created by the doctrine was identified by the Law Commission as one of the key defects in the operation of s 40.[7] Its effect was that '*an oral contract for sale can readily and unilaterally be rendered enforceable and the provisions of section 40 left to beat the air*'.[8] It was considered a '*blunt instrument for doing justice*'[9] where formality requirements have not been complied with. Its abolition was therefore a key recommendation in the Law Commission's report. Although nothing in the terms of s 2 of the LP(MP)A 1989 expressly abolishes the doctrine, no such provision is necessary. Its abolition was recognized by the

---

[4] Law of Property Act 1925, s 40(1), provided as follows: '*No action may be brought upon any contract for the sale or other disposition of land or any interest in land, unless the agreement upon which such action is brought, or some memorandum or note thereof, is in writing, and signed by the party to be charged or by some other person thereunto by him lawfully authorised.*'

[5] The application of part performance was expressly provided for by the Law of Property Act 1925, s 40(2).

[6] For an example of the operation of part performance, see *Steadman v Steadman* [1976] AC 536.

[7] Law Commission Report No 164 (1987, [1.9]).

[8] Ibid.

[9] Ibid.

Law Commission as inherent in the requirement for a contract to be in writing.[10] The abolition of the doctrine has generally been given effect by the courts,[11] although it was doubted
in *Singh v Beggs*[12] and the doctrine has continued to attract limited academic support.[13]

Under s 2, the written contract may take one of two forms: a single document signed by
both parties; or separate documents signed by each party and exchanged. The document—or
each document, in the case of an exchange—must contain all of the terms expressly agreed
by the parties. The terms may be contained in the signed document—or documents, in the
case of exchange—or be contained in a separate document that is incorporated by reference.
Three main issues arise for discussion: the circumstances in which s 2 applies; the concept of
an exchange; and the requirement of a signature.

3.1 WHEN DOES S 2 APPLY?

Section 2 of the LP(MP)A 1989 applies to all contracts for the creation or transfer of an
interest in land.[14] Although, in this chapter, we are concerned specifically with the acquisition of legal rights, it should be noted that s 2 applies equally to equitable interests.[15] In
McCausland v Duncan Lawrie Ltd,[16] it was held that s 2 also applies to the variation of an
existing contract. As a result, unless the variation complies with s 2, the terms of the contract
as originally agreed remain enforceable. In that case, an attempt to vary the completion date
in a contract failed for non-compliance with s 2, with the effect that the vendor's attempt to
rescind the contract was premature.[17]

Section 2 does not apply to a contract that relates to land without involving the sale or
disposition of an interest in land. In *Pitt v PHH Asset Management Ltd*,[18] it was held that
a 'lock-out' agreement, through which a vendor agreed not to negotiate with anyone other
than the purchaser for a fixed period of time, was not a contract for sale of land and therefore
s 2 did not need to be complied with. The contract locked the parties into negotiations, but
with no obligation that a contract for sale would be entered.

A specific issue has arisen as regards the application of s 2 to an option to purchase. An
option to purchase land consists of two stages: in the first stage, the option is granted; in
the second, the option is exercised by the grantee. Following the enactment of the LP(MP)
A 1989, Adams suggested that the exercise of the option by the grantee would need to comply with s 2:[19] an outcome that would run counter to commercial practice[20] and that, Stark
suggested, would give the provision 'seismic effect', by leaving the exercise of options to 'the

---

[10] Law Commission Report No 164 (1987, [4.13]).
[11] See, e.g., *United Bank of Kuwait v Sahib* [1997] Ch 107. In that case, it was acknowledged that the abolition of part performance prevented the practice of creating a mortgage by the deposit of title deeds.
[12] (1996) 71 P & CR 120. See Swann, 'Part Performance: Back from the Dead' [1997] Conv 293.
[13] Griffiths, 'Part Performance: Still Trying to Replace the Irreplaceable' [2002] Conv 216.
[14] Law Commission Report No 164 (1987, [4.3]).
[15] While the creation of equitable interests generally arises informally and is exempt from formality
requirements, s 2 will apply to the transfer of an equitable interest: e.g., a contract to transfer a beneficial
interest. See Law Commission Report No 164 (1987, [4.4]).
[16] [1997] 1 WLR 38.
[17] The case is further discussed by Thompson, 'Mere Formalities' [1996] Conv 366.
[18] [1994] 1 WLR 327.
[19] Adams, 'You've No Option: More Consequences of Section 2 of the Law of Property (Miscellaneous
Provisions) Act 1989' [1990] Conv 9.
[20] Ibid.

whim of the vendor'.[21] The issue soon arose for decision in the following case, which arose from an option granted a matter of weeks after s 2 came into force.

Spiro v Glencrown Properties Ltd [1991] Ch 537, HC

Facts: The vendor granted the purchaser an option to purchase land, exercisable the same day by notice in writing. The grant of the option complied with s 2(1), but was exercisable by unilateral notice by the purchaser. The purchaser exercised the option, but failed to complete and the vendor had been awarded damages for breach of contract. In an action for judgment against the purchaser's guarantor, the question arose whether the exercise of the option was required to comply with s 2(1).

Hoffmann J

At 541

Apart from authority, it seems to me plain enough that section 2 was intended to apply to the agreement which created the option and not to the notice by which it was exercised. Section 2, which replaced section 40 of the Law of Property Act 1925, was intended to pre-vent disputes over whether the parties had entered into a binding agreement or over what terms they had agreed. It prescribes the formalities for recording their mutual consent. But only the grant of the option depends upon consent. The exercise of the option is a unilateral act. It would destroy the very purpose of the option if the purchaser had to obtain the vend-or's countersignature to the notice by which it was exercised. The only way in which the concept of an option to buy land could survive section 2 would be if the purchaser ensured that the vendor not only signed the agreement by which the option was granted but also at the same time provided him with a countersigned form to use if he decided to exercise it. There seems no conceivable reason why the legislature should have required this additional formality.

The language of section 2 places no obstacle in the way of construing the grant of the option as the relevant contract. An option to buy land can properly be described as a contract for the sale of that land conditional on the exercise of the option. A number of eminent judges have so described it.

Following a review of authorities, Hoffmann J concluded that nothing prevented him from interpreting s 2 in that way. Hence, while the grant of an option must comply with s 2, the exercise of the option is a unilateral act by the purchaser.

The decision has been welcomed as regards the practical operation of options under s 2, although the 'conditional contract' analysis of options taken by Hoffmann J to achieve this may be more problematic in other contexts.[22]

3.2 THE CONCEPT OF AN EXCHANGE

As has been noted, under s 2 of the 1989 Act, a contract may take the form of an exchange of documents. Prior to that Act, it was possible for a contract for sale of land to come into

---

[21] Stark, 'The Option to Purchase: A Legal Chameleon' [1992] JBL 296, 296.
[22] Ibid; Smith, 'Options to Purchase: A Nasty Twist' [1991] Conv 140, 144.

existence though correspondence between the parties—the correspondence providing the written evidence of the contract required by s 40 of the LPA 1925. Parties could prevent their correspondence from being interpreted this way by indorsing it 'subject to contract'. In its report, the Law Commission anticipated that contracts by correspondence would remain possible[23]—but in the following case, the Court of Appeal held that s 2 of the LP(MP)A 1989 goes further than the Law Commission anticipated in this regard.

Commission for the New Towns v Cooper [1995] Ch 259, CA

Stuart-Smith LJ

At 287

But there were in fact three problems under the old law [...] and endless difficulties in determining when, and if so on what terms, a contract was entered into in correspondence. I can see no reason why Parliament should not have gone further than the Law Commission recommendation and required a greater degree of formality in this very important area of the law where it is crucial that the parties know for certain when they are bound and on what terms.

The decision in *Commission for the New Towns v Cooper* runs counter to a previous Court of Appeal case, *Hooper v Sherman*,[24] but its authority has not been doubted. As Oakley notes, a contract may still arise by correspondence, but only in the unlikely event that the parties' correspondence results in a document (or documents) that comply with the requirements of s 2: for example, if each party signs the same document, thus removing the need for an exchange.[25]

Hence, while the LP(MP)A 1989 enables contracts by exchange, the process of exchange must be distinguished from mere correspondence. The nature of an exchange was also considered in *Commission for the New Towns v Cooper*.

Commission for the New Towns v Cooper [1995] Ch 259, CA

Stuart-Smith LJ

At 285

In my opinion, the authorities show that, even if the expression "exchange of contracts" is not a term of art, it is a well-recognised concept understood both by lawyers and laymen which has the following features.

1. Each party draws up or is given a document which incorporates all the terms which they have agreed, and which is intended to record their proposed contract. The terms that have been agreed may have been agreed either orally or in writing or partly orally or partly in writing.

2. The documents are referred to as "contracts" or "parts of contract," although they need not be so entitled. They are intended to take effect as formal documents of title and must be capable on their face of being fairly described as contracts having that effect.

---

[23] Law Commission Report No 164 (1987, [4.15]).
[24] [1994] NPC 153. See Thomson, 'Contracts by Correspondence' [1995] Conv 319.
[25] Oakley, 'Conveyancing Contracts by Exchange of Letters' [1995] CLJ 502, 504.

3. Each party signs his part in the expectation that the other party has also executed or will execute a corresponding part incorporating the same terms.

4. At the time of execution neither party is bound by the terms of the document which he has executed, it being their mutual intention that neither will be bound until the executed parts are exchanged.

5. The act of exchange is a formal delivery by each party of its part into the actual or constructive possession of the other with the intention that the parties will become actually bound when exchange occurs, but not before.

6. The manner of exchange may be agreed and determined by the parties. The traditional method was by mutual exchange across the table, both parties or their solicitors being present. It also commonly takes place by post, especially where the parties or their solicitors are at a distance. In such a case exchange is sequential and does not take place until the second document to be dispatched has been received or posted: *Eccles v. Bryant and Pollock* [1948] Ch. 93, 97–98, *per* Lord Greene M.R. Exchange can also take place by telephone, in which case it will be simultaneous: *Domb v. Isoz* [1980] Ch. 548, 558, *per* Buckley L.J.

Therefore, an exchange is qualitatively different from correspondence; the difference is marked most clearly by the parties' mutual intentions as regards the documents and the 'formal delivery' by way of exchange.

3.3 THE REQUIREMENT OF A SIGNATURE

To constitute a contract within s 2 of the LP(MP)A 1989, the 'document' itself must be signed. Problems may arise in identifying what constitutes the document. In the following case, an Ordnance Survey plan was attached to a letter that purported to record an agreement for sale of land.[26] The vendor signed the letter and the plan, but the purchaser signed only the plan. It was held that the 'document' requiring signature for s 2 was the letter alone, the plan being a separate document incorporated into the letter by reference. Peter Gibson LJ acknowledged that the identification of the document was '*largely one of first impression*', but, on the facts, the 'natural' interpretation was to treat the letter alone as the document.[27] In the absence of the purchaser's handwritten signature on the letter, the question arose whether the requirement of a signature was met by the appearance of his printed or typed name. This had been considered sufficient to constitute a signature under s 40 of the LPA 1925 and its predecessor, the Statute of Frauds 1677.

Firstpost Homes Ltd v Johnson [1995] 1 WLR 1567, CA

Peter Gibson LJ

At 1575–6

In my judgment, it is an artificial use of language to describe the printing or the typing of the name of an addressee in the letter as the signature by the addressee when he has printed or

---

[26] In fact, it was held that the letter did not constitute a contract, because it failed to contain an obligation to buy: [1995] 1 WLR 1567.
[27] [1995] 1 WLR 1567, 1573.

typed that document. Ordinary language does not, it seems to me, extend so far; and for this there appears to be the powerful support of Sir Raymond Evershed M.R. in *Goodman v. J. Eban Ltd.* [1954] 1 Q.B. 550, 555 and of Denning L.J., who said, at p. 561:

"In modern English usage, when a document is required to be 'signed by' someone, that means that he must write his name with his own hand upon it."

In any event, I do not accept that authorities on what was a sufficient signature for the purposes of the Statute of Frauds 1677 and section 40 of the Act of 1925 should continue to govern the interpretation of the word "signed" in section 2 of the Act of 1989. Prior to the Act of 1989 the courts viewed with some disfavour those who made oral contracts but did not abide by them. The courts were prepared to interpret the statutory requirements generously to enable contracts to be enforced and in relation to the question whether there was a sufficient memorandum evidencing an agreement extrinsic evidence was admissible.

There are statements by judges who were called upon to consider what was a signature for the purpose of those statutory provisions which suggest that they regarded the interpretation by earlier courts, in the generous manner that I have indicated, as not being what they themselves would have decided if not constrained by authority. In particular, in *Durrell v. Evans* (1862) 1 H. & C. 174 both Crompton and Blackburn JJ. expressed their doubts as to the way the matter had been interpreted by earlier courts. I have already referred to the remark of Cave J. in *Evans v. Hoare* [1892] 1 Q.B. 593 in the first sentence of the passage which I cited from his judgment and that supports the view that a liberal interpretation had been placed by the courts on the statutory requirements. The Act of 1989 seems to me to have a new and different philosophy from that which the Statute of Frauds 1677 and section 40 of the Act of 1925 had. Oral contracts are no longer permitted. To my mind it is clear that Parliament intended that questions as to whether there was a contract, and what were the terms of the contract, should be readily ascertained by looking at the single document said to constitute the contract.

To accept Mr. Seymour's contentions would be to allow the courts to consider matters outside the claimed contractual document such as what the parties subjectively intended by the document or by the name to be found on it or who prepared the document. For my part, I do not see why it is right to encumber the new Act with so much ancient baggage, particularly when it does not leave the "signed" with a meaning which the ordinary man would understand it to have. This decision is of course limited to a case where the party whose signature is said to appear on a contract is only named as the addressee of a letter prepared by him. No doubt other considerations will apply in other circumstances. I therefore do not accept Mr. Seymour's contention that a signature of the purchaser appears on the letter.

Peter Gibson LJ's clear limitation of his judgment leaves the matter open to discussion in other circumstances, although with the clear message that the requirement of a signature will be interpreted differently now from that in which it was under s 40 of the LPA 1925.

3.4 THE EFFECT OF NON-COMPLIANCE

As has been noted, the effect of non-compliance with s 2 of the LP(MP)A 1989 is that there is no contract. The Law Commission acknowledged that: '*While it is important not to undermine the general rule that the formalities should be observed, it is equally important that the law should not be so inflexible as to cause unacceptable hardship in cases of non-compliance.*'[28]

---

[28] Law Commission Report No 164 (1987, [5.1]).

There are two possible responses to non-compliance. Where the parties have written and signed a document—or documents, in the case of exchange—but the terms are absent or wrong, rectification or the finding of a collateral contract may be invoked to create a contract that complies with s 2.[29] Alternatively, rather than seeking to establish a valid contract (or where there is no prospect of one being established, for example, through an absence of writing) a non-contractual remedy may be sought. The Law Commission specifically anticipated the doctrine of proprietary estoppel playing a role in this regard,[30] although, as will be seen, this has proved problematic.

Arguments relating to the validity of a contract cannot be raised once the contract has been executed by the creation or transfer of the legal right.

Tootal Clothing Ltd v Guinea Property Management Ltd (1992) 64 P & CR 452, CA

Facts: The parties had entered two agreements on the same day: firstly, a lease agreement, for the grant to the tenant, Tootal, of a 25-year lease of commercial premises; secondly, a 'supplemental agreement' that the landlord, Guinea, would pay Tootal £30,000 on completion of work by Tootal to fit the premises for use as a shop. The lease was granted, but Guinea refused to pay Tootal for its work. Guinea argued, unsuccessfully, that the term was part of the bargain for the grant of the lease and was therefore not enforceable for its exclusion from the lease agreement.

Scott LJ

However, section 2 is of relevance only to executory contracts. It has no relevance to contracts which have been completed. If parties choose to complete an oral land contract or a land contract that does not in some respect or other comply with section 2, they are at liberty to do so. Once they have done so, it becomes irrelevant that the contract they have completed may not have been in accordance with section 2.

In the present case, the parties having agreed all the terms under which the new 25 year lease would be granted, including those relating to the shop-fitting works and the contribution by Guinea Properties of £30,000 towards the cost incurred by Tootal in carrying out the shop-fitting works, chose to incorporate the terms in two documents instead of one, namely the lease agreement and the supplemental agreement. They then completed the lease agreement. The lease agreement thereupon ceased to be an executory contract. The question whether section 2 of the 1989 Act would, because not all the terms of the contractual bargain had been incorporated into the lease agreement, have rendered the lease agreement unenforceable became irrelevant. All that was left was the supplemental agreement. The supplemental agreement was not and is not by itself a land contract, or, at least, if it is, by incorporation therein of the terms of the lease agreement, a land contract, then there is no issue in the case that need detain the court. But on the footing that the supplemental agreement by itself is not a land contract, which is the contention of Mr. Ritchie for Guinea Properties, there was no longer, after the completion of the lease agreement, any executory

---

[29] The possibility of each claim was recognized by the Law Commission: Law Commission Report No 164 (1987, [5.6]–[5.8]).

[30] Law Commission Report No 164 (1987, [5.4]–[5.5]).

land contract in existence to which section 2 of the 1989 Act could apply. There was simply a contract recorded in writing, signed by each party, for the payment of £30,000 in a certain event by one party to the other.

Hence, following execution of the contract, Guinea could not raise compliance with s 2 to question the enforceability of its agreement to pay Tootal for its works.

As Wilde notes,[31] the decision is of limited practical significance. It is relevant only in cases in which contractual obligations remain following the creation or transfer of the legal right in issue. This does not affect the possibility of an action for damages for breach of contract where a term of the contract is not complied with in its execution.[32]

3.5 COLLATERAL CONTRACTS

Section 2 of the LP(MP)A 1989 requires a contract for sale of land to contain all of the terms agreed by the parties. Hence, if a term is omitted, there is no contract, even where there is a written and signed document (or documents, in the case of exchange). If the absent term can be construed as a separate or collateral contract, then this difficulty is overcome. The parties' agreement constitutes a valid contract within s 2, minus the absent term, which is enforceable (if at all) as a separate contract. If the collateral contract does not itself constitute a contract for the sale of land, then it does not need to comply with s 2. A collateral contract must, however, have all of the elements of an ordinary contract—that is, offer, acceptance, and consideration.

The possibility of a collateral contract was an alternative ground for the decision in *Tootal Clothing*. In that case, as we have seen, the Court held that no question of compliance with s 2 could be raised, because the contract for the grant of a lease had been executed. Alternatively, the Court suggested that the landlord's supplemental agreement to pay the tenant £30,000 on completion by the tenant of works could be constructed as collateral to the main agreement for the grant of a lease.

Tootal Clothing Ltd v Guinea Property Management Ltd (1992) 64 P & CR 452, CA

Scott LJ

At 456

I am of the opinion, speaking for myself, that even before completion of the lease agreement on August 31, 1990, section 2 would not have prevented the enforcement of the lease agreement. If parties choose to hive off part of the terms of their composite bargain into a separate contract distinct from the written land contract that incorporates the rest of the terms, I can see nothing in section 2 that provides an answer to an action for enforcement of the land contract, on the one hand, or of the separate contract on the other hand. Each has become, by the contractual choice of the parties, a separate contract.

---

[31] Wilde, 'Contracts for the Sale or Disposition of Land' (1993) 109 LQR 191.
[32] See, e.g., *Robert Leonard Developments v Wright* [1994] NPC 49.

The device of a collateral contract was used in *Record v Bell*.[33] In that case, a vendor had been unable to provide the purchaser with an office copy of the registered title at the time of exchange. To enable exchange to proceed, the vendor provided a warranty of title. The purchaser subsequently failed to complete and argued that the parties' agreement did not comply with s 2, because it did not contain the warranty of title. Judge Paul Baker QC held that the warranty was a collateral contract. The warranty had been offered to 'induce' exchange and was accepted by exchange taking place.[34] He noted the utility of the device in ensuring that common transactions do not fail for non-compliance with s 2.[35]

The notion of 'hiving off' part of the parties' agreement to save an agreement from non-compliance with s 2(1) was, however, criticized by the Court of Appeal in the following case.

Grossman v Hooper [2001] EWCA Civ 615, CA

Facts: Mr Hooper and Miss Grossman had separated after a period of cohabitation. The parties had both signed an agreement, whereby Mr Hooper undertook to transfer legal title to the parties' home to Miss Grossman. The agreement was contained in a single document, signed by both parties. Mr Hooper subsequently argued that the agreement did not constitute a contract under s 2(1), because it omitted a term whereby Miss Grossman agreed to repay a loan for £10,000 to a Mr Modi.

Chadwick LJ

At [19]–[23]

I do not, myself, find it helpful to ask whether the arrangement between the appellant and the respondent in relation to the discharge of the Modi loan was to be described as a collateral agreement. The correct starting point, as it seems to me, is to examine the words used in section 2 of the 1989 Act. Subsection (1) requires that "all the terms which the parties have expressly agreed" must be incorporated in one document—or, where contracts are exchanged, in each of the documents exchanged. In that context, "the terms which the parties have expressly agreed" means the terms (so far as they are not to be implied) upon which the parties to the sale or other disposition have agreed that the relevant interest in land shall be sold or otherwise disposed of. The words do not refer to terms upon which the parties have agreed (albeit contemporaneously) that some other transaction should be entered. [. . .]

The relevant inquiry, therefore, is (i) upon what terms did the parties agree that the land (or interest in land) was to be sold, and (ii) are all those terms incorporated in the document which the parties have signed. Or, to elide the two stages of the enquiry: did the terms upon which the parties agreed that the land was to be sold include a term (or terms) which have not been incorporated in the document which they have signed?

The point can be illustrated by an example. Suppose that A wishes to purchase a house from B; and wishes, also, to purchase the carpets and curtains that are in the house. Before anything is put in writing A and B negotiate a price for the house, say £500,000, and a separate

---

[33] [1991] 1 WLR 853.
[34] [1991] 1 WLR 853, 862.
[35] Ibid.

price for the carpets and curtains, say £50,000. But the negotiation for the sale of the house is made subject to contract; and it is implicit neither A nor B intends to become bound to a purchase and sale of the carpets and curtains (if at all) until after the terms for the sale of the house have been put in writing and signed. A contract for the sale of the house at a price of £500,000 is drawn up and is signed by both A and B. The document contains no reference to the sale of carpets or curtains. The question, in such a case, in the context of section 2(1) of the 1989 Act, is whether it was a term of the contract for the sale of the house that A would purchase and B would sell the carpets and curtains. That is a question of fact in each case. It would have been open to A and B to agree that the sale of the house was independent of any sale of the carpets and curtains; so that A was to buy the house whether or not he bought the carpets and curtains as well. It would, equally, have been open to A and B to agree that the sale of the house was conditional upon a sale of the carpets and curtains; so that A would not be obliged to buy the house, nor B to sell it, unless the carpets and curtains were sold also. In the first case, the requirements of section 2(1) of the 1989 Act would be satisfied; in the second case those requirements would not be satisfied. The requirements would not be satisfied in the second case because, upon a true understanding of the bargain between the parties, it was a term of the contract for the sale of the house that A would purchase and B would sell the carpets and curtains; and that term was not incorporated in the document signed by the parties.

The question of fact, in such a case, is not answered by asking whether the agreement to sell the carpets and curtains was "a collateral contract"; unless, by that term, it is intended to refer only to a contract the existence, or nonexistence of which has no effect upon the efficacy of the principal contract. Nor, it may be noted, is that question answered by asking whether or not the contract for the sale of the carpets and curtains is conditional upon the sale of the house. It is obvious that (save in the most exceptional circumstances) if a contract for the sale of the carpets and curtains has been made in advance of the contract for the sale of the house, it will be conditional upon the sale of the house. The question is whether the contract for the sale of the house is conditional upon the sale of the carpets and curtains.

In the present case, therefore, the relevant question is whether the respondent's undertaking to discharge the Modi loan was a term of the sale by the appellant to the respondent of his interest in 77d Nightingale Lane. The judge held that it was not. In my view he was entitled to reach that conclusion. [...]

Sir Christoper Staughton

At [35]–[37]

[...] If the parties are allowed by a simple device to avoid the effects of section 2 of the Law of Property (Miscellaneous Provisions) Act 1989 , what was the point of Parliament enacting it? [...]

So if there was a term in the contractual agreement that Miss Grossman would pay off Mr Modi, and if that was part and parcel of an agreement for the transfer of property, I am by no means sure that it can be hived off, as Scott LJ put it, into a separate contract.

But in the event it is unnecessary in this case for Miss Grossman to establish a collateral contract. There was in my judgment no term of any contract whether integral or collateral, that she should pay off Mr Modi. That was simply a matter of concurrence common to them both. They were in agreement that it would happen, as appears from the passage in the judgment which I first cited. There was no need for any contractual term about it and no such term was created.

In the view of the Court of Appeal, an agreement is either part of the contract for the sale of land, or it is not. If it is, then it must be contained in the parties' written document to ensure compliance with s 2; it cannot be 'hived off' as a collateral contract. If it is not part of the agreement for the sale of land, then it is not a collateral contract, but simply a wholly separate transaction, the existence of which has no bearing on whether s 2 is complied with. The classification of the agreement is dependent on the terms of Chadwick LJ's judgment. The essential question appears to be this: did the parties intend that the sale of the land would go ahead even in the absence of the agreement in question? If so, then the agreement is not part of the contract for sale of land.

This is a strict approach that casts doubt on the future use of collateral contracts and, implicitly, on the correctness of the decision in *Record v Bell*. Notably, that case is not referred to in the judgments. By reference to [21], however, it is difficult to avoid the conclusion that the warranty of title in that case *was* part of the contract for sale of land: in the absence of the warranty, the sale of the land would not have proceeded. If this is so, then, contrary to the decision in the case, the contract should have been void for non-compliance with s 2.

The cases may be distinguished by reference to the subject matter of the agreements in question. In *Grossman v Hooper*, the subject matter of the agreement was distinct from the land to be transferred: it concerned the discharge of an unsecured debt. Similarly, the example discussed by Chadwick LJ in his judgment involves distinct subject matter: carpets and curtains. It is difficult to apply the Court's reasoning to *Record v Bell* when the agreement related to the title of the land being transferred.

One consequence of the strict approach to collateral contracts signposted by *Grossman v Hooper* is that the ability of parties to establish a valid contract within s 2 through rectification becomes more significant.

3.6 RECTIFICATION

Where the parties have reached an agreement, but the terms are not all recorded in the document (or documents, in the case of exchange), or are recorded wrongly, the court may order rectification, with the result that the document then satisfies s 2 of the LP(MP)A 1989. The possibility of rectification is specifically referred to in s 2(4), which confers on the court discretion to determine the time at which the contract comes into being. This is to enable the court to take into account the possible effect of rectification on third parties who enter a transaction between the date of the original 'contract' (void at the time for non-compliance with s 2) and the court's decision to rectify the agreement.[36]

It is established as a matter of contract law that rectification may be awarded where there is a prior agreement or common intention to contract on specified terms, and convincing proof[37] that the written agreement does not reflect those terms.[38] More controversially, rectification may also be available in cases of unilateral mistake, but only where the party not mistaken has acted unconscionably.[39] To date, there is little authority on the use of

---

[36] Law Commission Report No 164 (1987, [5.6]).

[37] See Thompson, 'Blowing Hot and Cold' [1995] Conv 484. He suggests that this may be diluted to a test based on the balance of probabilities.

[38] *Josceleyne v Nissen* [1970] 2 QB 86.

[39] For example, through estoppel, fraud, undue influence, breach of fiduciary duty, or though actual knowledge of the mistake. In *Commission for the New Towns v Cooper* [1995] Ch 259, 277–82, it was suggested, obiter, that it would also be sufficient if one party merely suspects the other to be mistaken and intends them to be so, without proof of inducement.

rectification in relation to contracts for sale of land. But the courts' reticence towards the use of collateral contracts expressed in *Grossman v Hooper* implicitly increases the likelihood of claims to rectification.

The remedy was adopted in *Robert Leonard Developments Ltd v Wright*.[40] In that case, a purchaser had agreed to buy a show flat, the price of which was to include carpets and furnishings. This term was not included in both written contracts on exchange and the vendor removed the furniture. The contract was executed by the transfer of the lease of the flat and therefore the validity of the contract could no longer be questioned—but the purchaser sought damages for breach of contract. The Court of Appeal considered that there was no separate or collateral contract for the sale of the furnishings; it was part of one package for the sale of the flat. Instead, the Court held that the contract should be rectified to include the omitted term.

Rectification is not available in all cases in which a written document does not include all of the terms agreed by the parties. Interpreted in such a broad manner, it would have the potential to undermine the operation of s 2 of the 1989 Act.

Oun v Ahmad [2008] EWHC 545

Facts: Mr Ahmad and Mr Oun signed an agreement (referred to in the judgment as the 'first document') for the sale of premises comprising a residential flat and an off-licence. The sale was never completed and the question arose as to whether a valid contract for sale had been entered. The agreement signed by the parties did not refer to an apportionment of the purchase price between the building, fixtures, and fittings, and the business goodwill. This matter was instead recorded by the parties in a second document. Mr Oun, the proposed purchaser, argued that the parties' agreement should be rectified to include this term.

Morgan J

At [35]

Section 2(4) of the 1989 Act expressly contemplates that a court can order rectification in some cases where the written document does not incorporate all of the terms expressly agreed. However, there is an important issue in the present appeal as to the cases in which rectification is available. Is it every case where the written document does not incorporate all of the terms expressly agreed (whatever the reason for that might be) or is it only those cases where, applying conventional principles, the equity of rectification is available? [...]

At [39]

Although the process of rectification in this context is an unusual form of rectification, it seems to be the case that one applies the usual rules as to the availability of rectification. In the *Robert Leonard* case, Henry LJ adopted a passage in the Law Commission Report (Law Com No. 164) at paragraph 5.6 which dealt with the possibility of rectification. Reference to the Law Commission Report itself shows that the footnotes to paragraph 5.6 refer to the general law as to rectification as set out in *Snell's Equity* and in well known cases dealing with rectification. [...]

---

[40] [1994] NPC 49.

At [41]–[43]

Rectification: further discussion

Because of the arguments addressed to me, it is necessary to consider the possibility of rectification in more detail. I will distinguish between two types of case.

In the first type of case, the written document does not incorporate all the terms expressly agreed, by reason of a mistake in the recording of the agreement. In such a case, the court can rectify the written document so as to incorporate all the terms expressly agreed and then the document as rectified complies with section 2.

The second (rather more unusual) type of case is as follows. Say the parties expressly agree upon five terms of their agreement. They agree to record four of them in a written document and they do so. They agree that the fifth term shall remain unrecorded in writing. The result is that the written document does not comply with section 2 and is of no effect. Can one party seek an order for rectification to the effect that the fifth term should be incorporated into the written document so that the written document will then comply with section 2? Will the position be different if the court finds that the parties believed that they had made a binding contract and that it was unnecessary for them to record the fifth term in writing? [. . .]

At [48]

It appears from the above formulation that the court can order rectification where the relevant mistake is as to the meaning or effect of the words used in the instrument and, indeed, as to the legal effect of the instrument as a whole. [. . .]

At [51]

But rectification is not available where the parties have executed the document they intended to execute and the mistake is as to the legal consequences of that document. In *Allnutt v Wilding*, the parties had created a discretionary trust. They believed that the creation of a discretionary trust would be a potentially exempt transfer for the purposes of inheritance tax. It was not. If they had appreciated that legal consequence, their claim was that they would have created an interest in possession trust. It was held that a change in the document from one which created a discretionary trust into one which created an interest in possession trust was outside the ambit of rectification. [. . .]

At [55]

In my judgment, this express agreement to omit the term means that there is no defect or mistake in the recording of, or the expression of, the arrangement and it is beyond the ambit of rectification to write into the written agreement a term which the parties expressly agreed should not be so recorded. I reach this conclusion applying what I understand to be conventional principles as to the availability of rectification and not some special set of rules as to rectification for the purposes of section 2(4) of the 1989 Act. In my judgment, this approach serves the legislative objective of section 2 of the 1989 Act. [. . .]

On the facts, Morgan J considered that the parties had agreed on the apportionment of the purchase price at the time that the first document was signed and had further agreed that this should not be included in the document. Both parties had mistakenly considered that, notwithstanding the absence of the term, the document would still be a valid contract. This mistake was beyond the scope of rectification and therefore there was no contract for sale of the premises.

3.7 ESTOPPEL

The doctrine of proprietary estoppel has application in a wide range of circumstances, in many of which (for example, promises of a gift or an inheritance) there is no question of the existence of a contract. The doctrine is discussed in Chapter 13, where we will see that a recent decision of the House of Lords in *Yeoman's Row Management Ltd v Cobbe*[41] has challenged our conventional understanding of the doctrine. Contrary to the long-standing view of the effect of the doctrine, the House of Lords considered that it does not, in fact, operate as an independent means by which a claimant may acquire rights; instead (like other types of estoppel), it simply operates to prevent one party from denying that the other has a right, or from asserting their rights against that other party. A full analysis of that decision is provided in Chapter 13. In this chapter, we are concerned with a specific point regarding the operation of proprietary estoppel: can the doctrine (in whatever form it exists) be invoked by a claimant where a contract has failed for non-compliance with s 2(1) of the LP(MP)A 1989?

The Law Commission specifically envisaged the use of estoppel in appropriate cases in which formality requirements for a contract for sale were not complied with. Indeed, this prospect played a central role in the Law Commission's acknowledgment that the effect of its recommendations was that the doctrine of part performance would cease to have effect.[42]

Law Commission Report No 164, *Transfer of Land Formalities for Contracts for Sale etc of Land* (1987, [5.4]–[5.5])

We have already pointed out that it is implicit in our recommendation that a contract will no longer be enforceable simply because one party has performed some or all of his obligations under it. We believe this not to be a consequence to be regretted. [...] Nevertheless there are clearly circumstances in which injustice could be caused through the inability to plead part performance. [...] Are there other solutions than that which might have been provided by part performance? We believe that there are, and that the courts would use doctrines of estoppel to achieve very similar results where appropriate to those of part performance.

We see no cause to fear that the recommended repeal and replacement of the present section as to the formalities for contracts for sale or other disposition of land will inhibit the courts in the exercise of the equitable discretion to do justice between parties in individual otherwise hard cases.

The ability to invoke estoppel was, however, subsequently called into question in the following case. Two key issues were central to the Court of Appeal's discussion: firstly, a 'public policy principle' that estoppel could not be used to render valid a transaction that legislation has enacted is to be invalid;[43] secondly, the scope of s 2(5) of the 1989 Act. That provision (extracted above) provides a saving for the operation of resulting and constructive

---

[41] [2008] 1 WLR 1752.

[42] Law Commission Report No 164 (1987, [5.4]–[5.5]). See further, Bently and Coughlan, 'Informal Dealings with Land after Section 2' (1990) 10 LS 325.

[43] The principle is cited by Robert Walker LJ [2000] Ch 162, 172–3, from *Halsbury's Laws of England: Vol 16* (4th edn, reissue, 1992): '*The doctrine of estoppel may not be invoked to render valid a transaction which the legislature has, on grounds of general public policy, enacted is to be invalid.*'

trusts, but makes no reference to proprietary estoppel. This second issue, in turn, raised the question of the relationship between estoppel and constructive trusts.[44]

Yaxley v Gotts [2000] 1 Ch 162, CA

Facts: Mr Yaxley, a builder, found a property ripe for redevelopment. He entered an oral agreement, described as a 'gentleman's agreement', with his friend, Mr Brownie Gotts. The terms of the agreement were that Brownie would purchase the property, and that Mr Yaxley would undertake the redevelopment and manage the building, in return for which he would be given the two ground-floor flats. The property was, in fact, purchased in the name of Brownie's son, Mr Alan Gotts. Mr Yaxley carried out the works, but, following a falling out between the friends, Alan refused to transfer the flats to Mr Yaxley. At first instance, the judge had found that Mr Yaxley could invoke proprietary estoppel and ordered a long lease of the flats to be granted to him. On appeal, the Gotts argued that the agreement with Mr Yaxley was void for non-compliance with s 2(1) of the LP(MP)A 1989 and estoppel could not be invoked to give effect to the void agreement.

Robert Walker LJ

At 174–80

Recent cases on section 2 and estoppel

[...] I have no hesitation in agreeing with what I take to be the views of Peter Gibson L.J., Neill L.J., and Morritt L.J., that the doctrine of estoppel may operate to modify (and sometimes perhaps even counteract) the effect of section 2 of the Act of 1989. The circumstances in which section 2 has to be complied with are so various, and the scope of the doctrine of estoppel is so flexible, that any general assertion of section 2 as a "no-go area" for estoppel would be unsustainable. Nevertheless the impact of the public policy principle to which Sir John Balcombe drew attention in *Godden v. Merthyr Tydfil Housing Association* does call for serious consideration. It is not concerned with illegality (some confusion may have arisen from the inadequate report or note shown to this court in *Bankers Trust Co. v. Namdar*) but with what Viscount Radcliffe in *Kok Hoong v. Leong Cheong Kweng Mines Ltd.* [1964] A.C. 993, 1016, called a principle of general social policy,

> "to ask whether the law that confronts the estoppel can be seen to represent a social policy to which the court must give effect in the interests of the public generally or some section of the public, despite any rules of evidence as between themselves that the parties may have created by their conduct or otherwise."

In this case that principle must of course be applied consistently with the terms in which section 2 of the Act of 1989 has been enacted, including the saving at the end of section 2(5).

Parliament's requirement that any contract for the disposition of an interest in land must be made in a particular documentary form, and will otherwise be void, does not have such an obviously social aim as statutory provisions relating to contracts by or with moneylenders, infants, or protected tenants. Nevertheless it can be seen as embodying Parliament's

---

[44] The nature of constructive trusts is discussed in Chapter 14, section 4. The specific type of constructive trust discussed in this section is the common intention constructive trust, which is considered in Chapter 18.

conclusion, in the general public interest, that the need for certainty as to the formation of contracts of this type must in general outweigh the disappointment of those who make informal bargains in ignorance of the statutory requirement. If an estoppel would have the effect of enforcing a void contract and subverting Parliament's purpose it may have to yield to the statutory law which confronts it, except so far as the statute's saving for a constructive trust provides a means of reconciliation of the apparent conflict.

None of the recent authorities referred to by counsel is determinative of this appeal [...] Nor can anything in the Law Commission's report (or its earlier working paper) be decisive. The report and the working paper are invaluable guides to the old law and to the problems which constituted the "mischief" at which section 2 of the Act of 1989 is directed, but they cannot be conclusive as to how section 2, as enacted, is to be construed and applied.

Proprietary estoppel and constructive trusts

At a high level of generality, there is much common ground between the doctrines of proprietary estoppel and the constructive trust, just as there is between proprietary estoppel and part performance. All are concerned with equity's intervention to provide relief against unconscionable conduct, whether as between neighbouring landowners, or vendor and purchaser, or relatives who make informal arrangements for sharing a home, or a fiduciary and the beneficiary or client to whom he owes a fiduciary obligation. The overlap between estoppel and part performance has been thoroughly examined in the defendants' written submissions, with a survey of authorities from *Gregory v. Mighell* (1811) 18 Ves. 328 to *Take Harvest Ltd. v. Liu* [1993] A.C. 552.

The overlap between estoppel and the constructive trust was less fully covered in counsel's submissions but seems to me to be of central importance to the determination of this appeal. Plainly there are large areas where the two concepts do not overlap: when a landowner stands by while his neighbour mistakenly builds on the former's land the situation is far removed (except for the element of unconscionable conduct) from that of a fiduciary who derives an improper advantage from his client. But in the area of a joint enterprise for the acquisition of land (which may be, but is not necessarily, the matrimonial home) the two concepts coincide [...]

In this case the judge did not make any finding as to the existence of a constructive trust. He was not asked to do so, because it was not then seen as an issue in the case. But on the findings of fact which the judge did make it was not disputed that a proprietary estoppel arose, and that the appropriate remedy was the grant to Mr. Yaxley, in satisfaction of his equitable entitlement, of a long leasehold interest, rent free, of the ground floor of the property. Those findings do in my judgment equally provide the basis for the conclusion that Mr. Yaxley was entitled to such an interest under a constructive trust. The oral bargain which the judge found to have been made between Mr. Yaxley and Mr. Brownie Gotts, and to have been adopted by Mr. Alan Gotts, was definite enough to meet the test stated by Lord Bridge in *Lloyds Bank Plc. v. Rosset* [1991] 1 A.C. 107, 132.

The saving in section 2(5)

To recapitulate briefly: the species of constructive trust based on "common intention" is established by what Lord Bridge in *Lloyds Bank Plc. v. Rosset* [1991] 1 A.C. 107, 132, called an "agreement, arrangement or understanding" actually reached between the parties, and relied on and acted on by the claimant. A constructive trust of that sort is closely akin to, if not indistinguishable from, proprietary estoppel. Equity enforces it because it would be unconscionable for the other party to disregard the claimant's rights. Section 2(5) expressly saves the creation and operation of a constructive trust.

[...] To give [section 2(5)] what I take to be its natural meaning, comparable to that of section 53(2) of the Law of Property Act 1925 in relation to section 53(1), would not create a huge and unexpected gap in section 2. It would allow a limited exception, expressly contemplated by Parliament, for those cases in which a supposed bargain has been so fully performed by one side, and the general circumstances of the matter are such, that it would be inequitable to disregard the claimant's expectations, and insufficient to grant him no more than a restitutionary remedy.

Clarke LJ

At 181–2

Proprietary estoppel and the Law Commission

The Act of 1989 expressly refers to resulting, implied or constructive trusts but it does not expressly refer to proprietary estoppel, in so far as its principles are different from those relating to constructive trusts. The Act neither expressly saves the operation of the doctrine of proprietary estoppel nor expressly provides that it should have no application. Whether the principles of proprietary (or indeed other classes of estoppel) can be invoked will no doubt depend upon the principle which Robert Walker L.J. has quoted from *Halsbury's Laws of England*, 4th ed. reissue, vol. 16, pp. 849–850, para. 962, namely that the doctrine of estoppel may not be invoked to render valid a transaction which the legislature, on grounds of general public policy, has enacted is to be invalid or void.

It seems to me that in considering whether a particular estoppel relied upon would offend the public policy behind a statute it is necessary to consider the mischief at which the statute is directed. Where a statute has been enacted as a result of the recommendations of the Law Commission, it is, as I see it, both appropriate and permissible for the court to consider those recommendations in order to help to identify both the mischief which the Act is designed to cure and the public policy underlying it. Indeed, although I agree with Robert Walker L.J. that they cannot be conclusive as to how a particular provision should be construed, I entirely agree with Beldam L.J. that the policy behind section 2 of the Act of 1989 can clearly be seen from the Law Commission Report to which he refers. In my opinion the contents of that report will be of the greatest assistance in deciding whether or not the principles of particular types of estoppel should be held to be contrary to the public policy underlying the Act. In this regard it seems to me that the answer is likely to depend upon the facts of the particular case. So, for example, an attempt to apply the principles of estoppel by convention is likely to fail, as in *Godden v. Merthyr Tydfil Housing Association* [1997] N.P.C. 1; Court of Appeal (Civil Division) Transcript No. 370 of 1997, whereas an attempt to apply the principles of proprietary estoppel might well succeed, depending upon the facts of the particular case.

Beldam LJ

At 190

In the present case the policy behind the Commission's proposals was as clearly stated as its intention that the proposal should not affect the power of the court to give effect in equity to the principles of proprietary estoppel and constructive trusts. Even if the use to be made of the Commission's report is to be confined to identifying the defect in the law which the proposals were intended to correct, in a case such as the present it is unrealistic to divorce the defect in the law from the policy adopted to correct it. The Commission's report makes it clear that in proposing legislation to exclude the uncertainty and complexities introduced into unregistered conveyancing by the doctrine of part performance, it did not intend to affect the availability of the equitable remedies to which it referred.

The general principle that a party cannot rely on an estoppel in the face of a statute depends upon the nature of the enactment, the purpose of the provision and the social policy behind it. This was not a provision aimed at prohibiting or outlawing agreements of a specific kind, though it had the effect of making agreements which did not comply with the required formalities void. This by itself is insufficient to raise such a significant public interest that an estoppel would be excluded. The closing words of section 2(5)—"nothing in this section affects the creation or operation of resulting, implied or constructive trusts"—are not to be read as if they merely qualified the terms of section 2(1). The effect of section 2(1) is that no contract for the sale or other disposition of land can come into existence if the parties fail to put it into writing; but the provision is not to prevent the creation or operation of equitable interests under resulting implied or constructive trusts, if the circumstances would give rise to them [. . .]

There are circumstances in which it is not possible to infer any agreement, arrangement or understanding that the property is to be shared beneficially but in which nevertheless equity has been prepared to hold that the conduct of an owner in allowing a claimant to expend money or act otherwise to his detriment will be precluded from denying that the claimant has a proprietary interest in the property. In such a case it could not be said that to give effect to a proprietary estoppel was contrary to the policy of section 2(1) of the Act of 1989. Yet it would be a strange policy which denied similar relief to a claimant who had acted on a clear promise or representation that he should have an interest in the property. Moreover claims based on proprietary estoppel are more likely to arise where the claimant has acted after an informal promise has been made to him [. . .]

For my part I cannot see that there is any reason to qualify the plain words of section 2(5). They were included to preserve the equitable remedies to which the Commission had referred. I do not think it inherent in a social policy of simplifying conveyancing by requiring the certainty of a written document that unconscionable conduct or equitable fraud should be allowed to prevail.

In my view the provision that nothing in section 2 of the Act of 1989 is to affect the creation or operation of resulting, implied or constructive trusts effectively excludes from the operation of the section cases in which an interest in land might equally well be claimed by relying on constructive trust or proprietary estoppel.

That, to my mind, is the case here. There was on the judge's findings, as I interpret them, a clear promise made by Brownie Gotts to the plaintiff that he would have a beneficial interest in the ground floor of the premises. That promise was known to Alan Gotts when he acquired the property and he permitted the plaintiff to carry out the whole of the work needed to the property and to convert the ground floor in the belief that he had such an interest. It would be unconscionable to allow either Alan or Brownie Gotts to resile from the representations made by Brownie Gotts and adopted by Alan Gotts. For my part I would hold that the plaintiff established facts on which a court of equity would find that Alan Gotts held the property subject to a constructive trust in favour of the plaintiff for an interest in the ground floor and that that interest should be satisfied by the grant of a 99-year lease. I consider the judge was entitled to reach the same conclusion by finding a proprietary estoppel in favour of the plaintiff [. . .]

The outcome of the case for Mr Yaxley is beyond doubt. The first instance judge had ordered a grant to him of a 99-year lease of the ground-floor flats and the Gotts' appeal against that ruling failed.

It is, however, much harder to identify a clear ratio for the decision. The differences between the judgments of Robert Walker and Beldam LJJ, and the issues to which these differences give rise, are highlighted by Moore.

Moore, 'Proprietary Estoppel, Constructive Trusts and Section 2 of the Law of Property (Miscellaneous Provisions) Act 1989' (2000) 63 MLR 912, 914

It appears that, according to Robert Walker LJ, proprietary estoppel does not survive as a separate and distinct remedy in a case where a claimant relies on an oral agreement. Proprietary estoppel survives only in so far as it overlaps with (and is subsumed within) the common intention constructive trust. By implication, an estoppel claim that cannot be framed alternatively as a constructive or resulting trust can not override section 2.

At first sight the approach of Beldam LJ appears to be more generous than that of Robert Walker LJ. Unlike Robert Walker LJ, Beldam LJ did not hesitate to rely upon the Law Commission papers to identify parliamentary policy and intent. His Lordship observed that the general principle raised by the appellants depended upon the nature and purpose of the statutory provision and the social policy behind it. The policy here was to exclude uncertainty and complexities introduced by the doctrine of part performance, and not to prohibit specific agreements. The mere fact that informal agreements were rendered void rather than unenforceable was not enough in itself to raise a public interest sufficient to exclude proprietary estoppel. Furthermore his Lordship commented that if the appellants' contention succeeded, a claimant raising a proprietary estoppel through mere standing-by and encouragement would be in a stronger position than a claimant relying on a clear oral agreement.

Following this reasoning, proprietary estoppel (and presumably other equitable remedies) could continue to operate notwithstanding a failure to comply with section 2. Since the intention of the reforms was not to abolish these remedies there would be no conflict between equitable remedies and statutory policy. There is thus no logical need to restrict estoppel remedies to cases already falling within the saving of section 2(5). Despite this, Beldam LJ's later comments appear to restrict the scope of his judgment. Firstly, Beldam LJ considered that section 2(5) was 'included to preserve the equitable remedies to which the Law Commission had referred', so apparently allying proprietary estoppel and constructive trusts. Secondly, the learned judge concluded 'the saving in section 2 effectively excludes cases where an interest might equally well be claimed by relying on a constructive trust or proprietary estoppel. That, to my mind, is the case here.' This appears to echo the approach of Robert Walker LJ. There is therefore some doubt whether, despite his reasoning, Beldam LJ intended to give a wider judgment than Robert Walker LJ.

As Moore subsequently identities, the issue that remains unanswered in *Yaxley v Gotts* is whether a claimant in Mr Yaxley's position succeeds on the basis of constructive trusts or estoppel. The issue may be crucial, given the existence of remedial discretion in estoppel. Even on the facts of *Yaxley v Gotts*, as Smith noted, it is far from clear that the grant of a lease can be explained on the basis of a constructive trust.[45]

[45] Smith, 'Oral Contracts for the Sale of Land: Estoppels and Constructive Trusts' (2000) 116 LQR 11, 12–13.

The relationship between estoppel and s 2 was further considered in the following case. While the decision offers some clarification of the application of estoppel, the Court of Appeal followed the approach in *Yaxley v Gotts* without offering further elucidation as to whether the claimant succeeds under estoppel or constructive trust.

Kinane v Mackie-Conteh [2005] EWCA Civ 45, CA

Facts: Mr Mackie-Conteh agreed to grant a charge over his home as security for a loan from Mr Kinane, but the charge was not formally executed. Mr Kinane provided the loan money, but Mr Mackie-Conteh argued that the charge was void for non-compliance with s 2. Mr Kinane therefore argued for an estoppel.

Arden LJ

At [28]–[29]

In my judgment, therefore, a party seeking to rely on proprietary estoppel as a basis for disapplying section 2(1) of the 1989 Act is not prevented from relying in support of his case on the agreement which section 2(1) would otherwise render invalid. Thus, the requirement that the defendant encouraged (or allowed) the claimant to believe that he would acquire an interest in land may (depending on the facts) consist in the defendant encouraging the claimant (by words or conduct) to believe that the agreement for the disposition of an interest in land (here a security interest) was valid and binding. Here, Mr Mackie-Conteh gave Mr Kinane that encouragement. Mr Kinane made it clear that he required security for his loan. Mr Mackie-Conteh responded by providing the security agreement and persuading him that, once he had got that letter (and the cheque for £15,000 had been banked), he should make the loan to Almack. By his conduct, Mr Mackie-Conteh thereby encouraged Mr Kinane to believe that the security agreement was valid and binding. He must stand by that conduct even if he himself misunderstood the effect of section 2(1) on the security agreement. Accordingly, the requirement for encouragement by Mr Mackie-Conteh of Mr Kinane in the erroneous belief that he would obtain a security interest over the property is satisfied.

It is to be noted that, even on this scenario, reliance on the unenforceable agreement only takes the claimant part of the way: he must still prove all the other components of proprietary estoppel. In particular, the requirement that the defendant encouraged or permitted the claimant in his erroneous belief is not satisfied simply by the admission of the invalid agreement in evidence. In this sort of case, the claimant has to show that the defendant represented to the claimant, by his words or conduct, including conduct in the provision or delivery of the agreement, that the agreement created an enforceable obligation. The cause of action in proprietary estoppel is thus not founded on the unenforceable agreement but upon the defendant's conduct which, when viewed in all relevant respects, is unconscionable. [...]

At [31]–[33]

Accordingly the issue here is whether the circumstances justify a finding of proprietary estoppel overlapping with constructive trust in the manner explained above. I have dealt with the question of encouragement above. Did Mr Kinane act in the belief that he had or would obtain a valid security? Did he act thereon to his detriment? The security agreement demonstrates an intention to create a security interest. Mr Kinane made it clear in his witness statement and when giving evidence that he was not prepared to make a loan without security. Having obtained the security agreement, he made a loan which, to his detriment, is now irrecoverable. In my judgment, the fact that he knew that the formal documentation had not been executed does not mean that proprietary estoppel cannot be established. The fact is that he drew no distinction between the security agreement and the formal document. He assumed that the security agreement was enforceable and thus he acted in the belief that he would be given a formal security. Thus I would reject Mr Jack's argument that it is fatal to Mr Kinane's case that the security agreement had not been executed. Likewise, in my judgment, it is immaterial that the reliance consisted in the single act of making the loan. That act had significant consequences on its own, and is thus of itself sufficient to give rise to proprietary estoppel.

As I see it, the policy of section 2(1) of the 1989 Act is to protect the public by preventing parties from being bound by a contract for the disposition of an interest in land unless it has not been fully documented in writing. However, in section 2(5) Parliament has acknowledged that under section 2(1) there is a risk that one party will seek to take advantage of the sanction provided by that subsection when it is unconscionable for him so to do. To that extent, section 2(5) plays a role similar to that of part performance, although it operates more flexibly than that doctrine. Unconscionability on the part of the party seeking to rely on subsection (1) is the touchstone giving rise to a constructive trust. It will arise where a party led another party to believe that he would obtain an interest in property to another and then stands by while that other party acts to his detriment in reliance on that promise. The knowledge of the disadvantaged party is of less significance. Here Mr Mackie-Conteh induced Mr Kinane to make the loan before the formal documentation was executed. Even though the venture was abortive, Mr Mackie-Conteh benefited therefrom to the extent that he did not have to find another lender to get to the stage where FMBC could produce a letter of credit. The risk of the letter of credit at that stage not meeting the seller's requirements was one which, under the parties' agreement, Mr Mackie-Conteh and not Mr Kinane, had implicitly agreed to bear.

In proprietary estoppel, the court awards a remedy appropriate to satisfy the expectations that the defendant has induced. This need not be an interest in land. However, in my judgment, that is the appropriate remedy in this case and neither counsel has suggested otherwise.

Lord Neuberger

At [46]–[49]

There are observations in the speeches of Robert Walker and Beldam LJJ (with both of whom Clarke LJ agreed) in *Yaxley v Gotts* [2000] Ch. 174, to the effect that facts giving rise to an estoppel, could be sufficient (even if they do not give rise to a trust) to enable a claimant to avoid the rigours of Section 2(1) of the 1989 Act: see at 174F-G and 188F-9G. It is unnecessary to decide in this case whether those observations can survive in light of the reasoning of the House of Lords in *Actionstrength*. For the purposes of this appeal, I am content to assume, in favour of Mr Mackie-Conteh, that it would not be open to Mr Kinane to avoid the consequences of Section 2(1) of the 1989 Act if he could only establish a proprietary estoppel, and not a trust.

There are clearly circumstances which can give rise to an estoppel, but not a trust. This point was made clear by Robert Walker LJ in *Yaxley* at 176D where he said this of "estoppel and the constructive trust":

"Plainly there are large areas where the two concepts do not overlap: when a landowner stands by while his neighbour mistakenly builds on the former's land the situation is far removed (except for the element of unconscionable conduct) from that of a fiduciary who derives an improper advantage from his client."

He then went on to explain at 176E that, in light of cases such as *Gissing v Gissing* [1971] AC 886, it was well established that "the two concepts coincide" "in the area of a joint enterprise for the acquisition of land".

It initially appeared to me well arguable that the nature of the estoppel which could be established by Mr Kinane may not be such as to amount to a constructive trust. There is obviously a conceptual similarity between a person building on another's land in the false belief that he owns it, thereby conferring a benefit on the true owner, and a person who lends money to the owner of land, in the false belief that he has a mortgage over the land. In each case, the true owner of the land receives a benefit at the expense of a person who has spent money in the mistaken belief that he has an interest in the land.

However, I am persuaded that the reasoning, and the authorities cited, in *Yaxley* do lead to the conclusion that a constructive trust was created in the present case.

The case is notable as confirming that while the parties' agreement is void as a contract for non-compliance with s 2, it can, notwithstanding, form the basis of the agreement or assurance of rights for an estoppel claim. As Arden LJ explains, the other elements of estoppel must still be made out. It remains unclear, however, whether the claimant therefore succeeds on the basis of estoppel or constructive trust. Both Arden and Neuberger LJJ appear to adopt a narrow approach to estoppel that echoes Robert Walker LJ's judgment in *Yaxley v Gotts*. Hence, Arden LJ identifies the question as whether Mr Kinane can demonstrate an estoppel 'overlapping' with a constructive trust. Neuberger LJ proceeds on the basis that Mr Kinane's claim would fail under s 2 if he could only establish an estoppel, but not a constructive trust.

Arguably, such a narrow approach is unnecessary. It is beyond doubt that estoppel cannot be used to enforce an otherwise invalid contract.[46] Lord Scott expressed this point in unequivocal terms in an obiter comment in the following case.

Yeoman's Row Management Ltd v Cobbe [2008] 1 WLR 1752, HL

Lord Scott

At [29]

The question arises, therefore, whether a complete agreement for the acquisition of an interest in land that does not comply with the section 2 prescribed formalities, but would be specifically enforceable if it did can become enforceable via the route of proprietary estoppel. It is not necessary in the present case to answer this question [...] My present view, however, is that proprietary estoppel cannot be prayed in aid in order to render enforceable an agreement that statute has declared to be void. The proposition that an owner of land can be estopped from asserting that an agreement is void for want of compliance with the requirements of section 2 is, in my opinion, unacceptable. The assertion is no more than the statute provides. Equity can surely not contradict the statute.

But the purpose of an estoppel claim is not to enforce the parties' agreement. As Arden LJ acknowledges in *Kinane v Mackie-Conteh*, the claim is founded on the prevention of

---

[46] Dixon, 'Invalid Contracts, Estoppel and Constructive Trusts' [2005] Conv 247, 250.

unconscionability, not on the unenforceable agreement.[47] Academic commentators have argued that s 2 should not preclude estoppel claims, even in circumstances under which the estoppel does not overlap with a constructive trust. But differences of opinion remain as to the application of estoppel in this context. McFarlane notes that s 2 has only been raised as a bar to estoppel in cases such as *Yaxley v Gotts* (described in the following extract as 'group 2' cases), in which the lack of formalities alone prevents a contractual claim. The provision has not been raised as a bar in 'group 1' cases, in which a failure of formalities is just one reason preventing a contractual claim.

McFarlane, 'Proprietary Estoppel and Failed Contractual Negotiations'
[2005] Conv 501, 512–3

It is only in Group 2 cases that counsel have argued for s.2's imposing a restriction on the operation of proprietary estoppel. The submission, originally made in *Yaxley v Gotts* but also put in *Kinane v Mackie-Conteh*, is that proprietary estoppel cannot be used to rescue a contract rendered void by virtue of s.2. Such an argument clearly does not apply if, independently of s.2, there is no contract between the parties. However, this argument is flawed. It raises an unacceptable paradox: if s.2 has no effect in the Group 1 cases, why should it bar a claim in the Group 2 cases? Why should B suffer as a result of having come closer to a binding contractual agreement? Once it is accepted that s.2 has no role to play in the Group 1 cases, it must logically follow that it can have no impact in a Group 2 case. [...]

The basic point therefore seems to be that, unless one is prepared to say that the policy of s.2 is strong enough to bar any proprietary estoppel claim based on a belief that B will acquire an interest in A's land, one cannot argue that the policy blocks proprietary estoppel claims in Group 2 cases. Put simply, s.2, which deals with contractual validity, has no effect on proprietary estoppel claims. This conclusion is of course bolstered by the Law Commission's intention, made clear in the Report leading to the 1989 Act, that proprietary estoppel should be available as a means to protect those relying on informal agreements.

Dixon has argued that estoppel should be available in failed agreement cases in which there is a 'double assurance'—that is, where the representor assures the estoppel claimant both that he or she has rights over the representor's land, and that these rights will exist despite non-compliance with statutory formalities.

Dixon, 'Proprietary Estoppel and Formalities in Land Law and the Land Registration Act 2002: A Theory of Unconscionability' in *Modern Studies in Property Law: Vol 2* (ed Cooke, 2003, pp 180–1)

In so far as the general law requires the creation, transfer or enforcement of proprietary rights to be undertaken in a certain form, estoppel can be used to side-step these requirements only when there is a clear justification. That it would be 'unconscionable' for one of the parties to rely on the absence of the formality is that justification. [...] '[U]nconscionability' *can* explain why the absence of formality may be ignored—in the sense that a right still ensues for the claimant—if the concept is tied to the formality rules. Hence, it will be unconscionable

---

[47] *Kinane v Mackie-Conteh* [2005] EWCA Civ 45, [29] (extracted above).

for a representor to withdraw an assurance, relied on to detriment, if the assurance of the right carries with it (expressly or impliedly) a further assurance that the right will indeed be granted despite the absence of the formality that is normally required to create, transfer or enforce it. Thus a successful estoppel can be triggered only by a 'double assurance': an assurance that the claimant will have some right over the representor's land combined with an assurance that the right will ensue even if the formalities necessary to convey the rights are not complied with. It is the withdrawal of the promise of the right after the second assurance (assuming detrimental reliance) that constitutes the unconscionability required for a successful claim in estoppel.

At this stage, the relationship between proprietary estoppel and s 2 remains unresolved.

4 CREATION AND TRANSFER

Once a contract for the sale or other disposition of an interest in land is created, it is executed by the creation or transfer of the interest concerned. As we have noted, once the contract is executed, no question of compliance with s 2 of the LP(MP)A 1989 can be raised. The formality requirements necessary for the creation or transfer of the legal right, and their exceptions, are provided by ss 52 and 54 of the LPA 1925.

Law of Property Act 1925, ss 52 and 54

52 (1) All conveyances of land or of any interest therein are void for the purpose of conveying or creating a legal estate unless made by deed.

(2) This section does not apply to— [. . .]

    (d) leases or tenancies or other assurances not required by law to be made in writing; [. . .]

    (g) conveyances taking effect by operation of law.

54 (1) All interests in land created by parol and not put in writing and signed by the persons so creating the same, or by their agents thereunto lawfully authorised in writing, have, notwithstanding any consideration having been given for the same, the force and effect of interests at will only.

(2) Nothing in the foregoing provisions of this Part of this Act shall affect the creation by parol of leases taking effect in possession for a term not exceeding three years (whether or not the lessee is given power to extend the term) at the best rent which can be reasonably obtained without taking a fine.

Hence, save in exceptional cases, the creation or transfer of a legal right requires the execution of a deed. The effect of non-compliance is that legal title does not pass. The intended recipient of the rights may have a claim in equity. For example, where there is a contract for sale, but s 52 is not complied with, an equitable interest may arise under the doctrine of anticipation (discussed further in Chapter 12).

The most notable exception to the need for a deed is that contained in s 54(2) for short leases. This is limited by the terms of the provision to leases at market rent, without a premium, and taking effect in possession. It has been held that possession must be immediate.[48]

The requirements of a deed are provided in s 1 of the LP(MP)A 1989.

Law of Property (Miscellaneous Provisions) Act 1989, s 1

Deeds and their execution

(1) Any rule of law which—

(a) restricts the substances on which a deed may be written;

(b) requires a seal for the valid execution of an instrument as a deed by an individual; or

(c) requires authority by one person to another to deliver an instrument as a deed on his behalf to be given by deed,

is abolished.

(2) An instrument shall not be a deed unless—

(a) it makes it clear on its face that it is intended to be a deed by the person making it or, as the case may be, by the parties to it (whether by describing itself as a deed or expressing itself to be executed or signed as a deed or otherwise); and

(b) it is validly executed as a deed—

(i) by that person or a person authorised to execute it in the name or on behalf of that person, or

(ii) by one or more of those parties or a person authorised to execute it in the name or on behalf of one or more of those parties.

(2A) For the purposes of subsection (2)(a) above, an instrument shall not be taken to make it clear on its face that it is intended to be a deed merely because it is executed under seal.

(3) An instrument is validly executed as a deed by an individual if, and only if—

(a) it is signed—

(i) by him in the presence of a witness who attests the signature; or

(ii) at his direction and in his presence and the presence of two witnesses who each attest the signature; and

(b) it is delivered as a deed.

(4) In subsections (2) and (3) above "sign", in relation to an instrument, includes

(a) an individual signing the name of the person or party on whose behalf he executes the instrument; and

(b) making one's mark on the instrument,

and "signature" is to be construed accordingly.

(4A) Subsection (3) above applies in the case of an instrument executed by an individual in the name or on behalf of another person whether or not that person is also an individual.

---

[48] *Long v Tower Hamlets LBC* [1998] Ch 197. The implications of the decision are considered by Bright, 'Beware the Informal Lease: The (Very) Narrow Scope of S.54(2) Law of Property Act 1925' [1998] Conv 229.

This section, like s 2 of the 1989 Act concerning contracts, implements recommendations by the Law Commission.[49] It represents a modernization of the requirements for a deed. Under the provision, the key requirements for a document to be a deed are that it is signed and attested, and that it specifies on its face that it is a deed. The specific need for attestation, explained in s 1(3)(a)(i), is that the document is signed '*in the presence of a witness*', who then signs the deed him or herself. This requirement is not met, for example, if a witness who was not present when the party executing the deed signed it signs the document. Non-compliance with this requirement is most likely to be known by the party executing the deed, who may, in any event, be estopped from seeking to invalidate it on this basis.[50]

A deed takes effect when it is 'delivered as a deed'.[51] This will be immediate if the document specifies that it is 'signed and delivered' as a deed; in other cases, there will need to be a subsequent delivery. Delivery originally denoted a physical act, but the requirement has evolved to relate to an intention to be bound.

Vincent v Premo Enterprises (Voucher Sales) Ltd [1969] 2 QB 609, CA

Lord Denning MR

At 619

The law as to "delivery" of a deed is of ancient date. But it is reasonably clear. A deed is very different from a contract. On a contract for the sale of land, the contract is not binding on the parties until they have exchanged their parts. But with a deed it is different. A deed is binding on the maker of it, even though the parts have not been exchanged, as long as it has been signed, [...] and delivered. "Delivery" in this connection does not mean "handed over" to the other side. It means delivered in the old legal sense, namely, an act done so as to evince an intention to be bound. Even though the deed remains in the possession of the maker, or of his solicitor, he is bound by it if he has done some act evincing an intention to be bound, as by saying: "I deliver this my act and deed." He may, however, make the "delivery" conditional: in which case the deed is called an "escrow" which becomes binding when the condition is fulfilled.

Yale doubts the antiquity of this rule, highlighting the artificiality of continued reference to delivery.

Yale, 'The Delivery of a Deed' [1970] CLJ 52, 73–4

It is perhaps too harsh to say that fact has been replaced by fiction, for a man's state of mind is as much a fact as the state of his paper [...] But the element of fiction is truly present in the use of the word "delivery" in the mouths of modern judges. It is not the case that a word of lay usage has been appropriated to an artificial sense for purposes of legal definition and application; it is the case that one legal content has been emptied out of "delivery" and replaced by another. The wine has been changed (for better or for worse) but the bottle bears the same label.

---

[49] Law Commission Report No 163, *Deeds and Escrows* (1987).
[50] *Shah v Shah* [2002] QB 35.
[51] Section 1(3)(b) of the 1989 Act.

Intention becomes significant where, in the ordinary course of transactions, deeds are prepared and signed in advance of an anticipated completion of creation or transfer. Following *Longman v Viscount Chelsea*,[52] a deed that has been signed, but not delivered, may be classified in one of two ways: as an escrow, or as a 'non-deed'.[53]

The different legal consequence of these possibilities was considered in that case.

Longman v Viscount Chelsea (1989) 58 P & CR 189, CA

Nourse LJ

At 195

A writing cannot become a deed unless it is signed, [...] and delivered as a deed. Having reached that stage, it is correctly described as having been "executed" as a deed. Having been signed [...], it may be delivered in one of three ways. First, it may be delivered as an unconditional deed, being irrevocable and taking immediate effect. Secondly, it may be delivered as an escrow, being irrevocable but not taking effect unless and until the condition or conditions of the escrow are fulfilled. Thirdly, it may be handed to an agent of the maker with instructions to deal with it in a certain way in a certain event, being revocable and of no effect unless and until it is so dealt with, whereupon it is delivered and takes effect [...]

Whether a deed is within the second or third category is dependent on the intention of the party executing the deed. In that case, Mrs Longman, who held a long lease of a residential property, had negotiated with her landlord, the Cadogan Estate, for the surrender of her existing lease and the grant of a new one with an extended term. Each part of the transaction required a deed and both parties had signed deeds in preparation for completion. Following delays by the landlord, they then withdrew and made a fresh offer for a new lease at a vastly increased cost. Mrs Longman argued that the deed granting the new lease had been delivered as an escrow and that the remaining conditions had been, or could be, fulfilled. Her claim failed, because there was no intent on the part of the landlord to deliver the deed. This was evident by the fact that the parties' negotiations had been expressly conducted subject to the formal execution of the deeds. The Court was critical of the conduct of the landlord, which was considered 'deplorable',[54] but conscious that, in everyday conveyancing, it is usual for deeds to be signed in advance of completion with no intention of being irrevocable.

Longman v Viscount Chelsea (1989) 58 P & CR 189, CA

Nourse LJ

At 193

[T]he negotiations did not differ in substance from those which are conducted between solicitors all round the country every day of the week. In an area where there has already

---

52 (1989) 58 P & CR 189. The case is discussed further by Clarke, 'Delivery of a Deed: Recent Cases, New Statutes and Altered Practice' [1990] Conv 85.

53 A term used by Sparkes, *A New Land Law* (2nd edn, 2003, [7–08]).

54 (1989) 58 P & CR 189, 199, *per* Taylor LJ.

been some tendency to allow hard cases to make bad law we must recognise that our deci-sion will have equal effect on everyday transactions of varying and unpredictable merits, in respect of which settled and expedient practices ought to be more highly regarded than the merits of individual cases.

5 REGISTRATION OF TITLE

In most cases, the formal transfer of a legal estate is not complete until title is registered.[55] Either the legal title being transferred will already be subject to registration, or the transfer in question will trigger compulsory first registration. Where registration is required, failure to do so carries the consequence that legal title will not be transferred. Title remains with the transferor, although, in the case of a sale, it will be held in trust for the transferee under the doctrine of anticipation discussed in Chapter 12.[56]

Registration of title is now governed by the Land Registration Act 2002 (LRA 2002), which repealed and replaced the Land Registration Act 1925 (LRA 1925). The 2002 Act is based on recommendations by the Law Commission.[57] While the Act is a revolution in its own terms, it also marks the latest stage in the *evolution* of registered land, the origins of which can be traced back to the eighteenth century.[58] Over the course of time, the system has devel-oped from a mechanical means of registration of title, based on the substantive principles of unregistered land law, to an independent system of 'title by registration'.[59]

Cooke, *The New Law of Land Registration* (2003, p 31)

[In] the Land Registration Act 2002 and the Law Commission documents that preceded it we find the divergence of registered from unregistered title affirmed with confidence and reinforced. It has finally been appreciated that title registration can be used to manipulate the nature of title; for the first time we see real legislative enthusiasm for title registration not merely because of its accuracy or its potential benefit to conveyancers, but also because of its ability to change the law relating to land ownership.

5.1 WHY REGISTRATION OF TITLE?

It is common to refer to 'registered land' in contra-distinction to unregistered land, although 'registration of title' is more accurate, because it is titles that are registered. More

---

[55] The scope of registration is discussed below. The principle exception relates to leases of seven years' duration or less.

[56] No trust will be imposed in the case of a transfer by gift as a result of the maxim that 'equity does not complete an incomplete gift'.

[57] Law Commission Report No 271, *Land Registration for the Twenty-First Century: A Conveyancing Revolution* (2001).

[58] The history is traced by Ruoff et al, *Registered Conveyancing* (1986, ch 1).

[59] The Law Commission's Consultation Paper, which preceded the final Report, noted the aim to bring about '*not a system of registration of title but a system of title by registration*': Law Commission Report No 254, *Land Registration for the Twenty-First Century: A Consultative Document* (1998, [10.43]). The clearest illus-tration of the shift to title by registration is found in how the 2002 Act governs claims to adverse possession of registered land. This is considered in Chapter 10.

than one title may subsist in relation to the same piece of land and be registered as separate titles: in particular, a freehold and leasehold. Registration of title is considered desirable, both because of the positive attributes of registration and the defects of alternative systems. Unregistered conveyancing is cumbersome and repetitive: title must be investigated fresh on every transfer through an examination of the title deeds. Registration of title obviates this process by providing a single, updated record of title. An alternative system of deeds registration has successfully been adopted in some jurisdictions, and operated in Yorkshire and Middlesex before being replaced by registration of title.[60] It ensures that an accurate record of deeds is available to investigate title, but maintains the mechanism, and therefore the disadvantages, of unregistered conveyancing.

The 1857 Royal Commission considered registration of title to be the only answer to the following problem:

Royal Commission, *Registration of Title* (1857, 23–4)

By what means, consistently with the preservation of existing rights, can we now obtain such a system of registration as will enable owners to deal with land in as simple and easy a manner, as far as the title is concerned, and the difference in the nature and the subject matter may allow, as they now can deal with movable chattels or stock? No-one doubts that it would be a great benefit to the proprietors of land if they were able to convey it with the same facility as the owners of ships or of stocks or railway shares can now assign their property in any of them. The questions is, can this be accomplished?—and if so how?

The provision of a system of registration of title based on the 1857 Royal Commission report was first provided by the Land Transfer Act 1875.[61] Despite this, even at the time of the 1925 legislation, registered land was still seen as experimental. The intention was to operate both registered and unregistered systems for a ten-year period, before adopting '*whichever system should be found more safe, simple, speedy and economic*'.[62] Although no formal decision on the matter was ever taken, the system of registration was gradually extended.

In replacing the LRA 1925, the primary focus of the LRA 2002 is to lay the foundations for the implementation of e-conveyancing.

Law Commission Report No 271, *Land Registration for the Twenty-First Century: A Conveyancing Revolution*
(2001, [1.5]–[1.6])

The fundamental objective of the Bill is that, under the system of electronic dealing with land that it seeks to create, the register should be a complete and accurate reflection of the state of the title of the land at any given time, so that it is possible to investigate title to land on line, with the absolute minimum of additional enquiries and inspections.

---

60 For further explanation, see Cooke, *The New Law of Land Registration* (2003, pp 5–7). She notes that the system is successfully used within the USA, South Africa, and Scotland.

61 A previous system under the Land Registry Act 1862 had departed from those recommendations and was superseded by the 1875 Act: see Ruoff et al (1986, [1-03]).

62 Ruoff et al (1986, [1-05]).

Although that ultimate objective may seem an obvious one, its implications are considerable, and virtually all the changes that the Bill makes to the present law flow directly from it. [...]

E-conveyancing itself has not yet been achieved (and is discussed in section 6 below), but the changes made to facilitate its introduction are far reaching in their own right.

The Law Commission noted that the legislation called for a shift in attitude and perception.

Law Commission Report No 271, *Land Registration for the Twenty-First Century: A Conveyancing Revolution* (2001, [1.09]–[1.10])

To achieve the goals [of the report] will also require a change in attitude. There is a widely held perception that it is unreasonable to expect people to register their rights over land. We find this puzzling given the overwhelming prevalence of registered title. Furthermore, the law has long required compliance with certain formal requirements for the transfer of interests in land and for contracts to sell or dispose of such interests. The wisdom of these requirements is not seriously questioned. We cannot see why the further step of registration should be regarded as so onerous. In any event, under the system of electronic conveyancing that we envisage (and for which the Bill makes provision), not only will the process of registration become very much easier, but the execution of the transaction in electronic form and its simultaneous registration will be inextricably linked.

These changes will necessarily alter the perception of title to land. It will be the fact of registration and registration alone that confers title. This is entirely in accordance with the fundamental principle of a conclusive register which underpins the Bill.

The changes introduced by the LRA 2002 impact, in particular, on the operation of priority rules in registered land, discussed in Chapter 16, and on adverse possession of registered land, discussed in Chapter 10. We return to evaluate the operation of the 2002 Act in Chapter 17.

5.2 THE PRINCIPLES OF REGISTRATION OF TITLE

Registration of title is not unique to English law. Its introduction matched a parallel development in Australia, in the introduction to New South Wales of the Torrens system of registration, pioneered by Sir Robert Torrens. The principles underlying systems of registered title are identified in the following seminal work.

Ruoff, *An Englishman Looks at the Torrens System* (1957, pp 7–14)

The essential features of every system of registered title are that the State authoritatively establishes title by declaring, under a guarantee of indemnity, that it is vested in a named person or persons, subject to specified incumbrances and qualifications. Anterior defects of title are cured, and thenceforth all investigation of the history of how the named owner came to be entitled is ruled out for ever and all future transactions are carried out by simple forms and simple machinery. No transaction is effective until it has been entered on the official record kept by the State, but once this has happened it cannot (apart from fraud) be upset—that is the broad theory.

It remains for me to indicate what I believe to be the merits or faults of this system. I suggest that in each particular country or state it succeeds or fails according to the degree with which the local law and the local administration accord, or do not accord, with certain fundamental principles. I will call these:

1. The mirror principle.
2. The curtain principle.
3. The insurance principle.

The mirror principle involves the proposition that the register of title is a mirror which reflects accurately and completely and beyond all argument the current facts that are material to a man's title. [...]

The curtain principle is one which provides that the register is the sole source of information for proposing purchasers, who need not and, indeed, must not concern themselves with trusts and equities which lie behind the curtain. [...]

The true [insurance] principle is this, that the mirror that is the register is deemed to give an absolutely correct reflection of title but if, through human frailty, a flaw appears, anyone who thereby suffers loss must be put in the same position, so far as money can do it, as if the reflection were a true one. A lost right is converted into hard cash.

Achieving the 'mirror principle' has been a continuous goal of registration of title. It is reflected in the 'fundamental objective' of the LRA 2002 extracted above. Ruoff acknowledged that '*in this imperfect world the mirror does not invariably give a completely reliable reflection*'.[63] Tension remains, in particular, as regards the balance between the mirror principle and the category of 'overriding interests'—that is, those not entered on the register, but necessarily binding against purchasers. This category of interest is discussed in Chapter 16.

The 'curtain principle' is ensured through the process of overreaching, whereby (as long as certain conditions are met) purchasers take land free from beneficial interests under a trust. The mechanism is discussed in Chapter 20.

The 'insurance principle' is reflected in the provision for payment of an indemnity, now governed by Sch 8 of the 2002 Act, for those suffering loss as a result of a rectification of the register (or a mistake, the correction of which would involve rectification), or through mistakes made by the Land Registry. It is closely connected to the issue of indefeasibility of title, which is discussed below.

5.3 THE SCOPE OF REGISTRATION

When registration of title was first introduced, it operated on a voluntary basis. The Land Transfer Act 1897 was the first to make provision for compulsory registration.

Compulsory registration is a two-stage process: firstly, an area is declared (by Order in Council) to be subject to compulsory registration of title; secondly, title is registered for the first time on the occurrence of an event that triggers registration. Compulsory registration began in London and spread piecemeal. The last remaining districts were made subject to

---

63 Ruoff, *An Englishman Looks at the Torrens System* (1957, Sydney: The Lawbook Co, p 9).

compulsory registration on 1 December 1990.[64] Hence, title to all land in England and Wales is now either registered, or will be registered for the first time on the next triggering event.

Voluntary registration is possible under s 3 of the LRA 2002. To assist in the completion of the register, financial incentives have been provided by the reduction of fees for voluntary registration.[65] The Act further encourages voluntary registration through making a registered title qualitatively superior to its unregistered counterpart[66]—in particular, through its limited vulnerability to claims to adverse possession (discussed in Chapter 10).

It is estimated that as much as 40 per cent of land in England and Wales remains unregistered.[67] Because much of this is likely to be rural land, the percentage of titles that remain unregistered is considerably lower. The Law Commission identified 'total registration' as a goal:[68] '[U]nregistered land has had its day. In the comparatively near future, it will be necessary to take steps to bring what is left of it on to the register.'[69] But the recommendations for the 2002 Act did not include provisions to achieve this goal, for which three reasons were given.[70] Firstly, the Law Commission noted that it would be premature to do so before existing provisions were given the opportunity to work (including an anticipated rise in voluntary registration under the LRA 2002).

Secondly, it was felt that the triggers for compulsory registration catch the principal dispositions of land and extension of compulsion beyond this may be heavy handed.

Thirdly, concerns were expressed at further stretching the Land Registry's resources following the changes introduced by the 2002 Act.

The Law Commission suggested that the matter should be subject to a future review.

5.3.1 Registrable titles and first registration

The scope of registration of title is outlined in s 2 of the LRA 2002.

Land Registration Act 2002, s 2

This Act makes provision about the registration of title to—

(a) unregistered legal estates which are interests of any of the following kinds—

(i) an estate in land,

(ii) a rentcharge,

(iii) a franchise,

(iv) a profit à prendre in gross, and

(v) any other interest or charge which subsists for the benefit of, or is a charge on, an interest the title to which is registered; and

(b) interests capable of subsisting at law which are created by a disposition of an interest the title to which is registered.

---

64 Registration of Title Order 1989, SI 1989/1347.
65 Land Registration Fee Order 2006 (SI No 1332, art 2(6)) provides for a 25 per cent discount.
66 Law Commission Report No 271 (2001, [2.10]).
67 http://www.landregistry.gov.uk/www/wps/portal/PrimaryWebsite.
68 Law Commission Report No 271 (2001, [2.13]).
69 Ibid, [1.6].
70 Ibid, [2.10]–[2.12].

Of most significance is s 2(1)(a), through which registration applies to the two legal estates in land: the freehold and leasehold. As regards leases, ss 2 and 3 (which make provision for first registration of title) limit the application of registration to those of more than seven years' duration. The true scope of registration of title is therefore freeholds and leaseholds of more than seven years' duration. These are the only rights that are subject to compulsory registration. Rentcharges, franchises,[71] and profits *à prendre* in gross[72] may be registered voluntarily, but there is never an obligation to do so. Although economically valuable, these rights are of limited significance in understanding the operation of registered titles and they are not further discussed in this chapter.

Sections 3 and 4 of the LRA 2002 make provision for first registration of title. Section 3 concerns voluntary registration, enabling the proprietor of a freehold and of a lease with more than seven years left to run to apply to have the title registered. Section 4 then identifies the events that trigger compulsory registration.

Land Registration Act 2002, s 4

(1) The requirement of registration applies on the occurrence of any of the following events—

(a) the transfer of a qualifying estate—

(i) for valuable or other consideration, by way of gift or in pursuance of an order of any court, or

(ii) by means of an assent (including a vesting assent); [...]

(c) the grant out of a qualifying estate of an estate in land—

(i) for a term of years absolute of more than seven years from the date of the grant, and

(ii) for valuable or other consideration, by way of gift or in pursuance of an order of any court;

(d) the grant out of a qualifying estate of an estate in land for a term of years absolute to take effect in possession after the end of the period of three months beginning with the date of the grant; [...]

(f) the grant of a lease out of an unregistered legal estate in land in such circumstances as are mentioned in paragraph (b);

(g) the creation of a protected first legal mortgage of a qualifying estate.

(2) For the purposes of subsection (1), a qualifying estate is an unregistered legal estate which is—

(a) a freehold estate in land, or

(b) a leasehold estate in land for a term which, at the time of the transfer, grant or creation, has more than seven years to run.

Hence, registration is compulsory for freehold titles and for leases of more than seven years' duration. The events triggering first registration relate to the transfer of a freehold and the creation or transfer of a lease or mortgage.

---

[71] This category covers certain privileges, such as the grant of a right to hold a market.

[72] A profit is a right to take something from land. It exists in gross where it is not attached to a dominant estate. The category includes, e.g., a right to hunt and shoot game.

5.3.2 Grades of title

On first registration, a freehold estate is registered with absolute, qualified, or possessory title. 'Absolute' title is the usual expectation, and vests the estate in the proprietor subject principally to burdens on the register and overriding interests.[73] 'Qualified' or 'possessory' title may be awarded (respectively) where there is a possible defect in the applicant's title or insufficient documentary proof. Registration is additionally subject to estates, rights, or interests that are excepted from registration (in the case of qualified title), or are subsisting or capable of arising at the date of registration (possessory title).[74]

A fourfold scheme applies to leasehold title.[75] Absolute, qualified, and possessory leasehold titles have analogous effect to those grades of freehold title, with additional provision that they are subject to covenants, obligations, and liabilities in the lease.[76] Absolute leasehold is only available, however, where the freehold is also registered or proved to the satisfaction of the Registrar. Where this is not the case, good leasehold title is granted, leaving open a possible challenge against the estate out of which the lease was granted.[77]

5.3.3 Subsequent dispositions

It is essential that the register is kept up to date. Hence, once a title has been brought onto the register through voluntary or compulsory first registration, subsequent dealings must be completed by registration.

Land Registration Act 2002, s 27

(1) If a disposition of a registered estate or registered charge is required to be completed by registration, it does not operate at law until the relevant registration requirements are met.

(2) In the case of a registered estate, the following are the dispositions which are required to be completed by registration—

  (a) a transfer,

  (b) where the registered estate is an estate in land, the grant of a term of years absolute—

    (i) for a term of more than seven years from the date of the grant,

    (ii) to take effect in possession after the end of the period of three months beginning with the date of the grant,

    (iii) under which the right to possession is discontinuous,

    (iv) in pursuance of Part 5 of the Housing Act 1985 (c. 68) (the right to buy), or

    (v) in circumstances where section 171A of that Act applies (disposal by landlord which leads to a person no longer being a secure tenant),

  (c) where the registered estate is a franchise or manor, the grant of a lease,

---

[73] Land Registration Act 2002, s 11(3)–(5).
[74] Ibid, s 11(6)–(7).
[75] Ibid, s 12.
[76] Ibid, s 12(4).
[77] Ibid, s 12(7).

(d) the express grant or reservation of an interest of a kind falling within section 1(2)(a) of the Law of Property Act 1925 (c. 20), other than one which is capable of being registered under the Commons Registration Act 1965 (c. 64),

(e) the express grant or reservation of an interest of a kind falling within section 1(2)(b) or (e) of the Law of Property Act 1925, and

(f) the grant of a legal charge.

There is a logical symmetry between the scope of registered dispositions and events triggering compulsory first registration. Hence, the transfer of a registered freehold or leasehold title, and the creation of a lease or more than seven years' duration, are all included in the list of registrable dispositions.

It should be noted that the transfer of a registered lease requires registration even if there is less than seven years of the term left to run. The effect of non-compliance is specified in s 27(1): legal title does not pass unless and until completed by registration.[78]

5.4 THE REGISTRATION GAP

Inherent within s 27(1) of the LRA 2002 is the existence of a 'registration gap'—that is, a period between completion of a transfer by execution of a deed and the vesting of legal title by registration. During this period, legal title is held on trust for the purchaser through the doctrine of anticipation discussed in Chapter 12. But the purchaser remains vulnerable to third-party rights arising during this period, or further dealings affecting the title being carried out by the vendor.

Brown & Root Technology Ltd v Sun Alliance and London Assurance Co Ltd [2001] Ch 733, CA

Facts: Brown & Root Technology Ltd (Technology) was registered proprietor of a lease. Clause 8.1 conferred on it a personal break clause, enabling it to bring the lease to an end by notice. Technology assigned the lease to its parent company, B & R, but the assignment was not registered. Under the predecessor to s 27(1) of the 2002 Act in the Land Registration Act 1925, this meant that legal title had not vested in the assignee. Technology sought to exercise the break clause.

Mummery LJ

In my judgment, Technology were entitled, on the correct construction of clause 8.4 of the lease, to serve the notice terminating the lease. [...] My reasons are:

1. Clause 8.4 had two purposes: first, that the right to terminate should be unassignable; secondly, that, if there was an assignment of the lease, the personal right to terminate

---

[78] Under the Land Registration Act 2002, s 74, the entry has effect from the date of the application for registration.

conferred on Technology should cease to have effect. The second purpose is relevant to the resolution of this appeal, which turns on the identification of the precise event occasioning Technology's cesser of the right to invoke the break clause. The critical question is: has there been an assignment of the lease by the lessee and, if so, when did that event occur?

2. It is common ground that there has been no transfer (and therefore no assignment) of the legal title to the lease; that, as between Technology and B & R, the equitable title to the lease was capable of passing by virtue of a specifically enforceable contract to assign the lease; that, if this were unregistered land, the assignment would occur on the execution of the deed of assignment and the conveyance of the legal estate thereby, and not on the conclusion of the contract to assign; and that, depending on the context, the passing of the equitable or beneficial interest may amount to a transfer or assignment of the property in question, even though there has been no registration of the transfer, as required by statute, to perfect the legal title. The judge referred to the cases of *In re Rose* [1949] Ch 78 and *In re Rose* [1952] Ch 499 as instances of a bequest of shares and an inter vivos gift of shares which took effect as between donor and donee and in accordance with donative intent before the registration of the transfers of the shares pursuant to the provisions of the Companies Act. Until registration there was no transfer so far as the company was concerned, but that did not prevent the gift from being effective as between others.

3. This case is not a matter of beneficial ownership between parties to the transfer of the lease: the issue of assignment or no assignment affects the legal position of a third party, the lessors, who have given their licence to assign but are not a party to the transfer. As was observed by Jenkins LJ in *In re Rose* [1952] Ch 499, 518 it is necessary to keep clear and distinct the position between the transferor and the transferee and the position of a third party. Transfer of the beneficial title is not, in this context, relevant to the legal relationship between the lessees and the lessors. The issue is not what rights Technology and B & R have against each other, but what rights Technology and Sun Alliance have against each other. That is a question of legal, not equitable, rights.

4. As between lessors and lessees, there is binding Court of Appeal authority in *Gentle v Faulkner* [1990] 2 QB 267 for the proposition that assignment means, in the absence of a context showing an extended meaning, an assignment of the legal estate, and not of the beneficial interest, e g by declaration of trust of the lease. It is not a matter of intention to assign, a point highly relevant to the passing of beneficial title, but of whether a defined event has occurred. That event is not completion, as Mr Dowding contended; it is the transfer of the legal title to the lease, so as to create the legal relationship of lessor and lessee between B & R and Sun Alliance.

The facts of the case are unusual. The companies were the claimants in the action and had brought proceedings against the landlord, who had refused to accept the exercise of the break clause. Technology was owned by B & R and, following the assignment of the lease, falling rental values meant that the lease was commercially unattractive. B & R's non-registration therefore operated to its advantage. Technology's exercise of the break clause effectively enabled B & R to escape an unwanted lease.

The case illustrates, however, the vulnerability of a purchaser or assignee pending registration. The loss of a property right may, more usually, be the last thing wanted by a purchaser: for example, if the companies were not related and the exercise of the break clause was motivated by spite against the assignee. In such a case, personal remedies may lie against

TITLE NUMBER : CS72510 PROPERTY REGISTER

CORNSHIRE : MARADON

1. (29 August 1974) The Freehold land shown edged with red on the plan of the above Title filed at the Registry and being 23 Cottage Lane, Kerwick, (PL14 3JP).
2. (29 August 1974) The land tinted yellow on the title plan has the benefit of the following rights granted by the Conveyance dated 27 July 1968 referred to in the charges register:—
   "TOGETHER WITH the benefit of a right of way on foot only over that part of the shared accessway belonging to 25 Cottage Lane."
3. (29 August 1974) The land has the benefit of the rights granted by the Transfer dated 21 August 1974 referred to in the Charges Register.

END OF PROPERTY REGISTER

TITLE NUMBER : CS72510 PROPRIETORSHIP REGISTER—ABSOLUTE FREEHOLD

1. (18 December 2001): PROPRIETOR: PETER ANDREW BARTRAM and SUSAN HELEN BARTRAM of 23 Cottage Lane, Kerwick, (PL14 3JP).
2. (18 December 2001) The price stated to have been paid on 3 December 2001 was £128,000.
3. (18 December 2001) Except under an order of the registrar no disposition by the proprietor of the land is to be registered without the consent of the proprietor of the charge dated 3 December 2001 in favour of the Ilkingham Building Society referred to in the Charges Register.

END OF PROPRIETORSHIP REGISTER

TITLE NUMBER : CS72510 CHARGES REGISTER- ABSOLUTE FREEHOLD

1. (29 August 1974) A Conveyance of the land tinted pink on the title plan dated 14 February 1965 made between (1) Archibald Henry Dawson (Vendor) and (2) Thomas Yorke (Purchaser) contains the following covenants:—
   "THE Purchaser hereby covenants with the Vendor so as to bind the land hereby conveyed into whosoever hands the same may come that the Purchaser and his successors in title will not use the premises hereby conveyed for the retail sale of grocery or as a butchers shop."
2. (29 August 1974) The land in this title is subject to the following rights reserved by a Conveyance dated 27 July 1968 made between (1) Maradon Borough Council (Vendor) and (2) John Robertson (Purchaser):—
   "subject to
   (i) An exception and reservation in favour of the Vendor of the right to enter upon the land hereby conveyed for the purpose of constructing a public sewer the approximate line of which is shown coloured red on the plan annexed hereto and at all times hereafter for the purpose of inspecting cleaning repairing or renewing the said sewer."
   NOTE:—The red line referred to is shown by a blue broken line on the title plan.
3. (29 August 1974) A Transfer of the land in this title dated 21 August 1974 made between (1) Henry Smith and (2) David Stanley Charles and Susan Charles contains restrictive covenants.
   NOTE: Copy in Certificate.
4. REGISTERED CHARGE dated 3 December 2001 to secure the moneys including the further advances therein mentioned.
   PROPRIETOR Ilkingham Building Society of 101 Cambridge Street, Ilkingham IL1 3FC.

Figure 5 Sample register (Source: http://www.landregistry.gov.uk, accessed 30 October 2008)

the vendor (or assignor),[79] although the utility of these is dependent on the vendor's where-abouts and ability to pay.

The registration gap will be removed by e-conveyancing, because completion and registration will occur simultaneously.[80] The Law Commission flagged possible solutions to apply in the meantime,[81] but considered that personal liability sufficed.[82]

5.5 OUTLINE OF A REGISTERED TITLE

A sample registered title is provided in Figure 5. Each registered title is given a unique title number. The information recorded is divided into three parts.

- The *property register* identifies the title as freehold or leasehold, and, in the case of a lease, provides brief details of its terms. It identifies the land by a description, usually the address, and by reference to the official plan. It also lists rights that benefit the title, such as the benefit of an easement.

- The *proprietorship register* gives the name and address of the registered proprietor(s) and any restrictions on their ability to deal with the land.[83] It may also state the price paid for the title.

- The *charges register* contains information on registered mortgages and other secured interests, and any other burdens affecting the title: for example, leases, easements, and covenants to which the land is subject.

5.6 INDEFEASABILITY

Ruoff, in the extract at section 5.2 above, identifies as an essential requirement of title registration the idea that, once title is entered on the register, '*it cannot (apart from fraud) be upset*'. This encapsulates both the suggestion that a registered title is indefeasible and that indefeasibility is not absolute, because it is subject to an exception for fraud.

Cooke describes 'indefeasibility' as the affirmative warranty of title provided by registration.[84] The warranty is backed by an indemnity through the insurance principle. The approach adopted to indefeasibility is significant, because it determines how secure a registered title is.

Cooke, *The New Law of Land Registration* (2003, pp 99–100)

The question behind a discussion of indefeasibility, or security, or the affirmative warranty, is: can I be sure that, if I purchase a registered estate, I will be able to keep it without fear that I will lose it because of something already existing that I do not know about? Indefeasibility is a

---

[79] For example, because the legal title is held on trust, an action may lie for breach of trust.

[80] Law Commission Report No 271 (2001, [1.20]).

[81] Law Commission Report No 254 (1998, [11.26]–[11.29]).

[82] Law Commission Report No 271 (2001, [1.20]).

[83] The entry and removal of restrictions is governed by the 2002 Act, ss 40–47. They are considered in Chapter 16.

[84] Cooke (2003, p 99).

policy issue. The shape of the law, and the answer to any ambiguities in it, must depend upon whether preference is to be given to a proprietor of land or to a purchaser; that is, to static or dynamic security. Dynamic security means that the purchaser can be confident that he will get a good title, and this generates a confident market; static security means that someone who owns or has an interest in land can be sure he will not be deprived of it against his will. The two are in tension. If we say that an innocent purchaser P, who has obtained registration of a forged transfer, must be able to keep his land (while compensating O who has lost it due to fraud or forgery by a third party, who of course is not worth suing), P may be happy now, but he will be less happy if another rogue forges P's signature and transfers the land to P2, to whom the same principle will also give a good title, while compensating P. The system must therefore find an acceptable compromise between dynamic and static security; but different systems find the balance at different points.

Cooke argues that determining the approach to indefeasibility is now the 'biggest challenge' for the English system, because the provisions of the 2002 Act leave the matter open to interpretation.[85]

In Torrens systems, two approaches to indefeasibility have been identified: immediate indefeasibility supports dynamic security, by favouring the purchaser's title;[86] deferred indefeasibility supports static security, by giving preference to the former proprietor. Immediate indefeasibility has now been adopted in Australia and New Zealand. Cooke argues that the policy of the LRA 2002 requires a move towards the Torrens system and therefore to immediate indefeasibility[87]—but this is subject to special protection that is provided to a proprietor in possession.[88] The Law Commission termed its approach 'qualified indefeasibility'.[89]

5.6.1 Alteration, rectification, and indemnity

The scheme of the LRA 2002 is to permit, in circumstances specified in Sch 4 to the Act, an 'alteration' of the register. An alteration may be made by order of a court or by the Registrar. The circumstances in which a court or the Registrar may alter the register are the same, except for an additional power on the part of the Registrar to remove superfluous entries.[90] The other circumstances are given in Sch 4, para 2, in relation to a court and in para 3 in relation to the Registrar.

---

[85] Ibid, p 11.

[86] See, however, O'Connor, 'Registration of Title in England and Australia: A Theoretical and Comparative Analysis' in *Modern Studies in Property Law: Vol 2* (ed Cooke, 2003, p 86). She notes that equating dynamic security with protection of purchasers is too simplistic. It also benefits owners because '*Without it, owner's titles can be disturbed years after purchase if a defect in their title or a prior interest comes to light within the relevant limitation period*'.

[87] Cooke (2003, p 101).

[88] Ibid. The term 'proprietor in possession' is defined in s 131 of the 2002 Act. It covers proprietors who are physically in occupation themselves, or where the land is occupied by a party in a specified relationship to the proprietor: e.g., trustees and landlords are treated as proprietors in possession where the land is physically occupied by (respectively) their beneficiaries or tenants.

[89] Law Commission Report No 271 (2001, [10.13]).

[90] Schedule 4, para 5(d), of the 2002 Act.

Land Registration Act 2002, Sch 4, para 2

(1) The court may make an order for alteration of the register for the purpose of—

(a) correcting a mistake,

(b) bringing the register up to date, or

(c) giving effect to any estate, right or interest excepted from the effect of registration.

(2) An order under this paragraph has effect when served on the registrar to impose a duty on him to give effect to it.

The same provision is made for alterations by the Registrar in Sch 4, para 5(a)–(c). 'Rectification' is the term given to one specific type of alteration.

Land Registration Act 2002, Sch 4, para 1

In this Schedule, references to rectification, in relation to alteration of the register, are to alteration which—

(a) involves the correction of a mistake, and

(b) prejudicially affects the title of a registered proprietor.

Rectification is significant in understanding the extent to which a title is indefeasible, because it is an alteration that 'prejudicially affects' the registered title. It is directly linked to the availability of an indemnity under Sch 8 of the 2002 Act.

Land Registration Act 2002, Sch 8, para 1

(1) A person is entitled to be indemnified by the registrar if he suffers loss by reason of—

(a) rectification of the register,

(b) a mistake whose correction would involve rectification of the register, [...]

(2) For the purposes of sub-paragraph (1)(a)— [...]

(b) the proprietor of a registered estate or charge claiming in good faith under a forged disposition is, where the register is rectified, to be regarded as having suffered loss by reason of such rectification as if the disposition had not been forged.

These provisions therefore ensure that where a decision is made as regards the rectification of the register, the party who loses as a result of that decision receives an indemnity. Subparagraph 2(b) precludes an argument that no 'loss' is suffered where rectification is made pursuant to a forged disposition, because such a transaction has no effect.[91] Paragraph 5 of Sch 8 limits the availability of an indemnity to 'innocent' parties.[92]

---

[91] The provision maintains the reversal of *Re Odell* [1906] 2 Ch 47, enacted in the 1925 Act.

[92] Apart from instances of rectification, Land Registration Act 2002, Sch 8, provides for an indemnity to be payable as a consequence of various mistakes, errors, and omissions connected with the register that are not connected to an alteration of the register.

Land Registration Act 2002, Sch 8, para 5

(1) No indemnity is payable under this Schedule on account of any loss suffered by a claimant—

    (a) wholly or partly as a result of his own fraud, or

    (b) wholly as a result of his own lack of proper care.

(2) Where any loss is suffered by a claimant partly as a result of his own lack of proper care, any indemnity payable to him is to be reduced to such extent as is fair having regard to his share in the responsibility for the loss.

The special protection afforded to a proprietor in possession is provided in Sch 4, paras 3 (as regards alterations by a court) and 6 (as regards alterations by the Registrar).

Land Registration Act 2002, Sch 4, para 3

(1) This paragraph applies to the power under paragraph 2, so far as relating to rectification.

(2) If alteration affects the title of the proprietor of a registered estate in land, no order may be made under paragraph 2 without the proprietor's consent in relation to land in his possession unless—

    (a) he has by fraud or lack of proper care caused or substantially contributed to the mistake, or

    (b) it would for any other reason be unjust for the alteration not to be made.

(3) If in any proceedings the court has power to make an order under paragraph 2, it must do so, unless there are exceptional circumstances which justify its not doing so.

(4) In sub-paragraph (2), the reference to the title of the proprietor of a registered estate in land includes his title to any registered estate which subsists for the benefit of the estate in land.

The same provision is repeated in para 6 as regards alterations by the Registrar. Hence, the special protection afforded to the proprietor in possession is limited to rectification (not other alterations of the Registrar) and to the 'innocent' proprietor. A proprietor in possession has no special protection against an alteration that does not constitute rectification. Such an alteration may include amending the register to reflect an easement acquired through prescription, or a right binding against the proprietor as an overriding interest.[93]

5.6.2 Indefeasibility in action

To understand the scope of these provisions and, in particular, the 'qualified indefeasibility' conferred on a proprietor in possession, it is helpful to consider their application to a number of examples. The examples are based on the transfer of a registered title from A to B, or the grant of a registered charge to B. It transpires that the transfer is the result of forgery of A's signature, or fraud conducted against A, which includes the situation in which A signs a

---

[93] Law Commission Report No 271 (2001, [10.7] and [10.16]).

transfer as a result of undue influence. B may be the perpetrator of the forgery or fraud, or may be innocent—the wrong being committed by a third party (typically, a person who was jointly registered proprietor of the title with A).

The distinction between 'forgery' and 'fraud' is a significant one. The special protection afforded to a proprietor in possession applies only in relation to a rectification (Sch 4, para 3) and the register is only rectified if it is altered to correct a mistake (Sch 4, para 1). The availability of an indemnity (in Sch 8) is, in turn, linked to rectification. 'Mistake' is not defined in the LRA 2002. To determine whether a mistake has been made, it is necessary to consider the effect of a transaction as a matter of the general law. A forged transaction is void and does not, under the general law, pass title to B. Hence, if B is entered on the register pursuant to a forged transaction, then there is a mistake, because B did not, in fact, hold title. Removing B from the register constitutes rectification.

But fraud (such as undue influence) renders a transaction voidable by A. Title passes to B under the general law and therefore no mistake is made in registering B as proprietor: B holds the title at the time of registration. If the voidable transfer is rescinded by A, then removing B from the register does not involve rectification. It is an alteration of the register to bring it up to date (within Sch 4, para 2(1)(b)), with the setting aside of the transaction.[94]

With this distinction in mind, the examples can now be discussed. In each case, it is assumed that following B's entry on the register as proprietor, A seeks to be reinstated.

B forges A's signature

The register is rectified to correct the mistake made by B's registration following a void transaction. B's fraud precludes him or her from benefiting from indefeasibility, even if B is now a proprietor in possession (Sch 4, para 3(2)(a)), or from claiming an indemnity (Sch 8, para 5).

B procures A's signature through fraud (such as undue influence)

The effect of the fraud under the general law is that the transaction is voidable and A has an equity to rescind the transaction against B. When the transaction is set aside, the register is altered to bring it up to date. Because there is no rectification here, no issue arises of B being protected as a proprietor in possession or of an indemnity being payable.

A's signature is forged by a third party

The registration of B is a mistake, because it has been made pursuant to a void transaction. Alteration of the register therefore constitutes rectification. If the register is rectified, then B is indemnified under Sch 8, para 1(1)(a); if not, then A is indemnified under Sch 8, para 1(1) (b). Nothing in the terms of Sch 4 dictates the approach to be taken, although immediate indefeasibility (leaving B as registered proprietor) is consistent with the policy identified by Cooke of moving closer to the Torrens system.[95]

The position changes, however, if B is a proprietor in possession. B then benefits from the special protection afforded to proprietors in possession under Sch 4, para 3(2). The register is unlikely to be rectified against B, leaving A to a financial indemnity. This exemplifies the Law Commission's concept of 'qualified indefeasibility'.

---

[94] Law Commission Report No 271 (2001, [10.7], fn 23).
[95] Cooke (2003, p 101).

*A's signature is procured by fraud (such as undue influence)
perpetrated by a third party*

As in the previous example of forgery, there is no mistake in B's registration pursuant to a voidable transaction. There is therefore no rectification of the register and no issue of payment of an indemnity. The register may be altered to bring it up to date within Sch 4, para 2(1) (b), if the transaction is rescinded as against B.

The difference between this situation and that in which the fraud is perpetrated by B relates to the likelihood of rescission being available against B, and therefore to the likelihood of any alteration being made to the register. This, in turn, relates to the operation of the general law on undue influence rather than the statutory provisions on alteration of the register. Rescission will be available against B only if B is 'infected' by the undue influence exerted against A by the third party:[96] for example, if B, a bank, were to fail to take the steps necessary under *Royal Bank of Scotland v Etridge (No 2)*[97] to avoid being infected by undue influence exerted against A by her husband, the third party, in procuring A's signature on a mortgage application.

6 THE FUTURE: E-CONVEYANCING

The fundamental objective of the LRA 2002 (contained in [1.5] of the Law Commission report, extracted in section 5.1 above) is directly connected to the introduction of e-conveyancing. The Law Commission further described providing the framework for its introduction as '*the most important single function*' of the Act.[98]

Harpum, who, as Law Commissioner, was one of the architects of the 2002 Act, notes the close connection between the procedural and substantive changes introduced by the Act, and the political significance of e-conveyancing.

Harpum, 'Property in an Electronic Age' in *Modern Studies in Property Law: Vol 1* (ed Cooke, 2001, p 3)

The mechanisms by which property is transferred are undergoing a revolution, namely, the move from paper-based to dematerialised dealings. [. . .] Because of the time that the business of conveyancing takes and its expense, it has become a significant political issue. These fundamental changes in the ways in which conveyancing is conducted, remarkable though they are in themselves, will necessarily bring equally significant changes in substantive land law in their wake. The substantive law must be harmonised to fit the new conveyancing order.

None of this should come as any great surprise. Changes in the manner in which conveyancing is conducted have in the past acted as a catalyst for much wider changes, both legal and otherwise.

Cooke further describes e-conveyancing as the 'magic carpet' that transported the Bill through Parliament by making it politically attractive.[99]

---

[96] The operation of undue influence is discussed in Chapter 30.
[97] [2002] 2 AC 773.
[98] Law Commission Report No 271 (2001, [13.1]).
[99] Cooke (2003, p 158).

Two observations may be made about the relationship between the substantive and procedural changes provided for by the LRA 2002. The first observation is the scale of the substantive changes, on the one hand, and the uncertainty of the procedural ones, on the other. Despite its centrality to the 'conveyancing revolution' of the Act, e-conveyancing remains a work in progress—but a number of important steps have been taken. There is already electronic access to the register and provision for electronic searches. An electronic application can be made to make non-dispositionary changes to the register (for example, a change of the name of a current registered proprietor), and by a lender to discharge a registered charge. Introduction of the first electronic deed is imminent and will enable mortgages to be registered online.

Secondly, as will be seen, once e-conveyancing is introduced, the relationship between the process of registration and substantive property law is set to change.

6.1 ELECTRONIC DISPOSITIONS: THE LEGAL IMPACT

The legal effect of e-conveyancing is provided in s 93 of the LRA 2002.

Land Registration Act 2002, s 93

(1) This section applies to a disposition of—

   (a) a registered estate or charge, or

   (b) an interest which is the subject of a notice in the register,

where the disposition is of a description specified by rules.

(2) A disposition to which this section applies, or a contract to make such a disposition, only has effect if it is made by means of a document in electronic form and if, when the document purports to take effect—

   (a) it is electronically communicated to the registrar, and

   (b) the relevant registration requirements are met.

As a result of this section, a contract for the disposition of a registered estate and the disposition (for example, a contract to transfer the freehold of a house or to create a lease of more than seven years) has no effect unless made in electronic form.

As Howell notes,[100] up to now registration has been seen as an 'add-on' to pre-existing interests. Rights are transferred under the general law and then registered (with the acquisition of legal title alone dependent on the final step). Hence, in this chapter, it has been possible to discuss separately creation and transfer, on the one hand, and registration, on the other. Under e-conveyancing, such separation of the substantive law and the process of creation or transfer will cease to be possible.

The wording of s 93(2) is to be contrasted with s 27(1), which currently governs paper-based registered dispositions (and the application of which will be superseded by s 93).[101] Under s 27, a disposition '*does not operate*' at law' until registration requirements are met. This enables *equitable* title to pass (through the doctrine of anticipation) as soon as a specifically enforceable contract is in existence. Under s 93(2), a disposition 'only has effect' on registration; there is no qualification to its effect at law.

---

[100] 'Land Law in an E-Conveyancing World' [2006] Conv 553, 563.
[101] Land Registration Act 2002, s 93(4).

The consequence of s 93(2) is that the registration gap that currently exists between creation or transfer and registration is removed: creation or transfer and registration will occur simultaneously. The entry into a contract remains a separate stage, although the contract also becomes an electronic document.

At this stage, the likely response of the courts to the attempt to crush equitable intervention is a matter of speculation. Dixon has suggested that the application of s 91 will result in an 'estoppel boom'.[102]

Dixon, 'Proprietary Estoppel and Formalities in Land Law and the Land Registration Act 2002: A Theory of Unconscionability' in *Modern Studies in Property Law: Vol 2* (ed Cooke, 2003, pp 170–1)

First, it is anticipated that the great majority of proprietary rights will be subject to section 93 LRA 2002 in due course [...] Of course, the point is precisely to ensure that virtually all expressly created rights appear on the register. Thus, if they do not appear, they do not exist and resort to estoppel may be the only hope for a disappointed claimant. Secondly, we cannot assume that all property professionals immediately will understand that material deeds and contracts are to be completely ineffective, and a remedy in negligence will not secure the proprietary right denied by section 93 LRA 2002. Thirdly, registration (ie the act of creation or transfer) will be electronic, and only authorised persons will be able to transact. Thus, not only is it likely that individuals will continue to deal with each other without the benefit of legal advice and hence without understanding the relevant formality rules (as in *Yaxley v Gotts*), even if they did comprehend section 93 LRA 2002, how would they ensure the registration of their right? [...] Fourthly, and perhaps most importantly, it is now clear [...] that an 'estoppel' is a proprietary right capable of binding a third party as an overriding interest [...] Thus, whereas the failed creation or transfer of a proprietary right under the rubric of electronic conveyancing will be of no effect at all (s 93 LRA 2002), and so cannot trigger an 'interest that overrides' [...] a successful estoppel can do just this [...] How tempting then to use estoppel both to acquire the right despite the absence of compliance with sections 91 or 93 LRA 2002 [...] and then when the estoppel is established to ally it with actual occupation to make it binding against a third party. In other words, estoppel may well come to be the single most effective way of creating, transferring and enforcing property rights outside of electronic formalities. The greater the injunction to use electronic measures, the greater the scope for claims in estoppel.

But while acknowledging the possible reticence of the courts to allow perceived injustices to go unchecked, Cooke urges a restrictive approach to estoppel.

Cooke, *The New Law of Land Registration* (2003, pp 163–4)

Law and Equity have fused, but both traditions remain very much alive; the courts' will to intervene when the law works injustice will hardly vanish overnight. What the courts have found very difficult, of course, is the interaction of their equity jurisdiction with statute. It is

---

[102] Dixon, 'Proprietary Estoppel and Formalities in Land Law and the Land Registration Act 2002: A Theory of Unconscionability' in *Modern Studies in Property Law: Vol 2* (ed Cooke, 2003, p 170).

one thing to counter a common law injustice with an equitable maxim and its out-workings; it is quite another to override the expressed will of the legislature in a statute. Yet equity has ancient roots as the response to circumstances that the legislator had not thought of, so that modification of a statute by the courts is not inherently impossible, although the courts have become increasingly reluctant to do it. [...] Will the courts use their equitable jurisdiction, including the law of estoppel, to combat electronic conveyancing and conveyancing provisions? There is a very difficult line to be drawn here. The courts have the power to sabotage the new system, and it is to be hoped that they will find ways to balance the wish to remedy injustice in the individual case with the need to uphold the policy of the statute, reserving estoppel as a means of reversing injustice in cases involving unusual hardship or fraudulent behaviour, and interpreting fraud quite strictly.

6.2 ELECTRONIC DISPOSITIONS: FORMALITIES

As has been seen in section 4 of this chapter, creation or transfer requires a deed, the requirements of which are provided by s 1 of the LP(MP)A 1989. For electronic transactions, this will be superseded by an electronic document.

Land Registration Act 2002, s 91

(1) This section applies to a document in electronic form where—

   (a) the document purports to effect a disposition which falls within subsection (2), and

   (b) the conditions in subsection (3) are met.

(2) A disposition falls within this subsection if it is—

   (a) a disposition of a registered estate or charge,

   (b) a disposition of an interest which is the subject of a notice in the register, or

   (c) a disposition which triggers the requirement of registration, which is of a kind specified by rules.

(3) The conditions referred to above are that—

   (a) the document makes provision for the time and date when it takes effect,

   (b) the document has the electronic signature of each person by whom it purports to be authenticated,

   (c) each electronic signature is certified, and

   (d) such other conditions as rules may provide are met.

(4) A document to which this section applies is to be regarded as—

   (a) in writing, and

   (b) signed by each individual, and sealed by each corporation, whose electronic signature it has.

(5) A document to which this section applies is to be regarded for the purposes of any enactment as a deed.

(6) If a document to which this section applies is authenticated by a person as agent, it is to be regarded for the purposes of any enactment as authenticated by him under the written authority of his principal.

[...]

(10) In this section, references to an electronic signature and to the certification of such a signature are to be read in accordance with section 7(2) and (3) of the Electronic Communications Act 2000 (c. 7).

6.3 ELECTRONIC SIGNATURES

Central to the validity of the document in s 91 of the LRA 2002 is an electronic signature, the operation of which is explained by Capps.

Capps, 'Conveyancing in the 21st Century: An Outline of Electronic Conveyancing and Electronic Signatures' [2002] Conv 443, 447–9

Electronic Signatures are based on what is technically known as dual key cryptography. When an electronic signature is created two "keys" are created with it: a private key and a public key. These keys are mathematical codes that are different from each other, but inextricably linked. The private key remains with the person who owns the electronic signature and is kept secret; whereas the public key is distributed freely. The relevance of these keys to an electronic signature is best explained by way of an example.

X wishes to send Y an email that he wants to sign electronically. He composes the email and electronically signs it by attaching his digital certificate. X also attaches his public key. When X sends the email, his private key encrypts his signature. When the email is received, Y will use X's public key to decode the encrypted signature. Once the signature has been unencrypted, Y will be able to confirm that it was X who sent the email. This confirmation process is known as authentication. If, therefore, X was accepting an offer by Y, then the use of his electronic signature would be the same as signing a contract manually along the dotted line. [...]

Conveyancers will make their public keys available to others involved in a client's property transaction, either by emailing the key on demand or perhaps, by depositing their public key in a database accessible to others involved with the electronic conveyance. This will allow the free exchange of confidential information between parties to a transaction, which ensures that banks and building societies can electronically send copies of mortgage offers and property surveys to the relevant conveyancer; and to allow conveyancers to send copies of contracts to the other side with the confidence that the information is secure.

Security of the private key is a significant consideration. While paper-based conveyancing is also susceptible to fraud, e-conveyancing appears more vulnerable. Firstly, as Cooke notes, electronic forgery removes the need for the manual skill involved in copying a handwritten signature: '*I cannot forge a signature on a paper transfer; I can swipe my card* [containing the private key] *and press the button.*'[103] The authentication (or verification) process referred to by Capps confirms only that the sender had access to the private key. It cannot guarantee that the sender was the holder of the key or was acting honestly at the time.

[103] Cooke (2003, p 164).

Secondly, the private key is only as secure as the computer system on which it is used. It is vulnerable to lapses in security by the holder of the key (for example, in leaving a computer unattended) and to more sophisticated attacks, such as malicious software enabling the signature to be hijacked by a third party.[104]

QUESTIONS

1. Are formality requirements necessary?

2. Assess the role of rectification, collateral contracts, and proprietary estoppel under s 2 of the Law of Property (Miscellaneous Provisions) Act 1989.

3. Compare and contrast a deed, a 'non-deed', and an escrow.

4. What are the key advantages of registration of title?

5. What is the 'registration gap' and how will it be closed by e-conveyancing?

6. What do you understand by 'indefeasibility' of title? To what extent is a title registered under the Land Registration Act 2002 indefeasible?

7. What impact will the introduction of e-conveyancing have on existing formality requirements?

FURTHER READING

Bently and Coughlan, 'Informal Dealings with Land after Section 2' (1990) 10 LS 325

Capps, 'Conveyancing in the 21st Century: An Outline of Electronic Conveyancing and Electronic Signatures' [2002] Conv 443

Cooke, *The New Law of Land Registration* (Oxford: Hart, 2003)

Critchley, 'Taking Formalities Seriously' in Bright and Dewar (eds) *Land Law: Themes and Perspectives* (Oxford: OUP, 1998)

Dixon, 'Proprietary Estoppel and Formalities in Land Law and the Land Registration Act 2002: A Theory of Unconscionability' in *Modern Studies in Property Law: Vol 2* (ed Cooke, Oxford: Hart, 2003)

Grinlinton (ed), *Torrens in the Twenty-First Century* (Wellington: LexisNexis, 2003)

Harpum, 'Property in and Electronic Age' in *Modern Studies in Property Law: Vol 1* (ed Cooke, Oxford: Hart, 2001)

Law Commission Report No 164, *Transfer of Land Formalities for Contracts for Sale etc of Land* (1987)

Law Commission Report No 271, *Land Registration for the Twenty-First Century: A Conveyancing Revolution* (2001)

McFarlane, 'Proprietary Estoppel and Failed Contractual Negotiations' [2005] Conv 501

---

104 Mason and Bohm, 'The Signature in Electronic Conveyancing: An Unresolved Issue' [2003] Conv 460. The authors provide these and other examples of the vulnerability of the electronic signature.

O'Connor, 'Registration of Title in England and Australia: A Theoretical and Comparative Analysis' in *Modern Studies in Property Law: Vol 2* (ed Cooke, Oxford: Hart, 2003)

Ruoff, *An Englishman Looks at the Torrens System* (Sydney: The Lawbook Co, 1957)

Yale, 'The Delivery of a Deed' [1970] CLJ 52

10

INFORMAL METHODS OF ACQUISITION: ADVERSE POSSESSION

CENTRAL ISSUES

1. The principal means of the informal acquisition of legal rights are adverse possession, which enables the acquisition of a legal estate, and rules providing for the informal grant of legal easements.

2. An adverse possession claim has two stages. The first stage—establishing 'adverse possession'—has rules that are common to registered and unregistered land. The second—the consequences of adverse possession—operates differently in relation to registered and unregistered land.

3. Adverse possession has its roots in the concepts of title by possession and relativity of title, combined with the operation of rules on limitation of actions. Its operation reflects ideas underlying unregistered titles.

4. Adverse possession is incompatible with registration of title. The Land Registration Act 1925 sought to align registered land with unregistered land, but the Land Registration Act 2002 has departed from this approach.

5. Under the 2002 Act, it is not possible to acquire title automatically by adverse possession; instead, a claimant has access to a procedure, the outcome of which may be the award of title by registration. The scheme is, however, heavily weighted against claims, except in limited circumstances in which adverse possession is considered still to play a legitimate role.

6. Adverse possession rules have been held to be human rights compliant.

7. Specific issues arise where adverse possession takes place against a leasehold title.

1 INTRODUCTION

In Chapter 3, we saw that legal estates and interests in land can be acquired *dependently*, where they are granted by a person with property rights in land, and *independently*, by the unilateral conduct of the person acquiring the right. In Chapter 9, we considered the formality requirements that govern the dependent acquisition of legal estates and interests. We have seen that the creation of some legal rights is exempt from the statutory formality requirements: in particular, the grant of a lease for a term of three years or less is exempt from the requirement of a deed.[1] Apart from these specific exemptions, however, legal estates and interests cannot be created though informal *dependent* acquisition. Generally, informal dependent acquisition is the provenance of equitable intervention. We consider the acquisition of equitable interests in land in Chapters 11–14 and 18.

Legal rights may, however, be acquired informally through *independent* acquisition. There are two means through which such rights may arise: firstly, the rules of adverse possession, which provide a means of acquiring a legal estate; secondly, a number of doctrines enable the informal acquisition of a legal easement. The basis for the acquisition of a legal estate by adverse possession is *long use*. This basis is shared by *prescription*, which is one of the sources of an informally acquired easement. If a claimant uses land, or exercises a right with the characteristics of an easement over land, for a period of time, then he or she may obtain legal title, or a legal easement, by virtue of that use.

The similarity between adverse possession and prescription begins and ends with their common foundation in long use.[2] The doctrines differ in how long use is analysed as conferring rights. On the one hand, adverse possession has historically viewed long use as having a *negative* effect—of extinguishing previous titles. This remains the case in relation to unregistered land, although, as we will see, the Land Registration Act 2002 (LRA 2002) adopts a different approach to the effect of adverse possession. Prescription, on the other hand, views long use as having a *positive* effect—of implying the grant of a legal easement.

In *Buckingham County Council v Moran*,[3] Nourse LJ explained the essential difference between the claims as being that prescription requires possession 'as of right', while adverse possession concerns possession 'as of wrong'. This, in turn, means that, in prescription, the intention of the grantor may be significant, while, as will be seen, in adverse possession, the focus is on the intention of the claimant.[4] For the remainder of this chapter, our discussion is confined to adverse possession. Prescription and the other doctrines enabling the informal acquisition of legal easements are considered in Chapter 26.[5]

The English law of adverse possession came under close scrutiny in the *Pye* litigation, which plays a central role in this chapter. The first case, the House of Lords' decision in *JA Pye (Oxford) Ltd v Graham*,[6] concerned a successful claim to adverse possession by Mr and Mrs Graham to valuable development land of which Pye was the registered proprietor. Following the loss of its land, Pye brought an action against the UK before the European Court of Human Rights. It argued that the English law on adverse possession was contrary to the European Convention on Human Rights (ECHR) and that, as a result, it should receive financial compensation for the loss of its land. The Grand Chamber of the European Court of Human Rights rejected Pye's claim.[7] The decision of that Court has been discussed

---

[1] Law of Property Act 1925, s 52(2).

[2] A point made judicially in *Lovett v Fairclough* (1991) 61 P&CR 385, 398, *per* Mummery J.

[3] [1990] Ch 623, 644.

[4] Ibid.

[5] A conjoined discussion of the doctrines is provided by Hopkins, *The Informal Acquisition of Rights in Land* (2000, ch 10). For a general discussion of long use and proprietary rights, see Goymour, 'The Acquisition of Rights in Property by the Effluxion of Time' in *Modern Studies in Property Law: Vol 4* (ed Cooke, 2007).

[6] [2003] 1 AC 419.

[7] *JA Pye (Oxford) Ltd v UK* (App No 44302/02) [2008] 1 EHRLR 132.

in Chapter 5, but it is necessary to return to the decision in this chapter in order to place it in the context of the substantive laws challenged by *Pye* and how those laws have been changed by the LRA 2002.

2 IS ADVERSE POSSESSION JUSTIFIED?

We have noted that the basis on which rights are acquired by adverse possession is long use. As Howard and Hill explain, this is not an obvious basis for conferring rights on a claimant.

Howard and Hill, 'The Informal Creation of Interests in Land'
(1995) 15 LS 356, 372–3

The fact that a claimant has enjoyed a gratuitous benefit for a period in excess [of the statutory requirements] is not in itself a justification for allowing the claimant to continue to enjoy that benefit. If, for example, a newsagent does not object when each week a stranger comes into his shop and takes a Sunday newspaper without paying for it, does the passage of time enable the stranger to assert a right to a Sunday newspaper when the newsagent's good-nature is finally exhausted?

Why, then, is long use seen as sufficient to confer a legal right in land?

Holmes[8] suggested that what lies at the heart of justifications is '*the deepest instincts of man*'. He explained: '*A thing which you have enjoyed and used as your own for a long time [...] takes root in your being and cannot be torn away without your resenting the act and trying to defend yourself, however you came by it.*'[9] Holmes emphasized the need to look at limitation rules from the position of the person who gains a right, not that of the 'loser'. In this respect, long use has a 'curative' effect[10] through which the courts clothe fact with right.

Hopkins, *The Informal Acquisition of Rights in Land* (2000, p 219)

The initial difficulty in justifying [adverse possession and prescription] stems from a perspective of seeing them as "taking" from the legal owner. The difficulties become less apparent if the rules are viewed in terms of "confirming" to [the claimant] that he has the rights he has been exercising. The rules ensure that formal ownership of land reflects actual occupation and use. Reality is given preference above formal legal ownership.

Dockray[11] discussed four reasons why adverse possession is needed. Adverse possession forms part of the general law of limitation of actions—that is, rules that place a long stop on the time during which a claimant may commence proceedings to assert his or her rights.

---

8 'The Path of the Law' (1897) 10 Harv LR 457, 477.
9 Ibid.
10 Goodman, 'Adverse Possession of Land: Morality and Motive' (1970) 33 MLR 281.
11 'Why Do We Need Adverse Possession?' [1985] Conv 272.

Therefore, Dockray took as a starting point the general justifications for the operation of limitation periods, drawn from the Law Reform Committee.

Law Reform Committee 21st Report, *Final Report on Limitation of Actions*
(1977, Cmnd 6923, [1.7])

[...]

1. to protect defendants from stale claims

2. to encourage plaintiffs not to sleep on their rights; and

3. to ensure that a person may feel confident, after the lapse of a given period of time, that an incident which might have led to a claim against him is finally closed.

Dockray concluded that these objectives themselves, while relevant, do not fully explain the limitation of actions to recover land. The rules of adverse possession do not operate in a manner that is wholly consistent with any of the three objectives, while, in relation to the third, there is also insufficient evidence that it has influenced the development of the law. Dockray suggested that a fourth objective is at work, which he identified as facilitating the investigation of title to unregistered land.[12]

Dockray, 'Why do we Need Adverse Possession?' [1985] Conv 272, 277–8

To outline the policy, it is necessary to start by recalling that a vendor of unregistered land is obliged nowadays (subject to contrary agreement) to prove his title over a period of at least 15 years starting from a good root. However, as Professor J.T. Farrand points out in *Contract and Conveyance*, this does not require the vendor to give anything like a complete history, the account may not be of ownership at all, some third party being the true owner all the time.

But if this is possible why, it might be asked, does the legislation only require (and why are purchasers generally content only to require) a vendor to prove his title over a minimum period of 15 years. The answer, according to the theory on which the Statute of Limitations is based, is that this is because it is reasonably safe to do so, And it is reasonably safe to do so, according to the same theory, because the Statute was designed to and does provide a kind of qualified guarantee that any outstanding claims to ownership by third parties are time-barred.

The Law Commission considered this to be the 'strongest justification' for adverse possession.[13] The identification of this objective is significant, because, if the justification is rooted in the operation of unregistered land, an obvious question arises as to its applicability in registered land. As we will see, the incompatibility of adverse possession with principles of registered land resulted in significant reforms in the LRA 2002.

---

[12] See also Goodman (1970, 282–3).

[13] Law Commission Report No 254, *Land Registration for the Twenty-First Century: A Consultative Document* (1998, [10.9]–[10.10]).

3 AN OUTLINE OF THE OPERATION OF ADVERSE POSSESSION

Adverse possession has its roots in the concept of relativity of title[14] and the operation of limitation periods. The paradigm case, on which the following explanation is based, is adverse possession by the claimant (C) in unregistered land, of which the title, traced through the title deeds, belongs to the paper owner (PO). In English law, there is no concept of absolute title: title is relative and is based on possession. In a dispute between two parties, the court determines which party has the stronger claim to possession. As soon as C enters into adverse possession, he or she obtains a freehold title to the land. In Chapter 3, section 4, we saw that the idea of possession providing a means of independent acquisition of property rights applies both to land and personal property. In this case, it is C's possession alone that generates his or her freehold.

Swadling, 'Property' in *English Private Law* (2nd edn, ed Burrows, 2007, [4.414]–[4.417])

The mere act of taking possession—*occupatio* is the Roman term– bestows a right to exclusive possession, a title good against the whole world save a person with a better title. This is true of all things capable of being physically possessed, viz land and goods. In the leading case of *Armory v Delamirie* a chimney-sweep's boy acquired a right to exclusive possession of a brooch merely by the act of taking possession of it. Pratt CJ said:

[T]he finder of a jewel, though he does not by such finding acquire an absolute property or ownership, yet he has such a property as will enable him to keep it against all but the rightful owner and consequently may maintain trover.

The words 'against all but the rightful owner' are not perfectly accurate. As between the goldsmith who refused to return the brooch and the boy, the boy had the better right to possession, because he had the earlier factual possession. As between the boy and the title-holder of the house where it was found, it is likely that the latter would have had the better title, not because he was 'the rightful owner', but because his possession of his house included possession of the brooch in the chimney and antedated the possession obtained by the boy.

Asher v Whitlock teaches the same lesson in relation to land. The mere act of taking possession of a parcel of land gives the actor a right to exclusive possession of that land good against all save those with a superior right to possession. It should be stressed that the interest acquired by the possessor in a case such as *Armory v Delamirie* or *Asher v Whitlock* is legal and not equitable, for both cases involved successful actions in common law courts.

Logically, the freehold title obtained by possession should be classified as legal. As Swadling notes, both cases that he discusses arose in common law courts—but some doubt as to the classification of the right has been expressed.[15]

---

[14] For a general analysis of this concept in property law, see Fox, 'Relativity of Title at Law and in Equity' (2006) 65 CLJ 330.

[15] The different views are summarized by Cooke, 'Adverse Possession: Problems of Title in Registered Land' (1994) 14 LS 1, 4–5.

C's right to possession is stronger than that of any subsequent possessor, but is vulnerable to earlier claims. Hence, PO can bring an action against C to recover the land, relying on its earlier claim to possession evidenced by the paper title. In other words, in a dispute between the parties, PO has the relatively stronger title. But s 15 of the Limitation Act 1980 provides a twelve-year limitation period for actions to recover land. If PO does not take action within that time, then its claim is time-barred. Section 17 of the Limitation Act 1980 provides that, once time-barred, PO's title is extinguished. There is no transfer of PO's title to C. Once the limitation period has expired, however, the title that C obtained by the inception of adverse possession becomes unimpeachable by PO (and anyone claiming through PO's title).

The acquisition of title by adverse possession therefore consists of two distinct stages: firstly, the inception of adverse possession; and secondly, the operation of limitation rules at the end of the requisite period of adverse possession. The principles applying to the inception of adverse possession apply uniformly to registered and unregistered land. Differences emerge, however, in the operation of limitation rules. The concept of title being acquired by possession and extinguished at the end of the limitation period makes no sense in the context of registered land. In registered land, as we have seen in Chapter 9, titles are acquired by registration. A registered title is indefeasible and could not be 'extinguished' for so long as the proprietor is registered as holder of the estate. The Land Registration Act 1925 (LRA 1925) sought to align registered land with the operation of adverse possession in unregistered land. Hence, it enabled title to be acquired automatically in registered land by adverse possession, using the device of a trust to reconcile the extinguishment of a title with registered land principles. The LRA 2002 provides a significant departure from the previous law. There is no concept of title being acquired by adverse possession, or of a limitation period at the end of which the assertion of title is automatically time-barred. Instead, adverse possession provides access to a procedure though which the claimant may acquire title by registration.

In the next part of this chapter, we consider the rules governing the inception of adverse possession; these rules remain applicable to all claims. We will then consider the effect of adverse possession: by the operation of limitation rules in unregistered land and registered land under the LRA 1925, and the new scheme provided for registered land by the LRA 2002. We then consider the human rights challenge to adverse possession and, finally, specific issues that arise where adverse possession is commenced against the holder of a leasehold title.

4 THE INCEPTION OF ADVERSE POSSESSION

The key date to identify is the date at which a cause of action accrues against the paper owner. In unregistered land (and registered land under the LRA 1925), that is the date from which the limitation period begins to run.[16] In registered land, under the LRA 2002, that is the date from which a person is treated as being in adverse possession.[17] The events that trigger the accrual of a right of action are provided by the Limitation Act 1980.

---

[16] Limitation Act 1980, s 15(1).
[17] Land Registration Act 2002, Sch 6, para 11.

Limitation Act 1980, Sch 1, paras 1 and 8

1 Where the person bringing an action to recover land, or some person through whom he claims, has been in possession of the land, and has while entitled to the land been dispossessed or discontinued his possession, the right of action shall be treated as having accrued on the date of the dispossession or discontinuance.

8 (1) No right of action to recover land shall be treated as accruing unless the land is in the possession of some person in whose favour the period of limitation can run (referred to below in this paragraph as 'adverse possession'); and where under the preceding provisions of this Schedule any such right of action is treated as accruing on a certain date and no person is in adverse possession on that date, the right of action shall not be treated as accruing unless and until adverse possession is taken of the land.

Hence the inception of adverse possession is dependent on demonstrating either dispossession of the paper owner or its discontinuance in possession. In the latter case, it will be necessary to show separately that the claimant has moved into adverse possession. In relation to the former, as will be seen below, the commencement of adverse possession by the claimant is inherent in the definition of dispossession.

Discontinuance arises where 'the person in possession abandons possession and another then takes it'.[18] Discontinuance in *possession* is not demonstrated by discontinuance in physical *occupation*; rather, it is analogous to abandonment of land. In *Powell v McFarlane*,[19] Slade J noted that 'merely very slight acts by an owner in relation to the land are sufficient to negative discontinuance'. Dispossession arises by 'a person coming in and putting another out of possession'.[20]

The meaning of dispossession was considered by the House of Lords in the following case, the facts of which it is useful to set out at this stage. In this case, whether the Grahams had dispossessed Pye was identified as one of two key issues that determined the outcome of the case.[21]

JA Pye (Oxford) Ltd v Graham [2003] 1 AC 419, HL

Facts: Pye was the registered proprietor of development land that adjoined the Graham's farm. The land was enclosed by hedges, except for a gate, to which the Grahams held the only key, and a public footpath and highway. Pye had initially granted the Grahams a short grazing agreement to use the land. On the expiry of the agreement, Pye refused a request for renewal, because it was concerned that the existence of an agreement could adversely affect its application for planning permission. The Grahams continued to use the land for their farm, including uses that went beyond the original agreement. Initially, the Grahams continued to seek a renewal of the licence, but their requests went unanswered. Pye did nothing in relation to the land and the Grahams argued that they had acquired title by adverse possession. The House of Lords considered that the claim depended on whether the Grahams had dispossessed Pye (there being no suggestion

---

18 *Powell v McFarlane* (1979) 38 P&CR 452, 468, *per* Slade J.
19 Ibid.
20 Ibid.
21 [2003] 1 AC 491, [27]–[28].

that Pye had discontinued in possession) and, if so, whether the Grahams had remained in possession for the requisite limitation period.

Lord Browne-Wilkinson

At 36

[...] The question is simply whether the defendant squatter has dispossessed the paper owner by going into ordinary possession of the land for the requisite period without the consent of the owner. [...]

At 38

It is sometimes said that ouster by the squatter is necessary to constitute dispossession: see for example *Rains v Buxton* (1880) 14 Ch D 537, 539 *per* Fry J. The word "ouster" is derived from the old law of adverse possession and has overtones of confrontational, knowing removal of the true owner from possession. Such an approach is quite incorrect. There will be a "dispossession" of the paper owner in any case where (there being no discontinuance of possession by the paper owner) a squatter assumes possession in the ordinary sense of the word. Except in the case of joint possessors, possession is single and exclusive. Therefore if the squatter is in possession the paper owner cannot be. If the paper owner was at one stage in possession of the land but the squatter's subsequent occupation of it in law constitutes possession the squatter must have "dispossessed" the true owner for the purposes of Schedule 1, paragraph 1 [...]

Hence, in a case of dispossession, the right of action accrues at the date at which the claimant commences possession. Therefore, the answer to the question of whether the Grahams had dispossessed Pye lay in determining whether the Grahams could establish that they were in possession of the land.

Before considering the meaning of 'possession', it is useful to consider the definition of 'adverse'.

4.1 'ADVERSE' POSSESSION DEFINED

A claimant's possession is not adverse if he or she is present with the licence of the paper owner. In the following case, a claim to adverse possession failed, because the paper owner had unilaterally granted a licence.

BP Properties Ltd v Buckler (1988) 55 P & CR 337, CA

Facts: The appellant's parents had been in adverse possession of their home by remaining in occupation at the end of their lease. An order of possession was obtained within the limitation period, but was not enforced. BP Properties then purchased the freehold and wrote to Mrs Buckler, informing her that she could remain in the property rent-free for her life. Mrs Buckler neither accepted nor rejected the terms of the letter. Following her death, the appellant sought to establish that his parents had obtained title by adverse possession.

Dillon LJ

At 346–7

The claim that a unilateral licence can stop time running is a new one. It may be of some general importance in that it would enable a person who is not prepared to incur the obloquy of bringing proceedings for possession, or of enforcing a possession order, to keep his title alive for very many years until it suits him to evict. It might be thought that for title to be kept alive in this way was contrary to the policy of the statute as exemplified by section 13 of the 1939 Act which reproduced earlier statutory provision to the same effect and prevented any right of action to recover land being preserved by formal entry or continual claim.

So far as the facts are concerned, it would in my judgment be artificial to say that Mrs. Buckler "accepted" the terms set out in the two letters; B.P. Properties Ltd. neither sought nor waited for her acceptance. It would be equally artificial to say that there was any consideration in law for those terms.

It may be that the result would have been different if Mrs. Buckler had, as soon as she learned of the letters, plainly told B.P. Properties Ltd. that she did not accept the letters, and maintained her claims to be already the owner of the property; she did not however do that. She accepted her solicitors' advice that as the warrant for possession had been withdrawn, she should do nothing while the 12-year period from the date of the possession order of December 11, 1962 expired. In essence she was not asserting during the time from the receipt of the letters until after December 11, 1974—or indeed thereafter—any claim to ownership of the farmhouse and garden, or any intention to exclude the owner of the paper title.

Whether B.P. Properties Ltd. could or could not in law, in the absence of consideration have sought to determine in her lifetime the licence granted to Mrs. Buckler by the two letters, they did not in fact seek to do so. Had they sought to do so, they would in the absence of any repudiation of the letters by Mrs. Buckler have had to give Mrs. Buckler a reasonable time to quit as with any licensee.

The nature of Mrs. Buckler's possession after receipt of the letters cannot be decided just by looking at what was locked up in her own mind. It must depend even more, on this aspect of the case, on the position as seen from the standpoint of the person with the paper title. What could that person have done? The rule that possession is not adverse if it can be referred to a lawful title applies even if the person in possession did not know of the lawful title; the lawful title would still preclude the person with the paper title from evicting the person in possession. So far as Mrs. Buckler was concerned, even though she did not "accept" the terms of the letters, B.P. Properties Ltd. would, in the absence of any repudiation by her of the two letters, have been bound to treat her as in possession as licensee on the terms of the letters. They could not have evicted her (if they could have done so at all) without determining the licence.

I can see no escape therefore from the conclusion that, whether she liked it or not, from the time of her receipt of the letters, Mrs. Buckler was in possession of the farmhouse and garden by the licence of B.P. Properties Ltd., and her possession was no longer adverse within the meaning of section 10 of the 1939 Act.

The paper owner in that case therefore expressly granted the licence.

In the following case, the Court of Appeal considered that, in certain circumstances, a licence could be implied, thus defeating a claim to adverse possession on the basis that the claimant's possession is not 'adverse'.

Wallis's Cayton Bay Holiday Camp Ltd v Shell-Mex and BP Ltd [1975] 1 QB 94, CA

Facts: Shell-Mex had acquired land fronting the proposed site of a new road. The owners of the holiday camp had used the land as a farm and subsequently as a frontage to their camp. When the Council abandoned plans for the road, Shell-Mex wrote to the Wallises, offering to sell the land to them. The Wallises did not reply to this or a subsequent letter, but waited until their use exceeded twelve years, whereupon they argued that they had obtained title by adverse possession.

Lord Denning MR

At 103

When the true owner of land intends to use it for a particular purpose in the future, but meanwhile has no immediate use for it, and so leaves it unoccupied, he does not lose his title to it simply because some other person enters on it and uses it for some temporary purpose, like stacking materials; or for some seasonal purpose, like growing vegetables. Not even if this temporary or seasonal purpose continues year after year for 12 years, or more: see *Leigh v. Jack* (1879) 5 Ex.D. 264; *Williams Brothers Direct Supply Ltd. v. Raftery* [1958] 1 Q.B. 159; and *Tecbild Ltd. v. Chamberlain* (1969) 20 P. & C.R. 633. The reason is not because the user does not amount to actual possession. The line between acts of user and acts of possession is too fine for words. The reason behind the decisions is because it does not lie in that other person's mouth to assert that he used the land of his own wrong as a trespasser. Rather his user is to be ascribed to the licence or permission of the true owner. By using the land, knowing that it does not belong to him, he impliedly assumes that the owner will permit it: and the owner, by not turning him off, impliedly gives permission. and it has been held many times in this court that acts done under licence or permitted by the owner do not give a licensee a title under the Limitation Act 1939. They do not amount to adverse possession

In *Pye v Graham*, the decision in the *Wallis's* case was seen as stemming from a concept of 'non-adverse possession': arising where a claimant entered into possession of the paper owner's land, but did not 'oust' the paper owner by carrying out acts inconsistent with the paper title.[22] The general concept of non-adverse possession was removed from English law by the Real Property Limitation Act 1833 and the House of Lords considered that it had not been reintroduced by a 'side wind' by the specific requirement of 'adverse possession' in Sch 1, para 8, of the Limitation Act 1980 (or its predecessor in the Limitation Act 1939).[23] The specific manifestation of the concept in the *Wallis's* case was reversed by the Limitation Act 1980.

Limitation Act 1980, Sch 1, para 8(4)

(4) For the purpose of determining whether a person occupying any land is in adverse possession of the land it shall not be assumed by implication of law that his occupation is by

---

22 [2003] 1 AC 419, [33].
23 Ibid, [32].

permission of the person entitled to the land merely by virtue of the fact that his occupation is not inconsistent with the latter's present or future enjoyment of the land.

This provision does not preclude the implication of a licence in a genuine case, but ensures that a licence is not implied merely by reason of the fact that the adverse possessor's actions are not inconsistent with the paper owner's intended use of the land.

The implication of a licence where the adverse possessor's acts are not inconsistent with the intended use of the land by the paper owner received a brief revival in *Beaulane Properties Ltd v Palmer*.[24] In that case, the court held that the operation of adverse possession in registered land under the Land Registration Act 1925 was contrary to the ECHR. As a result, the court was required, by s 3 of the Human Rights Act 1998 (HRA 1998), to interpret the law, as far as possible, in a manner consistent with the Convention. The court considered that this could be achieved by interpreting adverse possession for the purposes of the LRA 1925 as requiring acts inconsistent with the paper owner's intended use—that is, the manner in which adverse possession would have been understood at the time that the 1925 statute was enacted.[25] On the facts of the case, the claimant had not used the land in a manner inconsistent with the paper owner's title and it was therefore held that his possession was not adverse to that of the paper owner. Judge Nicholas Strauss QC noted the House of Lords' warning in *Pye v Graham* (above) against the reintroduction of the concept of 'non-adverse possession', but considered that the House of Lords did not have in mind the possibility of that interpretation being required under the HRA.

Subsequent to *Beaulane Properties Ltd v Palmer*, it has been established by a decision of the European Court of Human Rights that the operation of adverse possession under the LRA 1925 is, in fact, compatible with the Convention. This litigation is discussed at section 5.4 below. Although *Beaulane Properties* has not formally been overruled, the finding of incompatibility in that case should not now be followed. In the absence of such a finding, there can be no justification for the reintroduction of the concept of non-adverse possession.

4.2 'POSSESSION' DEFINED

As has been noted, in *Pye v Graham*, the House of Lords considered that the Grahams would establish that they had dispossessed Pye by demonstrating that they had entered into possession of the land. This, in turn, raised the question of the meaning of 'possession'.

Defining this term forms the bedrock of case law on adverse possession. Although the term is being defined for a particular purpose, Green argues that the courts are influenced by, and construct, a particular concept of landowner.

Green, 'Citizens and Squatters' in *Land Law: Themes and Perspectives*
(eds Bright and Dewar, 1998, p 230)

In each case of adverse possession, the judges have to decide whether what the claimant did to the land amounts to possession of it. In making these decisions, they are, little by little,

---

[24] [2006] Ch 79.
[25] Ibid, [213].

fleshing out the character and activities of 'the landowner', while at the same time his pre-existing mythical figure is affecting their decisions. This is because such mythical figures as 'the landowner' 'resonate across space and over time' to anchor a philosophy of having and being 'which can influence events, behaviour and perception'. The judges are thus stabiliz-ing and making transparent the boundaries not only on the surface of the land but also in the ideology of ownership.

In *Pye v Graham*, the House of Lords confirmed that 'possession' is to be understood in the *'ordinary sense of the word'*.[26] The House of Lords defined it in a manner closely following an analysis by Slade J in *Powell v McFarlane*.[27]

JA Pye (Oxford) Ltd v Graham [2003] 1 AC 419, HL

Lord Browne-Wilkinson

At 40

[There] are two elements necessary for legal possession: (1) a sufficient degree of physical custody and control ("factual possession"); (2) an intention to exercise such custody and control on one's own behalf and for one's own benefit ("intention to possess"). What is cru-cial is to understand that, without the requisite intention, in law there can be no possession. [...] [There] has always, both in Roman law and in common law, been a requirement to show an intention to possess in addition to objective acts of physical possession. Such intention may be, and frequently is, deduced from the physical acts themselves. But there is no doubt in my judgment that there are two separate elements in legal possession. So far as English law is concerned intention as a separate element is obviously necessary. Suppose a case where A is found to be in occupation of a locked house. He may be there as a squatter, as an overnight trespasser, or as a friend looking after the house of the paper owner during his absence on holiday. The acts done by A in any given period do not tell you whether there is legal possession. If A is there as a squatter he intends to stay as long as he can for his own benefit: his intention is an intention to possess. But if he only intends to trespass for the night or has expressly agreed to look after the house for his friend he does not have possession. It is not the nature of the acts which A does but the intention with which he does them which determines whether or not he is in possession.

It is necessary to address each of these elements separately—that is the approach taken by the courts in determining claims to adverse possession—but it should be borne in mind at the outset that the two are closely interconnected.

Green, 'Citizens and Squatters' in *Land Law: Themes and Perspectives* (eds Bright and Dewar, 1998, pp 235–6)

In reality, the human body and mind, actions and thoughts, are fully interdependent: interpret-ation of the one is dependent on an understanding of the other. An ambiguous action may be

---

26 [2003] 1 AC 419, [36]–[39].
27 (1979) 38 P&CR 452, 470.

given unambiguous meaning when viewed in the light of the intention with which it is done, and the interpretation of an action which appears to have an unequivocal meaning may be changed by the additions of a particular human will. On their own, neither actions nor intentions have any necessary meaning.

[...] The real key to adverse possession lies not in discrete acts and intentions but in the effect of the claimant on the object of the claim (the land), and on the world beyond.

As we will see, ultimately, a claimant's acts provide the strongest evidence of his or her intent. Indeed, such is the connection between them that there is some doubt as to whether intent, in fact, exists as a free-standing element.

4.2.1 Factual possession

In *Pye v Graham*, the House of Lords approved a definition of factual possession given by Slade J in the following case.

Powell v McFarlane (1979) 38 P & CR 452, HC

Facts: The claimant, Mr Powell, lived on a farm with his grandparents. As a 14-year-old boy, he had started to use neighbouring land for purposes connected with the farm. In particular, he cut hay and made 'rough and ready' repairs to the boundary fence, so that the land could be used to graze the family's cow. The paper owner, Mr McFarlane, was working overseas and, on his return, Mr Powell argued that he had obtained title to the land by adverse possession.

Slade J

At 470–1

Factual possession signifies an appropriate degree of physical control. It must be a single and [exclusive] possession, though there can be a single possession exercised by or on behalf of several persons jointly. Thus an owner of land and a person intruding on that land without his consent cannot both be in possession of the land at the same time. The question what acts constitute a sufficient degree of exclusive physical control must depend on the circumstances, in particular the nature of the land and the manner in which land of that nature is commonly used or enjoyed. In the case of open land, absolute physical control is normally impracticable, if only because it is generally impossible to secure every part of a boundary so as to prevent intrusion. [...] Everything must depend on the particular circumstances, but broadly, I think what must be shown as constituting factual possession is that the alleged possessor has been dealing with the land in question as an occupying owner might have been expected to deal with it and that no-one else has done so.

Mr Powell's claim to adverse possession failed on the basis that he could not demonstrate an intention to possess (that aspect of the case is considered below). No specific findings were made in relation to factual possession. In *Pye v Graham*, it was held that the Grahams were in occupation of the land with exclusive physical control. Pye was physically excluded by the hedges and by the lack of a key to the only gate.[28] Therefore, factual possession was established.

---

[28] [2003] 1 AC 419, [41].

4.2.2 Intention to possess

In *Pye v Graham*, the House of Lords approved the decision in *Buckinghamshire County Council v Moran*,[29] in which an intention to possess had been distinguished from an intention to 'own'.[30] Adopting the formulation of the judge at first instance, the Court of Appeal in *Moran* held that what is required is '*not an intention to own or even an intention to acquire ownership but an intention to possess*'.[31] The distinction had been significant on the facts of that case. The council had acquired the disputed land for future use as part of a road. The land adjoined the claimant's garden and he used the land as an extension of his garden. The only access to the land was through the claimant's garden, or by a gate, which the claimant had locked. The claimant had conceded that he would have been obliged to leave the land if it was required for the road. This may have defeated an intention to 'own' the land, but it did not preclude the claimant demonstrating that he intended to possess the land, for the time being, to the exclusion of all others.[32]

Similarly, in *Pye v Graham*, the Grahams' willingness to enter into another agreement with Pye and to pay for the use of the land may have defeated an intention to own, but did not preclude an intention to possess. Lord Browne-Wilkinson explained: '[An] *admission of title by the squatter is not inconsistent with the squatter being in possession in the meantime.*'[33]

It is necessary to show an intention to exclude the world at large, including the paper owner.[34] For the duration of the limitation period, however, the claimant remains vulnerable to the paper owner's assertion of its stronger title. With this in mind, the requirement of intention was reformulated in *Powell v McFarlane*, in a manner approved by the House of Lords in *Pye v Graham*.[35]

Powell v McFarlane (1979) 38 P & CR 452, HC

Slade J

At 471–2

What is really meant, in my judgment, is that, the *animus possidendi* involves the intention, in one's own name and on one's own behalf, to exclude the world at large, including the owner with the paper title [. . .] so far as is reasonably practicable and so far as the processes of the law will allow.

As has been noted, in *Powell v McFarlane*, the claim to adverse possession failed on the basis of intention. Slade J considered Mr Powell's acts to be equivocal, in the sense that they

---

[29] [1990] Ch 623.

[30] This formulation was rejected by Tee, who argued that an intention to own should be required: 'Adverse Possession and the Intention to Possess' [2000] Conv 113. Her argument is countered by Harpum and Radley-Gardner, 'Adverse Possession and the Intention to Possess: A Reply' [2001] Conv 155.

[31] [1990] Ch 623, 643.

[32] Ibid, 642–3.

[33] [2003] 1 AC 419, [46].

[34] *Littledale v Liverpool College* [1990] 1 Ch 19, 23. For examples of cases that have failed on this point, see *Battersea Property Co v London Borough of Wandsworth* [2001] 19 EG 148 (no intention to exclude the world where the claimant provided access to the land to holders of allotments) and *Batt v Adams* [2001] 32 EG 90 (claimant did not intend to exclude the person that he wrongly believed to be the paper owner).

[35] [2003] 1 AC 419, [43].

were open to interpretation as demonstrating intent merely to use the land for so long as the paper owner took no steps to prevent the use, without intending to appropriate the land.[36] The claimant's age at the time that his acts began appeared to be a significant consideration in this regard.[37] Subsequently, Mr Powell had erected signs on the land and parked lorries on it in connection with his business. Slade J acknowledged that, at that later stage, the claimant may have established an intention to possess, but these acts occurred within the limitation period.

In *Pye v Graham*, the House of Lords held that the Grahams could establish an intention to possess. In continuing to use the land at the expiry of the original grazing agreement, they had acted in a way that they knew to be contrary to the wishes of Pye. They had made such use of the land as they had wished, including for purposes beyond the scope of the original grazing agreement. In essence, the Grahams had used the land '*for all practical purposes* [...] *as their own and in a way normal for an owner to use it*'.[38]

How to prove intent, and the relationship between intent and factual possession, remains unclear. In *Powell*, as has been seen, the failure of intent related directly to the nature of the claimant's acts: his acts were not sufficient, in qualitative terms, to establish intent. Further, it appears that the only way in which Mr Powell could have established intent would have been to show that he had done more. Slade LJ indicated that little weight would be afforded to self-serving declarations by a claimant as to his or her intent.[39] Similarly, in *Pye v Graham*, the claimants succeeded in establishing intent because their acts were qualitatively strong: they had used the land as an owner would. This gives rise to the question of whether intent is a free-standing requirement or is simply derived from the claimant's acts.

In *Pye v Graham*,[40] Lord Browne-Wilkinson acknowledged that intent may be deduced by the claimant's physical acts. Lord Hutton suggested that where the claimant makes full use of the land as if he or she were the owner, the claimant's conduct is sufficient to establish intent. The burden then shifts to the paper owner to provide evidence that points to the contrary.[41] In *Powell v McFarlane*, Slade J suggested that 'unequivocal' acts by the claimant established intent, unless the paper owner could demonstrate otherwise. Such acts include enclosure, which has been described as the strongest evidence of intent,[42] the cultivation of agricultural land, placing and enforcing 'keep out' notices, and locking or blocking the only means of access.[43] Where the claimant's acts are equivocal (as they were considered to be in that case), the claimant will need to adduce additional evidence to demonstrate his or her intent.[44]

On the face of it, this suggests that, in some cases, intent will be determined by reference to the claimant's acts, while in others, the claimant will be invited positively to prove his or her intent. Given the courts' (understandable) reticence to give weight to self-serving statements by claimants as to their intent, however, it is difficult to know what evidence, other than the claimant's acts, could be adduced.

[36] (1979) 38 P&CR 452, 478.

[37] Ibid, 480.

[38] [2003] 1 AC 419, [61], *per* Lord Browne-Wilkinson.

[39] (1979) 38 P&CR 452, 476.

[40] At [40] of his judgment extracted above.

[41] [2003] 1 AC 419, [75]–[76].

[42] *Seddon v Smith* (1877) 36 LT 168. See further the discussion of enclosure in *Buckingham County Council v Moran* [1990] Ch 623 and *Powell v McFarlane* (1979) 38 P & CR 452.

[43] (1979) 38 P & CR 452, 478.

[44] Ibid; *Pye v Graham* [2003] 1 AC 419, [76].

Radley-Gardner questions whether intent is, in fact, a free-standing requirement. He distinguishes between 'strong' will theory (in which intent is a free-standing requirement) and 'weak' will theory (in which intent is derived from the claimant's acts).

Radley-Gardner, 'Civilized Squatting' (2005) 25 OJLS 727, 745–7

It has to be said that the flirtations in English adverse possession cases with the 'strong' intentions theory, requiring animus as a discrete component, have not been successes. This has been a back-door method for introducing inquiries as to motive into the post-1833 law to inject some moral fibre into what has been described as 'a major inducement to steal land'. Yet such inquiries are irrelevant to the operation of possession, which is a question of fact and not morality. [...]

A weaker form of animus can, however, produce beneficial results. The unhappy consequences of stronger will theories might make a weaker version of animus more attractive, in which it is treated not as an independent component requiring separate proof, but rather arises as a rebuttable presumption arising from conduct. This would be beneficial in those rare cases where a squatter makes a statement against his own interest, denying that he intended to be in possession. In cases of that nature, there is no practical reason why the court should not deny possession. [...] Except, then, in this attenuated form, where the squatter effectively waives his possession, conduct alone should be the crux of possession in English law.

In *Purbrick v London Borough of Hackney*,[45] Neuberger J emphasized the need to assess the claim on the basis of what the claimant has done. The fact that the claimant could have done more does not defeat a claim if what he or she has done is sufficient to demonstrate factual possession and an intention to possess.

Similarly, in *Topplan Estates v Townley*,[46] the claimant's acts were sufficient to establish intent even though his use of the land did not change following the expiry of a previous grazing agreement, which, on its terms, purported not to grant possession. The acts fell to be assessed on their own merits and were not 'diluted or denatured' by reference to the parties' previous dealings.[47]

4.2.3 The rule in *Leigh v Jack*

We have seen that, in the *Wallis's* case, the Court of Appeal held that a licence would be implied where a person enters into possession, but does not act in a manner inconsistent with the holder of the paper title, although that decision has since been reversed by Sch 1, para 8(4), of the Limitation Act 1980. The *Wallis's* case was based on a more specific doctrine derived from *Leigh v Jack*.[48] In that case, it was held that there is no 'dispossession' of the paper owner by a claimant whose acts are not inconsistent with the paper owner's future use of the land. On the facts, the claimant's use of land for storage connected with his business was held not to constitute a dispossession of the paper owner, because the acts were not inconsistent with the paper owner's intention to dedicate the land to the public as a

---

[45] [2003] EWHC 1871, [20]–[23].
[46] [2004] EWCA 1369.
[47] Ibid, [79], *per* Jonathan Parker LJ.
[48] (1879) 5 Ex D 264.

road. Doubt has been expressed about whether this rule is reversed by Sch 1, para 8(4), of the Limitation Act 1980,[49] but it has been held, in any event, to be wrong as a matter of law.[50]

The underlying difficulty with the rule is that the sufficiency of the claimant's acts is made dependent upon the paper owner's intent. In this way, the rule focuses on the intention of the paper owner and not the intention of the adverse possessor. In *Pye v Graham*, Lord Browne-Wilkinson commented that '*the suggestion that the sufficiency of the possession can depend on the intention not of the squatter but of the true owner is heretical and wrong*'.[51] This is not to say, however, that the paper owner's intended use of the land is invariably irrelevant.

JA Pye (Oxford) Ltd v Graham [2003] 1 AC 419, HL

Lord Browne-Wilkinson

At 45

The highest it can be put is that, if the squatter is aware of a special purpose for which the paper owner uses or intends to use the land and the use made by the squatter does not conflict with that use, that may provide some support for a finding as a question of fact that the squatter had no intention to possess the land in the ordinary sense but only an intention to occupy it until needed by the paper owner. For myself I think there will be few occasions in which such inference could be properly drawn in cases where the true owner has been physically excluded from the land. But it remains a possible, if improbable, inference in some cases.

In this way, Lord Browne-Wilkinson refocused *Leigh v Jack* on the intention of the claimant: the paper owner's intended use of the land may be relevant, but only to the extent that it sheds light on the intention of the claimant. The decision on the facts of *Leigh v Jack* is generally considered to have been correct. It has been suggested that either the paper owner was not dispossessed, because he had continued to carry out repairs to a fence,[52] or that the adverse possessor, who was aware of the intended use of the land, thereby fell short of demonstrating factual possession or an intention to possess.[53]

5 THE EFFECT OF ADVERSE POSSESSION

As has been noted, the effect of adverse possession differs between unregistered land, registered land claims governed by the LRA 1925, and registered land claims governed by the LRA 2002.

5.1 UNREGISTERED LAND

Unregistered land displays the purity and simplicity of the operation of adverse possession in a system of relative titles. The general limitation period of twelve years is provided in

[49] Dockray, 'Adverse Possession and Intention II' [1982] Conv 345.
[50] *Pye v Graham* [2003] 1 AC 419, [45].
[51] Ibid.
[52] Ibid.
[53] *Buckingham County Council v Moran* [1990] Ch 623, 639–40.

s 15 of the Limitation Act 1980. Once adverse possession has continued for the twelve-year limitation period, the paper owner's title is extinguished by the operation of limitation of actions.

Limitation Act 1980, s 17

[...] at the expiration of the period prescribed by this Act for any person to bring an action to recover land (including a redemption action) the title of that person to the land shall be extinguished.

The twelve-year period may be completed by a single adverse possessor, or by two or more adverse possessors in succession: for example, where one adverse possessor is him or herself dispossessed by another before the expiry of the twelve-year period. At this stage, the adverse possessor's title is relatively superior to that of the paper owner, or persons claiming title through the paper owner.[54] There is no 'statutory conveyance' of the paper owner's title to the adverse possessor.[55] The effect of the statute is entirely negative.

Fairweather v St Marylebone Property Co Ltd [1963] AC 510, HL

Lord Radcliffe

At 535

It is necessary to start, I think, by recalling the principle that defines a squatter's rights. He is not at any stage of his possession a successor to the title of the man he has dispossessed. He comes in and remains in always by right of possession, which in due course becomes incapable of disturbance as time exhausts the one or more periods allowed by statute for successful intervention. His title, therefore, is never derived through but arises always in spite of the dispossessed owner.

The adverse possessor acquires an independent freehold title from the time at which he or she commenced adverse possession. The effect of the limitation rules, combined with relativity of title, is that the adverse possessor's title becomes inviolable by the paper owner. But the adverse possessor is not a purchaser for value of the land and therefore will be bound by pre-existing property rights affecting the paper owner's title: for example, the adverse possessor is bound by any easements or restrictive covenants affecting use of the land.[56]

Exceptions to the operation of the twelve-year limitation period are provided in a number of special cases, including: the mental incapacity of the paper owner;[57] fraud and

---

[54] In a case of successive adverse possessors, where C1 is dispossessed by C2, C1's title remains superior to that of C2 for twelve years from the date of dispossession. This is a consequence of relativity of title, discussed at section 3 of this chapter.

[55] *Tichborne v Weir* (1892) 67 LTR 735, 737.

[56] *Re Nisbet and Potts Contract* [1906] 1 Ch 386.

[57] Limitation Act 1980, s 28. A paper owner who is under a disability when the right of action accrues and regains capacity after the twelve-year limitation period had expired has six years from the time at which he

concealment on the part of the adverse possessor and cases of mistake;[58] acts between parties to a trust of land;[59] Crown lands and the foreshore.[60] Further, a period of adverse possession is ended by an acknowledgment of the paper owner's title.[61]

5.2 REGISTERED LAND: LAND REGISTRATION ACT 1925

As has been noted, the LRA 1925 sought to align registered land with the operation of adverse possession in unregistered land. Registered land was subject to the same limitation rules, except the extinguishment of title was replaced by s 75 of the Act.

Land Registration Act 1925, s 75

(1) The Limitation Acts shall apply to registered land in the same manner and to the same extent as those Acts apply to land not registered, except that where, if the land were not registered, the estate of the person registered would be extinguished, such estate shall not be extinguished but shall be deemed to be held by the proprietor for the time being in trust for the person who, by virtue of the said Acts, has acquired title against any proprietor, but without prejudice to the estates and interests of any other person interested in the land whose estate or interest is not extinguished by those Acts.

(2) Any person claiming to have acquired a title under the Limitation Acts to a registered estate in the land may apply to be registered as proprietor thereof.

(3) The registrar shall, on being satisfied as to the applicant's title, enter the applicant as proprietor either with absolute, good leasehold, qualified or possessory title, as the case may require, but without prejudice to any estate or interest protected by any entry on the register which may not have been extinguished under the Limitation Acts, and such registration shall, subject as aforesaid, have the same effect as the registration of a first proprietor; but the proprietor or the applicant or any other person interested may apply to the court for the determination of any question arising under this section.

At first sight, the imposition of a trust appears to be an expedient means of reconciling the idea of title being extinguished with registered land principles. As Cooke notes:[62] '[A] *trust is the English lawyer's natural response to a situation where true ownership and paper title diverge.*' In fact, however, the Law Commission noted that a trust was not necessary. All that was required was provision for the adverse possessor to apply for registration.[63]

---

or she regains capacity to bring an action. This is subject to a long stop of thirty years from the date at which the right of action accrued.

58 Limitation Act 1980, s 32. The limitation period commences from the date at which the claimant discovers the fraud, concealment, or mistake, or could have done so through reasonable diligence. Beyond concealment, there is no obligation on the part of the adverse possessor to bring its acts to the attention of the paper owner. See, e.g., *Topplan Estates Ltd v Townley* [2004] EWCA 1369, [85]–[86].

59 Limitation Act 1980, Sch 1, para 9, prevents a right of action accruing in favour of one beneficiary or a trustee against another beneficiary.

60 Limitation Act 1980, Sch 1, para 10, provides for a thirty-year limitation period for adverse possession against the Crown and para 11 provides for a sixty-year period in relation to the foreshore.

61 Limitation Act 1980, s 29. See, e.g., *Lambeth LBC v Bigden* (2001) 33 HLR 478 and *Lambeth LBC v Archangel* (2001) 33 HLR 490.

62 *The New Law of Land Registration* (2003, p 136).

63 Law Commission Report No 254 (1998, [10.27]).

The imposition of a trust was a source of confusion. It had the potential to confer a windfall on the adverse possessor, by providing a choice of enforcing his or her rights against the land, or enforcing personal liability against the dispossessed registered proprietor as trustee.[64] More generally, the trust raised questions as regards the relationship between the adverse possessor and the registered proprietor.

Cooke, 'Adverse Possession: Problems of Title in Registered Land' (1994) 14 LS 1, 3–4

Indeed, the whole concept of a trust, once its fiduciary implications are explored, begins to feel very uncomfortable. We are accustomed to trusts imposed upon a trustee against his will and even, initially, without his knowledge, in the context of resulting and constructive trusts. But in such cases the trust operates to prevent injustice to an innocent and often vulnerable beneficiary. To impose a trust, with the same implications and consequences, on the dispossessed proprietor to protect the erstwhile trespasser seems inappropriate [. . .]

A separate issue arising from the imposition of the trust is the nature of the interest acquired by the adverse possessor. In registered land, as in unregistered land, the claimant obtains a freehold title from the inception of the adverse possession. This title is independent from the title held by the registered proprietor. Once the trust is imposed by s 75(1) of the LRA 1925, however, the adverse possessor necessarily has a beneficial interest in the registered proprietor's estate. Therefore, the adverse possessor of registered land appears to have two distinct interests in the land: the independently acquired freehold title, and a beneficial interest in the registered proprietor's estate.[65]

As Cooke explains, this has consequences for understanding the nature of the right with which the adverse possessor should be registered if he or she applies under s 75(2) of the LRA 1925.

Cooke, 'Adverse Possession: Problems of Title in Registered Land' (1994) 14 LS 1, 5–6

Once the limitation period has expired, the well-advised squatter will apply to be registered as proprietor. As we have seen, under s 75(2) 'any person claiming to have acquired a title under the Limitation Acts to a registered estate in the land may apply to be registered as proprietor thereof.'

Does 'thereof' mean 'of the land' or 'of the registered estate to which he claims to have acquired title'? In either case, does it mean that X is to be registered as proprietor 'of the fee simple arising by adverse possession' or 'of X's already registered estate, to which he has the equitable title by virtue of the trust imposed by s 75'?

In unregistered land, there is no question of the squatter's acquiring the dispossessed owner's estate by a 'parliamentary conveyance.' The fact that it is land registry practice to give S a new title number indicates that S is getting something new, and that he is being registered with title to his own independent fee simple so as to mirror his position in unregistered land. This is of course what the position should be.

---

[64] Ibid, [10.30].
[65] Cooke, 'Adverse Possession: Problems of Title in Registered Land' (1994) 14 LS 1, 5.

It is debatable whether the 1925 Act provided for a parliamentary conveyance. The opening of a new title by the Land Registry suggests that this is not the case. Under the LRA 1925 (as in unregistered land cases), the adverse possessor obtained an independent freehold title, although he or she remained bound by property rights affecting the previous registered title.[66] The final closing of the registered proprietor's title produced a result analogous to the extinction of an unregistered title.

Notwithstanding, in *Fairweather v St Marylebone Property Co Ltd*,[67] a case involving unregistered land, Lord Radcliffe suggested obiter that s 75 of the LRA 1925 achieved a parliamentary conveyance. This analysis was subsequently taken in a first instance decision involving registered land.[68] But both of those cases concerned adverse possession against a leasehold estate. Specific difficulties arise in that context, which we return to consider below.

The LRA 2002 preserves the rights of adverse possessors acquired under the 1925 Act, but removes the s 75 trust. That section is repealed (without any saving) and transitional provisions are provided in Sch 12 of the 2002 Act.

Land Registration Act 2002, Sch 12, para 18

(1) Where a registered estate in land is held in trust for a person by virtue of section 75(1) of the Land Registration Act 1925 immediately before the coming into force of section 97, he is entitled to be registered as the proprietor of the estate.

(2) A person has a defence to any action for the possession of land (in addition to any other defence he may have) if he is entitled under this paragraph to be registered as the proprietor of an estate in the land.

The LRA 2002 came into force on 13 October 2003. As a result of Sch 12, para 18(1), the rights of a claimant who had completed twelve years of adverse possession (so that the s 75(1) trust had come into existence) on or before 12 October 2003 are preserved. The trust is removed by the repeal of s 75 of the 1925 Act, but the adverse possessor retains the right (originally conferred by s 75(2)) to be registered as proprietor. The entitlement to be registered as proprietor 'of the estate' confirms that a statutory transfer takes place.

5.3 REGISTERED LAND: LAND REGISTRATION ACT 2002

The LRA 2002 provides a new scheme of adverse possession. The scheme applies to adverse possessors in registered land who had not completed twelve years of adverse possession on or before the 12 October 2003.[69] It marks a clean break from attempting to transplant the operation of adverse possession in unregistered land into registered land. Instead, it takes as its starting point the underlying principle that, in registered land, registration alone confers

---

[66] Land Registration Act 1925, s 75(3), extracted above.
[67] [1963] AC 510, 542.
[68] *Central London Commercial Estates Ltd v Kato Kagaku Co Ltd* [1998] EWHC 314.
[69] It is not necessary that the title was registered throughout the period of adverse possession: Land Registration Act 2002, Sch 6, para 1(4). Hence the scheme will apply where a claimant enters into possession of unregistered land, but the title is registered before being extinguished by the expiry of the limitation period.

title, and seeks to provide a more appropriate balance between the registered proprietor and adverse possessor.[70]

The Law Commission explains the aims of the scheme.

Law Commission Report No 271, *Land Registration for the Twenty-First Century: A Conveyancing Revolution* (2001, [14.6])

The aims of the scheme are as follows.

1. Registration should of itself provide a means of protection against adverse possession, though it should not be unlimited protection. Title to registered land is not possession-based as is title to unregistered land. It is registration that vests the legal estate in the owner and that person's ownership is apparent from the register. The registered proprietor and other interested persons, such as the proprietor of a registered charge, are therefore given the opportunity to oppose an application by a squatter to be registered as proprietor.

2. If the application is not opposed, however, whether because the registered proprietor has disappeared or is unwilling to take steps to evict the squatter, the squatter will be registered as proprietor instead. This ensures that land which has (say) been abandoned by the proprietor, or which he or she does not consider to be worth the price of possession proceedings, will remain in commerce.

3. If the registered proprietor (or other interested person) opposes the registration, then it is incumbent on him or her to ensure that the squatter is either evicted or his or her position regularised within two years. If the squatter remains in adverse possession for two years after such objection has been made, he or she will be entitled to apply once again to be registered, and this time the registered proprietor will not be able to object. In other words, the scheme provides a registered proprietor with one chance, but only one chance, to prevent a squatter from acquiring title to his or her land. The proprietor who fails to take appropriate action following his or her objection will lose the land to the squatter.

4. Consistently with the approach set out above, a registered proprietor who takes possession proceedings against a squatter will succeed, unless the squatter can bring him or herself within some very limited exceptions.

It will be apparent from this summary that one of the essential features of the scheme is that it must produce a decisive result. Either the squatter is evicted or otherwise ceases to be in *adverse* possession, or he or she is registered as proprietor of the land.

Under the 2002 Act, there is no concept of title being acquired by adverse possession or of a limitation period barring the assertion of a registered proprietor's title. Sections 15 and 17 of the Limitation Act 1980, which provide the twelve-year limitation period for an action to recover land, and 'extinguish' title at the end of that period, are disapplied in relation to registered land.[71] Instead, the completion of a minimum of ten years' adverse possession[72]

---

[70] Law Commission Report No 254 (1998, [10.43]); Law Commission Report No 271, *Land Registration for the Twenty-First Century: A Conveyancing Revolution* (2001, [14.4]).

[71] Land Registration Act 2002, s 96.

[72] Ibid, Sch 6, para 1, extracted below. The adoption of ten years as the requisite period reflects separate recommendations made by the Law Commission for reform of limitation of actions: Law Commission Report No 271 (2001, [14.19]).

enables the claimant to access a procedure that will result in one of two outcomes: either with the claimant acquiring title to the land *by registration* (not by adverse possession itself); or with the assertion of title by the registered proprietor. Where the adverse possessor acquires title, there is a 'statutory transfer' of the registered proprietor's estate.

Sch 6 of the LRA 2002 provides the scheme. We will first outline the operation of the procedure and then assess the impact of the 2002 Act on adverse possession.

5.3.1 The new scheme of adverse possession

Land Registration Act 2002, Sch 6, paras 1–4

1 (1) A person may apply to the registrar to be registered as the proprietor of a registered estate in land if he has been in adverse possession of the estate for the period of ten years ending on the date of the application. [...]

2 (1) The registrar must give notice of an application under paragraph 1 to—

(a) the proprietor of the estate to which the application relates,

(b) the proprietor of any registered charge on the estate,

(c) where the estate is leasehold, the proprietor of any superior registered estate,

(d) any person who is registered in accordance with rules as a person to be notified under this paragraph, and

(e) such other persons as rules may provide.

(2) Notice under this paragraph shall include notice of the effect of paragraph 4.

3 (1) A person given notice under paragraph 2 may require that the application to which the notice relates be dealt with under paragraph 5.

(2) The right under this paragraph is exercisable by notice to the registrar given before the end of such period as rules may provide.

4 If an application under paragraph 1 is not required to be dealt with under paragraph 5, the applicant is entitled to be entered in the register as the new proprietor of the estate.

By virtue of Sch 6, adverse possession has no effect unless or until an application for registration is made. Adverse possession must have been maintained for at least ten years immediately prior to the application. Further, the applicant must generally have completed the adverse possession; successive periods of adverse possession by different squatters cannot be added together.[73] This ensures that if the adverse possessor succeeds in obtaining registration, his or her title is not vulnerable to challenge by a prior possessor. Security of the adverse possessor's title is preferred over the continued recognition of relativity of title, consistent with the underlying acceptance that title is based on registration, not possession. The general period of ten years provided in para 1(1) is subject to exceptions: in particular, an application cannot be made against a registered proprietor who is incapacitated by mental

---

[73] This is in contrast to the position in unregistered land explained at section 5.1 above. Successive periods of adverse possession were also possible in registered land under the 1925 Act. Limited exceptions to the bar on successive periods of adverse possession are provided by the 2002 Act, Sch 6, para 11(2). This includes where the applicant is the successor in title to a previous adverse possessor. For further discussion of these, see Law Commission Report No 271 (2001, [14.20]–[14.21]).

disability.[74] Applications relating to Crown foreshore land can be made only after a period of sixty years' adverse possession.[75]

Once an application for registration is made, the registered proprietor (and the other persons specified in para 2) are notified of the application by the Registrar. The onus then shifts to the registered proprietor to take steps to assert his or her title by issuing a counter-notice requiring the application to be dealt with under para 5. The period that has been provided in which the registered proprietor can do so under para 3(2) is sixty-five business days from the date of issue of the notification.[76] If the proprietor fails to issue a counter-notice within that period, then, by para 4, a statutory transfer of the estate is affected to the adverse possessor. The adverse possessor thereby acquires title to the land by registration.

If a counter-notice is issued, then (save in three exceptional cases in para 5, discussed below) the application for registration is rejected. Under para 6, the registered proprietor has two years in which to commence proceedings for possession of the land. If no such proceedings are commenced within that period, then the adverse possessor may make a further application for registration.[77] This application does not instigate a new system of notifications. On making this application, the adverse possessor is immediately entitled to be registered as proprietor of the estate.[78]

The exceptional circumstances, in which the adverse possessor's application will be successful despite the issue of a counter-notice, are given in para 5(2)–(4).

Land Registration Act 2002, Sch 6, para 5(2)–(4)

(2) The first condition is that—

  (a) it would be unconscionable because of an equity by estoppel for the registered proprietor to seek to dispossess the applicant, and

  (b) the circumstances are such that the applicant ought to be registered as the proprietor.

(3) The second condition is that the applicant is for some other reason entitled to be registered as the proprietor of the estate.

(4) The third condition is that—

  (a) the land to which the application relates is adjacent to land belonging to the applicant,

  (b) the exact line of the boundary between the two has not been determined under rules under section 60,

  (c) for at least ten years of the period of adverse possession ending on the date of the application, the applicant (or any predecessor in title) reasonably believed that the land to which the application relates belonged to him, and

  (d) the estate to which the application relates was registered more than one year prior to the date of the application.

---

[74] Land Registration Act 2002, Sch 6, para 8(2). Other exceptions are provided for registered proprietors who are enemies or are detained in enemy territory.

[75] Ibid, Sch 6, para 13.

[76] Land Registration Rules 2003 (SI 2003/1417), r 189.

[77] Land Registration Act 2002, Sch 6, para 6(1).

[78] Ibid, para 7.

The third of these is the only true exception. In each of the other situations, the underlying assumption is that the adverse possessor, in fact, has a separate claim to the land.[79] The third exception reflects what the Law Commission acknowledged to be a legitimate conveyancing justification for adverse possession in registered land.[80] The register is not conclusive as to boundaries and therefore there is no conflict with the concept of title by registration to enable adverse possession to be used to settle genuine boundary disputes.

We have seen that, in unregistered land, and in registered land under the LRA 1925, even though the adverse possessor acquires an independent freehold title, the title is subject to burdens affecting the old title. The position is clearer in the LRA 2002 where there is a statutory transfer of the exiting title. Schedule 6, para 9, confirms that the registration of the adverse possessor does not affect the priority of interests affecting the estate. An exception is, however, made as regards registered charges. A registered chargee is notified by the Registrar of the adverse possessor's application for registration, and has the same opportunity as the registered proprietor to issue a counter-notice and bring proceedings for possession against the adverse possessor.[81] If a chargee fails to do so, then there is no justification for enabling him or her to enforce his or her charge against an adverse possessor who obtains registration.

5.3.2 Assessment of the Land Registration Act 2002

As we have noted, one of the Law Commission's aims in its recommendations for adverse possession is to provide a more appropriate balance between adverse possessors and the registered proprietor. In fact, the new system is heavily weighted in favour of the registered proprietor. The LRA 2002 has been described as the 'emasculation' of adverse possession[82] and as making registered land 'virtually squatter proof'.[83] The role of adverse possession is reduced to settling boundary disputes and ensuring the marketability of abandoned land.[84] This is a deliberate policy choice to make registered land more secure and, in so doing, encourage voluntary registration.[85]

While the Act favours the registered proprietor, there is an underlying obligation of personal responsibility. To benefit from the protection afforded by Sch 6, registered proprietors must act on receipt of a notification by the Registrar and, in order to do so, must have systems in place to manage their land. This may pose few difficulties for the individual homeowner, but presents more of a challenge to large landowners, including some local authorities that have failed to protect their interests under the LRA 1925.[86]

Bogusz argues that the approach taken by the 2002 Act is to be welcomed.

[79] The relationship between estoppel and adverse possession is considered by Nield, 'Adverse Possession and Estoppel' [2004] Conv 123. As Cooke notes (2003, p 142), the utility of combining estoppel with adverse possession is unclear. The Law Commission Report No 271 (2001, [14.43]) suggested that the second exception could apply where the adverse possessor is entitled to the land under the will or intestacy of the registered proprietor, or where a sale of land had not been formally completed, but purchase money has been paid, so that the registered proprietor, in fact, holds the land on trust for the adverse possessor.

[80] Law Commission Report No 271 (2001, [14.3]).

[81] Ibid, [14.74].

[82] Dixon, 'The Reform of Property Law and the Land Registration Act 2002: A Risk Assessment' [2003] Conv 136, 150.

[83] Cooke (2003, p 139).

[84] Ibid, p 133.

[85] Law Commission Report No 271 (2001, [2.10]). See further Chapter 9, section 5.1.

[86] Cobb and Fox, 'Living Outside the System? The (Im)morality of Urban Squatting after the Land Registration Act 2002' (2007) 27 LS 236, 239. The authors suggest that the Law Commission's proposals were 'heavily influenced' by media criticism of the loss of local authority housing by adverse possession.

Bogusz, 'Bringing Land Registration into the Twenty-First Century: The Land Registration Act 2002' (2002) 65 MLR 556, 563

From a legal perspective, the Act reflects the true position that the basis of title to registered land is the fact of registration and is not based (as is the case in unregistered land) on the concept of possession. The Act intends to ensure an accurate register and restricting adverse possession in this way is necessary to achieve this. Adverse possession is therefore difficult to validate in the way it perhaps was in 1925. Arguments justifying adverse possession such as preventing the neglect of land or that there was a social need for wider land ownership are not so relevant today in a property owning democracy. Land ownership is not limited to a small proportion of the population, who, as was progressively becoming the case, did not have the resources to maintain the quality and value of their land. Adverse possession had a role to play when feudal landowners could no longer manage the estates they owned and when there was a need for some form of land redistribution.

Adverse possession with this egalitarian dimension is difficult to justify, at least in its present form, within a jurisdiction where land prices are high and the commercial market in land is particularly buoyant. The concept of alienability of land, which went to the heart of 1925 legislation, is very much a reality today. The economic reality of land being an important commercial commodity, that is freely and widely traded, makes adverse possession appear to be a very outdated concept. In this sense the LRA 2002 has very much lived up to the objectives of the Law Commission's Consultation Document of 1998 and as far as adverse possession is concerned, brought land registration into the twenty-first century.

Bogusz suggests that the reforms are equally welcome from a moral perspective.

Dixon, meanwhile, emphasizes that the approach taken by the LRA 2002 is not an inevitable one, but represents a policy choice.

Dixon, 'The Reform of Property Law and the Land Registration Act 2002: A Risk Assessment' [2003] Conv 136, 151–2

[The reform of adverse possession] is also a reflection of a political philosophy that sees adverse possession as "land theft" and as inherently inconsistent with a registration system. Of course, there is merit in both these views: modern expositions of the law on adverse possession appear to have favoured the rights of possessors over the rights of paper owners and the existence of an off-register mechanism for destroying titles seems to make a mockery of the state guarantee of title. On the other hand, the social and economic justifications for principles of adverse possession have been well documented and instead of "land theft", adverse possession can be seen as encouraging "productive land use". Again, there is nothing inherently contradictory in having principles of adverse possession operate in registered land, at least if those principles are seen positively as a method of transferring title from one person to another instead of a method of unfairly snatching it from them. It is a matter of perception, not of incontrovertible logic. Consequently, given that the Act has chosen to emasculate adverse possession—and so favours one policy perspective—we must be alive to the possibility that there will be some creative interpretation of the relevant provisions by a differently minded judiciary. [. . .]

Picking up on Dixon's acknowledgment of the importance of perception, Cobb and Fox are highly critical of the Law Commission's presentation of the morality of adverse possession.

Focusing on the position of urban squatters—that is, people who deliberately move in to empty residential properties—the authors argue that the Law Commission relies on too simplistic a presentation of an undeserving adverse possessor and a blameless registered proprietor.

Cobb and Fox, 'Living Outside the System? The (Im)morality of Urban Squatting after the Land Registration Act 2002' (2007) 27 LS 236, 242–3 and 249

The first component of the Commission's argument sought to highlight the 'undeserving' nature of many claims for title through adverse possession. It accepted the importance of protecting certain categories of 'inadvertent' squatter from hardship [...] In contrast to this, however, the Commission was highly critical of those squatters who deliberately take possession of land [...] Significantly, by focusing upon the construction of advertent squatting as 'land theft', the Law Commission has introduced, for the first time in England and Wales, an important moral distinction between good and bad faith adverse possession. The basis of moral opprobrium, quite simply, is the squatter's own knowledge of his or her occupation, which—like mens rea under the criminal law—renders the otherwise innocent act a culpable one.

The second, and arguably more implicit, component of the Commission's moral analysis was an emphasis upon the blamelessness of the dispossessed landowner. On the one hand, the Commission identified certain landowners as blameworthy, for example a landowner who encouraged an inadvertent squatter to rely on his representations [...] and proposed an exception to deal with this scenario. More importantly though, [...] the Commission pointed out that landowners who lose title to deliberate squatters are often unaware of the presence of squatters on their property until it is too late. In these circumstances—deliberate squatting unnoticed as a result of the inadvertence of the landowner—the Commission considered it unfair to allow a squatter to gain title to the property. [...]

The Law Commission's proposals implicitly constructed the moral debate over the doctrine of adverse possession around a binary division between 'good faith' and 'bad faith' squatters. Yet, while the 'land theft' approach to adverse possession appears, prima facie, to provide a convincing justificatory basis for the Law Commission's agenda in relation to registered land, the Commission should not simply be accepted as having the final word on the morality of 'bad faith' squatting, particularly in light of its apparent lack of engagement with the traditional justificatory theories. The actions of the 'bad faith' squatter in an unsupervised property can be usefully conceptualised through the alternative perspectives of labour-desert theory, personhood theory and utilitarianism. Each of these frameworks allows for the possibility that, in certain contexts—specifically, in the case of an advertent squatter—the consequences of unauthorised occupation by a squatter may negate the original title holder's moral claim and provide a moral justification for the conduct of the squatter.

We have noted that the LRA 2002 seeks to provide a scheme of adverse possession that is consistent with the underlying principle of title by registration. Cooke[87] notes that, under the Act, *proof of title has been divorced from proof of possession* and that relativity of title, a concept central to unregistered land, is no longer important.[88] These concepts have not been removed from registered land. The adverse possessor still relies on the inception of possession as the foundation of his or her claim. It is still recognized that adverse possession

---

[87] *Land Law* (2006, p 211).
[88] Ibid, p 203.

confers an independent freehold title from the moment at which possession begins. Hence, Sch 6, para 9, of the 2002 Act provides that this title (in contradistinction to that of the registered proprietor) is 'extinguished' when the adverse possessor becomes registered proprietor of the estate.

But these concepts retain only a ghostly existence. Their operation is overshadowed by the overarching principle that the adverse possessor remains vulnerable to the assertion of the registered title unless and until that title is acquired by the adverse possessor by registration.

5.4 HUMAN RIGHTS AND ADVERSE POSSESSION

Following the decision in *Pye v Graham*, Pye commenced proceedings in the European Court of Human Rights. It argued that the loss of its land was an infringement of its right of property under Art 1 of the First Protocol to the ECHR, for which it was entitled to compensation from the government. The Human Rights Act 1998 (HRA 1998), which incorporates the ECHR into domestic law, was not applicable to *Pye v Graham*, because the cause of action arose before that Act came into force.[89] Hence a direct action in the Strasbourg Court was the only means through which the human rights argument could be raised. The financial stakes were high, with Pye assessing its loss at £10m (a sum disputed by the government). The legal stakes were higher, with the legitimacy of rules of adverse possession called into question. The case focused on the operation of limitation periods under the LRA 1925, the scheme applied in *Pye v Graham*, although raised more generally the justification for adverse possession claims in a system of registered title.

In *Pye v UK*, the Grand Chamber of the European Court of Human Rights ultimately rejected Pye's claim by ten votes to seven.[90] This decision reversed that of the ordinary Chamber, in which Pye had succeeded by the narrowest of margins (four to three votes).[91] We have seen, in Chapter 5, the different stages of a claim under Art 1 of the First Protocol. Firstly, it must be established that the provision of the ECHR is engaged, and secondly, if it is, the possibility of justification must be considered. As we have seen in Chapter 5, the Grand Chamber agreed that Art 1 was engaged, and considered the operation of limitation rules to be concerned with the control of possessions, rather than with deprivation. The Court then turned its attention to the possibility of justification, considering, firstly, whether the limitation period serves a legitimate aim.

JA Pye (Oxford) Ltd v UK (App No 44302/02) [2008] 1 EHRLR 132, Grand Chamber

At [74]

It is a characteristic of property that different countries regulate its use and transfer in a variety of ways. The relevant rules reflect social policies against the background of the local conception of the importance and role of property. Even where title to real property is registered, it must be open to the legislature to attach more weight to lengthy, unchallenged possession than to the formal fact of registration. The Court accepts that to extinguish title where the

---

89 See Chapter 5, section 2.5.
90 (App No 44302/02) [2008] 1 EHRLR 132.
91 (App No 44302/02) (2006) 43 EHRR 3.

former owner is prevented, as a consequence of the application of the law, from recovering possession of land cannot be said to be manifestly without reasonable foundation. There existed therefore a general interest in both the limitation period itself and the extinguishment of title at the end of the period.

Applying its justification formula,[92] the Court held that the rules struck a fair balance between the general interest and the interest of the individuals. The absence of provision for compensation in domestic law was not considered significant in the context of limitation rules, while adequate procedural protection was available to Pye to enforce its rights. The Court was not swayed in its conclusions by the extent of Pye's loss and the corresponding gain enjoyed by the Grahams.

JA Pye (Oxford) Ltd v UK (App No 44302/02) [2008] 1 EHRLR 132, Grand Chamber

At [83]–[84]

The applicant companies contended that their loss was so great, and the windfall to the Grahams so significant, that the fair balance required by Article 1 of Protocol No. 1 was upset. The Court would first note that, in the case of *James*, the Court found that the view taken by Parliament as to the tenant's "moral entitlement" to ownership of the houses at issue fell within the State's margin of appreciation. In the present case, too, whilst it would be strained to talk of the "acquired rights" of an adverse possessor during the currency of the limitation period, it must be recalled that the registered land regime in the United Kingdom is a reflection of a long-established system in which a term of years' possession gave sufficient title to sell. Such arrangements fall within the State's margin of appreciation, unless they give rise to results which are so anomalous as to render the legislation unacceptable. The acquisition of unassailable rights by the adverse possessor must go hand in hand with a corresponding loss of property rights for the former owner. In *James and Others*, the possibility of "undeserving" tenants being able to make "windfall profits" did not affect the overall assessment of the proportionality of the legislation (*James and Others* judgment, referred to above, § 69), and any windfall for the Grahams must be regarded in the same light in the present case.

As to the loss for the applicant companies, it is not disputed that the land lost by them, especially those parts with development potential, will have been worth a substantial sum of money. However, limitation periods, if they are to fulfil their purpose (see paragraphs 67—74 above), must apply regardless of the size of the claim. The value of the land cannot therefore be of any consequence to the outcome of the present case.

It was on the issue of a fair balance that five of the seven dissenting judges disagreed with the majority.[93] In this respect, they highlighted the difference between unregistered and registered land.

---

[92] See Chapter 5, section 2.4.

[93] The other two dissenting judges considered that the application of the limitation rules in the context of registered land did not serve a legitimate function. They further considered that even if a legitimate function was served, the rules provided by the 1925 Act were disproportionate.

JA Pye (Oxford) Ltd v UK (App No 44302/02) [2008] 1 EHRLR 132, Grand Chamber

At [10]–[11] of the first dissenting judgment

In the case of unregistered land, title was made out by establishing a number of years' possession. Title deeds served only as evidence in support of possession, and could be defeated by a person who could prove actual (adverse) possession for the requisite number of years. In such a system, the extinguishment of title at the end of the limitation period could be seen as a coherent element in the rules on acquisition of title. [. . .]

In the case of registered land, however, title depends not on possession, but on registration as the proprietor. A potential purchaser of land can ascertain the owner of the land by searching the register, and there is no need for a potential vendor to establish title by proving possession. As pointed out by the Law Commission, the traditional reasons advanced to justify a law of adverse possession which resulted in the extinguishment of title on expiry of the limitation period had lost much of their cogency. This view was shared in the circumstances of the present case both by Lord Bingham and by Neuberger J., who found that the uncertainties which sometimes arose in relation to the ownership of land were very unlikely to arise in the context of a system of land ownership where the owner of the land was readily identifiable by inspecting the proprietorship register.

In the view of these dissenting judges, the absence of compensation carried a requirement of strong measures of protection for registered proprietors, which were not provided by the LRA 1925. In this respect, they contrasted the 1925 Act with the new safeguards provided by the LRA 2002 through the Sch 6 notification procedure.

Although based on the 1925 Act, it is implicit in the judgment of the Grand Chamber that the operation of adverse possession in unregistered land, and in registered land under the 2002 Act, is also human rights compliant.[94] The Grand Chamber accepted the legitimacy of limitation rules and hence the crucial issue is that of fair balance. The holder of unregistered land enjoys the same level of procedural protection as his LRA 1925 counterpart. The acceptance of the scheme under the 1925 Act necessarily means that the LRA 2002, with its additional protection for registered proprietors, would satisfy this test. This is implicit even in the joint judgment of five of the seven dissenting judges.

Jones argues further that the Grand Chamber was wrong to consider that Art 1 of the First Protocol was engaged.

Jones, 'Out with the Owners! The Eurasian Sequels to *JA Pye (Oxford) Ltd v United Kingdom*' (2008) 27 CJQ 260, 265–6

This [the conclusion that article 1, protocol 1 is engaged] is mistaken. The key term in Art.1 is "possessions". Article 1 is ultimately bound by its ordinary meaning, i.e. things which a person holds, according to the circumstances in which they were acquired. Thus, Art.1 merely confers a right to retain property in manner in which it has come to be held. The provision cannot be used to broaden the original scope of ownership. For this would have it confer a right, not to retention, but to acquisition of property, on more generous terms that did not,

---

[94] Jones, 'Out with the Owners! The Eurasian Sequels to *JA Pye (Oxford) Ltd v United Kingdom*' (2008) 27 Civil Justice Quarterly 260.

on the facts, emerge. As the Grand Chamber itself stated, "[i]t does not [...] guarantee the right to acquire property".

Paradoxically, this is precisely what the Grand Chamber's conclusion allows. As it indicated, the applicants' title to the Berkshire land was, "necessarily limited by the various rules of statute and common law applicable to real estate", including "the various rules on adverse possession". Thus, when "the applicant companies lost the beneficial ownership of [the land]", title had simply lapsed according to the terms on which it was acquired. The process was no more objectionable than the expiration of a lease by the effluxion of time. It could not attract the protection of Art.1, without suggesting that the provision guarantees the right to acquire title free from the possibility of adverse possession. As indicated, the provision does not go this far. In short, it was anything but "inescapable [...] that Article 1 of Protocol No 1 is applicable".

Jones' point is that once the issue goes to the matter of a fair balance, the division of opinion in the Grand Chamber (and, previously, in the ordinary Chamber judgment) shows that there is an element of subjectivity.

His argument has resonance with the approach of the House of Lords in a different context in *Aston Cantlow Parochial Church Council v Wallbank*.[95] In that case, as we have seen in Chapter 5, section 3.1.1, it was held that liability for chancel repairs did not engage Art 1, because it was an encumbrance that defined the nature of the possession. There is, however, an analytical difference between an encumbrance, as a right held by a third party affecting ownership, and the possibility of losing ownership through limitation of actions.

The Grand Chamber decision in *Pye v UK* is not technically binding on English courts, but it has since been followed by the Court of Appeal in the following case.[96] The Court rejected an argument that the justification for the operation of adverse possession is a matter that arises for reconsideration where a claim is distinguishable on the facts from *Pye v Graham*.

Ofulue v Bossert [2008] EWCA Civ 7, CA

Arden LJ

At [52]–[53]

The written submissions of the Ofulues proceed on the basis that it is open to this court to distinguish the decision in *Pye* on its facts or by reference to the applicability of the policy reasons for adverse possession identified by the Law Commission. In my judgment, this approach fundamentally misunderstands the purpose of the doctrine of the margin of appreciation. The Strasbourg Court accepted that the national authorities could in general determine the rules for the extinction of title as a result of the occupation of the land by a person who was not the true owner. That determination applies to all decisions on adverse possession and it is not open to this court not to follow that determination because the case is distinguishable on its facts. For the doctrine of the margin of appreciation to be inapplicable, the results would have to be so anomalous as to render the legislation unacceptable (see [83] of

---

95 [2003] UKHL 37, [2004] 1 AC 546.
96 See also Dixon, 'Human Rights and Adverse Possession: The Final Nail' [2008] Conv 160.

the judgment of the Strasbourg Court set out above), and in my judgment that has not been demonstrated in this case (see further [55] below).

The Ofulues' submissions additionally proceed on the basis that this court must apply the test of legitimate aim and proportionality to each different case of adverse possession which arises. Again, in my judgment this fundamentally misunderstands the function of this court. The Strasbourg Court considered the compatibility with the Convention of the limitation period in the case of adverse possession with Art.1 of Protocol No.1 and assessed its legitimate aim and proportionality as a general rule and not simply in the context of the specific facts of the *Pye* case. It would not therefore be appropriate for this court to proceed to examine the questions of legitimate aim and proportionality simply from the perspective of the facts of this case and the relationship between them and the policy considerations in the Law Commission's Consultation Paper.

6 ADVERSE POSSESSION AND LEASEHOLD TITLES

As we have seen in section 3 above, a claimant who moves into adverse possession thereby immediately obtains a freehold title. This is so even if the land is leased at the time at which the claimant commences adverse possession. In such a case, however, the adverse possession operates against the leasehold estate; the claim does not affect the title of the landlord (the holder of the freehold title). At the expiry of the term of the lease, the landlord can assert his or her freehold title against the adverse possessor. To defeat the landlord's title, a fresh claim to adverse possession is required.

The additional complexity of adverse possession in the leasehold context has given rise to a number of questions regarding the nature of the right acquired by the adverse possessor, the extent to which an estate is extinguished by the operation of limitation rules, and the relationship between the adverse possessor and the freeholder. The specific context in which these questions have arisen is the surrender of a lease by a tenant who has lost his or her title by adverse possession: is such a surrender effective to enable the landlord immediately to assert its freehold title against the adverse possessor, without the need to wait for the expiration of the term of the lease? Different answers to this question have been given in unregistered and registered land.

In unregistered land, the possibility of surrender of a lease is met with the immediate objection that the leasehold title is extinguished by adverse possession. It therefore appears illogical to suggest that the lease can be surrendered. Despite this apparent difficulty, the House of Lords has held that surrender was effective.

Fairweather v St Marylebone Property Co Ltd [1963] AC 510, HL

Facts: The freeholder of adjoining plots of land built a shed across the boundary of the two plots. The entrance to the shed was on No 311, but 75 per cent of the shed was on No 315. Long leases were granted of both plots. It was accepted that the owner of No 311 had obtained title to the land on No 315 occupied by the shed through adverse possession. The tenant of No 315 surrendered the lease and the freeholder sought to assert its title against the adverse possessor.

Lord Radcliffe

At 538–40

On one view, which seems not an implausible one having regard to the structure of the respective sections, the right or title extinguished is coterminous with the right of action the barring of which is the occasion of the extinguishment. This would mean that, when a squatter dispossesses a lessee for the statutory period, it is the lessee's right and title as against the squatter that is finally destroyed but not his right or title as against persons who are not or do not take through the adverse possessor. On the other view, that upon which the appellant's case depends, the lessee's right and title to the premises becomes extinguished for all purposes and in all relations, so that as between himself and the lessor, for instance, he has thereafter no estate or interest in the land demised. [...]

I think, therefore, that it is a false approach to the provisions of the Limitation Acts to regard the "extinguishment of title" as extinguishing more than the title of the dispossessed against the dispossessor. Where the person dispossessed is a lessee, I do not think it right to try to build legal conclusions on the assumption that the nexus between him and his lessor has been destroyed; or, consequently, that, once adverse possession has been completed, he ceases to hold the term of years and estate in it granted to him by his lessor. [...]

I conclude, therefore, that the effect of the "extinguishment" sections of the Limitation Acts is not to destroy the lessee's estate as between himself and the lessor; and that it would be incorrect to say that if he offers a surrender to the lessor he has nothing to surrender to him in respect of the land in the possession of the squatter. *Nemo dat quod non habet*, and I daresay that he does not, but, as Pearson L.J. indicated in the Court of Appeal, the question here is not whether there are any exceptions from that general principle but whether, as a principle, it is relevant to the situation that we have here. In my opinion it is not.

Hence, the extinguishment of title operated only as regards the relationship between the tenant and the adverse possessor. Because the lease continued in existence between the tenant and landlord, the surrender of the lease was effective to enable the landlord immediately to assert the freehold title against the adverse possessor.

In registered land, under s 75 of the LRA 1925, we have seen that title was not extinguished by adverse possession, but instead was held on trust. By s 75(2), the adverse possessor was then entitled to apply to be 'registered as proprietor thereof'. A question arose as regards with what estate the adverse possessor should be registered: the freehold title acquired by the inception of adverse possession, or the leasehold estate held on trust by s 75(2)? This, in turn, appeared to affect the issue of the effectiveness of a surrender of the lease.

In the following case, Mrs David was the registered proprietor of a long lease granted by Spectrum Investment. The defendant had been in adverse possession against Mrs David and, following the expiration of the limitation period, applied for registration. The Registrar closed Mrs David's title and registered the defendant as proprietor of a new leasehold estate. In these circumstances, a surrender by Mrs David was considered to be ineffective. Browne-Wilkinson J held that, because the surrender of a lease is a registered disposition, it was clear that, once Mrs David's title had been closed, she lacked the ability to execute a surrender. Browne-Wilkinson J was satisfied that the registration of the defendant with a lease had been correct.

Spectrum Investment Co v Holmes [1981] 1 WLR 221, HC

Browne-Wilkinson J

At 230

To my mind the words are clear and unequivocal: the squatter claims to have acquired a title to "a registered estate in the land" (i.e. the leasehold interest) and applies to be registered as a proprietor "*thereof*" (my emphasis). Therefore under section 75 (2), references to the squatter having acquired title to a registered estate must include the rights which under the Limitation Act 1939 the squatter acquires in relation to leasehold interests. Section 75 (2) then refers to the squatter applying to be registered as proprietor "thereof." This word can, in my judgment, only refer back to the registered estate in the land against which the squatter has acquired title under the Act of 1939, i.e. the leasehold interest. The clear words of the Act therefore seem to require that, once the 12 years have run, the squatter is entitled to be registered as proprietor of the lease itself, and is bound to be so registered if he applies for registration. It follows that in my judgment the defendant (as the squatter) is correctly registered as proprietor of the lease itself in accordance with the clear requirements of section 75. If that is right, Mrs. David cannot be entitled to rectification of the register as against the defendant, and she can therefore never get into a position in which she is competent to surrender the lease to the plaintiff.

Cooke identified difficulties with this result.

Cooke, 'Adverse Possession: Problems of Title in Registered Land' (1994) 14 LS 1, 9

The decision in Spectrum is unsatisfactory, while being correct on its facts, and has generated much academic distress. So glaring an inconsistency with unregistered land is unfortunate in itself; from a practical point of view, it imposes on the parties a relationship of landlord and tenant which neither has chosen. It raises technical queries. What has happened, for example, to S's independent fee simple, arising from his adverse possession of the land? He becomes the registered proprietor of the estate which the dispossessed owner held on trust for him; his fee simple has disappeared without trace.

Cooke argued that while *Spectrum Investment* was the correct decision on the facts, the registration of the adverse possessor with a leasehold title should not take place. She argued that the adverse possessor should be registered with a freehold title, to reflect the title acquired by possession. This prevented the relationship of landlord and tenant being forced upon the freeholder and adverse possessor.

In *St Marylebone*, Lord Radcliffe had also expressed doubt that the adverse possessor would be registered with the leasehold title.

Fairweather v St Marylebone Property Co Ltd [1963] AC 510, HL

Lord Radcliffe

At 543

[...] the trust of the dispossessed owner's title under subsection (1) must somehow be reconciled with the provision under subsection (2) for the squatter to apply to register his own title, which would presumably be his independent possessory title acquired by the adverse possession.

If the adverse possessor is registered with freehold title, then, as in unregistered land, the leasehold title continues to exist as between the landlord and dispossessed tenant, enabling the effective surrender of the lease.

But Browne-Wilkinson J's analysis of s 75 of the LRA 1925 was supported in a subsequent decision.

Central London Commercial Estates Ltd v Kato Kagaku Co Ltd [1998] EWHC 314

Sedley J

At [36]

To split the leasehold interest after 12 years' adverse possession into an element related entirely to the freehold and another related solely to the squatter, as is now known to happen with unregistered land, does not seem to me to marry up with either the purpose or the operation of section 75(1). The squatter, unlike an underlessee, has no legal relationship at all with the leaseholder during the 12 initial years of trespass (except in the negative sense that the leaseholder may at any time evict him and claim damages); and at the end of the 12 years, by operation of law, the leaseholder's right and title to do even this are extinguished wherever the Limitation Acts apply. At law the squatter is then in a position to make a good title, independent of the lease, although always subject to the freeholder's eventual reversion. In relation to a registered leasehold, however, section 75 lifts the extinguishing effect of the Limitation Act 1980 and substitutes a trust of the leasehold interest, benefits and burdens alike, from the moment of extinction of the leasehold title. The squatter becomes entitled, without regard to merits, to be placed in the same relationship with the freeholder as had previously been enjoyed by the leaseholder. The trust preserves not the squatter's common law title but a new statutory right to be substituted by registration for the leaseholder—carrying with it, as Mr Nugee accepts, an obligation to indemnify the leaseholder against outgoings. This is to all appearances a statutory conveyance of the entire leasehold interest.

In that case, the question that arose was whether a tenant in registered land that had lost its title by adverse possession could surrender the lease prior to the adverse possessor becoming registered and, therefore, while the s 75 trust remained in existence. This possibility had not arisen on the facts of *Spectrum Investment*, although Browne-Wilkinson J had noted the possibility that the tenant may remain free to deal with the title during this period. In *Kato Kagaku*, the answer followed logically from the court's refusal to 'split' the estate. A surrender of the lease passed the leasehold title back to the freeholder, but subject to the adverse possessor's beneficial interest.

As we have seen, the LRA 2002 preserves the rights of adverse possessors who completed twelve years of adverse possession at the time that the Act came into force, but removes the s 75 trust. The transitional provision in Sch 12, para 18, confers on the adverse possessor an entitlement to be registered as the proprietor of 'the estate'. This appears to confirm the approach adopted in *Spectrum Investment* and *Kato Kagaku* in so far as the adverse possessor is entitled to be registered with the lease. Once registered, the factual position mirrors that in *Spectrum Investment* and therefore the possibility of a surrender by the dispossessed tenant is removed. Doubt may arise, however, as regards the position prior to registration. In the absence of a trust, there may be nothing to prevent the dispossessed proprietor executing a surrender of the lease.

As regards claims to adverse possession under the 2002 Act, the position is placed beyond doubt. Title remains vested in the tenant unless and until the adverse possessor successfully applies for registration under Sch 6. A successful application will result in the claimant being registered as proprietor of the lease,[97] thus again removing the possibility of a surrender.

7 CONCLUSION

The LRA 2002 brings the modern law of adverse possession in line with principles of registration of title. In so doing, its practical impact is to reduce the role of adverse possession and reduce the significance of concepts that have long underlined English land law: title by possession and relativity of title.

At the outset of our discussion of possession, we noted Green's suggestion that, in defining this concept, the case law is influenced by, and constructs, the concept of an ideal landowner. Green identifies the characteristics of that individual.

Green, 'Citizens and Squatters' in *Land Law: Themes and Perspectives*
(eds Bright and Dewar, 1998, p 241)

The ideal landowner constructed by the laws of adverse possession is clearly no threat to civilised society. On the contrary, he is settled and stable, and honours both man-made and natural laws. His cultivation involves hard work. The sturdy figure of the ideal English landowner as reflected and maintained in adverse possession law invests his physical, intellectual, and emotional energies in the ground: he has entirely committed himself, through his engagement with the earth, to his plot of land. He wants to be a fixture in the landscape. He fences his land and locks his gates in order to exclude those who might detract from his hard labour—addressing the world outside as well as the land within his boundaries.

Green draws comparisons between the ideal landowner and the ideal citizen. She notes that, by drawing an ideal, the law also has an exclusionary effect. Green highlights that the most successful adverse possessors are those who already own land (and therefore, are already included) and are trying to extend their boundaries. The successful claimants in the leading cases of *Pye v Graham* and *Moran* clearly fit within this category. The least successful (on Green's analysis) are the 'have nots' who want to join the 'haves'. The unsuccessful claimant in *Powell* may be so described: he is presented in the court's judgment as a strong-willed rebellious teenager, acting despite (rather than in pursuance of) the wishes of his elderly, landowning grandparents.

Cobb and Fox further highlight the exclusionary effect of adverse possession.[98] They argue that, by setting the odds against claims, the LRA 2002 encourages urban squatters to

---

[97] Land Registration Act 2002, Sch 6, paras 4 and 7, both provide for a successful application to result in registration as proprietor of 'the estate'.

[98] Cobb and Fox, 'Living Outside the System? The (Im)morality of Urban Squatting after the Land Registration Act 2002' (2007) 27 LS 236.

lie low and not draw attention to their actions by applying for registration—that is, in this way, to live 'outside the system'.

While the practical role of adverse possession may therefore have been reduced and reformed by the 2002 Act, this is an area of law that continues to have resonance with important issues for land law and law in general: issues of ownership and use of land, and of inclusion and exclusion.

QUESTIONS

1. What do you understand by the concepts of 'title by possession', 'relativity of title', and the 'extinguishment' of a title by limitations?

2. To what extent are the concepts in the above question compatible with registration of title? Consider how any differences that may you identify are reflected in the operation of adverse possession in registered land.

3. How is adverse possession established? To what extent is this dependent on the intention of the adverse possessor and the paper owner/registered proprietor?

4. Do you consider the maintenance of rules of adverse possession to be justified?

FURTHER READING

Cobb and Fox, 'Living Outside the System? The (Im)morality of Urban Squatting after the Land Registration Act 2002' (2007) 27 LS 236

Cooke, *The New Law of Land Registration* (Oxford: Hart, 2003, ch 7)

Dockray, 'Why do we Need Adverse Possession?' [1985] Conv 272

Green, 'Citizens and Squatters' in *Land Law: Themes and Perspectives* (eds Bright and Dewar, Oxford: OUP, 1998)

Hopkins, *The Informal Acquisition of Rights in Land* (London: Sweet & Maxwell, 2000, ch 10)

Jones, 'Out with the Owners! The Eurasian Sequels to *JA Pye (Oxford) Ltd v United Kingdom*' (2008) 27 CJQ 260

O'Mahony and Cobb, 'Taxonomies of Squatting: Unlawful Occupation in a New Legal Order' (2008) 71 MLR 878

Radley-Gardner, 'Civilized Squatting' (2005) 25 OJLS 727

PART B2

THE ACQUISITION OF AN EQUITABLE INTEREST IN LAND

11

INTRODUCTION

CENTRAL ISSUES

1. In Chapters 9 and 10, we looked at the general rules regulating how a party can acquire a legal estate or legal interest in land. As we noted in Chapter 4, however, the *acquisition* question is answered differently depending on whether a party claims to have acquired a legal property right or an equitable property right. In Chapter 4, sections 4 and 6, we began to examine some of the general rules applying to the acquisition of equitable property rights. In Chapters 12–14, we will examine some of the specific rules regulating how a party can acquire an equitable interest in land. In Chapter 18, we will look at how some of those rules apply in the particular context of the family home.

2. The purpose of this introductory chapter is to set out some of the general themes that we will examine in Chapters 12–14 (as well as in Chapter 18). In particular, we will examine how the rules relating to the acquisition of an equitable interest in land may differ from those relating to the acquisition of a legal estate or interest. This chapter therefore develops the brief discussion of equity in Chapter 2, section 4: it asks *how* and *why* the *acquisition* question may be answered differently in equity as opposed to at common law.

3. The first theme emphasized in this chapter is *informality*. As we will see in Chapters 12–14, there are a number of important situations in which an equitable interest in land can arise *informally*: B can acquire such a right even if there have been no formal dealings between A and B.

4. The second theme emphasized in this chapter is *diversity*. As we will see in Chapters 12–14, there are a number of *different* principles on which B may be able to rely to show that he or she has acquired an equitable interest in land.

5. It is important to bear in mind that informality and diversity also have a role to play at common law: for example, in Chapter 10, we saw that it is sometimes possible for B to acquire a legal estate in land even if he or she has had no formal dealings with A. The point made in this chapter is not that informality and diversity are important *only* in equity; rather, it is that those themes are *more prominent* in equity than at common law.

1 THE ACQUISITION OF EQUITABLE INTERESTS: A REMINDER

In Chapter 4, we saw some examples of how a party can acquire an equitable interest in land. It is useful to remind ourselves of three of those examples.

- In *Hodgson v Marks*,[1] Mrs Marks transferred her freehold to Mr Evans, her lodger. There was no written evidence that Mr Evans was intended to hold that right on trust for Mrs Marks; nonetheless, both Ungoed-Thomas J and the Court of Appeal held that, due to the circumstances surrounding the transfer of the freehold to Mr Evans, he held that right on trust for Mrs Marks. Mrs Marks thus acquired an equitable interest from the moment at which Mr Evans acquired his freehold.

- In *Williams & Glyn's Bank v Boland*,[2] Mrs Boland had a right under a trust of a freehold held by her husband. In that case, Mrs Boland's equitable property right arose as a result of the financial contribution that she had made to Mr Boland's purchase of that freehold. Mrs Boland thus acquired an equitable interest in land from the moment at which Mr Boland acquired his freehold.

- In *Attorney-General of Hong Kong v Reid*,[3] Mr Reid acted as a prosecutor for the Hong Kong government. He accepted a bribe to act contrary to his duties to the government. The Privy Council found that Mr Reid held the bribe on trust for the government; thus he also held freeholds later bought with that bribe on trust for the government. The government thus acquired an equitable interest in land from the moment at which Mr Reid acquired his freeholds.

In considering these examples, it is possible to discern two important themes. The first is *informality*: in each case, B (Mrs Marks; Mrs Boland; the Hong Kong government) acquired an equitable property right even though no one (not Mr Evans; not Mr Boland; certainly not Mr Reid) exercised a power formally to give B that right. In contrast, as we saw in Chapter 9, it is generally true to say that, if B claims to have acquired a *legal* property right in land, he or she needs to show that particular formality rules have been satisfied (e.g. that A has used a deed; that B has registered his or her right).

The second theme is *diversity*: there is no single, specific principle that lies behind each of the three examples. In each case, there may well be a good reason for a court to find that B has acquired an equitable interest in land, but the good reason used in each case may differ from the good reason relied on in each of the other cases. Indeed, as we saw in Chapter 4, section 4, there was some judicial disagreement about the precise reason why Mrs Marks acquired her equitable interest. Ungoed-Thomas J, deciding the case at first instance, focused on the potentially fraudulent conduct of Mr Evans; Russell LJ, in the Court of Appeal, instead emphasized that Mrs Marks did not intend Mr Evans to be free to use the transferred freehold for his own benefit. This strongly suggests that there may be a number of *diverse* means by which B can acquire an equitable interest in land. In contrast, as we saw in Chapter 9, B's claim to have acquired a legal estate or interest in land is almost always based on the simple fact of A having exercised a power to give B such a right: for example, as where B acquires a legal freehold by showing that A has successfully transferred that right to B.

---

[1] [1971] Ch 892, Ch D and CA.
[2] [1981] AC 813.
[3] [1994] 1 AC 324.

Before going on to examine the themes of informality and diversity, we need to be aware of the risk of exaggerating the differences between common law and equity. As we saw in Chapter 10, it is sometimes possible for B to acquire a legal property in land through informal means: for example, by taking physical control of land, B can acquire a freehold of that land. Further, the doctrine of prescription allows B to acquire an easement without a formal grant from A. And, as we will see in Chapter 23, section 3.1.2, it is possible for B to acquire a short lease from A without registration, a deed, or even any writing. These examples show that informality and diversity are also present when considering the acquisition of legal estates and interests in land. Nonetheless, it is clear that those two themes are *more prominent* when considering the acquisition of equitable interests in land.

So, whilst it is wrong to think that informality and diversity are important *only* in equity, it is accurate to say that one of the distinctive features of equity is the prominence that it gives to informal and diverse means of acquiring an interest relating to land.

2 INFORMALITY

In Chapter 9, section 1, we considered why formality requirements are particularly prominent in land law. It would be a serious mistake to think that formality rules are irrelevant to the acquisition of an equitable interest in land. In fact, whilst informality is an important theme in the acquisition of such rights, it can operate only so far as it is consistent with three important formality rules, each of which regulates the acquisition of equitable interests.

2.1 THE THREE FORMALITY RULES

The three formality rules of particular importance to the acquisition of equitable interests in land are:

- s 53(1)(a) of the Law of Property Act 1925 (LPA 1925);
- s 53(1)(b) of the LPA 1925; and
- s 2 of the Law of Property (Miscellaneous Provisions) Act 1989 (LP(MP)A 1989).

2.1.1 Section 53(1)(a) and (b) of the Law of Property Act 1925

In Chapter 4, sections 6 and 4, respectively, we noted the rules set out by s 53(1)(a) and (b) of the LPA 1925.

Law of Property Act 1925, s 53

Instruments required to be in writing

(1) Subject to the provision hereinafter contained with respect to the creation of interests in land by parol—

  (a) no interest in land can be created or disposed of except by writing signed by the person creating or conveying the same, or by his agent thereunto lawfully authorised in writing, or by will, or by operation of law.

(b) a declaration of trust respecting any land or any interest therein must be manifested and proved by some writing signed by some person who is able to declare such trust or by his will;

(c) [...]

(2) This section does not affect the creation or operation of resulting, implied or constructive trusts.

Section 53(1)(a) sets out a general formality rule: the default position is that, whenever B claims to have acquired an equitable interest in land, B needs to show that A, the party from whom he or she has acquired that right, has used signed writing to give him or her that right.

Section 53(1)(b) modifies that rule where B claims a particular type of equitable interest in land: a right under a trust. B can *acquire* a right under a trust even if no writing has been used, but to *prove* that he or she has such a right, B will need to produce some writing signed by a party capable of setting up the trust.[4]

The two rules are thus different: for example, if A orally declares a trust of his or her freehold in B's favour, and then A *later* signs some writing acknowledging the trust, B will be able to prove that his or her equitable interest has existed from the moment of A's initial declaration. As the following extract shows, this can have an important practical effect.

Gardner v Rowe (1827–28) 5 Russ 258, High Court of Chancery

Facts: Mr Wilkinson, who lived in Newcastle-under-Lyme, was granted a 21-year mining lease of land known as 'The Wheal Regent Sett'. Mr Wilkinson later committed acts of bankruptcy. On his bankruptcy, Mr Gardner made a claim (on behalf of Mr Wilkinson's creditors) that the mining lease, as one of Mr Wilkinson's assets, should be available to meet his debts. Mr Rowe claimed that Mr Wilkinson, in fact, held that lease, from the moment at which he acquired it, on trust for Mr Rowe. Mr Rowe therefore claimed that, due to his equitable interest existing before Mr Wilkinson's bankruptcy, the lease could be used only for Mr Rowe's benefit. At the time of Mr Wilkinson's bankruptcy, there was no written record of the trust in favour of Mr Rowe. After his bankruptcy, however, Mr Wilkinson executed a deed declaring that, from the moment at which he had acquired the lease, he had held it on trust for Mr Rowe. A jury, after looking at all of the available evidence, found that Mr Wilkinson had, indeed, intended to acquire the lease as a trustee for Mr Rowe. But Mr Gardner claimed that, given the absence of signed writing at that point, the trust could not be shown to have existed at the moment of Mr Wilkinson's bankruptcy. Mr Gardner's argument was rejected by the court.

At the time, the relevant formality rule was set out by s 7 of the Statute of Frauds 1677. That section had a similar form to that of its successor, s 53(1)(b) of the Law of Property Act 1925: it meant that a declaration of trust of land had to be proved by signed writing.

---

[4] In a case in which B claims that A set up a trust by transferring a right to a trustee to hold on trust for B, the signed writing may be provided by either A or the trustee: see, e.g., *Forster v Hale* (1783) 3 Ves Jr 696. For discussion, see Youdan, 'Formalities for Trusts of Land and the Doctrine in *Rochefoucauld v Boustead*' [1984] CLJ 306, 315–20.

Lord Lyndhurst LC

At 261–2

The principal point insisted upon, on the part of [Gardner], related to the deed executed by Wilkinson, containing the declaration of trust, and which, executed after he committed an act of bankruptcy, was contended to be inoperative and void. The case upon the point was fully argued before the Vice-Chancellor, and I see no reason to differ from the opinion expressed upon it by that learned judge. Assuming the bankrupt to have been a trustee for Mr Rowe there was nothing, I think, to prevent him from making a valid declaration of trust, notwithstanding his bankruptcy.

It is true that the property of a trader cannot be assigned by him after his bankruptcy: the property is no longer his, it is vested in his assignees.[5] But property held in trust, is not the property of the bankrupt; it does not pass to his assignees. The only question, therefore, as it appears to me, in this case is, whether the declaration contained in the deed was founded upon a previous trust, or was altogether fraudulent. That question, however, has been decided in substance by the jury upon the trial of the issue; for they have found that the name of Wilkinson was used in the original deed as trustee for Rowe.

The result in *Gardner v Rowe* may seem harsh on Mr Wilkinson's creditors: after all, when dealing with Mr Wilkinson (before his bankruptcy), it will have been very difficult for them to discover that he, in fact, held the mining lease on trust for Mr Rowe. In fact, some of his creditors may even have been induced to lend to Mr Wilkinson on the assumption that the value of the mining lease would be available, if necessary, to meet Mr Wilkinson's debts.

The result in the case is, however, clearly demanded by the wording of the formality rule. As counsel for Mr Rowe made very clear when arguing before the Vice Chancellor, the rule does *not* state that a declaration of trust must be made in writing.

Gardner v Rowe (1825) 2 Sim & St 346

At 348–9

[Instead, it] merely enacts that all declarations of trust [relating to land] shall be *manifested and proved* by some writing signed by the party who is enabled by law to declare such trust [. . .] It is not required that a trust shall be *created*, but merely that it should be *proved* by writing [. . .] Nor does the statute fix any time beyond which a trust cannot be declared: it may be evidenced in writing at any time after its creation.

2.1.2 Section 2 of the Law of Property (Miscellaneous Provisions) Act 1989

In Chapter 9, section 3, we examined the formality rule set out by s 2 of the LP(MP)A 1989. That rule applies to contracts for the transfer or creation of legal or equitable property rights in land. As we saw in Chapter 9, the rule can therefore be relevant when considering the acquisition of a *legal* estate or interest in land: a contract between A and B is often the first

---

[5] [Or, as occurs in modern practice on the insolvency of an individual, in his trustee in bankruptcy.]

stage in a transaction by which B eventually acquires a legal property right in land. The rule also has an important effect on the acquisition of an *equitable* interest in land.

For example, in Chapter 4, section 6, we noted the decision in *Walsh v Lonsdale*.[6] Mr Lonsdale had made a contractual agreement to grant Mr Walsh a seven-year lease. Mr Lonsdale did not, in fact, get around to granting a formal lease, made by deed, to Mr Walsh. As a result, Mr Walsh did not have a legal lease. Nonetheless, the Court of Appeal held that Mr Walsh had an *equitable* lease, arising as a result of Mr Lonsdale's contractual duty to grant Mr Walsh the promised legal lease.

We will examine *Walsh v Lonsdale* in detail in Chapter 12. One point is, however, worth noting here: the Court of Appeal's finding that Mr Walsh had an equitable property right depended on the fact that Mr Lonsdale had a *contractual* duty to grant a lease to Mr Walsh—and, nowadays, s 2 of the 1989 Act may have an important impact on the key question of when such a contractual duty can arise. An equitable lease can still be acquired without the use of a deed, and without registration, but if B's claim to an equitable lease depends on showing that A is under a *contractual* duty to grant him that lease, B must show that A's contractual promise has been made in writing signed by both A and B, as required by the s 2 formality rule.

2.2 ROOM FOR INFORMALITY?

Each of the three examples that we noted in section 1 (*Hodgson v Marks*; *Williams & Glyn's Bank v Boland*; *Attorney General of Hong Kong v Reid*) demonstrates that it may be possible for B to acquire an equitable interest in land without any formal dealings with A. And yet we have seen, in section 2.1 above, that three important formality rules regulate the acquisition of equitable interests in land.

These two facts can be reconciled, because each of the three formality rules leaves scope for B to acquire an equitable interest in land *without* any formality. Firstly, s 53(1)(a) of the LPA 1925 expressly permits B to acquire an equitable interest informally *if* B's right arises 'by operation of law'. So, if B can show that he acquired his right not simply because A chose to give it to him, but rather because the law steps in to impose a duty on A, B can show that he has acquired that right 'by operation of law' and therefore that no signed writing is required. For example, in Chapter 13, we will examine a number of cases in which the doctrine of proprietary estoppel seems to have allowed B to acquire an equitable interest informally. It may be possible to reconcile these cases with s 53(1)(a) by analysing B's right as arising 'by operation of law': on one view at least, the doctrine of proprietary estoppel does not depend on A successfully giving B a right; instead, it allows the courts to impose a duty on A in order to protect B.

Similarly, s 2 of the LP(MP)A 1989 applies only to *contracts* for the sale or other disposition of an interest in land. This means that, if B can show that he or she acquired his or her right not simply because A chose to enter a contract with B, but rather because the law steps in to impose a *non-contractual* duty on A, the need for writing signed by both A and B should not apply. As we will see in Chapter 13, this point is important in explaining why, if A makes an unwritten promise to give B an interest in land, it may still be possible for the doctrine of proprietary estoppel to impose a duty on A and thus give B an equitable interest.

---

[6] (1882) LR 21 Ch D 9.

Further, each of s 53(1)(a) and (b) of the 1925 Act *and* s 2 of the 1989 Act has an exception for '*the operation of resulting, implied or constructive trusts*'. As we will see in Chapter 14, this means that the absence of writing will not stand in B's way if he or she can show that his or her right arises under such a trust. The significance of this exception, of course, depends on the meaning of the terms 'resulting', 'implied', and 'constructive'. The unifying element of such trusts, as we will see in Chapter 14, section 1, seems simply to be that they are not 'express' trusts—that is, they do *not* arise simply as a result of A exercising his or her power to set up a trust.

This brief analysis suggests that, when examining the acquisition of equitable interests in Chapters 12–14, cases in which B acquires such a right informally will fall into one of three groups:

- those in which B's right arises 'by operation of law', rather than as a result of A choosing to give B a right;
- those in which B's right arises as a result of A coming under a non-contractual duty to B, rather than a contractual duty; and
- those in which B's right arises under a resulting, implied, or constructive trust, rather than a trust arising as a result of A's exercise of a power to set up a trust in B's favour.

2.3 JUSTIFYING INFORMALITY?

It is clear, then, that each of the three formality rules regulating the acquisition of equitable interests in land allows room for the informal acquisition of such a right. But *why* is such room allowed by the statutory rules? After all, as we saw in Chapter 9, section 1, there are good reasons for imposing formality requirements when B claims to have acquired a legal or equitable property right in land.

This is a question that we have to consider in detail in Chapters 12–14 (as well as in Chapter 18). At this stage, it may be useful to highlight two possible approaches. Each approach can be linked to one of the two models set out by Harris and examined in Chapter 1, section 5.2: the first can be linked to the 'doctrine model'; the second, to the 'utility model'.

The first, doctrinal, approach is based on the fact that a common factor seems to lie behind the three situations, set out above, in which B may be able to acquire an equitable interest in land informally. In each case, B's right does *not* depend on A simply choosing to give B a right. It may be that this demonstrates a wider point about the doctrinal nature of formality rules in land law, as suggested in the following two extracts.

Hopkins, *The Informal Acquisition of Rights in Land* (2000, p 256)

The formality requirements for the express grant of proprietary rights are 'facilitative'. They enable the grant of recognised proprietary rights to give effect to the intentions of parties in their dealings with land. Informal acquisition is, in contrast, reactive. Proprietary rights are acquired as a reaction to the words and conduct of parties in relation to land. The right acquired will not necessarily reflect the intentions of the parties. Rarely would it be expected for parties consciously to choose to rely on informal acquisition. The primary role of informal acquisition is to enable rights to be acquired where parties have not executed a formal grant.

McFarlane, *The Structure of Property Law* (2008, p 101)

Within the property law system, the basic function of a formality rule is to *regulate a party's power to give another party a right*. A formality rule achieves that function by requiring that a party's exercise of his power to give another a right *must be expressed or recorded in a particular form*. If B's claim to a right depends on showing that such a power has been exercised, formality rules *may* apply [...] But if B's claim does *not* depend on showing that a party has exercised a power to give B a right, formality rules *cannot* apply.

The second, utility-based, approach looks not to the doctrinal limits of formality rules, but to the practical reasons that may justify the informal acquisition of equitable interests in land. It can be seen in the following extract.

Hopkins, *The Informal Acquisition of Rights in Land* (2000, pp 5–6)

The concept of informal acquisition represents, in essence, a policy judgment that in some situations the desire to enable a proprietary right to be acquired outweighs the reason for generally imposing formalities. The judgment may be based on a number of factors. The guarantees provided by formality requirements may be provided through other means. For example, the existence and scope of a proprietary right may be apparent because it has been exercised over a period of time. Or, it may be that to insist on formalities will defeat, rather than achieve, the purpose for which the requirements are imposed. This is particularly the case where proprietary rights are acquired to prevent fraudulent reliance on non-compliance with formalities. The desire to prevent certain types of conduct which may be classified as fraudulent or unconscionable may also represent policy goals superior to the desire for formality, with the effect that the latter gives way to the former. In this respect, informal acquisition enables a balance to be achieved between competing policy interests.

It should be stressed that the two approaches set out here are not contradictory: after all, Hopkins' analysis is consistent with each approach. Taken together, they may provide a powerful justification for the informal acquisition of equitable interests in land. Indeed, it is worth noting that the doctrinal and policy arguments, if correct, must apply not only to equity, but also to the common law. After all, as we noted in Chapters 9 and 10, it may be possible for B to acquire a *legal* estate or interest in land informally. In some cases, this can be explained by the fact that B's claim to such a right does not depend on A having exercised a power to give B that right, but rather on B's own conduct: this is the case, for example, when B takes adverse possession of A's land. In other cases, informality may be allowed by policy concerns: for example, s 54(2) of the LPA 1925 allows A orally to grant B certain forms of short legal lease. In Chapter 23, section 3.1.2, we will consider the possible policy justifications for that exception to the need for formality.

3 DIVERSITY

3.1 DIVERSITY AND UNCONSCIONABILITY

In Chapters 12–14 (as well as Chapter 18), we will consider a number of different means by which B can acquire an equitable interest in land: some depend on B showing that a formality rule has been satisfied; others do not. It would be wrong to think that one clear principle can be used to explain all of these different means by which B can acquire an equitable interest in land. After all, it seems that it would be beyond any one principle to explain even the three examples noted in section 1 above (*Hodgson v Marks*; *Williams & Glyn's Bank v Boland*; *Attorney-General of Hong Kong v Reid*).

It is sometimes suggested that the rules governing the acquisition of equitable interests in land, like *all* equitable rules, depend on the need to prevent unconscionable conduct.[7] Certainly, as we saw in Chapter 2, section 4, the concept of 'conscience' played an important role in the development of equitable principles. And, as we will see in Chapters 13 and 14, it may be that *specific* notions of unconscionable conduct can help us to understand *particular* means by which B can acquire an equitable interest in land. It may also be possible to argue that the underlying notion of 'conscience' explains why equity has been willing to expand the list of means by which B can acquire an equitable interest in land.

It is clear, however, that the *general* concept of unconscionability is far too vague to provide a meaningful test for the circumstances in which B can acquire such a right. That point is forcefully made in the following extract.

Cowcher v Cowcher [1972] 1 WLR 425, Ch D

Facts: Mr and Mrs Cowcher married in 1953. Ten years later, Mr Cowcher acquired a freehold of a home. Mr and Mrs Cowcher lived there together, before divorcing in 1971. Mrs Cowcher had made financial contributions to the acquisition of the freehold, and it was accepted that, as a result of those contributions, Mr Cowcher held his freehold on trust for both himself and his wife. Mrs Cowcher claimed that, under that trust, she and her husband each had an equal share of the benefit of his freehold. Mr Cowcher instead claimed that his wife's share was limited to one third, because that reflected the extent of her financial contributions to the purchase price of the freehold.

Bagnall J found in favour of Mr Cowcher. The law relating to trusts of the family home has moved on since 1972 and we will examine it in detail in Chapter 18. Nonetheless, one comment of Bagnall J continues to have resonance.

Bagnall J

At 429–30

Rights of property are not to be determined according to what is reasonable and fair or just in all the circumstances [. . .] In any individual case the application of [the relevant principles] may produce a result which appears unfair. So be it; in my view, that is not an injustice. I am convinced that in determining rights, particularly property rights, the only justice that can be attained by mortals, who are fallible and not omniscient, is justice according to law; the justice which flows from the application of sure and settled principles to proved or admitted facts. So in the field of equity the length of the Chancellor's foot has been measured or is capable of measurement. This does not mean that equity is past childbearing; simply that its progeny must be legitimate—by precedent out of principle. It is well that this should be so;

---

[7] For examples related to the law of trusts, see, e.g., *per* Lord Denning MR in *Hussey v Palmer* [1972] 1 WLR 1286, 1289–90; *per* Lord Browne-Wilkinson in *Westdeutsche Landesbank Girozentrale v Islington LBC* [1996] AC 669, 705–6; *per* Arden LJ in *Pennington v Waine* [2002] 1 WLR 2075, 2088–90.

otherwise no lawyer could safely advise on his client's title and every quarrel would lead to
a law suit.

As we will see in Chapter 18, there may be strong arguments in favour of the courts taking a
less restrictive approach when dealing with the special issues raised by disputes over a family home. Certainly, other judges have, on occasion, been willing to give ideas of justice and
conscience a larger role than that admitted by Bagnall J.[8] But it is clearly the case that B can
never go to court and claim that he or she has acquired an equitable property right *simply*
because A has acted 'unconscionably'; rather, B must make a more specific claim, by showing
precisely *why* A's conduct has led to B's acquisition of such a right.[9]

3.2 DIVERSITY AND DUTIES

In Chapter 4, section 1, we saw that equitable property rights, unlike legal property rights,
are necessarily based on A's being under a duty to B. This means that, at a very general
level, there is a common factor in cases such as *Hodgson v Marks*, *Williams & Glyn's Bank v
Boland*, and *Attorney-General of Hong Kong v Reid*: in each, A, due to his conduct, has come
under a duty to B.

At the same time, this point can explain the diversity of the means by which B can acquire
an equitable property right:

- there are many different means by which B can come under a duty to A; *and*

- to acquire an equitable interest in land, B needs to show that A is under a duty to B; *so*

- there are many different means by which B can acquire an equitable interest in land.

Of course, this does not mean that B acquires an equitable interest in land *whenever* A is
under a duty to B. For example, as we saw, in Chapter 8, section 3.3, if A is under a contractual duty to allow B to share occupation of land with A, B does *not* have an equitable interest
in land. But that is due to the *content* question: in such a case, the right acquired by B (a contractual licence) does not count as an equitable interest in land. When focusing on the *acquisition* question, as we will do in Chapters 12–14, we do not need to examine the *content* of A's
possible duty to B; instead, we can focus on the question of *whether* A is under such a duty.

As we noted in Chapter 4, section 1, Lionel Smith has made the link between duties and
equitable property rights. In the next extract, he again emphasizes that link. The particular
discussion centres on constructive trusts, but the analysis can apply to all equitable property
rights.

Smith, 'Unravelling Proprietary Restitution' (2004) 40 CBLJ 317, 322–3

Constructive trusts can be understood to arise for a range of reasons. We can start by reiterating that all trusts share the following common thread: the trustee holds property and owes

---

[8] In Chapter 18, we will consider how far the approach adopted by the House of Lords in *Stack v Dowden*
[2007] 2 AC 432 is based on wider notions of unconscionability.
[9] As has been noted by Lionel Smith, the concept of unconscionability is generally used as a conclusion, not
as a test: see 'Fusion and Tradition' in *Equity and Commercial Law* (eds Degeling and Edelman, 2005, p 24).

certain kinds of obligation with respect to that particular property. Then we can inquire as to why the obligations came into existence. If they arose because the trustee voluntarily undertook to hold the property in trust, we call it an express trust. Otherwise, the trust arises by operation of law and is either called resulting or constructive. So among all constructive trusts, the common thread is that the defendant trustee holds property and owes certain kinds of obligations with respect to that particular property; they are obligations that have effects on third parties and that are not voluntarily undertaken. But this allows us to see that while there is a common thread, there are important differences among constructive trusts. In particular, the obligation owed by the defendant may come from any one of a number of sources.

When we consider the law of obligations, we distinguish contract, tort, unjust enrichment; in other words, we distinguish obligations by their source. Some obligations arise from consent, some from wrongdoing, and some from unjust enrichment. Every constructive trust has at its core an obligation, and that obligation has a source, which in turn can be understood as the source of the trust.

3.3 DIVERSITY, DUTIES, AND INFORMALITY

A focus on duties may also help us to understand when an equitable interest in land can arise informally. The key point is to examine the *reason* for which A's duty is said to arise. In some cases, A's duty depends on A *choosing* to come under a duty to B. This is the case, for example, if A chooses to set up a trust of land in B's favour, or if A chooses to make a contractual promise to transfer an interest in land to B. In those cases, as we saw in section 2.1 above, formality rules govern B's assertion of an equitable property right.

In other cases, A's duty arises *not* because A has chosen to come under a duty to B, but for some other reason—that is, because A's conduct is such that equitable rules impose a duty on A to B. In these cases, as suggested in the extracts from Hopkins and McFarlane set out in section 2.3 above, formality rules may well be irrelevant. The crucial question, then, is *when* will A's conduct lead to a duty being imposed on A? That is one of the key questions that we will examine in Chapters 12–14, and in Chapter 18.

> **QUESTIONS**
> 1. In general terms, how do the rules relating to the acquisition of equitable interests in land differ from those applying to the acquisition of legal estates and interests in land? Can the differences be justified?
> 2. The cases demonstrate that there a number of different means by which a party can acquire an equitable interest in land. Should we expect those means of acquisition to have anything in common with each other?
> 3. What role should the concept of 'unconscionability' have to play in relation to the acquisition of equitable interests in land?
> 4. What formality rules govern the acquisition of equitable interests in land? What are the main exceptions to those rules?
> 5. Why might it be useful to view the acquisition of an equitable interest in land as depending on one party coming under a duty to another?

FURTHER READING

Burrows, 'We Do This at Common Law But That in Equity' (2002) 22 OJLS 1

Hopkins, *The Informal Acquisition of Rights in Land* (London: Sweet & Maxwell, 2000)

McFarlane, *The Structure of Property Law* (Oxford: Hart, 2008, Pts C1 and C3)

Smith, 'Fusion and Tradition' in *Equity in Commercial Law* (eds Degeling and Edelman, Sydney: Lawbook Co, 2005)

Smith, 'Unravelling Proprietary Restitution' (2004) 40 CBLJ 317

12

THE DOCTRINE OF ANTICIPATION: *WALSH V LONSDALE*

CENTRAL ISSUES

1. Equitable rights arise under the doctrine of anticipation where parties enter a specifically enforceable contract for the creation or transfer of legal estates and interests in land.

2. The doctrine is based on the maxim 'equity looks on as done that which ought to be done'. The availability of specific performance is the trigger for the application of the doctrine as providing the basis upon which the contract 'ought' to be performed.

3. Where the contract is for the transfer of an existing estate (the sale of a freehold or assignment of a lease), the effect of the doctrine is to separate legal and equitable entitlement to the same estate. The vendor therefore holds the estate on constructive trust for the purchaser, although the trust has some unusual features.

4. The doctrine of anticipation is of practical significance, in particular in determining the rights and duties of parties during the course of a transaction. Its application is, however, in decline and the need to rely on the doctrine will be curtailed by the introduction of e-conveyancing.

1 INTRODUCTION

In this chapter, we consider how equitable interests may arise through the application of the maxim 'equity looks on as done that which ought to be done'. The acquisition of equitable rights through this maxim is attributed to the decision in *Walsh v Lonsdale*,[1] although it has been afforded a much broader application than the specific context in which it was applied in that case. It is sometimes referred to as the 'doctrine of conversion', but we have adopted the nomenclature of the 'doctrine of anticipation' as a clearer description of the basis for the acquisition of rights.

[1] (1882) LR 21 Ch D 9.

The doctrine applies where a party is under a duty to grant another a legal property right, but has not yet done so. Equity anticipates the grant of those legal rights by conferring on the intended grantee an equitable interest mirroring the legal right in question. These equitable rights are generally temporal in duration, existing only in the period between the time at which legal rights 'ought' to be granted and the time at which such rights are, in fact, granted. But the rights are practically important, both in determining the rights and obligations of the grantor and grantee during this period, and in providing the grantee with proprietary rights that may be enforceable against third parties (under the priority rules discussed in Part B3) prior to the completion of the legal grant.

2   *WALSH V LONSDALE* IN CONTEXT

Walsh v Lonsdale (1882) LR 21 Ch D 9, CA

Facts: Lonsdale agreed to grant a lease of a mill to Walsh for seven years. The rent payable depended on the number of looms operated, but this was subject to a minimum number and rent based on that number was payable yearly in advance. No lease was granted, but Walsh moved in and started paying rent quarterly in arrears. Lonsdale demanded payment in advance and levied distress for non-payment of rent. Whether Lonsdale had acted lawfully in doing so depended on whether the terms of the parties' agreement were enforceable.

Jessel MR

At 14–15

There is an agreement for a lease under which possession has been given. Now since the Judicature Act the possession is held under the agreement. There are not two estates as there were formerly, one estate at common law by reason of the payment of the rent from year to year, and an estate in equity under the agreement. There is only one Court, and the equity rules prevail in it. The tenant holds under an agreement for a lease. He holds, therefore, under the same terms in equity as if a lease had been granted, it being a case in which both parties admit that relief is capable of being given by specific performance. That being so, he cannot complain of the exercise by the landlord of the same rights as the landlord would have had if a lease had been granted. On the other hand, he is protected in the same way as if a lease had been granted; he cannot be turned out by six months' notice as a tenant from year to year.

The context of the case lies in the merger of law and equity by the Judicature Acts 1873–75. The specific issue was the effect of the Acts on the position of a tenant who moves into possession and starts to pay rent in the absence of a formally granted lease. At common law, such facts gave rise to an implied periodic tenancy. If such a tenancy was present on the facts of the case, then Walsh was only liable for rent in arrears (as had been paid) and Lonsdale's distress for non-payment of rent in advance was illegal. In equity, it was already established that the effect of the maxim 'equity looks on as done that which ought to be done' was that the parties would be treated as though the lease had been granted,[2] with the effect that all of the terms of the parties' agreement were enforceable. Applying the Judicature Acts, the Court gave precedence to equity's analysis. The agreement for the grant of a legal lease created an equitable lease under which the parties were bound by the same terms as their intended grant. Jessel MR's judgment is generally considered to be too broad a statement of the effect of the Judicature Acts,[3] although the doctrine of anticipation attributed to the case is well established and beyond doubt.

The principle espoused in the case has significance beyond the factual context of an agreement to grant a lease. The doctrine applies in two distinct circumstances.[4] The first, exemplified by *Walsh v Lonsdale*, is a contract to create a lease (a new legal estate) or to assign an existing legal interest.

Hopkins, *The Informal Acquisition of Rights in Land* (2000, p 63)

[In *Walsh v Lonsdale*, the] uncompleted sale of the legal lease became the source for the creation of a lease in equity. Similarly, specifically enforceable contracts to create an interest in land are treated as creating the corresponding interest in equity. Hence, for example, a specifically enforceable contract to create a legal easement creates an equitable easement; a specifically enforceable contract to create a legal mortgage creates an equitable mortgage. In the same way, effect will be given to a specifically enforceable contract to transfer an existing legal interest.

The second situation in which the doctrine in *Walsh v Lonsdale* applies is an agreement for the sale of an existing legal estate: the transfer of a freehold or assignment of an existing lease. Its application in this situation is of particular practical significance, because it means that the doctrine is invoked as part of the usual conveyancing process for the sale and purchase of land. As we have seen in Chapter 9, the typical conveyance of land is divided into three stages: the entry into a contract for sale; execution of the contract by transfer of title; the application by the purchaser for registration. Legal title does not pass until registration. The doctrine of anticipation, however, operates as soon as there is a specifically enforceable contract.[5] From that time, equity treats the parties as though the contract has been executed.

Oakley explains the effect of the doctrine in this situation.

Oakley, *Constructive Trusts* (3rd edn, 1997, p 275)

[The] effect of the operation of the doctrine is to separate the legal and beneficial ownership of the property and it is only to be expected that equity therefore regards the vendor as a

---

[2] *Parker v Taswell* (1858) 2 De G & J 559.

[3] In upholding the use of a legal remedy (distress) for rent payable under an equitable lease, the decision is considered to go beyond mere procedural fusion generally attributed to the Judicature Acts. On this aspect of the case, see Sparkes, '*Walsh v Lonsdale*: The Non-Fusion Fallacy' (1988) 8 OJLS 350.

[4] Hopkins, *The Informal Acquisition of Rights in Land* (2000, pp 62–5).

[5] *Lysaght v Edwards* (1876) 2 Ch D 499. The equitable interest created by the doctrine arises when the vendor makes title according to the contract, or the purchaser agrees to accept the vendor's title, but is then backdated to the time of the contract. See further Oakley, *Constructive Trusts* (3rd edn, 1997, pp 282–5).

> trustee of the property for the purchaser pending performance of the contract. No corre-
> sponding trust of the purchase money will arise simply because such a trust would lack the
> necessary certainty of subject matter. However, the vendor acquires a lien or charge on the
> property for the unpaid purchase money.

The trust is generally classified as a constructive trust. The nature of the trust changes once
the purchase money has been paid in full, at the second stage of the usual conveyancing
process—that is, the execution of the contract. At that stage, the vendor ceases to have any
charge or lien on the property, and the trust becomes a bare trust.

In principle, the doctrine of anticipation applies equally to contracts relating to equitable
interests.[6] Where the contract is for the sale of an existing beneficial interest, the application
of the doctrine creates a sub-trust.

The doctrine of anticipation has also been applied where the duty to grant a property
right has arisen otherwise than under a contract: for example, where a court orders a transfer of property and the transfer has not yet taken place.[7] The use of the doctrine in respect of
a non-contractual duty has been considered in Chapter 4, section 6.

3 THE SIGNIFICANCE OF SPECIFIC PERFORMANCE

For the doctrine of anticipation to apply, it must be established that the parties' agreement
is capable of specific performance. The availability of specific performance renders the execution of a contract inevitable and is the basis upon which equity considers that the agreement 'ought' to be performed. Not all specifically enforceable agreements that *relate* to land
attract the application of the doctrine. It applies only to specifically enforceable contracts to
create a recognized proprietary right in land.

The distinction between a contract relating to land and a contract creating, or transferring,
a proprietary right in land has been noted in Chapter 9, section 3.1. Specific performance is
not capable of turning a personal right into a proprietary right. This point is explained, in
relation to the doctrine of anticipation, in the following extract.

McFarlane, 'Identifying Property Rights: A Reply to Mr Watt' [2003] Conv 473, 474

It is important to distinguish between two different senses in which the availability of specific performance is said to be relevant to the proprietary status of a right. The first is under
a generally accepted equitable doctrine, which can be called the "doctrine of anticipation".
Where A enters a contract with B to confer a recognised property right on B, if specific performance of that contract is available, then B can gain an equitable equivalent of that property
right which takes effect before, and continues in the absence of, the contemplated conferral

---

[6] The leading authority is *Oughtred v IRC* [1960] AC 206, which concerned a contract for sale of the beneficial interest under a trust of personal property (shares in a private company) rather than land. The application of the doctrine to equitable interests is not without controversy and is discussed by Oakley (1997, pp
278–80) and Hopkins (2000, pp 65–8).

[7] *Mountney v Treharne* [2003] Ch 135.

of the right by A. This doctrine is irrelevant when it comes to determining the proprietary status of a particular right, as it depends for its operation on A's being under a binding obligation to confer on B a right which is independently recognised as proprietary. Indeed, the doctrine of anticipation is concerned only with the methods by which property rights can be acquired: it allows such a right to be claimed without A's completing the planned transaction. The doctrine thus extends the list of means by which property rights can be acquired, not the list of rights which have proprietary status. Hence, as Swadling has emphasised, the doctrine of anticipation cannot, by itself, be used to confer proprietary status on rights otherwise regarded as personal.

An agreement to create or transfer a legal estate or interest will be specifically enforceable if three requirements are met. Firstly, there must be a valid contract. This means that there must be a contract that meets the formality requirements of s 2 of the Law of Property (Miscellaneous Provisions) Act 1989 (LP(MP)A 1989), as discussed in Chapter 9.

Secondly, consideration must have been provided; specific performance is an equitable remedy and equity does not assist a volunteer.

Thirdly, the circumstances must not reveal a defence to an action for specific performance. Defences include mistake (by the party seeking specific performance), undue hardship caused by ordering performance, delay, and misconduct. In particular, the party claiming specific performance must not have acted inequitably, because 'he who seeks the assistance of equity must come to court with clean hands'.

The dependence of the doctrine of anticipation on the availability of specific performance means that no rights are acquired until the requirements of specific performance are met. Moreover, once acquired, the rights remain dependent on the continuing availability of specific performance. This appears to make the equitable rights precarious: in particular, they are vulnerable to challenge on the basis of misconduct of delay.

The precarious nature of such rights leads Gardner to doubt that the ongoing availability of specific performance can, in fact, be a requirement of the doctrine.[8]

Gardner, 'Equity, Estate Contracts and the Judicature Acts: *Walsh v Lonsdale* Revisited' (1987) 7 OJLS 60, 64–5 and 74

According to the orthodoxy, then, the subsistence of estate contracts [acquired under *Walsh v Lonsdale*] is circumscribed at two levels: first, by the law of contract in general; and secondly, within that, by the law on the remedy of specific performance in particular. Now it is fundamentally implausible that a property right could be constituted in this way. The law of contract, with its doctrine of privity, is obviously at variance with the *in rem* quality of a proprietary interest; and the injection of the parameters of specific performance into its definition would give it an intermittent, discretionary nature quite at odds with the stability which is needed in an institution which has to be capable of recognition and application other than *ad hoc* and *inter partes*. This was the message of Lord Wilberforce's classic *dictum* that a property right must be 'definable, identifiable by third parties, capable in its nature of assumption by third parties, and have some degree of permanence and stability'.

[...] The applications of estate contracts are wide and varied. They involve many of considerable importance as property interests, for which a high degree of stability is of the

---

[8] A view shared by McFarlane, *The Structure of Property Law* (2008, pp 235–7 and 705).

essence. And the more applications to which they are put, the more they take on the aspect of a wholly pervasive institution, so conducing to their application in yet further contexts, in a self-propelling development. Overall, the doctrinal load which they have come to be expected- indeed, known- to bear is so large and multifarious that it appears in large measure to have been found incompatible with the maintenance of the orthodox requirement that specific performance must be available between the present parties in their present question. The proprietary nature which estate contracts are in practice evidently conceived to possess is fundamentally irreconcilable with the orthodoxy, and in reality is rather commonly upheld at the latter's expense.

Gardner suggests that rather than the interest acquired under the doctrine of anticipation being dependent on the availability of specific performance, the relationship between the two is reversed: specific performance is available to vindicate the right acquired under *Walsh v Lonsdale*, which is itself derived from another source.[9] Gardner's concern with the precarious nature of a right dependent upon the continuing availability of specific performance appears to be a legitimate one—but it begs the question: if the doctrine is not dependent on specific performance, on what basis 'ought' an agreement be performed?

Hopkins suggests that, other than specific performance, an agreement ought to be performed where the purchaser has paid the consideration in full.

Hopkins, *The Informal Acquisition of Rights in Land* (2000, pp 74–5)

For a contract to be specifically enforceable, it is necessary for the purchaser to have provided some consideration. The rights and obligations of the parties change when the purchaser has paid the consideration in full. This change can be illustrated by reference to the sale of a legal estate. On the conventional analysis, once full payment is made, the vendor becomes a bare trustee of the land for the purchaser, and the purchaser is entitled to any benefit derived from the land. [...] It is submitted that the effect of full payment of consideration by the purchaser is now twofold. [...] Secondly the purchaser's right is no longer dependent upon specific performance. This is significant because the absence of the need to rely on specific performance removes the element of precariousness that otherwise characterises the purchaser's right. Before full payment of consideration, it is the availability of specific performance that enables the application of equity's maxim "equity regards as done that which ought to be done" by demonstrating that the contract "ought" to be performed. However, once the consideration has been paid, the fact of full payment itself provides a sufficient basis to assert that the contract "ought" to be performed.

The purpose of Hopkins' analysis is twofold. Firstly, he argues that a right acquired under the doctrine of anticipation that is initially dependent on the availability of specific performance of a contract may mature and cease to be so dependent once full consideration is paid. Secondly, he suggests that the doctrine of anticipation may apply where a purchaser provides full consideration in the absence of a valid contract. Payment pursuant to an oral agreement may also reveal the elements of a claim to proprietary estoppel—but an ability to claim rights under the doctrine of anticipation would be advantageous. In particular, as we

[9] Gardner, 'Equity, Estate Contracts and the Judicature Acts: *Walsh v Lonsdale* Revisited' (1987) 7 OJLS 60, 74.

have seen in Chapter 9, doubt exists as to the availability of estoppel where a contract for sale of land is invalid for non-compliance with s 2 of the LP(MP)A 1989.

Full payment of consideration undoubtedly has an effect on the nature of the rights acquired under the doctrine of anticipation: for example, in rendering the vendor a bare trustee. It has not, however, had the wider impact advocated by Hopkins.[10] In particular, in *Lloyds Bank plc v Carrick*[11] (a case that is discussed further below), the Court of Appeal rejected an argument that a right acquired by entering a specifically enforceable contract ceased to be dependent on that contract once the consideration had been paid in full. Despite Gardner's analysis of the case law demonstrating to the contrary, the orthodox view remains that rights acquired under the doctrine of anticipation are dependent on the parties' contract and, therefore, on the continuing availability of specific performance of that contract.

4 THE NATURE OF THE RIGHTS ACQUIRED

As we have seen, the type of right acquired under the doctrine of anticipation is dependent on the nature of the agreement from which they are derived. Where the agreement concerns the creation of a lease or of an interest in land, the purchaser obtains the equitable equivalent of the intended right: an agreement for a lease gives rise to an equitable lease and an agreement for a mortgage gives rise to an equitable mortgage, etc. Where the agreement is for the transfer of an existing legal estate, the effect of the doctrine is that the estate is held on trust for the purchaser. In all cases, the right acquired is distinct from the legal right intended to be granted. This is readily apparent where the effect of the doctrine is to create a trust and so the contract for sale of the legal estate creates an equitable interest. It is less apparent, although is still the case, where the doctrine confers the equitable equivalent of the intended right.

In *Walsh v Lonsdale*, in the extract from his judgment above, Jessel MR considered that the parties hold under the same terms as if a lease had been granted. In *Chan v Cresdon Proprietary Ltd*,[12] the High Court of Australia emphasized that the equitable lease acquired is a distinct proprietary right from the legal lease that the tenant has contracted to buy. In that case, in the context of an intended grant of a legal lease to a tenant, the appellants agreed to act as guarantors for the tenant's obligations 'under this lease'. No legal lease was granted, because registration provisions had not been complied with. On the assumption that an equitable lease arose under the doctrine of anticipation, the Court held that the appellants were not liable as guarantors. The equitable lease was distinct from the legal lease and therefore obligations arising under it did not arise 'under this lease'.

Two further issues arise as regards the nature of the right acquired: firstly, the basis upon which rights acquired under the doctrine are enforceable against third parties; secondly, where the doctrine is given effect by the creation of a trust, the rights and obligations of the parties under the trust.

4.1 ENFORCEABILITY OF RIGHTS AGAINST THIRD PARTIES

As we have seen, on an orthodox approach, rights acquired under the doctrine of anticipation are dependent upon the existence of a contract and on the availability of specific

---

[10] For an analysis of the authorities, see Hopkins (2000, pp 79–83).
[11] (1997) 73 P & CR 314. See Hopkins (2000, p 78).
[12] (1989) 168 CLR 350.

performance of that contract. Similarly—at least, in most instances—the enforcement of the rights against third parties is dependent on the enforceability of the contract. A contract to convey or create a legal estate is an estate contract—itself a property right capable of binding third parties under the priority rules discussed in Part B3 of this book. In registered land, estate contracts may be enforceable against third parties by entry of a Land Registry notice or as an overriding interest where the beneficiary of the contract is in actual occupation; in unregistered land, estate contracts are registrable as a Class C(iv) land charge.[13] Hence, where the doctrine of anticipation applies, there may be two proprietary rights: the estate contract and the equitable rights acquired under the doctrine. At least as regards the enforcement of the rights against third parties, however, it seems that the latter has no existence independent from the former.

Where the contract is for the creation of a lease or a legal interest (such as an easement or mortgage), this may make little practical difference, because the priority rules applicable to the equitable easement or mortgage are the same as those applicable to an estate contract.[14] The difference is more evident in a contract for sale of an existing legal estate, where the doctrine of anticipation gives rise to a trust. The priority rules applicable to beneficial interests under a trust differ from those applicable to the underlying estate contract.

Lloyds Bank plc v Carrick (1997) 73 P & CR 314, CA

Facts: Following the death of her husband, Mrs Carrick agreed to buy the remaining term of a lease of a maisonette from Mr Carrick, her brother-in-law. The agreement was specifically enforceable and Mrs Carrick had paid the full purchase price, but no assignment of the lease had been executed. Mr Carrick subsequently used the lease as security for a loan. On his default, the bank argued that Mrs Carrick's interest constituted an estate contract, which (the land being unregistered) was void against it for non-registration as a land charge.

Morritt LJ

At 320–2

Thus the issue argued on this appeal was whether Mrs Carrick had an interest in the maisonette separate and distinct from that which arose under the unregistered estate contract which was capable of binding the Bank as successor in title to Mr Carrick. For Mrs Carrick it was submitted that she did. [. . .]

The argument for Mrs Carrick relied on the relative position at law and in equity as I have described it to found the argument that such an absolute equitable interest was not itself registrable but bound the bank as they had constructive notice of it. Counsel for Mrs Carrick accepted that such interest came or started from the contract but, he contended, it matured into an interest separate and distinct from the contract as soon as the purchase price was paid in full.

---

[13] Land Charges Act 1972, s 2(4)(iv); Land Registration Act 2002, ss 32–39 and Sch 3. For full discussion of these priority rules, see Part B3.

[14] In unregistered land, differences may arise in relation to the category of registrable land charge in issue. An equitable easement acquired under the doctrine of anticipation may be registered under Class D(iii) and an equitable mortgage under Class C(iii). In both cases, however, registration of the contract under Class C(iv) is also possible in the alternative. See Hopkins (2000, p 72).

> For my part I am unable to accept this analysis. The payment of £19,000 by Mrs Carrick to Mr Carrick did not as such and without more give her any interest in the maisonette. Nor, prior to the conclusion of the contract, were the circumstances such that Mrs Carrick could assert that her brother-in-law held the maisonette on any trust for her benefit. The source and origin of the trust was the contract; the payment of the price by Mrs Carrick served only to make it a bare trust by removing any beneficial interest of Mr Carrick. Section 4(6) of the Land Charges Act 1972 avoids that contract as against the bank. The result, in my judgment, must be that Mrs Carrick is unable to establish the bare trust as against the bank for it has no existence except as the equitable consequence of the contract. Accordingly I reject the contention founded on the bare trust. [...]
>
> In this case there was a trust of the maisonette for the benefit of Mrs Carrick precisely because there had been an agreement between her and Mr Carrick which, for her part, she had substantially if not wholly performed. As between her and Mr Carrick such trust subsisted at all times after November 1982. I agree with counsel for the bank that there is no room in those circumstances for the implication or imposition of any further trust of the maisonette for the benefit of Mrs Carrick.

The enforcement of Mrs Carrick's interest acquired under the doctrine of anticipation was therefore wholly dependent on the priority rules applicable to estate contracts, not those applicable to trusts. On the facts, Mrs Carrick's interest was void against the bank because she had not registered her estate contract as a Class C(iv) land charge. In this respect, rights acquired under the doctrine of anticipation appear parasitic in nature: they are dependent for their enforceability on the underlying contract from which they are derived. Further, the Court held that the existence of the estate contract precluded Mrs Carrick from seeking to establish property rights under other equitable doctrines, including estoppel (discussed in Chapter 13) and the common intention constructive trust (discussed in Chapter 18). Because interests arising under these doctrines would have been binding against the bank, the existence of the contract, and the consequent application of the doctrine of anticipation, left Mrs Carrick in a worse position than would otherwise have been the case.[15]

4.2 THE NATURE OF THE TRUST

As we have seen, where parties enter into a contract to convey an existing legal estate the effect of the doctrine of anticipation is to separate legal and equitable entitlement to the same estate. In such cases, the vendor has generally been regarded as becoming construct-ive trustee for the purchaser. The trust has been described as being '*of an extremely unusual nature*'.[16] Until full payment of the purchase money on completion, the trustee (the vendor) remains in possession, has a significant interest in the land, is entitled to income generated from the land, and is responsible for outgoings. The purchaser (the beneficiary under the trust) becomes entitled to capital benefits, such as any increase in the value of the land. In principle, risks pass to the purchaser, although these may be passed back to the vendor by the terms of the contract.[17]

---

[15] A point acknowledged by the court: *Lloyds Bank plc v Carrick* (1997) 73 P & CR 314, 322. For further discussion, see Ferguson, 'Estate Contracts, Constructive Trusts and the Land Charges Act' (1996) 112 LQR 549.

[16] Oakley (1997, p 277).

[17] The rights and duties of the parties are explored ibid, pp 292–304.

The trust therefore serves a very practical role in determining the respective rights and obligations of the parties during the period of the transaction, but, as Harpum notes, it is an inelegant mechanism with which to do so.

Harpum, 'The Uses and Abuses of Constructive Trusts: The Experience of England and Wales' (1997) 1 Edin LR 437, 457

Of course English law will not now abandon the constructive trust that arises out of a specifically enforceable contract. It is of ancient origin and is too much part of the weft and warp of our conveyancing law. In practice it is workable if inelegant. But it is not a cloth that any legal system would weave if it was starting de novo.

Viewed in the broader context of the doctrine of anticipation, the imposition of the trust creates a lack of doctrinal cohesion. The application of the same doctrine has a different effect depending on the type of contract entered. Only in those situations in which a constructive trust is imposed does the doctrine create fiduciary obligations.

It is difficult to justify why a contract to assign an existing lease places the vendor under fiduciary obligations to the purchaser as constructive trustee, while a contract to grant a new lease (such as that in *Walsh v Lonsdale*) does not. The basis for the imposition of the constructive trust (as is acknowledged by Oakley) is simply the division of legal and equitable entitlement to the same estate.[18] In *Westdeutsche Landesbank Gorozentrale v Islington LBC*,[19] the House of Lords denied that the division of entitlement necessarily requires a trust.

Hopkins suggests that the case may be used to rationalize the doctrine of anticipation.

Hopkins, *The Informal Acquisition of Rights in Land* (2000, pp 64–5)

Following *Westdeutsche Landesbank Gorozentrale v. Islington L.B.C.*, it is no longer necessary to see the imposition of fiduciary obligations as the inevitable consequence of the division of legal and equitable entitlement. [...] there are circumstances in which it is appropriate to accept that legal and equitable title is divided without the imposition of fiduciary obligations. However, adopting a broad definition, such situations could still be described as involving a trust. It may be more appropriate to treat the division of title that occurs by entering a specifically enforceable contract to sell a legal estate as not imposing fiduciary obligations. This would provide conceptual coherence to the application of equity's maxim by ensuring that the consequence of intervention is the same in all situations in which the rule is applied. In all situations, the purchaser acquires an equitable interest corresponding to the right he has contracted to buy. Where this results in the division of legal and equitable title to an estate, a form of trust may be imposed, but the vendor will not necessarily be placed under any fiduciary obligation towards the purchaser.

It may be questioned whether this solution, in fact, provides the rationalization that Hopkins suggests. It removes the initial disparity caused by the imposition of fiduciary obligations in those situations in which the doctrine of anticipation triggers the imposition of a

---

[18] Ibid, p 275, extracted above.
[19] [1996] AC 669, 705–7.

constructive trust—but, for so long as a trust is in place, the subsequent imposition of such obligations remains possible. Indeed, Hopkins suggests that fiduciary obligations should arise at the point in time that consideration has been paid in full, where the trust becomes a bare trust.[20] Arguably, full doctrinal cohesion could only be obtained by taking the doctrine outside the scope of constructive trusts. As Harpum acknowledges (in his comment quoted above), the trust is now too embedded in English law to do so.

5 CONCLUSION

The doctrine of anticipation applies where a party is under a duty to grant another a legal property right, but has not yet done so. In this chapter, we have focused on its application where the duty arises from a specifically enforceable contract for the creation or transfer of legal estates and interests in land. We have also noted (and explored further in Chapter 4, section 6) its application to non-contractual duties. The effect of the doctrine, reflecting the maxim 'equity looks on as done that which ought to be done', is to create equitable proprietary rights mirroring the legal rights that 'ought' to be granted. The doctrine is of practical significance in determining the rights and obligations of parties between contract and the grant of the legal right in question. The equitable rights created are unusual in two respects: firstly, on the orthodox view, they are precarious in their nature as dependent on the continuing availability of specific performance; secondly, their ability to bind third parties is dependent upon the enforceability of the underlying estate contract.

Despite its practical significance, the application of the doctrine in the context of contractual duties is in decline. Its scope has already been curtailed by s 2 of the LP(MP)A 1989. Only contracts that comply with the formality requirements provided in that section are capable of specific performance and therefore attract the application of the doctrine. In particular, this prevents the doctrine from applying to oral agreements.[21]

In future, its scope will be further curtailed by the introduction of e-conveyancing. As we have seen in Chapter 9, one impact of e-conveyancing will be to remove the 'registration gap' that currently exists between completion and registration—that is, the period during which the parties' rights are currently based on a bare trust subsisting under the doctrine of anticipation. Simultaneous completion and registration will remove the need to rely on the doctrine during this period, limiting its application to the period between entry into a specifically enforceable contract and completion.

QUESTIONS

1. Assess the relationship between the doctrine of anticipation and specific performance. Is there any other basis upon which an agreement 'ought' to be performed?

2. Compare and contrast the operation of the doctrine of anticipation to the following contracts: (i) a contract to grant a new lease; and (ii) a contract to assign an existing lease.

---

[20] Hopkins (2000, pp 74–5).

[21] A direct consequence of the 1989 Act was to prevent the doctrine of anticipation from being used to create an equitable mortgage by the deposit of title deeds—a previously common form of creating temporary security for a loan or overdraft: *United Bank of Kuwait plc v Sahib* [1996] 3 WLR 472.

3. Assess the role of the constructive trust in the operation of the doctrine of anticipation.

FURTHER READING

Gardner, 'Equity, Estate Contracts and the Judicature Acts: *Walsh v Lonsdale* Revisited' (1987) 7 OJLS 60

Hopkins, *The Informal Acquisition of Rights in Land* (London: Sweet & Maxwell, 2000, ch 5)

Oakley, *Constructive Trusts* (3rd edn, London: Sweet & Maxwell, 1997, ch 6)

Sparkes, '*Walsh v Lonsdale*: The Non-Fusion Fallacy' (1988) 8 OJLS 350

13

PROPRIETARY ESTOPPEL

CENTRAL ISSUES

1. Proprietary estoppel is a means by which a party (B) can gain some protection against an owner of land (A), even if he or she has no contract with A and even if A has not formally given B a property right in relation to A's land. A number of questions surround both *how* and *why* the doctrine allows B to acquire a right.[1]

2. The first set of questions relates to the *nature* of proprietary estoppel: is it an independent means by which B can acquire a right against A? Or is it simply an example of other forms of estoppel that: (i) prevent A from denying that B has a right; or (ii) prevent A from asserting a right against B?

3. The second set of questions relates to the *requirements* of proprietary estoppel: when will B be able to rely on the doctrine?

4. The third set of questions relates to the *extent of the right* acquired by B if he or she is able to make a successful proprietary estoppel claim: for example, if the doctrine applies, will A necessarily be

under a duty to keep a promise that he or she has made to B?

5. The fourth set of questions relates to the *effect of B's right on third parties*: for example, if B successfully claims a proprietary estoppel against A, will it ever be possible for B to rely on that same claim against C, a party who later acquires A's land? And, is that question decided by the priority rules discussed in Chapters 6–8, or do special rules apply to proprietary estoppel?

6. In examining these questions, we have to attend to two particular points: firstly, what is the impact of the House of Lords' recent decision in *Yeoman's Row Management Limited v Cobbe*;[1] secondly, what role does the concept of unconscionability have to play?

7. Each of the four sets of questions is important in practice, has recently been examined by the courts, and is the subject of academic disagreement. It is clear, then, that proprietary estoppel is an interesting, but difficult, topic.

---

[1] [2008] 1 WLR 1752. Another potentially important House of Lords decision, *Thorner v Majors and ors*, is expected before the publication of this book: see the companion website for analysis of this decision.

1 INTRODUCTION: PROPRIETARY ESTOPPEL IN PRACTICE

The best way to see the operation and importance of proprietary estoppel is to consider an example. In this section, we will focus on *Crabb v Arun District Council*.[2] As well as introducing proprietary estoppel, the case gives rise to a number of important questions: for example, there is a great deal of disagreement as to precisely *why* the defendant council was ordered by the court to allow Mr Crabb, for free, a right of way over the council's land. We will consider those questions later on in this chapter. In this introduction, our aim is more modest: it is to show the power of proprietary estoppel in allowing B (in this case, Mr Crabb) to acquire a valuable right over the land of A (in this case, the council), *even though* A did not formally grant B such a right, and even though there was no contract between A and B.

Crabb v Arun District Council [1976] Ch 179, CA

Facts: Victor Crabb owned a rectangular plot of land in a small village near Bognor Regis. Hook Lane, a public road, ran along the northern edge of the plot, and land owned by Arun District Council ran along the western edge. In 1967, Mr Crabb decided that he wanted to sell off the front half of his land, but keep the back half. If he sold the front half of the land and wanted access to Hook Lane from the back half of his land, he had two choices (as shown in Figure 6): (i) when selling the front half of the land, he could reserve a right of way over that land, allowing him to get from the back half of the land to Hook Lane; or (ii) he could sell the front half of the land without reserving such a right of way (allowing him to sell that front half for a higher price) and instead arrange for an alternative right of way over the council's land.

Mr Crabb preferred the second option and negotiated with the council for a right of way over its land. An agreement 'in principle' was reached: Mr Crabb would be given a right of way via 'Point B' (see Figure 6). The council did not formally grant Mr Crabb such an easement (no deed was used), and no formal contract was concluded between Mr Crabb and the council. But when the council later put up a fence separating Mr Crabb's land from its land, a gap was left at Point B and a gate was later installed there. Confident that he had, or would get, a right of way over the council's land, Mr Crabb sold the front half of his land *without* reserving a right of way over that land. Unfortunately for Mr Crabb, the council then took down the gate at Point B and built a wall over the gap. As a result, Mr Crabb had no means of getting from his retained land to Hook Lane; this meant that he was unable to continue with his commercial use of that land. The council offered to reopen the gap at Point B and give Mr Crabb a right of way—but only at a price of £3,000. Mr Crabb refused to pay and claimed that the council was *estopped* from denying him access over its land at Point B.

Lord Denning MR

At 187

When Mr Millett, for the plaintiff [Mr Crabb], said that he put his case on an estoppel, it shook me a little: because it is commonly supposed that estoppel is not itself a cause of action. But

---

[2] [1976] Ch 179.

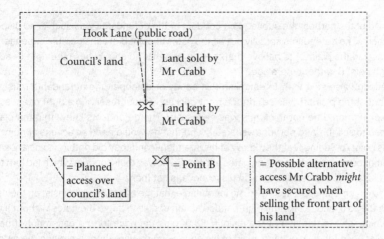

Figure 6 *Crabb v Arun DC*: The facts

that is because there are estoppels and estoppels. Some do give rise to a cause of action. Some do not. In the species of estoppel called proprietary estoppel, it does give rise to a cause of action [...] The new rights and interests, so created by estoppel, in or over land, will be protected by the courts and in this way give rise to a cause of action [...]

The basis of this proprietary estoppel—as indeed of promissory estoppel—is the interposition is equity. Equity comes in true to form to mitigate the rigours of the common law. The early cases did not speak of it as 'estoppel'. They spoke of it as 'raising an equity'. If I may expand what Lord Cairns LC said in *Hughes v. Metropolitan Railway Co* (1877) 2 App Cas 439, 448: 'it is the first principle upon which all courts of equity proceed,' that it will prevent a person from insisting on his strict legal rights—whether arising under a contract, or on his title deeds, or by statute—when it would be inequitable for him to do so having regard to the dealings which have taken place between the parties.

What then are the dealings which will preclude him from insisting on his strict legal rights? If he makes a binding contract that he will not insist on the strict legal position, a court of equity will hold him to his contract. Short of a binding contract, if he makes a promise that he will not insist upon his strict legal rights—then even though that promise may be unenforceable in point of law for want of consideration or want of writing—then, if he makes the promise knowing or intending that the other will act upon it, and he does act upon it, then again a court of equity will not allow him to go back on that promise.[3] Short of an actual promise, if he, by his words or conduct, so behaves as to lead another to believe that he will not insist on his strict legal rights—knowing or intending that the other will act on that belief—and he does so act, that again will raise an equity in favour [...]

At 188

The question then is: were the circumstances here such as to raise an equity in favour of the plaintiff? [...] The judge found that there was 'no definite assurance' by the defendants' representative, and 'no firm commitment,' but only an 'agreement in principle,' meaning I suppose that, as Mr. Alford [counsel for the council] said, there were 'some further processes' to be gone through before it would become binding. But if there were any such processes in

---

[3] [At this point, Lord Denning MR cited *Central London Property Trust Ltd v High Trees House Ltd* [1947] KB 130 and *Charles Rickards Ltd v Oppenhaim* [1950] 1 KB 616, 623.]

the mind of the parties, the subsequent conduct of the defendants was such as to dispense with them. The defendants actually put up the gates at point B at considerable expense. That certainly led the plaintiff to believe that they agreed that he should have the right of access through point B without more ado.

The judge also said that, to establish this equity or estoppel, the defendants must have known that the plaintiff was selling the front portion without reserving a right of access for the back portion. I do not think this was necessary. The defendants knew that the plaintiff *intended* to sell the two portions separately and that he would need an access at point B as well as point A. Seeing that they knew of his intention—and they did nothing to disabuse him but rather confirmed it by erecting gates at point B—it was their conduct which led him to act as he did: and this raises an equity in his favour against them.

In the circumstances it seems to me inequitable that the council should insist on their strict title as they did; and to take the high-handed action of pulling down the gates without a word of warning: and to demand of the plaintiff £3,000 as the price for the easement. If he had moved at once for an injunction in aid of his equity—to prevent them removing the gates—I think he should have been granted it. But he did not do so. He tried to negotiate terms, but these failing, the action has come for trial. And we have the question: in what way now should the equity be satisfied?

Here equity is displayed at its most flexible...because of the defendants' conduct, the back land has been landlocked. It has been sterile and rendered useless for five or six years: and the plaintiff has been unable to deal with it during that time. This loss to him can be taken into account. And at the present time, it seems to me that, in order to satisfy the equity, the plaintiff should have the right of access at point B without paying anything for it.

I would, therefore, hold that the plaintiff, as the owner of the back portion, has a right of access at point B over the verge on to Mill Park Road and a right of way along that road to Hook Lane without paying compensation. I would allow the appeal and declare that he has an easement, accordingly.

Scarman LJ

At 192

I agree that the appeal should be allowed [...] The plaintiff has no grant. He has the benefit of no enforceable contract. He has no prescriptive right. His case has to be that the defendants are estopped by their conduct from denying him a right of access over their land to the public highway. If the plaintiff has any right, it is an equity arising out of the conduct and relationship of the parties. In such a case I think it is now well settled law that the court, having analysed and assessed the conduct and relationship of the parties, has to answer three questions. First, is there an equity established? Secondly, what is the extent of the equity, if one is established? And, thirdly, what is the relief appropriate to satisfy the equity?

At 193

[...] I can conceive of cases in which it would be absolutely appropriate for a defendant to say: 'But you should not have acted to your detriment until you had had a word with me and I could have put you right.' But there are cases in which it is far too late for a defendant to get himself out of his pickle by putting upon the plaintiff that sort of duty; and this, in my judgment, is one of those cases [...]

Nothing had been done to disabuse the plaintiff of the expectation reasonably induced by what the defendants' engineer then said: and there had been the direct encouragement of the gates [...The sale] was detrimental to the interests of the plaintiff. He did it in the belief that he had or could enforce a right of way and access at point B in the southern land [...]

In the present case the court does have to consider what is necessary now in order to satisfy the plaintiff's equity. Had matters taken a different turn, I would without hesitation have
said that the plaintiff should be put upon terms to be agreed if possible with the defendants,
and, if not agreed, settled by the court. But [...] there has been a history of delay, and indeed
high-handedness, which it is impossible to disregard [...T]he defendants, for reasons which
no doubt they thought good at the time, without consulting the plaintiff, locked up his land
[...] I am not disposed to consider whether or not the defendants are to be blamed in moral
terms for what they did. I just do not know. But the effect of their action has been to sterilise
the plaintiff's land; and for the reasons which I have endeavoured to give, such action was
an infringement of an equitable right possessed by the plaintiff. It has involved him in loss,
which has not been measured; but, since it amounted to sterilisation of an industrial estate
for a very considerable period of time [...] I think therefore that nothing should now be paid
by the plaintiff and that he should receive at the hands of the court the belated protection of
the equity that he has established.

2 THE NATURE OF PROPRIETARY ESTOPPEL

In *Crabb*, the Court of Appeal clearly recognized that the council was under a duty to
Mr Crabb: a duty to allow him a right of way over its land. Why did that duty arise?

2.1 A CONTRACTUAL EXPLANATION?

Atiyah argued that, because of Mr Crabb's reliance on the council, the council was under
a *contractual* duty to Mr Crabb. Peter Millett QC (later Lord Millett) was counsel for
Mr Crabb and responded to that argument by pointing out that, on the orthodox understanding of the requirements of a contract, it had been impossible for Mr Crabb to argue that
he had made a contract with the council.

**Atiyah, 'When is an Enforceable Agreement Not a Contract? Answer:
When it is an Equity'** (1976) 92 LQR 174

At 174

The above riddle [the title of the case note] is suggested by the decision of the Court of
Appeal in *Crabb v Arun District Council* which once again illustrates the extraordinary conceptual morass into which English contract law is falling, largely because of outmoded ideas
about the purpose and nature of the doctrine of consideration [...]

At 177–8

[...] is there any reason why [Mr Crabb] should not have been able to set up his action in
reliance on the undertaking or agreement, as a valid consideration? The standard doctrine
is clear enough: consideration does not have to be a benefit to the promisor, it is enough
that there is a detriment to the promisee. Here, plainly, there was a detriment, *viz.* the
action of [Mr Crabb] in selling the northern portion of his land without reserving a right of
way. Why would that action in reliance not have been a sufficient detriment to constitute

a consideration? The only possible answer must be: because [Mr Crabb's] sale of the land was not requested or specified as the consideration required by [the council]. Although [the council] knew that [Mr Crabb] was contemplating the sale of part of his land the actual sale was made without [the council's] knowledge, or request. Now I have argued elsewhere that this limitation which the standard doctrine imposes on the doctrine of consideration makes little sense in itself; and makes still less sense when it is seen that the Courts are willing to by-pass the limitation by expanding the new doctrine of estoppel [...] The present case raises a further instructive point, namely that if, in some circumstances, it seems unjust to hold a party liable on a promise or representation because the promisee or representee has acted in a way which the promisor or representor did not expect, the injustice would be no less in estoppel than in contract [...] It seems clear then that the problem of what is, in any given case, a sufficient action in reliance to justify holding a party bound by an undertaking or promise or expectation he has created, cannot be magically wafted away by calling the case estoppel instead of contract. The problem is inescapably there, and it is the *same* problem, and deserves the *same* solution, whether the case is called estoppel or contract.

Millett, '*Crabb v Arun District Council*: A Riposte' (1976) 92 LQR 342

At 342

Professor Atiyah's interesting, if intemperate, note on *Crabb v Arun District Council* deserves a reply. He argues that the Court of Appeal reached the right result but for the wrong reasons. [Mr Crabb] he contends, had a simple remedy in contract, and there was no need to explore, let alone extend, the doctrine of equitable estoppel. In the writer's view, the argument cannot be sustained.

[Mr Crabb's] claim as originally pleaded did in fact rest on simple contract. It ran into immediate difficulties. When the defence was served, it denied the existence of any enforceable contract on at least four separate grounds, each of which appeared to be unassailable. These were: (i) there was in fact no agreement; (ii) that if there was an agreement it was unsupported by consideration; (iii) that there was neither evidence in writing to comply with section 40 of the Law of Property Act 1925 (which was undeniable) nor part performance of any such agreement;[4] and (iv) that in any event the alleged agreement had been entered into not with the defendant council but with its officers, who lacked any authority, actual or ostensible, to bind the council.

Since the absence of any contract was conceded in both courts, Professor Atiyah's criticism of their approach is misplaced. He is entitled to criticise the concession made by counsel, but not the approach of the courts which were bound by it. But was the concession wrongly made? Neither the trial judge nor the Court of Appeal thought so. At first instance, Sir John Pennycuick V-C said:

"Counsel for [Mr Crabb] did not attempt to support the allegation made in the Statement of Claim that there was any actual grant of an easement, or a contract for the grant of an easement; *it would be plainly impossible so to argue* in the absence of either writing or consideration."

4 [Note that s 40 of the Law of Property Act 1925 has now been replaced by s 2 of the Law of Property (Miscellaneous Provisions) Act 1989 (see Chapter 9, section 3). Applying the provisions of the 1989 Act to the facts of *Crabb v Arun DC*, it is clear that, due to the lack of writing signed by both Mr Crabb and the council, the council would *not* be under a contractual duty to give Mr Crabb a right of way.]

And in the Court of Appeal Scarman LJ said: "[Mr Crabb] has no grant. *He has the benefit of no enforceable contract.*"

The grounds for the concession may now be considered in turn [...]

At 344

[...] Professor Atiyah suggests that [Mr Crabb's] conduct in disposing of the northern portion of his land, which deprived the remaining portion of all access, could be regarded as constituting sufficient consideration for the grant of the new access which he had sought. This is not the place to consider whether the traditional definition of consideration may not be too narrow; but Professor Atiyah's suggestion appears to deprive it of all sensible meaning. [Mr Crabb's] disposal of his own land, and the terms of disposal, were matters of complete indifference to the defendant council. The disposal was not sought by, or even known to, the council. More to the point, it formed no part of the arrangements for the provision of the new access, and was in no sense a *quid pro quo*. [Mr Crabb] disposed of his land without reserving a right of way, not because he understood that this was part of any arrangement he had entered into with the council, but because he had been encouraged to believe that he already had, or would shortly be granted, a new access to his remaining land. Again, this is the language of estoppel, not of contract [...]

At 346

The case is an important one, precisely because there was no contract, and yet [Mr Crabb's] claim succeeded. It does no service to the law to proclaim that it 'ought' to have succeeded in contract. Both law and equity seek the same result, to do justice by refusing to allow a party to disappoint the legitimate expectations of another. But not all expectations are legitimate, and the law and equity do not necessarily draw the line in the same place. The gist of the claim in equity is prejudice; equity will not permit a party who has stood by while another prejudices his position in the belief, created or encouraged by him, that he has or will obtain a legal right, afterwards to deny that right.

The apparent similarity of the results achieved in the two cases is, however, deceptive. The claims are different, require different facts to be proved, and have different consequences. The contractual claim will always be the stronger. If there is a contract, it binds both parties *ab initio*; neither can resile from it without the consent of the other, whether or not the other has prejudiced his position in any way. And the [claimant] has a legal right to have what he bargained for, no more and no less. But if the claim rests only on estoppel, the [claimant] is not bound at all, unless he seeks relief and agrees to submit to any terms the court imposes; while the defendant is free to resile so long as the [claimant] has not prejudiced his position. Even then the remedy is at the discretion of the court; the [claimant] will obtain what it is just to give him, which is not necessarily the same as what he expected to receive.

2.2 PROPRIETARY ESTOPPEL AS AN INDEPENDENT MEANS OF ACQUIRING A RIGHT?

Despite Atiyah's analysis of the case, it is clear that the Court of Appeal judges in *Crabb v Arun DC* did not think that a contract existed between Mr Crabb and the council; rather, the council's duty was seen to arise as a result of *proprietary estoppel*. The term 'estoppel' is quite confusing. In general, it is used to refer to situations in which a party is *prevented*—that is, stopped or, in old French, *estopped*—from denying the truth of a particular matter of fact or law.

There are many different forms of estoppel. Here, we will look at the two forms that are most closely related to proprietary estoppel.

2.2.1 Estoppel by representation

In the following case, goods belonging to A were in the possession of X. A creditor of X seized the goods (as a means of executing a judgment given against X). The goods were subsequently sold to B. A knew that this sale was on the cards, but remained silent. A then brought a claim against B, alleging that B, by using the goods, had interfered with A's ownership of those goods. On the face of it, B had committed a wrong against A: he had used A's goods without A's permission and then refused to return those goods.

But there is a good reason for the courts to prevent A making a claim against B: (i) by failing to speak out before the sale, A led B to believe that A had no claim to the goods; and (ii) B relied on A's implied representation by buying the goods. Due to A's representation and B's reliance, it is said that *even though the goods still belong to A*, A is *estopped* (i.e. prevented) from using that fact to make a claim against B.

Pickard v Sears (1837) 6 Ad & El 469, Court of King's Bench

Lord Denman CJ

At 474

The rule of law is clear, that where one by his words or conduct wilfully causes another to believe the existence of a certain state of things, and induces him to act on that belief, so as to alter his own previous position, the former is concluded from averring against the latter a different state of things as existing at the same time [. . .]

A's failure to speak out before the sale thus meant that A was *estopped* (prevented) from subsequently asserting his ownership of the goods against B. This form of estoppel is often known as 'common law estoppel', or 'estoppel by representation'. It can be thought of as evidential: as against B, A is prevented from proving that he owns the goods.

There are two important points about this example: firstly, A's representation and B's reliance are clearly vital in preventing A from asserting his ownership of the bike against B; secondly, A's ownership of the bike is *not* transferred to B—it is simply the case that A cannot assert his right against B. This means that the estoppel, by itself, does not allow B to bring a claim against A: it simply *prevents* A from asserting a particular fact against B. To use Lord Denning MR's phrase in *Crabb v Arun DC*, estoppel by representation can thus '*prevent a person from insisting on his strict legal rights*'. It is therefore said that this form of estoppel—'estoppel by representation', or 'common law estoppel'—cannot, by itself, give B a cause of action.

2.2.2 Promissory estoppel

In the following case, A was a landlord, and B, a tenant. The building leased to B was damaged during the wartime bombing of London. As a result, A accepted B's proposal to pay lower rent. A then claimed the originally agreed rent, including back rent, arguing that: (i) B was under a contractual duty to pay the higher rent; and (ii) A's promise to accept a lower rent did not change that contractual duty, because B had provided no consideration for A's promise. On the face of it, A's argument was correct: Denning J accepted that B had provided nothing in return for A's promise.

But there is a good reason for the courts to prevent A from enforcing his contractual right against B: (i) A told B that he would be happy with the lower rent; and (ii) B relied on A's promise by paying that lower rent—and a demand for the higher sum (including back rent) would put a sudden burden on B.

Central London Property Trust Ltd v High Trees House [1947] KB 130

Denning J

At 134

With regard to estoppel, the representation made in relation to reducing the rent was not a representation of an existing fact. It was a representation, in effect, as to the future, namely, that payment of the rent would not be enforced at the full rate but only at the reduced rate. Such a representation would not give rise to an estoppel, because, as was said in *Jorden v. Money*,[5] a representation as to the future must be embodied as a contract or be nothing.

But what is the position in view of developments in the law in recent years? The law has not been standing still since *Jorden v. Money*. There has been a series of decisions over the last fifty years which, although they are said to be cases of estoppel, are not really such. They are cases in which a promise was made which was intended to create legal relations and which, to the knowledge of the person making the promise, was going to be acted on by the person to whom it was made and which was in fact so acted on. In such cases the courts have said that the promise must be honoured [...] As I have said they are not cases of estoppel in the strict sense. They are really promises—promises intended to be binding, intended to be acted on, and in fact acted on. *Jorden v. Money* can be distinguished, because there the promisor made it clear that she did not intend to be legally bound, whereas in the cases to which I refer the proper inference was that the promisor did intend to be bound. In each case the court held the promise to be binding on the party making it, even though under the old common law it might be difficult to find any consideration for it. The courts have not gone so far as to give a cause of action in damages for the breach of such a promise, but they have refused to allow the party making it to act inconsistently with it. It is in that sense, and that sense only, that such a promise gives rise to an estoppel.

Despite Denning J's doubts about the use of the term 'estoppel', the principle applied in *Central London Property Trust v High Trees* is now generally known as 'promissory estoppel', or 'equitable estoppel'.[6]

As Denning J made clear, it differs from estoppel by representation in at least three important ways. Firstly, it does not require A to make a representation about a matter of *existing* fact or law:[7] as in our example, it can be based on a promise by A as to how he will

---

[5] (1854) 5 HLC 185.

[6] For a recent example of that usage, see *Collier v Wright* [2008] 1 WLR 643.

[7] *Jordan v Money* (1854) 5 HL Cas 185 confirms that estoppel by representation can apply only where A makes such a representation.

act in the future. Secondly, it can never be used to support a claim by B against A; instead, it simply gives B a defence against A, by preventing A from asserting a particular right against B.[8] Thirdly—in some situations, at least—B's defence is only temporary: once B has the necessary time to adjust, his defence may disappear, so that A can then assert his right against B.[9]

Nonetheless, there are important similarities between estoppel by representation and promissory estoppel. Each doctrine: (i) depends on A's conduct and B's reliance; and (ii) cannot, by itself, give B a claim against A.

2.2.3 Proprietary estoppel: a special form of estoppel?

In *Crabb v Arun DC*, as in a case of estoppel by representation or promissory estoppel, A's conduct and B's reliance were vital. As Lord Denning MR noted, however, proprietary estoppel is allowed to *'give rise to a cause of action'*. On this view, there is a crucial difference between proprietary estoppel and those two other forms of estoppel: proprietary estoppel can, by itself, operate to give B a right against A. On this view, *Crabb* is not a case in which the council was simply *prevented* from asserting a fact or right against Mr Crabb; rather, the council came under a positive duty to Mr Crabb—a duty to grant him, for free, a right of way allowing him to get from his land to Hook Lane.[10]

It therefore seems that, when used as part of the term 'proprietary estoppel', the word 'estoppel' is misleading. True, like other forms of estoppel, proprietary estoppel is based on A's conduct and B's reliance—but in contrast to estoppel by representation or promissory estoppel, the doctrine of proprietary estoppel is not simply about preventing A from asserting a fact or right against B; instead, it can operate, by itself, to impose a duty on A to B.

This view, that proprietary estoppel can *'give rise to a cause of action'* has been the prevailing analysis of the doctrine since (at least) the time of the Court of Appeal's decision in *Crabb v Arun DC*.[11] As we will see in the next extract, however, the House of Lords has recently challenged that view.

2.3 PROPRIETARY ESTOPPEL AS A STANDARD FORM OF ESTOPPEL?

Yeoman's Row Management Ltd v Cobbe [2008] 1 WLR 1752, HL

Facts: Yeoman's Row Management Limited (YRML) held the registered freehold of land in Knightsbridge. Mr and Mrs Lisle-Mainwaring controlled the company. A building on the land contained thirteen flats. Mrs Lisle-Mainwaring hoped to redevelop the land: if planning permission could be obtained, six houses could be built, thereby greatly

---

8 See, e.g., *Combe v Combe* [1915] 2 KB 215.
9 See, e.g., *Tool Metal Manufacturing Co Ltd v Tungsten Electric Co Ltd* [1955] 1 WLR 761.
10 Scarman LJ, at 198, stated that Mr Crabb had a right *'either to an easement or to a licence upon terms to be agreed'*. But Lord Denning MR, at 190, stated that the court should declare that Mr Crabb had an easement; and Lawton LJ, at 192, agreed to the terms indicated by Lord Denning. The difficulty with Scarman LJ's suggestion that a licence might suffice is that, as we saw in Chapter 8, a licence would not protect Mr Crabb if the council were to sell its land to C.
11 See also *Inwards v Baker* [1965] 2 QB 29, 37, *per* Lord Denning MR.

increasing the value of the land. Mrs Lisle-Mainwaring, acting on behalf of YRML, entered into lengthy negotiations with Mr Cobbe, a property developer. They came to an oral agreement, with the following key points: (i) Mr Cobbe, at his own expense, would apply for planning permission to demolish the existing block of flats and to erect, in its place, a terrace of six houses; (ii) upon the grant of planning permission and the obtaining of vacant possession, YRML would sell its freehold to Mr Cobbe (or to a company nominated by him) for an up-front price of £12m; (iii) Mr Cobbe (or his nominee company) would develop the property in accordance with the planning permission; and (iv) Mr Cobbe (or his nominee company) would sell the six houses and pay to YRML 50 per cent of the amount, if any, by which the gross proceeds of sale exceeded £24m.[12]

The basics of the deal were thus clear: if Mr Cobbe were to fail to obtain planning permission, he would be paid nothing. But, if he were to succeed in getting planning permission, he and YRML would be able to share in the profits made from the redevelopment of the land. Mr Cobbe and Mrs Lisle-Mainwaring were both experienced business people: they both knew that the oral agreement was not legally binding and that a later, signed contract would have to be concluded, dealing with further issues not covered by the oral agreement. Nonetheless, Mr Cobbe, with the encouragement of Mrs Lisle-Mainwaring, spent considerable time and effort and incurred considerable expense, between late 2002 and March 2004, in applying for planning permission. By late 2003, Mrs Lisle-Mainwaring had formed an intention not to comply with the oral agreement, deciding instead to ask for more than £12m up-front before selling the freehold—but she hid her plan from Mr Cobbe, deliberately giving him the impression that, if planning permission were obtained, she would enter into a binding contract based on the oral agreement.

In March 2004, as a result of Mr Cobbe's efforts, planning permission was granted. As a result, before any redevelopment work had been started, it seems that YRML's freehold increased in value by around £4m. Mrs Lisle-Mainwaring then informed Mr Cobbe that she would only sell the land if he paid £20m up-front (as well as the agreed share of the proceeds should Mr Cobbe sell on for over £24m). Mr Cobbe objected and brought a claim against YRML. At first, he alleged a breach of contract—a claim that was doomed to fail, because no final agreement had been reached, and there was, in any case, no signed, written agreement between the parties complying with s 2 of the Law of Property (Miscellaneous Provisions) Act 1989 (LP(MP)A 1989) (see Chapter 9, section 3). Mr Cobbe then amended his pleadings to seek relief on the basis of proprietary estoppel, a constructive trust, or unjust enrichment.

At first instance, Etherton J found that Mr Cobbe did have a good proprietary estoppel claim; as a result, he ordered YRML to pay Mr Cobbe a sum equal to half of the increase in value of YRML's freehold caused by the grant of planning permission (as it turned out, this meant that YRML had to pay Mr Cobbe £2m). The Court of Appeal upheld that decision. The House of Lords, however, found that Mr Cobbe had *no* proprietary estoppel claim. It also found that he had not acquired a right under a constructive trust. The House of Lords did decide that he had a claim based on YRML's unjust enrichment, because YRML had received the benefit of his services without paying for them; but that claim allowed him to recover only his expenses in applying for planning permission, plus a reasonable fee to cover his professional services. As a result, Mr Cobbe was therefore limited to receiving only around £150,000—far less than the £2m awarded to him by Etherton J.

[12] [2008] 1 WLR 1752 at [6].

Our focus here is on the House of Lords' reasoning in rejecting Mr Cobbe's proprietary estoppel claim: it seems to be based on the view that proprietary estoppel, contrary to the view of Lord Denning MR in *Crabb*, is simply a standard form of estoppel and so does *not* operate as an independent means by which B can acquire a right.

Lord Scott

At [14]–[20]

Both the judge and the Court of Appeal regarded the relief granted as justified on the basis of proprietary estoppel. I respectfully disagree. The remedy to which, on the facts as found by the judge, Mr Cobbe is entitled can, in my opinion, be described neither as based on an estoppel nor as proprietary in character. There are several important authorities to which I want to refer but I want first to consider as a matter of principle the nature of a proprietary estoppel. An "estoppel" bars the object of it from asserting some fact or facts, or, sometimes, something that is a mixture of fact and law, that stands in the way of some right claimed by the person entitled to the benefit of the estoppel. The estoppel becomes a "proprietary" estoppel—a sub-species of a "promissory" estoppel—if the right claimed is a proprietary right, usually a right to or over land but, in principle, equally available in relation to chattels or choses in action. So, what is the fact or facts, or the matter of mixed fact and law, that, in the present case, [YRML] is said to be barred from asserting? And what is the proprietary right claimed by Mr Cobbe that the facts and matters [YRML] is barred from asserting might otherwise defeat?

The pleadings do not answer these questions [. . .] The terms of the oral "agreement in principle", the second agreement, relied on by Mr Cobbe are pleaded but it is accepted that there remained still for negotiation other terms. The second agreement was, contractually, an incomplete agreement. The terms that had already been agreed were regarded by the parties as being "binding in honour", but it follows that the parties knew they were not legally binding. So what is it that [YRML] is estopped from asserting or from denying? [YRML] cannot be said to be estopped from asserting that the second agreement was unenforceable for want of writing, for Mr Cobbe does not claim that it was enforceable; nor from denying that the second agreement covered all the terms that needed to be agreed between the parties, for Mr Cobbe does not claim that it did; nor from denying that, pre 18 March 2004, Mr Cobbe had acquired any proprietary interest in the property, for he has never alleged that he had. And what proprietary claim was Mr Cobbe making that an estoppel was necessary to protect? His originally pleaded claim to specific performance of the second agreement was abandoned at a very early stage in the trial and the proprietary claims that remained were claims that [YRML] held the property on trust for itself and Mr Cobbe. These remaining proprietary claims were presumably based on the proposition that a constructive trust of the property, with appropriate beneficial interests for [YRML] and Mr Cobbe, should, by reason of the unconscionable conduct of Mrs Lisle-Mainwaring, be imposed on the property. I must examine that proposition when dealing with constructive trust as a possible means of providing Mr Cobbe with a remedy, but the proposition is not one that requires or depends upon any estoppel.

It is relevant to notice that the amendments to Mr Cobbe's pleaded prayer for relief, made when the specific performance and damages for breach of contract claims were abandoned, include the following:

"(4) Alternatively, a declaration that [YRML and Mrs Lisle-Mainwaring] are estopped from denying that [Mr Cobbe] has such interest in the Property and/or the proceeds of sale thereof as the Court thinks fit."

This is the only pleaded formulation of the estoppel relied on by Mr Cobbe and, with respect to the pleader, is both meaningless and pointless. Etherton J concluded, in para.85 of his judgment,[13] that the facts of the case "gave rise to a proprietary estoppel in favour of Mr Cobbe", but nowhere identified the content of the estoppel. Mummery LJ agreed (paras.60 and 61 of his judgment, concurred in by Dyson LJ (para.120) and Sir Martin Nourse (para.141)),[14] but he, too, did not address the content of the estoppel. Both Etherton J and Mummery LJ regarded the proprietary estoppel conclusion as justified by the unconscionability of Mrs Lisle-Mainwaring's conduct. My Lords, unconscionability of conduct may well lead to a remedy but, in my opinion, proprietary estoppel cannot be the route to it unless the ingredients for a proprietary estoppel are present. These ingredients should include, in principle, a proprietary claim made by a claimant and an answer to that claim based on some fact, or some point of mixed fact and law, that the person against whom the claim is made can be estopped from asserting. To treat a "proprietary estoppel equity" as requiring neither a proprietary claim by the claimant nor an estoppel against the defendant but simply unconscionable behaviour is, in my respectful opinion, a recipe for confusion [...]

The problem (for Mr Cobbe's proprietary estoppel claim) is that when he made the planning application his expectation was, for proprietary estoppel purposes, the wrong sort of expectation. It was not an expectation that he would, if the planning application succeeded, become entitled to "a certain interest in land". His expectation was that he and Mrs Lisle-Mainwaring, or their respective legal advisers, would sit down and agree the outstanding contractual terms to be incorporated into the formal written agreement, which he justifiably believed would include the already agreed core financial terms, and that his purchase, and subsequently his development of the property, in accordance with that written agreement would follow.

At [27]–[28]

[...] It would be an unusually unsophisticated negotiator who was not well aware that oral agreements relating to [the transfer of estates in land] are by statute unenforceable and that no express reservation to make them so is needed. Mr Cobbe was an experienced property developer and Mrs Lisle-Mainwaring gives every impression of knowing her way around the negotiating table. Mr Cobbe did not spend his money and time on the planning application in the mistaken belief that the agreement was legally enforceable. He spent his money and time well aware that it was not. Mrs Lisle-Mainwaring did not encourage in him a belief that the second agreement was enforceable. She encouraged in him a belief that she would abide by it although it was not. Mr Cobbe's belief, or expectation, was always speculative. He knew she was not legally bound. He regarded her as bound "in honour" but that is an acknowledgement that she was not legally bound.

The reality of this case, in my opinion, is that Etherton J and the Court of Appeal regarded their finding that Mrs Lisle-Mainwaring's behaviour in repudiating, and seeking an improvement on, the core financial terms of the second agreement was unconscionable, an evaluation from which I do not in the least dissent, as sufficient to justify the creation of a "proprietary estoppel equity". As Mummery LJ said (para.123), she took unconscionable advantage of Mr Cobbe. The advantage taken was the benefit of his services, his time and his money, in obtaining planning permission for the property. The advantage was unconscionable because immediately following the grant of planning permission, she repudiated the financial terms on which Mr Cobbe had been expecting to be able to purchase the property. But to leap from

[13] [For Etherton J's decision, see [2005] EWHC 266 (Ch).]
[14] [For the Court of Appeal decision, see [2006] 1 WLR 2964.]

there to a conclusion that a proprietary estoppel case was made out was not, in my opinion, justified. Let it be supposed that Mrs Lisle-Mainwaring were to be held estopped from denying that the core financial terms of the second agreement were the financial terms on which Mr Cobbe was entitled to purchase the property. How would that help Mr Cobbe? He still would not have a complete agreement. Suppose Mrs Lisle-Mainwaring had simply said she had changed her mind and did not want the property to be sold after all. What would she be estopped from denying? Proprietary estoppel requires, in my opinion, clarity as to what it is that the object of the estoppel is to be estopped from denying, or asserting, and clarity as to the interest in the property in question that that denial, or assertion, would otherwise defeat. If these requirements are not recognised, proprietary estoppel will lose contact with its roots and risk becoming unprincipled and therefore unpredictable, if it has not already become so. This is not, in my opinion, a case in which a remedy can be granted to Mr Cobbe on the basis of proprietary estoppel.

Lord Walker

At [71]–[72]

So the judge found that Mr Cobbe believed that Mrs Lisle-Mainwaring was, and regarded herself as, bound in honour to enter into a formal written contract if planning permission was granted; and that Mr Cobbe regarded himself as similarly bound. It is implicit—in my view necessarily and deliberately implicit—in the judge's carefully chosen language that neither Mrs Lisle-Mainwaring nor Mr Cobbe regarded herself or himself as legally bound. They were both very experienced in property matters and they knew perfectly well that that was not the position.

Another unusual feature of this case is the judge's finding that Mr Cobbe believed that he would be reimbursed his reasonable expenditure if Mrs Lisle-Mainwaring decided to withdraw from the arrangement before planning permission was granted. This emphasis on the actual grant of planning permission as the crucial condition produces a strange result: would it be conscionable for Mrs Lisle-Mainwaring to withdraw (subject only to reimbursement) at a stage when 99% of the work necessary to obtain planning permission had been done, and success was virtually certain, but unconscionable to do so once success had actually been achieved? This feature of the arrangement emphasises the risk which Mr Cobbe was undertaking, in deciding to rely on Mrs Lisle-Mainwaring's sense of honour.

At [79]–[91]

Crabb v Arun District Council, the facts of which are well known, is a difficult case, not least because of different views taken by different members of the Court [...] The situation was that of a commercial negotiation in which both sides expected formal legal documents to be agreed and executed. The case is best explained, I think, by recognising that the Council's erection of the two sets of gates was an act so unequivocal that it led to Mr Crabb irretrievably altering his position, putting the matter beyond the stage at which it was open to negotiation [...]

[...] In my opinion none of these cases casts any doubt on the general principle laid down by this House in *Ramsden v Dyson* (1866) LR 1 HL 129, that conscious reliance on honour alone will not give rise to an estoppel. Nor do they cast doubt on the general principle that the court should be very slow to introduce uncertainty into commercial transactions by over-ready use of equitable concepts such as fiduciary obligations and equitable estoppel. That applies to commercial negotiations whether or not they are expressly stated to be subject to contract.

[...] The informal bargain made in this case was unusually complex, as both courts below acknowledged. When a claim based on equitable estoppel is made in a domestic setting the informal bargain or understanding is typically on the following lines: if you live here as my carer/companion/lover you will have a home for life. The expectation is of acquiring and keeping an interest in an identified property. In this case, by contrast, Mr Cobbe was expecting to get a contract. Under that contract he (or much more probably a company controlled by him) would have been entitled to acquire the property for a down-payment of £12m, but only as part of a deal under which the block of flats on the site was to be demolished, the site cleared, and six very expensive townhouses were to be erected instead, and sold for the best prices that they would fetch [...]

[...] Mr Cobbe's case seems to me to fail on the simple but fundamental point that, as persons experienced in the property world, both parties knew that there was no legally binding contract, and that either was therefore free to discontinue the negotiations without legal liability—that is liability in equity as well as at law [...] Mr Cobbe was therefore running a risk, but he stood to make a handsome profit if the deal went ahead, and the market stayed favourable. He may have thought that any attempt to get Mrs Lisle-Mainwaring to enter into a written contract before the grant of planning permission would be counter-productive. Whatever his reasons for doing so, the fact is that he ran a commercial risk, with his eyes open, and the outcome has proved unfortunate for him. It is true that he did not expressly state, at the time, that he was relying solely on Mrs Lisle-Mainwaring's sense of honour, but to draw that sort of distinction in a commercial context would be as unrealistic, in my opinion, as to draw a firm distinction depending on whether the formula "subject to contract" had or had not actually been used.

2.3.1 The decision itself

Although the House of Lords overturned the decisions of Etherton J and the Court of Appeal, the actual result in *Yeoman's Row* is not too surprising. It rests on the finding that Mr Cobbe, by undertaking work when he knew that there was no contract between him and YRML, was running a risk: the risk that, even if he did obtain planning permission, Mrs Lisle-Mainwaring (on behalf of YRML) might pull out of the planned contract. The House of Lords' assessment of the facts seems to be that: (i) it was perhaps dishonourable or immoral for Mrs Lisle-Mainwaring to lead on Mr Cobbe and then pull out of the planned agreement; but (ii) Mr Cobbe, an experienced property developer, should have been aware that business people do not always do the right thing.

This analysis means that, even on the previously prevailing view of the doctrine, Mr Cobbe would have no proprietary estoppel claim. For example, in *Attorney-General of Hong Kong v Humphrey's Estate*,[15] B started work on some land in the belief that A would sell that land to B. A and B had made a preliminary agreement for a sale, but that agreement was expressly 'subject to contract'. A thus made clear to B that, until a final contract was signed, A was not bound to transfer its ownership of the land to B. As a result, B acted at his own risk when undertaking the work and so proprietary estoppel did *not* impose a duty on A to B.

2.3.2 The wider consequences of the decision

To deny Mr Cobbe's proprietary estoppel claim, the House of Lords did *not* have to adopt a new view of the nature of proprietary estoppel. Yet that is precisely what the House of Lords

---

[15] [1987] 2 All ER 387.

did: it rejected the view, expressed by Lord Denning MR in *Crabb*, that proprietary estoppel can operate as a cause of action; instead, proprietary estoppel was seen simply as an application of standard estoppel principles—that is, of estoppel by representation and promissory estoppel.

That analysis has certain attractions. In particular, it removes the inconsistency inherent in saying that proprietary estoppel can operate as a cause of action, but other forms of estoppel cannot. It means that we no longer have to answer the difficult question of why B's reliance on A can give him a right where A makes a commitment relating to land, but not in other cases (e.g. where A makes a commitment to pay B money). But it is not the only way of removing that inconsistency: in Australia and many of the US states, for example, estoppel is allowed to operate as a cause of action *both* where A's commitment relates to land *and* in other cases.[16]

The chief disadvantage with the House of Lords' analysis in *Yeoman's Row* is that, whether or not is a good idea in theory, it is very hard to reconcile with some recent leading cases on proprietary estoppel—a point that is made in the following extract.

McFarlane and Robertson, 'The Death of Proprietary Estoppel' [2008] LMCLQ 449, 453–4

The reasoning of each of Lord Scott and Lord Walker (while differing one from the other) rests on what seems to be a dramatic re-interpretation of proprietary estoppel, as it has come to be commonly understood and applied. Lord Scott's re-interpretation essentially denies the existence of proprietary estoppel as a distinct doctrine. Its effect is that proprietary estoppel does not exist as an independent means by which B can acquire a right against A. Instead, it seems, "proprietary estoppel" simply consists of an application to particular facts of estoppel by representation or of promissory estoppel. First, like estoppel by representation, it can operate to prevent A from denying the truth of a matter of fact, or a mixed matter of fact and law. However, A's being bound to that fact is only of use to B if it assists B in establishing an independent cause of action (e.g. it allows B to show he has a contract with A; it allows B to show A has granted B a property right, etc). So, for example, it does not avail B to show that A is estopped from denying that A made a promise to give B a right: the mere fact of such a promise cannot give B a right against A. To acquire a right based on A's promise, B must show that A is estopped from denying the fact that A is under a *legal duty* to B to perform that promise. And, even then, where A's promise is part of a bargain under which A is to give B a right relating to land, A may still be able to rely on section 2 of the Law of Property (Miscellaneous Provisions) Act 1989 to show that he is under no contractual duty to B. Second, like promissory estoppel, proprietary estoppel can be used by B to prevent A (perhaps only temporarily) from asserting a particular right against B.

This analysis, as noted by Lord Scott, is consistent with the *name* of proprietary estoppel; however, it cannot be reconciled with the current operation of the doctrine. Whatever its roots, proprietary estoppel has been used, particularly since the 1960s, as an independent means by which B can acquire a right against A. As a result, many examples of its application cannot be explained on the basis put forward by the House of Lords in *Yeoman's Row*. For example, in the seminal case of *Crabb v Arun DC*, B acquired a right against A as a result of B's reasonable reliance on A's implied commitment to grant B an easement. Lord Scott

---

[16] For Australia, see, e.g., *Waltons Stores (Interstate Ltd) v Maher* (1988) 164 CLR 387. For the general position in the USA, see s 90 of the Restatement (Second) of Contracts.

analyses the decision as depending on a representation by A that B *already* had such a right;[17] not on a promise that B would acquire such a right in the future. However, that view is very difficult to reconcile with the facts of *Crabb*, or the analysis of the Court of Appeal in that case.[18] Moreover, even on Lord Scott's analysis of the case, it is not clear why Arun District Council could not rely on section 52 of the Law of Property Act 1925 to show that it had not, in fact, granted Mr Crabb an easement. If proprietary estoppel cannot be used to avoid the effect of section 2 of the 1989 Act, how can it be allowed to circumvent the effect of another formality rule?

When looking at other cases in this chapter, we will also need to ask if they can be reconciled with the *Yeoman's Row* analysis. If not, there are three possible reactions. The first is to say that the previous decisions must now be regarded as incorrect in the light of the House of Lords' view in *Yeoman's Row*.

The second is to say that the previous decisions must now be regarded as incorrect in having applied proprietary estoppel, but that the results in those cases can be justified on other grounds: for example, in some cases, it may be that the B's claim can be reanalysed as depending on the constructive trust principles that we will examine in Chapter 18, rather than on proprietary estoppel. Alternatively, as the House of Lords did in *Yeoman's Row* itself, we may be able to reanalyse B's claim as depending on A's unjust enrichment at B's expense.

The third reaction is to say that, to the extent that it is inconsistent with those previous decisions, the House of Lords' view of the nature of proprietary estoppel is incorrect. That route is possible, because we can see those views as unnecessary for the actual decision in *Yeoman's Row*.[19] The view that proprietary estoppel is an independent means of acquiring a right is consistent with the *result* in the case, because it can simply be said that, on the facts of the case, it was not reasonable for Mr Cobbe to rely on Mrs Lisle-Mainwaring, given that both parties knew that no contract had yet been concluded.[20]

3 THE TEST: THE REQUIREMENTS OF PROPRIETARY ESTOPPEL

3.1 INTRODUCTION

Prior to the House of Lords' decision in *Yeoman's Row*, it could be said that a party (B) must satisfy three requirements in order to show that proprietary estoppel imposes a duty on

---

[17] At [22].

[18] For example, Lord Denning MR, [1976] Ch 179 at 188, considers the situations in which B can acquire a right as a result of A leading B to believe that A will act in a particular way in the future; indeed, as noted by Lord Denning MR, at 186, the first instance judge stated that '*Mr Crabb believed that he had an assurance by the council that he* would *have access at point B*' (emphasis added). Indeed, at 187, Lord Denning MR directly states that proprietary estoppel, unlike some other forms of estoppel, '*does give rise to a cause of action*'.

[19] See further McFarlane and Robertson, 'The Death of Proprietary Estoppel' [2008] LMCLQ 449.

[20] The decision of the House of Lords in *Thorner v Majors and ors*, to be discussed on this book's comparison website, may play a very important role in determining the effect of the *Yeoman's Row* reasoning. For a narrow view of that effect see *Herbert v Doyle* [2008] EWHC 1950 at [13]–[15].

another party (A):

- A must be, in some way, responsible for a belief, held by B, that B already has a right in relation to A's land *or* that B will acquire such a right; *and*
- B must have reasonably relied on that belief—that is, he must have acted in a particular way on the faith of that belief; *and*
- B will suffer a detriment if A does not act consistently with that belief.

For example, in *Crabb v Arun DC*:

- by reaching an 'agreement in principle' with Mr Crabb (B) and then building a gate at Point B (the planned point of access from Mr Crabb's land to the council's neighbouring road), the council (A) was responsible for Mr Crabb's belief that he had (or would get) the planned right of way; *and*
- Mr Crabb relied on that belief by selling off the front part of his land without reserving a right of way over that land; *and*
- if the council were then free to act inconsistently with that belief by refusing to grant him a right of access, Mr Crabb would suffer a detriment, because he would be unable to make a commercial use of his retained land.

We will now look at three specific cases dealing with the requirements of proprietary estoppel. In doing so we have to bear two key questions in mind: (i) what effect will the House of Lords' decision in *Yeoman's Row* have on the test; and (ii) what role, if any, does the concept of unconscionability have to play in the test?

3.1.1 The effect of *Yeoman's Row*

On the reasoning adopted by the House of Lords in *Yeoman's Row*, the first part of the test as set out above is too generous to B. On that reasoning, it seems that proprietary estoppel can only apply if A is in some way responsible for a belief, held by B, that B *already has* a right in relation to A's land, *or* that A is under a legal duty to give B such a right. This means that proprietary estoppel cannot assist B in a case in which A leads B reasonably to believe that B will get a right in the future, without also leading B to believe that A has a *current* legal duty to give B such a right.

3.1.2 The role of unconscionability?

In considering the requirements of proprietary estoppel, it is also important to ask what role, if any, the concept of unconscionability has to play: for example, is it an additional, fourth requirement, so that B can only acquire a right through proprietary estoppel if he can show that it would be unconscionable for A to deny B such a right? Is it, instead, an alternative to the three requirements set out above, so that B can bypass those requirements and acquire a right simply by showing that it would be unconscionable for A to deny B such a right? Or is it, instead, an underlying concept that assists the court in understanding and applying the three requirements set out above?

3.2 CASE 1: *TAYLOR FASHIONS*

Taylor Fashions v Liverpool Victoria Trustees; Old & Campbell v Liverpool Victoria Friendly Society [1982] QB 133, CA

Facts: Each of Taylor Fashions (Taylors) and Old & Campbell (Olds) made a separate claim that it had a right to renew a lease of business premises. The landlord, Liverpool Victoria, denied that either Taylors or Olds had such a right. All of the parties had acted on the basis that both Taylors and Olds *did* have a right to renew the lease: they all assumed that an earlier lease that contained such a right bound Liverpool Victoria. As a result, Taylors and Olds had, for example, spent money on improving the premises. But that general assumption was mistaken: Liverpool Victoria was not bound by the earlier lease. Taylors and Olds, because each had acted in reliance on the mistaken belief that it had a right to renew, argued that Liverpool Victoria was now estopped from denying the existence of the right to renew. Liverpool Victoria argued that proprietary estoppel could not apply, because it had not acted unconscionably, nor had it tried to deceive Taylor or Olds: it, too, had genuinely believed that it was bound by the earlier lease.

Oliver J

At 144

This is the principal point upon which the parties divide. Mr Scott and Mr Essayan [counsel for Taylors and Olds, respectively] contend that what the court has to look at in relation to the party alleged to be estopped is only his conduct and its result, and not—or, at any rate, not necessarily—his state of mind. It then has to ask whether what that party is now seeking to do is unconscionable. Mr Millett [counsel for Liverpool Victoria] contends that it is an essential feature of this particular equitable doctrine that the party alleged to be estopped must, before the assertion of his strict rights can be considered unconscionable, be aware both of what his strict rights were and of the fact that the other party is acting in the belief that they will not be enforced against him [...]

[Mr Millett's contention was supported by the decision of Fry J in *Willmott v Barber*.[21] In that case, Fry J set out five criteria or 'probanda' for proprietary estoppel, one of which is that A, when making a representation to B that B has a particular right in relation to A's land, must be aware of his true rights against B.]

Now, convenient and attractive as I find Mr Millett's submissions as a matter of argument, I am not at all sure that so orderly and tidy a theory is really deducible from the authorities—certainly from the more recent authorities, which seem to me to support a much wider equitable jurisdiction to interfere in cases where the assertion of strict legal rights is found by the court to be unconscionable. It may well be (although I think that this must now be considered open to doubt) that the strict *Willmott v. Barber* probanda are applicable as necessary requirements in those cases where all that has happened is that the party alleged to be estopped has stood by without protest while his rights have been infringed...in a case of mere passivity, it is readily intelligible that there must be shown a duty to speak, protest or interfere which cannot normally arise in the absence of knowledge or at least a suspicion of the true position.

---

[21] (1880) 15 Ch D 96.

[Oliver J then examined a number of authorities, before continuing as follows.]

[...] the more recent cases indicate, in my judgment, that the application of the *Ramsden v Dyson* (1866) LR 1 HL 129 principle—whether you call it proprietary estoppel, estoppel by acquiescence or estoppel by encouragement is really immaterial—requires a very much broader approach which is directed rather at ascertaining whether, in particular individual circumstances, it would be unconscionable for a party to be permitted to deny that which knowingly, or unknowingly, he has allowed or encouraged another to assume to his detriment than to inquiring whether the circumstances can be fitted within the confines of some preconceived formula serving as a universal yardstick for every form of unconscionable behaviour.

So regarded, knowledge of the true position by the party alleged to be estopped becomes merely one of the relevant factors—it may even be a determining factor in certain cases—in the overall inquiry [...in] *Crabb v Arun District Council* [...] there was no mistake. Each party knew that the road was vested in the defendants and each knew that no formal grant had been made. Indeed I cannot see why in considering whether the defendants were behaving unconscionably, it should have made the slightest difference to the result if, at the time when [Mr Crabb] was encouraged to open his access to the road, the defendants had thought that they were bound to grant it. The fact was that he had been encouraged to alter his position irrevocably to his detriment on the faith of a belief, which was known to and encouraged by the defendants, that he was going to be given a particular right of access—a belief which, for all that appears, the defendants probably shared at that time.

[...] The inquiry which I have to make therefore, as it seems to me, is simply whether, in all the circumstances of this case, it was unconscionable for the defendants to seek to take advantage of the mistake which, at the material time, everybody shared, and, in approaching that, I must consider the cases of the two plaintiffs separately because it may be that quite different considerations apply to each.

Oliver J's conclusion was that Taylors' claim failed, but Olds' claim succeeded. The difficulties for Taylors were: (i) Liverpool Victoria had not encouraged Taylors to believe that it had a right to renew the lease; but instead, both parties had *assumed* that such a right existed; and (ii) it was not clear that the improvements made to the premises by Taylors were carried out in reliance on its belief that it had a right to renew the lease, because Taylors, in any case, benefited from those improvements by continuing to use the premises up to the end of its existing lease.

In contrast, Olds had been encouraged by Liverpool Victoria to spend a 'very large sum' on improving the premises precisely because of the belief that it would be able, at the end of the existing lease, to renew that lease and continue using the premises. As a result, Liverpool Victoria was ordered to allow Olds to renew its lease.

3.2.1 The decision itself

The success of Olds' claim demonstrates that proprietary estoppel can operate even if a landowner (A), when he encourages another party (B) to believe something, honestly believes that thing to be true. So, proprietary estoppel does not require A to deceive B by leading B to believe something that A knows to be false. There is, however, an important difference between: (i) a case in which a party (A) *actively encourages* another party (B) to believe something; and (ii) a case in which A simply goes along with, or fails to correct, B's belief. In the former case (as the success of Olds' claim shows), B can rely on proprietary estoppel even if A did not know that B's belief was false; in the latter case (as the failure of Taylors' claim shows), B cannot rely on proprietary estoppel. The point seems to be that, in such a case, it cannot be said that A is in any way *responsible* for B's belief: A did not encourage that belief; nor did he allow B to believe it even when A knew it to be false.

3.2.2 The wider significance of the decision: the effect of *Yeoman's Row*

The decision in *Taylor Fashions* is consistent both with the test for proprietary estoppel set out above and the reasoning of the House of Lords in *Yeoman's Row*. This is because each of Taylors and Olds believed that it *already* had a right in relation to Liverpool Victoria's land: the right to renew a lease.

3.2.3 The wider significance of the decision: the role of unconscionability

The decision in *Taylor* has been hailed as allowing an important relaxation in the requirements of proprietary estoppel: indeed, it has been called a '*watershed in the development of proprietary estoppel*'.[22] Certainly, Oliver J made clear that B can acquire a right through proprietary estoppel even if the five strict requirements laid down by *Willmott v Barber* have not all been fulfilled. And, in reaching that conclusion, Oliver J emphasized that proprietary estoppel, a doctrine developed by courts of equity, ultimately depends on the notion of unconscionability.

But we need to be careful. The decision certainly does not mean that, in a proprietary estoppel case, a judge can find in B's favour when the judge thinks that it would be 'fair' for B to win. After all, in *Taylor Fashions* itself, Oliver J rejected Taylors' claim: even though his Lordship clearly had a good deal of sympathy for that claim—dismissing it with 'regret'— he still found that the specific requirements of proprietary estoppel had not been satisfied. Further, in *Yeoman's Row*, Lord Scott emphasized that the established requirements of proprietary estoppel cannot be replaced with a simple test of unconscionability.[23]

In the following extract, Cooke takes a similar view, whilst also exploring what other roles unconscionability may play in cases such as *Taylor Fashions*.

Cooke, *The Modern Law of Estoppel* (2000, pp 85–6)

When we say that the court must decide whether or not it would be unconscionable to allow the representor [A] to go back on the impression he has given, the word 'unconscionable' does two jobs. First, it points us to the equity tradition and to the discretionary nature of the court's jurisdiction. Second, in the context of estoppel it indicates the issues relevant to the court's decision, namely detrimental reliance and, where appropriate, other factors [. . .] Where unconscionability is mentioned, we find it used in a number of different ways. At times it appears as a description of the whole process of the court's inquiry, without specifying what it involves, sometimes it is described as one item on a checklist of factors; more usually it is seen as summing up other factors, whether just detrimental reliance or a bundle involving at least detrimental reliance and other matters in addition [. . .]

---

[22] See Gray and Gray, *Elements of Land Law* (2nd edn, 1993, p 324), cited by Robert Walker LJ in *Gillett v Holt* [2001] Ch 210, 225. See now *Elements of Land Law* (5th edn, 2009, [9.2.36]).

[23] See [16] in the extract above.

Decisions involving unconscionability are not pure value judgments. There is a strong judicial resistance to any hint of 'palm-tree justice': a form of justice that is unacceptable because it is unpredictable. 'The court does not yet sit, as under a palm tree, to exercise a general discretion to do what the man in the street, on a general overview of the case, might regard as fair.' Thus, even where unconscionability is not spelt out in terms of detrimental reliance, with or without other factors, it will be found, it is submitted, that detrimental reliance is what the court actually examines. *Taylor Fashions Ltd v Liverpool Victoria Trustee Co Ltd* is a prime example of this. Oliver J, faced with a barrage of technical rules, used the idea of unconscionability as a way of stepping away from the rules. But his reasoning as to whether or not it would be unconscionable to allow the landlord to go back on his representation, to the two tenants, that the option was valid, was based firmly on what if anything the tenants believed as a result of the representation and what if anything they did by way of work and expenditure as a result—that is, what he examined was detrimental reliance.

3.3 CASE 2: *GILLETT V HOLT*

Gillett v Holt [2001] Ch 210, CA

Facts: Geoffrey Gillett first met Mr Holt at Woodhall Spa golf club in 1952, at which time, the former was a schoolboy aged 12 and the latter was a gentleman farmer (and a bachelor) aged 38. Geoffrey became Mr Holt's regular caddie and a friendship developed between them. In 1956, Geoffrey left school to start working on Mr Holt's farm (The Limes). He continued working for Mr Holt, taking on extra responsibilities, for over thirty-eight years. In 1971, Mr Gillett and his wife moved into a farmhouse (The Beeches), newly acquired by a company (KAHL) controlled by Mr Holt. In 1995, Mr Holt attempted to sack Mr Gillett and to remove him from The Beeches. Mr Holt also altered his will so that Mr Gillett was no longer the principal beneficiary.[24]

Mr Gillett claimed that Mr Holt was under a duty, arising as a result of proprietary estoppel: (i) not to remove him and his wife from The Beeches; and (ii) to transfer to him at least some of the The Limes. Mr Gillett claimed that, during the period from 1964 to 1989, Mr Holt gave seven 'specific assurances' that 'one day, he (Mr Gillett) would own the farm'. It was claimed that these assurances reflected a general understanding between Mr Gillett and Mr Holt, and were usually at significant events: for example, after Mr Gillett brought in his first harvest (1964) and at the christening of Mr Gillett's first child (1971).

Robert Walker LJ

At 225

Proprietary estoppel

[A]lthough the judgment is, for convenience, divided into several sections with headings which give a rough indication of the subject matter, it is important to note at the outset that

---

[24] The principal beneficiary instead was a Mr Wood, whom Mr Holt had met in 1992. According to the first instance judge in *Gillett v Holt*, '*Mr Holt's relationship with Mr Wood developed into something of an obsession, which was of concern to his family and other friends*': see [2001] Ch 210, 222.

the doctrine of proprietary estoppel cannot be treated as subdivided into three or four water-tight compartments. Both sides are agreed on that, and in the course of the oral argument in this court it repeatedly became apparent that the quality of the relevant assurances may influence the issue of reliance, that reliance and detriment are often intertwined, and that whether there is a distinct need for a "mutual understanding" may depend on how the other elements are formulated and understood. Moreover the fundamental principle that equity is concerned to prevent unconscionable conduct permeates all the elements of the doctrine. In the end the court must look at the matter in the round [...]

[I]n this case Mr Holt's assurances were repeated over a long period, usually before the assembled company on special family occasions, and some of them (such as "it was all going to be ours anyway" [in 1975]) were completely unambiguous [...] Plainly the assurances given on this occasion were intended to be relied on, and were in fact relied on.

At 231

Detriment

It is therefore necessary to go on to consider detriment [...] It is understandable that the judge devoted most attention to the issue of Mr Gillett being underpaid because that was the issue (affecting detriment) on which most time was spent in cross-examination [...] The judge said that he was not persuaded, on the evidence, that Mr Gillett did in fact receive less than a rea-sonable wage for his services as a manager, or that he did so as part of an understanding related to his expectations, and that conclusion has not been seriously challenged in this court.

Both sides agree that the element of detriment is an essential ingredient of proprietary estoppel [...] The overwhelming weight of authority shows that detriment is required. But the authorities also show that it is not a narrow or technical concept. The detriment need not consist of the expenditure of money or other quantifiable financial detriment, so long as it is something substantial. The requirement must be approached as part of a broad inquiry as to whether repudiation of an assurance is or is not unconscionable in all the circumstances.

[...] There must be sufficient causal link between the assurance relied on and the detri-ment asserted. The issue of detriment must be judged at the moment when the person who has given the assurance seeks to go back on it. Whether the detriment is sufficiently sub-stantial is to be tested by whether it would be unjust or inequitable to allow the assurance to be disregarded—that is, again, the essential test of unconscionability. The detriment alleged must be pleaded and proved [...]

The matters which Mr Gillett pleaded as detriment, and on which he adduced evidence of detriment, included, apart from the level of his remuneration, (i) his continuing in Mr Holt's employment (through KAHL) and not seeking or accepting offers of employment elsewhere, or going into business on his own account; (ii) carrying out tasks and spending time beyond the normal scope of an employee's duty; (iii) taking no substantial steps to secure his future wealth, either by larger pension contributions or otherwise; and (iv) expenditure on improv-ing The Beeches farmhouse which was, Mr Gillett said, barely habitable when it was first acquired by KAHL in 1971. That company paid for some structural work, with a local authority improvement grant, but Mr Gillett paid for new fittings and materials and carried out a good deal of the work himself [...]

[...] After listening to lengthy submissions about the judgment, and after reading much of Mr Gillett's evidence both in his witness statement and under cross-examination, I am left with the feeling that the judge, despite his very clear and careful judgment, did not stand back and look at the matter in the round. Had he done so I think he would have recognised that Mr Gillett's case on detriment (on the facts found by the judge, and on Mr Gillett's uncontra-dicted evidence) was an unusually compelling one.

[Having decided that the requirements of proprietary estoppel had been met, Robert Walker LJ went on to consider how to 'satisfy the equity'—that is, how to decide on the extent of Mr Gillett's right. It was held that Mr Holt and KAHL were under a duty to: (i) transfer to Mr Gillett the freehold of The Beeches (including the farmhouse and 42 hectares of attached land); and (ii) pay Mr Gillett £100,000 as compensation for not receiving any of The Limes.]

3.3.1 The decision itself

The success of Mr Gillett's claim shows the use of proprietary estoppel within the context of a close, domestic relationship. It also shows that a court can '*look at matters in the round*' when deciding whether a party (B) would suffer a detriment if the other party (A) were free to act inconsistently with B's belief. The Court of Appeal thus rejected the argument that detriment should be interpreted in a narrow, purely financial way.

That approach fits with the view of Lord Denning MR, as expressed in the following case.

Greasley v Cooke [1980] 3 All ER 710, CA

Lord Denning MR

At 713

It so happens that in many of these cases there has been expenditure of money. But that is not a necessary element [. . .] It is sufficient if the party, to whom the assurance is given, acts on the faith of it in such circumstances that it would be unjust and inequitable for the party making the assurance to go back on it [. . .]

Gillett also shows that B's reliance, in itself, does not need to be detriment; rather, the key question is whether, given B's reliance, he *would* suffer a detriment if he had no proprietary estoppel claim against A.[25]

Crabb v Arun DC provides a further example of this point. In that case, B's reliance consisted of selling off part of his land without reserving an easement over that land. If B had insisted on such an easement, he may well have had to sell that part of the land for a lower sum. So, in a sense, B initially *benefited* from his reliance: he received more money for that part of his land. The detriment test instead applies when A fails to meet his commitment to B: for example, in *Crabb*, when the council refused to grant B the planned easement. The court compares B's position at that point with B's position before A made any commitment to B.

3.3.2 The wider significance of the decision: the effect of *Yeoman's Row*

Gillett v Holt seems to be a case in which: (i) Mr Gillett believed that he *would* acquire a right in relation to the land of KAHL, or of Mr Holt; but (ii) Mr Holt did not make a commitment

---

[25] This point is made most clearly in an influential passage from the judgment of Dixon J in *Grundt v Great Boulder Pty Gold Mines Ltd* (1938) 59 CLR 641, 674–5. That passage was quoted with approval by Robert Walker LJ in *Gillett v Holt* [2001] Ch 210, 232–3.

that he was under a current legal duty to give Mr Gillett such a right. On that view, the decision in the case is consistent with the test for proprietary estoppel set out in section 3.1 above, but *not* with the reasoning of the House of Lords in *Yeoman's Row*.

In fact, *Gillett* is only one of a number of cases in which A made a commitment to give B a right relating to A's land upon A's death. In *Yeoman's Row* itself, Lord Walker (who, as Robert Walker LJ, gave the leading judgment in *Gillett v Holt*) attempted to explain these cases by drawing a distinction between the commercial context of a case such as *Yeoman's Row* and the domestic context of a case such as *Gillett*.

Yeoman's Row Management Ltd v Cobbe [2008] 1 WLR 1752, HL

Lord Walker

At [66]–[68]

[T]he young farm manager in *Gillett v Holt* [...] almost certainly did not take any legal advice until after the events relied on as creating the estoppel [... Mr Gillett] believed that the assurance on which [he] relied was binding and irrevocable [...]

In the commercial context, the claimant is typically a business person with access to legal advice and what he or she is expecting to get is a contract. In the domestic or family context, the typical claimant is not a business person and is not receiving legal advice. What he or she wants and expects to get is an interest in immovable property, often for long-term occupation as a home. The focus is not on intangible legal rights but on the tangible property which he or she expects to get. The typical domestic claimant does not stop to reflect (until disappointed expectations lead to litigation) whether some further legal transaction (such as a grant by deed, or the making of a will or codicil) is necessary to complete the promised title.

Lord Walker's point seems to be that a party such as Mr Gillett, unlike Mr Cobbe, can reasonably believe that A has made a legally binding commitment to give B a right relating to A's land even though A has not made that commitment in a written contract complying with the usual formality rules. If that view is correct, then the decision in a case such as *Gillett v Holt* can be reconciled to the *Yeoman's Row* approach: it is a case in which A led B to believe not only that A would give B a right in the future, but also that A was under a current legal duty to do so.

There are, however, a number of problems with this approach. Firstly, in the domestic context, is it likely that B will even think about whether A is under a binding legal duty to perform his promise to B? Secondly, even if B is aware that A is not under such a duty, does that necessarily mean B does not deserve any protection if he relies on A's commitment? After all, in practice, people regularly rely on each other's promises. Indeed, in *Gillett* itself, Mr Gillett admitted that he was aware that, even if Mr Holt were to make a will in his favour, that will could be revoked. The first instance judge in *Gillett* therefore found against Mr Gillett, applying the analysis of Judge Weeks QC in *Taylor v Dickens*[26] that a promise by A to leave property to B in a will could not give rise to a proprietary estoppel claim, because B should know that a will made in his favour can be revoked. But the Court of Appeal in *Gillett* rejected that argument, as we can see from the following extract from the judgment of Robert Walker LJ (as he then was).

---

[26] [1988] 1 FLR 806, 821.

Gillett v Holt [2001] Ch 210, CA

Robert Walker LJ

At 227–8

Taylor v Dickens has itself attracted a good deal of criticism: see for instance [1998] Conveyancer and Property Lawyer 210 (Professor M P Thompson) and [1998] Restitution Law Review 220 (W J Swadling); but compare the contrary view in [1999] Conveyancer and Property Lawyer 46 (M Dixon). Mr Swadling's comment is short and pithy:

> "This decision is clearly wrong, for the judge seems to have forgotten that the whole point of estoppel claims is that they concern promises which, since they are unsupported by consideration, are initially revocable. What later makes them binding, and therefore irrevocable, is the promisee's detrimental reliance on them. Once that occurs, there is simply no question of the promisor changing his or her mind."

Mr McDonnell [counsel for Mr Gillett] has added his voice to the criticism. In his skeleton argument he has submitted that *Taylor v Dickens* is 'simply wrong'. Mr Martin [counsel for Mr Holt and KAHL], while reminding the court that it is not hearing an appeal in *Taylor v Dickens*, has not given the case whole-hearted support. He has been inclined to concede that Judge Weeks should have focused on the promise which was made and whether it was of an irrevocable character, instead of looking for a second promise not to revoke a testamentary disposition.

In my judgment these criticisms of *Taylor v Dickens* are well-founded [...] the inherent revocability of testamentary dispositions (even if well understood by the parties, as Mr Gillett candidly accepted that it was by him) is irrelevant to a promise or assurance that 'all this will be yours' (the sort of language used on the occasion of the Beeches incident in 1975). Even when the promise or assurance is in terms linked to the making of a will (as at the 1974 Golf Hotel dinner) the circumstances may make clear that the assurance is more than a mere statement of present (revocable) intention, and is tantamount to a promise.

It therefore seems that, if the reasoning of the House of Lords in *Yeoman's Row* is accepted, *Gillett* can no longer be seen as a case of proprietary estoppel.[27]

One possibility may be to reanalyse *Gillett* as a case in which Mr Gillett acquired a right under a constructive trust. For example, in the following case, A made a promise to leave B, in her will, all of A's assets (including a cottage). B did not live with A, but regularly visited and cared for A, as well as spending some money in improving the cottage. A died before making a will and her rights passed to her personal representatives. Edward Nugee QC (sitting as a deputy High Court judge) found that, due to proprietary estoppel, those representatives held the rights received from A on trust for B. He drew an important link between proprietary estoppel and constructive trusts.

---

[27] The House of Lords recently had a chance to consider the application of proprietary estoppel (post-*Yeoman's Row*) to a case in which A made a testamentary promise in a domestic context: an appeal against the decision of the Court of Appeal in *Thorner v Curtis and ors* [2008] EWCA Civ 732 was head in January 2009: see this book's companion website for discussion of the decision.

Re Basham [1986] 1 WLR 1498

Edward Nugee QC

At 1503–4

[B] relies on proprietary estoppel, the principle of which, in its broadest form, may be stated as follows: where one person, [B], has acted to his detriment on the faith of a belief, which was known to and encouraged by another person, [A], that he either has or is going to be given a right in or over [A]'s property, [A] cannot insist on his strict legal rights if to do so would be inconsistent with [B]'s belief. The principle is commonly known as proprietary estoppel, and since the effect of it is that [A] is prevented from asserting his strict legal rights it has something in common with estoppel. But in my judgment, at all events where the belief is that [B] is going to be given a right in the future, it is properly to be regarded as giving rise to a species of constructive trust, which is the concept employed by a court of equity to prevent a person from relying on his legal rights where it would be unconscionable for him to do so. The rights to which proprietary estoppel gives rise, and the machinery by which effect is given to them, are similar in many respects to those involved in cases of secret trusts, mutual wills and other comparable cases in which property is vested in [A] on the faith of an understanding that it will be dealt with in a particular manner [...]

It is therefore important to consider whether, if a case like *Gillett* were to arise today, a court following the *Yeoman's Row* approach to proprietary estoppel could protect B by finding that a constructive trust has arisen. This depends on whether the facts of such a case can fit within the constructive trust principles explored in Chapters 14 and 18.

3.3.3 The wider significance of the decision: unconscionability

Robert Walker LJ's reasoning in *Gillett* is relevant to the wider question of how the courts should deal with proprietary estoppel. The approach in *Gillett* can be seen as consistent with that applied in *Taylor Fashions*: it recognizes the flexibility that a court has to '*look at matters in the round*' when asking if the requirements of proprietary estoppel have been satisfied. Certainly, Robert Walker LJ quoted with approval Oliver J's summary of the key question in a proprietary estoppel case: '[W]*hether, in particular individual circumstances, it would be unconscionable for a party to be permitted to deny that which, knowingly, or unknowingly, he has allowed or encouraged another to assume to his detriment.*'[28]

In *Yeoman's Row*, Lord Walker (as he now is) returned to the question of the role of unconscionability in a proprietary estoppel claim.

Yeoman's Row Management Limited v Cobbe [2008] 1 WLR 1752, HL

Lord Walker

At [92]

Mr Dowding [counsel for Mrs Lisle-Mainwaring] devoted a separate section of his printed case to arguing that even if the elements for an estoppel were in other respects present,

---

[28] [2001] Ch 210, 225–6, quoting from *Taylors Fashions Ltd v Liverpool Victoria Trustees Co Ltd* [1982] QB 133, 151–2.

it would not in any event be unconscionable for Mrs Lisle-Mainwaring to insist on her legal rights. That argument raises the question whether "unconscionability" is a separate element in making out a case of estoppel, or whether to regard it as a separate element would be what Professor Peter Birks once called "a fifth wheel on the coach".[29] But Birks was there criticising the use of "unconscionable" to describe a state of mind.[30] Here it is being used (as in my opinion it should always be used) as an objective value judgment on behaviour (regardless of the state of mind of the individual in question). As such it does in my opinion play a very important part in the doctrine of equitable estoppel, in unifying and confirming, as it were, the other elements. If the other elements appear to be present but the result does not shock the conscience of the court, the analysis needs to be looked at again. In this case Mrs Lisle-Mainwaring's conduct was unattractive. She chose to stand on her rights rather than respecting her non-binding assurances, while Mr Cobbe continued to spend time and effort, between Christmas 2003 and March 2004, in obtaining planning permission. But Mr Cobbe knew that she was bound in honour only, and so in the eyes of equity her conduct, although unattractive, was not unconscionable.

In contrast to Lord Scott's comments at [16] in *Yeoman's Row* (see section 2.3 above), Lord Walker thus seems to suggest that unconscionability may have a more active role to play in the test for proprietary estoppel.

There is some academic support for that suggestion.

Dixon, 'Proprietary Estoppel and Formalities in Land Law and the Land Registration Act 2002: A Theory of Unconscionability' in *Modern Studies in Property Law: Vol 2* (ed Cooke, 2002)

At p 175

The central role that unconscionability plays in the law of estoppel seems, at least to the present writer, to be in inverse proportion to the analysis devoted to it in the cases. All judges are agreed that unconscionability is vital, but few seem willing to share their understanding of the concept [...]

At p 177

[On one view of proprietary estoppel] 'unconscionability' has no independent existence for it is defined purely in terms of the three factual requirements. The corollary is, of course, that unconscionability exists *by definition* whenever there is an assurance, reliance and detriment, because non-performance of the assurance after detriment will always be unconscionable. Such a view is at odds with those who view unconscionability as at the heart of the doctrine—in the sense of providing its underlying rationale—because, quite simply it denies the concept of any discernible meaning. It is a non-definition.

If it is true that unconscionability is now to be regarded as no more than a function of assurance, reliance and detriment, this author submits that the approach is flawed and unprincipled.

---

[29] [See Birks in *Breach of Trust* (eds Birks and Pretto, 2002, p 226).]

[30] [The specific use of the term discussed by Birks comes from *Bank of Credit & Commerce International (Overseas) Ltd v Akindele* [2001] Ch 437, 455, *per* Nourse LJ. That case did not concern estoppel, but rather the question of whether a third party receiving a right held on trust can be liable, due to his 'knowing receipt' of the right, to account to the beneficiary of the trust.]

There are a number of reasons. First, and formally, this 'definition' of unconscionability is not supported by *Taylor Fashions* itself. A straightforward reading of Oliver J's judgment suggests that before an estoppel can be established, there must be an assurance, reliance and detriment (albeit holistically examined), but that this must occur in circumstances where the court is satisfied that it would be unconscionable to allow the party making the assurance to go back on it. Or, put shortly, *Taylor Fashions* suggests that assurance, reliance and detriment are necessary but not sufficient. Secondly, if unconscionability is simply the reflection of a withdrawn assurance after detrimental reliance, how does it justify the grant of an estoppel remedy in the formality cases, bearing in mind the point that estoppel is an exception to the normal formality rules? The whole point of the formality rules is to ensure that a representation about a property right shall be capable of enforcement only if it is in a proper form. If the proper form can be ignored simply because the representee has relied on the representation' to his detriment, that is tantamount to saying that the formality rules invalidate only 'voluntary' promises, being those where there is no detriment issuing from the promisee [...]

At p 180

In so far as the general law requires the creation, transfer or enforcement of proprietary rights to be undertaken in certain forms, estoppel can be used to side-step these requirements only where there is a clear justification. That it would be 'unconsionable' for one of the parties to rely on the absence of the required formality is that justification. This means that unconscionability cannot be merely a function of assurance, reliance and detriment (the factual elements of estoppel) for otherwise it is devoid of meaning [...] 'unconscionability' *can* explain why the absence of formality may be ignored—in the sense that a right still ensues for the claimant—if the concept is tied to the formality rules. Hence, it will be unconscionable for a representor to withdraw an assurance, relied on to detriment, if the assurance of the rights carries with it (expressly or impliedly) a further assurance that the right will ensue even if the formalities necessary to convey the right are not complied with. It is the withdrawal of the promise of the right after the second assurance (assuming detrimental reliance) that constitutes the unconscionability required for a successful claim in estoppel.

At p 182

Although it is submitted that unconscionability in the narrow sense just discussed must be present before a claim *can* succeed, that does not mean that the claim *must* then succeed. The 'double assurance', withdrawn after detrimental reliance is necessary but not sufficient. There still remains the broad equitable jurisdiction either to deny the remedy or modify the remedy because of the background circumstances of the case [...] Of course, this is not the unfettered and unprincipled discretion rejected by Robert Walker LJ in *Jennings v Rice* but it is in keeping with the use of estoppel as a remedy protecting those who cannot rely on formality and who instead must plead the favour of the court.

Dixon's main point is an important one. It goes back to the central question noted in section 1 above: given that A has not granted B a property right, nor made a contractual promise to B, why should the doctrine of proprietary estoppel impose a duty on A? After all, if it is a failure to satisfy a formality rule that means A has not granted B a property right, nor made a contractual promise to B, does giving B a proprietary estoppel claim undermine that formality rule (a question that was raised in Chapter 9, section 3.7)? The reasoning of the House of Lords in *Yeoman's Row* also provides some support for Dixon's 'double assurance' analysis: it suggests that it is not enough for A simply to promise to give B a right in the future; A must also lead B to believe that A is under a current legal duty to give B that right.

This does not mean that, to justify proprietary estoppel, we *must* agree with Dixon that unconscionability is an independent requirement of the doctrine; rather, it means that, if we take the view that A's duty arises simply because of A's commitment, B's reliance, and the prospect of B's detriment, we need to explain *why* those factors impose a duty on A to B. As Hopkins notes in the following extract, however, there is a risk that 'unconscionability', if not carefully defined, will not assist us in answering that key question.

Hopkins, 'Understanding Unconscionability in Proprietary Estoppel' (2004) JCL 210

At 221

Gillett v Holt suggests that unconscionability should be seen as an overriding or umbrella element of an estoppel claim. It feeds in to the assessment of an assurance, reliance and detriment (as it 'permeates the elements of a claim') but it also provides a general evaluative tool through which the court considers the claim 'in the round'. In practice, in subsequent cases, unconscionability has been discussed primarily in the context of detriment and as regards an 'in the round' evaluation. The shift in estoppel that has taken place through *Gillett v Holt* is subtle, but this does not detract from its significance. The courts' discretion remains structured insofar as estoppel is said to be dependent on finding an assurance, reliance and detriment. However, in emphasising the role of unconscionability, and showing greater willingness to discuss the concept expressly, the courts appear to have further liberalised the scope of estoppel.

At 222–3

The difficulty with the approach in these cases, which link the assessment of detriment directly with the question whether it is unconscionable for [A] to renege, is that the formula lacks transparency; what constitutes a sufficient detriment can be measured only by determining whether it is unconscionable for [A] to renege [...] the formula that has been adopted for detriment results in circularity: in the absence of detriment, it would not be unconscionable for [A] to renege; though whether [B] has acted to his or her detriment is determined by considering whether it is unconscionable for [A] to renege.

At 232

This [move to individualized, discretionary justice] gives rise to particular cause for concern as it comes at a time when the development of electronic conveyancing may in future place greater emphasis on the use of proprietary estoppel. Intervention through unconscionability by its nature involves discretion and flexibility. The challenge for the courts is to take advantage of these inherent characteristics whilst maintaining a principled approach. The lack of transparency and consistency in recent case law suggests that the courts are not successfully meeting this challenge. The resulting uncertainty and lack of guidelines will act as an incentive to litigation.

3.4 CASE 3: *WAYLING V JONES*

Wayling v Jones (1993) 69 P & CR 170, CA

Facts: Mr Wayling first met Mr Jones in 1967. In 1971, they started to live together in a homosexual relationship. At that time, Mr Wayling, a chef, was 21 years of age, while Mr Jones was aged 56. Over the following years, as well as living with Mr Jones, Mr Wayling worked in a number of Mr Jones' businesses. Mr Wayling received 'pocket money' and expenses, but was never given a standard salary for his work. Mr Jones made a will in which Mr Wayling was given a particular hotel (the Glen-y-Mor Hotel) owned by Mr Jones. That hotel was later sold and a different hotel bought (the Royal Hotel), but the will was never updated. So, when Mr Jones died in 1987, his will did not succeed in giving anything to Mr Wayling. Mr Wayling claimed that Mr Jones was under a duty (now binding on Mr Jones' executors), arising under the doctrine of proprietary estoppel, to give Mr Wayling ownership of the Royal Hotel.

Mr Jones had made a number of promises to Mr Wayling to leave him first ownership of the Glen-y-Mor Hotel, then ownership of the Royal Hotel on his death. The following exchange took place when Mr Wayling was cross-examined in court by counsel for Mr Jones' executors:

> 'Q: If he had not made that promise to you, would you still have stayed with him?
>
> A: Yes [. . .]
>
> Q: The promises were not the reason why you remained with the deceased?
>
> A: No, we got on very well together. He always wanted to reward me.'

The judge at first instance took this to mean that, because Mr Wayling would have acted in the same way even if he had never been promised Mr Jones' hotel, he could not show that he had relied on Mr Jones' assurances. But the Court of Appeal upheld Mr Wayling's appeal.

Balcombe LJ

At 1030

I am satisfied that [Mr Wayling's] conduct in helping [Mr Jones] run the café in Hastings Street and the Glen-y-Mor Hotel and managing the Royal Hotel for what was at best little more than pocket money [. . .] was conduct from which his reliance on [Mr Jones's] clear promises could be inferred. The question is whether [Mr Jones' executors] have established that [Mr Wayling] did not rely on these promises.

In his affidavit evidence [Mr Wayling] stated that he relied on [Mr Jones'] promises. In his oral evidence-in-chief he said:

> 'Q: One question, Mr Wayling. Assuming you were in the Royal Hotel bar before [Mr Jones's] death and [Mr Jones] was there, if [Mr Jones] had told you that he was not going to give the Royal Hotel to you but to somebody else after his death, what would you have done?
>
> A: I would have left.'

[. . .] I am satisfied that [Mr Wayling's] answers in cross-examination do not relate to the only question that mattered: "What would you have done if [Mr Jones] had told you that he was no longer prepared to implement his promises?".

[...] I am satisfied:

(a) that the promises were made;

(b) that [Mr Wayling's] conduct was of such a nature that inducement may be inferred;

(c) that [Mr Jones' executors] have not discharged the burden upon them of establishing that the plaintiff did not rely on the promises.

3.4.1 The decision itself

Mr Wayling was a deserving claimant because: (i) only a mistake (Mr Jones' failure to update his will) prevented him from acquiring the hotel as expected; and (ii) he had lived with, and worked for, Mr Jones as part of a long-term relationship—he had made sacrifices as a result of that relationship and was, to an extent, dependent on Mr Jones. Nowadays, as well as bringing a proprietary estoppel claim, a party in Mr Wayling's position can also bring a claim under the Inheritance (Provision for Family and Dependants) Act 1975. That Act gives the court a power to award a share of A's estate to B, an adult dependant of A, where adequate provision for B has not been made in A's will. When *Wayling v Jones* was decided, however, the Act did not give the court a power to make an order in favour of A's homosexual partner. So, proprietary estoppel was Mr Wayling's only recourse.

3.4.2 The wider significance of the decision

To bring a proprietary estoppel claim, B must show that he has relied on his belief that he will acquire a right in relation to A's land. That requirement is a key part of the test for proprietary estoppel, both on the test as set out in section 3.1 above and on the House of Lords' reasoning in *Yeoman's Row*. In theory, it might seem that reliance can be difficult to prove.

For example, in the following case, Ms Cooke lived in a home owned by Kenneth and Hedley Greasley. She was the partner of Kenneth and also cared for Clarice, another member of the family. Both Kenneth and Hedley had assured Ms Cooke that she would have 'a home for life', but Kenneth died without giving her any right to remain on the land and the current owners of the land wished to remove her. Ms Cooke's proprietary estoppel claim was based on the fact that, because of the assurances that she would have a 'home for life', she had remained there and cared for Clarice, rather than leaving to find paid work. It might seem difficult for her to prove such reliance: after all, because she was, in any case, 'one of the family', she may well have cared for Clarice even if she had not been given any assurances about remaining in the home. As Lord Denning MR pointed out in the following extract, however, it was not Ms Cooke's job to prove such reliance.

Greasley v Cooke [1980] 1 WLR 1306, CA

Lord Denning MR

At 713

The first point is on the burden of proof. [In *Brikom Investments Ltd v Carr* [1979] 2 All ER 753 at 759] I said that, when a person makes a representation intending that another should act on it—

'It is no answer for the maker to say: "You would have gone on with the transaction anyway." That must be mere speculation. No one can be sure what he would, or would not, have done in a hypothetical state of affairs which never took place [...] Once it is shown that a representation was calculated to influence the judgment of a reasonable man, the presumption is that he was so influenced.'

So here. These statements to [Ms Cooke] were calculated to influence her, so as to put her mind at rest, so that she should not worry about being turned out. No one can say what she would have done if Kenneth and Hedley had not made those statements. It is quite possible that she would have said to herself: 'I am not married to Kenneth. I am on my own. What will happen to me if anything happens to him? I had better look out for another job now rather than stay here where I have no security.' So, instead of looking for another job, she stayed on in the house looking after Kenneth and Clarice. There is a presumption that she did so relying on the assurances given to her by Kenneth and Hedley. The burden is not on her but on them to prove that she did not rely on their assurances. They did not prove it, neither did their representatives.

In *Wayling v Jones*, it could equally be presumed that Mr Wayling worked for low pay in reliance on Mr Jones's promises to leave the hotel to him. So the burden was on Mr Jones's executors to show otherwise. However, because Mr Wayling had *admitted* that he would have worked for low pay even if he had not been promised the hotel, it would seem that the executors had met that burden by proving that, in fact, Mr Wayling had not relied on Mr Jones's promises. Yet the Court of Appeal nonetheless allowed Mr Wayling's proprietary estoppel claim. As explained by Cooke in the following extract, this was done by applying an unusual test: to prove that Mr Wayling had not relied, the executors had to show that Mr Wayling would have continued to work for low pay *even if* he had been told by Mr Jones that Mr Jones intended to break his promise to leave the hotel to him.

Cooke, 'Reliance and Estoppel' [1995] 111 LQR 389, 391

That this is an unusual interpretation of reliance is best seen by comparing a case where it was held that there was no reliance. In *Coombes v. Smith* [1986] 1 W.L.R. 809 the plaintiff left her husband, moved into the defendant's house and bore his child. She claimed an interest in the property on the basis of proprietary estoppel. She failed for a number of reasons, among them the fact that she acted as she did, not in reliance upon the defendant's assurance that he would provide for her, but simply because she wanted to. Imagine her reaction if she had heard her partner say that he was not going to provide for her, in spite of his promise. Surely she would have left, because that would have undermined her relationship with him. She would thus have met the *Wayling* test. But it was held that she did not rely upon the assurance, because the giving of that assurance, and her expectation of an entitlement to the property, did not influence her actions.

Reliance is an aspect of causation. When we say that someone acted in reliance upon a promise we generally mean that he would not have so acted *but for* the making of the promise. We cannot say that of Wayling. Alternatively, it seems that reliance in the context of estoppel can mean that the plaintiff would not have acted as he did *but for* a belief, which was then encouraged by the promise, (as envisaged by Robert Goff J., as he then was, in *Amalgamated Investment & Property Co. Ltd. v. Texas Commerce International Bank Ltd.* [1982] Q.B. 84 at pp. 104–105). Wayling could not meet that test either, since he did not set up home with Jones in the belief that the latter would leave his property to him. He did so, and he stayed, because of his relationship with the defendant; because, as he put it, "he needed me". Obviously, if he had discovered that Jones was not going to change his will, the relationship would have been undermined, and he would have left. But any broken promise could have had the same effect.

The treatment of reliance in *Wayling v. Jones* is thus unusually generous. Despite the obvious justice of the result, the means of reaching it was inconsistent with earlier estoppel cases.

Cooke's analysis shows that the reasoning of the House of Lords in *Yeoman's Row* may be inconsistent with the test used for reliance in *Wayling*. That reasoning depends on proprietary estoppel being seen as a standard form of estoppel: this means that the standard test for reliance should apply, not the special test developed in *Wayling*.

One possible way of reconciling the *Wayling* test to the *Yeoman's Row* reasoning is to see *Wayling* as depending not on proprietary estoppel, but rather on constructive trust principles. The question then (which we will examine in Chapter 18, section 2.1.2) is whether the *Wayling* test is appropriate when considering constructive trusts.

4 THE EXTENT OF A'S DUTY TO B: RESPONDING TO A PROPRIETARY ESTOPPEL

4.1 INTRODUCTION

If B can show that proprietary estoppel imposes a duty on A, we then need to know the *extent* of A's duty. In any particular case, we could come up with a number of different possibilities. For example, it could be that:

- A is under a duty to *honour his commitment to B*—in such a case, the extent of A's duty depends on the extent of A's commitment to B; *or*

- A is under a duty to *ensure B suffers no detriment as a result of A's failure to honour his commitment*—in such a case, the extent of A's duty depends on the extent of B's potential detriment; *or*

- A is under a duty to *pay B the value of any benefit A has received as a result of B's reliance on A*—in such a case, the extent of A's duty is determined by the extent of the benefit that A has received at B's expense; *or*

- A is under a duty to do whatever is necessary to ensure that A does not act unconscionably—in such a case, the extent of A's duty depends on what a court determines that A must do to avoid behaving badly.

Of course, these are not the only four possibilities. As well as adopting a completely different approach, we could adopt an approach that mixes one or more of the four set out above. For example, in the first of two influential articles on the subject, Gardner[31] found evidence in the cases for the proposition that '*relief in proprietary estoppel ordinarily takes the form of expectation relief in specie, but that there is a discretion to give some other form of relief where*

---

[31] 'The Remedial Discretion in Proprietary Estoppel,' (1999) 115 LQR 438, 440.

this seems more appropriate'. That approach is based on the '*presumptive status of expectation relief*':[32] the stating point is that A's duty will be to honour his commitment to B. But the approach also gives the courts, in particular cases, a structured discretion[33] to reach a different result. That first article was published in 1999, before the important decision of the Court of Appeal in *Jennings v Rice*.

4.2 *JENNINGS V RICE*

Jennings v Rice [2003] 1 P & CR 100, CA

Facts: Mrs Royle, a childless widow, lived at Lawn House, Shapwick, in Somerset. She died in 1997. Mr Jennings had started to work for her in 1970 as a part-time gardener. He later began to do other work for her (e.g. running errands, taking her shopping, doing minor maintenance work). In the late 1980s, Mrs Royle stopped paying Mr Jennings for these services, but she provided him with £2,000 towards the purchase of a house. By the mid-1990s, Mr Jennings, at Mrs Royle's request, cared for her and stayed overnight at her house. In return, Mrs Royle assured him that, in her will, she would 'see him right'—but she died without leaving a will.

Mr Jennings claimed that, at her death, Mrs Royle was under a duty to Mr Jennings, arising as a result of proprietary estoppel. The first instance judge held that Mrs Royle (and so now Mr Rice, her personal representative) was under a duty to pay Mr Jennings £200,000. Mr Jennings appealed, claiming that Mr Rice was under a duty to give him the whole of Mrs Royle's estate (valued at £1.285m) or, at least, a sum equal to the value of Mrs Royle's house and its furniture (£435,000). The Court of Appeal upheld the award of the first instance judge: on her death, Mrs Royle was under a duty to pay Mr Jennings £200,000.

Aldous LJ

At [15]–[22]

The [first instance] judge then had to decide what was the appropriate relief. He started by referring to *Crabb v Arun DC*. He went on to refer to a number of authorities and concluded that he should be guided by the approach of Robert Walker LJ and the other members of the Court of Appeal in *Gillett v Holt*. He concluded that he had a discretion to be exercised judicially in the light of all the relevant circumstances. He took into account, first that Mr Jennings did not know the extent of Mrs Royle's wealth and second, that the value of her actual estate and even the part known to Mr Jennings was out of all proportion to what Mr Jennings might reasonably have charged for the services he provided free. He then considered whether it would be equitable for Mr Jennings to take the house and the furniture which were the minimum he expected, and also what the judge called the problem of proportionality. The judge reminded himself that the house was valued at £420,000 and was not a suitable house for Mr Jennings to reside in on his own and he took into account that Mrs Royle had no

---

[32] Ibid, e.g. at 464.

[33] Gardner rejects the idea that, having exceptionally decided that A is *not* under a duty to honour his or her commitment to B, the courts have a completely free discretion to set the extent of A's duty to B: see ibid, at 461–4.

special obligations to her family. He said that to reward an employee on the scale of £420,000 was excessive. He also compared the cost of full-time nursing care, which he estimated at £200,000, with the value of the house. He reasoned that Mr Jennings would probably need £150,000 to buy a house. He concluded:

'I do not think that he could complain that he had been unfairly treated if he had been left £200,000 in Mrs Royle's will. Most people would say that she would, at least, then have performed her promise to see him all right. The quality of her assurance affects not only questions of belief, encouragement, reliance and detriment, but also unconscionability and the extent of the equity.'

Mr Warner, who appeared for Mr Jennings, submitted that in a case like the present, where the claimant had established his claim of proprietary estoppel, the basic rule was that the established equity should be satisfied by making good the expectation. He accepted that there were exceptions, for example where there had been misconduct, but this case did not fall within any of them [...]

Miss Rich, who appeared for the respondents, supported the conclusion and reasoning of the judge. She submitted that to arrive at the correct award, the starting point was the claimant's expectation as that would indicate the maximum extent of the equity. However the court's task did not end there. The ultimate aim was to achieve justice. That was achieved by making the award proportionate to the expectation and the detriment suffered [...]

Before coming to the authorities which establish the approach necessary to arrive at the correct award, it is instructive to consider the basic principles of proprietary estoppel [...]

There can be no doubt that reliance and detriment are two of the requirements of proprietary estoppel and that the basis of the estoppel is, as Lord Denning MR said in *Crabb's* case, the interposition of equity: thus the requirement of unconscionability. If the conscience of the court is involved, it would be odd that the amount of the award should be set rigidly at the sum expected by the claimant.

Against that background I turn to consider the crucial question in this case, namely how to give effect to the estoppel. Mr Warner took us back to cases decided in the last century. For my part, I believe it is appropriate to start with *Crabb's* case, decided in 1976 [...]

At [36]–[38]

There is a clear line of authority from at least *Crabb's* case to the present day which establishes that once the elements of proprietary estoppel are established an equity arises. The value of that equity will depend upon all the circumstances including the expectation and the detriment. The task of the court is to do justice. The most essential requirement is that there must be proportionality between the expectation and the detriment.

Mr Warner warned against the conclusion I have reached. He submitted that it led to uncertainty and that the appropriate course was to satisfy the expectation. I accept that the flexible approach adopted in the past may mean that there is room for what has been referred to as a judicial discretion, but the rigidity of the approach advocated by Mr Warner can lead to injustice which could not form the basis of an equitable result. One only has to alter the facts of this case to illustrate the unsatisfactory nature of Mr Warner's submissions. The expectation was that Mr Jennings would receive the house and furniture valued at £435,000. If he had been left £5 or £50,000 or £200,000 in Mrs Royle's will, or she had died one month, one year or 20 years after making the representation relied on, should the court award the same sum? Yes, said Mr Warner. The result could then have been that Mr Jennings would receive £635,000 made up of the expectation and the legacy of £200,000, or perhaps, £435,000 in total, even when the detriment was say £800.

The judge was right to conclude that the award must be proportionate. He took into account the relevant factors as placed before him, namely the expectation, the detriment, the position of Mr Jennings and the amount available. His conclusion was the result of a judgment to which he was entitled to come. I would not interfere with it and would dismiss the appeal.

Robert Walker LJ

At [41]–[56]

I also agree that this appeal should be dismissed for the reasons given by Aldous LJ. Because of the general interest of this appeal I add some observations of my own.

It cannot be doubted that in this as in every other area of the law, the court must take a principled approach, and cannot exercise a completely unfettered discretion according to the individual judge's notion of what is fair in any particular case [. . .]

The need to search for the right principles cannot be avoided. But it is unlikely to be a short or simple search, because (as appears from both the English and the Australian authorities) proprietary estoppel can apply in a wide variety of factual situations, and any summary formula is likely to prove to be an over-simplification. The cases show a wide range of variation in both of the main elements, that is the quality of the assurances which give rise to the claimant's expectations and the extent of the claimant's detrimental reliance on the assurances. The doctrine applies only if these elements, in combination, make it unconscionable for the person giving the assurances (whom I will call the benefactor, although that may not always be an appropriate label) to go back on them.

Sometimes the assurances, and the claimant's reliance on them, have a consensual character falling not far short of an enforceable contract (if the only bar to the formation of a contract is non-compliance with s 2 of the Law of Property (Miscellaneous Provisions) Act 1989, the proprietary estoppel may become indistinguishable from a constructive trust: *Yaxley v Gotts*).[34] In a case of that sort both the claimant's expectations and the element of detriment to the claimant will have been defined with reasonable clarity. A typical case would be an elderly benefactor who reaches a clear understanding with the claimant (who may be a relative, a friend, or a remunerated companion or carer) that if the claimant resides with and cares for the benefactor, the claimant will inherit the benefactor's house (or will have a home for life). In a case like that the consensual element of what has happened suggests that the claimant and the benefactor probably regarded the expected benefit and the accepted detriment as being (in a general, imprecise way) equivalent, or at any rate not obviously disproportionate [. . .]

However the claimant's expectations may not be focused on any specific property. In *Re Basham* [see p 409 above] the deputy judge [. . .] rejected the submission that there must be some clearly identified piece of property, and that decision has been approved more than once in this court. Moreover (as the judge's findings in this case vividly illustrate) the claimant's expectations may have been formed on the basis of vague and inconsistent assurances. The judge said of Mrs Royle that she 'was prone to saying different things at different times and, perhaps deliberately, couched her promises in non-specific terms'. He made that observation in relation to the failure of the contract claim, but it is relevant to the estoppel claim also.

If the claimant's expectations are uncertain (as will be the case with many honest claimants) then their specific vindication cannot be the appropriate test. A similar problem arises if the court, although satisfied that the claimant has a genuine claim, is not satisfied that the high level of the claimant's expectations is fairly derived from his deceased patron's assurances, which may have justified only a lower level of expectation. In such cases the court

[34] [2000] Ch 162.

may still take the claimant's expectations (or the upper end of any range of expectations) as a starting point, but unless constrained by authority I would regard it as no more than a starting point.

I do not see that approach as being inconsistent with authority. On the contrary, I think it is supported by a substantial body of English authority. Scarman LJ's well-known reference to 'the minimum equity to do justice to the plaintiff'[35] must no doubt be read in the context of the rather unusual facts of that case, but it does not stand alone [...] Scarman LJ's reference to the minimum does not require the court to be constitutionally parsimonious, but it does implicitly recognise that the court must also do justice to the defendant.

It is no coincidence that these statements of principle refer to satisfying the equity (rather than satisfying, or vindicating, the claimant's expectations). The equity arises not from the claimant's expectations alone, but from the combination of expectations, detrimental reliance, and the unconscionableness of allowing the benefactor (or the deceased benefactor's estate) to go back on the assurances.

To recapitulate: there is a category of case in which the benefactor and the claimant have reached a mutual understanding which is in reasonably clear terms but does not amount to a contract. I have already referred to the typical case of a carer who has the expectation of coming into the benefactor's house, either outright or for life. In such a case the court's natural response is to fulfil the claimant's expectations. But if the claimant's expectations are uncertain, or extravagant, or out of all proportion to the detriment which the claimant has suffered, the court can and should recognise that the claimant's equity should be satisfied in another (and generally more limited) way.

But that does not mean that the court should in such a case abandon expectations completely, and look to the detriment suffered by the claimant as defining the appropriate measure of relief. Indeed in many cases the detriment may be even more difficult to quantify, in financial terms, than the claimant's expectations. Detriment can be quantified with reasonable precision if it consists solely of expenditure on improvements to another person's house, and in some cases of that sort an equitable charge for the expenditure may be sufficient to satisfy the equity.[36] But the detriment of an ever increasing burden of care for an elderly person, and of having to be subservient to his or her moods and wishes, is very difficult to quantify in money terms. Moreover the claimant may not be motivated solely by reliance on the benefactor's assurances, and may receive some countervailing benefits (such as free bed and board). In such circumstances the court has to exercise a wide judgmental discretion.

It would be unwise to attempt any comprehensive enumeration of the factors relevant to the exercise of the court's discretion, or to suggest any hierarchy of factors. In my view they include, but are not limited to, the factors mentioned in Dr Gardner's third hypothesis[37] (misconduct of the claimant as in *J Willis & Sons v Willis*[38] or particularly oppressive conduct on the part of the defendant, as in *Crabb's* case or *Pascoe v Turner*).[39] To these can safely be added: the court's recognition that it cannot compel people who have fallen out to live peaceably together, so that there may be a need for a clean break; alterations in the benefactor's assets and circumstances, especially where the benefactor's assurances have been given, and the claimant's detriment has been suffered, over a long period of years; the likely effect of taxation; and (to a limited degree) the other claims (legal or moral) on the benefactor or his

[35] *Crabb v Arun DC* [1976] Ch 179, 198.
[36] [Walker LJ here referred to *Snell's Equity* (30th edn, 2000, [39–21]) and the authorities mentioned in that paragraph.]
[37] [The reference here is to Gardner 'The Remedial Discretion in Proprietary Estoppel' (1999) 115 LQR 438.]
[38] [1986] 1 EGLR 62.
[39] [1979] 1 WLR 431.

or her estate. No doubt there are many other factors which it may be right for the court to take into account in particular factual situations.

[...] The essence of the doctrine of proprietary estoppel is to do what is necessary to avoid an unconscionable result, and a disproportionate remedy cannot be the right way of going about that.

4.2.1 The decision itself

On the approach adopted by the Court of Appeal in *Jennings*, proprietary estoppel does not always lead to A being under a duty to honour a commitment made to B. On the facts of *Jennings* itself, that approach seems to lead to a reasonable result. In particular, it was clear that Mrs Rice was not under a contractual duty to leave Mr Jennings the house: there was no signed writing necessary to satisfy s 2 of the LP(MP)A 1989. Mr Jennings was able to rely on proprietary estoppel because of his reliance on Mrs Rice's assurances—it therefore seems reasonable for the extent of that reliance to be taken into account when deciding the sum that Mrs Rice's personal representatives had to pay Mr Jennings.

But the difficulty posed by *Jennings* is clear: once we know that proprietary estoppel does not always lead to A being under a duty to honour a commitment to B, how do we know what duty will be imposed on A? In looking at that question, we must again consider both the impact of *Yeoman's Row* and the possible role of unconscionability.

4.2.2 The wider significance of the decision: the impact of *Yeoman's Row*

If the *Yeoman's Row* approach is applied to the facts of *Jennings*, it seems that three results are possible. Firstly, it could be said that Mr Jennings simply has no claim, because he did not believe that Mrs Rice was under a *legal duty* to leave him her house and its contents.

Secondly, it could be said that, whilst he has no proprietary estoppel claim, Mr Jennings had a different claim. As suggested above in relation to *Gillett v Holt*, that claim could be seen as based on a constructive trust. As we will see in Chapter 18, however, the usual position under a constructive trust is that the common understanding of A and B is enforced: this would mean that Mrs Rice's personal representatives would have held the house and its contents on trust for Mr Jennings. Instead, the Court of Appeal in *Jennings* found that he simply had a right to be paid £200,000. Alternatively, Mr Jennings' claim could be reanalysed as based on Mrs Rice's unjust enrichment at his expense: she received the benefit of his care and attention, and, given her broken promise to leave him the house and its contents, it would be unjust for her to keep that benefit without paying for it. The Court of Appeal in *Jennings* itself, of course, did not adopt this analysis—but it can explain why Mr Jennings had only a right to be paid £200,000, based on the value of the services that he gave to Mrs Rice. Further, it is consistent with the result reached by the House of Lords in *Yeoman's Row* itself: in that case, it was ordered that YRML had to pay Mr Cobbe a sum based on the value of his services to the company (estimated at £150,000).

Thirdly, it could be said that, on the facts of the case, Mr Jennings did have a proprietary estoppel claim, because he believed that Mrs Rice was under a legal duty to leave him the house and its contents. In *Yeoman's Row* itself, Lord Walker[40] seems to support

---

[40] At [66].

that analysis. But as we saw in section 3.3 above when considering *Gillett v Holt*, it would be surprising for Mr Jennings to believe that Mrs Rice was under such a duty. Further, if Lord Walker's suggestion is correct, then Mrs Rice (and so her personal representatives) should have been prevented from denying that she was under a legal duty to leave Mr Jennings the house and its contents, and so Mr Jennings' claim to be paid £435,000 should have succeeded.

4.2.3 The wider significance of the decision: the role of unconscionability

As we have seen, if the House of Lords' analysis in *Yeoman's Row* comes to be generally accepted, the *Jennings* approach may have to be rejected (or at least reanalysed as an approach based on unjust enrichment, rather than proprietary estoppel). It is, however, still important to understand the aim of the *Jennings* approach, and to see how it relates to the concept of unconscionability.

As we will see in the following extracts, commentators have interpreted the *Jennings* approach in different ways. In the first extract, Gardner draws an explicit link between that approach and the concept of unconscionability.

Gardner, 'The Remedial Discretion in Proprietary Estoppel—Again' (2006) 122 LQR 492, 498–500

Jennings v Rice tells us that the outcome should be "proportionate to" both expectation and detriment. The statements to this effect are not always cleanly put. For example, we read that "the task of the court is to do justice. The most essential requirement is that there must be proportionality between the expectation and the detriment." In itself, this says nothing about the scale of relief. The idea, however, is probably that there must be proportionality between the expectation, the detriment *and the outcome* [. . .]

Still, what does it mean to say that there must be "proportionality between" the expectation, the detriment and the outcome? It is hard to find anything beyond: "When the claimant's reliance and expectation interests differ, the judge should pitch the outcome somewhere between the two."

Notice one problem. To pitch the outcome somewhere between the reliance and the expectation, each of these must be quantifiable. But a valid estoppel claim may arise even though they are not. The claimant needs to have acted in detrimental reliance on his belief, but there is no requirement that the reliance has to take any particular form, and the current position is that "it is not a narrow or technical concept," and that it "need not consist of the expenditure of money or other quantifiable financial detriment." And it is well established that the right believed in need not be conceived by the claimant with any precision. It is thus perfectly possible for a successful estoppel claim to arise in circumstances where the claimant's detriment, or expectation, or both, cannot be valued. This was in fact the case in a number of modern authorities on relief. But in none of them did it prevent the court from reaching an outcome. The solution is presumably to pitch the outcome between the innermost values that the two interests may have.

There is a more fundamental problem, however. Imagine a judge asked "I understand that I am to pitch the remedy at a point somewhere between the value of the claimant's expectation and that of her detriment. And I understand that there is no single correct place for that point: that I must make a discretionary decision about it. But still, I do have to choose my place, and I have to do so as a representative of the law, not as a private individual. How am I supposed to go about it?" The question might well be an anxious one, for the facts generating estoppel claims often involve a wide difference between expectation and detriment. The authorities do not readily disclose the answer.

The information the judge seeks is the *aim* of the jurisdiction. It is the jurisdiction's aim that gives meaning to the assertion, which we require the judge to make in arriving at a discretionary outcome, "(in my view, though others may differ) this is the *best* response". The idea of a "best response" is meaningless unless we are told "best for what?" [...] and the "what" is the aim of the jurisdiction. It would make sense, for example, for a judge in a criminal trial to say "(in my view, though others may differ) this sentence best captures the defendant's deserts". It makes no sense for a judge in a proprietary estoppel case to say "(in my view, though others may differ) this outcome best pitches the remedy somewhere between the value of the claimant's expectation and that of his detriment". If the objective is simply to pitch the remedy at a point somewhere between the value of the claimant's expectation and that of his detriment, that objective is achieved equally well by the choice of any point between the two poles: there is nothing to make any particular point the "best" one.

In other words, "proportionality" cannot be not the aim of the jurisdiction. Rather, the aim is to rectify unconscionability, of a particular kind. The claimant's expectation and reliance are relevant because they are the essential ingredients of the unconscionability. The linkage is explicitly put in the famous dictum of Oliver J. in *Taylor Fashions Ltd v Liverpool Victoria Trustees Co Ltd*, posing the question "whether [...] it would be unconscionable for a party to be permitted to deny that which [...] he has allowed or encouraged another to assume to his detriment". Likewise in the dictum of Robert Walker L.J. in *Gillett v Holt*, stating that the finding of detrimental reliance "must be approached as part of a broad inquiry as to whether repudiation of an assurance is or is not unconscionable in all the circumstances".

So our judge should be told to seek the outcome that (in his or her view, though others might differ) best redresses the unconscionability. The essence of unconscionability, as the concept is used in property law contexts, is that the defendant has behaved *vis-à-vis* the claimant in a way which means that it would be morally reprehensible for him to insist on the current allocation of resources between them. More specifically, in proprietary estoppel, there is unconscionability where (and because) the defendant is responsible, by his encouragement or acquiescence, for an expectation on the part of the claimant, and for the reliance that the claimant has placed on that expectation, to his detriment. The aim of the jurisdiction is to redress the resulting state of affairs.

So the outcome our judge should seek will necessarily reflect the claimant's expectation and reliance interests, since these are essential to the unconscionability; and it will therefore normally (it should perhaps be, rather than necessarily) lie between the two in value. But that is not enough. For there to be unconscionability, the claimant's expectation and reliance must be ascribable to the defendant, via the encouragement, or acquiescence, that the defendant must have given. To redress the unconscionability, the outcome must therefore reflect *both* the claimant's expectation and reliance, *and* the degree to which these can be ascribed to the defendant, given his encouragement or acquiescence.

The role of unconscionability in determining the extent of B's right is also emphasized in the following extract.

Hopkins, 'Conscience, Discretion and the Creation of Property Rights' (2006) 26 LS 475, 495

[A]n examination of the case-law suggests that the renewed emphasis on unconscionability in establishing the existence of the estoppel claim since *Gillett v Holt* has started to spill over to the determination of the remedy. There is evidence of a shift in the underlying purpose of the remedy from expectations or reliance to a conscience-based approach. In this development, proportionality has been closely connected with unconscionability [. . .] Most explicitly, the prevailing view of the courts as to the purpose of the estoppel remedy is summarised by Arden LJ in *Ottey v Grundy*.[41] She explained:

> 'the purpose of proprietary estoppel is not to enforce an obligation that does not amount to a contract [expectations] nor yet to reverse the detriment which the claimant has suffered [reliance] but to grant an appropriate remedy in respect of the unconscionable conduct.'

A crucial point made by both Gardner and Hopkins is that, to understand what right B should acquire through proprietary estoppel, we need to understand *why* proprietary estoppel gives that claimant a right in the first place. That method is also adopted in the following extracts. But these extracts, rather than focusing on unconscionability, look to the need to prevent B from suffering a detriment as a result of his or her reliance on A.

Bright and McFarlane, 'Proprietary Estoppel and Property Rights' [2005] CLJ 449, 452–4

In order to determine the nature and extent of rights arising through proprietary estoppel it is crucial to ask why proprietary estoppel is recognized as a source of rights. Any account of the underlying purpose of the doctrine must be consistent both with the test for the availability of a proprietary estoppel claim, and with the extent of the rights awarded in response to such a claim. In particular cases proprietary estoppel may have the effect of allowing the informal grant of a property right; of enforcing a promise; or of reversing an unjust enrichment. Yet none of these three aims can constitute the basic purpose of the doctrine as, by itself, each fails to account both for the test for the availability of a claim and for the extent of the rights thereby gained by B.

On this approach, the only satisfactory theory of proprietary estoppel is one which explains proprietary estoppel as generating rights in order to protect B's reliance. Analysis of the case law shows that proprietary estoppel is concerned with reacting to and protecting B's reasonable reliance, where A can be said to be responsible for the expectation on which that reliance was based. This particular form of reliance seems to be the unifying feature which justifies the courts' view of proprietary estoppel as a single doctrine.

Moreover, this aim of protecting B's reliance explains the diverse range of responses to a proprietary estoppel claim. It does not follow that protecting reliance will limit B to recovering the direct financial cost of his reliance. This is no surprise: the reliance B needs to show in order to bring a claim is not limited to financial expenditure; hence the reliance protected by B's consequent right is not so limited. This can be seen in *Crabb v. Arun District Council*. B's reliance in that case consisted of selling part of his land without reserving a right of access to his remaining land. Were A then able to deny B his expected easement over A's land, B would

---

[41] [2003] EWCA Civ 1176, [61].

be left without access to that remaining land. That particular reliance could only be protected by allowing B to have the expected easement over A's land. In some cases, protecting B's reliance will require B's receiving a property right through an informal grant; in others it will require the enforcement of a promise by A; in others the reversal of A's unjust enrichment; in others the reimbursement of money spent by B. In each case, however, each response will not be a goal in itself but will rather be a means to the end of protecting B's reliance [...]

The use of proportionality in recent English decisions supports the view that the purpose of proprietary estoppel is to protect B's reliance: making a proportionate award, like finding the "minimum equity to do justice to [B]", entails recognizing that B has a right which adequately protects his reliance, but goes no further. The application of this principle in practice can be seen by a consideration of *Jennings v. Rice* [...] It is possible to take the [result in *Jennings*] as evidence of the wide discretion a court has when responding to an estoppel claim. Certainly, there is a tendency to equate the move away from the automatic enforcement of expectations with a move towards the courts having discretion to react to a proprietary estoppel as they see fit and even to re-distribute property rights. However [...] it is preferable to find specific principles which can be used to regulate that task: even when departing from expectations a court must, as Robert Walker L.J. emphasized in *Jennings v. Rice*, "take a principled approach". Admittedly, protecting B's reliance is a less predictable standard than routinely enforcing B's expectation: there will always be an element of judgement in gauging what is proportionate. The matter will not, however, be left to the unbridled discretion of the court: the crucial point is that the response to the estoppel will be guided by the goal of protecting B's reliance.

Robertson, 'The Reliance Basis of Proprietary Estoppel Remedies' [2008] Conv 295, 300–3

The outcomes of the English and Australian cases fall into a clear and consistent pattern. In most cases it is found that the claimant's equity can be satisfied only by granting expectation relief, either *in specie* or in monetary form. In a small but significant number of cases it is necessary to grant more limited relief in order to give effect to the minimum equity principle. In a few cases the courts seek to quantify the claimant's reliance loss by reference to a mathematical formula. In a similar number of cases the courts prefer to adopt a broadbrush approach to relief, framing the remedy by reference neither to the value of claimant's expectations nor the extent of his or her reliance loss. Together those two categories of case, the mathematical and the broad-brush, show that the proportionality principle is playing an important role in the determination of relief in proprietary estoppel cases [...]

The minimum equity principle requires that, in fashioning a remedy to give effect to proprietary estoppel, the court must go no further than is necessary to prevent detriment. This principle recognises reliance-based harm as the core of the estoppel equity: the touchstone in the determination of relief is the overriding goal of protecting against harm resulting from reliance on inconsistent conduct. The decision in *Jennings v Rice* was based on a rejection of the idea that the purpose of proprietary estoppel is to protect expectations or to enforce promises [...] In *Commonwealth v Verwayen*, Mason C.J. said that, in giving effect to an estoppel, "[i]t would be wholly inequitable and unjust to insist upon a disproportionate making good of the relevant assumption".[42] Mason C.J. did not, however, explain why it would be unjust

[42] (1990) 117 CLR 394, 413.

or inequitable to do so. If the expectation of a benefit and harm or potential harm, resulting from reliance, are both essential elements in the establishment of an estoppel, why should the claimant be limited to a remedy which protects his or her reliance interest? Why is it not necessary to protect the expectation interest? The answer is that both expectation loss and reliance loss are essential elements of the equity, and, once either the expectation is fulfilled or reliance loss is prevented, the relying party has no claim in estoppel. This is why it is said in estoppel cases that the relying party has nothing to complain about while the assumption is adhered to. It is also why even proprietary estoppel can, in some situations, have a suspensory effect: if the representor is able to and does give the relying party the opportunity to resume his or her original position, there is no longer an equity arising by way of estoppel. If either the expectation loss or the reliance loss is in one way or another avoided or taken away, the reason for the court's intervention comes to an end.

The reason reliance loss rather than expectation loss provides a loose cap on the remedy is simply that, where there is a discernable difference in value between the reliance interest and the expectation interest, the reliance interest is almost always the smaller. It usually makes no sense to expend £100 in the expectation of a benefit worth £50. Since both expectation loss and reliance loss are essential elements of an estoppel claim, the remedy must necessarily be limited by the smaller of the two measures. Once the lesser interest has been satisfied, an essential element of the claim has been removed. When the reliance-based harm has been prevented or compensated, there is no longer any need for the court to intervene. But just as we can say that, where there is no reliance loss, there is no claim, we can equally say that, where there is no expectation loss, there is no claim. For this reason, in the rare situation in which the claimant's reliance interest exceeds the value of the expectation, the expectation interest provides the upper limit of the remedy. *Baker v Baker* stands as authority for this proposition.[43] There, the claimant contributed £33,950 to the purchase of a house by his son's family in the expectation of having the right to occupy a room in the house for the rest of his life. The arrangement came to an end when the relationship between the parties broke down. The trial judge's award of (reliance-based) compensation in the amount of £33,950 was held on appeal to be unjustifiable because it exceeded the value of the expectation. The starting point should have been the value of the expectancy (the right to occupy), since that was less valuable than the reliance loss (the claimant's contribution to the purchase price).

In summary, then, the proportionality principle can be justified on the basis that both reliance loss and expectation loss are necessary to an estoppel claim. Where the lesser interest has been met, the equity is satisfied because an essential element of the claim has been removed. In those rare instances in which the expectation interest is less valuable, it will provide a cap on the claim. Almost invariably, however, the reliance interest is the smaller. That is why the minimum equity principle requires the courts to go no further in granting relief than is necessary to prevent reliance loss.

5 THE EFFECT OF PROPRIETARY ESTOPPEL ON A THIRD PARTY: THE PRIORITY QUESTION

5.1 INTRODUCTION

In land law, as we saw in Part A of this book, one of the most fundamental questions is as follows: if B acquires a right from A, when will it be possible for B to assert that right against C, a party

---

[43] (1993) 25 HLR 408.

later acquiring a right in relation to A's land? For example, we can go back to *Crabb v Arun DC*. In that case, no third party was involved: B simply made a claim against A. But what would have happened if the council had sold its land to C?

As we saw in Chapter 6, the first crucial question would then be whether B, at the time of the sale to C, had a property right in relation to A's land. In answering that question where proprietary estoppel is concerned, the usual approach is to distinguish between two situations: (i) where the sale to C occurs *after* a court has made an order in B's favour; and (ii) where the sale to C occurs *before* such an order.

5.2 B'S POSITION *AFTER* A COURT ORDER IN HIS OR HER FAVOUR

The position here seems to be clear: we simply need to see whether the court's order recognizes that, through proprietary estoppel, B has acquired a property right in relation to A's land. For example, in *Crabb v Arun DC*, the Court of Appeal ordered that A had to allow B a right of access over A's land. That right of access, in theory, could take the form of either a personal right against A (a licence) or a property right in relation to A's land (an easement). It seems that, to protect B fully, an easement was necessary. This means that A, as instructed by the Court of Appeal, was under a duty to grant B a legal easement. To acquire such a right, formality requirements have to be met, so it seems that the court order, by itself, cannot give B a *legal* easement. From at least the time of the court order, however, B has an equitable easement: A is under a specifically enforceable duty to give B a legal easement and so the doctrine of anticipation applies to give B an equitable easement (see Chapter 12).

In some cases, however, the court's order does not recognize that B has a property right. For example, in *Jennings v Rice*, Mrs Rice (and then her estate) was simply under a duty to pay Mr Jennings a sum of money: £200,000. Because that duty to pay money was not in any way secured on the land (e.g. by means of a charge—see Chapter 29), it could only give Mr Jennings a personal right. So it seems that if the land had been sold to C *after* the court order in favour of Mr Jennings, he would have no legal or equitable property right to assert against C.

A particular question arises where the court orders that B has a licence. As we saw in Chapter 8, section 4.3, the courts have, on occasion, suggested that a licence, if it arises through proprietary estoppel, can count as an equitable property right and so bind C. But we also saw that those suggestions were made at a time when some judges, at least, also regarded a contractual licence as an equitable property right in land. And, as noted by commentators such as Smith and Battersby,[44] it is very difficult to suggest that an estoppel licence, once recognized by a court, should be treated differently from a contractual licence.

5.3 B'S POSITION *BEFORE* A COURT ORDER IN HIS OR HER FAVOUR

The general view is that, before any court order is made in his or her favour, B has only an 'estoppel equity', or 'inchoate equity'—that is, a right to go to court. This is the case even if

---

[44] Smith, 'How Proprietary is Proprietary Estoppel' in *Consenus ad Idem: Essays in the Law of Contract in Honour of Guenther Treitel* (ed Rose, 1996, p 247); Battersby, 'Informally Created Interests in Land' in *Land Law: Themes and Perspectives* (eds Bright and Dewar, 1998, pp 503–4). See also McFarlane [2003] CLJ 661, 664–5, and Swadling, 'Property' in *English Private Law* (ed Burrows, 2nd edn, 2007, [4.128]).

the test for proprietary estoppel has been clearly satisfied, so that we know that A is under *some* form of duty to B. This means that, if A sells the land to C *after* B has relied to his or her detriment on a commitment made by A, but *before* a court has made any order in B's favour, the crucial question is whether B's 'estoppel equity' counts as a property right.

In relation to registered land, the position has now been clarified by s 116(a) of the Land Registration Act 2002 (LRA 2002).

Land Registration Act 2002, s 116

It is hereby declared for the avoidance of doubt that, in relation to registered land, each of the following:

(a) an equity by estoppel, and

(b) a mere equity

has effect from the time the equity arises as an interest capable of binding successors in title (subject to the rules about the effect of dispositions on priority).

The thinking behind this provision is explained in the following extract from the Law Commission Report that led to the 2002 Act.

Law Commission Report No 271, *Land Registration for the Twenty-First Century: A Conveyancing Revolution* (2001, [5.30])

Our concern was with the status of B's 'inchoate equity' that arises after he or she has acted to his or her detriment but before the court can make an order giving effect to it. Although the point is not finally settled, the weight of authority firmly favours the view that such an equity is a proprietary and not merely a personal right.[45] HM Land Registry treats it as such, permitting the entry of a caution or notice in relation to such equities. It has also been assumed that a person in actual occupation can protect such an equity in relation to land as an overriding interest. We pointed out in the Consultative Document that proprietary estoppel is increasingly important as a mechanism for the informal creation of property rights. To put the matter beyond doubt, we recommended that the proprietary status of an equity arising by estoppel should be confirmed in relation to registered land. It could therefore be protected by the entry of a notice in the register or, where the claimant was in actual occupation of the land in relation to which he or she claimed an equity, as an overriding interest. This recommendation was more contentious than our proposal in relation to rights of pre-emption. It was supported by 55 per cent of those who responded to the point (of whom there were not many). Those who opposed it were mainly academics, several of whom were defending their published views. On the other hand members of the legal profession generally supported the proposal. We have therefore decided to take the proposal forward, particularly as we consider that we are merely confirming what is probably the present law.

---

45 [The report here refers to *Megarry & Wade's Law of Real Property* (eds Harpum et al, 6th edn, 2000, [13-028]–[13-032]). Law Commission Consultation Paper No 254, which first suggested the provision to become s 116(a) of the Land Registration Act 2002, listed the following authorities at [3.35]: *Duke of Beaufort v Patrick* (1853) 17 Beav 60, 78; *Inwards v Baker* [1965] 2 QB 29, 37; *E R Ives Investment Ltd v High* [1967] 2 QB 379; *Voyce v Voyce* (1991) 62 P & CR 290, 294 and 296.]

It is important to note that s 116(a) does not mean that B's 'equity by estoppel' will *always* bind C. After all, as we saw in Chapter 6, any property right may be subject to defences. In particular, if C pays for and registers his or her right, C will have a defence against B's 'equity by estoppel' *unless*: (i) B has protected his or her equity by entering a notice on the register; (ii) *or* B can show that he or she was in actual occupation of the land at the relevant time. Nonetheless, the important point about s 116(a) is that, on the interpretation intended by the Law Commission, it means that B's 'equity by estoppel', like any property right, is *capable* of binding C.

But the Law Commission's view of the position prevailing before the Act (of course, that position still applies where B has an 'equity by estoppel' in relation to unregistered land) can be questioned. For example, there is no authority making clear that *every* 'equity by estoppel' is capable of binding a third party.[46] Indeed, in the following extract, Smith notes there are some doubts as to whether an 'equity by estoppel' should be capable of binding a third party. His first point relates to the discretion possessed by a court in deciding what right B has acquired through proprietary estoppel.

Smith, 'How Proprietary is Proprietary Estoppel', in *Consensus ad Idem: Essays on the Law of Contract in Honour of Guenther Treitel* (ed Rose, 1996, p 244)

Although most equities are claims to conventional property interests, the nature of the discretion is such that it cannot be argued that there is a right to this interest. It must, therefore, be recognised that, in saying that the equity binds a purchaser, the law is in substance accepting the principle that estoppels bind purchasers. It may well be argued that this is odd. Estoppels and contracts are rather similar, in that they are routes to providing remedies. Nobody seriously suggests that contracts bind purchasers, unless of course there is a contractual right to a legal estate (an estate contract). This seems correct: contracts as such do not represent rights to the land. The same can be argued of estoppels. Yet it has been seen that there is a large body of cases holding that proprietary estoppels bind successors in title. So it seems that the equity involved in an estoppel is a special and discrete property right, albeit one having respectably old origins [...]

The second and perhaps more forceful articulation of doubts is to argue that the position of purchasers is intolerable if it is impossible to discover what remedy B will be given. It is not enough to be informed that one is bound by an equity, when the practical effect of this cannot be foretold [...] Purchasers know what sort of rights to expect if there is, for example, an easement or a lease, but estoppels have no common content in terms of rights over the land. Next, it will be rare for an estoppel to be evidenced in writing, which necessarily makes it more difficult to ascertain the nature of the right claimed, quite apart from the strength of the claim. Similarly, the facts required to be prove an estoppel will often be in doubt: the average purchaser cannot be expected to investigate allegations of detriment. These points have little to do with discretion; they are features of any estoppel. Even once a purchaser knows about the expectation and the detriment, it will often be essential to know what remedy will be given in order to decide whether to proceed with a purchase. Many purchasers would withdraw from the purchase if B could reside in the property for life. On the other hand, monetary compensation for B could be reflected in an adjustment of the purchase price paid to A.

---

[46] For discussion of the authorities relied on by the Law Commission, see McFarlane, 'Proprietary Estoppel and Third Parties After the Land Registration Act 2002' [2003] CLJ 661. For a detailed analysis of *E R Ives Investment Ltd v High* [1967] 2 QB 379, showing (amongst other things) the difficulties in using that case as authority for the proposition that any 'equity by estoppel' can bind a third party, see Battersby, 'Informal Transactions in Land: Estoppel and Registration' (1995) 58 MLR 637.

> Yet these arguments have an air of unreality about them. In practice, most purchasers will run a mile on becoming aware of any form of estoppel claim. The typical response will be that the sale is off, unless A (the vendor) can persuade B to drop the claim. It would be very rare for the purchaser to want to investigate the claim and then proceed with the sale. It follows that uncertainty as to whether the claim can be made out and as to its exact scope is unlikely to be significant.

More fundamentally, it is also possible to challenge the very notion of the 'equity by estoppel'. The extract, which adopts an admittedly unorthodox view, argues that there is simply no need for the 'equity by estoppel': B's position should be the same both before and after any court order made in his or her favour.

McFarlane, *The Structure of Property Law* (2008, pp 468–70)

[The orthodox view] takes a *two-stage* approach to the acquisition of a right through proprietary estoppel. The first stage is complete once all the requirements of the doctrine have been met: B has relied on A's commitment, and has suffered, or would suffer, a detriment if A fails to honour that commitment. At that stage, we would expect B already to have a right against A: after all, the requirements of the doctrine have been met. However, on the orthodox view, B does not yet have a right against A. B has only an "equity by estoppel": a right to go to court [...]

So, in a case such as *Crabb v Arun DC*, if C acquires a right in relation to A's land *after* Stage 2 has begun [i.e. after the court order in B's favour] things are fairly clear. Due to the court order, A is under a duty to give B an Easement: A is thus under a duty in relation to a specific right and so C is *prima facie* bound by B's pre-existing Equitable Easement.

However, if C instead acquires his right during Stage 1 (i.e. *before* the court has made its order, but after B has relied on A's commitment) everything depends on the status of B's mysterious "equity by estoppel". C can be bound by B's proprietary estoppel claim if, and only if, the "equity by estoppel" counts as a persistent right.[47]

So, on the orthodox view, a choice has to be made: is an "equity by estoppel" capable of binding a third party or not? The consensus answer is Yes: and so the Law Commission, when preparing the draft provision that became s.116(a) of the LRA 2002, adopted that position [...]

The orthodox view treats proprietary estoppel in an odd way and therefore leads to odd results. First, as a matter of principle, it is strange to say that the doctrine works in two separate stages, and that B has no actual right until a court makes an order. Certainly, we do not talk of "inchoate" contracts, wrongs or unjust enrichments: the rule is that B's right arises as soon as all the relevant requirements for acquiring the right have been met. So, if A commits a wrong by carelessly running B over, B acquires a right against A immediately: there is no need to wait for a court order. Indeed, we do not usually think of courts as awarding rights to the parties: unless they have a special statutory jurisdiction, the job of the courts is not to confer new rights but to *recognise* rights the parties have already acquired. To say that, even after the requirements of proprietary estoppel have been met, B only has an "equity by estoppel" (a right to go to court) gives insufficient weight to the fact that B has relied on A's

---

47 ['Persistent right' here is used by the author to refer to rights usually called 'equitable property rights': see the discussion of this point in Chapter 4, section 7.]

commitment and would suffer a detriment if that commitment were not honoured: after all, vexatious litigants aside, *everyone* has the right to go to court. In fact, there are a number of cases in which the courts have recognised that B has a definite right *before* any court order has made in his favour.[48]

The special, two-stage view of proprietary estoppel *would* be defensible if the doctrine gave the courts an unfettered discretion to vary the rights of A and B. In such a world, it would be very difficult to say that B has a right before the court had exercised its discretion and awarded B a right. However [...] proprietary estoppel does *not* operate in that way: like contract, wrongs and unjust enrichment, it is a means of acquiring a right that has its own specific requirements. Indeed, the two-stage model seems to be based on an out-dated, seemingly medieval model of the law, where parties go cap in hand to an all-powerful representative of the monarch and hope that he will exercise his unregulated largesse in their favour.

The two-stage model, and the special treatment it accords proprietary estoppel, is thus over-complicated and unnecessary. There is simply no need for the "equity by estoppel": if B acquires a right through proprietary estoppel that right should arise immediately.

The view taken in that extract is inconsistent with the view of the Law Commission, seemingly now enshrined by statute in relation to registered land. This can be seen by considering a case such as *Jennings v Rice*. On the view taken in the extract above, Mr Jennings must have the same right both before and after a court order in his favour: a personal right, against Mrs Rice (and so her estate), to be paid £200,000. So, whether C acquires a right in Mrs Rice's land before or after such a court order, B's position is the same: he has no property right to assert against C.

The intended effect of s 116(a) of the LRA 2002 is that, before any court order was made in his favour, Mr Jennings had a right that was *capable* of binding a third party—that is, an 'equity by estoppel'. But after the court order was made in his favour, Mr Jennings presumably had only a personal right: a right to be paid £200,000 by Mrs Rice (and so then by her estate). It is not immediately clear what the justification is for this position—but, unless the courts decide to adopt a different (and strained interpretation) of s 116(a), it is certainly the law (at least in relation to registered land).

5.4 THE EFFECT OF *YEOMAN'S ROW*

It is not immediately clear that the reasoning of the House of Lords in *Yeoman's Row* is consistent with the usual two-stage approach to proprietary estoppel, in which B first acquires an 'equity by estoppel', and then a right from a court order satisfying that equity. Firstly, the usual 'equity by estoppel' analysis is applied only to proprietary estoppel and not to other forms of estoppel, whereas the *Yeoman's Row* reasoning sees proprietary estoppel as simply a standard form of estoppel.

Secondly, and related to this, the usual two-stage approach assumes that proprietary estoppel can operate as an independent means by which B can acquire a right. This allows for the possibility that B can use proprietary estoppel to acquire a right capable of binding C. But the *Yeoman's Row* reasoning challenges that assumption: it allows for the possibility that A may be estopped from denying that B has a property right—although that possibility alone does not explain why B should have any right capable of binding C. So, this is just one further

---

[48] [The example given in the text is *Voyce v Voyce* (1991) 62 P & CR 290, esp *per* Dillon LJ at 294.]

aspect of the law of proprietary estoppel in relation to which we may have to wait to see how later courts react to the reasoning in *Yeoman's Row*. In particular, the forthcoming House of Lords decision in *Thorner v Majors and ors*, which will be discussed on this book's companion website, will have an important role to play in determining the wider significance of the reasoning in *Yeoman's Row*. In this particular context, the problem faced by the courts is particularly acute—because the challenge is to reconcile the *Yeoman's Row* reasoning not only to previous judicial decisions, but also to a statute: s 116(a) of the LRA 2002.

QUESTIONS

1. In *Crabb v Arun District Council*, was the Court of Appeal right to give Mr Crabb some protection against the council, even though the council had made no contractual promise to Mr Crabb?

2. In *Yeoman's Row Management Ltd v Cobbe*, should Mr Cobbe have been entitled to at least some of the increase in value of YRML's land, given that his work was crucial in obtaining the planning permission that led to that increase?

3. What are the basic requirements of proprietary estoppel? Which of those requirements, if any, are affected by the decision of the House of Lords in *Yeoman's Row*?

4. Can proprietary estoppel apply even if A (the party against whom proprietary estoppel is used) has acted perfectly innocently? How does the decision in *Taylor Fashions v Liverpool Victoria Trustees* affect your answer?

5. Do you agree with the results reached by the Court of Appeal in *Gillett v Holt* and *Jennings v Rice*? Would the same results be reached in those cases by applying the reasoning of the House of Lords in *Yeoman's Row*?

6. Does s 116(a) of the Land Registration Act 2002 impose a potentially unfair burden on a third party acquiring land subject to a proprietary estoppel claim?

FURTHER READING

Bright and McFarlane, 'Proprietary Estoppel and Proprietary Rights' [2005] CLJ 449

Gardner, 'The Remedial Discretion in Proprietary Estoppel—Again' (2006) 122 LQR 462

McFarlane, 'Proprietary Estoppel and Third Parties After the Land Registration Act 2002' [2003] CLJ 661

McFarlane and Robertson, 'The Death of Proprietary Estoppel' [2008] LMCLQ 449

Robertson, 'The Reliance Basis of Proprietary Estoppel Remedies' [2008] Conv 295

Smith, 'How Proprietary is Proprietary Estoppel' in *Consensus ad Idem: Essays on the Law of Contract for Guenther Treitel* (ed Rose, London: Sweet & Maxwell, 2000, ch 11)

14

TRUSTS OF LAND

CENTRAL ISSUES

1. Beneficial interests under a trust of land may be acquired through an express, resulting, or constructive trust.

2. An express trust of land must be evidenced by signed writing to fulfil statutory formality requirements. Resulting and constructive trusts of land are exempt from this requirement.

3. A purchase money resulting trust arises where A purchases or contributes to the purchase of land in the name of B, or where land is purchased in the joint names of A and B, but with no express declaration as to their beneficial shares. The trust confers on the parties beneficial interests in proportion to their contribution. It is generally used to determine ownership of commercial property.

4. The basis of the resulting trust remains subject to debate. The trust arises either through a reluctance to assume that A intended a gift, or to prevent B's unjust enrichment at A's expense.

5. Constructive trusts arise in a number of circumstances in which, through the existence of specific factors, it is considered unconscionable for the legal owner to assert his or her own beneficial ownership, and to deny the beneficial interest of another.

6. There is no exhaustive definition of the circumstances giving rise to a constructive trust. Two types of constructive trust are considered in this chapter: those arising under the doctrine in *Rochefoucauld v Boustead*;[1] and those arising under the *Pallant v Morgan*[2] equity.

7. Constructive trusts arise under the doctrine in *Rochefoucauld v Boustead* where A transfers land to B on an oral trust in favour of A or transfers land to C on trust for B, a third party. The trust prevents B or C from fraudulently relying on the absence of compliance with formalities for an express trust to claim the land for him or herself.

8. Constructive trusts arise under the *Pallant v Morgan* equity where one party acquires land pursuant to an informal commercial joint venture and reneges on an agreement that another party will have an interest in the land. The non-acquiring party must have relied on the agreement, but it is not necessary that he or she acted to his or her detriment in so doing.

---

[1] [1897] 1 Ch 196, CA.   [2] [1953] 1 Ch 43.

1 INTRODUCTION

In this chapter, we consider how equitable interests are acquired by the creation of a trust of land. There are three principal categories of trust that need to be considered: express, resulting, and constructive. These categories of trust are differentiated by their method of creation and, specifically, by the different role afforded to the settlor's intention in the creation of the trust.

Snell's Equity (31st edn, ed McGhee, 2005, [19–07])

A classification of trusts in these terms [express, resulting, and constructive] refers to the extent to which the trust arises though the expression of the settlor's actual intention to create it, or by operation of law and irrespective of the intention of the person in whom the property is vested. The distinction between these classifications of trust is often a fine one, depending on a close analysis of the relevant transaction.

(a) *Express trust.* An express trust is created by the actual intention of the person in whom the property is vested, as where A declares himself a trustee of Whiteacre for B, or conveys it to C on trust for B. [. . .]

(b) *Resulting trust.* A resulting trust may arise by operation of law, though in response to a legal presumption about the intentions of the person who transfers the property which becomes subject to the trust. If A transfers property to B when it is unclear whether A intends B to have the beneficial interest in it, then B may hold the property on resulting trust for A. The trust arises by operation of law to give effect to a presumption that A did not intend B to take the property beneficially.

(c) *Constructive trust.* A constructive trust is imposed by operation of law, rather than through the express or presumed intention of the owner of the property to create a trust or to retain any beneficial interest for himself. The trust may even arise contrary to the actual intentions of the owner [. . .] In other cases the distinction between constructive and express trusts is less pronounced. So a constructive trust may be imposed on property to give enforce to a person's intention to make a gift to another or to act as a trustee, but where the necessary formalities to give effect to the gift or the trust relationship are not observed [sic].

Oakley succinctly explains the different role attributed to intent in each of these trusts.

Oakley, *Constructive Trusts* (3rd edn, 1996, p 29)

[An] express trust arises out of the intentional creation of the relationship, [of trustee and beneficiary] a resulting trust arises out of some other intentional act of the settlor and a constructive trust arises totally independently of the intention of anyone.

A fourth category—that of the 'implied trust'—may also exist, although the expression lacks a clear and consistent usage. It is sometimes used to refer to a trust created by a settlor, but where the settlor's intention is inferred, rather than express. This use of the implied trust has no application in relation to land,[3] where, as we will see, written evidence of intent is

---

[3] *Lewin on Trusts* (18th edn, ed Mobray, 2008, [7–04]).

required. At other times, the expression 'implied trust' is used simply as an umbrella term for resulting and constructive trusts, in contradistinction to express trusts.

More recently, an alternative means of classifying trusts has emerged. This classification is based on the causative event that triggers the imposition of the trust. This development should be seen in the broader context of the taxonomy of private law pioneered by Professor Peter Birks.[4] He demonstrated that obligations arise on the basis of consent, wrongs, unjust enrichment, and through a category of miscellaneous other events. The possibility of classifying trusts in these terms has garnered significant academic support.[5] This scheme appeals to a sense of logic and rationalization by aligning the creation of trusts with the creation of obligations in private law—but it is incompatible with current classifications of express, resulting, and constructive trusts.[6] Because (as we will see) the existing statutory scheme for trusts of land refers to the traditional classifications, a wholesale change to a scheme based on causative event appears unlikely.

Once a trust comes into existence, the method of creation and the consequent classification of the trust are of limited significance. Hence, the priority rules determining the enforcement of trusts against third parties (such as purchasers and those who lend money on security of the land) operate in the same way, regardless of how the trust came into existence. Those rules are discussed in Chapter 20. Equally, express, resulting, and constructive trusts of land are all 'trusts of land' within s 1(2)(a) of the Trusts of Land and Appointment of Trustees Act 1996 (TOLATA 1996). That Act, which is discussed in Chapter 19, sets out the general rights of beneficiaries and duties of the trustees for all trusts of land. It draws no distinction between different categories of trust, except that, where a trust is created expressly, the settlor may make specific provision as regards those rights and duties. In some instances, however, differences emerge through specific rules applicable to trusts arising in particular circumstances. For example, as we have seen in Chapter 12, the constructive trust arising under the doctrine of anticipation has unusual features stemming from its origin in a contract for sale of land. The classification of a trust therefore seems to be of secondary importance. In the beginning, it is more important to understand when a beneficial interest will arise than whether it is called an 'express', 'resulting', or 'constructive' trust.

Once these rules are understood, however, the issue of classification becomes more significant. The scope of resulting and constructive trusts ultimately lies in the development of doctrine by the courts. Rationalizing the basis on which these trusts come into existence can provide an important benchmark for distinguishing the uses and abuses of these doctrines. With this in mind, this chapter considers the application of express, resulting, and constructive trusts to land, and places this discussion in the broader context of current debate concerning those doctrines of trust.

2 EXPRESS TRUSTS

As we have seen, an express trust is one created by the actual intention of the settlor. The creation of express trusts of land is subject to compliance with formality requirements. These are provided in s 53(1)(b) of the Law of Property Act 1925 (LPA 1925), which, as we have seen

---

[4] Birks, *An Introduction to the Law of Restitution* (1985).

[5] This classification is adopted in *Snell's Equity* (31st edn, ed McGhee, 2005, [19.09]–[19.10]) and by Swadling, 'Property' in *English Private Law* (2nd edn, ed Burrows, 2007).

[6] A point acknowledged in *Snell's Equity* (2005, [19.09]–[19.10]).

in Chapter 11, is one of the main formality provisions governing the creation of equitable interests in land.

Law of Property Act 1925, s 53(1)(b) and (2)

(1) [...]

    (b) a declaration of trust respecting any land or any interest therein must be manifested and proved by some writing signed by some person who is able to declare such trust or by his will;

    [...]

(2) This section does not affect the creation or operation of resulting, implied or constructive trusts.

An express declaration of trust is conclusive as to the existence of the trust. If the declaration specifies the parties' respective beneficial shares, it is also conclusive in that respect;[7] otherwise, the parties' shares will be determined by the application of resulting and constructive trust principles.[8]

Debate arises as to whether a trust that the settlor intends to create, but which does not comply with s 53(1)(b) of the LPA 1925, should still be classified as 'express'. One instance of this debate is considered below, as regards the classification of the trust arising under the doctrine in *Rochefoucauld v Boustead*. The better view, it is suggested, is that a trust of land should be classified as an express trust only where s 53(1)(b) is complied with. In the absence of compliance, the trust should be classified as resulting or constructive to invoke the exception in s 53(2).

3 RESULTING TRUSTS

There are two main views on the scope of resulting trusts, each of which affords a different role to intent. The first, and traditional, view is that resulting trusts arise in two distinct categories: where A pays or contributes to the purchase of property in B's name (the 'presumed intention', or 'purchase money', resulting trust); and where A creates an express trust that does not exhaust the beneficial interest (an 'automatic' resulting trust).[9] The presumed trust arises through an assumption that A does not intend a gift. The role of intent in the automatic resulting trust is more contentious: it may play no role,[10] or the trust may arise because A does not intend the property to vest in the Crown as *bona vacantia*.[11]

The second view on the scope of resulting trusts is that they arise whenever B receives property in relation to which he or she was not intended to benefit. On this view, the trust

---

[7] *Goodman v Gallant* [1986] 2 WLR 236.

[8] The quantification of shares in such cases is considered in Chapter 18.

[9] The description of these as presumed and automatic is provided by Megarry J in *Re Vandervell's Trusts (No 2)* [1974] Ch 269, 294.

[10] The approach suggested ibid.

[11] Compare the discussion by Lord Browne-Wilkinson in *Westdeutsche v Landesbank Girozentrale v Islington LBC* [1996] AC 669, 708.

arises through A's (the transferor or purchaser) lack of intent to benefit B and the effect of the trust is to provide restitution for unjust enrichment.

Chambers, *Resulting Trusts* (1997, p 220)

There are two requirements for every resulting trust: (i) a transfer of property (ii) in circumstances in which the provider of that property did not intend to benefit the recipient. The property may be any interest in any type of property or asset, so long as it is capable of being the subject of the trust. The provider may be the previous owner of the property in question or someone who has contributed to the recipient's acquisition of that property. [...]

All resulting trusts effect restitution of what would otherwise be the unjust enrichment of the recipient. They are created neither by the consent of the recipient nor by the intention of the provider to create a trust. The resulting trust is not merely the passive preservation of the provider's pre-existing property interest, but is one of equity's active responses to non-voluntary transfer.

The broader view of the resulting trust was rejected by the House of Lords in *Westdeutsche v Landesbank Girozentrale v Islington LBC*.[12] The House of Lords preferred the traditional view, confining the trust to its two categories. Placing the resulting trust in the context of general principles of trust law, however, Lord Browne-Wilkinson considered that the trust could not arise until the trustees' conscience is affected by knowledge of the factors giving rise to the trust.[13]

That decision has not put an end to the debate and the restitutionary approach remains strongly advocated by Birks[14] and Chambers.[15] McFarlane suggests that the limitation of the resulting trust in *Westdeutsche* to the two traditional situations is arbitrary. Combining the analysis of Lord Browne-Wilkinson, on one hand, and Birks and Chambers, on the other, McFarlane argues that the resulting trust should arise to prevent unjust enrichment in cases outside the two traditional situations, but only where the trustee is aware, or ought to be aware, of the relevant facts.[16]

The practical differences between Lord Browne-Wilkinson's view of the resulting trust, on the one hand, and Birks' and Chambers' view, on the other, are twofold. Firstly, Lord Browne-Wilkinson confines the operation of the trust to its two traditional applications. The second difference relates to the timing of the trust: if an unjust enrichment analysis is applied, the trust dates from the time of receipt of the property (the time of the enrichment); on Lord Browne-Wilkinson's view, the trust does not arise until the trustee has knowledge of the factors that give rise to the trust. This difference in timing can be particularly significant where the recipient becomes bankrupt between the date of receipt and the date on which the trustee becomes aware of the relevant facts.[17]

---

[12] [1996] AC 669.

[13] [1996] AC 669, 709.

[14] See, e.g., Birks, 'Restitution and Resulting Trusts' in *Equity and Contemporary Legal Developments* (ed Goldstein, 1992).

[15] Chambers, *Resulting Trusts* (1997, p 220).

[16] McFarlane, *The Structure of Property Law* (2008, pp 314–22).

[17] See, e.g., the discussion of *Chase Manhattan Bank NA v Israel-British Bank (London) Ltd* [1981] Ch 105 in *Westdeutsche v Landesbank Girozentrale v Islington LBC* [1996] AC 669, 714–15.

In relation to land, the most significant application of the resulting trust is the purchase money resulting trust, arising where A purchases or contributes to the purchase of land in the name of B. In such a case, the analysis adopted may have no practical impact on the timing of the trust. The trust is within the two traditional categories and, because B will necessarily have knowledge of A's contribution, whichever analysis is taken, the trust will arise at the time of receipt. In view of this, and in line with prevailing judicial preference, the traditional analysis of the resulting trust is followed in the remainder of this chapter.

3.1 THE PURCHASE MONEY RESULTING TRUST

Where A purchases or contributes to the purchase of land in the name of B, a resulting trust arises, because it is presumed that A did not intend a gift. A classic exposition of the trust is contained in the following case.

Dyer v Dyer (1788) 2 Cox 92

Eyre CB

At 93

The clear result of all the cases, without a single exception, is that the trust of a legal estate whether freehold, copyhold, or leasehold, whether taken in the names of the purchaser and others jointly, or in the names of others without that of the purchaser, whether in one name or several, whether jointly or successive, results to the man who advances the purchase money.

The link between the trust and payment of purchase money is reflected in the quantification of shares under the resulting trust. Each party receives a share in proportion to their contribution.

The nature of the presumption is analysed by Swadling.

Swadling, 'Explaining Resulting Trusts' (2008) 124 LQR 72, 74

Presumptions properly so-called form part of the law of proof. Generally speaking, facts can be proved by admission, judicial notice, or evidence. In the absence of admission and judicial notice, the general rule is that facts must be proved by evidence, the burden of proving those facts lying on the party alleging them to have occurred. Very occasionally, however, proof by evidence of one fact, the "basic" or "primary" fact, gives that party to the litigation the benefit of another fact, the "secondary" fact, without any need to adduce evidence in proof. In such cases, the fact is proved by presumption. The burden then lies on the other party to adduce evidence to rebut the presumption. If they do not, the tribunal of fact must find the secondary fact proved.

In the resulting trust, the primary fact is A's contribution to the purchase. Swadling argues that the secondary fact (the fact presumed) is that A intended a declaration of trust.[18] On

---

[18] Swadling, 'Explaining Resulting Trusts' (2008) 124 LQR 72, 79.

Birks' and Chambers' unjust enrichment analysis, the fact presumed is the lack of intent to benefit the recipient.[19]

3.1.1 Presumption of advancement

In a limited number of circumstances, due to the relationship between A and B, no presumption of resulting trust is drawn; instead, it is presumed that A did, in fact, intend to make a gift of the land to B. These cases are described as involving a 'presumption of advancement', or a 'presumption of gift'. The relationships to which the presumption of advancement applies were established by the early twentieth century and reflect the prevailing views of relationships in which there is a moral obligation for A to provide for B. Hence, the presumption applies to transfers from a husband to his wife (but not from a wife to her husband, or between cohabiting partners), and from a father to his child. In *Laskar v Laskar*,[20] the Court of Appeal assumed that it would also apply to a transfer from a mother to her child (although counsel did not argue for its application on the facts).

The values on which the presumption of advancement is based now appear outdated. Its continuing application on a transfer from husband to wife has met with particular criticism. As we have seen in the context of the presumption of resulting trust, a presumption is no more than a means of proving the existence of a fact. As Lord Diplock explains, this means that a presumption is only as valid as the underlying assumptions upon which it is drawn.

Pettitt v Pettitt [1970] AC 777, HL

Lord Diplock

At 824

But the most likely inference as to a person's intention in the transactions of his everyday life depends upon the social environment in which he lives and the common habits of thought of those who live in it. The consensus of judicial opinion which gave rise to the presumptions of "advancement" and "resulting trust" in transactions between husband and wife is to be found in cases relating to the propertied classes of the nineteenth century and the first quarter of the twentieth century among whom marriage settlements were common, and it was unusual for the wife to contribute by her earnings to the family income. It was not until after World War II that the courts were required to consider the proprietary rights in family assets of a different social class. The advent of legal aid, the wider employment of married women in industry, commerce and the professions and the emergence of a property-owning, particularly a real-property-mortgaged-to-a-building- society-owning, democracy has compelled the courts to direct their attention to this during the last 20 years. It would, in my view, be an abuse of the legal technique for ascertaining or imputing intention to apply to transactions between the post-war generation of married couples "presumptions" which are based upon inferences of fact which an earlier generation of judges drew as to the most likely intentions of earlier generations of spouses belonging to the propertied classes of a different social era.

---

[19] See, e.g., Chambers (1997, p 21). The opposing views are discussed by Swadling (2008, pp 74–95).
[20] [2008] EWCA 347, [20].

Although the presumption of advancement still exists in a transfer from husband and wife, it will readily be rebutted. In *Stack v Dowden*,[21] Lord Neuberger noted: '[T]*he presumption of advancement, as between man and wife, which was so important in the 18th and 19th centuries has now become much weakened, although not quite to the point of disappearance.*'

3.1.2 Rebutting the presumptions: general principles

The presumptions of resulting trust and of advancement can be displaced by evidence of the actual intention of A.[22] Where the presumption of resulting trust is rebutted, A does not obtain a beneficial interest in the land despite his or her financial contribution to its purchase. Where the presumption of advancement is rebutted, the land is held on resulting trust for A, who provided the purchase money, despite A's relationship to B.

Debate has centred on the nature of the evidence required to rebut the presumption of resulting trust. As we have noted, the presumption that A intended a declaration of trust is drawn because of a reluctance to presume that A intended to make a gift of the land to B. Hence, evidence that a gift was, in fact, intended would clearly rebut the presumption of trust. But the presumption may be rebutted by a wider range of evidence, consistent with the view that the presumption drawn is that of a declaration of trust.

Swadling, 'A New Role for Resulting Trusts?' (1996) 16 LS 110, 116–17

The presumption of resulting trust which arises in the case of a transfer of property without consideration is not one of non-beneficial transfer. It is instead a presumption of transfer on trust for the transferor. And for that reason, evidence of a positive donative intent is not the only thing capable of rebutting the presumption. Any evidence which is inconsistent with the implication of an intended trust will do [. . .]

In *Westdeutsche v Landesbank Girozentrale v Islington LBC*,[23] Lord Browne-Wilkinson approved the statement that the presumption of trust is rebutted by evidence of any intention inconsistent with the trust. In doing so, he rejected the view (consistent with an unjust enrichment analysis) that the presumption is rebutted only by evidence of an intention to make a gift.[24]

3.1.3 Rebutting the presumptions: transfers for an illegal purpose

Where A transfers land to B, or contributes to the purchase of property in B's name, in order to facilitate an illegal activity, the illegal purpose cannot be invoked to rebut a presumption of advancement or trust. In the following case, a three–two majority of the House of Lords held that this does not prevent A from relying on the initial presumption, because A does not need to plead the illegality in order to do so.

---

[21] [2007] 2 AC 432, [101]. See further *Gissing v Gissing* [1971] AC 886, 907, in which Lord Diplock suggested that the presumption would seldom be decisive.

[22] *Snell's Equity* (2005, [23.09]).

[23] [1996] AC 669, 708.

[24] Ibid.

Tinsley v Milligan [1994] 1 AC 340, HL

Facts: Tinsley and Milligan, a lesbian couple, both contributed to the purchase of the house that they shared, but the house was transferred into Tinsley's sole name in order to facilitate fraudulent social security claims. Milligan subsequently repented and confessed to the frauds, following which, Tinsley moved out of the house. Tinsley then sought possession of the house and argued that she was solely entitled.

Lord Browne-Wilkinson

At 371–2

The presumption of a resulting trust is, in my view, crucial in considering the authorities. On that presumption (and on the contrary presumption of advancement) hinges the answer to the crucial question 'does a plaintiff claiming under a resulting trust have to rely on the underlying illegality?' Where the presumption of resulting trust applies, the plaintiff does not have to rely on the illegality. If he proves that the property is vested in the defendant alone but that the plaintiff provided part of the purchase money, or voluntarily transferred the property to the defendant, the plaintiff establishes his claim under a resulting trust unless either the contrary presumption of advancement displaces the presumption of resulting trust or the defendant leads evidence to rebut the presumption of resulting trust. Therefore, in cases where the presumption of advancement does not apply, a plaintiff can establish his equitable interest in the property without relying in any way on the underlying illegal transaction. In this case Miss Milligan as defendant simply pleaded the common intention that the property should belong to both of them and that she contributed to the purchase price: she claimed that in consequence the property belonged to them equally. To the same effect was her evidence in chief. Therefore Miss Milligan was not forced to rely on the illegality to prove her equitable interest. Only in the reply and the course of Miss Milligan's cross-examination did such illegality emerge: it was Miss Tinsley who had to rely on that illegality.

Although the presumption of advancement does not directly arise for consideration in this case, it is important when considering the decided cases to understand its operation. On a transfer from a man to his wife, children or others to whom he stands in loco parentis, equity presumes an intention to make a gift. Therefore in such a case, unlike the case where the presumption of resulting trust applies, in order to establish any claim the plaintiff has himself to lead evidence sufficient to rebut the presumption of gift and in so doing will normally have to plead, and give evidence of, the underlying illegal purpose.

Hence, Milligan could still invoke the presumption of resulting trust, because she did not need to rely on the illegal purpose of the purchase in Tinsley's sole name in order to do so. The outcome would have been different, however, if the case had involved a husband and wife, and the house had been purchased in the wife's name in order to facilitate social security fraud. In such a case, the initial presumption would be of a gift and therefore the husband would have to plead the illegal purpose in order to establish a resulting trust. This difference in outcome appears unsatisfactory, because the nature of the illegality in each case is identical.[25] The Law Commission[26] has noted the arbitrary and discriminatory effects

[25] Halliwell, 'Equitable Proprietary Claims and Dishonest Claimants: A Resolution' [1994] Conv 62.
[26] Consultation Paper No 154, *Illegal Transactions: The Effect of Illegality on Contracts and Torts* (1999, [3.5]–[3.31]).

of the presumption of advancement in the context of illegal transactions, and have recently published a consultative document on the matter.[27]

An exception to the principle that an illegal purpose cannot be raised to rebut a presumption was recognized in *Tribe v Tribe*.[28] In that case, a father transferred shares in a company to his son to preserve them for the benefit of the family in light of the father's possible liability for dilapidations under commercial leases. The liability did not materialize, but the son refused to re-transfer the shares. The relationship of father and son is one to which the presumption of advancement applies. The Court of Appeal noted the comments in *Tinsley v Milligan* that an illegal purpose could not be raised to rebut the presumption of advancement, but it was held that, because the illegal purpose had not been carried out, the father was not precluded from pleading the purpose of the transfer to claim a resulting trust of the shares.

3.2 THE SCOPE OF THE PURCHASE MONEY RESULTING TRUST

As we have seen, the presumption of resulting trust applies where A purchases or contributes to the purchase of land in B's name. The presumption also applies where land is purchased in the joint names of A and B, but there is no express declaration of trust regarding the parties' respective beneficial shares. In all cases, the presumption of resulting trust confers on the parties beneficial shares in proportion to their financial contribution to the purchase.

The scope of the purchase money resulting trust is curtailed by its relationship with the common intention constructive trust. Where A purchases or contributes to the purchase of land in B's name, or land is purchased in the joint names of A and B, but there is no express declaration of trust, a constructive trust may be imposed to give effect to the common intention of the parties. The practical difference between the constructive and resulting trusts relates to the quantification of the parties' respective beneficial shares. In the common intention constructive trust, beneficial shares are determined in accordance with the common intention of the parties. This may result in the acquisition of shares that are disproportionate to the parties' contributions.

The relationship between these types of trust has arisen principally in the context of determining ownership of a home. It is discussed fully in this context in Chapter 18. For the purposes of this chapter, it is sufficient to note that in an important decision in *Stack v Dowden*,[29] a majority of the House of Lords considered that the resulting trust should be confined in its application to commercial property, with the constructive trust favoured in relation to determining ownership of the home. The resulting trust is therefore the appropriate device to use where A and B are commercial parties.[30] In other cases, the distinction between domestic and commercial property is dependent on the purposes for which land is acquired, rather than the relationship between the parties. Hence, for example, ownership of a house purchased as a home by a husband and wife, or mother and daughter, is determined by the constructive trust, while ownership of a house purchased by the same parties as an investment is determined by the resulting trust. In *Laskar v Laskar*,[31] the resulting trust was therefore applied where a mother and daughter jointly purchased a house as a buy-to-let investment.

[27] Law Commission Consultation Paper No 189, *The Illegality Defence: A Consultative Report* (2009, Part 6).
[28] [1996] Ch 107.
[29] [2007] 2 AC 432.
[30] *Malayan Credit v Chia-Mph* [1986] AC 549 (PC).
[31] [2008] EWCA 347.

4 CONSTRUCTIVE TRUSTS

Constructive trusts represent the broadest and least clearly defined of the three categories of trust. In *Yeoman's Row*, Lord Scott explained.

Yeoman's Row Management Ltd v Cobbe [2008] UKHL 55

Lord Scott

At [30]

It is impossible to prescribe exhaustively the circumstances sufficient to create a constructive trust but it is possible to recognise particular factual circumstances that will do so and also to recognise other factual circumstances that will not.

Judicial attempts at definition have tended to be made at a high level of generality, as in the following case.

Paragon Finance plc v DB Thakerar & Co [1999] 1 All ER 400

Millett LJ

At 409

A constructive trust arises by operation of law whenever the circumstances are such that it would be unconscionable for the owner of property [. . .] to assert his own beneficial interest in the property and deny the beneficial interest of another.

The reference in this definition to unconscionability is significant, but of limited utility. In *Westdeutsche*, Lord Browne-Wilkinson considered unconscionability to be the foundation for the whole of the law of trusts. Notwithstanding, the constructive trust is the only category explicitly defined on this basis. The concept of unconscionability provides a common thread that ties together all trusts classified as constructive. The concept is of limited utility, however, because it does not operate at large. Indeed, in so far as it is indicative of a general discretionary jurisdiction to impose constructive trusts, it is entirely misleading. At best, it may be said that the combination of elements required for the imposition of a constructive trust in each particular application of the doctrine collectively establish conduct considered by the courts to be unconscionable.

4.1 INSTITUTIONAL AND REMEDIAL CONSTRUCTIVE TRUSTS

The key division in constructive trust doctrine is that between institutional and remedial versions of the trust. Lord Browne-Wilkinson explained the difference between these in *Westdeutsche*.

Westdeutsche Landesbank Girozentrale v Islington LBC [1996] AC 669, HL

Lord Browne-Wilkinson

At 714–15

Under an institutional constructive trust, the trust arises by operation of law as from the date of the circumstances which give rise to it: the function of the court is merely to declare that such trust has arisen in the past. The consequences that flow from such trust having arisen (including the possibly unfair consequences to third parties who in the interim have received the trust property) are also determined by rules of law, not under a discretion. A remedial constructive trust, as I understand it, is different. It is a judicial remedy giving rise to an enforceable equitable obligation: the extent to which it operates retrospectively to the prejudice of third parties lies in the discretion of the court.

This difference can be illustrated as follows. Assume that a claimant has fulfilled the elements of a claim to a constructive trust of land on 1 December 2006, but that a court does not decide the claim until 1 December 2009. If the trust is institutional, then the role of the court, having found the constituent elements of the claim to be established since 1 December 2006, is to declare that the trust arose on that date. Since that date, the claimant has had a proprietary interest in the land. If the defendant has sold the land since that date, or has become bankrupt, then the claimant's interest may bind the purchaser and the claimant will have priority in the bankruptcy against unsecured creditors. If, however, the trust is remedial, then the court has discretion to decide what affect, if any, it should have prior to its decision on 1 December 2009. The court therefore has a discretion to determine the claimant's ability to enforce his or her interest against a purchaser who has bought the land since 1 December 2006, and to determine whether the claimant should be treated as a secured creditor in a bankruptcy.

The remedial version of the trust has been embraced in North American jurisdictions, but its place in English law is uncertain. Undoubtedly, there are instances in which English courts impose a constructive trust as a remedy. Nield[32] highlights that a constructive trust imposed as the remedy for proprietary estoppel would be classified in this way. Outside such isolated incidences, however, attempts to develop the remedial constructive trust have faltered.

In the 1970s, Lord Denning advocated the development of a 'constructive trust of a new model'.[33]

Hussey v Palmer [1972] 1 WLR 1286, CA

Lord Denning MR

At 1289–90

[I]t is a trust imposed by law whenever justice and good conscience require it. It is a liberal process, founded upon large principles of equity, to be applied in cases where the

---

32 Nield, 'Constructive Trusts and Estoppel' (2003) 23 LS 311, 312.
33 *Eves v Eves* [1975] 1 WLR 1338, 1341.

legal owner cannot conscientiously keep the property for himself alone, but ought to allow another to have the property or the benefit of it or a share in it. The trust may arise at the outset when the property is acquired, or later on, as the circumstances may require. It is an equitable remedy by which the court can enable an aggrieved party to obtain restitution.

Lord Denning's new model constructive trust represents a particularly broad notion of the remedial trust and did not find favour in the courts. It was developed by Lord Denning in the context of determining ownership of the home: a matter that has subsequently been established as based on a much narrower form of institutional constructive trust.[34]

More recently, in *Westdeutsche*, Lord Browne-Wilkinson suggested that the remedial constructive trust could be used as a proprietary response to unjust enrichment. His comment was made in the context of his rejection of the unjust enrichment analysis of the resulting trust—but this suggestion has since been rejected by the Court of Appeal on a preliminary ruling in the following case, where the question was whether there was a seriously arguable case for the imposition of such a remedial trust.

Re Polly Peck International (No 2) [1998] 3 All ER 812, CA

Nourse LJ

At 830–1

Although [...] this court [...] and Lord Browne-Wilkinson in *Westdeutsche Landesbank* have accepted the possibility that the remedial constructive trust may become part of English law, such observations, being both obiter and tentative, can only be of limited assistance when the question has to be decided, as it does here. There being no earlier decision, we must return to principle. In doing so, we must recognise that the remedial constructive trust gives the court a discretion to vary proprietary rights. You cannot grant a property right to A, who has not had one beforehand, without taking some proprietary right away from B. No English court has ever had the power to do that, except with the authority of Parliament [...]

The underlying objection to the remedial constructive trust therefore lies in the discretion that it confers on the court to vary proprietary rights (as illustrated in the example discussed above). In *Re Polly Peck International*, the Court was being invited, in effect, to allow the claimants to 'leapfrog' other creditors on the company's insolvency. In those circumstances, the Court's reticence is unsurprising—but Nourse LJ considered that there would be no arguable case for a remedial trust even if the company had been solvent.

Currently, therefore, beyond isolated incidents of remedial trusts, the constructive trust recognized by English law is the institutional trust. There are four types of institutional constructive trust that are specifically concerned with the acquisition of beneficial interests in land:

- the common intention constructive trust that is used to determine ownership of the home;
- constructive trusts imposed on a vendor under a specifically enforceable contract for sale of land;

---

[34] The common intention constructive trust, discussed in Chapter 18.

- constructive trusts imposed under the doctrine in *Rochefoucauld v Boustead*;[35]
- constructive trusts arising under the *Pallant v Morgan*[36] equity.

The common intention constructive trust is considered in Chapter 18, while the trust imposed on a vendor has been considered in Chapter 12. In this chapter, we will consider constructive trusts arising under the doctrine in *Rochefoucauld v Boustead* and the *Pallant v Morgan* equity.

While these two types of constructive trust have developed separately and apply to different sets of facts, they are not unrelated. McFarlane suggests that they are both illustrations of the same principle.

McFarlane, *The Structure of Property Law* (2008, pp 270–1)

[T]he courts seem to apply a clear principle, which can be called the "receipt after a promise" principle [...] The principle means that if:

1. C makes a promise to come under a duty to B; *and*
2. C's promise relates to the use of a particular right; *and*
3. C acquires, as a result of that promise, an advantage in relation to the acquisition of that right; *then*
4. C is under a duty to B to keep that promise, as far as it relates to the right advantageously acquired by C.

[...] The principle thus allows C's promise, even though it was made to A, to be enforced by B, the party who benefits from the promise. It is important to note that B's right does *not* arise as a result of a contract between B and C. Rather, it is based on the principle that, having received a right on a particular basis (that he will allow B to make some use of that right), C is not then allowed to enjoy that right on a different basis."

We further consider this view in section 6 below after examining the operation of each of these types of constructive trust.

4.2 THE DOCTRINE IN *ROCHEFOUCAULD V BOUSTEAD*

The doctrine in *Rochefoucauld v Boustead* stems from the maxim that 'equity will not allow a statute to be used as an instrument of fraud'. Where land is transferred on trust, but the statutory requirements for an express trust are not complied with, a constructive trust is imposed to prevent the transferee from reneging on the trust and seeking to retain the property for him or herself. The paradigm case within the doctrine is a two-party case, in which land is transferred from A to B, to hold on trust for A. An extension to this paradigm is a three-party case, in which land is transferred from A to C, to hold on trust for a third party, B. These are illustrated in Figure 7.

---

[35] [1897] 1 Ch 196.
[36] [1953] Ch 43.

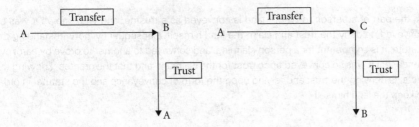

Figure 7 *Rochefoucauld v Boustead* in two and three-party cases

The doctrine has been further extended to situations in which A transfers land to C expressly 'subject to' rights in favour of B, where the rights intended to be enjoyed by B have either been proprietary rights that do not generally take effect under a trust,[37] or personal rights.[38] In such cases, the courts have, notwithstanding, held that a constructive trust may be imposed to prevent C reneging on the 'subject to' agreement. This extension of the doctrine has been particularly significant in cases in which A has conferred a contractual licence on B (a personal right) and wants to protect B's occupation on a transfer of the land to C. The imposition of a constructive trust pursuant to a 'subject to' transfer has been considered in Chapter 8 in the context of our discussion of licences. In this chapter, we consider the imposition of a constructive trust on a transfer of land from A to B on trust for A, or a transfer from A to C on trust for a third party, B.

4.3 THE TWO-PARTY CASE

The two-party case provides the factual context of the decision from which this doctrine takes its name.

Rochefoucauld v Boustead [1897] 1 Ch 196, CA

Facts: Rochefoucauld owned coffee estates in Ceylon, but had been unable to pay mortgages on the estates. She transferred the estates to Boustead, who had subsequently sold them. Rochefoucauld argued that the estates had been transferred to Boustead on trust for her and that the surplus proceeds of sale (after discharge of sums owed to Boustead) should therefore be paid to her. The Court doubted that there was written evidence of the trust, as was required under the Statute of Frauds 1677—the precursor to s 53 of the LPA 1925.

Lindley LJ

At 206

It is further established by a series of cases, the propriety of which cannot now be questioned, that the Statute of Frauds does not prevent the proof of a fraud; and that it is a fraud

---

[37] For example, *Lyus v Prowsa Developments Ltd* [1982] 1 WLR 1044, in which the transfer was made 'subject to' an option to purchase (an estate contract).

[38] For example, *Binions v Evans* [1972] Ch 359, in which the transfer was 'subject to' a contractual licence.

> on the part of a person to whom land is conveyed as a trustee, and who knows it was so conveyed, to deny the trust and claim the land himself. Consequently, notwithstanding the statute, it is competent for a person claiming land conveyed to another to prove by parol evidence that it was so conveyed upon trust for the claimant, and that the grantee, knowing the facts, is denying the trust and relying upon the form of conveyance and the statute, in order to keep the land himself.

The effect of the fraud was to enable oral evidence to be admitted as to the existence of the trust. On the facts, the Court was satisfied that the evidence established that the land had been transferred on trust in favour of Rochefouaculd.

4.3.1 Elements of the *Rochefoucauld v Boustead* constructive trust

The court's intervention is triggered by C's (the transferee's) denial of the trust pursuant to which the land was transferred. It is necessary only to establish that the land was transferred on trust and that the transferee has reneged on this agreement. In *Rochefoucauld v Boustead*, as we have seen in the extract above, Lindley LJ described Boustead's conduct as fraudulent. It is important to note that Lindley LJ's reference is to the concept of equitable fraud. In equity, fraud is a broad concept and has no inherent connection to an intention to cheat. Equitable fraud and unconscionability have been defined by reference to each other, and nothing turns on the classification of the conduct as 'fraudulent' as opposed to 'unconscionable'.[39] Discussing the terminology of fraud and unconscionability in another context (that of proprietary estoppel), Scarman LJ commented: '"[F]raud" was a word often in the mouths of those robust judges who adorned the bench in the 19th century. It is less often in mouths of the more wary judicial spirits today who sit upon the bench.'[40]

The key difficulty with the concept of fraud in *Rochefoucauld v Boustead* is that the fraud consists in denying the trust, which is the very thing that s 53(1)(b) of the LPA 1925 requires to be evidenced in writing.

Hopkins, *The Informal Acquisition of Rights in Land* (2000, pp 31–2)

> Applied broadly, *Rochefoucauld v. Boustead* has the effect that when land is transferred on trust, the trust is enforced as long as it is evidenced: in writing (within section 53(1)(b)); or orally. The effect of such a rule would be to reduce section 53(1)(b) to trusts declared by (current) holders of land. This would be a startling result for a rule purportedly based on the prevention of fraud. The underlying difficulty is in determining why the denial of an informal trust should, in some circumstances, be considered fraudulent [...] it may be argued that the fraud lies in the combination of the trustee's wrongdoing and the harm to the transferor. [...] However, it seems that such a definition does no more than beg the question as to the nature of the underlying wrongdoing and harm, in light of non-compliance with statutory formalities.

---

[39] See, e.g., *Nocton v Lord Ashburton* [1914] AC 932, 954; *Semiahmoo Indian Band v Canada* (1997) 148 DLR (4th) 523, 551–2. Further discussion of the relationship between these terms is provided by Hopkins, 'Understanding Unconscionability in Proprietary Estoppel' (2004) 20 JCL 210, 212–14.

[40] *Crabb v Arun DC* [1976] 1 Ch 179, 195.

A comparison can be drawn with the use of proprietary estoppel in the context of s 2 of the Law of Property (Miscellaneous Provisions) Act 1989 (LP(MP)A 1989). As we have seen in Chapter 9, in *Yaxley v Gotts*,[41] the Court of Appeal held that estoppel could not be used to render valid a transaction that legislation has enacted is to be invalid—but this is exactly what the doctrine of *Rochefoucauld v Boustead* appears to allow. The difference between this doctrine, operating in relation to s 53(1)(b) of the LPA 1925, and proprietary estoppel, operating in relation to s 2 of the LP(MP)A 1989, is that s 53(2) contains an explicit exception for constructive trusts. This difference is undoubtedly crucial. Notwithstanding, it is difficult to avoid the conclusion that *Rochefoucauld v Boustead* '*amounts to a drastic judicial modification*' of the statutory formalities.[42]

Three important points about the operation of the doctrine in *Rochefoucauld v Boustead* are derived from its application in the following case.[43]

Bannister v Bannister [1948] 2 All ER 133, CA

Facts: The defendant had inherited two cottages, one of which was her home, on the death of her husband. She transferred the cottages to the plaintiff, her brother-in-law, for less than the market value, pursuant to an oral agreement that she would remain living in her home, rent-free, for life. The plaintiff reneged on the agreement and sought possession of the defendant's home.

Scott LJ

At 136

It is, we think, clearly a mistake to suppose that the equitable principle on which a constructive trust is raised against a person who insists on the absolute character of a conveyance to himself for the purpose of defeating a beneficial interest, which, according to the true bargain, was to belong to another, is confined to cases in which the conveyance itself was fraudulently obtained. The fraud which brings the principle into play arises as soon as the absolute character of the conveyance is set up for the purpose of defeating the beneficial interest, and that is the fraud to cover which the Statute of Frauds or the corresponding provisions of the Law of Property Act, 1925 cannot be called in aid in cases in which no written evidence of the real bargain is available. Nor is it, in our opinion, necessary that the bargain on which the absolute conveyance is made should include any express stipulation that the grantee is in so many words to hold as trustee. It is enough that the bargain should have included a stipulation under which some sufficiently defined beneficial interest in the property was to be taken by another.

It is clear therefore that: firstly, the conveyance need not be obtained by fraud; secondly, the transfer need not use the technical language of trust; and thirdly, that no weight was given to the fact that the conveyance was at an undervalue. Intervention was triggered solely

---

[41] [2000] 1 Ch 162, CA.

[42] Youdan, 'Formalities for Trusts of Land, and the Doctrine in *Rochefoucauld v. Boustead*' (1984) 43 CLJ 306, 325, referring to the Statute of Frauds 1677, the precursor to the Law of Property Act 1925, s 53.

[43] Further discussion of this and related case law is provided in Chapter 7, section 2.3.

by the fraud consisting in the denial of the trust. As we will see below, this is significant in understanding the basis of intervention.

4.3.2 The classification of the trust: express or constructive?

In *Rochefoucauld v Boustead*, the Court classified the trust as an express trust. Without doubt, the trust was one that the parties intended to create. On that basis, Swadling considers that the trust is correctly considered to be express.[44] But the classification of the trust was discussed in the context of the prevailing Statute of Limitations. As McFarlane explains, the classification of a trust for that purpose is not conclusive.

**McFarlane, 'Constructive Trusts Arising on Receipt of Property
Sub Conditione' (2004) 120 LQR 667, 675**

[The] characterisation of trusts adopted when applying limitation statutes cannot be taken as definitive: to say that a trust is to be treated as an express trust "within the meaning" of a limitation statute is not the same as saying that trust is an express trust for all purposes. As far as the current inquiry is concerned, the critical question is: "what is the event which leads the court to recognise the new right arising on the transfer to C in *Rochefoucauld?*" On this point, there seems to be little controversy. On the constructive trust analysis, the trust does not arise simply because the former owner of the property so intended; rather, the trust arises to prevent C's reneging on the understanding subject to which he received the property. The trust is therefore constructive, and can arise without being manifested and proved by writing. It is thus possible to accept the view in *Rochefoucauld* that the trust is an express one for limitation purposes, as it was one that B (and C) intended to create, without admitting that the trust is an express one in the sense that this intention is by itself sufficient to create the trust.

While the parties in *Rochefoucauld v Boustead* intended a trust, this was not the basis upon which a trust was imposed: the trust was imposed to prevent Boustead's fraudulent denial of the agreement pursuant to which the land was transferred. As we have noted, nothing turns on the description of the conduct as fraudulent rather than unconscionable. The trust was therefore imposed to prevent unconscionable conduct and is therefore correctly classified as a constructive trust.[45] This was the classification adopted by the Court of Appeal (without discussion) in *Bannister v Bannister*.[46]

4.3.3 An alternative analysis: unjust enrichment

There is a tendency in the literature to subject the operation of the doctrine in *Rochefoucauld v Boustead* to an unjust enrichment analysis.[47] Sometimes, the analysis appears to relate to a broad sense of unjust enrichment, denoting no more than '*a state of affairs where*

---

[44] Swadling (2007, [4.207]).
[45] Hopkins, 'Conscience, Discretion and the Creation of Property Rights' (2006) 26 LS 475, 480.
[46] [1948] 2 All ER 133.
[47] See, e.g., Ames, 'Constructive Trusts Based on the Breach of an Express Oral Trust of Land' (1906–7) 29 Harv LR 549; Youdan (1984, p 328); Worthington, *Equity* (2006, pp 202–4).

the defendant can be said to have been enriched in circumstances of injustice'.[48] This is in contradistinction to the narrow sense of the term (the sense in which it is used in other references to the concept in this chapter) as denoting the existence of limited and specific factors on which a claimant can obtain restitution, because the defendant has been unjustly enriched at his or her expense.[49]

There are, however, difficulties in using either sense of unjust enrichment in relation to the doctrine in *Rochefoucauld v Boustead*. Used in a narrow sense, unjust enrichment requires a structured analysis of whether the transferee has been enriched at the transferor's expense and whether the enrichment is unjust by reference to specific unjust factors. There is no evidence of such an analysis being taken by the courts. It is doubtful, in particular, whether the facts of a claim within *Rochefoucauld v Boustead* fit within the scope of existing unjust factors.[50]

Used in a broad sense, the concept does not add to our understanding of the operation of the doctrine.

Hopkins, 'Conscience, Discretion and the Creation of Property Rights'
(2006) 26 LS 475, 481

In the broad sense of the term it may be accurate to say that a defendant who reneges on an agreement to hold on trust pursuant to which land is transferred would be unjustly enriched. However, at best this takes our understanding of intervention no further than the statement that it is unconscionable or fraudulent of the transferee to renege on the agreement.

Indeed, used in a broad sense, unjust enrichment can be detrimental to our understanding of the doctrine.

This is the sense in which Youdan appears to refer to unjust enrichment in a discussion of *Bannister v Bannister*. As we have seen, in that case, the transferee received a discount on the market value of the cottages in return for agreeing to allow the transferor to live in one cottage for the rest of her life.

Youdan, 'Formalities for Trusts of Land, and the Doctrine in *Rochefoucauld v. Boustead'* (1984) 43 CLJ 306, 328

Consider the position in *Bannister* if the making of the undertaking had been seriously disputed and the property had been sold for its full market value on a vacant possession basis. The enforcement of a mistaken or false allegation of an undertaking would have resulted in the woman being unjustly enriched by receiving both the full market value and the right to live in the property for the rest of her life. On the other hand, the non-enforcement of an undertaking that in fact was made would only have the result that the woman would not retain an expected gift—free living accommodation.

As Youdan acknowledges (and as has been noted above), the provision of the discount was not, in fact, considered significant. By focusing on the financial position of the

[48] Virgo, *The Principles of the Law of Restitution* (2nd edn, 2006, p 8).
[49] Ibid, pp 9–10.
[50] Hopkins (2006, pp 481–3).

parties, an unjust enrichment analysis loses sight of the essential element of the doctrine in *Rochefoucauld v Boustead*: the objection in the doctrine lies in the transferee reneging on the agreement pursuant to which the land was transferred.[51]

4.4 THE THREE-PARTY CASE

As we have noted, the three-party case involves a transfer of land from A to C on trust for B. This is only a slight extension from the paradigm two-party case and there is no doubt that the doctrine in *Rochefoucauld v Boustead* applies in this context.[52] The doctrine has been further applied beyond this factual matrix, where the agreement for the trust in favour of B is entered into between C (the transferee) and a party (X) providing finance for the purchase of land (Figure 8).

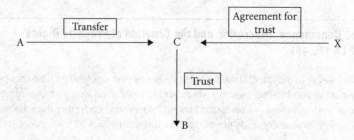

Figure 8 *Neale v Willis*

Neale v Willis (1968) 19 P & CR 836, CA

Facts: A husband obtained a loan from his mother-in-law in connection with the purchase of the house. The loan was made pursuant to an agreement that the house would be bought in the joint names of the husband and wife. The husband reneged on this agreement and bought the house in his sole name. Following the couple's divorce, the question arose as to the beneficial ownership of the house.

Lord Denning MR

At 839

This was a binding contract and a court of equity will not allow the husband to go back on it. It will enforce it by holding that the husband holds the property on a constructive trust for himself and his wife. This follows from *Bannister v Bannister*. That case shows that if a person who takes a conveyance to himself, which is absolute in form, nevertheless has made a bargain that he will give a beneficial interest to another, he will be held to be a constructive trustee for it for the other. He cannot insist on the absolute character of a conveyance to himself for the purpose of defeating a beneficial interest which according to the true bargain is to belong to another. So here we have a husband who is seeking to insist on the

---

[51] Ibid, p 481.
[52] See, e.g., Youdan (1984, p 326).

absolute character of the conveyance to himself and to him alone. He does it for the purpose of defeating a beneficial interest which according to the true bargain was to belong to his wife. He holds it on a constructive trust to carry out the bargain.

4.4.1 In whose favour does the constructive trust operate?

The key question that has arisen in three-party cases is whether the trust should operate in favour of B, the intended beneficiary, or A, the transferor. The debate has been complicated by the absence of clear authority, and the consequential impact on this issue of competing views as to the nature of the trust in issue and the basis of intervention. Hence, if *Rochefoucauld v Boustead* enforces the parties' express trust, then, in the three-party case, the trust necessarily operates in favour of B. If the doctrine is founded on unjust enrichment, then this necessarily dictates intervention in favour of A, as the party at whose expense C is otherwise unjustly enriched.[53]

But it has been suggested above that both of these views are incorrect: the doctrine imposes a constructive trust in response to C's fraudulent or unconscionable conduct. In a series of articles, Youdan and Feltham expressed opposing views: Youdan supporting the claim of B, and Feltham, that of A.

Youdan, 'Formalities for Trusts of Land, and the Doctrine in *Rochefoucauld v. Boustead'* (1984) 43 CLJ 306, 335–6

The claim of [B] is, I suggest, stronger for three main, related reasons. First, it seems inappropriate that [C], the trustee, should have the power to determine whether [B] or A should get the benefit of the property. Secondly, A has effectively divested himself of the property. It is he who is seeking equity to obtain the return of property he has given away on a valid trust. Thirdly, the allowance of [B's] claim is not contrary to the purpose of the formality requirement. If A had simply conveyed the land to [C] as a gift for [C] he obviously could not recover it since he effectively divested himself [. . .] There is no reason why A should be in a stronger position merely because the beneficial gift was to [B] with the interposition of [C's] trusteeship.

Feltham, 'Informal Trusts and Third Parties' [1987] Conv 246, 249

T. G. Youdan suggests three reasons why [B's] claim should be preferred to that of A. First, that it is inappropriate that [C], the trustee, should have the power to determine whether [B] or A should get the benefit of the property. But this goes rather to the proposition that lack of writing renders the transaction unenforceable rather than void. Secondly, that A has effectively divested himself of the property and is seeking the assistance of equity to obtain its return. But the only property of which A has effectively divested himself is the legal estate; the location of the equitable interest is what is at issue. Thirdly, that the allowance of [B's] claim is not contrary to the purpose of the formality requirement. But it has been argued

---

[53] See the example discussed by Worthington (2006, pp 203–4).

in the previous paragraph that the allowing of such claims does defeat the purpose of the formality requirement. Youdan's comparison with a direct conveyance by way of gift does not hold because he is assuming in the case of a direct conveyance that the relevant formal requirement (and the purpose behind it) has been satisfied.

Youdan, 'Informal Trusts and Third Parties: A Response'
[1988] Conv 267, 272–3

My three points were explicitly based on the assumption that it is "established that an oral trust of land is valid despite non-compliance with [the statutory formality requirement]; it is merely unenforceable. Consequently, where A conveys land to [C] on an oral trust for [B], A has ordinarily no right to restitution since [C] is holding the property on a valid trust for [B], and he may carry out that trust if he chooses to do so." I discuss, and indeed criticise, this principle in an earlier section of my article. Nevertheless, despite possible criticism of it, this principle does appear to be well established, as Feltham also seems to recognise at the beginning of his article.

My first point seems, therefore, to be accepted by Feltham if one accepts the assumption that lack of writing makes the transaction unenforceable rather than void. My second point is grounded on the same assumption and, on this basis, Feltham is wrong in saying "the only property of which A has effectively divested himself is the legal estate; the location of the equitable interest is what is at issue," since [C] is holding title to the property on a valid trust for [B]. Feltham is, however, justified in criticising the way I put my third point. I did overstate it when I said that the allowance of [B's] claim is not contrary to the purpose of the formality requirement. The *Rochefoucauld* doctrine as a whole substantially diminishes the policies of the formality requirement, and, as it was the main purpose of my article to show, the question becomes one of balancing the value of those policies against the injustice that may be caused by reliance on the formality requirement. Moreover, there is, as I recognised in my article, considerable merit in the view that restitution back to the transferor entails a less serious interference with the statute than enforcement in favour of the third party beneficiary.

However, I do maintain that my comparison with a direct gift to [C] is tenable, although perhaps too strongly stated.

On balance, the arguments appear weighted against B. The purpose of the doctrine is to prevent C's fraudulent or unconscionable conduct, and intervention should go no further than is necessary to achieve this purpose. B is a volunteer and 'equity does not assist a volunteer'. The imposition of a trust in favour of A provides A with a further opportunity to benefit B. Finally, intervention in favour of A does less violence to the formality requirement in s 53(1)(b) of the LPA 1925.[54]

In limited circumstances, however, intervention in favour of B may be justified.

Hopkins, *The Informal Acquisition of Rights in Land* (2000, pp 37–8)

First, there may be exceptional circumstances where intervention in [B's] favour is the only means of preventing fraud. This possibility is illustrated by *Neale v. Willis.* [...] it would not

---

[54] Youdan (1984, p 335); Worthington (2006, p 204).

have been appropriate for the land to be held in favour of the mother-in-law with whom the agreement had been entered. The agreement did not envisage that she, as a lender, should acquire rights in the house.

Secondly, an assumption underlying the reasoning against [B] is that A will have another opportunity to grant rights to [B]. There are circumstances in which no such opportunity in practice arises. The clearest example is where A has died. On a strict view this (unlike the first situation) does not alter the reasoning against [B]. The purpose of the rule, of preventing fraud, is still achieved by vesting the beneficial interest in A's estate. However, a concession in favour of [B] may be justified in terms of giving effect to A's intentions as he has died in the belief the gift was effective.

5 THE *PALLANT V MORGAN* CONSTRUCTIVE TRUST

Although taking its name from the decision in *Pallant v Morgan*,[55] the operation of this constructive trust received its most comprehensive judicial analysis and rationalisation in *Banner Homes Group plc v Luff Developments Ltd*.[56] As Nield has demonstrated, the origins of the trust ultimately lie in the doctrine of *Rochefoucauld v Boustead*.[57] As with the doctrine in *Rochefoucauld v Boustead*, the trigger for the imposition of the constructive trust lies in the transferee of land reneging on an agreement pursuant to which land is acquired—but the agreement arises in a different factual matrix and the finding of unconscionability is not based solely on the transferee reneging on the agreement.

5.1 THE ELEMENTS OF THE *PALLANT V MORGAN* CONSTRUCTIVE TRUST

The requirements of the claim were enumerated in *Banner Homes*.

Banner Homes Group plc v Luff Developments Ltd [2000] Ch 372, CA

Facts: Banner Homes (the claimant) and Luff Developments (the defendant) had commenced negotiations for a joint venture for the acquisition of development land. The parties had reached an agreement in principle for the joint venture, but no contract had been concluded, when the land was acquired by S Ltd, a wholly owned subsidiary of Luff. Unknown to Banner Homes, Luff had had second thoughts about the suitability of Banner Homes as a joint venture partner. Luff had not informed Banner Homes of this, out of concern that Banner Homes would mount a rival bid for the land. Banner Homes sought to establish entitlement to the land through a constructive trust.

---

[55] [1953] 1 Ch 43.
[56] [2000] Ch 372.
[57] Nield, 'Constructive Trusts and Estoppel' (2003) 23 LS 311, 315.

Chadwick LJ

At 397–400

It is important, however, to identify the features which will give rise to a *Pallant v. Morgan* equity and to define its scope; while keeping in mind that it is undesirable to attempt anything in the nature of an exhaustive classification. [. . .]

1. A *Pallant v. Morgan* equity may arise where the arrangement or understanding on which it is based precedes the acquisition of the relevant property by one party to that arrangement. It is the pre-acquisition arrangement which colours the subsequent acquisition by the defendant and leads to his being treated as a trustee if he seeks to act inconsistently with it. [. . .]

2. It is unnecessary that the arrangement or understanding should be contractually enforceable. Indeed, if there is an agreement which is enforceable as a contract, there is unlikely to be any need to invoke the *Pallant v. Morgan* equity; equity can act through the remedy of specific performance and will recognise the existence of a corresponding trust. [. . .]

3. It is necessary that the pre-acquisition arrangement or understanding should contemplate that one party ("the acquiring party") will take steps to acquire the relevant property; and that, if he does so, the other party ("the non-acquiring party") will obtain some interest in that property. Further, it is necessary that (whatever private reservations the acquiring party may have) he has not informed the non-acquiring party before the acquisition (or, perhaps more accurately, before it is too late for the parties to be restored to a position of no advantage/no detriment) that he no longer intends to honour the arrangement or understanding.

4. It is necessary that, in reliance on the arrangement or understanding, the non-acquiring party should do (or omit to do) something which confers an advantage on the acquiring party in relation to the acquisition of the property; or is detrimental to the ability of the non-acquiring party to acquire the property on equal terms. It is the existence of the advantage to the one, or detriment to the other, gained or suffered as a consequence of the arrangement or understanding, which leads to the conclusion that it would be inequitable or unconscionable to allow the acquiring party to retain the property for himself, in a manner inconsistent with the arrangement or understanding which enabled him to acquire it. *Pallant v. Morgan* [1953] Ch. 43 itself provides an illustration of this principle. There was nothing inequitable in allowing the defendant to retain for himself the lot (lot 15) in respect to which the plaintiff's agent had no instructions to bid. In many cases the advantage/detriment will be found in the agreement of the non-acquiring party to keep out of the market. That will usually be both to the advantage of the acquiring party—in that he can bid without competition from the non-acquiring party—and to the detriment of the non-acquiring party—in that he loses the opportunity to acquire the property for himself. But there may be advantage to the one without corresponding detriment to the other. Again, *Pallant v. Morgan* provides an illustration. The plaintiff's agreement (through his agent) to keep out of the bidding gave an advantage to the defendant—in that he was able to obtain the property for a lower price than would otherwise have been possible; but the failure of the plaintiff's agent to bid did not, in fact, cause detriment to the plaintiff—because, on the facts, the agent's instructions would not have permitted him to outbid the defendant. Nevertheless, the equity was invoked.

5. That leads, I think, to the further conclusions: (i) that although, in many cases, the advantage/detriment will be found in the agreement of the non-acquiring party to keep

out of the market, that is not a necessary feature; and (ii) that although there will usually be advantage to the one and correlative disadvantage to the other, the existence of
both advantage and detriment is not essential—either will do. What is essential is that
the circumstances make it inequitable for the acquiring party to retain the property for
himself in a manner inconsistent with the arrangement or understanding on which the
non-acquiring party has acted. Those circumstances may arise where the non-acquiring
party was never "in the market" for the whole of the property to be acquired; but (on
the faith of an arrangement or understanding that he shall have a part of that property)
provides support in relation to the acquisition of the whole which is of advantage to the
acquiring party. They may arise where the assistance provided to the acquiring party
(in pursuance of the arrangement or understanding) involves no detriment to the non-
acquiring party; or where the non-acquiring party acts to his detriment (in pursuance of
the arrangement or understanding) without the acquiring party obtaining any advantage
therefrom.

On the facts of the case, the requirements for the constructive trust were fulfilled. There was
a pre-acquisition agreement (falling short of a specifically enforceable contract) that a jointly
owned company would acquire the land. Banner Homes had relied on this agreement by
treating the site as 'out of play', as a potential acquisition in its own right.[58] This conferred an
advantage on Luff of keeping Banner Homes out of the market as a potential competitor. The
shares in S Ltd were therefore to be held on constructive trust for Banner Homes and Luff
equally, charged with the payment by Banner Homes of half the purchaser price.

The detailed factual matrix provided by Chadwick LJ enables the *Pallant v Morgan* constructive trust to be differentiated from other means of acquiring equitable interests in
land—in particular, proprietary estoppel (discussed in Chapter 13, where an assurance or
agreement is made by a party in relation to land currently owned),[59] and the common intention constructive trust applied in relation to joint ventures for the acquisition of a home
(discussed in Chapter 18).

In our discussion of the resulting trust, we noted that the distinction between domestic
and commercial property is dependent on the purposes for which land is acquired, rather
than the relationship between the parties. Hence, the *Pallant v Morgan* trust may be used
to determine ownership of investment property purchased by a cohabiting couple or family members where the circumstances surrounding the acquisition meet the elements of a
claim.

The trust was used in this context in *Cox v Jones*.[60] In that case, following the breakdown
of a relationship between the parties, the *Pallant v Morgan* trust was applied to determine
ownership of a flat purchased as an investment, while the common intention constructive
trust was used to ascertain ownership of a property bought as a home.[61]

---

58 [2000] Ch 372, 400, *per* Chadwick LJ.

59 An overlap between the doctrines does exist, however, in so far as a case that meets the elements of the
Pallant v Morgan trust may also display the requirements of proprietary estoppel. This is the case in which
the non-acquiring party has acted to his or her detriment: see Hopkins, 'The *Pallant v Morgan* "Equity"?'
[2002] Conv 35, 45–6.

60 [2004] EWHC 1486.

61 Compare *Kilcarne Holdings Ltd v Targetfellow (Birmingham) Ltd* [2005] EWCA 1355, in which both
types of trust are discussed in relation to a claim concerning commercial property, although the claim
failed on the facts. An initial suggestion that the *Pallant v Morgan* trust is an extension of the common
intention trust to commercial agreements was made by Thompson, 'Constructive Trusts and Non-Binding

To establish a claim, there appears to be little room for manoeuvre around the elements stated by Chadwick LJ. In *Yeoman's Row Management Ltd v Cobbe*,[62] the House of Lords held that *Pallant v Morgan* was not applicable, because the land in question was already owned by one of the parties to the joint venture agreement.

The Court of Appeal also noted this factor in rejecting a claim in *London & Regional Investments Ltd v TBI plc*.[63] In that case, in any event, the claim failed, because the negotiations between the parties had been conducted expressly 'subject to contract'. In these circumstances, it was not unconscionable for the party to withdraw from discussions following the acquisition of the land.[64]

In *Kilcarne Holdings Ltd v Targetfellow (Birmingham) Ltd*,[65] it was suggested that it was not essential for the non-acquiring party to have intended to obtain the land on their own account. The claim failed on the facts, however, because there was no agreement that the property would be acquired for the parties' joint benefit.

5.2 THE NATURE OF THE UNCONSCIONABILITY

As we have noted, the unconscionability on which the constructive trust is based does not lie solely in the trustee reneging on the agreement. It must also be demonstrated that the party in whose favour the trust is imposed had relied on the agreement. This is the fourth of the five elements of the trust in Chadwick LJ's judgment (extracted above). A requirement of reliance is found in other doctrines through which equitable interests may be acquired: for example, the common intention constructive trust and proprietary estoppel. In those doctrines, however, the requirement is explicitly one of detrimental reliance. The distinctive feature of the *Pallant v Morgan* constructive trust is that it suffices for the reliance to confer an advantage on the acquiring party, with no requirement of a corresponding detriment on the part of the non-acquiring party.

Nield highlights that the focus on the detriment or advantage in *Banner Homes* marks a development from the earlier cases.

Nield, 'Constructive Trusts and Estoppel' (2003) 23 LS 311, 324–5

[...] Earlier cases do not focus on this possible detriment or advantage, but upon the unconscionability inherent in the breach of trust and confidence that the non-acquiring party placed in the acquiring party to carry out their arrangements for the acquisition of certain property. This duty may be articulated as an agency, but it does not have to fit neatly within defined categories of fiduciary relationship, provided the central characteristics of a fiduciary relationship can be identified. For instance, commercial enterprises, husband and wife, relatives and neighbours have all been required by equity to adhere to their informal arrangements for the joint acquisition of property because of the trust and confidence placed in them to act not only in their own interests, but also the interests of the non-acquiring party. In this context

Agreements' [2001] Conv 265, but this is refuted by Hopkins (2002). As will be seen below, the nature of the reliance required in the *Pallant v Morgan* trust differentiates the doctrine.

[62] [2008] UKHL 55, [33].
[63] [2002] EWCA 355, [48].
[64] Ibid, [42].
[65] [2005] EWCA 1355, [21].

equity seems to demand remarkably high standards of conduct and perhaps what is surprising about the *Banner Homes* decision is the line drawn between acceptable commercial
tactics and a breach of duty justifying the imposition of one of equity's most potent weapons,
the constructive trust.

Hopkins also expresses concern with the ease with which *Banner Homes* provides for the
imposition of a constructive trust in the commercial context. His criticism is grounded in
the gain-based nature of the unconscionability involved.

Hopkins, 'The *Pallant v Morgan* "Equity?" ' [2002] Conv 35, 46–7

Constructive trusts are not usually imposed solely as a response to an unconscionable gain.
Constructive trusts are usually imposed only where the gain is the result of a particular breach
of duty; for example, in relation to gains made by a breach of fiduciary duty. On one level it
may seem attractive to suggest that the *Pallant v. Morgan* equity could be rationalised as
involving the breach of a fiduciary relationship and therefore as within an accepted category
of gain based constructive trust. The finding of agency in some of the earlier cases may
have provided an avenue for such an analysis. Such an approach would also be consistent
with Canadian law. In that jurisdiction, a constructive trust has been imposed following the
breakdown of a commercial joint venture based on beach of fiduciary duty or breach of confidence. The finding of fiduciary duties in a commercial context is contentious because of the
consequence such duties carry; i.e., the imposition of equitable doctrines, such as the constructive trust. In this respect, the decision in *Banner Homes* perhaps represents the worst
of both worlds. By providing for a gain based constructive trust, without an indication of a
breach of duty, the court circumvented difficult questions arising from the nature of fiduciary
relationships and the circumstances in which one commercial undertaking may owe fiduciary
duties to another.

In many cases that fulfil the requirements of the *Pallant v Morgan* trust, there will, in any
event, be detrimental reliance. In *Banner Homes*, the Court left open the issue of whether
Banner Homes had suffered a detriment on the facts.

Banner Homes Group plc v Luff Developments Ltd [2000] Ch 372, CA

Chadwick LJ

At 400–1

I am satisfied, also, that the judge was wrong to reject the constructive trust claim on the
grounds that Banner had failed to show that it had acted to its detriment in reliance on the
arrangement agreed on 14 July 1995. [...] In other words, Luff saw it as an advantage that
Banner's belief that the site was out of play should be maintained. Luff wanted to keep
Banner out of the market. In those circumstances, it does not lie easily in Luff's mouth to say
that Banner suffered no detriment. But whether or not Banner suffered detriment from the
fact that it never regarded itself as free to consider the site as a potential acquisition of its own
does not seem to me conclusive. Luff obtained the advantage which it sought.

In the context of proprietary estoppel, the requirement of detrimental reliance has been met where a claimant has linked his or her life and career to the defendant in reliance on an assurance of rights (typically, of an inheritance).[66] It may be suggested, by analogy, that detriment lies in the non-acquiring party resting his or her chance of obtaining an interest in the land on the proposed joint venture.[67]

The analogy has, however, been doubted by Nield.[68] Further, it is clear that *Pallant v Morgan* can operate where no detriment arises—a point illustrated by the facts of that case. In *Pallant v Morgan*, immediately before the start of an auction, agents acting for the parties agreed that the claimant would refrain from bidding and, if the defendant succeeded in acquiring the land, part would be sold on to the claimant. The defendant's agent obtained the land with a bid of £1,000, but the defendant then reneged on the agreement. The defendant's agent was authorized to bid up to £3,000, while the claimant's agent was authorized to bid to £2,000. On these facts, it is clear that the claimant suffered no detriment, because the land would not have been acquired even in the absence of the agreement—but the defendant obtained an advantage, because the land was acquired for half of the sum that would have been necessary to outbid the claimant. Judgment in the case is not given explicitly in terms of a constructive trust. The Court considered that the defendant's agent had acted for both parties at the auction. The defendant therefore held the land for himself and the claimant jointly, subject to agreement by the parties as to its division (with provision for a resale if no such agreement was reached).

6 TOWARDS A RATIONALIZATION OF CONSTRUCTIVE TRUSTS

In this chapter, we have considered two situations in which constructive trusts are imposed in relation to land: those arising under the doctrine in *Rochefoucauld v Boustead*; and those arising through the *Pallant v Morgan* equity. We have noted other constructive trusts that are discussed elsewhere in this book: a transfer of land from A to C 'subject to' rights in favour of B; the common intention constructive trust used to determine ownership of the home; and the constructive trust imposed on a vendor under the doctrine of anticipation. We have noted that constructive trusts share a common thread, because the trust is imposed in response to unconscionability, but that this concept is of limited utility in understanding the scope of constructive trust doctrine. Is there a further thread linking these trusts together, or must each simply been seen as a discrete operation of the constructive trust?

There are undoubtedly advantages in identifying common links. This rationalizes our understanding of the constructive trust and can assist us in understanding developments of the doctrine. An awareness of differences, as well as similarities, can, however, aid our understanding of individual applications of the trust. It must also be acknowledged that no single element ties together all constructive trusts. In particular, the common intention constructive trust is perhaps more closely related to proprietary estoppel than to other species of constructive trust. In Chapter 12, we highlighted the unusual features of the constructive trust imposed on a vendor of land.

---

[66] For example, *Gillett v Holt* [2001] Ch 210.
[67] Hopkins (2002, p 45).
[68] Nield, 'Constructive Trusts and Estoppel' (2003) 23 LS 311, 322–3.

At the outset of our discussion, we noted McFarlane's suggestion that these constructive trusts are illustrations of a 'receipt after promise' principle. There are undoubtedly advantages in the recognition of this principle: for example, it provides an explanation of the decision in *Neale v Willis*[69] (extracted above), which may otherwise appear an awkward deviation from the factual matrix of a claim within *Rochefoucauld v Boustead*.

But Hopkins questions whether the sense of unity provided by this common principle is an illusion.

Hopkins, 'Conscience, Discretion and the Creation of Property Rights' (2006) 26 LS 475, 487

It is submitted that there are difficulties in accepting McFarlane's common principle as a rationalisation for *Rochefoucauld v Boustead*. In seeking analogies with other cases, his analysis loses sight of the actual principle involved in that case. *Rochefoucauld v Boustead* enables the court to intervene to prevent a transferee on trust from reneging on the trust and claim the land for him or herself. [...] The provision for intervention solely on the basis of the transferee's attempt to deny the trust links together the application of *Rochefoucauld v Boustead* in both two- and three-party cases, and distinguishes this instance of unconscionability from other principles discussed by McFarlane.

In the present state of the authorities, it remains a moot point whether these applications of the constructive trust will remain discrete, or be brought within an umbrella principle.

QUESTIONS

1. Assess the different role afforded to the settlor's intention in the creation of express, resulting, and constructive trusts.

2. Would the following situations, each concerning the purchase of an investment property, give rise to a presumption of resulting trust or a presumption of advancement? Do your answers yield a logical result?

   (a) The property is purchased in the joint names of Mr and Mrs X, with the purchase money provided by Mr X.

   (b) The property is purchased in the joint names of Mr and Mrs X, with the purchase money provided by Mrs X.

   (c) The property is purchased in the joint names of Mr Y and his son, with the purchase money provided by Mr Y.

   (d) The property is purchased in the joint names of Mr Y and his son, with the purchase money provided by the son.

3. What is the nature of the unconscionable of fraudulent conduct that triggers the imposition of the constructive trust under the doctrine in *Rochefoucauld v Boustead*? Compare and contrast this with the conduct required for a trust under the *Pallant v Morgan* equity.

[69] (1968) 19 P & CR 836, 839.

4. In a three-party case within the doctrine in *Rochefoucauld v Boustead*, should the constructive trust arise in favour of A (the transferor) or B (the intended beneficiary)?

FURTHER READING

Chambers, *Resulting Trusts* (Oxford: Clarendon Press, 1997)

Hopkins, 'Conscience, Discretion and the Creation of Property Rights' (2006) 26 LS 475

Hopkins, *The Informal Acquisition of Rights in Land* (London: Sweet & Maxwell, 2000, ch 3)

Hopkins, 'The *Pallant v Morgan* "Equity?"' [2002] Conv 35

McFarlane, 'Constructive Trusts Arising on Receipt of Property Sub Conditione' (2004) 120 LQR 667

Oakley, *Constructive Trusts* (3rd edn, London: Sweet & Maxwell, 1996)

Swadling, 'A New Role for Resulting Trusts?' (1996) 16 LS 110

Youdan, 'Formalities for Trusts of Land, and the Doctrine in *Rochefoucauld v. Boustead*' (1984) 43 CLJ 306

PART B3

PRIORITY

15

UNREGISTERED LAND
AND PRIORITIES

CENTRAL ISSUES

1. Where A transfers land to C, priority questions arise as to whether B, who has pre-existing property rights, can enforce those rights against C. Property rights are capable of binding any third party later acquiring a right from A; therefore this issue is conceptualized as the *defences* question: does C have a defence against the enforcement of B's pre-existing property rights?

2. Priority rules differ between unregistered and registered land. The overreaching mechanism (discussed in Chapter 20) is the only rule that is common to both systems. This chapter considers the priority rules of unregistered land.

3. In unregistered land, the key distinction is between legal and equitable rights.

4. C generally has no defence against the enforcement of legal rights held by B.

5. The enforcement of equitable rights in unregistered land used to be governed by the doctrine of notice. C would have a defence only if he or she were a bona

fide purchaser for value without notice of B's equitable rights. The doctrine is perceived as being a fundamentally ethical means of resolving priority issues, but had fallen out of favour by the time of the 1925 legislation and has largely been replaced with more mechanical means of determining priorities.

6. A number of equitable interests, and one legal interest, are registrable as land charges under the Land Charges Act 1972. This is a limited register of interests in unregistered land. Land charges are registered against the name of the holder of the legal estate at the time of registration.

7. Where B's interest is registrable as a land charge, its enforcement against C is entirely dependent on the provisions of the 1972 Act; the defence of bona fide purchaser is irrelevant. Controversially, this has been held to mean that C has a defence against B's unregistered land charge even where C knows about B's interest.

1 INTRODUCTION

Where A transfers an estate in land to C, or creates a mortgage in C's favour, the question arises whether third parties, B, have property rights that are enforceable against C. This fundamental question gives rise to the priority triangle that was introduced in Chapter 6.

There are two distinct ways in which B may have rights that are binding on C. Firstly, the transfer from A to C may have created a new direct right in favour of B. The importance of new direct rights has been discussed in Chapter 7 and, in Chapter 8, we saw an example of new direct rights being created where the transfer is made 'subject to' rights in favour of B.

Secondly, B may have pre-existing property rights at the time of the transfer. Property rights are prima facie enforceable against third parties later acquiring a right from A; therefore property rights owned by B at the time of the transfer are prima facie enforceable against C.

The difference between these two scenarios is illustrated in Figure 9.

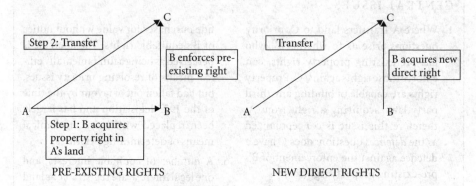

PRE-EXISTING RIGHTS   NEW DIRECT RIGHTS

Figure 9 The priority triangle and the creation of new direct rights

In this chapter, and in Chapter 16, we are concerned with the enforcement of B's pre-existing property rights. These are sometimes referred to in this context as 'incumbrances'. We examine the rules that determine whether B's pre-existing property rights are binding against C on a transfer of an estate in land. Because B's rights are prima facie binding, this is conceptualized as the *defences* question: does C have a defence to the enforcement of B's property rights? This question is answered through land law's priority rules. These rules determine whether C has priority over B's property rights, or is bound by them.

It is important to emphasize that we are concerned only with the enforcement of pre-existing *property* rights held by B—that is, legal and equitable estates and interests in land. These are the only rights that are prima facie enforceable against a third party. We are not concerned with any personal rights that B has against A at the time of the transfer: B's pre-existing personal rights are not enforceable against C. To obtain property rights enforceable against C, B would need to demonstrate that new direct rights were created on the transfer.

Different priority rules apply to unregistered and registered land. The unregistered land rules are considered in this chapter and those of registered land in Chapter 16. The practical significance of the unregistered land rules is diminishing, but they retain some importance. As we have seen in Chapter 9, all unregistered land is now subject to compulsory first registration on the occurrence of a triggering event. This includes the transfer (by sale or gift) of a legal estate, except the grant of a new legal lease of no more than seven years' duration, or the transfer of an existing legal lease with seven years or less remaining.[1]

The priority rules of unregistered land apply in two situations. Firstly, on a transfer of unregistered land that triggers compulsory first registration, title to the estate in question will be investigated through the unregistered land rules for the last time. Secondly, the rules will continue to apply to unregistered land as regards transfers of an estate that do not trigger compulsory first registration: for example, the creation of a legal lease for seven years or less, or the transfer of an existing legal lease with seven years or less remaining, or the transfer of an equitable interest (such as an assignment of an existing beneficial interest under a trust).

2 INVESTIGATION OF TITLE

To ascertain the existence of pre-existing property rights, C will investigate A's title to the land. The means of investigation is twofold. Firstly, C will investigate the documentary proof of A's title. In Chapter 9, we saw the written formality requirements that apply to the creation and transfer of rights in land. In unregistered land, there is no central record of title. A's documentary proof therefore consists of the bundle of deeds recording transactions carried out in relation to the land that have been executed to fulfil those formality requirements. C does not need to investigate the full history of the title, but must establish a good root of title. The period of time that must be investigated to establish good root of title has gradually been decreased. At the time of the 1925 legislation, it was necessary to investigate from the first conveyance that had taken place at least thirty years ago. Section 23 of the Law of Property Act 1969 (LPA 1969) reduced this period to fifteen years.

Secondly, C should undertake a physical inspection of the land. As we will see, each of these means of investigation has a particular role in the application of priority rules.

3 THE TWO BASIC PRIORITY RULES

In unregistered land, two basic priority rules are applied. The key distinction is that between legal and equitable rights. Firstly, legal rights bind all third parties who later acquire a right from A and therefore legal rights held by B are necessarily binding. C has no defence against the enforcement of these rights. The existence of legal rights will generally be apparent from the title deeds, although this is not invariably the case.[2]

Secondly, equitable rights bind any third party acquiring a right from A except a bona fide purchaser of legal estate without notice of the rights. Hence, equitable rights held by B are enforceable against C unless C can invoke the defence of bona fide purchaser. The 'doctrine of notice' is an important part of this defence. A person who successfully invokes this defence is sometimes described as 'equity's darling'—that is, as beyond the reproach of courts of equity.

The first rule is subject only to one limited exception. As we will see, the enforcement of a puisne mortgage, a specific type of legal mortgage, is now subject to registration under the

---

[1] Land Registration Act 2002, s 4.

[2] For example, there may be no record of short leases that are exempt from statutory formalities for their creation (Law of Property Act 1925, s 54(2)) or of legal easements created by implied grant.

Land Charges Act 1972 (LCA 1972). C may have a defence against this type of mortgage if it has not been registered under that Act. Apart from this exception, pre-existing legal property rights held by B do not require further discussion.

The second rule is subject to two significant exceptions. Firstly, the enforcement of a number of equitable property rights is subject to registration under the 1972 Act. The defence of bona fide purchaser has no application in relation to these rights, the enforcement of which is determined by the rules provided by that Act. Secondly, the enforcement against C of beneficial interests under a trust is subject to the operation of the overreaching mechanism. That mechanism, which applies equally to unregistered and registered land, is discussed in Chapter 20. Overreaching enables C to take the land free from beneficial interests as long as certain conditions are fulfilled: in particular, C must pay the purchase money to a minimum of two trustees or a trust corporation. If the conditions for overreaching are met, then C has a defence against the enforcement of beneficial interests held by B. As we will see in Chapter 20, B's interests are removed from the land and attach to the proceeds of sale held by the trustees (A). If the conditions for overreaching are not fulfilled (for example, because there is only one trustee of the trust), then the enforcement of beneficial interests is determined by the doctrine of notice. Hence, C will be bound by B's beneficial interest unless C can invoke the defence of bona fide purchaser.

As a result of these exceptions, the defence of bona fide purchaser plays a residual, but significant, role. In *Shiloh Spinners Ltd v Harding*,[3] Lord Wilberforce noted: '[T]*here may well be rights, of an equitable character, outside the provisions as to registration and which are incapable of being overreached.*' Such rights remain enforceable against C unless C can invoke the defence of bona fide purchaser.

4 THE DEFENCE OF BONA FIDE PURCHASER

The defence of bona fide purchaser is founded on equity's ideas of acting in good conscience. Equity would enforce its property rights against all those who could not, in good conscience, seek to take free from them. In this respect, the defence represents an essentially ethical rule.[4] But by the time of the 1925 legislation, the defence appeared too narrow. As is illustrated below in the debate arising from *Kingsnorth Finance v Tizard*,[5] its effect is to enforce rights against persons whose conduct it is difficult to call into question. As we will see, this is due, in particular, to the broad reach of constructive notice.

The effect of the defence, when successfully applied, is to provide the purchaser of a legal estate with an '*absolute, unqualified, unanswerable defence*' against the enforcement of B's equitable interest.[6] B's interest is not resurrected on a subsequent sale to a purchaser with notice.[7] The defence therefore seems to reflect a value judgment about the relative worth of legal and equitable rights; security of legal transfers is assisted at the cost of equitable proprietary rights.

The legitimacy of this value judgment is assessed by Worthington. She considers the defence in the context of its impact on a beneficiary, B, following the transfer of legal title from A to C.

---

3 [1973] AC 691, 721.
4 Compare Battersby, 'Informal Transactions in Land, Estoppel and Registration' (1995) 58 MLR 637.
5 [1986] 1 WLR 783.
6 (1871–72) LR 7 Ch App 259, 269, *per* James LJ.
7 *Wilkes v Spooner* [1911] 2 KB 473.

Worthington, *Equity* (2nd edn, 2006, p 96)

Although the bona fide purchaser rule is commonly justified by the need to make (legal) transfers of property secure, this rationalization presupposes that legal ownership is the pre-eminent property right. [...] In the face of this, it is sometimes suggested that the rule is not grounded in logic, but in the competitive jurisdictional politics that once existed between the Common Law and Chancery courts, and that Chancery was simple (but perhaps illogically) ceding jurisdiction to the Common Law courts. There is scope for logical justification, however. A trust presupposes that the beneficiary has left the trustee with all the incidents of title and the power (even if not the authority) to deal with the trust property. Given this, it may make sense to reassess the appropriate balance of risk between the beneficiary and an innocent third party, and sometimes (perhaps not always) favour the third party's security of transaction over the beneficiary's security of property. This forces the beneficiary, not the third party, to bear the risk of the defaulting trustee being unable to make the claims against him.

To invoke the defence, C must meet each of the composite elements.

4.1 'BONA FIDE'

C must act in good faith in the purchase. The requirement of good faith is closely related to an absence of notice, but it has been held to remain a distinct element.

Midland Bank Trust Co Ltd v Green [1981] AC 513, HL

Lord Wilberforce

At 528

My Lords, the character in the law known as the bona fide (good faith) purchaser for value without notice was the creation of equity. In order to affect a purchaser for value of a legal estate with some equity or equitable interest, equity fastened upon his conscience and the composite expression was used to epitomise the circumstances in which equity would or rather would not do so. I think that it would generally be true to say that the words "in good faith" related to the existence of notice. Equity, in other words, required not only absence of notice, but genuine and honest absence of notice. As the law developed, this requirement became crystallised in the doctrine of constructive notice which assumed a statutory form in the Conveyancing Act 1882, section 3. But, and so far I would be willing to accompany the respondents, it would be a mistake to suppose that the requirement of good faith extended only to the matter of notice, or that when notice came to be regulated by statute, the requirement of good faith became obsolete. Equity still retained its interest in and power over the purchaser's conscience. The classic judgment of James L.J. in *Pilcher v. Rawlins* (1872) L.R. 7 Ch.App. 259, 269 is clear authority that it did: good faith there is stated as a separate test which may have to be passed even though absence of notice is proved. and there are references in cases subsequent to 1882 which confirm the proposition that honesty or bona fides remained something which might be inquired into (see *Berwick & Co. v. Price* [1905] 1 Ch. 632, 639; *Taylor v. London and County Banking Co.* [1901] 2 Ch. 231, 256; *Oliver v. Hinton* [1899] 2 Ch. 264, 273).

While it is clear from this statement that bona fides is a separate requirement from notice, it is difficult to pinpoint what it adds to the defence.

In *Grindal v Hooper*,[8] the definition of a good faith purchaser arose for consideration in the context of a statute, rather than the defence of bona fide purchaser. Lord Wilberforce's statement was interpreted to mean that '*notice is an essential but not an exclusive aspect of good faith*'. Hence, a purchaser with notice would necessarily act in bad faith in denying the enforceability of B's rights, but an absence of notice does not guarantee that C acts in good faith in so doing.

4.2 'PURCHASER FOR VALUE'

To be a purchaser, C must acquire the estate by an act of the parties, rather than by operation of law. Hence, for example, a person who acquires a legal estate through adverse possession (as discussed in Chapter 10) is not a 'purchaser'.

The requirement of value precludes the defence being invoked where A transfers the land to C as a gift, whether during A's lifetime or on A's death. 'Equity will not assist a volunteer' and therefore the recipient of a gift is not placed in a better position than the donor. In *Midland Bank v Green*, in the context of discussing statutory definitions of purchaser, Lord Wilberforce considered that valuable consideration '*requires no definition: it is an expression denoting an advantage conferred or detriment suffered*'.[9] It is a general expression that, unless curtailed by statute, includes inadequate consideration[10] and even nominal consideration.[11] In that case, it was held that a purchaser who paid £500 for land valued at £40,000 had provided valuable consideration.[12]

4.3 'OF A LEGAL ESTATE'

The defence of bona fide purchaser is available only to purchasers of a legal estate—that is, a legal freehold or leasehold. If C purchases an equitable interest, such as an equitable lease or an existing beneficial interest, then C remains bound by all equitable interests affecting that interest.

4.4 'WITHOUT NOTICE'

The most significant aspect of the defence is the requirement that C does not have notice of B's equitable proprietary right. Notice can take three forms: actual, constructive, and imputed.

---

[8] Unreported, judgment 6 December 1999.

[9] [1981] AC 513, 531.

[10] *Basset v Nosworthy* (1673) 23 ER 55, 56, '*in Purchases the Question is not, whether the* Consideration be adequate, but whether 'tis valuable' (sic).

[11] Compare Lord Wilberforce's discussion in *Midland Bank Trust Co Ltd v Green* [1981] AC 513, 531–2. Lord Wilberforce defined nominal consideration and a nominal sum as '*terms of art,* [referring] *to a sum or consideration which can be mentioned as consideration but is not necessarily paid*'.

[12] Ibid. While the matter did not arise for consideration, Lord Wilberforce doubted that £500 would be classed as nominal consideration on the definition of that term which he provided.

4.4.1 Actual notice

Actual notice refers to those matters of which C is actually aware. If C knows of B's property rights, then C has no defence against their enforceability. The means by which C obtained notice are generally irrelevant: in particular, it is not necessary that notice is obtained from A or B.

The contrary was suggested to be the case in *Barnhart v Greenshields*.[13] In that case, it was held that '*a purchaser is not bound to attend to vague rumours to statements by mere strangers, but that a notice in order to be binding, must proceed from some person interested in the property*'.[14] While the irrelevance of rumours has not been doubted, a broader approach to the defence has been indicated.

Lloyd v Banks (1868) LR 3 Ch App 488

Lord Cairns LC

At 490–1

I do not think it would be consistent with the principles upon which this Court has always proceeded, or with the authorities which have been referred to, if I were to hold that under no circumstances could a trustee, without express notice from the incumbrancer, be fixed with knowledge of an incumbrance upon the fund of which he is the trustee so as to give the incumbrancer the same benefit which he would have had if he had himself given notice to the trustee. It must depend upon the facts of the case; but I am quite prepared to say that I think the Court would expect to find that those who alleged that the trustee had knowledge of the incumbrance had made it out, not by any evidence of casual conversations, much less by any proof of what would only be constructive notice—but by proof that the mind of the trustee has in some way been brought to an intelligent apprehension of the nature of the incumbrance which has come upon the property, so that a reasonable man, or an ordinary man of business, would act upon the information and would regulate his conduct by it in the execution of the trust.

4.4.2 Constructive notice

If C does not have actual notice of B's rights because of a failure to make reasonable inquiries, then C will be fixed with constructive notice and be precluded from invoking the defence. The Law of Property Act 1925 (LPA 1925) provides a statutory explanation of the scope of constructive notice.

Law of Property Act 1925, s 199

(1) A purchaser shall not be prejudicially affected by notice of—

[...]

---

[13] (1853) 9 Moo PCC 18.
[14] Ibid, 36, *per* The Rt Hon T Pemberton Leigh.

> (ii) any other instrument or matter or any fact or thing unless—
>
> > (a) it is within his own knowledge, or would have come to his knowledge if such inquiries and inspections had been made as ought reasonably to have been made by him;
> >
> > [...]

Howell explains the rationale for this form of notice.

Howell, 'The Doctrine of Notice: An Historical Perspective'
[1997] Conv 431, 432

It is constructive notice which has caused and continues to cause the most difficulty. The principle upon which it is based is eminently reasonable. If a purchaser is affected only by matters of which he actually knows, he will take care to ensure that he is without that knowledge. Since this could clearly lead to injustice, equity was prepared in certain circumstances to treat the purchaser as having knowledge which he did not in fact have. In order to satisfy the courts of equity, the purchaser was expected to inspect both the land itself and the documents of title to a standard of enquiry set by the courts, and that standard could be very high. [...] In general, however, the courts were concerned to confine constructive notice within the scope of those inspections and enquiries which it was reasonable to make, and not to put an over-stringent burden of enquiry on the purchaser.

Inevitably, what constitutes 'reasonable' inquiries has provided a fertile ground for litigation. In particular, this has centred on the protection afforded to those in occupation.

It is well established that B's occupation is sufficient to fix C with constructive notice of B's rights.[15] To have this effect, however, the fact of B's occupation must be ascertainable on reasonable enquiries. This gives rise to two issues: what constitutes occupation and what constitutes reasonable enquiries.

As we will see in Chapter 16, occupation is relevant to determining priorities in registered, as well as unregistered, land. In registered land, in *William & Glyn's Bank v Boland*,[16] the House of Lords interpreted 'occupation' broadly. In particular, it was held that there is no requirement that occupation must be inconsistent with the title offered by A. In taking this approach, the House of Lords declined to follow case law from unregistered land, including the following case, which signals a narrower definition of 'occupation'.

Caunce v Caunce [1969] 1 WLR 286, HC

Facts: Mr Caunce was the sole legal owner of a matrimonial home, which he held on trust for himself and his wife, who had paid towards the cost of the purchase. Mr Caunce used the home as security for loans and became bankrupt. Mrs Caunce argued that the banks had constructive notice of her beneficial interest, because she was in occupation.

---

[15] See, e.g., *Barnhart v Greenshields* (1853) 9 Moo PCC 18; *Hunt v Luck* [1902] 1 Ch 428.
[16] [1981] AC 487.

Stamp J

At 393–4

In my judgment, where the vendor or mortgagor is himself in possession and occupation of the property, the purchaser or the mortgagee is not affected with notice of the equitable interests of any other person who may be resident there, and whose presence is wholly consistent with the title offered. If you buy with vacant possession on completion and you know, or find out, that the vendor is himself in possession and occupation of the property, you are, in my judgment, by reason of your failure to make further inquiries on the premises, no more fixed with notice of the equitable interest of the vendor's wife who is living there with him than you would be affected with notice of the equitable interest of any other person who might also be resident on the premises, e.g., the vendor's father, his "Uncle Harry" or his "Aunt Matilda," any of whom, be it observed, might have contributed towards the purchase of the property. The reason is that the vendor being in possession, the presence of his wife or guest or lodger implies nothing to negative the title offered. It is otherwise if the vendor is not in occupation and you find another party whose presence demands an explanation and whose presence you ignore at your peril.

Caunce v Caunce has never been overruled. Its effect, if applied, is that where A is in occupation of the land, C is not fixed with constructive notice of property rights held by other persons in occupation whose presence is not inconsistent with A's title. In particular, this includes A's spouse.

As a matter of policy, the decision is unsatisfactory. It means that the level of protection afforded to a person's property rights is dependent on his or her relationship to A. At a broad level, it runs counter to the increasing recognition of the likelihood of co-ownership of the home. The practical effect of developing the doctrines of trust through which co-ownership may be established (discussed in Chapter 18) is weakened if due protection of those rights is denied simply on the basis of the parties' relationship. Therefore, it may be expected that, should the scope of occupation arise again in unregistered land, the court would prefer the wide approach taken in *Boland* and further discussed in Chapter 16.

The court considered the need for C's occupation to be ascertainable on reasonable inquiries in the following case.

Kingsnorth Finance Co Ltd v Tizard [1986] 1 WLR 783, HC

Facts: Mr Tizard held legal title to his house on trust for himself and his wife. Following the breakdown of their marriage, Mrs Tizard had stopped living in the home, while Mr Tizard had remained there with the couple's son and daughter. Most of Mrs Tizard's clothes remained in the house, which she visited every day to care for the children. Mrs Tizard slept at the house on the frequent occasions when her husband was away. Unknown to her, Mr Tizard used the house as security for a loan, the proceeds of which he used to emigrate with their son. The facts came to light when the loan was not repaid. The court held that Mrs Tizard was in occupation. Prior to the grant of the loan, an agent (Mr Marshall) had visited the house to undertake a valuation. The inspection had taken place on a Sunday afternoon, at a time arranged by Mr Tizard, who ensured that his wife took the children out for the day. Mr Marshall saw evidence of occupation by the children, but not of Mrs Tizard. Mr Tizard told Mr Marshall that he was separated from this wife, although he had described himself as single on his application form. The issue arose of whether Kingsnorth Finance had constructive notice of Mrs Tizard's beneficial interest.

Judge John Finlay QC

At 794–5

I return to the submissions made by Mr. Romer and Mr. Wigmore. Mr. Romer's submission is that as Mrs. Tizard was in fact in occupation, that circumstance itself fixed the plaintiffs with notice of such rights as she had; to the contrary is the submission made by Mr. Wigmore that, in the case of unregistered land, it is only where the purchaser or mortgagee finds the claimant to an equitable interest in occupation that he has notice.

I accept Mr. Wigmore's submission but subject to a significant qualification: if the purchaser or mortgagee carries out such inspections "as ought reasonably to be made" and does not either find the claimant in occupation or find evidence of that occupation reasonably sufficient to give notice of the occupation, then I am not persuaded that the purchaser or mortgagee is in such circumstances (and in the absence, which is not the case here, of other circumstances) fixed with notice of the claimant's rights. One of the circumstances, however, is that such inspection is made "as ought reasonably to be made."

Here Mr. Marshall carried out his inspection on a Sunday afternoon at a time arranged with Mr. Tizard. If the only purpose of such an inspection were to ascertain the physical state of the property, the time at which the inspection is made and whether or not that time is one agreed in advance with the vendor or mortgagor appears to me to be immaterial. Where, however, the object of the inspection (or one of the objects) is to ascertain who is in occupation, I cannot see that an inspection at a time pre-arranged with the vendor will necessarily attain that object. Such a pre-arranged inspection may achieve no more than an inquiry of the vendor or mortgagor and his answer to it. In the case of residential property an appointment for inspection will, in most cases, be essential so far as inspection of the interior is concerned. How then is a purchaser or mortgagee to carry out such inspection "as ought reasonably to have been made" for the purpose of determining whether the possession and occupation of the property accords with the title offered? What is such an inspection "as ought reasonably to be made" must, I think, depend on all the circumstances. In the circumstances of the present case I am not satisfied that the pre-arranged inspection on a Sunday afternoon fell within the category of "such inspections which ought reasonably to have been made," the words in section 199 of the Law of Property Act 1925 which I have already read. The plaintiffs not having established that they made such an inspection, the conclusion that I have reached by another route is, in my view, fortified. It follows that the plaintiffs' claim for possession fails.

Jackson notes that *Tizard* takes a broad approach to determining when occupation is apparent. On her analysis, there were two routes to the finding of constructive notice: in the following extract, she refers to 'latent' and 'patent' defects in A's title. Latent defects are those ascertainable on inquiry; patent defects are those that would be disclosed on a reasonable inspection of the land.[17]

---

[17] Jackson, 'Title by Registration and Concealed Overriding Interests: The Cause and Effect of Antipathy to Documentary Proof' (2003) 119 LQR 660, 672–3.

Jackson, 'Title by Registration and Concealed Overriding Interests: The Cause and Effect of Antipathy to Documentary Proof'
(2003) 119 LQR 660, 673–4

There were two grounds for the decision. First, under the "latent" aspect of constructive notice he [Judge Finlay] held that inquiries would have revealed the presence of an interest that encumbered Kingsnorth's title. Secondly, under the "patent" aspect of the doctrine, it was held that Kingsnorth had not made a reasonable inspection of the land. In relation to the latter, Judge Finlay observed that sufficient evidence of occupation was required before a purchaser would be bound by an equitable co-ownership right. Under s.199, occupiers' rights are protected to the extent that their occupation is patent, i.e. apparent on a reasonable inspection. That occupation then puts a purchaser on inquiry as to the possible existence of an adverse claim. A purchaser will take free from the interest of the occupier only if the purchaser could not establish that there was insufficient evidence of occupation. [...] By definition therefore, if Mrs Tizard's minimal constructive occupation would be considered to be apparent, the apparency requirement itself imposes a high standard of inspection on purchasers.

Thompson criticizes Judge Finlay's focus on whether Kingsnorth Finance had notice of Mrs Tizard's occupation. He notes that the issue under the bona fide purchaser defence is whether the company had notice of Mrs Tizard's beneficial interest, not of her occupation. This is in contrast to the position in registered land. There, as we will see in Chapter 16, the rights of persons in occupation are protected as 'overriding interests'. Statutory regulation of this category of interest is centred on the issue of occupation as the trigger for protecting B's rights.[18]

Once it is accepted that occupation confers constructive notice, however, some focus on determining when B is in occupation appears logical and necessary. The key question for the scope of constructive notice is whether the court has struck the right balance in its interpretation of what constitutes reasonable inquiries. This is the case whether those inquiries are focused towards discovering B's rights, or B's occupation. On this crucial issue, Thompson questions Judge Finlay's suggestion (in the extract from his judgment above) that a single inspection at a prearranged time is insufficient when the object is to ascertain who is in occupation.

Thompson, 'The Purchaser as Private Detective' [1986] Conv 283, 286

With respect, this seems to go too far. Suppose Mr. Marshall had asked where the mother of the children was and had been told either that she was dead or that she had left years ago and her present whereabouts, or even whether she was still alive, was unknown. What then is he supposed to do? Clearly, an inspection of the property should take place. If the mortgagor says this can take place at the weekend, can it really be supposed that the mortgagee's agent must insist on calling at an alternative, unannounced time to check whether the mortgagor is lying? Similarly must he insist upon rifling through drawers and cupboards, inevitably causing offence? It is submitted that such behaviour goes far beyond what are reasonable inquiries.

---

[18] Thompson, 'The Purchaser as Private Detective' [1986] Conv 283. Overriding interests are discussed in Chapter 16.

It is suggested that the onus on a purchaser of unregistered land is not this heavy. It is necessary that the vendor should be asked whether he shares the house with anyone else. Additionally he should be asked if he either is or was married. If the answers reveal the existence of anybody, then inquiries where possible should be made of that person. Further, an inspection of the property should be carried out. If such an inspection gives no cause to suspect adverse rights then, pace Judge Finlay, even if this inspection was performed at a time arranged with the vendor, the purchaser should be held to have done all that is required of him by section 199 of the Law of Property Act 1925. For the purchaser to insist on doing more carries the inevitable implication that he suspects the vendor of deceit. Such demands should not be considered to be within the scope of reasonable inquiries.

Ultimately, it must be recalled that the requirement is to make *reasonable* inquiries. What this entails must be dependent on the facts. In a case such as *Tizard*, in which a prearranged inspection brings to light irregularities, it may be reasonable to expect that these are followed up.

Where B is in occupation as a tenant, his or her occupation does not give C constructive notice of the rights of the landlord. Farwell J explained the position at first instance in the following case—a judgment that was upheld by the Court of Appeal[19] and remains authoritative.

Hunt v Luck [1901] 1 Ch 45

Facts: A solicitor transferred property to the defendant as security for a mortgage. The property consisted of a number of homes let out to tenants. Prior to the transfer, the defendant had been informed by the tenants that their rent was paid to a local estate agent, but did not make further inquiries to ascertain on whose behalf the rent was collected. The plaintiff argued that the defendant had constructive notice that the property was held on her behalf.

Farwell J

At 48–9

The plaintiff's contention, therefore, is that it was the duty of the mortgagees to direct their agent (1.) to inquire of the tenants, not merely whether they claimed any and what interest in their holdings, but also who was the person to whom their rents were paid; and (2.) having ascertained to whom the rents were paid, to inquire of the recipient on whose behalf those rents were received.

Now, in my opinion on the authorities as they stand, it is not the duty of a purchaser to ask the tenants to whom they pay their rents. The fact that a tenant is in occupation is notice of his own rights, but is not notice of the rights of the persons through whom he claims.

The matter is different if the purchaser has actual notice that rent is being paid to a person whose receipt is inconsistent with the vendor's title. In such circumstances, the purchaser has constructive notice of the recipient's property rights.[20]

---

[19] [1902] 1 Ch 428.
[20] [1901] 1 Ch 45, 51.

4.4.3 Imputed notice

This category concerns notice obtained by agents acting on C's behalf.[21] If C's agent—for example, C's solicitor—has notice of B's rights, whether actual or constructive, then the agent's notice is imputed to C.

Like constructive notice, a statutory explanation of the scope of imputed notice is provided by s 199 of the LPA 1925.

Law of Property Act 1925, s 199

(1) A purchaser shall not be prejudicially affected by notice of—

[. . .]

(ii) any other instrument or matter or any fact or thing unless—

[. . .]

(b) in the same transaction with respect to which a question of notice to the purchaser arises, it has come to the knowledge of his counsel, as such, or of his solicitor or other agent, as such, or would have come to the knowledge of his solicitor or other agent, as such, if such inquiries and inspections had been made as ought reasonably to have been made by the solicitor or other agent.

Tizard illustrates the operation of imputed notice. In that case, as we have seen, Mr Marshall undertook an inspection of the property. He was considered to have been acting as an agent for Kingsnorth Finance and therefore information that he obtained, that Mr Tizard was separated from his wife, was imputed to Kingsnorth Finance. It was on the basis of this imputed knowledge that Judge Finlay considered that Kingsnorth Finance should have made further inquiries.[22]

5 THE LAND CHARGES ACT 1972

A system for the registration of a limited number of interests in unregistered land was provided by the Land Charges Act 1925 (LCA 1925). The idea of registering land charges was not new, but had previously been confined to '*somewhat unusual charges which a purchaser might fail to discover in an ordinary investigation of title*'.[23] The 1925 Act extended the operation of registration to '*numerous everyday transactions*'.[24] That Act was replaced by the LCA 1972.

At first sight, it seems paradoxical to speak of *registration* in relation to *unregistered* land. It is important, therefore, to understand the limited scope of land charges registration and how this scheme differs from the system of registered land.

The 1972 Act provides for a number of equitable interests, and one legal interest, to be recorded on a register against the name of the holder of the legal estate. Registered land, as

---

[21] For further consideration of the nature of imputed notice, see Nield, 'Imputed Notice' [2000] Conv 196.

[22] [1986] 1 WLR 783, 794.

[23] *Megarry and Wade's The Law of Real Property* (6th edn, ed Harpum, 2000, [5–086]). This paragraph is referred to in [8–062] of the seventh edition, but is not repeated in the text.

[24] Ibid.

we have seen in Chapter 9, requires the registration of legal estates in land. Each estate is given a title number, with the name of the holder of the legal estate, and the holders of certain other legal and equitable interests in the land, recorded against that title number. Hence land charges registration is a system for the registration of *interests* in unregistered land against the *name* of the holder of the legal title; registered land provides for the registration of *legal estates* against a unique *title number*.

5.1 THE SCOPE OF THE LAND CHARGES ACT 1972

The interests registrable as land charges are listed in s 2 of the LCA 1972 in six classes: Classes A–F, with Classes C and D further subdivided. The most important land charges are those contained in Classes C(i) and C(iv), D(ii) and D(iii), and F. These are discussed below. Other classes cover various statutory and equitable financial obligations connected to land, including equitable mortgages (Class C(iii)) and statutory charges securing payment of tax (Class D(i)).

Land Charges Act 1972, s 2

(1) If a charge on or obligation affecting land falls into one of the classes described in this section, it may be registered in the register of land charges as a land charge of that class.

[…]

(4) A Class C land charge is any of the following (not being a local land charge), namely—

    (i) a puisne mortgage;

    […]

    (iv) an estate contract;

and for this purpose—

    (i) a puisne mortgage is a legal mortgage which is not protected by a deposit of documents relating to the legal estate affected;

    […]

    (iv) an estate contract is a contract by an estate owner or by a person entitled at the date of the contract to have a legal estate conveyed to him to convey or create a legal estate, including a contract conferring either expressly or by statutory implication a valid option to purchase, a right of pre-emption or any other like right.

(5) A Class D land charge is any of the following (not being a local land charge), namely—

    […]

    (ii) a restrictive covenant;

    (iii) an equitable easement;

and for this purpose—

    […]

    (ii) a restrictive covenant is a covenant or agreement (other than a covenant or agreement between a lessor and a lessee) restrictive of the user of land and entered into on or after 1st January 1926;

    (iii) an equitable easement is an easement, right or privilege over or affecting land created or arising on or after 1st January 1926, and being merely an equitable interest.

[...]

(7) A Class F land charge is a charge affecting any land by virtue of the Part IV of the Family Law Act 1996

The Class C(i) land charge, the puisne mortgage, is notable as the only legal interest registrable as a land charge and (as has been noted above) the only exception to the general priority rule that a purchaser of unregistered land is necessarily bound by legal interests. In unregistered land, the first legal mortgagee generally holds title deeds—hence registration is aimed at second and subsequent legal mortgages.

The estate contract in Class C(iv) has a broad application. Its scope may be sufficiently broad to cover all cases in which there is a specifically enforceable contact for the creation or transfer of legal estates and interests[25] in land that would attract the application of the doctrine of anticipation discussed in Chapter 12. It includes contracts for sale of a freehold, for the creation and assignment of a lease, and contracts to create a mortgage. It also includes a contract to create an easement,[26] although an equitable easement arising from the contract could be registered as a Class D(iii) land charge.

An estate contract arises in the ordinary course of a conveyance of a legal estate in unregistered land as soon as there is a specifically enforceable contract (the requirements of which are discussed in Chapter 9). Registration may not be usual where the period of time between contract and conveyance is short. This leaves the purchaser vulnerable to loss of his or her property right, although it does not affect contractual remedies. For example, if A contracts to sell land to B and, in breach of contract, sells to C (who has offered a higher price), B's estate contract is not enforceable against C unless registered, but A remains liable for damages for breach of contract.

Class D(iii) covers only equitable easements; legal easements are governed by the general priority rule that legal rights bind all third parties who acquire rights from A. The existence of legal easements should be apparent from the title deeds if expressly created, but, as we will see in Chapter 26, legal easements may also arise through an implied grant. The existence of such easements may be no more or less apparent on an inspection of the land than equitable easements. Hence the different treatment of these is not necessarily logical. The scope of Class D(iii) has been subject to debate. In *ER Ives Investment Ltd v High*,[27] Lord Denning MR suggested that it included only those easements that would have been categorized as legal before the 1925 legislation and became equitable as a result of the changes introduced by those Acts. This is an artificially narrow interpretation.[28] In *Shiloh Spinners Ltd v Harding*,[29] Lord Wilberforce said that it *'should be given its plain prima facie meaning'*.

Equitable easements and restrictive covenants (in Class D(ii)) are registrable only if created after the LCA 1925 came into force. The enforceability of those that pre-date the introduction of registration of land charges remains determined by the doctrine of notice. This limitation on the scope of Class D(ii) is significant, because easements and restrictive

---

[25] Although defined in the Land Charges Act 1972, s 2(4)(iv), as concerned with 'legal estates', s 17 provides for that expression to be given the same meaning as in the Law of Property Act 1925. 'Legal estates' is defined broadly in the 1925 Act, s 1(4), as *'estates, interests, and charges which under this section are authorised to subsist or to be conveyed or created at law'*. See Battersby (1995, p 646).

[26] Ibid.

[27] [1967] 2 QB 379.

[28] Battersby (1995).

[29] [1973] AC 691, 721.

covenants constitute some of the most important and enduring third-party rights, the creation of which was already common prior to 1925.

Class F concerns statutory rights of occupation conferred on certain spouses and civil partners who do not own legal title to their home. The scope of these occupation rights is considered in Chapter 18. The need to register has been described as a 'severe restriction' on the protection afforded by these statutory rights.[30] Registration is unlikely to be undertaken through lack of knowledge or advice, or where the claimant is *still living at home in peace with her husband*.[31] Notwithstanding, registration can be used as a potent weapon. In *Wroth v Tyler*,[32] the vendor's wife objected to her husband's plan to sell their house and relocate the family. She registered a Class F land charge between contract and conveyance, thus preventing her husband from completing the sale with vacant possession and leaving him liable for damages for breach of contract. On the facts, it was apparent that the consequence of such liability would be the bankruptcy of the husband and, through that, the loss of the home. Despite this, the wife refused the opportunity to cancel the land charge to enable the sale to go ahead.

5.2 THE EFFECT OF REGISTRATION AND NON-REGISTRATION

The effect of registration is given in clear and unequivocal terms in s 198 of the LPA 1925.

Law of Property Act 1925, s 198

(1) The registration of any instrument or matter [in any register kept under the Land Charges Act 1972 or any local land charges register], shall be deemed to constitute actual notice of such instrument or matter, and of the fact of such registration, to all persons and for all purposes connected with the land affected, as from the date of registration or other prescribed date and so long as the registration continues in force.

[…]

The effect of a failure to register is provided in s 4 of the LCA 1972. The general effect of non-registration is to provide a purchaser with a defence of lack of registration—the defence that we introduced in Chapter 6, section 3.2. Minor differences arise as regards when a purchaser can invoke the defence, depending on the class of registrable land charge.

Land Charges Act 1972, s 4

[…]

(5) A land charge of Class B and a land charge of Class C (other than an estate contract) created or arising on or after 1st January 1926 shall be void as against a purchaser of the land charged with it, or of any interest in such land, unless the land charge is registered in the appropriate register before the completion of the purchase.

---

[30] *Williams & Glyn's Bank v Boland* [1979] Ch 312, 328, *per* Lord Denning MR.
[31] Ibid.
[32] [1974] Ch 30.

(6) An estate contract and a land charge of Class D created or entered into on or after 1st January 1926 shall be void as against a purchaser for money or money's worth [or, in the case of a HM Revenue and Customs charge, a purchaser within the meaning of the Capital Transfer Tax Act 1984] of a legal estate in the land charged with it, unless the land charge is registered in the appropriate register before the completion of the purchase.

The effect of non-registration of land charges in Classes C(iv) and D therefore differs in two respects from non-registration of all other classes. Firstly, unregistered land charges in Classes C(iv) and D are void only against purchasers for money or money's worth. In the absence of a specific requirement, land charges in other classes are void for non-registration against purchasers for 'valuable consideration', within the general definition of 'purchaser' in s 17 of the 1972 Act. The practical difference between these is that marriage consideration constitutes value, but is not money or money's worth.

Secondly, unregistered land charges in Classes C(iv) and D are void only against purchasers of a legal estate. Unregistered land charges in other classes are void against purchasers of any interest in the land, which would include equitable interests.

As we will see below, there is no scope in these provisions to superimpose the doctrine of notice. Where B holds a property right that is registrable as a land charge and has not been registered, the statutory protection conferred by s 4 of the LCA 1972 provides the purchaser with a complete defence against the enforcement of B's property right.

5.3 THE MECHANICS OF REGISTRATION

The register maintained under the LCA 1972 is names-based.

Land Charges Act 1972, s 3

(1) A land charge shall be registered in the name of the estate owner whose estate in intended to be affected.

[…]

B registers his or her land charge against the name of the holder of the legal estate at the time of registration. The purchaser, C, searches the register against the names of all holders of the legal estate within the period of inspection necessary to establish a good root of title. The successful operation of the register is therefore dependent on B registering and C searching against the correct name. The correct name is the name of the estate owner, as disclosed by the conveyancing documents;[33] this is the name available to the purchaser when investigating title.

The need to register against the name of the holder of the legal estate gives rise to a particular difficulty on a sub-sale. In *Barrett v Hilton Developments*,[34] A contracted to buy land from X. Before the purchase was completed, A subcontracted to sell the land to B, who

---

[33] *Standard Property Investment plc v British Plastics Federation* (1987) 53 P & CR 25.
[34] (1975) 29 P & CR 300.

registered a Class C(iv) land charge against A's name. A subsequently acquired legal title, but sold the land to C (Figure 10).

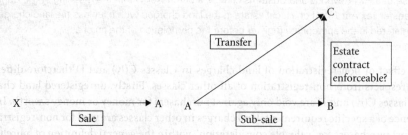

Figure 10 *Barrett v Hilton Developments*

B's registration against A's name was ineffective, because A was not the holder of the legal estate at the time of the registration. The Court of Appeal acknowledged the practical difficulties for B, who may have no means of knowing that A did not hold legal title—but the Court considered that that s 3(1) of the 1972 Act was not susceptible to a construction that would validate registration against anyone other than the current holder of legal title.

The purchaser is entitled to see the title deeds only once the contract for sale has been entered, although, in practice, they may be produced beforehand. The title deeds enable the purchaser to ascertain the names against which a search of the land charges register should be carried out, and it is usual conveyancing practice to search the register in the period between contract and completion. This means that C generally investigates title only after he or she has become contractually bound to purchase the land. The vendor will, however, have contracted to give good title free from undisclosed third party interests; hence, if good title is not shown, or undisclosed interests are discovered, then contractual remedies, including rescission, would be available to the purchaser. Provisions in the contract to the contrary are void.[35]

5.4 SEARCHING THE LAND CHARGES REGISTER

A purchaser may search the land charges register personally or requisition an official search.[36] An official search carries two significant advantages. Firstly, the certificate of search is deemed conclusive.

Land Charges Act 1972, s 10

[...]

(4) In favour of a purchaser or an intending purchaser, as against persons interested under or in respect of matters or documents entries of which are required or allowed as aforesaid, the certificate, according to its tenor, shall be conclusive, affirmatively or negatively, as the case may be.

---

[35] Law of Property Act 1969, s 24.
[36] Land Charges Act 1972, ss 9 and 10.

Hence, a correctly registered charge that is not revealed on the certificate of an official search is unenforceable against the purchaser. In such a case, the Registrar would be liable in negligence to the holder of the land charge.[37]

The second advantage of an official search is that it confers on the purchaser, for a limited 'priority period', protection against new charges registered between the time of search and completion of the conveyance.

Land Charges Act 1972, s 11

[...]

(5) Where a purchaser has obtained a certificate under section 10 above, any entry which is made in the register after the date of the certificate and before the completion of the purchase, and is not made pursuant to a priority notice entered on the register on or before the date of the certificate, shall not affect the purchaser if the purchase is completed before the expiration of the relevant number of days after the date of the certificate.

(6) The relevant number of days is—

(a) for the purposes of subsections [...] (5) above, fifteen;

[...]

or such other number as may be prescribed; but in reckoning the relevant number of days for any of the purposes of this section any days when the registry is not open to the public shall be excluded.

Land charges registered pursuant to a 'priority notice' are excluded from the protection afforded to purchasers during the priority period. Such land charges arise where notice of intent to register has been given to the Registrar prior to the creation of the land charge.

5.5 PROBLEMS WITH A NAMES-BASED REGISTER

The system of land charges registration is undermined by two flaws: firstly, it is susceptible to human error in registration and search; secondly, there is an inherent and unavoidable risk of registered charges being hidden behind a good root of title.

5.5.1 Errors in search and registration

As we have noted, land charges should be registered and searches made under the name of the holder of the legal estate as provided on the title deeds. Like any database or search engine, variations and misspellings of names will not be recognized. An official search against the correct name provides a purchaser with a defence against interests registered under an incorrect name. In *Diligent Finance Co Ltd v Alleyne*,[38] Mrs Alleyne registered her statutory rights of occupation as a Class F land charge against her husband as 'Erskine Allyene'. This was not revealed when Diligent Finance, prior to the grant of a mortgage,

---

[37] By analogy with *Ministry of Housing and Local Government v Sharp* [1970] 2 QB 223. In that case, a local authority was held vicariously liable for the negligence of its clerk in issuing an incorrect local land charges search certificate.

[38] (1972) 23 P & CR 346.

requisitioned an official search against 'Erskine *Owen* Alleyne', the name used on the conveyancing documents. The official search protected Diligent Finance against Mrs Alleyne's Class F land charge. Conversely, an official search against an incorrect name would offer no protection against a properly registered land charge: the certificate of an official search is only conclusive in relation to the names searched. In rare cases, errors occur at both stages of registration and search.

Oak Co-operative Building Society v Blackburn [1968] Ch 730, CA

Facts: Mr Blackburn granted an estate contract over his house to B. The estate contract was registered as a Class C(iv) land charge under the name 'Frank David Blackburn', Frank being the name by which Mr Blackburn was known. In fact, however, his correct name (used on the title deeds) was 'Francis David Blackburn'. Subsequently, Mr Blackburn used his house as security for a mortgage from the building society. An official search was requisitioned against the name 'Francis Davis Blackburn'; the building society's solicitor, a 'Mr Davis', apparently transposing his own name onto the search request. The certificate of official search showed a nil return and the mortgage was granted.

Russell LJ

At 743

We have come to the conclusion that the registration on this occasion ought not to be regarded as a nullity simply because the formal name of Blackburn was Francis and not Frank, and notwithstanding that Frank as a name is not merely an abbreviation or version of Francis but also a name in its own right, as are also for example Harry and Willie. We are not led to this conclusion by the fact that initials would seem to suffice for registration of a lis pendens: see *Dunn v. Chapman*—at least under the then legislation and rules: for presumably a request for search under a full name having the same initials should throw up all entries under those initials. We take a broader view that so far as possible the system should be made to work in favour of those who seek to make use of it in a sensible and practical way. If a proposing purchaser here had requested a search in the correct full names he would have got a clean certificate and a clear title under section 17 (3) of the Land Charges Act, 1925, and would have suffered no harm from the fact that the registration was not in such names: and a person registering who is not in a position to satisfy himself what are the correct full names runs that risk. But if there be registration in what may be fairly described as a version of the full names of the vendor, albeit not a version which is bound to be discovered on a search in the correct full names, we would not hold it a nullity against someone who does not search at all, or who (as here) searches in the wrong name.

Section 17 of the LCA 1925 is now replaced by the provisions for official searches in s 10 of the LCA 1972. The outcome of the case would have been the same if the building society had undertaken a personal search against the correct name. Russell LJ commented, obiter, that the courts would not protect a personal searcher 'from his folly'.[39]

---

[39] [1968] Ch 730, 744.

It is apparent from the decisions in *Oak Co-Operative Building Society v Blackburn* and *Diligent Finance Co Ltd v Alleyne* that registration of a land charge against an incorrect version of a name is not wholly ineffective. The land charge will still be enforceable against a purchaser who does not search, who searches personally, or who requisitions an official search against an incorrect name. A defence against the enforcement of an incorrectly registered land charge is available only to a purchaser who requisitions an official search against the correct name.

5.5.2 Registered charges hidden behind good root of title

As we have noted, good root of title is established by investigating title back to the first conveyance that is at least fifteen years old. The purchaser therefore receives title deeds relating to that period, from which he or she should requisition an official search against the names of the holders of legal estates. This will not reveal land charges registered against the names of those who held legal title at an earlier time: such land charges are hidden behind the good root of title. Notwithstanding, by the force of s 198 of the LPA 1925, a purchaser has no defence against the enforcement of the land charge.

This problem was inherent in the provision for land charges to be registered against the name of the holder of the legal estate. It was bound to arise as soon as the register had subsisted for a period longer than that constituted by good root of title. The matter was investigated by the Roxburgh Committee, which conceded that the problem was insoluble.

Report of the Committee on Land Charges (Cmd 9825, 1956, [22])

We are the inheritors of a transitory system which was bound to disclose this defect after 30 years of transition [the period of good root of title at the time of the LCA 1925] and it seems too late to disclaim our inheritance. [...] The only policy which we can recommend is to press on as quickly as may be with the extension of the system of compulsory registration of title.

The creation of such an inherently flawed system undoubtedly gives cause for concern.

Wade, 'Land Charges Registration Reviewed' [1956] CLJ 216, 216

If the inventions of one generation of legislators fail to justify themselves, the next generation should be able to amend them, at any rate where the difficulties are purely technical and there are no questions of policy. But Lord Birkenhead and Sir Benjamin Cherry appear to have succeeded in creating the conveyancing equivalent of a Frankenstein's monster, which with the passing years would become not only more dangerous but also more difficult to kill.

A pragmatic solution is provided by s 25 of the LPA 1969, which provides for financial compensation for the purchaser.

5.6 LAND CHARGES REGISTRATION AND THE DOCTRINE OF NOTICE

The statutory protection against unregistered land charges afforded to a purchaser leaves no room for the operation of the doctrine of notice. If A sells land to C, who has actual notice of B's registrable, but unregistered land charge, then B's property right is void against C as long as C meets the criteria of purchaser within s 4 of the LCA 1972. C's statutory protection confers an absolute defence against B.

This prompted the following criticism.

Wade, 'Land Charge Registration Reviewed' [1956] CLJ 216, 227

The policy of 1925 was to abandon the equitable principle of notice in favour of a mechanical principle of registration. This was a shift from a moral to an a-moral basis. Its justification was that the doctrines of constructive and imputed notice had been over-refined "to such an extent that it had become dangerous to employ in a purchase a solicitor of good practice and reputation." But those difficulties could be avoided without the defiance of ethics which occurs when a purchaser with *actual* notice is allowed to disregard a third party's rights.

The matter was put to the test in *Midland Bank Trust Co Ltd v Green*,[40] a case that we discussed in Chapter 6, which concerned an option to purchase (a Class C(iv) land charge) granted to Geoffrey Green by his father, Walter. Geoffrey did not register his option as a land charge and, aware of this fact, Walter colluded with his wife, Evelyne, to defeat Geoffrey's option. In order to do so, Walter conveyed the land, which had a market value of £40,000, to Evelyne for £500. Despite Evelyne's actual notice of Geoffrey's option, the House of Lords held that she had a defence against its enforcement because of Geoffrey's non-registration. Against this conclusion, it was argued that Evelyne could not benefit from the statutory protection against unregistered land charges, because she was not a purchaser in good faith.

As we have noted above, the House of Lords acknowledged notice of a right precluded a purchaser from acting in good faith. But the definition of purchaser provided in the LCA 1925 (and the LCA 1972) excludes a requirement of good faith. This is in contrast to the definitions given in the other statutes in the 1925 property legislation.

Was this omission deliberate?

Midland Bank Trust Co Ltd v Green [1981] AC 513, HL

Lord Wilberforce

At 530

My Lords, I recognise that the inquiring mind may put the question: why should there be an omission of the requirement of good faith in this particular context? I do not think there should be much doubt about the answer. Addition of a requirement that the purchaser should be in good faith would bring with it the necessity of inquiring into the purchaser's motives and state of mind. The present case is a good example of the difficulties which would exist. If the

---

[40] [1981] AC 513.

position was simply that the purchaser had notice of the option, and decided nevertheless to buy the land, relying on the absence of notification, nobody could contend that she would be lacking in good faith. She would merely be taking advantage of a situation, which the law has provided, and the addition of a profit motive could not create an absence of good faith. But suppose, and this is the respondents' argument, the purchaser's motive is to defeat the option, does this make any difference? Any advantage to oneself seems necessarily to involve a disadvantage for another: to make the validity of the purchase depend upon which aspect of the transaction was prevalent in the purchaser's mind seems to create distinctions equally difficult to analyse in law as to establish in fact: avarice and malice may be distinct sins, but in human conduct they are liable to be intertwined. The problem becomes even more acute if one supposes a mixture of motives. Suppose—and this may not be far from the truth—that the purchaser's motives were in part to take the farm from Geoffrey, and in part to distribute it between Geoffrey and his brothers and sisters, but not at all to obtain any benefit for herself, is this acting in "good faith" or not? Should family feeling be denied a protection afforded to simple greed? To eliminate the necessity for inquiries of this kind may well have been part of the legislative intention. Certainly there is here no argument for departing—violently—from the wording of the Act.

In the judgment of the House of Lords, therefore, the omission of a requirement of good faith purchase was deliberate. The underlying fault lay in the failure to register Geoffrey's estate contract as a land charge. As may often be the case, the fault was that of the solicitor: Geoffrey's solicitor had already accepted liability pending the outcome of the case.[41] A separate action, for the tort of conspiracy, lay against Geoffrey's parents.[42] That action is discussed in Chapter 7, section 2.4.

Commenting on *Green* and, more generally, on the move away from the doctrine of notice, Megarry and Wade echo Wade's earlier criticism.[43]

Megarry and Wade's The Law of Real Property (6th edn, ed Harpum, 2000, [5–120])

For centuries the courts had developed a policy based upon good faith and fair dealing under the doctrine of notice, the reasons for which were primarily ethical. Its refinements having grown too great for practical convenience, they were largely swept away [by the legislation in 1925 and since then] in favour of a mechanical system from which the ethical element was eliminated. Convenience was bought at the price of injustice in cases where the owners of registrable interests did not realise that they should register them (their solicitors usually making the omission) and so suffered loss. To allow the defeat of a prior interest by a later transaction is a failure on the part of the law, and a natural reluctance to enforce it has sometimes tempted judges to resist the policy of the legislation, clear-cut though it is. [...] The House of Lords [in *Green*] has now reasserted the stark policy of 1925, unethical and uncompromising but clear and simple, at least for those who are aware of it.

[41] Noted by Lord Wilberforce [1981] AC 513, 526. The existence of a cause of action in negligence was established in *Midland Bank Trust Co Ltd v Hett, Stubbs and Kemp* [1978] Ch 384.

[42] *Midland Bank Trust Co Ltd v Green (No 3)* [1982] 2 WLR 1.

[43] The paragraph extracted is omitted from the seventh edition.

It seems open to question whether the disparity between the doctrine of notice and land charges registration is as clear-cut as these authors suggest. Lord Wilberforce's discussion of the possible mixed motives at play in *Green* give at least some cause for caution in classifying the outcome dictated by the land charges mechanism as amoral or unethical. It is far from apparent that Lord Wilberforce viewed the outcome to which he was led in this way.

Gray and Gray suggest that the House of Lords' decision reflects a particular view of the function of property law.[44]

Gray and Gray, *Elements of Land Law* (4th edn, 2004)

At [12.116]

[…] The dominant ideology of modern property law places a clear emphasis upon the simple mechanics of contract and transfer, leaving the morality of exchange largely unquestioned. On this view, the principal purpose of the law of property is to provide clarity and procedural efficiency in the combined operation of bargain and disposition. In many ways the law of property implicitly assumes a world of assertive individualism in which all are presumed to be equal, self-determining and competent to protect their own self-interest. Land transactions therefore have no particularly significant moral dimension. There is, however, another perspective according to which the ultimate business of the law of property is, quite inescapably, the administration of distributive justice. In this context there is no such thing as moral neutrality. The priorities which we allow to govern the law of property simply reflect the moral sensitivity of an entire legal culture […]

At [12.296]

The decision of the House of Lords in *Midland Bank Trust Co Ltd v Green* is entirely consistent with the amoral approach to economic relations which infuses the market concept of property. The ruling confirmed the traditional inclination of the property lawyer to trade off justice in return for enhanced security and stability in commercial transactions. […]

The simple mechanisms favoured by property law extend beyond the LCA 1972 to the operation of overreaching as a means of protecting purchasers against the enforcement of beneficial interests under a trust. However desirable the ethical underpinnings of the bona fide purchaser defence are, it is too uncertain a means of resolving the question of priorities. The common theme underlying criticisms of the decision in *Green* by Megarry and Wade, and Gray and Gray, is their perception of the relationship between certainty and justice. The authors do not see these as diametrically opposed, but certainty is seen as necessarily detracting from justice. The relationship between these concepts is undoubtedly complex and the extent to which the case law reflects those authors' views remains open to debate.

5.7 FRAUDULENT TRANSACTIONS

In *Green*, the House of Lords considered that Evelyn Green did not act fraudulently by seeking to rely on her statutory rights.[45] The decision leaves open the position where there is,

---

44 The paragraphs extracted are omitted from the 5th edition (2009).
45 [1981] AC 513, 531.

in fact, fraud in the transaction.[46] Where a purchaser seeks to invoke a statutory defence against the enforcement of a pre-existing property right in circumstances amounting to fraud or other wrongdoing, two courses of action may be taken: firstly, the purchaser may be denied the statutory defence; or secondly, fresh obligations may arise under the general law. These fresh obligations may involve the imposition of personal liability on C towards B, or the creation of new direct rights in B's favour.

The appropriate response to fraud and other wrongdoing is of equal significance where the statutory defence concerns an unregistered land charge under the LCA 1972, or one of the defences provided in registered land by the Land Registration Act 2002 (LRA 2002). The issue is therefore discussed in Chapter 16.

5.8 CLAIMS TO ALTERNATIVE PROPERTY RIGHTS

In two notable cases, claimants whose land charges have been void against a purchaser for non-registration have sought to establish the existence of other property rights that, not being registrable, bind the purchaser as a purchaser with notice. The defence of lack of registration provides the purchaser with protection only against B's unregistered land charges; it does not protect a purchaser against two categories of rights: firstly, B's pre-existing rights that are not registrable as land charges and therefore remain governed by the doctrine of notice; secondly, new direct rights claimed by B.

As a matter of general law, where alternative claims are available, the claimant is entitled to choose the cause of action that is most favourable to him or herself. Complex questions may, however, arise as regards the relationship between the different property rights concerned.

In *Lloyds Bank v Carrick*,[47] B entered a specifically enforceable contract to buy a home from her brother-in-law (A). B moved into the home, but, unknown to her, A subsequently used the property as security for a loan obtained from C. B had not registered her contract as a Class C(iv) land charge and therefore it was void against C. The Court of Appeal held that the existence of the estate contract precluded B from claiming other property interests under a trust or estoppel, which may have been binding on C, as purchasers with notice, because B was in occupation. The objection to these alternative claims lay in the fact that their source and origin was the contract that was void for non-registration.

In *ER Ives Investment Ltd v High*,[48] A assured B of a right of way across A's land, in return for which B did not object to a trespass caused by the foundations of flats constructed by A. B did not register a land charge and A subsequently sold the land to C. Danckwerts and Winn LLJ accepted that B had an equitable easement that was registrable as a land charge and which was void for non-registration. But they held that B had also acquired rights through estoppel that were not registrable and bound C as purchasers with notice.[49]

In light of *Carrick*, the decision is open to the criticism that the source and origin of B's claim lay in the same facts that had generated the equitable easement. Lord Denning MR considered that B's equitable easement fell outside the classes of registrable land charge and itself bound C as purchasers with notice—but to reach this conclusion requires an

---

[46] Gray and Gray, *Elements of Land Law* (4th edn, 2004, [12.296]).

[47] [1996] 4 All ER 630.

[48] [1967] 2 QB 379.

[49] See further, Battersby, 'Informal Transactions in Land, Estoppel and Registration' (1995) 58 MLR 637 for an analysis based on the principle of mutual benefit and burden. See Chapter 7, section 2.5.

artificially restrictive interpretation of the scope of registrable land charges.[50] It is difficult to avoid the conclusion that the Court of Appeal in *Ives v High* (unlike the Court of Appeal in *Carrick* and the House of Lords in *Green*) was not prepared to accept the outcome in a hard case to uphold the policy of land charges registration. Lord Denning noted that a decision against B would perpetrate the 'grossest injustice'.[51]

6 CONCLUSION

Where A transfers unregistered land to C, or creates a mortgage in C's favour, pre-existing property rights held by B will bind C unless C has a defence against the enforcement of those rights. The key distinction is between legal and equitable rights held by B: C generally has no defence against the enforcement of legal rights held by B.

One exception to this rule arises in relation to the puisne mortgage, which is registrable as a Class C(i) land charge. C has the defence of lack of registration against the enforcement of a puisne mortgage in the following circumstances:[52]

- the mortgage has not been registered as a land charge;

- the mortgage has been registered against an incorrect name and C has requisitioned an official search against the correct name.

C has a defence against the enforcement of equitable rights held by B in the following circumstances.

- B's equitable right is registrable as a land charge and either:
  - has not been registered; or
  - has been registered against an incorrect name and C has requisitioned an official search against the correct name;[53]
- B's equitable right remains governed by the doctrine of notice and C is a bona fide purchaser for value without notice. Equitable rights within this category include, in particular:
  - beneficial interests under a trust—the defence of bona fide purchaser need be invoked only in relation to trusts with one trustee; where there are two or more trustees, the beneficial interests will be overreached on a sale under the mechanism discussed in Chapter 20;
  - an inchoate equity arising under a claim to proprietary estoppel;[54]
  - equitable easements and restrictive covenants created prior to 1 January 1926 and therefore falling outside the application of the LCA 1972.

---

[50] Compare the discussion of the scope of Class C(iv) and D(iii) at section 5.1 above. The equitable easement in the case in fact appears to be registrable as a Class C(iv) or D(iii) land charge. See further Battersby (1995).

[51] [1967] 2 QB 379, 396.

[52] B must be a purchaser for value within the Land Charges Act 1972, s 4(5).

[53] In both cases, subject to B meeting the requirements of the Land Charges Act 1972, s 4(5) or (6), depending on the class of land charge concerned.

[54] *ER Ives Investment Ltd v High* [1967] 2 QB 379. Proprietary estoppel is discussed in Chapter 13.

QUESTIONS

1. What do you understand by the defence of 'bona fide purchaser'? In what circumstances is this defence relevant to determining priority questions in unregistered land?

2. What difficulties arise from the use of a names-based register for the registration of land charges under the Land Charges Act 1972?

3. What do you consider to be the advantages and disadvantages of the 1972 Act as a means of determining priority questions compared with the defence of bona fide purchaser?

4. In what circumstances will the following pre-existing property rights held by C bind B, a purchaser of unregistered land?

    (a) A beneficial interest, assuming that B purchased the land from a single trustee.

    (b) A beneficial interest, assuming that B purchased the land from two trustees.

    (c) A legal mortgage.

    (d) An equitable easement created in 1930.

    (e) A restrictive covenant created in 1900.

FURTHER READING

Battersby, 'Informal Transactions in Land, Estoppel and Registration' (1995) 58 MLR 637

Howell, 'The Doctrine of Notice: An Historical Perspective' [1997] Conv 431

Wade, 'Land Charges Registration Reviewed' [1956] CLJ 216

16

REGISTERED LAND
AND PRIORITIES

CENTRAL ISSUES

1. Where A transfers land to C, priority questions arise as to whether B, who has pre-existing property rights, can enforce those rights against C. Property rights are capable of binding all third parties who acquire a right from A, therefore this issue is conceptualized as the *defences* question: does C have a defence against the enforcement of B's pre-existing property rights?

2. Priority rules differ between unregistered and registered land. The overreaching mechanism (discussed in Chapter 20) is the only rule that is common to both systems. This chapter considers the priority rules of registered land.

3. The Land Registration Act 2002 provides a distinct set of priority rules for one category of transaction: a registrable disposition of a registered estate for valuable consideration. This category incorporates the most common dealings with land, including an ordinary sale or mortgage.

4. In this category of transactions, C is provided with a defence against B's rights where: the disposition complies with limitations on A's owner's powers, which are entered on the register; and B's interest is not entered on the register; and B's interest is not within a category of overriding interests. These are interests that do not appear on the register, but which are, notwithstanding, enforceable against C.

5. The category of overriding interests includes property rights held by persons in actual occupation of the land at the time of the disposition. The meaning of 'occupation' for this purpose has been the subject of debate and the 2002 Act introduced a reasonable inspection qualification to the operation of this category.

6. Where the disposition to C involves fraud or other wrongdoing (but not such as to invalidate the transaction), the policy of the 2002 Act is to enable C still to invoke defences against B's property rights, but to rely on the general law to create new direct rights that are enforceable against C. This may involve C being held personally liable to B or the creation of new property rights in B's favour.

1   INTRODUCTION

In this chapter, we are concerned with how questions of priorities are answered in registered land. The priority triangle was introduced in Chapter 6 and, in Chapter 15, we considered the priority rules applied in unregistered land. It is useful, however, to recap the basic issue with which we are concerned.

Where A transfers land to C, or creates a mortgage in favour of C, the priority question asks whether C is bound by property rights held by a third party, B. This is illustrated in Figure 11.

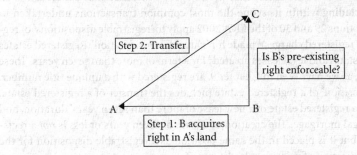

Figure 11 The priority triangle

It is important to emphasize that we are concerned with pre-existing rights held by B at the time of the transfer, and only with B's property rights. Because property rights are prima facie enforceable against all third parties who later acquire a right from A, we have conceptualized this as the *defences* question: on a transfer of land from A to C, does C have a defence against the enforcement of pre-existing property rights held by B?

The rules by which this question is answered differ between unregistered and registered land. The only priority rule common to both systems is overreaching. That mechanism, which is discussed in Chapter 20, enables C to take the land free from beneficial interests under a trust as long as certain conditions are fulfilled: in particular, C must pay any purchase money to two trustees or a trust corporation. If the conditions for overreaching are met, then C has a defence against the enforcement of beneficial interests held by B. As we will see in Chapter 20, B's interests are removed from the land and attach to the proceeds of sale held by the trustees (A).

2   AN OVERVIEW: PRIORITIES AND PRINCIPLES OF REGISTRATION OF TITLE

The starting point in understanding the approach of registered land to priorities is s 28 of the Land Registration Act 2002 (LRA 2002).

Land Registration Act 2002, s 28

(1) Except as provided by sections 29 and 30, the priority of an interest affecting a registered estate or charge is not affected by a disposition of the estate or charge.

> (2) It makes no difference for the purposes of this section whether the interest or disposition is registered.

The starting point therefore is that the 2002 Act does not alter how questions of priority are determined under the general law. The exception contained in ss 29 and 30 is, however, highly significant. Those sections (s 29 is extracted at section 2.2 below) refer to a category of transactions that are elevated out of the general law and provided with distinct priority rules.

It is important to note at the outset that the category of transactions concerned is an important one, including within its scope the most common transactions undertaken in relation to land. Sections 29 and 30 of the LRA 2002 apply to 'registrable dispositions' of registered estates (and registered charges)[1] made for 'valuable consideration'. Registered estates are legal freehold estates and legal leases created[2] for a term of more than seven years. These are the estates that, as we have seen in Chapter 9, are registered with a unique title number. A 'registrable disposition' of a registered estate includes the transfer of a registered estate, the creation out of a registered estate of a new lease of more than seven years' duration, and the creation of a legal mortgage. The creation of a lease of seven years or less is *not* a registrable disposition, but it is placed in the same position as a registrable disposition for the purposes of the application of priority rules.[3]

The requirement of 'valuable consideration' excludes from this scheme of priorities transfers by gift, for nominal consideration,[4] or through adverse possession.[5] The type of transactions to which the distinct scheme of priorities contained in ss 29 and 30 of the LRA 2002 applies therefore includes the ordinary sale or mortgage of registered land.[6]

To understand how questions of priority are answered in relation to registrable dispositions, it is necessary to understand two particular aspects of the operation of the 2002 Act: firstly, the powers of disposition conferred on A; secondly, the effect of a registered disposition to C. These aspects of the operation of registered land should be understood in light of two underlying principles: the *mirror principle* and the *curtain principle*.[7] The mirror principle is the proposition that the register constitutes an accurate reflection of facts material to the title; the curtain principle provides that a curtain is drawn across the register against any trusts.[8]

Cooke explains the combined effect of these principles.

---

[1] Land Registration Act 2002, s 30.

[2] Or with more than seven years remaining at the time of the transfer of an existing lease that triggers compulsory first registration.

[3] Land Registration Act 2002, s 29(4), extracted below.

[4] Valuable consideration is defined in s 132(1) of the 2002 Act.

[5] The scheme of priorities for registration following a successful application based on adverse possession is provided in the 2002 Act, Sch 6, para 9.

[6] The approach adopted by the 2002 Act to priorities is not intended to make major changes to the position under the Land Registration Act 1925, but to place prevailing rules on a statutory footing. A full explanation is provided in Law Commission Report No 271, *Land Registration for the Twenty-First Century: A Conveyancing Revolution* (2001, Pt V).

[7] These principles are explained in Chapter 9, section 5.2.

[8] Ruoff, *An Englishman Looks at the Torrens System* (1957, pp 7–14), extracted in Chapter 9, section 5.2.

Cooke, *The New Law of Land Registration* (2003, p 53)

[...] the mirror reveals, the curtain hides. The strange thing about this mirror is that it is an active one; what it reveals has been made true, at least to some extent, by the register itself. And just as domestic mirrors are designed to assist a specific type of viewer (humanoids with heads about 1.8 metres from the floor), so is the land register: it is designed to assist purchasers. It is designed so as to fashion and display that particular facet of truth which most tends to make a purchaser secure, although what it shows is also informative and useful to others. What the register hides are things that the purchaser does not need to know, because the law of registration has ensured that they cannot affect him, although they may be of first importance to others. [...]

These principles continue to influence the development of registered land. In particular, the desire for the register to provide '*a complete and accurate reflection of the state of the title at any given time*' was fundamental to the Law Commission's work[9] that led to the LRA 2002.

2.1 OWNER'S POWERS

Section 23 of the LRA 2002 confers on A, as a registered proprietor (or a person entitled to be registered as the proprietor),[10] 'owner's powers'.

Land Registration Act 2002, s 23(1) and (2)

(1) Owner's powers in relation to a registered estate consist of—

  (a) power to make a disposition of any kind permitted by the general law in relation to an interest of that description, other than a mortgage by demise or sub-demise, and

  (b) power to charge the estate at law with the payment of money.

(2) Owner's powers in relation to a registered charge consist of—

  (a) power to make a disposition of any kind permitted by the general law in relation to an interest of that description, other than a legal sub-mortgage, and

  (b) power to charge at law with the payment of money indebtedness secured by the registered charge.

Section 26 of the 2002 Act enables C to assume that A's owner's powers are free from any limitations, except those reflected by an entry on the register. It ensures that C's title is unaffected by any limitation on A's powers that do not appear on the register. The means of registering a limitation is through entry of a restriction.[11] As we will see, entry of a restriction is of particular relevance to priorities where B holds a beneficial interest under a trust.

---

9 Law Commission Report No 271 (2001, [1.5]).
10 Land Registration Act 2002, s 24.
11 Ibid, ss 40–47.

2.2 THE EFFECT OF A REGISTERED DISPOSITION

The effect of a registered disposition is explained in s 29 of the LRA 2002.

Land Registration Act 2002, s 29

(1) If a registrable disposition of a registered estate is made for valuable consideration, completion of the disposition by registration has the effect of postponing to the interest under the disposition any interest affecting the estate immediately before the disposition whose priority is not protected at the time of registration.

(2) For the purposes of subsection (1), the priority of an interest is protected—

  (a) in any case, if the interest—

    (i) is a registered charge or the subject of a notice in the register,

    (ii) falls within any of the paragraphs of Schedule 3, or

    (iii) appears from the register to be excepted from the effect of registration, and

  (b) in the case of a disposition of a leasehold estate, if the burden of the interest is incident to the estate.

(3) Subsection (2)(a)(ii) does not apply to an interest which has been the subject of a notice in the register at any time since the coming into force of this section.

(4) Where the grant of a leasehold estate in land out of a registered estate does not involve a registrable disposition, this section has effect as if—

  (a) the grant involved such a disposition, and

  (b) the disposition were registered at the time of the grant.

Section 30 makes equivalent provision to s 29 in relation to the disposition of a registered charge. Section 29(4) is notable, because it means that where C is granted a lease of seven years or less in duration (a grant that does not constitute a registrable disposition), C is, notwithstanding, able to invoke the protection afforded by s 29.

The effect of s 29 is that, on a registrable disposition, C has a defence against the enforcement of pre-existing property rights held by B except in two situations: firstly, where B's right is protected by entry on the register (the defence of lack of registration that we introduced in Chapter 6, section 3.2); secondly, where B's interest is an overriding interest within Sch 3 of the LRA 2002. The means by which B protects his or her right by entry on the register is the entry of a 'notice'.[12] It should be noted that this protection is afforded to C '*at the time of registration*'[13] against pre-existing rights held by B '*immediately before the disposition*' (completion of the sale or mortgage).[14] That is the time at which C will accept A's title. C is not afforded protection against property rights arising in favour of B in the gap between disposition and registration. C's vulnerability in this period will be cured only by the introduction of e-conveyancing.[15]

---

[12] Ibid, ss 32–39.
[13] B will be registered as the proprietor of the estate transferred or, where B is a mortgagee, as proprietor of the charge. The creation of mortgages in registered land is discussed in Chapter 29.
[14] Law Commission Report No 271 (2001, [5.10]).
[15] The registration gap is explored in Chapter 9.

Provision for entry on the register (of limitations on A's owner's powers and of B's rights) accords with the mirror principle: it enables C to discover the material facts about the title. The category of overriding interests provides 'a very significant impediment' to the accuracy of the register.[16] By definition, these are interests that do not appear on the register, but which are immune from the defence of lack of registration. In the report that led to the enactment of the LRA 2002, the Law Commission sought to advance the mirror principle further, both by simplifying the mechanisms available to B to protect his or her property rights, and by restricting the number of overriding interests.[17] The Law Commission expressed the expectation that the introduction of e-conveyancing[18] will further enhance the accuracy of the register.[19]

The cumulative effect of the provisions of the LRA 2002 governing owner's powers and the effect of a registered disposition can be summarized as follows. C has a defence against B's pre-existing legal rights where C has provided valuable consideration and:

- the disposition complies with any limitations on A's owner's powers entered on the register as a restriction; and
- B's interest is not protected on the register by entry of a notice; and
- B's interest is not within the category of overriding interests.

Hence, to understand the scheme of priorities provided for registrable dispositions, it is necessary to consider these three topics.

3 RESTRICTIONS ON OWNER'S POWERS

A 'restriction' is the means by which limitations on A's owner's powers are recorded on the register. A restriction may be entered by or with the consent of A, as registered proprietor (or a person entitled to be registered as proprietor),[20] by B, as a person with an interest or a claim to an interest in the land,[21] or by the Registrar.[22]

The nature and scope of restrictions is explained in s 40 of the LRA 2002.

Land Registration Act 2002, s 40

(1) A restriction is an entry in the register regulating the circumstances in which a disposition of a registered estate or charge may be the subject of an entry in the register.

(2) A restriction may, in particular—

  (a) prohibit the making of an entry in respect of any disposition, or a disposition of a kind specified in the restriction;

---

[16] Law Commission Report No 271 (2001, [2.24]).

[17] Ibid, [2.19] and [2.25].

[18] For further discussion of this, see Chapter 9.

[19] In particular, accuracy will be assisted by simultaneous creation and registration of interests other than the current registrable estates. See Law Commission Report No 271 (2001, [2.17] and [2.26]).

[20] Land Registration Act 2002, s 43(1)(a) and (b).

[21] Ibid, s 43(1)(c).

[22] Ibid, s 42.

(b) prohibit the making of an entry—

    (i)   indefinitely,

    (ii) for a period specified in the restriction, or

    (iii) until the occurrence of an event so specified.

(3 Without prejudice to the generality of subsection (2)(b)(iii), the events which may be specified include—

    (a) the giving of notice,

    (b) the obtaining of consent, and

    (c) the making of an order by the court or registrar.

(4) The entry of a restriction is to be made in relation to the registered estate or charge to which it relates.

In relation to priorities, the most significant use of a restriction is in relation to beneficial interests. As we have noted, on a transfer of land, the overreaching mechanism enables C to take the land free from B's beneficial interest, but only where C pays any purchase money to a minimum of two trustees or a trust corporation. Where land is held on trust, a restriction may be entered on the register to ensure that overreaching occurs on a disposition. Where there are two or more registered proprietors, the Registrar is obliged to enter a restriction to this effect.

Land Registration Act 2002, s 44(1)

If the registrar enters two or more persons in the register as the proprietor of a registered estate in land, he must also enter in the register such restrictions as rules may provide for the purpose of securing that interests which are capable of being overreached on a disposition of the estate are overreached.

The entry of this restriction ensures that overreaching takes place and therefore facilitates the operation of the curtain principle.

The effect of a restriction is explained in s 41 of the LRA 2002.

Land Registration Act 2002, s 41

(1) Where a restriction is entered in the register, no entry in respect of a disposition to which the restriction applies may be made in the register otherwise than in accordance with the terms of the restriction, subject to any order under subsection (2).

(2) The registrar may by order—

    (a) disapply a restriction in relation to a disposition specified in the order or dispositions of a kind so specified, or

    (b) provide that a restriction has effect, in relation to a disposition specified in the order or dispositions of a kind so specified, with modifications so specified.

(3) The power under subsection (2) is exercisable only on the application of a person who appears to the registrar to have a sufficient interest in the restriction.

It is important to note that the effect of a restriction is therefore confined to preventing registration of the disposition. On an ordinary sale or mortgage of registered land, where an application for registration proceeds from disposition (completion of the transfer), the restriction takes effect only at that final stage. Notwithstanding, as Cooke explains, failure to comply is disastrous for the purchaser or mortgagee.

Cooke, *The New Law of Land Registration* (2003, p 53)

It [a restriction] is a trip-wire to prevent the making of an *entry* of a disposition; it does not actually prevent the making of the disposition itself. Thus it does not prevent a transfer of a registered estate in contravention of the terms of the restriction; but the transfer could not then be registered, and so could not actually transfer the legal estate, would not overreach anything, and would not confer any protection on the purchaser pursuant to section 29. Contravention of a restriction does not prevent a disposition but makes the disposition disastrous for the purchaser.

In essence, failure to comply therefore has a twofold effect: firstly, it prevents legal title passing to C; secondly, it removes C from the protection afforded by the overreaching mechanism[23] and from the distinct priority rules applied to registrable dispositions. C would be left with an equitable title and, under the general law, bound by all pre-existing property rights held by B.[24] Given these consequences, a purchaser would not proceed with completion without ensuring compliance with restrictions: for example, ensuring purchase money is paid to two trustees.

4 ENTRY OF A NOTICE

A notice plays a distinct role from a restriction. As we have seen, entry of a restriction tells C something about A's owner's powers: specifically, it informs C of limitations on those powers. In contrast, entry of a *notice* tells C about property rights claimed by B. It informs C of rights that—if, in fact, they exist—will be enforceable against him or her.

Entry of a notice in registered land must not be confused with the *doctrine* of notice in unregistered land. As we have seen in Chapter 15, the doctrine of notice (or the defence of bona fide purchaser) governs the enforceability of certain equitable property rights against a purchaser of unregistered land. It is concerned with the whole process of the investigation of an unregistered title. Entry of a notice in registered land is used to secure the enforcement of legal and equitable property rights against C. It relates solely to the entry of a notice on the register. Sparkes avoids terminological confusion by referring to entry of a notice in registered land as a 'Land Registry notice'.[25]

---

[23] The relevance of the entry of a restriction to the operation of the overreaching mechanism is considered in Chapter 20.

[24] Under the general rule for competing equitable interests that priority is determined according to the order of creation.

[25] Sparkes, *A New Land Law* (2nd edn, 2003, [20.02]).

4.1 NATURE AND EFFECT

The nature and effect of a notice is provided by s 32 of the LRA 2002.

Land Registration Act 2002, s 32

(1) A notice is an entry in the register in respect of the burden of an interest affecting a registered estate or charge.

(2) The entry of a notice is to be made in relation to the registered estate or charge affected by the interest concerned.

(3) The fact that an interest is the subject of a notice does not necessarily mean that the interest is valid, but does mean that the priority of the interest, if valid, is protected for the purposes of sections 29 and 30.

Two points are notable in relation to this provision. Firstly, the description of a notice as entry of a 'burden' encapsulates the idea that the entry informs C of a third party's property right, subject to which he or she will take title to the land. This has a direct impact on the types of right in respect of which it is appropriate to enter a notice. Entry of a notice is confined to property rights that it is anticipated will bind C.[26]

Secondly, entry of a notice does not guarantee the validity of the property right claimed. This is in contrast to the effect of registration of title. Registration of A as proprietor of a legal estate operates to vest A with legal title. Entry of a notice by B to the effect (for example) that B has a restrictive covenant over A's land does not vest B with a restrictive covenant; instead, it ensures only that *if B in fact has a restrictive covenant*, that restrictive covenant will be enforceable against C.

Cooke suggests terminology to reflect this difference. She describes the entry of a notice as 'recording' an interest, in contradistinction to 'registration' of title.[27]

4.2 SCOPE

As has been noted above, the entry of a notice is confined to property rights held by B that are intended to bind C. The LRA 2002 does not attempt to provide an exhaustive list of property interests in respect of which entry of a notice is possible; instead, the Act defines interests that cannot be protected by the entry of a notice.

The most important of these are contained in s 33(a)–(c) of the 2002 Act.[28]

Land Registration Act 2002, s 33

No notice may be entered in the register in respect of any of the following—

    (a) an interest under—

---

[26] Law Commission Report No 271 (2001, [6.9]).

[27] Cooke, *The New Law of Land Registration* (2003, pp 4 and 72).

[28] An explanation of all property rights excluded from entry of a notice is provided in Law Commission Report No 271 (2001, [6.8]–[6.16]).

> (i)   a trust of land, or
>
> (ii) a settlement under the Settled Land Act 1925 (c. 18),
>
> (b) a leasehold estate in land which—
>
> (i)   is granted for a term of years of three years or less from the date of the grant, and
>
> (ii) is not required to be registered,
>
> (c) a restrictive covenant made between a lessor and lessee, so far as relating to the demised premises,

The rationale for each of these exclusions is different. Entry of a notice in respect of a trust is prohibited, because beneficial interests under a trust are not intended to bind C. The overreaching mechanism (supported by entry of a restriction) should ensure that C takes free from beneficial interests. Preventing entry of a notice in relation to a trust is therefore consistent with the curtain principle. Short leases, excluded from entry as a notice, are enforceable against C as overriding interests.[29] Leasehold covenants are excluded, because their enforcement is subject to a separate statutory scheme.[30]

With these exclusions in mind, the category of interests in respect of which notice may be entered is broad. It is an appropriate means of protection for any property right that is not specifically excluded. This includes, for example, equitable mortgages, restrictive covenants, legal and equitable easements, legal leases of more than three years (to a maximum of seven years),[31] estate contracts, rights to occupy conferred by the Family Law Act 1996 (FLA 1996),[32] and an inchoate equity arising from a claim to proprietary estoppel.

4.3 APPLICATION FOR ENTRY OF A NOTICE

As with a restriction, an application for entry of a notice may be made by the registered proprietor or a person claiming an interest in the land.[33] The Registrar may also enter a notice.[34] Notices are subdivided into 'agreed' and 'unilateral'. Each type of notice serves the same function: each ensures that B's property right binds C on a registrable disposition. A unilateral notice is entered where the registered proprietor has not given consent and the Registrar is not satisfied as to the validity of B's claim.[35] The Registrar will then notify the registered proprietor of the entry.[36] The registered proprietor may apply to have a unilateral notice cancelled.[37] The person whose interest is protected by the notice is informed of the application and given a limited timeframe in which to respond.[38] If no response is received, then the notice is cancelled.[39] If notice is received and agreement cannot be reached, the matter is

---

[29] Land Registration Act 2002, Sch 3, para 1.

[30] Contained in the Landlord and Tenant (Covenants) Act 1995. This Act is discussed in Chapter 25.

[31] Leases of more than seven years are registrable estates.

[32] These rights of occupation are explained in Chapter 18.

[33] Land Registration Act 2002, s 34.

[34] Ibid, s 37.

[35] Ibid, s 34(3).

[36] Ibid, s 35.

[37] Ibid, s 36.

[38] Ibid, 36(2).

[39] Ibid, s 36(3). Permitted time frames are given in the Land Registration Rules 2003 (SI 2003/1417), r 86(3).

referred to the adjudicator.[40] If the claim to a property right is made out, then an appropriate entry will be made.[41] A unilateral notice may also be cancelled by the beneficiary.[42]

The Registrar has the power to enter a notice in respect of a number of interests that would be enforceable against the transferee as overriding interests on first registration of title.[43] This power brings those property rights (against which C has no defence) onto the register. The Registrar has a duty to enter a notice on the estate that has the burden of an interest created by various dispositions.[44] For example, on the registration of a legal lease, the Registrar enters a notice of the lease on the freehold title out of which the lease has been created;[45] on the registration of a legal easement, the Registrar will enter a notice on the estate with the burden of the easement.[46]

5 OVERRIDING INTERESTS

As we have noted, overriding interests[47] constitutes a category of property rights that do not appear on the register, but which are immune from the defence of lack of registration. They have been described as the 'crack in the mirror' of title[48] and as making the idea of a perfect register a 'myth'.[49] The Law Commission's rationale for their continued existence is simple: the category acknowledges that there are circumstances in which it is unreasonable to expect B to register his or her property right to secure its enforcement.[50] The necessary breadth of the category in light of this rationale is more contentious. The LRA 2002 has reduced the number of overriding interests from the previous legislation. The policy adopted by the Act (as explained by the Law Commission) is that *interests should only have overriding status where protection against buyers was needed, but where it was neither reasonable to expect nor sensible to require any entry on the register*.[51]

The 2002 Act provides two distinct lists of overriding interests: those overriding at first registration (listed in Sch 1); and those overriding on a disposition of a registered estate (listed in Sch 3). First registration is treated separately, because the intention is to reflect the state of the title at that time. Whether C is bound by any overriding interests will have been determined prior to registration.[52] Our discussion focuses on interests overriding on a disposition of a registered estate—that is, those transfers that are subject to the distinct priority rules contained in ss 29 and 30 of the LRA 2002.

40 Land Registration Act 2002, s 73.

41 Law Commission Report No 271 (2001, [6.31]). This may take the form, e.g., of the entry of an agreed notice or of a restriction.

42 Land Registration Act 2002, s 35(3).

43 Ibid, s 37. The interests in relation to which this power is exercisable are listed ibid, Sch 1.

44 Ibid, s 38.

45 Ibid, s 27(2)(b).

46 Ibid, s 27(2)(d).

47 Ibid, Sch 3, refers to this category as *'interests which override registered dispositions'*. The expression 'overriding interests' is not used in the Act, but is the terminology of the Land Registration Act 1925 and remains a useful form of reference.

48 Hayton, *Registered Land* (3rd edn, 1981, p 76).

49 Cooke (2003, p 76).

50 Law Commission Report No 254, *Land Registration for the Twenty-First Century: A Consultative Document* (1998, [4.4]). For further discussion of this rationale, see Chapter 17.

51 Law Commission Report No 271 (2001, [8.6]).

52 For further discussion, see Law Commission Report No 271 (2001, [8.3]–[8.5]); Harpum. and Bignell, *Registered Land: The New Law* (2002, [2.47]).

The full list of these overriding interests is contained in Sch 3 of the 2002 Act. Our discussion is confined to those contained in paras 1–3 of the Schedule, short leases, property rights held by those in actual occupation, and legal easements and profits *à prendre*.

We begin with the most important and notorious[53] category.

5.1 PROPERTY RIGHTS HELD BY PERSONS IN OCCUPATION

Property rights held by persons in actual occupation are given the status of overriding interests in Sch 3, para 2. This category is different in its scope from all other categories. Those categories confer the status of overriding interest on a particular property right. This paragraph, instead, confers the status of overriding interest on any property right held by a person in occupation. Its focus is therefore on the factual position of the holder of the right, not the type of property right held.[54]

Land Registration Act 2002, Sch 3, para 2

An interest belonging at the time of the disposition to a person in actual occupation, so far as relating to land of which he is in actual occupation, except for—

(a) an interest under a settlement under the Settled Land Act 1925 (c. 18);

(b) an interest of a person of whom inquiry was made before the disposition and who failed to disclose the right when he could reasonably have been expected to do so;

(c) an interest—

   (i) which belongs to a person whose occupation would not have been obvious on a reasonably careful inspection of the land at the time of the disposition, and

   (ii) of which the person to whom the disposition is made does not have actual knowledge at that time;

(d) a leasehold estate in land granted to take effect in possession after the end of the period of three months beginning with the date of the grant and which has not taken effect in possession at the time of the disposition.

It should be noted that occupation is the trigger for protection, but not the subject of protection. The subject of protection is B's property rights. In most cases, B's property rights will have some connection to his or her occupation, but this not necessary.[55] Further, and importantly, if B is in occupation, but is not entitled to any property rights (for example, where B is a licensee), then B has nothing capable of binding C under Sch 3, para 2. The time of disposition (completion of the sale) is key: that is the time at which B's occupation is assessed and only those property rights held by B at the time of the disposition are protected.[56] Protection is confined to the geographical extent of B's occupation. This reverses

---

[53] Law Commission No 254 (1998, [5.56]).

[54] Cooke (2003, p 79).

[55] See, e.g., *Webb v Pollmount* [1966] Ch 584, in which a tenant's option to purchase the freehold reversion was protected as an overriding interest.

[56] Contrast the position under the Land Registration Act 1925. In *Abbey National Building Society v Cann* [1991] 1 AC 56, the House of Lords held that C's interests at the time of registration were protected as long as C was in occupation at the time of the disposition.

the decision under the Land Registration Act 1925 (LRA 1925) in *Ferrishurst Ltd v Wallcite Ltd*,[57] in which a property right (an option to purchase) extending over offices and a garage was protected even though B was in occupation of the offices only.

This category of overriding interest (and its predecessor in the 1925 Act) has provided a key role in enforcing beneficial interests against purchasers and, particularly, mortgagees, where the beneficial interests have not been overreached because there has been one trustee of the trust. In the typical case, this has arisen where one partner is the sole registered proprietor of the family home but his or her spouse, or cohabitee, has acquired a beneficial interest through a resulting or constructive trust (the operation of which in the context of the home is considered in Chapter 18). The immunity from the defence of lack of registration afforded to the property rights of occupiers is considered to be consistent with the policy underlying the recognition of these and other informal rights.[58] A person who has obtained their rights informally is unlikely to seek to protect those rights by entry on the register. The provision also accords with the expectations of those in occupation.[59]

Strand Securities Ltd v Caswell [1965] Ch 958, CA

Lord Denning MR

At 979–80

Fundamentally its object is to protect a person in actual occupation of land from having his rights lost in the welter of registration. He can stay there and do nothing. Yet he will be protected. No one can buy the land over his head and thereby take away or diminish his rights. It is up to every purchaser before he buys to make inquiry on the premises. If he fails to do so, it is at his own risk. He must take subject to whatever rights the occupier may have.

Prior to the LRA 2002, the property rights of occupiers were protected as overriding interests in s 70(1)(g) of the LRA 1925. Decisions made under that legislation remain of interest, although caution must be exercised, because the current provision has made substantive differences to the scope of the provision.

5.1.1 Actual occupation

The requirement of actual occupation was contained in s 70(1)(g) of the 1925 Act. The general principles developed in case law under that earlier provision may be expected to remain authoritative—but this is subject to the qualification (considered below) that Sch 3, para 2, has introduced a defence based on reasonable inspection.

Hayton identified two approaches to the interpretation of actual occupation.

Hayton, *Registered Land (3rd edn, 1981, p 87)

On the absolutist view [...] a person is absolutely bound by the rights of every person in actual occupation of the land [...] It matters not that it is unreasonably difficult to ascertain

---

[57] [1999] Ch 353.
[58] Law Commission Report No 254 (1998, [5.61]).
[59] Ibid, [5.61].

the actual occupier [...]; it matters not that it is unreasonable to expect someone to discover certain unusual rights of the occupier [...] Any traditional doctrine of notice is excluded from the self-contained paragraph.

The constitutionalist view of those accustomed to traditional conveyancing is that a person is only bound by the rights of every person in actual occupation [...] so far as such rights are binding according to traditional conveyancing principles (concerned with legal interests, equitable interests and the doctrine of notice, express, constructive and imputed) except as expressly limited or extended by statute.

In the following case, the House of Lords signalled the adoption of the absolutist approach.

Williams & Glyn's Bank v Boland [1981] AC 487, HL

Facts: Mr Boland was the sole registered proprietor of the home in which he lived together with his wife. He used the home as security for a loan from the bank and subsequently defaulted on the payments. Mrs Boland, in fact, had a beneficial interest in the home as a result of contributions that she had made to its purchase. She argued that, because she was in occupation of the home, her interest bound the bank as an overriding interest. The first question that arose was whether she was in actual occupation. (The case was a consolidated action arising from claims by the bank against Mrs Boland and, in the other case, a Mrs Brown.)

Lord Wilberforce

At 504–6

Were the wives here in "actual occupation"? These words are ordinary words of plain English, and should, in my opinion, be interpreted as such. [...]

Then, were the wives in actual occupation? I ask: why not? There was physical presence, with all the rights that occupiers have, including the right to exclude all others except those having similar rights. The house was a matrimonial home, intended to be occupied, and in fact occupied by both spouses, both of whom have an interest in it: it would require some special doctrine of law to avoid the result that each is in occupation. Three arguments were used for a contrary conclusion. First, it was said that if the vendor (I use this word to include a mortgagor) is in occupation, that is enough to prevent the application of the paragraph. This seems to be a proposition of general application, not limited to the case of husbands, and no doubt, if correct, would be very convenient for purchasers and intending mortgagees. But the presence of the vendor, with occupation, does not exclude the possibility of occupation of others. There are observations which suggest the contrary in the unregistered land case of *Caunce v. Caunce* [1969] 1 W.L.R. 286, but I agree with the disapproval of these, and with the assertion of the proposition I have just stated by Russell L.J. in *Hodgson v. Marks* [1971] Ch. 892, 934. Then it was suggested that the wife's occupation was nothing but the shadow of the husband's—a version I suppose of the doctrine of unity of husband and wife. This expression and the argument flowing from it was used by Templeman J. in *Bird v. Syme-Thomson* [1979] 1 W.L.R. 440, 444, a decision preceding and which he followed in the present case. The argument was also inherent in the judgment in *Caunce v. Caunce* [1969] 1 W.L.R. 286 which influenced the decisions of Templeman J. It somewhat faded from the arguments in the present case and appears to me to be heavily obsolete. The appellant's main and final position became in the end this: that, to come within the paragraph, the occupation in question must be apparently inconsistent with the title of the vendor. This, it was suggested, would exclude the wife of a husband-vendor because her apparent occupation would be satisfactorily accounted for by his. But, apart from the rewriting of the paragraph which this would involve, the suggestion is unacceptable. Consistency, or inconsistency, involves the absence, or presence, of an independent right to occupy, though I must observe that "inconsistency" in this context is an inappropriate word. But how can either quality be predicated of a wife, simply qua wife? A wife may, and everyone knows this, have rights of her own, particularly, many wives have a share in a matrimonial home. How can it be said that the presence of a wife in the house, as occupier, is consistent or inconsistent with the husband's rights until one knows what rights she has? and if she has rights, why, just because she is a wife (or in the converse case, just because an occupier is the husband), should these rights be denied protection under the paragraph? If one looks beyond the case or husband and wife, the difficulty of all these arguments stands out if one considers the case of a man living with a mistress, or of a man and a woman—or for that matter two persons of the same sex—living in a house in separate or partially shared rooms. Are these cases of apparently consistent occupation, so that the rights of the other person (other than the vendor) can be disregarded? The only solution which is consistent with the Act (section 70 (1) (g)) and with common sense is to read the paragraph for what it says. Occupation, existing as a fact, may protect rights if the person in occupation has rights. On this part of the case I have no difficulty in concluding that a spouse, living in a house, has an actual occupation capable of conferring protection, as an overriding interest, upon rights of that spouse.

The House of Lords held that Mrs Boland's beneficial interest was therefore enforceable against the bank as an overriding interest. The decision was controversial at the time, because it brought to light the previously unanticipated vulnerability of purchasers and mortgagees to beneficial interests being enforceable as overriding interests. Its significance has been highlighted in Chapter 1, in which the decision was examined as an illustration of the tensions in issue when questions arise as to the enforcement of property rights against banks.

The adoption of the absolutist approach to defining occupation was only one step in the decision that led to the enforcement of Mrs Boland's interest. While other aspects of the case have provided the focus of much subsequent discussion,[60] the approach to occupation was significant.

Tee, 'The Rights of Every Person in Actual Occupation: An Enquiry into Section 70(1)(g) of the Land Registration Act 1925' (1998) 57 CLJ 328, 345

The *Boland* judgments were uncompromising, and suggested that it would no longer be necessary or relevant to consider concepts of notice when assessing occupation [...]. However, such a radical departure from previously held assumptions is not generally successfully achieved by one case alone, even if that case emanates from the House of Lords.

Despite the decision in *Boland*, the constitutionalist view of occupation garnered support at Court of Appeal level.

---

60 In particular, the relationship between overreaching and overriding interests (discussed in Chapter 20), and the treatment of a beneficial interest under a trust for sale as an interest in land, contrary to the doctrine of conversion (discussed in Chapter 19, section 5.3).

Lloyds Bank plc v Rosset [1989] Ch 350, CA

Facts: Mr Rosset was the sole registered proprietor of a semi-derelict house that he and his wife were renovating and into which they were to move as their home. Builders were undertaking work on the house and Mrs Rosset was there almost daily, assisting in the decorating. Mr Rosset mortgaged the house and defaulted on the repayments. Mrs Rosset argued that she had a beneficial interest in the house that was enforceable against the bank as an overriding interest. In the Court of Appeal, Mrs Rosset's claim to a beneficial interest under a constructive trust was successful. The Court therefore considered whether she was in actual occupation.

Purchas LJ

At 403–4

The application of the words "in actual occupation" in section 70(1)(g) is the aspect of this appeal that has given me the most concern. The provisions of the section clearly were intended to import into the law relating to registered land the equitable concept of constructive notice. Thus, a purchaser or a chargee acquiring the title to or an interest in the land where the vendor was not in actual possession in order to protect his interest had to make appropriate inquiries if he found someone else in occupation of the property. [. . .]

In order for the wife's interest in the property to qualify as an overriding interest under section 70(1)(g) two things must be established: (a) was she in actual occupation? and (b) would appropriate inquiries made by the bank have elicited the fact of her interest?

The majority of the Court of Appeal held that Mrs Rosset was in occupation and had a beneficial interest enforceable against the bank. The case went on appeal to the House of Lords, where it was held that Mrs Rosset did not, in fact, have a beneficial interest.[61] She therefore did not have any property right capable of protection as an overriding interest and the issue of occupation did not arise for decision.

The difference between the absolutist and constitutionalist approach is of practical significance in marginal cases of occupation. The danger of the *Boland* approach is that it appeared to leave purchasers and mortgagees vulnerable to beneficial interests claimed by those whose occupation was not discoverable.

Sparkes suggested that the approaches to occupation in *Boland* and *Rosset* may have separate fields of application.

Sparkes, 'The Discoverability of Occupiers of Registered Land' [1989] Conv 342, 346–7

It remains to be seen how this notice-orientated test to the finding of actual occupation [in *Rosset*] is to be reconciled with the plain English test proposed by Lord Wilberforce in Boland. Lord Wilberforce was concerned with a person who clearly was in physical occupation albeit sharing with the mortgagor, and not a person whose occupation was marginal. It is tentatively submitted that his dictum should not be viewed as having binding force in these different circumstances.

---

[61] This aspect of the case is considered in Chapter 18.

The classic illustration of marginal occupation is undiscoverable occupation. The denial by Lord Wilberforce in *Williams & Glyn's Bank Ltd. v. Boland* of a link between overriding interests and notice occurred in a case in which occupation was obvious. It was left to academics to formulate hypothetical cases in which the issue would precisely arise for decision. Situations which five years ago had seemed fanciful products of the need for academic novelty have now emerged from the examination room to become the concern of practising conveyancers and the courts. A choice between absolutism or constitutionalism is likely to form the ratio of a decision very shortly, probably in relation to undiscoverable occupiers.

No such decision was forthcoming at the time of the LRA 2002. That Act has introduced, in Sch 3, para 2(c)(i) (extracted above), a qualification to the scope of protection afforded to occupiers based on reasonable inspection.

5.1.2 The reasonable inspection qualification

Schedule 3, para 2(c)(i), of the LRA 2002 protects C against overriding interests claimed by B, by virtue of actual occupation, where two conditions are met: firstly, that B's occupation is not obvious on a reasonably careful inspection; secondly, that C did not actually know of the existence of B's property right at the time of the disposition.

This provision steers a careful course between *Boland* and *Rosset*, and between the absolutist and constitutionalist views. The absolutist view is rejected, in so far as the rights of those in occupation do not necessarily bind a purchaser or mortgagee. But in mapping the scope of the exception, the Law Commission disavows the relevance of concepts derived from the doctrine of notice.

Law Commission Report No 254, *Land Registration for the Twenty-First Century: A Consultative Document* (1998, [5.71]–[5.72])

[…] Any requirement that [occupation should have to be apparent] it was said, would introduce into land registration the doctrine of notice. […] While we entirely agree that the doctrine of notice should not be introduced into registered land, we do not agree that limiting actual occupation to cases where it is apparent would have that effect.

[…] The test is whether the right is apparent on a reasonable inspection of the land, not whether the right would have been discovered if the purchaser had made all the enquiries which ought reasonably to have been made.

It is suggested that, subject to the exclusion of those whose occupation falls outside the qualitative requirement, *Boland* remains authoritative as the general approach to adopt to defining actual occupation.

Jackson argues that the reasonable inspection qualification is misconceived.

Jackson, 'Title by Registration and Concealed Overriding Interests: The Cause and Effect of Antipathy to Documentary Proof' (2003) 119 LQR 660, 665–7

Contrary to the reasoning of the Law Commission, it is submitted that a reasonable inspection defence will not limit the impact of occupational overriding interests upon the purchaser's registered estate. There are two arguments that support this view. First, there are other important observations that may be drawn from the differences in method of proof of title. A reasonable inspection requirement has no normative content. [...] the resurrection of the reasonable inspection defence provides no meaningful guidance to purchasers as to the fact or extent of the inspection required of them. In effect, such a defence will not preclude the concealed overriding interest. Although the Law Commission indicates the type of conduct that may amount to "actual occupation", in order to discover an adverse occupational right, a purchaser would require a type of knowledge that was neither based in law nor in fact. The normative guidance of the 2002 Act emphasises the conclusiveness of the register and online inspections. Thus, a purchaser may end up by being bound by an interest that was objectively apparent to the legally minded officious bystander but which was undiscoverable to the purchaser if only because he did not know what he was looking for.

Secondly, there is an implied premise behind the methodology employed by the 2002 Act to reduce the circumstances in which occupational interests will take effect as overriding the estate of a registered proprietor. This premise is the connection of ideas that a purchaser, under s.70(1)(g), risked taking his title subject to a concealed overriding interest because there was no reasonable inspection defence. This is a logically flawed connection. The Law Commission assumes that the absence of an apparency requirement within s.70(1) (g) resulted in the extension of overriding protection to the interests of undiscoverable occupants. It is undeniable that some constructions of the paragraph impose onerous duties of inspection on purchasers. However, these duties resulted from wide interpretations of the type of occupation that could be considered to be apparent and were not the consequence of the absence of such a requirement. This mistaken orthodoxy exists in both registered and unregistered conveyancing.

The underlying issue in debate as to the correct scope of protection afforded to occupiers lies in the tension between the desire for a conclusive register and the acknowledgment that there are circumstances in which a requirement of registration would be unreasonable. As Jackson explains, the reasonable inspection qualification does not make the register any more conclusive.[62]

5.1.3 Assessing occupation

In *Lloyds Bank v Rosset*,[63] the Court of Appeal acknowledged that occupation should be assessed by reference to the state of the property. Mrs Rosset's daily visits were sufficient to show occupation of a semi-derelict house: occupation does not require physical presence. In *Chhokar v Chhokar*,[64] a wife in hospital to have a baby was considered to remain in actual occupation of the home despite her physical absence. Her possessions evidenced her occupation.

In contrast, in *Stockholm Finance Ltd v Garden Holdings Inc*,[65] a Saudi princess was not considered to be in occupation of her London home, in which she had not 'set foot' for a year. In *Abbey National Building Society v Cann*,[66] preparatory acts of moving furniture into a home minutes before completion of the sale took place were not considered to establish

---

62 Jackson, 'Title by Registration and Concealed Overriding Interests: The Cause and Effect of Antipathy to Documentary Proof' (2003) 119 LQR 660, 675.

63 [1989] Ch 350, 377.

64 [1984] FLR 313.

65 [1995] NPC 162.

66 [1991] 1 AC 56.

occupation at the time of the disposition. The reasonable inspection qualification may be expected to produce the same outcomes in these cases, subject to the possibility of the occupation of an absent person being successfully hidden.[67]

5.1.4 Occupation by proxy

In *Lloyds Bank plc v Rosset*,[68] the Court of Appeal accepted that builders were in actual occupation on behalf of Mrs Rosset. Nicholls LJ suggested that whether occupation by an employee or agent sufficed depended on the '*function which the employee or agent is discharging*'. The difficulty with this test is that it shifts focus away from the nature of the occupation: B's resident housekeeper occupies on B's behalf, while B's licensee does not,[69] although the evidence of occupation in each case may be indistinguishable. In *Lloyd v Dugdale*,[70] Mr Dugdale used business premises in his capacity as managing director of a company in which he was also the majority shareholder. He was considered to be in occupation solely on behalf of the company and therefore a property right that he acquired in his personal capacity was not binding as an overriding interest when the premises were sold.

It is unclear what impact the reasonable inspection qualification may have on cases involving occupation by proxy. It may now be appropriate to ask, in each case, whether occupation by B is reasonably obvious on an inspection of the land that reveals the physical presence of an agent or employee. The adoption of this approach would have the advantage of shifting the focus away from the function of the occupier. But *Lloyd v Dugdale* raises a separate issue, because courts do not generally look behind the corporate veil.

5.1.5 Occupation by children

In *Boland*, in the passage of his judgment extracted above, Lord Wilberforce rejected the shadow doctrine as a means of denying Mrs Boland's occupation. The doctrine has its origins in unregistered land, but had been applied in registered land to deny a claim to an overriding interest by a spouse. Its effect can be shortly stated.

Bird v Syme-Thomson [1979] 1 WLR 440, HC

Templeman J

At 444

In my judgment, when a mortgagor is in actual occupation of the matrimonial home, it cannot be said that his wife also is in actual occupation. I hasten to add that, equally, if the mortgagor is the wife and the house is occupied as the matrimonial home, then it is the wife who is in actual occupation and not the husband.

A spouse in occupation with a sole legal owner was therefore not considered to occupy in his or her own right, but merely as the shadow of the owner.

---

[67] Compare *Kingsnorth Finance Ltd v Tizard* [1986] 1 WLR 783. The case is discussed in Chapter 15.
[68] [1989] Ch 350, 377.
[69] Compare the examples discussed by Nicholls LJ in *Lloyds Bank plc v Rosset* [1989] Ch 350, 377, and *Strand Securities v Caswell* [1965] Ch 958.
[70] [2002] 2 P & CR 13. See esp [42]–[49].

Despite its rejection in *Boland* in relation to a spouse, the shadow doctrine was applied in relation to minor children in *Hypo Mortgage Services Ltd v Robinson*.[71] Nourse LJ considered it 'axiomatic' that such children are not in actual occupation for the purposes of statutory provisions governing overriding interests, but are present '*as shadows of occupation of their parent*'.[72] Nourse LJ justified the application of the doctrine by difficulties of making inquiries of children. It has been argued that other means of circumventing this difficulty are available.[73] Ultimately, however, the likelihood of children having property rights is arguably too slim to justify changes in conveyancing practice.

5.1.6 The relevance of inquiry

Non-disclosure by B of his or her property rights prevents reliance on Sch 3, para 2 of the LRA 2002. The need for inquiries to be made directly of B replicates the position under the LRA 1925,[74] but the 2002 Act introduced a new limitation to this exception: B is only denied protection where disclosure could reasonably have been expected. The practical impact of this limitation is yet to become apparent. As we have noted, protecting the rights of occupiers as overriding interests is considered consistent with the policy underlying the recognition of informal rights. These rights are particularly significant in the context of the home, and often arise on the basis of the parties' intention and conduct during the course of their relationship. B may be unaware of the existence of a claim until the relationship is subjected to legal analysis at a time of crisis—including a priority dispute with C. If B does not know that he or she has a property right, then will non-disclosure prevent reliance on Sch 3, para 2?

The answer is not apparent on the face of the provision. On the one hand, by making inquiries, C has done all that the provision requires and B should be estopped[75] from asserting an undisclosed claim; on the other hand, it is inherent in the provision that making inquiries will not necessarily protect C against B's property rights.

Dixon suggests that, in some circumstances, ignorance may excuse non-disclosure, but acknowledges that the criterion is a source of uncertainty.

Dixon, 'The Reform of Property Law and the Land Registration Act 2002: A Risk Assessment' [2003] Conv 136, 146–7

Thus, the right holder loses overriding status (after failure to disclose) only if disclosure could reasonably be expected to be made. Such disclosure might not be reasonably expected where, say, the right holder did not know, and could not reasonably be expected to know, that they actually had a right (e.g. in cases of uncrystallised estoppel). While this is a welcome reform, there are uncertainties. For example, is it "reasonable" to expect disclosure when the right holder knows that the consequences of disclosure will be the loss of the family home because the purchaser will take steps to acquire the property free from the right?

---

[71] [1997] 2 FLR 71.

[72] Ibid, at 72.

[73] See, e.g., Cooke, 'Children and Real Property: Trusts, Interests and Considerations' [1998] Fam Law 349. She suggests that inquiries could be made of a person with parental responsibility.

[74] *Hodgson v Marks* [1971] Ch 892.

[75] This is the basis on which then operation of the provision is explained in Law Commission Report No 271 (2001, [8.60]).

Presumably it is, because otherwise it will always be permitted to withhold disclosure if that would result in the loss of a property right and that would defeat the point of the provision. However, the circumstances in which a person may be asked about their rights are many and varied, and the introduction of a reasonableness criterion must introduce uncertainty that can only be settled by litigation.

There is some cause to question whether the provision was actually intended by the Law Commission. The Law Commission did not describe the effect of inquiries as limited to B's reasonable disclosure, but instead referred to limiting C's obligation to that of making reasonable inquiries.[76] The Law Commission may have intended the latter,[77] but the former has been enacted. A limitation based on reasonable disclosure by B is substantively different from one based on reasonable inquiries by C.

5.2 SHORT LEASES

With some exceptions,[78] legal leases created for seven years or less are overriding interests within Sch 3, para 1, of the LRA 2002. This provision therefore covers legal leases that fall below the duration at which a lease becomes a registered estate. The combined effect of this paragraph and s 33 of the Act (concerned with entry of a notice) is to give a dual means of protection to legal leases of more than three years, but not greater than seven years. These leases may be protected by entry of a notice and are overriding interests in the absence of such an entry. Legal leases of three years' duration or less are protected only as overriding interests. Equitable leases fall outside the scope of Sch 3, para 1 (which is confined to 'leases *granted*'). An equitable lease that is not protected by entry of notice may be an overriding interest under Sch 3, para 2, where the tenant is in actual occupation.

5.3 EASEMENTS AND PROFITS À *PRENDRE*

Legal easements and profits are overriding interests under Sch 3, para 3, of the LRA 2002.

Land Registration Act 2002, Sch 3, para 3

(1) A legal easement or profit a prendre, except for an easement, or a profit a prendre which is not registered under the Commons Registration Act 1965 (c. 64), which at the time of the disposition—

(a) is not within the actual knowledge of the person to whom the disposition is made, and

(b) would not have been obvious on a reasonably careful inspection of the land over which the easement or profit is exercisable.

---

[76] Law Commission No 254 (1998, [5.69]); Law Commission No 271 (2001, [8.60]). The latter is equivocal. The paragraph is headed '*Rights not disclosed on reasonable inquiry*', although the text refers to a failure to disclose a right '*when* [C] *could reasonably have been expected to do so*'. The wording of the provision is unchanged to that contained in the Bill annexed to the report.

[77] The Law Commission did not intend to change the law, but to reflect an assumption underlying the requirement of inquiries in the Land Registration Act 1925: Law Commission No 254 (1998, [5.69]). A requirement of reasonable inquiries is consistent with this intent.

[78] Listed in the 2002 Act, Sch 3, para 1(a) and (b).

(2) The exception in sub-paragraph (1) does not apply if the person entitled to the easement or profit proves that it has been exercised in the period of one year ending with the day of the disposition.

The scope of this paragraph needs to be understood in light of the general treatment of easements within the 2002 Act. The express grant of a legal easement is a registered disposition and such easements necessarily appear on the register.[79] Paragraph 3 is therefore directed at legal easements that arise from an implied grant.[80] The limitation of the provision to legal easements is significant: the equivalent provision in the LRA 1925 had controversially been interpreted as including some equitable easements.[81] Equitable easements will now bind B only if protected by entry on the register.

The scope of the paragraph appears abstruse, but, unpackaged, it provides as follows: a legal easement arising from an implied grant is overriding if C has actual knowledge of its existence, or it is obvious on a reasonably careful inspection of the land, or it has been exercised in the year preceding the disposition. The latter is designed to ensure the protection of practically important, but 'invisible', easements, including drainage in an underground pipe.[82]

The provision has been tightly drawn and is intended to dovetail with inquiries made by C. The underlying goal is that C should become aware of binding easements prior to completion of the disposition.

Law Commission Report No 271, *Land Registration for the Twenty-First Century: A Conveyancing Revolution* (2001, [8.71])

What we wish to encourage is the creation of a straightforward system of standard inquiries as to easements and profits which will prompt sellers to disclose what they can reasonably be expected to know. This in turn will ensure that such rights are then registered. We anticipate that, prior to contract, a seller would be expected to disclose any unregistered easements or profits affecting his or her property of which he or she was aware, at least to the extent that they were not obvious on a reasonably careful inspection of the land. In particular, he or she would be asked to disclose any easements or profits that had been exercised in the year preceding the inquiry. The result of such inquiries is likely to be that the buyer will have actual knowledge of any unregistered legal easements and profits long before the transaction is completed.

6 INVESTIGATION OF REGISTERED TITLE AND SEARCH OF THE REGISTER

The investigation of title to registered land, like its unregistered counterpart, requires both a search of the register and a physical inspection of the land. Physical inspection is directed at discovering the existence of overriding interests. A search of the register will

---

79 Ibid, s 27(2)(e).
80 The rules governing the implied grant of easements are considered in Chapter 26.
81 Land Registration Act 1925, s 70(1)(a), as interpreted in *Celsteel Ltd v Alton House Holdings Ltd* [1985] 1 WLR 204.
82 Law Commission No 271 (2001, [8.70]).

reveal entries both of restrictions, informing the purchaser of limitations on A's owner's powers, which must be complied with to benefit from ss 29 and 30 of the LRA 2002, and of notices, informing B of pre-existing property rights that will be enforceable against him or her.

The defence against the enforcement of B's pre-existing rights (other than those entered on the register or binding as overriding interests) provided by ss 29 and 30 of the 2002 Act applies at the time of registration against interests held by B at the time of the disposition. C will search the register between contract and the completion of the disposition. There is a risk of property rights arising after the search has been made and before the disposition is completed. To offset this risk, provision is made for C to obtain an official search with priority protection. This prevents new entries being made on the register for thirty working days.[83]

7 REGISTRATION, FRAUD, AND LIABILITY

Sections 29 and 30 of the LRA 2002 place in a privileged position, as far as priorities are concerned, registrable dispositions of a registered estate made for valuable consideration. C is provided with a defence against the enforcement of B's pre-existing property rights that are not entered on the register or protected as overriding interests. Should C be able to utilize this protection if the transaction is tainted by fraud or other wrongdoing? Where fraud affects the validity of the transaction between A and C, the issue is one of indefeasibility of title. The rules governing the circumstances in which an alteration of the register is possible have been discussed in Chapter 9. In this chapter, we are concerned with fraud or other wrongdoing that does not affect the transaction between A and C, but which, if C can invoke ss 29 or 30, would confer on him or her a defence against a pre-existing property right held by B.[84] Few would argue that C's conduct should be left unchecked in such circumstances, but the appropriate response is more contentious.

Torrens systems of registration of title have a two-pronged response to transactions involving fraud and wrongdoing that would enable C to invoke a defence against pre-existing property rights.[85] Where the transaction is considered to constitute fraud (a term defined specifically for this purpose), C is denied statutory protection and is bound by B's pre-existing property rights. Where wrongdoing falls short of fraud, *in personam* liability is imposed. A new direct right is created between C and B, which may either involve C being held personally liable to B, or the creation of property rights in favour of B. Hence, the label *in personam* is misleading in so far as it appears to be a synonym for personal liability: in fact, the liability may be either personal or proprietary. The difference between these solutions is illustrated in Figure 12.

---

[83] Land Registration Act 2002, ss 70 and 72, and Land Registration Rules 2003 (SI 2003/1417), rr 147–154.

[84] The distinction between these two issues is highlighted by Cooke and O'Connor, 'Purchaser Liability to Third Parties in the English Land Registration System: A Comparative Perspective' (2004) 120 LQR 640, 640–3.

[85] This summary of the Torrens approach is based on the account provided ibid.

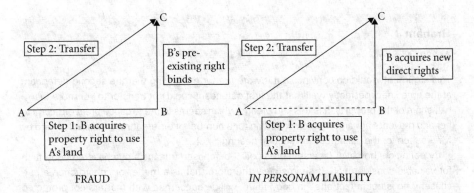

Figure 12 Torrens fraud and *in personam* liability

While English law has eschewed the explicit adoption of the same scheme of liability, the same choices arise: C can either be held bound by B's pre-existing property right, or a new direct right may be imposed. Where the latter is the case, that right may be personal or proprietary. Under the LRA 1925, a controversial decision in *Peffer v Rigg*[86] adopted the former solution. As we will see, however, the court's reasoning was erroneous and would not be possible under the LRA 2002. Instead, focus has been shifted to the imposition of new direct rights under the general law.

7.1 THE LAND REGISTRATION ACT 1925 AND THE DECISION IN *PEFFER V RIGG*

To understand the decision, it is necessary to explain briefly some of the provisions of the LRA 1925. Section 20 of the 1925 Act performed the function now found in s 29 of the LRA 2002. Section 59 of the 1925 Act, with exceptions, provided that purchasers were not concerned with matters not entered on the register, '*whether he has or has not notice thereof, express, implied or constructive*'. Section 74 of the 1925 Act provided that parties dealing with a registered estate were not '*affected with notice of a trust express, implied or constructive*'. Section 3 of the LRA 1925 defined a purchaser as '*a purchaser in good faith for valuable consideration*'.

Peffer v Rigg [1977] 1 WLR 285, HC

Facts: Mr Peffer and Mr Rigg had married two sisters, and therefore had a common relative in their mother-in-law. Mr Peffer and Mr Rigg jointly bought a house that was a home for their mother-in-law. The house was purchased in Mr Rigg's sole name, although he held on trust for himself and Mr Peffer. Following the breakdown of the Rigg's marriage, Mr Rigg transferred the house to his wife for £1 as part of their divorce settlement. Mrs Rigg knew of Mr Peffer's beneficial interest, but argued notwithstanding that it was unenforceable against her under the terms of the Act.

---

[86] [1977] 1 WLR 285.

Graham J

At 293–4

This argument would be convincing if it were not for my finding that the second defendant at the time knew perfectly well that the first defendant could not transfer to her more than a half share of the property. It is this knowledge which seems to me to cause great difficulty to her and prevents her argument succeeding for a number of different reasons put forward by Mr. Poulton for the plaintiff at the second hearing. [...]

By definition, however (see section 3 (xxi), "purchaser" means a purchaser in good faith for valuable consideration. It seems clear therefore that as a matter of construction a purchaser who is not in fact one "in good faith" will be concerned with matters not protected by a caution or other entry on the register, at any rate, as I hold, if he has notice thereof. If these sections 20 and 59 are read together in the context of the Act they can be reconciled by holding that if the "transferee" spoken of in section 20 is in fact a "purchaser" he will only be protected if he has given valuable consideration and is in good faith. He cannot in my judgment be in good faith if he has in fact notice of something which affects his title as in the present case. Of course if he and, a fortiori, if a purchaser from him has given valuable consideration and in fact has no notice he is under no obligation to go behind the register, and will in such a case be fully protected. This view of the matter seems to me to enable the two sections to be construed consistently together without producing the unreasonable result of permitting a transferee purchaser to take advantage of the Act, and divest himself of knowledge of defects in his own title, and secure to himself a flawless title which he ought not in justice to be allowed to obtain.

The principal difficulty with this judgment is that, in defining Mrs Rigg's actual knowledge as constituting bad faith, the decision apparently ignores provisions in the LRA 1925 that provided for notice to be irrelevant. Essential to the decision was the existence of a definition of purchaser as acting 'in good faith'.

In the subsequent unregistered land decision in *Midland Bank Trust Co Ltd v Green*[87] (which is discussed fully in Chapter 15), a purchaser with actual notice of an unregistered land charge was held to be able to rely on a defence provided in the Land Charges Act 1925 (LCA 1925), now the Land Charges Act 1972 (LCA 1972) against the enforcement of unregistered land charges. In holding that the purchaser's notice was irrelevant, the House of Lords relied on the absence of a requirement of good faith purchase in the LCA 1925.

Cooke and O'Connor suggest that, while the basis of the decision in *Peffer v Rigg* is wrong, the right result was achieved.

Cooke and O'Connor, 'Purchaser Liability to Third Parties in the English Land Registration System: A Comparative Perspective' (2004) 120 LQR 640, 653–4

The reasoning was wrong, while the result was right. The ratio, revealed in the words quoted above, was: this purchaser has notice, therefore she is not in good faith. This nullifies one of the main benefits of a title registration system, taking away from a purchaser with notice all the protection of a registered disposition and moving back to the position that obtained under the early English deeds registration statutes. Yet simply to condemn the decision as

[87] [1981] AC 513.

incorrect is unhelpful, for clearly this is not the sort of arms' length purchaser for whom the protection of the old s.20 was intended. It is unsatisfactory for Mrs Rigg to take free of Mr Peffer's interest.

There are two alternative bases on which the same outcome could have been achieved. Firstly, Graham J held that Mrs Rigg was not a purchaser for valuable consideration.[88] This, in itself, provided a means for precluding her from relying on the statutory protection.

Secondly, as we will see, Graham J considered, obiter, that a new direct right arose on the transfer to Mrs Rigg. Hence if she had not been bound by Mr Rigg's pre-existing property right, an alternative route to liability was available.

The enforcement of C's pre-existing property rights where C has actual notice has attracted some academic support as introducing an ethical element into registration.[89] But the Law Commission considered it to run counter to the policy of registration of title and doubted the weight of ethical concerns.[90]

Law Commission Report No 254, *Land Registration for the Twenty-First Century: A Consultative Document* (1998, [3.46])

[...] We have concluded—as the Law Commission has done on two previous occasions—that there should in general be no place for concepts of knowledge or notice in registered land. We have reached this conclusion for the following reasons—

1. It was intended that the system of registration under the Land Registration Act 1925 should displace the doctrine of notice.

2. There is little evidence of which we are aware that the absence of the doctrine of notice in dealings with registered land has been a cause of injustice in the seventy-two years in which the present system has been operative.

3. The ethical argument is weaker than at first sight it appears to be if the issue is considered in relation to those principles which should in our view, guide the development of land registration. Registration should be regarded as an integral part of the process of creating or transferring interests in registered land, closely akin to the formal requirement of using a deed (or in some cases, writing) in unregistered conveyancing. Just as a deed is required to convey or create a legal estate or interest in unregistered conveyancing, a disposition of registered land must be completed by registration if it is to confer a legal estate or interest. When electronic registration is introduced, it seems probable that many rights will be incapable of being created *except* by registering them.

4. In practice, if it were provided that unregistered rights in or over registered land were binding because a purchaser had *actual* knowledge of them, it would be very difficult to prevent the introduction by judicial interpretation of doctrines of *constructive* notice. If actual knowledge sufficed, the question would inevitably be asked: why not wilful blindness as well? In reality the boundary between actual knowledge and constructive notice is unclear and is, in our view, incapable of precise definition.

---

[88] [1977] 1 WLR 285, 293.

[89] Battersby, 'Informal Transactions in Land, Estoppel and Registration' (1995) 58 MLR 637, 655–6. The issue is discussed in Law Commission No 254 (1998, [3.44]–[3.46]).

[90] The recommendation endorsed in the paragraph extracted here was adopted in Law Commission No 271 (2001, [5.16]).

5. The mere fact that a purchaser *could* be bound if he or she had actual knowledge of an unregistered right or interest would inevitably weaken the security of title that registered land at present provides. Disappointed third parties, who found their rights apparently defeated by a purchaser, would threaten litigation. Because of the nuisance value of such threats, purchasers would often settle out of court.

Cooke and O'Connor argue that in focusing on notice-based liability the Law Commission lost sight of the possible role that could be played by a requirement of good faith, where a finding of bad faith requires something more than mere notice.

Cooke and O'Connor, 'Purchaser Liability to Third Parties in the English Land Registration System: A Comparative Perspective' (2004) 120 LQR 640, 657–8

Thus, a useful baby (purchaser-liability for Torrens fraud because of the absence of good faith) has been thrown out with the bathwater (purchaser-liability for notice). And all the argument is directed at the bathwater; arguments against imposing liability on the purchaser for Torrens fraud, or against requiring good faith on the purchaser's part, are simply not given. *Peffer v Rigg* has caused such a backlash that potentially good law has been rejected, because of the overwhelming need to reject the reasoning in *Peffer*.

It is clear that the reasoning adopted in *Peffer v Rigg* could not be followed under the LRA 2002. Central to that decision was the definition of purchaser in the LRA 1925 as a purchaser in good faith, and ss 29 and 30 of the 2002 Act require only that the disposition is for valuable consideration.

7.2 THE LAND REGISTRATION ACT 2002: A FOCUS ON NEW DIRECT RIGHTS

In rejecting the enforcement of B's pre-existing property rights against C on the basis that C has notice, the Law Commission emphasized the possibility of new direct rights arising on appropriate facts.

Law Commission Report No 254, *Land Registration for the Twenty-First Century: A Consultative Document* (1998, [3.48]–[3.49])

Furthermore, [...] the law provides a wide range of *personal* remedies against those who in some way behave improperly. The operation of these personal remedies can be demonstrated by four examples.

1. If A transfers trust property to [C] in breach of trust and [C] knows or (perhaps) has notice of this, [C] is liable as constructive trustee for "knowing receipt" of trust property. Liability is personal and not proprietary and the obligation is to make restitution for the loss suffered by the trust. It has been assumed that this form of liability may apply

where the trust property transferred is registered land and the rights of the beneficiaries have not been protected, so that as a matter of property law, the transferee takes the land free of the trust

2. If property is transferred by A to [C] expressly subject to some right of [B's] which will not in fact bind [C], a constructive trust may be imposed upon [C] if he refuses to give effect to [B's] right in circumstances in which that refusal is unconscionable. [C] can in this way be compelled to give effect to [B's] rights. [...]

3. There may be circumstances where tortious liability is imposed because A conspires with [C] to defeat [B's] proprietary rights.

4. If [C] induces A by misrepresentation or undue influence to charge his or her property to [B] to secure [C's] debts, A will be able to set the charge aside if [B] has notice of [C's] misconduct.

In each of these cases, a purchaser may acquire the registered land free from the rights of the third party, yet find himself personally liable for the loss suffered by that third party or subject to some personal equity, which enables the transaction to be set aside. [...]

Although described by the Law Commission as 'personal remedies', this is a misnomer. It is apparent from the examples given that the Law Commission, in fact, is referring to new direct rights that may either be personal (1, 3, and 4) or proprietary (2).

The creation of new direct rights has been discussed in Chapter 7. Land law does not exist in a vacuum and the possibility of such rights arising on a transfer is beyond doubt—but reliance on other principles is not without controversy or difficulty. The scope of liability is no longer dependent on the land law statutes and tension may arise where liability is imposed in circumstances that run contrary to land law principles: for example, if a new direct right were to arise on the basis of notice. The objection may be acute where the new liability was proprietary, although Thompson has argued further that purchasers should also be protected against personal liability in such circumstances.[91]

Reliance on the imposition of new direct rights causes difficulty simply because the application of these principles is not generally well developed in the land law context. This is particularly the case as regards personal liability, outside of undue influence (4), which has its own developed jurisprudence in relation to mortgages. The possibility of personal liability based on knowing receipt of trust property (1) was suggested, obiter, as an alternative basis for the decision in *Peffer v Rigg*.[92] Graham J considered that Mrs Rigg's knowledge of the trust was sufficient to render her personally liable to Mr Peffer even if his pre-existing interest did not bind her through lack of good faith.

The creation of new direct rights on a transfer 'subject to' some right of B (2) has been considered in Chapter 8 and is drawn from the doctrine in *Rochefoucauld v Boustead*,[93] which has been discussed in Chapter 14. Under the LRA 2002, the development of these principles may become more significant.

[91] Thompson, 'Registration, Fraud and Notice' (1985) 44 CLJ 280.
[92] [1977] 1 WLR 285, 294.
[93] [1897] 1 Ch 196.

8 CONCLUSION

The LRA 2002 provides a distinct scheme of priority rules for a category of transactions (registrable dispositions of registered estates for valuable consideration) that incorporates the most common dealings with land. C has a defence against the enforcement of B's pre-existing property rights, except those that are entered on the register by a notice (the defence of lack of registration) or binding as an overriding interest. The disposition must also comply with any limitations on A's owner's powers recorded on the register by entry of a restriction.

There is a need to find a satisfactory reconciliation between the operation of these statutory defences, and ensuring that fraud and wrongful conduct by C does not go unchecked. The policy of the 2002 Act is to rely on the creation of new direct rights arising under the general law. This may involve the imposition on C of personal liability to B, or the creation of new direct rights. But the scope of principles governing the imposition of new direct rights is largely undeveloped in the land law context.

QUESTIONS

1. What do you understand to be meant by a 'registrable disposition of a registered estate for valuable consideration'? What is the significance of this category of transaction for determining questions of priority in registered land?

2. To what extent do the priority rules in registered land implement the 'mirror' and 'curtain' principles?

3. Compare and contrast the scope and effect of entry of a restriction and entry of a notice.

4. How useful are the constitutionalist and absolutist views of the meaning of 'actual occupation' in determining the scope of Sch 3, para 2, of the Land Registration Act 2002?

5. Assess the advantages and disadvantages of responding to fraud or other wrong-doing in a disposition of land to B by: (i) preventing B from invoking statutory defences against C's property rights; and (ii) relying on the creation of new direct rights.

6. What action should the holder of the following property rights in registered land take? In what circumstances will a purchaser of the land have a defence against the enforcement of these rights?

    (a) A beneficial interest under a trust.

    (b) A legal lease created for five years.

    (c) A legal easement arising from an implied grant.

    (d) A restrictive covenant.

FURTHER READING

Cooke, *The New Law of Land Registration* (Oxford: Hart, 2003, chs 4–5)

Cooke and O'Connor, 'Purchaser Liability to Third Parties in the English Land Registration System: A Comparative Perspective' (2004) 120 LQR 640

Dixon, 'The Reform of Property Law and the Land Registration Act 2002: A Risk Assessment' [2003] Conv 136

Jackson, 'Title by Registration and Concealed Overriding Interests: The Cause and Effect of Antipathy to Documentary Proof' (2003) 119 LQR 660

Law Commission Report No 254, *Land Registration for the Twenty-First Century: A Consultative Document* (1998, Pts IV–VII)

Law Commission Report No 271, *Land Registration for the Twenty-First Century: A Conveyancing Revolution* (2001, Pts V, VI, and VIII)

Sparkes, 'The Discoverability of Occupiers of Registered Land' [1989] Conv 342

Thompson, 'Registration, Fraud and Notice' (1985) 44 CLJ 280

17

EVALUATING THE LAND
REGISTRATION ACT 2002

CENTRAL ISSUES

1. The provisions of the Land Registration Act 2002 have a profound effect in land law. We have seen in previous chapters that those provisions affect the acquisition of legal estates and interests in land (see especially Chapters 9 and 10), as well as the defences available to a pre-existing legal or equitable property right in land (see especially Chapters 6 and 16).

2. This chapter gives us a chance to stand back and examine the impact of the 2002 Act. Firstly, we will consider the possible purposes of a registration system and then the specific aims of the Act itself. Secondly, we will bring together some of the material covered in previous chapters in order to summarize the effect of the Act. Thirdly, we will evaluate the Act, by asking both whether the Act achieved its stated purpose and whether that purpose is, in any case, worthwhile.

3. In considering the effect of the 2002 Act, it is useful to look at the three questions that we considered in Chapter 1, section 3—that is, the *content*, *acquisition*, and *defences* questions. As we will see, the chief impact

of the Act is on the second and third of those questions.

4. In analysing the 2002 Act, we have to be careful to separate out its current and future effects. The Act was designed to facilitate a general system of e-conveyancing. That system is not yet fully in place. So we need to distinguish the current effect of the 2002 Act from the effect that it will have in the future, when a general system of e-conveyancing has been established and consequential changes have been made to the registration rules.

5. In evaluating the 2002 Act, we need to ask if we approve of the answers that it provides to the *acquisition* and *defences* questions. This is not simply a matter of comparing the provisions of the Act to its predecessor, the Land Registration Act 1925; rather, to evaluate the 2002 Act, we have to compare the results that it produces in particular situations with what we would regard as the best results in those cases. This, of course, raises the very difficult question of how we are to decide, in the abstract, what is the 'best possible result' in any particular case.

1 INTRODUCTION: THE AIMS OF THE LAND REGISTRATION ACT 2002

1.1 THE GENERAL AIMS OF REGISTRATION

When considering the possible aims of a registration system, it is important to bear in mind that the usefulness of registration is not confined to land law. The following extract refers to two examples in which rights unrelated to land may be registered. The first concerns the registration of company shares; the second, the registration of security interests over company assets.

McFarlane, *The Structure of Property Law* (2008, pp 82–3)

The central purpose of any register is to provide *publicity*. For example, a register of births, marriages and deaths gives interested parties the opportunity to discover important information about a community. The publicity provided by a register of rights may be useful to a number of different groups: for example, it may provide the State with information it can use when making tax assessments [...]

Registration can thus be particularly useful to C [a party acquiring a right from A], both in disputes about the use of a thing and in disputes about the use of a right. A registration system can protect C against the two chief risks he faces when attempting to acquire a right:

1. A, the party C deals with, may in fact lack the power to give C the right. This is the risk from which a register of rights, such as a register of company share-holders, aims to protect C.

2. Even if A does have the power to give C the right, B may have a pre-existing right that he can assert against C and that will thus reduce the value of C's right. This is the risk from which a register of pre-existing powers or rights, such as a register of floating charges against a company's rights,[1] aims to protect C.

[...] The publicity provided by a register of rights can never provide C with full protection: in practice, no such register can ever be completely accurate. In Example 1, a register may record A as the holder of some shares, but can C be sure that the register is correct? In Example 2, a register may make no mention of a pre-existing floating charge but, again, can C be sure that the register is correct? Of course, if the register is not complete, C may have to make his own enquiries as to whether A is indeed a holder of the shares; or whether there is a floating charge against A Co's assets. The usefulness of having a register will then be reduced: C will have to spend time and money on his own investigations; as a result the possible deal between A and C will be delayed, or perhaps even called off.

Ideally, C would like to have a *guarantee*. In Example 1, he wants a guarantee that: (i) if A is recorded as the holder of the shares, then (ii) A does indeed hold those shares. In Example 2, he wants a guarantee that: (i) if there is no floating charge recorded on the register; then (ii) no-one will be able to assert such a power against him. Such a guarantee can only be provided if *legal consequences* are attached to the fact that a right is, or is not, recorded on a register. Once those legal consequences exist, registration no longer operates neutrally, as a

---

[1] [As we will see in Chapter 29, section 3.4, a floating charge is a particular form of security interest: e.g., it can be used by a company to give a lender security over that company's current and future assets.]

simple record. Rather, registration begins to operate as a legal concept. This introduction of legal consequences allows registration systems to affect the basic structure of property law and hence to have a greater impact on resolving the **basic tension** [i.e. the tension between the wishes of B, on the one hand, and of C, on the other].

1.2 THE PROMINENCE OF REGISTRATION IN LAND LAW

If a party (A) has a legal freehold of land in England or Wales, or a legal lease of such land with more than seven years to run, A can[2] register with the Land Registry[3] as the holder of that legal estate. Indeed, the overwhelming majority of such freeholds and leases are now registered. This means that the rules imposed by the Land Registration Act 2002 (LRA 2002) will apply to regulate A's dealings with his or her registered estate. For example, as we saw in Chapter 9, a transfer of A's registered legal estate to C will only be complete once C is registered as the new holder of that legal estate. And, if C has provided something of value in return for that registered estate (e.g. if C has bought it from A), C may then gain protection against a pre-existing property right of B that has not been noted on the register. That protection comes from the lack of registration defence provided by the LRA 2002, which we considered in Chapter 6, section 3.2, and Chapter 16.[4]

In Chapter 6, section 3.2, as well as in Chapter 15,[5] we also noted that a form of registration scheme applies even if A's legal freehold or lease is *not* registered at the Land Registry. In relation to such unregistered land, the Land Charges Act 1972 (LCA 1972) may function to give C (a party acquiring a right from A) a defence against a pre-existing property right of B: the case of *Midland Bank Trust Co Ltd v Green*,[6] which we examined in Chapter 6, section 3.1, provides a memorable example.

It is therefore clear that registration is a particularly important concept in land law. As the following extract suggests, the prominence of registration can perhaps be explained by the special features of land (as examined in the extract from the same author set out in Chapter 1, section 4).

McFarlane, *The Structure of Property Law* (2008, pp 86–7)

Registration is particularly prominent in land law. We can explain this by looking at the special features of land [...]

1. Due to its fixed location, each piece of land is easy to identify. As a result, if a register exists, it is easy to look up a particular piece of land in that register.

---

[2] As we saw in Chapter 9, section 5, if A seeks to transfer to C an unregistered freehold or lease with more than seven years to run, then C will *have* to register in order to acquire a legal estate; it is not, however, compulsory for A, an unregistered holder of such a freehold or lease, to register that right.

[3] Formally titled Her Majesty's Land Registry, the organization now brands and refers to itself without a definite article—that is, as 'Land Registry' rather than 'the Land Registry'. In this book, however, we have used the more conventional appellation.

[4] See, e.g., Chapter 16, section 2.2.

[5] See, e.g., Chapter 15, section 5.8.

[6] [1981] AC 513.

2. Due to its capacity for multiple, simultaneous use, as well as its social importance, the list of [legal and equitable property rights in land] is longer than the list of such rights in things other than land. So, if C acquires a right in land from A, there is an increased risk to C of being bound by a pre-existing right of B.

3. Due to its permanence, there is an increased risk of a pre-existing [legal or equitable property right] existing in relation to a particular piece of land. So, if C acquires a right in land from A, there is an increased risk to C of being bound by a pre-existing right of B.

4. Due to its limited availability, land is already very expensive. As a result, there is a particularly strong desire to limit the time and cost C must expend in acquiring a right in land. The more expensive the process of buying land becomes, the more difficult it becomes for those of even average wealth to acquire the land they need to set up a home or run a business.

So, the special features of land both: (i) make a registration system possible; and (ii) justify the extra protection such a system can provide to C. However, this leaves open the question of *how* a land registration system should operate. The **basic tension** [between B and C] will govern not only *whether* the concept of registration applies, but also *how* it applies.

From one perspective, then, we can understand how a registration system can help to protect a party attempting to acquire a right in land (C) from both: (i) the risk that the party with whom he or she deals (A) may not have the power to give C such a right; *and* (ii) the risk that, even if A does have that power, another party (B) may have a pre-existing legal or equitable interest in land that binds C.

As the following extract notes, this 'conveyancing' perspective, focusing on the specific transaction between A and C, can be complemented, and broadened, by a consideration of the possible economic advantages of a registration scheme.

O'Connor, 'Registration of Title in England and Australia' in *Modern Studies in Property Law: Vol 2* (ed Cooke, 2003, pp 84–5)

While lawyers tend to view registration of title as a law reform project to overcome problems in common law conveyancing, governments and economists regard it as a market-supporting mechanism operated as a government program. The system is, as Mapp said, 'overwhelmingly administrative in operation',[7] with economic objects, namely, to improve security of title and to facilitate the transfer of interests in land. These two objects are found in the preamble to the very first English registration of title statute, the Land Registry Act 1862, which began: 'Whereas it is expedient to give certainty to the title to real estates and to facilitate the proof thereof and also to render the dealing with land more simple and economical'.

Economists have long recognised that secure property rights are a precondition for investment and economic growth. Puzzled by the difficulty of replicating the economic success of Western capitalism in the Third World, economists have in the past decade turned their attention to examining the nature of the legal institutions and property laws that underpin capitalism in developed countries. The new 'institutional economics' has rediscovered a long-overlooked connection between property laws and prosperity. Laws that ensure the

---

[7] Mapp, *Torrens' Elusive Title: Basic Principles of an Efficient Torrens System* (1978, p 63).

security and transferability of property establish the framework of incentives that enable the creation of new wealth from existing assets.

Secure titles have been found to contribute to economic growth in a multiplicity of ways. They provide owners with an incentive to invest in improving and developing their land, for they are assured of reaping the benefits for themselves. Owners who wish to invest are better able to obtain the development capital they need on favourable terms if they can offer a good title as collateral for a loan. If purchasers can easily satisfy themselves that the title they are acquiring is clear, the costs of transacting in land will fall. Lower transaction costs assist the market to allocate land assets to their most productive uses, by allowing them to pass to those who value them most highly.

1.3 THE AIMS OF A PARTICULAR LAND REGISTRATION SYSTEM

It is not enough simply to state that having *a* registration system can be useful in land law; we also have to ask what *sort* of registration system should apply. Certainly, it would be a mistake to think that all land registration systems are the same: even in the common law world,[8] the detail of the registration rules varies if we move from England and Wales to, for example, Australian or Canadian jurisdictions.

In particular, as the following extract explores, we need to ask how our registration system should balance the needs of a prior user of land (such as A or B) with those of a party later acquiring a right in relation to the land (such as C).

O'Connor, 'Registration of Title in England and Australia' in *Modern Studies in Property Law: Vol 2* (ed Cooke, 2003, pp 85–6)

A title to land is secure if it is at no risk, or no significant risk, of being found to be defective or subordinate to another interest. While economists assume that security of title is a good that property laws can bestow, it is, as Mapp said 'an elusive ideal',[9] for it incorporates contradictory elements. There are two competing aspects of security of title, that Demogue called 'static' and 'dynamic' security.[10]

Static security

The law of private conveyancing was based on the principle of static security, which protects the rights of existing owners at the expense, if necessary, of purchasers. This was achieved through rules such as *nemo dat quod non habet*,[11] the preference of both law and equity

---

[8] Of course, given that the special features of land are the same the world over, many civil law jurisdictions also have registration systems: for a useful survey of the position in other European jurisdictions, see Cooke, *The New Law of Land Registration* (2003, ch 9). In ch 1, Cooke notes, at p 2, that '*the ancient Egyptians, for example, kept a record of ownership in documentary form, so that land could be allocated accurately when it became accessible following the annual flooding of the Nile*'. She also notes that images of such a papyrus can be seen online, via the Duke (University) Papyrus Library: see now http://scriptorium.lib.duke.edu/papyrus/records/276r.html.

[9] Mapp, [n7 above] (1978, p 63).

[10] Demogue, 'Security' in *Modern French Legal Philosophy* (eds Fouillee et al, 1916).

[11] One many not grant a better title than one has.

for the interest first in time when adjudicating the priority of competing interests, and the doctrines of notice and equitable fraud. Equity's preference for the 'bona fide purchaser for value without notice' was an attempt to balance static security against the reasonable expectations of purchasers in good faith, but the standard of inquiry required of purchasers under the extended doctrine was onerous.

Conveyancing rules based on static security suited a society emerging from feudalism, where land ownership was confined to the privileged few, and was rarely traded. By the mid nineteenth century, England and Australia were developing market economies, in which value is captured through exchange. The old conveyancing rules inhibited exchange of land by imposing high transaction costs upon purchasers, and exposing them to the risk of acquiring defective or subordinate titles.

Dynamic security

The enactment of registration of title legislation in mid-nineteenth century England and Australia decisively shifted the conveyancing law towards the opposing principle of dynamic security. Dynamic security is provided by legal rules that protect the reasonable expectations of those who purchase in good faith. It facilitates exchange by reducing or eliminating the risk that the purchaser's title will be subject to unknown prior claims and title defects. This lowers transaction costs by limiting the inquiries that purchasers need to make. By relieving against risk, it also restores value to clouded titles [...]

The shift to dynamic security in the law of real and personal transactions was an essential condition for the operation of market capitalism. De Soto explains that, while the law in Western countries seeks to promote both types of security, dynamic security is favoured because of its greater economic importance:

'Although they are established to protect both the security of ownership and that of transactions, it is obvious that Western systems emphasize the latter. Security is principally focussed on producing trust in transactions so that people can more easily make their assets lead a parallel life as capital.'[12]

It is natural to equate dynamic security with protection for purchasers, but this is too simple. While dynamic security reduces purchasers' costs and risks in transactions, it also benefits owners. Without it, owners' titles can be disturbed years after purchase if a defect in their title or a prior interest comes to light within the relevant limitation period.

The 'security of title' object of registration refers to both static and dynamic security. The dilemma for the law is that the two stand in an inverse relationship. Measures that improve dynamic security tend to diminish static security to some extent, and vice versa. The law must determine how to balance dynamic and static security in the formulation of the rules, taking into account a range of policy considerations. Different evaluation of the considerations accounts for much of the variation and instability in the rules of registration of title systems.

It is clear that we have a number of choices to make when designing a registration system. Consider a case in which A is registered as holding a freehold of particular land. A then goes away for six months. X takes advantage of this by forging A's signature and claiming that A has transferred his registered freehold to X. X is registered as the new holder of A's freehold and then sells that estate to C. A returns and seeks possession of the land from C, as well as

---

[12] De Soto, *The Mystery of Capital* (2000, p 61).

asking to be reinstated to the register. This example raises the question of 'indefeasibility': how secure should C's position as registered proprietor be?

As we saw in Chapter 9, section 5.6, there are a number of possible approaches that a registration system can take to this question. For example, one solution could be to reinstate A as both possessor and registered owner, whilst ordering those in charge of the register and duped by X to pay compensation to C for the loss that C has incurred by relying on the register. Conversely, of course, A's claims for possession and reinstatement could be denied, but A could receive a compensation payment from those running the register.

Equally, consider a case in which B acquires a right of way, allowing B to get from a road to his land by walking or driving over A's neighbouring land. That right of way may be crucial to protecting the economic value of B's land. Certainly, it is capable of counting as an easement: a legal interest in land (see Chapter 3, sections 5 and 6, and Chapter 26). What should happen if B fails to register his easement and A then sells his estate to C? Static security may argue in B's favour; dynamic security favours C. And what if, although B's easement was unregistered, C did, in fact, *know* about B's right? In such a case, does C's knowledge make a difference? O'Connor notes, in the extract, above that: '*Dynamic security is provided by legal rules that protect the reasonable expectations of those who purchase in good faith.*' Yet, as we saw when examining *Midland Bank Trust Co Ltd v Green* in Chapter 6, section 3.1, it is also possible for a registration system to protect C even where C knows all about B's pre-existing, but unregistered, legal or equitable property right.

1.4 THE AIMS OF THE LAND REGISTRATION ACT 2002

So far, we have seen that: (i) there are good reasons why registration is particularly important in land law; and (ii) despite those reasons, a question remains as to precisely how a land registration system should operate. We can now focus on the LRA 2002 and its specific aims.

The 2002 Act resulted from the Law Commission's work: in the following extract, the Law Commission sets out its aims in producing the draft Bill that led to the Act. We considered parts of the following extract in Chapter 9, section 5.1, but given its importance in setting out the chief aim of the LRA 2002, it is worth seeing again—and in full.

Law Commission Report No 271, *Land Registration for the Twenty-First Century: A Conveyancing Revolution* (2001, [1.5]–[1.10])

The fundamental objective of the Bill is that, under the system of electronic dealing with land that it seeks to create, the register should be a complete and accurate reflection of the state of the title of the land at any given time, so that it is possible to investigate title to land on line, with the absolute minimum of additional enquiries and inspections.

Although that ultimate objective may seem an obvious one, its implications are considerable, and virtually all the changes that the Bill makes to the present law flow directly from it. The Bill is necessarily limited in its scope to registered land or to dealings with unregistered land in England and Wales that will trigger first registration. Although the great majority of titles are in fact now registered, there are still substantial amounts of land (particularly in rural areas) that are unregistered. However, as we explain in Part II, unregistered land has had its day. In the comparatively near future, it will be necessary to take steps to bring what is left of it on to the register.

The process of registration of title is conducted by the State through the agency of HM Land Registry. Indeed, the State guarantees the title to registered land. If, therefore, any person suffers loss as a result of some mistake or omission in the register of title, he or she is entitled to be indemnified for that loss. At present, there is no requirement that a disposition of registered land has to be entered in the register if it is to be effective. Even without registration, dispositions are valid not only between the parties to them, but as against many but not necessarily all third parties who subsequently acquire an interest in the same registered land. This is a necessity under the present law because there is a hiatus—called the "registration gap"—between the making of any disposition and its subsequent registration. The transfer or grant has to be submitted to the Land Registry for registration, which inevitably takes some time. It would be wholly unacceptable for the transfer or grant to have no legal effect in that interim period. It should be noted that there are some interests in registered land, presently known as overriding interests, which are not protected in the register at all but which nonetheless bind *any* person who subsequently acquires an interest in the land affected. This is so whether or not that person knew of, or could readily have discovered, the existence of these interests.

If it is to be possible to achieve the fundamental objective of the Bill mentioned [above]—

1. all express dispositions of registered land will have to be appropriately protected on the register unless there are very good reasons for not doing so;

2. the categories of overriding interests will have to be very significantly reduced in scope; and

3. dispositions of registered land will have to be registered simultaneously, so that it becomes impossible to make most dispositions of registered land except by registering them.

The aim stated in (3) will be possible only if conveyancing practitioners are authorised to initiate the process of registration when dispositions of registered land are made by their clients. This is a very significant departure from present practice.

To achieve the goals stated [above] will also require a change in attitude.

There is a widely-held perception that it is unreasonable to expect people to register their rights over land. We find this puzzling given the overwhelming prevalence of registered title. Furthermore, the law has long required compliance with certain formal requirements for the transfer of interests in land and for contracts to sell or dispose of such interests. The wisdom of these requirements is not seriously questioned. We cannot see why the further step of registration should be regarded as so onerous. In any event, under the system of electronic conveyancing that we envisage (and for which the Bill makes provision), not only will the process of registration become very much easier, but the execution of the transaction in electronic form and its simultaneous registration will be inextricably linked.

These changes will necessarily alter the perception of title to land. It will be the fact of registration and registration alone that confers title. This is entirely in accordance with the fundamental principle of a conclusive register which underpins the Bill.

In order to understand the LRA 2002, it is crucial to understand its basic aims, as stated by the Law Commission in the extract above. Firstly, the Act clearly aims to prioritize dynamic security: to protect a third party (C) attempting to acquire a legal property right in land from the risk of being bound by a pre-existing, but hidden, legal or equitable property right. So, in the first of the two examples given in section 1.3 above (where X fraudulently registers as the new holder of A's freehold and then sells to C), we would expect the Act to protect C rather than A. Indeed, if it is truly '*the fact of registration and registration alone that confers title*', we might even expect C to win if C *knew* about X's fraud. As we saw in Chapter 9, section 5.6, and as we will discuss in section 2.1.2 below, however, the 2002 Act does *not* adopt such an absolute position. Similarly, in the second of those two examples (where B fails to register an easement given to him by A), we would again expect the Act to protect C—this time, at B's expense. It would seem from the statements above that B should expect no sympathy for the failure to protect his or her right through registration, and that C will be protected even if C *knew* about B's right. But, as we saw in Chapter 16, section 5.3, and as we will discuss in section 2.1.4 below, the provisions of the 2002 Act do allow B, in certain circumstances, to assert an unregistered easement against C.

Secondly, it is clear that the standard use of e-conveyancing (and hence electronic registration) is a fundamental part of the scheme of the LRA 2002. Certainly, it is viewed as providing an important justification for protecting C against pre-existing, but unregistered, rights: the logic is that, because e-conveyancing makes it simpler for B to register a right, it becomes harder for B to excuse a failure to register, and thus fairer to protect C against any unregistered right of B. As we will see, e-conveyancing can also lead to the closing of the 'registration gap' referred to in the extract above: one depression of a key by A or C's solicitor or conveyancer can simultaneously finalize A's grant of a legal property right to C *and* C's registration as holder of that right.

Thirdly, and linked to the previous two points, is the fundamental idea that the registration system exists not to set out rights already acquired by parties such as A, B, and C, but, instead, to *create* those rights. In such a world, the register will *necessarily* be a '*complete and accurate reflection of the state of the title of the land at any given time*'. Indeed, there will be no external standard by which to check the accuracy of the register: anything on the register will be correct, simply because it *is* on the register.

Finally, it is important to remember that the Law Commission described its fundamental objective of a 'complete and accurate register' as an 'ultimate' objective. Certainly, the LRA 2002 did not aim to achieve its intended effects overnight. The most important outstanding step was, and remains, the standard use of e-conveyancing. This means that, when evaluating the Act, we need to be aware that its full impact cannot be determined unless and until that e-conveyancing system is fully operational. Nonetheless, the 2002 Act did make a number of very significant, immediate changes, taking effect independently of e-conveyancing. Those changes will be summarized in the next section and we will evaluate them in section 3.

Before discussing those changes, it is worth noting an important tension in the fundamental objective of the 2002 Act, as described by the Law Commission in the extract above. That tension stems from the notion that: (i) the register should be 'complete and accurate'; so that (ii) C can '*investigate title to land on line, with the absolute minimum of additional enquiries and inspections*'. Of course, if the register really were complete and accurate, there would be no need for *any* further investigation of title: such enquiries would be eliminated, rather than minimized. This tension suggests that the aim of making the register complete and accurate may not only be very difficult to achieve in practice, but may also be of dubious merit. Certainly, as we will see in the next section, it would be dangerous for C to think that he or she will *always* be fully protected from an unregistered, but pre-existing, property right of A or B.

2 THE IMPACT OF THE LAND REGISTRATION ACT 2002: A SUMMARY

In summarizing the impact of the LRA 2002, we need to distinguish between: (i) its immediate impact; and (ii) its possible future impact once the e-conveyancing system is fully operational. At each stage, a useful way to analyse the Act is to examine its effect on the ways in which B, a prior user of land, may attempt to assert a right against C, a party later acquiring a legal estate or interest in that land. Firstly, it is important to note that, as we saw in Chapter 7, the 2002 Act has *no* impact on the question of whether B can assert a new, direct right against C, arising as a result of C's conduct. This point is made clear in the Law Commission reports that led to the Act.[13] As a result, as we noted in Chapter 16, section 7.2, the possible means by which B can acquire a direct right against C (discussed in Chapter 7) are unaffected by the 2002 Act.

The focus of the LRA 2002 is therefore on the different question of whether B (or A) can assert a pre-existing legal or equitable property right against C. As we saw in Chapter 1, section 3, and Chapter 6, we can break that key question down into three specific questions.

1. The *content* question: does the right claimed by B count as such a property right?
2. The *acquisition* question: has B, in fact, acquired the right that he or she claims?
3. The *defences* question: if B does have a property right, does C have a defence to it?

In considering the immediate impact and future effect of the 2002 Act, we can focus on those three questions.

Before doing so, it is useful to remember an important effect of the LRA 2002, discussed in Chapter 10, section 5.3. There, we saw that the rules introduced by the Act make it impossible for an adverse possessor to claim that the lapse of time, by itself, has extinguished the legal estate of a registered proprietor. As a result, a registered proprietor is given far more effective protection against an adverse possessor than an unregistered holder of a legal estate. In evaluating the 2002 Act as a whole, it is important to take a view as to whether that particular change was desirable. To a large extent, that depends on a consideration of the merits of the claim of an adverse possessor—a question that we examined in Chapter 10, section 2. It is worth adding here, however, that the extra protection given to a registered proprietor against an adverse possessor may promote the Law Commission's goal of extending the number of registered titles: an unregistered holder of a freehold or long lease, even if he or she does not plan to deal with the land in the near future, may consider registering his or her legal estate so as to reduce the (admittedly small) risk of losing that estate due to another's adverse possession.

2.1 THE IMMEDIATE IMPACT OF THE LAND REGISTRATION ACT 2002

2.1.1 The *content* question

Dixon has pointed out that, in theory, we could have a registration system that simply ignores the fundamental divide between property rights and personal rights: it could, for

---

[13] See, e.g., Law Commission Report No 254, *Land Registration for the Twenty-First Century: A Consultative Document* (1998, [3.38]–[4.9]) and Law Commission Report No 271, *Land Registration for the Twenty-First Century: A Conveyancing Revolution* (2001, [4.11] and [7.7]).

example, stipulate that C can be bound by registered rights that are otherwise regarded as personal rights (e.g. contractual licences).[14] The LRA 2002 does *not* set out to do this: after all, given its chief aim is to give extra protection to C, it would be very surprising if it were systematically to allow personal rights to have an effect on C. But it is worth noting that, with the aim of promoting clarity, the Law Commission took a position on whether particular types of rights, the proprietary status of which is uncertain at best, are capable of binding C. And, thanks to what are now ss 115 and 116 of the 2002 Act, those rights (such as rights of pre-emption,[15] 'mere equities',[16] and 'equities by estoppel') are now prima facie binding on C.

Of course, even if B has such a right, it may still be possible for C to have a defence against it. Nonetheless, it is perhaps surprising that the Act has resolved these doubts in favour of B, rather than C. The Law Commission's position was not based on a particular policy, but rather on its view as to whether such rights were already recognized as equitable interests in land. As we saw in Chapter 13, section 5.3, however, when considering 'equities by estoppel', it may be that—in some cases, at least—the Law Commission's interpretation of the pre-existing law was overly generous to B.

2.1.2 The *acquisition* question: legal estates and interests

As we saw in Chapter 9, if a party (B or C) claims that A (a party with a registered freehold or lease) has granted B or C a legal estate or interest, the provisions of the LRA 2002 may be crucial. As we saw in Chapter 9, section 5.3.3, s 27 of the 2002 Act creates a category of 'registrable dispositions'—that is, certain dealings with A's registered estate that are not complete unless and until they are registered: for example, a transfer of A's registered estate is only complete if and when the transferee registers as the new holder of A's estate. And if A attempts to grant a legal lease of more than seven years,[17] the recipient of that lease again needs to register in order to acquire that legal estate. In addition, even if A's legal estate is *not* registered, certain dealings with that estate have to be registered before the other party can acquire a legal estate from A: for example, a transfer of an unregistered freehold is not complete until the transferee has registered that freehold. In this way, progress can be made to the Law Commission's goal of reducing the number of unregistered titles to land.

In those cases, registration can be seen to operate in a *negative* sense: if B or C fails to register a claimed legal estate, he or she fails to acquire that right. In some cases, this can, of course, assist C. For example, if C is registered as the new holder of A's freehold, B may claim that he or she has a pre-existing legal estate in the land, because A earlier transferred that freehold to B. But because B failed to register as the new holder of A's freehold, B's claim must fail: B's failure to register means that B failed to acquire A's freehold.

---

[14] Dixon, 'Proprietary and Non-Proprietary Rights in Modern Land Law' in *Land Law: Issues, Debates and Policy* (ed Tee, 2002, pp 26–8).

[15] Such as, e.g., a right of B to enter a contract with A *if* A chooses to sell his legal estate in land. For discussion of whether such a right counts as an equitable interest, see, e.g., *Pritchard v Briggs* [1980] Ch 338. For the Law Commission's discussion of whether such a right should be capable of binding C, see Law Commission Report No 271 (2001, [5.26]–[5.28]).

[16] Such as, e.g., a power of B to rescind a transfer of a legal estate to A, where that transfer was procured by an innocent misrepresentation of A. For the Law Commission's discussion of whether such a right should be capable of binding C, see Law Commission Report No 271 (2001, [5.32]–[5.36]).

[17] In addition, registration is also necessary in relation to certain exceptional forms of shorter lease: see Land Registration Act 2002, s 4(1)(b), (d), and (e) (cases of first registration) and s 27(2)(b)(ii)–(v) (where a lease is granted by a registered proprietor). See further Chapter 23, section 3.1.2.

In addition, in these cases, registration can also operate in a *positive* sense: if a party does register his or her legal estate, then that right is guaranteed—the fact of registration operates positively to mean that he or she has acquired that right. This result is produced by s 58 of the LRA 2002.

Land Registration Act 2002, s 58

Conclusiveness

(1) If, on the entry of a person in the register as the proprietor of a legal estate, the legal estate would not otherwise be vested in him, it shall be deemed to be vested in him as a result of the registration.

(2) Subsection (1) does not apply where the entry is made in pursuance of a registrable disposition in relation to which some other registration requirement remains to be met.

Section 58(1) thus has an important effect in the first example mentioned in section 1.3 above. If X manages to have herself registered as the new holder of A's freehold (even if that registration is fraudulent), then s 58 means that X is 'deemed' to have acquired a legal estate, simply as a result of her registration. Conversely, of course, because A is no longer registered as the holder of that freehold, A has lost his legal estate. This result seems very harsh on A: he surely does not deserve to lose his legal estate simply because X managed to trick the Land Registry by forging A's signature on the transfer documents?

This is where Sch 4 of the 2002 Act comes in. As we saw in Chapter 9, section 5.6.1, it is possible for the register to be changed: for example, a court (under Sch 4, para 2(1)(a)) or the Registrar (under Sch 4, para (5)(a)) can alter the register for the purpose of 'correcting a mistake'. It is true that Sch 4, para 6(2), sets out the basic position that a change affecting '*the title of the proprietor of a registered estate in land*' cannot be made without the consent of that proprietor (in our case, X) *if* that proprietor is in possession of the land. But Sch 4, para 6(2) (a), states that the basic position does not apply where the registered proprietor—like X in our cases—'*has by fraud or lack of proper care caused or substantially contributed to the mistake*'.

It is therefore clear that if A discovers X's fraud *before* X gives any rights to a third party, A's position will be secure. But what if, as in the first example mentioned in section 1.3 above, A discovers X's fraud only *after* X transfers X's registered freehold to C? The problem for A in such a case is that, under s 24 of the LRA 2002, X, whilst proprietor of the registered freehold, is able to 'exercise owner's powers' in relation to that legal estate. Those 'owner's powers' are set out by s 23 of the 2002 Act and include, for example, the power to transfer the registered estate. In such a case, we have a classic clash between 'static' and 'dynamic' security: A will argue that he should be reinstated on the register, just as he could have been if he had discovered X's fraud before the transfer to C; C will argue that, because he or she dealt with the registered proprietor and because the register should be regarded as conclusive, there are no grounds for A's reinstatement.

In such a case, if A's call for a change to the register succeeds, then, as long as C gave something in return when acquiring his estate from X, C will be entitled to an *indemnity* (see Chapter 9, section 5.6.1)—that is, a payment from the Registrar to compensate C for the loss that he or she will suffer as a result of the rectification of the register. A's claim for rectification can only succeed, however, if it is shown that C's registration is a 'mistake'.

Unfortunately, the meaning of that term is not clearly defined by the LRA 2002. The prevailing view (which we will consider further in section 3.1.1 below) is that the register will *not* be changed, because C's registration as the new proprietor involves no 'mistake': after all, despite her fraud, X *was* the registered proprietor when C dealt with her. As a result, X *was* able to exercise 'owner's powers', including the power to transfer the registered freehold to C. And, if C is in possession of the land, then Sch 4, para 6(2), means that A's application for reinstatement can only succeed if: (i) C '*has by fraud or lack of proper care caused or substantially contributed to the mistake*'; or (ii) '*it would for any other reason be unjust for the alteration not to be made*'.

If C does remain as registered proprietor, we would then expect A to receive an indemnity, as compensation for the loss caused to him by X's fraudulent registration. But there may be a slight difficulty here. A's most obvious route to an indemnity is Sch 8, para 1(1)(b), of the 2002 Act, which applies where A has suffered loss as a result of '*a mistake whose correction would involve rectification of the register*'. But if the argument against rectification is that, in fact, no mistake has been made (because X, by virtue of her registration, did have the power to transfer her estate to C), it is not immediately obvious that Sch 8, para 1(1)(b), applies. It is inconceivable that, in such a case, A will neither be reinstated nor receive an indemnity, but, to allow A an indemnity, a court or the Registrar may have to give the concept of 'correcting a mistake' one meaning when considering the powers to rectify under Sch 4, paras 2(1)(a) and 5(a) (there is no mistake to correct, because C's registration was not a mistake), and a different meaning when considering A's entitlement to an indemnity under Sch 8, para 1(1)(b) (there is a mistake to correct, because X's registration was a mistake).

2.1.3 The *acquisition* question: equitable interests

As it stands, the LRA 2002 does not affect the acquisition of equitable interests. This means that registration does not operate negatively: if B claims to have acquired an equitable interest from A, it is never necessary for B to show that his or her right has been recorded on the register. It also means that registration does not operate positively: B can never claim that he or she has acquired an equitable interest simply by virtue of having entered that right on the register. This does not, however, mean that registration is irrelevant when considering equitable interests: as we will see in section 2.1.4 below, if B fails to enter a notice on the register protecting his or her equitable interest, there is a risk that C, when later acquiring a right from A, will have a defence to B's right.

2.1.4 The *defences* question: legal estates and interests

As we noted in Chapter 6, section 3.2, and Chapter 16,[18] the LRA 2002 provides a very important defence: the lack of registration defence. If C acquires a legal estate or interest from A *and* if C provides something in return for that right, C may be able to use that defence against a pre-existing right of B. But it is only in the rarest cases that C can use the defence against a pre-existing *legal* estate or interest of B. Firstly, as we saw in section 2.1.2 above, B generally needs to register in order to *acquire* such a legal property right: C clearly cannot use the defence, because B's right, by definition, will be recorded on the register. For example, if B has acquired a legal ten-year lease from A, B must necessarily

---

[18] See, e.g., Chapter 16, section 2.2.

have registered that right. This means that, as far as legal property rights are concerned, the lack of registration defence is only relevant where B has managed to acquire such a right without registering it.

There are two principal situations in which this can occur: firstly, where B acquires a legal lease with a maximum period of seven years or less; secondly, where B acquires an easement that has not been expressly granted to him by A—it being possible for B to acquire a legal easement by means of an implied grant from A (see Chapter 26, section 3.2) or through the doctrine of prescription (see Chapter 26, section 3.3).

In the first case, in which B acquires a legal lease, B's right counts as an overriding interest under Sch 3, para 1, of the LRA 2002. It is therefore impossible for C to rely on the lack of registration defence against such a right.

In the second case, in which B acquires a legal easement, B's right will almost always count as such an overriding interest under Sch 3, para 3, of the 2002 Act. In this way, the Act essentially preserves the position applying in unregistered land: if B has a pre-existing *legal* property right, it is almost impossible for C to have a defence against that right.

2.1.5 The *defences* question: equitable interests

Where B has a pre-existing equitable interest, the lack of registration defence comes to the fore: for example, whilst a legal lease will count as an overriding interest, an equitable lease, in itself, does not; whilst a legal easement will almost always count as an overriding interest, an equitable easement, in itself, does not. As we saw in Chapter 16, section 5, an equitable interest of B, in itself, can never count as an overriding interest: it will only qualify if it is accompanied by B's actual occupation of the registered land.

2.2 THE FUTURE IMPACT OF THE LAND REGISTRATION ACT 2002: THE EFFECT OF E-CONVEYANCING

2.2.1 The *content* question

There is no suggestion that the introduction of e-conveyancing will lead to the introduction of registration rules that affect the fundamental question of whether or not B's pre-existing right counts as a personal right, on the one hand, or as a legal or equitable property right, on the other.

2.2.2 The *acquisition* question: legal estates and interests

The introduction of e-conveyancing will make a difference to the acquisition of legal estates and interests, but not a dramatic one. As we saw in section 2.1.2 above, it is already often the case that, to acquire a legal property right from A, a party (B or C) needs to register that right. In such cases, as we saw in Chapter 9, section 6.1, e-conveyancing will have the useful effect of removing the 'registration gap' that occurs between: (i) A's granting of a right to B or C; and (ii) B or C registering, and thus acquiring, that right. As we noted in Chapter 16, section 2.2, that gap can cause particular problems for C. For example, imagine that A transfers her registered freehold to C. If A then grants B a legal lease of seven years or less *after* the transfer to C, but *before* C has registered as the new holder of the freehold, B's legal lease will bind C: it is an overriding interest in existence at the moment of C's acquisition of the freehold. Under e-conveyancing, the transfer and registration of A's freehold will occur simultaneously, and C will no longer face that risk.

In addition, the introduction of e-conveyancing is likely to see an increase in the category of 'registrable dispositions'—that is, those dealings with a registered estate that, under s 27 of the LRA 2002, need to be completed by registration. For example, we have seen that, in general, B can currently acquire a legal lease of seven years or less without needing to register. The Law Commission, however, envisages that, when e-conveyancing makes it simpler for B to register, the registration requirement will be extended to any lease of more than three years. This will assist in reaching the 'fundamental objective' of a 'complete and accurate' register. The likelihood is that leases of three years or less will remain outside the scope of compulsory registration. This is no surprise: as we noted in Chapter 9, section 4, s 54(2) of the Law of Property Act 1925 (LPA 1925) permits such leases to be created without any formality at all, if certain further conditions are met (see further Chapter 23, section 3.1.2).

2.2.3 The *acquisition* question: equitable interests

As we noted in Chapter 9, section 6.1, the introduction of e-conveyancing is likely to make a dramatic difference to the acquisition of equitable interests in land. The crucial point is that, under s 93(2) of the LRA 2002, rules can be introduced requiring the electronic registration not only of registrable dispositions, but also of *contracts* to make such dispositions. As we saw in Chapter 12, when examining cases such as *Walsh v Lonsdale*,[19] B can acquire an immediate equitable interest if A is under a contractual duty to give B a legal or equitable property right in land. This particular means by which B can acquire an equitable interest is already regulated by a formality rule: as we noted in Chapter 9, section 3, s 2 of the Law of Property (Miscellaneous Provisions) Act 1989 (LP(MP)A 1989) already requires a contract for the '*sale or other disposition of an interest in land*' to be made in writing, signed by all of the contracting parties (see also Chapter 11, section 2.1.2). This means that rules passed under s 93(2) of the LRA 2002 would not be the first to apply formal requirements to contracts to transfer or create interests in land—but such rules would be the first to make the existence of such a contract depend on its *registration*.

The potential significance of rules passed under s 93(2) can be seen in a case in which B plans to buy A's freehold, and, as a result, A and B enter a contract, made in writing and signed by both parties, under which A is under a duty to transfer her freehold to B. B pays A the purchase price and takes up occupation of the land—but B neglects to have himself registered as the new holder of A's freehold. A, who remains as registered proprietor, takes advantage of her position by selling her registered estate to C, who does have himself registered as the new holder of A's freehold. Under the current law, B can assert a pre-existing equitable interest against C because: (i) as soon as A came under a contractual duty to transfer her freehold to B, B acquired an equitable interest (see Chapter 12); and (ii) because B was in actual occupation of the land at the relevant time, B has an overriding interest. C therefore cannot use the lack of registration defence against B (see Chapter 16, section 5). So, whilst B's failure to register as the new holder of A's freehold prevented him from acquiring a legal estate, it did not prevent him from asserting a right against C.

Now consider the same situation after the introduction of e-conveyancing rules. B's failure to have his contract with A electronically registered will mean that there is *no* contract between A and B. So, unless B can rely on some other means of showing that A is under

---

[19] (1882) LR 21 Ch D 9.

a duty to transfer her freehold to him, B will have *no* equitable interest. This means that, despite B's actual occupation of the land, B will have no pre-existing right to assert against C. B will thus be in the same position as Mrs Ainsworth in *National Provincial Bank v Ainsworth*[20] (see the discussion in Chapter 1, section 5.1, and Chapter 4, section 5.4): in the absence of a new, direct right arising as a result of C's conduct, B will have no right to remain in occupation. In such a case, as noted in Chapter 9, sections 3.7 and 6.1, B could try to rely on the doctrine of proprietary estoppel to show that, despite the absence of a contract, A was under a duty to transfer her freehold to B.[21] As we saw in Chapter 13, however, the approach taken by the House of Lords in *Yeoman's Row Management Limited v Cobbe*[22] means that that argument may now be a very difficult one for B to make.

2.2.4 The *defences* question: legal estates and interests

We saw in section 2.1.4 above that the lack of registration defence provided by the LRA 2002 very rarely protects C against the risk of being bound by a pre-existing *legal* property right of B. That position will be unchanged by the introduction of e-conveyancing.

2.2.5 The *defences* question: equitable interests

The introduction of e-conveyancing rules will not directly affect the application of the lack of registration defence to pre-existing equitable interests. The importance of those rules, as we saw in section 2.2.3 above, will instead lie in their effect on the acquisition of equitable interests. As a result, there will be cases (such as in the example given in section 2.2.3 above) in which B's actual occupation of registered land is of no use to him, because he has no underlying equitable interest that can be protected by that occupation.

3 EVALUATING THE LAND REGISTRATION ACT 2002

In this section, we will evaluate the immediate impact of the LRA 2002, as summarized in section 2.1 above, as well as considering the future effect of the Act, following the possible introduction of e-conveyancing rules.

3.1 A COMPLETE AND ACCURATE REGISTER?

The first question to consider is whether the LRA 2002 has lived up to the Law Commission's 'fundamental objective' of creating a 'complete and accurate' register. In considering this aim, we do need to be aware, as discussed in section 1.4 above, that the 2002 Act was not intended to achieve that aim overnight. Nonetheless, it is interesting to note that we have

---

[20] [1965] AC 1175.

[21] See Chapter 9, section 3.7, for a discussion of the possible use of proprietary estoppel in cases in which a formality rule has not been satisfied: note in particular the extract given there from Dixon, 'Proprietary Estoppel and Formalities in Land Law and the Land Registration Act 2002: A Theory of Unconscionability' in *Modern Studies in Property Law: Vol 2* (ed Cooke, 2003).

[22] [2008] 1 WLR 1752. But note the forthcoming House of Lords decision in *Thorner v Majors and ors* may change the position: see the companion website for details.

seen a number of situations in which the provisions of the Act diverge from this ultimate objective of a complete and accurate register.

3.1.1 Rectification

The possibility of rectification, defined by Sch 4, para 1, of the LRA 2002 as a change to the register that corrects a mistake and prejudicially affects the title of a registered proprietor, demonstrates that the register is never wholly 'complete and accurate'. This is not to suggest that rectification can ever be entirely eliminated: as we have seen, it would be very strange if, following X's fraudulent registration, it was impossible for A to be reinstated as registered proprietor. The crucial question is not as to the existence of rectification, but rather as to its *scope*. In particular, if A's claim to rectification depends on showing that a 'mistake' has been made, how we are to judge what counts as a mistake? As we saw in section 2.1.2 above, when considering the effect of a transfer by X to C, this question has important practical consequences.

Because 'mistake' is not defined by the 2002 Act, the possible scope of rectification will ultimately depend on judicial interpretation of that term. As a result, it is worth noting how judges approached rectification under the predecessor of the LRA 2002, the Land Registration Act 1925 (LRA 1925).

A good example is provided by the following extract. The facts of the case are essentially identical to those in our example in which C acquires a registered estate from X, who fraudulently registered as the new holder of A's registered estate.

Malory Enterprises Ltd v Cheshire Homes (UK) Ltd [2002] Ch 216, CA

Facts: Malory Enterprises Ltd, a company established in the British Virgin Islands, was the registered proprietor of a derelict development site behind a block of flats numbered 16–28 Wilbraham Road, Fallowfield, Manchester. The land was close to one of the sites for the XVIIth Commonwealth Games held in Manchester in July and August 2002. In 1996, a different, English company, also called Malory Enterprises Ltd, managed to obtain a land certificate in its name from the Land Registry. Using that certificate, the English company then sold the land to Cheshire Homes (UK) Ltd, which registered as the new holder of the estate in 1999. When the British Virgin Islands company ('Malory BVI') discovered this, it asked for rectification of the register and also claimed damages from Cheshire Homes (UK) Ltd, alleging that it had trespassed on the land.

Judge Maddocks found in favour of Malory BVI, ordering that the rectification should be deemed to have occurred from the moment of Cheshire Homes's registration in 1999. This meant that Cheshire Homes had thus committed trespass by using the land since that date. We will not examine the Court of Appeal's discussion of whether, under the LRA 1925, retrospective rectification was possible. Schedule 4, para 8 of the LRA 2002 makes very clear that, under the current Act, rectification can only take effect for the future.

Before the Court of Appeal, Cheshire Homes accepted that rectification should be allowed. Nonetheless, it is useful to consider the Court of Appeal's analysis of how, under the terms of the 1925 Act, rectification was possible. The Court of Appeal's analysis of s 69 of the 1925 Act (the nearest equivalent to s 58 of the 2002 Act) is particularly important.

Arden LJ

At 231–2

The starting point is the material parts of sections 5, 20 and 69 of the LRA 1925 [...]:

> s.69(1): 'The proprietor of land (whether he was registered before or after the commencement of this Act) shall be deemed to have vested in him without any conveyance, where the registered land is freehold, the legal estate in fee simple in possession, and where the registered land is leasehold, the legal term created by the registered lease, but subject to the overriding interests, if any, including any mortgage term or charge by way of legal mortgage created by or under the Law of Property Act 1925 or this Act or otherwise which has priority to the registered estate.'

Although Malory UK had no title to convey to Cheshire, the position of Cheshire once it is registered as proprietor is governed by section 69 of the LRA. Accordingly, when it became the registered proprietor of the rear land, Cheshire was deemed to have vested in it 'the legal estate in fee simple in possession'.

However, section 69 deals only with the legal estate. Unlike section 5 [of the Land Registration Act 1925], which deals with first registration, that registered estate is not vested in Cheshire 'together with all rights, privileges, and appurtenances'. Moreover, since the transfer to Cheshire could not in law be of any effect in itself, in my judgment it cannot constitute a 'disposition' of the rear land and accordingly section 20 [of the 1925 Act] cannot apply. In those circumstances, Cheshire's status as registered proprietor is subject to the rights of Malory BVI as beneficial owner [...] It follows that I accept that Malory BVI has sufficient standing to sue for trespass even without seeking rectification of the register because it is the true owner and has a better right to possession [...]

Clarke LJ

At 237

Subject to one potentially significant reservation for the future,[23] I agree with the reasoning and conclusions of Arden LJ in her very full judgment. Thus I entirely agree with her: (i) that Cheshire's status as registered proprietor was subject to the rights of Malory BVI as beneficial owner because section 69 of the Land Registration Act 1925 only has the effect of vesting in Cheshire 'the legal estate in fee simple in possession'; (ii) that Malory BVI has an overriding interest by virtue of its right to claim rectification; (iii) that the judge's conclusion that Malory BVI was in 'actual occupation' of the rear land within the meaning of section 70(1)(g) of the 1925 Act should not be disturbed, with the result that any rights of Cheshire were subject to Malory BVI's overriding interest; and (iv) that Malory BVI throughout had a sufficient possessory interest in the rear land to maintain an action in trespass against Cheshire.

For our present purposes, the significance of the decision in *Malory Enterprises Ltd* lies in the limited interpretation given by the Court of Appeal to s 69 of the LRA 1925. It was assumed that, whilst that section ensured that Cheshire Homes necessarily acquired a legal estate, it did not prevent Cheshire Homes from holding that estate on trust for the initial, and defrauded, registered proprietor, Malory Enterprises BVI. The presence of this trust is very significant: it means that the new registered proprietor is under a duty to use its right

---

[23] [That reservation related to the question of whether rectification under the Land Registration Act 1925 could take effect with retrospective effect.]

wholly for the benefit of the defrauded party. As a result, that defrauded party can exercise a power, as sole beneficiary of the trust, to force the registered proprietor to transfer its estate—a power that is sometimes associated with a well-known case in which it was recognized, *Saunders v Vautier*.[24]

In the following extract, Harpum suggests that the Court of Appeal's interpretation did not give full effect to the *purpose* of s 69(1).

Harpum, 'Registered Land: A Law Unto Itself?' in *Rationalizing Property, Equity and Trusts: Essays for Edward Burn* (ed Getzler, 2002, pp 195–9)

The effect of the subsection [s.69(1)] is that registration vests the legal estate in the registered proprietor: no significance is to be attached to the use of the word 'deemed'. Indeed it is registration alone that has this effect. Vesting occurs through registration 'without any conveyance', a process judicially referred to as 'statutory magic'.[25] Although the subsection [unlike s.5 of the LRA 1925] makes no reference to appurtenances, it does not need to do so. A *conveyance* of a legal estate in *unregistered land* will carry with it any appurtenances without express mention. LRA 1925 makes express provision [in s.20(1)] by which a *registered disposition of registered land* vests the relevant estate in the transferee or grantee 'together will all rights, privileges, and appurtenances belonging to or appurtenant thereto.' However, the statutory vesting of the legal state on registration must necessarily do likewise in any case where there was no registered disposition. The legal estate in the land in question carries any appurtenances with it [. . .]

If the registration merely vests the bare legal estate in the person who is registered as proprietor pursuant to the forged disposition and he holds it on a bare trust for the former registered proprietor, the following would appear to be the consequences:

1. By virtue of the rule in *Saunders v Vautier*, the former registered proprietor might require the new registered proprietor to transfer the registered estate to him [. . .]

2. If the rule in *Saunders v Vautier* can be applied in this manner, the scheme laid down in LRA 1925 for dealing with mistakes in the register by means of rectification and indemnity will be circumvented. The system of rectification and indemnity goes to the root of the system of registered conveyancing, and there could be grave hardship if it could be side-stepped in this way [. . .]

3. If the former registered proprietor were in actual occupation of the land vested in the new registered proprietor [as was found to be the case in *Malory Enterprises Ltd*], he would have an overriding interest, namely an interest under a bare trust protected by actual occupation.

This interpretation of LRA 1925, s.69(1) undermines, therefore, the essential structure of land registration without any compensating gains. Does the wording of LRA 1925, s.69(1) compel such an interpretation? It is suggested that, on a purposive construction of the subsection, it does not.

Of course, the decision in *Malory Enterprises Ltd* is not directly applicable to the position under the LRA 2002: s 69(1) of the LRA 1925 has now been replaced by s 58 of the 2002 Act.

---

[24] (1845) 4 Beav 115; affirmed (1845) Cr & Ph 240.
[25] *Argyle Building Society v Hammond* (1984) 49 P & CR 148,153, *per* Slade LJ.

As Harpum goes on to point out, its wording is different from that of s 69(1)[26] and so there may be no room for judges to give the same limited interpretation to s 58 that the Court of Appeal gave to s 69(1) in *Malory Enterprises Ltd*.

Malory Enterprises Ltd is, however, significant in a deeper way. As Harpum suggests, it was open to the Court of Appeal to give a wider interpretation to s 69(1), consistent with the general aim of the registration system to provide dynamic security by protecting the current registered proprietor (Cheshire Homes). Instead, the Court of Appeal opted for a more limited interpretation, preserving the usual preference of property law in favour of static security and thus ensuring that A, having been defrauded, did not lose the benefits of its legal estate. *Malory Enterprises Ltd* thus provides a useful example of how judges, when interpreting the provisions of a registration scheme, may be reluctant to discard the general principles of property law in favour of promoting the special rules of the scheme.

We saw another example of this point in Chapter 16, section 7.1, when examining *Peffer v Rigg*.[27] We saw that Graham J attempted to introduce a notice test into the lack of registration defence provided by the LRA 1925. As later noted by the Law Commission, in one of the reports leading to the LRA 2002, it is generally assumed that *'there should in general be no place for concepts of knowledge or notice in registered land'*. Certainly, the provisions of the 1925 Act seemed to be inconsistent with the approach taken by Graham J. Yet, the crucial point is that, even if the provisions of a land registration system seem to exclude the general principles of property law, judges, when applying that system, may be tempted to bring those general principles back into play. So, when interpreting terms used in the 2002 Act, such as 'mistake', it may be that judges will continue to rely on those general principles. It is therefore far from impossible that, in considering our example in which X is fraudulently registered as the holder of A's registered estate and then transfers that estate to C, a judge may be tempted to find that C's registration *is* a 'mistake' and then to order rectification in favour of A. This creates a risk that the Law Commission's goal of promoting dynamic security through protecting C may be undermined by judges reverting to the general principles of property law, which instead tend to favour static security.

In the following extract, Harpum (the Law Commissioner responsible for the reports leading to the 2002 Act) calls for judges to resist that temptation.

Harpum, 'Registered Land: A Law Unto Itself?' in *Rationalizing Property, Equity and Trusts: Essays for Edward Burn* (ed Getzler, 2002, p 203)

[Cases such as *Malory Enterprises Ltd*] show how the judiciary has not come to terms with the logic of the scheme of land registration and does not yet see it as a distinct set of rules that operate in a different way. Nor are these isolated examples, for many others could have been given. The enactment of LRA 2002 offers an opportunity for a fresh approach to land registration by the courts. It is a very different Act from its predecessor. First, it has the coherent objective of securing a conclusive register. Secondly, it creates a system under which, when electronic conveyancing is introduced, there will be title by registration rather than registration of title. Thirdly, it sets out to create a system of substantive law that reflects the principles of registered conveyancing. The two Law Commission reports, that respectively

---

[26] Harpum suggests that the wording of s 58 of the 2002 Act is 'significantly different' from that of s 69 of the 1925 Act, which perhaps overstates the case.

[27] [1977] 1 WLR 285.

preceded and accompanied the Land Registration Bill [Reports Nos 254 and 271], provide a substantial corpus of material to guide the courts in interpreting the new legislation and the mischief it is intended to remedy. Furthermore, the draftsman of LRA 2002 went to considerable trouble to define the relationship between land registration and the general principles of real property law. It is much clearer under the new Act than it is under LRA 1925. However, no draftsman, however good, can foresee all possibilities, nor address all those situations that he can. The modern approach to statutory interpretation is purposive and, it is suggested, principles that might be applicable in unregistered conveyancing should not be applied to dealings with registered land if to do so would be inconsistent with the scheme found in the new Act. In the final report that accompanied the draft Land Registration Bill, the Law Commission commented that 'unregistered land has had its day.'[28] If LRA 2002 is to achieve its objective the registered system has to be recognised in its own right and can no longer be regarded as mere gloss on the unregistered system.

It is therefore clear that the success of the LRA 2002 in achieving its 'ultimate objective' of a 'complete and accurate' title will depend, as noted in [1.9] of Law Commission Report No 271 (set out in section 1.4 above), on a 'change in attitude'—not only on the part of conveyancers and lawyers, but also on the part of the judges. The interpretation of terms such as 'mistake', as used in Sch 4 to regulate the scope of rectification, will be one of the testing grounds; as we will see in the next section, the interpretation of Sch 3, para 2, may be another.

3.1.2 Overriding interests

If the possibility of rectification is one dent in the idea of a 'complete and accurate' register, the concept of an overriding interest is another. The Law Commission's view of such interests is clear, as the following extract shows.

Law Commission Report No 271, *Land Registration for the Twenty-First Century: A Conveyancing Revolution* (2001, [8.6])

It is the fact that overriding interests do not appear on the register, yet bind any person who acquires any interest in registered land, that makes them such an unsatisfactory feature of the system of registered conveyancing. The existence of such rights means that inquiries as to title cannot be confined to a search of the register. We devoted a substantial part of the Consultative Document to a discussion of overriding interests and how their impact might be reduced without causing any disadvantage to those who have the benefit of them. Our conclusion was that interests should *only* have overriding status where protection against buyers was needed, but where it was neither reasonable to expect nor sensible to require any entry on the register. We suggested a number of strategies to ensure that the only overriding interests were those which met these criteria. As we have explained above, the introduction of electronic conveyancing will, of itself, substantially reduce the circumstances in which those criteria are met. As might be anticipated, our proposals attracted a good deal of interest and the responses were lively. However, for the most part they were supported. Where this was not so, or where better solutions were proposed, those contrary or better views have been adopted.

---

[28] Law Commission Report No 271 (2001, [1.6]).

Has the LRA 2002 achieved this aim of limiting overriding interests to situations in which B (a party with a pre-existing legal or equitable property right) cannot reasonably be expected to register that right? Clearly, it has not. For example, under Sch 3, para 2, *any* equitable interest of a party in actual occupation counts as an overriding interest (see Chapter 16, section 5.2). And, as McFarlane has pointed out,[29] *'the presence or absence of actual occupation is irrelevant to the question of whether B can be expected to register his right'*. So, as noted above, the 2002 Act currently allows B to have an overriding interest if: (i) he has bought land from A, and has failed to register as the new holder of A's legal estate; as long as (ii) B is in actual occupation of that land. In such a case, it is usually perfectly reasonable to expect B to register (he may well have been instructed by his solicitor or conveyancer to do so)—yet this does not prevent B from acquiring an overriding interest.

Of course, as noted in section 2.2.3 above, the result in our example may well change when e-conveyancing is operational: B's failure to register his *contract* with A may then deny him an equitable interest in the land. As we saw in Chapter 9, sections 3.7 and 6.1, however, even then, the courts will have to grapple with the question of whether B can acquire an equitable interest through the doctrines of proprietary estoppel or constructive trust. Again, this shows that the attitude of the judges will be decisive to the success, or otherwise, of the LRA 2002 in progressing towards a 'complete and accurate' register.

It is worth noting that the Law Commission attempted to limit the scope of 'actual occupation' overriding interests. For example, Sch 3, para 2(c), means that even if B is in actual occupation, his right will not be overriding if his *'occupation would not have been obvious on a reasonably careful inspection of the land at the time of the disposition'*, unless C, in any case, had 'actual knowledge' of B's right. As we noted in Chapter 16, section 5.1.2, this qualification aims to give extra protection to C—but the extent of that protection again rests with the judges who will have to give meaning to the term 'reasonably careful inspection'. And, as suggested by Jackson (see the extract in Chapter 16, section 5.1.2), it may well be the case that the width of the concept of 'actual occupation' under the LRA 1925 came not from any absence of such a qualification, but rather from the judges' willingness to protect important rights of B, even if those rights had not been noted on the register.

It is important to remember that the property rights of those in actual occupation of registered land are not the only form of overriding interest. For example, as we saw in Chapter 16, sections 5.2 and 5.3, Sch 3, para 1, gives overriding status to all non-exceptional legal leases of seven years or less, and Sch 3, para 3, does the same for almost all legal easements. In contrast, as we noted in section 2.1.5 above, an equitable lease or equitable easement can only be overriding if accompanied by actual occupation of the land that it burdens. Again, it is very hard to see how this can be reconciled to the Law Commission's view that B's right should be overriding only where it is unreasonable to expect B to register that right. For example, compare: (i) a case in which A, using a deed, grants B a seven-year lease of business premises; and (ii) a case in which A orally promises B that B already has a seven-year lease of residential property. In each case, B relies on this promise by incurring expenses in modifying the land: in which case is it more reasonable to expect B to register? The answer is clear—but it is only in the first case, not the second, that B's right is necessarily overriding.

As noted in section 2.2.2 above, the position is likely to change when e-conveyancing rules are introduced: it may well be the case that *any* lease of more than three years will have to be registered in order to count as a legal lease. There will thus be a reduction in the number of overriding interests that it is reasonable to expect B to register. Yet the point remains

---

[29] *The Structure of Property Law* (2008, p 488).

that many interests will still fail to be overriding, even though it is *not* necessarily reasonable to expect B to register. For example, no equitable interest acquired by B under the doctrine of proprietary estoppel (see Chapter 13, section 5.3) will be overriding in its own right: it can only count as an overriding interest if B is in actual occupation of the registered land at the relevant time.

We can also go back to the second example given in section 1.3 above: A, a registered freehold owner, grants B a right of way, allowing B to walk or drive over A's land in order to get from a public road to B's neighbouring land. That right of way is crucial to protecting the economic value of B's land, but B does not register it. A then sells her estate to C. In such a case, if A *expressly* granted B the easement, B's failure to register prevents him from acquiring a legal easement. He will have an equitable easement, but that right, in itself, does not count as an overriding interest. Imagine, however, that B's easement arose when A transferred part of her land to B. In such a case, it may that B acquired the easement not because A expressly gave it to B, but rather because it was implied into the transfer of a legal estate from A to B. In such a case, B's right *can* count as a legal easement and can therefore be an overriding interest. This may seem to accord with the Law Commission's rationale: certainly, it is reasonable to expect B to register an expressly granted easement. But this does not mean it is necessarily unreasonable to expect B to register an implied easement: after all, as we will see in Chapter 26, section 3.2.1, such an easement may arise because it is *necessary* to allow B to access his land. In such a case, B should clearly be aware that he has such a right. Given its importance to B, and given that it arises as part of the registered transfer of a legal estate from A to B, there is a strong argument that it is reasonable to expect B to register.

3.2 EVALUATING THE LAW COMMISSION'S AIM

One way in which to evaluate the LRA 2002 is to see how close it comes to achieving the Law Commission's aim of a 'complete and accurate' register; we have considered this in section 3.1 above. It is also important to evaluate that aim itself: for example, if the introduction of e-conveyancing rules assists in making it harder and harder for an unregistered right of B to bind C, is that necessarily a good thing? Further, even if the aim is a good one, are the means employed to achieve it proportionate? After all, it should be remembered that the registration system has to be paid for and that C, when registering as the new holder of A's registered estate, must pay a fee to the Land Registry.

It is clear from the Law Commission reports leading to the 2002 Act that the basic aim of the new system is to strengthen the protection of C, a party who acquires for value, and registers as the holder of, a legal estate in land. It is in the light of this aim, for example, that overriding interests are regarded as 'unsatisfactory'.

In the following extract, Dixon considers the possible justifications for the Law Commission's desire, given effect to in the 2002 Act, to limit the scope of overriding interests as formerly permitted by the LRA 1925.

Dixon, 'The Reform of Property Law and the Land Registration Act 2002: A Risk Assessment' [2002] Conv 136, 137–9

There is, perhaps, no other creation of the Land Registration Act 1925 that has aroused as much fierce comment as the infamous s.70(1) and its list of overriding interests. The fact that there is a category of property right that can bind a purchaser of a registered title without either that interest appearing on the register or necessarily being discoverable is thought by many to be anathema to the very idea of a registration system. To others, among which the present author can be counted, there is nothing inherently wrong with a category of non-registrable binding right, even in a system of land registration, provided that the category is well-bounded, well known and can be justified by reference to some stronger legal, social or economic need. Indeed, policy might well dictate that there should be a class of right that binds a registered title irrespective of registration. Obligations of general public utility, such as the burden of maintaining sea walls and public rights of way, are an obvious example. But, "policy" can mean more than this and it could be thought socially and economically politic to ensure that the property rights of those who do not have the protection of a formal acknowledgement of their rights, but who nevertheless occupy land as their home, should be protected without the need to register. For, theory aside, the act of registration "against" another's land, even when it is not the land of one's emotional partner, is readily seen as an hostile act.

Of course, it is unarguable that changes to land law and land use have turned s.70(1) of the LRA 1925 into a different creature from that envisaged by the drafters of 1925 Act. The development of principles permitting (some might say encouraging) the informal acquisition of interests in land—such as resulting and constructive trusts and proprietary estoppel—have dramatically increased both the chance that an adverse right might exist and that it might be undiscoverable, being neither materially recorded nor necessarily obvious to the prudent purchaser. Likewise, the rise of a different kind of "purchaser", the institutional mortgagee, and the importance of such lending to the domestic economy has both exposed the latent power of s.70(1) and released a tidal wave of litigation. So, despite the fact that the case against overriding interests is not watertight, there are powerful arguments in favour of reform even without the imperative of e-conveyancing. When that imperative is taken into account, with its goal of making the register both the evidence and the origin of a person's title achieved on-line with the absolute minimum of additional enquiries, it is clear that reform cannot be put off. The very point of e-conveyancing where the act of electronic registration is to be the act of creation or transfer of a property right would be undone if it were possible to claim protection for rights created off-register through a substantial category of overriding interests. Thus, it is with some justification that the Law Commission saw the existence of overriding interests as the "major obstacle" to its reforms and although there was a brief flirtation with the idea of abolishing the concept altogether, in the result the 2002 Act lays the axe to the tree with some vigour by both minimising the occasions on which an "interest that overrides" can affect a registered title and by encouraging the registration of interests that might otherwise take effect as such. Conversely, if these reforms are not effective, then the dream of e-conveyancing as it is currently set out in the Act will be unattainable.

Dixon identifies the tension between: (i) the importance to the overall scheme of the 2002 Act of limiting overriding interests; and (ii) opposing policy needs that may justify the protection of pre-existing, but unregistered, property rights.

In the following extract, it is argued that the Law Commission—at least in the rhetoric used when describing overriding interests—may have underestimated those opposing policy needs.

McFarlane, *The Structure of Property Law* (2008, p 487)

The purpose of a registration system is not simply to provide security for C, but is rather to balance the interests of C with those of B. Overriding interests form a vital part of that balance

[...N]o registration system would go so far as to say that B, a party with a pre-existing but unregistered property right or persistent right,[30] should *never* be able to assert that right against C. As a result, it is possible to take the opposite view to that of the Law Commission. The *very fact* that overriding interests give B the chance, in some circumstances, to assert his unregistered right against C, makes these interests a *crucial part* of the system of registered conveyancing.

The real question, therefore, is not whether the *general* concept of overriding interests is appropriate in a registration system. Rather, the question is whether *each particular type* of overriding interest ought to be capable, even though unregistered, of binding C. One point worth noting is that if C is bound by an overriding interest, *no* indemnity is payable to C. That is because any change to the register made as a result of B's overriding interest does *not* "prejudicially affect" C's right: C was *already* bound by B's right, even before the change to the register was made. We saw when considering rectification—the second gap in C's protection—that, in many situations, C will at least receive some compensation in return for being bound by B's right. However, the same is not true of where C is bound by an overriding interest. Similarly, if C can use the lack of registration defence against a pre-existing property right or persistent right of B, no indemnity is payable to B.

The extract raises a further means of resolving the tension, identified by Dixon, between, on the one hand, making the register 'complete and accurate' and, on the other, giving effect to policy concerns in favour of protecting an unregistered property right of B. That means would be to allow B to have an overriding interest, but, at the same time—in some cases, at least—to provide C with an indemnity.

The Law Commission briefly considered this possibility.[31] Of course, no indemnity would be payable in a case in which C could reasonably have discovered B's overriding interest (e.g. where B was in actual occupation of the land at the relevant time). But an indemnity could be justified if, for example, C is bound by an oral legal lease of B: a right that counts as an overriding interest even if B is not in actual occupation. The Law Commission quickly dismissed this possibility, however, in the consultative document preceding the full report and draft Bill that, in turn, led to the LRA 2002.[32]

Nonetheless, Roger Smith has canvassed it more seriously, as shown by the following extract.

Smith, 'The Role of Registration in Modern Land Law' in *Land Law: Issues, Debates. Policy* (ed Tee, 2002, p 52)

Indemnity

The third and final aspect of guaranteeing titles concerns the financial guarantee if loss is caused to the registered proprietor. However well structured the system, it is inevitable that rectification will sometimes deny or damage a registered title [...] There is no financial guarantee of titles in unregistered land, so indemnity is potentially a very significant benefit for purchasers of registered land. When I reviewed the position in the mid 1980s, I concluded

---

[30] [In this extract, 'property rights' refers to legal estates or interests in land; 'persistent rights' refers to equitable interests in land. See further Chapter 4, section 7.]

[31] Law Commission Report No 158, *Property Law: Third Report on Land Registration* (1987).

[32] See Law Commission No 254 (1998, [4.18]–[4.20]).

that just 0.18% of fee income [i.e. registration fees received by the Land Registry] went on indemnity claims, though I thought that a truer figure to take account of inflation and growth in the system would be 0.44%. How do those figures look 15 years on, when inflation is low and the system closer to a steady-state position?

Taking the last five years, the figure has increased to 0.61% of fee income [...] However the precise figures are viewed, it is clear that a minute part of the resources of registration is devoted to indemnity: its value to the average purchaser, in financial terms, is minimal. This may demonstrate that the Land Registry makes commendably few errors, but it also defeats any idea that indemnity can be seen as insurance for defects in title. A brave attempt was made by the Law Commission in the 1980s to extend indemnity to purchasers bound by overriding interests. Because of the impossibility of quantifying likely claims, that approach is now regarded as foolhardy and has been dropped by the Law Commission. It may well be that this was essential in order to advance more general reforms of land registration, but it severely limits the extent to which imaginative use is made of registration to guarantee a proprietor's title.

The point raised by Smith is a very important one. Given that such a small proportion of the income generated by land registration is currently paid out by way of indemnity, there is room to consider changes that allow such payments to be claimed more frequently. Certainly, the most recent figures published by the Land Registry show that the general financial position has not changed since Smith's survey. The Land Registry enjoyed a healthy operating surplus of £96.3m in 2006–07, with only £5.25m paid out by way of indemnity.[33] It is therefore possible to dispute the Law Commission's suggestion, referred to by Smith in the extract above, that allowing indemnity payments to C in some overriding interest cases would 'undoubtedly increase registration fees'.[34] The crucial point in favour of the reform is that the registration system would be able to take advantage—in some cases, at least—of a further way of resolving the tension between B and C. Indeed, it is even possible to argue that there could be cases (e.g. where it is unreasonable for B to register his right, but B is not in actual occupation) in which C should be able to use the lack of registration defence and B should receive an indemnity.[35]

This consideration of finance brings us to the question of proportionality. It is clear that, even though the register is not yet 'complete and accurate', the registration system does provide legally significant protection to C against the risk of being bound by a hidden, but pre-existing, property right. But that protection is bought at a cost: the general cost of maintaining a registration system, and the individual cost to C when he or she pays to register the legal estate acquired from A. For example, if A sells a registered freehold worth £215,000 to C, it will cost C £220 to register as the holder of that freehold.[36] So is the protection given to C worth the money: is it *practically* significant?

Smith considers this point in the following extract.

---

[33] Land Registry, *Annual Report and Accounts 2006–07*, pp 38 and 64.

[34] See Law Commission Report No 254 (1998, [4.18]–[4.20]).

[35] See, e.g., McFarlane, *The Structure of Property Law* (2008, pp 498–9).

[36] The fee is the same if A's freehold was unregistered so that C is applying for first registration. If A gives her registered freehold, worth £215,000, to C for free (e.g. by leaving it to C in her will), then C must pay a registration fee of £70. These figures were taken from Land Registry website in November 2008.

Smith, 'The Role of Registration in Modern Land Law' in *Land Law: Issues,*
Debates. Policy (ed Tee, 2002, pp 31–2)

The conveyancing dimension

This is, perhaps, the most obvious role of land registration: the principal reasons underpinning its introduction and extension have been to make conveyancing simpler, quicker
and cheaper. We are not here concerned with issues of security of title or protection
of interest holders, but rather the nuts and bolts of buying and selling land. Three sub-
issues emerge: the ease of conveying registered land, its cost and the potential for future
improvements.

Ease and cost

These issues will be dealt with together, as they are so closely linked in practice. I considered
them some 15 years ago[37] and concluded that registration offered relatively minor benefits.
The core point is that registration is all about the quality of the seller's title. In favour of
registration, it is plainly easier to see all the relevant information from a copy of the register
than to investigate complex deeds stretching over many years (and to make the necessary
land charges searches). Yet two factors have combined to diminish the significance of this.
First, unregistered conveyancing is much more straightforward than it used to be. Title has
to be searched for a minimum period of 15 years, and this relatively short period ensures
that few conveyances are likely to be involved. Indeed, the title may well consist of a single
conveyance. Not only this, but the style of modern conveyances is simpler than in the past:
reading the operative parts of a small number of modern conveyances is scarcely taxing [...]
Perhaps the best conclusion is that for the average transaction the benefits of registration
are decidedly minor, though on occasion they may be significant, especially where title is
unusually complex or the boundaries unusually uncertain. The second factor that has to be
considered in assessing the benefits of registration is that the title questions form a relatively small part of the work of a lawyer acting for the seller or purchaser of land. Questions
relating to local authority searches, inquiries before contract (dealing with many non-title
related issues), mortgage finance and the tying together of sales in a chain all take significant amounts of time. When one recalls that lawyers charge around 0.5% of the land value
for average house values, it is easy to see that title issues account for (let us say) 0.1%
of the land value. Even significant benefits in the title areas (and one may doubt whether
these are achieved in practice) are going to have little impact in terms of pounds and pence.
Registration has the potential for greater speed, but it is unclear that title questions contribute to the two or three months' delay often experienced between acceptance of an offer and
completion. Online access to the land register may save a couple of days in obtaining vital
information. This would be terribly important if other factors in the conveyancing process
enabled it to be completed virtually instantaneously. As is known only too well, this is not the
case. Perhaps the most obvious reasons for the present delays lie in the need to organise
a chain of conveyances (as well as mortgage finance) and the obtaining of information from
sources such as local authorities [...]

What about the cost of registration? In the mid-1980s, I concluded that registered conveyancing is more expensive because fees have to be paid to the Land Registry, whilst

---

[37] 'Land Registration: White Elephant or Way Forward?' [1986] CLP 111.

legal costs are virtually identical for registered and unregistered land. At that time, the Land Registry fee might be close to half the fees charged by the purchaser's legal advisers, so the extra amount was by no means trivial. Have things changed since then? [. . .] Sharp increases in housing costs bring additional revenue to the Land Registry, as the fees increase according to the value of the land [. . .]

Accordingly, we can say that the 1980s conclusion still stands: registration of title cannot be defended as a system that is more efficient, fast and inexpensive. This does not mean it does not possess advantages but rather that the inherent bureaucracy is bought at a not insignificant expense.

Smith goes on to point out that the widespread use of e-conveyancing could lead to some reduction in costs. Yet it is worth bearing in mind, as noted above, the large operating surplus of almost £100m made by the Land Registry in 2006–07, even after the payment of indemnities. The presence of this surplus makes clear that the registration system is not cost-neutral: fees paid by its users certainly generate a profit for the government.

Smith also makes the vital point that, whilst delays in the process of buying a house are well known and a constant source of frustration, those delays, even in an unregistered system, are not based on the need to check the seller's title; nor are they chiefly caused by the need to see whether any third parties have pre-existing legal or equitable property rights in relation to the seller's land. Rather, the most obvious causes of delay are: (i) the need for the purchaser to investigate the physical condition of the seller's land; (ii) the practice of offers to buy being accepted 'subject to contract', which gives both seller and purchaser the space to pull out of the planned transaction, or to insist on new contractual terms; (iii) the need for a purchaser to arrange mortgage finance; and (iv) in particular, the need for one sale in a chain to be completed before another can proceed.

As Smith goes on to note, the LRA 2002 does attempt to address the last of those problems. The Law Commission planned that, under the e-conveyancing system, a 'chain manager' could be appointed to monitor and manage the various links in a conveyancing chain: under Sch 5, para 9, of the 2002 Act, the Registrar (or a delegate) is given those powers to monitor and manage. But as the next extract suggests, it is not obvious how simply changing the rules of the registration system can reduce the other causes of delay.

McFarlane, *The Structure of Property Law* (2008, pp 496–7)

The basic aim of the [LRA 2002] is to simplify conveyancing; its chief tool for achieving this is the introduction of an electronic system. This means that the Act can only be fully evaluated by an empirical study, carried out once electronic conveyancing is fully operational, assessing the efficiency of the system. However, it is overwhelmingly likely that the Act will not succeed in silencing those who complain about the time and cost involved in buying a house. The chief cause of annoyance to purchasers does *not* come from the risk of being bound by a pre-existing right of B. Rather, it is the *process* of buying a house that causes problems. First, there is the problem that, before committing to a contract, a buyer needs to pay for a survey to check the condition of the vendor's land: that is the case even if another potential buyer has already paid for such a survey. The survey may be expensive and may in fact deter the buyer from proceeding with the sale. One solution to this would be to place responsibility on the vendor to carry out a survey and to include it in a "Home Information Pack"; however, that idea has now been rejected.[38] Second, there is the practice of offers to buy being accepted "subject to contract". This means that, whilst the potential buyer may feel reasonably secure once his offered price has been accepted, no binding agreement has been concluded and the vendor is free to impose further conditions or to pull out of the sale entirely. Unless some mechanism is introduced to deal with this uncertain period between acceptance of an offer and conclusion of a binding contract such as, perhaps, a deposit system,[39] buying a house in England and Wales[40] will continue, for those who can afford it, to be a fraught process.

This is not a direct criticism of the 2002 Act; rather, it suggests that changing the legal rules of the registration system can have only a limited practical effect. So, whilst the Law Commission heralded the reforms made by the LRA 2002 as a 'conveyancing revolution',[41] it is clear that further changes to conveyancing practice are needed in order to tackle the perennial frustration experienced by potential homebuyers.

QUESTIONS

1. What were the aims of the Land Registration Act 2002?

2. Following the enactment of the 2002 Act, is it true to say that the register is now 'complete and accurate'? If not, will it be so once e-conveyancing rules have been introduced?

3. Do you agree with the Law Commission that overriding interests are an inherently 'unsatisfactory' aspect of a registration system?

4. What impact will the full-scale introduction of e-conveyancing have on land law?

5. Does the success or failure of the 2002 Act lie in the hands of the judges who will interpret it?

6. Is it possible or desirable for the principles of a land registration system to be wholly separate from the general principles of land law?

FURTHER READING

Dixon, 'The Reform of Property Law and the Land Registration Act 2002: A Risk Assessment' [2003] Conv 136

Harpum, 'Registered Land: A Law Unto Itself?' in *Rationalizing Property, Equity and Trusts: Essays for Edward Burn* (ed Getzler, London: Butterworths, 2002)

---

[38] It has been compulsory, since December 2007, for a vendor of a home in England or Wales to provide a 'Home Information Pack'. But whilst a 'Home Condition Report' can be included as an optional document, a vendor has no duty to provide a survey of his land: see http://www.homeinformationpacks.gov.uk.

[39] In 1987, the Conveyancing Standing Committee issued a Practice Direction on pre-contract deposits. As discussed in [1988] Conv 80, the plan was that, on acceptance of an offer to purchase, both vendor and purchaser should pay a deposit equal to half of 1 per cent of the purchase price to a neutral third party. If the parties proceeded to reach a binding contract within four weeks, the deposits would be repaid; if one party withdrew for a reason not permitted by the deposit agreement, the other party would receive both deposits.

[40] The system is different in Scotland, as in most other European jurisdictions. In Scotland, sales are often conducted through a sealed bid system. Once a bid is accepted, then both vendor and purchaser are bound: see, e.g., the Scottish Executive's *Guide to House Purchase*, available from its website.

[41] 'A Conveyancing Revolution' is the subtitle of Law Commission Report No 271 (2001).

Jackson, 'Title by Registration and Concealed Overriding Interests: The Cause and Effect of Antipathy to Documentary Proof' (2003) 119 LQR 660

McFarlane, *The Structure of Property Law* (Oxford: Hart, 2008, Pts C2 and E5)

O'Connor, 'Registration of Title in England and Australia' in *Modern Studies in Property Law: Vol 2* (ed Cooke, Oxford: Hart, 2003)

Smith, 'The Role of Registration' in *Modern Land Law in Land Law: Debates, Issues. Policy* (ed Tee, Devon: Willan, 2002)

PART C

THE SHARED HOME

18

INTERESTS IN THE HOME

CENTRAL ISSUES

1. In most situations, ownership of the home falls to be determined by the application of property law principles. There is no special regime for determining rights in the home.

2. A person who does not own legal title to his or her home, and who is not a beneficiary under an express trust, may claim property rights in that home through the doctrines of resulting and constructive trust. These trusts differ in relation to how they are created and the means by which the parties' beneficial interests are quantified.

3. In *Stack v Dowden*,[1] the House of Lords signalled a preference in the 'domestic consumer context' for the constructive trust, which is the more flexible device. The creation of the trust and the quantification of the parties' shares are based on the 'common intention' of the parties.

4. Where there is sole legal ownership of the home, the initial presumption is of sole beneficial ownership. A claimant

may use the constructive trust both to establish the existence of a beneficial interest and to quantify his or her share.

5. Where there is joint legal ownership of the home, but no express declaration of the parties' respective beneficial shares, the initial presumption is of equal beneficial ownership. The constructive trust may be used to claim more than an equal share. In *Stack v Dowden*, however, it was considered that the presumption of equal beneficial ownership will be departed from only in 'very unusual' circumstances.

6. Reliance on property law principles to determine rights in the home has been criticized, particularly in the context of relationship breakdown between cohabitants. Law Commission recommendations, if enacted, will replace the application of the constructive trust (and other property principles) in this narrow category of case with a more flexible regime, where certain eligibility criteria are met.

---

[1] [2007] 2 AC 432, HL.

1 INTRODUCTION

This chapter is concerned with ownership of the home. We consider how a person who does not have property rights in his or her home—for example, as owner of the legal title or a beneficiary under an expressly created trust of land—may acquire rights through the doctrines of resulting and constructive trusts. While our principal concern is with ownership of the home, we also consider the statutory routes through which a person may claim a right to occupy his or her home, whether or not he or she has a property right in the home.

We have considered the general operation of resulting and constructive trusts in Chapter 14. Our discussion of these doctrines in this chapter is confined to their use in the context of the home. It is useful at the outset to state the key features of these doctrines, as are relevant for our discussion in this chapter.

- The *purchase money resulting trust* arises where the claimant to the trust pays or contributes to the purchase of property in another's name. The rationale for the trust is a presumed intent that the contributor did not intend a gift.

- *Constructive trusts* arise where, through the existence of defined elements, it is considered unconscionable for the legal owner of land to assert his or her own beneficial interest and deny the beneficial interest of the claimant. As a general doctrine, constructive trusts are considered to be imposed by operation of law, rather than through the express or presumed intention of the owner.

In addition to the doctrines of trust discussed in this chapter, interests in a home may also be obtained through a claim to proprietary estoppel, the scope and nature of which was considered in Chapter 13.

There are a number of circumstances under which it becomes necessary to determine ownership of the home. The Law Commission identified four key circumstances in which the issue may arise.

Law Commission Report No 278, *Sharing Homes: A Discussion Paper* (2002, [1.11])

[...]

1. The persons (two or more) who share a home cease to do so. Typically, one leaves. It may be that this follows the breakdown of a relationship between the sharers. It may be that the living arrangement is no longer convenient to the person who leaves, as they have obtained employment elsewhere. The question arises of whether the person who leaves is entitled to receive payment of a capital sum representing their share of the property, or indeed, in the event of no satisfaction being obtained, whether that person can force a sale thereof.

2. One of the persons who has been sharing the home dies. The question arises whether that person had an interest in the property, and, if so, what therefore is now to happen to it.

3. The home is subject to a mortgage securing a loan negotiated by its owner or owners to facilitate the acquisition of the property or to provide funds for other purposes. The borrower defaults on the mortgage, and the mortgagee seeks possession in order to

> realise its security by sale of the property. The question arises whether any of those living in the home can assert an interest in that property against the mortgagee, and whether they can successfully defend the proceedings for repossession.
>
> 4. A creditor whose debt is not secured over the property by way of mortgage seeks to have the property sold so that the demand can be satisfied. The question arises whether any person who has been sharing with the debtor can successfully hold out against the creditor's claim.

In most circumstances in which the issue of ownership arises, it falls to be determined by the application of the property rules discussed in this chapter. The principal exception is the breakdown of a marriage by divorce, or the dissolution of a civil partnership, in which statutory schemes enable the courts to make property adjustment orders between the parties.[2] Significantly, however, no equivalent legislation applies on the breakdown of a relationship between cohabitants who live together without having married or (as regards same-sex partners) having entered a civil partnership. Even in the case of marriage and civil partnerships, the statutory schemes are confined in their application to determining the parties' rights on a relationship breakdown. They do not apply, for example, where the parties' rights fall to be determined in a dispute between a mortgagor or creditor within the third or fourth situations, where property rules must be invoked.[3]

Where the issue of ownership arises as a matter of property law, the question for the court is what each party *actually* owns, not what they *ought* to own. As Dillon LJ commented:[4] '*The court does not as yet sit, as under a palm tree, to exercise a general discretion to do what the man in the street, on a general overview of the case, might regard as fair.*' Equally, English law does not have a special regime for determining rights to family property.[5] There has been increasing dissatisfaction with the operation of property rules to determine parties' rights in their home. This is particularly the case where the matter arises following the breakdown of a relationship between cohabitants, in which case the strict application of property rules stands in stark contrast to the property adjustment orders available on a divorce or the dissolution of a civil partnership. The Law Commission has noted[6] that the current law is generally accepted as being '*unduly complex, arbitrary and uncertain in its application. It is ill-suited to determining the property rights of those who, because of the informal nature of their relationship, may not have considered their respective entitlements*'. In response, the Law Commission has recommended a scheme that, if enacted, will replace the determination of the parties' property rights with a more flexible scheme to provide financial relief on the breakdown of a relationship between cohabitants who fulfil certain eligibility criteria.

---

[2] Matrimonial Causes Act 1973, s 23; Civil Partnership Act 2004, Sch 5, para 2.

[3] In most of the case law discussed in this chapter, the issue of ownership has, in fact, arisen in the context of relationship breakdown (the first situation). The third situation is exemplified by *Williams & Glyn's Bank v Boland* [1981] AC 487, HL, and subsequent case law, which is examined in Chapter 16. The fourth situation would arise on an application for sale under s 14 of the Trusts of Land and Appointment of Trustees Act 1996, the operation of which is considered in Chapter 21.

[4] *Springette v Defoe* (1993) 65 P & CR 1, 6.

[5] Compare Law Commission Report No 278, *Sharing Homes: A Discussion Paper* (2002, [1.18]), in which the Law Commission noted that English law does not have a special property regime even in relation to married couples. The major distinction between married couples (and couples with a civil partnership) and others is the applicable regime on the breakdown of the parties' relationship.

[6] Law Commission Report No 274, *Eighth Programme of Law Reform* (2001, p 7).

2 TRUSTS AND THE HOME

In Chapter 14, the basic rules for the acquisition of rights under a trust of land were outlined. As we saw, an express trust must be evidence by signed writing within s 53(1)(b) of the Law of Property Act 1925 (LPA 1925). But s 53(2) exempts from this requirement '*implied, resulting and constructive trusts*'.

Where an express trust exists, it is considered conclusive.[7] There is no room for the operation of resulting or constructive trusts. The preponderance of claims to these trusts thus arises through the failure of parties to determine expressly the ownership of their home, despite repeated pleas from the judiciary to legal advisers to encourage parties to do so.

Carlton v Goodman [2002] 2 FLR 259, CA

Ward LJ

At [44]

I ask in despair how often this court has to remind conveyancers that they would save their clients a great deal of later difficulty if only they would sit the purchasers down, explain the difference between a joint tenancy and a tenancy in common, ascertain what they want and then expressly declare in the conveyance or transfer how the beneficial interest is to be held because that will be conclusive and save all argument. When are conveyancers going to do this as a matter of invariable standard practice? This court has urged that time after time. Perhaps conveyancers do not read the law reports. I will try one more time: ALWAYS TRY TO AGREE ON AND THEN RECORD HOW THE BENEFICIAL INTEREST IS TO BE HELD. It is not very difficult to do.

The House of Lords recently considered the application of resulting and constructive trusts in the context of the home in *Stack v Dowden*.[8] In that case, the need to determine ownership of the home arose following the breakdown of the relationship between Mr Stack and Ms Dowden. The couple had cohabited for nearly twenty years and had four children. The home in question was registered in the joint names of the parties, but there was no express declaration of their respective beneficial shares. The purchase had been funded from the proceeds of sale of a previous home (held in Ms Dowden's sole name), money from Ms Dowden's bank account, and a joint loan. While both parties contributed to the discharge of the loan, Ms Dowden's contributions exceeded those of Mr Stack. Throughout the parties' relationship, they had kept their finances separate. The House of Lords unanimously agreed that Ms Dowden should be awarded 65 per cent of the beneficial interest—the percentage that she had claimed; Lord Neuberger, in a minority judgment, disagreed with the reasoning adopted by the other members of the House.

The decision in *Stack v Dowden* is significant both in terms of the House of Lords' judgment and the ethos that underpinned that decision. The decision of the majority, led by Baroness Hale, is underpinned with the belief that '*in law "context is everything" and the domestic context is very different from the commercial world*'.[9] The focus on context provided

---

[7] *Goodman v Gallant* [1986] Fam 106.
[8] [2007] 2 AC 432.
[9] Ibid, at [69], *per* Baroness Hale.

the key point of departure for Lord Neuberger's judgment. He was unconvinced that the domestic context requires 'a different approach in principle'.[10] On his view: 'In the absence of statutory provisions to the contrary, the same principles should apply to assess the apportionment of the beneficial interest as between legal co-owners, whether in a sexual, platonic, familial, amicable or commercial relationship.'[11]

Subsequent case law has clarified that the key factor in determining whether the approach of the majority in Stack v Dowden applies is whether the land was intended to be used as a home, rather than the relationship between the parties. Hence, the case was applied in Adekunle v Ritchie,[12] in which a mother and son jointly purchased a house as a home for the mother, but not in Lasker v Lasker,[13] in which a mother and daughter jointly purchased a flat as a buy-to-let investment.

In Stack v Dowden, the House of Lords identified two distinct circumstances in which resulting and constructive trusts may be claimed, and the starting point for legal analysis in each of these situations. The first situation comprises cases of sole legal ownership, in which legal title is conveyed to one person alone. The starting point is that the sole legal owner is also the sole beneficial owner. A claimant may use resulting or constructive trusts to establish that he or she is also beneficially entitled. If the trust is successfully established, the claimant's beneficial share must then be determined. Hence, in sole legal ownership cases, the trust is used both to determine whether the claimant has a beneficial interest, and, if so, to quantify the extent of his or her share.

The second situation concerns joint legal ownership cases, in which legal title is conveyed to the claimant and another person (or persons), but there is no declaration as regards the parties' respective beneficial shares. The majority of the House of Lords considered that the starting point in this case is that the parties are equally entitled to the beneficial interest.[14] In this case, the conveyance is conclusive as to the existence of a trust, but a resulting or constructive trust may be claimed to show that the beneficial interest is held in unequal shares. Hence, in joint legal ownership cases, the application of the trust is concerned only with the matter of quantification of the parties' shares.

The House of Lords' division between sole and joint legal ownership provides the basis of the structure of this part of the chapter.

2.1 SOLE LEGAL OWNER

As has been noted, where there is sole legal ownership, the claimant may use the resulting or constructive trust to establish that he or she also has a beneficial interest. If the claim to a trust is successful, then the claimant's beneficial interest must be quantified. Stack v Dowden itself arose in the context of joint legal ownership, where there was no declaration of the parties' beneficial shares. The only issue for the House of Lords to decide was therefore the quantification of the parties' shares. In some respects, the House of Lords is careful

---

10 Ibid, at [107].
11 Ibid.
12 Leeds County Court, judgment 21 August 2007.
13 [2008] 2 P & CR 14.
14 Lord Neuberger dissented on this point: [2007] 2 AC 432, [109]–[110]. He considered that where the parties contributed unequally, their beneficial interests should correspond to their respective contributions. This analysis is the consequence of Lord Neuberger's continued adoption of the resulting trust, which is considered at section 2.1.1 below. It is consistent with how the matter was understood prior to Stack v Dowden. See, e.g., Hopkins, The Informal Acquisition of Rights in Land (2000, p 92).

to distinguish this issue from the creation of a trust in cases of sole legal ownership,[15] but not all of the discussion is so confined.[16] Further, logical consistency of approach between sole and joint legal ownership cases will necessarily mean that some aspects of the decision will be carried over to sole legal ownership cases.

2.1.1 Resulting trust

Where the claimant has made a direct financial contribution to the purchase of property in another person's sole name, a purchase money resulting trust may be imposed. The rationale for the trust is a presumption that the claimant did not intend to make a gift of his or her contribution. This rationale is reflected in the division of the beneficial interest in proportion to each party's contribution. In *Stack v Dowden*, the majority of the House of Lords doubted the utility of the resulting trust in the context of determining proprietary rights in the home. Lord Walker suggested that it should not generally be used to determine ownership of the home, even in cases of sole legal ownership.[17] Its focus on the parties' financial contributions is considered to be more apt in a commercial context, with the constructive trust preferred in relation to domestic property. In a minority judgment, Lord Neuberger supported the application of the resulting trust in joint and sole ownership cases. On his view, the starting point for a claimant who has made a direct financial contribution to the purchase of property in another's name is that the claimant has a beneficial interest in proportion to his or her contribution through a resulting trust.

In a domestic context, where the claimant has made a direct financial contribution, it may be more appropriate (consistent with the majority decision in *Stack v Dowden*) to use this contribution as evidence of a constructive trust. The relationship between the resulting and constructive trust is considered further below, where it is suggested that the view of the majority is to be preferred. But even on this approach, there may be cases in which the resulting trust remains appropriate. In *Stack v Dowden*, Lord Walker indicated that it '*may still have a useful function in cases where two people have lived and worked together in what has amounted to both an emotional and a commercial relationship*'.[18]

Where a resulting trust is imposed, two issues may arise: firstly, the scope of direct financial contributions on which the trust is based—is the trust confined to cash contributions, or does it also take into account contributions to a mortgage? Secondly, how to quantify the claimant's beneficial share where each party's contribution cannot accurately be ascertained. Lord Neuberger discussed these matters.

Stack v Dowden [2007] 2 AC 432, HL

Lord Neuberger

At 117–21

There are two other aspects of the resulting trust analysis which I should like to mention. First, there is the effect of liability under a mortgage. This will normally be a relevant, often

---

[15] [2007] 2 AC 432, [63].
[16] See, e.g., Lord Walker's general consideration of the theoretical underpinning of the trust doctrines: [2007] 2 AC 432, [15] et seq.
[17] [2007] 2 AC 432, [31].
[18] [2007] 2 AC 432, [32].

a very important, factor, because, as Lord Walker points out, the overwhelming majority of houses and flats are acquired with the assistance of secured borrowing. There is attraction in the notion that liability under a mortgage should be equivalent to a cash contribution. On that basis, if a property is acquired for £300,000, which is made up of one party's contribution of £100,000, and both parties taking on joint liability for a £200,000 mortgage, the beneficial interest would be two-thirds owned by the party who made the contribution, and one-third by the other. If one party then repays more of the mortgage advance, equitable accounting might be invoked to adjust the beneficial ownerships at least in a suitable case. Such an adjustment would be consistent with the resulting trust analysis, as repayments of mortgage capital may be seen as retrospective contributions towards the cost of acquisition, or as payments which increase the value of the equity of redemption.

However, there is an argument that taking on liability under a mortgage should not be equivalent to a cash payment. The cash contribution is effectively equity, whereas the mortgage liability arises in relation to a secured loan. If the value of the property in the example just given had fallen by 25% when it came to be sold, the party who made the cash contribution would lose £75,000 of his £100,000, whereas the other party would lose nothing (unless he would be liable to pay £25,000 to the former, which seems intuitively improbable).

In *Ulrich v Ulrich and Felton* [1968] 1 WLR 180, an engaged couple (who subsequently married) had bought a house, she paying one-sixth of the acquisition cost in cash, and he raising the balance by a mortgage in his name. In passages at pp 186 and 189 (approved in *Pettitt v Pettitt* [1970] AC 777, 816 A), Lord Denning MR and Diplock LJ held it was wrong to treat a mortgage contribution as equivalent to a cash contribution.

Desirable though it is to give as much guidance as possible, this is not an appropriate case in which to express a view as to whether liability under a mortgage should be treated as the equivalent of a cash contribution for the purpose of assessing the shares in which the beneficial interest is held. Certainty, simplicity and first impression suggest a positive answer, perhaps particularly where a home is bought almost exclusively by means of a mortgage. More sophisticated economic and legal analysis may suggest otherwise, especially where the cash contributions are very different and, at least in the case of one party, substantial. The point has not been fully canvassed here, because, however one treats the mortgage, the outcome of the appeal is the same.

The final aspect I wish to deal with in relation to the resulting trust analysis is where the evidence is so unsatisfactory that it is impossible to reach a clear conclusion as to the parties' respective contributions to the purchase price. In many such cases, the evidence may be so hopeless or may suggest contributions of the same sort of order, and equality would be the appropriate outcome (as in *Rimmer v Rimmer* [1953] 1 QB 63, 72, approved in *Pettitt v Pettitt* [1970] AC 777, 804 A—B, 810 H, 815 H). However, in other cases (as here, in my opinion), the court may conclude that, while it is impossible to be precise as to the relative contributions, one party cannot have contributed more (or less) than Y%. In such cases, where Y is clearly below (or above) 50, to decide that the party concerned had more (or less) than Y% of the beneficial interest would be wrong.

2.1.2 Constructive trust

The specific type of constructive trust used to determine ownership of the home is the common intention constructive trust. The trust has its origins in the House of Lords' decisions in *Pettitt v Pettitt*[19] and *Gissing v Gissing*,[20] although the leading case on the elements

[19] [1971] AC 886.
[20] [1970] AC 777.

of a claim to the trust is *Lloyds Bank plc v Rosset*.[21] In that case, Lord Bridge drew a clear distinction between two distinct forms of the common intention constructive trust.

Lloyds Bank plc v Rosset [1991] 1 AC 107, HL

Facts: The claimant, Mrs Rosset, sought to establish a beneficial interest in the matrimonial home, which was solely owned by her husband. The house had been purchased in a semi-derelict condition with money from Mr Rosset's family trust and the trustees had insisted on his sole ownership. Mr Rosset had also funded the cost of the renovations. Mrs Rosset had made no financial contribution to the acquisition, or the cost of renovations, but she had assisted in the building works in various respects.

Lord Bridge

At 132–3

The first and fundamental question which must always be resolved is whether, independently of any inference to be drawn from the conduct of the parties in the course of sharing the house as their home and managing their joint affairs, there has at any time prior to acquisition, or exceptionally at some later date, been any agreement, arrangement or understanding reached between them that the property is to be shared beneficially. The finding of an agreement or arrangement to share in this sense can only, I think, be based on evidence of express discussions between the partners, however imperfectly remembered and however imprecise their terms may have been. Once a finding to this effect is made it will only be necessary for the partner asserting a claim to a beneficial interest against the partner entitled to the legal estate to show that he or she has acted to his or her detriment or significantly altered his or her position in reliance on the agreement in order to give rise to a constructive trust or a proprietary estoppel.

In sharp contrast with this situation is the very different one where there is no evidence to support a finding of an agreement or arrangement to share, however reasonable it might have been for the parties to reach such an arrangement if they had applied their minds to the question, and where the court must rely entirely on the conduct of the parties both as the basis from which to infer a common intention to share the property beneficially and as the conduct relied on to give rise to a constructive trust. In this situation direct contributions to the purchase price by the partner who is not the legal owner, whether initially or by payment of mortgage instalments, will readily justify the inference necessary to the creation of a constructive trust. But, as I read the authorities, it is at least extremely doubtful whether anything less will do.

Hence, the common intention constructive trust is divided into those founded on an express agreement and those in which the agreement between the parties is inferred. Where there is an express agreement, the claimant must also show detrimental reliance on the agreement, while in inferred agreement cases, the claimant's contribution serves the dual purpose of providing evidence of the agreement and of detrimental reliance. On the facts of the case, Mrs Rosset's claim failed: there was no express agreement between the parties

---

[21] [1991] 1 AC 107.

and Mrs Rosset had not made any direct contribution to the purchase, which Lord Bridge considered necessary for an agreement to be inferred.

Each type of common intention constructive trust will now be considered. Where a constructive trust is successfully claimed, the next question for the court is the quantification of the claimant's share. This issue also arises in joint legal ownership cases in which a constructive trust is invoked to displace the presumption of equal beneficial ownership. Therefore, the basis on which the courts quantify interests under a constructive trust is discussed in relation to both situations below. As will be seen, in *Stack v Dowden*, the House of Lords held that, in a constructive trust, the quantification of shares is determined by the common intention of the parties.

Inferred agreement constructive trust

An inferred agreement constructive trust arises where an agreement to share beneficial ownership is derived from what the parties have done, rather than what they have said. The courts' focus is on the conduct of the parties at the time of acquisition. While an agreement can be inferred from post-acquisition conduct, the courts have indicated that they will be 'slow' to do so.[22]

In *Stack v Dowden*, the House of Lords considered both what is meant by an 'inferred' agreement and the type of evidence from which an agreement may be inferred. In relation to the meaning of an inferred agreement, the Law Lords were again divided between the majority and Lord Neuberger. Lord Neuberger suggested that a distinction should be drawn between an inferred agreement and an imputed one.

Stack v Dowden [2007] 2 AC 432, HL

Lord Neuberger

At [125]–[127]

While an intention may be inferred as well as express, it may not, at least in my opinion, be imputed. That appears to me to be consistent both with normal principles and with the majority view of this House in *Pettitt v Pettitt*, as accepted by all but Lord Reid in *Gissing v Gissing* (see [1970] 2 All ER 780 at 783, 783–784, 786, 789, [1971] AC 886 at 897, 898, 900, 901, 904), and reiterated by the Court of Appeal in *Grant v Edwards* [1986] 2 All ER 426 at 434–435, [1986] Ch 638 at 651–653. The distinction between inference and imputation may appear a fine one (and in *Gissing v Gissing* [1970] 2 All ER 780 at 787–788, [1971] AC 886 at 902, Lord Pearson, who, on a fair reading I think rejected imputation, seems to have equated it with inference), but it is important.

An inferred intention is one which is objectively deduced to be the subjective actual intention of the parties, in the light of their actions and statements. An imputed intention is one which is attributed to the parties, even though no such actual intention can be deduced from their actions and statements, and even though they had no such intention. Imputation involves concluding what the parties would have intended, whereas inference involves concluding what they did intend.

To impute an intention would not only be wrong in principle and a departure from two decisions of your Lordships' House in this very area, but it also would involve a judge in an

---

[22] *James v Thomas* [2007] EWCA 1212, [24]; *Morris v Morris* [2008] EWCA 257, [19].

exercise which was difficult, subjective and uncertain. (Hence the advantage of the resulting trust presumption.) It would be difficult because the judge would be constructing an intention where none existed at the time, and where the parties may well not have been able to agree. It would be subjective for obvious reasons. It would be uncertain because it is unclear whether one considers a hypothetical negotiation between the actual parties, or what reasonable parties would have agreed. The former is more logical, but would redound to the advantage of an unreasonable party. The latter is more attractive, but is inconsistent with the principle, identified by Baroness Hale (at [61], above), that the court's view of fairness is not the correct yardstick for determining the parties' shares (and see *Pettitt v Pettitt* [1969] 2 All ER 385 at 395, 402, 416, [1970] AC 777 at 801, 809, 826).

The majority did not support the distinction between inferred and imputed agreements. Lord Walker suggested that, by endorsing Lord Bridge's explanation in *Rosset* of the inferred agreement constructive trust, the House of Lords had '*unanimously, if unostentiously,* [agreed] *that a "common intention" trust could be inferred even where there was no evidence of an actual agreement*'.[23] Baroness Hale did not directly address the distinction between inferred and imputed agreements, but she emphasized the need to determine the parties' shared intentions '*actual, inferred* or imputed'.[24] The difficulty with the distinction (as is acknowledged by Lord Neuberger) lies in identifying when an agreement can and cannot be inferred. The majority sidestepped this difficulty by taking an (artificially) broad approach to ascertaining the existence of a common intention. The effect of the majority's approach is that whether a common intention is found is dependent on considering the actions of the parties and the context in which those actions are undertaken. A common intention is inferred where relevant conduct has been undertaken in the domestic context. This raises the question of the nature of the conduct from which a common intention can be inferred.

In *Rosset*, Lord Bridge suggested that an agreement would only be inferred on the basis of a direct cash contribution, either initially or by contributions to a mortgage. In *Stack v Dowden*, in the context of a general discussion of the development of the constructive trust, Lord Walker doubted that this aspect of Lord Bridge's judgment took full account of conflicting views in *Gissing v Gissing*[25] and noted that it had attracted 'trenchant criticism' from academic commentators. He suggested that '*the law has moved on*'[26]—a comment that appeared to be indorsed by Baroness Hale.[27]

The extent to which the courts would, or should, move beyond direct financial contributions as the basis for an inferred agreement constructive trust is unclear. Lord Walker's reference to conflicting views in *Gissing v Gissing* relates specifically to the issue of *indirect* cash contributions. These arise where, through paying household bills and other expenses, the claimant enables the legal owner to discharge the mortgage. But the academic commentary to which Lord Walker refers goes far beyond this. In particular, Lord Walker cites Gray and Gray,[28] who criticize generally the courts' 'denigration' of conduct other than direct financial contributions, which has denied beneficial entitlement to 'long-serving mothers and homemakers'.[29]

---

[23] [2007] 2 AC 432, [25].
[24] Ibid, [60] (emphasis added).
[25] [1971] AC 886.
[26] [2007] 2 AC 432, [26].   [27] Ibid, [60].
[28] Gray and Gray, *Elements of Land Law* (4th edn, 2004, [10.132]–[10.137]).
[29] Ibid, [10.133] and [10.136].

As regards indirect financial contributions, the opposing views are aptly reflected in the judgments of Lord Reid and Lord Diplock in *Gissing v Gissing*.

Gissing v Gissing [1971] AC 886, HL

Lord Reid

At 896

As I understand it, the competing view is that, when the wife makes direct contributions to the purchase by paying something either to the vendor or to the building society which is financing the purchase, she gets a beneficial interest in the house although nothing was ever said or agreed about this at the time: but that, when her contributions are only indirect by way of paying sums which the husband would otherwise have had to pay, she gets nothing unless at the time of the acquisition there was some agreement that she should get a share. I can see no good reason for this distinction and I think that in many cases it would be unworkable. Suppose the spouses have a joint bank account. In accordance with their arrangement she pays in enough money to meet the household bills and so there is enough to pay the purchase price instalments and their bills as well as their personal expenses. They never discuss whose money is to go to pay for the house and whose is to go to pay for other things. How can anyone tell whether she has made a direct or only an indirect contribution to paying for the house? It cannot surely depend on who signs which cheques. Is she to be deprived of a share if she says 'I can pay in enough to pay for the household bills,' but given a share if she says 'I can pay in £10 per week regularly.'

Lord Diplock

At 909

Where the wife has made no initial contribution to the cash deposit and legal charges and no direct contribution to the mortgage instalments nor any adjustment to her contribution to other expenses of the household which it can be inferred was referable to the acquisition of the house, there is in the absence of evidence of an express agreement between the parties no material to justify the court in inferring that it was the common intention of the parties that she should have any beneficial interest in a matrimonial home conveyed into the sole name of the husband, merely because she continued to contribute out of her own earnings or private income to other expenses of the household. For such conduct is no less consistent with a common intention to share the day-to-day expenses of the household, while each spouse retains a separate interest in capital assets acquired with their own moneys or obtained by inheritance or gift. There is nothing here to rebut the prima facie inference that a purchaser of land who pays the purchase price and takes a conveyance and grants a mortgage in his own name intends to acquire the sole beneficial interest as well as the legal estate [. . .]

It is suggested that, as regards indirect financial contributions, it is difficult to disagree with the tenor of Lord Reid's judgment that the determination of rights in the home should not be dependent on the happenstance of how a family's finances are arranged. In light of the divergence in authorities on this point prior to *Lloyds Bank plc v Rosset* (as acknowledged in *Stack v Dowden*), such an extension of the inferred agreement constructive trust would be a modest development.

The argument for inferring an agreement from conduct beyond direct or indirect cash contributions appears to be far more contentious. Prior to *Stack v Dowden*, it had been accepted that there is a difference between contributions that may be taken into account in relation to the issue of quantification of a beneficial interest and those relevant to the creation of a trust.[30] As will be seen below, in *Stack v Dowden*, the House of Lords held that the issue of quantification is to be determined on the basis of the common intention of the parties. As a result, both the creation of a trust (in sole legal ownership cases) and the quantification of beneficial interests (in sole and joint legal ownership cases) are now based on the same criterion of common intent. It will be difficult to maintain that the same conduct (for example, the contribution of 'long-serving mothers and homemakers') can be used to infer an agreement for one purpose (quantification), but not for another (to create a trust). The consequences of inferring an agreement to create a trust from such conduct are far-reaching for the scope of constructive trust doctrine. It is certainly inconceivable that such a step could be taken on the basis of *Stack v Dowden* where the creation of a trust was not in issue. But such a step also has the potential to provide a welcome rationalization and simplification of the constructive trust. These consequences need to be explored in light of a full understanding of the current operation of the constructive trust and therefore we return to them below in section 2.5.

The relationship between the inferred agreement constructive trust and the resulting trust

An overlap exists between the inferred agreement constructive trust and the resulting trust, because both may arise on the basis of a direct financial contribution to the purchase of land. These two trusts are, however, also mutually exclusive, because the basis upon which the claimant's beneficial interest is quantified is different under each: in a resulting trust, as we have seen, the claimant obtains an interest in proportion to his or her contribution; in the constructive trust, the claimant's interest is quantified by reference to the common intention of the parties.

This difference in the method of quantifying the claimant's share reflects a conceptual difference in how the claimant's contribution is analysed under each doctrine. A resulting trust is imposed on the *negative* basis that the claimant did not intend (or is presumed not to have intended) to make a gift of his or her contribution to the legal owner. A constructive trust is imposed on the basis that the claimant's contribution infers a *positive* agreement between the parties to share the beneficial interest. The trust arises because it would be unconscionable for the legal owner to deny the claimant a share.

There are two possible bases for distinguishing the respective scope of operation of the resulting trust and inferred agreement constructive trust. The first, reflected by the majority of the House of Lords in *Stack v Dowden*, relies on the context of the claim. As we have seen, the majority considered the constructive trust to be the appropriate mechanism by which to determine ownership in the domestic context and the resulting trust to be more apt in the commercial sphere. Applying this approach:

- a direct financial contribution made in the domestic context is used to infer the parties' common intention for a constructive trust;
- a direct financial contribution made in a commercial context is used as the basis of a resulting trust.

---

30 See, in particular, *Oxley v Hiscock* [2004] EWCA Civ 546; *Grant v Edwards* [1986] Ch 638, 646.

This distinction, which appears to be purely pragmatic, enables the more flexible approach to quantification under the constructive trust to be used in domestic contexts.

The second approach, reflected in Lord Neuberger's analysis, is to rely on the doctrinal differences between the trusts as a means of distinguishing their scope of application. On this basis:

- direct financial contributions lead to a constructive trust where, regardless of context, a common intention can be inferred;
- direct financial contributions lead to a resulting trust where, regardless of context, the contribution has been made, but no common intention can be inferred.

This approach reflects Lord Neuberger's distinction between inferred and imputed agreements, which, as we have seen, is difficult to maintain. In practical terms, it may be that an agreement is more likely to be inferred where a direct contribution is made in a domestic context. If this is the case, then the view of the majority may be preferred as providing a more direct explanation of when each type of trust will be applied.

Express agreement constructive trust

An express agreement constructive trust will be imposed where there is an agreement to share the beneficial interest, in reliance on which the claimant has acted to his or her detriment. In *Rosset*, Lord Bridge held that the agreement must be based on '*evidence of express discussions between the partners, however imperfectly remembered and however imprecise their terms may have been*'. Further, he suggested that the agreement must be reached prior to acquisition, or only exceptionally at a later date. Applied strictly, this latter requirement would preclude the trust arising where the claimant moves into a home already purchased by the legal owner. In practice, post-acquisition express agreements have been accepted, without reference to a requirement that the case must be 'exceptional'.[31]

The requirement of 'express discussions' appears to be unrealistic in the domestic context. In *Pettitt v Pettitt*, Lord Hodson noted:[32] '*The conception of a normal married couple spending the long winter evenings hammering out agreements about their possessions appears grotesque.*' As the following extract illustrates, there is a sense of artificiality in the courts' detailed examination of the parties' relationship in the search for evidence of an agreement.

Hammond v Mitchell [1991] 1 WLR 1127, HC

Waite J

At 1139

[The] tenderest exchanges of a common law courtship may assume an unforeseen significance many years later when they are brought under equity's microscope and subjected to an analysis under which many thousands of pounds of value may be liable to turn on fine questions as to whether the relevant words were spoken in earnest or in dalliance and with or without representational intent.

---

[31] See, e.g., *Hammond v Mitchell* [1991] 1 WLR 1127.
[32] [1971] AC 777, 810.

The artificiality of the search for an agreement is highlighted by Lord Bridge's acceptance in *Rosset* of *Eves v Eves*[33] and *Grant v Edwards*[34] as 'outstanding examples' of agreements.[35] In these cases, an agreement was found in the fact that the legal owner had given the claimant an 'excuse' for not placing the property in the parties' joint names: in *Eves v Eves*, the claimant had been told that, but for the fact she was under the age of 21 (the age of majority at the time), the house would have been placed in the parties' joint names; in *Grant v Edwards*, the claimant was told that the house was not put in joint names because this could prejudice her own divorce proceedings. Lord Bridge suggested that such excuses provide evidence of an agreement, because the claimant '*had been clearly led by the* [legal owner] *to believe, when they set up home together, that the property would belong to them jointly*'.[36]

Gardner casts doubt on this interpretation of an excuse.

Gardner, 'Rethinking Family Property' (1993) 109 LQR 263, 265

But the fact that the men's statements were excuses (i.e. neither objectively valid nor even sincerely uttered) does not mean that the men were thereby acknowledging an agreement whereby the woman should have a share. If I give an excuse for rejecting an invitation to what I expect to be a dull party, it does not mean that I thereby agree to come: on the contrary, it means that I do not agree to come, but for one reason or another find it hard to say so outright. The fallacious quality of the reasoning in *Eves v. Eves* and *Grant v. Edwards* is thus clear. It is hard to think that the judges concerned really believed in it. One can only conclude that they too were engaged in the business of inventing agreements on women's behalf [. . .]

Gardner's analysis is, however, doubted by Glover and Todd, on the one hand, and Mee, on the other.

Glover and Todd suggest that there is a fallacy in Gardner's analysis. In the following extract, they refer to the sole legal owner as 'A' and the claimant to a beneficial interest as 'B'.

Glover and Todd, 'The Myth of Common Intention' (1996) 16 LS 325, 331

Once it is appreciated that the test for intention is objective, then we can see the fallacy of Gardner's argument that A did not really intend to declare himself a trustee in favour of B, in *Eves v Eves* and *Grant v Edwards*. It is not necessary for A to intend subjectively, merely that a reasonable person would assume that A was declaring himself trustee. In both cases the property was identified, and the statements could be taken as statements of immediate and irrevocable intention to hold the property for both of them. In both cases, B might reasonably have thought that A intended to hold the land on trust for himself and herself, but was prevented from doing so merely because of some formality. In neither case was there any reason for the declaration not to take immediate and irrevocable effect.

[33] [1975] 1 WLR 1338.
[34] [1986] Ch 638.
[35] [1991] 1 AC 107, 133.
[36] Ibid.

This criticism is made in the context of an argument that the express agreement cases should be classified as express trusts, which, as a matter of general trust law, arise on the basis of an objective declaration by the settler (the legal owner). The basis of Glover and Todd's argument is therefore removed if it is accepted (as the case law currently indicates) that the constructive trust is a discrete type of trust based on the common intention of the parties, not on a declaration of trust by one of them.

Mee suggests that, while the judges in *Eves* and *Grant* may have been generous in their view of the facts, Gardner goes too far in describing their reasoning as fallacious.

Mee, *The Property Rights of Cohabitees* (1999, p 123)

The answer to Gardner's argument (which emerges clearly from the relevant passages in Grant and Eves) lies in the difference between legal and equitable ownership. Gardner does not appear to advert to the possibility that the woman in each case reasonably understood from her partner's representation that, while it was agreed between the parties that (beneficial) ownership was to be shared, there was some technical obstacle which prevented her being given *legal* ownership of the property. This, after all, is the nature of any "common intention" within the terms of the doctrine under discussion; it is understood between the parties that beneficial ownership is (or will be) shared, notwithstanding the fact that this is not reflected in the legal title. To put the point in Gardner's terms: naturally, the guest's excuse will not make the dull hostess believe that he is really coming to the party; however, depending on the nature of the excuse and the manner in which it is made, she might be led to believe other things about her relationship with the guest, for example, that he finds her company delightful.

Ultimately, as Mee suggests, the appropriate interpretation of an excuse seems to be dependent on the facts of the case and the circumstances in which it is made.

Once an express agreement has been found, it is necessary to consider whether the claimant has relied on the agreement to his or her detriment.

Detriment

The requirement of detriment is concerned with what acts the claimant has done. It is assessed objectively.[37] The most authoritative judicial discussion of what acts constitute sufficient detriment is contained in *Grant v Edwards*. Nourse LJ gave the leading judgment in the case. While Mustill LJ and Browne-Wilkinson VC indicated their agreement, in fact, there are some differences in each judge's approach to detriment.

Grant v Edwards [1986] Ch 638, CA

Facts: Mrs Grant and Mr Edwards were cohabitants. As we have noted above, Mr Edwards had given Mrs Grant an excuse for not conveying their home into their joint names and this constituted an express agreement for the purposes of a constructive trust. Mr Edwards had paid a deposit and the mortgage instalments for the house, while Mrs Grant had made substantial contributions to the general household expenses

---

[37] Lawson, 'The Things We Do for Love: Detrimental Reliance in the Family Home' [1996] LS 218, 219.

and to bringing up the parties' children. It was clear from the evidence that Mr Edwards would have been unable to maintain payments on two mortgages secured over the home without Mrs Grant's contributions. The Court of Appeal held that Mrs Grant had acted sufficiently to her detriment (and had done so in reliance on the agreement) for her claim to a constructive trust to succeed.

Nourse LJ

At 649–50

It seems therefore, on the authorities as they stand, that a distinction is to be made between conduct from which the common intention can be inferred on the one hand and conduct which amounts to an acting upon it on the other. There remains this difficult question: what is the quality of conduct required for the latter purpose? The difficulty is caused, I think because although the common intention has been made plain, everything else remains a matter of inference. Let me illustrate it in this way. It would be possible to take the view that the mere moving into the house by the woman amounted to an acting upon the common intention. But that was evidently not the view of the majority in *Eves v. Eves* [1975] 1 W.L.R. 1338. and the reason for that may be that, in the absence of evidence, the law is not so cynical as to infer that a woman will only go to live with a man to whom she is not married if she understands that she is to have an interest in their home. So what sort of conduct is required? In my judgment it must be conduct on which the woman could not reasonably have been expected to embark unless she was to have an interest in the house. If she was not to have such an interest, she could reasonably be expected to go and live with her lover, but not, for example, to wield a 14-lb. sledge hammer in the front garden. In adopting the latter kind of conduct she is seen to act to her detriment on the faith of the common intention. [...]

In the circumstances, it seems that it may properly be inferred that the plaintiff did make substantial indirect contributions to the instalments payable under both mortgages. This is a point which seems to have escaped the judge, but I think that there is an explanation for that. He was concentrating, as no doubt were counsel, on the plaintiff's claim that she herself had paid all the instalments under the second mortgage. It seems very likely that the indirect consequences of her very substantial contribution to the other expenses were not fully explored.

Was the conduct of the plaintiff in making substantial indirect contributions to the instalments payable under both mortgages conduct upon which she could not reasonably have been expected to embark unless she was to have an interest in the house? I answer that question in the affirmative. I cannot see upon what other basis she could reasonably have been expected to give the defendant such substantial assistance in paying off mortgages on his house. I therefore conclude that the plaintiff did act to her detriment on the faith of the common intention between her and the defendant that she was to have some sort of proprietary interest in the house.

Mustill LJ

At 652–3

(4) For present purposes, the event happening on acquisition may take one of the following shapes. (a) An express bargain whereby the proprietor promises the claimant an interest in the property, in return for an explicit undertaking by the claimant to act in a certain way. (b) An express but incomplete bargain whereby the proprietor promises the claimant an interest in the property, on the basis that the claimant will do something in return. The parties do not

themselves make explicit what the claimant is to do. The court therefore has to complete the bargain for them by means of implication, when it comes to decide whether the proprietor's promise has been matched by conduct falling within whatever undertaking the claimant must be taken to have given sub silentio. (c) An explicit promise by the proprietor that the claimant will have an interest in the property, unaccompanied by any express or tacit agreement as to a quid pro quo. (d) A common intention, not made explicit, to the effect that the claimant will have an interest in the property, if she subsequently acts in a particular way. [...]

The propositions do not touch two questions of general importance. [...] The second question is closer to the present case: namely, whether a promise by the proprietor to confer an interest, but with no element of mutuality (i.e. situation (c) above) can effectively confer an interest if the claimant relies upon it by acting to her detriment. This question was not directly addressed in *Gissing v. Gissing* [1971] A.C. 886, although the speech of Lord Diplock, at p. 905, supports an affirmative answer. The plaintiff's case was not argued on this footing in the present appeal, and since the appeal can be decided on other grounds, I prefer not to express an opinion on this important point.

Browne-Wilkinson VC

At 656–7

There is little guidance in the authorities on constructive trusts as to what is necessary to prove that the claimant so acted to her detriment. What "link" has to be shown between the common intention and the actions relied on? Does there have to be positive evidence that the claimant did the acts in conscious reliance on the common intention? Does the court have to be satisfied that she would not have done the acts relied on but for the common intention, e.g. would not the claimant have contributed to household expenses out of affection for the legal owner and as part of their joint life together even if she had no interest in the house? Do the acts relied on as a detriment have to be inherently referable to the house, e.g. contribution to the purchase or physical labour on the house?

I do not think it is necessary to express any concluded view on these questions in order to decide this case. [...]

As at present advised, once it has been shown that there was a common intention that the claimant should have an interest in the house, any act done by her to her detriment relating to the joint lives of the parties is, in my judgment, sufficient detriment to qualify. The acts do not have to be inherently referable to the house.

Mustill LJ's approach is notable as looking for a quid pro quo between the parties. This reflects the basis of the trust in the parties' common intention. While a clear bargain may be unusual, where one exists, it seems legitimate for the court to treat the bargained-for acts as sufficient detriment.[38]

There is a significance difference, however, between the approaches adopted by Nourse LJ and Browne-Wilkinson VC. On Nourse LJ's test, detriment requires conduct on the part of the claimant that he or she could not reasonably be expected to do unless he or she was to have an interest in the house. In contrast, Browne-Wilkinson VC's accepts as detriment all acts done by the claimant as part of the parties' joint lives. Subsequent decisions

[38] Compare *Jennings v Rice* [2002] EWCA Civ 159, [45], in which, in the context of exercising remedial discretion in proprietary estoppel, Robert Walker LJ indicated that where the claimant's expectations and detriment have been defined with reasonable clarity, the consensual character of the case would justify the award of expectations.

have favoured Nourse LJ's test, which has required courts to reject conduct that the court considers it 'reasonable' for the claimant to have undertaken by reason of the parties' relationship (unless explicitly done as part of a quid pro quo).

The assumption underlying this test is highlighted by Lawson.

Lawson, 'The Things We Do for Love: Detrimental Reliance in the Family Home' (1996) LS 218, 219–20

Nourse LJ's test rests on the assumption that certain types of behaviour can reasonably be expected of people who believe that they have an interest in their home, but not of people who have no such belief. If the behaviour is of a type that can reasonably be expected of people acting purely out of love and affection or the desire to live in pleasant, comfortable surroundings, it will not normally be considered detrimental. It may be so regarded, however, if it was actually requested by the legal owner as the quid pro quo for the beneficial interest. If conduct of a type judges might ordinarily expect of a claimant motivated by love and affection has been requested by the legal owner, judges will be prepared to assume that, had it not been for the promise of the beneficial interest, the claimant would not have performed the conduct.

Direct contributions to the purchase of property, which would be sufficient for the courts to infer an agreement to share, would necessarily be sufficient to constitute detriment where there is an express agreement between the parties. Indirect financial contributions, as illustrated in *Grant v Edwards*, are also accepted as detriment, regardless of the debate as to whether such contributions should also be a sufficient basis for the courts to infer an agreement. Substantial improvements to property will also suffice,[39] but not redecoration of a more 'ephemeral'[40] nature. Beyond such clear examples, it has been difficult for the courts to assess what conduct the claimant could not reasonably be expected to perform unless he or she was to obtain an interest in the home.

Unfortunately, in making such assessments, courts have tended to draw on outdated stereotypes of what conduct it is reasonable to expect of a man or woman. Because most claimants have been women, the most significant effect of this approach has been the rejection of domestic work and childcare as constituting acts of detriment.

A powerful feminist critique of the courts' approach is reflected in the comments of Flynn and Lawson. The examples to which they refer in the following extract draw on case law covering both constructive trusts and proprietary estoppel, which shares the requirements of reliance and detriment.[41]

Flynn and Lawson, 'Gender, Sexuality and the Doctrine of Detrimental Reliance' [1995] Fem Leg Stud 105, 106, 117–18

The status of women in Western, market-economy societies is intimately dependent on their position in the public world of the market and in the private domestic sphere, and on

---

[39] *Eves v Eves* [1975] 1 WLR 1338.

[40] *Pettitt v Pettitt* [1970] AC 777, 796, *per* Lord Reid.

[41] Although the point is not without controversy, there seems little, if any, distinction between how these requirements are met under the constructive trust and proprietary estoppel. For consideration of this point, see Ferguson, 'Constructive Trusts: A Note of Caution' (1993) 109 LQR 114, 115–20.

the relationship between those arenas as constructed in opposition to one another. Feminist lawyers now possess a coherent, (almost) canonical account of the relationship between 'separate spheres' ideology and the legitimation of inequality for women in our society. This model sees the legal system participating in the active segregation of the domestic world of the household from the public space of the market and gendering the qualities of each, notwithstanding women's on-going presence in and contributions to both. The domestic arena is anointed as fit and proper for women to occupy, and its defining qualities of care, intimacy and selflessness held out as the binary opposite of the market characterised by self-centred, arms-length bargaining. The household and the feminine qualities which are associated with it in this schema are simultaneously exalted and demeaned. In this ideological framework, the qualities of the domestic sphere are represented as a justification of appropriate female behaviour and treatment and as an explanation of its consequences. [. . .]

If a claimant's behaviour is taken by the court to consist of nothing more than normal, everyday actions, then her claim will not succeed because she will not have acted to her detriment. In their construction of normality, the decision of the courts display the tenacious hold of 'separate spheres' ideology. All the behaviour which is placed in the realm of the domestic, no matter how arduous, will not amount to detriment because it can be expected of any woman in an intimate relationship with a man. Behaviour which takes the claimant outside the domestic realm is categorised as abnormal, and, in order to explain it, it must be placed in the context of a market-like transaction giving rise to a property interest. According to the authorities one cannot expect women, out of the love they have for their partners or of the desire to live in a comfortable place, to pay towards mortgage instalments. Nor is it reasonable to expect them to spend small sums on improvements, at least when those small sums represent a quarter or all their worldly wealth and their partner is a relatively rich man. A woman cannot be reasonably expected to wield 14-lb sledge-hammers or work cement mixers out of love or the desire for more pleasant surroundings. Prompted by such motives, however, it is reasonable to expect women to leave their husbands, move in with their lovers, bear their babies, refrain from seeking employment, wallpaper, paint, and generally decorate and design their lovers' houses, and to organize builders working on those same houses, even when this includes the purchase and delivery of the building materials. In order to succeed, female claimants must show that they "did much more than most women would do", or rather that they did more than the judges would expect most women to do. If a claimant's conduct [is] of a type regarded by judges as "the most natural thing in the world for a wife" to have done, she will not succeed. The use of the stereotype as a norm, from which deviation has to be established, is an almost inevitable consequence of the adoption of Nourse L.J.'s test.

The effect of the courts' approach is illustrated by comparing the claims to detriment in two cases: *Wayling v Jones*[42] and *Hammond v Mitchell*.[43] In *Wayling v Jones*, the issue of detriment was discussed in the context of proprietary estoppel. The claim arose from a homosexual relationship throughout which Mr Wayling had acted as 'companion and chauffeur' to his partner, in addition to assisting in business ventures for which he was paid 'pocket money' rather than a full wage. His acts were accepted as sufficient detriment.

Flynn and Lawson highlight the disparity between the court's treatment of Mr Wayling's conduct as detriment and the general attitude of the courts towards domestic activities undertaken by women.

[42] (1995) 69 P & CR 170, CA.
[43] [1991] 1 WLR 1127.

Flynn and Lawson, 'Gender, Sexuality and the Doctrine of Detrimental Reliance' [1995] Fem Leg Stud 105, 118–19

[When] the normalcy-dependent test of detriment is applied to male-male relationships the unnatural qualities of these relations between men can operate in favour of the cohabiting claimant. In the separate spheres ideology which resurfaces in this field, it is not normal for a man to undertake caring, domestic duties. As a result, it is necessary for Balcombe L.J. to explain (and to elevate) Wayling's domestic behaviour in the description of him acting as companion and chauffeur in exchange for monetary support. Wayling's activities have a visibility here which no woman's would possess. However, the Court of Appeal does not dwell on this aspect of the case because it can turn to a more conventional pattern of behaviour. Wayling has also engaged in non-domestic activity with Jones, and his work in the various hotels and restaurants which they ran is deemed to constitute detrimental behaviour. Wayling, a man who lives with another gay man, who works inside and outside the domestic sphere, is visible in a way in which a woman living with Jones would not have been. All of his private behaviour is unnatural and so could amount to detriment in the eyes of a court. All of his public behaviour in the market is conventional and familiar; he does the type of things which men do which are the foundation of contracts and property transactions.

In *Hammond v Mitchell*, the sole form of detriment identified by the Court of Appeal was that Miss Mitchell had participated wholeheartedly in speculative business ventures, which, had they gone badly, would have resulted in the loss of the home that she shared with Mr Mitchell, who was the sole legal owner. Her support had included subordinating any interest she may have in the property to mortgagees, to enable finance for the business ventures to be secured over the home.

As O'Hagan notes, there is an underlying difficulty in accepting as detriment Miss Mitchell's willingness to risk losing the home. (In the following extract, O'Hagan refers to Miss Mitchell as 'F' and to Mr Mitchell as 'M'.)

O'Hagan, 'Indirect Contributions to the Purchase of Property' (1993) 56 MLR 224, 226

It seems that the court felt that F's agreement to postpone any interest in the property, followed by her agreement to subject the property to risk, constituted an act of detriment which was referable to the property. Until she had agreed to postpone any rights she may have had in the property to those of the bank, and proceeded to support M's entrepreneurial activities, she was a bare licensee. However, by agreeing to risk a bare licence, F obtained a proprietary interest. It is suggested, with respect, that the better view is that a party can only suffer detriment if he or she has something to lose. When F supported M in his business venture she had no *interest* in land to put at risk. Certainly F would have suffered had the bank sought to enforce its security, but she would not have lost any rights in the property because she had none to lose.

It may be argued that Miss Mitchell's commercial endeavours, like Mr Wayling's domestic work, had an increased visibility because each claimant was operating outside of his or her 'expected' sphere. As Flynn and Lawson highlight in the extract above, Mr Wayling's domestic activities were visible because he was a man acting in the domestic sphere. Equally,

Miss Mitchell's shared enjoyment of the masculine-based commercial sphere, and her willingness to risk loss of her home for commercial success, runs counter to the ideological norm of a woman's attachment to her home.[44]

It is not suggested that *all* domestic conduct by a male claimant and *all* commercial activities by a female claimant are given an undue emphasis by the courts in assessing detriment. A male claimant who has stayed at home caring for the parties' children would not be considered to have acted to his detriment any more than would a female claimant who undertakes the role of homemaker. On the current test, the actions of the claimants would be considered no more than is reasonable in light of their relationship. *Wayling v Jones* and *Hammond v Mitchell* suggest, however, that, in marginal or atypical cases, undue emphasis may be placed on conduct that falls outside gender stereotypes.

Reliance

While detriment focuses objectively on what acts the claimant has done, the element of reliance focuses subjectively on the claimant's motive in doing those acts.[45] For a constructive trust to arise, there must be a causative link between the common intention and the detriment. The leading authority on how this requirement is fulfilled is the proprietary estoppel case of *Wayling v Jones*, in which Balcombe LJ drew jointly on constructive trust and estoppel cases to summarize how the requirement of reliance is fulfilled.[46]

Wayling v Jones (1995) 69 P & CR 170, CA

Balcombe LJ

At 173

1. There must be a sufficient link between the promises relied upon and the conduct which constitutes the detriment—see *Eves v. Eves*, in particular *per* Brightman J. *Grant v. Edwards, per* Nourse L.J. and *per* Browne-Wilkinson V.-C. and in particular the passage where he equates the principles applicable in cases of constructive trust to those of proprietary estoppel.

2. The promises relied upon do not have to be the sole inducement for the conduct: it is sufficient if they are an inducement—*Amalgamated Property Co. v. Texas Bank.*

3. Once it has been established that promises were made, and that there has been conduct by the plaintiff of such a nature that inducement may be inferred then the burden of proof shifts to the defendants to establish that he did not rely on the promises—*Greasley v. Cooke; Grant v. Edwards.*

The question that arises from Balcombe LJ's third point is this: once the burden of proof has shifted to the defendant, how can reliance be disproved?

As we have seen, in *Wayling v Jones*, Mr Wayling was held to have acted to his detriment by acting as 'companion and chauffeur' to his partner, and working without full remuneration within his partner's businesses. In his evidence, he acknowledged that he would have acted

---

44 Hopkins (2000, p 113).

45 Lawson (1996, p 219).

46 For the relationship between proprietary estoppel and constructive trusts as regards the requirements of detriment and reliance, see fn 44 above.

the same way if no promise of a property right had been made. At first instance, the judge considered this to be fatal to his claim, as demonstrating that he had not acted in reliance on the promise. This decision was overruled on appeal. The Court of Appeal held that it was not sufficient to show that Mr Wayling would have acted the same way if no promise had been made. To discharge the burden of proof, the defendant must show that Mr Wayling would have acted the same way if the promise, once made, had been revoked. Mr Wayling had stated in his evidence that, in such circumstances, he would have left Mr Jones and therefore the burden of disproving reliance had not been discharged.

The test of reliance has not been specifically discussed in the context of a constructive trust claim subsequent to the decision in *Wayling v Jones*. Some restatement is required to apply the test to a constructive trust to reflect the existence of a common intention, rather than a promise. It is suggested that, in a claim to a constructive trust, once the burden shifts to the defendant in order to disprove reliance, he or she would have to demonstrate that the claimant would have acted the same way even if informed that the defendant would not comply with the parties' initial common intention.

2.2 JOINT LEGAL OWNERS

Where legal title to a home is conveyed into the joint names of the parties, the conveyance is conclusive as to the existence of a trust. If the conveyance identifies the parties' respective shares, then it is also conclusive as to those shares. In such cases, there is no room for arguments based on constructive trusts.[47] This leaves the exceptional case of joint ownership in which, as in *Stack v Dowden*, a conveyance into joint names is silent as to the parties' respective shares.[48]

As we have seen, in that case, the majority of the House of Lords held that the starting point is equal beneficial ownership. This was preferred to the presumption of resulting trust, which would confer beneficial interests in proportion to each party's contribution to the acquisition. A party who wishes to claim more than an equal share may, however, do so on the basis of a constructive trust—but Baroness Hale warned that the task is not one that should be undertaken lightly by the claimant.

Stack v Dowden [2007] 2 AC 432, HL

Baroness Hale

At [68]

In family disputes, strong feelings are aroused when couples split up. These often lead the parties, honestly but mistakenly, to reinterpret the past in self-exculpatory or vengeful terms. They also lead people to spend far more on the legal battle than is warranted by the sums actually at stake. A full examination of the facts is likely to involve disproportionate costs. In joint names cases it is also unlikely to lead to a different result unless the facts are very unusual.

---

[47] *Goodman v Gallant* [1986] Fam 106.
[48] In *Stack v Dowden* [2007] 2 AC 432, [52], Baroness Hale noted that the incidence of such transfers should be reduced, because the standard form completed by joint transferees of registered land (form TR1) provides them with the opportunity to specify their respective shares.

At present, there is little guidance on the types of factor that would make a case 'unusual' enough to justify a departure from the presumption of equal beneficial ownership.

In *Stack v Dowden*, in concluding that the facts of the case were unusual, Baroness Hale emphasized the rigid separation of the couple's financial affairs throughout their long relationship.[49] In *Adekunle v Ritchie*,[50] the court considered that it may be easier to find that circumstances are unusual where the parties are not living together as a couple. In that case, a son jointly purchased a house with his mother. The mother qualified for a substantial discount on the purchase price of her council home under 'right to buy' legislation, but was unable to obtain a mortgage alone to fund the purchase. The court noted that, like the parties in *Stack v Dowden*, the mother and son's financial affairs were kept separate. Further, the son was one of ten children and there was no reason to believe the mother would have wanted to benefit him on her death to the exclusion of his siblings.[51]

In contrast, in *Fowler v Barron*,[52] the Court of Appeal rejected Mr Barron's claim to depart from the presumption of equal beneficial ownership. In that case, the parties' home had been placed in their joint names, although Mr Barron alone provided the deposit and paid the mortgage instalments. Miss Fowler's income was used to meet day-to-day expenses, and additional expenditure towards such matters as school trips, holidays, and special occasions. Arden LJ considered that this was tantamount to the parties treating their income as '*one pool from which household expenses will be paid*'. There was nothing unusual to justify departing from the presumption.

Where the constructive trust is invoked in a joint legal ownership case, it is used solely to quantify the claimant's share. The existence of the trust is established by the fact of conveyance into joint names. The basis on which interests should be quantified was central to the decision in *Stack v Dowden*.

2.3 QUANTIFICATION OF BENEFICIAL INTERESTS UNDER A CONSTRUCTIVE TRUST

The issue of quantification of a beneficial interest under a constructive trust may arise in two circumstances: firstly, in all cases of sole legal ownership, once a constructive trust has been established the claimant's share must be quantified; secondly, following *Stack v Dowden*, the issue of quantification will arise in a joint legal ownership case in which the conveyance is silent as to the parties' beneficial shares and one party wishes to claim more than an equal share.

In *Stack v Dowden*, the House of Lords noted a curious (and perhaps unintended) distinction that had emerged in previous case law. In sole ownership cases, a flexible approach to quantification of beneficial shares had developed through the application of the constructive trust.[53] In joint ownership cases, the courts had appeared to prefer basing decisions on the resulting trust, with its rigid approach to quantification as a proportion of each party's contribution.[54] By rejecting the resulting trust as a starting point in joint ownership cases,

---

[49] [2007] 2 AC 432, [92].

[50] Leeds County Court, judgment 14 October 2008, [65].

[51] Ibid, [66]–[68].

[52] [2008] EWCA 377, [46].

[53] See, in particular, *Stokes v Anderson* [1991] 1 FLR 391; *Midland Bank plc v Cooke* [1995] 4 All ER 562; *Drake v Whipp* [1996] 1 FLR 826; *Oxley v Hiscock* [2005] Fam 211.

[54] In this respect, Baroness Hale highlighted the decisions in *Walker v Hall* [1984] 1 FLR 126, *Springette v Defoe* [1992] 2 FLR 388, and *Huntingford v Hobbs* [1993] 1 FLR 736. She held that, to the extent that these

the House of Lords paved the way to the adoption of the more flexible constructive trust approach to quantification in all cases. Baroness Hale noted:[55] 'The approach to quantification in cases where the home is conveyed into joint names should certainly be no stricter than the approach to quantification in cases where it has been conveyed into the name of one only.' The House of Lords then proceeded to state and develop the basis on which quantification is determined.

Prior to *Stack v Dowden*, the Court of Appeal had comprehensively addressed the issue of quantification in the following case, involving a sole legal owner.

Oxley v Hiscock [2005] Fam 211, CA

Facts: The parties were cohabitants whose home was in the sole legal ownership of Mr Hiscock. Both parties had provided a cash contribution to the purchase (approximately 28 per cent by Mrs Oxley and 48 per cent by Mr Hiscock), with the remainder raised by a mortgage. Throughout the parties' relationship, they had both contributed to the household expenditure, including the discharge of the mortgage, and to improvements and maintenance. On the breakdown of the relationship, Mrs Oxley claimed 50 per cent of the proceeds of sale. Following a review of the authorities, Chadwick LJ summarized the principles governing quantification. Chadwick LJ referred to this as the 'second question'—arising once the existence of a constructive trust (the first question) has been established.

Chadwick LJ

At [69]

In those circumstances, the second question to be answered in cases of this nature is 'what is the extent of the parties' respective beneficial interests in the property?'. Again, in many such cases, the answer will be provided by evidence of what they said and did at the time of the acquisition. But, in a case where there is no evidence of any discussion between them as to the amount of the share which each was to have—and even in a case where the evidence is that there was no discussion on that point—the question still requires an answer. It must now be accepted that (at least in this court and below) the answer is that each is entitled to that share which the court considers fair having regard to the whole course of dealing between them in relation to the property. And, in that context, 'the whole course of dealing between them in relation to the property' includes the arrangements which they make from time to time in order to meet the outgoings (for example, mortgage contributions, council tax and utilities, repairs, insurance and housekeeping) which have to be met if they are to live in the property as their home.

On the facts of the case, the Court of Appeal held that Mrs Oxley was entitled to a 40 per cent beneficial share. An equal share was considered disproportionate in light of the difference in the parties' initial cash contributions.

---

decisions hold that a stricter approach to quantification applies in joint ownership cases, they should not be followed: *Stack v Dowden* [2007] 2 AC 432, [65].

55 Ibid.

In *Stack v Dowden*, Baroness Hale referred to Chadwick LJ's formula before shifting the emphasis away from 'fairness' towards the parties' common intention.

Stack v Dowden [2007] 2 AC 432, HL

Baroness Hale

At [61]

[...] *Oxley v Hiscock* has been hailed by Gray and Gray as 'An important breakthrough' (see p 931 (para 10.138)). The passage quoted is very similar to the view of the Law Commission in *Sharing Homes: A Discussion Paper* (Law Com no 278) p 69 (para 4.27) on the quantification of beneficial entitlement:

> 'If the question really is one of the parties' "common intention", we believe that there is much to be said for adopting what has been called a "holistic approach" to quantification, undertaking a survey of the whole course of dealing between the parties and taking account of all conduct which throws light on the question what shares were intended.'

That may be the preferable way of expressing what is essentially the same thought, for two reasons. First, it emphasises that the search is still for the result which reflects what the parties must, in the light of their conduct, be taken to have intended. Second, therefore, it does not enable the court to abandon that search in favour of the result which the court itself considers fair. For the court to impose its own view of what is fair upon the situation in which the parties find themselves would be to return to the days before *Pettitt v Pettitt* [1969] 2 All ER 385, [1970] AC 777 without even the fig leaf of s 17 of the 1882 Act. [...]

At [69]–[70]

In law, 'context is everything' and the domestic context is very different from the commercial world. Each case will turn on its own facts. Many more factors than financial contributions may be relevant to divining the parties' true intentions. These include: any advice or discussions at the time of the transfer which cast light upon their intentions then; the reasons why the home was acquired in their joint names; the reasons why (if it be the case) the survivor was authorised to give a receipt for the capital moneys; the purpose for which the home was acquired; the nature of the parties' relationship; whether they had children for whom they both had responsibility to provide a home; how the purchase was financed, both initially and subsequently; how the parties arranged their finances, whether separately or together or a bit of both; how they discharged the outgoings on the property and their other household expenses. When a couple are joint owners of the home and jointly liable for the mortgage, the inferences to be drawn from who pays for what may be very different from the inferences to be drawn when only one is owner of the home. The arithmetical calculation of how much was paid by each is also likely to be less important. It will be easier to draw the inference that they intended that each should contribute as much to the household as they reasonably could and that they would share the eventual benefit or burden equally. The parties' individual characters and personalities may also be a factor in deciding where their true intentions lay. In the cohabitation context, mercenary considerations may be more to the fore than they would be in marriage, but it should not be assumed that they always take pride of place over natural love and affection. At the end of the day, having taken all this into account, cases in which the joint legal owners are to be taken to have intended that their beneficial interests should be different from their legal interests will be very unusual.

> This is not, of course, an exhaustive list. There may also be reason to conclude that, whatever the parties' intentions at the outset, these have now changed. An example might be where one party has financed (or constructed himself) an extension or substantial improvement to the property, so that what they have now is significantly different from what they had then.

Baroness Hale's formula represents the view of the majority of the House of Lords.[56] The issue of quantification is therefore addressed by reference to the *'whole course of dealings between the parties'* (as stated in *Oxley v Hiscock*), but with a view to establishing the common intention of the parties, rather than determining what would constitute a 'fair' share.

In *Fowler v Barron*,[57] the Court of Appeal emphasized that the parties' shared intention alone is relevant. Mr Barron argued that the parties' home had been placed in their joint names to ensure that Miss Fowler (who was considerably younger than him) would benefit on his death, on the assumption that the couple were still together at that time. He had not appreciated that the effect of joint ownership was to confer an immediate beneficial interest on Miss Fowler. This 'secret intention',[58] which was not communicated to Miss Fowler, had no affect on the initial presumption of equal beneficial ownership.

Two final consequences of Baroness Hale's approach to quantification should be noted. Firstly, no distinction is drawn between acts at the time of acquisition and the subsequent conduct of the parties. The claimant can draw on all factors relating to the course of conduct between the parties in order to rebut the presumption of equal ownership. This is apparent from the types of factors listed in [69]–[70] of her judgment. Further, Baroness Hale accepts that the parties' intentions may change over time,[59] the relevant intention being that prevailing at the time that the issue of quantification arises. This feature of the constructive trust is encapsulated in Lord Hoffmann's characterization of it as 'ambulatory'.[60]

Secondly, while quantification will now be decided by reference to the same principles in both sole and joint legal ownership cases, the application of these may still lead to different outcomes. This is because the starting point in each case differs. Again, this point is acknowledged in [69] of Baroness Hale's judgment. The extent of any variation in the courts' approach may only become apparent as the principles developed in *Stack v Dowden* begin to be applied.

2.4 A CRITIQUE OF THE COMMON INTENTION

Following *Stack v Dowden*, the parties' common intention now provides the basis of both the creation of a constructive trust and the quantification of shares under the trust. Academic opinion has been divided on whether the parties' common intention provides an

---

[56] While Lord Neuberger also considered quantification under the constructive trust to be based on the parties' intention, his approach to quantification differs in key respects. As a result of his rejection of the relevance of imputed intent, his approach to ascertaining the parties' common intention is narrower than that of the majority. Further, he considers the course of dealings between the parties to be relevant only as background information in ascertaining their intentions (narrowly defined).

[57] [2008] EWCA 377.

[58] Ibid, [36].

[59] [2007] 2 AC 432, [62].

[60] This characterization of the trust by Lord Hoffmann was made in argument in *Stack v Dowden* [2007] 2 AC 432, and is noted by Baroness Hale at [62] and Lord Neuberger at [138].

appropriate rationale for the constructive trust.[61] The common intention has been variously described as a myth[62] and a phantom.[63]

While academic commentators have suggested alternative bases for intervention, however, no clear consensus has developed.[64] Alternative schemes may simply raise different concerns. The Law Commission abandoned its own attempt to replace the parties' common intention as the basis of determining property rights in the home,[65] noting that its 'uncompromising rejection of intention was ultimately impossible to justify' and could prejudice many of those who would obtain an interest under the current law.[66]

Bottomley, who had previously argued that the requirement of a common intention led to discrimination against female claimants,[67] became an unlikely proponent for this approach. This support comes from a specific understanding of what is involved in finding a common intention.

Bottomley, 'Women and Trust(s): Portraying the Family in the Gallery of the Law' in _Land Law: Themes and Perspectives_ (eds Bright and Dewar, 1998, pp 206, 227–8)

"I would contend that neither the Courts of Law nor the Courts of Criticism could continue to function if we really let go of the notion of an intended meaning."[68]

Gombrich, in accepting that a work of art may 'hold' many readings, recognizes a more complex picture of the artist/author than one which assumes that authorial knowledge or control is absolute. Value may be given to a work in a series of readings which 'mean' more than the artist/author might have intended or foreseen. However he is holding, as a historian, to a basic need to attempt to draw a distinction between drawing a meaning from a work of art and attributing that meaning to the creator. In a sense it is a recovery of the artist, but with a clear recognition that this is only one mode of analysis, of normative and functional value, rather than a simple reality to be asserted (imposed) to the exclusion of all else. [...]

The value of intention returns us to the value of 'intended meaning'. It focuses on a need to try and attribute to actors a purpose to their actions which was within their own foresight. As policy in law, this gives credence to individuals and also, as a broader statement, encourages in individuals the need to take responsibility for their actions. [...]

The importance of holding to the idea of 'intended meaning' seems, to me, to be crucial both for women and for feminists when faced with the alternatives of being rewarded (protected) on the basis of status or arguments based on economic exchange or presumed mutuality. It ascribes to us the freedom we seek to make our own decisions; what the law

---

[61] See, e.g., the contrasting views on _Grant v Edwards_ [1986] Ch 638 by Montgomery, 'A Question of Intention' [1987] Conv 16 (supporting common intention) and Eekelaar, 'A Woman's Place: A Conflict between Law and Social Values' [1987] Conv 93 (against common intention).

[62] Glover and Todd, 'The Myth of Common Intention' (1996) LS 325.

[63] _Pettkus v Becker_ (1980) 117 DLR (3d) 257, _per_ Dixon J.

[64] See, e.g., Gardner, 'Rethinking Family Property' (1993) 109 LQR 263 (relationship-based approach) and Barlow and Lind, 'A Matter of Trust: The Allocation of Rights in the Family Home' (1999) 19 LS 468 (a form of community property).

[65] Law Commission Report No 278, _Sharing Homes: A Discussion Paper_ (2006, [1.11]).

[66] Ibid, [3.76]–[3.78].

[67] Bottomley, 'Self and Subjectivities: Languages of Claim in Property Law' in _Feminist Theory and Legal Strategy_ (eds Bottomley and Conaghan, 1993).

[68] [Gombrich, _Gombrich on The Renaissance_ (3rd edn, London, Phaidon, 1984, p ii).]

> must act to mitigate are those situations which circumscribe our freedom through the power relations emanating from, and creating, economic or emotional dependency. [sic]

Much, therefore, may lie on how the requirement of common intention is understood. As we have seen, the majority of the House of Lords in *Stack v Dowden* took a broad approach, to acknowledge that a common intention can be found even where there is no suggestion of an actual agreement between the parties (and therefore, no need artificially to construct one). This seems close to the understanding of an intention on which Bottomley bases her conversion.

Piska suggests that intention and fairness may, in substance, be the same.

Piska, 'Intention, Fairness and the Presumption of Resulting Trust after *Stack v Dowden*' (2008) 71 MLR 120, 128

> The search is for the parties' intentions but, as these are only discoverable through words and conduct, and conduct cannot provide arithmetical answers to quantification, the parties' intentions are determined according to what is fair. That this is what Baroness Hale contemplated is indicated by her statement that the search is for 'the result which reflects what the parties must, in the light of their conduct, be taken to have intended'. The importance of this is that whilst the substance of the fairness approach in *Oxley v Hiscock* is in effect affirmed, Chadwick LJ's view of the reasoning that underpins the principle (fairness) is abandoned in favour of the artificial fiction that he rejected in that case—that the result is what the parties must be taken to have intended. Consequently the majority clothe fairness in the language of intention without providing explicit guidance for determining the content of either.

One attempt at providing content to determining common intention, specifically imputed intention, has been made by Gardner. He suggests that the key factor is whether the parties have a 'materially communal relationship'. Only if this is the case will the courts impute an intention of equal shares; in other cases, the parties' shares will be proportionate to their contributions.

Gardner, 'Family Property Today' (2008) 124 LQR 422, 431–2

> A "materially communal" relationship is one in which C and D in practical terms pool all their material resources (including money, other assets, and labour), rather than keeping separate tallies. The presence of a joint bank account will strongly, almost conclusively, suggest a materially communal relationship, but its absence will not particularly prove the opposite. The parties' having, or not having, a sexual relationship will prove nothing either way; likewise even their having children together, though in this event it is probably commoner for their relationship to be materially communal. If they are married or civil partners, their relationship will necessarily be regarded as materially communal, regardless of the nature and scale of their contributions to the family economy: that is the basis on which the law proceeds under the Matrimonial Causes Act 1973. But an unmarried couple could operate likewise, once again regardless of their contributions to the family economy; though if D is the sole wage-earner, while C keeps house and perhaps looks after their children, it is hard to see their relationship otherwise than as materially communal.

> A non-materially communal relationship is one without this profile. That is not to say that it may not be close in other respects; the parties may even pool their material resources in one or more areas, as where a couple both shop for groceries or maybe even buy a car together; but it lacks the key characteristic of a practical pooling of their material resources across the board. For present purposes, however, the parties must at least both contribute to the acquisition of the house (albeit that their contributions may be indirect, as where C meets the household bills while D pays off the mortgage): for in the case of a non-materially communal relationship, it is these contributions that generate the imputed common intention, giving the parties shares in the house in proportion to them.

Gardner acknowledges that current case law offers only equivocal support for this thesis.[69] One difficulty with Gardner's suggestion is that it is based on determining whether parties should be imputed with a common intention of equal beneficial ownership or ownership in other proportions. But under *Stack v Dowden*, in cases of joint legal ownership, equal beneficial ownership is the starting point. To this extent, the factors discussed by Gardner may be more apt to determine whether the circumstances are sufficiently unusual to depart from this initial presumption.

2.5 CAN *STACK V DOWDEN* BE USED TO RATIONALIZE TRUSTS OF THE HOME?

The decision in *Stack v Dowden* concerns the quantification of beneficial interests in cases of joint legal ownership. While the ratio of the decision is confined to this issue, we have noted its likely effect on the creation of a trust in sole ownership cases. In this regard, two aspects of the decision, in particular, may be highlighted. Firstly, the rejection of the utility of resulting trust principles in the domestic context inevitably seems to mean that the resulting trust will not, in general, be considered an appropriate basis on which a party can claim a share in cases of sole legal ownership. This has been explored in our discussion of the resulting trust above.

Secondly, both the creation of a constructive trust and the quantification of shares under the trust are now founded on the common intention of the parties. Prior to *Stack v Dowden*, the courts maintained a distinction between conduct from which an agreement to share the beneficial interest could be inferred, a broader category of conduct that could constitute detrimental reliance on an express agreement, and, broader still, the type of conduct that could be taken into account to quantify a claimant's share once the existence of the trust was established. Hence while, for example, domestic work does not generally constitute a detriment, it could still be taken into account when quantifying a claimant's share.[70] This is illustrated by *Midland Bank v Cooke*,[71] in which, in holding the parties entitled to equal shares despite significant differences in their financial contributions, Waite LJ noted that the parties had shared everything equally, including '*the upbringing of their children*'.

The distinction between conduct relevant to establishing a trust and conduct relevant only to quantification could be maintained when each was based on different criteria:

---

[69] Gardner, 'Family Property Today' (2008) 124 LQR 422, 432.
[70] Hopkins (2000, pp 118–24).
[71] (1995) 27 HLR 733, 747.

common intention for creation, and 'fairness' for quantification.[72] Now that both are founded on common intention, such distinctions will be difficult to maintain. It is this aspect of the judgment that potentially has the most significant implications for the future development of the constructive trust. Potentially, all conduct by the parties could be considered by the court to determine the parties' common intention, both in relation to the creation of a trust and quantification of their shares.

The most radical aspect of this suggestion is that conduct that is not currently considered sufficient detriment in reliance on an express agreement would become relevant to determining the existence of an inferred or imputed common intention to create a trust. As we have seen, however, the current approach to detriment has been criticized for its denigration of domestic activities. That appears to be the consequence of adopting Nourse LJ's 'reasonable expectations' test of detriment in *Grant v Edwards*, rather than Browne-Wilkinson VC's broader acceptance of acts done for the parties' joint lives.[73] Further, it would not necessarily be the case that domestic conduct alone would be considered a sufficient basis on which to ascertain a common intention to share the beneficial interest: such conduct would be taken into account only as part of the whole course of dealings between the parties.

Adoption of this broad approach to the constructive trust would bring one further welcome rationale: it would reduce the need for the courts to search for evidence of express discussions for an express agreement constructive trust, and hence remove criticism of the artificiality of this exercise that we have seen in the 'excuses' cases. The broader the range of conduct from which a common intention can be inferred or imputed, the less need there is to search for an express agreement.[74] While it may still seem artificial to insist that the trust is based on the common intention of the parties, we have seen 'common intention' defined broadly by the House of Lords as not requiring evidence of an actual agreement. Acting on the basis of a common intention, broadly defined, may be a more accurate description of the basis of intervention than insisting that evidence of an 'express agreement' is present.

At present, the authorities appear equivocal as regards extending the general approach of *Stack v Dowden* to determining the existence of a trust in cases of sole legal ownership. Shortly after the House of Lords' decision in that case, in *Abbott v Abbott*,[75] the Privy Council considered disputed ownership of a home in the context of sole legal ownership. The parties in the case were married, but, in the jurisdiction from which the case was referred (Antigua and Barbuda), entitlement fell to be determined as a matter of property law. Three members of the Board (Lords Walker and Neuberger, and Baroness Hale) had also decided *Stack v Dowden* and the Opinion of the Board was delivered by Baroness Hale, who noted that '*the law has indeed moved on*' since *Lloyds Bank v Rosset*.[76] As regards determining ownership of the home, Baroness Hale explained:[77] '*The parties' whole course of conduct in relation to the property must be taken into account in determining their shared intentions as to its ownership.*'

---

[72] The criterion used in *Oxley v Hiscock* [2005] Fam 211.

[73] See section 2.1.2 above.

[74] See, e.g., Gardner, 'Rethinking Family Property' (1993) 109 LQR 263, 265. He suggests that, in the excuses cases, the courts '*were engaged in the business of inventing agreements on women's behalf*' because, in the absence of a direct financial contribution, this was the only way in which a beneficial interest could be conferred.

[75] [2007] UKPC 53.

[76] Ibid, [20].

[77] Ibid.

This suggests that the approach to quantification of shares provided in *Stack v Dowden* will be carried over to determine the existence of a constructive trust in cases of sole legal ownership. As a decision of the Privy Council, it is not, however, binding on English law. Further, on the facts of the case, Mr Abbott did not dispute that Mrs Abbott should obtain a share of the beneficial interest; the dispute concerned the extent of her share.[78]

In *Holman v Howes*,[79] the Court of Appeal suggested that there is not necessarily any difference between cases of joint legal ownership and those of sole legal ownership in which it is not disputed that the claimant is entitled to some share of the beneficial interest. In both cases, the only issue for determination is the quantification of the parties' shares. The application of *Stack v Dowden* to determine the existence of a constructive trust will be tested only where the claimant's argument for a beneficial interest is disputed by the sole legal owner.

In *James v Thomas*,[80] a claim to a beneficial interest failed. Miss James had worked in her cohabitee's business and had become a partner in the business. The Court of Appeal held that this did not give rise to a common intention to share the beneficial interest in the parties' home. Miss James's assistance was considered to be explicable on the basis that the couple were dependent on the success of the business to meet their outgoings. In that context, it was 'not at all surprising' that she did what she could to make the business prosper.[81] The decision is not *inconsistent* with an extension of *Stack v Dowden*, but, at this stage, it seems that a claimant has not successfully invoked *Stack v Dowden* in order to establish the existence of a constructive trust in circumstances under which the claim would have failed under the criteria of *Lloyds Bank v Rosset*.

3 OCCUPATION RIGHTS

A right to occupy a home may be claimed in two ways. Firstly, it may be claimed by virtue of holding a property right of a type that confers a right to occupy. In this respect, where the home is held on trust (whether an express trust or a trust arising under the principles discussed in this chapter), the trust will be a trust of land within the Trusts of Land and Appointment of Trustees Act 1996 (TOLATA 1996). Section 12 of that Act confers a right to occupy on beneficiaries as long as specified preconditions are met. The scope of this right to occupy is considered in Chapter 19. The trustees regulate exercise of the right, in the first instance, with an application to the court under ss 14–15 of that Act in the event of any dispute.

Secondly, a statutory right to occupy is conferred on certain categories of person under the Family Law Act 1996 (FLA 1996), irrespective of holding a property right. In some instances, the right arises automatically; in others, it is dependent on an application to the court. Rights to occupy derived from the FLA 1996 are regulated by applications to the court under that Act.

The FLA 1996 confers an automatic right to occupy (referred to as 'home rights') on a spouse or civil partner in circumstances outlined in s 30. No equivalent rights are conferred on cohabitants.

---

[78] Ibid, [19].
[79] [2007] EWCA 877, [28].
[80] [2008] 1 FLR 1598.
[81] Ibid, [27], *per* Sir John Chadwick.

Family Law Act 1996, s 30(1) and (9)

(1) This section applies if—

    (a) one spouse or civil partner ("A") is entitled to occupy a dwelling-house by virtue of—

        (i) a beneficial estate or interest or contract; or

        (ii) any enactment giving A the right to remain in occupation; and

    (b) the other spouse or civil partner ("B") is not so entitled.

[...]

(9) It is hereby declared that [a person]—

    (a) who has an equitable interest in a dwelling-house or in its proceeds of sale, but

    (b) is not [a person] in whom there is vested (whether solely or as joint tenant) a legal estate in fee simple or a legal term of years absolute in the dwelling-house,

is to be treated, only for the purpose of determining whether he has home rights, as not being entitled to occupy the dwelling-house by virtue of that interest.

Hence, B obtains a right to occupy in two circumstances: firstly, where B has no proprietary, statutory, or contractual right to occupy outside of the Act (and B's spouse or civil partner does enjoy such rights); secondly, where B's only proprietary right is as a beneficiary and B does not also hold legal title. In this instance, B may also have a right to occupy under the TOLATA 1996 by virtue of holding a beneficial interest. The scope of the rights conferred by each statute is, however, different. The 'home rights' conferred by the FLA 1996 are confined to the right, if in occupation, not be evicted by his or her spouse or civil partner and, if not in occupation, to enter and occupy with the leave of the court.[82] They are generally limited in duration to the subsistence of the marriage or civil partnership and the continuance of A's own right to occupy.[83]

A right to occupy may be obtained on application to the court by a former spouse or civil partner (s 35) or a former cohabitant (s 35). As with the automatic home rights conferred on spouses and civil partners, applications are confined to parties who cannot claim a right to occupy outside of the Act, or whose only claim is as a beneficiary.[84] The rights are further limited to houses that were occupied, or intended by the parties to be occupied, as their home.[85] Any right to occupy obtained by an application under ss 35 or 36 is temporary, with an absolute maximum duration of one year.[86]

4 RECOMMENDATIONS FOR REFORM

The Law Commission first indicated that it was considering the property rights of home sharers in 1995.[87] The intervening period has seen a significant shift in the focus of the Law Commission's work. Its initial aim was to provide a scheme to determine the property

---

[82] Family Law Act 1996, s 30(2).

[83] Ibid, s 30(8). The rights may be extended by the court under s 33(5).

[84] Ibid, ss 35(1) and (11), and 36(1) and (11).

[85] Ibid, ss 35(1)(c) and 36(1)(c).

[86] Ibid, ss 35(10) and 36(10). The maximum length of a court order is six months, with the possibility of extension on one further application for another maximum of six months.

[87] Law Commision Report No 234, *Sixth Programme of Law Reform* (1995, item 8).

rights of all those who share their home, including married and unmarried couples, and others who share homes as friends, relatives, or for companionship or support.[88] The Law Commission explored the possibility of developing a single scheme to determine ownership of the home in all circumstances in which the issue arose[89] (except cases of relationship breakdown covered by existing statutory schemes), and to the exclusion of claims based on the doctrines of trust (discussed in this chapter) and estoppel (examined in Chapter 13). The Law Commission published its conclusions on this work in *Sharing Homes: A Discussion Paper*.[90] The Law Commission concluded that such a scheme simply is not possible:[91] the diversity of situations in which people share homes precludes a uniform approach to determining their property rights.

Subsequently, the focus of the Law Commission's work shifted. It narrowed the scope of its work to consider only the position of cohabitants *'living as a couple in a joint household'*[92] (who have not married or entered a civil partnership) and principally in the context of relationship breakdown.[93] Within this narrow context, however, the Law Commission's work has moved outside the confines of determining property ownership to consider more broadly the financial consequences of relationship breakdown. Its recommendations are published in the report *Cohabitation: The Financial Consequences of Relationship Breakdown*.[94]

The application of the current property rules on the breakdown of a relationship has long provided the focus of criticism—in part, due to the contrast from the statutory scheme applicable to married couples who divorce. The disparity in treatment received further attention during the passage through Parliament of the Civil Partnership Act 2004, which contains its own scheme for property adjustment orders on the dissolution of a civil partnership.[95]

In *Stack v Dowden*, Baroness Hale highlighted the social significance of rules applicable on the breakdown of a relationship between cohabitants, and the clear divergence between how property rights are *actually* resolved and how many people *believe* that such issues are resolved.

Stack v Dowden [2007] 2 AC 432, HL

Baroness Hale

At [41]–[42]

[...] The first development is, of course, the huge expansion in home ownership which has taken place since the Second World War and was given a further boost by the 'right to buy' legislation of the 1980s. Coupled with this has been continuing house price inflation, albeit

---

88 Law Commission Report No 278, *Sharing Homes: A Discussion Paper* (2006, p vi).

89 That is, the four circumstances outlined by the Law Commission in the extract in section 1 above.

90 Law Commission Report No 278 (2006).

91 Ibid, [15] of the Executive Summary and Pt VI of the Discussion Paper.

92 Law Commission Report No 307, *Cohabitation: The Financial Consequence of Relationship Breakdown* (2007, [3.13]). This expression is intended, *in substance*, to denote parties living together as though they were married or in a civil partnership, whilst deliberately avoiding the *language* of relationships 'analogous' to marriage or a civil partnership.

93 Consequential changes are also proposed to the Inheritance (Provision for Family and Dependents) Act 1975 where a relationship ends through the death of a cohabitant.

94 Law Commission Report No 307 (2007). The report was preceded by Law Commission Consultation Paper No 179, *Cohabitation: The Financial Consequences of Relationship Breakdown* (2006).

95 Civil Partnership Act 2004, Sch 5, Pt II. It was this disparity that led to a request to the Law Commission to undertake the work that led to the current proposals: Law Commission Report No 307 (2007, [1.18]).

with occasional interruptions such as occurred at the end of the 1980s. This has meant that it is almost always more advantageous for someone who has contributed to the acquisition of the home to claim a share in its ownership rather than the return of the money contributed, even with interest.

Another development has been the recognition in the courts that, to put it at its lowest, the interpretation to be put on the behaviour of people living together in an intimate relationship may be different from the interpretation to be put upon similar behaviour between commercial men. To put it at its highest, an outcome which might seem just in a purely commercial transaction may appear highly unjust in a transaction between husband and wife or cohabitant and cohabitant [. . .]

At [44]–[45]

Inter vivos disputes between unmarried cohabiting couples are still governed by the ordinary law. These disputes have become increasingly visible in recent years as more and more couples live together without marrying. The full picture has recently been painted by the Law Commission in *Cohabitation: The Financial Consequences of Relationship Breakdown—A Consultation Paper* (Law Com Consultation Paper no 179) (2006) Pt 2, and its Overview paper, paras 2.3 to 2.11. For example, the 2001 census recorded over 10 million married couples in England and Wales, with over 7 5 million dependent children; but it also recorded over two million cohabiting couples, with over one-and-a-quarter million children dependent upon them. This was a 67% increase in cohabitation over the previous ten years and a doubling of the numbers of such households with dependent children. The Government Actuaries Department predicts that the proportion of couples cohabiting will continue to grow, from the present one in six of all couples to one in four by 2031.

Cohabitation comes in many different shapes and sizes. People embarking on their first serious relationship more commonly cohabit than marry. Many of these relationships may be quite short lived and childless. But most people these days cohabit before marriage—in 2003, 78.7% of spouses gave identical addresses before marriage, and the figures are even higher for second marriages. So many couples are cohabiting with a view to marriage at some later date—as long ago as 1998 the British Household Panel Survey found that 75% of current cohabitants expected to marry, although only a third had firm plans (see J Ermisch 'Personal Relationships and Marriage Expectations: Evidence from the 1998 British Household Panel' (2000) Working Papers of the Institute of Social and Economic Research: Paper 2000–27). Cohabitation is much more likely to end in separation than is marriage, and cohabitations which end in separation tend to last for a shorter time than marriages which end in divorce. But increasing numbers of couples cohabit for long periods without marrying and their reasons for doing so vary from conscious rejection of marriage as a legal institution to regarding themselves 'as good as married' anyway (see Law Com Consultation Paper no 179, Pt 2, p 39 (para 2.45)). There is evidence of a wide-spread myth of the 'common law marriage' in which unmarried couples acquire the same rights as married after a period of cohabitation (see A Barlow et al 'Just a Piece of Paper? Marriage and Cohabitation', in A Park et al *British Social Attitudes: Public policy, social ties. The 18th Report* (2001), pp 29–57). There is also evidence that 'the legal implications of marriage are a long way down the list of most couples' considerations when deciding whether to marry' (see Law Com Consultation Paper no 179, Pt 5, p 96 (para 5.10)).

In developing proposals for reform, an underlying issue has been the extent to which any new scheme applicable to cohabitants should mirror the statutory schemes applicable on divorce and on the dissolution of a civil partnership. Those schemes reflect a different ethos to the application of the property rules discussed in this chapter.

Miles highlights the essence of this difference.[96]

Miles, 'Property Law v Family Law: Resolving the Problems of Family Property' (2003) LS 624, 627

Property law, it may be said, is concerned simply with identifying in an 'unpurposive and formalist' manner existing rights to property (most importantly, beneficial ownership of land) in accordance with pre-determined rules. The basic question underlying property law's approach to the acquisition of property rights might be said to be 'what do I have to do?' to get them. [...]

Family law, by contrast, is very much concerned with the status of the parties, in particular the relationship between them, and the economic and other consequences of that relationship. Indeed, it is the existence of a prescribed type of relationship that gives family law its jurisdiction over the issue. A key initial question is not 'what do I have to do?' but 'who do I have to be?' Moreover, unlike property law's backward-looking focus—seeking evidence of past conduct which has automatically generated property rights—family law tends to be forward-looking and discretion-based, typically primarily concerned to cater for future needs created by the relationship between the parties, and is prepared by way of court order to adjust patterns of ownership formally determined by the law of property in relation to assets owned by the parties in order to cater for those needs.

In its report on cohabitation, the Law Commission has recommended a scheme to provide financial relief to cohabitants on the breakdown of their relationship. The proposed scheme will provide a more flexible approach than the property rules discussed in this chapter, but is intentionally not modelled on existing schemes applicable to divorce or the dissolution of a civil partnership.[97] The scheme will apply where cohabitants meet specified eligibility criteria. These are that *either* the cohabitants have a child together, *or* they have cohabited for a minimum duration, which the Law Commission recommends is set between two and five years. It will be possible for cohabitants to opt out of the scheme.[98] This must be achieved through a signed agreement between the parties, which '*makes clear the parties' intention to disapply the statute*'.[99] Notably, an express declaration of trust will not, without more, constitute such an opt-out. The proposed scheme will still apply unless the parties have also made it clear that they intend to disapply the new scheme.[100]

The Law Commission explains, in the following extract, the basis on which relief is determined and the form that the relief may take.

---

[96] See also *Hammond v Mitchell* [1991] 1 WLR 1127, in which, Waite J compared the 'forward-looking' approach of family law to the 'painfully detailed retrospect' required to ascertain the parties' property rights.

[97] Law Commission Report No 307 (2007, [1.2]).

[98] Ibid, Pt 5.

[99] Ibid, [5.56].

[100] Ibid, [5.64].

Law Commission Report No 307, *Cohabitation: The Financial Consequences of Relationship Breakdown* (2007, [4.32]–[4.41])

We recommend that financial relief on separation should be granted in accordance with a statutory scheme based upon the economic impact of cohabitation, to the following effect.

An eligible cohabitant applying for relief following separation ("the applicant") must prove that:

1. the respondent has a retained benefit; or

2. the applicant has an economic disadvantage;

as a result of qualifying contributions the applicant has made.

A qualifying contribution is any contribution arising from the cohabiting relationship which is made to the parties' shared lives or to the welfare of members of their families. Contributions are not limited to financial contributions, and include future contributions, in particular to the care of the parties' children following separation.

A retained benefit may take the form of capital, income or earning capacity that has been acquired, retained or enhanced.

An economic disadvantage is a present or future loss. It may include a diminution in current savings as a result of expenditure or of earnings lost during the relationship, lost future earnings, or the future cost of paid childcare.

The court may make an order to adjust the retained benefit, if any, by reversing it in so far as that is reasonable and practicable having regard to the discretionary factors listed below. If, after the reversal of any retained benefit, the applicant would still bear an economic disadvantage, the court may make an order sharing that loss equally between the parties, in so far as it is reasonable and practicable to do so, having regard to the discretionary factors.

The discretionary factors are:

1. the welfare while a minor of any child of both parties who has not attained the age of eighteen;

2. the financial needs and obligations of both parties;

3. the extent and nature of the financial resources which each party has or is likely to have in the foreseeable future;

4. the welfare of any children who live with, or might reasonably be expected to live with, either party; and

5. the conduct of each party, defined restrictively but so as to include cases where a qualifying contribution can be shown to have been made despite the express disagreement of the other party.

Of these discretionary factors, item (1) above shall be the court's first consideration.

In making an order to share economic disadvantage, the court shall not place the applicant, for the foreseeable future, in a stronger economic position than the respondent.

The following range of orders should be available to the court:

1. lump sums, including payment by instalment, secured lump sums, lump sums paid by way of pensions attachment, and interim payments;

2. property transfers;

3. property settlements;

4. orders for sale; and

5. pension sharing.

Unlike on divorce, periodical payments should not generally be available.

In so far as the scheme is engaged, it should apply between the parties to the exclusion of the general law of implied trusts, estoppel and contract.

It should be emphasized that the proposed scheme moves the enquiry away from determining the parties' ownership of property. Where the scheme applies, issues of ownership become otiose. It is consistent with this that the scheme will operate to the exclusion of claims based on the property principles discussed in this chapter. If adopted, there will be a clear demarcation between circumstances in which the scheme applies and circumstances in which parties' ownership of their home will need to be determined under the property rules discussed in this chapter.

Table 3 Scope of the Law Commission's Proposals

When the Law Commission's scheme will apply (if implemented)	When ownership will continue to be determined using property law principles discussed in this chapter
(i) Cohabitants have been living as a couple in a joint household; *and* (ii) the eligibility criteria are met; *and* (iii) the parties have not executed a valid opt out; *and* (iv) an application for financial relief is made by one of the parties following the breakdown of their relationship.	(i) The parties are not cohabitants living as a couple in a joint household. This will include relatives and friends who share a home, and those who live together to provide care or companionship; *or* (ii) cohabitants have lived together as a couple in a joint household, but do not meet the eligibility criteria; *or* (iii) the parties have executed a valid opt-out; *or* (iv) in all cases in which the parties' rights need to be determined in circumstances other than relationship breakdown.

QUESTIONS

1. Compare and contrast resulting and constructive trusts. Why do you think the majority of the House of Lords in *Stack v Dowden* preferred the constructive trust as a means of determining rights in the home?

2. What do you understand is meant by the 'common intention' of the parties in the context of the constructive trust? Does the parties' common intention provide a satisfactory basis for ascertaining ownership of the home?

3. Are the problems of gender stereotypes that have been encountered in ascertaining the existence of detriment inherent in the adoption of the test provided by Nourse LJ in *Grant v Edwards*? Is Browne-Wilkinson VC's test (in the same case) preferable?

4. To what extent do you consider it desirable to extend the reasoning in *Stack v Dowden* to determine the creation of a trust in sole legal owner cases?

5. What are the advantages and disadvantages of determining ownership of the home through the application of property law principles? Is the Law Commission

justified in singling out relationship breakdown between cohabitants as a situation to be dealt with outside property law principles?

FURTHER READING

Bottomley, 'Women and Trust(s): Portraying the Family in the Gallery of the Law' in *Land Law: Themes and Perspectives* (eds Bright and Dewar, Oxford: OUP, 1998)

Etherton, 'Constructive Trusts: A New Model for Equity and Unjust Enrichment' (2008) 67 CLJ 265

Gardner, 'Family Property Today' (2008) 124 LQR 422

Gardner, 'Rethinking Family Property' (1993) 109 LQR 263

Law Commission Report No 307, *Cohabitation: The Financial Consequence of Relationship Breakdown* (2007)

Mee, *The Property Rights of Cohabitees* (Oxford: Hart, 1999)

Miles, 'Property Law v Family Law: Resolving the Problems of Family Property' (2003) LS 624

Piska, 'Intention, Fairness and the Presumption of Resulting Trust after *Stack v Dowden*' (2008) 71 MLR 120

Probert, 'Equality in the Family Home?' (2007) 15 FLS 341

19

REGULATING CO-OWNERSHIP

CENTRAL ISSUES

1. Through the existence of express and implied trusts (particularly constructive trusts arising under the principles discussed in Chapter 18), it is common for the home to be co-owned.

2. English law has two forms of co-ownership: the *joint tenancy* and the *tenancy in common*. The legal position of the co-owners as between themselves differs under each form.

3. The distinguishing feature of the joint tenancy is the operation of survivorship on the death of a joint tenant.

4. A joint tenant can become a tenant in common through severance of the joint tenancy. This may occur unilaterally, by the individual act of one or

more joint tenants, or mutually, by all of the joint tenants.

5. In both forms of co-ownership, the rights and duties of the co-owners are regulated through the imposition of a trust of land, governed by the Trusts of Land and Appointment of Trustees Act 1996.

6. The 1996 Act confers powers on the trustees in relation to the management of the land and rights on the beneficiaries. In particular, it confers on certain beneficiaries a right to occupy the land.

7. The 1996 Act provides a procedure through which disputes between the co-owners are resolved by an application to court.

1 INTRODUCTION

Co-ownership describes the situation in which two or more people are concurrently entitled to legal and/or beneficial title to an estate in land. Co-ownership may arise either in relation to a freehold or leasehold estate, and is of particular relevance in understanding the legal regulation of the home. The home may be co-owned either through the existence of an express trust, or through a successful claim to ownership of the home being made under the constructive or resulting trust discussed in Chapter 18. The defining characteristic of co-ownership is that the parties have 'unity of possession'—that is, they are each entitled to possession of the whole of the land. It is unity of possession that distinguishes co-ownership from successive ownership (which is considered in Chapter 22), in which possession is enjoyed consecutively, and separate ownership of neighbouring plots of land.

The presence of co-ownership gives rise both to internal issues, in relation to the relationship between the co-owners themselves, and external issues, as regards the relationship between the co-owners and third parties. The purpose of this chapter is to consider the internal regulation of co-ownership. It is concerned with the *content* question: the relationship between the co-owners themselves, including their rights and duties in relation to each other, and whether one co-owner can insist on a sale of the land against the wishes of another. Chapters 20 and 21 consider external issues of priority between the co-owners and third-party purchasers of the land, and applications for sale of the land by third parties.

The internal regulation of co-ownership is dominated by two features of English law: firstly, the recognition of two distinct types of co-ownership—the *joint tenancy* and the *tenancy in common*; and secondly, the imposition of a trust in all cases of co-ownership. When considering the internal regulation of co-ownership, the trust is best seen as a device through which the powers of management and disposition of the land are separated from the enjoyment of the land, whether 'enjoyment' takes the form of occupation, or receipt of profits and the proceeds of sale. Through the imposition of the trust, the powers of management and disposition are vested in the legal owner or co-owners as trustee(s), while enjoyment of the land vests in the beneficial or equitable owners. Even when the same people are both trustees and beneficiaries, it is important to differentiate the capacity in which a person is exercising his or her rights and duties in relation to the land.

2 JOINT TENANTS AND TENANTS IN COMMON

Co-ownership may take the form of a joint tenancy or a tenancy in common. The essence of a *joint tenancy* is that each joint tenant is wholly entitled to the land when acting collectively, but that, individually, no single joint tenant has any 'share' in the land with which he or she can separately deal. This is reflected in Coke's[1] description of the joint tenancy: '[E]*ach joint tenant holds the whole and holds nothing, that is, he holds the whole jointly and nothing separately.*' The practical consequence of each joint tenant holding 'the whole' is that, when one dies, there is no 'share' to pass by will or intestacy. Title simply 'survives' in the remaining joint tenants through the process of survivorship: there is no passing or vesting of title in the remaining joint tenants, because they were already 'wholly entitled' themselves. The operation of survivorship is the key practical difference between the joint tenancy and the tenancy in common.

Tenants in common hold what are described as 'undivided shares' in the land. Lawson and Rudden explain this concept using the analogy of a company.

Lawson and Rudden, *The Law of Property* (3rd edn, 2002, p 93)

The simplest way to grasp the idea [of tenants in common] is to think of shares in a company. The shareholders each have a separate thing which they can alienate or leave to pass on their death, but none of them can go to the company's head office, point at a particular room and

---

[1] *Coke upon Littleton* (19th edn, 1832, p 186a).

say 'I claim my share'. So if there are two owners in common of a house each has a separate, though intangible, asset: it is the house which is not divided into distinct 'shares'.

Each tenant in common may deal with his or her share individually during his or her life-time (for example, by selling the share to another co-owner, or to a third party). On the death of a tenant in common, his or her share passes through his or her will or under the rules of intestacy. In sum, it may be said that while joint tenants can act only *collectively* and their acts necessarily affect the whole of the co-owned estate, tenants in common can also act *individually* in relation to their own undivided shares in the estate.

Where co-owners start out as joint tenants, one or more of the co-owners may subse-quently become a tenant in common through the process of severance. Co-ownership of a legal estate is, however, subject to a particular statutory framework that, through a series of provisions, confines the creation of legal co-ownership to a joint tenancy, precludes any subsequent severance of that joint tenancy, and imposes a maximum number of four joint legal owners.

Law of Property Act 1925, s 1(6)

(6) A legal estate is not capable of subsisting or of being created in an undivided share in land [...]

Law of Property Act 1925, s 36(2)

(2) No severance of a joint tenancy of a legal estate, so as to create a tenancy in common in land, shall be permissible, whether by operation of law or otherwise, but this subsection does not affect the right of a joint tenant to release his interest to the other joint tenants, or the right to server a joint tenancy in an equitable interest whether or not the legal estate is vested in the joint tenants [...]

Trustee Act 1925, s 34(2)

(2) In the case of settlements and dispositions [creating trusts of land] made or coming into operation after the commencement of this Act—

  (a) the number of trustees thereof shall not in any case exceed four, and where more than four persons are named as such trustees, the four first named (who are able and willing to act) shall alone be the trustees, and the other persons named shall not be trustees unless appointed on the occurrence of a vacancy;

  (b) the number of the trustees shall not be increased beyond four.

Hence, s 1(6) of the Law of Property Act 1925 (LPA 1925) prohibits legal tenancies in common ('undivided shares'), while s 34(2) of the Trustee Act 1925 imposes a limit of four trustees or owners of the legal title. The effect of these provisions is to create a single and indivisible legal title, held by (and registered in the names of) a maximum of four co-owners. The prohibition of severance—a logical consequence of s 1(6) of the LPA 1925—is put beyond doubt by s 36(2) of that Act. Because legal title cannot be fragmented through severance, purchasers can deal confidently with the legal owners as collective managers of the sole legal title. The certainty provided to purchasers does not come at the expense of flexibility for the co-owners: flexibility is ensured through the fact that co-ownership necessarily arises under a trust.

These provisions affect only the legal title held by the trustees. Beneficial co-owners remain free to choose between the joint tenancy and tenancy in common, with no limitation on their number.

So what happens if, contrary to these provisions, land is purported to be transferred as a legal tenancy in common? This possibility is dealt with by s 34(2) of the LPA 1925.

Law of Property Act 1925, s 34(2)

(2) Where, after the commencement of this Act, land is expressed to be conveyed to any persons in undivided shares and those persons are of full age, the conveyance shall (notwithstanding anything to the contrary in this Act) operate as if the land had been expressed to be conveyed to the grantees, or, if there are more than four grantees, to the four first named in the conveyance, as joint tenants in trust for the persons interested in the land [...]

2.1 IDENTIFYING JOINT TENANTS AND TENANTS IN COMMON

While legal title must be held as a joint tenancy, in equity, the beneficiaries may be either joint tenants or tenants in common. So how do we know whether co-owners are joint tenants or tenants in common?

Three factors may determine this. Firstly, the joint tenancy is characterized by four 'unities', which must be present for the beneficiaries to be joint tenants. In addition to unity of *possession*, these are unity of *interest* (the joint tenants have the same interest in the land), unity of *title* (the joint tenants must derive their title from the same act, for example, of adverse possession, or document), and unity of *time* (joint tenants derive their title at the same time). But while the presence of all four unities is a prerequisite for a joint tenancy, it is not determinative. A tenancy in common may still be found where the unities are present.[2]

Secondly, in an express trust, the parties may declare the capacity in which beneficial entitlement is held. In *Goodman v Gallant*,[3] the court held that such a declaration is conclusive. In *Cowcher v Cowcher*,[4] Bagnell J considered that '*A trust for A and B without further definition creates an equitable joint interest*'. In registered land, joint transferees have the opportunity to indicate on the transfer form TR1 whether equitable title is to be held as a joint tenancy—but completion of that part of the form is not mandatory and therefore issues of interpretation will continue to arise as to whether the terms of a trust are sufficient to

---

[2] Smith, *Plural Ownership* (2005, p 27).
[3] [1986] Fam 106.
[4] [1972] 1 WLR 425, 430.

declare a joint tenancy.[5] In *Robertson v Fraser*,[6] Lord Hatherley LC noted: '*I cannot doubt, having regard to the authorities respecting the effect of such words as amongst and respectively that anything which in the slightest degree indicates an intention to divide the property must be held to abrogate the idea of a joint tenancy, and to create a tenancy in common.*' A declaration that a survivor can give a valid receipt for capital moneys has been held insufficient to establish an express joint tenancy.[7]

Thirdly, in the absence of an express declaration by the parties, the status of co-owners is determined by the application of legal presumptions. The starting point is the general presumption that equity follows the law. In *Stack v Dowden*,[8] the majority of the House of Lords considered that, in the 'domestic consumer context', this presumption will only be rebutted where the contrary is proved through a common intention constructive trust (in the manner discussed in Chapter 18). Further, it was considered that cases in which the presumption would be rebutted in this way would be 'very unusual'.[9] Prior to that decision, equity was considered to favour the tenancy in common as crediting parties with a share reflecting their actual contribution and avoiding the capricious effect of survivorship that the longest survivor gains all. Hence, the initial presumption of a joint tenancy was considered to be readily rebutted where parties contributed to the purchase of land in unequal shares. Lord Neuberger preferred this approach in his dissenting judgment in *Stack v Dowden*.[10]

It may be questioned whether a strong presumption of joint tenancy (and the consequent application of survivorship) will always be appropriate in the 'domestic consumer context'. In *Stack v Dowden*, the parties were in an intimate relationship. The presumption has since been applied, in *Ritchie v Ritchie*,[11] to a house purchased by a mother and son. In that case, an initial presumption of a joint tenancy was drawn despite the fact that the parties had contributed unequally. The facts of the case (as in *Stack v Dowden*) were, however, ultimately found to be sufficiently unusual for the presumption to be rebutted.

In *Stack v Dowden*, the status of the co-owners as joint tenants or tenants in common was addressed by the House of Lords only in relation to cases of joint legal ownership. The decision does not indicate the status of parties in a case of sole legal ownership where another party (or parties) establish a beneficial interest through a contribution to the purchase. Prior to the decision, as with cases of joint legal ownership, the status of the parties would be dependent on whether they contributed equally or unequally: equal contributions were considered to be consistent with a joint tenancy. In cases of sole legal ownership, there is no initial presumption of co-ownership; the initial presumption is of sole beneficial ownership. This may be sufficient to differentiate such cases and leave the existing presumptions intact. But *Stack v Dowden* moves the ethos in determining rights in the home away from contributions (and the resulting trust) to the parties' common intention (through the constructive trust). It is consistent with this to suggest that, in sole legal ownership cases, parties should be joint tenants where, on a constructive trust analysis, there is a common intention to share equally.

---

5 *Stack v Dowden* [2007] UKHL 17, [52]–[53].

6 (1870–71) LR 6 Ch App 696.

7 *Stack v Dowden* [2007] UKHL 17, [51], approving the Court of Appeal decisions in this respect in *Harwood v Harwood* [1991] 2 FLR 274 and *Huntingford v Hobbs* [1993] 1 FLR 736.

8 [2007] UKHL 17, [58], *per* Baroness Hale.

9 Ibid, [68], *per* Baroness Hale.

10 Ibid, [109]–[110]. The presumption of a tenancy in common where parties contribute unequally remains intact in commercial cases. See, e.g., *Malayan Credit v Jack Chia* [1986] AC 549, PC.

11 Unreported, 17 August 2007. The decision is discussed by Dixon, 'The Never-Ending Story: Co-ownership After *Stack v Dowden*' [2007] Conv 456, 459–60.

2.2 SURVIVORSHIP

As has been noted, survivorship operates in a joint tenancy, with the effect that, on the death of one co-owner, title simply remains in the survivors. Through this process, the longest surviving co-owner becomes the sole owner. Practical difficulties that would arise where the co-owners die jointly are precluded by an arbitrary rule in s 184 of the LPA 1925.

Law of Property Act 1925, s 184

In all cases where, after the commencement of this Act, two or more persons have died in circumstances rendering it uncertain which of them survived the other or others, such deaths shall (subject to any order of the court), for all purposes affecting the title to property, be presumed to have occurred in order of seniority, and accordingly the younger shall be deemed to have survived the elder.

The effect of this provision is that, in the event of simultaneous deaths of joint tenants, the land passes wholly under the terms of the will (or rules of intestacy) of the youngest co-owner.

2.3 SEVERANCE

Severance is the process through which a beneficial joint tenant may become a tenant in common. By doing so, the severing joint tenant obtains an undivided share in the land that can be separately dealt with and which, on his or her death, will pass under the terms of their will or through statutory rules applicable to intestacy. The severing joint tenant is no longer affected by survivorship, which continues to operate as between any remaining joint tenants. Severance is irreversible. Because survivorship operates immediately upon the joint tenants' death, severance must take place during their lifetime. In particular, this carries the consequence that severance cannot take place by will. The severing joint tenant is invariably credited with an equal share.[12]

Four methods of severance exist. One is provided by statute in s 36(2) of the LPA 1925. That subsection also preserves the operation of other methods of severance. Three other methods have developed through case law and were summarized in the following case.

Williams v Hensman (1861) 1 J&H 546

Page-Wood VC

At 557

A joint-tenancy may be severed in three ways: in the first place, an act of any one of the persons interested operating upon his own share may create a severance as to that share. The right of each joint-tenant is a right by survivorship only in the event of no severance having

---

[12] *Goodman v Gallant* [1986] Fam 106.

taken place of the share which is claimed under the *jus accrescendi*. Each one is at liberty to dispose of his own interest in such manner as to sever it from the joint fund—losing, of course, at the same time, his own right of survivorship. Secondly, a joint-tenancy may be severed by mutual agreement. And, in the third pace, there may be a severance by any course of dealing sufficient to intimate that the interests of all were mutually treated as constituting a tenancy in common. When the severance depends on an inference of this kind without any express act of severance, it will not suffice to rely on an intention, with respect to the particular share, declared only behind the backs of the other persons interested. You must find in this class of cases a course of dealing by which the shares of all the parties to the context have been effected [...]

The methods identified by Page-Wood VC may be referred to, respectively, as an act of a joint tenant operating on his or her share, mutual agreement, and severance by a course of dealing. Of these four methods, a joint tenant may use the first two (statutory severance and an act operating on a share) unilaterally. For so long as there are two or more joint tenants, their joint tenancy remains intact between them and exists side by side with the severed tenant in common. The effect of such unilateral severance is illustrated in Figure 13.

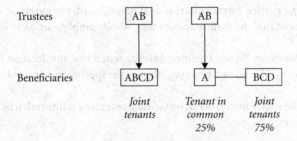

Figure 13 Unilateral severance by one joint tenant (A)

The other two methods (mutual agreement and course of dealing) necessarily involve the participation of all of the joint tenants and, if applied, bring the joint tenancy to an end by turning all of the beneficiaries into tenants in common. These methods of severance cannot be used, for example, by two of four joint tenants to sever their joint tenancy, but leave the joint tenancy intact as between the others.

In addition to these methods, severance may also arise as a consequence of the unlawful killing of one joint tenant by another.

2.3.1 Statutory severance

The statutory method of severance is found in the proviso to s 36(2) of the LPA 1925.

Law of Property Act 1925, s 36(2)

(2) Provided that, where a legal estate (not being settled land) is vested in joint tenants beneficially, and any tenant desires to sever the joint tenancy in equity, he shall give to the other joint tenants a notice in writing of such desire or do such other acts or things as would, in the

case of personal estate, have been effectual to sever the tenancy in equity, and thereupon [the land shall be held in trust on terms] which would have been requisite for giving effect to the beneficial interests if there had been an actual severance.

It is important to note that, to be effective, written notice must be served on all of the joint tenants. Written notice that is not served on all of the joint tenants will not constitute severance under this provision.

Two key issues have arisen in the application of s 36(2): firstly, what constitutes written notice; and secondly, how to identify the point in time at which notice is validly served.

What constitutes written notice?

While there is no particular form that the notice must take,[13] it must express an immediate severance and must relate to the ownership (rather than use) of the land or proceeds of sale. The latter point is highlighted by *Nielson-Jones v Fedden*.[14] In that case, severance was held not to have taken place, because the written notice dealt with use, rather than ownership, of the proceeds of sale. The notice, which took the form of a memorandum agreed between the parties, directed the husband to '*use his entire discretion and free will*' to decide whether to sell the parties' former matrimonial home in order to purchase a home for himself. Walton J noted that the memorandum was 'wholly ambiguous' as to ownership of the proceeds of sale.[15]

In *Burgess v Rawnsley*,[16] Lord Denning MR suggested that the decision in *Nielson-Jones v Fedden* was wrong. He did not, however, discuss the specific issue regarding a declaration of use.

The need for the notice to express an immediate severance is illustrated by contrasting the two following cases.

Re Draper's Conveyance [1969] 1 Ch 486, HC

Facts: A husband and wife were joint tenants of their matrimonial home. Following their divorce, the wife issued a summons under s 17 of the Married Woman's Property Act 1882 for an order that the house be sold, and the proceeds distributed equally between her and her husband—a request reflected in an affidavit sworn by her in support of her application. An order for possession and sale, and equal division of the proceeds, was made, but the husband remained in possession until his death. The question then arose as to whether severance had occurred.

Plowman J

At 492–4

The summons, coupled with the affidavit in support of it, clearly evinced an intention on the part of the plaintiff that she wished the property to be sold and the proceeds distributed, a

---

[13] There is no requirement that the notice is signed: *Re Draper's Conveyance* [1969] 1 Ch 486, 492.

[14] [1975] Ch 222.

[15] Ibid, at 229.

[16] [1975] Ch 429. See further Prichard, 'Joint Tenancies: Severance' [1975] CLJ 28, 30–1.

half to her and a half to the deceased. It seems to me that that is wholly inconsistent with the notion that a beneficial joint tenancy in that property is to continue, and therefore, apart from these objections to which I will refer in a moment, I feel little doubt that in one way or the other this joint tenancy was severed in equity before the end of February, 1966, as a result of the summons which was served on the plaintiff's then husband and as a result of what the plaintiff stated in her affidavit in support of the summons of Feb. 11, 1966 [...]

Counsel for the plaintiff took another point. Counsel for the defendants, in argument, having indicated that he relied not only on the summons as operating to sever the joint tenancy but on the orders as well, counsel for the plaintiff submitted on the authority of *Bedson v. Bedson* that there was no power in the court by an order made under the Married Women's Property Act, 1882, to sever a beneficial joint tenancy. He submitted that the power of the court was to declare what the rights of the parties were and not to alter those rights. That may well be so—for the purposes of my judgment I am prepared to assume that counsel for the plaintiff is right about that—but the view which I take is that the question does not arise here. The severance, in my judgment, is effected by the summons and the affidavit, not by any order that was made. Accordingly, in my judgment, the beneficial joint tenancy was severed by the plaintiff in the lifetime of the deceased husband, and I propose to declare that on the true construction of the above-mentioned conveyance and s. 36 of the Law of Property Act, 1925, and in the events which have happened, the plaintiff, as trustee, holds the beneficial interest in any proceeds of sale of the property after discharge of incumbrances and costs for herself and the estate of the deceased as tenants in common in equal shares.

Harris v Goddard [1983] 3 All ER 242, CA

Facts: As in *Re Draper's Conveyance*, a husband and wife were joint tenants of their matrimonial home. Following the breakdown of the relationship, the wife petitioned for divorce and requested, under the Matrimonial Causes Act 1973, '*That such order may be made by way of transfer of property and/or settlement in respect of the former matrimonial home* [...] *and otherwise as may be just*'. The husband was subsequently killed in an accident and the question arose whether this petition had acted to sever the joint tenancy.

Lawton LJ

At 246

When a notice in writing of a desire to sever is served pursuant to s. 36(2) it takes effect forthwith. It follows that a desire to sever must evince an intention to bring about the wanted result immediately. A notice in writing which expresses a desire to bring about the wanted result as some time in the future is not, in my judgment, a notice in writing within s. 36(2). Further, the notice must be one which shows an intent to bring about the consequences set out in s. 36(2), namely that the net proceeds of the statutory trust for sale "[...] shall be held upon the trust which would have been requisite for giving effect to the beneficial interests if there had been an actual severance". I am unable to accept Mr Berry's submission that a notice in writing which shows no more than a desire to bring the existing interest to an end is a good notice. It must be a desire to sever which is intended to have the statutory consequences. Paragraph 3 of the prayer to the petition does no more than invite the court to consider at some future time whether to exercise its jurisdiction under s. 24 of the 1973 Act or, if it does, to do so in one or more of three different ways. Orders under s. 24(1)(a) and (b) could bring co-ownership to an end by ways other than by severance. It follows, in my judgment, that para. 3 of the prayer of the petition did not operate as a notice in writing to sever the joint tenancy in equity. This tenancy had not been severed when Mr Harris died with the consequence that Mrs Harris is entitled to the whole of the fund held by the first and second defendants as trustees. I wish to stress that all I am saying is that para. 3 in the petition under consideration in this case did not operate as a notice of severance.

The key difference between the cases is that that the petition in *Harris v Goddard* did not evince an *immediate* desire to sever. It should be emphasized that, in *Re Draper's Conveyance*, the court acknowledged that severance was caused by the summons and affidavit, not the order of the court. Hence, where the application constitutes written notice, severance occurs regardless of whether the application is heard or, if it is, regardless of the outcome. The courts' reliance on the summons and affidavit in *Re Draper's Conveyance* caused doubt to be cast on the decision. In *Nielson-Jones v Fedden*,[17] Walton J noted that, until a court order is made, proceedings can be withdrawn. He considered that notice under s 36(2) of the LPA 1925 must be irrevocable, and therefore doubted that a summons and affidavit could suffice. This doubt was cast aside in *Harris v Goddard*.[18] Lawton LJ noted that the revocable nature of court proceedings is simply a factor for the court to consider in all of the circumstances when determining whether, on the facts of the case, notice has been served within s 36(2).

Whether it is necessary for the notice to be irrevocable appears to remain unsettled. Notably, in responding to Walton J's judgment, Lawton LJ does not explicitly reject such a requirement. But Smith suggests that the indorsement of *Re Draper's Conveyance* by the Court of Appeal, both in *Harris v Goddard* and in a further decision,[19] suffices to dispel the need to show that notice is irrevocable.[20]

When is notice of severance validly served?

Whether notice of severance has been validly served is a matter of importance, as it is from that moment that the joint tenancy is irreversibly severed, the severing joint tenant becomes a tenant in common and, as such, is no longer subject to survivorship. In most cases, this issue does not cause difficulties: written notice is sent and received, and the matter is beyond doubt. But understanding when notice is validly served may be crucial where a death occurs in close proximity of time or a joint tenant, having issued notice, seeks to intercept it following a change of mind.

The requirement in s 36(2) of the LPA 1925 is that the notice is given to the joint tenants. General guidelines on service of a notice are provided in s 196 of the Act. These have been applied to s 36(2), 'given' and 'served' being considered in this context to be synonymous.[21]

---

17 [1975] Ch 222, 236.
18 [1983] 1 WLR 1203, 1210–11.
19 *Burgess v Rawnsley* [1975] Ch 429.
20 Smith (2005, p 51).
21 *Re 88 Berkeley Road* [1971] 1 All ER 254.

Law of Property Act 1925, s 196(3) and (4)

(3) Any notice required or authorised by this Act to be served shall be sufficiently served if it is left at the last-known place of abode or business in the United Kingdom of the lessee, lessor, mortgagee, mortgagor, or other person to be served, or, in case of a notice required or authorised to be served on a lessee or mortgagor, is affixed or left for him on the land or any house or building comprised in the lease or mortgage, or, in case of a mining lease, is left for the lessee at the office or counting-house of the mine.

(4) Any notice required or authorised by this Act to be served shall also be sufficiently served, if it is sent by post in a registered letter addressed to the lessee, lessor, mortgagee, mortgagor, or other person to be served, by name, at the aforesaid place of abode or business, office, or counting-house, and if that letter is not returned [by the postal operator (within the meaning of the Postal Services Act 2000) concerned] undelivered; and that service shall be deemed to be made at the time at which the registered letter would in the ordinary course be delivered.

It should be noted that there is no requirement that the notice is actually *received* or seen by the intended recipient. It is sufficient that it reaches (or is deemed to have reached) the joint tenant's last known address. Where notice is sent by ordinary post, it is served within s 196(3) when the postman delivers the letter, because this constitutes leaving the notice at the '*last known place of abode*'.

This was held in the following case, which contains the most thorough judicial analysis of when written notice is served. As Neuberger J highlights, the seemingly unending possible factual permutations justify a clear rule.

Kinch v Bullard [1999] 1 WLR 423, HC

Facts: Mr and Mrs Johnson were beneficial joint tenants of their matrimonial home. The parties were divorcing and Mrs Johnson, who was terminally ill, sent a notice of severance to Mr Johnson by ordinary first-class post. The letter was duly delivered, but, before seeing it, Mr Johnson suffered a serious heart attack. Realizing that she was now likely to outlive her husband, Mrs Johnson destroyed the letter. Mr Johnson died a couple of weeks later, followed, in a matter of months, by Mrs Johnson. An action was brought by the parties' respective executors to determine whether the notice—delivered, but then destroyed—had operated to sever the joint tenancy. If it had, then each party had a 50 per cent share to pass under the terms of their respective wills; if not, survivorship would have operated on Mr Johnson's death, leaving the entire property to pass under Mrs Johnson's will.

Neuberger J

At 427–30

Section 196(4) deems service on the premises to have taken place if the requirements of sending by registered post and non-return by the Post Office are satisfied, even if it can be shown that physical service did not in fact take place on those premises. Section 196(3), on the other hand, requires it to be established that physical service did in fact take place on the appropriate premises, before any deemed service can arise. It appears to me that the natural meaning of s 196(3) is that if a notice can be shown to have been left at the last known abode or place of business of the addressee, then that constitutes good service, even if the addressee does not actually receive it. [. . .]

Thirdly, it was contended on behalf of the defendants that the fact that Mrs Johnson changed her mind and no longer '(desired) to sever the joint tenancy' by the time that the notice might otherwise have been said to have been 'given' (ie by the time that the notice arrived at the property) meant that the notice was ineffective to effect such severance. This argument is based on the language of s 36(2). Assuming that the notice was validly 'given' pursuant to s 196(3), the giving of the notice only occurred when it was actually delivered to the property, and at that time Mrs Johnson no longer 'desire[d] to sever the joint tenancy'. Accordingly, it is said that the statutory precondition for the giving of a valid notice was not, at the date it was given, satisfied, because at that date Mrs Johnson did not have the necessary 'desire'.

In my judgment, this argument is not correct. The function of the relevant part of s 36(2) is to instruct any joint tenant who desires to sever the joint tenancy how to do it: he is to give the appropriate notice (or do such other things as are prescribed by the section). Clear words would be required, in my judgment, before a provision such as s 36(2) could be construed as requiring the court to inquire into the state of mind of the sender of the notice. Once the sender has served the requisite notice, the deed is done and cannot be undone. The position is the same as with a contractual right to determine a lease, which normally entitles either or both parties to serve notice to determine the lease if it desires to put an end to the term. Once the procedure has been set in train, and the relevant notice has been served, it is not open to the giver of the notice to withdraw the notice, and I have never heard it suggested that a change of mind before the notice is given would render it ineffective.

I reach this conclusion based on the proper construction of s 36(2). However, it appears to me that it is also correct as a matter of policy. If it were possible for a notice of severance or any other notice to be ineffective because, between the sender putting it in the post and the addressee receiving it, the sender changed his mind, it would be inconvenient and potentially unfair. The addressee would not be able to rely confidently upon a notice after it had been received, because he might subsequently be faced with the argument that the sender had changed his mind after sending it and before its receipt. Further, as I have already mentioned, it is scarcely realistic to think that the legislature intended that the court could be required to inquire into the state of mind of the sender of the notice in order to decide whether the notice was valid.

I am inclined to think that the position would be different if, before the notice was 'given', the sender had informed the addressee that he wished to revoke it. In such a case, it appears to me that the notice would have been withdrawn before it had been 'given'. After all, as is clear from the reasoning at first instance and in the Court of Appeal in *Holwell Securities Ltd v Hughes* [1973] 2 All ER 476 at 481, [1973] 1 WLR 757 at 761–762; [1974] 1 All ER 161 at 164, 166–167, [1974] 1 WLR 155 at 158–159, 160–162, a notice sent by post is not 'served' in accordance with s 196(3) until it arrives at the premises to which it has been addressed. Accordingly, it seems to me that, while the notice is still in the post, it has not been given, and, until it is given, the sender has in effect a locus poenitentiae whereby he can withdraw the notice, but only provided his withdrawal is communicated to the addressee before the notice is given to, or served on, the addressee. I should emphasise, however, that this is no more than a tentative view.

Fourthly, it is said that, in the present case, the notice was not 'left' at the property within the meaning of s 196(3). Assuming that, before the notice was actually posted through the letter box, Mrs Johnson had decided that she would pick it up and destroy it, and bearing in mind that she was the person whose notice it was, it is said that the notice was never really 'left' for Mr Johnson at the property. In my judgment, that argument is wrong as a matter of principle, and would be inconvenient to apply in practice.

So far as the principle is concerned, it seems to me that, by putting the notice in the post, Mrs Johnson effectively left it to the Post Office to serve the notice on her behalf. One therefore has to ask oneself whether the person who was, in effect, appointed by Mrs Johnson to serve the notice, acted in accordance with the test propounded by Russell LJ in Lord Newborough's case. In my judgment, by posting the envelope containing the notice, and addressed to Mr Johnson at the property, through the letter box of the property, the postman served the notice in accordance with that test. I do not think that it is right to test the matter by reference to what Mrs Johnson thought or intended, because, she left it to the Post Office to serve the notice. Accordingly, subject to any other arguments, once the notice was posted through the letter box, it had been 'served' in accordance with s 196(3), and therefore 'given' in accordance with s 36(2), and, as I have mentioned, such a notice cannot be 'un-served' or 'un-given'.

So far as convenience is concerned, I consider that, if s 196(3) is satisfied once it is shown that the relevant document was bona fide delivered to the last-known place of abode or business of the addressee, then, although it might lead to an unfair result in an exceptional case, the law is at least simple and clear. On the other hand, if the court starts implying exceptions into the clear and simple statutory procedure, confusion and uncertainty could result. Thus, if, by picking up the notice after it was posted through the front door of the property, Mrs Johnson might have prevented the notice being 'served', problems could arise. Would there be a maximum time within which Mrs Johnson would have to pick up the notice before it would be held to be validly served? Would it make any difference if Mr Johnson had seen the envelope containing the notice on the mat? What if Mrs Johnson had picked up the notice and had kept it but not destroyed it? What if she had picked up the notice intending to destroy it but had changed her mind? What if she had picked up the notice and tried to destroy it, but Mr Johnson had seen her doing it, or had seen and read the imperfectly burnt notice?

Hence, notice was served at the time that the letter was delivered. Once this had occurred, it was too late for Mrs Johnson to seek to change her mind.

Similarly, in the earlier case of *Re 88 Berkeley Road*,[22] severance was held to have occurred when written notice was sent by registered post and signed for on delivery by the sender without, it seems, ever being passed on to the other joint tenant.

2.3.2 An act of a joint tenant operating on his or her share

An act of a joint tenant severs the joint tenancy by destroying one or more of the unities of title, time, and interest.[23] This first head of severance, identified in *Williams v Hensman*,[24] runs into the immediate logical difficulty that joint tenants do not have 'shares': on what basis can a joint tenant 'act' upon a share that he or she does not have? Logical difficulties are sidestepped by treating the act itself as causing severance and so freeing up the share as the subject matter of the act in question.[25]

---

[22] [1971] 1 All ER 254.
[23] Prichard (1975, p 29) (referring specifically to destruction of unity of title).
[24] (1861) J&H 546, (1861) 70 ER 862.
[25] Crown, 'Severance of Joint Tenancy by Partial Alienation' (2001) 117 LQR 477, 478.

In *Williams v Hensman*, Page-Wood VC referred to an act of disposition. The disposition may be voluntary—for example, through the sale of a share—or involuntary—as where a joint tenant's bankruptcy causes his or her share to vest in their trustee in bankruptcy. Despite the terms of Page-Wood VC's judgment, an actual disposition appears unnecessary. Joint tenants have also been held to have acted on their share by, for example, entering a contract for sale[26] or simply through acquiring a greater share than other joint tenants.[27]

The position is more complex if one joint tenant buys out the share of another. In such a case, the purchasing joint tenant is a tenant in common as regards the newly acquired share, but remains a joint tenant in relation to his or her original interest. Hence, just as the joint tenancy and tenancy in common can subsist side by side, the same beneficiary may be a joint tenant in relation to his or her initial interest and a tenant in common as regards a subsequently acquired interest (see Figure 14).

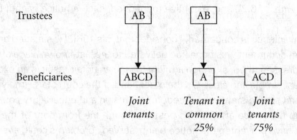

Figure 14 Severance by one joint tenant (B) selling his or her share to another joint tenant (A)

The ultimate limit on the scope of this head of severance is that there must be *an act* operating on the share. A unilateral declaration of intent to sever by a joint tenant is not effective. In the absence of an act operating on his or her share, the joint tenant must follow the requirements of s 36(2) of the LPA 1925 and serve written notice in order to affect severance. In *Nielson-Jones v Fedden*,[28] Walton J considered there to be 'no conceivable ground' for suggesting that a unilateral declaration can ever be effective to sever.

Voluntary dispositions

An outright transfer of a share by a joint tenant by sale or gift, whether to another joint tenant or a third party, is the clearest example of an act operating on a share. More contentious is the effect of a partial alienation, where the transferring joint tenant retains an interest and the transfer itself may have only temporal effect.[29]

The most significant practical example of partial alienation is a mortgage or charge of an equitable share. The beneficiary-mortgagor retains an interest in property and (subject to an action for default) the mortgage will eventually be discharged. Such mortgages may

---

[26] *Brown v Raindle* (1796) 3 Ves 296, (1796) 30 ER 998.

[27] *Megarry and Wade: The Law of Real Property* (7th edn, eds Harpum et al, 2008, [13–041]).

[28] [1975] Ch 222, 230. Previous judicial acceptance to the contrary is criticised by Baker (1968) 84 LQR 462. See further, *Burgess v Rawnsley* [1975] Ch 429, 448, where, in a summary of principles, Sir John Pennycuick noted: 'An uncommunicated declaration by one party to the other or indeed a mere verbal notice by one party to another clearly cannot operate as a severance.'

[29] Crown (2001, pp 479–80).

be unlikely to be granted expressly, because the security of a beneficial share may not be commercially attractive, but they arise, not infrequently, as the result of a failed attempt by a single joint tenant to mortgage the legal title through, for example, forgery or undue influence committed against the other co-owners.[30] Such a mortgage has no effect on the legal title, but operates as a mortgage of the joint tenant's beneficial interest: does such a mortgage affect a severance? The issue is of importance, because, if severance does not take place, the mortgagee '*joins the survivorship wheel of fortune*', with his or her security interest over the property lost on the death of the mortgagor.[31]

In *First National Security v Hegerty*,[32] a husband forged his wife's signature on a legal charge to use the property as security for a loan. Bingham J considered this to constitute a disposition of the husband's beneficial share, which severed the beneficial joint tenancy and created a valid equitable charge over the husband's share. While this remains the current position, the matter was not argued in the case (it being unclear whether the parties were joint tenants or tenants in common) and academic doubt has since been cast on the issue.

Nield suggests that the distinction between a mortgage and a charge may be crucial in this context. A mortgage of an equitable interest necessarily takes effect as an assignment of the interest and therefore involves a disposition.[33] In contrast, she argues that the inherent nature of a charge means that an equitable charge should not affect severance.

Nield, 'To Sever or Not to Sever: The Effect of a Mortgage by One Joint Tenant' [2001] Conv 462, 469–70

However the historical and comparative evidence against severance by equitable charge is strong. At common law, although alienation was preferred over survivorship, survivorship was preferred over the creation of a mere encumbrance. It has long been asserted that easements and rentcharges do not effect a severance. They are encumbrances and as such are said not to be inconsistent with the nature of a joint tenancy, even though they may create a distinction between the interests of the joint tenants. For instance, it has been suggested that a rentcharge would not disturb the joint tenancy for it could be paid out of the joint tenant's portion of the income from the land, even though re-entry might follow if payments were not made. An easement granted by one joint tenant will only effect the interest held by that joint tenant and the right granted thus must be exercised in common with the rights of the other joint tenant.

Equitable charges are mere encumbrances that give no right to possession. The chargee may apply to court for an order for sale or the appointment of a receiver over the charged property. It is accepted that an equitable charge creates some sort of interest that is proprietary in nature but there is considerable hesitation in acknowledging this interest as an interest in the land itself. There are thus even weaker grounds for claiming that an equitable charge should effect a severance, because it destroys the unities, than in the case of a rentcharge or easement, which are clearly interests in land.

---

[30] Nield, 'To Sever or not to Sever: The Effect of a Mortgage by One Joint Tenant' [2001] Conv 462, 462–3.

[31] Ibid, p 463. The debt remains and will need to be met from the mortgagor's estate.

[32] [1965] 1 QB 850.

[33] Nield (2001, p 467).

In contrast, Crown considers that the issue of severance should not be left to technical questions as to whether alienation occurs. He suggests the matter should be addressed by considering whether there are policy reasons for preferring one approach to the other.

Crown, 'Severance of a Joint Tenancy of Land by Partial Alienation' (2001) 117 LQR 477, 483

One can easily imagine a situation where A and B are joint tenants in law and equity of land. A grants an equitable mortgage of his "share". If the approach of *Re Sharer* is adopted, this severs the joint tenancy in equity, but B may know nothing about it. Suppose A repays the loan with the result that the mortgage is discharged, and subsequently B dies. B's personal representatives will have no way of finding out about the creation of the mortgage and the result will be that A will succeed to the entire estate by virtue of the doctrine of survivorship. If A were to die first, however, a different result might well occur. A's personal representatives may well find documentary evidence of the creation of the mortgage while going through his papers. They will then be able to argue successfully that the joint tenancy was severed with the result that they will succeed to half the estate. Policy considerations therefore point strongly towards adopting the view that the grant of an equitable mortgage will not sever a joint tenancy.

Underlying Crown's concern is the risk of a mortgage of an equitable interest causing severance without the knowledge of other joint tenants. While the example he gives is not an attractive outcome, however, it is acknowledged as a unique feature of this head of severance that it enables a joint tenant to sever in secret, without the participation of, or giving of notice to, the other joint tenants.[34]

A novel approach to severance has been suggested in relation to a different example of partial alienation: the unilateral grant of a lease by one joint tenant. As with a mortgage, the joint tenant retains an interest in the land and the status quo is returned to at the end of the lease. As will be seen in Chapter 23, the essential characteristic of a lease is exclusive possession. The effect of a single joint tenant granting a lease is therefore to confer on the tenant of the lease exclusive possession against all persons other than those joint tenants who did not take part in the grant.[35] There is no clear authority determining whether the grant of a lease by one joint tenant constitutes an act of severance.[36] One possibility in such a case is that the joint tenancy is suspended for the duration of the lease, but is resurrected when the lease expires. The suspension of the joint tenancy ensures that if the grantor of the lease dies during its duration, survivorship does not operate, which ensures that the tenant's lease is unaffected by the death.

The possibility of the joint tenancy being suspended is explored by Crown.

---

[34] Smith (2005, p 58).

[35] Crown (2001, p 484).

[36] Ibid, pp 485–90. He notes that while sixteenth-century cases indicate that the grant of a lease by one joint tenant of a leasehold estate affects a severance, there is no authority dealing with the grant of a lease by one joint tenant of a freehold estate. Courts in other jurisdictions have reached different conclusions on the matter.

Crown, 'Severance of a Joint Tenancy of Land by Partial Alienation' (2001) 117 LQR 477, 488

The notion of a suspension of the joint tenancy has, however, been criticised on the ground that "once a severance, albeit temporary, has occurred, surely the unity of interest of the joint tenants is destroyed, and the co-owners cannot afterward be regarded as enjoying unity of title and time". This argument has a certain attraction, but one needs to bear in mind that the very idea of severance by alienation is based on a logical fallacy, as pointed out at the beginning of this article. Joint tenants do not have separate shares in the land. The alienor disposes of an interest that he does not actually have and this "transfer" creates the very interest, which was supposedly the subject-matter of the transfer in the first place. The truth of the matter is that modern lawyers accept the idea of severance by alienation not because it makes any logical sense, but simply because it is enshrined in the case law. The notion of suspension of a joint tenancy may not be so solidly rooted in the case law, but it is not a new idea and can be supported by reference to the earlier literature preceding Dixon J.'s remarks in *Wright v. Gibbons*. Moreover, it is by no means clear that the co-owners should not be regarded as enjoying unity of title, time and interest after the expiry of the lease. So far as unity of title is concerned, the co-owners still claim title to the land under the same act or document. So far as unity of time is concerned, the interest of each co-owner did indeed vest at the same time. So far as unity of interest is concerned, once the lease has come to an end, the interest of each joint tenant is the same in extent, nature and duration.

Perhaps the strongest argument for the idea of suspension of the joint tenancy in leasehold cases arises out of practical considerations. It has been argued here that the existence of a simple method of severance under modern statute law means that there is no need to increase the number of cases of severance in equity. Indeed, it is undesirable to do so where there is a risk that this might make it possible for one co-owner to sever behind the back of his fellow co-owner. Such a risk may indeed exist in the case of leases.

Fox also supports the suspension of the joint tenancy.[37] If accepted, could the same solution be adopted to the more practically important case of a mortgage? Crown highlights that leases are different from mortgages, because a lease must come to an end, while a mortgage carries the risk that the security will be enforced. He suggests that this may explain the different effect each has on severance. Nield, however considers the suspension of the joint tenancy (or some other means of modifying survivorship) to *provide tantalising compromises to balance the interests of the mortgagee and joint tenants and deserve serious consideration*.[38]

A final example of partial alienation is a declaration by a joint tenant of a trust of his or her share. In this instance, severance seems likely to arise by analogy with the effect of a contract to sell the share outright. Such a contract gives rise to a constructive trust through the maxim 'equity looks on as done that which ought to be done'. If a constructive trust effects severance, it necessarily follows that an express trust must also do so.[39]

---

[37] Fox, 'Unilateral Demise by a Joint Tenant: Does it Effect a Severance?' [2000] Conv 208.
[38] Nield (2001, p 474).
[39] Smith (2005, pp 59–60); Crown (2001, pp 490–2).

Involuntary disposition

The most likely instance of severance by an involuntary disposition is the bankruptcy of a joint tenant. While bankruptcy undoubtedly causes severance, debate continues as to the time at which severance occurs. This can be significant where the bankrupt (or another joint tenant) dies during the course of the bankruptcy. If death pre-dates the time of severance, then survivorship operates, taking the beneficial interest beyond the reach of the creditors.

There are three possible dates from which severance may take effect: the date of the act of bankruptcy; the date on which the joint tenant is declared bankrupt; and the date of appointment of the trustee in bankruptcy.

The date of the act of bankruptcy was favoured by the common law and was applied under the Bankruptcy Act 1914 in *Re Dennis*.[40] In that case, the bankrupt and his wife were joint tenants of their home. Between the date of the act of bankruptcy (by failing to comply with a bankruptcy notice) and the declaration of bankruptcy, the wife died. The court held that severance occurred at the date of the act of bankruptcy. This meant that, on her death, the wife was a tenant in common of a 50 per cent share, which passed to the couple's children. If the date of the declaration of bankruptcy had been chosen, survivorship would have operated on the wife's death, leaving the bankrupt as sole owner and the entire house therefore available to his creditors.

In *Re Palmer*,[41] which was decided under the Insolvency Act 1986, a different analysis was taken. Under s 306 of that Act, the bankrupt's estate vests in the trustee in bankruptcy immediately upon appointment; from the time of the declaration of bankruptcy, however, the Official Receiver holds the estate in trust. The court held that severance therefore occurs at the time of the declaration of bankruptcy. In that case, Mr Palmer was declared bankrupt after his death. In such a case, the declaration dates back to the day of death, so the bankrupt's estate on that day vests in the trustee in bankruptcy. The court held, however, that this did not include a joint tenancy that the bankrupt had at the start of the day, but which ceased to exist at the moment of his death through survivorship. Through survivorship, Mr Palmer's wife became solely entitled to the home, which was protected from the effect of the bankruptcy.

Both decisions produce results that are sympathetic to the bankrupt's family. The courts' choice as to the date of severance conflicts and, while factually distinct, there is no logical reason for treating the date of severance as different, according to whether bankruptcy occurs during the bankrupt's lifetime, or after his or her death. The analysis in *Re Palmer* should now be followed in all cases, because it applies the current legislation. If applied to the facts of *Re Dennis*, it would appear to reverse the decision in that case.

Subsequent to the decision in *Re Palmer*, the Insolvency Act 2000 inserted s 421A into the Insolvency Act 1986. The effect of that provision is that where a joint tenant is declared bankrupt after his or her death (so that survivorship operates in favour of the remaining joint tenants), the survivors may be required by the court, on an application by the trustee in bankruptcy, to compensate the bankrupt's estate by payment of a sum not exceeding the value lost through survivorship. Hence, while the operation of severance remains governed by *Re Palmer*, the financial consequences of the decision may be reversed by an application under s 421A.

---

[40] [1996] Ch 80.
[41] [1994] Ch 316.

2.3.3 Severance through mutual agreement

The scope of the second category of severance identified by Page-Wood VC in *Williams v Hensman* is difficult to pinpoint in the abstract: it is sandwiched between the stricter requirement of an 'act' and the more liberal third category of a course of dealings. Collectively, mutual agreement and a course of dealings differ from statutory severance and an act operating on a share, because they only enable severance by all of the joint tenants. They differ from the other common law methods of severance as regards the rationale for severance. As we have noted, an act operating on a share effects severance by the destruction of one or more of the unities of title, time, and interest.[42] In cases of mutual agreement and a course of dealings, the rationale for severance is the common intentions of the parties. Destruction of a unity is the result of the severance, not the cause of it.[43]

The Court of Appeal applied severance by mutual agreement in the following case. Browne LJ's judgment demonstrates both the similarities and differences between this method and the other two recognized in *Williams v Hensman*.

Burgess v Rawnsley [1975] Ch 429, CA

Facts: Mr Honick and Mrs Rawnsley were joint tenants of a house occupied by Mr Honick alone. The property had been purchased in the expectation that the parties would both live there, but while Mr Honick anticipated marriage, Mrs Rawnsley intended to live alone in the upstairs flat. The parties' mismatched expectations came to light after the purchase. Mrs Rawnsley did not move in, but reached an oral agreement to sell her share to Mr Honick for £750. She then changed her mind and sought a higher price. Matters stood this way at Mr Honick's death, whereupon the house was sold and Mrs Burgess, his administratrix, sought to establish that severance had occurred, leaving his estate entitled to 50 per cent of the proceeds of sale.

Browne LJ

At 443–4

Counsel for Mrs Rawnsley conceded, as is clearly right, that if there had been an enforceable agreement by Mrs Rawnsley to sell her share to Mr Honick, that would produce a severance of the joint tenancy; but he says that an oral agreement, unenforceable because of s 40 of the Law of Property Act 1925, is not enough. Section 40 merely makes a contract for the disposition of an interest in land unenforceable by action in the absence of writing. It does not make it void. But here Mrs Burgess is not seeking to enforce by action the agreement by Mrs Rawnsley to sell her share to Mr Honick. She relies on it as effecting the severance in equity of the joint tenancy. An agreement to sever can be inferred from a course of dealing (see Lefroy B in *Wilson v Bell* and Stirling J in *Re Wilks*) and there would in such a case ex hypothesi be no express agreement but only an inferred, tacit agreement, in respect of which there would seldom if ever be writing sufficient to satisfy s 40. It seems to me that the point is that the agreement establishes that the parties no longer intended the tenancy to operate as a joint tenancy and that automatically effects a severance. I think the reference in *Megarry*

---

[42] See section 2.3.2 above.
[43] Prichard (1975, pp 29–30).

and Wade to specifically enforceable contracts only applies where the suggestion is that the joint tenancy has been severed by an alienation by one joint tenant to a third party, and does not apply to severance by agreement between joint tenants. I agree with counsel for Mrs Burgess that s 40 ought to have been pleaded, but I should be very reluctant to decide this case on a pleading point.

The result is that I would uphold the county court judge's judgment on his second ground, namely, that the joint tenancy was severed by an agreement between Mrs Rawnsley and Mr Honick that she would sell her share to him for £750. In my view her subsequent repudiation of that agreement makes no difference. I would dismiss the appeal on this ground.

Section 40 of the LPA 1925 has since between replaced by s 2(1) of the Law of Property (Miscellaneous Provisions) Act 1989 (LP(MP)A 1989), under which an oral contract for sale of land is void. This change does not, however, alter the decision in the case. Browne LJ's judgment demonstrates that there was no act operating on a share in the absence of a specifically enforceable contract; there was, instead, an informal agreement, drawn from the parties' course of dealing. It is emphasized, however, that severance was based on mutual agreement, not on the course of dealings itself. The Court of Appeal was unanimous that severance had occurred under this method, while, as will be seen, the judges were divided on the possible application of course of dealings as an alternative basis for severance. Browne LJ's judgment leaves that method of severance to apply where the course of dealings falls short of even an informal agreement.

In *Hunter v Babbage*,[44] although an informal agreement was found on the facts, the court suggested that such agreement is not necessary for this method of severance. Drawing on comments in the judgment of *Williams v Hensman*, Deputy Judge John McDonnell QC considered that it would be sufficient if it could be inferred that the parties had mutually treated their interests as a tenancy in common.[45]

2.3.4 Severance through a course of dealings

Actions between parties falling short of establishing a mutual agreement will still sever if there is a sufficient course of dealings to intimate that the parties regarded themselves as tenants in common. The exact demarcation of this method with mutual agreement may be difficult to identify with certainty, particularly if, as has been suggested, mutual agreement can include cases falling short of an actual agreement. Practically, nothing may turn on any overlap between the categories. It is more important to note, as was emphasized by Pennycuick LJ in *Burgess v Rawnsley*,[46] that this method of severance is distinct from mutual agreement, not merely a subheading of that category.

In that case, the judges were divided on whether a course of dealings provided an alternative means of severance on the facts.

---

[44] (1995) 69 P & CR 548.
[45] Ibid, at 554.
[46] [1975] Ch 429, 447.

Burgess v Rawnsley [1975] Ch 429, CA

Lord Denning MR

At 440

Even if there was not any firm agreement but only a course of dealing, it clearly evinced an intention by both parties that the property should henceforth be held in common and not jointly.

Pennycuick LJ

At 447

I do not doubt myself that where one tenant negotiates with another for some rearrangement of interest, it may be possible to infer from the particular facts a common intention to sever even though the negotiations break down. Whether such an inference can be drawn must I think depend on the particular facts. In the present case the negotiations between Mr Honick and Mrs Rawnsley, if they can be properly described as negotiations at all, fall, it seems to me, far short of warranting an inference. One could not ascribe to joint tenants an intention to sever merely because one offers to buy out the other for £X and the other makes a counter-offer of £Y.

Browne LJ expressed no final opinion on the matter. The key issue appears to be when negotiations falling short of an agreement are sufficient to effect severance. Lord Denning MR appears to take a broad view of this issue, reflected both in his decision in *Burgess v Rawnsley* and in his discussion, in his judgment in that case, of *Nielson-Jones v Fedden*.[47] In that case, as has been seen,[48] a memorandum granting the husband discretion to sell the house was considered insufficient to sever under s 36(2) of the LPA 1925 on the basis that it dealt with use, rather than ownership of the proceeds of sale. At the time of the husband's death, a contract for sale had been entered and a deposit paid by the purchaser. It was argued, as an alternative to s 36(2), that the parties' discussions, as regards their financial arrangements and the distribution of part of the deposit, constituted severance. Walton J rejected this argument, on the basis that no agreement could be drawn from the parties' ongoing negotiations.

We have seen that Lord Denning MR considered the decision to be wrong in relation to s 36(2). He further suggested that severance had occurred through a course of dealings:[49] '*The husband and wife entered on a course of dealing sufficient to sever the joint tenancy. They entered into negotiations that the property should be sold. Each received £200 out of the deposit paid by the purchaser. That was sufficient.*' To the extent that reliance is placed on negotiations, these should be accepted only where the agreement, if reached, would have been sufficient to sever within the category of mutual conduct. If the agreement would have been insufficient to affect severance, it necessarily follows that negotiations for the agreement cannot do so.[50]

---

[47] [1975] Ch 222.
[48] See section 2.3.1 above.
[49] *Burgess v Rawnsley* [1975] Ch 429, 440.
[50] *Hunter v Babbage* (1995) 69 P & CR 548, 560.

2.3.5 Severance through unlawful killing

Public policy prevents a person responsible for the unlawful death of another from benefiting from their death. Such benefit could arise through the operation of survivorship where one joint tenant is responsible for the death of another. The public policy rule is achieved through forfeiture under the Forfeiture Act 1982, with the possibility of relief.

In *Re K*,[51] Vinelott J accepted the view of counsel that '*the forfeiture rule unless modified under the Act of 1982 applies in effect to sever the joint tenancy in the proceeds of sale and in the rents and profits until sale*'. This implies that, where relief is awarded, the correct analysis is that severance does not occur, leaving survivorship to operate. Hence, it is the availability of relief that determines whether severance occurs.[52] In *Re K*, relief was awarded where a battered wife, who had unintentionally shot and killed her husband (her intention had been merely to threaten him), had been convicted of manslaughter.

The culpability of the defendant has since been confirmed as the principal factor in determining relief.[53]

2.3.6 Are the current severance rules satisfactory?

In 1985, in its Working Paper on *Trusts of Land*, the Law Commission considered two radical reforms of severance: firstly, limiting severance to the statutory method of written notice; secondly, enabling severance by will.[54] Reform of severance was not carried over into the subsequent final report on *Trusts of Land*, on the basis that the issue is also relevant to personal property; instead, the Law Commission indicated that the matter would form the basis of a separate, future report.[55] The Law Commission has, in fact, carried out no further work in this respect. Notwithstanding, its suggestions have continued to attract academic attention in discussions of possible reforms.[56]

The limitation of severance to written notice necessarily carries the consequence of the abolition of the *Williams v Hensman* methods of severance. We have seen that these methods of severance do cause difficulties in interpretation and application. The underlying question, therefore, is whether these difficulties are sufficient to support the extreme response of abolition—a question addressed by Tee, together with the other reform discussed by the Law Commission: the introduction of severance by will.

Tee, 'Severance Revisited' [1995] Conv 105, 110–13

The abolition of severance by acting upon one's share has a certain attraction in logic—there has always been an intellectual sleight of hand which allows the alienation both to transform and transfer the interest, but it would effectively prevent a joint tenant from dealing with his equitable interest in any way. Voluntary alienation, whether by sale or mortgage

---

[51] [1985] Ch 85, 100.

[52] The practical focus on the availability of relief is noted by Bridge, 'Assisting Suicide Rendered Financially Painless' [1998] CLJ 31, 32.

[53] *Dunbar v Plant* [1998] Ch 412, in which relief was awarded to the survivor of a suicide pact who was clearly criminally complicit in the suicide of her fiancé, although had not been charged.

[54] Law Commission Working Paper No 94, *Trusts of Land* (1985, [16.11]–[16.14]).

[55] Law Commission Report No 181, *Transfer of Land: Trusts of Land* (1989, [1.3]).

[56] Tee, 'Severance Revisited' [1995] Conv 105; Smith (2005, pp 79–82).

would be impossible, unless there had been a prior severance. Thus, for example, an inno-cent mortgagee would only obtain an unsecured debt if a determined rogue "mortgaged" his unsevered "share". Involuntary alienation, as, for example, in bankruptcy, would also be affected. At present, the vesting of the debtor's estate in the trustee in bankruptcy automat-ically severs the debtor's joint tenancy and vests the resultant tenancy in common in the trustee. An absolute requirement of written notice would complicate an already difficult area of the law and could result in unfairness to creditors where the bankrupt held property as a beneficial joint tenant.

The abolition of severance by mutual agreement or by mutual conduct would have fewer legal repercussions. It is arguable that severance on such grounds has been found so rarely by the courts over the last 50 years that the abolition of these methods would not in practice amount to a serious limitation, and would produce much needed certainty. When personal representatives feel obliged to go to court to discover the beneficial entitlement to a home after the death of an erstwhile joint tenant, land law is shown in a poor light; the stress of any litigation is self-evident, and the timing, shortly after a death, and the subject matter, a home, must only compound the unhappiness for the parties involved.

What is uncertain, however, is how often severance on one of these grounds has been rec-ognised and accepted by practitioners without resort to court. The Working Paper suggests that "if either has behaved as though the joint tenancy does not exist and treated the property as his own, it seems right that the law should accept that [...]" If indeed people often act in this way, then the abolition of informal methods of severance could result in widespread unfairness. The advantage of permitting informal methods, in terms of fairness to lay people, has to be weighed against the disadvantage of the uncertainty engendered by the possibility of informal severance having taken place.

(c) The introduction of severance by will

This is a radical suggestion, which runs counter to the whole concept of joint tenancy with its right of survivorship. This right is its distinctive feature, and is why equity in general favours the less capricious tenancy in common. Thus the arguments in favour of introducing sever-ance by will must be carefully examined. The Working Paper mentions that in a matrimonial breakdown a spouse may be anxious to sever but unwilling to serve a notice and thereby aggravate negotiations over, for example, access to the children. The argument has a cer-tain force, but the period during which such considerations hold sway should be quite short. In any relationship breakdown negotiations over children and property may be delicate and fraught, but they still need to be pursued and any property arrangement would be incomplete without an explicit decision as to the beneficial ownership of the home.

A more persuasive argument is that severance by will would prevent undesired devolution of property. There must be many cases where a beneficial joint tenant leaves his property by will, fondly (and not unreasonably) imagining that thereby the "half share" in the house will go to his children, his new loved one or whomever. No doubt the testator was told about the right of survivorship and the methods of severance when he originally bought the house, but that could have been many years ago. Presumably, the deceased testator is never aware that his wishes have been frustrated. The cases do not come to court because the law is clear: one cannot bequeath a beneficial joint tenancy. Although the problem would not occur if a testator took proper legal advice before making a will, this frequently does not happen.

The counter argument is two-fold: first, it would be unfair to allow severance by will and second, difficult questions of construction would arise. The first argument is that a "rogue" beneficial joint tenant could secretly sever by will and then enjoy the possibility of the right of survivorship without any risk to his estate. If he survived his co-tenant, he would take all, and if he pre-deceased, his chosen beneficiaries would inherit his share. Thus he could both "have his cake and eat it". His co-tenant, meanwhile, would not know of his severance by will, and would assume that the right of survivorship was going to operate. By the time she discovered her mistake (after the rogue's death), it would be too late for her to rearrange her affairs. Or she might die first, never knowing that she had been duped. It is possible to riposte that she must have been content that the rogue should take the house or she, too, would have made a will to the contrary, or would previously have severed inter vivos. Also, although she might have relied financially upon acquiring the rogue's "share" after his death, such reliance would not have been secure anyway—up until the moment of death, the rogue could have served a notice of severance—and the family provision legislation should cure any dependancy problems. But still one's immediate reaction is that the law should not facilitate such apparently unscrupulous behaviour, or permit a joint tenant to break faith with his co-tenants with impunity. A sophisticated argument that the unfairness is more apparent than real is not the basis upon which to apply legislative reform, especially one which directly affects so many people.

The other difficulty with severance by will is a practical one—the construction of the will. The Working Paper states that severance by will should be specified and explicit: "Severance should not be implied by a gift, for example, of all the residue to a charity, but a gift of 'my halfshare of Blackacre' should be sufficiently explicit to sever". Those examples seem clear enough, but the gift of all the residue to the testator's children, or indeed of "all to mother", would be far more problematic. At present, it is sometimes uncertain whether inter vivos severance has taken place; the additional possibility of severance by will would no doubt result in still more uncertainty for the survivors and a succession of applications to the court. The question to be decided is whether the real problem of undesired property devolution is sufficiently serious to warrant a reform which will in turn produce problems both of principle and practice.

While both reforms discussed by the Law Commission are drawn from dissatisfaction with the operation of the current rules, they provide polarized responses that strengthen or weaken the role of survivorship. Abolition of the *Williams v Hensman* methods of severance would inevitably appear to increase the incidence of survivorship; in contrast, the introduction of severance by will would enable joint tenants to undermine the very essence of the joint tenancy as a gamble on survivorship. Because survivorship is the key difference between the two forms of co-ownership, perhaps the underlying issue is the desirability of the beneficial joint tenancy. The scope and purpose of any reform must logically reflect a policy decision as to the desirability of the joint tenancy. Without this, there is a danger of focusing on the symptoms, whilst ignoring the disease.

We return to this issue at the end of this part of the chapter, after first noting the methods through which co-ownership is brought to an end.

3 TERMINATION OF CO-OWNERSHIP

Co-ownership comes to an end once there is a sole legal and equitable owner. Where the same person is entitled in law and equity, this also marks the end of the trust. Where the legal and equitable owners are different (for example, if *T* is the sole legal owner and *B* the sole beneficial owner), a bare trust remains.

Termination of co-ownership in this way may arise through a variety of circumstances. In a joint tenancy, the longest surviving co-owner will become solely entitled through survivorship. A sole beneficiary who is of full age and capacity may insist that legal co-owners transfer legal title to him or her through the rule in *Saunders v Vautier*.[57] It should be noted, however, that where co-owned land is sold to a single purchaser, even assuming that the beneficial interests do not bind the purchaser under the priority rules discussed in Chapter 20, co-ownership is not terminated. While the purchaser solely owns the land, the co-owner's interests (whether as joint tenants or tenants in common) shift from the land into the proceeds of sale.

Co-ownership may also be brought to an end through the process of partition, as provided for by s 7 of TOLATA 1996. This is a process through which the trustees may physically divide the land and transfer separate plots into the sole ownership of the beneficiaries. The beneficiaries thus cease to be co-owners, with unity of possession over the land, and become sole owners of their separate parcels of land.

Trusts of Land and Appointment of Trustees Act 1996, s 7(1)–(5)

(1) The trustees of land may, where beneficiaries of full age are absolutely entitled in undivided shares to land subject to the trust, partition the land, or any part of it, and provide (by way of mortgage or otherwise) for the payment of any equality money.

(2) The trustees shall give effect to any such partition by conveying the partitioned land in severalty (whether or not subject to any legal mortgage created for raising equality money), either absolutely or in trust, in accordance with the rights of those beneficiaries.

(3) Before exercising their powers under subsection (2) the trustees shall obtain the consent of each of those beneficiaries.

(4) Where a share in the land is affected by an incumbrance, the trustees may either give effect to it or provide for its discharge from the property allotted to that share as they think fit.

(5) If a share in the land is absolutely vested in a minor, subsections (1) to (4) apply as if he were of full age, except that the trustees may act on his behalf and retain land or other property representing his share in trust for him.

It should be noted that partition is limited to circumstances in which the beneficiaries are tenants in common. This precludes the trustees from interfering with the consequences of survivorship while joint tenants remain. While it is also initially restricted to trusts in which the beneficiaries are of full age (subs (1)), subs (5) enables the trustees to partition even where there are minor beneficiaries—in which case, the minor's land is held on trust by the trustees.

4 IS THE BENEFICIAL JOINT TENANCY DESIRABLE?

The operation of survivorship is the key practical difference between the joint tenancy and the tenancy in common. As has been noted, the two reforms of the severance rules discussed by the Law Commission would strengthen or weaken the role of survivorship. It was

---

[57] (1841) 4 Beav 115.

suggested, therefore, that the reforms raise an underlying issue of the desirability of the beneficial joint tenancy. Difficulties and uncertainties in the application of severance rules would be removed at a stroke by confining equitable ownership to the tenancy in common. But because this would come at the expense of the loss of survivorship, is this a price worth paying?

The operation of survivorship is most obviously consistent with the likely intentions of parties embarking on what they anticipate will be a lifelong relationship. Smith notes that relationship breakdown, where survivorship ceases match the parties' intentions, now provides the factual context for the 'great majority' of severance cases[58]—but he also notes that the abolition of the joint tenancy will not resolve problems.

Smith, *Plural Ownership* (2005, pp 87–8)

We now need to investigate the broken down relationship in more details. This context is the major source of concern as far as the operation of the joint tenancy is concerned. How well would the law operate if there were no joint tenancy? Obviously, if the parties never wanted survivorship, then the tenancy in common works well. However, in most relationships the parties are likely to want the survivor to get the property. We have just seen that this can cause problems if one dies during the relationship without making a will. The tenancy in common demands that wills be made in order to that the parties' intentions are fulfilled. What happens if a will has been made and then the relationship breaks down? In theory, the answer is simple: a new will should be made. In practice, the obvious danger is that this will be overlooked (as with joint tenancies, unexpected deaths pose the greatest problems) so that on death the property passes to the estranged spouse or partner. This is exactly the same outcome as with an unsevered joint tenancy. The lawyer who sees the problem is as likely to sever a joint tenancy as to urge the making of a new will. In other words, the problems will be just as severe whether a joint tenancy or tenancy in common is employed. Any legal structure which provides for property to go a particular person is apt to malfunction if the relationship with that person has broken down. It is difficult to avoid the conclusion that positive steps must be taken to change the destination of the property and that those steps are in fact not taken in many cases. Indeed, one may argue that joint tenancy is much more likely to produce the correct result because of the court's ability to find a suitable agreement or course of dealing to achieve severance; implying terms into wills is far more difficult. [...]

The main advantages of joint tenancies lie in fulfilling the wishes of co-owners when one dies during the relationship. Both joint tenancy and tenancy in common can cause inappropriate results once the relationship breaks down. It seems likely that breakdown of relationships has become more common. This is reflected in the growth of divorce rates and is likely to be related to greater numbers living together outside marriage. These changes tend to reduce the advantages of the joint tenancy.

As this extract shows, the underlying problem is not with the joint tenancy itself, but with the failure of the parties to utilize legal devices to ensure that their intentions are met. While the joint tenancy remains apt to give effect to the parties' intentions where the relationship continues at the time of death, the tenancy in common places the onus on the parties, in all cases, to ensure that their intentions are reflected in an up-to-date will. The arguments for and against abolition of the beneficial joint tenancy appear finely balanced and dependent

[58] Smith (2005, p 85).

on many variables. Smith suggests that the case for abolition has not been made out,[59] but he acknowledges that evidence as to the true intentions of purchasers, the incidence of relationship breakdown, and the use of wills may all affect our perception of where the balance currently lies.[60]

5 TRUSTS AND CO-OWNERSHIP

Whenever land is co-owned, whether co-ownership arises in relation to the legal title, the beneficial interests, or both, the land is held on trust. As was noted in section 1, the imposition of a trust in all cases is a dominant feature of the regulation of co-ownership in English law. All co-ownership trusts now constitute 'trusts of land' and are governed by the TOLATA 1996—an Act that originated in Law Commission recommendations.[61] Of its time, and in terms of its effect on the conceptual scheme of land law, the Act was described as *'the most significant measure of property law reform since the legislation of 1925'.*[62] Prior to the 1996 Act, co-ownership trusts were almost invariably classified as 'trusts for sale'—a form of trust regulated by the LPA 1925. To understand the significance of the TOLATA 1996, it is therefore necessary to consider how the trust of land differs from this previous form of regulation.

The Law Commission succinctly highlighted the key differences, both in substance and ethos in its report.

Law Commission Report No 181, *Transfer of Land: Trusts of Land* (1989, [3.1]–[3.5])

PART II

THE TRUST OF LAND

Concurrent interests

At present, most concurrent interests fall under a trust for sale, either expressly or by implication. The defining feature of the trust for sale, at least as it was originally designed, is that the trustees are under a duty to sell the trust land. Implicit in this is the notion that this land should be held primarily as an investment asset rather than as a 'use' asset.

This formulation may well have been suitable or convenient for the purposes which it was designed to serve. However, since the passing of the 1925 property legislation, social conditions have altered to such an extent that the invariable imposition of a duty to sell now seems wholly artificial. This is largely because the incidence of owner-occupation has, over the last sixty-three years, risen to such a level that most dwellings are now owner-occupied. Most of these are occupied by joint owners. One consequence of this is that the imposition

---

[59] Ibid, p 89.

[60] Ibid.

[61] Law Commission No 181 (1989). For general discussions of the Act, see Oakley, 'Towards a Law of Trusts for the Twenty-First Century' [1996] Conv 401; Hopkins, 'The Trusts of Land and Appointment of Trustees Act 1996' [1996] Conv 411; Clements, 'The Changing Face of Trusts: The Trusts of Land and Appointment of Trustees Act 1996' (1998) 61 MLR 56.

[62] Harpum, 'The Law Commission and Land Law' in *Land Law Themes and Perspectives* (eds Bright and Dewar, 1998, p 169).

of a duty to sell seems clearly inconsistent with the interests and intentions of the majority of those who acquire land as co-owners. In such cases the intention will rarely be that the land should be held pending a sale; it is much more probable that it will be retained primarily for occupation. In other words, the property will not be held simply as an investment asset, but rather as a 'use' asset.

The courts have sought to neutralise this artificiality by developing the principle that, where the 'collateral purpose' of the trust is, for example, to provide a family of matrimonial home, and where that purpose still subsists, the court may, in the exercise of its discretion under section 30 of the Law of Property Act 1925, refuse to order a sale. In that a single trustee is no longer able to force a sale (as against occupiers' interests) the 'use' value of the property is given recognition. It is, however, somewhat illogical that the courts should be required to develop and maintain a doctrine which takes as its foundation the artificiality of the trust for sale.

As a corollary of the duty to sell, and in accordance with the doctrine of conversion, any interest held under a trust for sale is an interest in the proceeds of the sale of the land. Consequently, the beneficiaries are deemed not to have an interest in the land as such. Once again, the courts have intervened to mitigate the artificiality of the position. This intervention has, however, resulted in an unsatisfactory division between those circumstances in which an interest under a trust for sale will be held to be an interest in land and certain others in which it will not, or might not.

Our proposals in relation to concurrent interests are focused upon two features of the trust for sale. Our principal recommendations are, firstly, that all land which previously would have been held under an implied trust for sale should now be held under the new system by trustees with a power to retain and a power to sell, and, secondly, that the doctrine of conversion should cease to apply. Thus, the main purpose of the trust will no longer be the realisation of the capital value of the land. Although this purpose is often seen as a merely notional one, judicial interpretation has not been so consistent as to exclude the occasional reappearance of the 'old' approach. The new system will be more readily intelligible to non-lawyers than the trust for sale. The point here is not simply that it should be easier for practitioners to explain the law to their clients, but also that co-ownership should take a form which non-lawyers can make sense of for themselves.

Section 30 of the LPA 1925 concerning the powers of the court under a trust for sale, referred to in this extract, has been repealed by the TOLATA 1996, and replaced by ss 14 and 15 of that Act.

Hence, as a matter of policy, the trust of land represents a shift to a form of regulation that is more suited to the use of land as a home, reflecting modern trends of home ownership. This shift is marked, in particular, by the removal of the duty to sell—the defining characteristic of the trust for sale—together with the abolition, in this context,[63] of the doctrine of conversion (which is further discussed in section 5.3 below). Against this background, the key provisions of the 1996 Act can be considered.

---

[63] Ibid, p 173. He notes that the sidenote to the Trusts of Land and Appointment of Trustees Act 1996, s 3, which reads *'Abolition of doctrine of conversion'* has *'excited some attention amongst academic commentators'*. In fact, the Act only purports to abolish the doctrine in the specific context of its application to trusts for sale.

5.1 SCOPE OF THE TRUST OF LAND

While we are considering trusts of land in the context of co-ownership trusts, it is important to note that the trust of land itself is broader in scope. One of the principal objectives of
the Law Commission was to replace the prevailing tripartite scheme with a single form of
regulation for all trusts of land.[64] Prior to the TOLATA 1996, in addition to the trust for sale
governing (principally) co-ownership trusts, trusts under which the beneficiaries are entitled in succession (discussed in Chapter 22) were usually regulated by the Settled Land Act
1925.[65] Bare trusts, in which there is one adult beneficiary, fell outside both of these schemes
of regulation.

The scope of the trust of land is defined in s 1 of the TOLATA 1996.

Trusts of Land and Appointment of Trustees Act 1996, s 1

(1) In this Act—

(a) "trust of land" means (subject to subsection (3)) any trust of property which consists
of or includes land; and

(b) "trustees of land" means trustees of a trust of land.

(2) The reference in subsection (1)(a) to a trust—

(a) is to any description of trust (whether express, implied, resulting or constructive),
including a trust for sale and a bare trust, and

(b) includes a trust created, or arising, before the commencement of this Act.

(3) The reference to land in subsection (1)(a) does not include land which (despite section 2) is settled land or which is land to which the Universities and College Estates Act 1925
applies.

Through this section, all trusts that consist of or include land are brought within the scope
of the 1996 Act, whether express or created, for example, through the doctrines of resulting and constructive trust considered in Chapters 14 and 18. The application of the Act
was extended to trusts in existence at the date of its commencement (1 January 1997). All
trusts for sale and bare trusts in existence at that date were turned into trusts of land. But
by s 1(3), existing successive interest trusts governed by the Settled Land Act 1925 remain
unaffected.

5.2 TRUSTEES' POWERS

The powers of trustees of land are set out in broad terms in s 6 of the TOLATA 1996.

---

[64] Law Commission No 181 (1989, [8.1]).

[65] Settled Land Act 1925, s 1(7), precluded the application of that Act to trusts for sale, enabling
successive interest trusts to be expressly created as trusts for sale.

Trusts of Land and Appointment of Trustees Act 1996, s 6

(1) For the purpose of exercising their functions as trustees, the trustees of land have in relation to the land subject to the trust all the powers of an absolute owner.

[...]

(3) The trustees of land have power to acquire land under the power conferred by section 8 of the Trustee Act 2000.

[...]

(5) In exercising the powers conferred by this section trustees shall have regard to the rights of the beneficiaries.

(6) The powers conferred by this section shall not be exercised in contravention of, or of any order made in pursuance of, any other enactment or any rule of law or equity.

(7) The reference in subsection (6) to an order includes an order of any court or of the [Charity Commission]

(8) Where any enactment other than this section confers on trustees authority to act subject to any restriction, limitation or condition, trustees of land may not exercise the powers conferred by this section to do any act which they are prevented from doing under the other enactment by reason of the restriction, limitation or condition.

(9) The duty of care under section 1 of the Trustee Act 2000 applies to trustees of land when exercising the powers conferred by this section.

The Law Commission acknowledged that many trustees, particularly of a co-owned home, considered themselves to be 'owners'. Hence, s 6 represents an attempt to reflect this, while ensuring that general equitable duties imposed on trustees are respected.[66] The trustees have the same powers as an absolute owner, but these are conferred on them specifically in their capacity as trustees of the land, not as absolute owners entitled to enjoy the land (by occupation or receipt or profits) themselves.[67] Hence, the powers are to be exercised with regard to the rights of the beneficiaries and in a manner consistent with any other enactment or rule of law or equity.

Section 8 of the TOLATA 1996 enables further limitations to be imposed on the trustees' powers where the trust is expressly created.[68] Under that section, the settlor of the trust may remove or restrict the trustees' powers, or make their exercise subject to obtaining consent.

Section 6 has the effect of removing the duty to sell imposed under a trust for sale: the powers of an owner include the power to sell or to retain the land.[69] While these are equally weighted, the Act is, in fact, biased against sale,[70] reflecting the recognition that land is commonly held on trust for use as a home, rather than as an investment. Section 8 conceivably enables the settlor of a trust to exclude the power of sale and, by so doing, make land

---

[66] Law Commission No 181 (1989, [10.4]).

[67] Hopkins (1996, p 413).

[68] Trusts of Land and Appointment of Trustees Act 1996, s 8, applies to trusts 'created by a disposition'. This may not, in fact, cover all express trusts. As Clements notes (1998, p 58), the need for a 'disposition' may exclude the situation in which a settlor declares him or herself to be holding on trust. The section would then be confined to express trusts created where the settlor transfers the land to trustees on trust. There is, however, no logical reason for drawing such a distinction.

[69] Law Commission No 181 (1989, [10.6]).

[70] Hopkins (1996, p 414).

inalienable. In contrast, a settlor cannot compel trustees to sell. While a duty to sell can be expressly imposed, in any such trust, s 4 of the Act provides the trustees with a power to postpone the sale and indefinite protection against liability for so doing.[71]

The limitations on the trustees' powers—both general, within s 6, and any expressly imposed by the terms of the trust, through s 8—have a limited impact on purchasers of the land. In this respect, a clear distinction is drawn between the internal regulation of the trust and its effect on third parties. Trustees who act contrary to limitations on their powers may be held personally liable to the beneficiaries for breach of trust. As regards purchasers, s 16 provides specific protection in the context of unregistered land. Purchasers are not concerned with whether s 6(5) has been complied with, and are protected against a conveyance carried out in contravention of ss 6(6) and (8) or contrary to limitations on the trustees' powers imposed through s 8, unless they have actual notice of the contravention or limitation. Section 16 does not apply to registered land where, under the general operation of the Land Registration Act 2002 (LRA 2002), a purchaser would be affected only by a limitation on the trustees' powers entered as a restriction on the register.[72]

5.3 BENEFICIARIES' RIGHTS

The TOLATA 1996 confers two key rights on beneficiaries. Firstly, it confers a right to be consulted by the trustees, who are directed in s 11(1)(b) to give effect to the wishes of the majority (in terms of the parties' beneficial shares) 'so far as consistent with the general interest of the trust'. By s 11(1)(a), this right is enjoyed by all adult co-owners. It is of practical significance to a beneficiary who is not also a legal owner and who does not therefore play a direct role in the management of the trust: for example, where A holds the parties' home on trust for A and B, s 11(1)(a) requires A to consult B in the exercise of his or her powers as trustee. The right to be consulted may be excluded in express trusts.[73] It does not apply to all trusts that were in existence at the commencement of the 1996 Act.[74]

Secondly, the most important right conferred on beneficiaries is the right to occupy the land. Where co-owners hold their home on trust, it seems remarkable to have to question whether, as beneficiaries, they have a right to occupy—but the imposition of a trust *for sale* brought the beneficiaries' right to occupy into question. As the Law Commission noted in [3.4] of its report (extracted above), the doctrine of conversion had the effect that beneficiaries under a trust for sale had an interest in the proceeds of sale, not in the land. The application of the doctrine arose through a combination of the trustees' duty to sell and equity's maxim 'equity looks upon as done that which ought to be done'. Because the trustees *ought* to sell, equity treated the parties as though sale had already taken place. So if the beneficiaries had no interest in the land, on what basis could they claim a right to occupy?

---

[71] Ibid.

[72] Full discussion of the purchaser protection provisions is provided in Chapter 20, section 4.2.

[73] As with the Trusts of Land and Appointment of Trustees Act 1996, s 8, s 11(2)(a) applies where a trust is 'created by a disposition'. Whether this includes all express trusts is dependent on the same comment made in relation to the previous provision above.

[74] Trusts of Land and Appointment of Trustees Act 1996, s 11(2)(b) and (3), excludes the requirement of consultation from express trusts (with provision for the settlors of those trusts to opt in to the new arrangements) and will trusts created prior to the commencement of the Act. This ensures that settlors who relied on the previous law (where a duty to consult would not be imposed unless expressly provided) are respected.

In practice, the courts did not invariably apply the doctrine of conversion.[75] It was clear that trustees for sale, in the exercise of their powers of management, could allow the beneficiaries to occupy. Further, a right to occupy was acknowledged to exist in leading case law,[76] although the basis of the right was uncertain. In particular, it remained unresolved as to whether occupation was a right enjoyed by all beneficial co-owners, or only in circumstances in which the trust had been created for the purpose of his or her occupation.[77] The abolition of the doctrine of conversion, and the shift to a scheme of regulation focused on the use of trust land as a home, paved the way for the introduction of a statutory right to occupy. This is provided for in s 12 of the TOLATA 1996.

Trusts of Land and Appointment of Trustees Act 1996, s 12

(1) A beneficiary who is beneficially entitled to an interest in possession in land subject to a trust of land is entitled by reason of his interest to occupy the land at any time if at that time—

(a) the purposes of the trust include making the land available for his occupation (or for the occupation of beneficiaries of a class of which he is a member or of beneficiaries in general), or

(b) the land is held by the trustees so as to be so available.

(2) Subsection (1) does not confer on a beneficiary a right to occupy land if it is either unavailable or unsuitable for occupation by him.

(3) This section is subject to section 13.

Hence, the existence of a right to occupy is dependent on the criteria in s 12(1) and (2) being fulfilled. As regards the interpretation of these criteria, the purpose of the trust may be derived from the declaration of an express trust, or be ascertained by the circumstances. The alternative criterion of availability enables the right to be claimed where the land is available for occupation, even if this is not within the purposes of the trust. For the trustees to make land available for occupation contrary to the express wishes of the settlor would, however, constitute a breach of trust and therefore would be outside the trustees' powers within s 6(6).[78] The additional requirement, in all cases, that the land is 'suitable' for occupation enables the subjective characteristics of the beneficiaries to be taken into account: for example, no right to occupy will arise if the land is a farm and the beneficiary is not a farmer.[79]

Where two or more beneficiaries are entitled to occupy, s 13 of the 1996 Act enables the trustees to exclude or restrict one or more of those entitled, but at least one qualifying bene-

---

[75] For example, in *Williams v Glyn's Bank v Boland* [1981] AC 487, the House of Lords held that Mrs Boland's beneficial interest under a trust for sale was an 'interest in land' protected as an overriding interest through her occupation.

[76] The existence of the right was acknowledged by the House of Lords in *Williams v Glyn's Bank v Boland* [1981] AC 487 and *City of London Building Society v Flegg* [1988] AC 54.

[77] Ross Martyn, 'Co-owners and their Entitlement to Occupy their Land Before and After the Trusts of Land and Appointment of Trustees Act 1996: Theoretical Doubts are Replaced by Practical Difficulties' [1997] Conv 254.

[78] Hopkins (1996, p 421); Pascoe, 'Right to Occupy Under a Trust of Land: Muddled Legislative Logic' [2006] Conv 54, 59.

[79] This has been a popular example in highlighting the interpretation of the right since first raised by Smith 'Trusts of Land Reform' [1989] Conv 12, 19. See further Pascoe (2006, p 62).

ficiary must be allowed to occupy. In exercising their powers, trustees may impose 'reasonable conditions'[80] on the beneficiary or beneficiaries in occupation, including the payment of compensation to those excluded from occupation.[81] This marks a change from the previous law, under which payment of compensation to a non-occupying beneficiary was seen as exceptional and confined to cases in which a beneficiary had been 'ousted' by those in occupation: for example, where one co-owner left the home through the domestic violence of the other.[82] Section 13 is concerned only with compensation payable by an occupying beneficiary to a non-occupying beneficiary who has a right of occupation under s 12 of the 1996 Act.

Liability to compensate other parties may arise outside of the provisions of the Act. In *French v Barcham*,[83] an occupying beneficiary was held liable to make compensation payments to her husband's trustee in bankruptcy, to reflect her continued occupation from the time of the bankruptcy. The court rejected an argument that ss 12–15 of the 1996 Act provide an exclusive regime for compensation.[84] A trustee in bankruptcy could not qualify for compensation under the Act, because neither the trustee nor the creditors themselves have a right to occupy.

A novel question on the application of s 13 arose in the following case: does the section enable trustees to restrict each beneficiary to occupying part of the trust land?

Rodway v Landy [2001] Ch 703, CA

Facts: Drs Rodway and Landy held the premises of their surgery on trust for themselves in equal shares. In proceedings following the termination of their business partnership, Dr Landy suggested that each of the parties should be given exclusive occupation of part of the surgery.

Peter Gibson LJ

At 712–13

I accept that the limitation on the power to exclude or restrict is expressed as a limitation on the number of beneficiaries who may be excluded or restricted. Plainly it would make no sense if there was no beneficiary left entitled to occupy land subject to a trust of land as a result of the exercise of the power under section 13. That is the force of the words "(but not all)". But if an estate consisting of adjoining properties, Blackacre and Whiteacre, was held subject to a trust of land and A and B were entitled to occupy the estate, it would be very surprising if the trustees were not able under section 13 to exclude or restrict B's entitlement to occupy Blackacre and at the same time to exclude or restrict A's entitlement to occupy Whiteacre, thereby leaving A alone entitled to occupy Blackacre and B Whiteacre. So also I do not see why, in relation to a single building which lends itself to physical partition, the trustees could not exclude or restrict one beneficiary's entitlement to occupy one part and at the same time exclude or restrict the other beneficiary's entitlement to occupy the other part.

---

[80] Trusts of Land and Appointment of Trustees Act 1996, s 13(3).
[81] Ibid, s 13(6).
[82] *Dennis v McDonald* [1982] Fam 63. For further discussion of the Trusts of Land and Appointment of Trustees Act 1996, s 13, and comparison with the previous law, see *Murphy v Gooch* [2007] EWCA 603.
[83] [2008] EWHC 1505.
[84] Ibid, [18].

Each part is land subject to a trust of land and the beneficiaries are entitled to occupy that part until the entitlement of a beneficiary is excluded or restricted by the exercise of the power under section 13. So construed section 13(1) seems to me to make good sense and to provide a useful power which trustees might well wish to exercise in appropriate circumstances so as to be even-handed between beneficiaries. In contrast, I can see no good reason why Parliament should want to confine the trustees to the all or nothing approach [. . .]

The Court ordered that the premises should be divided to provide each of the doctors with a self-contained surgery.[85]

In exercising their powers under s 13 of the TOLATA 1996, the trustees must act reasonably and with regard to the intentions of the settlor (in an express trust), the purposes for which land is held, and the circumstances and wishes of beneficiaries who have a right to occupy.[86] Occupying beneficiaries may be required to make monetary payments to those excluded.[87] In all cases, the trustees may also impose reasonable conditions on beneficiaries in occupation, including, for example, requiring them to meet any expenses arising in relation to the land.[88]

Section 12 remains controversial, both as regards the interpretation of its terms and, more broadly, whether a statutory right of occupation was, in fact, necessary.[89] Pascoe considers the value of the introduction of this right, in its broader context.

Pascoe, 'Right to Occupy Under a Trust of Land: Muddled Legislative Logic' [2006] Conv 54, 55–7

The introduction of a statutory right may be viewed as mirroring social, cultural and economic developments in society, reflecting a contemporary concern with the maximisation of material welfare. The significance of the imperative of an increasingly secular and materialistic age is revealingly, if unconsciously, reflected in the very language of the post-war European Convention on Human Rights, which guarantees the entitlement of every natural or legal person to the "peaceful enjoyment of his possessions". The emphasis is thus on the "use" value of property rather than the "exchange" or capital value and the changing social consensus on the importance of residential utility and residential security has led to the materialisation of this statutory right. Property law is the basic legal expression of the nature of economic life in all its aspects and this development has to be understood in relation to the social context in which it gains its significance as a mode of regulating behaviour. [. . .]

The right to occupy represents part of a shift in power from trustees to beneficiaries. With the abolition of conversion, this right emphasises that beneficiaries under trusts of land have rights in the land. Gray and Gray term this the democratisation of the trust. Where the

---

[85] The outcome in this case may be contrasted with partition of the land under the Trusts of Land and Appointment of Trustees Act 1996, s 7. Partition would have involved the physical subdivision of the surgery into two separate properties, each with its own legal title, with the parties receiving legal title to their part of the property. The trust would therefore come to an end.

[86] Ibid, s 13(2) and (4).

[87] Ibid, s 13(6).

[88] Ibid, s 13(6).

[89] Barnsley, 'Co-owners' Rights to Occupy Trust Land' (1998) 57 CLJ 123. He argues that, in fact, a broader right to occupy was available under the previous law (as not subject to the conditions imposed by s 12) and that beneficiaries' may still seek to invoke non-statutory rights of occupation.

doctrine of conversion prevailed under trusts for sale, consistency dictated that the trustees would remain the prime decision-makers, but with increasing judicial emphasis on the "use" value of property, the emancipation of beneficiaries inevitably followed as a logical consequence of this progression.

As Pascoe illustrates, in so far as the right to occupy shifts power from the trustees to the beneficiaries, it is logically consistent with the ethos of the trust of land as emphasizing the use value, rather than the investment value, of land. But Pascoe convincingly demonstrates the absence of doctrinal cohesiveness underlying the new right. This arises largely as a result of the preconditions of the right provided in s 12(1) and (2): that either the purposes of the trust include occupation, or the land is held by the trustees to be available for occupation, and, in all cases, that it is suitable for occupation.

Pascoe, 'Right to Occupy Under a Trust of Land: Muddled Legislative Logic' [2006] Conv 54, 63

Section 12 represents an amalgam and jumble of principles derived from the old law intermingled with explicitly new concepts of availability and suitability to constitute a qualified right, which may be the subject of great uncertainty and thus litigation due to the impreciseness of drafting of the section. The merits of such a hotchpotch of concepts challenges the sagacity and utility of instituting a new right which displays three conflicting characteristics: beneficiary autonomy, trustee authoritarianism and settlor interposition.

As was noted above, under the trust for sale, uncertainty remained as to whether a right to occupy was conferred on all beneficiaries, or only those for whom the purposes of the trust anticipated occupation.

The TOLATA 1996 continues to send conflicting messages. The right to occupy is conferred by s 12(1) on a beneficiary '*by reason of his interest*', but this is immediately made conditional on an assessment of the purpose of the trust, or the availability of the land for occupation, and its suitability for occupation by the beneficiaries.

Ross Martyn explains the effect of this.

Ross Martyn, 'Co-owners and their Entitlement to Occupy their Land Before and After the Trusts of Land and Appointment of Trustees Act 1996: Theoretical Doubts are Replaced by Practical Difficulties' [1997] Conv 254, 260

Inevitably trustees will form their own judgment as to whether or not land is unavailable or unsuitable for a particular beneficiary who requests occupation. In doing so, they will be carrying out much the same process as trustees carried out before the 1996 Act, when exercising their discretion whether or not to accede to the request of a beneficiary to go into occupation. They would have made their decision on the basis of whether they thought the land was or was not available and suitable for occupation by the beneficiary in question.

The crucial difference now is that paragraph (b) of section 12(1) and section 12(2) treat unavailability and unsuitability as objective criteria, depriving a beneficiary of an entitlement that he would otherwise have, and not as considerations for the exercise of a discretion.

The beneficiaries' position is made more certain by s 12, in so far as their right to occupy is now derived from statute. Practically, however, their position may be no more secure than under the trust for sale. They have a right to occupy subject to meeting criteria that will be assessed, in the first instance, by the trustees, with disputes resolved by the court under s 15 of the TOLATA 1996.

5.4 OCCUPATION, THE TRUSTS OF LAND AND APPOINTMENT OF TRUSTEES ACT 1996, AND THE FAMILY LAW ACT 1996

As we have seen in Chapter 18, rights to occupy a home may be derived from the Family Law Act 1996 (FLA 1996). There is an overlap between the FLA 1996 and the TOLATA 1996 in two respects. Firstly (as noted in Chapter 18), a spouse or civil partner who is a beneficiary, but does not own legal title, may be entitled to a right to occupy ('home rights') under the FLA 1996.

Secondly, s 33 of the FLA 1996 enables the court to regulate occupation of a house that is, or has been, or was intended to be, the home of the applicant and '*another person with whom he is associated*'. This expression covers a wide range of people, including existing (and former) married couples, civil partners and cohabitants, and others who have shared a home otherwise than through a commercial relationship.[90]

An application may be made to the court under s 33 by (amongst others) a person entitled to occupy as a beneficiary or through holding 'home rights' conferred by the FLA 1996.[91] Hence, a beneficiary who is entitled to occupy a home under the TOLATA 1996 may apply to the court for an order regulating occupation under the FLA 1996. An overlap in jurisdictions arises because occupation by beneficiaries is also subject to regulation by the court under ss 13 and 14 of the TOLATA 1996.

The range of orders that can be made by the court, and the factors that the court is directed to take into account, differ under each statute. How should this overlap be resolved?

Chan v Leung, unreported 30 November 2001, HC

Facts: The case arose following the breakdown of a relationship between Miss Chan and Mr Leung, in the course of which, for a period of time, they had lived together in a house that was the subject of the action. Miss Chan had remained in the house and was pursuing university studies. The court held that Miss Chan had a beneficial interest in the house and then considered what order should be made in relation to occupation. The issue arose whether this matter should be dealt with under the Trusts of Land and Appointment of Trustees Act 1996 or the Family Law Act 1996.

HH Judge McGonigal

Where a court is addressing the question of occupation of a house subject to a trust or the alternative of sale, in my view the court should approach it primarily in the context of s 33 of the Family Law Act 1996. It is in this Act that Parliament addresses the question of

---

[90] Family Law Act 1996, s 62(3).
[91] Ibid, s 33(1).

occupation of the home in most detail. The court is required by s 33(6) to have regard to all the circumstances. These will include the fact that it is a trust property, so that ss 14 and 15 apply to it. Accordingly, the matters specifically referred to in s 15 of the Trusts of Land and Appointment of Trustees Act 1996 and any other relevant consideration arising from the fact that it is a trust property, including the terms of the trust, should be taken into account by the court when considering the question of continued occupation or sale.

Hence, where the jurisdictions overlap, precedence is afforded to the FLA 1996—but the matters that the court would be required to refer to under the TOLATA 1996 are taken into account as part of the circumstances of the case. On the facts, the court issued an order enabling Miss Chan to continue to occupy, to the exclusion of Mr Leung, for the duration of her current studies, following which the house would be sold.

The judge's order was affirmed on appeal, although without discussion by the Court of Appeal of the overlap between the jurisdictions.[92]

5.5 APPLICATIONS TO COURT

Section 14 of the TOLATA 1996 enables an application to be made to the court by a trustee or a person with an interest in the trust property '*relating to the exercise by the trustees of any of their functions*'. Section 15 then provides guidance to the court of the factors for the court to take into account when making decisions.

Trusts of Land and Appointment of Trustees Act 1996, s 15

(1) The matters to which the court is to have regard in determining an application for an order under section 14 include—

  (a) the intentions of the person or persons (if any) who created the trust,

  (b) the purposes for which the property subject to the trust is held,

  (c) the welfare of any minor who occupies or might reasonably be expected to occupy any land subject to the trust as his home, and

  (d) the interests of any secured creditor of any beneficiary.

(2) In the case of an application relating to the exercise in relation to any land of the powers conferred on the trustees by section 13 the matters to which the court is to have regard also include the circumstances and wishes of each of the beneficiaries who is (or apart from any previous exercise by the trustees of those powers would be) entitled to occupy the land under section 12.

(3) In the case of any other application, other than one relating to the exercise of the power mentioned in section 6(2), the matters to which the court is to have regard also include the circumstances and wishes of any beneficiaries of full age and entitled to an interest in possession in property subject to the trust or (in case of dispute) of the majority (according to the value of their combined interests).

---

[92] *Chan v Leung* [2003] 1 FLR 23.

> (4) This section does not apply to an application if section 335A of the Insolvency Act 1986 (which is inserted by Schedule 3 and relates to applications by a trustee of a bankrupt) applies to it.

A wide range of matters may be referred to the court under s 14. It was on the basis of s 14, for example, that the court resolved the issue of the beneficiaries' occupation in *Rodway v Landy*. In particular, however, s 14 is the basis on which the courts will consider disputes as to whether the land should be sold. In Chapter 21, we consider applications for sale brought by third parties to the trust: in particular, creditors and trustees in bankruptcy of the beneficiaries. In this chapter, however, we are concerned with how disputed sales are determined when the parties to the trust refer the matter to the court themselves. This may arise, for example, where A and B are co-owners of their home, and, following a breakdown of the parties' relationship, A wishes to remain in the home (either alone or with children), while B wants the house to be sold.

In addition to their practical importance, such disputes may also raise directly the tension between the house as a home and as an investment. Ultimately, in the example outlined, the question that arises is in what circumstances A's desire to remain in the home takes precedence over B's wish to realize his or her capital investment. To answer this question, it is necessary first to consider the general principles and then to address specifically situations in which the welfare of minor children need to be taken into account through s 15(1)(c). We will then consider the extent to which s 15 represents a change in the law from the position under the trust for sale. This is a matter to which we return in Chapter 21, where we consider whether s 15 has changed the law from the position under the trust for sale if the application for sale is made by a third party, such as a creditor, rather than by one of the beneficiaries themselves.

5.5.1 General principles

In all applications, s 15 of the TOLATA 1996 directs the court to have regard to the intentions of the persons who created the trust (s 15(1)(a)), the purposes for which the property is held (s 15(1)(b)), and the interests of secured creditors (s 15(1)(d)).

Arden LJ considered the interpretation of the first two of these factors, and the difference between them, in the following case.

White v White [2003] EWCA 924, CA

Facts: Mr and Mrs White were co-owners of their home. Following the breakdown of their relationship, Mr White remained in occupation of the home with the couple's young daughters. Mrs White sought an application for sale of the home. The welfare of the children fell to be considered under s 15(1)(c) and this aspect of the decision is considered below. In this extract, Arden LJ considers whether the provision of a home for the children constituted the intentions of the Whites within s 15(1)(a), or the purposes for which they held the home within s 15(1)(b). The home had been purchased before the children were born.

Arden LJ

At [22]–[24]

[Arden LJ cited s 15 and continued...] Where more than one person created the trust, the intention for the purposes of section 15(1)(a) must, as I see it, be the intention of all the persons who created the trust and be an intention which they had in common. This is because the subsection speaks of "the intentions of the person or persons [...] who created the trust". This may be contrasted with the reference in section 15(1)(c) to the welfare of "any minor". The use of the definite article and the word "person" or "persons" in subsection (1) (a) to my mind make it clear that the intention referred to in section 15(1)(a) must be the intention of the persons who created the trust if more than one in common.

The question then remains whether the intention could include intention subsequently come to, as Mr Routley submits. I do not myself consider that this is the correct construction. Parliament has used the word "intention" which speaks naturally to the intentions of persons prior to the creation of the trust. If that were not its meaning, then it is not clear whether the court should be looking at the parties' intention at the date of the hearing or at some other antecedent point in time and, if so, what date. If Parliament meant the present intention, it would have used some such word as "wishes" rather than the word "intention" which implies some statement or opinion as to the future. In all the circumstances, I consider that the appellant's submissions on the point of law on this point are not correct.

I turn now to what I have termed the third point of law, and it was put in this way. It is that the judge had failed to deal with a submission by the father that there was an additional purpose come to after the property was purchased and the parties had been living there. This was based primarily on paragraph 11 of the father's statement of 22nd February 2001, in which he stated that the trust was entered into to provide a home for the mother and himself but subsequently there arose an additional purpose, namely to provide a home for the children. I would accept that, for the purposes of section 15(1)(b), purposes could have been formulated informally, but they must be the purposes subject to which the property is held. The purpose established at the outset of the trust which, on the judge's finding, did not include the provision of a home for children, could only change if both parties agreed. There was no evidence from which the judge could find that the mother agreed to the additional purpose spoken to by the father. Nor was the assertion that there was such a purpose ever put to the mother. Notwithstanding Mr Routley's submission, I would not accept the argument that the judge's omission to deal with the additional purpose undermines his decision.

Hence, while the 'intentions' of the persons who created the trust are fixed and determined at the time of creation, the purposes can change by agreement of the parties. In *Rodway v Landy*, the Court of Appeal noted that the relevant purposes are those in existence at the time that the application is considered.[93] As we will see below, the interests of the children in *White v White* were still taken into account by the Court through the specific reference to the welfare of children in s 15(1)(c).

As regards the interests of secured creditors, it is important to note that these are relevant even in applications brought by the parties to the trust. In *Anneveld v Robinson*,[94] the practical impossibility of a large mortgage being paid by one of the parties, if allowed to remain in occupation, was a significant factor in the court's order of sale on the breakdown of their relationship.

[93] [2001] Ch 703, 711.
[94] [2005] WL 3142400 (county court), judgment 12 August 2005.

In addition to the factors mentioned in s 15, the court should have regard to any other relevant matter. The matters referred to in s 15 are non-exhaustive. In *White v White*, for example, the Court had regard to Mrs White's circumstances and her wish to raise money to provide a home for herself. Arden LJ explained that there is no weighting of the factors within s 15:[95] the responsibility lies with judges to determine how much weight to afford to all relevant factors, including those not specifically referred to in s 15.

5.5.2 Disputed sales and child welfare

Section 15(1)(c) specifically directs the court to have regard to the welfare of minor children who are in occupation of the home, or may be expected to be so. This ensures that the needs of such children are taken into account even where, as in *White v White*, the provision of a home for them was not the intention of the parties and is not an agreed, current purpose of the trust. Section 15(1)(c) is significant in so far as it ensures that the welfare of children is considered. It is consistent with the underlying ethos of the TOLATA 1996 as providing a scheme of regulation for trusts that reflects the fact that much co-owned land is the parties' home.

As we have noted, however, the factors for the court to be take into account in determining applications are not weighted. Other factors may favour sale despite the occupation of children. In *White v White*, the Court of Appeal confirmed an order of sale by the judge at first instance. The Court noted that the judge had correctly taken into account both the interests of the children in remaining in their home and Mrs White's need to realize her only capital asset. In that case, the judge was also satisfied that, following the sale, cheaper suitable accommodation would be available.

5.5.3 Has s 15 changed the law?

Prior to the TOLATA 1996, under the trust for sale, disputes as to sale were considered by the court under s 30 of the LPA 1925. Against the background of the duty to sell, the starting point for the courts was that sale should be ordered unless the trustees unanimously agreed to exercise their power to postpone sale.[96] This was, however, significantly qualified by the courts' recognition that trusts for sale were often created for a purpose other than sale (often referred to as the 'secondary', or 'collateral', purpose of the trust, but, in fact, representing its *primary* purpose). As a general principle, sale would not be ordered for so long as a collateral purpose could still be achieved.[97] Hence, the key issues for the courts in settling disputes was the identification of the purposes of the trust and an assessment of whether any of those purposes could still be achieved. Where children were present, a particularly contentious issue was whether the provision of a home for children formed part of the purposes of the trust.

In its recommendations that led to s 15, the Law Commission considered the relationship between the new provision and the secondary purpose case law.

---

[95] [2003] EWCA 924, [26].
[96] *Re Mayo* [1943] 1 Ch 302.
[97] *Jones v Challenger* [1960] 2 WLR 695.

Law Commission Report No 181, *Transfer of Land: Trusts of Land* (1989, [12.9])

As regards the exercise of these powers [i.e., the powers conferred by s 14 of the Trusts of Land and Appointment of Trustees Act 1996], it is our view that the court's discretion should be developed along the same lines as the current 'primary purpose' doctrine. This approach was moulded to practical requirements, and we consider that it gets the balance more or less right. Nevertheless, we recommend that [s 15] should set out some guidelines for the exercise of the court's discretion, the aim being to consolidate and rationalise the current approach. The criteria which the courts have evolved for settling disputes over trusts for sale are ones which will continue to have validity in the context of the new system. One function of the guidelines will be to put these criteria on a statutory footing. [...]

In *Mortgage Corporation v Shaire*,[98] in an application for sale brought by a creditor, the court concluded that s 15 of the TOLATA 1996 had changed the law. But where an application to court is made by one of the parties to the trust themselves, it seems at least questionable whether the result of cases is likely to be significantly different. It is possible that the existence of the duty to sell had a greater impact on the reasoning employed by the courts than on the outcome of the cases.

This point is explored by Smith, who draws the following conclusions on the likely impact of the 1996 Act.

Smith, *Plural Ownership* (2005, pp 166–7)

Leaving aside the welfare of minors, does any of this impact on the general conclusions from the cases that sale will be refused if there is a continuing purpose, but ordered if the purpose has ended? Taking the former first, there appears to be little reason why purposes should be significantly less important. Given that they constitute just one factor today, it is possible that they may be somewhat less powerful. This might be relevant where there are multiple purposes (exemplified by *Bedson*) and would allow other factors, such as the needs of the party seeking sale, to be more prominent. However, any changes as a result of [the Trusts of Land and Appointment of Trustees Act 1996] are likely to be marginal. More problematic is the leaning towards sale where purposes have ended. In the past, the courts reasoned that the trust for sale re-asserted itself in these circumstances, so that the land should be sold. Now that trusts for sale are no longer the normal form of trust of land, this reasoning falls to the ground. However, too much should not be read into this. If land is purchased for a purpose and that purpose fails, then (absent special factors) sale seems the appropriate outcome: the project has been frustrated. Accordingly, the result reached by the cases is appropriate even though the reasoning today would be significantly different: we obviously cannot say today that the law leans towards sale. Though other factors may be taken into account, avoidance of sale is likely to require exceptional circumstances, at least where no minors are involved.

Hence, as regards the general approach, it is likely that the purpose of the trust will remain a significant influence. Although the purposes for which the land is held is now only one factor for the court to consider, once the purpose has ended (for example, on the breakdown

[98] [2001] Ch 743, 760.

of the relationship between the co-owners), an application by one party to recoup his or her capital investment may be compelling.

Smith's conclusions exclude those cases in which the welfare of minors is in issue. Under the trust for sale, doubt remained as to whether the purposes of a trust would include the provision of a home for children, or whether their interests were 'only incidentally to be taken into consideration [...] so far as they affect the matter between the two persons entitled to the beneficial interests'.[99] Both views could claim support from conflicting Court of Appeal judgments.[100] The balance of the authorities suggested that, where a house was occupied by one of the beneficiaries with minor children, sale would not be ordered unless alternative (cheaper) accommodation could then be provided.[101] The decision in White v White, discussed above, mirrors this approach. It suggests that, in cases involving minors as well, the difference under s 15 may be more one of reasoning than result. The importance of s 15(1)(c) may lie in the fact that it confirms the relevance of the welfare of children.

5.6 REGULATION OF CO-OWNERSHIP OUTSIDE OF THE TRUSTS OF LAND AND APPOINTMENT OF TRUSTEES ACT 1996

This chapter has focused on the regulation of co-ownership as a matter of property law through the TOLATA 1996. The rights of co-owners may also fall to be regulated by other legislation: for example, within the regime of family law. The general principle appears to be that broader powers conferred on the court through such legislation should be applied in priority to the general scheme of the 1996 Act.[102]

There are three main situations when such an overlap may occur:

- as we have seen in section 5.4, where a co-owner derives a right of occupation under the FLA 1996;

- on the breakdown of a marriage or civil partnership, courts have broad powers to make property adjustment orders between the parties that may also affect ownership and sale;[103]

- under Sch 1 of the Children Act 1989, courts may make orders relating to parents' property for the benefit of their children.

These orders may have consequential effects on the exercise of powers under TOLATA 1996, as is illustrated by White v White.[104] In that case, as has been seen in section 5.5.1, the court ordered sale of a home on an application by Mrs White despite the fact that the house remained occupied by Mr White and the couple's young daughters. Mr White had

---

[99] Burke v Burke [1974] 1 WLR 1063, 1067, per Buckley LJ.

[100] In Browne v Pritchard [1975] 1 WLR 1366, Williams v Williams [1976] 3 WLR 494, and Re Evers' Trust [1980] 1 WLR 1327, sale was refused where, following the breakdown of the parties' relationship, a home was occupied by one beneficiary and children. Burke v Burke [1974] 1 WLR 1063 stands alone as a case in which sale was ordered in such circumstances. This approach was also supported in Re Holliday [1981] Ch 405, although the case itself concerned an application by a trustee in bankruptcy, rather than by one of the parties to the trust.

[101] Williams v Williams [1976] 3 WLR 494, 499.

[102] Smith (2005, pp 179–81).

[103] Matrimonial Causes Act 1973, s 24; Civil Partnership Act 2004, Sch 5, paras 2 and 3. See further, Cretney et al, Principles of Family Law (7th edn, 2002, [14.092]–[14.098]).

[104] [2003] EWCA 924.

applied under the Children Act 1989 for a transfer of Mrs White's beneficial interest during their daughters' minority. That application had been suspended pending the outcome of Mrs White's case under the TOLATA 1996.[105] The consequence of the order for sale was to resurrect Mr White's application. If successful, it would necessarily appear to override the order for sale, because Mrs White would no longer hold the beneficial interest that provided the linchpin of her claim.

QUESTIONS

1. What do you consider to be the main advantages and disadvantages of the joint tenancy and tenancy in common as forms of co-ownership? What factors would you take into account in advising co-owners whether to hold their home as beneficial joint tenants or tenants in common?

2. Assess the methods by which a joint tenancy may be severed: (i) unilaterally, by one joint tenant; and (ii) mutually, by all of the joint tenants. What changes, if any, do you consider desirable to simplify the current law?

3. How does the underlying ethos of the trust of land differ from that of the trust for sale? To what extent is this change in ethos reflected in the rights of the beneficiaries?

4. In what circumstances is the court likely to order sale of a home on an application by one co-owner?

FURTHER READING

Barnsley, 'Co-owners' Rights to Occupy Trust Land' (1998) 57 CLJ 123

Clements, 'The Changing Face of Trusts: The Trusts of Land and Appointment of Trustees Act 1996' (1998) 61 MLR 56

Cooke, *Land Law* (Oxford: OUP, 2006, ch 5)

Hopkins, 'The Trusts of Land and Appointment of Trustees Act 1996' [1996] Conv 411

Law Commission Report No 181, *Transfer of Land: Trusts of Land* (1989)

Oakley, 'Towards a Law of Trusts for the Twenty-First Century' [1996] Conv 401

Smith, *Plural Ownership* (Oxford: OUP, 2005, chs 3–8)

---

[105] Ibid, [5]. Thorpe LJ criticized the suspension of the proceedings. He considered that the applications should, in fact, have been conjoined, or the Children Act application given priority, given the courts' broader powers under that Act.

20

CO-OWNERSHIP AND THIRD PARTIES: PRIORITIES

CENTRAL ISSUES

1. Where co-owned land is sold or mortgaged, a question of priority may arise between a beneficiary who is not a party to the transaction and the purchaser. In co-owned land, priority is determined primarily by the mechanism of overreaching.

2. This mechanism, which applies to registered and unregistered land, enables the purchaser to take free from beneficial interests as long as certain conditions are met As noted in Chapter 6, section 3.3, it can therefore operate as a defence to a pre-existing equitable interest in land. The beneficiaries' interests are removed from the land and attach to the proceeds of sale.

3. Where overreaching does not occur, priority between the beneficiary and purchaser is determined using the separate rules of registered and unregistered land.

4. The preconditions for overreaching include a requirement that any

purchase money is paid to a minimum of two trustees. As a result, a practical distinction is drawn between one and two trustee trusts. In two-trustee trusts, priority is determined by overreaching, while in one-trustee trusts, the separate priority rules of unregistered and registered land are applied.

5. The prevailing view is that the basis of overreaching lies in the trustees' powers of disposition and its operation is therefore dependent on the trustees acting within their powers.

6. Purchasers and mortgagees may often benefit from statutory protection even where trustees have acted ultra vires, although the level of protection differs between registered and unregistered land.

7. The operation of overreaching against beneficiaries in occupation continues to be contentious and may remain vulnerable to challenge under the Human Rights Act 1998.

1 INTRODUCTION

This chapter is concerned with the priority rules applicable where co-owned land is sold or mortgaged. It considers the circumstances in which the beneficial interests of those who are not party to the sale or mortgage as legal owners are binding against the purchaser or mortgagee. In this book, we have conceptualized priority rules as part of the *defences* question (see Chapter 6, section 3). In that respect, this chapter is concerned with when a purchaser or mortgagee has a defence against the enforcement of pre-existing beneficial interests.

The priority between beneficiaries and third parties is determined primarily by the mechanism of *overreaching*. Overreaching is a mechanism enabling purchasers to take title free from certain property interests, particularly beneficial interests under a trust. In other words, as we noted in Chapter 6, section 3.3, it provides the purchaser or mortgagee with a defence against the enforcement of those interests. The interests are removed from the land and attached instead to the proceeds of sale.

Overreaching applies in relation to both personal property and land, although we are concerned only with its application to land. It applies as long as two conditions are met: firstly, the interest must be capable of being overreached; and secondly, the transaction must be one that has overreaching effect. Where these conditions are met, overreaching applies to the exclusion of other priority rules. Importantly, it applies both to registered and unregistered land. Only where one of the conditions is not met is the enforcement of the beneficial interest against the purchaser determined by the separate priority rules of registered and unregistered land that have been examined in Chapters 15 and 16. The priority rules discussed in those chapters are therefore wholly subsidiary to the overreaching mechanism.

In this chapter, we will focus on the particular form of overreaching that applies where a purchaser or mortgagee deals with land held on trust. In such cases, a key element of the requirement that a transaction has overreaching effect is that any capital money is paid to a minimum of two trustees. The practical effect of overreaching is thus to draw a division between transactions undertaken by a single trustee and those executed by two or more trustees. Where there are two or more trustees, issues of priority between a purchaser and beneficiary are determined by overreaching. Where there is a single trustee, priority between a purchaser and the beneficiaries generally falls to be considered under the separate priority rules governing registered and unregistered land.

This chapter focuses on the operation of the overreaching mechanism. The final part of the chapter, section 7, then briefly notes how issues of priority are determined where overreaching does not take place and addresses a specific issue that arises on a sale by a sole surviving legal joint tenant.

2 OVERREACHING

The effect of overreaching is explained in Wolstenholme and Cherry in the following terms.

Wolstenholme and Cherry's Conveyancing Statutes:Vol I
(12th edn, ed Farrand, 1972, p 51)

In such cases [where overreaching operates] the purchaser is not concerned with the title to the equitable interest or power, or to obtain the concurrence of the owner thereof. On the other hand, the equitable interest or power is not defeated or destroyed by the disposition, but is shifted so as to become a corresponding interest or power in or over the proceeds [...] The conveyance to the purchaser is then said to 'overreach' the equitable interest or power

> [...] An overreaching conveyance must be distinguished from one which wholly destroys some interest or right.

The key aspect of this explanation lies in the idea that overreaching operates to *shift* the interest from an interest in land to an interest in the proceeds of the conveyance. The purchaser or mortgagee thus obtains title to the land unencumbered by the interest. The holder of the overreached interest no longer has any proprietary claim in the land, but a beneficial interest in the moneys received by the trustees. His or her interest has shifted from an interest in land to an interest in money. In this way, overreaching draws a clear distinction between the beneficiaries' rights against purchasers, on the one hand, and their rights against their trustees, on the other.

Overreaching operates within a complex statutory framework and implements fundamental principles of the trust curtain and security of transactions, both for purchasers and, more particularly (in the leading cases), mortgage lenders. Because the application of the mechanism has been stretched to (and, some would argue, beyond) its legitimate limits, its continuing fitness for purpose is being called into question, together with its compliance with the Human Rights Act 1998 (HRA 1998).

So why do we have overreaching? In the following case, it was considered that the consequences of not giving full effect to overreaching would be as follows.

City of London Building Society v Flegg [1988] 1 AC 54

Lord Oliver

At 76–7

[To reverse, by judicial decision] the legislative policy of the 1925 legislation of keeping the interests of beneficiaries behind the curtain and confining the investigation of title to the devolution of the legal estate [...] financial institutions advancing money on the security of land will face hitherto unsuspected hazards, whether they are dealing with registered or unregistered land.

This comment reflects the twin objectives of implementing the trust curtain and ensuring security of transactions.

In this chapter, we first consider the general scope of overreaching, and then address the operation of overreaching in two particular circumstances: where the beneficiaries are in occupation of the land, and where the transaction is executed ultra vires (outside) the trustees' powers or in breach of trust. Following an assessment of whether overreaching remains fit for its purpose, we consider the future of the mechanism.

2.1 THE SCOPE OF OVERREACHING

For overreaching to take place, two conditions must be met: firstly, the interest must be capable of being overreached; secondly the transaction must be one that has overreaching effect. Both of these requirements are apparent from the terms of s 2 of the Law of Property Act 1925 (LPA 1925).

Law of Property Act 1925, s 2

(1) A conveyance to a purchaser of a legal estate in land shall overreach any equitable interest or power affecting that estate, whether or not he has notice thereof, if—

(i) the conveyance is made under the powers conferred by the Settled Land Act, 1925, or any additional powers conferred by a settlement, and the equitable interest or power is capable of being overreached thereby, and the statutory requirements respecting the payment of capital money arising under the settlement are complied with;

(ii) the conveyance is made by trustees of land and the equitable interest or power is at the date of the conveyance capable of being overreached by such trustees under the provisions of subsection (2) of this section or independently of that subsection, and the requirements of section 27 of this Act respecting the payment of capital money arising on such a conveyance are complied with;

(iii) the conveyance is made by a mortgagee or personal representative in the exercise of his paramount powers, and the equitable interest or power is capable of being over-reached by such conveyance, and any capital money arising from the transaction is paid to the mortgagee or personal representative;

(iv) the conveyance is made under an order of the court and the equitable interest or power is bound by such order, and any capital money arising from the transaction is paid into, or in accordance with the order of, the court.

(1A) An equitable interest in land subject to a trust of land which remains in, or is to revert to, the settlor shall (subject to any contrary intention) be overreached by the conveyance if it would be so overreached were it an interest under the trust.

(2) Where the legal estate affected is subject to [a trust of land], then if at the date of a conveyance made after the commencement of this Act by the trustees, the trustees (whether original or substituted) are either—

(a) two or more individuals approved or appointed by the court or the successors in office of the individuals so approved or appointed; or

(b) a trust corporation,

any equitable interest or power having priority to the trust shall, notwithstanding any stipulation to the contrary, be overreached by the conveyance, and shall, according to its priority, take effect as if created or arising by means of a primary trust affecting the proceeds of sale and the income of the land until sale.

(3) The following equitable interests and powers are excepted from the operation of subsection (2) of this section, namely—

(i) Any equitable interest protected by a deposit of documents relating to the legal estate affected;

(ii) The benefit of any covenant or agreement restrictive of the user of land;

(iii) Any easement, liberty, or privilege over or affecting land and being merely an equitable interest (in this Act referred to as an "equitable easement");

(iv) The benefit of any contract (in this Act referred to as an "estate contract") to convey or create a legal estate, including a contract conferring either expressly or by statutory implication a valid option to purchase, a right of pre-emption, or any other like right;

(v) Any equitable interest protected by registration under the Land Charges Act, 1925, other than—

(a) an annuity within the meaning of Part II, of that Act;

(b) a limited owner's charge or a general equitable charge within the meaning of that Act.

(4) Subject to the protection afforded by this section to the purchaser of a legal estate, nothing contained in this section shall deprive a person entitled to an equitable charge of any of his rights or remedies for enforcing the same.

(5) So far as regards the following interests, created before the commencement of this Act (which accordingly are not within the provisions of the Land Charges Act, 1925), namely—

(a) the benefit of any covenant or agreement restrictive of the user of the land;

(b) any equitable easement;

(c) the interest under a puisne mortgage within the meaning of the Land Charges Act, 1925, unless and until acquired under a transfer made after the commencement of this Act;

(d) the benefit of an estate contract, unless and until the same is acquired under a conveyance made after the commencement of this Act;

a purchaser of a legal estate shall only take subject thereto if he has notice thereof, and the same are not overreached under the provisions contained or in the manner referred to in this section.

2.2 INTERESTS CAPABLE OF BEING OVERREACHED

The remainder of the section substantially curtails the initially broad statement in s 2(1) of the LPA 1925. Firstly, subs (3) excludes certain equitable interests from the scope of overreaching. The general effect of this subsection is to remove from the operation of overreaching most equitable interests that do not take effect under a trust. Discussing the scope of overreaching in *Birmingham Midshires Mortgage Services Ltd v Sabherwal*,[1] Robert Walker LJ indorsed a distinction drawn by Megarry and Wade[2] between 'commercial' and 'family' interests. Family interests, such as beneficial interests under a trust, can readily be represented by money; in contrast, commercial interests (which Robert Walker LJ considered to be exemplified by equitable easements and rights of entry) 'cannot sensibly shift from the land'. They are logically inseparable from the land over which they are intended to be exercised. In this respect, the effect of subs (3) is to exclude such commercial interests from the initially broad wording of s 2(1).

The second respect in which the broad statement in s 2(1) of the 1925 Act is curtailed is that an interest must be 'capable of being overreached' through the particular transactions listed in s 2(1)(i)–(iii).[3] Hence, it is necessary to identify which interests are 'capable of being overreached' by each type of transaction mentioned. Paragraphs (i) and (iii) can be dealt

---

[1] (2000) 80 P & CR 256 at [28].

[2] Citing from *Megarry and Wade: The Law of Real Property* (5th edn, ed Harpum, 1984, p 409).

[3] The analogous requirement in para (iv) is found in the requirement that the interest is 'bound by' the court order.

with briefly in this regard. As regards para (i), the interests capable of being overreached by a conveyance made under the Settled Land Act 1925 are identified by s 72 of that Act. This includes (but is not limited to) the beneficial interests under the settlement. It is not discussed further, because, as we will see in Chapter 22, the Settled Land Act 1925 is in the process of being phased out.[4]

As regards para (iii), in relation to mortgages, this provision ensures that an exercise of the power of sale overreaches the mortgagor's equity of redemption and any subsequent mortgages.[5] Its operation is further discussed in Chapter 31, section 3.1.2.[6]

Of much greater significance is para (ii), which provides for overreaching on a conveyance by trustees of land. Beneficial interests under a trust of land are 'capable of being overreached' on a conveyance by the trustees where overreaching is provided for by s 2(2) or 'independently of that subsection'. Section 2(2) provides for overreaching of interests already in existence at the time the trust was created. This is a concept of extended overreaching that may be invoked only by a trust corporation, or by trustees approved or appointed by the court for the purpose. Section 2(2) does not, however, provide for overreaching of the beneficial interests under the trust: the most common and practically significant use of the mechanism, and the use with which we are concerned in this chapter. The basis for overreaching beneficial interests under a trust of land must therefore be found outside the terms of s 2.

On what basis are the beneficial interests under a trust of land 'capable of being overreached'? Four theories have been advanced, three of which are consistent with the view that overreaching has the same basis and scope in registered and unregistered land. These three theories are:

- that overreaching is provided for by s 27(1) of the LPA 1925;
- that it is based on the doctrine of conversion; or
- that overreaching is inherent in the trustees' powers of disposition.

It will be seen that only the last of these provides a convincing basis for overreaching of the beneficial interests under a trust of land.

The fourth theory is that, while the trustees' powers of disposition provide the basis of overreaching in unregistered land, the Land Registration Act 1925 (LRA 1925) provided— and the Land Registration Act 2002 (LRA 2002) now provides—its own basis for the operation of the mechanism in registered land. On this fourth view, the basis of overreaching and, as a consequence, its scope differs between registered and unregistered land.

2.2.1 Overreaching and s 27(1) of the Law of Property Act 1925

The first theory is that s 27(1) of the LPA 1925 provides the basis of overreaching.

---

[4] A full discussion of the scope of the Settled Land Act, s 72, is provided in *Megarry and Wade: The Law of Real Property* (7th edn, eds Harpum et al, 2008, [A-093]–[A-100]).

[5] Personal representatives have the same functions as trustees of land (by virtue of the Administration of Estates Act 1925, s 9(1)(ii)) and therefore the interests capable of being overreached on an exercise of these powers are the same as those overreached on a sale by trustees of land.

[6] The effect of such overreaching is considered in *Horsham Properties Group Ltd v Clark* [2008] EWHC 2327, [50]–[51].

Law of Property Act 1925, s 27(1)

(1) A purchaser of a legal estate from trustees of land shall not be concerned with the trusts affecting the land, the net income of the land or the proceeds of sale of the land whether or not those trusts are declared by the same instrument as that by which the trust of land is created.

From Harpum's seminal analysis of overreaching[7] (parts of which are extracted below), it is apparent that there are at least two difficulties with using s 27(1) as the basis of the mechanism. Firstly, while we are concerned only with the operation of overreaching in relation to land, the same mechanism is applied to trusts of personal property. Therefore, it cannot have its basis in legislation, such as s 27(1), which is applicable only to land. Secondly, overreaching itself pre-dates the 1925 legislation and therefore its basis must be found outside that legislation.[8]

What, then, is the effect of s 27(1)? It appears to serve two purposes. Firstly, it seems likely that it was intended merely as a declaration of the existing law.[9] It provides a statement of the effect of a conveyance that complies with the conditions of overreaching, but it does not provide the basis for the mechanism itself, nor does it negate the need to show that those conditions have been complied with.[10] Secondly, it absolves the purchasers from any need to ensure that the trustees apply the purchase money in accordance with the terms of the trust.

2.2.2 Overreaching and the doctrine of conversion

The second theory is that the basis of overreaching lies in the doctrine of conversion. That doctrine, which applied to trusts for sale, had the effect that, from the inception of the trust, the beneficiaries were considered to have an interest in the proceeds of sale of the land, rather than the land itself.[11] The doctrine was abolished by s 3 of the Trusts of Land and Appointment of Trustees Act 1996 (TOLATA 1996).

If the doctrine of conversion provided the basis of overreaching of beneficial interests under a trust for sale, then overreaching should not be possible where trustees hold land under a trust of land, rather than under a trust for sale. This would mean that the 1996 Act, in removing the statutory trust for sale formerly imposed in cases of co-ownership of land, would have dramatically limited the applicability of overreaching. Such a consequence would be wholly unintended. In its report that led to the 1996 Act, the Law Commission specifically envisaged the application of overreaching to trusts of land.[12]

On an initial analysis, there appears to be a logical connection between the doctrine of conversion, providing that beneficiaries have only an interest in proceeds of sale from the inception of the trust, and overreaching, which leaves beneficiaries with a claim against the proceeds on sale. But despite this apparent connection between conversion and

---

[7] Harpum, 'Overreaching, Trusteees' Powers and the Reform of the 1925 Legislation' (1990) 49 CLJ 277.

[8] Ibid, p 278.

[9] Explained in the annotation of the section provided by Wolstenholme and Cherry, *Conveyancing Statutes* (11th edn, 1932).

[10] Hopkins, 'Overreaching and the Trusts of Land and Appointment of Trustees Act 1996' [1997] Conv 81, 82.

[11] The doctrine is further explained in Chapter 19, section 5.3.

[12] Law Commission Report No 181, *Transfer of Land: Trusts of Land* (1989, [6.1]).

overreaching, it seems that conversion did not, in fact, provide the basis on which over-reaching took place within a trust for sale. Indeed, Harpum dismissed any suggestion of a connection between the doctrines as a misconception.

Harpum, 'Overreaching, Trustees' Powers and the Reform of the 1925 Legislation' (1990) 49 CLJ 277, 278–9

The second misconception is that overreaching is connected with the doctrine of conversion, at least in relation to trusts for sale. Because of that doctrine, it is said that the interests of the beneficiaries are from the inception of the trust in the proceeds of sale. Such a view is untenable as an explanation of overreaching. First, a disposition under a mere *power* of sale will overreach just as much as a disposition under a trust for sale, and this is so even though the doctrine of conversion has no application to powers of sale. Secondly, the doctrine of conversion is usually relevant to determine whether beneficial interests are in land or in personalty. Overreaching applies as much to trusts for sale of personalty as to trusts of realty. Thirdly, overreaching is concerned to transfer trusts from the original subject-matter of the trust to the *actual* proceeds *after* sale. The beneficial interests of those entitled under a trust for sale, by reason of the doctrine of conversion, are regarded for certain purposes as interests in the *notional* proceeds of sale *from the date of the creation of the trust*. There is no inevitability about the application of the doctrine of conversion to trusts for sale, and indeed the doctrine suffers from inherent logical flaws. The correct approach in every case is, it is suggested, to ask whether, as a matter of policy and for the particular purpose in issue, the interests of the beneficiaries should be regarded as interests in the subject matter of the trust or in the proceeds. It is not easy to predict whether the doctrine of conversion will ever again be used to explain overreaching. Lord Oliver, who in analysing the interests of tenants in common in *City of London Building Society v. Flegg*, favoured a strict application of the doctrine of conversion, certainly assumed that overreaching occurred on sale, but at the same time cited with approval the statement that "[t]he whole purpose of the trust for sale is to make sure, by shifting the equitable interests away from the land and into the proceeds of sale, that a purchaser of the land takes free from the equitable interests".

2.2.3 Overreaching and trustees' powers of disposition

The third theory is that the basis of overreaching of beneficial interests under a trust is the trustees' powers of disposition. Harpum, who describes overreaching as a 'necessary concomitant' of such powers, favours this theory.[13] In relation to trusts of land, this means that the basis of overreaching of beneficial interests under such trusts is the powers of disposition conferred on trustees by s 6 of the TOLATA 1996.

Locating the basis of overreaching in the trustees' powers has now attracted a significant degree of acceptance.[14] Ultimately, in view of the shortfalls identified in the other two theories, this view provides the most satisfactory explanation of the basis of overreaching of beneficial interests under a trust of land that can be applied to both registered and unregistered land. The theory is not, however, without its own difficulties. For example, as Sparkes

---

[13] Harpum (1990, p 277).

[14] See, e.g., *Snell's Equity* (31st edn, ed McGhee, 2005, [4.16]); Smith, *Plural Ownership* (2005, pp 184–5), Fox, 'Overreaching' in *Breach of Trust* (ed Birks and Pretto, 2002, ch 4); McFarlane, *The Structure of Property Law* (2008, pp 394–404).

notes,[15] there is nothing in the 1996 Act to say that trustees, having exercised a power of sale, hold the proceeds on trust for the beneficiaries. There is no doubt that such a trust exists, because the trustees cannot take the proceeds themselves, but because the trust is the necessary consequence of overreaching, this omission appears odd if the exercise of powers conferred by the 1996 Act provides the basis through which the mechanism operates.[16]

Further, using the trustees' powers as the basis of overreaching has also given rise to one of the key remaining issues on the scope of the mechanism. If the basis of overreaching lies in the trustees' powers, it follows that overreaching can take place only when the trustees are acting *within* those powers. We consider below the different arguments that have been raised as regards dispositions by trustees that are ultra vires their powers of disposition.

2.2.4 Overreaching in registered land

The final theory to consider is that the LRA 1925 provided its own basis of overreaching for registered land, which has been carried over into the LRA 2002.

Jackson has advanced this argument.[17]

Jackson, 'Overreaching in Registered Land Law' (2006) 69 MLR 214, 227–8

Any purchaser from a trustee also takes a title under section 20 [of the Land Registration Act 1925], *whether he has notice* of adverse equities or not: 'and the disposition shall operate in like manner as if the registered transferor or grantor were [...] entitled to the registered land in fee simple in possession for his own benefit'. Benjamin Cherry, in his evidence to the *Royal Commission on the Land Transfer Acts*, describes this as the 'overreaching' effect of registration. Apart from restrictions, which prevented registration of a transfer that did not comply with their terms, trusts were kept off the face of title. Section 94(1) of the Land Registration Act 1925 provided that trustees are registered as proprietors, not as trustees. There was also a direction in section 74 to keep trusts, as far as possible, off the face of the register. [...]

The effect of sections 20, 74 and 94 is to bring about a substantive alteration in the nature of the beneficial interest from a proprietary claim to a claim solely against the substitute property or proceeds of sale in the hands of the trustee(s). Some minor interests could become burdens on the land by registration against the title. Other matters could not be protected against a purchaser in this way, such as interests under a trust for sale or settlements. Such interests could be protected by entries on the register that restricted the registered owner's freedom to deal with the land. The intention behind these restrictions was to ensure that the land was dealt with in accordance with the terms of the trust or settlement. The nature of the beneficiary's interest changed from a proprietary right to a mere restriction or 'restraint on alienation'. But the default position was that trustee proprietors would be able to deal with the land as any ordinary proprietor could.

---

[15] Sparkes, *A New Land Law* (2nd edn, 2003, [13.51]). He notes the contrast with the trust for sale, where a trust of the proceeds was express within the terms of the trust.

[16] Although see the explanation provided by McFarlane (2008, pp 400–1).

[17] This argument is not without support in previous literature. For example, see the discussion of the Land Registration Act 1925, s 18, by Harpum (1990, p 308). His comments on s 18 were, however, rejected by Ferris and Battersby, 'The Impact of the Trusts of Land and Appointment of Trustees Act 1996 on Purchasers of Registered Land' (1998) Conv 168, 180–4, further developed in their subsequent work 'Overreaching and the Trusts of Land and Appointment of Trustees Act 1996: A Reply to Mr Dixon' [2001] Conv 221 and 'General Principles of Overreaching and the Reforms of the 1925 Legislation' (2002) 118 LQR 270, 281–2.

In essence, Jackson's argument is that, in registered land, overreaching arises through the process of registration itself. It is the cumulative effect of provisions aimed at keeping trusts off the register and those protecting purchasers from matters that have not been entered on the register as a restriction on how land can be dealt with. While the statutory provisions upon which Jackson's argument is based have changed in the LRA 2002, she suggests that the same scheme of overreaching has been maintained.[18]

If Jackson is correct, a chasm has been created between the operation of overreaching in registered and unregistered land. The basis and scope of overreaching in each would need to be separated. Two significant practical consequences follow. Firstly, if overreaching is not based on the trustees' powers of disposition, then it arises regardless of whether the trustees are acting within their powers.[19] The discussion of this matter (in section 4 below) would be an issue only for unregistered land.

Secondly, a disposition by a single trustee in registered land would overreach beneficial interests. The need for any capital money to be paid to two trustees would not apply to registered land unless, again, entered as a restriction on the register. The discussion (below) of this requirement would also be confined to unregistered land.[20]

Jackson's theory, as she acknowledges, is against the current authorities and the 'universally unquestioned' view that ss 2 and 27 of the LPA 1925 apply equally to registered and unregistered land.[21] To date, courts have not differentiated the operation of overreaching in each scheme of land. To do so now (with the practical consequences that would follow) would require a fundamental reversal of current understanding. It is notable that Jackson's argument is developed around the LRA 1925. If that Act was intended to provide a self-contained scheme of overreaching, which has therefore not been properly applied by the courts, the LRA 2002 provided an opportunity to reassess the position. In the absence of any clarification provided by that Act, it seems unlikely that Jackson's argument will find acceptance by the courts. Therefore, it is suggested that the better view remains that, for both registered and unregistered land, the basis of overreaching lies in the trustees' powers of disposition.

2.2.5 Other interests capable of being overreached

In addition to the interests for which overreaching is provided in s 2 of the LPA 1925, it has been accepted that some interests claimed under proprietary estoppel must also be capable of being overreached.

Birmingham Midshires Mortgage Services Ltd v Sabherwal
(2000) 80 P & CR 256, CA

Facts: Mrs Sabherwal lived in a house with her two sons and their families. Legal title to the house was vested in the sons who had defaulted on charges granted to BMMS to raise

---

[18] Jackson, 'Overreaching in Registered Land Law' (2006) 69 MLR 214, 241, fn 183.

[19] A consequence confirmed by Jackson, 'Overreaching and Unauthorised Disposition of Registered Land' [2007] Conv 120. She says, at 129: '*I contend that an unauthorised disposition by trustees of registered land would always overreach.*'

[20] In this respect, it should be noted that while the Law of Property Act 1925, s 2(1)(ii), refers to a conveyance by 'trustees of land' in the plural, this is no bar to an argument for overreaching by a single trustee. The Interpretation Act 1978, s 6(c), provides '*words in the singular include the plural and words in the plural include the singular*'.

[21] Jackson (2007, p 229).

money to support their business ventures. Mrs Sabherwal sought to establish that she had a proprietary interest in the house binding against BMMS. One argument made was that she had an interest through proprietary estoppel, which, in contrast to a beneficial interest under a trust of land, was not capable of being overreached.

Robert Walker LJ

At [24]–[32]

On the facts of this case, Mrs Sabherwal plainly made a substantial financial contribution to all the properties successively owned by the family. She could rely on a resulting trust and had no need to rely on proprietary estoppel (if and so far as the two are, in the context of the family home, distinct doctrines: see the observations of Sir Nicolas Browne-Wilkinson V-C in *Grant v Edwards* [1986] 1 Ch 638, [1986] 2 All ER 426 at 656 of the former report). If she had made no financial contribution, but had nevertheless acted to her detriment in reliance on her sons promises, she might have obtained (through the medium of estoppel rather than through the medium of a trust) equitable rights of a proprietary nature. Her actual occupation of the house would then have promoted those rights into an overriding interest. That, I think, is not conceded by counsel for the respondents but I assume that to be the case. On that basis, it would have been a remarkable result if those more precarious rights were incapable of being overreached, on a sale by trustees, under s 2(1)(ii) of the Law of Property Act 1925.

Mr Beaumont has however contended for that result, citing what Lord Wilberforce said in *Shiloh Spinners v Harding* [1973] AC 691, [1973] 1 All ER 90 at 721 of the former report:

> "All this seems to show that there may well be rights, of an equitable character, outside the provisions as to registration and which are incapable of being overreached."

Lord Wilberforce had just before referred to *ER Ives Investment Ltd v High* [1967] 2 QB 379, [1967] 1 All ER 504. In that case a boundary dispute between neighbours had been settled by an informal agreement including the grant of a right of way. The agreement about the right of way was never completed by a deed of grant, and was never registered. The Court of Appeal held that it was binding despite the lack of registration. Similarly, *Shiloh Spinners v Harding* was concerned with an equitable right of entry for enforcement of a covenant arising in what Lord Wilberforce called a dispute [...] of a commonplace character between neighbours.

Equitable interests of that character ought not to be overreached, since they are rights which an adjoining owner enjoys over the land itself, regardless of its ownership from time to time. The principle is in my view correctly stated in Megarry and Wade, *The Law of Real Property* 5th ed p 409:

> "In fact the only examples of such equities likely to occur are commercial (as opposed to family) interests, which it is absurd to speak of overreaching. Two instances are an equitable right of way which is yet not an equitable easement, and an equitable right of entry to secure performance of a covenant, and there are probably others. To overreach such interests is to destroy them [...]"

The footnotes to this passage refer to *ER Ives Investment Ltd v High* and *Shiloh Spinners v Harding* (cases which were cited to the House of Lords in *Flegg*—see especially counsels argument at p 63—but are not referred to in any of the speeches of their Lordships). The essential distinction is, as the authors of Megarry and Wade note, between commercial and family interests. An equitable easement or an equitable right of entry cannot sensibly shift from the land affected by it to the proceeds of sale. An equitable interest as a tenant in common can do so, even if accompanied by the promise of a home for life, since the proceeds of sale can be used to acquire another home.

Mr Beaumont has also argued that, although in *Grant v Edwards* the Vice-Chancellor regarded interests in the family home created by equitable estoppel or by a constructive trust as closely similar, if not interchangeable, his remarks do not apply to a resulting trust arising from a monetary contribution. This is an area of the law in which the terminology is unfortunately far from uniform, but I do not accept that the Vice-Chancellors remarks were limited in that way. On the contrary, immediately after his reference to proprietary estoppel he said (see [1986] Ch 657, H-658A):

"Identifiable contributions to the purchase [price] of the house will of course be an important factor in many cases."

Similarly, in *Lloyds Bank v Rosset* [1991] 1 AC 107, [1990] 1 All ER 1111 Lord Bridge (in a very well-known passage at pp 132–3 of the former report) referred to direct contributions to the purchase price by [a party] who is not the legal owner, as readily justifying the creation of a constructive trust. Such a trust, however labelled, does not then leave room for a separate interest by way of equitable estoppel: compare the remarks of Morritt LJ in *Lloyds Bank v Carrick* [1996] 4 All ER 630, [1996] 2 FLR 600 at p 639C-E of the former report. To do so would cause vast confusion in an area which is already quite difficult enough. The confusion is avoided if what Lord Wilberforce said in *Shiloh Spinners v Harding* is limited, as in my judgment it must be, to some unusual types of equitable interest arising in commercial situations. In this type of family situation, the concepts of trust and equitable estoppel are almost interchangeable, and both are affected in the same way by the statutory mechanism of overreaching, the substance of which is not affected by the 1996 Act.

In these circumstances I do not find it necessary to consider how far the judges findings in this area (which were largely limited to a general acceptance of Mrs Sabherwal's evidence) would establish the necessary conditions for proprietary estoppel. I assume in favour of Mrs Sabherwal that they would do so.

On the basis of this decision, family interests under a proprietary estoppel are capable of being overreached, while commercial interests are not. To have held otherwise would have created a significant lacuna in the operation of overreaching: the mechanism could be avoided simply by claiming an interest through proprietary estoppel rather than constructive trust. To that extent, the decision seems correct—but questions may still arise as to its scope and therefore to the extent to which interests claimed through proprietary estoppel can be overreached. It is unclear whether the category of 'family' interests to which overreaching is extended is limited to those circumstances, exemplified by the facts of *Sabherwal*, in which claims to estoppel and constructive trusts coincide, or could apply to other circumstances in which estoppel claims arise in relation to a home. Robert Walker LJ's definition of a family interest is sufficiently broad to cover such cases.

Harpum considered the scope of the judgment. Although generally adopting a restrictive approach, his comment implies that the case is not limited to situations in which trusts and estoppel coincide.

Harpum, 'Overreaching, Trusts of Land and Proprietary Estoppel'
(2000) 116 LQR 341, 344–5

Thus in determining whether an inchoate equity arising by estoppel is overreached by a disposition to two or more owners, it is necessary to consider the manner in which the court might have given effect to that equity. Robert Walker L.J. considered that the essential difference was between "commercial and family interests". The latter but not the former were overreachable. That may, however, be an oversimplification. If effect would be given to the equity by the creation or transfer of a legal estate in land or by the grant of a legal or equitable right over land, then the equity should be incapable of being overreached. However, if the appropriate way of giving effect to the equity was by means of an interest that could properly be converted into money on sale, such as an interest under a trust of land or a lien, the equity should be overreachable.

The scope of *Sabherwal* must be considered to remain uncertain. Overreaching of interests claimed through estoppel where a constructive trust would not also be available appears to be outside the ratio of the decision. Because the basis of overreaching is the trustees' powers of disposition, there is a difficulty in extending the operation of the mechanism to situations in which no trust could be claimed. On that view, there is simply no basis on which an equitable interest not arising under a trust can be overreached. Indeed, even if overreaching is limited in that way, it is not necessary to extend overreaching to interests under estoppel. The same result can be achieved by reliance on the suggestion in *Lloyds Bank v Carrick*[22] (referred to in the judgment extracted above and discussed in Chapter 15, section 5.8) that the existence of a constructive (or resulting) trust precludes any further claim to an interest through estoppel.

2.3 TRANSACTIONS WITH OVERREACHING EFFECT

Once it is established that an interest is capable of being overreached, overreaching will take place only if the transaction is one that has such effect. Three requirements must be met. Firstly, there is an overarching requirement, reflecting the fact that overreaching has its basis within the trustees' powers, that the transaction is one that is within the powers of the trustees. We consider below the effect of transactions that do not fulfil this requirement.

The second and third requirements are drawn from the LPA 1925. The second requirement is that the transaction must be one of those listed in s 2(1)(i)–(iv) of the Act (extracted above) as having overreaching effect. The third is that s 2(1)(i) and (ii) provides that, to overreach beneficial interests under a trust, statutory requirements as regards payment of capital money must be complied with. These requirements are contained in s 27(2) of the 1925 Act.

Law of Property Act 1925, s 27(2)

(2) Notwithstanding anything to the contrary in the instrument (if any) creating a trust of land or in any trust affecting the net proceeds of sale of the land if it is sold, the proceeds of sale or other capital money shall not be paid to or applied by the direction of fewer than two persons as [trustees], except where the trustee is a trust corporation, but this subsection does not affect the right of a sole personal representative as such to give valid receipts for, or direct the application of, proceeds of sale or other capital money, nor, except where capital money arises on the transaction, render it necessary to have more than one trustee.

[22] [1996] 4 All ER 630.

This provision, like s 2, applies equally to registered and unregistered land. In registered land, trustees should enter a restriction on the register preventing a disposition unless s 27(2) is complied with. But (contrary to Jackson's argument, discussed above) the absence of a restriction does not remove the need for the requirement to be complied with in order for a purchaser to rely on the overreaching mechanism.

Neither ss 2 nor 27 state in their terms that there must be capital money for overreaching to take place. They impose requirements to be met when such money does arise. The fact that capital money will be paid may be thought to be inherent in overreaching as a process of 'shifting' beneficial interests from the land to money: if no money is paid, into what can the beneficial interests shift? In identifying the trustees powers of disposition as the basis of overreaching of the beneficial interests under a trust, however, Harpum indicated that this was not, in fact, the case.

Harpum, 'Overreaching, Trusteees' Powers and the Reform of the 1925 Legislation' (1990) 49 CLJ 277, 282

[T]he interest created or the estate granted by the exercise of the power takes priority over the estates and interests under the settlement. The exercise of a power which does not give rise to any capital monies—such as an exchange of land—overreaches just as much as a transaction which does.

This statement proved prescient when the application of overreaching to a transaction in which no capital money arose came to be decided in the following case. The Court of Appeal cited Harpum's comment with approval in holding that such a transaction still has overreaching effect.

State Bank of India v Sood [1997] Ch 276, CA

Facts: Mr and Mrs Sood were registered proprietors of their home. They granted a charge over the home for existing and future liabilities of themselves and their business. No capital money was advanced contemporaneously with this disposition, but, over a period of time, Mr and Mrs Sood accrued debts of over £1m and the State Bank of India (to which the benefit of the charge had been assigned by the Punjab National Bank) sought to enforce the charge. The five children of the couple (the third to seventh defendants) argued that they were beneficiaries under a trust of land and that their beneficial interests had not been overreached.

Peter Gibson LJ

At 279–90

The question can be formulated in this way: where two trustees for sale hold registered land for themselves and other beneficiaries and mortgage the land as security for existing and future liabilities of themselves and other persons, are the equitable interests of the beneficiaries overreached, notwithstanding that no money was advanced by the mortgagee to or at the direction of the trustees contemporaneously with the mortgage? The judge in effect answered that question in the negative. [. . .]

There is no dispute that the equitable interests of the third to seventh defendants were at the date of the legal charge capable of being overreached. That condition of section 2(1)(ii) was therefore satisfied. Most of the argument has turned on the final condition of that paragraph relating to compliance with the statutory requirements respecting the payment of capital money. [...]

I accept that a novel and important point of law is raised by this appeal. Lending institutions regularly take security from businessmen in the form of a legal charge on property (which very frequently means that the matrimonial home is charged) to secure existing and future indebtedness, and very commonly that property will be registered land held by two registered proprietors on trust for sale with no restriction registered in respect of their power to transfer or mortgage that property. It was not suggested that it had ever been the practice of mortgagees to make inquiries of occupiers of the property as to any claimed rights. Yet if the third to seventh defendants are right, that is what the mortgagees must do if they are not to take subject to the beneficial interests of the occupiers. [...]

The crucial issue is the true construction of the final condition of section 2(1)(ii) relating to compliance with statutory requirements respecting the payment of capital money. There is no dispute that if capital money does arise under a conveyance by trustees for sale to a purchaser it must be paid to or applied as section 27(2) dictates. But for overreaching to occur, does capital money have to arise on and contemporaneously with the conveyance?

The judge appears to have assumed that there could be no overreaching if no capital money arose.

He said:

> "we have to look to see whether capital money was paid [to] or applied by the direction of the two trustees. If it was, then the defendants have no defence; if it was not, then the bank cannot overreach and they have an arguable defence on the evidence."

Mr. Havey and Mr. Williams submitted that was indeed the position and they said that the arising of capital money on the conveyance was the assumption on which section 2(1)(ii) was drafted. Mr. Crawford's initial submission accorded with that view, but he sought to escape the consequences by contending that capital money arose whenever the Punjab National Bank advanced money, even if before the legal charge was executed. However, I cannot accept that what was done prior to the legal charge has any relevance to the condition that "the statutory requirements respecting the payment of capital money arising under a disposition upon trust for sale are complied with." Nor can I accept Mr. Crawford's further submission that the debt existing at the date of the legal charge was not materially different from the secured debt which existed at the date of the mortgage in *Flegg* and was discharged in that case out of the money raised. The circumstances are wholly different.

Mr. Crawford however had recourse to a further submission, adopting a point suggested by the court, that the relevant condition in section 2(1)(ii) should be construed as applying only to those cases where there was capital money arising under a disposition upon trust for sale, the statutory requirements of section 27(2) being simply irrelevant to a transaction under which no capital money arises. There are several types of conveyance to a purchaser (within the statutory meanings of those terms) other than a charge to secure existing and future debt which do not give rise to capital money, for example, an exchange or a lease not at a premium. Why should the legislature have intended to exclude such conveyances from having an overreaching effect? It is interesting to note that the precursor of section 2(1), viz. section 3(2)(ii) of the Law of Property Act 1922, used as one of the conditions for overreaching to occur the formula "If any capital money arises from the transaction [...] the requirements of this Act respecting the payment of capital money arising under a trust for sale [...] are complied with." However the form of section 3(2) differed in a number of respects from section

2(1) of the Act of 1925 and it may not be safe to infer that the later provision was intended to re-enact the substance of the earlier provision. But it points to the relevant condition of section 2(1) being worded in surprisingly oblique fashion if what was intended was that capital money must arise so that the statutory requirements can be complied with. Mr. Havey drew attention to the word "any" in connection with "capital money" in section 2(1)(iii) and (iv) and suggested that its omission from the reference to "capital money" in section 2(1)(i) and (ii) was significant. But the structure of those paragraphs is quite different from section 2(1)(iii) and (iv) and the draftsman could not have achieved the effect of section 3(2) of the Act of 1922 by adding "any" before "capital money" in section 2(1)(i) or (ii).

The relevant condition in section 2(1)(ii) is the same as that in section 2(1)(i). The overreaching powers conferred by the Settled Land Act 1925 include power to convey by an exchange or lease as well as by a mortgage or charge where capital money may not arise (see section 72 of that Act). The statutory requirements governing capital money (to be paid to or applied by the direction of not less than two individuals or a trust corporation: sections 94 and 95 of that Act) can only apply to those conveyances giving rise to capital money. The same interpretation must apply to the condition in section 2(1)(i) as it does to the conveyancing condition in section 2(1)(ii).

A more substantial argument of policy advanced on behalf of the third to seventh defendants is that if overreaching occurs where no capital money arises, the beneficiaries' interests may be reduced by the conveyance leaving nothing to which the interests can attach by way of replacement save the equity of redemption, and that may be or become valueless. I see considerable force in this point, but I am not persuaded that it suffices to defeat what I see to be the policy of the legislation, to allow valid dispositions to overreach equitable interests. In my judgment on its true construction section 2(1)(ii) only requires compliance with the statutory requirements respecting the payment of capital money if capital money arises. Accordingly I would hold that capital money did not have to arise under the conveyance.

The judge further said:

"I consider that overreaching must take place at the time of the execution. I think that the plaintiff does not object to that in principle, but says that the defendants' right simply attaches to the equity of redemption; but I do not think one can have a condition of over-reaching on moneys which may or may not be drawn down later. For overreaching to take effect all parts of section 27(2) must be complied with; it is a two stage process which requires, first, the existence of either proceeds of sale or capital moneys and, secondly, those are either to be paid to the two trustees or applied at their discretion. The plaintiff says it does not matter-because there was a general direction for application in the charge-if it comes into existence or is applied at a subsequent time. I think that is wrong; it is necessary for the moneys to be in existence at the time of the charge so that those moneys can either be received or applied at the trustees' directions."

[…]

Both Mr. Harvey and Mr. Williams supported the judge's conclusion that some capital money must arise contemporaneously with the conveyance for there to be overreaching. They said that if a conveyance provided only for deferred payment, that would not suffice. They further submitted that provided some capital money arose contemporaneously with the conveyance and section 27(2) was complied with, overreaching would occur even though other money was subsequently advanced under the conveyance. Thus if a £1m facility was secured by a mortgage and in the course of time was fully drawn on but at the time of the mortgage only £100 was advanced, there would nevertheless be overreaching in respect of the whole £1m thereby secured, whereas if the £100 had not been advanced at the time of the mortgage, there would have been no overreaching. I do not believe that the statutory language supports a requirement producing such a surprising and illogical result. Mr. Havey drew our attention to a large number of provisions in the Settled Land Act 1925 which, he said, showed that money arising from a transaction must be received or applied at the same time as the transaction. I cannot agree, though I of course accept that to be paid or applied, capital money must be in hand. If and to the extent that capital money arises after the conveyance, section 27(2) must be complied with for the mortgagee to obtain a good receipt. If it is not, for example if an advance is made after a mortgage has been executed but under a facility provided for by the mortgage but is not paid to or at the direction of two or more trustees or a trust corporation, that would not affect the overreaching which would have occurred on the mortgage. [...]

The correct analysis of the position in the present case is that on the execution of the legal charge, the interests of the third to seventh defendants were overreached and attached to the equity of redemption. The legal estate in the property was by the legal charge made subject to the rights thereunder of the Punjab National Bank which were subsequently assigned to the plaintiff, including the right to sell the property. The value of the equity of redemption on the execution of the legal charge would reflect the then existing liabilities thereby secured. That value would be further reduced as further liabilities arose and were secured under the legal charge. In the light of *City of London Building Society v. Flegg* [1986] Ch. 605; [1988] A.C. 54 it follows from the overreaching that section 70(1)(g) does not avail the third to seventh defendants and that their defence on this point cannot succeed and should be struck out. On the assumption that they were not consulted about the legal charge by the first and second defendants, it may be that they have the right to obtain redress against the trustees.

Much though I value the principle of overreaching as having aided the simplification of conveyancing, I cannot pretend that I regard the resulting position in the present case as entirely satisfactory. The safeguard for beneficiaries under the existing legislation is largely limited to having two trustees or a trust corporation where capital money falls to be received. But that is no safeguard at all, as this case has shown, when no capital money is received on and contemporaneously with the conveyance. Further, even when it is received by two trustees as in *City of London Building Society v. Flegg* [1986] Ch. 605; [1988] A.C. 54, it might be thought that beneficiaries in occupation are insufficiently protected. Hence the recommendation for reform in the Law Commission's report, "Transfer of Land, Overreaching: Beneficiaries in Occupation" (1989) (Law Com. No. 188), that a conveyance should not overreach the interest of a sui juris beneficiary in occupation unless he gives his consent. Mr. Harpum in the article to which reference has been made proposed an alternative reform, limiting the power of trustees to mortgage. Whether the legislature will reform the law remains to be seen. I should add for completeness that we were assured by counsel that the recent Trusts of Land and Appointment of Trustees Act 1996 was of no assistance and we have not considered its effect.

In the absence of capital money, there may still be a shifting of the beneficial interests. In *Sood*, the interests shifted to the equity of redemption. To the extent that this may be valueless, where the debt equals or exceeds the value of the property, the result is no harsher than that in a case, exemplified by *City of London Building Society v Flegg*,[23] in which capital money is paid to the trustees, but is dissipated by them.

In *Sood*, two trustees executed the charge. If s 27(2) applies only to dispositions in which capital money is paid, however, it seems that a sole trustee (in registered and unregistered land) can overreach beneficial interests through dispositions that do not involve payment of

---

23 [1986] Ch. 605, [1988] AC 54.

capital money.[24] There is no independent statutory requirement that the transaction must be undertaken by at least two trustees.[25] It is, however, worth noting that if the third party provides *nothing* in return for the right received from the trustees, overreaching will not occur, because the third party has not acquired a right 'for valuable consideration'.[26]

Commenting on the decision in *Sood*, Thompson suggested that the outcome prevents the need to distinguish between different types of mortgage and thus avoids the 'strange results' that Peter Gibson LJ's judgment highlights would result from drawing such distinctions.[27] But if a single trustee can overreach beneficial interests through mortgages (and other dispositions) that do not involve payment of capital money, then the effect of *Sood* is that it is, in fact, necessary to distinguish between such mortgages. The 'strange results' avoided by the decision in trusts with at least two trustees will arise in sole-trustee trusts. Hence, for example, a mortgage by a sole trustee, with £100 advanced at the outset and debts of £1m subsequently accrued, would not overreach (because the application of s 27(2) would be triggered by the initial payment of capital money), while a mortgage in which the level of borrowing reached the same amount, but with no initial advanced payment, *would* overreach, because the absence of capital money precludes the application of s 27(2). While it must be doubted that such results are intended, there is no statutory basis for limiting overreaching to transactions undertaken by at least two trustees unless s 27(2) is applied. The unfortunate result is that transactions in which beneficiaries appear most vulnerable are also those in which they are least protected.

Having outlined the general scope of overreaching, we can now consider its application in the specific context of a home occupied by the beneficiaries under a trust of land.

3 CO-OWNERSHIP, OVERREACHING, AND OCCUPYING BENEFICIARIES

We have seen that one of the interests capable of being overreached is the beneficial interest under a trust of land. Indeed, overreaching of such interests is probably the most common and practically important use of the mechanism. The shifting of beneficial interests from land to money appears neither controversial, nor problematic, where the function of the trust property is to provide an investment fund for the beneficiaries. The physical identity of the trust property itself is, then, not of central concern; what is more important is the wealth that it represents. It is of no particular significance to the beneficiaries whether their interest is in any particular piece of land or other type of property; what is important is that the value of the trust fund is maintained by the profitable sale of the land and the reinvestment of the proceeds in other lucrative investments. The trustees' equitable and statutory duties under the Trustee Act 2000 are defined with that objective in mind.

But a trust of land will also arise where co-owners hold land with the intention that they will occupy it as their home. In the common situation in which a couple purchase a home

---

[24] See, e.g., McFarlane (2008, pp 397–400).

[25] Statutory references to 'trustees', e.g. in the Law of Property Act 1925, s 2, may considered by reference to the Interpretation Act 1978, s 6(3), to include a single trustee.

[26] Section 2(1) limits overreaching to cases in which the third party is a '*purchaser of a legal estate in land*' (this includes a mortgagee); s 205(1)(xxi) of the Law of Property Act 1925 states that, unless the context otherwise requires, a 'purchaser' means a purchaser for 'valuable consideration'.

[27] Thompson, 'Overreaching without Payment' [1997] Conv 134.

in their joint names, they are both the legal and beneficial co-owners, and this trust creates no difficulties. Indeed, the couple is likely to be unaware that they deal with the property as trustees for the benefit of themselves as beneficial co-owners.

By contrast, a very real tension can arise where co-owners hold the legal estate on express or implied trust for themselves and others. This is a situation that can occur, for example, where a home is purchased for an extended family, where individuals within the family take the legal estate on trust for themselves and the remaining family members take as beneficial co-owners. The beneficiaries may be concerned not only with the value of their trust property, but also with its identity as their home. Yet overreaching does not recognize this concern. Their interests are assumed to be adequately protected, firstly, by the continued representation of their proprietary rights in the proceeds of sale by the process of overreaching itself, and secondly, by the requirement that at least two trustees receive those proceeds to guard against a misappropriation of the trust property or other breach of duty. If a misappropriation or other breach of duty does occur, the beneficiaries' proprietary interests are placed in jeopardy against a purchaser by overreaching, but the beneficiaries retain their personal remedies against the trustees to redress any loss in value of the trust fund.

The tension between trust property as a home for beneficiaries and the wealth that it represents came to a head in the following case. The Fleggs' main arguments focused on the need to afford protection to their occupation of the trust property as their home, by treating investment and occupation trusts differently. They argued, relying on *William & Glyn's Bank v Boland*,[28] that their beneficial interests bound the mortgagees as an overriding interest, and that an overriding beneficial interest should not be overreached. Further, they suggested that s 14 of the LPA 1925 operated to protect the interests of occupiers. If the land had been unregistered, the Fleggs would have argued that their occupation gave a purchaser constructive notice of their interest, so as to confer priority under the doctrine of notice. The House of Lords rejected these arguments. Overreaching operated, provided that the statutory conditions were satisfied. At that point, the Fleggs' beneficial interest in their home was transferred to the proceeds of sale so that there simply was no interest in the land that their occupation (or, indeed, any entry on the register) could protect.

City of London Building Society v Flegg [1988] AC 54, HL

Facts: Mr and Mrs Flegg sold their home of twenty-eight years and, in 1982, contributed the £18,000 proceeds to the purchase of Bleak House as a new home for themselves, and their daughter and son-in-law, Mrs and Mrs Maxwell-Brown. The balance of the £34,000 purchase price was funded by a mortgage. Despite their solicitor's advice that Bleak House should be registered in the names of all four parties, it was, in fact, registered in the joint names of Mr and Mrs Maxwell-Brown, who, given the Fleggs' contribution to the purchase price, held the house as joint tenants on resulting trust for themselves and Mr and Mrs Flegg. Bleak House was occupied and became the home of all four parties. The Maxwell-Browns ran into financial difficulties and, without the knowledge or consent of the Flegg's, remortgaged the house to the City of London Building Society to raise £37,500. The Fleggs must have been suspicious and, before the mortgage could be registered, they entered a caution against dealings at the Land Registry. Unfortunately, the Maxwell-Browns were unable to meet the repayments under the mortgage, and the

---

[28] [1981] 1 AC 487.

building society sought a declaration that the mortgage bound and could be enforced against the Fleggs' interest, and an order for possession.

Lord Templeman

At 71–4

The respondents resist the claim of the appellants to possession of Bleak House and rely on section 14 of the Law of Property Act 1925. Sections 27 and 28 of that Act which overreach the interests of the respondents under the trust for sale of Bleak House are to be found in Part I of the Act. Section 14 provides:

"This Part of this Act shall not prejudicially affect the interest of any person in possession or in actual occupation of land to which he may be entitled in right of such possession or occupation."

The respondents were in actual occupation of Bleak House at the date of the legal charge. It is argued that their beneficial interests under the trust for sale were not overreached by the legal charge or that the respondents were entitled to remain in occupation after the legal charge and against the appellants despite the overreaching of their interests. [...]

If the argument for the respondents is correct, a purchaser from trustees for sale must ensure that a beneficiary in actual occupation is not only consulted but consents to the sale. Section 14 of the Law of Property Act 1925 is not apt to confer on a tenant in common of land held on trust for sale, who happens to be in occupation, rights which are different from and superior to the rights of tenants in common, who are not in occupation on the date when the interests of all tenants in common are overreached by a sale or mortgage by trustees for sale. [...]

In my view the object of section 70 was to reproduce for registered land the same limitations as section 14 of the Law of Property Act 1925 produced for land whether registered or unregistered. The respondents claim to be entitled to overriding interests because they were in actual occupation of Bleak House on the date of the legal charge. But the interests of the respondents cannot at one and the same time be overreached and overridden and at the same time be overriding interests. The appellants cannot at one and the same time take free from all the interests of the respondents yet at the same time be subject to some of those interests. The right of the respondents to be and remain in actual occupation of Bleak House ceased when the respondents' interests were overreached by the legal charge save in so far as their rights were transferred to the equity of redemption. As persons interested under the trust for sale the respondents had no right to possession as against the appellants and the fact that the respondents were in actual occupation at the date of the legal charge did not create a new right or transfer an old right so as to make the right enforceable against the appellants.

One of the main objects of the legislation of 1925 was to effect a compromise between on the one hand the interests of the public in securing that land held in trust is freely marketable and, on the other hand, the interests of the beneficiaries in preserving their rights under the trusts. By the Settled Land Act 1925 a tenant for life may convey the settled land discharged from all the trusts powers and provisions of the settlement. By the Law of Property Act 1925 trustees for sale may convey land held on trust for sale discharged from the trusts affecting the proceeds of sale and rents and profits until sale. Under both forms of trust the protection and the only protection of the beneficiaries is that capital money must be paid to at least two trustees or a trust corporation. Section 14 of the Law of Property Act 1925 and section 70 of the Land Registration Act 1925 cannot have been intended to frustrate this compromise and to subject the purchaser to some beneficial interests but not others depending on the way-wardness of actual occupation. The Court of Appeal took a different view, largely in reliance on the decision of this House in *Williams & Glyn's Bank Ltd. v. Boland* [1981] A.C. 487. In that case the sole proprietor of registered land held the land as sole trustee upon trust for sale and to stand possessed of the net proceeds of sale and rents and profits until sale upon trust for himself and his wife as tenants in common. This House held that the wife's beneficial interest coupled with actual possession by her constituted an overriding interest and that a mortgagee from the husband, despite the concluding words of section 20(1), took subject to the wife's overriding interest. But in that case the interest of the wife was not overreached or overridden because the mortgagee advanced capital moneys to a sole trustee. If the wife's interest had been overreached by the mortgagee advancing capital moneys to two trustees there would have been nothing to justify the wife in remaining in occupation as against the mortgagee. There must be a combination of an interest which justifies continuing occupation plus actual occupation to constitute an overriding interest. Actual occupation is not an interest in itself.

Lord Oliver

At 80–1

My Lords, the ambit of section 14 is a matter which has puzzled conveyancers ever since the Law of Property Act was enacted [. . .] For my part, I think that it is unnecessary for present purposes to seek to resolve the conundrum. What section 14 does not do, on any analysis, is to enlarge or add to whatever interest it is that the occupant has "in right of his occupation" and in my judgment the argument that places reliance upon it in the instant case founds itself upon an assumption about the nature of the occupying co-owners' interest that cannot in fact be substantiated. The section cannot of itself create an interest which survives the exe-cution of the trust under which it arises or answer the logically anterior question of what, if any, interest in the land is conferred by the possession or occupation [. . .] the section cannot, in my judgment, have the effect of preserving, as equitable interests in the land, interests which are overreached by the exercise of the trustees' powers or of bringing onto the title which the purchaser from trustees for sale is required to investigate the equitable interest of every beneficiary who happens to be in occupation of the land. That would be to defeat the manifest purpose of the legislature in enacting the sections to which reference has already been made. [. . .]

At 90–1

Considered in the context of a transaction complying with the statutory requirements of the Law of Property Act 1925 the question of the effect of section 70(1)(g) of the Land Registration Act 1925 must, in my judgment, be approached by asking first what are the "rights" of the person in occupation and whether they are, at the material time, subsisting in reference to the land. In the instant case the exercise by the registered proprietors of the powers conferred on trustees for sale by section 28(1) of the Law of Property Act 1925 had the effect of overreaching the interests of the respondents under the statutory trusts upon which depended their right to continue in occupation of the land. The appellants took free from those trusts (section 27) and were not, in any event, concerned to see that the respond-ents' consent to the transaction was obtained (section 26). If, then, one asks what were the subsisting rights of the respondents referable to their occupation, the answer must, in my judgment, be that they were rights which, vis-à-vis the appellants, were, eo instante with the creation of the charge, overreached and therefore subsisted only in relation to the equity of redemption. I do not, for my part, find in *Boland's case* [1981] A.C. 487 anything which compels a contrary conclusion. Granted that the interest of a co-owner pending the execution of the statutory trust for sale is, despite the equitable doctrine of conversion, an interest subsisting in reference to the land the subject matter of the trust and granted also that Boland's case establishes that such an interest, although falling within the definition of minor interest and so liable to be overriden by a registered disposition, will, so long as it subsists, be elevated to the status of an overriding interest if there exists also the additional element of occupation by the co-owner, I cannot for my part accept that, once what I may call the parent interest, by which alone the occupation can be justified, has been overreached and thus subordinated to a legal estate properly created by the trustees under their statutory powers, it can, in relation to the proprietor of the legal estate so created, be any longer said to be a right "for the time being subsisting." Section 70(1)(g) protects only the rights in reference to the land of the occupier whatever they are at the material time—in the instant case the right to enjoy in specie the rents and profits of the land held in trust for him. Once the beneficiary's rights have been shifted from the land to capital moneys in the hands of the trustees, there is no longer an interest in the land to which the occupation can be referred or which it can protect. If the trustees sell in accordance with the statutory provisions and so overreach the beneficial interests in reference to the land, nothing remains to which a right of occupation can attach and the same result must, in my judgment, follow vis-à-vis a chargee by way of legal mortgage so long as the transaction is carried out in the manner prescribed by the Law of Property Act 1925, overreaching the beneficial interests by subordinating them to the estate of the chargee which is no longer "affected" by them so as to become subject to them on registration pursuant to section 20(1) of the Land Registration Act 1925. In the instant case, therefore, I would, for my part, hold that the charge created in favour of the appellants overreached the beneficial interests of the respondents and that there is nothing in section 70(1)(g) of the Land Registration Act 1925 or in Boland's case which has the effect of preserving against the appellants any rights of the respondents to occupy the land by virtue of their beneficial interests in the equity of redemption which remains vested in the trustees.

Although the decision in *Flegg* remains the leading authority on the application of overreaching against the overriding interests of occupiers, the framework of the law has moved on. The TOLATA 1996 has reformed trusts of land, including co-ownership trusts. The Fleggs would no longer hold a beneficial interest under a trust for sale, but under a trust of land, and their beneficial interests would be clearly in the land, in respect of which they would have a right of occupation.[29]

The Court of Appeal in *Sabherwal* confirmed that the 1996 Act does not affect the application of overreaching.

Birmingham Midshires Mortgage Services Ltd v Sabherwal
(2000) 80 P & CR 256, CA

Walker LJ

At 261

The judge gave ten reasons for concluding that the decision in Flegg has not been affected by the 1996 Act. Since that conclusion is not directly challenged in this court, at any rate on

---

[29] Trusts of Land and Appointment of Trustees Act 1996, ss 5, 12, and 13. The beneficiaries' right to occupy is considered in Chapter 19, section 5.3.

the grounds that the judge considered, it is sufficient to mention three of the most cogent of his reasons. First, the overreaching effect of the legal charges took place when they were executed in July 1990, and cannot be ousted by the coming into force of the 1996 Act over six years later. Second, the 1996 Act contains nothing to exclude the essential overreaching provision contained in section 2(1)(ii) of the Law of Property Act 1925. On the contrary, that provision is amended so as to meet the new terminology of the 1996 Act (see section 25(1) and Schedule 3 paragraph 4(1)) and so is in effect confirmed, with that new terminology, by the 1996 Act. Third, the abolition of the doctrine of conversion (by section 3 of the 1996 Act) is irrelevant for reasons stated by Lord Oliver in *Flegg*. However, the abolition of that doctrine does explain the amendment of s.27(1) of the Law of Property Act 1925, on which some reliance has been placed.

The 1996 Act does confer wider implied powers of disposition upon trustees[30] than were conferred by the LPA 1925 and, furthermore, provides protection to the purchasers of unregistered land from the trustees.[31] The LRA 2002 replaces the LRA 1925 and preserves the protection afforded to the interests of occupiers as an overriding interest.[32] It also defines the abilities of the registered owner, including trustees, to dispose of the registered land[33] and provides protection to purchasers dealing with the registered owner, even where the registered owner is a trustee.[34]

4 OVERREACHING AND BREACH OF TRUST

The interplay between a breach of trust and overreaching has been the subject of considerable academic debate.[35] The fact that overreaching is founded upon the trustees' powers of disposition places in question its operation where the trustees are acting in breach of their powers or the duties to which they are required to adhere when exercising those powers. Almost all of the cases on overreaching have concerned unauthorized mortgages by trustees, which have been entered into to raise finance unconnected with the purchase of the property. Unauthorized sales by trustees tend not to lead to the same problems for occupying beneficiaries, although the danger from overreaching exists. A purchaser of land will generally wish to obtain vacant possession of the land and will conduct enquiries to that end, thus invariably revealing the occupying beneficiaries. The purchaser can then take steps to ensure that the occupying beneficiaries are prepared to vacate the property before proceeding with their purchase.[36]

---

[30] Ibid, s 6.
[31] Ibid, s 16.
[32] Ibid, Sch 3, para 2.
[33] Land Registration Act 2002, s 23.
[34] Ibid, s 26.
[35] The debate is led by a series of articles by Ferris and Battersby: 'The Impact of the Trusts of Land and Appointment of Trustees Act 1996 on Purchasers of Registered Land' (1998) Conv 168; 'Overreaching and the Trusts of Land and Appointment of Trustees Act 1996: A Reply to Mr Dixon' (2001) Conv 221; 'General Principles of Overreaching and the Reforms of the 1925 Legislation' (2002) 118 LQR 270; 'The General Principles of Overreaching and the Modern Legislative Reforms 1996–2002' (2003) 119 LQR 94; and Ferris, 'Making Sense of Section 26 of the Land Registration Act 2002' in *Modern Studies in Property Law: Vol 2* (ed Cooke, 2003, p 101). See also Dixon, 'Overreaching and the Trusts of Land and Appointment of Trustees Act 1996' [2000] Conv 267 and Pascoe, 'Improving Conveyancing by Redrafting Section 16' [2005] Conv 140.
[36] Harpum (1990, p 312).

4.1 TRUSTEES' ABILITY, AUTHORITY, AND DUTIES

Ferris and Battersby[37] make the crucial point that it is important, at the outset, to understand the different ways in which we refer to trustees' powers and the different consequences that result from a misuse of these powers. A reference to the powers of trustees may be used to define the ability of the trustees to undertake a certain disposition. Trustees as holders of the legal estate are able to deal with that estate, but they do not have ability to deal with the beneficiaries' equitable interests unless given authority to do so on behalf of the beneficiaries, either by the terms of the trust instrument or by statute. Thus, when we are talking about trustees' powers, we are usually referring to their authority to affect the beneficiaries' equitable interests rather than their ability to deal with the legal estate.[38]

Harpum demonstrated that it has long been the law that a disposition beyond the trustees' authority (ultra vires) cannot overreach the beneficial interests and nor can the purchaser claim the protection of s 2 of the LPA 1925.[39] Other mechanisms are thus necessary if a purchaser is to be protected against the risk that a trustee is acting ultra vires his or her authority.

Trustees may also act within their authority, but, in so doing, misapply the trust property or otherwise breach their duties as trustees. For example, we have seen that, in *Flegg*, the Maxwell-Browns, although they had authority to mortgage Bleak House, acted in breach of trust in doing so without consulting the Fleggs and with the object of discharging their own personal debts, rather than in pursuance of their duty to act for the benefit of the trust.

Trustees may also fail to act in accordance with their statutory duty of care, as defined by s 1 of the Trustee Act 2000, or they may breach their equitable fiduciary duties. For example, the trustees may fail to exercise due care in obtaining the true market value for the property, or they may allow their personal interests to conflict with their fiduciary duty to give undivided loyalty to the beneficiaries' interests by dealing with the land for their own benefit. The TOLATA 1996 underlines both the need for the trustees to act in the interests of the beneficiaries, and in accordance with their legal and equitable duties, by reiterating these duties in s 6(5) and (6). These types of breach of duty are sometimes referred to as 'intra vires' breaches of trust, because they are within the ability and authority of the trustees, but are nevertheless proscribed. Ferris and Battersby[40] suggest that overreaching is unaffected by breaches of trust of this nature, because the purchaser can look to the protection of s 2 of the LPA 1925. Where the trust moneys are misapplied, the protections provided both by s 27(1) of that Act and of s 17 of the Trustee Act 1925 should absolve a purchaser from liability.[41]

Being clear about the ability and authority of the trustees to act, on the one hand, and their duties when acting in exercise of that ability or authority, on the other, underlines the matters upon which we need to concentrate when considering the impact of a breach of duty on overreaching. Firstly, the dispositive powers of the trustees are important in defining their authority to deal with the equitable estate and so overreach the beneficial interests. Secondly, if a purchaser cannot rely on the protection of s 2 of the LPA 1925, because the trustees have acted ultra vires, then we need to look at what other protection is available to them.

[37] Ferris and Battersby (2002) 118 LQR 270, 273–80.

[38] Contrast the mortgagee's power of sale, discussed in Chapter 31. Mortgagees must be given both the ability to deal with the legal estate and the authority to deal with the borrower's equity of redemption.

[39] Harpum (1990, pp 283–5, 294–6).

[40] Ferris and Battersby (2002, pp 283–94). Smith (2005, p 198) suggests that such protection is unnecessary.

[41] Harpum (1990, p 309).

4.1.1 The source of trustees' powers of disposition

The trustees' authority is defined by the trust instrument and/or implied by statute. Originally, s 28 of the LPA 1925 granted trustees for sale all of the powers that were conferred upon a tenant for life and trustees under the Settled Land Act 1925, so that the purchaser would not necessarily have to examine the trust instrument in order to determine the width of the trustees' authority.[42]

Section 28 of the LPA 1925 has now been repealed and replaced by s 6 of the TOLATA 1996. As we have seen in Chapter 19, section 5.2, s 6(1) of the 1996 Act confers on the trustees *all the powers of an absolute owner'*, though these powers must be exercised for the benefit of the trust and in a manner consistent with any other enactment of law or equity. Hence, in contrast to the previous law, rather than limiting the trustee's powers by authorizing only particular transactions, the 1996 Act authorizes all types of transaction. Consequently, at first sight, it might be thought that ultra vires transactions are less likely to result. But s 6(1) does not stand alone: s 8 enables a settlor to limit the width of the authority conferred by s 6(1).

Trusts of Land and Appointment of Trustees Act 1996, s 8

(1) Sections 6 and 7 do not apply in the case of a trust of land created by a disposition in so far as provision to the effect that they do not apply is made by the disposition.

(2) If the disposition creating such a trust makes provision requiring any consent to be obtained to the exercise of any power conferred by section 6 or 7, the power may not be exercised without that consent.

Thus, s 8 enables the settlor to limit the trustees' powers by, for example, providing that the trustees cannot act without the consent of a third party, or even by limiting or entirely excluding the implied statutory powers. Thus, where the statutory powers have been limited pursuant to s 8, a sale or mortgage that exceeds these powers will not overreach the beneficial interests and the purchaser or mortgagee will have to find protection elsewhere.

The changes made to the trustees' powers of disposition by the TOLATA 1996 may have a direct impact on the likelihood of an ultra vires disposition arising in the context of a co-owned home. Where co-ownership arises through the joint purchase of a home, the owners are unlikely to limit their own powers as trustees under s 8. As a result, an ultra vires disposition is unlikely to arise. An *intra* vires breach of duty or the misapplication of trust property, as exemplified by *Flegg*, is more likely to arise in such trusts. This is, however, subject to one further argument advanced by Ferris and Battersby.[43] They argue, although others disagree,[44] that the powers conferred by s 6(1) are also circumscribed by further statutory conditions: in particular, s 6(6), which provides that the powers of the trustees conferred by s 6(1) shall not be exercised in contravention of any rule of law or equity, and s 11, which imposes a duty of consultation upon the trustees. Thus, they suggest, the apparent

---

[42] Ibid, p 290. If the disposition contemplated was outside the s 28 (Law of Property Act 1925) powers, the purchaser could demand to see the trust instrument to check if the disposition was nevertheless within the express authority conferred by the trust deed.

[43] Ferris and Battersby (2002, pp 283–94). Smith (2005, p 198) suggests that such protection is unnecessary.

[44] Pascoe (2005); Smith (2005, p 196); Dixon (2000).

wide authority conferred by s 6(1) is illusory and there is, in fact, a greater risk of transactions that are ultra vires the trustees' authority and thus unable to overreach the beneficial interests.[45]

4.2 PROTECTION OF PURCHASERS

Prior to the 1925 legislation, purchasers were in a particularly vulnerable position.[46] In order to overreach the beneficial interests, the purchaser had to be satisfied that the sale was intra vires and that the sale moneys were to be properly applied in accordance with the trust. The burden placed on purchasers was indeed onerous, particularly because they could be fixed with constructive notice of a breach of trust that the law considered they should have discovered. The LPA 1925 did not relieve a purchaser of the need to check the trustees' authority to sell, but it did try to ensure that purchasers, once they knew that they were dealing with trustees, could easily satisfy themselves of the trustee's authority by relying on the s 28 powers.

A purchaser could, however, be protected from the more difficult to discover intra vires breaches of trust by sheltering under the protection of s 2, provided that he or she followed the prescribed overreaching machinery by paying any capital moneys to two trustees.[47] This sophisticated framework came under strain with the increased prevalence of implied trusts (particularly of domestic property) that emerged in the latter half of the twentieth century. Where the trust is implied, purchasers may not know they are dealing with trustees and may thus be unaware that they should satisfy themselves that the trustees are acting within their authority.[48]

Differing statutory provisions, depending upon whether the land is unregistered or registered, have addressed this need for greater purchaser protection.

4.2.1 Unregistered land

The protection of purchasers is governed by s 16 of the TOLATA 1996.

Trusts of Land and Appointment of Trustees Act 1996, s 16

(1) A purchaser of land which is or has been subject to a trust need not be concerned to see that any requirement imposed on the trustees by section 6(5), 7(3) or 11(1) has been complied with.

(2) Where—

   (a) trustees of land who convey land which (immediately before it is conveyed) is subject to the trust contravene section 6(6) or (8) but

   (b) the purchaser of the land from the trustees has no actual notice of the contravention,

the contravention does not invalidate the conveyance.

---

[45] 'The Impact of the Trusts of Land and Appointment of Trustees Act 1996 on Purchasers of Registered Land' [1998] Conv 168, 169–76, developed further in 'The General Principles of Overreaching and the Modern Legislative Reforms 1996–2002' (2003) LQR 94, 95–108.

[46] Harpum (1990, pp 283–7).

[47] Ibid, and Ferris and Battersby (2002).

[48] Ferris and Battersby (2002, pp 297–301).

(3) Where the powers of trustees of land are limited by virtue of section 8—

    (a) the trustees shall take all reasonable steps to bring the limitation to the notice of any purchaser of the land from them, but

    (b) the limitation does not invalidate any conveyance by the trustees to a purchaser who has no actual notice of the limitation.

(4) Where trustees of land convey land which (immediately before it is conveyed) is subject to the trust to persons believed by them to be beneficiaries absolutely entitled to the land under the trust and of full age and capacity—

    (a) the trustees shall execute a deed declaring that they are discharged from the trust in relation to that land, and

    (b) if they fail to do so, the court may make an order requiring them to do so.

(5) A purchaser of land to which a deed under subsection (4) relates is entitled to assume that, as from the date of the deed, the land is not subject to the trust unless he has actual notice that the trustees were mistaken in their belief that the land was conveyed to beneficiaries absolutely entitled to the land under the trust and of full age and capacity.

(6) Subsections (2) and (3) do not apply to land held on charitable, ecclesiastical or public trusts.

(7) This section does not apply to registered land.

Hence, purchasers of unregistered land from trustees are protected by the terms of s 16 provided that they do not have actual knowledge of the trustees' breach of trust. The terms of s 16 have, however, been subject to some criticism and are certainly not framed in the clearest terms.[49]

4.2.2 Registered land

Much of the controversy that has, in the past, surrounded the protection of purchasers of registered land[50] has been sidelined by the enactment of ss 23 and 26 of the LRA 2002.[51]

Land Registration Act 2002, s 23

(1) Owner's powers in relation to a registered estate consist of—

    (a) power to make a disposition of any kind permitted by the general law in relation to an interest of that description, other than a mortgage by demise or sub-demise, and

    (b) power to charge the estate at law with the payment of money.

(2) Owner's powers in relation to a registered charge consist of—

    (a) power to make a disposition of any kind permitted by the general law in relation to an interest of that description, other than a legal sub-mortgage, and

---

[49] Ferris and Battersby (2003, pp 108–19); Pascoe (2005); Smith (2005, p 197).
[50] Harpum (1990, pp 304–9); Ferris and Battersby (2002, pp 283–94); Dixon (2000).
[51] Land Registration Act 2002, s 52, which deals with dispositions by a registered chargee, is considered in Chapter 31, section 3.2.6.

(b) power to charge at law with the payment of money indebtedness secured by the registered charge.

(3) In subsection (2)(a), "legal sub-mortgage" means—

(a) a transfer by way of mortgage,

(b) a sub-mortgage by sub-demise, and

(c) a charge by way of legal mortgage.

Land Registration Act 2002, s 26

(1) Subject to subsection (2), a person's right to exercise owner's powers in relation to a registered estate or charge is to be taken to be free from any limitation affecting the validity of a disposition.

(2) Subsection (1) does not apply to a limitation—

(a) reflected by an entry in the register, or

(b) imposed by, or under, this Act.

(3) This section has effect only for the purpose of preventing the title of a disponee being questioned (and so does not affect the lawfulness of a disposition).

Hence, s 23 confers upon the registered owner almost unfettered ability to dispose of the registered estate. Section 26 provides that no limitation upon a person's right to exercise an owner's power of disposition, including a trustee's authority to deal with the registered estate, will affect a purchaser unless that limitation is protected by the entry of a restriction on the register. The purchaser is thus no longer concerned with any ultra vires lack of authority that is not revealed by the entry of a restriction.

The wide terms of s 26 have already been noted:[52] in particular, the section provides no saving for overriding interests, nor does it call for the purchaser or other person dealing with the trustees to be registered. The provision does not specify that the purchaser must provide value to be protected and therefore appears to provide volunteers with the same degree of protection as purchasers. But a purchaser must provide value to qualify for over-reaching under s 2 of the LPA 1925.[53] Further, the defence of lack of registration (including as regards the entry of a restriction) is conferred by s 29 of the LRA 2002 only in respect of registered dispositions made for valuable consideration. Through these routes, it may, in fact, be confined in its scope to purchasers.

4.3 SUMMARY

The liability of a buyer purchasing, or a lender taking a mortgage, from trustees who are acting ultra vires is no longer dependent upon the trustees' powers of disposition, but upon the protection afforded by statute. The nature of that protection differs according to whether the land is registered or unregistered. A person purchasing, or acquiring an interest in, registered land will be protected against an ultra vires breach of trust unless the

---

[52] Ferris (2003, p 101). See also Smith (2005, p 194).
[53] See above, fn 26.

limitation of the trustees' authority is recorded on the register by the entry of a restriction. Common restrictions call for the purchase money to be paid to two trustees, thus triggering overreaching, or a requirement to obtain the consent of a third party. In the absence of a restriction on the register, overreaching will continue to operate, even though the person dealing with the trustees has knowledge of a limitation upon the trustees' authority. By contrast, a purchaser of unregistered land will only be protected if he or she has no actual notice that the trustees are acting in excess of their authority. Actual notice is unlikely where the trust is implied, because the trustees will enjoy the unlimited powers of disposition enjoyed by an absolute owner conferred by the TOLATA 1996. Even where the trust is express, the purchaser is not required to scrutinize the trust instrument to confirm the nature of the trustees' authority.

Purchasers, but not volunteers, of both registered and unregistered land continue to be protected against intra vires breaches of trust by s 2 of the LPA 1925 provided that any capital moneys are paid to two trustees. It has been suggested (but is not yet established) that s 26 of the LRA 2002 might also provide protection to both purchasers and volunteers against intra vires breaches of trust.[54] Doubt is placed on whether a volunteer would be protected under s 26 by the framework of provisions within which the provision operates.

5 IS OVERREACHING JUSTIFIED?

We have noted that overreaching serves the twin objectives of implementing the trust curtain and ensuring security of transactions. Purchasers need not investigate the existence or terms of any trust affecting land. Title is taken unencumbered from such interests as long as overreaching occurs. We have further seen that where land is held on trust as an investment, the shifting of the beneficial interests from land to money is not problematic. In such cases, the effect of overreaching is entirely consistent with the purpose of the trust, because the beneficiaries' key concern is with the maintenance of the trust fund, rather than any particular item of property.

Overreaching is, however, more contentious when it is applied to land held on trust to be used as a home. Even in this context, the mechanism is problematic only in those cases, such as *Flegg*, in which the home is held on trust for the legal owners and others, and a sale or (typically) mortgage is arranged without the knowledge or consent of all of the beneficiaries. It is in these situations that the effect of overreaching, and the underlying assumption that the beneficiaries' concern lies in the maintenance of a fund, clashes with the purpose of the trust.

The spread of co-ownership of the home could not have been predicted at the time of the 1925 legislation. Both the trust for sale and the overreaching mechanism reflected the use of land as an investment. The shift from investment trusts to trusts of the home was a key impetus in the replacement of the trust for sale with the trust of land through the TOLATA 1996.[55] But in making the recommendations that led to that Act, the Law Commission envisaged the continuing operation of overreaching. This matter has since been placed beyond any doubt by the decision of the Court of Appeal in *Sabherwal*. The Law Commission did, however, identify the need to consider separately the impact of overreaching on beneficiaries in occupation and published these recommendations in a separate report.

---

[54] Cooke, *The New Law of Land Registration* (2003, p 60).
[55] Chapter 19, section 5.

Law Commission Report No 188, *Transfer of Land. Overreaching:*
Beneficiaries in Occupation (1989, [3.1]–[3.3], [4.1]–[4.3])

PART III

NEED FOR REFORM

Change of circumstances

The 1925 legislation compromise between the need to protect beneficiaries under trusts of land and the demand for certainty and simplicity in conveyancing was satisfactory, and perhaps ideal, in the circumstances in which it was intended to operate. A purchaser from the trustees could ignore the beneficial interests so long as he was careful to observe simple precautions in paying the price. This successfully hid the terms of the settlement "behind the curtain". Buying from trustees became as simple as buying from a single beneficial legal owner which it certainly had not been previously. At the same time, the financial interest of the beneficiary was safeguarded by transferring his claim to the proceeds of sale. So long as the trustees properly conducted the affairs of the settlement, it was not important to the beneficiary by what assets his interest was secured.

Doubts about these provisions arise now because, over the years, the patterns of land ownership and the use of settlements have changed. Although the rules with which we are concerned affect all types of real property, the changes relating to residential property are most significant. Since 1925, both the number of dwellings in England and Wales and the percentage of them which are owner-occupied have jumped dramatically. Couples have increasingly bought owner-occupied housing in their joint names, and this trend was accelerated by the decision in *Williams & Glyn's Bank Ltd v. Boland*, following which lending institutions encouraged borrowers to buy jointly so that they, the institutions, had the advantage of the statutory overreaching rules. These couples are technically trustees for sale, whether they hold on trust only for themselves, as is often the case, or whether there are others with beneficial interests.

For this reason, there is now a very large number of cases in which trust beneficiaries occupy trust property as their homes. Sometimes, also, the trust property is where they carry on business. Generally, the trust is a conveyancing technicality, imposed by the Law of Property Act 1925 as part of the scheme to confine normal conveyancing to legal estates. Most individuals in this position would be surprised to hear themselves referred to as trustees or as beneficiaries; they regard themselves simply as joint owners. The changes in circumstances have exposed the 1925 rules for the device which they are. "If the framers of the property legislation in 1925 had been able to foresee the growth in joint ownership of property which, coupled with the vast increase in the breakdown of marriage, has exposed the artificiality of the statutory trust for sale, they might have made clearer provision for the protection of beneficial interests without widening the enquiries needed to be made by a purchaser".

PART IV

REFORM PROPOSALS

Principal recommendation

We have concluded that the present protection of the interests of equitable owners in occupation of property is, in some circumstances, inadequate. The owner of an equitable interest which carries a right of occupation is entitled to two distinct benefits: a right to the value of the interest and that right to enjoy occupation. When the owner of a legal estate is in a similar position, the law protects each right separately: if the owner opts to remain in possession, he cannot be obliged to rely solely on the alternative financial right. The effect of overreaching is, however, to oblige the equitable owner to surrender his occupation right in favour of his financial one, without the chance to make a choice. We see no reason why equitable owners should be at a disadvantage in this respect

We are, however, conscious of the need to maintain arrangements which will not unduly interfere with conveyancing. This leads us to place our emphasis on protecting the rights of owners of equitable interests who are in actual occupation of the property. That very fact of occupation can be used to alert prospective purchasers and mortgagees to the claims of the equitable owners. It means that the protection of occupation rights does not extend to those who, while they are entitled to occupy, are not currently exercising the right. While that means that equitable owners will sometimes be at a disadvantage, when compared with legal owners, it seems to us to be a reasonable compromise. It offers the right to continue in occupation, to those who are already there, so it is likely to extend the new protection to those who most need it, and of course protection extends to those who enter later.

Our principal recommendation, to protect the occupation rights of those with an equitable interest in property, can be succinctly stated:

A conveyance of a legal estate in property should not have the effect of overreaching the interest of anyone of full age and capacity who is entitled to a beneficial interest in the property and who has a right to occupy it and is in actual occupation of it at the date of the conveyance, unless that person consents.

We examine below the detailed effects of the recommendation.

The Law Commission's proposals represent a logical extension of the reasoning underlying the introduction of the TOLATA 1996. In this report, as in its report leading to the Act, the Law Commission sought to provide a scheme of regulation for land held on trust that reflects the likely use of that land as a home. The government announced however, that the recommendations on overreaching would not be implemented.[56]

It must be questioned why there is resistance to this proposal. As Smith highlights,[57] a requirement of obtaining consent is not necessarily onerous. Indeed, making enquiries of occupiers is standard procedure in other aspects of conveyancing practice. It is one of the ways in which a balance is sought between protecting the interests of beneficiaries (and other persons with subsisting property rights) and purchasers. It may be suggested that, where overreaching is concerned, there is a clear imbalance in favour of purchasers. The importance of the trust curtain and security of transactions has, it seems, superseded any concerns at the mismatch between a trust of a home and the investments ideals that underpin overreaching.

6 THE FUTURE OF OVERREACHING

We conclude this discussion of overreaching by considering possible future developments of overreaching and the rules affecting the broader context in which the mechanism operates. Firstly, we consider how the scope of overreaching could be restricted or qualified; secondly,

---

[56] (1998) 587 HL Deb WA213.
[57] Smith (2005, p 191).

we highlight recent arguments as to whether overreaching is compliant with the HRA 1998; finally, we consider alternative causes of action that may be available to beneficiaries.

6.1 QUALIFYING AND RESTRICTING THE SCOPE OF OVERREACHING

We have seen that the Law Commission's recommendation to qualify the operation of overreaching in relation to a particular type of beneficiary (those in actual occupation), through the imposition of a requirement of consent, has been rejected. Harpum has suggested an alternative means of qualifying the mechanism. If the rationale for overreaching is found in the powers of disposition of the trustees, a more logical means of qualification might lie in restricting those powers. It has already been pointed out, and the cases demonstrate, that the most acute tension between overreaching and the interests of the beneficiaries occurs where the trustees utilize the land, which the beneficiaries occupy as their home, as security for a loan that is applied to discharge personal or business debts, rather than towards the acquisition or improvement of the property. Harpum advocated limiting the trustees' power to mortgage the land to first mortgages to secure the purchase, improvement, or repair of the land.[58]

Harpum, 'Overreaching, Trustees Powers and The Reform of the 1925 Legislation' (1990) 49 CLJ 277, 330–1

[T]he Law Commission has been forced to take the path of requiring the consent of beneficiaries in actual occupation because it has failed to appreciate the basis on which overreaching rests. Overreaching is the necessary concomitant of a power of disposition. If the trustees have no power to make a disposition, that disposition will not overreach. The present writer believes that this principle could provide a more effective means of securing the objectives which the Law Commission seeks.

[...]

The powers of the trustees could be limited [...] these powers would draw a distinction between those transactions which should be facilitated and which are unlikely be detrimental to the interest of beneficiaries, and those dispositions which should not be encouraged and which may harm those interested in the land. There seems no reason to restrict the trustees' powers to sell and lease. If the trustees have to give vacant possession they will necessarily have to obtain the consent of persons in actual occupation who will thereby be involved in the decision-making process. [...] The mortgaging powers of the trustees would however be limited. The principal mortgaging powers that should be given to trustees would be to execute a first mortgage of the land to enable them to purchase the land, and a power to raise money for the improvement or repair of the property. There should be no power to execute a second mortgage.

Neither the TOLATA 1996 nor the LRA 2002 has adopted the approach advocated by Harpum. As we have seen, the 1996 Act confers upon trustees all of the powers of an absolute owner, unless expressly restricted, whilst the 2002 Act protects a purchaser against any

---

[58] See also Thompson (1997). Smith (2005, p 191) suggests a hybrid approach depending both upon a limitation of the trustees' powers of disposition and the consent of occupiers.

express limitation of the trustees' powers, which is not evident by way of a restriction on the register.

6.2 HUMAN RIGHTS AND OVERREACHING

Given that the policy of overreaching with regard to occupying beneficiaries has raised concerns, it is no surprise that it has attracted attention as potentially incompatible with fundamental human rights contained in Art 8 (respect for the home) and Art 1 of the First Protocol (deprivation of property) of the European Convention on Human Rights.

The issue was raised both in *Sabherwal*[59] and in *National Westminster Bank Plc v Malhan*.[60] The court rejected the submission in both cases on the simple ground that the HRA 1998 did not have retrospective effect and thus could not affect either of the mortgages, which were both entered into before the Act came into force.[61] Whilst Robert Walker LJ showed little sympathy with the substantive force of human rights in *Sabherwal*, Morritt VC in *Malhan* lent a more sympathetic ear '*finding much force in the submissions*', although his comments were obiter, because Mrs Malhan was unable to establish a beneficial interest.

As we have seen in Chapter 5, a claim based upon a breach of the 1998 Act needs to clear a number of hurdles: firstly, we need to establish the horizontal effect of that Act; secondly, we need to prove that one of the Articles of the ECHR is engaged; and finally, we need to examine whether the interference can be justified by the stated qualifications to the enshrined rights. These lie within the government's margin of appreciation, with a requirement that the interference is proportionate in both its aim and in the procedure adopted to achieve that aim.

The horizontal effect of the HRA 1998 is established by the dictates of s 3, which requires the court to interpret legislation in a manner that is compatible with the ECHR '[s]*o far as it is possible to do so*'. Further, s 4 empowers a court to declare a statutory provision incompatible with the ECHR. We have examined a number of statutory provisions upon which overreaching and its effect on purchasers is dependent. Sections 2 and 27 of the LPA 1925 define the scope of overreaching. In the TOLATA 1996, we find, in s 6, the authority of the trustees to overreach by the exercise of their powers of disposition, and in s 16, the protection of purchasers of unregistered land against the effects of an unauthorized disposition. The protection of the purchasers of registered land against an unauthorized disposition is found in s 26 of the LRA 2002. There is thus considerable scope for the courts to examine the compatibility of overreaching with the ECHR.

Article 8 and Art 1 of the First Protocol are the prime targets for engagement. But the argument in *Malhan* was based upon the discriminatory effect of overreaching where there are two trustees in comparison with the failure of overreaching where there is only one trustee. Article 8 and Art 1 of the First Protocol were thus to be read with Art 14 (prohibition of discrimination). In the past, this difference in treatment has been justified by the protection said to be afforded to beneficiaries by two trustees: firstly, as a guard against the commission of a breach of trust; and secondly, by providing two, rather than one, pockets against which to pursue any personal claim for damages. In reality, this so-called 'protection' has proved illusory. This is the case, for example, where the trust is implied and the trustees are ignorant of their responsibilities. Equally, the protection is illusory where, in

---

59 (2000) 80 P & CR 256.
60 [2004] EWHC 847.
61 *Wilson v Secretary of State for Trade & Industry* [2003] UKHL 40.

the face of financial difficulties, an action for breach against the trustees (who may be family members) is worthless. But we have seen that the need for two trustees has been questioned both in the *Sood* situation, in which there are no capital moneys, and possibly (although less convincingly) where, in the absence of an appropriate restriction, a sole proprietor of a registered title deals with the land. The picture is thus rather more complex than the argument in *Malhan* suggests.

In *Malhan*, counsel was driven to rely on Art 14 because it had conceded that a submission based upon Art 8 or Art 1 of the First Protocol alone would not succeed. In the light of more recent cases, this concession may not have been prudent.[62]

Possession proceedings against a beneficiary in occupation by a purchaser or mortgagee claiming the benefit of overreaching should engage Art 8. The appropriate enquiry is whether there is a justification for that interference on the grounds either of the economic well-being of the country, in maintaining a well-balanced property and lending market, or the protection of the rights and freedoms of others—namely, purchasers and mortgagees.

Likewise, the operation of overreaching by shifting the beneficial interest from the land to the capital moneys (if any) may be capable of engaging Art 1 of the First Protocol as a deprivation of property, although the issue has not been resolved.[63] It will be recalled from Chapter 5 that a deprivation of property encompasses both the loss of ownership and controls over the use of property that interfere with the peaceful enjoyment of property.[64] Overreaching shifts, but does not terminate, the beneficiary's interest. This is the case even though, either because there are no proceeds (as in *Sood*) or the proceeds are dissipated (as in *Flegg*), the property to which the interest notionally shifts is of no value to the beneficiaries. Overreaching will effect the peaceful enjoyment of property by controlling the identity of the property in which the beneficial interest vests and against which attendant ownership rights can be asserted. An occupying beneficiary's occupation of his or her home is disturbed, because his or her interest is no longer in the land, but in the capital moneys (if any).

If Art 1 of the First Protocol is engaged, then both the operation of overreaching, by depriving the beneficiary of his or her property, and the process by which that deprivation is achieved must be justified as being in the public interest: for example, in securing a fair and efficient conveyancing system.

Any justification, whether required under Art 8 or Art 1 of the First Protocol, must strike a proportionate balance, within the State's margin of appreciation, between the interests of the beneficiary (particularly the beneficiary in occupation) and the purchaser or mortgagee. Furthermore, the processes by which that balance is achieved falls to be considered.

Whether the courts will be inclined to question the justification of overreaching, under Art 8 and/or Art 1 of the First Protocol, is a most difficult issue. But the House of Lords in *Kay v Lambeth LBC*,[65] in the context of a local authority's possession proceedings against a tenant, indicated that it would be a considerable task to persuade them of the incompatibility of the current rules of property law, which have evolved over many centuries and which, in the case of statutory rules, have been considered by Parliament. Both the TOLATA 1996 and the LRA 2002 have enabled a recent appraisal of overreaching both by the Law Commission

---

[62] *Kay v Lambeth LBC; Leeds CC v Price* [2006] UKHL 10, [2006] 2 WLR 570 (re Art 8); *JR Pye (Oxford) Ltd v UK* (2006) 43 EHRR 3 (re Art 1 of the First Protocol).

[63] See Goymour, 'Proprietary Claims and Human Rights: A Reservoir of Entitlement?' (2006) 65 CLJ 696, 714–5.

[64] See *Sporrong and Lonroth v Sweden* (1982) 8 EHRR 123, explored in Chapter 5.

[65] [2006] 2 WLR 570.

and Parliament. Thus the courts are likely to be particularly cautious, despite remaining concern with overreaching expressed by the judiciary.[66]

If a challenge were to be mounted, there are two respects in which overreaching appears vulnerable:[67] firstly, the width of the trustees' powers of disposition under s 6 of the 1996 Act, coupled with the width of the protection of purchasers conferred by s 26 of the 2002 Act (for registered land), particularly when contrasted with s 16 of the 1996 Act (for unregistered land). The variation in protection between registered and unregistered land might itself provide a possible ground for a challenge based on discrimination under Art 14.

Secondly, the automatic trigger of overreaching by the payment of any capital moneys to two trustees might also be challenged, not only on the basis raised in *Malhan*, but also as a process that provides no opportunity for the rights of a beneficiary occupying the trust property as his or her home to be protected, or to be balanced against those of the purchaser or mortgagee.

6.3 ALTERNATIVE CAUSES OF ACTION

Overreaching does not exist in a legal vacuum. In Chapter 16, in the context of our discussion of the priority rules of registered land, we highlighted the possibility of new direct rights being imposed on a purchaser on a transfer of land. These rights, arising from a myriad of alternative causes of action, include *personal* liability being imposed on the trustees and other parties where the sale constituted a breach of trust, and *proprietary* claims over assets purchased by trustees using the proceeds of sale. Hence, one partial solution to concerns as regards the scope of overreaching is to ensure that these alternatives are developed and used. As we will see, however, each of these actions has its own limitations.

6.3.1 Breach of trust

Trustees who act in breach of trust are personally liable to the beneficiaries. In practice, however, the utility of this form of liability is dependent on the financial circumstances of the trustees. For example, we have noted that, in *Flegg*, the Maxwell-Browns acted in breach of trust towards the Fleggs in mortgaging the parties' joint home—but, as a result of the Maxwell-Brown's financial circumstances, an action against them for this breach was of no practical use.

6.3.2 Knowing (or unconscionable) receipt and dishonest assistance

A purchaser who takes trust property knowing that it is dealt with in breach of trust, or some other person who dishonestly assists in the breach of trust itself, may find him or herself called upon personally to account for the loss suffered by the trust through the equitable doctrines of knowing receipt and dishonest assistance. The beneficial interests continue to be overreached, but a distinct personal liability is imposed, which requires the purchaser or interfering third party to be held to account as if he or she were the trustee committing the breach of trust.[68]

---

[66] See, in particular, *State Bank of India v Sood* [1997] Ch 276 and *National Westminster Bank plc v Malhan* [2004] EWHC 847.

[67] See, however, McFarlane (2008, p 404), who is sceptical as to the likely success of human rights challenges to overreaching.

[68] This basis for liability is suggested by Dixon (2000, p 270) and although initially disputed by Ferris and Battersby (see [2001] Conv 221, p 224), they subsequently acknowledged its availability (see (2003) 119 LQR 94, 122). See also Pascoe (2005).

A detailed examination of the scope and basis of these doctrines lies outside this work. It is sufficient to note that the key debate has surrounded the threshold requirement for imposing liability. While the imposition of liability on those who assist in a breach of trust (without receiving trust property) has now settled on a requirement of dishonesty,[69] the position as regards recipients of trust property remains undetermined. The possible alternative bases are knowledge of the breach of trust, unconscionability, and strict liability on receipt.[70] With regards to the liability of a recipient, it is also possible to argue that if the recipient has a defence to the beneficiaries' equitable rights, then the recipient cannot come under a personal liability to those beneficiaries.[71] If that is the case, the presence of overreaching would also protect a purchaser or mortgagee from any personal liability based on his or her receipt.

6.3.3 Tracing

Tracing is the process by which beneficiaries can track their proprietary interest into a substitute asset that the trustees may have acquired with the proceeds of sale, following a disposition by the trustees in breach of trust.[72] Once the beneficiaries have done so, they may be able to claim proprietary interests in those substitute assets.

Tracing may be available to beneficiaries in two situations, although the process will only be of any practical assistance to a beneficiary where there are substitute assets. Furthermore, any claim that the beneficiaries may have in relation to those assets is subject to a significant limitation through the defence of bona fide purchaser.

The first situation in which tracing is available is that in which trustees make a disposition that is an ultra vires breach of trust. An unauthorized disposition will not overreach, but, in light of the protection available to purchasers, a beneficiary is unlikely to be able to assert his or her interest in the property disposed of. A beneficiary may be able to trace the proceeds of sale of an unauthorized disposition received by the trustees into any substitute asset acquired with those proceeds.[73]

Secondly, tracing may also assist the beneficiaries once overreaching has occurred and the trustees hold proceeds of sale on trust. Overreaching shifts the beneficial interests into the proceeds of sale. If the trustees then apply those proceeds in breach of trust, the beneficiaries may be able to trace their proprietary interest into assets acquired through that breach. As we have seen, s 27(1) of the LPA 1925 absolves the purchaser of any liability in this regard.

As Fox explains, the effect of tracing looks very similar to overreaching's effect in allowing a beneficiary a claim against the proceeds of sale acquired by the trustees.[74] There are, however, important differences between the mechanisms, particularly as regards their effect on the beneficiaries' title. Where overreaching takes place, the beneficiaries have the same interest in the proceeds of sale as they previously had in the land and that interest vests immediately upon overreaching. Where beneficiaries trace funds into a substitute asset,

---

[69] *Royal Brunei Airlines v Tan* [1995] 2 AC 378 and *Twinsectra v Yardley* [2002] UKHL 12.

[70] Watt, 'Personal Liability for Receipt of Trust Property: Allocating the Risks' in *Modern Studies in Property Law: Vol 3* (ed Cooke, 2003, p 91); Lord Nicholls, 'Knowing Receipt: The Need for a New Landmark' in *Restitution Past, Present and Future* (ed Cornish et al, 1998).

[71] See, e.g., the High Court of Australia in *Farah Constructions Pty Ltd v Say-Dee Pty Ltd* [2007] HCA 22 (denying recipient liability where the recipient was able to rely on the lack of registration defence against the beneficiaries' equitable interests); McFarlane (2008, p 418).

[72] *Foskett v McKeown* [2001] AC 102.

[73] See ibid, *Cave v Cave* (1880) 15 Ch D 639, and *Ffrench's Estate* (1887) 21 LR (Ir) 283, referred to by Fox (2002).

[74] Fox (2002). See also McFarlane (2008, pp 400–1).

they have a right to elect between a beneficial interest in the asset (a proportionate share of an asset purchased in part with trust finds) or a lien to enforce their personal claim against the trustees for breach of trust.[75] It will not be until they have made that election that their appropriate interest will vest and, prior to that election, their interest is inchoate.

7 PRIORITY RULES WHERE OVERREACHING DOES NOT TAKE PLACE

Where overreaching does not take place, the rules determining the enforcement of a beneficial interest are dependent on whether the title is registered or unregistered. In unregistered land, enforcement of a beneficial interest is determined by the doctrine of notice (see Chapter 15, section 4). Occupation of the home by the beneficiary may be sufficient to fix the purchaser with constructive notice of the interest.[76] In registered land, the curtain principle precludes entry of a notice of a beneficial interest on the register.[77] A beneficial interest that is not overreached may bind a purchaser as an overriding interest where the beneficiary is in occupation (see Chapter 16, section 5.1).[78]

A specific issue arises where, through the process of survivorship (discussed in Chapter 19, section 2.2), legal title remains in a sole surviving joint tenant. A beneficiary may have severed his or her equitable joint tenancy prior to his or her death. A transfer by the sole trustee will not have overreaching effect, leaving a purchaser vulnerable to a claim that the severed beneficial interest is binding against him or her through notice (in unregistered land) or as overriding interests (in registered land). In unregistered land, a statutory solution is provided.

Law of Property (Joint Tenants) Act 1964, s 1

(1) For the purposes of section 36(2) of the Law of Property Act 1925, as amended by section 7 of and the Schedule to the Law of Property (Amendment) Act 1926, the survivor of two or more joint tenants shall, in favour of a purchaser of the legal estate, be deemed to be solely and beneficially interested if [. . .] the conveyance includes a statement that he is so interested.

Provided that the foregoing provisions of this subsection shall not apply if, at any time before the date of the conveyance by the survivor—

(a) a memorandum of severance (that is to say a note or memorandum signed by the joint tenants or one of them and recording that the joint tenancy was severed in equity on a date therein specified) had been endorsed on or annexed to the conveyance by virtue of which the legal estate was vested in the joint tenants; or

(b) a bankruptcy order made against any of the joint tenants, or a petition for such an order, had been registered under the Land Charges Act 1925, being an order or petition of which the purchaser has notice, by virtue of the registration, on the date of the conveyance by the survivor.

---

75 Fox (2002, p 102).
76 *Kingsnorth Finance Co v Tizard* [1986] 1 WLR 783.
77 Land Registration Act 2002, s 33(a).
78 Ibid, Sch 3, para 2.

> (2) The foregoing provisions of this section shall apply with the necessary modifications in relation to a conveyance by the personal representatives of the survivor of joint tenants as they apply in relation to a conveyance by such a survivor.

Hence, as long as the purchaser falls outside of the provisos to s 1(1), he or she is protected against a priority claim by a beneficiary. Although not so described in the statute, Cooke notes[79] that the effect of the provision is that the beneficial interest is overreached, because the beneficiary would have a claim against the proceeds of sale.

The Law of Property (Joint Tenants) Act 1964 is confined in its application to unregistered land. No equivalent statutory protection is provided to a purchaser of registered land. This may be an oversight, explicable on the basis that the prospect of a beneficial interest binding a purchaser in registered land as an overriding interest became apparent only with the decision in *Williams & Glyn's Bank v Boland*,[80] some years after the enactment of the 1964 Act.

Cooke suggests that the problem is a small one and that the solution is simple.

Cooke, 'Beneficial Joint Tenants and the Protection of Purchasers: An Unsolved Problem' [2004] Conv 41, 48

Obviously a simple extension of the 1964 Act to registered land by repealing s.3 will not work; there is no way of making a memorandum of severance on the conveyance or transfer to the vendor and the deceased joint tenant, nor could the purchaser see that memorandum, since he has access only to the register and not to previous title deeds. All that is needed is a corresponding provision to the effect that the surviving joint tenant vendor will be deemed to be solely and beneficially entitled if:

(a) the transfer states that the vendor is solely and beneficially interested in the land;

(b) the purchaser obtains a clean bankruptcy search, exactly as in the 1964 Act;

(c) there is no restriction on the register preventing a disposition by the survivor of the two trustees.

The requirement of the absence of a memorandum of severance is thus matched by the requirement of the absence of a restriction. Neither is in fact conclusive; in unregistered land, severance could have been effected without the making of a memorandum, just as in registered land there could be a severance without the entry of a restriction. In both cases something inconclusive is deemed, for the protection of a purchaser, to be conclusive.

The application of the Act appears to have been qualified by the following case—the first in which a purchaser sought to rely on the protection provided.

Grindal v Hooper, unreported judgment 6 December 1999, HC

Facts: Two sisters, Vera and Sheila, were legal and beneficial joint tenants of a house occupied by Vera. She severed the beneficial joint tenancy by written notice, and, on her death, left her estate to her brother, Brian and other siblings. Sheila, as sole legal owner

---

[79] Cooke, 'Beneficial Joint Tenants and the Protection of Purchasers: An Unsolved Problem' [2004] Conv 41, 42.
[80] [1981] AC 487.

through survivorship, sold the house to Brian for £600, the market value being in the region of £70,000. Brian knew of the trust and of the severance, but no memorandum had been placed on the conveyance to Vera and Sheila. Following Brian's death, the question arose whether, under the 1964 Act, he was solely entitled to the house (so that it would pass under the terms of his will), or whether he held title on trust for himself and Vera's estate, each estate now entitled to a 50 per cent share.

Judge Jarvis QC

Mr Charman says that Brian in these circumstances is the purchaser of the legal estate, and in order to be a purchaser who is protected by the assumptions given by law under s.1 of the 1964 Act he must fall within the definition of a purchaser under s.205 of the Law of Property Act 1925. At definition 21 a purchaser is defined to mean:

> "a purchaser in good faith for valuable consideration [...] and valuable consideration includes marriage but does not include a nominal consideration in money."

In short, Mr Charman says that Brian had notice of the severance before he entered into the agreement to purchase the property. Notice of severance is in these circumstances a notice of the fact that the property was no longer jointly held and therefore that Sheila held the property on trust as to one half for herself and one half for Vera. In those circumstances, where a person has actual notice of circumstances he cannot be said to take in good faith. [...]

It seems to me that on the facts of this case Brian had full notice of the fact that Vera's interest was held on trust by Sheila, and that to acquire the property in these circumstances could not satisfy the definition of a purchaser for good faith under the Act. He, without doubt, purchased the property at a gross under value with actual notice of the estate's interest, and the only inference that I can draw is that that was a transaction which would be designed to deprive the estate of its interest in the property. I conclude that in any event Brian's estate could not take this property without being bound by the equitable interest of Vera's estate.

As Gravells notes, it is doubtful whether actual notice alone should deny the purchaser statutory protection.

Gravells, 'Co-ownership, Severance and Purchasers: The Law of Property (Joint Tenants) Act 1964 on Trial' [2000] Conv 461, 470

[It] might be questioned whether actual notice is or should be sufficient in itself to negative good faith. It might be argued that, in so far as the operation of section 1(1) is excluded where there is an endorsement of the notice of severance, the 1964 Act provides a means of protection for a beneficial tenant in common following the severance of the joint tenancy; that such endorsement may be seen as a form of "quasi-registration"; and that, if the beneficial tenant in common fails to take advantage of that protection, a purchaser should not be bound by the beneficial interest on the basis of actual notice without more. The view that a purchaser who has actual notice of a protectable but unprotected interest cannot be in good faith has been severely criticised and rejected in analogous circumstances.

As is apparent from the observation at the end of the extract from Gravells, the question of the relationship between good faith and actual notice is not unique to the Law of Property

(Joint Tenants) Act 1964. We have explored the relationship between those concepts further in Chapter 15 in our discussion of *Midland Bank plc v Green*.[81]

QUESTIONS

1. Outline the rules that would be used to determine the enforcement of a beneficial interest against a purchaser where purchase money is paid to: (i) one trustee; and (ii) two trustees.

2. To what extent does the requirement that purchase money must be paid to two trustees for overreaching to take place protect the beneficiaries against dissipation of funds by trustees?

3. Does a disposition by trustees in breach of trust (ultra vires or intra vires) have overreaching effect? What is the position of the purchaser following such a disposition?

4. Assess the arguments for and against enabling overreaching of the interests of beneficiaries in occupation. What advice would you give an occupying beneficiary who is concerned that his or her trustee(s) may sell the land?

5. What are the dangers for a purchaser who buys land from a sole surviving joint tenant? To what extent have these dangers been overcome?

FURTHER READING

Cooke, *Land Law* (Oxford: OUP, 2006, ch 3)

Ferris, 'Making Sense of Section 26 of the Land Registration Act 2002' in *Modern Studies in Property Law: Vol 2* (ed Cooke, Oxford: Hart, 2003)

Ferris and Battersby, 'General Principles of Overreaching and the Reforms of the 1925 Legislation' (2002) 118 LQR 270

Ferris and Battersby, 'The General Principles of Overreaching and the Modern Legislative Reforms 1996–2002' (2003) 119 LQR 94

Harpum, 'Overreaching, Trustees' Powers and the Reform of the 1925 Legislation' (1990) 49 CLJ 277

Jackson, 'Overreaching and Unauthorised Disposition of Registered Land' [2007] Conv 120

Jackson, 'Overreaching in Registered Land Law' (2006) 69 MLR 214

Pascoe, 'Improving Conveyancing by Redrafting Section 16' [2005] Conv 140

---

[81] [1981] AC 513. See Chapter 15, section 5.6.

21

CO-OWNERSHIP AND THIRD PARTIES: APPLICATIONS FOR SALE

CENTRAL ISSUES

1. Third parties may make an application for sale of co-owned land to a trust and a creditor or trustee typically makes such applications on the occasion of the bankruptcy of one of the beneficiaries.

2. Since the Trusts of Land and Appointment of Trustees Act 1996, applications made by creditors are considered under the general provisions of that Act, while those by trustees in bankruptcy are considered under the Insolvency Act 1986.

3. As regards applications by creditors, there has been judicial acknowledgment that the 1996 Act has changed the law from the previous practice, which was heavily weighted in favour

of sale. The outcome of cases, however, casts doubt on the extent of any such change.

4. In relation to trustees in bankruptcy, under the Insolvency Act 1986, there is a presumption in favour of sale after an initial one-year adjustment period. Sale may be postponed if there are exceptional circumstances, although this criterion has been narrowly construed.

5. The absence of a discretion in applications by trustees in bankruptcy where no exceptional circumstances are present has led to questions as to the compatibility of the Insolvency Act 1996 with the Human Rights Act 1998.

1 INTRODUCTION

In Chapter 19, we considered how the courts determine applications for the sale of co-owned land where the application is brought by one of the co-owners. It may be recalled that applications for sale (like all other applications relating to the exercise of their functions by trustees of land) are made to the court under s 14 of the Trusts of Land and Appointment of Trustees Act 1996 (TOLATA 1996). Section 15 provides a non-exhaustive list of factors for the court to take into account. In this chapter, we consider applications for sale that are brought by third parties to the trust. Any person with 'an interest in property subject to a trust of land' may bring an application under s 14. Other than the co-owners themselves, the most likely persons to have an interest in the property are creditors who have a security interest over the share of a beneficiary and trustees in bankruptcy of one of the co-owners.

The ability of creditors and trustees in bankruptcy to apply for sale means that, even where a beneficial interest in the home has been established using the doctrines of trust in Chapter 18 and the beneficiary has priority over a creditor or mortgagee under the rules discussed in Chapter 20, their ability to remain in occupation of the home is not guaranteed. A beneficial interest that binds a creditor under the priority rules is separable from the asset (the home) held on trust. On an application for sale by a creditor or trustee in bankruptcy, the court must decide whether the beneficiary should be able to remain in the home, or whether the home should be sold to enable debts to be paid. The resulting case law raises interesting policy questions as to the relative weight that should be given to the desire to remain in the home and the purely financial interests of creditor. An appropriate balance between these interests is all the more difficult to determine given the factual context in which disputes typically arise. The beneficiary resisting sale and the applicant for sale may both be 'victims' of another co-owner's fraud or undue influence, or may be suffering the fallout caused by that co-owner's financial crisis.

As far as creditors are concerned, it is possible for a beneficial tenant in common to grant an equitable charge (or mortgage) over his or her share, but such arrangements are not necessarily commercially attractive to lenders. As will be seen in the case law in this chapter, such interests are more likely to arise because a purported grant of a legal mortgage over the entire estate fails: for example, because one co-owner (A) has exerted undue influence over the other (B),[1] or has forged B's signature to procure a mortgage.[2] The result of the undue influence or forgery is that the charge takes effect only against A's beneficial share. On a sale of the home, B obtains proceeds in proportion to the extent of his or her beneficial share.[3] The proceeds representing A's share alone are used to discharge the debt. If the co-owners were joint tenants at the time, then creating the charge could constitute an act operating on the joint tenant's share to sever the joint tenancy (as discussed in Chapter 19).

Where a co-owner becomes bankrupt, all of his or her property vests in the trustee in bankruptcy, who is under a statutory duty to realize the assets. As is the case with creditors, on a sale, only the proceeds of sale representing the bankrupt's share are used to discharge his or her debts. Where the beneficiary is a joint tenant, we have seen in Chapter 19 that bankruptcy also severs the joint tenancy as an (involuntary) act operating on the joint tenant's share.

The starting point in determining an application by a third party is s 15 of the TOLATA 1996.

---

[1] For example, First National Bank plc v Achampong [2003] EWCA 487, in which a presumption of undue influence was drawn under the tests provided in Royal Bank of Scotland v Etridge (No 2) [2001] UKHL 44.

[2] For example, Mortgage Corporation v Shaire [2001] 4 All ER 364.

[3] An exceptional decision is Bank of Ireland Home Mortgages Ltd v Bell [2001] 2 FLR 908. In that case, an equitable charge arising as the result of Mr Bell's forgery of his wife's signature was, notwithstanding, held to have priority over both parties' beneficial shares. This meant that, on a sale of the home, the debt would be paid out of the full proceeds, not only the part representing Mr Bell's beneficial interest. The Court of Appeal doubted the decision of the first instance judge in this respect, but that aspect of his decision was not subject to appeal.

Trusts of Land and Appointment of Trustees Act 1996, s 15

(1) The matters to which the court is to have regard in determining an application for an order under section 14 include—

   (a) the intentions of the person or persons (if any) who created the trust,

   (b) the purposes for which the property subject to the trust is held,

   (c) the welfare of any minor who occupies or might reasonably be expected to occupy any land subject to the trust as his home, and

   (d) the interests of any secured creditor of any beneficiary.

[...]

(3) In the case of any other application, other than one relating to the exercise of the power mentioned in section 6(2), the matters to which the court is to have regard also include the circumstances and wishes of any beneficiaries of full age and entitled to an interest in possession in property subject to the trust or (in case of dispute) of the majority (according to the value of their combined interests).

(4) This section does not apply to an application if section 335A of the Insolvency Act 1986 (which is inserted by Schedule 3 and relates to applications by a trustee of a bankrupt) applies to it.

The effect of s 15 is that applications by creditors and trustees in bankruptcy are treated differently. The court deals with applications by creditors under s 15. By virtue of s 15(4), however, applications by a trustee in bankruptcy fall to be decided under s 335A of the Insolvency Act 1986. Therefore, each type of application must be considered separately.

To an extent, however, applications by creditors and trustees in bankruptcy raise the same policy considerations. It is useful to highlight these before analysing the case law concerning the different applicants for sale.

2 POLICY CONSIDERATIONS

In Chapter 19, we noted that the policy underlying the TOLATA 1996 was to provide a form of regulation for trusts of land more suited than the trust for sale to the use of a land as a home. We noted that where a dispute as to sale arises between the co-owners, this raises the tension between one party's wish to maintain his or her 'home' and the other's desire to realize his or her investment. The tension between the 'use' and 'investment' functions of a home are all the more apparent when the application for sale is brought by a creditor or trustee in bankruptcy of a co-owner, for whom the property has only ever represented a commercial investment.

Fox highlights the opposing concerns of creditors, on the one hand, and of co-owners, on the other, and is critical of the law's track record in protecting the home.

Fox, *Conceptualising Home: Theories, Laws and Policies*
(2007, pp 14–15, 23–5)

The concerns of the creditor

It is a truism that, in disputes between creditors and occupiers, the creditor almost invariably wins. Legislative and judicial policy makers have routinely favoured the interests of creditors over those of occupiers, thus demonstrating the greater weight attributed to the concerns of creditors over those of occupiers. It is not difficult to understand why this has been the case. For one thing, the creditor has a legitimate expectation, when he lends money against the security of real property, that the debt will be satisfied or the security honoured. Furthermore, there are a series of policy arguments to bolster the creditor's case, for example, the potentially adverse consequences of diminishing the legal protection of creditors; interests on the availability of credit secured against domestic property, either for acquisition of the property itself or as business capital. By contrast, the occupier's interest in the property which a creditor is seeking to realise as a home is not only inconvenient—operating as it could to subjugate the claims of creditors, whose economic clout weights heavily on the balancing scales—but also difficult to ascertain or represent, relative to the creditor's interest. While the creditor's concerns, which essentially revolve around their economic claim on the property as capital, are relatively straightforward, the occupier's interest in retaining the home for use and occupation is much more complex, and, with its many dimensions—financial, practical, emotional, psychological, social and so on—more difficult to quantify. [...]

The concerns of the occupier

While the creditor's concerns are relatively straightforward, the home interests of occupiers are much more complex and difficult to quantify. [...] By drawing upon understandings of the meaning of 'home' as they have developed in other disciplines, legal scholars can begin to appreciate that an occupier's desire to retain the property for use and occupation as a home is not merely sentimental but may also encompass multi-emotional, psychological, social and cultural matters. These meanings can operate to intensify the occupier's attachment to their home, and to exacerbate the experience of losing the home through actions at the hands of a creditor.

However, attempts to argue 'home' interests in law, particularly when positioned against financial interests, are beset by difficulties. Although interdisciplinary research has established the authenticity of home meanings, the relationship between an occupier and his or her home—inherently intangible and difficult to define—is not readily comprehensible to lawyers. For one thing, as home scholars in other disciplines have recognised, an occupier's interest in his or her home is:

> a relative concept, not an absolute one that can be defined in a dictionary or by a linguist. Given that it transcends quantitative, measurable dimensions and includes qualitative subjective ones, it is a complex, ambiguous concept that generates confusion.

It is often difficult to verbalise ideas about home, since they are highly personal, and this adds to the analytical obstacles. Perhaps even more significantly, particularly in the legal domain, the idea of personal attachment to one's home can be portrayed as sentimental and emotional, and as a consequence can become trivialised, particularly when measured against the objective and quantifiable claims of creditors to the capital value of the property. These characteristics provide a ready argument against attempts to develop a coherent legal concept of home. Nevertheless, even setting aside our instinctive appreciation of the importance of home, the proposition that home is a meaningful site and the authenticity of the attachment of occupiers to their homes have been firmly established in other disciplines. In light of this scholarship and the centrality of home to legal discourse, the idea that the subject of 'home' is too difficult for law to comprehend is indefensible.

While Fox refers to creditors, the concerns of the parties are the same whether the application for sale is brought by the creditors themselves or by a trustee in bankruptcy. As we will see, however, under the applicable statutory schemes, the ability of the court to take into account the concerns of the occupier is greater in a dispute with a creditor.

3 APPLICATIONS BY CREDITORS

Applications for sale by a creditor are considered under s 15 of the TOLATA 1996. In applying that section, the responsibility lies with the judge to determine how much weight to afford to each of the factors listed in the provision and all other relevant matters.[4] This includes, but is not limited to, the interest of secured creditors (s 15(1)(d)) and the provision of a home for one or more of the co-owners, in so far as that reflects the parties' intentions at the time that the trust was created (s 15(1)(a)) or the purposes for which the land is held (s 15(1)(b)).

Prior to the 1996 Act, applications for sale by creditors and trustees in bankruptcy were considered by courts under s 30 of the Law of Property Act 1925 (LPA 1925). In applying that provision, it was held that no distinction should be made between the applications. It had been established, in *Re Citro*,[5] that, on an application by a trustee in bankruptcy, sale would be ordered unless the circumstances were exceptional (a criterion that is discussed at sections 4.1 and 4.2 below). In *Lloyds Bank v Byrne*,[6] the Court of Appeal considered that the same rule should apply in relation to creditors.

The 1996 Act distinguishes between these applications, because those by creditors are considered under s 15 of that Act, while applications for sale by trustees in bankruptcy are now dealt with under s 335A of the Insolvency Act 1986. Against this background, Neuberger J considered in the following case whether s 15 of the TOLATA 1996 had changed the law.

Mortgage Corporation v Shaire [2001] 4 All ER 364, HC

Facts: Mrs Shaire and Mr Fox were joint legal owners of their home. Unknown to Mrs Shaire, Mr Fox had forged her signature to secure mortgages over the house. As a result of the forgery, these took effect only against his beneficial share, which the court assessed as being 25 per cent. Following Mr Fox's death, the mortgagee sought sale of the house.

Neuberger J

At 378–80

To my mind, for a number of reasons, Mr Asif is correct in his submission, on behalf of Mrs Shaire, that s 15 has changed the law.

---

[4] *White v White* [2003] EWCA 924, [26]. See further the discussion in Chapter 19, section 5.5.1.
[5] [1991] Ch 142.
[6] [1993] 1 FLR 369.

First, there is the rather trite point that if there was no intention to change the law, it is hard to see why Parliament has set out in s 15(2) and, indeed, on one view, s 15(3), the factors which have to be taken into account specifically, albeit not exclusively, when the court is asked to exercise its jurisdiction to order a sale.

Secondly, it is hard to reconcile the contention that Parliament intended to confirm the law as laid down in *Byrne's case* with the fact that, while the interest of a chargee is one of the four specified factors to be taken into account in s 15(1)(d), there is no suggestion that it is to be given any more importance than the interests of the children residing in the house (see s 15(1)(c)). As is clear from the passage I have quoted from the judgment of Nourse LJ in *Re Citro* as applied to a case such as this in light of *Byrne's case*, that would appear to represent a change in the law.

Thirdly, the very name 'trust for sale' and the law as it has been developed by the courts suggests that under the old law, in the absence of a strong reason to the contrary, the court should order sale. Nothing in the language of the new code as found in the 1996 Act supports that approach.

Fourthly, it is clear from the reasons in *Byrne's case* and indeed the later two first instance cases to which I have referred, that the law, as developed under s 30 of the Law of Property Act 1925, was that the court should adopt precisely the same approach in a case where one of the co-owners was bankrupt (*Re Citro*) and a case where one of the co-owners had charged his interest (*Byrne's case*). It is quite clear that Parliament now considers that a different approach is appropriate in the two cases-compare ss 15(2) and 15(3) of the 1996 Act with s 15(4) and the new s 335A of the Insolvency Act 1986.

Fifthly, an indication from the Court of Appeal that the 1996 Act was intended to change the law is to be found in (an albeit plainly obiter) sentence in the judgment of Peter Gibson LJ in *Banker's Trust Co v Namdar* [1997] CA Transcript 349. Having come to the conclusion that the wife's appeal against an order for sale had to be refused in light of the reasoning in *Re Citro* and *Byrne's case*, Peter Gibson LJ said:

> 'It is unfortunate for Mrs Namdar, that the very recent Trusts of Land and Appointment of Trustees Act 1996 was not in force at the relevant time [i.e. at the time of the hearing at first instance...]

Of course it would be dangerous to build too much on that observation, but it is an indication from the Court of Appeal and indeed from a former chairman of the Law Commission, as to the perceived effect of the 1996 Act.

Sixthly, the leading textbooks support the view that I have reached. In *Megarry & Wade on the Law of Real Property* p 510 (para 9–064) one finds this:

> 'Although the authorities on the law prior to 1997 will therefore continue to provide guidance, the outcome will not in all cases be the same as it would have been under the previous law. This is because the legislature was much more specific as to the matters which a court is required to take into account.'

Emmet on Title (19th edn, January 1999 release) para 22–035, contains this:

> 'Cases decided on pre-1997 law may be disregarded as of little, if any, assistance [...] because the starting point [...] was necessarily a trust for sale implied or expressed as a conveyancing device enabling the convenient co-ownership of the property [...]'

Seventhly, the Law Commission report which gave rise to the 1996 Act, *Transfer of Land, Trusts of Land* (Law Com No 181, 8 June 1989), tends to support this view as well. It is fair to say that the Law Commission did not propose a new section in a new Act such as s 15 of the 1996 Act, but a new s 30 of the Law of Property Act 1925. It is also fair to say that the terms of the proposed new s 30 were slightly different from those of s 15. However, in my judgment, the way in which the terms of the 1996 Act, and in particular s 15, have been drafted suggests that the Law Commission's proposals were very much in the mind of, and were substantially adopted by, the legislature. In para 12.9 of the report, the Law Commission describe the aim as being to 'consolidate *and rationalise*' (my emphasis) the current approach. When commenting on the proposed equivalents of what are now s 15(2) and (3), the Law Commission said (note 143):

'Clearly, the terms of these guidelines may influence the exercise of the discretion in some way. For example, it may be that the courts' approach to creditors' interests will be altered by the framing of the guideline as to the welfare of children. If the welfare of children is seen as a factor to be considered independently of the beneficiaries' holdings, the court may be less ready to order the sale of the home than they are at present.'

Finally, the Law Commission said (para 13.6):

'Within the new system, beneficiaries will be in a comparatively better position than bene-ficiaries of current trusts of land. For example, given that the terms governing applications under section 30 will be less restrictive than they are at present, beneficiaries will have greater scope to challenge the decisions of the trustees and generally influence the management of the trust land.'

Eighthly, to put it at its lowest, it does not seem to me unlikely that the legislature intended to relax the fetters on the way in which the court exercised its discretion in cases such as *Re Citro* and *Byrne's case*, and so as to tip the balance somewhat more in favour of families and against banks and other chargees. Although the law under s 30 was clear following *Re Citro* and *Byrne's case*, there were indications of judicial dissatisfaction with the state of the law at that time. Although Bingham LJ agreed with Nourse LJ in *Re Citro*, he expressed unhappi-ness with the result ([1990] 3 All ER 952 at 965, [1991] Ch 142 at 161), and Sir George Waller's dissatisfaction went so far as led him to dissent ([1990] 3 All ER 952 at 965–966, [1991] Ch 142 at 161–163). Furthermore, there is a decision of the Court of Appeal in *Abbey National plc v Moss* [1994] 2 FCR 587, which suggests a desire for a new approach.

All these factors, to my mind, when taken together point very strongly to the conclusion that s 15 has changed the law. As a result of s 15, the court has greater flexibility than here-tofore, as to how it exercises its jurisdiction on an application for an order for sale on facts such as those in *Re Citro* and *Byrne's case*. There are certain factors which must be taken into account (see s 15(1) and, subject to the next point, s 15(3)). There may be other factors in a particular case which the court can, indeed should, take into account. Once the relevant factors to be taken into account have been identified, it is a matter for the court as to what weight to give to each factor in a particular case.

The only indication the other way is a decision of Judge Wroath in the Newport, Isle of Wight, County Court in *TSB plc v Marshall* [1998] 2 FLR 769 at 771–772, where he said this, having referred to *Byrne's*, *Moss'*, and *Hendricks'* cases:

'Those three cases were all decided where the applications to the court were under s 30 of the Law of Property Act. However, it has been submitted that the principles established are applic-able to an application under s 14, and I accept that submission.'

It does not appear clear to what extent the matter was argued before him, or, indeed, whether it was argued before him. With all due respect to Judge Wroath, I disagree with his conclusion.

A difficult question, having arrived at this conclusion, is the extent to which the old author-ities are of assistance, and it is no surprise to find differing views expressed in the two textbooks from which I have quoted. On the one hand, to throw over all the wealth of learning and thought given by so many eminent judges to the problem which is raised on an application for sale of a house where competing interests exist seems somewhat arrogant and possibly rash. On the other hand, where one has concluded that the law has changed in a significant respect so that the court's discretion is significantly less fettered than it was, there are obvious dangers in relying on authorities which proceeded on the basis that the court's discretion was more fettered than it now is. I think it would be wrong to throw over all the earlier cases without paying them any regard. However, they have to be treated with caution, in light of the change in the law, and in many cases they are unlikely to be of great, let alone decisive, assistance.

Applying s 15 of the 1996 Act, Neuberger J noted that the intentions of Mrs Shaire and Mr Fox when the house was acquired (within s 15(1)(a)) were to provide a home for themselves and for Mrs Shaire's son from a previous relationship. The property was now held (within s 15(1)(b)) both as a home and an asset for Mrs Shaire, with 75 per cent of the beneficial interest, and as security for the loan as regards Mr Fox's 25 per cent share. The interest of the creditor fell to be considered under s 15(1)(d), while Mrs Fox's son was now an adult and therefore his position could not be taken into account. Under s 15(3), it was also relevant that Mrs Shaire had the majority of the beneficial interest.

Weighing up these factors, Neuberger J noted,[7] on the one hand, that for Mrs Shaire to leave her home of nearly twenty-five years '*would be a real and significant hardship, but not an enormous one*'; on the other hand, for the mortgagee to be '*locked into a quarter of the equity of a property would be a significant disadvantage unless they had a proper return and a proper protection as far as insurance and repair is concerned*'. He therefore proposed a solution under which the mortgage would be converted into a loan, on which Mrs Shaire would pay interest pending any future sale. Failing agreement on this (or Mrs Shaire's ability to pay), sale would be ordered.

The careful balancing act conducted by Neuberger J stands in contrast to how applications for sale by creditors were considered prior to the TOLATA 1996 under s 30 of the LPA 1925. There is no doubt that the facts of the case do not demonstrate 'exceptional circumstances' such as would have prevented sale under s 30.

Pascoe is critical of Neuberger J's decision. The Law Commission had envisaged that s 15 of the 1996 Act would consolidate and rationalize the approach developed by the courts under s 30 of the 1925 Act.[8] Against this background, Pascoe considers that Neuberger J's conclusion that s 15 has changed the law is likely to be read with '*some surprise and bewilderment*'.[9] Her concern lies with the consequences of the decision for secured creditors and, in particular, whether these consequences have been fully considered.

Pascoe, 'Section 15 of the Trusts of Land and Appointment of Trustees Act 1996: A Change in the Law' [2000] Conv 315, 327–8

Neuberger J.'s approach is radical: it recognises more rights for beneficiaries and their children in relation to the land which is arguably a more accurate reflection of the ideals and

---

[7] [2001] 4 All ER 364, 383.

[8] Law Commission Report No 181, *Transfer of Land: Trusts of Land* (1989, [12.9]) (the paragraph is extracted in Chapter 19, section 5.5.3).

[9] Pascoe, 'Section 15 of the Trusts of Land and Appointment of Trustees Act 1996: A Change in the Law' [2000] Conv 315, 316.

purposes behind modern home ownership. In his view, section 15 has done more than to codify judicial practice which had been working in the restrictive framework of the 1925 legislation. The new trust of land will therefore better reflect and protect the different expectations which have arisen with the change in our perception of the social role of land. Neuberger J's approach is not one of consolidation and rationalisation; rather he is wiping the slate clean and starting afresh with secured creditors the likely casualties of the new approach. It will be a welcome change in the law for spouses, partners and children living in the property, but an inexpedient, prejudicial and financially detrimental development if one is a secured creditor. Secured creditors must be asking whether the guidelines in section 15 were enacted with proper consideration and deliberation. It must be questionable whether section 15 has abdicated too much responsibility to the judiciary. Perhaps policy should have been formulated by Parliament, rather than relying on ad hoc developments in case law. This will inevitably have commercial and financial repercussions as creditors absorb the effects of the change. Only time will tell if judges are prepared to implement the consequences of Neuberger J.'s judgment and let a fresh wind blow away the remnants of the harshness for families of section 30 of the Law of Property Act 1925 when faced with applications by secured creditors.

Has s 15 of the TOLATA 1996 changed the law? Neuberger J's arguments may appear persuasive, although Pascoe raises legitimate concerns. To the extent that *Shaire* indicates a more sympathetic approach to beneficiaries in actions by creditors, the decision may have been a false dawn. Despite Mrs Shaire's 75 per cent beneficial interest and long-term occupation of the house as her home, sale would only be prevented if the mortgagee's interest could satisfactorily be protected.

3.1 APPLICATIONS FOR SALE BY CREDITORS POST-*SHAIRE*

It is useful to compare the contrasting outcomes in the subsequent cases of *First National Bank plc v Achampong*[10] and *Bank of Ireland Home Mortgages Ltd v Bell*,[11] on the one hand, and *Edwards v Lloyds TSB*,[12] on the other. The following extracts from these decisions show how the courts have exercised their discretion under s 15 of the TOLATA 1996. Analysed together with *Shaire*, the significance attached by the courts to the interest of the secured creditor in determining applications for sale becomes apparent.

First National Bank plc v Achampong [2003] EWCA 487, CA

Facts: Mrs and Mrs Achampong were co-owners of their home. The parties had granted a mortgage over their home, but Mrs Achampong successfully argued that her agreement had been obtained through the presumed undue influence of her husband. As a result, the mortgage took effect only against his 50 per cent beneficial share. Mr Achampong had returned to Ghana, leaving Mrs Achampong in occupation of the home, with two of the parties' adult children (one of whom was mentally disabled) and three infant grandchildren. Blackburne J considered whether sale should be ordered under s 14 of the 1996 Act.

10 [2003] EWCA 487.
11 [2001] 2 FLR 809.
12 [2004] EWHC 1745.

Blackburne J

At [65]

[...] I regard it as plain that an order for sale should be made. Prominent among the considerations which lead to that conclusion is that, unless an order for sale is made, the bank will be kept waiting indefinitely for any payment out of what is, for all practical purposes, its own share of the property. While it is relevant to consider the interests of the infant grandchildren in occupation of the property, it is difficult to attach much if any weight to their position in the absence of any evidence as to how their welfare may be adversely affected if an order for sale is now made. It is for the person who resists an order for sale in reliance on section 15(1)(c) to adduce the relevant evidence. Insofar as the Achampongs' intention in creating the trust of the property was to provide themselves with a matrimonial home, and insofar as that was the purpose for which the property was held on trust, that consideration is now spent. Given the many years' absence of contact between Mr and Mrs Achampong, the fact that there has not yet been a divorce cannot disguise the reality that theirs is a marriage which has effectively come to an end. The possibility, therefore, that the property may yet serve again as the matrimonial home can be ignored. Insofar as the purpose of the trust—and the intention of the Achampongs in creating it—was to provide a family home and insofar as that is a purpose which goes wider than simply the provision of a matrimonial home, I am unpersuaded that it is a consideration to which much if any weight should be attached. The children of the marriage have long since reached adulthood. One of them is no longer in occupation. It is true that the elder daughter, Rosemary, is a person under mental disability and remains in occupation but to what extent that fact is material to her continued occupation of the property and therefore to the exercise of any discretion under section 14 is not apparent.

Bank of Ireland Home Mortgages v Bell [2001] 2 FLR 809, CA

Facts: Mr and Mrs Bell were co-owners of their home with, respectively, a 90 per cent and 10 per cent beneficial share. Mr Bell forged Mrs Bell's signature to obtain a mortgage. He had subsequently left the property and the parties had divorced. Mrs Bell, who was in poor health, remained in occupation, with the parties' son. At first instance, the judge had refused an order of sale. This was overturned on appeal.

Peter Gibson LJ

At [26]–[31]

Further, the judge does not mention the fact that the debt was at the time of the trial some £300,000, and increasing daily, no payment of either capital or interest having been received from Mr Bell (or Mrs Bell for that matter) since June 1992. Mrs Bell's beneficial interest is only about 10 per cent at the very most, as Mr De la Rosa conceded, and there is no equity in the property which would be realised for her on a sale of the property. In effect, therefore, the bank would take all the proceeds on a sale. That is a most material consideration to which the judge should have given great weight.

Second, the judge referred to the property being purchased as a family home. Let me accept that as a finding of fact, although Mr Jackson was able to point to other inconsistent evidence from Mrs Bell as to why the property was purchased. Let me assume that the judge thereby had regard to section 15(1)(a), the intentions of the persons creating the trust.

But that purpose ceased to be operative once Mr Bell left the family, either in 1991 or at any rate by 1992 when possession proceedings started. Mrs Bell is now divorced from Mr Bell. Therefore that purpose is not a matter to which the judge could properly have regard.

Third, the judge referred to the occupation of the property by Mrs Bell and her son. Let me assume that thereby the judge was referring to section 15(1)(b), the purposes for which the property is held. But that is not an operative purpose of the trust since the departure of Mr Bell. The reference to the son may also be a reflection of section 15(1)(c), the welfare of a minor occupying the property. But the son at the time of the trial was not far short of 18 and therefore that should only have been a very slight consideration.

Fourth, the judge referred to Mrs Bell's poor health. At the time of the trial she was facing an operation. I accept that the judge could properly have regard to this, but it would provide a reason for postponing a sale rather than refusing sale.

Fifth, the judge referred to Lloyds Bank as second chargee. But in my judgment that was not a relevant consideration. There was no obligation to give notice to a subsequent encumbrancer. Nor has it ever been the practice of the court when giving effect to a mortgagee's request for an order for sale to hear the views of subsequent encumbrancers. In theory a subsequent encumbrancer might wish to redeem the prior encumbrance, but in practice there was no possibility of that in the circumstances of the present case given the size of the debt.

Prior to the 1996 Act the courts under section 30 of the Law of Property Act 1925 would order the sale of a matrimonial home at the request of the trustee in bankruptcy of a spouse or at the request of the creditor chargee of a spouse, considering that the creditors' interest should prevail over that of the other spouse and the spouse's family save in exceptional circumstances. The 1996 Act, by requiring the court to have regard to the particular matters specified in section 15, appears to me to have given scope for some change in the court's practice. Nevertheless, a powerful consideration is and ought to be whether the creditor is receiving proper recompense for being kept out of his money, repayment of which is overdue (see *The Mortgage Corporation v Shaire*, a decision of Neuberger J on 25th February 2000). In the present case it is plain that by refusing sale the judge has condemned the bank to go on waiting for its money with no prospect of recovery from Mr and Mrs Bell and with the debt increasing all the time, that debt already exceeding what could be realised on a sale. That seems to me to be very unfair to the bank.

Edwards v Lloyds TSB [2004] EWHC 1745

Facts: Mr and Mrs Edwards were co-owners of their home. Following the parties' separation, Mrs Edwards remained in occupation of the home, with the couple's children (now aged 15 and 13). Mr Edwards had forged his wife's signature on a mortgage of the property, which therefore took effect only against his 50 per cent share. Mr Edwards could no longer be traced. The bank sought an application for sale. Park J held that sale should be postponed for five years, until the youngest child reached the age of 18.

Park J

At [31]–[33]

In this case the bank has applied for an order for sale, and Mrs Edwards has opposed the application. I must weigh up the various factors which are relevant and do the best I can to reach a balanced conclusion. I mention now two particular points on the facts of this case which were (I believe) not present in any of the three cases to which I was referred. First, if the house was sold now it is hard to see how Mrs Edwards could find the money to buy another smaller one. In the other cases it appears to have been different. For example in *The Mortgage Corporation v Shaire* (supra) Neuberger J said that if the house was sold Mrs Shaire would still have a substantial sum which she could put towards a smaller home. In the present case, in contrast, the house is a two-bedroom house in which Mrs Edwards already has to share a bedroom with her daughter. The house is obviously at the lower end of the range of prices for houses in the area where she lives. If there was a sale and the husband's debt to the bank was taken out of half of the net proceeds before the balance was available to Mrs Edwards, I very much doubt that she would be able to find another house which she could afford to buy and which would be adequate to accommodate her and her children.

Second, whereas in the other three cases it appears that the debt owed to the bank already exceeded the value of the interest over which the bank had an equitable charge, in the present case that is not so. On the figures which I gave in paragraph 12 above the value of the bank's security (a 50% interest in the house) would be (if the entirety were sold) about £70,000. The husband's debt to the bank (£15,000 plus interest plus costs) is unlikely at present to be more than £40,000. It is true that interest is not currently being paid to the bank on the debt owed to it, but interest continues to accrue on the debt, and now and for some time to come the security will be sufficient to cover the increasing amount of the debt.

In the circumstances I do not want to order an immediate sale, because I believe that that would be unacceptably severe in its consequences upon Mrs Edwards and her children. But equally I believe that I should make some order which, admittedly later rather than sooner, should enable the bank to recover its debt with accrued interest upon it.

Two points are notable about these decisions. The first point to note is the courts' differing approach to the purposes of the trusts. In *Achampong*, Blackburne J was not prepared to afford weight to any subsisting purposes of the trust of providing a 'family' home following the effective termination of the marriage by Mr Achampong's return to Ghana. Similarly, in *Bell*, the departure of Mr Bell was considered to have ended the purpose of the trust. In contrast, in *Edwards*, Park J was satisfied that, following Mr Edwards' departure, '*in part the purpose still survives, because the house is still the home for Mrs Edwards and the two children*'.[13] These differing attitudes to the purpose are significant, because the continuing purpose of the trust is the factor that enables the occupying beneficiary to have his or her interests weighed against those of the creditors under s 15 of the 1996 Act. Where the purpose is considered to have come to an end, the likelihood of sale being postponed appears remote, unless there are children present whose interests fall for consideration under s 15(1)(c).

Probert considered the consequences of the narrow approach to the purpose of the trust in *Achampong* and *Bell* in a discussion of the latter case.

Probert, 'Creditors and Section 15 of the Trusts of Land and Appointment of Trustees Act 1996: First Among Equals' [2002] Conv 61, 66–7

The danger in the reasoning lies in the way that it downgrades the purpose of providing a family home as against the interests of the creditors. If the purpose of providing a family home

---

[13] *Edwards v Lloyds TSB* [2004] EWHC 1745, [29].

comes to an end upon the departure of one of the parties and only the original purposes are to be taken into account, then where one party has left the property and there are no children, the only relevant factor remaining is the interests of the creditors. Even where there are children the dispute is reduced to a straightforward contest between the welfare of any minors who might wish to occupy the property and the interests of the creditors. If these two factors are given equal weight then it is possible that either may prevail in the short term. In the long term, the minors will grow up and their interests will cease to be a relevant concern. Moreover, if the interests of those nearing 18 are "only a very slight consideration" then the creditors' interests may prevail even before the former reach adulthood. If the statement that the creditors interests are a "powerful consideration" indicates that more weight is given to this factor than any other, then there is the risk that the interests of creditors will trump the rights of even very young children, once the factors listed in (a) and (b) are negated. If this interpretation of section 15 prevails then the wind has changed and blown us back to where we started.

Does the wider approach to the purpose of the trust adopted in *Edwards* ensure that the interests of the occupying beneficiary (in addition to the welfare of children) are weighed against those of the creditor? The difficulty with the decision lies in understanding when the wider approach to the purpose will be taken. Objectively, the only difference between the three cases as regards the courts' identification of the purpose is the continuing occupation, in *Edwards*, of the couple's young children. It seems likely that this affected the courts' attitude towards the purpose of the trust, despite the fact that the welfare of children should be taken into account independently through s 15(1)(c) of the TOLATA 1996. Even under *Edwards* it remains unlikely that the purpose of providing a family home will be considered to continue where one beneficiary remains in occupation without children. In such cases, as Probert notes, the only remaining factor under s 15 is the interests of the creditors.

The second notable point about the decisions is the differing position of the creditors in each case, as highlighted by Park J in *Edwards*. In *Shaire*, as we have seen, the decision not to order sale was dependent on an arrangement being reached under which the creditor would not be prejudiced; in *Edwards*, it was clear that this criterion was also met. In contrast, in *Achampong*, the debt had reached a level of £180,000. It was enforceable against only a 50 per cent share of the home, which, at the time of the judgment, had a full value of only £195,000; similarly, in *Bell*, as we have noted, the debt already exceeded the value of the house. It may be suggested that, while the interests of creditors is only one factor for the court to take into account, these cases indicate that it will be difficult to resist sale unless the creditor will not be prejudiced.

3.2 HAS S 15 OF THE TRUSTS OF LAND AND APPOINTMENT OF TRUSTEES ACT 1996 CHANGED THE LAW?

On the basis of this analysis of applications for sale by creditors post-*Shaire*, we can assess Neuberger J's conclusion that s 15 of the TOLATA 1996 has 'changed the law' from the courts' previous practice under s 30 of the LPA 1925. The decisions in these cases may cast doubt on the extent of any such change. As we have noted, in applications for sale by a creditor under s 30 of the 1925 Act, *Re Citro* established that sale would be ordered unless the circumstances were exceptional. As we will see below, at the time of that decision, the only reported case in which this criterion was met was one in which a postponement of sale would not prejudice the interest of the creditor.[14] In view of this, it seems that the decisions in *Achampong*, *Bell*, and *Edwards* are entirely consistent with the courts' previous practice. Despite Neuberger J's conclusion in *Shaire*, the decision in that case may stand alone as one in which the 1996 Act has made a practical difference to the outcome.[15]

Two factors may account for the pattern of decisions since *Shaire*. Firstly, the utility of developing a flexible approach under s 15 of the 1996 Act is dependent on creditors bringing their applications under that provision. It was predicted at the time of the Act that s 15 would operate as an incentive for creditors to obtain an order of bankruptcy, enabling them to rely on the more favourable provision in s 335A of the Insolvency Act 1986.[16] Radley-Gardner[17] notes that, by the time of the decision in *Achampong*, the ability of mortgagors to circumvent s 15 by making the defaulting beneficiary bankrupt had become apparent. This is illustrated by *Alliance and Leicester plc v Slayford*,[18] in which a wife's beneficial interest was binding against a mortgagee, because she had entered into a transaction through her husband's undue influence. The court held that it was not an abuse of process for the mortgagee to sue the husband on his personal covenant to pay the debt, with a view to bankrupting him and bringing an application for sale under the Insolvency Act 1986. Hence, as Radley-Gardner explains: '[E]*ven if a more flexible approach had emerged under section 15, it would have been a paper tiger, easily undercut by recourse to the insolvency regime.*'

Secondly, the decisions in the cases echo Fox's comment, in the extract above, of the difficulty in balancing the qualitative and emotional concerns of occupiers against the quantitative and financial interests of the creditor. In the balancing exercise under s 15, creditors have nothing to prove: their interest in obtaining sale is unarguable. Pitted against this are the more nebulous concepts of the intentions and purposes of the trust, and the 'welfare' of children. In *Achampong*, for example, little weight was attached to the occupying grandchildren in the absence of evidence as to *how* their welfare would be affected by sale.

4 APPLICATIONS BY TRUSTEES IN BANKRUPTCY

Where there is a trust of land, applications for sale by a trustee in bankruptcy are considered by the court under s 335A of the Insolvency Act 1985.

Insolvency Act 1986, s 335A

(1) Any application by a trustee of a bankrupt's estate under section 14 of the Trusts of Land and Appointment of Trustees Act 1996 powers of court in relation to trusts of land) for an order under that section for the sale of land shall be made to the court having jurisdiction in relation to the bankruptcy.

---

[14] *Re Holliday* [1981] Ch 405.

[15] The decision in *Edwards v Lloyds TSB* [2004] EWHC 1745 may be contentious in this regard. The case shares some analogies with *Re Citro* [1991] Ch 142 (in which sale was ordered under s 30) in so far as the application was made despite the continuing purpose of the trust, but the fact the creditors in *Edwards* would not be prejudiced may have been sufficient, in light of *Re Holliday* [1981] Ch 405, to distinguish the cases even under s 30.

[16] Hopkins, 'The Trusts of Land and Appointment of Trustees Act 1996' [1996] Conv 411, 425.

[17] Radley-Gardner, 'Section 15 of TOLATA, or, the Importance of Being Earners' [2003] 5 Web JCLI.

[18] (2001) 33 HLR 66.

(2) On such an application the court shall make such order as it thinks just and reasonable having regard to—

(a) the interests of the bankrupt's creditors,

(b) where the application is made in respect of land which includes a dwelling house which is or has been the home of the bankrupt or the bankrupt's spouse or civil partner or former spouse or former civil partner—

(i) the conduct of the [spouse, civil partner, former spouse, or former civil partner], so far as contributing to the bankruptcy,

(ii) the needs and financial resources of the [spouse, civil partner, former spouse, or former civil partner], and

(iii) the needs of any children; and

(c) all the circumstances of the case other than the needs of the bankrupt.

(3) Where such an application is made after the end of the period of one year beginning with the first vesting under Chapter IV of this Part of the bankrupt's estate in a trustee, the court shall assume, unless the circumstances of the case are exceptional, that the interests of the bankrupt's creditors outweigh all other considerations.

(4) The powers conferred on the court by this section are exercisable on an application whether it is made before or after the commencement of this section.

The circumstances to be taken into account under s 335A of the 1986 Act therefore differ from those under s 15 of the TOLATA 1996. In particular, the intentions of the settlors and the purposes for which the land is held (the criteria contained in s 15(1)(a) and (b) of the 1996 Act) cease to be relevant on bankruptcy. Moreover, through s 335A(3) of the Insolvency Act 1986, as long as the application for sale is brought at least a year after the bankruptcy, the interests of the creditors prevail and sale is therefore ordered unless the circumstances are exceptional. Only if exceptional circumstances are present is the court required to balance the factors listed in the provision.[19]

Although s 335A was inserted into the Insolvency Act 1986 by the TOLATA 1996, it is an extension of a provision contained in the original Act, the origins of which lie with the Cork Report. The discussion of the family home in that report remains instructive in understanding the policy represented by s 335A.

Insolvency Law and Practice: Report of the Review Committee (The Cork Report) (Cmnd 8558, 1982, [1118], [1120]–[1123])

THE FAMILY HOME

It would be clearly wrong to allow a debtor or his family to continue to live in lavish style at the expense of the debtor's creditors for an extended period. Nevertheless considerable personal hardship can be caused to the debtor's family by a sudden or premature eviction,

---

[19] Compare Dixon, 'Trusts of Land, Bankruptcy and Human Rights' [2005] Conv 161, 164. He notes that this is the manner in which the courts have, in fact, approached s 335A, although he suggests that a 'less preconceived interpretation' would be that the factors listed should always be balanced, even though the 'scales are heavily tilted' in favour of sale after the initial one-year period.

and we believe it to be consonant with present social attitudes to alleviate the personal hardships of those who are dependent on the debtor but not responsible for his insolvency, if this can be achieved by delaying for an acceptable time the sale of the family home. We propose therefore to delay, but not to cancel, enforcement of the creditors' rights.

[...]

Nevertheless we consider that any new Insolvency Act should confer on the Court a specific power to postpone a trustee's rights of possession and sale of the family home. In exercising this power the Court should have particular regard to the welfare of any children of the family and of any adult members of the family who are ailing or elderly [...] Giving this power to the Court will, we hope and expect, serve to support the natural inclination of the usually sympathetic [trustee in bankruptcy], and to protect the debtor's family in those cases where lack of sympathy with, or anger at, the debtor produces unfortunate and undeserved consequences for his family.

Where there are dependents, the Court should not order an immediate sale unless satisfied that no avoidable hardship to them will be caused by the sale of the family home. That is not to say that application need be made to the Court in every case; once the correct principles have been established, we believe that in only a very small minority of cases will the Court be concerned.

When an application does come before the Court, we consider that the Court must have wide discretion to enable it to make whatever order may be just and equitable in the great variety of circumstances that may arise. While the Court will first consider the dependants—and the greater their vulnerability the greater will be the protection needed—creditors' rights should be postponed only in order to prevent injury to the welfare of those dependants; not to preserve for them any particular standard of life.

No two cases will be alike; the Court must therefore have complete discretion to do what seems to it to be appropriate. Such guidelines as can be given must of necessity be in the most general terms and, indeed, little more than an indication of the factors for consideration. While some of us have considered that there should be a statutory limit on the length of time for which a postponement could be ordered, all of us are agreed that, in practice, any very lengthy postponement should be rare. The majority of us have concluded that the Court's powers should not be limited in duration. In the reported cases, both under the matrimonial legislation and (more rarely) under the bankruptcy law, much importance has been attached to the ages, welfare and educational prospects of the children.

The report undoubtedly envisages a less prescriptive regime than that provided for in s 335A,[20] while acknowledging the strength of the creditors' claims following bankruptcy. But s 335A does reflect the underlying idea in this extract of alleviating the hardship of a sudden eviction. The effect of s 335A is to provide the bankrupt (and his or her family) with an initial one-year adjustment period, following which the financial claim of the creditors becomes paramount.

Section 335A of the Insolvency Act 1986 must now be read in conjunction with ss 283A and 313A. These provisions were introduced into the Act by the Enterprise Act 2002 and reflect the policy of that Act of providing a 'fresh start' for bankrupts. Under s 283A of the

---

20 Compare, e.g., the 'wide discretion' and the 'complete discretion to do what seems [...] appropriate' in the extract with the actual provision in the Insolvency Act 1986, s 335A. Further, as is noted by Omar, 'Security Over Co-Owned Property and the Creditor's Paramount Status in Recovery Proceedings' [2006] Conv 157, 168, some of the factors the Cork Committee specifically envisaged being taken into account were held in Re Citro [1991] Ch 142 not to constitute exceptional circumstances.

1986 Act, the beneficiary's share in his or her home is returned to him or her after three years if the trustee in bankruptcy has not applied for sale (or dealt with the share in other ways provided by the Act). Read in conjunction with s 335A, the practical effect of this is that the trustee in bankruptcy has a two-year period during which sale will be ordered in the absence of exceptional circumstances. Under s 313A, sale will not be ordered where the value of the bankrupt's share is below a prescribed level and therefore of marginal benefit to the creditors.[21]

The key issue of interpretation arising from s 335A is the meaning of 'exceptional circumstances', which may result in the postponement of sale after the initial year. We will first consider the courts' general approach to defining 'exceptional circumstances' and then address a developing argument that human rights considerations may require the courts to extend this general interpretation.

4.1 THE COURTS' GENERAL APPROACH TO DEFINING 'EXCEPTIONAL CIRCUMSTANCES'

The test of exceptional circumstances has its origins in the courts' case law under s 30 of the LPA 1925. In applications under that section, *Re Citro* established the general principle that, on an application by a trustee in bankruptcy, sale would be ordered unless there are exceptional circumstances. In doing so, Nourse LJ offered the following definition.

Re Citro [1991] Ch 142, CA

Nourse LJ

At 157

What then are exceptional circumstances? As the cases show, it is not uncommon for a wife with young children to be faced with eviction in circumstances where the realisation of her beneficial interest will not produce enough to buy a comparable home in the same neighbourhood, or indeed elsewhere. And, if she has to move elsewhere, there may be problems over schooling and so forth. Such circumstances, while engendering a natural sympathy in all who hear of them, cannot be described as exceptional. They are the melancholy consequences of debt and improvidence with which every civilised society has been familiar. It was only in *In re Holliday* [1981] Ch. 405 that they helped the wife's voice to prevail, and then only, as I believe, because of one special feature of that case. One of the reasons for the decision given by Sir David Cairns was that it was highly unlikely that postponement of payment of the debts would cause any great hardship to any of the creditors, a matter of which Buckley L.J. no doubt took account as well.

Implicit in Nourse LJ's definition is that 'exceptional' requires something '*out of the ordinary course, or unusual, or special, or uncommon*'.[22]

In the following case, Judge Sumption QC explained further.

---

21 Ibid, pp 169–70.
22 *Hosking v Michaelides* [2004] All ER (D) 147, *per* Judge Morgan QC.

Re Bremner [1999] 1 FLR 912

Judge Sumption QC

At 915

The test is whether the problems which would result from an eviction are within the broad range of problems, necessarily distressing, which can be expected to arise from the process of bankruptcy and the resultant realisation of the bankrupt's assets, or whether they lie wholly outside that range.

The clearest example of exceptional circumstances is chronic ill health on the part of the bankrupt, or the bankrupt's spouse or partner. In *Claughton v Charalambous*,[23] the bankrupt and his wife were beneficial co-owners of their home. Mrs Charalambous was in poor health, with consequential mobility problems that the couples' home had been altered to accommodate. She had a reduced life expectancy. The judge considered these circumstances to be exceptional and postponed sale for so long as Mrs Charalambous continued to live in the property.[24] In *Re Bremner*, the bankrupt himself was elderly and terminally ill with inoperable cancer. This case raised a specific issue because, under s 335A, the interests of the bankrupt are not themselves a relevant consideration.[25] But the court accepted that the bankrupt's wife, who was also his carer, had a distinct need to continue to provide that care in their home. Sale was postponed until three months after the bankrupt's death.

In the extract from *Re Citro* (above), Nourse LJ notes that, in *Re Holliday*[26] (the only reported case at the time in which exceptional circumstances had been found), the creditors would not be prejudiced by the postponement of sale. In that case, sale was postponed for five years until the bankrupt's children reached 17 years of age, at which point, the proceeds of sale represented by the bankrupt's beneficial share would still be sufficient to pay his debts with interest. An immediate sale, however, would leave his former wife with insufficient funds to obtain alternative accommodation.

The fact that creditors will not be prejudiced by a sale is not, in itself, an exceptional circumstance enabling courts to postpone sale.[27] Where exceptional circumstances are present, however, the impact of any delay on the creditors remains a significant factor in the courts' willingness to postpone sale under s 335A. A review of case law under s 335A suggests that the protection of creditors is a point of synergy between applications under that provision and those by creditors under s 15 of the TOLATA 1996.

In *Re Bremner*, the court noted that sale would not necessarily have been delayed if the bankrupt had been younger, or less ill, or had a longer life expectancy. The expected short period of the delay meant that any prejudice to creditors was likely to be modest.[28]

---

23 [1999] 1 FLR 740.

24 Contrast *Foenander v Allan* [2006] BPIR 1392. The bankrupt co-owned his home with his brother, who was suffering from progressive dementia. This was not sufficient to postpone sale. Judge Strauss QC noted, at [34], that the house was the only asset available in the bankruptcy and that the Registrar had left open the possibility of sale being delayed as long as necessary to ensure alternative accommodation was provided. Sale was, however, postponed on other grounds discussed below.

25 There was no co-ownership trust in this case, because Mr Bremner was the sole owner of the home. The case was decided under the Insolvency Act 1986, s 336, which is identical in all relevant respects to s 335A.

26 [1981] Ch 40.

27 *Donohoe v Ingram* [2006] EWHC 282.

28 The eventual sale of the house would still provide sufficient proceeds with which to pay the secured creditors the sum due, plus interest, and pay unsecured creditors, with the loss of statutory interest.

In *Foenander v Allan*[29] and *Martin-Sklan v White*,[30] a postponement of sale in light of exceptional circumstances was not expected to prejudice creditors, because the sum realized on sale would still be sufficient to repay the outstanding debt. In *Martin-Sklan*, the postponement maintained the 'web of support' provided to the bankrupt's partner, an alcoholic; *Foenander* is an unusual case in which the exceptional circumstances were financial, rather than personal. In that case, an immediate sale would raise sufficient proceeds to repay creditors with a modest surplus. Sale was postponed on condition that an insurance claim for subsidence was likely to be met in a reasonable period. This would significantly increase the value of the home, enhancing the surplus available to the bankrupt and his brother, with whom the house was co-owned.

In *Nicholls v Lan*,[31] sale was delayed for a minimum of eighteen months to give the bankrupt's wife, a chronic schizophrenic, an opportunity to raise funds by the sale of another property, which would enable her to buy out the bankrupt's share. Her medical circumstances meant that a forced sale could have specific psychiatric effects. The case is notable in so far as the sale was postponed despite the fact that the proceeds realized by sale would be insufficient to pay the outstanding debts.

4.2 EXCEPTIONAL CIRCUMSTANCES: THE HUMAN RIGHTS DIMENSION

In *Barca v Mears*,[32] a novel argument was made that the application of s 335A of the Insolvency Act 1986 may, in some circumstances, constitute an infringement of Art 8 of the European Convention on Human Rights (the right to respect for private and family life). We have examined that Article in Chapter 5. As we have seen, the right is not absolute, although any interference must be for a legitimate aim and must be proportionate to that aim. We have also seen in Chapter 5 that s 3 of the Human Rights Act 1998 (HRA 1998) requires courts to interpret legislation, in so far as it is possible to do so, in a manner that is consistent with the ECHR. Under s 335A of the Insolvency Act 1986, a presumption in favour of the creditors arises after one year, unless there are exceptional circumstances. The courts have defined that requirement narrowly, as meaning circumstances outside those expected to arise on a bankruptcy. The argument raised in *Barca v Mears* was that the resulting absence of any ability by the court to undertake a proper balancing of interests under s 335A constituted an infringement of Art 8. This argument attracted support by the court, although, on the facts, it was not sufficient to prevent sale.

Barca v Mears [2004] EWHC 2170, HC

Judge Strauss QC

At [39]–[42]

Clearly, in many or perhaps most cases, the sale of a bankrupt's property in accordance with bankruptcy law will be justifiable on the basis that it is necessary to protect the rights

---

[29] [2006] BPIR 1392.
[30] [2006] EWHC 3313.
[31] [2006] EWHC 1255.
[32] [2004] EWHC 2170.

of others, namely the creditors, and will not be a breach of the Convention. Nevertheless, it does seem to me to be questionable whether the narrow approach as to what may be 'exceptional circumstances' adopted in *Re Citro (Domenico) (a Bankrupt)* [1991] Ch 142, is consistent with the Convention. It requires the court to adopt an almost universal rule, which prefers the property rights of the bankrupt's creditors to the property and/or personal rights of third parties, members of his family, who owe the creditors nothing. I think that there is considerable force in what is said by Ms Deborah Rook in *Property Law and Human Rights* (Blackstone Press, 2001), at pp 203–205 to which Mr Gibbon very fairly referred me:

'It is arguable that, in some circumstances, [s 335A(3)] may result in an infringement of Article 8. The mortgagor's partner and children have the right to respect their home and family life under Article 8 even though they may have no proprietary interest in the house [...] therefore it is possible that the presumption of sale in s 335A and the way that the courts have interpreted it, so that in the majority of cases an innocent partner and the children are evicted from the home, violates Convention rights [...]'

The eviction of the family from their home, an event that naturally ensues from the operation of the presumption of sale in s 335A, could be considered to be an infringement of the right to respect of the home and family life under Article 8 if the presumption is given absolute priority without sufficient consideration being given to the Convention rights of the affected family. Allen [Mr T Allen in "The Human Rights Act (UK) and Property Law" in *Property and the Constitution* (Hart Publishing, 1999), at p 163] observes that:

"As the law currently stands, the right to respect for family life and the home receives almost no consideration after the one year period. Whether such a strict limitation is compatible with the Convention is doubtful".

[...] it may be that the courts, in applying s 335A [...] will need to adopt a more sympathetic approach to defining what constitutes "exceptional circumstances". If an immediate sale of the property would violate the family's rights under Article 8, the court may be required in compliance with its duty under s 3 of the HRA 1988 to adopt a broad interpretation of "exceptional circumstances" [...] to ensure the compatibility of this legislation with Convention rights.'

In particular, it may be incompatible with Convention rights to follow the approach taken by the majority in *Re Citro (Domenico) (a Bankrupt)* [1991] Ch 142, in drawing a distinction between what is exceptional, in the sense of being unusual, and what Nourse LJ refers to as the 'usual melancholy consequences' of a bankruptcy. This approach leads to the conclusion that, however disastrous the consequences may be to family life, if they are of the usual kind then they cannot be relied on under s 335A; they will qualify as 'exceptional' only if they are of an unusual kind, for example where a terminal illness is involved.

It seems to me that a shift in emphasis in the interpretation of the statute may be necessary to achieve compatibility with the Convention. There is nothing in the wording of s 335A, or the corresponding wording of ss 336 and 337, to require an interpretation which excludes from the ambit of 'exceptional circumstances' cases in which the consequences of the bankruptcy are of the usual kind, but exceptionally severe. Nor is there anything in the wording to require a court to say that a case may not be exceptional, if it is one of the rare cases in which, on the facts, relatively slight loss which the creditors will suffer as a result of the postponement of the sale would be outweighed by disruption, even if of the usual kind, which will be caused in the lives of the bankrupt and his family. Indeed, on one view, this is what the Court of Appeal decided in *Re Holliday (a Bankrupt) ex parte Trustee of the Property of the Bankrupt v Holliday and Another* [1981] Ch 405.

> Thus it may be that, on a reconsideration of the sections in the light of the Convention, they are to be regarded as merely recognising that, in the general run of cases, the creditors' interests will outweigh all other interests, but leaving it open to a court to find that, on a proper consideration of the facts of a particular case, it is one of the exceptional cases in which this proposition is not true. So interpreted, and without the possibly undue bias in favour of the creditors' property interests embodied in the pre-1998 case-law, these sections would be compatible with the Convention.

It is important to emphasize that the objection raised to s 335A is essentially procedural. The possible incompatibility with Art 8 arises where the court is unable to balance the bankrupt's interests against those of the creditors because of the absence of exceptional circumstances. In *Nicholls v Lan*,[33] in which exceptional circumstances were present, Judge Morgan suggested that the balancing exercise that he was therefore required to undertake under s 335A '*precisely captures what is required*' by Art 8. In view of this, while the objection raised is *procedural*, the solution may lie in a *substantive* alteration of the definition of exceptional circumstances. By finding that such circumstances are present, the court has access to the discretion conferred by s 335A of the Insolvency Act 1986 and is therefore able to undertake the balancing exercise required by Art 8 of the ECHR.

Because the underlying objection is procedural, issues of incompatibility with Art 8 are unlikely to arise in relation to s 15 of the TOLATA 1996 when an application for sale is made by a creditor. That section requires a proper balancing of interests to take place in every case. There is no precondition that exceptional circumstances are present.

The consequences of *Barca v Mears* are considered by Dixon. He notes that it will not necessarily lead to an erosion of the current preference for commercial claims.

Dixon, 'Trusts of Land, Bankruptcy and Human Rights' [2005] Conv 161, 166–7

If *Barca v Mears* lights the future way, what will it mean? Certainly, it suggests that a court can no longer simply refuse sale within a year and then order sale after a year without genuinely considering the factors specified in s.335A. A genuine exercise of judicial discretion is called for. Yet, this is not wholly disadvantageous to creditors who might now achieve a sale within the period of grace, something that might become more desirable given the time and financial limits imposed by the Enterprise Act 2002 on the trustee in bankruptcy's ability to seek a sale. Likewise, the case suggests that even after the expiry of one year, the court should not refuse to consider the factors listed in the section simply because it cannot be shown that there is an exceptional circumstance. Rather the court should still weigh all the specified factors, even after a year, but it may legitimately presume that the creditor's rights outweigh all else unless there is something exceptional, either in the sense of an individual circumstance or when taking all the other circumstances weighed together. Again, there is nothing to fear here, save only that this different emphasis may uncover some cases where a sale should not be ordered because the substantive inquiry has revealed an exceptional circumstance that might otherwise have lay hidden. Thirdly, and perhaps most significantly, what amounts to "exceptional circumstances" should be broadened because the Convention requires the court to have regard to the private and family life of all occupiers and to ensure respect for property rights. Any unusual consequences of a sale—that is, over and above the "normal"

---

[33] [2006] EWHC 1255, [43].

tragedy of losing one's home—would remain "exceptional circumstances", but severe consequences of the usual type might now also fall within the definition, especially if little or no hardship would be caused to the creditors by further postponement. Indeed, many might argue that this change in the interpretation of s.335A actually restores the original parliamentary intention. It has never been immediately apparent why such a narrow view of the section should have been adopted, save perhaps that the pervasive influence of *Re Citro* exerted a force too powerful to resist, even though that case did not turn on s.335A.

To date, the human rights argument remains undeveloped. It was raised in *Donohoe v Ingram*,[34] in which, as in *Barca v Mears*, the court considered that, even on a broad approach to exceptional circumstances, sale would still be ordered.

5 APPLICATIONS FOR SALE BY CREDITORS AND TRUSTEES IN BANKRUPTCY: A SUMMARY

Applications for sale by creditors are decided under s 15 of the TOLATA 1996, which confers discretion on the court in every case. We have seen that the courts are unlikely to consider the purpose of provision of a home to continue once one of the parties has left, unless children are present. The interests of children, in any event, are given independent consideration. Further, it will be difficult for a beneficiary to resist sale unless the interests of creditors are protected.

Applications by trustees in bankruptcy are determined under s 335A of the Insolvency Act 1986. That section anticipates an initial adjustment period of one year, following which sale will be ordered, unless there are exceptional circumstances. Even where such circumstances are present, the impact on creditors of any postponement of sale remains a significant factor. 'Exceptional' is currently defined as requiring something out of the ordinary—but a need to demonstrate exceptional circumstances as a precondition to the existence of discretion has left s 335A vulnerable to challenge as being incompatible with Art 8 of the ECHR. A broadening of this definition, to confer discretion on the court, may meet this concern.

QUESTIONS

1. Compare and contrast the rules applicable to applications for sale made by creditors and those made by trustees in bankruptcy. Do you consider differences between the applications to be justified by the status of the applicants?

2. In considering applications for sale by creditors, have the courts paid sufficient regard to the interests of beneficiaries who wish to prevent sale of their home? In what circumstances do you consider beneficiaries to be most vulnerable to a sale of their home being ordered?

3. How (if at all) would you advise the courts to change their interpretation of the test of 'exceptional circumstances' to ensure compatibility with the Human Rights Act 1998? Would your proposed change necessarily lead to a different outcome in cases?

---

[34] [2006] EWHC 282, [23].

FURTHER READING

Fox, *Conceptualising Home: Theories, Laws and Policies* (Oxford: Hart, 2007)

Fox, 'Creditors and the Concept of a "Family Home": A Functional Analysis' (2005) 25 LS 201

Omar, 'Equitable Interests and the Secured Creditor: Determining Priorities' [2006] Conv 509

Omar, 'Security Over Co-Owned Property and the Creditor's Paramount Status in Recovery Proceedings' [2006] Conv 157

22

SUCCESSIVE OWNERSHIP

CENTRAL ISSUES

1. Successive ownership arises under a trust in which the beneficiaries are entitled to possession in succession, rather than concurrently. While it retains practical significance, successive ownership has been superseded by co-ownership in social and economic importance.

2. Central to successive ownership is the existence of a life estate—that is, a period of ownership of land measured by the life of the beneficiary entitled in possession. The life estate is commercially unattractive and other devices can be used to confer rights of ownership or occupation for life.

3. Successive interest trusts can be created in the same way as other trusts of land. Those created after the commencement of the Trusts of Land and Appointment of Trustees Act 1996 are regulated by that Act.

1 INTRODUCTION

In Chapter 19, we examined the regulation of co-ownership, arising where two or more people are concurrently entitled to legal or beneficial title to land. We saw that the defining characteristic of co-ownership is *unity of possession*: each co-owner is concurrently entitled to possession of the whole of the land. Successive ownership arises where two or more people are entitled to possession of land in succession to each other, rather than concurrently: for example, where land is held on trust for A for life and thereafter for B. In such a case, A alone is entitled to possession of the land for his or her life (the nature of A's 'life interest' is considered in section 4 below) and, on A's death, B's interest comes into possession. Successive ownership necessarily arises under a trust of the legal estate with A and B's interests arising in equity. Therefore, this chapter is concerned with successive *beneficial* ownership.

Beyond its own practical significance, an understanding of the operation of successive ownership enhances our appreciation of the concept of ownership of an estate in land (discussed in Chapter 3). It is the recognition, through the doctrine of estates, that ownership can be divided by periods of time that makes it possible to divide ownership of land successively. Further, successive ownership provides a useful bridge between our current focus on the home and Part D of this book, in which our attention moves to leases and commonholds. This is because some of the arrangements for ownership of land that would previously have been achieved through successive ownership of an estate may now be achieved through leasehold arrangements, as illustrated by *Ingram v Inland Revenue Commissioners*.[1] In that case, Lady Ingram wished to make a gift of her land during her lifetime to avoid inheritance tax, whilst simultaneously securing her own occupation until her death. Lifetime occupation could be secured through a lease or through successive beneficial ownership, but the former alone protected the estate from inheritance tax.[2]

2 THE SIGNIFICANCE OF SUCCESSIVE OWNERSHIP

Historically, the regulation of successive ownership was an important feature of land law. At its core, lay the family 'strict settlement' within which the forms of successive ownership (considered in section 3 below) were used in combination to keep land within the family for generation after generation.[3]

As Simpson explains, the rules governing settlements were developed by lawyers with conflicting desires to create a market in land to buy, but then retain that land within the family.[4] Additionally, however, the family settlement provided an important means of protecting women at a time of legal subservience. While the social and legal environments in which successive ownership and co-ownership have flourished are very different, in this respect alone, there is some parallel between their legal histories.

Simpson, *A History of the Land Law* (2nd edn, 1986, p 209)

Many settlements of property were created on the occasion of a marriage between dynastic families, and here what was needed was compromise between the interests of the families concerned. Given the legal subservience of women, the bride's family required of property law some security both for their daughter and for her children and grandchildren. This could only be achieved if the husband's rights over the family land were in some degree restricted, so that the landed endowment of the family would pass down to the next generation. Indeed the whole history of settlements can only be made intelligible if we remember that although the family as such was not treated as a legal entity by the common law, which dealt only in individual property rights, landed society did nevertheless view property as ultimately belonging to the family in some moral sense, and the legal system reflected this.

The historical significance of the strict settlement appears beyond doubt even though, as Simpson acknowledges, its precise effects remain uncertain.

---

[1] [1999] 1 AC 293.

[2] Ibid, at 300. The effect of the decision was subsequently reversed by statute. For discussion of this, see Lee, 'Inheritance Tax: An Equitable Tax No Longer—Time for Abolition?' [2007] LS 678, 686.

[3] A simplified example of a typical strict settlement is outlined by Simpson, *A History of the Land Law* (2nd edn, 1986, pp 236–7).

[4] Ibid, p 209.

Simpson, *A History of the Land Law* (2nd edn, 1986, p 239)

> The strict settlement, by perpetuating and consolidating the wealth and power of the wealthy families, and by preserving their estates intact through the years, had an immense effect upon the social and political life of the country until very recent times. Precisely what effect is somewhat controversial. The settlement was the legal regime of the landed interest, powerful in both national and local political life; there is inevitably a problem in saying whether the legal institution was cause or effect of the political and social phenomenon. Death duties have in this century brought about the destruction of the social structure which the strict settlement enshrined, though the institution still lingers on.

As regards fiscal regulation, 'death duties' have been replaced by inheritance tax, which has retained disadvantageous treatment for successive interests. In particular, on the death of a lifetime beneficiary, inheritance tax is calculated on the basis that he or she was entitled to the entire estate.[5]

The decline in the significance of the strict settlement is mirrored by the growth of co-ownership. In modern law, co-ownership has superseded the strict settlement both in its social and economic importance. Despite the decline of the strict settlement, other instances of successive ownership remain of practical significance. A simple instance may arise in which, on the death of a sole owner, a home is left on trust for the deceased's spouse for life and thereafter to the couples' children.

3 FORMS OF SUCCESSIVE OWNERSHIP

Since the Trusts of Land and Appointment of Trustees Act 1996 (TOLATA 1996) came into force on 1 January 1997, trusts of successive interests take two principal forms: firstly, a legal estate in land may be held on trust for A for life, remainder to B; secondly, a legal estate may be held on trust for A for life and then revert back to the settlor of the trust.

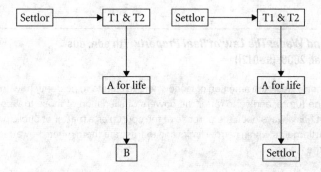

Figure 15 Successive interests in remainder and in reversion

In both examples, the trustees hold legal title as legal joint tenants.[6] A and B (in the first example), or A and the settlor (in the second example), have successive interests. In both

---

[5] Inheritance Tax Act 1984, s 49.

[6] Legal title is vested in the trustees under the scheme of regulation provided by the Trusts of Land and Appointment of Trustees Act 1996, which is examined in section 6 below. As has been seen in Chapter 19, section 2, legal co-owners are necessarily joint tenants.

examples, A has a life estate (or life interest) in possession. In the first, on A's death, the freehold estate is held on trust for B, who is described during A's life as having an interest 'in remainder'. This form of trust may be used, for example, on the settlor's death, to provide for his or her spouse for life and thereafter for their child.

In the second example, on A's death, the trust returns the freehold estate to the settlor. During A's life, the settlor is described as having an interest 'in reversion', because the estate will revert or return back to the settlor on A's death. Such a trust may be used, for example, to provide housing for an elderly relative.

In each example, on A's death, B's interest 'in remainder', or the settlor's interest 'in reversion', becomes an interest 'in possession'.

Numerous variations on these basic examples are possible. Hence, the settlor may declare him or herself trustee of the trust and the number of trustees may vary, subject to the maximum number of four legal owners.[7] The successive interests of A and B (or of A and the settlor) may be combined with co-ownership of their respective estates. For example, adapting the first example, the freehold estate may be held on trust for A and X for their lives (ending on the death of the longest surviving), with remainder to B and Y. More than one life estate may be granted in succession before the remainder or reversion. Hence, in a different variation of our first example, a settlor may create a trust for A (his or her child) for life, then to B (A's child) before granting the remainder to C. But attempts to use successive interests in this way to keep land within generations of a family are likely to fall foul of the rule against perpetuities.

3.1 THE RULE AGAINST PERPETUITIES

The rule against perpetuities places a limit on the period of time within which a future interest in property may vest or take effect, from the time of the disposition creating the interest. The rule is borne from an ongoing battle between settlors, who wish to continue to exercise control of their property from beyond the grave, and courts keen to ensure alienation of land.

Megarry and Wade: The Law of Real Property (7th edn, eds Harpum et al, 2008, [9–012])

It has commonly been the ambition of landowners to dictate to posterity how their land is to devolve in the future, and so to fetter the powers of alienation of those to whom they may give it; and it has always been the purpose of the courts, as a matter of public policy, to confine such settlements within narrow limits and to frustrate them when they attempt to reach too far into the future.

A full discussion of the rule against perpetuities, which applies both to trusts of land and those of personal property, lies beyond the scope of this book.[8]

---

[7] Trustee Act 1925, s 34(2). This provision is discussed in Chapter 19, section 2.

[8] A full account is provided in *Megarry and Wade: The Law of Real Property* (7th edn, Harpum et al, 2008, [9-012]–[9-136]); *Cheshire and Burn's Modern Law of Real Property* (17th edn, eds Burn and Cartwright, 2006, ch 16).

The Law Commission gives a useful outline of the rules. As it explains in the following extract, two sets of rules, in fact, exist. Which rules apply in a particular case is dependent on whether the instrument that creates the future interest took effect before or after the coming into force of the Perpetuities and Accumulations Act 1964. The operation of both sets of rules revolves around the identity of 'lives in being'. The relevant lives in being must be living or conceived at the time that the instrument takes effect. The settlor may identify them, in the absence of which they are determined by rules.

Law Commission Report No 251, *The Rules Against Perpetuities and Excessive Accumulations* (1998)

The rule against perpetuities has to be stated in two parts. For dispositions made before the 1964 Act came into force on 16 July 1964, the rule is as follows—

1. A future interest in any type of property will be void from the date that the instrument which attempts to create it takes effect, if there is any possibility that the interest *may* vest or commence outside the perpetuity period.

2. For these purposes, the perpetuity period consists of one or more lives in being plus a period of 21 years and, where relevant, a period of gestation.

Where an instrument creates a future interest after 15 July 1964—

1. that interest will only be void where it *must* vest or take effect (if at all) outside the perpetuity period;

2. it is therefore necessary to "wait and see", if need be for the whole perpetuity period, to determine whether the interest is valid; and

3. an alternative perpetuity period of up to 80 years may be employed instead of a life in being plus 21 years. [. . .]

The Perpetuities and Accumulations Act 1964 also introduced a number of measures to save gifts that would otherwise fail. The Law Commission considered that some form of perpetuities rule should continue to apply to successive interests in property. The Law Commission recommended replacing the current rules with a single period of 125 years, adopting the 'wait and see' principle. These recommendations have not, however, been implemented.

Smith states succinctly the practical impact of the current rules (assuming the application of the Perpetuities and Accumulations Act 1964) on an attempt to create successive interests in land.

Smith, *Plural Ownership* (2004, p 18)

In general terms, gifts to children of a living person are likely to be valid (so long as there is no age qualification greater than twenty-one years) but gifts to grandchildren of living persons are likely to be void. The possibilities may be regarded as preposterous by [the settlor], but that is irrelevant.

Hence, returning to our first example, a trust created by the settlor for A (his child) for life, remainder to B (A's child), is unproblematic, so long as B's interest is not made contingent or conditional on B reaching an age beyond 21 years. A variation of this example, extending the scope of the trust by a further generation to B's child, C, is, however, likely to fall foul of perpetuities. If it does, then the gift to C is void. But B's own life estate is not affected and, on B's death, the freehold reverts to the settlor of the trust. If the settlor is dead (as is likely in our example), the land passes under his or her will, or the rules governing intestacy.

3.2 ENTAILED INTERESTS

A third form of successive ownership is the 'entailed interest'. The TOLATA 1996 prohibits the creation of new entailed interests, although those in existence remain unaffected by that Act.[9]

The entailed interest is an estate in land that passes successively through direct lineal descendants. It represents the clearest attempt to keep land tied up for future generations. In this respect, its chief advantage over the creation of successive life interests is that the entail lies outside the scope of the rule against perpetuities. In its most traditional form, the entailed interest follows the primogeniture principles exemplified by the passing of the British Crown: from eldest surviving son to eldest surviving son, passing to the eldest surviving daughter only where there is no male heir. Variations may limit the estate to the male or female line.

4 THE NATURE OF THE LIFE ESTATE

Central to successive ownership is the existence of a life estate. As has been seen in Chapter 3, an estate denotes the period of time for which rights of ownership are enjoyed in relation to land. A life estate therefore denotes a period of ownership measured by the life of the party entitled in possession. A life estate can exist only in equity and is given effect under a trust of the legal title.[10] Since the coming into force of the 1996 Act, the trust is a trust of land, and the rights and duties of the trustees and beneficiaries are governed by the terms of that Act. These have been discussed in Chapter 19 and their specific application to successive ownership trusts is highlighted in section 6 below.

The limited nature and uncertain duration of the life estate impact both the rights of the beneficiary and the commercial value of the estate. The nature of a life estate can be understood by analogy with a trust of money. If trustees hold £100,000 on trust for A for life, remainder to B, then A and B's rights are located respectively in the income generated from the fund (A) and the capital sum on A's death (B). In essence, the same distinction between income and capital denotes the respective rights of A and B where the trust consists of land. A alone is entitled in possession of the land (akin to the income) for his or her life. A's right to possession may be enjoyed through physical occupation, or through receipt of rents and profits generated from the land. If the land is sold, then A is entitled to the income generated from the proceeds of sale. The land (the capital) or the proceeds of sale of the land must, however, be preserved for B. A's life estate is a property right, with which A is free to deal in

---

[9] Trusts of Land and Appointment of Trustees Act 1996, Sch 1, para 5. Whether the provision does, in fact, prevent the creation of new entailed interests is doubted by Pascoe, 'Solicitors: Be Bold: Create Entailed Interests' [2001] Conv 396.

[10] Law of Property Act 1925, s 1(1), provides that only the freehold and leasehold estates are capable of existing at law. By virtue of s 1(3), all other estates are equitable. This provision is discussed in Chapter 3.

the same way as any other estate in land: for example, A can sell his or her life estate, transfer it as a gift, or use it as security for a loan. Practically, however, the uncertain duration of the estate imposes a limit on its commercial value. Where a life estate is sold or transferred to a third party, the purchaser or transferee is described as holding an estate *pur autre vie* (for the life of another).

McCaffery compares the rights of the holder of a life estate with those of the holder of the freehold by reference to six incidents of ownership identified by Pound. (The numbers listed in the extract below refer to the six rights of ownership listed by Pound.)

McCaffery, 'Must We Have a Right to Waste?' in *New Essays in the Legal and Political Theory of Property* (ed Munzer, 2001, p 79)

Most of the six rights readily extend to a life estate owner, or to any other present interest of limited duration. A life estate holder can possess the property (1), exclude others from it (2), dispose of her life estate (3), use the property (4), and enjoy its fruits or profits (5). One can think of these as the present-oriented rights of ownership, for they use or affect the present interest.

A fee simple absolute adds but two powers to the life estate. One is the power to direct where the property is to go on the termination of the life estate: that is, a *jus disponendi* (3) as to the remainder, or future, interest. Two is the *jus abutendi* or right of waste (6). We could add a third difference—the right to sell or alienate the entire estate in fee simple absolute. But although the ability to sell the whole property is of immense practical importance, it is entailed in the rights set out above. One can sell what one has. A life estate owner already has the *jus disponendi* as to her life estate. What she lacks is the right of disposition as to the remainder, which, when combined with what it is that she does have, would give her a right of disposing of the whole.

This all follows from the fact that the fee simple absolute owner owns the remainder interest, but the life estate holder does not. The *jus disponendi* as to the whole and the *jus abutendi* are rights that affect the remainder interest as well as the present one—one can think of them as the future-oriented rights of ownership. Under a life estate conception of ownership, the property holder cannot waste the property or direct where the remainder is to go.

One of the key differences between the estates therefore consists in what McCaffery refers to as the 'right to waste'. The purpose of McCaffery's essay is to encourage a rethinking of ownership in which a life estate is seen as an attractive form.[11] In this respect, he argues that a right to waste should not be recognized.[12] As McCaffery notes,[13] waste is usually understood in the negative, as a doctrine *against* waste. Waste generally denotes an act or omission that affects the value of the freehold (negatively or positively), or changes the nature of the land.[14] Historically, waste determined the rights of the holder of a life estate, together with the relationship between him or her and the holder of the interest in remainder or reversion. The holder of a life estate would be liable to the holder of the estate in remainder or reversion for some types of waste (for example, conduct that reduces the value of the land),

---

[11] McCaffery, 'Must We Have a Right to Waste?' in *New Essays in the Legal and Political Theory of Property* (ed Munzer, 2001, pp 78–9).

[12] Ibid, p 105.

[13] Ibid, p 84.

[14] McCaffery's own concept of waste is broader: ibid, p 77.

but not others (including permissive waste, resulting from an omission to keep the land in good repair).[15]

In modern law, the provisions of the TOLATA 1996 govern the relationship between the parties. The broad powers of management conferred on trustees appear effectively to preclude resort to the law of waste.[16]

5 THE CREATION OF SUCCESSIVE INTERESTS

Successive interests take effect under a trust and can be created in the same way as any other trust of land. Hence, a successive ownership trust can be created expressly through compliance with s 53(1)(b) of the Law of Property Act 1925 (LPA 1925), which requires the declaration of trust to be evidenced in writing, signed by the settlor, or through a validly executed will. Successive interest trusts may also arise impliedly: for example, through a common intention constructive trust of the type that we have considered in Chapter 18 in relation to co-ownership.

As we have seen in Chapter 18, the elements of the common intention trust are an agreement to share beneficial ownership, coupled with detrimental reliance on the part of the claimant. In most cases, the agreement to share will reflect an intention to co-own the home, but, exceptionally, an agreement will be consistent with successive ownership.

Ungurian v Lesnoff [1990] Ch 206, HC

Facts: At the time that the relevant facts took place, Poland was under Communist rule. Mrs Lesnoff, a Polish national, gave up her Polish nationality, a flat in Poland in which she could have remained in occupation for her life, and her career, to move to London to live with Mr Ungurian. The couple lived in a house, registered in Mr Ungurian's sole name, together with Mrs Lesnoff's sons and one of Mr Ungurian's sons, Paul. During the course of the parties' four-year relationship, Mrs Lesnoff carried out considerable improvements to the property. On the breakdown of the relationship, Mrs Lesnoff argued that the house was held on trust for her or, at the least, that she was entitled to remain in occupation for her life.

Vinelott J

At 223–4

In summary, therefore, I am not satisfied that the house was bought by Mr. Ungurian with the intention that it would belong to Mrs. Lesnoff, either immediately or when she gave up her flat in Poland and obtained permission to live permanently abroad; but I am satisfied that it was bought with the common intention that Mrs. Lesnoff would be entitled to live there with her children, sharing it with Mr. Ungurian when he was in England, and with any of his children who were here for the purpose of being educated. I am satisfied that Mrs. Lesnoff went through with this plan, initiated in Beirut and later elaborated, in the expectation that Mr. Ungurian would provide her with a secure home and that she burnt her boats by giving up her flat in Wraclow

---

[15] A brief summary is provided by Smith, *Plural Ownership* (2004, p 20).

[16] Ibid, pp 20–1.

in the belief that he had done so. The question is whether these facts, and the work subsequently done by Mrs. Lesnoff, give rise, either to a constructive trust under which Mrs. Lesnoff became entitled to a beneficial interest in the house, or to a licence to reside, or to an estoppel preventing Mr. Ungurian from denying her right to reside in the house. [...]

In my judgment, the inference to be drawn from the circumstances in which the property was purchased and the subsequent conduct of the parties—the intention to be attributed to them—is that Mrs. Lesnoff was to have the right to reside in the house during her life. It would be to that extent her house, and although the expectation was that Mr. Ungurian would live there with her when he was in England, and that Paul, and possibly in due course his younger son also, would be accommodated there while they were being educated, that result would flow from the continued relationship between Mrs. Lesnoff and Mr. Ungurian and would be dependent on it. It must be borne in mind that Mr. Ungurian was a man of considerable means with flats in Beirut, Amman and Switzerland. He was providing a house as a home for a woman much younger than himself who would be likely to survive him. I do not think that full effect would be given to this common intention by inferring no more than an irrevocable licence to occupy the house. I think the legal consequences which flow from the intention to be imputed to the parties was that Mr. Ungurian held the house on trust to permit Mrs. Lesnoff to reside in it during her life unless and until Mr. Ungurian, with her consent, sold the property and bought another residence for her in substitution for it.

The factual background to *Ungurian v Lesnoff* is unusual. The extreme lengths required of Mrs Lesnoff to be able to leave Poland during the time of Communist rule highlighted her particular need for security of accommodation. The case also illustrates that there are different ways in which occupation for life can be given effect. Vinelott J notes the possibility of finding a constructive trust, a licence, or a claim to estoppel. As regards estoppel, if Vinelott J were to have found that Mr Ungurian was estopped from denying Mrs Lesnoff a right to reside, he would then have had a discretion as to the appropriate remedy to award in satisfaction of the claim.[17] The remedy could take the form, for example, of a licence or a trust. Lifetime occupation may also be given effect through the grant of a lease, with provision for the lease to be terminated on an individual's death.[18]

Prior to the TOLATA 1996, the informal creation of a life estate gave rise to a trust governed by the Settled Land Act 1925. Such a trust was imposed in *Ungurian v Lesnoff*. The effect of the Settled Land Act 1925 is considered in section 6 below. It is sufficient to note that it conferred upon the holder of the life estate greater powers of management over the land than may have been appropriate.[19] The TOLATA 1996 has superseded that legislation. That Act removes the difficulties encountered under the Settled Land Act 1925 and the informal creation of a successive ownership trust is therefore less problematic. But the question still arises whether a life estate, licence, or lease is the most appropriate means of securing occupation for life. As Table 4 shows, each differs as regards the method of creation and the extent of security conferred on the occupier.

[17] The nature of the courts' discretion is considered in Chapter 13.

[18] A lease 'for life' is not itself valid, because a lease must have a fixed maximum duration. This requirement is considered in Chapter 23.

[19] A full discussion of the debate surrounding the application of the Settled Land Act 1925 to life occupancy is now largely of historical interest. Useful discussions of *Ungurian v Lesnoff* [1990] Ch 206 that highlight the issues are provided by Hill, 'The Settled Land Act 1925: Unresolved Problems' (1991) 107 LQR 596, 596–600, and Sparkes, 'Beneficial Interest or Licence for Life' [1990] Conv 223. For discussion of the earlier case law, see Hornby, 'Tenancy or Life or Licence' (1977) 93 LQR 561.

Table 4 Legal mechanisms to provide occupation and/or ownership of land for life

	Life estate	Licence to occupy for life	Lease determinable on death
Legal status	Proprietary estate—equitable, given effect under trust	Personal	Proprietary—legal or equitable
Duration	Life	Life	Fixed term, with provision for determination by freeholder (landlord) on tenant's death
Creation	Express trust (during settlor's lifetime or by will) Implied trust, e.g. constructive trust	No specific formality requirements	Legal—dependent on duration of fixed term, but likely to require deed and registration (Law of Property Act 1925, ss 52 and 54; Land Registration Act 2002, s.4) Equitable—through existence of valid contract to create a lease, in compliance with Law of Property (Miscellaneous Provisions) Act 1989, s 2 *See discussion of lease formalities in Chapter 23*
Enforcement against third parties	Overreached on sale if requirements of overreaching are met. Possible enforcement only if not overreached: • registered land—possible protection as an overriding interest within Land Registration Act 2002, Sch 3, para 2; • unregistered land—doctrine of notice.	Not enforceable against third parties, but note possible imposition of constructive trust on sale *See Chapter 8*	Registered land—dependent on duration of fixed term, but possible entry as Land Registry notice (Land Registration Act 2002, ss 32 and 33(b)), or protection as an overriding interest within Land Registration Act 2002, Sch 3, paras 1 and 2

	Life estate	Licence to occupy for life	Lease determinable on death
	See Chapters 15, 16, and 20		Unregistered land— legal lease binds all purchasers; equitable lease, an estate contract governed by Land Charges Act 1972, Class C(iv) *See Chapters 15 and 16*
Principal source of regulation	Trusts of Land and Appointment of Trustees Act 1996 *See Chapter 19 and section 6 below*	Personal agreement	Terms of lease/implied covenants *See Chapter 25*

6 REGULATION OF SUCCESSIVE OWNERSHIP

Prior to the TOLATA 1996, trusts involving successive ownership were generally regulated by the Settled Land Act 1925. That Act applied to all instances of successive ownership (whether created through an express trust or arising informally through, for example, a constructive trust)[20] unless the trust was expressly created as a trust for sale.[21] One of the key aims of the 1996 Act was to provide a single scheme of regulation for all trusts of land, including both co-ownership and successive ownership trusts.[22] The scheme of regulation under the Settled Land Act 1925 differed from the trust for sale as regards the *location* of the legal title and powers of management over the land.[23] In a trust for sale—and, now, under a trust of land—legal title is vested in the trustees, who exercise powers of management. Under the Settled Land Act 1925, legal title and the powers of management were vested in the 'tenant for life'—that is, the beneficiary currently entitled in possession.[24] The trustees of the settlement exercised specific functions (including executing a deed of discharge on the termination of the settlement), received and held capital moneys on sale, and played a general supervisory role.[25]

---

[20] The application of the Settled Land Act 1925 to informal trusts was controversial, because it circumvented the strict formality requirements otherwise specified in s 4 of the Act. But *Ungurian v Lesnoff* [1990] Ch 206 is one of a number of cases in which the Act was applied to an informally created settlement. For further discussion of this point, see the literature listed at fn 19 above.

[21] Settled Land Act 1925, s 1(1) and (7).

[22] Law Commission Report No 181, *Transfer of Land: Trusts of Land* (1989, [1.4]).

[23] The content of the powers was the same, because trustees for sale were conferred with the same powers of management as a tenant for life in relation to land held on trust: Law of Property Act 1925, s 28(1) (repealed by the Trusts of Land and Appointment of Trustees Act 1996).

[24] Settled Land Act 1925, s 19(1). Where the beneficiary was a minor, the powers of management were vested in other persons by s 26.

[25] For a full list of the functions of trustees of the settlement, see *Megarry and Wade* (2008, [A-092]).

This scheme of regulation was subject to specific criticism for the position of the tenant for life.

Law Commission Report No 181, *Transfer of Land: Trusts of Land*
(1989, [1.3], citing Law Commission Working Paper No 94,
Trusts of Land, 1985, [3.16])

Conflict of interest. It has been suggested that there is an inherent conflict involved in the position of the tenant for life. The legal estate and all the powers of dealing with it are vested in him and under s.16 of the Settled Land Act 1925 he is a trustee. Yet he is, at the same time, the principal beneficiary. While it is quite usual for a trustee to be a beneficiary, given the lack of any other restraints on the tenant's powers, the conflict may become real. It seems that where there is a conflict of interests, the tenant of life is not treated like an ordinary trustee. It has been held that the court will not intervene if the tenant for life allows the estate to become derelict, but only if there is evidence that he has refused to exercise his powers. Thus the remaindermen may inherit an estate much diminished in value and have no remedy. Similarly the interests of the remaindermen may be adversely affected by a sale of the settled land at a low price. Again, they may have no effective remedy as they may not discover the sale until years after it took place and, even if they could establish a breach of trust, the tenant for life may be dead and his estate not worth suing. While it is clear that the courts, recognising the risks arising from conflicts of interest, usually make the purchase of trust property by a trustee virtually impossible, in one case where the tenant for life purchased the settled land without the proper procedure being adopted, the sale was simply allowed to stand.

Successive ownership trusts created on or after the commencement of the TOLATA 1996 are trusts of land and are within the scheme of regulation provided by that Act.[26] Successive ownership trusts that were in existence on the date of commencement of that Act, and which were governed by the Settled Land Act 1925 at that time, remain regulated by the 1925 Act.[27] Hence the 1925 Act has not been repealed, but it is in the process of being phased out.

The scheme of regulation provided under the 1996 Act has been examined in Chapter 19 in the context of co-ownership trusts. It has been seen that the Act confers certain powers on the trustees as regards the management and sale of the land, and confers rights on the beneficiaries. A full discussion of the trustees' powers and the beneficiaries' rights is provided in Chapter 19, sections 5.2 and 5.3; in this chapter, it is necessary only to outline how these powers and rights apply in the specific context of successive ownership.

Under the 1996 Act, the legal title and powers of management are vested in the trustees of land. This removes the conflict of interest for the beneficiary entitled in possession created by the Settled Land Act 1925. As we have seen in Chapter 19, section 5.2, trustees of land are vested with '*all the powers of an absolute owner*'. These powers must be exercised with regard to the rights of the beneficiaries (s 6(5) of the 1996 Act) and in a manner that is consistent with any other enactment or rule of law or equity (s 6(6)). The settlor of an express trust may also impose limitations on the trustees' powers.[28]

---

[26] Trusts of Land and Appointment of Trustees Act 1996, s 1(2)(a) and (3).

[27] Successive ownership trusts expressly created as a trust for sale prior to the commencement of the 1996 Act, like all express trusts for sale, became trusts of land on 1 January 1997: Trusts of Land and Appointment of Trustees Act 1996, s 1(2)(b).

[28] Ibid, s 8.

The courts have not yet considered the application of these provisions in the context of successive ownership. It is suggested that difficulties may arise in applying the general limitations on trustees' powers in the context of successive owners: what 'rights' are enjoyed by beneficiaries whose interest is in remainder or reversion? We have seen, in Chapter 19, section 5.3, that the 1996 Act confers two key rights on beneficiaries: a right to be consulted by the trustees, and a right to occupy the trust land. These rights are conferred on those beneficiaries who are '*beneficially entitled to an interest in possession in the land*'.[29] Hence, these rights are limited to the holder(s) of the life estate in possession, to the exclusion of those whose interest is in reversion or remainder. The rights of beneficiaries to which the trustees must have regard in the exercise of their powers by virtue of s 6(5) are not necessarily confined to the rights conferred by the Act.[30] There is, however, no clear source of rights outside of the 1996 Act, beyond any specific rights that may be conferred by the settlor of an express trust. Beneficiaries with an interest in remainder or reversion may have to rely on the general equitable duties imposed on trustees, to which the trustees must have regard through s 6(6), in order to safeguard their interest.

We have seen, in Chapter 19, section 5.4, that disputes relating to the exercise of powers by trustees may be referred to the court on an application under s 14 of the 1996 Act. An application may be made (amongst others) by '*any person who* [...] *has an interest in property subject to a trust of land*'. This provision is not confined to parties with an interest in possession. Therefore, a beneficiary with an interest in remainder or reversion may bring an application to court under s 14: for example, this would enable such a beneficiary to bring an action to challenge a decision by the trustees to sell the land. But it remains open to question how much emphasis the courts will place on the wishes of a beneficiary with an interest in remainder or reversion. Although not exhaustive of the factors that may be taken into account by the court, s 15(3) directs the court to consider the wishes of beneficiaries with an interest in possession.

QUESTIONS

1. Compare and contrast successive ownership and concurrent ownership. While both take effect under a trust regulated by the Trusts of Land and Appointment of Trustees Act 1996, what differences may remain in the application of that Act to each type of trust?

2. When might it be appropriate to confer: (i) a life estate; (ii) a licence to occupy; and (iii) a lease determinable on death?

FURTHER READING

Cheshire and Burn's Modern Law of Real Property (17th edn, eds Burn and Cartwright, Oxford: OUP, 2006, ch 16)

---

[29] Ibid, ss 11(1)(a) and 12(1). (The right to be consulted is further limited by s 11(1)(a) to beneficiaries of full age.)

[30] See the annotation to ibid, s 6(5), by Kenny and Kenny, in *Current Law Statutes* (1997). The annotation suggests that the 'rights' referred to would include those conferred by the settlor of the trust. This implicitly accepts that the rights of the beneficiaries to which the trustees are to have regard are not confined to those conferred by the Act.

Law Commission Report No 251, *The Rules Against Perpetuities and Excessive Accumulations* (1998)

McCaffery, 'Must We Have a Right to Waste?' in *New Essays in the Legal and Political Theory of Property* (ed Munzer, Cambridge: CUP, 2001)

Simpson, *A History of the Land Law* (2nd edn, Oxford: OUP, 1986)

Smith, *Plural Ownership* (Oxford: OUP, 2004, ch 2)

PART D

LEASES

23

THE LEASE

CENTRAL ISSUES

1. Over the next three chapters, we will examine the lease in detail. In this chapter, we will concentrate on a key feature of a lease: its ability to count as a property right. We will look at the three principal questions that apply to any property right: the *content* question (when will B's right count as a lease?); the *acquisition* question (how can B acquire a lease?); and the *defences* question (if B has a lease of A's land, when can C, a party later acquiring a right from A, have a defence to B's lease?). In considering the *content* question, we will see how a lease differs from a licence (see Chapter 8 for an examination of licences).

2. Before examining those questions, we will consider why B may wish to show that he or she has a lease. One important consequence of having a legal or equitable lease, of course, is that such a right is capable of binding C, a third party who later acquires a right from A. In addition, if B can show that he or she has a lease, this may mean that additional duties are imposed on A: in particular, such duties may be imposed by statutes that provide protection to B *if* B has a lease.

3. In Chapter 24, we will consider in more detail the statutory protection potentially available to B if he or she has a lease. We will see there that, in some cases, B can be seen as having a lease (at least, in the sense used by a particular statute) even if B has no property right. This suggests that there are two sorts of leases: a proprietary lease, and a non-proprietary lease. In this chapter, we will concentrate on the former type of lease and will see if the judges' approach to defining the content of a proprietary lease may have been influenced by the presence of such statutory protection.

4. A lease, in the sense of a property right, will often arise as part of an agreement imposing a number of duties on both A and B. In some cases, those duties, even if positive, can bind not only A and B, but also parties later acquiring the rights of A and B. We will examine this phenomenon in Chapter 25, by looking at the concept of a leasehold covenant. In Chapter 24, we will consider in more detail the statutory protection potentially available to B if he or she has a lease. In this chapter, we will see how the judges' approach

to defining the content of a lease *as a property right* may have been influenced by the presence of such statutory protection.

5. The content of a lease can be simply defined: B has a lease if he or she has a right to exclusive possession of land for a limited period. In practice, however, there may be difficulties in applying this simple test: for example, how should we deal with cases in which B1 and B2 occupy land together? And what is the effect of a term inserted by A into an occupation agreement with B with the sole purpose of denying B exclusive possession of land?

6. In considering the *acquisition* and *defences* questions, we will see the impact of the Land Registration Act 2002 on leases. We considered the

general effect of that Act in Chapters 16 and 17. When considering the *acquisition* and *defences* questions, we will also need to bear in mind the possibility of B's having an equitable, rather than a legal, lease.

7. Finally, in section 5 below, we will consider a recurrent debate about the conceptual nature of a lease: should it be seen as primarily a contractual right, or, instead, as primarily a property right? It will be suggested that the debate rests on a misconception: there is no reason why a right cannot be both contractual—that is, acquired as a result of a contractual agreement between A and B—and also proprietary—that is, having a content that means it can count as a legal property right.

1 INTRODUCTION: THE IMPORTANCE OF THE LEASE

1.1 THE EFFECT OF A LEASE

Imagine a case in which A, who holds a registered legal estate in land, makes a contractual agreement with B. A promises to allow B to occupy A's land for a year; in return, B promises to pay A £200 a week. In such a case, B clearly has a permission to use A's land: he or she has, at the very least, a contractual licence (see Chapter 8, section 3). Why might B want to claim that his or her agreement with A instead gives him or her a lease of A's land?

We can answer this question by considering three different types of situation, matching the different situations that we examined in Chapter 8 when considering the effect of a licence. In the first set of situations, B wants to make a claim against A. In the second set of situations, B wants to make a claim against X, a stranger who has not acquired a right in A's land, but who has, in some way, interfered with B's use of that land. In the third set, B wants to make a claim against C, a third party who has acquired a right in A's land.

1.1.1 The effect of a lease on A

In Chapter 8, section 3.1, we saw that, even if B has a contractual licence rather than a lease, his or her position as against A is fairly secure. In our example in which A has promised to allow B to occupy A's land for a year, it is quite possible that, if A were to threaten to remove B early, B could obtain a court order preventing A from thus breaching his or her contractual duty to B.[1] Nonetheless, if B can show he or she has acquired a lease, A may come under *extra* duties to B, going beyond the express terms of the parties' agreement.

Firstly, if B has a lease, A and B can be said to be in a 'landlord–tenant relationship'. The common law may then impose particular duties on the parties, even if they did not expressly undertake those duties when making their contractual agreement. These implied duties are, however, very limited:[2] for example, B has a duty not permanently to alter the physical character of the land;[3] and A's implied duties include a duty to allow B 'quiet enjoyment' of the land, meaning that A has a duty not to interfere physically with B's expected use of the land, or to interfere substantially with B's enjoyment of the land.

Secondly, and much more importantly in practice, particular statutes may operate to impose duties on A *if and only if* A has given B a lease. We will look at the scope of this statutory protection in more detail in Chapter 24, but its existence is crucial to understanding the context of a number of cases that we will examine in this chapter.

It is certainly apparent in the case from which the following extract is taken. The extract given below is a long one, but the length of the extract is commensurate with the importance of the decision. Lord Templeman's analysis provides the key starting point for any attempt to define the content of a lease or to distinguish a lease from a contractual licence.

Street v Mountford [1985] AC 809, HL

Facts: Roger Street, a solicitor from Bournemouth, owned No 5, St Clement's Gardens, Boscombe. On 7 March 1983, he entered a signed written agreement with Wendy Mountford, allowing her a right to exclusive occupation of two rooms in that house (Rooms 5 and 6). Under the terms of the agreement, Mrs Mountford was under a duty to pay £37 a week to Mr Street and either party was free was to terminate the agreement by giving fourteen days' notice. The agreement described itself throughout as a licence: for example, the £37 payment was described as a 'licence fee'. Under the terms of the Rent Act 1977, if the agreement gave Mrs Mountford a lease, then Mr Street was obliged to accept whatever rent was set as a fair rent by an independent officer or tribunal. Mrs Mountford claimed that the agreement did, indeed, give her a lease and applied for a fair rent to be assessed. Mr Street then applied to the county court for a declaration that Mrs Mountford had only a licence. If it were found that Mrs Mountford had a lease, the Rent Act 1977 would also limit the grounds on which Mr Street could end her occupation and would thus prevent him bringing her occupation to an end by simply giving fourteen days' notice. The county court judge found that Mrs Mountford did, indeed, have a lease. The Court of Appeal upheld Mr Street's appeal, on the basis that the written agreement made clear that Mr Street did not intend to grant Mrs Mountford a lease. But the House of Lords held that, the contrary intention notwithstanding, the agreement between Mr Street and Mrs Mountford did give her a lease. Lord Templeman, with whom all of their Lordships agreed, gave the only reasoned speech. In it, the term 'tenancy' is used interchangeably with 'lease'.

---

[1] See, e.g., *Verrall v Great Yarmouth Borough Council* [1981] QB 202, although note *Thompson v Park* [1944] KB 408. Both cases are discussed in Chapter 8, section 3.1.2.

[2] Judges in other jurisdictions have been more willing to impose duties on A: see, e.g., *Javins v First National Realty* (1970) 428 F 2d 1071 (District of Columbia Court of Appeals). For a comparison between the English and US approaches, see Bright, *Landlord and Tenant Law in Context* (2007, pp 30–5).

[3] See, e.g., *Marsden v Edward Heyes* [1927] 2 KB 1, applying *Horsefall v Mather* (1815) Holt NP 7.

Lord Templeman

At 814

A tenancy is a term of years absolute. This expression, by section 205(1)(xxvii) of the Law of Property Act 1925, reproducing the common law, includes a term from week to week in possession at a rent and liable to determination by notice or re-entry. Originally a term of years was not an estate in land, the lessee having merely a personal action against his lessor. But a legal estate in leaseholds was created by the Statute of Gloucester 1278 and the Act of 1529 21 Hen. VIII, c. 15. Now by section 1 of the Law of Property Act 1925 a term of years absolute is an estate in land capable of subsisting as a legal estate. In the present case if the agreement dated 7 March 1983 created a tenancy, Mrs. Mountford having entered into possession and made weekly payments acquired a legal estate in land. If the agreement is a tenancy, the occupation of Mrs. Mountford is protected by the Rent Acts.

A licence in connection with land while entitling the licensee to use the land for the purposes authorised by the licence does not create an estate in the land. If the agreement dated 7 March 1983 created a licence for Mrs. Mountford to occupy the premises, she did not acquire any estate in the land. If the agreement is a licence then Mrs. Mountford's right of occupation is not protected by the Rent Acts. Hence the practical importance of distinguishing between a tenancy and a licence.

At 816–9

On behalf of Mrs. Mountford her counsel, Mr. Hicks Q.C., seeks to reaffirm and re-establish the traditional view that an occupier of land for a term at a rent is a tenant providing the occupier is granted exclusive possession. It is conceded on behalf of Mr. Street that the agreement dated 7 March 1983 granted exclusive possession to Mrs. Mountford. The traditional view that the grant of exclusive possession for a term at a rent creates a tenancy is consistent with the elevation of a tenancy into an estate in land. The tenant possessing exclusive possession is able to exercise the rights of an owner of land, which is in the real sense his land albeit temporarily and subject to certain restrictions. A tenant armed with exclusive possession can keep out strangers and keep out the landlord unless the landlord is exercising limited rights reserved to him by the tenancy agreement to enter and view and repair. A licensee lacking exclusive possession can in no sense call the land his own and cannot be said to own any estate in the land. The licence does not create an estate in the land to which it relates but only makes an act lawful which would otherwise be unlawful.

On behalf of Mr. Street his counsel, Mr. Goodhart Q.C., relies on recent authorities which, he submits, demonstrate that an occupier granted exclusive possession for a term at a rent may nevertheless be a licensee if, in the words of Slade L.J. in the present case:

'there is manifested the clear intention of both parties that the rights granted are to be merely those of a personal right of occupation and not those of a tenant.'[4]

My Lords, there is no doubt that the traditional distinction between a tenancy and a licence of land lay in the grant of land for a term at a rent with exclusive possession. In some cases it was not clear at first sight whether exclusive possession was in fact granted. For example, an owner of land could grant a licence to cut and remove standing timber. Alternatively the owner could grant a tenancy of the land with the right to cut and remove standing timber during the term of the tenancy. The grant of rights relating to standing timber therefore required careful consideration in order to decide whether the grant conferred exclusive possession of

---

4 [1985] 49 P & CR 324, 332.

the land for a term at a rent and was therefore a tenancy or whether it merely conferred a bare licence to remove the timber [...]

In the case of residential accommodation there is no difficulty in deciding whether the grant confers exclusive possession. An occupier of residential accommodation at a rent for a term is either a lodger or a tenant. The occupier is a lodger if the landlord provides attendance or services which require the landlord or his servants to exercise unrestricted access to and use of the premises. A lodger is entitled to live in the premises but cannot call the place his own. In *Allan v. Liverpool Overseers* Blackburn J. said:[5]

'A lodger in a house, although he has the exclusive use of rooms in the house, in the sense that nobody else is to be there, and though his goods are stowed there, yet he is not in exclusive occupation in that sense, because the landlord is there for the purpose of being able, as landlords commonly do in the case of lodgings, to have his own servants to look after the house and the furniture, and has retained to himself the occupation, though he has agreed to give the exclusive enjoyment of the occupation to the lodger.'

If on the other hand residential accommodation is granted for a term at a rent with exclusive possession, the landlord providing neither attendance nor services, the grant is a tenancy; any express reservation to the landlord of limited rights to enter and view the state of the premises and to repair and maintain the premises only serves to emphasise the fact that the grantee is entitled to exclusive possession and is a tenant. In the present case it is conceded that Mrs. Mountford is entitled to exclusive possession and is not a lodger. Mr. Street provided neither attendance nor services and only reserved the limited rights of inspection and maintenance and the like set forth in clause 3 of the agreement. On the traditional view of the matter, Mrs. Mountford not being a lodger must be a tenant.

There can be no tenancy unless the occupier enjoys exclusive possession; but an occupier who enjoys exclusive possession is not necessarily a tenant. He may be owner in fee simple, a trespasser, a mortgagee in possession, an object of charity or a service occupier. To constitute a tenancy the occupier must be granted exclusive possession for a fixed or periodic term certain in consideration of a premium or periodical payments. The grant may be express, or may be inferred where the owner accepts weekly or other periodical payments from the occupier.

In the present case, the agreement dated 7 March 1983 professed an intention by both parties to create a licence and their belief that they had in fact created a licence. It was submitted on behalf of Mr. Street that the court cannot in these circumstances decide that the agreement created a tenancy without interfering with the freedom of contract enjoyed by both parties. My Lords, Mr. Street enjoyed freedom to offer Mrs. Mountford the right to occupy the rooms comprised in the agreement on such lawful terms as Mr. Street pleased. Mrs. Mountford enjoyed freedom to negotiate with Mr. Street to obtain different terms. Both parties enjoyed freedom to contract or not to contract and both parties exercised that freedom by contracting on the terms set forth in the written agreement and on no other terms. But the consequences in law of the agreement, once concluded, can only be determined by consideration of the effect of the agreement. If the agreement satisfied all the requirements of a tenancy, then the agreement produced a tenancy and the parties cannot alter the effect of the agreement by insisting that they only created a licence. The manufacture of a five-pronged implement for manual digging results in a fork even if the manufacturer, unfamiliar with the English language, insists that he intended to make and has made a spade.

It was also submitted that in deciding whether the agreement created a tenancy or a licence, the court should ignore the Rent Acts. If Mr. Street has succeeded, where owners

5 (1874) LR 9 QB 180, 191–2.

have failed these past 70 years, in driving a coach and horses through the Rent Acts, he must be left to enjoy the benefit of his ingenuity unless and until Parliament intervenes. I accept that the Rent Acts are irrelevant to the problem of determining the legal effect of the rights granted by the agreement. Like the professed intention of the parties, the Rent Acts cannot alter the effect of the agreement.

At 826–7

My Lords, the only intention which is relevant is the intention demonstrated by the agreement to grant exclusive possession for a term at a rent. Sometimes it may be difficult to discover whether, on the true construction of an agreement, exclusive possession is conferred. Sometimes it may appear from the surrounding circumstances that there was no intention to create legal relationships. Sometimes it may appear from the surrounding circumstances that the right to exclusive possession is referable to a legal relationship other than a tenancy. Legal relationships to which the grant of exclusive possession might be referable and which would or might negative the grant of an estate or interest in the land include occupancy under a contract for the sale of the land, occupancy pursuant to a contract of employment or occupancy referable to the holding of an office. But where as in the present case the only circumstances are that residential accommodation is offered and accepted with exclusive possession for a term at a rent, the result is a tenancy.

The position was well summarised by Windeyer J. sitting in the High Court of Australia in *Radaich v. Smith* where he said:[6]

'What then is the fundamental right which a tenant has that distinguishes his position from that of a licensee? It is an interest in land as distinct from a personal permission to enter the land and use it for some stipulated purpose or purposes. And how is it to be ascertained whether such an interest in land has been given? By seeing whether the grantee was given a legal right of exclusive possession of the land for a term or from year to year or for a life or lives. If he was, he is a tenant. And he cannot be other than a tenant, because a legal right of exclusive possession is a tenancy and the creation of such a right is a demise. To say that a man who has by agreement with a landlord, a right of exclusive possession of land for a term is not a tenant is simply to contradict the first proposition by the second. A right of exclusive possession is secured by the right of a lessee to maintain ejectment and, after his entry, trespass. A reservation to the landlord, either by contract or statute, of a limited right of entry, as for example to view or repair, is, of course, not inconsistent with the grant of exclusive possession. Subject to such reservations, a tenant for a term or from year to year or for a life or lives can exclude his landlord as well as strangers from the demised premises. All this is long established law [. . .]'

My Lords, I gratefully adopt the logic and the language of Windeyer J. Henceforth the courts which deal with these problems will, save in exceptional circumstances, only be concerned to inquire whether as a result of an agreement relating to residential accommodation the occupier is a lodger or a tenant. In the present case I am satisfied that Mrs. Mountford is a tenant, that the appeal should be allowed, that the order of the Court of Appeal should be set aside and that [Mr Street] should be ordered to pay the costs of [Mrs Mountford] here and below.

In *Street v Mountford*, Lord Templeman thus set out a seemingly simple test for the existence of a lease: B can only have a lease if he or she has exclusive possession of land for a term (i.e. for a limited period). In the extract above, Lord Templeman does refer to the payment of

---

[6] (1959) 101 CLR 209, 222.

rent: nothing turned on that in *Street* itself and, as we will see in section 1.1.2 below, it is now accepted that B can have a lease even if no rent is paid. We will examine the content of a lease and Lord Templeman's test in more detail in section 2 below.

Street also raises the important question of whether and, if so, how the courts' approach to defining a lease has been affected by the fact that various forms of statutory protection are, or have been, available *only* in cases in which B has a lease. This question may raise the tension between *doctrine* and *utility* that we considered in Chapter 1, section 5.2: if B, according to the doctrinal rules does (or does not) have a lease, should a court bend those rules in order to deny (or give) B the statutory protection that depends on B's having a lease?

For present purposes, however, the key lesson from *Street* is a simple one: like Mrs Mountford, B may claim that he or she has a lease in order to show that A is under extra, statutory duties to B. As we will see in Chapter 24, the particular statutory duties imposed by the Rent Act 1977 are now of marginal relevance. Nowadays, a private landlord, such as Mr Street, has very little to fear from a lease: he can grant a party, such as Mrs Mountford, an 'assured shorthold tenancy'—that is, a form of lease that gives rise to no fair rent duties and places no substantial limits on Mr Street's ability to remove the tenant at the end of the agreed period.

Nonetheless, even where private landlords are concerned, there are still some statutory duties that apply if and only if B has a lease. For example, as we will see in Chapter 24, s 11 of the Landlord and Tenant Act 1985 can impose a duty on a private landlord (A) to keep in repair the structure and exterior of a dwelling house occupied by B. This particular statutory duty (which cannot be varied by the express terms of a lease) provides the context for another important House of Lords decision, *Bruton v London and Quadrant Housing Trust*,[7] which we will consider in section 2.6 below. It is important to note here that, in *Bruton*, the House of Lords held that Mr Bruton had a lease, at least for the purposes of the Landlord and Tenant Act 1985, even though his agreement with A did not give him a property right. The idea that B can have a lease even if he has no property right is a controversial and important one: we will examine it further in Chapter 24, section 3—but we will not consider it in this chapter, because our focus here is on the role of a lease *as a property right in land*.

Statutory protection continues to be important in cases not involving private landlords. As we will see in Chapter 24, if B can show that he or she has a lease from a local authority, the Housing Act 1985 will apply to impose extra duties on that local authority. For example, the statute limits the grounds on which B can be removed and thus confers on a tenant (but not a licensee) a form of security of tenure. And if B has a lease of business premises, Pt II of the Landlord and Tenant Act 1954 may impose a statutory duty on A to renew B's lease when it reaches the end of the initially agreed period. In contrast, if B has only a licence, A is under no such statutory duty.

1.1.2 The effect of a lease on X

We have seen that the distinction between a lease and a licence can be crucial in deciding whether extra statutory duties will be imposed on A. There is a further, more fundamental distinction between a lease and a licence: a lease, unlike a licence, can count as a property right in land.

As we saw in Chapters 3 and 4, the key feature of a property right is that it is capable of binding parties other than A. In particular, if B has a *legal* estate or interest (such as a legal

---

[7] [2000] 1 AC 406.

lease), then the rest of the world is under a prima facie duty not to interfere with B's use of the land. The consequences of such a duty can be seen in the following extract.

Hunter and ors v Canary Wharf Ltd [1997] AC 665, HL

Facts: Patricia Hunter lived on the Isle of Dogs, in East London. Along with hundreds of other claimants living in that area, she claimed that her television reception had been affected by the construction, on land belonging to Canary Wharf Ltd, of the Canary Wharf Tower.[8] It was claimed that the interference began in 1989, during the construction of the tower, and continued until a relay transmitter was put up in 1991. It seems that the interference was particularly bad in Poplar, to the north of Canary Wharf, as the tower lay between that area and the BBC's at Crystal Palace transmitter. It was claimed that, by causing this interference, Canary Wharf Ltd had committed the tort of nuisance. In a separate action, brought against the London Docklands Development Corporation (LDDC), Ms Hunter and the other claimants sought compensation for damage caused by the dust produced by the LDDC in building the Limehouse Link Road. That separate action alleged that LDDC had committed the torts of negligence and nuisance.

The claims raised a number of difficult legal issues, which were tried as preliminary issues of law. By the time that the case reached the House of Lords, two issues remained. In the words of Lord Goff of Chieveley, they were: '(1) whether interference with television reception is capable of constituting an actionable nuisance, and (2) whether it is necessary to have an interest in property to claim in private nuisance and, if so, what interest in property will satisfy this requirement.'[9] The House of Lords held that: (1) interference with television reception, at least when caused by the construction of a building on the defendant's land, cannot amount to a nuisance;[10] and (2) to sue in nuisance, a claimant must have a property right in land, and that property right must give the claimant exclusive possession of land. The claims made by Ms Hunter and other residents of the Isle of Dogs against Canary Wharf Ltd therefore failed. The claims made against LDDC succeeded, but only in relation to those claimants with a right to exclusive possession of land. As we will see in the extracts below, this meant that if Ms Hunter simply had a *licence* of the land that she occupied as her home, she could not bring a nuisance claim in respect of damage caused by the dust; whereas, if she had a *lease* of that land, she could do so.

Lord Goff

At 687

The basic position is, in my opinion, most clearly expressed in Professor Newark's classic article on *The Boundaries of Nuisance* (1949) 65 L.Q.R. 480 when he stated, at p. 482, that

---

[8] Also known by its address, 'One Canada Square', the tower rises 235 m from ground level and remains the tallest building in the UK. Taller buildings are, however, under construction: for example, Riverside Tower 1, on another part of the general Canary Wharf site, is due to be 1 m taller.

[9] [1997] AC 665, 684.

[10] One issue considered by the House of Lords was whether it is possible for a party to have an easement to receive television signals, and, if so, whether such an easement could be acquired over the passage of time through the doctrine of prescription. This point is examined in Chapter 26, section 3.3.

the essence of nuisance was that 'it was a tort to land. Or to be more accurate it was a tort directed against the plaintiff's enjoyment of rights over land [...]'

[Lord Goff then examined the relevant authorities, finding that they supported Newark's view.][11]

At 692–4

It follows that, on the authorities as they stand, an action in private nuisance will only lie at the suit of a person who has a right to the land affected. Ordinarily, such a person can only sue if he has the right to exclusive possession of the land, such as a freeholder or tenant in possession, or even a licensee with exclusive possession. Exceptionally however, as *Foster v. Warblington Urban District Council*[12] shows, this category may include a person in actual possession who has no right to be there; and in any event a reversioner [e.g. a landlord] can sue in so far his reversionary interest is affected. But a mere licensee on the land has no right to sue.

[...A]ny such departure from the established law on this subject, such as that adopted by the Court of Appeal in the present case, faces the problem of defining the category of persons who would have the right to sue. The Court of Appeal adopted the not easily identifiable category of those who have a 'substantial link' with the land, regarding a person who occupied the premises 'as a home' as having a sufficient link for this purpose. But who is to be included in this category? It was plainly intended to include husbands and wives, or partners, and their children, and even other relatives living with them. But is the category also to include the lodger upstairs, or the au pair girl or resident nurse caring for an invalid who makes her home in the house while she works there? If the latter, it seems strange that the category should not extend to include places where people work as well as places where they live, where nuisances such as noise can be just as unpleasant or distracting. In any event, the extension of the tort in this way would transform it from a tort to land into a tort to the person, in which damages could be recovered in respect of something less serious than personal injury and the criteria for liability were founded not upon negligence but upon striking a balance between the interests of neighbours in the use of their land. This is, in my opinion, not an acceptable way in which to develop the law.

It was suggested in the course of argument that at least the spouse of a husband or wife who, for example as freeholder or tenant, had exclusive possession of the matrimonial home should be entitled to sue in private nuisance. For the purposes of this submission, your Lordships were referred to the relevant legislation, notably the Matrimonial Homes Act 1983 and the Family Law Act 1996.[13] I do not however consider it necessary to go through the statutory provisions. As I understand the position, it is as follows. If under the relevant legislation a spouse becomes entitled to possession of the matrimonial home or part of it, there is no reason why he or she should not be able to sue in private nuisance in the ordinary way. But I do not see how a spouse who has no interest in the matrimonial home has, simply by virtue of his or her cohabiting in the matrimonial home with his or her wife or husband whose freehold or leasehold property it is, a right to sue. No distinction can sensibly be drawn between such spouses and other cohabitees in the home, such as children, or grandparents. Nor do

---

[11] An exception was *Khorasandijan v Bush* [1993] QB 727, in which the Court of Appeal found that the defendant had committed the tort of nuisance by pestering the claimant with unwelcome telephone calls. In *Hunter v Canary Wharf*, the House of Lords rejected the nuisance analysis, noting that the need to prevent such behaviour can be met through use of the Protection from Harassment Act 1997, or by holding that the defendant commits a tort when intentionally causing distress: see, e.g., *per* Lord Hoffmann at 707.

[12] [1906] 1 KB 648.

[13] [For discussion of the statutory licence that may arise under the Family Law Act 1996, see Chapter 8, section 5.]

I see any great disadvantage flowing from this state of affairs. If a nuisance should occur, then the spouse who has an interest in the property can bring the necessary proceedings to bring the nuisance to an end, and can recover any damages in respect of the discomfort or inconvenience caused by the nuisance. Even if he or she is away from home, nowadays the necessary authority to commence proceedings for an injunction can usually be obtained by telephone. Moreover, if the other spouse suffers personal injury, including injury to health, he or she may, like anybody else, be able to recover damages in negligence.

Lord Hoffmann

At 702–3

In the dust action it is not disputed that, in principle, activities which cause dust to be deposited on the plaintiff's property can constitute an actionable nuisance. The question raised by the preliminary issue is: who can sue? In order to answer this question, it is necessary to decide what exactly he is suing for. Since these questions are fundamental to the scope of the tort of nuisance, I shall deal with them first.

Up to about 20 years ago, no one would have had the slightest doubt about who could sue. Nuisance is a tort against land, including interests in land such as easements and profits. A plaintiff must therefore have an interest in the land affected by the nuisance...An example of an action for nuisance by a de facto possessor is *Foster v. Warblington Urban District Council*[14] in which the plaintiff sued the council for discharging sewage so as to pollute his oyster ponds on the foreshore. He had some difficulty in proving any title to the soil but Vaughan Williams L.J. said, at pp. 659–660:

> 'But, even if title could not be proved, in my judgment there has been such an occupation of these beds for such a length of time—not that the length of time is really material for this purpose—as would entitle the plaintiff as against the defendants, who have no interest in the foreshore, to sustain this action for the injury which is alleged has been done by the sewage to his oysters so kept in those beds.'

Thus even a possession which is wrongful against the true owner can found an action for trespass or nuisance against someone else: *Asher v. Whitlock*.[15] In each case, however, the plaintiff (or joint plaintiffs) must be enjoying or asserting exclusive possession of the land: see *per* Blackburn J. in *Allan v. Liverpool Overseers*.[16] Exclusive possession distinguishes an occupier who may in due course acquire title under the Limitation Act 1980 from a mere trespasser. It distinguishes a tenant holding a leasehold estate from a mere licensee. Exclusive possession de jure or de facto, now or in the future, is the bedrock of English land law.

The decision of the House of Lords in *Hunter v Canary Wharf* reveals a point that we examined in Chapter 3, section 1: the key feature of a legal property right is that it imposes a duty on the rest of the world. So, if B has a legal lease of A's land,[17] the rest of the world is under

---

[14] [1906] 1 KB 648.

[15] (1865) LR 1 QB 1.

[16] (1874) LR 9 QB 180.

[17] An interesting question arises where B has an *equitable* lease rather than a legal lease. As noted in Chapter 4, section 7, it seems that equitable interests, whilst they can bind a third party who later acquires a right in the affected land, do *not* impose a duty on the rest of the world. This suggests that a party with an equitable lease *cannot* bring a nuisance claim. In *Hunter v Canary Wharf*, however, Lord Hoffmann does make the contrary (but obiter) suggestion (at 708) that a party with an equitable interest under a trust of a family home can bring a nuisance claim.

a prima facie duty to B not to interfere with B's use of that land. As a result, B, if he or she has a legal lease, can, for example, bring a nuisance claim against a third party whose activities interfere with B's reasonable enjoyment of the land. In contrast, if B has only a licence to use A's land (even a contractual licence), then, as we saw in Chapter 8, B does *not* have a right that he or she can assert against a third party later acquiring a right in the land. And, as shown by *Hunter v Canary Wharf*, if B has only a licence, then the rest of the world is not under a duty to B.

One point in Lord Goff's judgment may seem puzzling: his Lordship stated that a 'licensee with exclusive possession' may be able to sue in nuisance. As we saw in section 1.1.1 above, *Street v Mountford* establishes the presence of exclusive possession as the key test for the presence of a lease. So it may seem odd that a party can both be a licensee (rather than a tenant) *and* have exclusive possession. But this problem disappears when we distinguish between two types of exclusive possession. The first type is the form of exclusive possession that matters when considering the test for a lease: it is a right to exclusive possession for a limited period arising as a result of B's agreement with A. If B is a licensee, then he or she will not have such a right. There is, however, also a second form of exclusive possession. Consider a case such as *National Provincial Bank v Ainsworth*.[18] A has a freehold of a home and lives there with his partner, B. A then moves out, but B remains in occupation. At each stage, B has a licence: certainly, there is no agreement between A and B giving B a right to exclusive possession of the land. But when A moves out, B occupies alone and so assumes sole *factual* control of the land. At that point, B acquires the second type of exclusive possession: a right to exclusive possession arising as a result of B's conduct in having sole physical control of land. As we saw in Chapter 8, sections 2.2 and 3.2, B's factual control of the land then means that third parties come under a duty to B. That duty arises because, as we saw in Chapter 10, section 3, the *fact* of B's exclusive physical control gives B a legal estate in land: a freehold.[19]

In such a case, B's freehold is the same type of right as held by the claimant in *Foster v. Warblington Urban District Council*[20] (referred to by Lords Goff and Hoffmann in the extract above). It is not given to B by A, but is instead acquired independently (see Chapter 3, section 4, for discussion of the concept of independent acquisition).[21] This means that, once A leaves and B takes sole physical control of the land, B not only has a licence (arising as a result of A's permission for B to remain on the land), but also a legal freehold (arising as a result of B's physical control of the land). It is in such a case that B, in Lord Goff's words, is a 'licensee with exclusive possession'. B's ability to sue in nuisance thus comes from his or her legal freehold, not from his or her licence.

1.1.3 The effect of a lease on C

When considering B's position as against C (a party who later acquires a right in relation to A's land), it is vital to bear in mind the key difference between a lease and a licence—that

---

[18] [1965] AC 1175. See Chapter 1, section 5, and Chapter 4, section 5.4.

[19] We noted in Chapter 10, section 3, that there is some academic doubt as to whether B's property right is legal or equitable, but, as we saw there, the cases strongly favour the view that B has a legal freehold.

[20] [1906] 1 KB 648.

[21] Because B's freehold is independently acquired, it arises *after* A's legal estate and so A (or C, a party later acquiring a right from A) can, of course, remove B from the land (see Chapter 6, section 2, for the importance of timing when considering conflicting property rights). Of course, if B has a defence to A or C's prior property right, then B will be protected (such a defence could be based, for example, on B's long possession of the land: see Chapter 10).

is, that the licence, unlike the lease, can count as a property right in land. So, as we saw in Chapter 4, section 7, an equitable lease, as well as a legal lease, is capable of binding a third party, such as C, who later acquires a right from A.

Ashburn Anstalt v Arnold [1989] Ch 1, CA

Facts: We examined this case in Chapter 8, section 3.3.1. Arnold & Co had a lease of business premises. It sold that lease to Matlodge Ltd in 1973. As part of the sale, Matlodge made a promise, in clause 5 of the contract with Arnold & Co, that Arnold & Co could remain in occupation of the land until it was needed for redevelopment. Cavendish Land Co Ltd then acquired both a freehold and the lease of the land, and took on Matlodge's contractual duties to Arnold & Co. Cavendish was later taken over by Legal & General Assurance Society Ltd, which also took on the contractual duties to Arnold & Co. Legal & General (A) then sold its freehold to Ashburn Anstalt (C).

As we saw in Chapter 8, section 3.3.1, under the terms of the sale contract, C took its freehold 'subject to' the contractual rights of Arnold & Co (B) against A, arising as a result of the original agreement with Matlodge. This gave rise to the question of whether B had a new, direct right against C, arising as a result of C's promise to take 'subject to' B's rights. As we saw, the Court of Appeal decided that C's promise did *not* give B such a right: it was not intended to impose a new duty on C.

But the Court of Appeal nonetheless found in B's favour. It held that: (i) the contractual agreement between A and B gave B a lease; and (ii) C had no defence to B's lease.

Fox LJ

At 9–10

It is said on behalf of Arnold & Co. that the interest conferred by clause 5 of the 1973 agreement is a lease and therefore a true property interest which is protected [as an overriding interest by virtue of Arnold & Co's actual occupation: see Chapter 6, section 3.2 and Chapter 16, section 5. The first question, therefore, is whether clause 5 did create a tenancy or merely a licence. The deputy judge held that it created a licence.

In *Street v. Mountford*[22] Lord Templeman, who gave the leading speech, regarded three hallmarks as decisive in favour of a tenancy of residential accommodation, namely exclusive possession, for a term, at a rent.[23] In the present case it is common ground that Arnold & Co. was always in exclusive occupation of the premises from 28 February 1973, as it was before that date. As regards rent, Arnold & Co. was not required to pay a rent under the provisions of clause 5, nor did it do so. It may be that the sum paid to Arnold & Co. for its leasehold interest took account of the freedom from rent under clause 5. There is, however, no evidence of that. We treat the case as one where no rent was payable. Did that prevent the provisions of clause 5 from creating a tenancy? We do not think so. We are unable to read Lord Templeman's speech in *Street v. Mountford* as laying down a principle of "no rent, no lease." In the first place, that would be inconsistent with section 205(1) (xxvii) of the Law of Property Act 1925, which defines "Term of years absolute" as "a term of years (taking effect either in possession or in reversion whether or not at a rent) [. . .]". Secondly, it would be inconsistent

---

[22] [1985] AC 809.
[23] *Ibid* at 826E, 825C, and 826G.

with the judgment of Windeyer J. in *Radaich v. Smith*,[24] which was expressly approved by Lord Templeman in *Street v. Mountford*, at p. 827:

> "What then is the fundamental right which a tenant has which distinguishes his position from that of a licensee? It is an interest in land as distinct from a personal permission to enter the land and use it for some stipulated purpose or purposes. And how is it to be ascertained whether such an interest in land has been given? By seeing whether the grantee was given a legal right of exclusive possession of the land for a term or from year to year or for a life or lives. If he was, he is a tenant."

Windeyer J. in this passage makes no reference to a rent.

In the circumstances I conclude that the reservation of a rent is not necessary for the creation of a tenancy. That conclusion involves no departure from Lord Templeman's proposition in *Street v. Mountford*, at p. 825:

> "If exclusive possession at a rent for a term does not constitute a tenancy then the distinction between a contractual tenancy and a contractual licence of land becomes wholly unidentifiable."

We are saying only that we do not think that Lord Templeman was stating the quite different proposition that you cannot have a tenancy without a rent.

There remains the question of the existence of a term. It is [Ashburn Anstalt's] case that clause 5 created no term sufficiently identifiable to be capable of recognition by the law, and that accordingly no tenancy was created.

The Court of Appeal's decision that B can have a lease even if no rent is paid must be correct. After all, if A has a freehold, he or she can, if he or she wishes, transfer that freehold to B for free. There is no reason why A should not similarly be able to give B a lease for free. But the Court of Appeal also went on to reject Ashburn Anstalt's contention as to the absence of a term: it held that the agreement for B to occupy '*until the land is needed for redevelopment*' *did* give B exclusive possession for a certain term.

As we will see in section 2.7 below, however, that aspect of the decision no longer represents good law: it was reversed by the House of Lords in *Prudential Assurance v London Residuary Body Ltd*.[25] Nonetheless, the decision in *Ashburn Anstalt* still demonstrates one of the key advantages, to B, of a lease: it gives B a right that is capable of binding parties other than A.

1.2 THE PRACTICAL IMPORTANCE AND DIVERSITY OF LEASES

Leases are tremendously important in a number of different practical contexts. There is, of course, the residential sector: for many residents, a lease is the property right they hold in the land they call their home. When considering the residential sector, a number of subdivisions can be made. For example, long residential leases are often isolated as a specific category: certainly, there is a clear practical distinction between, on the one hand, a party with a 999-year lease of a flat who acquired that lease by paying a large up-front price and then pays a very small rent, and, on the other, a party with a weekly, monthly, or yearly tenancy

[24] (1959) 101 CLR 209, 222 (a decision of the High Court of Australia).
[25] [1992] 2 AC 386.

of a flat, who pays a regular market rent. Around 30 per cent of homes in England and Wales are leased in this second way. Those shorter leases can be divided into three groups, roughly equal in terms of numbers, according to the nature of the landlord: private, local authority, or social (e.g. housing association).[26] As we will see in Chapter 24, the statutory rules applying to private landlords (such as Mr Street) are very different from those applying to public landlords, such as local authorities or housing associations.

But it would be a mistake to focus solely on the residential sector. Leases are also very important in other areas: for example, many businesses hold leases of their premises; and many farmers hold leases of their agricultural land. Again, as we will see in Chapter 24, statute has intervened in those areas to give some extra protection to business and agricultural tenants.

The following extract emphasizes the importance and diversity of leases. As demonstrated by the extract, a number of different terms can be used to describe a party with a lease: 'tenant', 'lessee', etc.; the party granting a lease can be referred to as a 'landlord', or 'lessor'; and the property right retained by the landlord or lessor is referred to as a 'reversion', on the basis that, at the end of the lease, a right to exclusive possession of the land goes back to the landlord.

Bright, *Landlord and Tenant Law in Context* (2007, pp 5–6)

The variety of letting arrangements

There is a wide variety within the landlord and tenant relationship. A lease of a house is likely to be very different from a lease of a department store. A tenant who rents a house in order to let out individual rooms to others has quite a different perspective from a tenant renting the house to provide a home for his family. Some tenancies may be intended to last for only a short period, such as a let of holiday accommodation, and some may be for extremely long periods, such as a 999 year lease. Some may be granted in return for a substantial capital payment (known as a premium) and only a nominal rent, others for no premium but for a market rent. Some landlords are motivated primarily by financial considerations, others by social concerns.

It is important to have an overview of how leases are used in practice as different types of lease raise very different legal issues. The student renting a room for the year would, for example, rightly expect the landlord to be responsible for solving the problem of a leaking roof. In contrast, the commercial tenant with a 125 year lease of an entire building would usually be responsible for the maintenance and repair of the property itself. For the landlord, also, the length of the lease will affect its expectations; with a short lease the freehold (or reversion) has a high capital value and so the landlord may take an active role in managing the property in order to preserve this capital value, but with very long term leases the capital value of the reversion will be minimal, and so the landlord may show less interest in managing the property.

At the risk of over-generalisation, there are three broad categories of lease that can be identified based on the length of the lease. The expectations of landlords and tenants in terms of what the relationship provides will differ according to which category the lease comes within.

---

[26] The annual Housing Review published by the Chartered Institute of Housing and the Council of Mortgage Lenders provides up-to-date figures: see, e.g., Wilcox, *UK Housing Review 2007/08*.

First, there are tenancies for short term occupation which usually involve the payment of a market rent and will be either periodic (weekly, monthly or annual) or for a fixed term up to five years (commercial) or seven years (residential). The tenant pays for occupation and exclusive possession for the term, while the landlord's reversion retains all, or nearly all, of the capital value of the property. Second, medium term leases are generally used to provide occupation for the tenant for up to, say, 25 years for commercial leases and 21 years for residential leases. Again, these leases will usually be at a market rent, with provision for the rent to be reviewed at regular intervals. A premium (a capital sum) may be paid for the grant of the lease, but this would be unusual. The reversion again continues to have a substantial value. In the last category, long leases, there is a greater divergence between the commercial and residential models. The longer commercial lease, typically, for a term of 125 years, may involve the payment of a 'ground rent', that is, a market rent that reflects the value of the land only (the site value). In this arrangement, the lessee will often construct the buildings on the site, and the cost of doing so will be written off over the life of the lease, with the expectation that the building's useful life will draw to an end as the lease does. Notwithstanding the length of the lease, the reversion will carry a significant capital value because of the substantial and reviewable ground rent. In contrast, the long residential lease is typically granted for terms of 99, 125 or 999 years and a substantial premium will be paid to purchase this interest, similar to the amount that would be paid to buy a freehold interest. Here, it is the lease that will have a significant capital value, rather than the reversion. Indeed, the leaseholder will usually perceive of himself as the 'owner' of the property, as a purchaser rather than a renter or tenant. The lease is primarily being used in this context because it enables covenants, such as obligations to repair and financial commitments to contribute towards the cost of shared facilities, to be enforced against successive owners (English common law does not permit positive covenants to be attached to freehold land).

The rights and responsibilities of the landlord and tenant will be most affected by the type of letting, whether it is short term rented housing, a home purchased on a long lease, commercial property or agricultural land. Within these main divisions, there will be further differentiation according to the status of the landlord.

This passage also sets out some of the reasons why a party may acquire a lease, rather than a freehold. In Chapter 28, section 1, we will examine why a party buying a flat will almost always acquire a long lease of that flat rather than a freehold: as explained by Bright, the key point is that, if a lease is used, the 'owner' of each flat can take the benefit and burden of *positive* duties (such as duties to keep the flat in good repair). In Chapter 28, we will also examine the concept of a *commonhold*—that is, a mechanism introduced with the aim of allowing such duties to bind flat 'owners' without the necessity for each such owner to have a lease of his or her flat.

In other cases, the key attraction of a lease is often that it involves a shorter commitment: for example, if moving to a town to study there for three years, B has no need to incur the extra expense necessary in acquiring a freehold. Similarly, if B is starting up a business and is unsure of its long-term prospects, a freehold is an unattractive option. In some cases, however, B may wish to establish a long-term home, but be unable to find the finance needed to acquire a freehold. In such cases, financial necessity may lead B to acquire a shorter residential lease. There is a risk in such cases that B's need for a home, and relatively weak bargaining position, may give A an opportunity to exploit B. As we saw in section 1.1.1 above, this has led to statutory intervention in B's favour: we will consider that intervention further in Chapter 24.

1.3 THE LANDLORD–TENANT RELATIONSHIP

As is made clear by the decision of the House of Lords in *Street v Mountford*, an agreement can only count as a lease if it gives B a right to exclusive possession of land for a limited period. As we saw in sections 1.1.2 and 1.1.3 above, once A has given B that core right, third parties can then also come under a duty, during that period, not to interfere with B's right to exclusive possession. In practice, of course, a standard lease agreement will generally include many other terms, imposing additional duties on A (e.g. duties to undertake major repairs), as well as duties on B (e.g. a duty to pay rent). And, in certain circumstances, those additional duties can also affect third parties: for example, it may be that, if A owns other, neighbouring land, he or she will make a binding promise to B not to use that other land in a particular way (e.g. not to build on that land, not to run a business on that land that will compete with the business B plans to operate from the leased premises, etc.). In such a case, A's promise can give B an equitable interest in A's other land: a restrictive covenant (see Chapter 27). Like any equitable interest, that restrictive covenant will be capable of binding C, a third party who later acquires a right in A's other land.

There is a further, important way in which third parties can be affected by the additional duties assumed by A or B in a lease agreement: if the contractual promise giving rise to the duty counts as a 'leasehold covenant', it can bind other parties who later step into the shoes of A or B, and thereby also enter a landlord–tenant relationship. For example, it may be possible for B to assign (i.e. to transfer) his or her lease to another party (B2). In such a case, B's contractual promise to pay A rent will bind B2. If A then transfers his or her reversion (i.e. A's legal estate) to A2, then B2 will be under a duty to pay rent to A2; and, due to the promise to repair made by A in the initial lease, A2 will be under a duty to B2 to do such repairs. In this way, later parties who step into the landlord–tenant relationship will also take the benefit and burden of at least some of the additional duties originally agreed to by A and B. A key question, of course, is *which* of those additional duties should be seen as part of the landlord–tenant relationship, and thus capable of benefiting and binding later parties. We will consider that question, and others, in Chapter 25, when looking in detail at leasehold covenants.[27]

2 THE *CONTENT* QUESTION

In this chapter, our focus is on the lease as a property right. In Chapter 1, section 3, we saw that there are three key questions when considering property rights. The first of these, the *content* question, focuses on the nature of B's right to use land. Section 1 of the Law of Property Act 1925 (LPA 1925) makes clear that a lease, referred to there as a 'term of years absolute', can count as a legal estate in land. But how do we tell if an agreement made between A and B, under which B has a right to occupy A's land, counts as a lease?

2.1 WHERE A DOES NOT INTEND TO GRANT A LEASE

The first question to ask is whether B's right can count as a lease *even if* A, when making the agreement with B, makes it clear that he or she does not intend to grant B a lease. As we saw in section 1.1.1 above, that question was answered by the House of Lords in *Street v*

---

[27] In that chapter, the party here referred to as 'B2' (i.e. the party acquiring B's lease) is referred to as 'TA' (i.e. tenant's assignee). Similarly, 'A2' (i.e. the party acquiring A's estate) is referred to as 'LA' (i.e. landlord's assignee).

Mountford: A's lack of intention to grant B a lease does *not* necessarily prevent B's right from counting as a lease.

As evidenced by the following extract, this result came as a surprise to Mr Street.

Street, 'Coach and Horses Trip Cancelled? Rent Act Avoidance after *Street v Mountford*' [1985] Conv 328, 328–9

The Rent Acts are grossly unfair to landlords. A stranger obtains a weekly tenancy of a house: half a century may pass before the owner can have his property again. In the meantime he can only charge a so-called 'fair' rent which in many cases does little more than cover the cost of keeping the property in repair. As a result of all this the capital value of the property drops to between one-third and one-half of its vacant possession value. Little wonder that over the years landlords and their legal advisers have sought various ways of avoiding the potentially horrendous consequences of being caught by the legislation [...]

In *Street v. Mountford* the plaintiff was—in the eyes of some—a double rogue, a landlord and a lawyer. He had studied the Court of Appeal decisions of the late 1970s which appeared to confirm a shift of emphasis from status to contract. The traditional view had been that exclusive possession meant a tenancy had been created (subject to one or two well-recognised exceptions), but the approach in the more recent cases suggested the ultimate test was one of intention. Lord Denning's judgments in particular seemed to show this development very clearly. By 1977 he felt able to say:

'What *is* the test to see whether the occupier of one room in a house is a tenant or a licensee? It does not depend on whether he or she has exclusive possession or not [...The test is] Was it intended that the occupier should have a stake in the room or did he have only permission for himself personally to *occupy* the room, whether under a contract or not, in which case he is a licensee?'

In 1979 the writer decided to take the Court of Appeal at its word and drafted a document, using the simplest possible terms, expressed to be a personal non-assignable licence. A declaration was appended to underline the fact that it was not the intention of the parties to create a tenancy, which would be protected by the Rent Acts. No attempt was made to avoid granting the licensee exclusive possession, as this was not seen as the dominant factor. The document was to mean what it said, the licensee was to have an exclusive right to occupy a room, but this would be revocable on notice and would be outside the scope of the statutory protection afforded to tenants. The writer employed the document from 1979 to 1983 with no problems arising [...]

[When the case came to the Court of Appeal] Slade LJ stated:

'Having regard to the form of the document and the declaration at the foot of it, I do not see how [Mr Street] could have made much clearer his intention that what was being offered to [Mrs Mountford] was a mere licence to occupy and not an interest in the premises as tenant. And I do not see how [Mrs Mountford] could have made clearer her acceptance of that offer than by her two signatures.'

The House of Lords unanimously reversed this decision [...] Lord Templeman's judgment, with which Lords Scarman, Keith, Bridge and Brightman concurred, turned the clock back more than a quarter of a century, and in doing so expressly disapproved of a number of decisions in recent years. The ancient wisdom is reinstated: save in exceptional 'special category' cases (e.g. master and service occupier, vendor and purchaser) the grant of exclusive possession for a fixed or periodic term in consideration of periodic payments will create a tenancy.

It is, of course, rare to see an article about a reported decision written by one of the very parties to that decision.[28] There is, of course, a question about the writer's objectivity—but Roger Street is certainly correct in pointing out that, prior to the decision of the House of Lords in *Street*, the Court of Appeal had developed a rule that, if A did not intend to grant B a lease, no lease would arise. The question is whether the House of Lords had good reason to depart from that rule.

As noted in Chapter 1, section 5.2, we can approach this question from the perspective of *doctrine*, or from the perspective of *utility*. The following extract argues that the House of Lords' approach in *Street v Mountford* can be justified only from the latter perspective.

Hill, 'Intention and the Creation of Proprietary Rights: Are Leases Different?' [1996] LS 200

To what extent can the parties effectively deny proprietary effect to an interest which, in terms of its characteristics and in terms of the rights and obligations of the parties *inter se*, has the appearances of an interest to which the law grants proprietary consequences? To what extent can [A] grant to [B] an interest which has the substance of a proprietary interest but determine that the agreement is purely personal to the parties?

There is a group of authorities which suggest that an interest which has the substantive characteristics of a proprietary interest will, nevertheless, not be binding on a purchaser of the property to which the interest relates if there is a sufficient indication that the parties to the transaction which establishes the interest intended to create only personal rights. Perhaps the clearest authority is *IDC Group v Clark*, which concerns the boundary between easements and contractual licences. In this case [A] and [B] were the owners of adjoining buildings. By means of a formal document [A] granted [B] the right to make an opening in a party wall so as to create a fire escape from B's property. Subsequently C acquired a lease of A's property and B2 acquired the other building from B. When the fire escape was blocked off, B2 sought to enforce against C the right granted to B by A. B2 attempted to rely on the fact that the right being claimed was in the nature of an easement which was binding on A's successors in title. C, however, argued that because in the original transaction between A and B the parties had used the words 'grant licence' the right conferred on B was in the nature of a personal licence, the burden of which did not pass.

Although the right granted by A was capable of being the subject-matter of an easement, the Court of Appeal thought that, in view of the fact that 'the simple expression "grant licence" is not one which would have been used by a conveyancer of any experience as the means of creating an easement', the grantor 'intended to grant a licence properly so called and no more.'[29] the court held that the deed created only a personal licence, the burden of which was not binding on C [...]

[Hill then goes on to examine a number of other cases in which A's intention, expressed in an agreement with B, is effective to ensure that B's right, whilst matching the content of a particular legal or equitable property right, takes effect only as a personal right against A.]

The pattern of authorities supports the view that as a general rule the parties to an agreement may render personal rights which, in the normal course of events, would have proprietary consequences. An exception exists, however, with regard to leases. Can the exception be explained or justified?

---

[28] Articles by *counsel* of one of the parties are more common: see, e.g., Chapter 13, section 2.1.
[29] *Per* Nourse LJ at 183–4.

[Hill then notes that, prior to *Street v Mountford*, the Court of Appeal had developed the rule that A's intention not to grant a lease could prevent B from acquiring a property right, even if the agreement between A and B gave B a right to exclusive possession for a term.]

[...] This is not to deny the validity of the courts' intervention in *Street v Mountford* or the desirability of the result achieved. The point is rather that the true rationale underlying the decision is to some extent obscured by Lord Templeman's assertion that 'the Rent Acts must not be allowed to alter or influence the construction of an agreement.'[30]

The context in which the distinction between leases and licences has been most relevant is the private sector of the housing market. In *Street v Mountford* the statement in the agreement between the parties that the occupier was a licensee rather than a tenant was not motivated by any desire to ensure that the occupier's interest would not be binding on nay subsequent purchaser of the land; it was an attempt to avoid the statutory controls contained in the Rent Acts. In a market in which there is a severe shortage of residential accommodation for rent, the prospective occupier is in a very weak bargaining position vis-à-vis the owner. It is often the case that the prospective occupiers of residential property are desperate to find somewhere to live and have no knowledge of the scope of the protective legislation [...]

[T]he most honest approach to the lease/licence distinction would be for the courts to recognise more explicitly the basis of their intervention. Unless external factors suggest that the parties' expressed wished should be overridden, there is no reason why an agreement which confers exclusive possession for a term at a rent should not take effect as a licence if that is what the parties intend to create. Where a transaction is freely entered into on the basis of commercial considerations there is no justification for the law's disregard of the parties' intentions.

However, where there is inequality between the parties—as is the case in the private sector of the housing market—the law is entitled to look behind the form of the agreement [...] It is widely recognised that '[f]reedom of contract [...] is a particularly inappropriate model when dealing with the consumer as a contracting party.' Accordingly, it seems reasonable to look at the lease/licence distinction from the consumer law perspective rather than purely as an aspect of the law relating to real property.

Hill makes the very important point that, as shown by the decision of the Court of Appeal in *IDC Group v Clark*,[31] there are other areas of land law in which A *is* permitted to give B a personal right that matches the content of a recognized property right (such as an easement). His argument is that the same general, doctrinal approach had been adopted to leases by the Court of Appeal, but that such an approach was inappropriate for dealing with the special problems caused by residential occupation. So, in *Street v Mountford*, the House of Lords created a special exception to that general approach, departing from doctrine to uphold a policy of protecting vulnerable residential occupiers.

The next extract takes a different approach. It argues that there are sound doctrinal reasons for treating leases as different from other forms of property right, such as easements. On this view, the decision in *Street v Mountford* can be justified from a doctrinal perspective, as well as from a utility perspective.

30 [1985] AC 809, 825.
31 (1992) 65 P & CR 179.

McFarlane, *The Structure of Property Law* (2008, pp 661–2)

If the rights given by A to B entitle B to exclusive control of the land for a limited period then, providing he satisfies the acquisition question, B will have a Lease. This is the case *even if A did not intend to give B a Lease*. A's intention is of course crucial when we ask the first question: what rights does the agreement give to B? However, A's intention is irrelevant when we ask the second question: do the rights given to B amount to a Lease? There are two points here. First, it is for the land law system, not A, to define a Lease. That point is not specific to property law. For example, let's say A makes an oral promise to give B £100 in two weeks' time. A and B both call the promise "a contract" and intend it to be binding. However, it does *not* give B a contractual right against A: no consideration has been provided by B. As the law's test for a contract has not been satisfied, A and B's intention to have a contract is irrelevant.

The second point that it is simply not possible for A *both* to (i) give B a right to exclusive control of a thing; and (ii) to deny that B has a property right. This point is specific to property law. It shows that (i) *if* A gives B a right to exclusive control of a thing; *then* (ii) A's intention to give B only a personal right is irrelevant. Of course, this does not mean A is trapped into giving B a Lease. If A is keen to ensure that B does not acquire a Lease, A simply needs to ensure that the rights he gives B under agreement do not amount to a right to exclusive control.

We can draw an analogy with cooking. A can choose his own ingredients when cooking: his intention is therefore crucial to what he produces. But if A chooses to (i) mix together flour, eggs, sugar, butter and baking powder; and (ii) put the mixture in a tin and heat it in the oven; then (iii) whether he likes it or not, A makes a cake. It does not matter that A intended to make a casserole: he is judged by what he produces and he has produced a cake. If A wants to make a casserole, the solution is simple: he needs to choose the right ingredients.

[. . . The decision of the House of Lords in *Street v Mountford*] might seem to be an example of a court bending the rules to thwart A's unscrupulous attempt to avoid giving B the statutory protection available under the Rent Acts. However, the decision is perfectly correct as a matter of doctrine: it is conceptually impossible for A to give B a right to exclusive control for a limited period and then to claim that B has only a licence.

On the view taken in this extract, the decision of the House of Lords in *Street* returns to the traditional, doctrinal position that, if A's agreement with B gives B a right to exclusive possession, B can acquire a lease even if A does not intend to give B a property right. Indeed, on this view, it was the Court of Appeal, in cases prior to *Street*, which departed from doctrine in order to uphold a policy: a policy of *allowing* owners of land to escape the onerous statutory duties imposed by giving an occupier a lease.[32]

2.2 INTENTION TO CREATE LEGAL RELATIONS

To have a lease, B must show he or she has been given a *right* to exclusive possession. If A and B make an agreement allowing B to occupy A's land, but that agreement is not intended to be legally binding, then A has not given B such a right. This flows from the general rule of

---

[32] Certainly, Lord Denning MR openly admitted that the Court of Appeal's approach was affected by the statutory regime: see, e.g., *Cobb v Lane* [1952] 1 TLR 1037, 1041; *Marcroft Wagons v Smith* [1051] 2 KB 496. See also *Marchant v Charters* [1977] 1 WLR 1181, 1184. See also Chapter 8, section 3.3.2 at pp 247–8.

contract law: as *Treitel* has put it,[33] '*An agreement, though supported by consideration, is not binding as a contract if it was made without any intention of creating relations*'. For example, in *Booker v Palmer*,[34] Mr Palmer agreed with a friend that an evacuee could occupy a cottage owned by Mr Palmer. The Court of Appeal found that the evacuee did not have a lease: the informal agreement, under which Mr Palmer received no rent, was not intended to create legal rights. Lord Greene MR stated:[35] '*There is one golden rule which is of very general application, namely, that the law does not impute intention to enter into legal relationships where the circumstances and the conduct of the parties negative any intention of the kind.*'

This requirement for a lease is entirely consistent with doctrine: it is simply a requirement for the creation of contractual rights. As has been noted in other contexts, however, there is scope for the courts to manipulate that requirement:[36] so, if a court wishes to hold, for a particular policy reason, that B does not have a lease, it may then be inclined to find, as a matter of fact, that the agreement between A and B was not intended to create legal relations. Certainly, in *Street v Mountford*, Lord Templeman makes a very flexible use of the concept when attempting to explain the results of past cases in which B was found to have no lease.[37]

2.3 A RIGHT TO EXCLUSIVE POSSESSION: GENERAL POSITION

Where A and B's agreement does create contractual rights, it is necessary to see if its terms give B a right to exclusive possession of the land: in the absence of such a right, B cannot have a lease. As we have seen, in *Street v Mountford*, Lord Templeman was confident that the exclusive possession test would be simple to apply in residential cases.

Street v Mountford [1985] AC 809, HL

Lord Templeman

At 817–18

In the case of residential accommodation there is no difficulty in deciding whether the grant confers exclusive possession. An occupier of residential accommodation at a rent for a term is either a lodger or a tenant. The occupier is a lodger if the landlord provides attendance or services which require the landlord or his servants to exercise unrestricted access to and use of the premises. A lodger is entitled to live in the premises but cannot call the place his own.

As explained by Lord Templeman, a right to exclusive possession is synonymous with ownership for a limited period: at one point in *Street*, his Lordship states: '*The tenant*

---

[33] *Treitel's Law of Contract* (12th edn, ed Peel, 2007, [4–001]).
[34] [1942] 2 All ER 674, CA.
[35] Ibid, at 676.
[36] See, e.g., Hepple, 'Intention to Create Legal Relations' (1970) 28 CLJ 122.
[37] For example, Bright, *Landlord and Tenant in Context* (2007, p 69) notes that: '*In* Street v Mountford *Lord Templeman explained the finding of no tenancy in* Marcroft Wagons [*v Smith* [1951] 2 KB 496, CA] *as being due to the fact that the parties did not intend to contract at all.*'

possessing exclusive possession is able to exercise the rights of an owner of land, which is in the real sense his land albeit temporarily and subject to certain restrictions.[38]

As we noted in Chapter 3, section 3.2, this analysis supports the view of Harris[39] that the concept of ownership is vital to understanding the content of the two legal estates in land permitted by s 1 of the LPA 1925: the freehold and the lease. According to Harris, a key aspect of any ownership interest is that it gives its holder an *open-ended* set of use privileged and control powers in relation to a resource.

As the following extract shows, that analysis seems to be reflected in the test for a lease, even in a case involving commercial premises: if the agreement between A and B gives B only a limited set of rights (e.g. if it permits B only to use the land in a specific way), B cannot have a lease.

Hunts Refuse Disposals Ltd v Norfolk Environmental Waste Services Ltd [1997] 1 EGLR 16, CA

Facts: In 1974, Norfolk Environmental Waste Services Ltd (NEWS), the waste disposal arm of Norfolk County Council, entered into an agreement with Hunts Refuse Disposals Ltd (HRD), owners of Priory Farm, Blackborough End, Kings Lynn in Norfolk. Clause 1 of that agreement gave NEWS an *'exclusive licence and full liberty to use the relevant Site for depositing waste* [...] *for a period of 21 years'*. NEWS argued that it had a lease: if so, it acquired a statutory opportunity to renew the lease, arising under Pt II of the Landlord and Tenant Act 1954. HRD claimed that the agreement gave NEWS only a licence and so NEWS had no right to renew the agreement when, in 1995, it came to an end. The first instance judge held that NEWS did *not* have a lease; the Court of Appeal upheld that decision.

Hutchison LJ

At 18

At a stage in his judgment when [the first instance judge] was summarising the principles to be derived from *Street v Mountford* and the other authorities to which he had been referred, and had accepted (rightly) that 'similar principles apply in the case of both residential and business premises' he went on to observe:

> 'It is right to say however that while general principle is immutable, its effect in practice may be very different when one is considering an agreement relating to the use of a 31-acre rubbish tip as opposed to the occupancy of a two-bedroomed residential flat.'

The judge was here recognising, realistically and correctly, that the analysis to determine whether an agreement constitutes a licence or a tenancy, while of course it involves giving close attention to the terms of the agreement, is not to be undertaken in a vacuum but rather with a proper regard to the context in which the issue arises. Thus, while one would ordinarily expect that someone in occupation of a small house for a fixed term at a rent had exclusive possession, one would I suggest have no such preconceptions about a person given the right to tip rubbish in the excavated parts of a large plot of land, on other parts of which, it seems, quarrying was continuing.

---

[38] [1985] AC 809, 816.
[39] Harris, *Property and Justice* (1996, pp 72–3). See Chapter 3, section 2.

Morritt LJ

At 20

This case concerns a 31-acre site on which, at the time of the execution of the deeds, quarrying or mineral extraction operations were taking place and likely to continue. The deeds did not grant the exclusive licence and full liberty to use the site at all times and for any purpose for which it might be suitable. Rather it granted the exclusive licence and full liberty to use the site for depositing waste. Thus it was exclusive only for that purpose. It prevented the grantor from granting a competing right to any one else, but did not exclude the grantors from continuing with their quarrying and mineral extraction operations on the site or from using it or allowing others to use it for any purpose which did not inhibit the exercise by [NEWS] or their predecessor of the exclusive rights granted.

The reasoning of Hutchison LJ may suggest that the result in *Hunts Refuse* depends on the fact that it involved commercial premises, rather than residential occupation. In each case, however, the underlying test is the same: there is no lease unless A has given B a right to exclusive possession. The point is that, in a commercial context, it is factually more likely that an agreement may give B a limited right (e.g. a right to use a quarry *only* for the purpose of dumping waste) rather than the open-ended rights that constitute exclusive possession. This does not mean that a different underlying test applies in commercial cases. And, as the following extract shows, it does not mean that a residential occupier will necessarily have a right to exclusive possession.

Westminster City Council v Clarke [1992] 2 AC 288, HL

Facts: Westminster City Council owned the Cambridge Street Hostel, Cambridge Street, London. Mr Clarke occupied Room 133E. He was provided with that room under an agreement with the council. The agreement was headed 'Licence to occupy'. It stated that Mr Clarke was permitted '*to occupy in common with the council and any other persons to whom the same right is granted accommodation at the single persons hostel at 131–137, Cambridge Street, S.W.1 in the City of Westminster*'. The first clause of the agreement stated:

This licence does not give you and is not intended to give you any of the rights or to impose upon you any of the obligations of a tenant nor does it give you the right of exclusive occupation of any particular accommodation or room which may be allotted to you or which you may be allowed to use nor does it create the relationship of landlord and tenant. The accommodation allotted to you may be changed from time to time without notice as the council directs and you may be required to share such accommodation with any other person as required by the council.

Following complaints by other residents of the hostel, the council sought to remove Mr Clarke. Mr Clarke argued that his agreement gave him a lease, that he therefore had a secure tenancy under Pt IV of the Housing Act 1985, and that the council could therefore only remove him if one of the grounds permitted by the Housing Act applied. Mr Clarke's argument failed at first instance, but was accepted by the Court of Appeal. The council then appealed successfully to the House of Lords.

Lord Templeman

At 296

The council own a terrace of houses 131–137, Cambridge Street. The premises are used by the council as a hostel. There are 31 single rooms each with a bed and limited cooking facilities. There was originally a common room which has since been vandalised. The occupiers of the hostel are homeless single men, including men with personality disorders or physical disabilities, sometimes eccentric, sometimes frail, sometimes evicted from domestic accommodation or discharged from hospital or from prison. Experience has shown the possibility that the hostel may have to cope with an occupier who is suicidal or alcoholic or addicted to drugs. There is a warden supported by a resettlement team of social workers. The hope is that after a period of rehabilitation and supervision in the hostel, each occupier will be able to move on to permanent accommodation where he will be independent and look after himself. In the case of Mr. Clarke, the hostel was designed to be a halfway house for rehabilitation and treatment en route to an independent home [...]

At 300–2

The question is whether upon the true construction of the licence to occupy and in the circumstances in which Mr. Clarke was allowed to occupy room E, there was a grant by the council to Mr. Clarke of exclusive possession of room E.

From the point of view of the council the grant of exclusive possession would be inconsistent with the purposes for which the council provided the accommodation at Cambridge Street. It was in the interests of Mr. Clarke and each of the occupiers of the hostel that the council should retain possession of each room. If one room became uninhabitable another room could be shared between two occupiers. If one room became unsuitable for an occupier he could be moved elsewhere. If the occupier of one room became a nuisance he could be compelled to move to another room where his actions might be less troublesome to his neighbours. If the occupier of a room had exclusive possession he could prevent the council from entering the room save for the purpose of protecting the council's interests and not for the purpose of supervising and controlling the conduct of the occupier in his interests. If the occupier of a room had exclusive possession he could not be obliged to comply with the terms and the conditions of occupation. Mr. Clarke could not, for example, be obliged to comply with the directions of the warden or to exclude visitors or to comply with any of the other conditions of occupation which are designed to help Mr. Clarke and the other occupiers of the hostel and to enable the hostel to be conducted in an efficient and harmonious manner. The only remedy of the council for breaches of the conditions of occupation would be the lengthy and uncertain procedure required by the [Housing Act 1985] to be operated for the purpose of obtaining possession from a secure tenant. In the circumstances of the present case I consider that the council legitimately and effectively retained for themselves possession of room E and that Mr. Clarke was only a licensee with rights corresponding to the rights of a lodger. In reaching this conclusion I take into account the object of the council, namely the provision of accommodation for vulnerable homeless persons, the necessity for the council to retain possession of all the rooms in order to make and administer arrangements for the suitable accommodation of all the occupiers and the need for the council to retain possession of every room not only in the interests of the council as the owners of the terrace but also for the purpose of providing for the occupiers supervision and assistance. For many obvious reasons it was highly undesirable for the council to grant to any occupier of a room exclusive possession which obstructed the use by the council of all the rooms of the hostel in the interests of every occupier. By the terms of the licence to occupy Mr. Clarke was not entitled to any particular room, he could be required to share with any other person as required by the council and he was only entitled to "occupy accommodation in common with the council whose representative may enter the accommodation at any time." It is accepted that these provisions of the licence to occupy were inserted to enable the council to discharge its responsibilities to the vulnerable persons accommodated at the Cambridge Street terrace and were not inserted for the purpose of enabling the council to avoid the creation of a secure tenancy. The conditions of occupancy support the view that Mr. Clarke was not in exclusive occupation of room E. He was expressly limited in his enjoyment of any accommodation provided for him. He was forbidden to entertain visitors without the approval of the council staff and was bound to comply with the council's warden or other staff in charge of the hostel. These limitations confirmed that the council retained possession of all the rooms of the hostel in order to supervise and control the activities of the occupiers, including Mr. Clarke. Although Mr. Clarke physically occupied room E he did not enjoy possession exclusively of the council.

   This is a very special case which depends on the peculiar nature of the hostel maintained by the council, the use of the hostel by the council, the totality, immediacy, and objectives of the powers exercisable by the council and the restrictions imposed on Mr. Clarke. The decision in this case will not allow a landlord, private or public, to free himself from the Rent Acts or from the restrictions of a secure tenancy merely by adopting or adapting the language of the licence to occupy. The provisions of the licence to occupy and the circumstances in which that licence was granted and continued lead to the conclusion that Mr. Clarke has never enjoyed that exclusive possession which he claims. I would therefore allow the appeal and restore the order for possession made by the trial judge.

The decision in *Westminster City Council* provides an interesting contrast with that in *Street v Mountford*, not least because, in each case, Lord Templeman provides the only reasoned speech. Again, there is a question of whether the decision is best viewed from the perspective of doctrine or utility. From the latter point of view, there is no doubt that the different context of *Westminster City Council* may have influenced their Lordships: there certainly seems to be more sympathy for the objectives of the council than for those of Mr Street. But there is also an important doctrinal difference between the two cases: in *Street v Mountford*, Mr Street (as he admits in the extract in section 2.1 above) quite readily gave Mrs Mountford a right to exclusive possession; in contrast, in *Westminster City Council*, the council was careful *not* to give Mr Clarke such a right. The contextual factors identified by Lord Templeman explain *why* the council chose not to give Mr Clarke a right to exclusive possession—but from a doctrinal perspective, the only relevant point is the fact that no such right was granted.

2.4 A RIGHT TO EXCLUSIVE POSSESSION: SHAMS AND PRETENCES

The comparison between *Street v Mountford*, on the one hand, and *Westminster City Council v Clarke*, on the other, gives rise to a further question: if a party such as Mr Street wishes to avoid granting an occupier a lease, can he simply insert a term in the agreement that denies the occupier a right to exclusive possession? The first point to remember, noted in section 1.1.1 above, is that a private landlord no longer has any real need to avoid granting a lease: he can simply grant an 'assured shorthold tenancy'—that is, a form of lease that gives the tenant only trifling statutory protection.

Under the previous statutory regimes, however, private landlords did, indeed, react to *Street* by inserting terms for the purpose of denying an occupier exclusive possession. As the next extract shows, that tactic was not always successful: in some cases, courts showed themselves to be willing, when asking if the agreement gave B a right to exclusive possession, to disregard particular terms inserted with the purpose of denying B such a right.

AG Securities v Vaughan and ors; Antoniades v Villiers and anor [1990] 1 AC 417, HL

Facts: Two separate appeals were heard together by the House of Lords. In the first case, AG Securities (an unlimited company) had a long lease of a flat: No 25 Linden Mansions, Hornsey Lane, London. That flat had four bedrooms, as well as communal areas, and it was rented out to four occupiers: Nigel Vaughan and three others. The four had not moved in as a group: each moved in as and when a former occupier left and a room became available. Mr Vaughan had arrived in 1982; two of the other occupiers, in 1984; the fourth occupier, in 1985. In May 1985, AG Securities attempted to terminate the occupation of the four. The four claimed that, acting together, they jointly held a lease, arising from the terms of their agreements with AG Securities, and therefore qualified for statutory protection. AG Securities sought a declaration that the occupiers each had an individual licence. The first instance judge granted that declaration, but the Court of Appeal (Sir George Waller dissenting) held that the occupiers, acting jointly, had a lease. The House of Lords upheld AG Securities' appeal, holding that the occupiers were, indeed, licensees.

In the second case, Mr Antoniades had a long lease of the top flat at No 6, Whiteley Road, Upper Norwood, London. That flat had a bedroom, a room described as a bed–sitting room, a kitchen, and a bathroom. It was rented out to two occupiers: Mr Villiers and Miss Bridger. They were a couple and moved in together, signing separate, but identical, agreements with Mr Antoniades on the same day: 9 February 1985. Each agreement contained a term (Clause 16) stating that: *'The licensor shall be entitled at any time to use the rooms together with the licensee and permit other persons to use all of the rooms together with the licensee.'* In 1986, Mr Antoniades claimed possession of the flat. The occupiers claimed that, acting jointly, they had a lease, arising as a result of their agreements with Mr Antoniades. If they were found to have a lease, they would qualify for statutory protection and Mr Antoniades' power to remove them would be limited by statute. The first instance judge found that the occupiers did have a lease, but the Court of Appeal held that they were licensees and so allowed Mr Antoniades' appeal. The House of Lords took a different view, restoring the order of the first instance judge, and holding that Mr Villiers and Miss Bridger, acting together, had a lease.

Lord Templeman

At 458–465

My Lords, ever since 1915 the Rent Acts have protected some tenants of residential accommodation with security of tenure and maximum rents. The scope and effect of the Rent Acts have been altered from time to time and the current legislative protection is contained in the Rent Act 1977 [...] Parties to an agreement cannot contract out of the Rent Acts; if they were able to do so the Acts would be a dead letter because in a state of housing shortage a person seeking residential accommodation may agree to anything to obtain shelter. The Rent Acts protect a tenant but they do not protect a licensee. Since parties to an agreement cannot contract out of the Rent Acts, a document which expresses the intention, genuine or bogus, of both parties or of one party to create a licence will nevertheless create a tenancy if the rights and obligations enjoyed and imposed satisfy the legal requirements of a tenancy. A person seeking residential accommodation may concur in any expression of intention in order to obtain shelter. Since parties to an agreement cannot contract out of the Rent Acts, a document expressed in the language of a licence must nevertheless be examined and construed by the court in order to decide whether the rights and obligations enjoyed and imposed create a licence or a tenancy. A person seeking residential accommodation may sign a document couched in any language in order to obtain shelter. Since parties to an agreement cannot contract out of the Rent Acts, the grant of a tenancy to two persons jointly cannot be concealed, accidentally or by design, by the creation of two documents in the form of licences. Two persons seeking residential accommodation may sign any number of documents in order to obtain joint shelter. In considering one or more documents for the purpose of deciding whether a tenancy has been created, the court must consider the surrounding circumstances including any relationship between the prospective occupiers, the course of negotiations and the nature and extent of the accommodation and the intended and actual mode of occupation of the accommodation. If the owner of a one-bedroomed flat granted a licence to a husband to occupy the flat provided he shared the flat with his wife and nobody else and granted a similar licence to the wife provided she shared the flat with the husband and nobody else, the court would be bound to consider the effect of both documents together. If the licence to the husband required him to pay a licence fee of £50 per month and the licence to the wife required her to pay a further licence fee of £50 per month, the two documents read together in the light of the property to be occupied and the obvious intended mode of occupation would confer exclusive occupation on the husband and wife jointly and a tenancy at the rent of £100.

Landlords dislike the Rent Acts and wish to enjoy the benefits of letting property without the burden of the restrictions imposed by the Acts. Landlords believe that the Rent Acts unfairly interfere with freedom of contract and exacerbate the housing shortage. Tenants on the other hand believe that the Acts are a necessary protection against the exploitation of people who do not own the freehold or long leases of their homes. The court lacks the knowledge and the power to form any judgment on these arguments which fall to be considered and determined by Parliament. The duty of the court is to enforce the Acts and in so doing to observe one principle which is inherent in the Acts and has been long recognised, the principle that parties cannot contract out of the Acts [. . .]

Where residential accommodation is occupied by two or more persons the occupiers may be licensees or tenants of the whole or each occupier may be a separate tenant of part. In the present appeals the only question raised is whether the occupiers are licensees or tenants of the whole [. . .]

[In *AG Securities v Vaughan*, the Court of Appeal] concluded that the four [occupiers] were jointly entitled to exclusive occupation of the flat. I am unable to agree. If a landlord who owns a three-bedroom flat enters into three separate independent tenancies with three independent tenants each of whom is entitled to one bedroom and to share the common parts, then the three tenants, if they agree, can exclude anyone else from the flat. But they do not enjoy exclusive occupation of the flat jointly under the terms of their tenancies. In the present case, if the four [occupiers] had been jointly entitled to exclusive occupation of the flat then, on the death of one of [the occupiers], the remaining three would be entitled to joint and exclusive occupation. But, in fact, on the death of one [occupier] the remaining three would not be entitled to joint and exclusive occupation of the flat. They could not exclude a fourth person nominated by the company. I would allow the appeal.

In the first appeal the four agreements were independent of one another. In the second appeal [*Antoniades v Villiers*] the two agreements were interdependent. Both would have been signed or neither. The two agreements must therefore be read together. Mr. Villiers and Miss Bridger applied to rent the flat jointly and sought and enjoyed joint and exclusive occupation of the whole of the flat. They shared the rights and the obligations imposed by the terms of their occupation. They acquired joint and exclusive occupation of the flat in consideration of periodical payments and they therefore acquired a tenancy jointly. Mr. Antoniades required each of them, Mr. Villiers and Miss Bridger, to agree to pay one half of each aggregate periodical payment, but this circumstance cannot convert a tenancy into a licence. A tenancy remains a tenancy even though the landlord may choose to require each of two joint tenants to agree expressly to pay one half of the rent. The tenancy conferred on Mr. Villiers and Miss Bridger the right to occupy the whole flat as their dwelling. Clause 16 reserved to Mr. Antoniades the power at any time to go into occupation of the flat jointly with Mr. Villiers and Miss Bridger. The exercise of that power would at common law put an end to the exclusive occupation of the flat by Mr. Villiers and Miss Bridger, terminate the tenancy of Mr. Villiers and Miss Bridger, and convert Mr. Villiers and Miss Bridges into licensees. But the powers reserved to Mr. Antoniades by clause 16 cannot be lawfully exercised because they are inconsistent with the provisions of the Rent Acts [. . .]

Clause 16 is a reservation to Mr. Antoniades of the right to go into occupation or to nominate others to enjoy occupation of the whole of the flat jointly with Mr. Villiers and Miss Bridger. Until that power is exercised Mr. Villiers and Miss Bridger are jointly in exclusive occupation of the whole of the flat making periodical payments and they are therefore tenants. The Rent Acts prevent the exercise of a power which would destroy the tenancy of Mr. Villiers and Miss Bridger and would deprive them of the exclusive occupation of the flat which they are now enjoying. Clause 16 is inconsistent with the provisions of the Rent Acts.

There is a separate and alternative reason why clause 16 must be ignored. Clause 16 was not a genuine reservation to Mr. Antoniades of a power to share the flat and a power to authorise other persons to share the flat. Mr. Antoniades did not genuinely intend to exercise the powers save possibly to bring pressure to bear to obtain possession. Clause 16 was only intended to deprive Mr. Villiers and Miss Bridger of the protection of the Rent Acts. Mr. Villiers and Miss Bridger had no choice in the matter.

In the notes of [the first instance judge], Mr. Villiers is reported as saying that: 'He [Mr. Antoniades] kept going on about it being a licence and not in the Rent Act. I didn't know either but was pleased to have a place after three or four months of chasing.' The notes of Miss Bridger's evidence include this passage: 'I didn't understand what was meant by exclusive possession or licence. Signed because so glad to move in. Had been looking for three months.'

In *Street v. Mountford*, I said:

'Although the Rent Acts must not be allowed to alter or influence the construction of an agreement, the court should, in my opinion, be astute to detect and frustrate sham devices and artificial transactions whose only object is to disguise the grant of a tenancy and to evade the Rent Acts.'[40]

It would have been more accurate and less liable to give rise to misunderstandings if I had substituted the word 'pretence' for the references to 'sham devices' and 'artificial transactions.'

---

[40] [1985] AC 809, 825.

Street v. Mountford was not a case which involved a pretence concerning exclusive possession. The agreement did not mention exclusive possession and the owner conceded that the occupier enjoyed exclusive possession. In *Somma v. Hazelhurst*[41] and other cases considered in *Street v. Mountford*, the owner wished to let residential accommodation but to avoid the Rent Acts. The occupiers wished to take a letting of residential accommodation. The owner stipulated for the execution of agreements which pretended that exclusive possession was not to be enjoyed by the occupiers. The occupiers were obliged to acquiesce with this pretence in order to obtain the accommodation. In my opinion the occupiers either did not understand the language of the agreements or assumed, justifiably, that in practice the owner would not violate their privacy. The owner's real intention was to rely on the language of the agreement to escape the Rent Acts. The owner allowed the occupiers to enjoy jointly exclusive occupation and accepted rent. A tenancy was created. *Street v. Mountford* reasserted three principles. First, parties to an agreement cannot contract out of the Rent Acts. Secondly, in the absence of special circumstances, not here relevant, the enjoyment of exclusive occupation for a term in consideration of periodic payments creates a tenancy. Thirdly, where the language of licence contradicts the reality of lease, the facts must prevail. The facts must prevail over the language in order that the parties may not contract out of the Rent Acts. In the present case clause 16 was a pretence.

The fact that clause 16 was a pretence appears from its terms and from the negotiations. Clause 16 in terms conferred on Mr. Antoniades and other persons the right to share the bedroom occupied by Mr. Villiers and Miss Bridger. Clause 16 conferred power on Mr. Antoniades to convert the sitting-room occupied by Mr. Villiers and Miss Bridger into a bedroom which could be jointly occupied by Mr. Villiers, Miss Bridger, Mr. Antoniades and any person or persons nominated by Mr. Antoniades. The facilities in the flat were not suitable for sharing between strangers. The flat, situated in an attic with a sloping roof, was too small for sharing between strangers. If clause 16 had been genuine there would have been some discussion between Mr. Antoniades, Mr. Villiers and Miss Bridger as to how clause 16 might be operated in practice and in whose favour it was likely to be operated. The addendum imposed on Mr. Villiers and Miss Bridger sought to add plausibility to the pretence of sharing by forfeiting the right of Mr. Villiers and Miss Bridger to continue to occupy the flat if their double-bedded romance blossomed into wedding bells. Finally and significantly, Mr. Antoniades never made any attempt to obtain increased income from the flat by exercising the powers which clause 16 purported to reserve to him. Clause 16 was only designed to disguise the grant of a tenancy and to contract out of the Rent Acts. In this case in the Court of Appeal Bingham L.J. said:

> 'The written agreements cannot possibly be construed as giving the occupants, jointly or severally, exclusive possession of the flat or any part of it. They stipulate with reiterated emphasis that the occupants shall not have exclusive possession.'[42]

My Lords, in *Street v. Mountford*, this House stipulated with reiterated emphasis that an express statement of intention is not decisive and that the court must pay attention to the facts and surrounding circumstances and to what people do as well as to what people say.

My Lords, in each of the cases which were disapproved by this House in *Street v. Mountford* and in the second appeal now under consideration, there was, in my opinion, the grant of a joint tenancy for the following reasons. (1) The applicants for the flat applied to rent the flat jointly and to enjoy exclusive occupation. (2) The landlord allowed the applicants jointly

---

[41] [1978] 1 WLR 1014.
[42] [1988] 3 WLR 139, 148.

to enjoy exclusive occupation and accepted rent. A tenancy was created. (3) The power reserved to the landlord to deprive the applicants of exclusive occupation was inconsistent with the provisions of the Rent Acts. (4) Moreover in all the circumstances the power which the landlord insisted upon to deprive the applicants of exclusive occupation was a pretence only intended to deprive the applicants of the protection of the Rent Acts.

Lord Oliver [addressing *Antoniades v Villiers*]

At 468–70

The document is clearly based upon the form of document which was upheld by the Court of Appeal as an effective licence in *Somma v. Hazelhurst*. That case, which rested on what was said to be the impossibility of the two licensees having between them exclusive possession, was overruled in *Street v. Mountford*. It was, however, a case which related to a single room and it is suggested that a similar agreement relating to premises containing space which could, albeit uncomfortably, accommodate another person is not necessarily governed by the same principle. On the other hand, the trial judge found that apart from the few visits by [Mr Antoniades] (who, on all but one occasion, sought admission by knocking on the door) no one shared with [the occupiers] and that they had exclusive possession. He held that the licences were 'artificial transactions designed to evade the Rent Acts,' that a tenancy was created and that [the occupiers] occupied as joint tenants.

His decision was reversed by the Court of Appeal on, broadly, the grounds that he had erred in treating the subsequent conduct of the parties as admissible as an aid to construction of the agreements and that in so far as the holding above referred to constituted a finding that the licences were a sham, that was unsupported by the evidence inasmuch as [the occupiers'] intention that they should enjoy exclusive possession was not shared by [Mr Antoniades]. The licences could not, therefore, be said to mask the real intention of the parties and fell to be construed by reference to what they said in terms.

If the documents fall to be taken seriously at their face value and to be construed according to their terms, I see, for my part, no escape from the conclusion at which the Court of Appeal arrived. If it is once accepted that [Mr Antoniades] enjoyed the right—whether he exercised it or not—to share the accommodation with [the occupiers], either himself or by introducing one or more other persons to use the flat with them, it is, as it seems to me, incontestable that the [occupiers] cannot claim to have had exclusive possession. [The occupiers'] case therefore rests, as [counsel for the occupiers] frankly admits, upon upholding the judge's approach that the true transaction contemplated was that [the occupiers] should jointly enjoy exclusive possession and that the licences were mere sham or window-dressing to indicate legal incidents which were never seriously intended in fact, but which would be inconsistent with the application to that transaction of the Rent Acts. Now to begin with, I do not, for my part, read the notes of the judge's judgment as showing that he construed the agreement in the light of what the parties subsequently did. I agree entirely with the Court of Appeal that if he did that he was in error. But though subsequent conduct is irrelevant as an aid to construction, it is certainly admissible as evidence on the question of whether the documents were or were not genuine documents giving effect to the parties' true intentions. Broadly what is said by [counsel for the occupiers] is that nobody acquainted with the circumstances in which the parties had come together and with the physical lay-out and size of the premises could seriously have imagined that the clauses in the licence which, on the face of them, contemplate [Mr Antoniades] and an apparently limitless number of other persons moving in to share the whole of the available accommodation, including the bedroom, with what, to all intents and purposes, was a married couple committed to paying £174 a month in advance, were anything other than a smoke-screen; and the fact [Mr Antoniades], who might be assumed to want to make the maximum profit out of the premises, never sought to introduce anyone else is at least some indication that that is exactly what it was [...]

The judge was, in my judgment, entitled to conclude that [the occupiers] had exclusive possession of the premises. I read his finding that, 'the licences are artificial transactions designed to evade the Rent Acts' as a finding that they were sham documents designed to conceal the true nature of the transaction. There was, in my judgment, material on which he could properly reach this conclusion and I, too, would allow the appeal.

Each of *AG Securities v Vaughan* and *Antoniades v Villiers* raises questions about how multiple occupiers of land can claim a lease. We will examine that issue in detail in section 2.5 below. For present purposes, we can focus on the appeal in *Antoniades* and the decision that the agreement created a lease even though the clear effect of Clause 16 was to deny the occupiers a right to exclusive possession.

The decision of the House of Lords can only be justified if it is permissible, when deciding if B (or B1 and B2) has a right to exclusive possession, to *disregard* particular contractual terms. In examining this question, we again have to consider both the doctrinal perspective and the utility approach.

From a doctrinal perspective, it is clear that an apparent contractual term can be disregarded if it is not, in fact, contractually binding. One well-established example occurs if an apparent contractual term is a 'sham' (a term used by Lord Templeman in *Street v Mountford* when referring to 'sham devices').[43] Diplock LJ provided the commonly used definition of a sham, in the contractual context at least, in the following case.[44]

Snook v London and West Ridings Investments Ltd [1967] 2 QB 786, CA

Diplock LJ

At 802

If it has any legal meaning, the term 'sham' means acts done or documents executed by the parties to the 'sham' which are intended by them to give to third parties or to the court the appearance of creating between the parties legal rights and obligations different from the actual legal rights and obligations (if any) which the parties intended to create [...] for acts or documents to be a 'sham', with whatever legal consequences follow from this, all the parties thereto must have a common intention that the acts or documents are not to create the legal rights and obligations which they give the appearance of creating. No unexpressed intentions of a 'shammer' affect the rights of a party whom he deceived.

As is made clear by that definition, a term can only be dismissed as a sham if *neither* party intends that the term should create genuine legal rights. One example occurs if A sells a painting to B for £10,000, but, to minimize her tax bill, persuades B to sign a contract of

---

43 [1985] AC 809, 825.

44 The reference to documents cannot mean that either all of a document is sham, or none of it: see *Hitch v Stone* [2001] STC 214. Rather, each apparent term within a document must be seen as a relevant 'act', and will only be valid if accompanied by the necessary intention that the term should genuinely create contractual rights.

sale recording the price as £100. In such a case, each party intends that B should be under a legal duty to pay £10,000; neither party intends that B's duty is to pay only £100. The written 'contract' is therefore of no legal effect: it is not genuinely intended to create legal rights.

It is clear that this model is of very little use in a case such as *Antoniades v Villiers*. In that case, it was abundantly clear that Mr Antoniades *did* intend for Clause 16 to create genuine legal rights: the whole point of the clause was to ensure that the occupiers did not have a right to exclusive possession. It is therefore no surprise that, in *Antoniades*, Lord Templeman did not base his decision on the sham concept; instead, his Lordship based his decision to disregard the sharing clause (Clause 16) on two separate grounds. As suggested in the extract below, those grounds are not free from difficulty.

McFarlane and Simpson, 'Tackling Avoidance' in *Rationalizing Property, Equity and Trusts: Essays in Honour of Edward Burn* (ed Getzler, 2003)

At 151–2

Lord Templeman provides two grounds for denying effect to the sharing clause. First, it was said that Mr Antoniades could never insert others into occupation as [the Rent Acts prevent him from exercising his power to do so]. This reasoning cannot be supported, as it assumes the very thing it purports to prove. The Rent Acts can only apply if the occupiers are lessees, which will only be the case if they have a right to exclusive possession. As the Rent Acts can therefore only apply if the sharing clause, which seems to deny such a right to exclusive possession, is found to be invalid, those Acts cannot also be the means by which such invalidity is proved [...]

Secondly, Lord Templeman held that the clause was [...] "a pretence [...] only designed to disguise the grant of a tenancy and to contract out of the Rent Acts". This reasoning is crucial as it aims to provide a means, independent of the Rent Acts, to render the sharing clause ineffective. It also seems clear that Lord Templeman contemplates going beyond the sham doctrine, as conventionally understood. First, his Lordship prefers to condemn the clause as a "pretence", rather than as a "sham device or artificial transaction." Whilst the concepts of pretence and sham had been used interchangeably in the past, Lord Templeman's explicit preference for the former term does suggest that it involves the adoption of a new means by which a clause may be rendered ineffective. Certainly, Lord Templeman's application of the concept of pretence in *Villiers* goes beyond [...] the orthodox 'sham test'.

At 157–8

[...A suggested justification for the 'pretence' test is that] terms can be disregarded where they are inserted for the purpose of avoiding the Rent Acts by denying a right to exclusive possession. It is true that, at a number of points in his judgment in *Villiers*, Lord Templeman emphasises that this was the owner's aim in including clause 16 in the written agreement...Nonetheless, the courts have repeatedly rejected any suggestion that they have a general, non-statutory power to disregard agreed terms simply because those terms have been agreed in order to avoid a particular characterisation of the parties' dealings. Any number of examples can be given.

First, the courts have frequently had to consider situations in which parties have, for various reasons, chosen to set up a hire-purchase transaction rather than a simple loan on the security of goods. As long as the parties have genuinely intended to create the legal rights characteristic of hire-purchase, then, even if the only reason for preferring that mechanism has been the desire to avoid creating a secured loan, the agreement will be taken at face-value by the court.[45] The validity of this approach has been upheld in cases dealing with attempts to avoid the very legislation considered in *Antoniades v Villiers*. In *Kaye v Massbetter*,[46] an owner insisted that a tenancy agreement be made with a company created for that purpose, rather than with the individual who was to occupy the property. The only reason for doing so was to avoid the Rent Acts, which do not protect company tenants, yet this device was upheld by the Court of Appeal.

From a doctrinal perspective, then, it seems that the 'pretence' test, if it amounts to disregarding terms inserted for the *purpose* of denying an occupier exclusive possession, cannot be justified. After all, if A simply decides not to grant B exclusive possession, he is perfectly free to do so. In *Antoniades v Villiers* itself, it may nonetheless be possible to reconcile the decision of the House of Lords with doctrine. Lord Oliver's speech does not rely on the pretence test and can perhaps be explained on a standard contractual principle: a term is only binding on B if A reasonably believes that B is agreeing to be bound by that term. Usually, of course, B's signature of a written document ensures that it *is* reasonable for A to believe that B is agreeing to be bound by all of the terms set out in the document. But if the surrounding factual circumstances serve to make a term as set out in the document wholly implausible, it may just be possible for B to argue that such a term is not binding. This seems to be the point that Lord Oliver makes in the extract above, when stating that no reasonable person *'acquainted with the circumstances in which the parties had come together and with the physical lay-out and size of the premises'* could genuinely believe that Mr Antoniades had a legal right to share occupation of the flat.

The difficulty with this attempt to exclude the pretence test, however, is that the Court of Appeal adopted that test in cases following *Antoniades*. One example is provided by the combined judgment of the Court of Appeal in the cases of *Aslan v Murphy (Nos 1 & 2); Duke v Wynne*.[47] In each case, occupation of residential premises occurred under an agreement that permitted A to share occupation, or to insert other occupiers. In *Aslan*, the agreement also included a term that *'the licensor licenses the licensee to use (but not exclusively) all the furnished room [...] on each day between the hours of midnight and 10.30am and between noon and midnight, but at no other times'*. In *Aslan*, B occupied a small basement room in Redcliffe Gardens, London.

In *Duke*, B1 and B2, a married couple, occupied a three-bedroom house in Dunkeld Road, South Norwood, along with their two young sons. The Court of Appeal found that, in each case, a lease had been granted. Lord Donaldson MR, referring to the concept of a pretence, regarded it as important that, in each case, A had not, in practice, attempted to exercise his rights to share occupation, or, in *Aslan*, to remove B from the land between 10.30 a.m. and noon.

Such decisions can only be seen as doctrinally justified if it is possible to find a rationale for the wider pretence test. One such rationale is proposed in the following extract.

---

[45] See, e.g., *Helby v Matthews* [1895] AC 471, 475; *Re George Inglefield Ltd* [1933] Ch 1, *per* Romer LJ; *Yorkshire Railway Co v Maclure* (1882) 21 Ch D 309, *per* Lindley LJ.

[46] [1991] 2 EGLR 97.

[47] [1990] 1 WLR 766.

Bright, 'Avoiding Tenancy Legislation: Sham and Contracting Out Revisited' [2002] CLJ 146

At 152–3

In practice, the need for a common intention and for a whole transaction to be a sham limits the usefulness of the doctrine. There could not, for example, have been a sham in this strict sense in *Antoniades v. Villiers* where a couple were asked to sign separate licence agreements containing a provision, clause 16, which stated that the "licensor shall be entitled at any time to use the rooms together with the licensee and permit other persons to use all of the rooms together with the licensee [...]" Given the size and layout of the accommodation, and the relationship between the couple, it was obvious that the "licensor" would not exercise this right. In holding the couple to have a tenancy and not separate licences, the House of Lords used a variety of language to explain why clause 16 should not be given its face value. Only Lord Oliver spoke of sham [...] In moving away from the language of sham to pretence there is the chance to introduce greater flexibility. Essentially, pretence will be found where there is no genuine intention to implement the agreement as it stands. This can also be said of sham, but there are not the same constraints about the need for a common intention and for the whole document to be a lie. Lord Donaldson M.R. clearly saw the two concepts operating differently in *Aslan*:

> '[...] parties may succumb to the temptation to agree to pretend to have particular rights and duties which are not in fact any part of the true bargain [... The] courts would be acting unrealistically if they did not keep a weather eye open for pretences, taking due account of how the parties have acted in performance of their apparent bargain. This identification and exposure of such pretences does not necessarily lead to the conclusion that their agreement is a sham, but only to the conclusion that the terms of the true bargain are not wholly the same as that of the bargain appearing on the face of the agreement.'

Throughout the speeches in *Antoniades* it is clear that the reason why the licences were found to be non-genuine was because there was never any intention to rely on clause 16. Had they been applying the *Snook* concept of sham the House of Lords would have had to find a mutuality of intention to mislead, but there is no discussion in the speeches of whether both parties intended for clause 16 not to operate, nor was there a third party that they intended to mislead. Nor did it matter that the focus was on two aspects of the transaction rather than the transaction as a whole. The essence of pretence is that the agreement is a smokescreen. It is not sufficient to strike down a device on the grounds that it was intended or designed for the sole purpose of avoiding protective legislation, even if there is no other purpose served by it. As with sham, motive is irrelevant. It does not matter that the only reason why a particular route, however tortuous, is selected is to avoid statutory provisions: the test is simply one of whether or not the device is seriously intended. The transaction must be taken at face value unless it is shown that it was not genuine in the sense that the parties never intended to rely on that device.

At 157–9

Much of value was lost when the dicta of Diplock L.J. in *Snook* became hardened law and it is clear that in *AG Securities* the House of Lords, and Lord Templeman in particular, was seeking to break away from these confines. Both sham and pretence are to do with the same thing, that is, to enable the true nature of a transaction to be revealed. The case law, although rather thin on this, does support a more sophisticated account of sham than is usually given and which accords better with "legal principle and morality". Whatever it is called, this refined doctrine of sham would be able to subsume within it the doctrine of pretence.

Where it is found that documents entered into give the appearance of creating legal rights and obligations between the parties that are not genuine, in the sense that there is no intention of honouring these obligations or enjoying the rights, then:

1. where there is a common intention to deceive, that document will be void as between those parties. It is this automatic consequence of voidness, and possible impact upon third parties, that accounts for the reluctance of courts to find a sham and the need for very clear evidence that the provisions are not genuine. If an innocent third party has relied upon the form of the document, the parties may be estopped from setting up the invalidity of the documents

2. where only one of the parties intended to deceive or inserted provisions which he had no intention of honouring and the other party was ignorant of this (or did not 'know or care') or simply went along with it through absence of choice, the party with the deceitful (non-genuine) intent:

   (i) will not be allowed to take advantage of the formal appearance of rights to the disadvantage of an 'innocent' party. This means that a person innocent of the sham will be allowed to rely upon external evidence to prove that the formal agreement is a sham/non-genuine. Similarly, when applied to the residential tenancy cases, the occupier is allowed to prove that the 'licensor' never had any intention of relying upon clauses which prevent a tenancy arising, as, for example, with the 'sharing clause' in *AG Securities* or the clause requiring a daily 90 minute departure in *Aslan*. As Lord Donaldson M.R. said in *Aslan*, it 'is the true rather than the apparent bargain which determines the question: tenant or lodger?'

   (ii) will not be allowed to set aside the formal document by proving it is a sham and thereby rely on the real/true agreement if an innocent person has relied upon the formal agreement. *Snook* [is an example]...the court held that there was no sham because there was no common intention to deceive but the effect was the same as saying that the 'shammer' could not set aside the sham document to the detriment of the innocent party.

Bright's argument is that the pretence test is *not* a special feature of the law of leases, developed to ensure that statutory protection is available to deserving or vulnerable occupiers. Bright instead argues that the pretence test is a logical corollary of the sham test and, indeed, can be subsumed within it. On this view, cases such as *Antoniades* and *Aslan* are simply applying standard contractual principles. The validity of that view therefore depends on a more general question about contract law: is it the case that, for a term to be contractually binding, the parties must intend *not only* that the term should create legal rights, *but also* that the term will be enforced in practice?[48]

Whatever the answer to that question, it may still be possible to justify the pretence test from the perspective of utility rather than doctrine. For example, in section 2.1 above, we

---

[48] For a view that a contractual term is, in general, binding even if the parties did not intend to enforce it in practice, see McFarlane and Simpson, 'Tackling Avoidance' in *Rationalizing Property, Equity and Trusts: Essays in Honour of Edward Burn* (ed Getzler, 2003, pp 160–3) and McFarlane, *The Structure of Property Law* (2008, p 665).

saw Hill's suggestion that policy, rather than doctrine, can justify the decision in *Street v Mountford* that a lease can be created even when A does not intend to give B a property right. In that article, Hill suggests:[49] '*The drafting of a residential agreement as a licence rather than a lease is analogous to the inclusion of an unfair contractual term in a consumer sale.*' On this view, the pretence doctrine is simply a means to an end: it gives judges the power (usually only given by statutes such as the Unfair Contract Terms Act 1977) to disregard terms that, whilst notionally agreed, have been forced on a reluctant occupier. Certainly, as noted by Hill, Lord Templeman did refer in *Antoniades* to the fact that '*a person seeking residential accommodation may concur in any expression of intention* [. . . and] *may sign a document couched in any language in order to obtain shelter*'.[50]

This analysis raises an important point about the utility approach: one that we encountered in Chapter 1, section 5.7. There, we saw Harris's observation that a choice as to whether the doctrinal or utility approach is to be preferred may depend on your view as to the proper role of judges. For example, it may be plausible take the view that whilst it is important, in a case such as *Antoniades*, to protect an occupier and to ensure that the relevant statutory protection applies, it is not for judges to take on the power to disregard terms that, according to the usual doctrinal tests, are contractually binding. On that view, it is for Parliament to make a change to the law: for example, by extending the statutory protection beyond those with leases to parties who occupy their home under a contractual licence. Indeed, as we will see in Chapter 24, section 4, the Law Commission has recently suggested just that change: the remaining statutory protection (of course, now much diminished in the private rental sector) should not be limited to tenants, but should also be extended to licensees.

2.5 A RIGHT TO EXCLUSIVE POSSESSION: MULTIPLE OCCUPANCY

In each of *AG Securities* and *Antioniades*, more than one person occupied land. In such a case, it could, in theory, be possible for each occupier to claim a right to exclusive possession of a *particular part* of the land (e.g. of a particular room in a flat). But the occupiers did not pursue that argument in either case; instead, it was argued (unsuccessfully in *AG Securities*, but successfully in *Antoniades*) that the occupiers, seen as a unit, had a single right to exclusive possession. This is a claim to co-ownership of the whole of the land: a claim that the individual occupiers, acting a team, held a single legal estate. We examined co-ownership in Chapter 19, in section 2 of which we saw that there are two possible forms of co-ownership: the joint tenancy and the tenancy in common. In each case, there is 'unity of possession' amongst the co-owners: each is prima facie entitled to occupy all of the land. In a tenancy in common, unlike a joint tenancy, each co-owner also has an 'undivided share': a right to a particular, individual share of the benefits of the co-owned land. We also saw there that, due to s 1(6) of the LPA 1925, it is impossible for a legal estate (such as a legal lease) to be held by tenants in common: in such a case, the only permitted form of co-ownership is a joint tenancy. So, what happens if A transfers a freehold to B1 and B2, stating that B1 is to have a 40 per cent share and B2 is to have a 60 per cent share? Despite the parties' intentions, B1 and B2 hold the legal freehold as joint tenants (without an individual share). But, under s 34(2) of the 1925 Act,

---

49 (1996) 16 LS 200, 217.
50 [1990] 1 AC 417, 458.

a trust is imposed: B1 and B2 hold that legal freehold as joint tenants, but each also has an individual share to the benefit of that legal right, arising under a trust.

In *AG Securities*, however, the House of Lords adopted a different approach to the specific question of co-ownership of a lease. It was held that the four occupiers had a lease only if they could show that, acting together, they *genuinely* had a joint tenancy of that lease. The assumption is that, if B1, B2, B3, and B4 had intended to receive a right to exclusive possession as tenants in common, no lease would arise: s 34(2) cannot operate to save the lease by allowing B1, B2, B3, and B4 to hold a legal lease as joint tenants on trust for themselves. This approach causes real problems for joint occupiers. As we saw in Chapter 19, section 2, to establish a tenancy in common, it is necessary for the occupiers to show *only* that they have 'unity of possession'—that is, that each is entitled to occupy all of the land. To establish a *genuine* joint tenancy (rather than one imposed by s 34(2)), however, the occupiers also need to show that they have '*unity of interest, time and title*'. This means that they must show that they acquired the lease together: without individual shares, at the same time, and in the same way.

In *AG Securities*, it was impossible for the occupiers to show a genuine joint tenancy: it was clearly not the case that they had acquired a lease together, because they had not moved into the land at the same time; rather, they were part of a 'fluctuating population' of occupiers, each of whom moved in whenever an individual room happened to be vacant. In *Antoniades*, Mr Villiers and Miss Bridger had signed separate agreements with Mr Antoniades. Nonetheless, they were able to show that they had acquired a lease together: the agreements were identical and signed on the same day, and Mr Villiers and Miss Bridger moved in together, as a couple. The cases thus reflect an important difference between: (i) cases in which rooms in a house or flat are occupied by individuals who move in and move out at different times; and (ii) cases in which the house or flat itself is occupied together by a couple (or group) who move in together and who would expect to move out together. In particular, the *decision* in *AG Securities* seems correct, because, on the facts, it was not plausible to see the four occupiers as a group, co-operating to claim exclusive possession of the entire property.

The *reasoning* in *AG Securities*, however, with its insistence on a joint tenancy requirement, can cause problems even in a case in which a couple or group *do* move in together and exercise joint exclusive control of the property (and thus have unity of possession). As the following extract shows, the difficulties arise if the occupiers undertake individual and separate duties to pay rent (and thus have no unity of interest).

Mikeover v Brady [1989] 3 All ER 618, CA

Facts: Mikeover Ltd had a long lease of the top floor flat at 179 Southgate Road, London N1. It advertised the flat as available for occupation by two people. The flat consisted of a front room, which had a cooker and refrigerator in it, and a back room, which had a sink in it. In addition, there was a bathroom and lavatory in the attic. Mr Brady and Miss Guile, a couple, responded to the advert and moved into the flat together. Each signed a separate, but identical, agreement, headed as a licence agreement, allowing each of them to share occupation of the flat for six months, in return for paying a monthly rent of £86.66. Once that initial six months had expired, the occupiers were allowed to remain in the flat, on the same terms as set out in the initial agreements. Early in 1986, Miss Guile moved out of the flat. She informed Mr Ferster (a director of Mikeover Ltd, and the party with whom she and Mr Brady had dealt) of this in April 1986. Mr Brady wished to remain and offered to pay £173.32 as monthly rent. Mr Ferster declined that offer, stating: '*I can't accept it. I'll hold you responsible for your share only.*' Nonetheless, even on the basis that he had to pay only £86.66 a month, Mr Brady fell into arrears on the rent payment and, in early 1987, Mikeover Ltd sought to remove him from the flat. Mr Brady claimed that, as a result of the initial agreements signed by the parties, he and Miss Guile had, acting together, acquired a lease of the flat. If that were correct, Mr Brady would then qualify for statutory protection under the Rent Acts. The first instance judge, however, rejected that argument and held that the initial agreements gave each party only a licence. Mr Brady appealed unsuccessfully to the Court of Appeal.

Slade LJ

At 623–7

[Slade LJ found that the agreements should be interpreted together and against the factual background that '*the layout of the flat was such that it was clearly only suitable for occupation by persons who were personally acceptable to one another*'. On that basis:] It follows that, in our judgment, [Mr Brady's] agreement on its true construction conferred on him the right (by cl 1) to exclusive occupation of the flat in common only with Miss Guile during its currency [...]

It is, however, well settled that four unities must be present for the creation of a joint tenancy, namely the unities of possession, interest, title and time [...] In the present case there is no dispute that the two agreements of 6 June 1984 operated to confer on the defendant and Miss Guile unity of possession and title. Likewise, there was unity of time in that each of their interests arose simultaneously and was expressed to endure for six months. The dispute concerns unity of interest. The general principle, as stated in *Megarry and Wade* is:[51]

> 'The interest of each joint tenant is the same in extent, nature and duration, for in theory of law they hold but one estate.'

'Interest' in this context must, in our judgment, include the bundle of rights and obligations representing that interest. The difficulty, from the defendant's point of view, is that the two agreements, instead of imposing a joint liability on him and Miss Guile to pay a deposit of £80 and monthly payments of £173.32, on their face imposed on each of them individual and separate obligations to pay only a deposit of £40 and monthly payments of only £86.66. On the face of it, the absence of joint obligations of payment is inconsistent with the existence of a joint tenancy.

Counsel for [Mr Brady] sought to meet this difficulty in three ways. First, he contended that the two agreements were, as he put it, 'interdependent' and must be read together. When so read, he submitted, they should be construed as placing on the two parties joint obligations. However, it seems to us quite impossible to rewrite the two agreements in this manner as a matter of construction [...o]ne cannot add up two several [i.e. separate] obligations to pay £X so as to construct a joint obligation to pay £2X.

Next counsel for [Mr Brady], as we understood him, contended that, in so far as the two agreements purported to render each of the defendant and Miss Guile merely individually liable for the payment of a deposit of £40 and monthly payments of £86·66, they were 'shams'. The true intention of the parties, he submitted, to be inferred from all the circumstances, was

---

[51] [The reference in the case is to the 5th edn (1984): see now *Megarry and Wade's Law of Real Property* (7th edn, eds Harpum et al, 2008, [13–006]).]

that they should be jointly liable to make monthly payments of £173.32 and to pay a deposit of £80 (to the return of which they should be jointly entitled in due course).

In this context, the subsequent conduct of the parties is admissible in evidence, not for the purpose of construing the agreements but on the question whether the documents were or were not genuine documents giving effect to the parties' true intentions [...]

However, the onus of proving a sham falls on the defendant and, in our judgment, the parties' subsequent conduct affords no support, or at least no sufficient support, to his case in this respect [...] we see no sufficient grounds for disturbing the judge's finding that the receipts of sums by [Mikeover Ltd] from [Mr Brady] after Miss Guile left the flat represented no more than was due from him on the footing that he was liable only for monthly payments of £86.66 [...Mikeover Ltd's] failure to accept [Mr Brady's] offer to pay the higher monthly sum does not in any way assist [Mr Brady's] contention that the provisions for payment contained in the two agreements were shams.

On these authorities, it appears to us that unity of interest imports the existence of joint rights and joint obligations. We therefore conclude that the provisions for payment contained in these two agreements (which were genuinely intended to impose and did impose on each party an obligation to pay no more than the sums reserved to [Mikeover Ltd] by his or her separate agreement) were incapable in law of creating a joint tenancy, because the monetary obligations of the two parties were not joint obligations and there was accordingly no complete unity of interest. It follows that there was no joint tenancy.

Mikeover v Brady nicely illustrates the problem caused to occupiers by the approach adopted in *AG Securities*. In *Mikeover*, the individual rent obligation would *not* have prevented Mr Brady from showing that he and Miss Guile held a lease as tenants in common, each with a 50 per cent share of the lease—but it did prevent him from showing that they held a lease as joint tenants (i.e. only as a team and without any individual share), and, under the *AG Securities* approach, it then follows that the occupiers did not have a lease.

As explained in the following extract, it is not obvious why the courts should insist on there being a *genuine* joint tenancy of a lease when, as we have seen, there is no such requirement when parties acquire a freehold together.

Sparkes, 'Co-Tenants, Joint Tenants and Tenants in Common' (1989) 18 AALR 151

At 155

In the light of Lord Templeman's speech [in *AG Securities v Vaughan*], it must be asked whether a tenancy in common can exist in an informal tenancy. The House of Lords simply assumed that this could not be the case. The question is by no means easy to answer in view of the well-known inadequacy of the provisions of the Law of Property Act 1925 concerned with the imposition of a statutory [trust of land] on co-ownership.[52] Before 1926, legal tenants could be either joint tenants or tenants in common. Equally landlords could hold in common, so that for example one landlord could serve a notice to quit that was effectual in respect of his undivided share, while leaving intact the term in respect of the undivided shares of other landlords. An informal tenancy could then have created a legal leasehold

---

[52] [The author here refers to a statutory trust for sale, because the article was written before the Trusts of Land and Appointment of Trustees Act 1996. As to the effect of that Act, see Chapter 19, section 5.]

estate held by tenants in common. Such a tenancy, if it could exist today, would fall squarely within the definition of a protected tenancy.

After 1925, a legal estate must be held by joint tenants. A statutory [trust of land] arises and the beneficial owners might be either joint tenants or tenants in common beneficially. These rules should apply to any legal estate, whether the estate is freehold or leasehold [...]

Business tenancies must often exist as equitable tenancies in common, since such tenancies are frequently held by partnerships. A business lease is likely to contain an express declaration of a beneficial tenancy in common, which is best suited for business partnership. In the absence of an express declaration, equity would presume the intention to create a beneficial tenancy in common. Similar considerations apply to agricultural holdings. The question is therefore whether there is something special about residential tenancies which marks them out as uniquely confined to joint tenancies in the technical sense. The Rent Act 1977 contains no express prohibition; nor does the Housing Act 1988 for the assured tenancy present and future [...]

At 163–4

Nothing is clear in the field of co-ownership of short term leases. The courts have confidently equated a co-ownership joint tenancy and a co-tenancy under the Rent Act 1977. It is tentatively submitted that it is wrong to equate these two separate concepts.

In *AG Securities v. Vaughan* the House of Lords decided that four occupiers who were free to leave independently of each other were licensees and not co-tenants. The main ground relied upon was that the occupiers did not together share exclusive possession. Some dicta rest this decision on a different ground—that is the absence of unity of interest. In the absence of this unity at most a tenancy in common was created. This now forms the ratio decidendi of the Court of Appeal decision, *Mikeover v Brady*.

In both cases, it was important to establish whether or not there was a concurrent interest in the four occupiers. If it was concurrent, whether it was a joint tenancy or a tenancy in common or some other kind of relationship was (until the death of one of the parties)[53] quite irrelevant. For a tenancy in common to exist, only one of the four unities—that is unity of possession—would be necessary. An informal tenancy in common might create a statutory trust [...] or it might stand altogether outside conventional property law. There is no need to search for the remaining unities—that is time, title and interest.

The court should look to see whether there has been a joint grant of the right to exclusive occupation of the property, or in shorthand, joint exclusive possession. The opinions delivered in *AG Securities v Vaughan* are quite consistent with the general view that it is the substantive existence of a joint right to exclusive possession that is determinative of the existence of a tenancy.

Sparkes' view is thus that the approach in *Mikeover v Brady* cannot be justified as a matter of doctrine.

There are some challenges to that view: for example, Roger Smith[54] has argued that the structure of the LPA 1925 may support the approach; McFarlane[55] has argued that if, as in

---

[53] [As we saw in Chapter 19, section 2.2, the doctrine of survivorship means that the death of a joint tenant has consequences differing from those arising on the death of a tenant in common.]

[54] See Smith, *Plural Ownership* (2005, pp 24–6).

[55] McFarlane, *The Structure of Property Law* (2008, pp 714–15). The general rule applying to contractual rights is shown by, for example, Coke, *Commentaries on Littleton* (1628, p 198a) and *Re McKerrell* [1912] 2 Ch 648.

Mikeover, the occupiers claim that a contractual agreement has given rise to a lease, then they must claim as joint tenants, because, as a matter of general contract law, it is impossible for a contractual right to be held by tenants in common. Whatever your final view on the doctrinal question, however, it is also important to consider the *AG Securities* approach from the utility perspective. From that point of view, the approach, as exemplified by the decision in *Mikeover v Brady*, certainly contrasts with the more generous stance taken towards occupiers in cases such as *Street v Mountford* and *Antoniades v Villiers*.

2.6 A PROPRIETARY RIGHT TO EXCLUSIVE POSSESSION

If I were to make a contractual promise allowing you exclusive possession of Buckingham Palace for five years, recorded in a deed, could that promise give you a property right in Buckingham Palace? Clearly not. The problem is that, whilst you have a right *against me* to have exclusive possession of the Palace, I am simply not in a position to give you a property right in relation to that land. Nonetheless, the reasoning of the House of Lords in *Bruton v London & Quadrant Housing Trust Ltd*[56] appears to mean that, in such a case, our contractual agreement does give you a lease.

Not surprisingly, as we will see when examining *Bruton* in Chapter 24, section 3, that decision has attracted a lot of disapproval. It is, however, very important to note that the House of Lords in *Bruton* made clear that, in our example, the contractual agreement does *not* give you a property right. The controversy excited by the decision is about the very idea that B can have a 'lease' *even though* he or she does not have a property right. In effect, *Bruton* means that there are now two sorts of leases: standard leases, which give their holder (B) a property right in land; and contractual leases, which give their holder (B) only a personal right against A. We will therefore postpone our consideration of *Bruton* to Chapter 24; in this chapter, our focus is on the standard, proprietary lease.

2.7 A RIGHT TO EXCLUSIVE POSSESSION FOR A LIMITED PERIOD

In section 1.1.3 above, we saw that, in *Ashburn Anstalt v Arnold*, the Court of Appeal held that B acquired a lease as a result of A's agreement to give B exclusive possession of land until that land was needed for re-development. In doing so, however, the Court of Appeal followed an earlier case (*In re Midland Railway Co's Agreement*),[57] which had departed from the orthodox position that, to have a lease, B needs to have a right to exclusive possession *for a limited period*. This requirement is reflected in the very phrase used, in s 1 of the LPA 1925, to define a lease—that is, a 'term of years absolute'. In that context, the word 'term'—like 'terminus', or 'terminal'—indicates an end or a limit. The problem in *Ashburn Anstalt* was that there was a chance that the land would *never* be needed for re-development; as a result, the agreement between A and B did not necessarily give B a right to exclusive possession for a limited period.

The House of Lords noted that problem in the following case, which restored the orthodox position and thus overruled *Ashburn Anstalt* (albeit only on the specific question of whether a lease needs to be for a limited period).

---

56 [2000] 1 AC 406.
57 [1971] Ch 725. Lord Denning MR was *not* on the panel.

Prudential Assurance Ltd v London Residuary Body [1992] 2 AC 386, HL

Facts: Prior to 1930, Mr. Nathan owned shop premises: Nos 263–265, Walworth Road, Southwark, London. The London City Council (LCC) owned the road itself. LCC planned to widen the road: this would lead to it encroaching on part of the strip of land, owned by Mr Nathan, then separating his shop from the road. So the LCC bought Mr Nathan's freehold of that strip of land, agreeing, however, that Mr Nathan could continue to use it until the road-widening project went ahead. The agreement stated the strip was leased back to Mr Nathan for continued use, with the rest of 263–265 Walworth Road, until required for road widening; in return, Mr Nathan agreed to pay £30 a year in rent. It was clear that both parties intended this to be a temporary arrangement, because both believed that the road-widening project would soon go ahead. So, for example, there was no provision to allow the rent to be increased.

By 1988, however, the road widening had not occurred. The London Residuary Body (LRB), a successor of LCC, now held the freehold of the strip of land, and Nos 263–265 were owned by Prudential Assurance Ltd, which also had the benefit of the 1930 agreement. LRB attempted, by giving notice, to end Prudential's right to use the strip of land. It was agreed by valuers acting for each side that the current commercial rent for the strip of land (valuable because it allowed Nos 263–265 to have a shop frontage) was £10,000 per annum rather than the £30 that Prudential was paying under the 1930 agreement. Prudential, however, argued that LRB could not regain possession of the strip, because the land was not yet needed for road widening. Millett J found in favour of Prudential; LRB[58] appealed directly to the House of Lords.[59]

Lord Templeman

At 390–6

A demise for years is a contract for the exclusive possession and profit of land for some determinate period [...] The Law of Property Act 1925 [...] provided, by section 1(1), that:

'The only estates in land which are capable of subsisting or of being conveyed or created at law are—(a) An estate in fee simple absolute in possession; (b) A term of years absolute.'

Section 205(1)(xxvii) was in these terms:

'"Term of years absolute" means a term of years [...] either certain or liable to determination by notice, re-entry, operation of law, or by a provision for cesser on redemption, or in any other event (other than the dropping of a life, or the determination of a determinable life interest); [...] and in this definition the expression 'term of years' includes a term for less than a year, or for a year or years and a fraction of a year or from year to year; [...]'

The term expressed to be granted by the agreement in the present case does not fall within this definition [...]

---

58 After giving the notice to quit, LRB sold its freehold, so, technically, the new freehold owners brought the appeal.

59 Such a 'leapfrog' appeal is permitted where, for example, an appellant wishes to challenge the validity of previous Court of Appeal authority: in this case, *Ashburn Anstalt v Arnold* [1989] Ch 1. There is no point appealing first to the Court of Appeal because, unlike the House of Lords, it will simply be bound by that Court of Appeal authority.

When the agreement in the present case was made, it failed to grant an estate in the land. The tenant however entered into possession and paid the yearly rent of £30 reserved by the agreement. The tenant entering under a void lease became by virtue of possession and the payment of a yearly rent, a yearly tenant holding on the terms of the agreement so far as those terms were consistent with the yearly tenancy. A yearly tenancy is determinable by the landlord or the tenant at the end of the first or any subsequent year of the tenancy by six months' notice unless the agreement between the parties provides otherwise [. . .]

Now it is said that when in the present case the tenant entered pursuant to the agreement and paid a yearly rent he became a tenant from year to year on the terms of the agreement including clause 6 which prevents the landlord from giving notice to quit until the land is required for road widening. This submission would make a nonsense of the rule that a grant for an uncertain term does not create a lease and would make nonsense of the concept of a tenancy from year to year because it is of the essence of a tenancy from year to year that both the landlord and the tenant shall be entitled to give notice determining the tenancy.

[. . . T]he agreement in the present case did not create a lease and that the tenancy from year to year enjoyed by the tenant as a result of entering into possession and paying a yearly rent can be determined by six months' notice by either landlord or tenant. The landlord has admittedly served such a notice [. . .]

A tenancy from year to year is saved from being uncertain because each party has power by notice to determine at the end of any year. The term continues until determined as if both parties made a new agreement at the end of each year for a new term for the ensuing year. A power for nobody to determine or for one party only to be able to determine is inconsistent with the concept of a term from year to year [. . .] principle and precedent dictate that it is beyond the power of the landlord and the tenant to create a term which is uncertain [. . .]

In the present case the Court of Appeal were bound by the decisions in *In re Midland Railway Co.'s Agreement* and *Ashburn's case*. In my opinion both these cases were wrongly decided. A grant for an uncertain term does not create a lease. A grant for an uncertain term which takes the form of a yearly tenancy which cannot be determined by the landlord does not create a lease. I would allow the appeal.

Lord Browne-Wilkinson

At 396–7

As a result of our decision Mr. Nathan's successor in title will be left with the freehold of the remainder of No. 263–265 which, though retail premises, will have no frontage to a shopping street: the L.C.C.'s successors in title will have the freehold to a strip of land with a road frontage but probably incapable of being used save in conjunction with the land from which it was severed in 1930, i.e. the remainder of No. 263–265.

It is difficult to think of a more unsatisfactory outcome or one further away from what the parties to the 1930 agreement can ever have contemplated. Certainly it was not a result their contract, if given effect to, could ever have produced. If the 1930 agreement had taken effect fully, there could never have come a time when the freehold to the remainder of No. 263–265 would be left without a road frontage.

This bizarre outcome results from the application of an ancient and technical rule of law which requires the maximum duration of a term of years to be ascertainable from the outset. No one has produced any satisfactory rationale for the genesis of this rule. No one has been able to point to any useful purpose that it serves at the present day. If, by overruling the existing authorities, this House were able to change the law for the future only I would have urged your Lordships to do so.

> But for this House to depart from a rule relating to land law which has been established for many centuries might upset long established titles. I must therefore confine myself to expressing the hope that the Law Commission might look at the subject to see whether there is in fact any good reason now for maintaining a rule which operates to defeat contractually agreed arrangements between the parties (of which all successors in title are aware) and which is capable of producing such an extraordinary result as that in the present case.

There are a number of points to note about the decision of the House of Lords in *Prudential Assurance*. Firstly, whilst the *contractual agreement* entered into in 1930 did not create a lease, because it did not give Mr Nathan a right to exclusive possession for a limited period, he (and, later, Prudential) nonetheless did acquire a lease. That lease did not arise under the agreement, but instead resulted from Mr Nathan's payment of rent and the LCC's acceptance of that rent. This form of lease is known as an 'implied periodic tenancy': it provides a particular means by which B can acquire a lease and so we will examine it in section 3.1.2 below. As Lord Templeman noted, the important point about the lease held by Prudential was that it could be terminated by the giving of notice by the landlord: because it was not based on the initial contractual agreement between LCC and Mr Nathan, it did not give Prudential a right to use the land until it was needed for road widening. It may be the case that, had LCC tried to prevent Mr Nathan using the strip of land, Mr Nathan could then have relied on LCC's promise to allow him to use the land until road widening: after all, that promise gave Mr Nathan a contractual, personal right against LCC.[60] But it was clear that Prudential had no such personal right against LRB.

Secondly, we can analyze the decision from both the doctrinal and the utility perspectives. Lord Browne-Wilkinson's speech is particularly interesting. His Lordship states that he is bound to make a decision on established, doctrinal grounds and so to apply the orthodox rule that a lease must be for a limited period. This is combined, however, with a view that the orthodox rule has no good justification and may lead to 'bizarre' or 'extraordinary' results that certainly do not increase utility. Certainly, the rule is relatively easy to avoid: for example, as noted by Lord Templeman,[61] there is nothing to prevent A from giving B a lease 'for 999 years, to determine if and when the land is need for road-widening'—such a lease is for a limited period, because 999 years provides a clear maximum duration for the lease. Indeed, this tactic has been adopted by statute to save certain types of intended lease.

Law of Property Act 1925, s 149(6)

Any lease or underlease, at a rent, or in consideration of a fine, for life or lives or for any term of years determinable with life or lives, or on the marriage of the lessee, or any contract therefor, made before or after the commencement of this Act, or created by virtue of Part V. of the

---

[60] As we saw in Chapter 8, section 3.1, the courts will generally prevent A (a contractual licensor) from breaching his or her contractual promise to allow B to make a particular use of A's land. It has been suggested that a promise to allow B to occupy for an indefinite period, if intended as part of a valid lease, does *not* impose a contractual duty on A and so does not give B even a personal right against A: see, e.g., *Lace v Chantler* [1944] KB 368, at 372, *per* Lord Greene MR. But as explained by Bright, *Landlord and Tenant Law in Context* (2007, pp 75–6), that suggestion is not convincing.

[61] [1992] 2 AC 386, 395.

Law of Property Act, 1922, shall take effect as a lease, underlease or contract therefor, for a term of ninety years determinable after the death or marriage (as the case may be) of the original lessee, or of the survivor of the original lessees, by at least one month's notice in writing given to determine the same on one of the quarter days applicable to the tenancy, either by the lessor or the persons deriving title under him, to the person entitled to the leasehold interest, or if no such person is in existence by affixing the same to the premises, or by the lessee or other persons in whom the leasehold interest is vested to the lessor or the persons deriving title under him:

Provided that [. . .]

There are further provisos to s 149(6) of the LPA 1925, but the key point for our purposes is that certain forms of lease (e.g. a lease for B's life) are validated by interpreting the lease as a lease for a fixed term (ninety years), determinable on a particular event (e.g. B's death). It may then seem strange to insist on a rule that can easily be avoided and for which, according to Lord Browne-Wilkinson, there is no 'satisfactory rationale'.

The following extracts consider possible reasons for the rule. The first focuses on a doctrinal explanation; the second, finding that explanation unconvincing, suggests that the rule, in some cases at least, may serve a useful policy purpose.

McFarlane, *The Structure of Property Law* (2008, pp 677–8)

A Lease consists of a right to exclusive control of land for a limited period. So, if A gives B a right to exclusive control of land "until England win the football World Cup" that right does not count as a Lease. The problem is *not* that the parties will be unable to tell if the specified event has happened: if and when England win the football World Cup, they (and everyone else) will know about it. The problem is rather that it is impossible for A to know *if and when* he can regain his right to exclusive control of the land. And that uncertainty is simply incompatible with a Lease. A Lease arises where A retains his property right in the land and grants B a new property right. So, if A grants B a Lease, A does *not* lose his property right in the land. But if it were possible to have a Lease in which A does not know if and when he will again have a right to exclusive control of the land, A's property right will, in effect, be meaningless [. . .]

[In *Prudential Assurance*] Lord Browne-Wilkinson expressed frustration that the rationale for the rule was unclear, stating that "No one has produced any satisfactory rationale for the genesis of the rule" that "the maximum duration of a [Lease must be] ascertainable from the outset". However, the problem may lie with his Lordship's formulation of the rule. It is *not* the case that the maximum length of the Lease must be known at the outset: the important point is that A must be able to tell if and when he will be able to assert his right to exclusive control of the land. The rule therefore has a valid doctrinal purpose.

Bright, *Landlord and Tenant Law in Context* (2007, pp 73–4)

The explanation for the certainty requirement is sometimes said to rest in the fact that it serves to distinguish leases, as determinate interests, from freeholds, which are of uncertain duration (such as for life, indefinitely, or until the happening of some future event). There are, however, difficulties with accepting this as a continuing justification for the rule. As seen, statute clearly accepts the notion of a *lease for life* as it provides that it is to be converted into a fixed period lease determinable on death, and this makes it therefore difficult to argue that determinancy can tell us on which side of the line an interest falls. Further, there are usually other ways of knowing if an interest is freehold or leasehold, especially as it is common (though not universal) for a rent to be paid if there is a lease. It has also been argued that the rule is simply part of the *numerus clausus* principle in land law (the idea that there is a closed list of rights that can exist as property rights) and the certainty requirement draws a line which marks the boundary between property and contract rights. At one level, this is clearly true but it does not tell why the line is drawn where it is. The rule has also been supported for promoting careful drafting, but this would need only a rule requiring linguistic certainty.

None of these explanations provides a convincing justification for retaining a rule which strikes down otherwise good commercial arrangements. Why should a landlord not be able to agree with a tenant that he can occupy a workshop 'until planning permission is obtained to redevelop the site'? [...] Although not designed for this purpose, the rule can have the benefit of releasing the landlord from what turns out to have been an improvident bargain. The commercial intention behind the workshop example is that the tenant occupies the workshop as an interim measure [...] The risk [...] is that it may become clear that planning permission will never be given, thereby creating a perpetual lease [...] This risk materialised in *Prudential Assurance* itself. The lease was to end when the land was needed for road widening. Circumstances changed, and the road was never widened. The 'lease' that had been intended to only be of short duration when granted in 1930 for a fixed rent of £30 per annum was still running in 1992, by which time the current rental value was in excess of £10,000 per annum. The fact that the letting was intended by the parties to be fairly short term and was drafted on that basis means that the arrangement, initially evenly balanced, became heavily slanted against the landlord over time. By declaring the lease void the court opens up the relationship so that it can be renegotiated to reflect current property values [...] But it is unlikely that the certainty rule was ever intended to facilitate contractual variation; and the problem remains that it strikes down not only the leases that have become unfair over time, but all leases with an unknown end-date.

Bright's view, in contrast to McFarlane's, is thus that there is no clear doctrinal justification for the limited period requirement. From the utility perspective, it may have a useful role to play in certain cases (such as *Prudential Assurance* itself), but the policy of allowing a party to escape an improvident long-term contract, if valid, should be enforced directly rather than through the clumsy mechanism of the limited period rule.

2.8 EXCEPTIONS?

The discussion so far suggests that there is a relatively simple test for the content of a lease: does B have a right to exclusive possession of land for a limited period? In *Street v Mountford*, however, Lord Templeman set out a number of exceptions: situations in which B can have a right to exclusive possession without having a lease. We need to ask if those situations really do constitute exceptions to the basic rule.

Bruton v London and Quadrant Housing Trust [1988] QB 834, CA[62]

Millett LJ

At 843

In *Street v Mountford* Lord Templeman gave only three examples of exceptional circumstances where the grant of exclusive possession does not create a tenancy. First, where the circumstances negative any intention to create legal relations at all. Secondly, where the possession of the grantee is referable to some other legal relationship such as vendor and purchaser or master and servant. Thirdly, where the grantor has no power to create a tenancy, as in the case of a requisitioning authority. As I pointed out in *Camden London Borough v Shortlife Community Housing*,[63] the first and third of these are not exceptions to a general rule. The relationship of landlord and tenant is a legal relationship. It cannot be brought into existence by an arrangement which is not intended to create legal relations at all or by a body which has no power to create it. The existence of these two categories is due to the fact that the creation of a tenancy requires the grant of a legal right to exclusive possession.

On the view of Millett LJ, which seems to be correct, we need to focus our attention on cases in which '*possession of* [B] *is referable to some other legal relationship such as vendor and purchaser or master and servant*'. In *Street v Mountford*,[64] Lord Templeman stated that: '*an occupier who enjoys exclusive possession is not necessarily a tenant. He may be owner in fee simple, a trespasser, a mortgagee in possession, an object of charity or a service occupier.*'

In the first three of those cases we can explain the absence of a lease by simply pointing to the absence of a term: B may have exclusive possession, but he does not have it for a limited period.[65] The 'object of charity' exception may admit of two explanations. Firstly, it may be that, as in *Booker v Palmer*[66] (see section 2.2 above), A's charitable motive means that he does not intend to enter legal relations with B. This may well be the case, where, for example, B pays no rent. In that case, the absence of a lease is easy to explain.

Secondly, in *Gray v Taylor*,[67] Mrs Taylor occupied an almshouse under an agreement with the trustees of a charity. Sir John Vinelott stated:[68] '*A person who is selected as an almsperson becomes a beneficiary under the trusts of the charity and enjoys the privilege of occupation of rooms in the almshouses as beneficiary.*' As noted by Barr,[69] the analysis here seems to be that the occupier's rights come from her *status* as a 'beneficiary' of the charitable trust. The argument seems to be that the agreement between the parties, by itself, did not define Mrs Taylor's right to occupy; rather, that right flowed from, and depended on the continuation of, the charity's decision to regard her as a suitable recipient of its generosity. Equally, of course, this approach promotes a policy of ensuring that landlords acting with altruistic motives are not hampered by the statutory protection that may be available to B if he or she

---

62 See Chapter 24, section 3, for discussion of the facts of the case and the decision of the House of Lords.

63 (1992) 25 HLR 330.

64 [1985] AC 809, 825.

65 See, e.g., McFarlane, *The Structure of Property Law* (2008, p 670).

66 [1942] 2 All ER 674.

67 [1998] 4 All ER 17.

68 Ibid, at 21.

69 Barr, 'Charitable Lettings and their Legal Pitfalls' in *Modern Studies in Property Law* (ed Cooke, 2001, pp 247–9).

is found to have a lease. Certainly, in *Gray v Taylor*, Sir John Vinelott noted that it would be absurd if, due to that statutory protection, the charity were prevented from ending the occupation of a party who, for example, won the lottery.

The final case, of a service occupier, can also be explained without needing to create an exception to the basic test for a lease. There is a general principle, not confined to land law, that an employee in possession of property in the course of his or her employment does not hold that possession in his or her own right, but instead it holds it on behalf of on his or her employer.[70] That principle may now seem outdated and can certainly be attacked,[71] but, as long as it continues to exist, it ensures that a contractual agreement between an employer and an employee simply cannot give the employee a right to exclusive possession of property *if* that property is to be used by the employee in the course of his or her employment.

2.9 SUMMARY

It seems that, despite the supposed 'exceptional categories' noted by Lord Templeman in *Street v Mountford*, B has a lease (in the sense of a property right in land) *if and only if* he or she has a right to exclusive possession of land for a limited period, given to him or her by A, a party who has the power to give B such a property right.

The main complications arise from two sources. Firstly, it is necessary to analyse the agreement between A and B to see what legal rights it creates. It may be that, when asking if B has a right to exclusive possession, an apparent contractual term can be disregarded if it is a 'pretence'—that is, if it is clear that A had no intention to enforce that term in practice. As we saw in section 2.4 above, the court's power to disregard such apparent terms is, on one view, doctrinally justified: it is simply an application of a general concept (the 'sham' concept), which, when properly understood, makes such terms invalid as a matter of contract law. On another view, the disregarding of such terms is not doctrinally justified, and can be justified, if at all, only from a utility perspective: it denies A an easy means of withholding the statutory protection available, in some circumstances, to parties with a lease.

The second complication occurs where B1 and B2, acting together, claim to have a lease. It is currently the law that B1 and B2 can only have a lease if they are *genuinely* joint tenants— that is, if the four unities of possession, interest, time, and title are all present. On one view, this restriction is doctrinally justified;[72] on another, more widespread, view it is not: it overlooks the possibility that B1 and B2, acting together, can acquire a lease as tenants in common and thus without the need to show unity of interest, time, or title.[73] Certainly, from the utility perspective, it is hard to find a convincing policy argument for the restriction.

As we have seen throughout this section, it is important to remember that the courts' approach to the content of a lease may be shaped by the fact that, if B has such a right, he or she may qualify (or have qualified) for significant statutory protection. On the summary given above, this utility concern may (perhaps) have been an influential factor in the development of the 'pretence' test. As we will see in Chapter 24, section 3 it may also have affected

---

[70] See, e.g., *Parker v British Airways Board* [1984] QB 1004, 1017, *per* Donaldson LJ; Bridge, *Personal Property* (3rd edn, 2002, p 20).

[71] See, e.g., ibid, pp 20–1; McFarlane, *The Structure of Property Law* (2008, p 156).

[72] See Smith, *Plural Ownership* (2004, pp 24–6); McFarlane, *The Structure of Property Law* (2008, pp 714–15).

[73] See Sparkes (1989) 18 AALR 151; Bright (1993) 13 LS 38.

an important House of Lords' decision that has also had an impact on the definition of a lease: *Bruton v London & Quadrant Housing Trust*[74].

3 THE *ACQUISITION* QUESTION

To show that he or she has a lease, B must show that he or she has *acquired* a right to exclusive possession of land for a limited period. In considering the *acquisition* question, it is vital to distinguish between *legal* leases and *equitable* leases.

3.1 LEGAL LEASES

As we saw in Chapter 3, section 4, there are, in general, two different ways in which B may acquire a legal property right: firstly, and most commonly, B can acquire such a right through a dependent acquisition: by showing that A gave him or her the right; secondly, and more rarely, B can acquire a legal property right by an independent acquisition—that is, simply by relying on his or her own conduct. For example, as noted in section 1.1.2 above, as well as in Chapter 10, section 3, if B takes possession of land, so that he or she has exclusive physical control of that land, B independently acquires a legal freehold. It is, however, very difficult to see how B could ever independently acquire a lease: firstly, a lease consists of a right to exclusive possession for a *limited period*—if B simply takes control of land, he or she is not asserting such a limited right; secondly, a lease depends on a relationship between A and B, as landlord and tenant—and it is hard to see how such a relationship can arise solely because of B's conduct.

Nonetheless, under the provisions of the Land Registration Act 2002 (LRA 2002), it is now possible for B to acquire a lease independently.[75] As we saw in Chapter 10, section 6, if B can successfully show adverse possession of land subject to a registered lease, B can apply to be registered as the new holder of that lease. From a doctrinal point of view, this is a very strange result: B's possession of the land gives him or her a freehold, but he or she then acquires a lease by applying to the Registrar.[76] From the utility perspective, however, there may be something to be said for this result: it essentially represents a compromise solution to the difficult practical and theoretical questions raised by the adverse possession of land subject to a lease.[77]

In any case, in looking at the acquisition of leases, we can concentrate on the case of dependent acquisition—that in which B claims that A has given him a lease.

3.1.1 Basic formality requirements

As we saw in Chapter 9, B's claim that A has given him or her a legal property right, such as a lease, may be affected by formality rules.

---

[74] [2000] 1 AC 406.
[75] For the background to this change, see Law Com No 271 at [14.66]–[14.73].
[76] This point is made by, e.g., McFarlane, *The Structure of Property Law* (2008, pp 684–5).
[77] See Chapter 10, section 6, for discussion of those problems.

1. A contract to grant a lease, like a contract to grant a freehold, must, in general, satisfy the need for writing signed by both A and B, as required by s 2 of the Law of Property (Miscellaneous Provisions) Act 1989 (LP(MP)A 1989) (see Chapter 9, section 3).

2. A's grant of the lease to B must, in general, be made in a deed, as required by s 52 of the LPA 1925 (see Chapter 9, section 4).

3. Again, in general, the transaction will not be complete, and B will not acquire a legal lease, unless and until B is registered as the holder of that lease. That registration requirement is imposed by s 4 of the LRA 2002 in a case in which A does not hold a registered estate and s 27 of that Act in a case in which A does hold a registered estate (see Chapter 9, section 5).

It is important to note that exceptions are provided to each of these three rules. In some cases, of course, none of those exceptions applies.

In considering the exceptions, it is useful to distinguish between: (i) cases in which A gives B a new legal lease; and (ii) cases in which B1 transfers his or her existing legal lease to B2.

3.1.2 Where A attempts to give B a new legal lease

If A attempts to give B a new legal lease of more than seven years, the full set of formality requirements applies: in particular, B does not acquire that legal lease unless and until he or she registers as its holder. As we will see in section 3.2 below, B's failure to register will not prevent him or her from acquiring an equitable lease—but there may be disadvantages to B in having only an equitable lease: in particular, an equitable lease can only count as an overriding interest if B is in actual occupation of the land; in contrast, as legal lease *always* counts as an overriding interest (see Chapter 16, section 5.2, and section 4.1 below). Further, as we saw in Chapter 17, section 2.1.2, once B has registered as the holder of a legal estate, s 58 of the LRA 2002 operates to vest that right conclusively in B. So, unless and until the register is changed, B is secure in knowing that he or she has a legal lease. And, indeed, even if the register is rectified, B, if he or she has not acted fraudulently or carelessly, is very likely to qualify for an indemnity payment from the Land Registry.

There is an exceptional category of leases that, even if given for seven years or less, must be registered. The leases falling within this category are defined by ss 4(1)(d)–(f) and 27(2)(b) (ii)–(v) of the 2002 Act. One example consists of a lease taking effect only after a gap of more than three months from the date of its grant by A to B.[78] In that particular case, it seems that the registration requirement is imposed as such a legal lease could otherwise cause a trap for C, a party acquiring a right from A during the period after the grant of a lease, but before it has taken effect.

If A attempts to grant B a non-exceptional lease of seven years or less, B can acquire a legal lease without needing to register his or her right. As we have seen, the general rule under s 52 of the LPA 1925 is that A must use a deed to grant B a legal lease. There is, however, an exception to the need for a deed, provided by s 54(2) of the 1925 Act.

---

[78] Other examples are a discontinuous lease (such as a time-share lease, in which B has a right to exclusive possession only for a limited part of each year) and leases that, under the provisions of the Housing Act 1985, would, in any case, require registration.

Law of Property Act 1925, s 54(2)

Nothing in the foregoing provisions of this Part of this Act shall affect the creation by parol of leases taking effect in possession for a term not exceeding three years (whether or not the lessee is given power to extend the term) at the best rent which can reasonably be obtained without taking a fine.

If the requirements of s 54(2) are met, B can acquire a legal lease as a result of a purely oral grant from A: registration is not needed; nor a deed; nor even any writing. The basic policy of the exception is clear: as a matter of convenience, parties should be free to enter relatively short-lived arrangements without having to express their intentions in a particular form.

It is, however, important to note that the length of the lease is only *one* of the requirements of the exception. To acquire a legal lease without a deed, B needs to show that the lease:

- is for three years or less; *and*
- takes effect in possession; *and*
- is at the best rent reasonably obtainable without taking a fine.

The third requirement will be satisfied if B is paying a reasonable market rent rather than, for example, acquiring the lease by paying a one-off premium. This requirement may be seen as a means of protecting C, a party to whom A might later transfer A's estate in the land. The problem for C is that B's oral, but legal, lease may be hard to discover. Of course, in practice, B may well be in occupation of the land—but, as we saw in Chapter 16, section 5.2, B's legal lease counts as an overriding interest in its own right and so is immune from the lack of registration defence even if B is not in actual occupation of the land. The rent requirement in s 54(2) provides some protection for C: even if he or she is bound by B's oral lease, he or she will at least, receive a reasonable rent from B.

In the following case, the second of the three requirements was decisive.

Long v Tower Hamlets London Borough Council [1998] Ch 197

Facts: Tower Hamlets LBC had a freehold of No 21 Turners Road, consisting of a ground-floor shop and a maisonette. It gave Mr Long permission to occupy the shop; Mr Long later decided to occupy the maisonette as well. As far as the shop was concerned, Mr Long, before moving in, had received a letter setting out the terms of occupation. The letter was sent in early September 1975 and stated that Mr Long's right of occupation would begin on 29 September. Mr Long indorsed and returned the letter on 8 September. At some point (claimed by Mr Long to be in 1977), Mr Long stopped paying rent. In 1995, Mr Long claimed that, because he had been occupying both the shop and maisonette, without Tower Hamlets' consent, for over twelve years, the doctrine of adverse possession extinguished Tower Hamlet LBC's freehold of that land (see Chapter 10 for a discussion of that doctrine). According to Sch 1, para 5, of the Limitation Act 1980, if Tower Hamlets LBC could show that Mr Long had occupied under a 'lease in writing', Mr Long's adverse possession claim would fail, because the twelve-year limitation period would have begun in 1984 and so would not yet have expired. But if Tower Hamlets could not show that Mr Long had a 'lease in writing', the twelve-year clock would have begun to count down from an earlier point (when Mr Long stopped paying rent) and so Mr Long's adverse possession claim could succeed. The case was therefore slightly unusual: the claim of a lease was made not by the occupier, but rather by the party granting the rights of occupation.

Tower Hamlets LBC applied for an order striking out Mr Long's adverse possession claim, on the basis that, because he had been given 'a lease in writing', the limitation period only began to run against Tower Hamlets LBC in 1984. James Munby QC, sitting as a deputy High Court judge, rejected that argument, holding that Mr Long had *not* been given a 'lease in writing'.

James Munby QC (sitting as a Deputy High Court judge)

At 205

At common law a lease could be granted in any way, even orally [. . .] Moreover, there was at common law no restraint upon the grant of a reversionary lease, that is, a lease to take effect in reversion on some future day, however distant, and conferring no right to take possession in the meantime. Such a lease [. . .] gave the lessee an immediate vested legal *interest* in the land, that interest being known as an interesse termini, though until the date when the lease was due to take effect this interest was vested in interest and not in possession. On the other hand, the lessee under a reversionary lease acquired no *estate* in the land until he had actually entered, that is, taken possession in accordance with the lease; until then all he had was an interesse termini [. . .]

At 216–17

In the first place, the words 'in possession,' when used as part of the phrase 'taking effect in possession for a term not exceeding three years,' in my judgment have their normal legal meaning. They connote an estate or interest in the land which is vested 'in possession' rather than merely vested 'in interest.' This reading is powerfully reinforced by the distinction drawn in section 205(1)(xxvii) of the Law of Property Act 1925 between a 'term of years taking effect in possession' and a 'term of years taking effect in reversion.' The words 'taking effect in possession' in section 54(2) are, in my judgment, used in the same sense in which those words are used in section 205(1)(xxvii) and thus, and this is the critical point, in distinction to the words 'taking effect in reversion.' This, as it seems to me, demonstrates that [. . .] reversionary leases were not intended to come within the ambit of section 54(2).

Moreover, there has been omitted from section 54(2) any express reference to the date of 'the making' of the lease. Thus, if [counsel for Tower Hamlets'] argument is correct, there is no limit expressed in section 54(2) to the period which may elapse before the lease 'tak[es] effect in possession,' the only requirement being that the lease, when eventually it does 'tak[e] effect in possession,' must be 'for a term not exceeding three years.'

As interpreted in *Long v Tower Hamlets LBC*, the requirement that the lease must 'take effect in possession' can also be seen as providing some protection for C: a lease under which B has no right to immediate possession may be particularly hard for C to discover.[79]

But whilst the decision must be correct as a matter of statutory interpretation, it reveals that the s 54(2) exception has only a limited practical impact.

---

[79] It should be noted, however, that a lease can 'take effect in possession' even if B does not immediately go into occupation; the question is whether B has an immediate *right* to exclusive possession.

Bright, 'Beware the Informal Lease: The (Very) Narrow Scope of s 54(2) Law of Property Act 1925' [1998] Conv 229, 232–3

Whilst the reasoning behind [*Long v Tower Hamlets*] is hard to fault, the practical implications of the decision are absurd. It is easy to state that, to be safe, all leases should be entered into by deed, but this is unrealistic. Another option is to say that where there is an informal lease, the term date should be stated to pre-date the date of the agreement (presumably it is the term commencement that indicates whether a lease is in possession). This again is an unrealistic option for in most situations the parties want a binding commitment prior to the commencement date. The absurdity of the subsection is revealed when we consider what the policy is underlying it. There are many reasons why formalities may be required in land transactions but underlying section 52 is the benefit it secures for the parties to the transaction (creating evidence, warning of legal effects, protecting against outside influences) and for the court (evidential). Given the advantages of formality in this context, why are short leases exempted? The answer in part is probably that many short leases are, in fact, entered into without legal advice and if a formality requirement were imposed many parties would remain in ignorance of it. In addition to non-compliance through ignorance there is likely to be a high level of non-compliance through fear of costs. Deeds are likely to involve instructing lawyers, which means expense and delay. The disadvantages of requiring a deed outweigh the advantages to be gained from requiring one. If these ideas explain why the law permits the creation of short leases by parol, the exemption should not be restricted to those taking effect immediately in possession. Instead, the exemption should apply to those leases that are most likely to be entered into without the benefit of legal advice, informally, and where the costs of a deed would discourage compliance. Looked at in this light, the exemption should apply to short leases which are to take effect in possession within a reasonable period, and perhaps twelve months would provide a sensible cut-off.

There is another form of short legal lease that can be acquired by B without a deed, or any writing. As we saw when considering *Prudential Assurance Ltd v London Residuary Body* in section 2.7 above, B's payment and A's acceptance of rent can give rise to an *implied periodic tenancy*. In such a case, the conduct of the parties leads a court to imply, or assume, that A granted a lease to B; there is no need for any formal proof of that grant. In practice, B may occupy land for a long time under a succession of periodic tenancies (in *Prudential Assurance*, for example, the House of Lords held that the strip of land in question had been occupied in that way for over sixty years). The maximum duration of any individual periodic tenancy is, however, a year. The length of the term depends on how B pays rent: if B pays weekly, a weekly tenancy will be implied; if B pays monthly, a monthly tenancy will result; and if the frequency is calculated by reference to a year (e.g. if B pays quarterly), B will have a yearly periodic tenancy. To terminate the lease, either party needs to give notice of an intention not to renew it at the end of the current period. A week's notice is needed in the case of a weekly tenancy; a month's notice for a monthly tenancy; six months' notice is required for a yearly tenancy.

Given that the maximum length of a periodic tenancy is a year and that B will necessarily have a right to immediate possession, it may seem that any implied periodic tenancy will fall within the s 54(2) exception. Because an implied periodic tenancy can arise even if B does *not* pay a reasonable market rent, however, it seems that it provides an independent exception to the general rule that a legal interest in land can only be acquired where a deed is used.

The position can be summarized as in Table 5.

Table 5 Formality requirements for legal leases

Type of legal lease	Deed required?	Registration required?
For more than seven years *or* in an exceptional category *	Yes	Yes
For three years or less, *and* taking effect in possession, *and* at a reasonable market rent	No	No
All other leases	Yes	No

* See Land Registration Act 2002, ss 4 and 27, for the exceptional categories (e.g. a lease taking effect in possession more than three months from the time of the grant).

3.1.3 Where B1 attempts to transfer an existing legal lease to B2

Imagine that A has a legal estate in land and then grants B1 a legal lease. It is then possible for B1 to retain his or her lease and to grant B2 a new lease (a sublease): in such a case, the formality requirements will apply in the way set out above. It is also possible for B1 to transfer his or her lease to B2. In that case, the formality requirements apply in a slightly different way:[80] firstly, if B1's lease is registered, B2 cannot acquire that right until he or she registers as its new holder; second, if B1's lease is not registered (e.g. because it is a lease of less than seven years), B1 *must* use a deed to transfer the lease to B2. That rule applies even if B1 acquired his or her lease orally, by relying on the s 54(2) exception. The Court of Appeal confirmed this in *Crago v Julian*.[81]

It is clear, as a matter of statutory interpretation, that the s 54(2) exception does *not* apply to the transfer of an existing lease; it applies only to the creation of a new lease. Yet this can cause problems in practice, because, if B1 has acquired his or her lease orally, he or she may be unaware that the lease can only be transferred by using a deed.

3.2 EQUITABLE LEASES

It was suggested in Chapter 4, section 1, and Chapter 11, section 3.2, that all equitable interests depend on A's being under a duty to B. Certainly, it seems that, to acquire an equitable lease, B needs to show that A is under a duty to grant B a lease. In Chapter 12, when considering *Walsh v Lonsdale*,[82] we saw that B can acquire an equitable lease when A comes under a *contractual* duty to grant B a lease. As we saw in Chapter 9, section 3, A can only come under such a duty if the formality rule set out by s 2 of the LP(MP)A 1989 has been satisfied. Further, it is generally assumed that B will only acquire an equitable lease if A's duty to grant

---

[80] The terms of B1's lease may attempt to prevent B1 from granting a sublease to B2 or from transferring his or her lease to B2. In such a case, the sublease or transfer does still occur (see *Old Grovebury Manor Farm Ltd v W Seymour Plant Sales and Hire Ltd (No 2)* [1979] 1 WLR 1397), but B1's breach may give A a power to forfeit the lease (see Chapter 25, section 6.4).

[81] [1992] 1 WLR 372.

[82] (1882) 21 Ch D 9.

a lease can be enforced by an order of specific performance—but, as we saw in Chapter 12, section 3, it is not entirely clear that the specific performance requirement is justified, either as a matter of history or of principle.

There may be situations in which A has not made a contractual promise to give B a lease but, instead, has simply tried and failed to make an immediate grant of a lease: for example, A may attempt to grant B a five-year lease, but fail to use a deed. In such a case, if B provided something in return for the failed grant (e.g. money), A will be regarded as under a duty to give B a lease and B can thus acquire an equitable lease: *Parker v Taswell*[83] provides an example of this principle. Further, in line with the discussion in Chapter 11, section 2.2, B may well be able to acquire an equitable lease if he or she can show that the doctrine of proprietary estoppel imposes a duty on A to grant B a lease. It seems that B acquired such an equitable lease in *Lloyd v Dugdale*.[84] As we saw in Chapter 13, however, the reasoning of the House of Lords in *Yeoman's Row Management Ltd v Cobbe*[85] may now restrict B's ability to use proprietary estoppel to impose a positive duty on A to give B a lease.

If B1 has an equitable lease, arising as a result of A being under a duty to grant B1 a lease, it should also be possible for B1 to transfer that equitable lease to B2. In such a case, the basic formality rule set out by s 53(1)(a) of the LPA 1925 (see Chapter 11, section 2.1.1) will apply: the transfer must be made in writing signed by B1.

It is sometimes suggested that an equitable lease is 'as good as' a legal lease. Certainly, if B has an equitable lease, this will generally be enough to entitle him or her to any statutory protection available to a holder of a lease (see section 1.1.1 above). Further, an equitable lease is capable of binding a third party who later acquires a right in relation to the land from A (see section 1.1.3 above). But certain advantages do come with a legal lease. Firstly, as we have noted, a legal lease, unlike an equitable lease, *necessarily* counts as an overriding interest and so C, a party later acquiring a right from A, will not be able to use the lack of registration defence against B's right.

Secondly, if B acquires a legal lease for value, then, under s 29 of the LRA 2002, B may him or herself be able to use the lack of registration defence against a pre-existing property right (such as a prior equitable lease created by A in favour of Z).[86] But if B has only an equitable lease, he or she cannot use that defence.

Thirdly, if B acquires a legal lease from A, B will also be able to rely on s 62 of the LPA 1925, which can imply the grant of additional rights by A (such as easements—see Chapter 26, section 3.2) into the creation of B's legal lease. But if B has only an equitable lease, s 62 cannot apply.

---

[83] (1858) 2 De G & J 559.

[84] [2002] 2 P & CR 13. See further Bright and McFarlane, 'Proprietary Estoppel and Property Rights' [2005] CLJ 449. The problem for B (Mr Dugdale) was that, because he was in not in actual occupation of the land when A transferred his freehold to C, C had a defence to B's pre-existing equitable lease. B therefore tried to assert a new, direct right against C, arising as a result of a promise made by C when acquiring the freehold: we discussed that aspect of the case in Chapter 7, section 2.3.

[85] [2008] 1 WLR 1752.

[86] Usually, B needs to register his or her own right if he or she wishes to rely on the lack of registration defence. But s 29(4) of the Land Registration Act 2002 means that B can rely on that defence if he or she has been *granted* a lease that cannot be registered (e.g. a non-exceptional lease of seven years or less). The term 'grant' is crucial, because it excludes a party with only an equitable lease: if B has only an equitable lease, he or she has not been granted a right; rather, A is under a duty to make such a grant (see Chapter 6, section 3.6).

4 THE *DEFENCES* QUESTION

If B acquires a legal or equitable lease of A's land, his or her right will be prima facie bind-ing on C, a third party later acquiring a right relating to that land from A. As we noted in Chapter 6, however, it may be possible for C to have a defence to a pre-existing property right of B. In practice, the key defence is the lack of registration defence, provided (in relation to unregistered land) by the Land Charges Act 1972 (LCA 1972) and (in relation to registered land) by the LRA 2002.

In considering the defence, we again need to distinguish between cases in which B has a legal lease and those in which B's lease is equitable.

4.1 B HAS A LEGAL LEASE

To acquire a legal lease of seven years or more of registered land, B must register as the holder of that right (see section 3.1 above). In such a case, C clearly will not be able to rely on the lack of registration defence. B can, however, acquire a shorter legal lease without needing to register as the holder of that right. Even in such a case, it is still impossible for C to rely on the lack of registration defence, because Sch 3, para 1, of the LRA 2002 ensures that B's right counts as an overriding interest: that is the case even if B is not in actual occupation of the land. If A has an unregistered legal estate and grants B a legal lease, it may be the case that, when A transfers his or her estate to C, C will register that estate for the first time. In such a case, B's legal lease is again overriding, this time under Sch 1, para 1, of the 2002 Act.

If B has a legal lease of unregistered land, then, as we saw in Chapter 15, section 3, it is impossible for C to rely on the lack of registration defence provided by the LCA 1972: the general position is that a legal estate or interest does *not* count as a registrable land charge for the purposes of the 1972 Act. This means that, as far as legal leases are concerned, the pic-ture is clear: C will never be able to use the lack of registration defence against a pre-existing legal lease.

4.2 B HAS AN EQUITABLE LEASE

Where B has an equitable lease of registered land, it is possible for B to protect that right by entering a notice on the register. As noted above, the entry of a notice does not guarantee B's equitable right—but it does prevent C, when later acquiring a right, from using the lack of registration defence against B's right. If B fails to protect his or her equitable lease by entering a notice, that right will be vulnerable to the lack of registration defence *unless* B is in actual occupation of the land under Sch 3, para 2 of the LRA 2002 (where C registers a legal estate for the first time, Sch 1, para 2, of that Act has the same effect). But if B is *not* in actual occupation at the relevant time, he or she has *no* overriding interest. Unlike a legal lease, an equitable lease, by itself, does not count as an overriding interest. This flows from the fact that Sch 3, para 1 (like Sch 1, para 1) protects only 'A *leasehold estate in land granted for a term* [...]'. As confirmed by the Court of Appeal in *City Permanent Building Society v Miller*,[87] a grant necessarily implies the acquisition of a *legal* property right: if B has an

---

[87] [1952] Ch 840.

equitable lease, he or she has not been granted a lease by A; rather, A is instead under a duty to make such a grant.[88]

If B has an equitable lease of unregistered land, the applicability of the lack of registration defence provided by the LCA 1972 will depend on the means by which B acquired that equitable lease. If it arises as a result of A's contractual promise to give B a lease (or under the principle in *Parker v Taswell*),[89] B's right counts as an 'estate contract': as we saw when examining *Midland Bank Trust Co Ltd v Green*[90] in Chapter 6, section 3.1, B's failure to register such a right as a land charge[91] gives C the chance to use the lack of registration defence provided by the 1972 Act. If, however, B's equitable lease arises because A is under a *non-contractual* duty to grant B a lease, that lack of registration defence cannot apply and C will instead have to attempt to rely on the general 'bona fide purchaser' defence, as discussed in Chapter 15, section 4.

5 THE CONTRACTUAL ASPECT OF A LEASE

In this chapter, we have been examining the lease *as a property right* and have therefore asked the three key questions relating to such rights: the *content*, *acquisition*, and *defences* questions. There are, however, other aspects to a lease. In Chapter 24, we will examine how a lease can confer *status*, by allowing B to qualify for important statutory protection. In addition, it is sometimes stated that, due to developments in the law occurring in the last thirty years or so, the lease has become more 'contractualized'. It is certainly true that, *as well as* functioning as a property right in land, a lease almost always has an important contractual aspect. As the following extract suggests, however, we have to be very careful when framing a debate about the nature of leases as a conflict between property, on one hand, and contract, on the other.

McFarlane, *The Structure of Property Law* (2008, pp 697–8)

It is often said that there is a tension between two different views of the Lease. On the first view, the Lease is seen as primarily a *property right*; on the second, it is seen as chiefly a *contractual right* [...]

However, this tension is an illusion. There is *no* conflict between property rights on the one hand and contractual rights on the other. The classification of a right as a property right depends on the **content question**: does B's right impose a *prima facie* duty on the rest of the world not to interfere with B's use of a thing? The classification of a right as a contractual right depends on the **acquisition question**: does B's right arise as a result of a promise which, because it was made in an agreement for which consideration was provided, binds A? It is therefore perfectly possible for B to have a right that is *both* (i) a property right; *and* (ii) a contractual right. An example occurs where A, by means of a sale, transfers his Ownership of a bike to B. B acquires a property right; and that right arises as a result of the contractual bargain between A and B.

---

[88] Compare fn 86, discussing the effect of the term 'grant' in s 29(4) of the Land Registration Act 2002.
[89] (1858) 2 De G & J 559. See section 3.2 above.
[90] [1981] AC 813.
[91] Land Charges Act 1972, s 2(4)(iv), makes clear that an estate contract counts as a registrable land charge.

Indeed, in almost all cases where he has a Lease, B's right to exclusive control of land for a limited period is *both* (i) a property right; *and* (ii) a contractual right. It is a property right because it is a right, relating to a thing, that imposes a *prima facie* duty on the rest of the world. It is a contractual right as B acquires that right as a result of a promise made to B in return for which B provided consideration. In fact, B usually acquires a number of different contractual rights: (i) a right to exclusive control of the land for a limited period; (ii) the benefit of contractually agreed leasehold covenants (rights that can be enforced against parties later acquiring A's estate); and (iii) personal rights against A. All those rights are **acquired** in the same way; but their **content** differs.

This analysis does not mean that a Lease *must* arise as a result of a contract. It is possible for a Lease to arise purely by consent: A can exercise his power to grant B a Lease *without* coming under any contractual duties to B.[92] However, it does mean that it is misleading to say that there is a tension between the proprietary view of the Lease and the contractual view of the Lease. A Lease is simply a property right that can, and almost always does, arise through a contract. Indeed, when analysing the practical problems that are often said to depend on a choice between the 'proprietary' and 'contractual' views, that false opposition only obscures the solution to the problems.

So, what does it mean to say that the lease has been 'contractualized'? In a very controversial decision, the House of Lords has stated that the term 'lease' can be extended to cases in which A, even if he or she has no property right in land, makes a binding promise to give B exclusive possession of that land for a limited period. In such a case, B has a lease even though the core feature examined in this chapter, B's acquisition of a property right, is missing. We will examine this decision (*Bruton v London & Quadrant Housing Trust*) in Chapter 24, section 3. In other cases, however, the 'contractualization' amounts not to a denial of the proprietary status of a lease, but rather to the recognition that, where A grants B a lease, the *purpose* of the parties' contract extends beyond the simple acquisition of a property right by B.

This point has been made by Bright,[93] who has argued that the key issue relates to the *characterization* of a contract granting B a lease. The question is whether B's acquisition of a property right should be seen as: (i) the *sole* aim of the parties' contract; or (ii) only one of the aims of the contract, or even as a means to a more important end (e.g. the provision of a home or business premises). In Bright's words, is the contract: (i) for possession only; or (ii) for possession 'plus'?[94]

The traditional view of a lease, it seems, favoured the former analysis. This affected the application to the lease of normal contractual principles and, as a result, had a number of important practical consequences. Firstly, it meant that judges were very reluctant to use the particular purpose for which a lease was acquired (e.g. to give B a home) as a reason to imply contractual terms into that lease. As noted in section 1.1.1 above, certain minimal duties are implied as a result of B's acquisition of a property right (e.g. A is under a duty not to interfere with B's 'quiet enjoyment' of the land), but the courts would not go beyond those duties by looking to the particular factual circumstances in which the lease was granted.

---

92 See *per* Millett LJ (dissenting) in *Ingram v IRC* [1997] 4 All ER 395, 421–2: '*There is no doubt that a lease is property. It is a legal estate in land. It may be created by grant or attornment as well as by contract and need not contain any covenants at all.*' There was a successful appeal against the decision of the majority of the Court of Appeal ([2000]1 AC 293): Lord Hutton, at 310, expressly agreed with Millett LJ's analysis of the nature of a lease.

93 See Bright, *Landlord and Tenant Law in Context* (2007, pp 30–3).

94 Ibid, p 31.

Secondly, it meant that the doctrine of frustration was not applied to leases: even if there was a radical change in circumstances, frustrating the particular purpose for which B acquired his or her lease, B would still have a property right and so, on the traditional view, B would still have his or her bargained-for benefit.

Thirdly, and similarly, it meant that a significant breach by A of one of his or her continuing duties under the contract (e.g. to provide repairs) could never allow B to terminate the contract: after all, B would still have a property right and hence his or her bargained-for benefit.

Over time, the courts have recognized that, in many circumstances, it is unrealistic to view A and B's lease agreement as *solely* a means for B to acquire a property right in land. This has led to a reversal of each of the three consequences, set out above, of that former view. Firstly, in *Liverpool City Council v Irwin*,[95] the House of Lords recognized that, where A gave B a lease of a flat in a tower block, the obvious purpose of providing B with accommodation meant that, under normal contractual principles, terms could be implied allowing B to use other parts of the block (such as the lift and stairs) and imposing a duty on A to make reasonable efforts to keep those parts working and usable by B.

Secondly, in *National Carriers Ltd v Panalpina (Northern) Ltd*,[96] the House of Lords acknowledged that, where A gave B a lease of a warehouse for storage, the obvious commercial purpose of the contract meant that, under normal contractual principles, the closure of the only road giving access to the warehouse could, if continuing for a long enough period, lead to the parties' contract being frustrated.[97]

Thirdly, in *Hussein v Mehlman*,[98] Stephen Sedley QC, sitting as an assistant recorder, held that, where A gave B a lease of a house, A's serious breaches of his duty to repair, rendering the house unfit to live in, interfered with the 'central purpose'[99] of the contract and so allowed B to terminate the contract by moving out and ceasing to pay rent.[100]

These developments have proceeded on the eminently reasonable basis that, in many situations, the acquisition of a property right in land, whilst fundamental, is not the *only* purpose that B has in mind when entering a lease agreement with A. As we will see in the next chapter, its effect in giving B a property right is only *one* of the lease's key features.

QUESTIONS

1. If A makes a contractual agreement to allow B to occupy land, why might B want to claim that the agreement gives him or her a lease?

2. In *Street v Mountford*, the House of Lords held that A's contractual agreement with B can give B a lease even if A clearly did not intend the agreement to have that effect. Can that aspect of the decision be defended, either from a doctrinal or policy perspective?

---

[95] [1977] AC 239.

[96] [1981] AC 675.

[97] In the case itself, the contract was *not* frustrated: the road was closed only for twenty months of a ten-year lease.

[98] [1992] 2 EGLR 87 (County Court).

[99] Ibid, at 91.

[100] That reasoning has since been confirmed by the Court of Appeal: see *Chartered Trust plc v Davies* [1997] 2 EGLR 83.

3. In *Antoniades v Villiers*, the House of Lords, in deciding that Mr Villiers and Miss Bridger had a joint right to exclusive possession, disregarded a term in an agreement signed by both Mr Villiers and Miss Bridger. Can that aspect of the decision be defended, either from a doctrinal or policy perspective?

4. In *AG Securities v Vaughan*, the House of Lords assumed that it is impossible for B1 and B2 to acquire a lease as tenants in common. Is that assumption correct?

5. Are there any genuine exceptions to the rule that if A gives B a right to exclusive possession of land for a limited period, B has a lease?

6. Do you agree with Lord Browne-Wilkinson that the result reached by the House of Lords in *Prudential Assurance Ltd v London Residuary Body* had a 'bizarre' practical outcome?

FURTHER READING

Bright, 'Avoiding Tenancy Legislation: Sham and Contracting Out Revisited' [2002] CLJ 146

Bright, *Landlord and Tenant Law in Context* (Oxford: Hart, 2007, esp chs 1–3)

Bright, '*Street v Mountford* Revisited' in *Landlord and Tenant Law: Past, Present and Future* (ed Bright, Oxford: Hart, 2006)

Hill, 'Intention and the Creation of Proprietary Rights: Are Leases Different?' [1996] LS 200

McFarlane, *The Structure of Property Law* (Oxford: Hart, 2008, Pt G1B)

Sparkes, 'Co-Tenants, Joint Tenants and Tenants in Common' (1989) 18 AALR 151

24

REGULATING LEASES AND
PROTECTING OCCUPIERS

CENTRAL ISSUES

1. In Chapter 23, we concentrated on a key
   feature of a lease: its ability to count as
   a property right. This can be referred to
   as the *property right-conferring* aspect
   of a lease. We also saw, in Chapter 23,
   section 5, that the conferral of a property right is not the *only* key feature of a
   lease: as now recognized by the courts,
   a contract giving B a lease can also be a
   means for B to achieve a further practical end, such as to have a home in
   which to live, or premises from which
   to run a business.

2. In Chapter 23, we also saw that the
   applicability of various forms of
   important statutory protection may
   be dependent on B showing that he
   or she has a lease. In this chapter, we
   will examine that statutory protection
   in more detail. Such protection can
   be important in a number of different
   contexts, such as, for example, if B has
   an agricultural or commercial lease. In
   this chapter, we will focus on the protection available to B where he or she
   occupies land as his or her home. The
   degree of statutory protection available to B depends on the identity of B's
   landlord: A. If A is a private individual,
   the statutory protection available to B

   is now very slight; where A is a local
   authority, however, significant statutory protection is still available to B, in
   the form of a 'secure tenancy'.

3. In examining this statutory protection, we will see that a lease can give
   B *status*: the status of a party qualifying for statutory protection. This
   demonstrates a further key feature of
   a lease: its *status-conferring* aspect. It
   also raises a fundamental question: is
   it possible for an agreement between
   A and B to give B the status of a party
   with a lease *without* giving B a property right? A key recommendation of
   the Law Commission's recent review
   of the area is that the statutory protection available to B, a party occupying
   land, a home and paying rent, should
   no longer depend on whether or not B
   has a property right in that land.

4. Having focused on the *property
   right-conferring* aspect of a lease in
   Chapter 23, and its *status-conferring*
   aspect in this chapter, we will then
   move on, in Chapter 25, to examine its
   relationship-creating aspect. There, we
   will see that the landlord–tenant relationship arising when A gives B a lease
   may impose duties and confer rights

not only on A and B, but also on later parties stepping into the shoes of A or B, and thus entering into a landlord–tenant relationship. In Chapter 25, section 6, we will also see how the courts have given B some protection against the risk of losing his or her lease due to a breach of one of his or her duties to A.

1 INTRODUCTION

In Chapter 23, we focused on a particular aspect of the lease: its ability to confer a property right on B. In this chapter, we will also consider the *status-conferring* aspect of a lease—that is, its ability, in certain circumstances, to allow B to qualify for important statutory protection.

Bridge, 'Leases: Contract, Property and Status' in *Land Law: Issues, Debates, Policy* (ed Tee, 2002, pp 98–9)

The lease straddles the worlds of contract and property. It is an estate the duration of which is determined by the agreement of the landlord and the tenant. It is also highly significant as a status, tenants enjoying rights and incurring obligations that are denied to others. The law of leases is extraordinarily complex, and the search for order out of the inherent chaos can at times seem an almost futile exercise. The student of land law [...] tends to concentrate on the 'general principles' affecting the leasehold relationship [...] It is inevitable that this emphasis on 'general principles' provides a view of the law of landlord and tenant which is some way removed from the practical realities of the leasehold relationship. One obvious divergence relates to security of tenure. It may be that according to the 'general principles', a lease can be terminated by notice, but there may be statutory restrictions on such termination, nor does it necessarily follow that recovery of possession ensues upon termination of the lease. The landlord and tenant practitioner must be aware that specific types of lease are dealt with by statute in very different ways, and that engrafted on to the 'general part' are principles which may or may not apply according to the specific kind of lease.

The 'general principles' referred to in the extract can be seen as the principles, set out in Chapter 23, that govern the *property right-conferring* aspect of a lease. If we analyse a lease as no more than a grant by A to B of a property right, giving B a right to exclusive possession of land (and thus ownership powers over land) for a limited period, then the positions of A and B seem clear. Each is free to pursue his or her own self-interest: B, by making use of the land during the period of the lease; A, by recovering possession of the land when the agreed period ends. If either party wants to control the actions of the other, the basic position is that he or she can only do so by convincing the other party to agree to that limit and thus making it a term of the parties' contractual agreement. As we will see in this chapter, there are many situations in which that simple model of a lease has been found wanting.

2 THE *STATUS-CONFERRING* ASPECT OF A LEASE: BACKGROUND

The first important challenge to the simple model of a lease set out above comes from Parliament: as noted by Bridge, statutory intervention means that, in many cases, we have to look beyond the *property right-conferring* aspect of a lease. Again, it is useful to refer back to the contrasting approaches that we noted in Chapter 1, section 5.2. From the perspective of *doctrine*, the simple model of a lease, with its emphasis on the parties' property rights and their freedom of contract, may seem perfectly adequate—but from the perspective of *utility*, Parliament has accepted that the simple model may fail to secure important policy goals.

In very broad terms, there are two general reasons why Parliament may have decided that A and B cannot simply be left to determine their respective rights: firstly, it may be that the use of land is sufficiently important that a particular party's individual wishes can be overridden; secondly, it may be that differences in the parties' relative bargaining positions mean that, absent statutory protection, one may be left at the mercy of the other. In particular, given the limited availability of land (see Chapter 1, section 4), it may be that A holds too powerful an advantage when negotiating the terms of a lease with B: even if B finds the proposed terms unattractive, it may not be possible, in practice, for B to walk away and negotiate better terms elsewhere.

Of course, the particular policy goals that Parliament wishes to advance will vary according to the particular context in question. This means that, as Bridge notes in the extract above, B's position may vary according to the particular context in which he or she has acquired his or her lease.

For the purpose of considering the statutory regulation of leases, we can distinguish between four broad types of lease:

- agricultural leases;
- commercial leases;
- long-term residential leases;
- short-term residential leases.

In line with the approach taken in Part C of this book (see Chapters 18–22), our focus will be on the protection that may be available to B where he or she occupies land as his or her *home*.

In Chapter 28, section 2.1, we will see how the statutory protection applicable to long-term residential leases may be useful to B where, generally by having paid a large purchase price, he or she has acquired a long lease (e.g. 99 or 125 years) of a flat. The central problem for B, in such a case, is that B may reasonably regard himself or herself as 'the owner' of the flat: B may have made significant financial investments in the land, as well as establishing his or her home there. Yet as time passes, and the period remaining on the lease grows shorter, the prospect of B losing his or her right to exclusive possession of the land undermines B's position. Of course, if we apply the simple doctrinal model set out above, in which A and B's positions are to be determined entirely by their property rights and the agreed terms of their contract, B's loss of the land at the end of the agreed period will be unavoidable. Nonetheless, as we will see in Chapter 28, section 2.2, Parliament has intervened on policy grounds to ensure that B is protected even at the end of his or her lease.

A very similar form of intervention forms the background to *James v UK*,[1] a case that we considered in Chapter 5 (see especially section 2.4.2). That case concerned the effect of the Leasehold Reform Act 1967. That Act does not apply to flats, but it protects B where he or she holds a long lease, at a low rent, of a house. B is given a statutory power to 'enfranchise'—that is, to purchase A's freehold at a price set by a statutory formula.[2] The Duke of Westminster (who was obliged by the 1967 Act to sell a number of freeholds) claimed that the 1967 Act infringed his right, protected by Art 1 of the First Protocol of the European Convention on Human Rights, to the '*peaceful enjoyment of his possessions*'. Certainly, the Act departed from the simple model in which A and B's positions are to be determined entirely by their property rights and the agreed terms of their contract. Nonetheless, as we saw in Chapter 5, the Court found that the UK had *not* infringed the Duke's Art 1 right. Taking into the account the 'margin of appreciation' afforded to the UK (see Chapter 5, section 2.4.2), the Court recognized that the Act employed a proportionate means of pursuing a legitimate aim: to give effect to B's 'moral entitlement' to the ownership of the house and thus to remedy the 'social injustice' inherent in the precariousness of B's position.[3] Whilst dealing with a specific form of statutory intervention, applying only to long-term residential leases, the *James* case also reveals the tension inherent whenever Parliament intervenes to protect B at A's expense. In some cases, at least, it seems that wider policy goals can justify a departure from the simple model based on the parties' property rights and their freedom to contract.

In this chapter, our focus is on short-term residential leases. Around 30 per cent of all homes in England and Wales are occupied by tenants with such leases.[4] The protection available to such tenants may come from many different sources: for example, the criminal law prohibits certain forms of harassment by a landlord;[5] local authorities also have regulatory powers to ensure that certain minimum housing and public health standards are maintained.[6] In addition, in around one third of all short-term residential leases, A (the landlord) is a local authority.[7] This means that public law may also limit A's exercise of its property rights as landlord: in particular, as a public body, a local authority has a basic duty not to act inconsistently with B's rights under the ECHR. A number of the cases that we examined in Chapter 5, exploring the extent of those rights, concerned the position of residential occupiers of land owned by a local authority.

In addition, as we saw in Chapter 23, section 5, general contractual rules, when applied to leases, may provide B with some protection: for example, A's incentive to comply with his or her statutory repairing duty may be increased by the prospect of B, in the event of a serious breach by A, being able to terminate the lease (and thus being free to move out and cease paying rent).[8]

Further, statutory regulation applying to all contracts will also apply to leases and thus provide some protection to B:[9] for example, B may able to rely on the Unfair Terms in

---

[1] (1986) 8 EHRR 123.

[2] A power of enfranchisement (or instead to extend the length of the lease) was extended to a holder of a long residential lease of a flat only with the introduction of the Leasehold Reform Housing and Urban Development Act 1993: see Chapter 28, section 2.2.

[3] (1986) 8 EHRR 123, 47.

[4] See Wilcox, *UK Housing Review 2006/07*, Table 17b.

[5] See the Protection from Eviction Act 1977.

[6] See, e.g., the Environmental Protection Act 1990, esp ss 79–82.

[7] See Wilcox, *UK Housing Review 2006/07*, Table 17b.

[8] See *Hussein v Mehlman* [1997] 2 EGLR 87 (County Court), considered in Chapter 23, section 5.

[9] It is clear that the Unfair Terms in Consumer Contracts Regulations 1999 (SI 1999/2083) may apply to leases: this was confirmed by the Court of Appeal in *Khatun v Newham LBC* [2005] QB 37. In contrast, the

Consumer Contracts Regulations 1999[10] to show that 'non-core' terms of the lease contract are unfair and hence not binding on B.[11] Indeed, the Office of Fair Trading produces useful guidance as to terms that, if included in a lease without being individually negotiated, may be regarded as 'unfair'.[12]

Clearly, in this chapter, we cannot consider the full scope of the protection available to a short-term residential tenant. As noted in Chapter 1, section 2, our focus is not on all of the legal rules that affect the use of land; rather, our primary concern is with property rights relating to land. In this context, it is with the statutory protection that is made available to B *because* B has a property right in the land: a lease.

In considering that protection, we can start by noting that there is a clear difference between short-term residential leases and their long-term equivalents. Generally, to acquire a long-term residential lease, B will pay a large purchase price and then a very low, often nominal, rent. In contrast, a short-term residential lease generally involves no such premium, but, instead, a duty on B to pay regular, more significant sums as rent. Of course, some tenants opt for a short-term residential lease simply as a matter of convenience: they do not wish to make a long-term commitment to a particular property or area. But the absence of a purchase price may mean that many tenants acquire a short-term residential lease out of financial necessity rather than choice: such a tenant may well wish to establish a permanent home, but lack the money needed to acquire a freehold or long-term lease. As a result—in those cases, at least—there may be a particularly strong case for statutory intervention in favour of a tenant with a short-term residential lease. Certainly, as we saw in Chapter 23, the Rent Act 1977 gave significant protection to such a tenant: that was precisely why private landlords such as Mr Street (see Chapter 23, section 1.1.1) and Mr Antoniades (see Chapter 23, section 2.4) went to such lengths to try to deny B a lease. This was not because they wanted to deny B a property right—their concern was not with whether B would have a right capable of binding third parties; rather, it was because they wished to deny B the *status* that would come with a lease—that status which enabled B to qualify for statutory protection.

In the following extract, Bridge develops the idea of the *status-conferring* aspect of a lease. He also explains how the statutory protection available to a short-term residential tenant has changed, very significantly, since the time of the Rent Act 1977.

Bridge, 'Leases: Contract, Property and Status' in *Land Law: Issues, Debates, Policy* (ed Tee, 2002, pp 105–8)

The lease as status

The status-conferring dimension of the landlord-tenant relationship is given little attention in modern land law courses. Yet [...] the leading cases have frequently been motivated by

---

Unfair Contract Terms Act 1977 does *not* apply to leases (due to an express exemption: see Sch 1, para 1(b), of the Act). The 1977 Act can, however, apply to licences: this is a rare situation in which the availability of particular statutory protection depends on B *not* having a lease.

[10] These Regulations also apply to the terms of a mortgage contract and can thus provide protection to a mortgage borrower: see Chapter 30, section 4.1.3.

[11] Core terms are not subject to the fairness test: as a result, the Unfair Terms in Consumer Contracts Regulations 1999 cannot be used to challenge, e.g., the level of the agreed rent.

[12] The website of the Office of Fair Trading (http://www.oft.gov.uk) is a useful starting point for a tenant wishing to claim that a non-individually negotiated term in the lease agreement is unfair and so not binding on the tenant.

a desire on the part of the landlord to avoid legislative status and [...] there are many other cases where the courts have been faced with the interaction of the general principles of landlord and tenant law with specific statutory provisions that apply to certain kinds of lease. The landlord-tenant relationship does not exist within a vacuum, it exists within a factual context, and the type of property let (a house, a flat, a farm, an office), for instance, will make considerable differences to the legal regime applicable. There is insufficient space here to do justice to the multifarious forms of statutory intervention in the landlord-tenant relationship. However, it may be useful to mention three particular areas in an attempt to show how the legal background has moved on, even since the days of *Street v Mountford*, to illustrate why it is that private sector residential landlords have changed their practices, and to compare the operation of principle in the residential sector of property with that in the commercial field.

Part 1 of the Housing Act 1988 came into force on 15 January 1989, less than four years after the decision in *Street v Mountford*. The Conservative government had taken the view that the decline in the private rented sector of residential property was attributable to the impact of rent control, and that any revival would require landlords to obtain a commercial return for their investment. The 1988 Act sought to phase out the Rent Acts by providing that tenancies granted after the legislation came into force would be taken out of the operation of the Acts altogether. Instead, a new regime of letting, known as the 'assured tenancy', would apply to them, pursuant to which landlords could charge whatever rent the tenant agreed to pay. The assured tenant was given statutory security and a limited form of succession on death was also enacted. Eight years later, by the Housing Act 1996, the statutory security of private sector tenants was dealt a further blow. As from 28 February 1997, any new tenancy was to take effect as an 'assured shorthold tenancy', unless the parties expressly agreed otherwise, under which the landlord can recover possession once any fixed term has expired by giving notice of a sufficient length. The legislative matrix is extremely convoluted, but the sum effect is clear. Since the enactment of the Housing Act 1988 there has been a highly significant diminution in the statutory rights of the tenant of residential property in the private sector. The spectre of the Rent Acts, which cast a long shadow over residential lettings, has been vanquished, and market forces are now allowed to prevail. Over the course of the last decade, private sector landlords have ceased to care whether they grant tenancies or licences.

[...] The public sector of housing has never been subjected to the regime of the Rent Acts, as it was for many years assumed that local authorities would act in the interests of their rate-paying tenants and not be influenced by unseemly market forces. Council tenants were therefore left to resort to public law remedies in cases where they fell into dispute with their local authority landlords over matters such as the negotiation of council rents. The systematic conferment of security of tenure on public sector tenants was initiated by Margaret Thatcher's first Conservative administration, contemporaneously with its highly publicised promotion of the tenant's right to buy the reversion of their landlord. Thus there arose, in the public sector, the status of 'secure tenant', conferring security of tenure, rights to exchange tenancies, and succession rights on death.

It is therefore clear that the policy adopted by Parliament can change over time. There may be a number of reasons for this. Firstly, it may be felt that giving significant protection to tenants can be counterproductive. As noted in the extract above, if the level of that protection means that potential landlords are deterred from renting out their land, the supply of available housing will be reduced. In this way, the cost of protecting those in need of accommodation *and* fortunate enough to have found it already may be that others, also in need of accommodation, find it more difficult to acquire.

Secondly, there is a political question. Parliament's willingness to enforce a departure from the simple model of a lease (for example, by preventing A from regaining exclusive possession at the end of the agreed lease period) will depend on its view of the importance of the parties' property rights and their freedom to contract. Certainly, the political consensus from the mid-1990s or so has been broadly in favour of reduced state intervention and greater deregulation: as we will see in Chapter 30, that consensus has also shaped the degree of protection available to a mortgage borrower.

The current scheme of regulation centres on the identity of A: the landlord. Where A is a private party and B is an individual, rather than a company, B's short-term lease may be an 'assured shorthold tenancy', *or* an 'assured tenancy'.[13] A has a choice as to which tenancy to give B: the default position is that it will be an assured shorthold tenancy. As noted in the extract above, that form of lease is only very lightly regulated: certainly, B acquires no security of tenure. So parties such as Mr Street or Mr Antoniadas, who once went to such lengths to avoid granting a lease, are now perfectly content to grant B an assured shorthold tenancy. In contrast, if B has an assured tenancy, the grounds on which A can regain exclusive possession of the land (even after the end of the agreed lease period) are limited by statute.

Bright, *Landlord and Tenant Law in Context* (2007, p 187)

The assured shorthold has now become the main tenancy found in new private rental sector lettings, as the landlord effectively has the legal right to recover possession whether or not there is any tenant default [...A]lmost 63 per cent of all private sector lettings are assured shortholds, only 10 per cent are assured tenancies[14] [...] If only market rentals available to members of the public are taken into account, then the proportion of assured shortholds is much higher. A survey conducted for ARLA [the Association of Residential Letting Agents] and its panel of mortgage lenders found that 87 per cent of new tenancies were assured shortholds and 11 per cent were 'non Housing Act' tenancies (company lets) [and thus not subject to statutory regulation under the Housing Act 1988]. The assured tenancy is now mainly used by Registered Social Landlords (RSLs).

Even if B has only an assured shorthold tenancy, statute can still have an effect, however, to impose certain limited repairing duties on A. Section 11 of the Landlord and Tenant Act 1985 essentially[15] ensures that, where B has a lease, for less than seven years, of a dwelling, A is under the following duties.

Landlord and Tenant Act 1985, s 11

[...]

    (a) to keep in repair the structure and exterior of the dwelling-house (including drains, gutters and external pipes);

    (b) to keep in repair and proper working order the installations in the dwelling-house for the supply of water, gas and electricity and for sanitation (including basins, sinks, baths and

---

13 These forms of tenancy can also arise where a number of individuals (e.g. B1 and B2) acquire a lease as joint tenants.

14 [Other categories include: (i) 'regulated tenancies' (leases granted under the former Rent Act 1977 regime, which have continued), accounting for 5 per cent; and (ii) those in which the landlord is resident (in which cases, the tenant has no statutory protection.]

15 There are some exceptional situations in which the duty does not arise: see Landlord and Tenant Act 1985, s 14.

sanitary conveniences, but not other fixtures, fittings and appliances for making use of the supply of water, gas or electricity), and

(c) to keep in repair and proper working order the installations in the dwelling-house for space heating and heating water.

The policy behind this statutory duty seems clear: if B has a short-term lease, it seems unreasonable for B to have to bear the cost of repairs that may ultimately benefit A when A regains exclusive possession of the land. In addition, having rented a home in a particular condition, B may reasonably expect a certain basic level of maintenance and repair. In practice, it may be that B's need for accommodation and relatively weak bargaining position makes it impossible to leave the matter to the parties' freedom to contract: hence the mandatory statutory duty. Those policy concerns would also seem to apply in a case in which B has a licence rather than a lease—it is difficult to see how B's acquisition of a property right makes him or her more deserving of the protection afforded by s 11. Nonetheless, the statute makes clear that the duty it imposes can only be implied into a *lease*. It is in this way that B's acquisition of a lease gives him or her the *status* needed to qualify for the statutory protection.

If A is not a private landlord, more significant protection may be available to B. A registered social landlord, such as a housing association, may be required by the terms of its registration to grant B an 'assured tenancy'. In particular, if A is a local authority, then, as noted by Bridge in the extract above, B's lease will necessarily be a 'secure tenancy'. B *does* then acquire significant statutory protection: in particular, the grounds on which B can be removed from the land (even after the expiry of the agree lease period) are limited and subject to control by a court. The key provision is s 79(1) of the Housing Act 1985, which states that 'A *tenancy under which a dwelling-house is let as a separate dwelling*' counts as a secure tenancy where A is a local authority[16] and B is '*an individual and occupies the dwelling-house as his only or principal home*'.[17] It is important to note that s 79(3) of that Act states that the secure tenancy rules also '*apply in relation to a licence to occupy a dwelling-house (whether or not granted for consideration) as they apply in relation to a tenancy*'.

In *Westminster City Council v Clarke*,[18] which we examined in Chapter 23, section 2.3, however, the House of Lords explained that s 79(3) was intended to deal only with those cases in which, under the approach to the definition of a lease applying before *Street v Mountford*,[19] B could have a licence involving exclusive possession (see Chapter 23, section 1.1.1). In practice, then, the protection given to a secure tenant, like the statutory duty to repair imposed by the Landlord and Tenant Act 1985, can apply only where B has a lease. That was precisely why, in *Westminster City Council v Clarke*, it was vital to decide if B had a right to exclusive possession of the land for a limited period. Again, it could well be argued that the policy behind the secure tenancy (in particular, the need to allow B to be and feel secure in his or her home) applies equally where B occupies as a licensee, lacking a right to exclusive possession. Crucially, however, it is only B's acquisition of a *lease* that gives B the statutory status of a secure tenant.

[16] A secure tenancy may also arise where A is not a local authority, but is, instead, another one of the bodies listed by s 80 of the Housing Act 1985 (e.g. an urban development corporation). In practice, the local authority secure tenancy is by far the most significant.

[17] Where there is a joint tenancy, it will be a secure tenancy if each of B1 and B2 is an individual and '*at least one of them occupies the dwelling-house as his only or principal home*': Housing Act 1985, s 81.

[18] [1992] AC 288.

[19] [1985] AC 809.

3 THE *STATUS-CONFERRING* ASPECT OF A LEASE: PRACTICE

We have seen two reasons why B, a short-term residential tenant, may wish to rely on the *status-conferring* aspect of a lease: firstly, he or she may wish to show that A is under the statutory repairing duty set out by s 11 of the Landlord and Tenant Act 1985; secondly, where A is a local authority, B may wish to show that he or she has a secure tenancy and therefore can only be removed from the land on limited grounds.

The extract below is from a case in which the first reason initially motivated B's claim to a lease.

Bruton v London & Quadrant Housing Trust Ltd [2000] 1 AC 406, HL

Facts: The London Borough of Lambeth ('the council') owned a block of flats, Oval House, in Brixton, London. It planned to demolish the block and build new flats, but there were delays to that project. In the meantime, the council gave the London & Quadrant Housing Trust, a charitable body that sought to provide accommodation to the homeless and those in need, a licence to use the flats for that purpose. It was clear that its agreement with the council gave the Trust only a licence: in particular, the council had no statutory power, in the circumstances, to give the Trust a lease. Mr Bruton was one of the parties housed by the Trust in Oval House. The agreement entered into by Mr Bruton and the Trust was described as a licence. It stated that:

> The trust has the property on licence from [the council] who acquired the property for development [. . .] and pending this development, it is being used to provide temporary housing accommodation. It is offered to you on the condition that you will vacate upon receiving reasonable notice from the trust, which will not normally be less than four weeks.

Mr Bruton claimed that his agreement with the Trust, in fact, gave him a lease; that the Trust was therefore under a statutory repairing duty, imposed by s 11 of the Landlord and Tenant Act 1985; and that the Trust had failed to perform that duty. The Trust argued that Mr Bruton could not have a lease: the Trust had no power to grant Mr Bruton a property right in the land because it had no such right itself (it had only a licence from the council). Judge James, sitting at Lambeth county court, found in favour of the Trust. The Court of Appeal dismissed Mr Bruton's appeal (Sir Brian Neill dissenting)—but the House of Lords found that Mr Bruton did have a lease and thus that the Trust was under the statutory repairing duty.

Lord Hoffmann

At 413–6

Did this agreement create a 'lease' or 'tenancy' within the meaning of the Landlord and Tenant Act 1985 or any other legislation which refers to a lease or tenancy? The decision of this House in *Street v. Mountford*[20] is authority for the proposition that a 'lease' or 'tenancy'

---

[20] [1985] AC 809.

is a contractually binding agreement, not referable to any other relationship between the parties, by which one person gives another the right to exclusive occupation of land for a fixed or renewable period or periods of time, usually in return for a periodic payment in money. An agreement having these characteristics creates a relationship of landlord and tenant to which the common law or statute may then attach various incidents. The fact that the parties use language more appropriate to a different kind of agreement, such as a licence, is irrelevant if upon its true construction it has the identifying characteristics of a lease. The meaning of the agreement, for example, as to the extent of the possession which it grants, depends upon the intention of the parties, objectively ascertained by reference to the language and relevant background. The decision of your Lordships' House in *Westminster City Council v. Clarke* is a good example of the importance of background in deciding whether the agreement grants exclusive possession or not. But the classification of the agreement as a lease does not depend upon any intention additional to that expressed in the choice of terms. It is simply a question of characterising the terms which the parties have agreed. This is a question of law.

In this case, it seems to me that the agreement, construed against the relevant background, plainly gave Mr. Bruton a right to exclusive possession. There is nothing to suggest that he was to share possession with the trust, the council or anyone else. The trust did not retain such control over the premises as was inconsistent with Mr. Bruton having exclusive possession as was the case in *Westminster City Council v. Clarke*. The only rights which it reserved were for itself and the council to enter at certain times and for limited purposes. As Lord Templeman said in *Street v. Mountford* such an express reservation 'only serves to emphasise the fact that the grantee is entitled to exclusive possession and is a tenant.'[21] Nor was there any other relationship between the parties to which Mr. Bruton's exclusive possession could be referable.

Mr. Henderson, who appeared for the trust, submitted that there were 'special circumstances' in this case which enabled one to construe the agreement as a licence despite the presence of all the characteristics identified in *Street v. Mountford*. These circumstances were that the trust was a responsible landlord performing socially valuable functions, it had agreed with the council not to grant tenancies, Mr. Bruton had agreed that he was not to have a tenancy and the trust had no estate out of which it could grant one.

In my opinion none of these circumstances can make an agreement to grant exclusive possession something other than a tenancy. The character of the landlord is irrelevant because although the Rent Acts and other Landlord and Tenant Acts do make distinctions between different kinds of landlords, it is not by saying that what would be a tenancy if granted by one landlord will be something else if granted by another. The alleged breach of the trust's licence is irrelevant because there is no suggestion that the grant of a tenancy would have been ultra vires either the trust or the council [. . .] If it was a breach of a term of the licence from the council, that would have been because it was a tenancy. The licence could not have turned it into something else. Mr. Bruton's agreement is irrelevant because one cannot contract out of the statute. The trust's lack of title is also irrelevant, but I shall consider this point at a later stage. In *Family Housing Association v. Jones*,[22] where the facts were very similar to those in the present case, the Court of Appeal construed the 'licence' as a tenancy. Slade L.J. gave careful consideration to whether any exceptional ground existed for making an exception to the principle in *Street v. Mountford* and came to the conclusion that there was not. I respectfully agree. For these reasons I consider that the agreement between

---

[21] Ibid, at 818.
[22] [1990] 1 WLR 779.

the trust and Mr. Bruton was a lease within the meaning of section 11 of the Landlord and Tenant Act 1985.

My Lords, in my opinion, that is the end of the matter. But the Court of Appeal did not stop at that point. In the leading majority judgment, Millett L.J. said that an agreement could not be a lease unless it had a further characteristic, namely that it created a legal estate in the land which 'binds the whole world.'[23] If, as in this case, the grantor had no legal estate, the agreement could not create one and therefore did not qualify as a lease. The only exception was the case in which the grantor was estopped from denying that he could not create a legal estate. In that case, a 'tenancy by estoppel' came into existence. But an estoppel depended upon the grantor having purported to grant a lease and in this case the trust had not done so. It had made it clear that it was only purporting to grant a licence.

My Lords, I hope that this summary does justice to the closely reasoned judgment of Millett L.J. But I fear that I must respectfully differ at three critical steps in the argument.

First, the term 'lease' or 'tenancy' describes a relationship between two parties who are designated landlord and tenant. It is not concerned with the question of whether the agreement creates an estate or other proprietary interest which may be binding upon third parties. A lease may, and usually does, create a proprietary interest called a leasehold estate or, technically, a 'term of years absolute.' This will depend upon whether the landlord had an interest out of which he could grant it. *Nemo dat quod non habet.*[24] But it is the fact that the agreement is a lease which creates the proprietary interest. It is putting the cart before the horse to say that whether the agreement is a lease depends upon whether it creates a proprietary interest [...]

Secondly, I think that Millett L.J. may have been misled by the ancient phrase 'tenancy by estoppel' into thinking that it described an agreement which would not otherwise be a lease or tenancy but which was treated as being one by virtue of an estoppel. In fact, as the authorities show, it is not the estoppel which creates the tenancy, but the tenancy which creates the estoppel. The estoppel arises when one or other of the parties wants to deny one of the ordinary incidents or obligations of the tenancy on the ground that the landlord had no legal estate. The basis of the estoppel is that having entered into an agreement which constitutes a lease or tenancy, he cannot repudiate that incident or obligation [...] Thus it is the fact that the agreement between the parties constitutes a tenancy that gives rise to an estoppel and not the other way round. It therefore seems to me that the question of tenancy by estoppel does not arise in this case. The issue is simply whether the agreement is a tenancy. It is not whether either party is entitled to deny some obligation or incident of the tenancy on the ground that the trust had no title.

Thirdly, I cannot agree that there is no inconsistency between what the trust purported to do and its denial of the existence of a tenancy. This seems to me to fly in the face of *Street v. Mountford.* In my opinion, the trust plainly did purport to grant a tenancy. It entered into an agreement on terms which constituted a tenancy. It may have agreed with Mr. Bruton to say that it was not a tenancy. But the parties cannot contract out of the Rent Acts or other landlord and tenant statutes by such devices. Nor in my view can they be used by a landlord to avoid being estopped from denying that he entered into the agreement he actually made.

For these reasons I would allow the appeal and declare that Mr. Bruton was a tenant. I should add that I express no view on whether he was a secure tenant or on the rights of the council to recover possession of the flat.

---

[23] [1998] QB 834, 845.
[24] [No one can give what he does not have.]

Lord Hobhouse

At 417–8

The claim made in the action seeks to enforce a contractual cause of action. The breach of contract alleged against the defendant housing trust is the failure to maintain and keep in repair the flat in which the plaintiff, Mr. Bruton is living. He relies upon a written agreement between himself and the housing trust dated 31 January 1989. The written agreement does not contain any undertaking by the housing trust to repair the flat. But Mr. Bruton alleges that the agreement creates a relationship of landlord and tenant between the housing trust and himself and that therefore an undertaking to repair by the housing trust is compulsorily implied by statute—section 11 of the Landlord and Tenant Act 1985.

Counsel for the housing trust accepted before your Lordships that a contractual relationship of landlord and tenant suffices to make the provisions of the Act applicable. The question therefore is whether the agreement creates such a relationship. The answer to this question is, in my judgment, determined by the decision in *Street v. Mountford*. The agreement was an agreement to give Mr. Bruton the exclusive possession of the flat for a period or periods of time in return for the periodic payment of money; the grant of exclusive possession was not referable to any other relationship between the parties. It follows that the relationship created was that of landlord and tenant and the provisions of the Act apply to the agreement. Mr. Bruton is entitled to succeed [. . .]

The Court of Appeal were influenced by the way in which the case for Mr. Bruton was argued before them. They understood that his case depended upon establishing a tenancy by estoppel. This was not a correct analysis. He needed to do no more than rely upon the written agreement he had with the housing trust and its legal effect. The only concept of estoppel which was possibly relevant was that which arises from the agreement [. . .] The present case does not depend upon the establishing of an estoppel nor does any problem arise from the fact that the housing trust did not have a legal estate. The case of Mr. Bruton depends upon his establishing that his agreement with the housing trust has the legal effect of creating a relationship of tenant and landlord between them. That is all. It does not depend upon his establishing a proprietary title good against all the world or against the council. It is not necessary for him to show that the council had conveyed a legal estate to the housing trust. I therefore cannot agree with the reasoning of the Court of Appeal and would allow this appeal.

The decision of the House of Lords in *Bruton* has proved to be controversial, to say the least. The essential point is that, prior to the decision, it had been assumed that, to take advantage of the *status-conferring* aspect of a lease, B necessarily had to have a property right—but the House of Lords departed from that assumption. It was held that Mr Bruton's agreement with the Trust, *even if it did not give him a property right in the land*, could nonetheless give Mr Bruton the status of a tenant and therefore allow him to take advantage of s 11 of the Landlord and Tenant Act 1985.

As Bright notes in the following extract, this suggests that there are two forms of lease: the standard proprietary lease, and a new, purely contractual, lease.

Bright, 'Leases, Exclusive Possession and Estates' (2000) 116 LQR 7, 8–9

Certain propositions emerge clearly from the speeches in the House of Lords:

1. Mr Bruton had a right to exclusive possession;

2. the relationship of landlord and tenant existed between Mr Bruton and the Housing Trust;

3. this relationship does not give a title good against all the world; and

4. the fact that the Housing Trust had no estate did not matter.

Cumulatively, these propositions illustrate an understanding about the essential nature of leases that was not shared by the Court of Appeal. Although both courts agree that exclusive possession is necessary in order for there to be a lease, there are contrasting views as to whether this is an absolute or relative concept. In the House of Lords, exclusive possession was found on the basis of the contractual agreement between Mr Bruton and the Housing Trust. The agreement gave Mr Bruton the right to exclusive possession: he did not have to share possession with anyone else, and the Housing Trust retained only limited rights over the premises. The Housing Trust's lack of title is not relevant. In contrast, Millett L.J. regarded exclusive possession as looking beyond the relationship between the two contracting parties. According to this view, exclusive possession, meaning possession to the exclusion of the whole world, is essential for a lease; if 'the grantor has no power to exclude the true owner from possession, he has no power to grant a legal right to exclusive possession and his grant cannot take effect as a tenancy'.[25] This means that Mr Bruton could not have exclusive possession and, thus, he could not have a lease. If it is possible to have exclusive possession in the relational sense referred to in the House of Lords, the further question arises as to the nature of the resulting relationship. We are told that it is a relationship of landlord and tenant but not whether it is an "estate". Given that relativity of title is a fundamental aspect of English land law, it could be classified as an estate in this relative sense. This is hard to accept, however. For derivative title, at least, the principle of *nemo dat quod non habet*—no one can convey what he does not own—is also fundamental to English land law. The Housing Trust did not have an estate, and so could not grant an estate to Mr Bruton. Indeed, this is implied when Lord Hoffmann states that a 'lease may, and *usually does*, create a proprietary interest called a leasehold estate [...] This will depend upon whether the landlord had an interest out of which he could grant it' (emphasis added). If usually, then it must be that sometimes there can be a lease which is not an estate.

On this point, too, the Court of Appeal had differed. The premise in the Court of Appeal was that a lease is (always) a proprietary concept: 'A tenancy is a legal estate'.[26] There is much to be said for this view. Although there can be tenancies of sorts which do not confer estates, the tenancy at will and the tenancy by estoppel, these are generally treated as special cases and would not be described as 'leases' without qualification. Moreover, much previous case law proceeds on the assumption that all leases are estates in land, an assumption which has, on occasion, been made explicit: 'I myself find it impossible to conceive of a relationship of landlord and tenant that has not got that essential element of tenure in it, and that implies that the tenant holds of his landlord, and he can only do that if the landlord has a reversion. You cannot have a purely contractual tenure.'[27] More recently, Neuberger J. stated that "a lease involves not only a contract, but also an estate in land".[28] ... It is, therefore, a surprise that both Lord Hoffmann and Lord Hobhouse of Woodborough state clearly in *Bruton*, with little discussion of the point, that, though usual, an estate in land is not an essential element of a lease. A lease, in the words of Lord Hoffmann 'describes a relationship

---

[25] [1998] QB 834, 845, *per* Millett LJ.
[26] Ibid.
[27] *Milmo v Carreras* [1946] KB 306, 310, *per* Lord Greene MR.
[28] *Re Friends Provident Life Office* [1999] 1 All ER (Comm.) 28, 36.

between two parties who are designated landlord and tenant. It is not concerned with the question of whether the agreement creates an estate or other proprietary interest which may be binding upon third parties'.

If this is a correct reading of what Lord Hoffmann says and it is possible to have leases which are not estates, contractual rights of occupation will need to be classified as either proprietary leases giving an estate in land and enforceable against all third parties, or as contractual leases conferring exclusive possession and giving rights against all who interfere with possession other than those who can show a better right to possession, or as licences. There will be consequential issues to be addressed. Will 'contractual leases' count as leases for all statutory purposes? Can 'contractual leases' be created informally? It would appear so, as the formality requirements set out in the Law of Property Act 1925, ss.52 and 54, and the Law of Property (Miscellaneous Provisions) Act 1989, s.2, apply only to interests in land. The rules on certainty of term presumably apply to 'contractual leases'—otherwise the outcome in *Prudential Assurance Co. Ltd v. London Residuary Body* [1992] 2 A.C. 386 would have been different and the agreement upheld as a contractual tenancy [. . .] What status will a "contractual lease" have vis-à-vis third parties?

The essence of the House of Lords' decision in *Bruton* is that B can have the status of a tenant even if his or her agreement with A does not give B a property right: B may instead have a 'non-estate tenancy'.[29]

In the following extract, it is suggested that the House of Lords could have reached that conclusion in a more conventional way: by utilizing the well-established notion of a 'tenancy by estoppel'.

Routley, 'Tenancies and Estoppel: After *Bruton v London & Quadrant Housing Trust*' (2000) 63 MLR 424, 424–8

As generally understood, a tenancy by estoppel results where a person purports to grant a tenancy of land, but does not in fact have a sufficient interest in the land to create a tenancy: he is then estopped from denying that the relationship of landlord and tenant exists between him and the grantee [. . .] As between the parties it is as though they are actually landlord and tenant *even though in fact they are not.*

The authorities describe a tenancy by estoppel as a different creature from the more familiar estoppel by representation, as a development from the doctrine of estoppel by deed, but extended in the field of landlord and tenant to all grants whether merely written or oral. A tenancy by estoppel could be said to be the result of the operation of estoppel by grant. Unlike its cousin, estoppel by grant does not rely upon any express representation as to title: 'It is the product of a fundamental principle of the common law which precludes a grantor from disputing the validity of his own grant.'[30]

[. . .] Confusion between the doctrines of estoppel by representation and estoppel by grant gave rise to some of the difficulties in *Bruton* [. . .] Millett LJ [in the Court of Appeal] found that there is no estoppel 'unless the grantor's denial of title is inconsistent with his grant.'[31]

---

[29] To use the term applied by Lord Scott when considering the *Bruton* tenancy in *Kay v Lambeth London Borough Council* [2006] 2 AC 465, [145]–[147]. We examined the human rights aspects of that case in Chapter 5, section 4.2.2.

[30] *Per* Millett LJ in *Bruton* in the Court of Appeal: [1998] QB 834, 844.

[31] Ibid, at 845.

There was no estoppel here, because there was no inconsistency between the nature of the alleged grant (a licence), and therefore there could not be any tenancy. The principles of estoppel and of *Street v Mountford* were irreconcilable:

> '*Street v Mountford* rejects the professed intentions of the parties in favour of the true effect of the transaction. Estoppel by convention gives effect to the professed intentions of the parties. Any attempt to combine them produces a hopeless circularity.'[32]

I fear that Millett LJ may have been too bemused by the elegance of that conundrum to notice its flaws: it is an oversimplification to say that estoppel 'gives effect to the professed intentions of the parties'. While Millett LJ acknowledges the difference described above between estoppel by representation and by grant, he then applies the 'representation' test to the facts of the case before him, basing his conclusion of no estoppel on a finding of no misrepresentation.

The flaw in that reasoning is that this estoppel does not arise from a representation, but from the grant, and if one correctly concludes via *Street v Mountford* that the grant was in fact the grant of a tenancy, then the Trust's denial of title *is* inconsistent with that grant, and, despite the fact that both the Trust and [Mr Bruton] thought that a licence was being granted, a tenancy by estoppel arises [...]

The whole corpus of law relating to landlord and tenant derives from the status of landlord and tenant, from privity of estate, from the fact of ownership of a proprietary interest in land, not from the fact of having entered into an agreement which might or might not have created such a proprietary interest.

An agreement in the form of a lease, but which does not create a proprietary interest, cannot be a lease. And the order of cart and horse is not as Lord Hoffmann would have it, but as it has always been.

Which is precisely why the common law imposes an estoppel upon the man who purports to grant a lease by means of an agreement in the form of a lease which purports to create one: to prevent him from saying 'I did not have the interest out of which to create a lease, therefore I could not have granted one, therefore the grantee is not my tenant, and I am not bound by any obligations as landlord.' But it must never be overlooked that a 'tenancy by estoppel' is not a tenancy: not a proprietary interest.

Routley's argument is that the House of Lords in *Bruton* reached the correct result, but by the wrong route. Certainly, given the policy behind s 11 of the Landlord and Tenant Act 1985, it would seem unreasonable for the Trust to use its own lack of a property right as a means to escape a statutory repairing duty. Routley suggests that the unfairness comes from the fact that the Trust entered an agreement seemingly giving Mr Bruton exclusive possession of the land for a limited period: as a result, the Trust should now be prevented from denying that Mr Bruton has a lease. This form of estoppel thus has the same effect as the estoppel by representation that we examined in Chapter 13, section 2.2.1: it does not, in fact, give B a lease, but it prevents A from denying that B has a lease. That reasoning could thus have been used to prevent the Trust denying its statutory repairing duty.

Routley's argument is convincing—but, as he admits, it does not fit with the reasoning of the House of Lords. The key aspect of that reasoning seems to be the separation of the *status-conferring* and *property right-conferring* aspects of the lease. The agreement between Mr Bruton and the Trust, whilst it could not give Mr Bruton a property right in the land, *did*

[32] Ibid.

give him the status needed to qualify for statutory protection. The validity of that approach can be seen as a question of statutory interpretation: when Parliament used the word 'lease' to define the scope of the repairing duty, did it intend that term to be confined to cases in which B has a property right in land?

This suggestion is pursued in the following extract.

McFarlane and Simpson, 'Tackling Avoidance' in *Rationalizing Property, Equity and Trusts: Essays for Edward Burn*
(ed Getzler, 2002, pp 175–6)

[It may] be significant that Lord Hoffmann posed the question: 'Did this agreement create a 'lease' or 'tenancy' within the meaning of the Landlord and Tenant Act 1985 or any other legislation which refers to a lease or tenancy?'[33] and also that counsel for the housing trust, in the words of Lord Hobhouse, accepted that 'a contractual relationship of landlord and tenant suffices to make the provisions of the Act applicable.'[34] It can be argued that *Bruton* [...] does not involve a re-working of the general test for a lease but rather involves an attempt to further the presumed purpose of a legislative scheme by looking not for a lease in the technical sense of a legal right to exclusive possession but instead for a lease in the wider, non-juristic sense of an arrangement which confers practical control of property. The decision can thus be seen as based on an implicit assumption that the legislature's use of the concept of a tenancy to determine the bounds of particular protection for occupiers is simply a means to achieve an underlying purpose of giving such protection to those who, in practice, occupy property as one occupies a home. Provided such occupation exists, the precise legal rights enjoyed by the occupier are therefore not decisive in determining the application of the statute [...]

Hence, it may just be possible to justify the decision in *Bruton* by arguing that "lease" and "tenancy", when used in the Landlord and Tenant Act 1985, include an occupier under an agreement which only fails to confer a legal right to exclusive possession because of the grantor's lack of title. It could be said that the purpose of the legislation is to regulate the relationship between grantor and occupier, and the lack of title of the grantor, whilst it will prevent the occupier gaining rights against the true owner or those claiming through him, should not deny the occupier the protection of the Act: put simply, in such a situation the fact that the occupation agreement is technically unable to confer a lease in the full legal sense is not the fault of the occupier [...]

McFarlane and Simpson also explore whether this 'statutory interpretation' approach can be used to explain the 'pretence' concept applied by the House of Lords in *Antoniades v Villiers*.[35] As we saw in Chapter 23, section 2.4, there is a debate as to whether that concept provides a doctrinal justification for ignoring terms in the parties' contract that, if valid, would prevent B from acquiring a right to exclusive possession of the land. McFarlane and Simpson suggest that, in *Antoniades*, the House of Lords may have been motivated by an understandable desire to ensure that the statutory protection then provided by the Rent Acts should extend not only to parties with a legal right to exclusive possession, but also to parties, such as Mr Villiers and Miss Bridger, who, *in practice*, enjoyed exclusive control of a

---

[33] [2000] 1 AC 406, 413.
[34] Ibid, at 417.
[35] [1990] 1 AC 417.

home in return for paying rent. As the authors go on to note in the following passage, however, this approach to statutory interpretation, whilst it may be able to explain the results in *Bruton* and *Antoniades*, seems to be inconsistent with the seminal decision of the House of Lords in *Street v Mountford*.[36]

McFarlane and Simpson, 'Tackling Avoidance' in *Rationalizing Property, Equity and Trusts: Essays for Edward Burn*
(ed Getzler, 2002, p 177)

Lord Templeman's [speech in *Street v Mountford*] is founded on a rejection of the previously prevailing idea that the term 'tenancy' could be given an unorthodox meaning when used in the Rent Acts. A heresy had sprung up in the Court of Appeal which allowed an owner wishing to avoid the burdens of such legislation to do so provided he demonstrated an intention not to grant a lease. It seems clear that this heresy was motivated by sympathy towards such an owner, and a consequent willingness to narrow the application of the Rent Acts. Lord Templeman firmly emphasises that the orthodox, traditional definition of a lease as the grant of exclusive possession is the true test to apply. This can be defended on the simple grounds that when Parliament selects a concept such as 'lease' or 'tenancy', with an established juridical meaning, to communicate with judges there is no reason to believe it intends an unorthodox meaning of that term to be applied. Therefore whilst the result in *Street* may be favourable to occupiers rather than owners, its methodology is avowedly neutral.

The authors of the extract go on to make the point that, if the terms 'lease' or 'tenancy' can be interpreted in a novel way when used in a statute, this will not necessarily lead to an *increase* in the availability of statutory protection. For example, a court could find that, because of the special duties imposed on A if B has a lease, the term should be given a particularly narrow definition. Indeed, as we noted in Chapter 23, section 2.1, the Court of Appeal seemed to adopt just such an approach in the period leading up to *Street v Mountford*. Even if it is agreed that a judge, when interpreting a statute, should try to advance its purpose, we have to ask *how* a judge should discern that purpose. After all, as noted above, it may seem that the policy underlying s 11 of the Landlord and Tenant Act 1985 should apply even if B's agreement with A has not given B a property right. But it is doubtful that a court can make that decision given that: (i) the statute expressly limits its scope to cases in which B has a 'lease'; and (ii) as noted by the authors of all three extracts above, the term 'lease' is generally understood as applying only where A's agreement with B gives B a property right in land.

The solution, of course, is for Parliament to make its policy clearer. One resolution would be for the statutory protection currently available to those with leases to be extended to parties with licences. The lease would then be left to play its role as a concept conferring a property right; it would not have to perform the further task of conferring the status needed to qualify for statutory protection. In fact, as we will see in the next section, the Law Commission has proposed just such a change.

[36] [1985] AC 809.

4 THE *STATUS-CONFERRING* ASPECT OF A LEASE: REFORM?

There have long been calls for the reform of the statutory regulation of short-term residential leases. One of the central complaints has been that the law is too complex, with occupiers and landlords often unsure of their positions. Certainly, any protection that the law aims to provide for occupiers will be undermined if, in practice, those occupiers are unaware of their legal rights.[37]

In 2006, the Law Commission, following what it described as '*one of the largest consultation exercises* [it had] *ever undertaken*',[38] published its report on *Renting Homes*. The report considered the statutory protection available to short-term residential tenants and suggested significant changes, based on three objectives of '*simplification, increased comprehensibility, and flexibility*'.[39] It produced a very detailed draft Bill (the Rented Homes Bill) and stated that its proposals were based on '*two radical changes to the legislative approach to the regulation of rented housing*'. Those changes are set out in the extract below:

Law Commission Report No 297, *Renting Homes* (2006, [1.4]–[1.6])

First, we recommend the creation of a single social tenure. At present, local authorities can only let on secure tenancies; registered social landlords only on assured tenancies. Our recommendations are 'landlord-neutral'. They enable social housing providers, referred to in the Bill as 'community landlords', and those private sector landlords who so wish to rent on identical terms. This has long been sought by local authorities and registered social landlords. This offers the prize of vastly increased flexibility both to policy makers and landlords in the provision and management of social housing.

Secondly, we recommend a new 'consumer protection' approach which focuses on the contract between the landlord and the occupier (the contract-holder), incorporating consumer protection principles of fairness and transparency. Thus our recommended scheme does not depend on technical legal issues of whether or not there is a tenancy as opposed to a licence (as has usually been the case in the past). This ensures that both landlords and occupiers have a much clearer understanding of their rights and obligations.

The terms of the contract, underpinned by our statutory scheme, will be set out in model contracts that we anticipate will be free and easily downloadable. They will benefit landlords by explaining their rights and obligations, thus reducing the ignorance many landlords have about their responsibilities. They will benefit occupiers who will also have a clear statement of their rights and obligations, which sets out the basis on which they occupy accommodation, and the circumstances in which their rights to occupy may come to an end.

The aim of simplification is achieved in a number of ways. Firstly, the current focus on the identity of the landlord, and, with it, the different statutory categories of lease (e.g. 'assured shorthold tenancy', 'assured tenancy', 'secure tenancy', etc.), would be removed. Secondly, and most importantly for our current purposes, the *status-conferring*

---

[37] For a good example of this problem, exploring occupiers' ignorance of the legal protection given to them by the Protection from Eviction Act 1977, see Cowan [2001] Conv 249.

[38] Law Commission Report No 297, *Renting Homes* (2006, [1.3]).

[39] Ibid, at [1.9].

aspect of a lease would be lost: to qualify for statutory protection, it would no longer be necessary for B to show that he or she has a lease. The new scheme would instead regulate 'occupation contracts'. There would be two forms of such contract: the 'standard contract', lightly regulated and offering no security of tenure (similar to the current assured short-hold tenancy), and the 'secure contract', more heavily regulated and providing security of tenure, to be used (like the current secure tenancy and assured tenancy) by local authorities or social landlords.

Law Commission Report No 297, *Renting Homes* (2006)

At [3.9]

A number of points about the definition of "occupation contract" should be noted at the outset.

1. It is specifically provided that an occupation contract can be either a tenancy or a licence. This avoids historic complications whereby statutory schemes only applied where premises were "let". This definition recognizes that the distinction between a lease/tenancy and a licence exists. This will often be important. For example, where a landlord sells their legal estate in a property to another, it is highly relevant whether that estate is subject to a lease or a licence. These issues continue to be determined by application of the current law. We also make explicit that, where an occupation contract is a tenancy, any land registration requirements must be satisfied.

2. The contract must be made between a landlord and an individual (the "contract-holder"). The contract must confer the right to occupy premises as a home. Where the contract is made with two or more persons, at least one must be an individual. Contracts relating to the occupation of premises for purposes other than occupation as a home fall outside the scope of our scheme. In many situations, such agreements fall within the scope of other statutory schemes, for example business tenancies [...]

3. Despite the breadth of the definition, not all contracts which confer the right to occupy premises as a home fall within the scope of the Bill [...][40]

4. Most of the ancillary tests currently used to define the scope of statutory protection are removed. Thus, there is no requirement that the rent should be above or below a defined rent limit. Nor is there any requirement that the premises must be occupied as the 'only or principal home'.

5. Most importantly in the context of the social rented sector, there is no 'landlord condition'. Our emphasis on the principle of landlord neutrality means that the scheme will, for the first time, enable the creation of a single type of contract that can apply throughout the social rented sector, irrespective of the identity of the landlord.

6. Once created, an occupation contract continues in existence either until it is terminated in accordance with the provisions of the scheme, or unless the premises or the contract come within the scope of the exceptions listed in paragraph 3 of schedule 1[41] [...]

[40] [One example of a type of contract not covered by the Bill occurs where B pays to *share* occupation of A's land with A.]

[41] [That is, if a change in circumstances means that the contract now falls into one of those types not covered by the Bill.]

At [3.18]–[3.21]

In place of the current multiplicity of statutory statuses, the scheme provides for just two types of occupation contract: secure and standard.

Secure contracts

Secure contracts are modelled on secure tenancies which currently can only be created by local authorities. As with secure tenancies, secure contracts have a high degree of security of tenure protected by the Bill. They can be created only on a periodic basis. The reason for this is that in the context of the high security of tenure granted by the Bill for a secure contract, having a fixed term would not be useful [...] The idea of the secure contract is to provide a security gold standard for use in the social sector. To allow fixed term secure contracts would at best muddle the picture, and at worst, undercut that objective.

Standard contracts

Standard contracts are modelled on the current assured shorthold tenancy granted by private landlords. Although they have a low degree of security of tenure protected by statute, there is nothing preventing landlords entering contracts which have a greater degree of security than the Bill requires. Often this happens because it is in the landlord's interest to do so, for example to minimize void letting periods. Standard contracts can be either fixed term or periodic.

In the case of standard contracts only, the Bill provides that a landlord is able to specify periods where, notwithstanding the existence of the contract, the premises cannot be used for occupation. The purpose of this provision is to enable, for example, universities to enter occupation contracts with their students for the whole academic year, but also enable them to regain possession during vacation periods when the accommodation is needed for conferences. It would be a disproportionate administrative burden for there to be separate contracts for each academic term or semester.

Under the proposals, A would be obliged to give B a written copy of any occupation contract.[42] Such a contract would include four classes of 'matters' or 'terms': (i) key matters; (ii) fundamental terms; (iii) supplementary terms; and (iv) additional terms.[43]

Contractual terms regulating the key matters (the identity of the land; the date when occupation is to start; the sums to be paid by B as rent or as other payments; the period of the rent) would be exempt from regulation under the Unfair Terms in Consumer Contracts Regulations 1999, because those Regulations do not permit a party to challenge core contractual terms.

Fundamental terms would be those imposed by statute: the parties could not vary them. One such term would replicate the statutory repairing duty currently imposed by s 11 of the Landlord and Tenant Act 1985. Of course, under the Law Commission's proposals, that duty would no longer depend on B showing that he or she has a lease from A.

Supplementary terms would be those required in the contract as a result of a decision by an appropriate authority, rather than under the statute itself.

Additional terms would be any added by the parties. Control over those terms would come from the 'consumer protection' approach and, in particular, by the application of the Unfair Terms in Consumer Contracts Regulations 1999. As we noted at the start of section

---

42 Law Commission Report No 297 (2006, [2.7]–[2.9]).
43 Ibid, at [2.10].

2 above, those Regulations can currently apply both to lease and to licence agreements. But their operation is restricted by: (i) the need for A to be *'acting for purposes relating to his trade, business or profession'*;[44] and (ii) the fact that the unfairness test does not apply to terms individually negotiated by A and B. Under the Law Commission's proposals, those two restrictions would no longer apply where A and B enter an occupation contracts.

The Law Commission's proposals have not been enacted:[45] certainly, the reform of the statutory regulation of leases is a daunting task. Nonetheless, as noted in the following extract, the proposals have had a positive reception.

Bright, *Landlord and Tenant Law in Context* (2007, p 224)

These reform proposals have received widespread support. Many organizations have for some time been arguing that there should be a single form of tenancy available for all social lettings, irrespective of landlord type. Further, the emphasis placed on transparency and fairness through requiring a written contract which sets out the rights and obligations of both parties should help foster a 'mind-set' in which tenants are seen as consumers with rights and expectations, and landlords as service providers opting in to a regulated regime. Whether or not the proposals will progress to become law will depend, of course, on the political process. Legislation of this sort is complex and not politically eye-catching but it would be most unfortunate if these very welcome proposals never make it to the statute book.

For our present purposes, the key aspect of the Law Commission's proposals consists in the decision to decouple statutory protection from the presence of a property right. The thinking behind the decision to regulate occupation contracts, rather than only leases, is set out in one of the Consultation Papers that preceded the report.

Law Commission Consultation Paper No 162, *Renting Homes 1: Status and Security* (2002, [9.39]–[9.40])

We have thought very carefully about whether the lease-licence distinction should be retained as a means to determine which agreements should fall within our proposed scheme, and those which should fall outside. Considerable conceptual difficulties are caused by the distinction between exclusive occupation and exclusive possession. It is not readily understandable by the public at large.

As we have already argued, we regard the contract between the landlord and the occupier as central to the operation of our scheme. We see no reason why any distinction should be drawn between a contract which comprises a lease and a contract which comprises a licence. This distinction is essential where the proprietary consequences of the contract are concerned, and should remain so, but it should not affect the statutory regulation of the contract as between the contracting parties themselves.

---

[44] Unfair Terms in Consumer Contracts Regulations 1999, reg 3. In addition, B must be acting *'for purposes which are outside his trade, business or profession'*: that will always be the case in relation to short-term residential agreements.

[45] Under the Housing and Regeneration Act 2008, however, local authorities are to have the power, in certain circumstances, to grant non-secure tenancies: this introduces into local authority letting some of the flexibility called for by the Law Commission.

Certainly, one advantage of the Law Commission's scheme would be the elimination of the current *status-conferring* aspect of the lease. In addition to its practical benefits, such a change could have an important conceptual effect: it would permit the courts to consider the doctrinal definition of the lease (as a property right in land), free from the concern that the same definition may also have to be used to advance the policy goals behind a particular statute.

QUESTIONS

1. Why might Parliament intervene to give a tenant extra rights beyond those expressly agreed between that tenant and his or her landlord?

2. '*The distinction between a lease and a licence should only matter if a third party is involved: it should make no difference when considering the positions of A (the landlord/licensor) and B (the tenant/licensee).*' Do you agree?

3. What is a 'tenancy by estoppel'? Should the House of Lords in *Bruton v London & Quadrant Housing Trust* have found that Mr Bruton had a tenancy by estoppel?

4. Does the Law Commission's 'consumer protection' model provide the best way in which to regulate short-term residential leases?

FURTHER READING

Bridge, 'Leases: Contract, Property and Status' in *Land Law: Issues, Debates, Policy* (ed Tee, Devon: Willan, 2002)

Bright, *Landlord and Tenant Law in Context* (Oxford: Hart, 2007, chs 5 and 6)

Dixon, 'The Non-Proprietary Lease: The Rise of the Feudal Phoenix' [2000] CLJ 25

Law Commission Report No 297, *Renting Homes* (2006, especially Pts 1 and 2)

McFarlane and Simpson, 'Tackling Avoidance' in *Rationalizing Property, Equity & Trusts: Essays for Edward Burn* (ed Getzler, London: LexisNexis, 2002)

Pawlowski, 'The *Bruton* Tenancy: Clarity or More Confusion' [2005] Conv 262

25

LEASEHOLD COVENANTS

CENTRAL ISSUES

1. Both the positive and negative obligations of landlord and leaseholder have long been enforceable by the principle of privity of estate. The appropriate legal framework now differs according to whether the lease was granted before or after the enactment of the Landlord and Tenant (Covenants) Act 1995 on 1 January 1996.

2. *Pre-1996 leases (the burden)* A leaseholder's covenants (provided that they touch and concern the lease) are enforceable against a purchaser of the lease by privity of estate (see *Spencer's Case*).[1] The burden of the landlord's covenants (provided that they relate to the subject matter of the lease) is enforceable against the purchaser of the freehold reversion by s 142 of the Law of Property Act 1925.

3. *Pre-1996 leases (the benefit)* The leaseholder's covenants and the landlord's covenants (both having reference to the subject matter of the lease) are enforceable by a purchaser of the freehold reversion and by a purchaser of

the lease, respectively, under ss 141 and 142 of the 1925 Act.

4. *Pre-1996 leases* The contractual liability of the original parties to the lease continues throughout the term of the lease.

5. *Post-1996 leases* The benefit and burden of the leaseholder's and landlord's covenants (provided that they are not expressed to be personal) are enforceable against and by purchasers of the lease and the freehold reversion under s 3 of the 1995 Act.

6. *Post-1996 leases* The original leaseholder is automatically released from contractual liability upon his or her assignment of the lease under s 5 of the 1995 Act, and the original landlord may apply for a release from his or her liability upon his or her assignment of the freehold reversion under ss 6 and 8 of the Act.

7. A sub-lessee is not within the privity of estate relationship, but is obliged (inter alia) to observe the negative leaseholder

---

[1] (1583) 5 Co Rep 16a.

covenants in the head lease under the doctrine in *Tulk v Moxhay*.[2]

8. The primary remedy for breach of a leasehold covenant that has not been waived is for the landlord to exercise a right of re-entry to forfeit the lease.

9. The landlord may re-enter peacefully or by serving proceedings for possession. Before a landlord is able exercise a right of re-entry for breach of covenant (other than to pay rent), a notice must be served in accordance with s 146(1) of the 1925 Act.

10. A tenant (and subtenant or mortgagee) may apply for relief from forfeiture based upon a breach of either the covenant to pay rent or a breach of any other of the tenant's covenants.

1 INTRODUCTION

A lease will not only contain the grant of the leasehold term by the landlord to the tenant, but also covenants detailing the respective obligations of the landlord and the tenant. Certain covenants are implied, but, in a written lease, these covenants will be supplemented by often extensive and detailed covenants stipulating the tenant's obligations to the landlord and the landlord's, often more limited, obligations to the tenant. The landlord's covenants will include a covenant for quiet possession, and may also include obligations to repair and insure; a tenant's covenants will include a covenant to pay the rent and covenants governing his or her use of the premises, as well as covenants detailing the tenant's responsibilities for repair and maintenance, and to meet the cost of the landlord's obligations in this regard, by paying a management or service charge.

In this chapter, we will examine the mechanisms by which both negative and positive leasehold covenants bind, on the one hand, subsequent purchasers of the lease from the original tenant and, on the other, subsequent purchasers of the freehold reversion from the landlord. We will also consider the law governing the enforcement of leasehold covenants and, in particular, the process of forfeiture by which a landlord can bring the lease to an end for a failure by the tenant to perform the tenant's covenants.

The legal regulation of leasehold covenants is applicable to all leases that are capable of assignment. As we saw in Chapter 24, most short-term tenancy agreements of residential accommodation will contain a restriction on assignment of, or otherwise dealing with, the leasehold term. If an existing tenant wishes to leave the premises, he or she will normally surrender his or her tenancy to the landlord, who can then let the premises to another tenant.

The most common types of lease in which the enforcement of leasehold covenants is important are in the commercial context or in the ownership of flats, where the long lease structure is employed. Indeed, in Chapter 28, we will see that the long lease is employed in the ownership of flats, precisely because it provides a mechanism whereby positive obligations can be enforced against subsequent flat owners. In the commercial context, a lease of business premises will usually be capable of assignment (unless it is for a very short term), although it is common for the tenant's ability to assign or otherwise dispose of his or her term to be qualified by the need to obtain the landlord's consent, which cannot be unreasonably refused. Many of the cases that we will be considering are set in the commercial context, perhaps because commercial landlords and tenants are more inclined to litigate. Our focus will, however, be on the residential long lease.

[2] (1848) 2 Ph 774.

1.1 LEASEHOLD COVENANT TERMINOLOGY

Where a lease or a freehold reversion is assigned, it is necessary to determine whether or not the covenants given by the original tenant (TO) to the original landlord (LO) in the lease (the tenant's covenants) may be enforced by a purchaser of the freehold reversion (the landlord's assignee, or LA) against TO and any purchaser of the lease (the tenant's assignee, or TA). Likewise, it is also necessary to establish whether TO and TA can enforce against LA the covenants granted by LO to TO in the original lease (the landlord's covenants). This web of relationships can be depicted as shown in Figure 16.

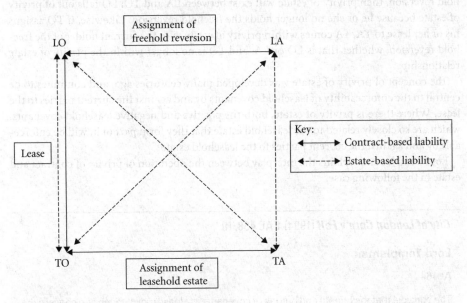

Figure 16 Leasehold covenant relationships

The answer to these central questions on the enforceability of both the landlord's and tenant's covenant depends on when the lease was granted. This is because the law was amended and codified by the Landlord and Tenant (Covenants) Act 1995, but the amendments enacted apply only to those leases granted on or after 1 January 1996. There are, of course, many leases granted before 1 January 1996 that still have many years to run and which will continue to be governed by the old law. It is thus necessary to look at the law governing leases entered into before 1 January 1996 ('pre-1996 leases') and the law regulating leases entered into on or after 1 January 1996 ('post-1995 leases').

1.2 CONTRACT AND ESTATE-BASED LIABILITY

We saw in Chapter 23 that a lease has a dual personality: firstly, as a contract between the original parties; and secondly, as a proprietary interest in the form of a leasehold estate in the land, which may be transferred or left by will. Liability on the landlord's covenants and the tenant's covenants in the lease is based either upon the contractual relationship between LO and TO, or upon the leasehold estate that will vested in TA, upon his or her purchase of the lease, or the freehold reversion (subject to the lease), which likewise may be transferred by LO to LA. Where the parties fall within this leasehold relationship, we say that there is *privity of estate*.

Students of contract law will recognize that, between LO and TO, there is *privity of contract*, which is unaffected if and when LO and/or TO assign their interests to LA and TA, respectively. The lease contract continues between the original parties throughout the term of the lease.

Privity of estate exists between the current parties to the leasehold estate. It can thus vary during the leasehold term, depending on in whom the lease and the freehold reversion are vested. Initially, LO and TO are the parties to the leasehold estate. If LO assigns the freehold reversion, then privity of estate will exist between LA and TO: LO falls out of privity of estate because he or she no longer holds the freehold reversion. Likewise, if TO assigns his or her lease to TA, TA comes within privity of estate with the current holder of the freehold reversion, whether that is LO or LA, and TO is no longer within the privity of estate relationship.

The concept of privity of estate was developed many centuries ago, and continues to be central to the enforceability of leasehold covenants by and against the current parties to the lease. Where there is privity of estate, both the positive and negative leasehold covenants, which are so closely related to the leasehold estate that they form part of it, will be enforceable by and against the current parties to the leasehold estate.

Lord Templeman explains the interplay between the operation of privity of contract and estate in the following case.

City of London Corp v Fell [1994] 1 AC 458, HL

Lord Templeman

At 464

The principle that the benefit and burden of covenants in a lease which touch and concern the land run with the term and with the reversion is necessary for the effective operation of the law of landlord and tenant. Common law, and statute following the common law, recognise two forms of legal estate in land, a fee simple absolute in possession and a term of years absolute: see section 1 of the Act of 1925. Common law, and statute following the common law, were faced with the problem of rendering effective the obligations under a lease which might endure for a period of 999 years or more beyond the control of any covenantor. The solution was to annex to the term and the reversion the benefit and burden of covenants which touch and concern the land. The covenants having been annexed, every legal owner of the term granted by the lease and every legal owner of the reversion from time to time holds his estate with the benefit of and subject to the covenants which touch and concern the land. The system of leasehold tenure requires that the obligations in the lease shall be enforceable throughout the term, whether those obligations are affirmative or negative. The owner of a reversion must be able to enforce the positive covenants to pay rent and keep in repair against an assignee who in turn must be able to enforce any positive covenants entered into by the original landlord. Common law retained the ancient rule that the burden of a covenant does not run with the land of the covenantor except in the case of a lease, but even that rule was radically modified by equity so far as negative covenants were concerned: see *Tulk v. Moxhay* (1848) 2 Ph. 774.

The effect of common law and statute on a lease is to create rights and obligations which are independent of the parallel rights and obligations of the original human covenantor who and whose heirs may fail or the parallel rights and obligations of a corporate covenantor which may be dissolved. Common law and statute achieve that effect by annexing those rights and obligations so far as they touch and concern the land to the term and to the reversion. Nourse L.J. neatly summarised the position when he said in an impeccable judgment [1993] Q.B. 589, 604:

> "The contractual obligations which touch and concern the land having become imprinted on the estate, the tenancy is capable of existence as a species of property independently of the contract."

The common law did not release the original tenant from liability for breaches of covenant committed after an assignment because of the sacred character of covenant in English law [...] This only means that the fortunate English landlord has two remedies after an assignment, namely his remedy against the assignee and his remedy against the original tenant. It does not follow that if the liability of the original tenant is released or otherwise disappears then the term granted by the lease will disappear or that the assignee will cease to be liable on the covenants.

As between landlord and assignee the landlord cannot enforce a covenant against the assignee because the assignee does not covenant. The landlord enforces against the assignee the provisions of a covenant entered into by the original tenant, being provisions which touch and concern the land, because those provisions are annexed by the lease to the term demised by the lease. The assignee is not liable for a breach of covenant committed after the assignee has himself in turn assigned the lease because once he has assigned over he has ceased to be the owner of the term to which the covenants are annexed.

2 THE ORIGINAL PARTIES (LO AND TO) AND CONTRACTUAL ENFORCEABILITY

2.1 PRE-1996 LAW

LO and TO remain contractually liable on their leasehold covenants throughout the term of the lease, even though they may have disposed of their respective interests, unless they have expressly agreed to limit their respective liabilities in their original covenants.

This contractual liability can operate harshly particularly against TO, who, many years after he or she has assigned the lease, can find him or herself sued in respect of a breach of the tenant's covenants (usually a failure to pay the rent or service charge) committed by TA. For example, the current landlord will be tempted to rely on this contractual liability where TA is insolvent.[3] Although this liability is more often relied upon in commercial leases, where rentals reflect market levels, the principles are equally applicable to residential long leases.

Lord Nicholls explained the problems in the following case.

---

[3] The economic downturn of the late 1980s and early 1990s resulted in a number of well-publicized and criticized cases in which original leaseholders were successfully held liable.

Hindcastle Ltd v Barbara Attenborough & Associates Ltd [1997] AC 70, HL

Lord Nicholls

At 83

The insolvency may occur many years after the lease was granted, long after the original tenant parted with his interest in the lease. He paid the rent until he left, and then took on the responsibility of other premises. A person of modest means is understandably shocked when out of the blue he receives a rent demand from the landlord of the property he once leased. Unlike the landlord, he had no control over the identity of assignees down the line. He had no opportunity to reject them as financially unsound.

TO does have the benefit of an indemnity covenant for the performance of the tenant's covenant from TA, which will build up a chain of indemnity covenants following each assignment of the lease,[4] and also a restitutionary action for any damages that TO may have to pay as a result of the default of another (i.e. TA).[5] But these actions will be of little value where the defaulter is insolvent or the chain of indemnity covenants has been broken.[6]

In a series of decisions, the courts added further to TO's woes by confirming that his or her liability could be affected by a variation in the lease terms (e.g. an upward rent review), where that variation was made in pursuance of the terms of the lease.[7] A variation would not affect TO where it resulted from the separate agreement of the current parties to the lease, whether that variation resulted in a renewal or extension of the leasehold term,[8] or was to the terms upon which the lease was held.[9]

This contractual liability was the target of criticism by the Law Commission.

Law Commission Report No 174, *Landlord and Tenant Law: Privity of Contract and Estate* (1988, [3.1]–[3.3])

In Part III of the Working Paper, we identified the following criticisms of the present law:

(a) It is intrinsically unfair that anyone should bear burdens under a contract in respect of which they derive no benefit and over which they have no control: contractual obligations undertaken in a lease should only regulate relations between current owners with interests in the property.

(b) When demand is made under continuing liability of the original tenant it will often not only be unexpected, but beyond the means of the former tenant; there is no logical way

---

[4] See Law of Property Act 1925, s 77(1)(c), and Land Registration Act 2002, Sch 12, para 20. The indemnity is implied into each assignment of the lease and so can build up a chain of indemnity covenants to pass liability down to the defaulting leaseholder. As to the operation of indemnity covenants, see Chapter 27, section 2.4.2.

[5] *Moule v Garrett* (1872) LR 7 EX 101.

[6] *RHP Ltd v Mirror Group Newspapers and Mirror Group Holdings* (1992) 65 P & CR 252.

[7] See *Centrovincial Estates plc v Bulk Storage Ltd* (1983) 46 P & CR 393, in which the leaseholder was liable for rent varied from £17,000 to £40,000 pursuant to a rent review clause contained in the original lease, and *Selous Street Properties Ltd v Oronel Fabrics Ltd* (1984) 270 EG 643, in which the rent review took into account unauthorized alterations that were subsequently approved by the landlord.

[8] *City of London Corp v Fell* [1994] 1 AC 458.

[9] *Friends Provident Life Office v British Railways Board* (1997) 73 P & CR 9.

in which a former tenant who does understand that there is a contingent liability can estimate the amount.

(c) A single lease can contain some covenants of which the burden automatically passes to an assignee, by privity of estate, and others of which the burden does not pass automatically. This contrast in a single document, which is not apparent from its wording is unsatisfactory [...]

(d) Many laymen do not realise that the original parties have a continuing liability and most leases do not make this clear on their face.

(e) Where a lease contains a rent review clause, the original tenant's liability, under privity of contract, normally extends to payment of the higher rents after revision. For this reason, privity of contract sometimes results in the original tenant having a greater liability then he understood he was assuming. While this may merely reflect the increase in value of the premises it can cast on a former tenant a burden resulting from an increased value from which he has derived no benefit.

(f) Landlords who are in practice the main beneficiaries of the privity of contract principle are unduly protected. They have the ability to enforce obligations undertaken by tenants by action against both the original tenant and the current tenant [...] This makes the principle one-sided, and unreasonably multiplies the remedies available to landlords.

(g) Original tenants against whom covenants are enforced after they have assigned the lease are not adequately protected, nor do they have adequate means of reimbursement. They are not released even if the tenant in possession agrees materially to vary the extent of liability, they are not entitled to notice of default and they have no right to take back possession of the property. Former tenants are therefore often deprived of the opportunity to limit their liability by taking prompt remedial action. Faced with demands that they must meet, they are often unable even to have recourse to the property to recoup any losses.

(h) The contingent liability which privity of contract imposes in an original tenant who has parted with his interest in the property can create difficulty in winding-up and distributing the estates of tenants who have died. The response to the Working Paper suggests that this difficulty is more theoretical than practical.

[...]

Against these criticisms we pointed out that continuing liability of the parties to leases is a matter of contract. They are free to vary the normal rule. This is sometimes done, but not frequently. Some feel that a heavy burden lies on those who propose any further restriction on freedom of contract, but others question whether there is any true freedom here because there is widely thought to be an inequality of bargaining power between landlords and tenants, favouring landlords.

These criticisms have, in part, been addressed by the Landlord and Tenant (Covenants) Act 1995. The reforms of the 1995 Act affecting pre-1996 leases address only the worst excesses of privity of contract. The original parties' liability under post-1995 leases is subject to more far-reaching reform, which is considered below.

Section 18 of the 1995 Act provides that TO's liability to pay an amount due under the lease will not be altered by a variation of the lease, which the landlord had an absolute right to refuse, made after the time at which he or she has disposed of his or her interest.

Section 17 of the Act provides that the current landlord, who wishes to recover a fixed sum from TO, must give notice of the amount that he or she is intending to recover within six months of the sum becoming due.[10] Where TO complies with this notice, he or she may claim an overriding lease to secure any sums that he or she has been required to pay. An overriding lease takes effect as a statutory lease interposed between the current landlord and the current defaulting leaseholder. As such, it will enable TO to enforce the tenant's covenants, for example, by claiming the rental due and seeking forfeiture if the rent is not paid.[11] Thus TO is at least given a warning of his or her potential contractual liability for fixed sums, which should not exceed six months' rental or other charges, and is provided with a mechanism to try to recover the sums that he or she has had to meet. His or her contractual liability for unliquidated sums, however, is undiminished.

2.2 POST-1995 LAW

2.2.1 Release of TO

Section 5 of the Landlord and Tenant (Covenants) Act 1995 releases TO from contractual liability once he or she has assigned his or her lease. It also confirms TA's release from liability should he or she, in turn, dispose of the leasehold estate.

Landlord and Tenant (Covenants) Act 1995, s 5

Tenant released from covenants on assignment of tenancy

(1) This section applies where a tenant assigns premises demised to him under a tenancy.

(2) If the tenant assigns the whole of the premises demised to him, he—

    (a) is released from the tenant covenants of the tenancy, and

    (b) ceases to be entitled to the benefit of the landlord covenants of the tenancy,

as from the assignment.

Where the tenant requires the consent of the landlord to assign the lease, however, a landlord may refuse his or her consent unless the tenant enters into an authorized guarantee agreement, under which the tenant guarantees the assignee's payment of the rent and performance of the other tenant's covenants.[12] A landlord's consent to assign is a common feature of commercial leases, but not of residential long leases.

2.2.2 Release of LO

LO can also be released from his or her contractual liability, although a release is not available from liabilities that are expressed to be personal to LO.[13] LO's release does not operate automatically upon assignment of the reversion, but must be requested by LO serving a notice on TO, within four weeks of the assignment of his or her reversion.

---

[10] Landlord and Tenant (Covenants) Act 1995, s 17. This notice must be in statutory form (see s 27) and is commonly referred to as a 'problem notice'.

[11] Ibid, s 19.

[12] Ibid, s 16.

[13] *BHP Petroleum Great Britain Ltd v Chesterfield Properties Ltd* [2002] Ch 194: see section 3.2.2 below.

Landlord and Tenant (Covenants) Act 1995, s 6

Landlord may be released from covenants on assignment of reversion

(1) This section applies where a landlord assigns the reversion in premises of which he is the landlord under a tenancy.

(2) If the landlord assigns the reversion in the whole of the premises of which he is the landlord—

(a) he may apply to be released from the landlord covenants of the tenancy in accordance with section 8; and

(b) if he is so released from all of those covenants, he ceases to be entitled to the benefit of the tenant covenants of the tenancy as from the assignment.

The process is governed by s 8, which provides that, where TO refuses to grant a release, the county court may grant a release where it is reasonable to do so.

Landlord and Tenant (Covenants) Act 1995, s 8

Procedure for seeking release from a covenant under section 6 or 7

(1) For the purposes of section 6 or 7 an application for the release of a covenant to any extent is made by serving on the tenant, either before or within the period of four weeks beginning with the date of the assignment in question, a notice informing him of—

(a) the proposed assignment or (as the case may be) the fact that the assignment has taken place, and

(b) the request for the covenant to be released to that extent.

(2) Where an application for the release of a covenant is made in accordance with subsection (1), the covenant is released to the extent mentioned in the notice if—

(a) the tenant does not, within the period of four weeks beginning with the day on which the notice is served, serve on the landlord or former landlord a notice in writing objecting to the release, or

(b) the tenant does so serve such a notice but the court, on the application of the landlord or former landlord, makes a declaration that it is reasonable for the covenant to be so released, or

(c) the tenant serves on the landlord or former landlord a notice in writing consenting to the release and, if he has previously served a notice objecting to it, stating that that notice is withdrawn.

The provisions of the 1995 Act cannot be excluded or varied.[14] But the House of Lords has held that a limitation of liability contained in the terms of the original covenant does not fall foul of this prohibition. In so doing, the Lords explained the purpose and effect of the Act's limitation of LO and TO's contractual liability.

---

[14] Landlord and Tenant (Covenants) Act 1995, s 25.

London Diocesan Fund v Phithwa [2005] 1 WLR 3956, HL

Facts: A lease provided that the original landlord (Avonridge Property Co Ltd) would not be liable for the payment of rent under the head lease after it assigned the reversion. After Avonridge assigned its leasehold reversion, the head lease was forfeited as a result of its assignee's failure to pay the rent under the head lease; the sub-lessees obtained relief from forfeiture, but had to pay the arrears of rent. They unsuccessfully claimed that the limitation of Avonridge's liability in the head lease was void under s 25 of the 1995 Act.

Lord Nicholls

At [13]–[21]

So sections 6 to 8 of the Act provide a landlord with a means which may result in his being released from the landlord covenants but will not necessarily do so. If the landlord assigns the whole of the premises of which he is landlord he may apply to be released from the landlord covenants of the tenancy. A landlord covenant is a covenant falling to be complied with by the landlord of the premises demised by a tenancy. An application for release is made by the landlord serving an appropriate notice on the tenant requesting a release of the landlord covenant wholly or in part. Where the landlord makes such an application the covenant is released to the requested extent if the tenant consents, or if he fails to object, or if he does object but the court decides it is reasonable for the covenant to be released: section 8.

These statutory provisions might readily be stultified if the parties to a lease could exclude their operation. In particular, the provision for automatic release of tenant covenants on assignment of a lease would be a weak instrument if it were open to a landlord to provide that the original tenant's contractual liability should continue for the whole term notwithstanding section 5. So the Act, in section 25, enacts a comprehensive anti-avoidance provision. Subsection (1) relevantly provides:

> "Any agreement relating to a tenancy is void to the extent that- (a) it would apart from this section have effect to exclude, modify or otherwise frustrate the operation of any provision of this Act, or (b) it provides for- (i) the termination or surrender of the tenancy, or (ii) the imposition on the tenant of any penalty, disability, or liability, in the event of the operation of any provision of this Act [...]"

The words in parenthesis in Avonridge's covenant in clause 6 of each sublease are an "agreement relating to a tenancy" within the meaning of this section: section 25(4). But does this agreement "frustrate the operation" of any provision of the Act? That is the key question.

The subtenants submit it does. The limited release provisions in sections 6 to 8 were intended to be the sole means whereby an original landlord could obtain a release from the landlord covenants when he assigned the reversion. The parenthetical words in clause 6 would frustrate that statutory purpose if they were allowed to have effect according to their tenor.

I am unable to agree. Where I part company with this submission is its statement of the statutory purpose. Sections 5 to 8 are relieving provisions. They are intended to benefit tenants, or landlords, as the case may be. That is their purpose. That is how they are meant to operate. These sections introduced a means, which cannot be ousted, whereby in certain circumstances, without the agreement of the other party, a tenant or landlord can be released from a liability he has assumed. The object of the legislation was that on lawful assignment of a tenancy or reversion, and irrespective of the terms of the tenancy, the tenant or the landlord should have an exit route from his future liabilities. This route should be available in accordance with the statutory provisions.

Thus the mischief at which the statute was aimed was the *absence* in practice of any such exit route. Consistently with this the legislation was not intended to close any *other* exit route already open to the parties: in particular, that by agreement their liability could be curtailed from the outset or later released or waived. The possibility that by agreement the parties may limit their liability in this way was not, it seems, perceived as having unfair consequences in practice, even though landlords normally have greater bargaining power than tenants. So there was no call for legislation to exclude the parties' capacity to make such an agreement, ending their liability in circumstances other than those provided in the Act.

Section 25 is of course to be interpreted generously, so as to ensure the operation of the Act is not frustrated, either directly or indirectly. But there is nothing in the language or scheme of the Act to suggest the statute was intended to exclude the parties' ability to limit liability under their covenants from the outset in whatever way they may agree. An agreed limitation of this nature does not impinge upon the operation of the statutory provisions.

[. . .] Whatever its form, an agreed limitation of liability does not impinge upon the operation of the statutory provisions because, as already noted, the statutory provisions are intended to operate to relieve tenants and landlords from a liability which would otherwise exist. They are not intended to impose a liability which otherwise would be absent. They are not intended to enlarge the liability either of a tenant or landlord. The Act does not compel a landlord to enter into a covenant with his tenant to pay the rent under a headlease. The Act does not compel this, even though it may be eminently reasonable that a landlord should do so. Nor do the statutory restrictions on the circumstances where a landlord can end his liability without his tenant's consent carry any implication that a tenant may not agree to end his landlord's liability in other circumstances. Such an implication would be inconsistent with the underlying scheme of these provisions.

This appraisal accords with the thrust of the Law Commission's report [. . .]

Nor do the events in this case exemplify a loophole in the Act Parliament cannot have intended. The risks involved were not obscure or concealed. They were evident on the face of the subleases. The sublessees were to pay up-front a capitalised rent for the whole term of the subleases. But clause 6 enabled Avonridge to shake off all its landlord obligations at will. Any competent conveyancer would, or should, have warned the sublessees of the risks, clearly and forcefully.

The decision does provide an escape route, particularly for landlords, who can use their bargaining power and superior knowledge of the law to limit their liability when negotiating the term of the lease.

Not all of the Law Lords were happy to accept this possibility.

London Diocesan Fund v Phithwa [2005] 1 WLR 3956, HL

Lord Walker (dissenting)

At 35

I am driven to the conclusion that although the general legislative purpose of the Act was to effect the release from liability of landlords and tenants on their assignment of their interests, subject to and in accordance with the provisions of the Act, section 25 is expressed in terms wide enough to interfere with the freedom of contract which was available to the parties in negotiating a tenancy before the coming into force of the Act. By restricting the parties' freedom of contract, the Act (in a case such as the present) does operate to make it more difficult for a landlord to escape liability on landlord covenants (within the meaning of the Act). I would accept the submission of Mr Wells, for the respondents, that that can be done only by the procedure laid down in section 8 of the Act. To that limited extent the Act does operate, as it seems to me, to shut off what my noble and learned friend, Lord Nicholls of Birkenhead, has described as "any other exit route" previously open to the parties.

3 ASSIGNEES (LA AND TA) AND ESTATE-BASED LIABILITY

3.1 PRE-1996 LAW

The benefit and burden of the landlord's covenants and the tenant's covenants have run with the freehold reversion and the leasehold estate since the sixteenth century. Statute has conferred upon LA the right to sue upon the tenant's covenant given to LO and has imposed upon LA the obligation to observe the landlord's covenant's given by LO in the original lease. The current statutory provisions are now found in ss 141 and 142 of the Law of Property Act 1925 (LPA 1925).[15]

3.1.1 The landlord's covenants

Law of Property Act 1925, s 142(1)

Obligation of lessor's covenants to run with reversion

(1) The obligation under a condition or of a covenant entered into by a lessor with reference to the subject-matter of the lease shall, if and as far as the lessor has power to bind the reversionary estate immediately expectant on the term granted by the lease, be annexed and incident to and shall go with that reversionary estate, or the several parts thereof, notwithstanding severance of that reversionary estate, and may be taken advantage of and enforced by the person in whom the term is from time to time vested by conveyance, devolution in law, or otherwise; and, if and as far as the lessor has power to bind the person from time to time entitled to that reversionary estate, the obligation aforesaid may be taken advantage of and enforced against any person so entitled.

Section 142 relates both to the benefit and to the burden of the landlord's covenants given by LO to TO, by imposing upon LA the obligation to perform these covenants and conferring upon TA the right to enforce these covenants. Thus TO can sue LA and TA can sue LO or LA, as appropriate (see Figure 17).

---

[15] They were originally contained in the Grantee of Reversions Act 1540 and amended by the Conveyancing Acts of 1881 and 1911.

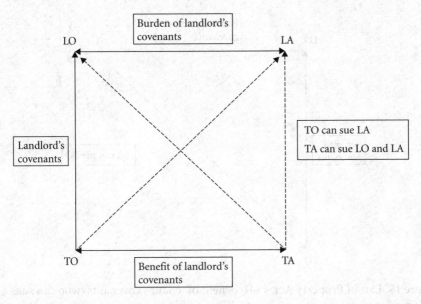

Figure 17 Law of Property Act 1925, s 142: benefit (who can sue) and burden (who can be sued) of landlord's covenants

3.1.2 The tenant's covenants

Law of Property Act 1925, s 141

Rent and benefit of lessee's covenants to run with the reversion

(1) Rent reserved by a lease, and the benefit of every covenant or provision therein contained, having reference to the subject-matter thereof, and on the lessee's part to be observed or performed, and every condition of re-entry and other condition therein contained, shall be annexed and incident to and shall go with the reversionary estate in the land, or in any part thereof, immediately expectant on the term granted by the lease, notwithstanding severance of that reversionary estate, and without prejudice to any liability affecting a covenantor or his estate.

(2) Any such rent, covenant or provision shall be capable of being recovered, received, enforced, and taken advantage of, by the person from time to time entitled, subject to the term, to the income of the whole or any part, as the case may require, of the land leased.

Section 141 relates to the benefit of the tenant's covenants, and confers upon LA the right to sue for the rent and upon the other covenants given by TO to LO in the original lease. Thus LA can sue TO (see Figure 18).

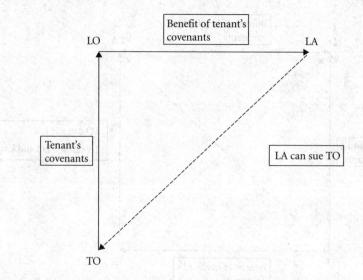

Figure 18 Law of Property Act, s 141: benefit of tenant's covenants (who can sue)

The missing link in the enforceability matrix is provided, not by statute, but by *Spencer's Case*,[16] which imposes upon TA the obligation to perform the tenant's covenants given by TO, including the covenant to pay rent.[17] Thus LO and LA can sue TA (see Figure 19).

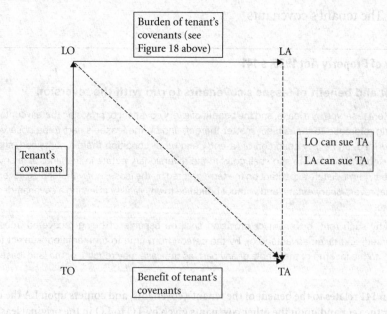

Figure 19 Spencer's Case: burden of tenant's covenants (who can be sued)

---

[16] (1583) 5 Co Rep 16a.

[17] The omission of this link from the statutory framework is a result of 'parliamentary fumbling': see Sparkes, *A New Landlord and Tenant* (2001, p 749–52).

Spencer's Case (1583) 5 Co Rep 16a

If lessee for years covenants to repair the houses during the term, it shall bind all others as a thing which is appurtenant, and goeth with the land in whose hands soever the term shall come, as well those who come to it by act in law, as by the act of the party, for all is one having regard to the lessor. And if the law should not be such, great prejudice might accrue to him; and reason requires, that they, who shall take benefit of such covenant when the lessor makes it with the lessee, should on the other side be bound by the like covenant when the lessee makes it with the lessor.

3.1.3 Covenants that touch and concern, or have reference to the subject matter of, the lease

Sections 141 and 142 relate to covenants that '*have reference to the subject matter of the lease*', whilst *Spencer's Case* refers to covenants that '*touch and concern the land*'. The expressions have identical meaning,[18] but that meaning has proved somewhat elusive.

Lord Oliver provides the clearest explanation in the following case.[19]

P&A Swift Investments v Combined English Stores Group plc [1989] AC 632, HL

Lord Oliver

At 642

In my opinion the question of whether a surety's covenant in a lease touches and concerns the land falls to be determined by the same test as that applicable to the tenant's covenant.

Formulations of definitive tests are always dangerous, but it seems to me that, without claiming to expound an exhaustive guide, the following provides a satisfactory working test for whether, in any given case, a covenant touches and concerns the land: (1) the covenant benefits only the reversioner for time being, and if separated from the reversion ceases to be of benefit to the covenantee; (2) the covenant affects the nature, quality, mode of user or value of the land of the reversioner; (3) the covenant is not expressed to be personal (that is to say neither being given only to a specific reversioner nor in respect of the obligations only of a specific tenant); (4) the fact that a covenant is to pay a sum of money will not prevent it from touching and concerning the land so long as the three foregoing conditions are satisfied and the covenant is connected with something to be done on to or in relation to the land.

There should be no difficulty in the common covenants found in the long leases of flats satisfying this test: covenants for quiet enjoyment; the payment of rent or service charge; for repair and insurance; or relating to the user of the flat or the common areas and facilities.

More difficult questions have tended to arise with commercial leases. Here, the application of test has led to '*arbitrary and inconsistent outcome(s)*'.[20] A surety's covenant runs with

---

[18] See *Caern Motor Services Ltd v Texaco Ltd* [1994] 1 WLR 1249.

[19] And *Coronation Street Industrial Properties Ltd v Ignall Industries Ltd* [1989] 1 WLR 304. These cases concerned a surety's covenant, rather than leasehold covenants, but the test has been subsequently applied to leasehold covenants in *Caern Motor Services Ltd v Texeco Ltd* [1994] 1 WLR 1249 and *Cardwell v Walker* [2003] EWHC 3117.

[20] Gray and Gray, *Elements of Land Law* (5th edn, 2009, [4.5.52]).

the land,[21] but a covenant to repay a deposit does not;[22] an option for a tenant to purchase the reversion does not touch and concern with the land,[23] but an option to renew the lease does;[24] a covenant to sell only the landlord's products is a covenant that touches and concerns the land,[25] but a non-competition covenant by a landlord does not.[26]

3.1.4 Equitable leases and assignments

A further qualification affects the running of the burden of the tenant's covenants to TA under *Spencer's Case*, although not the passing of the benefit and burden under ss 141 and 142 of the LPA 1925. *Spencer's Case* operates where the leaseholder's covenants form part of leaseholder's legal estate in the land. Thus it has been held that the burden of the leaseholder's covenants will not pass to TA where the lease[27] or the assignment[28] to TA is equitable. This limitation has been described as *'anomalous and inconvenient'*,[29] and various other approaches have been suggested.[30]

Boyer v Warbey [1953] 1 QB 234, CA

Denning LJ

At 246

[...] since the fusion of law and equity [by the Judicature Act 1873], the position is different. The distinction between agreements under hand and agreements under seal has largely been obliterated. There is no valid reason nowadays why the doctrine of covenants running with the land—or with the reversion—should not apply equally to agreements under hand as to covenants under seal; and I think we should so hold.

This view, whilst attractive, rather stretches the effect of the Judicature Act 1871. A more satisfactory route to overcome the problem could be based upon finding a separate contractual nexus, or even legal periodic tenancy, between LO (or LA) and TA, from the fact of TA's possession and payment of rent, and LO (or LA's) acceptance of that rent by way of acknowledgment of TA's position as tenant.

LO or LA are not without redress: they can still exercise a right to forfeit the lease in the event of a breach of covenant (see section 6.4 below), or, where the covenant is negative, rely upon its enforceability as a restrictive covenant under the doctrine of *Tulk v Moxhay*.[31]

---

[21] See *Kumar v Dunning* [1989] QB 193 and *P&A Swift Investments v Combined English Stores Group plc* [1989] AC 632.

[22] *Hua Chiao Commercial Bank Ltd v Chiap Hua Industries Ltd* [1987] AC 99.

[23] *Woodall v Clifton* [1905] 2 Ch 257, 279.

[24] *Phillips v Mobil Oil Co Ltd* [1989] 1 WLR 888, 891, *per* Nicholls LJ, who excuses the anomaly only on established practice.

[25] *Caern Motor Services Ltd v Texeco Ltd* [1994] 1 WLR 1249 and *Cardwell v Walker* [2003] EWHC 3117.

[26] *Thomas v Hayward* (1869) LR 4 Ex 311.

[27] *Purchase v Lichfield Brewery Co* [1915] 1 KB 184.

[28] *Cox v Bishop* (1857) 8 De GM&G 815.

[29] Gray and Gray *Elements of Land Law* (5th edn, 2009, [4.5.86]).

[30] Smith, 'The Running of Covenants in Equitable Leases and Equitable Assignments of Legal Leases' [1978] CLJ 98.

[31] See Chapter 27, section 2.

3.2 POST-1995 LEASES

3.2.1 The Landlord and Tenant (Covenants) Act 1995 framework of enforceability

The Landlord and Tenant (Covenants) Act 1995 provides a statutory framework for passing the benefit and burden of the landlord's and the tenant's covenants. TA is entitled to sue upon the landlord's covenants and is bound by the tenant's covenants by s 3(2), and LA becomes entitled to sue upon the tenant's covenants[32] and is bound by the landlord's covenants by s 3(3).

Landlord and Tenant (Covenants) Act 1995, s 3

Transmission of benefit and burden of covenants

(1) The benefit and burden of all landlord and tenant covenants of a tenancy—

    (a) shall be annexed and incident to the whole, and to each and every part, of the premises demised by the tenancy and of the reversion in them, and

    (b) shall in accordance with this section pass on an assignment of the whole or any part of those premises or of the reversion in them.

(2) Where the assignment is by the tenant under the tenancy, then as from the assignment the assignee—

    (a) becomes bound by the tenant covenants of the tenancy except to the extent that—

        (i) immediately before the assignment they did not bind the assignor, or

        (ii) they fall to be complied with in relation to any demised premises not comprised in the assignment; and

    (b) becomes entitled to the benefit of the landlord covenants of the tenancy except to the extent that they fall to be complied with in relation to any such premises.

(3) Where the assignment is by the landlord under the tenancy, then as from the assignment the assignee—

    (a) becomes bound by the landlord covenants of the tenancy except to the extent that—

        (i) immediately before the assignment they did not bind the assignor, or

        (ii) they fall to be complied with in relation to any demised premises not comprised in the assignment; and

    (b) becomes entitled to the benefit of the tenant covenants of the tenancy except to the extent that they fall to be complied with in relation to any such premises.

[...]

(6) Nothing in this section shall operate—

    (a) in the case of a covenant which (in whatever terms) is expressed to be personal to any person, to make the covenant enforceable by or (as the case may be) against any other person; or

---

[32] Landlord and Tenant (Covenants) Act 1995, s 4, provides that the landlord's right of re-entry will also pass.

(b) to make a covenant enforceable against any person if, apart from this section, it would not be enforceable against him by reason of its not having been registered under the Land Registration Act 2002 or the Land Charges Act 1972.

3.2.2 All but personal covenants

The 1995 Act also removes any distinction between legal and equitable leases, and between covenants that touch and concern the land, and those that do not. All that is required is that the covenant is contained (either expressly or impliedly) in a legal or equitable lease and that the covenant is not expressed to be personal to any particular person.

Landlord and Tenant (Covenants) Act 1995, s 2

Covenants to which the Act applies

(1) This Act applies to a landlord covenant or a tenant covenant of a tenancy—

(a) whether or not the covenant has reference to the subject matter of the tenancy, and

(b) whether the covenant is express, implied or imposed by law

[...]

Landlord and Tenant (Covenants) Act 1995, s 28(1)

Interpretation

"landlord covenant", in relation to a tenancy, means a covenant falling to be complied with by the landlord of premises demised by the tenancy;

[...]

"tenancy" means any lease or other tenancy and includes—

(a) a sub-tenancy, and

(b) an agreement for a tenancy,

but does not include a mortgage term;

"tenant covenant", in relation to a tenancy, means a covenant falling to be complied with by the tenant of premises demised by the tenancy.

There is thus a shift in emphasis. There is no need to prove that a covenant touches and concerns the land: all covenants are transmissible, unless the parties specifically agree that they should not be so because they are expressed to be personal.[33]

---

[33] It seems extraordinary that a purely personal obligation can be transmissible because the parties do not expressly identify it as such: see Clarke and Kohler, *Property Law: Commentary and Material* (2005, p 647).

BHP Petroleum Great Britain Ltd v Chesterfield Properties Ltd
[2002] 2 Ch 195, CA

Facts: Chesterfield had covenanted personally to carry out certain remedial works to premises leased by BHP. It then transferred its reversion to an associated company and served a notice under s 8, seeking a release from its contractual liability on the covenant, to which BHP did not respond. Chesterfield unsuccessfully claimed that it had been released from its covenant when it was called upon to carry out repairs under the covenant.

Jonathan Parker LJ

At [59]–[62]

The crux, as we see it, is the definition of "landlord" in section 28(1) as meaning "the person *for the time being* entitled to the reversion expectant on the term of the tenancy". (My emphasis.) We find it impossible to read that definition as meaning only the original landlord. [...] we consider that those words clearly connote the person who may from time to time be entitled to the reversion on the tenancy. It follows that, transposing that definition into the definition of the expression "landlord covenant", what one has is an obligation "falling to be complied with by [the person who may from time to time be entitled to the reversion on the tenancy]". An obligation which (that is to say, the burden of which) is personal to the original landlord is, by definition, not such an obligation, since it does not fall to be performed by the person who may from time to time be entitled to the reversion on the tenancy.

It follows that in our judgment Chesterfield's obligations in clause 12 of the agreement, being expressed to be personal to Chesterfield, are not "landlord covenants" within the meaning of the 1995 Act, and that the notice was accordingly ineffective to release Chesterfield from such obligations.

With respect to Mr Lewison, Chesterfield's argument on the 1995 Act issue seems to us to be based on the fallacy that there is a direct antithesis between a personal covenant (that is to say a covenant which is personal in the sense that the burden of it is expressed to be personal to the covenantor) on the one hand and a covenant which "touches and concerns", or which relates to, the land on the other. As Mr Barnes correctly submits, there is no such direct antithesis. A covenant which relates to the land may nevertheless be expressed to be personal to one or other or both of the parties to it. That is a matter for the contracting parties.

Nor can we see anything in the 1995 Act to fetter the freedom of contracting parties to place a contractual limit on the transmissibility of the benefit or burden of obligations under a tenancy. On the contrary, that no such fetter was intended by Parliament is clearly demonstrated, in our judgment, by section 3(6)(a) (quoted earlier).

The decision seems, on the face of it, correct, but it could lead to unfortunate consequences. In *BHP*, it was the landlord who was denied a release from contractual liability, but the same reasoning might equally be applied to the tenant's covenants. If a tenant's covenant is expressed to be personal, then TO will be unable to obtain a release from his or her contractual liability, unless he or she can negotiate an express release from his or her current landlord.[34]

---

[34] Kenny [2007] Conv 1.

Slessinger, 'Precedents Editor's notes' [2007] Conv 198, 199

If the argument stands up, the whole purpose of the 1995 Act is destroyed. The primary mischief at which it was aimed was the continuing liability of tenants despite assignment of the lease.

[Slessinger goes onto to suggest that, to avoid this result, the courts might be tempted to conclude...] that there are certain covenants which are essential to the lease and cannot be made personal. Unfortunately the covenant in the *BHP* case was, essentially, a landlord's repairing covenant, so it would be difficult to distinguish the decision on that basis. In any case, such a distinction runs the risk of reintroducing the concept of covenants which "touch and concern" the lease by the back door when this too was intended to be swept away by the 1995 Act.

A subtler version of the distinction would be for the courts to say that it is not for the parties to define what is a personal covenant merely by sticking a label on it (see, for example, the court's attitude to documents labelled "licences"). To be a personal obligation there must be some reason why this landlord or this tenant is peculiarly in a position to perform it.

The crux of the matter is the extent to which the 1995 Act provides a complete code or merely interferes with existing concepts of privity of contract and estate, as shaped by the parties' (or their draughtsmen's) expressed intentions.

This tension is also evident in the distinct views expressed by the majority and minority in *London Diocesan Fund v Phithwa*,[35] in respect of which Dixon makes the following observation.

Dixon, 'A Failure of Statutory Purpose or a Failure of Professional Advice?' [2006] Conv 79

[...] a chance was missed, possibly deliberately, to establish the 1995 Act as a self contained scheme free from the dictates of privity of estate and privity of contract. So it seems that, after all, the 1995 Act is another example of piecemeal intervention in the landlord and tenant relationship and an intervention that can be sidestepped—in some circumstances—by careful draughtmanship.

4 THE CONTINUING LIABILITY FOR BREACHES OF COVENANT

An assignee's liability under privity of estate ends when he or she no longer holds the estate upon which enforceability depends.[36] Thus neither LA nor TA is liable for breaches of covenant that occur after they have disposed of their respective estates. They will also not be liable for breaches that occurred before they acquired their respective estates, unless those breaches are of a continuing nature.

---

[35] [2005] UKHL 70.
[36] *Onslow v Corriw* (1817) 2 Madd 330.

This position is reflected by s 23 of the 1995 Act, as well as ss 5 and 6, which we have already considered.

Landlord and Tenant (Covenants) Act 1995, s 23

Effects of becoming subject to liability under, or entitled to benefit of, covenant etc.

(1) Where as a result of an assignment a person becomes, by virtue of this Act, bound by or entitled to the benefit of a covenant, he shall not by virtue of this Act have any liability or rights under the covenant in relation to any time falling before the assignment.

(2) Subsection (1) does not preclude any such rights being expressly assigned to the person in question.

(3) Where as a result of an assignment a person becomes, by virtue of this Act, entitled to a right of re-entry contained in a tenancy, that right shall be exercisable in relation to any breach of a covenant of the tenancy occurring before the assignment as in relation to one occurring thereafter, unless by reason of any waiver or release it was not so exercisable immediately before the assignment.

4.1 CONTINUING RIGHTS TO ENFORCE BREACHES OF COVENANT

Where a breach of covenant occurs before the lease, or freehold reversion, is assigned, the question is who may sue for that breach: is it the assignee (e.g. LA or TA, as appropriate), or does the right to sue remain with the assignor (e.g. LO or TO, as appropriate)? The answer again differs according to whether or not the lease is governed by the Landlord and Tenant (Covenants) Act 1995.

4.1.1 Pre-1996 law

A landlord is not able to sue in respect of a breach that has occurred after he or she has sold his or her reversion, because he or she has suffered no damage, nor can he or she do so in respect of a breach of the tenant's covenants that occurred before the assignment. This result flows from the interpretation of s 141 in the following case.

Re King [1963] Ch 459, CA

Facts: Mr King had owned a factory, the lease of which required him to repair and insure, and to lay out any insurance moneys successfully claimed in reinstating, the factory. The factory was destroyed during the Second World War, but, after the war, the land was resumed by the government and a housing estate built. Mr King's estate sought directions as to whether it remained liable for breach of the covenant to repair, insure, and reinstate the factory.

UpJohn LJ

At 487

I turn, then, to a consideration of the meaning of section 141 and construe the language used in its ordinary and natural meaning, which seems to me quite plain and clear. To illustrate this, consider the case of a lease containing a covenant to build a house according to certain detailed specifications before a certain day. Let me suppose that after that certain day the then lessor assigns the benefit of the reversion to an assignee, and at the time of the assignment the lessee has failed to perform the covenant to build. Who can sue the lessee for breach of covenant? It seems to me clear that the assignee alone can sue. Upon the assignment the benefit of every covenant on the lessee's part to be observed and performed is annexed and incident to and goes with the reversionary estate. The benefit of that covenant to build, therefore, passed; as it had been broken, the right to sue also passed as part of the benefit of the covenant and, incidentally, also the right to re-enter, if that has not been waived. I protest against the argument that because a right to sue is itself a chose in action it, therefore, has become severed from, and independent of, the parent covenant; on the contrary it remains part of it. The right to sue on breach is merely one of the bundle of rights that are contained in the concept "benefit of every covenant." [. . .] Suppose the right to sue for breach of that covenant did not pass, and that right remained in the assignor, then the assignee would take the lease without the benefit of that covenant and he could never enforce it. So he has not got the benefit of every covenant contained in the lease and the words of the section are not satisfied. That cannot be right. The obligation to build being (as I have assumed) clearly defined by detailed specifications in the lease, it seems to me quite plain that the assignee could bring an action for specific performance compelling the lessee to perform his covenant to build. That is one of the rights which passed to him when the benefit of that covenant passed. The assignor has by the operation of section 141 assigned his right to the benefit of the covenant and so has lost his remedy against the lessee. Of course, the assignor and assignee can always agree that the benefit of the covenant shall not pass, in which case the assignor can still sue, if necessary, in the name of the assignee.

This view has been followed in *London & County (A&D) Ltd v Wilfred Sportsman Ltd*[37] in respect of the right to recover rent. Accordingly, under s141 of the 1995 Act, the right to sue for arrears of rent due before the assignment will pass to the landlord's assignee and cannot be recovered by the assignor landlord.

This approach is to be contrasted with the interpretation of s 142, which preserves the rights of the tenant to continue to sue, after he or she has disposed of his or her leasehold term, in respect of a breach that occurred before the assignment.

City and Metropolitan Properties Ltd v Greycroft Ltd [1987] 1 WLR 1085, HC

Facts: Greycroft was in serious breach of its covenant to repair premises leased by City. After abortive attempts to sell the property, City successfully took action against Greycroft to carry out the much-needed repairs. It was then able to sell its lease, but also sought damages against Greycroft for the damages that it had suffered in its earlier, but abortive, sale attempt.

---

[37] [1971] Ch 764 and, in so doing, has disapproved the pre-s 141 decision of *Flight v Bentley* (1835) 7 Sim 149.

Mowbray QC

At 1086

The landlord's first defence is that, when the tenant assigned the lease, all its rights passed to the assignee, including any right to damages such as are claimed under the pre-existing specially indorsed writ, so the tenant has no cause of action left to support its claim. In my view that defence is not well founded. No authority was cited on the precise question whether a tenant who has assigned his lease can afterwards recover damages from the landlord for breaches of the landlord's covenants committed while the tenant held the lease. It is common ground, though, that a tenant (not the original lessee) who has assigned his lease again remains liable to the landlord for breaches of covenant which he committed while tenant [...] Both this liability and the benefit of the landlord's covenants run with the lease at common law by privity of estate under *Spencer's Case* (1583) 5 Co.Rep. 16 a: see *Smith's Leading Cases*, 13th ed. (1929), vol. 1, p. 51. There is a close analogy between the two. I take the view that, by this analogy, the landlord's liability to the tenant for existing breaches survives the assignment of the lease, in the same way as the tenant's liability to the landlord.

Mr. Moss argued for the landlord here that the tenant's rights against the landlord did not survive the assignment of the lease, because on the assignment section 142(1) of the Law of Property Act 1925 made a statutory transfer of the tenant's rights to the assignee of the lease. [...]

He pointed out that the Court of Appeal has held section 141(1) to make a statutory transfer of the whole benefit of a tenant's covenant to an assignee of the reversion: *In re King, decd.* [1963] Ch. 459 and *London and County (A. & D.) Ltd. v. Wilfred Sportsman Ltd.* [1971] Ch. 764. He asked me to apply that principle by analogy to an assignment of the lease.

It is not possible to apply those decisions. They turned on words corresponding to the first part of section 142(1), "shall [...] be annexed and incident to and shall go with that reversionary estate." The middle passage of section 142(1) is quite different. [...] If the intention had been to effect a statutory transfer of the right to an assignee of the term, I should have expected words to have been used similar to those in section 141(1) and the beginning of section 142(1) itself.

4.1.2 Post-1995 law

The divergence evident in *Re King* and *Greycroft* is resolved by s 23 of the 1995 Act in favour of the *Greycroft* solution. The right to sue in respect of a breach committed before an assignment of the lease or the freehold reversion remains with the assignor, although the benefit of the right to sue may be expressly assigned to the purchaser.

5 SUB-LESSEES

Where a tenant grants a lease for a shorter term than he or she enjoys, even if it is only a day shorter, he or she grants a new estate that is called a 'sublease', or 'underlease'. The sub-lessee is bound by covenants in the sublease by way of privity of contract, but he or she is not within the privity of estate of the head lease and thus is not bound by, or able to enforce, the covenants in the head lease on this basis. A sub-lessee cannot, however, ignore the covenants in the head lease.

Firstly, a well-drafted sublease will include a covenant that the sub-lessee must observe and perform the covenants contained in the head lease. The head tenant, as landlord of the sublease, can thus enforce this covenant by way of privity of contract to ensure that the sub-lessee acts in a manner that does not place the head lease in jeopardy. A carefully drafted covenant to this effect may also confer the benefit of the sub-lessee's covenant upon the head landlord, who, although not within privity of contract, may be able to rely upon s 56 of the LPA 1925, or the Contracts (Rights of Third Parties) Act 1999, to enforce the covenant directly against the sub-lessee. An action based upon s 56 failed in *Amsprop Trading Ltd v Harris Distribution Ltd*[38] on the wording of the covenant, which was not expressed (as the section requires) as made with the head landlord. The Contracts (Rights of Third Parties) Act 1999 is less restrictive and could enable a head landlord to rely upon a covenant in the sublease where it is merely made for his or her benefit.[39]

Secondly, if the covenants in the head lease are not observed, the head landlord may forfeit the head lease. A forfeiture of the head lease will trigger the automatic extinction of the sub-lease, unless the sub-lessee successfully applies for relief from forfeiture. Relief will usually only be granted on condition that the sub-lessee remedies the breach.[40]

Thirdly, the restrictive covenants in the head lease have independent proprietary status and may be enforced in accordance with the principles that we will examine in Chapter 27. The head landlord may thus require the sub-lessee (or, indeed, any occupier of the land) to observe the restrictive covenants in the head lease under the doctrine of *Tulk v Moxhay*. The requirement of land to be benefited by the covenant has traditionally been identified as the landlord's reversionary interest,[41] although Gardner suggest an alternative rationale and, in so doing, controversially questions the whole exclusion of sub-lessees from privity of estate.

Gardner, *An Introduction to Land Law* (2007, p 226)

This special application of the restrictive covenant rule involves a radical departure from the rules original thrust [...] the rule in its standard form makes obligations operate in rem if, *and because*, they protect the standard of amenity prevailing between neighbouring plots of (necessarily) physical land. By not conforming to that factual pattern, the special application therefore cannot rest on the same justification. It must have a basis of its own, on the lines that the distinction between assignee and sub-tenant [...] is unimportant: the protection of the landlord's reversionary interest requires the lease terms be effective against both. Contrary to the assumption made by the idea of privity of estate, that seems a very reasonable position, resting on the idea that a tenant, on sub-leasing, should not be able to confer more (in the sense of an interest with fewer obligations to the landlord) then he himself has [...] and that idea makes as much sense for positive obligations as it does for negative ones. This lesson can best be absorbed, however, not by extending the restrictive covenant rule to positive as well as negative obligations, but by attacking the fundamental problem—privity of estate—itself.

The 1995 Act confirms the operation of *Tulk v Moxhay* to post-1995 leases in s 3(5).

---

[38] [1997] 1 WLR 1025.
[39] See Contracts (Rights of Third Parties) Act 1999, s 1(b), and Chapter 27, section 3.3.3.
[40] See section 6.4 below.
[41] *Hall v Ewin* (1887) 37 Ch D 74.

Landlord and Tenant (Covenants) Act 1995, s 3(5)

Any landlord or tenant covenant of a tenancy which is restrictive of the user of land shall, as well as being capable of enforcement against an assignee, be capable of being enforced against any other person who is the owner or occupier of any demised premises to which the covenant relates, even though there is no express provision in the tenancy to that effect.

The principle was applied in the following case to enforce a covenant prohibiting assignment and underletting against a sub-lessee. The action was for a mandatory injunction requiring the sub-lessee to execute a surrender of its sublease, which afforded the sub-lessee no opportunity to seek relief from the loss of its sublease.[42]

Hemingway Securities Ltd v Dunraven Ltd (1996) 71 P & CR 30, HC

Jacob J

At 33

I should say that the plaintiffs put their case also on the doctrine of *Tulk v. Moxhay*. They say here is a restrictive covenant; it is well settled that a restrictive covenant for the benefit of the landlords' reversion counts for the purposes for the doctrine of *Tulk v. Moxhay*; the restrictive covenant accordingly runs with the land; it accordingly binds the second defendants; they are acting in breach of it and, therefore, again, an injunction to compel them to stop acting in breach of it and in effect to gain a mandatory injunction should be granted.

Again, I do not see the answer to this way of putting the plaintiff's case. It was suggested that a covenant against alienation is not a restrictive covenant for the purposes of the *Tulk v. Moxhay* doctrine. That doctrine was limited to covenants in respect of the mode of user of property. No direct authority was cited to that effect and I do not see why, in principle, it should be so. One can have covenants subject to the doctrine not to build things without showing plans first; covenants against multiple occupation; and I do not see why this particular restrictive covenant against alienation should be treated differently.

The subsection may not, however, be employed to allow a sub-lessee to enforce a covenant in the head lease against the head landlord.[43]

In a block of flats in which the flat leases are all granted subject to the same covenants, the principles of a building scheme may also be applied to create a letting scheme, with the head lease covenants creating a local law for the development, binding upon and enforceable by all leaseholders within the block.[44] This local law might also encompass sub-lessees.[45]

---

42 See Wilkie and Luxton, 'Who Needs s 146? Injunctive Relief for Landlords' [1995] Conv 416.
43 *Oceanic Village Ltd v United Attractions Ltd* [2000] Ch 234 ('demised premises' refers to the land under the head lease and not the sublease).
44 *Williams v Kiley (t/a CK Supermarkets Ltd) (No 1)* [2003] L & TR 20.
45 See *Brunner v Greenslade* [1971] Ch 993.

6 REMEDIES FOR BREACH OF LEASEHOLD COVENANTS

In addition to the usually contractual remedies of common law damages, and the equitable discretionary remedies of specific performance and injunction, the breach of a tenant's covenant may lead to the forfeiture of the lease, or, where the breach is a failure to pay rent, the possibility of recovering rent by seizing the tenant's goods, previously governed by the law of distress. It may be possible for a lease to be terminated as a result of a breach that deprives the innocent party of substantially the whole benefit of the lease.[46] In this section, we will concentrate on forfeiture, as the most common measure with which to compel performance of the tenant's covenants.

6.1 DAMAGES

Damages are recoverable, in accordance with usually contractual principles, either by a landlord or tenant, for the loss occasioned by a breach of a covenant.

A landlord's recovery of damages for breach by the tenant of a repairing obligation is, however, limited by statute. Firstly, s 18 of the Landlord and Tenant Act 1927 limits the amount recoverable to the loss in value to the landlord's reversion and provides that no damages are recoverable where the premises are demolished or the premises are so altered that the repairs are valueless.

Secondly, the landlord of a lease granted for more than seven years, and which has at least three years left to run, is precluded by the Leasehold Property (Repairs) Act 1938 from seeking damages for breach of a tenant's repairing covenant, unless notice is served under s 146 of the LPA 1925, which is extracted and considered below. This notice must include a statement that the tenant may serve a counter-notice, which will have the effect of prohibiting any further proceedings without leave of the court. This latter provision has caused difficulties where the landlord carries out the repairs and seeks to recover the cost of doing so from the tenant,[47] although where the landlord does so pursuant to a suitably drafted 'self-help' clause in the lease, it has been held that his or her recovery falls outside the Act as an action for a debt.[48]

A tenant suffering damage as a result of a landlord's breach of a repairing covenant cannot simply refuse to pay the rent.[49] He or she may resort to self-help by arranging for the necessary repairs and recovering the cost from the landlord, either by direct action or by offsetting the cost against the rent.[50] This convenient route to redress may, however, be excluded by the clear terms of the lease.[51] We will consider the more far-reaching issues of ensuring effective and efficient management of flats later in Chapter 28.

---

[46] i.e. to repudiate the lease; see Gray and Gray, *Elements of Land Law* (5th edn, 2009) [4.2.142].

[47] *SEDAC Investments Ltd v Tanner* [1982] 1 WLR 1342.

[48] See *Jervis v Harris* [1996] 1 ALL ER 303, overruling *Swallow Securities Ltd v Brand* (1981) 45 P & CR 328, noted at [1997] Conv 299.

[49] *Melville v Grapelodge Developments Ltd* (1978) 39 P & CR 179. It should also be noted that recovery may lie for breach of statutory duty under the Defective Premises Act 1972.

[50] *Lee Parker v Izzet* [1971] 1 WLR 1688; *British Anzani (Felixstowe) Ltd v International Marine Management (UK) Ltd* [1980] QB 137.

[51] *HSBC v Kloeckner* [1990] 2 QB 514, but see *Connaught Restaurants Ltd v Indoor Leisure Ltd* [1994] 1 WLR 501.

6.2 SPECIFIC PERFORMANCE

It is now clear that, where damages are an inadequate remedy, there is inherent jurisdiction, and also statutory jurisdiction limited to residential leases, for the court to award specific performance of a landlord's repairing obligations.[52] Specific performance may also be ordered of a tenant's obligations, although this jurisdiction is likely to be only rarely exercised.[53] Forfeiture is likely to remain the more appropriate remedy against a tenant.

6.3 DISTRESS AND TAKING CONTROL OF THE TENANT'S GOODS

The ancient law of distress permits seizure and sale of the tenant's (and other person's) goods that are at the premises in order to pay arrears of rent. Distress has long been in the firing line of reformers given not only its antiquity and resulting complexity, but also the priority that it confers upon a landlord's claims over those of other creditors and its almost certain incompatibility with the Human Rights Act 1998 (HRA 1998). It is thus in the process of abolition and replacement by an alternative process by the Tribunals, Courts and Enforcement Act 2007.

Part 3 of this new statute abolishes the previous common law and statutory provisions, and enacts a new statutory code. In particular, distress for rent is abolished[54] and a new remedy termed 'commercial rent arrears recovery' is introduced.[55] As its name suggests, the remedy is unavailable to landlords of domestic premises, who entirely lose their right to seize goods to enforce rent arrears; they must rely on their right to sue for recovery of rent or rely upon forfeiture.

6.4 FORFEITURE

6.4.1 Introduction

Forfeiture is the process by which a landlord can extinguish a lease by exercising a right to re-enter the premises. A right of re-entry must be expressly granted,[56] as it invariably is, by the lease and it exists as a separate legal interest of the landlord.[57] An agreement for a lease will, however, imply (as a usual covenant) a right of re-entry, which the landlord can insist is included in the lease itself.[58]

A right of re-entry is generally expressed to be exercisable if the tenant fails to pay the rent, or if the tenant fails to observe or perform any of the other covenants contained in the lease. Occasionally, a right of re-entry may be triggered by some other specified event: for example,

---

52 See *Jeune v Queen's Cross Properties Ltd* [1974] Ch 97, and Landlord and Tenant Act 1985, ss 17 and 32.

53 See *Rainbow Estates Ltd v Tokenhold Ltd* 1999] Ch 64, noted at [1998] Conv 495 and [1998] JBL 564. The Law Commission has recommended that this jurisdiction be afforded a statutory basis: see Law Commission Report No 238, *Responsibility for State and Condition of Property* (1996, [11.33]–[11.34]).

54 Tribunals, Courts and Enforcement Act 2007, s 71.

55 See ibid, ss 72–80.

56 A right to re-enter for denying the landlord's title is implied.

57 See Law of Property Act 1925, s 1(1)(e).

58 *Chester v Buckingham Travel Ltd* [1981] 1 WLR 96.

the tenant's bankruptcy, in the case of an individual tenant, or entry into one of the corporate insolvency regimes, where the tenant is a company.[59]

A common form of a right of re-entry is set out below.

Encyclopaedia of Forms and Precedents, Landlord and Tenant (Residential Tenancies): Vol 23(2) (2002, Form 9)

Recovery of possession

(1) The Landlord's rights under this clause arise if and whenever during this Term:

  (i) the rent, or any part of it, or any other sum reserved as rent by this lease, lawfully due from the Tenant is unpaid [14 days] after becoming due, whether formally demanded or not, or

  (ii) the Tenant breaches any covenant, condition or other term of this lease.

(2) If and whenever during the Term any of the above events occurs, the Landlord may bring an action to recover possession from the Tenant and re-enter the Property subject:

  (i) in the case of unpaid rent to the Tenant's right to relief on payment of the arrears and costs, and

  (ii) in the case of a breach of any obligation other than to pay rent, to his obligations to serve notice on the Tenant specifying the breach complained of, requiring its remedy if it is capable of remedy, and requiring the Tenant to pay compensation in any case, and to allow the Tenant a reasonable time to remedy a breach that is capable of remedy.

On the making of a court order for possession this tenancy shall cease absolutely, but without prejudice to any rights or remedies that may have accrued to the Landlord against the Tenant, or to the Tenant against the Landlord in respect of any breach of covenant or other term of this lease, including the breach in respect of which the re-entry is made.

The law has taken a broad approach to what constitutes a right of re-entry. Thus, for example, a right of the landlord to serve notice to terminate the lease upon a breach by the tenant of his or her obligations under the lease has been interpreted as a right of re-entry.[60]

Forfeiture provides '*an essential management tool, particularly in relation to commercial and long residential leases*',[61] but it can also be a heavy-handed response. It is possible for a tenant holding for a long term to lose his or her whole interest because of a comparatively minor breach. What is more, any derivative interest granted out of that lease—for example, a sublease or mortgage—will also be lost. Forfeiture should thus only be employed as a long-stop remedy.

Clarke, 'Property Law' (1992) 45(1) CLP 81, 104

Forfeiture displays the best and worst features of a self help remedy. When exercised extra-judicially it is a fast and effective remedy for breach, and it is sufficiently drastic in effect to deter breaches. In fact it has been so successful in this jurisdiction that it has developed at

---

[59] A right of re-entry on bankruptcy or insolvency is unlikely to be regarded as usual covenant: see ibid.
[60] *Richard Clarke & Co Ltd v Widnall* [1976] 1 WLR 845 and Law of Property Act 1925, s 146(7).
[61] Gravells [2006] JBL 830.

the expense of the doctrines of repudiatory breach and frustration. On the other hand, its bad features are, first, that it affects the interests of third parties, who may have had no knowledge of the breach and no means of preventing it, and secondly that its effects between the parties bears no relation to the effects of the breach: it can inflict loss on the tenant quite disproportionate to the blameworthiness of the breach, and it can produce a windfall profit for the landlord.

The draconian nature of forfeiture is tempered, firstly, by the law's attitude to the ease with which a landlord is deemed to have waived a right of re-entry (see section 6.4.3 below), secondly, by the procedural steps that must be followed (see sections 6.4.4 and 6.4.5 below), and lastly, by the court's jurisdiction to grant relief from forfeiture (see section 6.4.6 below). In addition, certain short-term residential leases cannot be forfeited and the forfeiture of residential long leases is subject to additional controls, which we will examine when looking more closely at such leases.[62]

In the following case, Lord Templeman explains how the law has tempered the operation of forfeiture.

Billson v Residential Apartments Ltd [1992] 1 AC 494, HL

Lord Templeman

At 534

By the common law, when a tenant commits a breach of covenant and the lease contains a proviso for forfeiture, the landlord at his option may either waive the breach or determine the lease. In order to exercise his option to determine the lease the landlord must either re-enter the premises in conformity with the proviso or must issue and serve a writ claiming possession. The bringing of an action to recover possession is equivalent to an entry for the forfeiture [...]

Before the intervention of Parliament, if a landlord forfeited by entering into possession or by issuing and serving a writ for possession, equity could relieve the tenant against forfeiture but only in cases under the general principles of equity whereby a party may be relieved from the consequences of fraud, accident or mistake or in cases where the breach of covenant entitling the landlord to forfeit was a breach of the covenant for payment of rent [...]

In 1881 Parliament interfered to supplement equity and to enable any tenant to be relieved from forfeiture. The need for such intervention was and is manifest because otherwise a tenant who had paid a large premium for a 999-year lease at a low rent could lose his asset by a breach of covenant which was remediable or which caused the landlord no damage. The forfeiture of any lease, however short, may unjustly enrich the landlord at the expense of the tenant. In creating a power to relieve against forfeiture for breach of covenant Parliament protected the landlord by conferring on the court a wide discretion to grant relief on terms or to refuse relief altogether. In practice this discretion is exercised with the object of ensuring that the landlord is not substantially prejudiced or damaged by the revival of the lease [...]

Section 146(1) prevents the landlord from enforcing a right of re-entry or forfeiture by action or otherwise so that the landlord cannot determine the lease by issuing and serving

---

62 See Chapter 24 and Chapter 28, section 2.6.

a writ or by re-entering the premises until the tenant has failed within a reasonable time to remedy the breach and make reasonable compensation. Section 146(2) enables the tenant to apply to the court for relief where the landlord "is proceeding, by action or otherwise" to enforce his right of re-entry or forfeiture. If the landlord "is proceeding" to determine the lease by issuing and serving a writ, the tenant may apply for relief after the writ has been served. If the landlord "is proceeding" to determine the lease by re-entering into possession, the tenant may apply for relief after the landlord has re-entered.

After considering the effect of forfeiture more closely, we will go on to examine each of these ways in which the law regulates its operation, before finally looking at the current proposals for reform in the light of the Law Commission's conclusion that the law governing forfeiture '*is complex, it lacks coherence, and it can lead to injustice*'.[63]

6.4.2 The effect of forfeiture

As Lord Templeman explains, where the tenant has breached a leasehold covenant, the landlord has a choice: he or she may either elect to ignore the breach, or he or she may exercise his or her right of re-entry and so trigger forfeiture. The lease will be brought to an end, but the landlord must then recover possession either by peacefully gaining entry to the premises, or by issuing and serving on the tenant proceedings for possession. It is the landlord's decision to re-enter, either peacefully or by court process, which forfeits the lease and not the court's order for possession.[64] From the time of the landlord's re-entry, the tenant is a trespasser and no longer liable to pay rent. Instead, the landlord may claim mesne profits—being damages for the tenant's use of the land—which is calculated according the current rental value of the land.

The Law Commission explains the artificiality of this process.

Law Commission Report No 303, *Termination of Tenancies for Tenant Default* (2006, [1.9])

When a landlord commences court proceedings with a view to forfeiting the tenancy and recovering possession, a "constructive" re-entry takes place. This means, counter-intuitively, that the tenancy terminates not when the court makes an order to such effect, but on the date the proceedings are served on the tenant. This has several highly artificial consequences. First, the tenancy ends before there has been any opportunity for the parties to make representations to the court. Secondly, the tenant's obligations to pay the rent and observe the covenants are extinguished. Thirdly, the landlord's proceedings are not to terminate the tenancy (as forfeiture has technically already occurred) but are instead to recover possession of the premises. Fourthly, if the former tenant wishes the tenancy to continue, it is incumbent upon the tenant to bring a claim for "relief" in order retrospectively to revive the tenancy that has been forfeited.

---

[63] Law Commission Report No 174, *Landlord and Tenant: Privity of Contract and Estate—Executive Summary* (2004).

[64] *Canas Property Co Ltd v KL Television Services Ltd* [1970] 2 QB 433.

We have described the lease as being extinguished by forfeiture, but until the proceedings for possession and, in particular, any claim for relief is decided, that is not quite accurate.[65]

Meadows v Clerical Medical & General Life Assurance Society [1981] Ch 70, HC

Sir Robert Megarry VC

At 75

There are, of course, curiosities in the status of a forfeited lease which is the subject of an application for relief against forfeiture. Until the application has been decided, it will not be known whether the lease will remain forfeited or whether it will be restored as if it had never been forfeited [...] The tenancy has a trance-like existence pendente lite; none can assert with assurance whether it is alive or dead.

Bignall describes the unsatisfactory position of the parties during this 'twilight period'[66] between the service of the landlord's application for possession and the determination of the proceedings.

Bignell, 'Forfeiture: A Long Overdue Reform?' [2007] L&T Rev 140, 142

Such historic hangovers from the early days of forfeiture by physical re-entry mean the status of the occupier is now unclear during this time. Such a period may be a lengthy one. This is disadvantageous for landlords, tenants and those with derivative interests. Until matters are resolved one way or the other, the tenant is no longer bound by the covenants in the tenancy, including the obligation to pay rent, or to repair. If the tenant remains in possession, the landlord cannot rely on the covenants in the lease so as to make a claim for an interim injunction, or claim damages for dilapidation which have accrued during the "twilight period". There is no good reason for this and the practical consequences may be very serious for the landlord. By contrast, because the tenant has not elected to treat the lease as at an end, the tenant is entitled to seek an injunction to enforce the landlord's covenants, to pursue a claim for a new tenancy [...] and to collect rent from a sub-tenant.

Further in the event that the tenant remains in possession whilst court proceedings are conducted, the tenant becomes a trespasser whose continuing use and occupation of the premises simply entitle the landlord to recover mesne profits, or damages, from the date of actual or notional re-entry. Where the rent payable under the tenancy represents the fair market value of the property, the mesne profits will be payable at the same rate. If the fair market rental value is higher or lower than the rent, the mesne profits will be different. The quantification of this claim to damages may lead to another round of litigation, and will compound any financial hardship suffered by a landlord who has receive no income at all from the property whilst the forfeiture proceedings have run their course.

---

65 See also *Driscoll v Church Commissioners* [1957] Ch 70; *Ivory Gate Ltd v Spetale* (1999) 77 P & CR 141; *Maryland Estate v Joseph* [1991] 1 WLR 83; *Twinsectra Ltd v Hynes* [(1995) 71 P & CR 145.

66 This expression was used by Lightman J in *GS Fashions Ltd v B&Q plc* [1995] 1 WLR 1088, 1093.

6.4.3 Waiver

Landlords cannot rely on a breach of covenant to forfeit the lease where he or she has waived his or her right of re-entry. A waiver of a right of re-entry will occur where the landlord, with knowledge of the breach of covenant, acts in some way that recognizes the continued existence of the lease.[67] The most common action is the demand or acceptance of the rent payable under the lease.[68]

The effect of waiver has been criticized as operating unfairly to landlords, bearing in mind that a tenant may avoid the harsh consequences of forfeiture by applying for relief.

Smith, *Property Law* (3rd edn, 2006, p 408)

Three criticisms may be made of this rule. First, one must feel sympathy for the position of L [the landlord] who can claim neither rent nor mesne profits until the action is heard. Secondly, rent is usually accepted because of some mistake within L's offices: it is not as if a conscious decision has been made to keep the lease alive. Thirdly, and most damning, it does not matter that T [the tenant] is well aware that L has no intention of waiving the forfeiture.

Waiver is less of an issue where the breach is continuing in nature: the landlord can simply rely upon a subsequent breach. An example of a continuing breach is a breach of a covenant to repair,[69] or, as in the following case, a covenant that restricts the user of the premises.

Segal Securities Ltd v Thoseby [1963] 1 QB 887, HC

Facts: Mrs Thoseby rented a maisonette under a 21-year lease for a rent of £300 a year, which was payable quarterly in advance. The lease contained a covenant that it should be used only as a residence for one household. After the death of her husband, Mrs Thoseby shared her accommodation with two other women, one of whom was a friend and the other, a paying guest. The landlord alleged that she had breached the user covenant and served the required statutory notice at the beginning of June. It demanded the rent that was payable in advance on the next quarter day at the end of June; its demand was expressed to be 'without prejudice' to any breaches. Mrs Thoseby, in the landlord's action for possession, unsuccessfully claimed that the landlord had waived the breach of the user covenant. The breach was continuing and, although the right to re-enter flowing from breaches occurring before the date of service of the notice had been waived, the demand for rent did not waive future breaches.

Sachs J

At 897

When one approaches the law relating to waiver of forfeiture, one comes upon a field—one might say a minefield—in which it is necessary to tread with diffidence and warily. That is to

---

[67] *Matthews v Smallwood* [1910] 1 Ch 777; *Central Estates (Belgravia) Ltd v Woolgar (No 2)* [1972] 1 WLR 1048; *Cornillie v Saha* (1996) 72 P & CR 147.

[68] The acceptance of rent due before the breach will not operate as a waiver.

[69] *Penton v Barnett* [1898] 1 QB 276.

no small degree due to the number of points in that field that are of a highly technical nature, originating in the days before the court was able to give relief, if at all, with such freedom as it can nowadays.

[...] In this field of law, one point, however, is plain and was conceded by counsel for the landlord. The law as to the effect of the acceptance of rent "without prejudice" must be taken as that stated in a classic passage in the judgment of Parker J. in *Matthews v. Smallwood* [1910] 1 Ch 777 at 786 [...]:

> "It is also, I think, reasonably clear upon the cases that whether the act, coupled with the know-ledge, constitutes a waiver is a question which the law decides, and therefore it is not open to a lessor who has knowledge of the breach to say 'I will treat the tenancy as existing, and I will receive the rent, or I will take advantage of my power as landlord to distrain; but I tell you that all I shall do will be without prejudice to my right to re-enter, which I intend to reserve.' That is a position which he is not entitled to take up. If, knowing of the breach, he does distrain, or does receive the rent, then by law he waives the breach, and nothing which he can say by way of pro-test against the law will avail him anything."

[...] It is thus a matter of law that once rent is accepted a waiver results [...] Where forfeiture is involved, in essence once the landlord has knowledge of a past breach, the law thus treats the rent as a piece of cake equivalent to the land out of which it derives: its nutritional qualities in the landlord's hands being unaffected by attaching to it the label "without prejudice," the law treats that attachment as having no effect.

Whether a demand for rent made without prejudice similarly operates as a waiver has, apparently, not been specifically decided. [...] As both demand and acceptance respectively are in law merely different forms of a notification by a landlord of election not to avoid or for-feit the lease, to my mind no distinction can nowadays be drawn between them in relation to a question whether the label "without prejudice" affects their quality as an election. [...]

At this stage it is right to mention that there was for a long time much able argument before me, and much discussion of authorities on the question whether the continued breach of cov-enant in the present case was a series of continuing breaches within the meaning of those words as they apply to breaches of covenants to repair, or whether, on the other hand, once it was discovered and known to the landlord that the tenant was in breach the landlord only had a single election. It was urged by counsel for the tenant that once the landlord had thus accepted rent he could not in future play cat and mouse with the tenant and bide the time for enforcing a forfeiture. At the very last moment, however, of his concluding address, counsel for the landlord cited *Doe d. Ambler v. Woodbridge*, a judgment of a strong court presided over by Lord Tenterden in which it was held that user by a lodger was a continuing breach: thereafter counsel for the tenant felt unable to press the argument that here the tenant was not guilty of a continuing breach [...]

One thus has to consider the position on the basis that this is a case where, according to the rule in *Penton v. Barnett*, [1898] 1 QB 276 there were a fresh series of breaches after July 6 of which the landlord is entitled, subject to any waiver, to take advantage without serving a further notice under section 146 of the Law of Property Act, 1925.

With that rule in mind, I now turn to the important and decisive question as to the circum-stances in which a demand for or acceptance of rent payable in advance constitutes a waiver of breaches during the period covered by the rent demanded. Clearly it cannot be a waiver of future breaches of which the landlord has no advance knowledge: *Ellis v. Rowbotham* [1900] 1 QB 740 which relates to a default in payment of rent in advance, seems to illustrate this point, despite being an Apportionment Act case. Equally clearly, an acceptance of rent in advance does waive a once and for all—that is to say, a non-continuing—breach in the past: such a waiver applies both to the past and to the period covered by the rent.

As regards continuing breaches, it seems to me that, in the absence of express agreement, the acceptance of rent in advance can at highest only waive those breaches that are at the time of demand known to be continuing, and to waive them for such period as it is definitely known they will continue. When it is a question of estimating the chances as to whether the tenant's breach will continue, the position is, in my view, different, irrespective of whether those chances are high or low. The object of a covenant by which rent has to be paid in advance is to obtain a certain security for that payment: *Ellis v. Rowbotham* points to the nature and effect of that covenant. A landlord cannot, to my mind, lightly be deprived of the benefit of such rights: he cannot be put in the position of having to wait until the end of the period covered by the rent before demanding or accepting it merely because there are chances that the tenant may so break or continue in breach of covenant as to render himself liable to forfeiture.

6.4.4 Notice

The reason for requiring the landlord to give notice of a breach of covenant is explained in the following case.

Horsey Estate Ltd v Steiger [1899] 2 QB 79, CA

Lord Russell

At 91

The object seems to be to require in the defined cases (1.) that a notice shall precede any proceeding to enforce a forfeiture, (2.) that the notice shall be such as to give the tenant precise information of what is alleged against him and what is demanded from him, and (3.) that a reasonable time shall after notice be allowed the tenant to act before an action is brought. The reason is clear: he ought to have the opportunity of considering whether he can admit the breach alleged; whether it is capable of remedy; whether he ought to offer any, and, if so, what, compensation; and, finally, if the case is one for relief, whether he ought or ought not promptly to apply for such relief. In short, the notice is intended to give to the person whose interest it is sought to forfeit the opportunity of considering his position before an action is brought against him.

When considering a landlord's obligation to warn the tenant of his or her intention to exercise his or her right of re-entry, we must distinguish between a re-entry based upon a tenant's failure to pay the rent and that based on a breach of another leasehold covenant.

Breach for non-payment of rent

Rent must be formally demanded before a right of re-entry can be exercised, unless, as is invariably the case, the right excludes the need for a formal demand.[70] The right of re-entry extracted at section 6.4.1 above provides an example in clause (1)(i).[71]

---

[70] Common Law Procedure Act 1852, s 210, also dispenses with the need for a formal demand where the rent is six months in arrears and there are insufficient goods at the premises to distrain for the arrears.

[71] *Encyclopaedia of Forms and Precedents, Landlord and Tenant (Residential Tenancies): Vol 23(2)* (2002, Form 9).

Breach of covenants other than to pay rent

Where a breach of another covenant in the lease is relied upon,[72] the landlord must serve a notice under s 146(1) of the LPA 1925. A notice that fails to comply with the subsection is void and the landlord will have to serve another notice before re-entering.

Law of Property Act 1925, s 146(1)

Restrictions on and relief against forfeiture of leases and underleases

(1) A right of re-entry or forfeiture under any proviso or stipulation in a lease for a breach of any covenant or condition in the lease shall not be enforceable, by action or otherwise, unless and until the lessor serves on the lessee a notice—

(a) specifying the particular breach complained of; and

(b) if the breach is capable of remedy, requiring the lessee to remedy the breach; and

(c) in any case, requiring the lessee to make compensation in money for the breach;

and the lessee fails, within a reasonable time thereafter, to remedy the breach, if it is capable of remedy, and to make reasonable compensation in money, to the satisfaction of the lessor, for the breach.

The purpose of the notice, as Lord Russell explains in his point (2) of the above extract, is not only to warn the tenant, but also to let them know what they must do to avoid forfeiture. The nature of the breach must thus be accurately and sufficiently stated.

Akici v LR Butlin Ltd [2006] 1 WLR 201, CA

Facts: Mr Akici acquired a lease of commercial premises that contained a covenant 'not to charge assign [...] underlet or part with possession of a part of the demised premises [...] nor to share possession of the whole or any part of the [...] premises nor to part with possession of the whole of the [...] premises'. Mr Akici operated a takeaway pizza business at the premises, through a company owned by another. Butlin, as landlord, served a s 146 notice, alleging 'assignment or alternatively subletting or alternatively parting with possession of the premises without the landlord's consent'. The Court decided that Mr Akici was sharing (but had not parted with possession of) the premises with the company, although this breach of covenant had not been adequately identified in the s 146 notice.

Neuberger LJ

At [54]–[58]

I accept the submission that the approach of the majority of the House of Lords in *Mannai [Investment Co Ltd v Eagle Star Life Assurance Co Ltd* [1997] AC 749] to contractual notices

---

[72] Save for certain cases in which re-entry is based upon the tenant's bankruptcy: see Law of Property Act 1925, s 146(9) and (10).

would apply to section 146 notices, despite Mr Butler's submission to the contrary. However, I have none the less come to the conclusion that Mr Lloyd's defence of the notice cannot stand. Even applying the *Mannai* case the notice has to comply with the requirements of section 146(1) of the 1925 Act, and if, as appears pretty plainly to be the case, it does not specify the right breach, then nothing in the *Mannai* case can save it.

Quite apart from this, if, on its true construction, the section 146 notice did not specify sharing possession as a breach complained of, it can be said with considerable force that it neither informed the recipient of the breach complained of, nor indicated to him whether, and if so how, he must remedy any breach. On the basis that there was a sharing of possession, a reasonable recipient of the section 146 notice would have been entitled to take the view that he need do nothing, because the lessors were only complaining about the presence of the company if there was a parting with possession (or assigning or underletting) by Mr Akici to it.

Accordingly, a reasonable recipient in this case (and it is the understanding of such a hypothetical person by reference to which the validity of the notice is to be assessed according to the *Mannai* case) could, to put it at its lowest, reasonably have taken the view that the lessors were not objecting to any sharing of possession, and consequently that no steps need to be taken, either with a view to remedying the breach or with a view to improving the prospects of obtaining relief from forfeiture.

We were referred to authorities relating to the validity of notices served under section 146 and its statutory predecessor. I do not consider that they provide much assistance on the point that we have to determine in the present case. It is, however, appropriate to mention the decision of the House of Lords in *Fox v Jolly* [1916] 1 AC 1, 23 where the last sentence of the speech of Lord Parmoor appears to me to encapsulate the proper approach to section 146 notices and, it may be said, to notices generally:

"I think that the notice should be construed as a whole in a common-sense way, and that no lessee could have any reasonable doubt as to the particular breaches which are specified."

In this case I think it is impossible to say that no lessee would have been in any doubt but that the lessors were not contending that he was sharing possession of the premises.

It is not necessary for the landlord to specify compensation if he or she is not seeking compensation,[73] but it is the requirements of s 146(1)(b) of the 1925 Act that have proved problematic. Where the breach is capable of remedy, the notice must call for the breach to be remedied. It is only where the breach is incapable of remedy that the landlord's notice can overlook s 146(1)(b). It is relatively easy for landlords to avoid the difficulty in distinguishing between those breaches that are capable of remedy and those that are not: they merely have to call for the breach to be remedy 'if it is capable of remedy'. Where a landlord has failed to use this convenient wording, it is vital to establish whether a particular breach is capable of remedy. As we will see, the question is also of significance when the court exercises its discretion to grant relief.

It could be argued that no breach can be remedied, in the sense that it is impossible to put the clock back to before the breach, but the courts have taken a wider approach by asking whether or not the harm occasioned by the breach can be remedied.

---

[73] *Rugby School (Governors) v Tannahill* [1935] 1 KB 87.

Savva v Hussein (1997) 73 P & CR 150, CA

Facts: The lessees holding under a twelve-year lease of commercial premises in London carried out various alterations, including changing the sign and facia to the premises, without obtaining the prior consent of the landlords as they were required to do by the terms of the lease. In holding that the landlord's s 146 notice was invalid, the Court held that the breaches were capable of remedy.

Staughton LJ

At 154

[...T]he question is: whether the remedy referred to is the process of restoring the situation to what it would have been if the covenant had never been broken, or whether it is sufficient that the mischief resulting from a breach of the covenant can be removed. When something has been done without consent, it is not possible to restore the matter wholly to the situation which it was in before the breach. The moving finger writes and cannot be recalled. That is not to my mind what is meant by a remedy, it is a remedy if the mischief caused by the breach can be removed. In the case of a covenant not to make alterations without consent or not to display signs without consent, if there is a breach of that, the mischief can be removed by removing the signs or restoring the property to the state it was in before the alterations.

The courts have tended to draw a distinction between positive and negative covenants. A positive covenant is generally capable of remedy, whether it relates to a once-and-for-all breach or a continuing breach: for example, a covenant to repair is generally capable of being remedied by carrying out the necessary repairs.

Expert Clothing Service & Sales Ltd v Hillgate House Ltd [1986] Ch 340, CA

Facts: Hillgate was granted a lease of premises, which it agreed to convert either into office space, or into a gym and health club. The conversion work was to be substantially completed by 28 September 1982—but, by this date, the work had not even started. The landlord served a s 146(1) notice on Hillgate, which claimed that its breach of covenant was incapable for remedy. The Court disagreed.

Slade LJ

At 351

In a case where the breach is "capable of remedy" within the meaning of the section, the principal object of the notice procedure provided for by section 146(1), as I read it, is to afford the lessee two opportunities before the lessor actually proceeds to enforce his right of re-entry, namely (1) the opportunity to remedy the breach within a reasonable time after service of the notice, and (2) the opportunity to apply to the court for relief from forfeiture. In a case where the breach is not "capable of remedy," there is clearly no point in affording the first of these two opportunities; the object of the notice procedure is thus simply to give the lessee the opportunity to apply for relief.

At 354

[After reviewing the authorities, Slade LJ continued] Mr. Neuberger, on behalf of the defendants, did not feel able to go so far as to support the view of MacKinnon J. that the breach of a positive covenant is *always* capable of remedy. He accepted, for example, that the breach of a covenant to insure might be incapable of remedy at a time when the premises had already been burnt down. Another example might be the breach of a positive covenant which in the event would be only capable of being fully performed, if at all, after the expiration of the relevant term.

Nevertheless, I would, for my part, accept Mr. Neuberger's submission that the breach of a positive covenant (whether it be a continuing breach or a once and for all breach) will ordinarily be capable of remedy. As Bristow J. pointed out in the course of argument, the concept of capability of remedy for the purpose of section 146 must surely be directed to the question whether the harm that has been done to the landlord by the relevant breach is for practicable purposes capable of being retrieved. In the ordinary case, the breach of a promise to do something by a certain time can for practical purposes be remedied by the thing being done, even out of time. For these reasons I reject the plaintiffs' argument that the breach of the covenant to reconstruct by 28 September 1982 was not capable of remedy *merely* because it was not a continuing breach [...]

In contrast with breaches of negative user covenants, the breach of a positive covenant to do something (such as to decorate or build) can ordinarily, for practical purposes, be remedied by the thing being actually done if a reasonable time for its performance (running from the service of the section 146 notice) is duly allowed by the landlord following such service and the tenant duly does it within such time [...]

In my judgment, on the remediability issue, the ultimate question for the court was this: if the section 146 notice had required the lessee to remedy the breach and the lessors had then allowed a reasonable time to elapse to enable the lessee fully to comply with the relevant covenant, would such compliance, coupled with the payment of any appropriate monetary compensation, have effectively remedied the harm which the lessors had suffered or were likely to suffer from the breach? If, but only if, the answer to this question was "No," would the failure of the section 146 notice to require remedy of the breach have been justifiable. In *Rugby School (Governors) v. Tannahill* [1935] 1 K.B. 87; *Egerton v. Esplanade Hotels, London Ltd.* [1947] 2 All E.R. 88 and *Hoffmann v. Fineberg* [1949] Ch. 245 the answer to this question plainly would have been "No." In the present case, however, for the reasons already stated, I think the answer to it must have been "Yes."

By contrast, it has been suggested that a negative covenant is incapable of remedy. For example, MacKinnon J, at first instance in *Rugby School (Governors) v Tannahill*,[74] raised this possibility, although the Court of Appeal refused to indorse his view.[75] The Court did accept, however, that a covenant against an immoral or illegal user could be incapable of remedy where the breach carries a continuing stigma from which the premises cannot easily be cleansed. In *Tannahill*, the premises had been used for prostitution.[76] In the later case of

---

[74] [1934] 1 KB 695, 701.

[75] [1935] 1 KB 87, 90, *per* Greer LJ.

[76] See also *Egerton v Esplanade Hotel, London Ltd* [1947] 2 All ER 88; *Glass v Kencakes* [1966] 1 QB 611; *Central Estates (Belgravia) Ltd v Woolgar (No 2)* [1972] 1 WLR 1048; *British Petroleum Pension Trust Ltd v Behrendt* (1985) 52 P & CR 117. Other 'stigma' cases have related to: gambling (*Hoffman v Fineberg* [1949] Ch 245); pornography (*Dunraven Securities Ltd v Hollaway* [1982] 2 EGLR 47); and spying (*Van Haarlam v Kasner* (1992) 64 P & CR 214).

Scala House & District Property Co Ltd v Forbes,[77] the Court of Appeal also decided that a once-and-for-all breach of a negative covenant against subletting, without the prior consent of the landlord, was incapable of remedy.

The Court of Appeal has subsequently backtracked from broad statements that negative covenants are incapable of remedy. In *Expert Clothing*, the decision in *Scala* was doubted and limited to covenants against subletting. This change in approach has gone hand in hand with an appreciation of the wider meaning of remedy explained in *Savva*, in which Aldous LJ also doubted the usefulness of distinguishing between positive and negative covenants.[78]

Neuberger LJ outlined the current approach in his dicta comments in the following case, in which he went so far as he was able, in the light of authority, to explain that all breaches of positive or negative covenants should be capable of remedy unless falling within the authority of *Scala* or the stigma cases.

Akici v LR Butlin Ltd [2006] 1 WLR 201, CA

Neuberger LJ

At [64]–[75]

In those circumstances it seems to me that the proper approach to the question of whether or not a breach is capable of remedy should be practical rather than technical. In a sense it could be said that any breach of covenant is, strictly speaking, incapable of remedy. Thus, where a lessee has covenanted to paint the exterior of demised premises every five years, his failure to paint during the fifth year is incapable of remedy, because painting in the sixth year is not the same as painting in the fifth year, an argument rejected in *Hoffmann v Fineberg* [1949] Ch 245, 253, cited with approval by this court in *Expert Clothing Service and Sales Ltd v Hillgate House Ltd* [1986] Ch 340, 351c-d. Equally it might be said that where a covenant to use premises only for residential purpose is breached by use as a doctor's consulting room, there is an irremediable breach because even stopping the use will not, as it were, result in the premises having been unused as a doctor's consulting room during the period of breach. Such arguments, as I see it, are unrealistically technical.

In principle I would have thought that the great majority of breaches of covenant should be capable of remedy, in the same way as repairing or most user covenant breaches. Even where stopping, or putting right, the breach may leave the lessors out of pocket for some reason, it does not seem to me that there is any problem in concluding that the breach is remediable. That is because section 146(1) entitles the lessors to "compensation in money... for the breach" and, indeed, appears to distinguish between remedying the breach and paying such compensation.

On this basis I consider that it would follow, as a matter of both principle and practicality, that breaches of covenants involving parting with or sharing possession should be capable of remedy. One can see an argument, albeit that it strikes me as somewhat technical, for saying that the breach of covenant against assigning or subletting is incapable of remedy, because such a breach involves the creation or transfer of an interest in land, and a surrender or assignment back does not alter the fact that an interest in land has been created or transferred. Were the point free of authority, I would see much force in the contention that such an

---

[77] [1974] QB 575.
[78] (1996) 73 P & CR 150, 157.

analysis is over-technical, and I would be attracted to the view that a surrender or assignment back could be a sufficient remedy, at least in most cases, for the purposes of section 146.

So far as the authorities are concerned it appears to me that, at least short of the House of Lords, there are two types of breach of covenant which are as a matter of principle incapable of remedy. The first is a covenant against subletting: that is the effect of the reasoning of this court in the *Scala House case* [1974] QB 575. At least part of the reasoning in the leading judgment of Russell LJ, at p 588, justifying that conclusion is defective, as was explained by O'Connor LJ in the *Expert Clothing case* [1986] Ch 340, 364e-f in a judgment with which Bristow J agreed (at p 365c). However, as O'Connor LJ also said, the *Scala House case* is a decision which is binding on this court. In terms of principle (which may not be a wholly safe touchstone in this field) this is, I think, based on the proposition that one cannot, as it were, uncreate an underlease. It therefore appears to me that it should very probably follow that the general assumption that an unlawful assignment also constitutes an irremediable breach is correct. (This would suggest that breach of a covenant against charging a lease is irremediable, which strikes me as arguably unsatisfactory; failure to comply with a covenant to give notice of a charge, a somewhat different breach, is remediable: see the *Expert Clothing case* at p 355d).

The other type of breach of covenant which is incapable of remedy is a breach involving illegal or immoral use: see *Rugby School (Governors) v Tannahill* [1935] 1 KB 87 and *British Petroleum Pension Trust Ltd v Behrendt* [1985] 2 EGLR 97. This has been justified on the basis of illegal or immoral user fixing the premises with some sort of irremovable "stigma", which results in the breach being incapable of remedy. Especially in the light of the provision for damages in section 146, it is not entirely easy to justify this, particularly as it does not appear to apply where the lessee himself does not know of the illegal or immoral user: see *Glass v Kencakes Ltd* [1966] 1 QB 611. However, in terms of policy there is force in the view that a lessee, who has used premises for an illegal or immoral purpose, should not be able to avoid the risk of forfeiture simply by ceasing that use on being given notice of it, particularly as relief from forfeiture would still be available. Another example, mentioned in the *Expert Clothing case* [1986] Ch 340, 355a, might be a breach of covenant to insure against damage by fire, where the property burns down before insurance can be effected.

In the *Expert Clothing case* itself the Court of Appeal held that a covenant to carry out substantial building works was capable of remedy at the time of the service of the section 146 notice, even though the work should have been completed by the date of service and had not even been started. Slade LJ said, at p 357, that breach of a positive covenant could "ordinarily, for practical purposes, be remedied by the thing being actually done". However, the notion that any breach of a negative covenant will be irremediable plainly cannot be right, as is demonstrable by considering an innocuous and innocent breach of a user covenant.

There are three types of classification of covenants. They are (a) positive and negative (relevant to the transmission of the burden of freehold covenants, equitable in origin), (b) continuing and "once and for all" (relevant to waiver of forfeiture, with a common law origin), and (c) remediable and irremediable (relevant for section 146, and thus statutory in origin). These three types of classification are thus for different purposes and have different origins. Attempting to equate one class of one type with one class of a different type is therefore likely to be worse than unhelpful.

Any idea that negative covenants are by their nature irremediable has been put to rest by the decision of this court in *Savva v Hussein* (1996) 73 P & CR 150. In that case the breach of covenant consisted of carrying out alterations in breach of a covenant not to do so. After quoting the passage I have just cited from the *Expert Clothing case*, Aldous LJ said, at p 157, that he could "see no reason why similar reasoning should not apply to some negative covenants". He went on to quote with approval of a subsequent passage in Slade LJ's judgment [1986] Ch 340, 358:

> "if the section 146 notice had required the lessee to remedy the breach and the lessors had then allowed a reasonable time to elapse to enable the lessee fully to comply with the relevant covenant, would such compliance, coupled with the payment of any appropriate monetary compensation, have effectively remedied the harm which the lessors had suffered or were likely to suffer from the breach?"

As Aldous LJ, with whom Sir John May agreed, then went on to say 73 P & CR 150, 157: "It is only if the answer to that question is 'no' it can be said that the breach is not capable of being remedied."

In these circumstances it appears to me that, unless there is some binding authority, which either calls into question the conclusion or renders it impermissible, both the plain purpose of section 146(1) and the general principles laid down in two relatively recent decisions in this court, namely the *Expert Clothing* [1986] Ch 340 and *Savva* 73 P & CR 150 cases, point strongly to the conclusion that, at least in the absence of special circumstances, a breach of covenant against parting with possession or sharing possession, falling short of creating or transferring of legal interest, are breaches of covenant which are capable of remedy within the meaning of section 146.

The only authority which could be cited to call that conclusion into question is the *Scala House case* [1974] QB 575 itself, but that does not deter me from my conclusion. First, it was only concerned with underletting; secondly, the reasoning of the leading judgment in the case is, at least in part, demonstrably fallacious and inconsistent with common sense and many other authorities; thirdly, it has been overtaken and marginalised by the *Expert Clothing* and *Savva* cases; fourthly, there is no reason of logic or principle why the reasoning or conclusion in the *Scala House case* should be extended to apply to a breach which falls short of creating a legal interest.

It is true that Slade LJ said in the *Expert Clothing case* [1986] Ch 340, 354g that the principle in the *Scala House case* extends to parting with possession, as well as assigning and underletting. That was an obiter observation, which I do not regard as binding. Bristow J, at p 365c, agreed with Slade LJ's judgment but he also agreed with the judgment of O'Connor LJ who, at p 365a-b, said that the *Scala House case*, while authority for the proposition that breach of a covenant against underletting was irremediable, was not "authority for any wider proposition". As I have indicated, my present view is an intermediate one. I think that principle and precedent probably require one to go along with Slade LJ and conclude that the *Scala House case* applies to assigning but, in agreement with O'Connor LJ, I certainly do not see why it extends to parting with (let alone sharing) possession.

Once a valid notice has been served, the tenant must be given a reasonable time to remedy the breach, if it is capable of remedy, or to pay any compensation. A reasonable time will depend primarily on the nature of the breach and the time frame of the dispute, including the remaining residue of the lease.[79]

Slade LJ explained the significance of allowing a reasonable time.

---

[79] See the general guideline of three months to remedy the breach of a repairing covenant expressed in *Bhojwani v Kingsley Investment Trust Ltd* [1992] EGLR 70, 73.

Expert Clothing Service & Sales Ltd v Hillgate House Ltd [1986] Ch 340. CA

Slade LJ

At 358

An important purpose of the section 146 procedure is to give even tenants who have hitherto lacked the will or the means to comply with their obligations one last chance to summon up that will or find the necessary means before the landlord re-enters. In considering what "reasonable time" to allow the defendants, the plaintiffs, in serving their section 146 notice, would, in my opinion, have been entitled to take into account the fact that the defendants already had enjoyed 15 months in which to fulfil their contractual obligations to reconstruct and to subject the defendants to a correspondingly tight timetable running from the date of service of the notice, though, at the same time, always bearing in mind that the contractual obligation to reconstruct did not even arise until 29 June 1981, and that as at 8 October 1982 the defendants had been in actual breach of it for only some 10 days. However, I think they were not entitled to say, in effect: "We are not going to allow you any time at all to remedy the breach, because you have had so long to do the work already."

If the tenant does respond to the notice and remedies the breach, the landlord cannot forfeit the lease, even though the tenant's record in performing his or her leasehold obligations has been poor.[80]

Where the breach is incapable of remedy, the landlord must allow the tenant a short period before proceeding to forfeiting the lease; fourteen days is usually considered sufficient time for the tenant to prepare to accept his or her fate or plea for relief.[81]

6.4.5 Peaceful re-entry

The prospect of criminal liability under s 6 of the Criminal Law Act 1977, for forcible entry, or under the Protection from Eviction Act 1977, which prohibits the forfeiture of the lease of an occupied dwelling house other than by court order, discourages landlords from trying to enter peacefully, unless the premises are used for commercial purposes and they are empty. Despite these dangers, there was once an incentive for a landlord to try to re-enter peacefully, because it was believed that the tenant was then unable to apply to the court for relief from forfeiture under s 146(2) of the LPA 1925. The House of Lords held this belief to be erroneous in *Billson v Residential Apartments Ltd*,[82] a decision that we shall examine in more detail shortly. The decision also reflects a move away from self-help remedies, which have led to proposals for reform that we will examine below.

Gray and Gray, *Elements of Land Law* (5th edn, 2009, [4.4.25])

There is nowadays a widespread apprehension that, although forfeiture by actual re-entry remains lawful at common law, it is 'undesirable to encourage landlords to self-help'. The

---

[80] Law Commission Report No 302 *Termination of Tenancies for Tenant Default* (2006), [1.12.6]).
[81] *Scala House & District Property Co Ltd v Forbes* [1974] QB 575, but see *Horsey Estates Ltd v Steiger* [1899] 2 QB 79.
[82] [1992] 1 AC 494.

gathering perception can only be intensified by the statutory assimilation of the European Convention guarantee of the right to a 'fair and public hearing' [...] The clear trend of modern human rights jurisprudence is to castigate the resort to self-help remedies as 'inimical to a society in which the rule of law prevails'. It is highly unlikely that the landlord's remedy of peaceable re-entry without court order can survive much longer as a general feature of the English law of landlord and tenant.

6.4.6 Relief from forfeiture

The draconian nature of forfeiture is tempered by the tenant's ability to apply for relief from forfeiture. Relief operates to recharacterize forfeiture from a tool of expropriation of the tenant's term to a security for the tenant's performance of the covenants contained in the lease. The rules governing relief are, however, complicated by the interplay between the courts' original equitable jurisdiction to grant relief and subsequent statutory measures. Furthermore, we again see a distinction drawn between different types of breach: namely, a failure to pay rent and breaches of other covenants. There are also differences in the treatment of the original tenant's right to relief and the rights to relief of holders of derivative interests: for example, under-lessees and sub-lessees; mortgagees and chargees.

Relief for non-payment of rent

Equity has long granted relief from forfeiture for non-payment of rent upon payment of the arrears and any costs, provided that it is equitable to grant relief.[83] This jurisdiction is overlain by various statutory measures. The result is 'an intricate maze'[84] of absolute and discretionary rights that differ according to whether the application is made before or after possession is ordered or the landlord has re-entered (whether peacefully or otherwise), and depend upon whether proceedings are brought in the High or county courts.[85]

In the High Court, relief before trial is available under s 212 of the Common Law Procedure Act 1852, which confers an absolute right to relief, and the continuance of the original lease, where the tenant pays the rent arrears and costs before trial. Under s 210 of the 1852 Act, the tenant may also claim similar relief after the hearing, provided that the claim is made within six months of execution of the order for possession. Relief under the 1852 Act is rather bizarrely only available where the rent is at least six months in arrears and there are no goods on the premises that would satisfy a landlord's claim for distress.[86] It is also unavailable where the landlord has re-entered peacefully.

Where proceedings are brought in the county court, s 138(2) of the County Court Act 1984 confers an absolute right to relief where the tenant pays the arrears and costs at least five days before the hearing. Under s 138(3), the court must allow at least four weeks before an order for possession can be executed. This period may be extended.[87] Where the possession order has been executed or where the landlord has re-entered peacefully, the tenant

---

[83] *Howard v Fanshawe* [1895] 2 Ch 581, 588, *per* Stirling J; *Ladup Ltd v William & Glynns Bank plc* [1985] 1 WLR 851, 860, *per* Warner J. This jurisdiction is available for a failure to pay other charges, for example, a service charge, where those charges are expressed to be paid by way of rent: see *Escalus Properties Ltd v Robinson* [1996] QB 231.

[84] Luxton [1994] JBL 37.

[85] The county court has unlimited jurisdiction in forfeiture and relief proceedings.

[86] *Billson v Residential Apartments Ltd* [1992] 1 AC 494, 529, *per* Nicholls LJ.

[87] County Court Act 1984, s 138(4).

may apply for relief from forfeiture provided that his or her application is made within six months of the date on which the landlord regained physical possession.[88]

Where statutory relief is unavailable, the court's equitable jurisdiction may assist. The manner in which the court will exercise its discretion under its equitable jurisdiction is explained in the following case. Similar considerations apply where the court is exercising its discretion to grant relief under it statutory jurisdiction.[89]

Gill v Lewis [1956] 2 QB 1, CA

Jenkins LJ

At 13

As to the conclusion of the whole matter, in my view, save in exceptional circumstances, the function of the court in exercising this equitable jurisdiction is to grant relief when all that is due for rent and cost has been paid up, and (in general) to disregard any other causes of complaint that the landlord may have against the tenant. The question is whether, provided all is paid up, the landlord will not have been fully compensated; and the view taken by the court is that is he gets the whole of his rent and costs, then he has got all he is entitled to so far as rent is concerned, and extraneous matters of breach of covenants, and so forth, are generally speaking irrelevant.

Exceptional circumstances may exist where the landlord has, not unreasonably, altered his or her position, or where a third party's interest would be affected.[90] The poor payment record of the tenant is irrelevant.

Where relief is granted after completion of forfeiture, whether by possession order or the landlord's peaceful re-entry, the lease will be restored and the landlord placed in the same position as if there had been no forfeiture.[91]

Relief from breach of other covenants

A tenant's right to relief, from a right of re-entry based upon a breach of the other covenants contained in the lease, is governed by s 146(2) of the LPA 1925.

Law of Property Act 1925, s 146(2)

Where a lessor is proceeding, by action or otherwise, to enforce such a right of re-entry or forfeiture, the lessee may, in the lessor's action, if any, or in any action brought by himself, apply to the court for relief; and the court may grant or refuse relief, as the court, having regard to the proceedings and conduct of the parties under the foregoing provisions of this section, and to all the other circumstances, thinks fit; and in case of relief may grant it on such terms, if any, as to costs, expenses, damages, compensation, penalty, or otherwise,

---

[88] Ibid, ss 138(9A) and 139(2). See *United Dominions Trust Ltd v Shellpoint Trustees Ltd* [1993] 4 All ER 310.

[89] *Howard v Fanshawe* [1895] 2 Ch 581 and *Lovelock v Margo* [1963] 2 QB 786.

[90] See *Gill v Lewis* [1956] 2 QB 1, 9–10, *per* Jenkins LJ, referring to *Stanhope v Haworth* (1886) 3 TLR 34.

[91] *Bland v Ingrams Estates Ltd* [2001] EWCA Civ 1088, [13]–[15].

including the granting of an injunction to restrain any like breach in the future, as the court, in the circumstances of each case, thinks fit.

The right to relief is available where the landlord has entered peacefully,[92] but not where the landlord has entered into possession pursuant to a court order. In the latter case, the tenant must apply for relief during the possession proceedings.

Billson v Residential Apartments Ltd [1992] 1 AC 494, HL

Facts: In breach of covenant, Residential Apartments had made substantial alterations to the property without the written permission of Billson as landlord. Billson served notice under s 146(1) and, fourteen days later, at 6 a.m., peaceably re-entered the premises before workmen of Residential Apartments retook possession four hours later. At the centre of the dispute was whether Residential Apartments could apply for relief under s 146(2) of the 1925 Act.

Lord Templeman

At 535

Mr. Reid submitted and referred to authority for the proposition that on the true construction of section 146(2) a tenant cannot apply for relief against forfeiture after the landlord has re-entered without obtaining a court order. Thereafter the landlord is no longer "proceeding" to enforce his rights; he has succeeded in enforcing them. The proposition is in my opinion historically unsound because the effect of issuing and serving a writ is precisely the same as the effect of re-entry; in each case the lease is determined. The landlord is entitled to remain in possession if he has re-entered and he is entitled to possession if he has issued and served a writ because the lease no longer exists. In each case the tenant seeks relief because the lease has been forfeited. The proposition is also inconsistent with the language of section 146(2). The tenant may apply for relief where the landlord is "proceeding, by action or otherwise" to enforce his rights. The tenant may apply for relief where the landlord is "proceeding" by action and also where the landlord is proceeding "otherwise" than by action. This can only mean that the tenant may apply for relief where the landlord is proceeding to forfeit by re-entry after the expiry of a section 146 notice. If re-entry bars relief, the right of the tenant to apply for relief where the landlord is proceeding otherwise than by action is substantially inoperative and the words "or otherwise" in section 146(2) have no application. In my opinion those words must have been included because Parliament intended that a tenant should be able to obtain relief against a landlord whether the landlord has asserted his rights by a writ or by re-entering. It is said that a tenant served with a section 146 notice could during and after the expiration of the notice apply for relief under section 146(2) but if he fails to do so he is at the mercy of the landlord who decides to re-enter and whose rights are therefore, it is said, quite unaffected by the provisions of section 146(2) designed to relieve tenants from the consequences of breach of covenant. In my opinion the ambiguous words "is proceeding" can mean "proceeds" and should not be construed so as to produce the result that a tenant

---

[92] In *Billson v Residential Apartments (No 2)* [1993] EGCS 155, the court warned that it may be more disposed to grant relief where landlords have entered peacefully without the sanction of a court order for possession.

served with a section 146 notice can only ensure that he will be able to apply for relief if he does so before he knows whether or not the landlord intends to proceed at all or whether, if the landlord decides to proceed, he will issue and serve a writ or will attempt to re-enter.

When a tenant receives a section 146 notice he will not know whether the landlord can be persuaded that there is no breach or persuaded to accept in due course that any breach has been remedied and that he has been offered adequate and satisfactory compensation or whether the landlord will seek to determine the lease by issuing and serving a writ or will seek to determine the lease by re-entering the premises. The tenant will not wish to institute proceedings seeking relief from forfeiture if those proceedings will be aggressive and hostile and may be premature and unnecessary. Parliament cannot have intended that if the landlord employs the civilised method of determining the lease by issuing and serving a writ, then the tenant will be entitled to apply for relief, but if the landlord employs the dubious and dangerous method of determining the lease by re-entering the premises, then the tenant will be debarred from applying for relief.

Mr. Reid concedes that re-entry can only avail the landlord if the entry is lawful. Re-entry is unlawful where the premises are occupied by the tenant but not unlawful where the premises are occupied by the tenant's goods. If the argument of the landlords is correct, section 146 provides a method by which a landlord can sneak up on a shop at night, break into the shop, and install new locks so that the tenant loses his lease and can only press his nose against the shop window being unable to obtain the assistance of the court because he has become a trespasser entitled to no rights and to no relief. The farce in the present case when the landlords occupied the premises for four hours should not be allowed to defeat the statutory rights of the tenants.

The right conferred by section 146(2) on a tenant to apply for relief against forfeiture may without violence to the language, be construed as a right to apply "where a lessor *proceeds*, by action or otherwise" to enforce a right of re-entry. So construed, section 146(2) enables the tenant to apply for relief whenever and however the landlord claims that the lease has been determined for breach of covenant. I have no doubt that this was the object and intention and is the effect of section 146.

[His Lordship considered past authorities, which suggested the contrary conclusion, but which he held had not decided the point in issue.]

My Lords, I accept that it is now settled law that a tenant cannot apply for relief after the landlord has recovered judgment for possession and has re-entered in reliance on that judgment. But I do not accept that any court has deprived or is entitled to deprive a tenant of any right to apply for relief if the landlord proceeds to forfeit otherwise than by an action instituted for that purpose [. . .]

The landlords or their advisers, perhaps incensed by the activities of the tenants in the present case, conceived and carried out a dawn raid which fortunately did not result in bloodshed. Since the decision of the Court of Appeal in the instant case there has been a proliferation of section 146 notices followed by pressure on tenants to surrender on terms favourable to the landlord. If this appeal were not allowed, the only safe advice for a tenant would be to issue proceedings for relief against forfeiture as soon as a section 146 notice is received at a time when the tenant cannot know whether relief will be necessary. A tenant ignorant of the development in the law pioneered by the landlords in the present case will be at the mercy of an aggressive landlord. The conclusions which I have reached will not entail these consequences and will not again involve Parliament in correcting judicial constructions of statute by further legislation.

The results of section 146 and the authorities are as follows. A tenant may apply for appropriate declarations and for relief from forfeiture under section 146(2) after the issue of a section 146 notice but he is not prejudiced if he does not do so. A tenant cannot apply for relief after a landlord has forfeited a lease by issuing and serving a writ, has recovered judgment and has entered into possession pursuant to that judgment. If the judgment is set aside or successfully appealed the tenant will be able to apply for relief in the landlord's action but the court in deciding whether to grant relief will take into account any consequences of the original order and repossession and the delay of the tenant. A tenant may apply for relief after a landlord has forfeited by re-entry without first obtaining a court order for that purpose but the court in deciding whether to grant relief will take into account all the circumstances, including delay, on the part of the tenant. Any past judicial observations which might suggest that a tenant is debarred from applying for relief after the landlord has re-entered without first obtaining a court order for that purpose are not to be so construed.

Given this interpretation of s 146(2) of the LPA 1925, it was unnecessary for the House of Lords to consider whether the subsection provided a complete statutory code or whether there was a residual equitable jurisdiction to grant relief to a tenant from a breach of covenant, other than to pay rent. The majority of the Court of Appeal in *Billson* had decided that s 146(2) was a complete statutory code. The question remains significant to the holder of a derivative interest seeking relief under s 146(4), which we will consider below.

The court's jurisdiction to grant relief is wide and unfettered.[93] All of the circumstances of the case are to be considered, but particularly significant are the gravity of the breach, the conduct of the parties, the question of whether or not the breach can be remedied, and the disparity between the loss caused to the landlord by the breach and the loss caused to the tenant should the lease be forfeited.[94] Relief will rarely be granted where the breach is intentional or cannot be remedied, unless the breach is trivial and the damage to the landlord's reversion insignificant.[95] Here, we thus see an interface with the question of whether or not a breach can be remedied for the purposes of a s 146(1) notice.

Relief and derivative interests

We have already noted that the forfeiture of a lease will also extinguish interests that are carved out of that lease: namely, underleases (of the whole of the lease premises), sub-leases (of part of the leased premises), mortgages, and charges. It is thus important that persons holding such interests are also able to claim relief. There is a confusing array of possibilities.

The primary jurisdiction is found in s 146(4) of the LPA 1925, which provides a right for under-lessees and sub-lessees, mortgagees and legal chargees,[96] to apply for relief against forfeiture based upon a breach of a covenant, both to pay rent and other covenants. Equitable chargees are excluded.[97]

---

[93] *Rose v Hyman* [1912] AC 623, 631.

[94] See, e.g., *Ropemaker Properties Ltd v Noonhaven Ltd* [1989] 2 EGLR 50, in which relief was granted, even though the breach was serious, because the financial loss to the tenants would be out of proportion to the loss suffered by the landlords.

[95] See, e.g., *Central Estates (Belgravia) Ltd v Woolgar (No 2)* [1972] 1 WLR 1048 and *Van Haarlam v Kasner* (1992) 64 P & CR 214.

[96] *Grand Junction Co Ltd v Bates* [1954] 2 QB 160.

[97] *Bland v Ingram Estates Ltd (No 2)* [2002] Ch 177.

Law of Property Act 1925, s 146(4)

Where a lessor is proceeding by action or otherwise to enforce a right of re-entry or forfeiture under any covenant, proviso, or stipulation in a lease, or for non-payment of rent, the court may, on application by any person claiming as under-lessee any estate or interest in the property comprised in the lease or any part thereof, either in the lessor's action (if any) or in any action brought by such person for that purpose, make an order vesting, for the whole term of the lease or any less term, the property comprised in the lease or any part thereof in any person entitled as under-lessee to any estate or interest in such property upon such conditions as to execution of any deed or other document, payment of rent, costs, expenses, damages, compensation, giving security, or otherwise, as the court in the circumstances of each case may think fit, but in no case shall any such under-lessee be entitled to require a lease to be granted to him for any longer term than he had under his original sub-lease.

A successful application will result in the grant of a new lease held directly from the head landlord. Where relief is grant to a mortgagee, the expectation is that the new lease will be held on the same terms as the original lease. Where relief is grant to an under-lessee or sub-lessee, the new lease cannot exceed the length of the original term and where a sublease is in issue, the new sublease will also be limited to the relevant part of the premises.[98] If there is a difference in rental between the head and under/sublease, the higher rental will prevail.[99] The courts' discretion is exercised in a similar manner to relief granted under s 146(2), with an expectation that the breach will be remedied.[100] The court may also be circumspect in imposing upon the landlord a tenant that he or she has not chosen.

A derivative interest holder may also apply for relief from forfeiture based upon a breach of a covenant other than to pay rent under s 146(2), which we considered above.[101] The right is based upon the definition of 'lessee' found in s 146(5)(b).

Law of Property Act 1925, s 146(5)

(5) For the purposes of this section [...]

 (b) "Lessee" includes an original or derivative under-lessee, and the persons deriving title under a lessee; also a grantee under any such grant as aforesaid and the persons deriving title under him;

 [...]

The difference between relief granted under s 146(2) and the general ground in s 146(4) is that, under s 146(2), the existing lease will continue, whilst under s 146(4), a new lease is granted.

Relief from the breach of a covenant to pay rent is also available to a the holder of a derivative interest under the provisions of the Common Law Procedure Act 1852 and the County Court Act 1984, considered above.

---

[98] *Cadogan v Dimovic* [1984] 1 WLR 609.
[99] *Ewart v Fryer* [1901] 1 Ch 499.
[100] *Hill v Griffin* [1987] 1 EGLR 81.
[101] *Escalus Properties Ltd v Robinson* [1996] QB 231.

Where the court is persuaded to exercise its jurisdiction to grant relief, the expectation is that the breaches will be made good in respect of the affected premises.[102]

Despite these various statutory routes to relief, there are still gaps. It is thought that the approach adopted in *Billson* will also apply to applications for relief by the holders of derivative interests, whether under s 146(2) or (4). Accordingly, the right will be lost where the landlord has obtained possession pursuant to a court order, although not where the landlord has entered peacefully. This possibility presents a real danger to lenders who, not being in possession, may well be unaware of the head landlord's proceedings. Equitable chargees also fall through the safety net provided by s 146(2) and (4), and the Common Law Procedure Act 1852. Equitable chargees can rely upon the county court jurisdiction, or, alternatively, may insist that the tenant asserts his or her right to relief in order to protect the security.[103]

These statutory gaps in the relief available to holders of derivative interests might be plugged if resort can be made to the courts' equitable jurisdiction. We have noted that the court has long exercised an equitable jurisdiction that provides relief from a breach of covenant to pay rent. The ability of the court to grant relief from forfeiture based upon breach of another covenant was doubted until the House of Lords decision in *Shiloh Spinners Ltd v Harding*.[104] But the House, whilst holding that such an inherent equitable jurisdiction did exist, indicated that the jurisdiction would not prevail where Parliament has made statutory provision covering the particular case. The question thus turns upon whether s 146 provides a complete statutory code. As we have already noted, the Lords in *Billson* did not provide an answer to this question, although the signs from the Court of Appeal are not hopeful.[105]

Billson v Residential Apartments Ltd [1991] 3 WLR 264, CA

Browne-Wilkinson V–C

At 279

From the early 19th century until *Shiloh Spinners Ltd. v. Harding* [1973] A.C. 691 it was thought that the court had no inherent jurisdiction to grant relief from forfeiture for "wilful" breach of covenant other than the covenant to pay rent or some other specified sum of money. This is a point of central importance in the present case. The decision in *Shiloh Spinners* disclosed, retrospectively, that the view so held for 150 years had been erroneous. The court had originally had an inherent jurisdiction to relieve in such cases (though such jurisdiction was to be exercised with great caution). However, the House of Lords recognised that, in certain areas, such inherent jurisdiction might have been implicitly removed by Parliament in conferring on the court statutory powers of relief.

In *Shiloh Spinners* it was argued that, although the covenant and forfeiture provision there in question did not arise as between landlord and tenant, the statutory provisions for relief from forfeiture as between landlord and tenant contained in section 146 of the Law of Property Act 1925 and its predecessors had impliedly removed the whole equitable jurisdiction to

---

102 *Chatham Empire Theatres (1955) Ltd v Ultrans Ltd* [1961] 1 WLR 817.
103 *Bland v Ingrams Estates Ltd* [2001] Ch 767.
104 [1973] AC 691.
105 See also *Official Custodian for Charities v Parway Estates Development Ltd* [1984] 3 WLR 525. There is conflicting first instance authority to the contrary in *Abbey National Building Society v Maybeech* [1985] Ch 190, which was heard at the same time, but without reference to *Parway*.

relieve in such cases. The House of Lords rejected this argument. After mentioning some of the statutes dealing with relief in cases between landlord and tenant, Lord Wilberforce said, at p. 725:

"In my opinion where the courts have established a general principle of law or equity, and the legislature steps in with particular legislation in a particular area, it must, unless showing a contrary intention, be taken to have left cases outside that area where they were under the influence of the general law [...]"

The question therefore is whether the legislature has stepped into the area of relief against forfeiture for wilful breach of covenant (other than to pay rent) as between landlord and tenant so as to have excluded the old equitable jurisdiction to relieve in that area [...]

However, I have reluctantly come to the conclusion that the inherent equitable jurisdiction as between landlord and tenant to relieve from forfeiture for wilful breach of covenant (other than a covenant for the payment of rent) has been extinguished by reason of Parliament having legislated comprehensively in that field.

First, the question is whether Parliament has impliedly shown an intention to exclude the inherent jurisdiction. In one sense, it is impossible logically to find any such intention: since, at the time all the legislation was passed, no one (including Parliament) thought that the courts had any such jurisdiction, Parliament could not have intended to exclude such jurisdiction. However, in my judgment, that is to take too narrow a view. Since, at the relevant times, no one thought that there was an inherent jurisdiction, the intention of Parliament in legislating must have been to lay down a comprehensive and exclusive code setting out the circumstances in which relief could be given.

Rexhaven Ltd v Nurse[106] raises one further possibility for the derivative interest holder where the landlord has executed a possession order against the tenant—that is, to apply to have the possession order set aside on the basis that he or she has a good claim to relief, which he or she has been unable to present to the court, for example, because of his or her ignorance of the possession proceedings.

6.4.7 Reform

It should come as no surprise that there have long been calls for reform of the law governing forfeiture. The Law Commission first mooted reform in 1968,[107] although it was not until 1985 that its first report on the question was published.[108] Implementation of these proposals was delayed by other projects and developments—most notably, title registration, the HRA 1998, and changes to the civil procedure rules—but, in 2006, a further report was issued.[109]

The proposals are to replace the existing forfeiture schemes for non-payment of rent and breaches of other covenants with a single scheme for the termination of leases based upon any relevant default by the tenant. This scheme is outlined in the Executive Summary to the report.

---

106 (1995) 28 HLR 241.
107 Law Commission Working Paper No 16 (1968).
108 Law Commission Report No 142, *Forfeiture of Tenancies* (1985).
109 Law Commission Report No 303, *Termination of Tenancies for Tenant Default* (2006), following the favourable response to its Consultation Paper No 174 (2004).

Law Commission Report No 303, *Termination of Tenancies for Tenant Default: Executive Summary* (2006, [1.9]–[1.24])

Tenant default

The scheme introduces a new concept of "tenant default" to define the circumstances in which a landlord may seek to terminate the tenancy before the end of its term. In simple terms, tenant default is a breach by the tenant of a covenant or condition of the tenancy. There is no need for a forfeiture clause or right of re-entry to be included in a tenancy agreement entered into post implementation, although the tenant should be given an "explanatory statement" explaining what can happen in the event of tenant default.

It is open to the parties to agree that the breach of one or more covenants will not comprise tenant default and so exclude or limit the application of the scheme. It is no longer possible for the landlord to "waive" the breach (either intentionally or inadvertently).

Tenant default notice

The scheme requires the landlord wishing to proceed to warn the tenant of the impending action by giving a written notice. The tenant default notice must set out the details of the breach, any remedial action required and the date by which it should be completed. The scheme limits the period after a tenant default during which a tenant can be served with a tenant default notice.

The tenant default notice must also be served on those who hold qualifying interests deriving out of the tenancy of which the landlord has knowledge (principally mortgagees and sub-tenants).

The primary purpose of the tenant default notice is to ensure that the tenant complies with the obligations under the tenancy. It can also provide a period for negotiation by the parties. For a minimum period of seven days, or until the date for remedy set out in the notice expires, the landlord cannot take any further steps in the process that might culminate in the termination of the tenancy.

Making a termination claim

If the service of a tenant default notice fails in its primary purpose, the landlord may make a termination claim. The claim is served on the tenant and on all qualifying interest holders who have previously been served with a tenant default notice.

The orders available to the court

Once the court is satisfied that the tenant default has occurred, it may make such order that it thinks appropriate and proportionate in all the circumstances. In arriving at this decision the court is required to take into account a number of considerations. These include the conduct of the landlord and the tenant, whether any action can be or has been taken to remedy the default and whether the deadline by which it was to be remedied was reasonable.

A **termination order** ends the tenancy and any interests deriving out of it on a date specified in the order.

A **remedial order** will set out what the tenant must do to remedy the default and the date by which it must be remedied. The order does not affect the continued existence of the tenancy. It stays the landlord's claim for a termination order for a period of three months from the day by which the tenant is required to have carried out the work. During that period the landlord can apply to lift the stay and proceed with the termination claim. On lifting the stay, the court may make any order available to it, including a termination order.

An **order for sale** requires that the tenancy is sold and the proceeds distributed. This may be appropriate where the tenancy has a significant capital value and a termination order would provide a disproportionate windfall to the landlord.

There are two orders that can only be sought by qualifying interest holders. The first is the **transfer order**. This requires the tenancy to be transferred to the applicant or a third party (for example, a tenants' management company). The second is the **new tenancy order** which grants the applicant a new tenancy of all or part of the demised premises [...]

[...]

Summary termination procedure

The scheme provides an alternative procedure under which the landlord can bring a tenancy to an end without applying to the court. It is intended for use in cases where the tenant would have no realistic prospect of resisting a termination order or where premises have been abandoned. The procedure cannot be used concurrently with the court-based procedure; the landlord must elect which route to take.

The procedure cannot be used where (1) someone is lawfully residing in the premises, (2) the unexpired term exceeds 25 years, or (3) the tenancy was granted for a term in excess of seven years and there are three or more years unexpired, and the default is breach of a repairing covenant.

The procedure is commenced by service of a summary termination notice and operates to bring the tenancy and all interests deriving out of it to an end one month after the notice is served. However, the tenant or any qualifying interest holder can resist the summary termination by applying to court to discharge the notice. This application suspends the termination of the tenancy until it has been decided. The landlord must rebut the presumption that the notice should be discharged by showing that, on a termination claim being made, the tenant would have no realistic prospect of persuading the court not to make a termination order and that there is no other reason why the matter should be disposed of by way of a hearing of a termination claim.

For six months after summary termination of a tenancy, the former tenant (or a former qualifying interest holder) can apply to court for a "post-termination order". This may be any order in connection with the tenancy that the court thinks appropriate and proportionate and includes the grant of a new tenancy to the applicant or the payment of compensation. However, the court cannot in any circumstances revive the terminated tenancy.

QUESTIONS

1. Explain what we mean by 'privity of estate'? Why does a sub-lessee fall outside the privity of estate matrix of the head lease and does this matter?

2. Why is the contractual liability of the original parties to a long lease unfair? How does the Landlord and Tenant (Covenants) Act 1995 address the problem? In any event, did this contractual liability present so much of a problem for long leases of flats?

3. Is it easier for the benefit and burden of a tenant's and landlord's covenants to pass in a post-1995 lease than in a pre-1996 lease?

4. The Landlord and Tenants (Covenants) Act 1995 abandons the concepts of a covenant 'touching and concerning', and 'having reference to the subject matter' of the lease. Is it sensible for it to do so?

5. How draconian a remedy is forfeiture?

6. Why does a 'twilight period' occur during the process of forfeiture?

7. Can a negative leasehold covenant be remedied?

8. Is there any role for equity's inherent jurisdiction to provide relief from forfeiture or does the statutory right to relief provided by s 146 of the Law of Property Act 1925 provide a complete code?

FURTHER READING

Bridge, 'Former Tenants, Future Liabilities and the Privity of Contract Principle' (1996) 55 CLJ 313

Clarke, 'Property Law' (1992) 45(1) CLP 81

Davey, 'Privity of Contract and Leases: Reform at Last' (1996) 59 MLR 78

Gravells, 'Forfeiture of Leases for Breach of Covenant' [2006] JBL 830

Law Commission Report No 174, *Landlord and Tenant Law: Privity of Contract and Estate* (1988)

Law Commission Report No 303, *Termination of Tenancies for Tenant Default* (2006)

Luxton, 'Waiver of Forfeiture: Time to Shake Away the Doctrine of Election' [1991] JBL 342

PART E

NEIGHBOURS AND NEIGHBOURHOODS

26

EASEMENTS

CENTRAL ISSUES

1. An easement is the proprietary right to enjoy limited use of the land of another, which may exist in both positive and negative form.

2. The defining characteristics of an easement are: (i) there must be a dominant and a servient tenement; (ii) each of the tenements must be in separate occupation; (iii) the easement must accommodate the dominant tenement; and (iv) the easement must be capable of being the subject matter of a grant.

3. Easements may be created by express, implied, or presumed grant.

4. An implied grant of an easement may arise: (i) by necessity; (ii) by common intention; (iii) under the rule in *Wheeldon v Burrows*;[1] or (iv) by the

   operation of s 62 of the Law of Property Act 1925.

5. A grant of an easement may be presumed by prescription as a result of long user as of right either at common law, or under the doctrine of lost modern grant or the Prescription Act 1832.

6. The status of easements as overriding interests presents a challenge to a complete register, which has been addressed by the Land Registration Act 2002.

7. An easement may be extinguished by common ownership of the dominant and servient tenement, by release, by abandonment, or by excessive user (in extreme cases).

---

[1] (1879) 12 LR Ch D 31.

1 INTRODUCTION

1.1 WHAT ARE EASEMENTS?

An easement is the right of a landowner to enjoy limited use of the land of another land-owner.[2] There is thus a need for two pieces of land: the *dominant* land, to which the right is attached, and the *servient* land, over which the right is exercised and which must thus suffer the burden of the right. In England and Wales, easements are very common. Land Registry figures reveal that 65 per cent of existing registered freehold titles and 24 per cent of existing registered leasehold titles are subject to an easement.[3]

Easements may be positive or negative in nature. A positive easement will allow the owner of the dominant land to go onto the servient land to use some facility. The most common positive easement is a right of way to use a path or road on the servient land. A negative ease-ment is a right to receive something from the servient land: for example, a right to receive light or air flowing from the servient land. It is negative in nature both because the dominant owner is not entitled to do anything over the servient land, and because the servient owner is not permitted to interfere with the right.

Easements are proprietary rights that exist for a defined estate.[4] They are thus capable of accruing to the benefit of purchasers of the dominant land and will bind purchasers of the servient land.[5] In this respect, they differ from licences, which, as mere gratuitous or contractual permissions, allow a landowner to use another's land without committing a trespass, but will only bind the parties personally.[6] We saw, in Chapters 3 and 4, that the boundary between personal and proprietary rights is strictly patrolled and that only rights over the land of another that display certain characteristics are accepted as easements. Those that fail to display these characteristics may operate as licences.

We will confine our attention in this chapter to easements, but easements sit within a range of other limited rights over the land of another. There are a number of public rights that are not dependent on owning land: for example, we all have a right to use the public highways and many will gain access to their properties directly from a public road.[7] The utility companies enjoy 'way-leaves' granted by statute to run the services that they provide over land in order to supply mains gas, electricity, water, and sewage services.[8] Landowners may also claim the benefit of natural rights of support from neighbouring land and, where appropriate, the right to water flowing naturally in a river or stream. Profits *à prendre* are private rights to take the natural produce from another's land: for example, the right to fish or take game. Profits are very similar to easements, save that they do not have to be con-nected with the use of any dominant land, but may be held purely for the benefit of a par-ticular individual. In our next chapter, we will be looking at restrictive covenants, which can

---

[2] See Chapter 3, sections 5 and 6.

[3] See Law Commission Consultation Paper No 186, *Easements, Covenants and Profits à Prendre* (2008, Appendix A). This percentage is based upon statistics for the years 2003–04 and 2004–05.

[4] To exist at law, an easement must be held for a freehold or leasehold estate. An easement for life can only exist in equity.

[5] See section 4 below.

[6] See Chapter 8.

[7] The public also has rights of access to certain commons: see, e.g., Law of Property Act 1925, s 193; the Countryside and Rights of Way Act 2000 now confers rights of public access to some areas of private land.

[8] For example, under the Water Industry Act 1991, Electricity Act 1989, Gas Act 1986, and Telecommunications Act 1984.

operate negatively to regulate the user of land for the benefit of adjacent land. As such, they are similar to easements—particularly negative easements.

In this chapter, we will examine the defining characteristics of easements, before looking at how they operate as proprietary interests in terms of their mode of creation, their effect on third parties, and the manner in which they may be extinguished. Before we do so, however, we should note the underlying concerns that have shaped the law governing easements.

1.2 THE UTILITY BALANCE

Easements have a long history. They were known to medieval lawyers, but their essential characteristics remained rudimentary until the nineteenth century, when easements became increasingly prominent as a result of the agricultural and industrial revolutions that underpin much of our modern way of life.[9] It is no coincidence that it was in 1839 that Gale wrote an influential book on easements, which remains the leading text today.[10]

Gardner explains the reason why the nineteenth century saw a growth in the importance of easements when, to maximize its economic utility, communally owned land was divided into smaller areas of individual ownership. These imperatives remain relevant today as the intensity of land use continues to grow.

Gardner, *Introduction to Land Law* (2007, p 158–60)

Division into sealed packets has a great merit: at a basic level, it gives the owner of each packet the maximum opportunity and incentive to exploit his own packet to the full. But a given packet of land may in practice not be self sufficient in the things required for its optimal exploitation. It may lack efficient access for example. Greater benefit can be extracted by running the land in question co-operatively with neighbouring packets, from which additional requirements can be sourced [. . .]

The English law of easements thus developed most during the 19th century. During the first three quarters of that century, English agricultural land was being divided into sealed packets, in a process known as 'enclosure'. Previously, the land had been operated much more communally. Enclosure was born of a realisation that the old communal approach impeded the land's maximum exploitation. But easements were developed out of a realisation, in turn, that even greater exploitation was possible if one could have it both ways. At about the same period, too, intensive building was taking place, centred on the mills, factories and so on which were perceived as the most effective tools by which to exploit downstream resources. Maximum intensity was achieved by introducing easements to allow the collaborative use of neighbouring plots of land.

Care is needed, however. Cross-exploitation does harm as well as good for it erodes the benefits to be had from dividing land into sealed packets. The less my land becomes simply 'mine' because there are obligations such as easements affecting its use, the further I shall be from having the maximum opportunity and incentive to exploit it, by growing crops myself, or building houses, or whatever. So the establishment of easements needs to be restricted to the situations in which sealed packets does more good than harm. The law does this by rules that limit the forms of benefit that can be associated with easements, favouring those that are traditional, ordinary, agricultural, and as a matter of business rather than recreation, and its rule limiting easements to rights that do not deprive me of 'any reasonable use' of my land.

---

[9] See Holdsworth, *Historical Introduction to the Land Law* (1927, p 265).

[10] Now in its 17th edition: see *Gale on Easements* (eds Gaunt and Morgan, 2002).

As Gardner highlights, there is a need to balance the benefit of exploiting the dominant land against the burden placed upon the servient land. This balance is central in determining what characteristics a right must satisfy to qualify as an easement.

A further balance that must be struck is between the desirability of implying an easement to promote utility and the conveyancing problems that arise where such rights are difficult to trace. This question was in minds of the architects of the Land Registration Act 2002 (LRA 2002) and we will consider their solution later in the chapter.[11]

2 THE *CONTENT* QUESTION

The leading case of *Re Ellenborough Park* summarizes the essential characteristics of an easement.

Re Ellenborough Park [1956] Ch 131, CA

Facts: Ellenborough Park is a development of houses surrounding a park. Each house was sold together with the right to full enjoyment of the park. During the Second World War, the park was requisitioned and a dispute arose as to who was entitled to the compensation payable as a result. If the house owners' right to use the park was an easement, they were entitled to share the compensation. It was held that the house owners' right to use the park was an easement, because it satisfied the legal characteristics of an easement, and they were entitled to share the compensation.

Evershed MR

At 163

For the purposes of the argument before us Mr Cross and Mr Goff were content to adopt, as correct, the four characteristics formulated in *Dr Cheshire's Modern Real Property* 7th ed pp456 et seq. They are (1) there must be a dominant tenement and a servient tenement: (2) an easement must "accommodate" the dominant tenement: (3) dominant and servient owners must be different persons, and (4) a right over land cannot amount to an easement, unless it is capable of forming the subject matter of a grant.

We will use these four characteristics as our guide to explore the characteristics of easements, although we will look at them in a slightly different order.

2.1 'THERE MUST BE A DOMINANT TENEMENT AND A SERVIENT TENEMENT'

There must be two pieces of land: the servient tenement, over which the right is exercised, and the dominant tenement, which benefits from the right.

---

[11] See section 4 below.

2.1.1 Should we have easements in gross?

In some jurisdictions, it is possible for there only to be a servient tenement, over which the right is exercised by a person who is not required to be the owner of any land. The easement is then said to exist *in gross*. English law accepts the possibility that profits may exist in gross and statutory way-leaves confer upon certain bodies what are, in effect, easements in gross. For example, service suppliers, such as the gas, electricity, water, and telephone companies, enjoy way-leaves to run their pipes and wires over and under land to maintain the national supply of these services.

Sturley has argued that easements in gross should also be permitted in English law.[12] He believes that the requirement for a dominant tenement is *'without authority or justification'*,[13] and that the arguments against easements in gross, in terms of imposing a potentially excessive or unjustified burden on the servient tenement, can be overcome.

Sturley, 'Easements in Gross' (1980) 96 LQR 557

At 562

Though no justification is given against the rule against easements in gross in the cases which establish it, it may nevertheless be possible to justify it after the fact. Two possibilities, both of which are suggested by nineteenth century cases, should be considered. The first, which may be labelled the "surcharge argument," holds that an easement in gross, not being limited to the needs of the dominant tenement is likely to burden the servient tenement with excessive use. The second and somewhat more convincing, which may be labelled the "clogs on title argument," holds that an easement in gross is likely to be an unjustified incumbrance on the title of the servient tenement [. . .]

At 563

Certainly surcharge concerns are genuine, but they should not be overemphasised. Though not limited by reference to the dominant tenement, an easement in gross would still be limited by the terms of its grant [. . .] The problem of an easement in gross passing to too many people could also be solved by a limitation in the grant if the parties consider it appropriate. The interpretation of such limitations is neither new nor unfamiliar.

Even if the grant fails to make any provision for the problem other limitations are available. Many easements are self limiting [. . .] Possibilities of surcharge have long existed, both in profits and easements, but there have not been problems sufficient to justify the total prohibition of the interests. It seems the same should be true of easements in gross.

If further protection should be necessary, a convenient solution might be an extension of section 84 of the Law of Property Act 1925. This provision enables any interested person to apply to the Lands Tribunal for the discharge or modification of a restrictive covenant in some circumstances [. . .] Were the tribunal to have similar jurisdiction over easements in gross, an unjustified surcharge could be eliminated if any problems arose. Such an approach would deal only with the actual problem cases while allowing useful easements in gross to exist.

The clogs on title argument may be seen as an underlying rationale of *Keppel v Bailey* and *Hill v Tupper* where it was decided that novel rights cannot be annexed to land. The concern

---

12 See also McClean, 'The Nature of an Easement' (1996) 5 West LR 32, 36–42.
13 Sturley, 'Easements in Gross' (1980) 96 LQR 557, 568.

in both cases, however, is the type of right held rather than the means of holding it, and thus they properly relate to Cheshire's fourth characteristic of an easement, the subject matter of a grant. With respect to easements in gross the argument suggests not that anything is wrong with the right, per se, but that the owner in gross may be difficult to discover, thus making any right an unjustified clog on title when held in gross [. . .]

At 566

A solution, it seems, is to be found in the Land Charges Act [1972 or Land Registration Act 2002] scheme. If an easement in gross has to be registered, it is not very different from an appurtenant easement from the point of view of the clogs on title argument.

The Law Commission has considered whether, as a matter of policy, easements in gross should be permitted, but, whilst acknowledging the arguments made by Sturley, its view is that the requirement for a dominant tenement should not be relaxed.[14] To do so would also require a rethink of the fundamental need for an easement to accommodate the dominant tenement.[15]

2.1.2 The need to identify the dominant tenement

The extent of the dominant tenement must be clearly established at the time that the easement is to be granted.

London & Blenheim Estates Ltd v Ladbroke Retail Parks Ltd [1994] 1 WLR 31, CA

Facts: Leicestershire Co-op sold part of its land (the dominant tenement) to London & Blenheim, together with the right to park cars on land retained by the Co-op (the servient land). The agreement also included a provision that, in the event of London & Blenheim acquiring additional land, it should be entitled to give notice to the Co-op for that additional land (the alleged additional dominant tenement) to acquire similar parking rights. Before any notice was given, the servient land came into the ownership of Ladbrooke. London & Blenheim failed in its claim to a right to park for the benefit of the additional land that it had acquired, because, at the time that the servient land was sold by the Co-op, the alleged dominant tenement was not adequately identified.

Peter Gibson LJ

At 37

If one asks why the law should require that there should be a dominant tenement before there can be a grant, or a contract for the grant, of an easement sufficient to create an interest in land binding successors in title to the servient land, the answer would appear to lie in the policy against encumbering land with burdens of a uncertain extent. As was said by Fox LJ in *Ashburn Ansalt v Arnold* [1989] 1 Ch 26, "In matters relating to the title to land, certainty is of prime importance." A further related answer lies in the reluctance of the law to recognise

---

[14] Law Commission Consultation Paper No 186 (2008, [3.16]).
[15] See also Lawson, 'Easements' in *Land Law: Issues, Debates, Policy* (ed Tee, 2002, p 71).

new forms of burden on property conferring more than contractual rights. Thus in *Ackroyd v Smith* (1850) 10 CB 164, 188 Cresswell J., giving judgment of the judges of Common Pleas, after referring to the impossibility of a grant of a right of way in gross said "nor can the owner of the land render it subject to a new species of burden, so as to bind it in the hands of an assignee." "Incidents of a novel kind cannot be devised, and attached to property, at the fancy and caprice of any owner:" per Lord Brougham LC in *Keppel v Bailey* (1834) 2 Myl & K 517. A right intended as an easement and attached to a servient tenement before the dominant tenement is identified would in my view be an incident of a novel kind.

2.1.3 The rule in *Harris v Flower*[16]

A dominant owner, who acquires additional land adjacent to or close by the dominant land, may wish to use the easement that he or she enjoys for the benefit of that additional land. In general, he or she will be unable to do so without committing a trespass to the servient land. This prohibition is known as the 'rule in *Harris v Flower*', outlined by Romer LJ in the case of the same name as: '[I]*f a right of way be granted for the enjoyment of Close A, the grantee because he owns or acquires Close B cannot use the way in substance for passing over the Close A to Close B* [...]'[17]

Harris v Flower envisages the additional land being adjacent to the dominant land, so it is necessary to pass from the servient land to access the dominant land and then over the dominant land to access the additional land. Whilst it is perfectly acceptable for the dominant owner to use the right of way to access the dominant land, his or her use of the right of way will become unacceptable if he or she uses it to gain access to the additional land. The situation may be represented as in Figure 20.

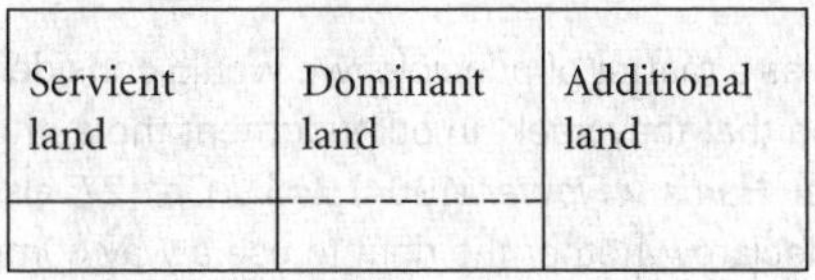

Servient land	Dominant land	Additional land

Figure 20 *Harris v Flower*: Situation 1

An alternative situation may arise where the additional land does not lie beyond the dominant land, but to the side, or close by: there is then no need for the dominant owner to pass over the dominant land to gain access to the servient land. The situation may be represented as in Figure 21.

This is what happened in *Das v Linden Mews*,[18] in which mews houses in London enjoyed a right of way along a privately owned street. Two of the owners acquired ground at the end of the street on which to park their cars. The owners of the street (the servient land) successful argued that the rule in *Harris v Flower* prohibited the house owners from exercising the right of way attached to their house to drive along the street to the land that they had acquired for parking.

The rationale for the rule lies in keeping within the terms of the easement, rather than excessive use of the servient tenement.

---

[16] (1904) 74 LJ Ch 127.
[17] Ibid, at 127.
[18] [2002] EWCA Civ 590, [2003] 2 P & CR 4.

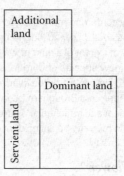

Figure 21 *Harris v Flower*: Situation 2

Peacock v Custins [2002] 1 WLR 1815, CA

Facts: Peacock owned a field ('the red land', i.e. the dominant land), which was accessed by a right of way over land owned by Custins ('the yellow strip', i.e. the servient land). Peacock also owned another field adjacent to the dominant land ('the blue land'), but he failed to prove that he could use his right of way over the servient land once or twice a year to access the additional field.

Schiebsmann LJ

At [25]

Considering the position as a matter of principle, we would consider that the defendants are entitled to the declaration that they seek. In our judgment the authorities to which we have referred, and in particular *Harris v Flower* (1904) 74 LJ Ch 127, also confirm that, where a court is being asked to declare whether the right to use a way comprises a right to use it to facilitate the cultivation of land other than the dominant tenement, the court is not concerned with any comparison between the amount of use made or to be made of the servient tenement and the amount of use made or that might lawfully be made within the scope of the grant. It is concerned with declaring the scope of the grant, having regard to its purposes and the identity of the dominant tenement. The authorities indicate that the burden on the owner of the servient tenement is not to be increased without his consent. But burden in this context does not refer to the number of journeys or the weight of the vehicles. Any use of the way is, in contemplation of law, a burden and one must ask whether the grantor agreed to the grantee making use of the way for that purpose [...]

At [27]

It is in our judgment clear that the grantor did not authorise the use of the way for the purpose of cultivating the blue land. This cannot sensibly be described as ancillary to the cultivation of the red land. We therefore allow the appeal and declare that the claimants are not entitled to use the yellow strip for the purpose of obtaining access to the blue land in order to cultivate it.

It has to be remembered that the dominant owner is perfectly entitled to use the right in connection with his or her enjoyment of the dominant land, and it may be that he or she goes onto, or makes some use of, the additional land, which is merely ancillary to his or her use of the dominant land.

Schiebsman LJ makes reference to this possibility earlier in his judgment.

Peacock v Custins [2002] 1 WLR 1815, CA

Schiebsmann LJ

At [22]

The law is clear at the extremes. To use the track for the sole purpose of accessing the blue land is outside the scope of the grant. However in some circumstances a person who uses the way to access the dominant land but then goes off the dominant land, for instance to picnic on the neighbouring land, is not going outside the scope of the grant.

Such ancillary use will thus not fall foul of the rule in *Harris v Flower*. Whilst the cultivation of the 'blue land', or the use of the car park, was held not to be ancillary to the use of the dominant land in either *Peacock v Custins* or *Das v Linden Mews*, there are cases in which the use of the additional land has been considered ancillary. For example, in *Massey v Boulden*,[19] the Masseys claimed a prescriptive easement over a village green to gain access to their house. Their house had been extended by the addition of two rooms from an adjoining property. They had used the access to their original house for the required prescription period, but they had acquired the additional rooms just short of that period. It was nevertheless held that their use of the two additional rooms was ancillary to their use of their original house and thus fell within the prescriptive easement.[20]

The scope of the ancillary use exception is not easy to identify. The possible principles underlying ancillary use were explored in the following case, in which the court sought to reconcile the authorities by identifying that a use will be ancillary where the use is not 'in substance' for the benefit of non-dominant land, either because there is no benefit to the non-dominant land, or because any benefit is insubstantial.

Macepark (Whittlebury) Ltd v Sargeant (No 2) [2003] 1 WLR 2284, HC

Facts: A hotel close to Silverstone race circuit was leased with the benefit of a right of way along a path across adjoining land. A wood lay between the hotel and Silverstone. With the agreement of the owners of the wood, Macepark planned a short cut through the wood as a direct link to Silverstone. The hotel unsuccessfully claimed that the right of way could be used by hotel guests to drive from the hotel, and along the short cut through the wood, to Silverstone. The use of the right of way would not merely benefit of the hotel as the dominant land, but would also substantially benefit the owners of the wood and Silverstone. The owners of the wood could charge for the short cut over their land and Silverstone would benefit from an additional access route.

---

[19] [2003] 1 WLR 1792.
[20] See also *National Trust v White* [1987] 1 WLR 907, in which the use of a car park was held to be ancillary to the enjoyment of the ancient site of Figsbury Rings.

Gabriel Moss QC (sitting as a High Court judge)

At [35]–[38]

The principle underlying the "ancillary" exception is not spelt out.

There seem to be at least two possibilities. One is that a use of the right of way to go on to non-dominant land can be ancillary where it is *insubstantial*, as in the case of going on to non-dominant land for a picnic, but cannot be ancillary if it is *substantial*, as where the access is used for going on to non-dominant land in order to cultivate another field or to store on the dominant land timber grown and felled on non-dominant land.

A second approach, which would often coincide with the first, would be that a use can be ancillary if it does not *benefit* the non-dominant land, ie does not *in effect extend the domin-ant land*. The picnic for example concerned a situation where the use of the right of access involved going on to non-dominant land but not benefiting it [...] By contrast, non-dominant land is benefited if the access is used to enable it or to facilitate it to be cultivated or logged.

A third approach would be to say that a use was ancillary if it were *either* insubstantial *or* not a benefit [...]

At [47]–[52]

In accepting and applying the "ancillary" doctrine I must assume that the Court of Appeal in *Massey v Boulden* [2003] 1 WLR 1792 chose to follow the approach in *Peacock v Custins* [2002] 1 WLR 1815 rather than *Das v Linden Mews Ltd* [2002] 2 EGLR 76, since both cases are referred to in the judgment of Simon Brown LJ [2003] 1 WLR 1792, 1803, para 37. I must accept, therefore, that there is an "ancillary" doctrine.

The apparent clash with *Harris v Flower* (1904) 74 LJ Ch 127 is more difficult to resolve. The facts seem essentially similar. Moreover, there seems no doubt that in *Massey v Boulden* the access was used for the benefit of the non-dominant land as well as the dominant land. The only way, therefore, in which the Court of Appeal could have regarded the use of the access to benefit the non-dominant land as "ancillary" is if they regarded it as insubstantial: compare the use of the phrase "in substance" by Romer LJ in *Harris v Flower* at 132 and Morritt LJ in *Jobson v Record* [1998] 1 EGLR 113 at 114. The additional rooms which extended the domin-ant land appear to have been regarded as mere appendages to the dominant land, so that the use of the access could be seen as being *in substance* for the benefit of the dominant land and not in substance for the benefit of the non-dominant land.

If I have reconciled the apparently conflicting authorities on the question of ancillary use successfully, the result seems to be as follows. (1) There is a doctrine of "ancillary use". (2) It applies where the use of the access for the benefit of the non-dominant land in addition to the benefit of the dominant land is insubstantial, e g where it is used to reach rooms which are mere appendages to the dominant property. (3) It also applies where the use of the access to reach the dominant land and then go on to non-dominant land does not benefit the non-dominant land, e g where there is a picnic on the non-dominant land. (4) With regard to the question of what "benefits" the non-dominant land, where the access makes the use of the non-dominant land profitable, that access is being used to benefit the non-dominant land. For example, where the access, by an arrangement between the owner of the dominant land and the owner of the non-dominant land, is used to enable a profit to be made out of the use of the non-dominant land, there is a benefit to the non-dominant land.

Summary of the law

On the basis that I have accurately understood the current standing of the "ancillary" doc-trine, the following propositions now seem to be correct. (1) An easement must be used for the benefit of the dominant land. (2) It must not "in substance" be used for the benefit of non-dominant land. (3) Under the "ancillary" doctrine, use is not "in substance" use for the benefit of the non-dominant land if (a) there is no benefit to the non-dominant land or if (b) the extent of the use for the benefit of the non-dominant land is insubstantial, ie it can still be said that in substance the access is used for the benefit of the dominant land and not for the benefit of both the dominant land and the non-dominant land. (d) "Benefit" in this context includes use of an access in such a way that a profit may be made out of the use of the non-dominant land, e g as a result of an arrangement with the owner of the dominant land.

The application of these principles can involve potentially difficult questions of fact and degree.

One significant factor, identified by the Court of Appeal in *Peacock v Custins* at para 24, is whether the benefit to the non-dominant land is likely to have its own "commercial value". It also seems from *Peacock v Custins* that it is not necessary to prove that separate value if it can be regarded as "self-evident".

A further feature of *Macepark* is that the court paid no regard to the fact that the hotel (as the dominant land), and the wood and race circuit (as the non-dominant, additional land), were in separate ownership.

The rule in *Harris v Flower* has been the subject of criticism.

Paton and Seabourne, 'Can't Get There From Here? Permissible Use of Easements After *Das*' [2003] Conv 127, 132

If the rule is to be justified purely on grounds of doctrinal "neatness", then it must be recognised that its application, and the concept of "bona fide" or "colourable" use of a right of way for a particular purpose, produces some odd doctrinal consequences. It introduces something like "guilt by intention" to the law of trespass in this area. Conduct which externally is wholly consistent with the lawful exercise of right of way to land A—for example, the tractors driving along the way in *Peacock v Custins*—is made unlawful by the presence of an *intention* to carry on through A to B, land in which the servient owner has no legal or practical interest.

Yet in such cases where the right of way serving A is the only means of access to A and B, the courts have noticeably stopped short of the logical conclusion that land B is thereby landlocked and effectively sterilised. In *Peacock v Custins*, Schiemann L.J. suggested that the owner of land A could still go from A to B, perhaps for a picnic. What he could presumably not do was use the right of way serving A with that ultimate purpose (going to B) in mind. In other words, excursions from A to B, for picnics or otherwise, must be spontaneous, the idea originating once the owner is safely ensconced in A, having used the way to get there first. If, however, the servient owner one day spies the owner driving along the way with his car packed full of hampers, then sees him picnicking on B later that day, a trespass will have been committed [...]

The implication of this [...] is not a logically inevitable analysis. If lands A and B are contiguous and in common ownership, one of the most elementary incidents of such ownership must be the owner's right to *move freely between the two*. He needs no externally granted "right" to do this. There is no reason why use of the right of way to go to B via A can not be seen as a two stage process: use of the right of way to get to A, followed by access from A to B along the owner's own land as an incident of his ownership of both.

> [...] In cases other than "passing through" ones, the above argument is not possible, but nor is it necessary. If the *only* threatened use of additional land B is by the owner/occupier of the land A which has the benefit of the right, such use of B is either ancillary or necessarily connected to the use of A, and the use of B generates no risk of increased user of the way, it is difficult to see any justification for a further, prohibitive rule.

Paton and Seabourne instead advocate that the determining principle should be based upon the concept of excessive user.[21] Their call has been taken up by the Law Commission.[22]

Paton and Seabourne, 'Can't Get There From Here? Permissible Use of Easements After *Das*' [2003] Conv 127, 134

A modified rule: excessive user

[...] As a controlling principle, excessive user is clearly related to the law of nuisance, in which the courts are more accustomed to balancing the competing activities, rights and convenience of neighbours, and giving some degree of latitude to worthwhile or productive uses of land. A court considering a claim of excessive user can have regard to the likely duration and nature of the proposed user, and the likelihood and severity of any actual or threatened damage, and can impose temporary or permanent conditions/restrictions on any relief granted.

The "rule in *Harris v Flower*", by contrast, originates in the strict construction of deeds and the conceptualisation of the law of easements around identifiable dominant and servient tenements. Ultimately, it is unnecessary. It can be qualified without collapsing the principle of appurtenance to an identified dominant tenement into "easements in gross". So long as the proposed additional activity bears *some* connection to the original dominant tenement, and does not generate excessive user or damage, the servient owner is protected. No further policy is served, or interest protected, by maintaining the strict rule for the sake of doctrinal purity.

2.2 THE DOMINANT AND SERVIENT TENEMENTS MUST BE IN SEPARATE OWNERSHIP AND OCCUPATION

It is not possible to have an easement over your own land.[23] Any rights that are exercised over two adjoining pieces of land that you own are exercised as a result of your ownership. Accordingly, where the dominant and servient tenement come into the same ownership and occupation, the easement is extinguished, although if the dominant tenement is sold off, an easement may once again be created by implied grant.[24] If the dominant and servient tenement come only into the same occupation—for example, because a tenant takes

---

[21] See section 5 below.
[22] See Law Commission Consultation Paper No 186 (2008, [5.64]–[5.71]).
[23] *Roe v Siddons* (1889) 22 QBD 224, 236; *Metropolitan Railway Co v Fowler* [1892] 1 QB 165; *Kilgour v Gaddes* [1904] 1 KB 457, 461. The rule can be inconvenient when a housing estate is being developed, because the developer will be unable to create easements between the plots whilst the plots remain in their common ownership. The Law Commission has suggested relaxing the rule where the servient and dominant land are registered under separate titles: see Law Commission Consultation Paper No 186 (2008, [3.56]–[3.66]).
[24] See the rule in *Wheeldon v Burrows*: section 3.2 below.

a lease of both pieces of land—the easement is suspended until the common occupation comes to an end.

It must be remembered that an easement is attached to the estate in the land and thus it is perfectly possibly for a tenant taking a lease to be granted an easement for the term of the lease over servient land retained by his or her landlord. Likewise, a landlord may wish to reserve an easement over land that he or she has leased for the benefit of adjoining dominant land that he or she owns.

2.3 AN EASEMENT MUST ACCOMMODATE THE DOMINANT LAND

The right must benefit the land, as opposed to an individual owner of the land, if it is to have the necessary proprietary character to qualify as an easement. The concept of the land being able to enjoy rights is somewhat strained when it is the use of the land by its occupier that derives any benefit. The import of the requirement thus relates to the benefit enjoyed by the owner for the time being of the land, rather than a personal advantage of a particular owner. The point has been explained in the following case.

Moody v Steggles (1879) 12 Ch D 261

Fry J

At 266

It is said that the easement in question relates, not to the tenement, but to the business of the occupant of the tenement, and that therefore I cannot tie the easement to the house. It appears to me that that argument is of too refined a nature to prevail, and for this reason, that the house can only be used by an occupant, and that the occupant only uses the house for the business he pursues, therefore in some manner (direct or indirect) an easement is more or less connected with the mode in which the occupant of the house uses it.

A right that was held to confer only a personal advantage is found in the early case of *Hill v Tupper*.[25] As we saw in Chapter 3, section 1, a canal company leased land beside the canal to Mr Hill and granted to him the exclusive right to put or use boats on the canal. Mr Tupper owned a pub situated beside the canal and, when he also rented out boats to be used on the canal, Mr Hill objected. The court held that his exclusive right to put boats on the canal was not an easement, but a personal advantage. In the following case, Evershed MR explained why.

Re Ellenborough Park [1956] Ch 131, CA

Evershed MR

At 175

It is clear that what the plaintiff was trying to do was to set up, under the guise of an easement, a monopoly which had no normal connexion with the ordinary use of his land, but

---

[25] (1863) 2 H & C 121.

which was merely an independent business enterprise. So far from the right claimed sub-serving or accommodating the land, the land was but a convenient incident to the exercise of the right.

The question of accommodation was of central importance in *Re Ellenborough Park* when the Court decided that the right to use the communal gardens satisfied the test.

Re Ellenborough Park [1956] Ch 131, CA

Evershed MR

At 173

Can it be said, then, of the right of full enjoyment of the park in question, which was granted by the conveyance of December 23, 1864, and which, for reasons already given, was, in our view, intended to be annexed to the property conveyed to Mr. Porter, that it accommodated and served that property? It is clear that the right did, in some degree, enhance the value of the property, and this consideration cannot be dismissed as wholly irrelevant. It is, of course, a point to be noted; but we agree with Mr. Cross's submission that it is in no way decisive of the problem; it is not sufficient to show that the right increased the value of the property conveyed, unless it is also shown that it was connected with the normal enjoyment of that property. It appears to us that the question whether or not this connexion exists is primarily one of fact, and depends largely on the nature of the alleged dominant tenement and the nature of the right granted. As to the former, it was in the contemplation of the parties to the conveyance of 1864 that the property conveyed should be used for residential and not commercial purposes [. . .] We have already stated that the purchasers of all the plots, which actually abutted on the park, were granted the right to enjoy the use of it, as were also the purchasers of some of the plots which, although not fronting upon the park, were only a short distance away from it. As to the nature of the right granted, the conveyance of 1864 shows that the park was to be kept and maintained as a pleasure ground or ornamental garden, and that it was contemplated that it should at all times be kept in good order and condition and well stocked with plants and shrubs; and the vendors covenanted that they would not at any time thereafter erect or permit to be erected any dwelling-house or other building (except a grotto, bower, summer-house, flower-stand, fountain, music-stand or other ornamental erection) within or on any part of the pleasure ground. On these facts Mr. Cross submitted that the requisite connexion between the right to use the park and the normal enjoyment of the houses which were built around it or near it had not been established. He likened the position to a right granted to the purchaser of a house to use the Zoological Gardens free of charge or to attend Lord's Cricket Ground without payment. Such a right would undoubtedly, he said, increase the value of the property conveyed but could not run with it at law as an easement, because there was no sufficient nexus between the enjoyment of the right and the use of the house. It is probably true, we think, that in neither of Mr. Cross's illustrations would the supposed right constitute an easement, for it would be wholly extraneous to, and independent of, the use of a house as a house, namely, as a place in which the householder and his family live and make their home; and it is for this reason that the analogy which Mr. Cross sought to establish between his illustrations and the present case cannot, in our opinion, be supported. A much closer analogy, as it seems to us, is the case of a man selling the freehold of part of his house and granting to the purchaser, his heirs and assigns, the right, appurtenant to such part, to use the garden in common with the vendor and his assigns. In such a case, the test of connexion, or accommodation, would be amply satisfied; for just as the use of a garden undoubtedly enhances, and is connected with, the normal enjoyment of the house to which it belongs, so also would the right granted, in the case supposed, be closely connected with the use and enjoyment of the part of the premises sold. Such, we think, is in substance the position in the present case. The park became a communal garden for the benefit and enjoyment of those whose houses adjoined it or were in its close proximity. Its flower beds, lawns and walks were calculated to afford all the amenities which it is the purpose of the garden of a house to provide; and, apart from the fact that these amenities extended to a number of householders, instead of being confined to one (which on this aspect of the case is immaterial), we can see no difference in principle between Ellenborough Park and a garden in the ordinary signification of that word. It is the collective garden of the neighbouring houses, to whose use it was dedicated by the owners of the estate and as such amply satisfied, in our judgment, the requirement of connexion with the dominant tenements to which it is appurtenant. The result is not affected by the circumstance that the right to the park is in this case enjoyed by some few houses which are not immediately fronting on the park. The test for present purposes, no doubt, is that the park should constitute in a real and intelligible sense the garden (albeit the communal garden) of the houses to which its enjoyment is annexed. But we think that the test is satisfied as regards these few neighbouring, though not adjacent, houses. We think that the extension of the right of enjoyment to these few houses does not negative the presence of the necessary "nexus" between the subject-matter enjoyed and the premises to which the enjoyment is expressed to belong.

It is evident from Evershed's judgment that there must be some physical proximity between the servient and dominant tenements for the necessary benefit to arise, although it was no objection that some of the houses did not immediately border the park, but were a short distance away.

It is also clear that an increase in economic value of the dominant tenement, whilst influential, is not the sole yardstick. The issue is whether or not the normal enjoyment of the land is enhanced, which is a question of fact to be determined by considering both the nature of the dominant tenement and the right itself.[26] Thus a right to use a communal garden will accommodate a residence, but is most unlikely to accommodate a factory or farm. Where the land is used for commercial purposes, the right may enhance the business conducted on the land. Thus, in the case of *Moody v Steggles*,[27] a right to erect a sign to announce and promote a public house on the dominant land was held to be an easement.

Although labelled a test of fact, there are value judgments to be made, taking into account current social conditions, technical advances, and accepted modes of use of property. It has been suggested that a right of recreation and amusement cannot qualify as an easement. The Court of Appeal considered the question in *Re Ellenborough Park*, when it rejected the claim that the right to use the garden was a right of mere recreation and amusement. It did so as part of the fourth requirement that the right must be capable of being the subject matter of a grant, but, because the question relates to issues of benefit, it falls more appropriately within Cheshire's second condition.

---

[26] Lawson (2002, p 73).
[27] (1879) 12 Ch D 261.

Re Ellenborough Park [1956] Ch 131, CA

Evershed MR

At 177–8

The third of the questions embraced in Dr. Cheshire's fourth condition rests primarily on a proposition stated in *Theobald's The Law of Land*, 2nd ed. (1929), at p. 263, where it is said that an easement "must be a right of utility and benefit and not one of mere recreation and amusement." It does not appear that a proposition in similar terms is stated by Gale.

[The Court considered the authorities quoted by Theobald in support being, *Mounsey v. Ismay*,[28] *Dyce v Lady James Hay*,[29] and *Dempster v Cleghorn*.[30]].

In any case, if the proposition be well-founded, we do not think that the right to use a garden of the character with which we are concerned in this case can be called one of mere recreation and amusement [...] No doubt a garden is a pleasure—on high authority, it is the purest of pleasures—but, in our judgment, it is not a right having no quality either of utility or benefit as those words should be understood. The right here in suit is, for reasons already given, one appurtenant to the surrounding houses as such, and constitutes a beneficial attribute of residence in a house as ordinarily understood. Its use for the purposes, not only of exercise and rest but also for such domestic purposes as were suggested in argument— for example, for taking out small children in perambulators or otherwise—is not fairly to be described as one of mere recreation or amusement, and is clearly beneficial to the premises to which it is attached [...] the right in suit is, in point of utility, fairly analogous to a right of way passing over fields to, say, the railway station, which would be none the less a good right, even though it provided a longer route to the objective. We think, therefore, that the statement [...] must at least be confined to exclusion of rights to indulge in such recreations as [...] horse racing or perhaps playing games, and has no application to the facts of the present case.

It may well be that an aversion to rights of recreation and amusement are a reflection of social conditions of the time (Theobald was writing in 1929),[31] and that, where recreational rights are adequately defined, they now may be accepted as easements.

Gray and Gray, *Elements of Land Law* (5th edn, 2009, [5.1.39])

The judicial animus against recreational easements has undoubtedly receded in recent times. It may be an index of a more hedonistic (or even more health conscious) age that it no longer seems inappropriate to acknowledge the easement character of certain recreational facilities annexed to dominant land. This is particularly the case where the claim of easement refers to a defined area over which a right of recreational enjoyment has been given not to the public but to a limited number of lot holders.

---

[28] (1865) 3 H & C 486.
[29] (1852) 1 Macq 305.
[30] (1813) 2 Dow 40.
[31] Theobald, *The Law of Land* (2nd edn, 1929, p 263).

2.4 THE RIGHT MUST BE CAPABLE OF BEING THE SUBJECT MATTER OF A GRANT

Cheshire's fourth condition has been described as '*both obscure and unhelpful*'.[32] At one level, the condition is deceptively simple: as a legal interest in land, an easement must be capable of being granted by deed. There must be a grantor and grantee, who have the necessary capacity and who enjoy the necessary title to create the easement in question. If the grantor does not hold the appropriate title, the easement can only operate to estop the grantor denying the right as against the grantee.

In fact, the condition hides '*an inept shorthand*'[33] for a number of criteria, the common features of which operate to circumscribe the effect upon the servient land of those rights that qualify as easements. We will examine these criteria under four headings:[34]

1. the requirement for certainty in the scope of the grant;

2. the requirement that the right places no positive burden on the servient owner;

3. the limitations on new easements;

4. the 'ouster' principle, which prohibits rights that amount to a claim to exclusive or joint ownership.

2.4.1 Certainty in the scope of the grant

Certainty is a constant refrain of the law when defining parties' rights and obligations. It must be clear what the dominant owner is entitled to do, and what is the nature and extent of the burden to which the servient owner must submit. The call for certainty is particularly insistent when rights are proprietary and thus capable of binding third parties. In the case of easements, certainty can be elusive when there are a wide variety of rights that can operate over another's land. There is thus a '*heightened emphasis on rigorous definitional clarity*'.[35]

There is no right to an uninterrupted right to light or air; such a right can only operate through a defined channel.[36] Nor is there a right to a view,[37] or to uninterrupted television reception.[38] In *Re Ellenborough Park*, the Court of Appeal drew a distinction between the certainty of a right to use a communal garden attached to dominant residential land, and the uncertainty of a right to wander at will over a large and ill-defined area.[39]

---

[32] McClean, 'The Nature of an Easement' (1966) 5 West LR 32, 61. The Court of Appeal in *Re Ellenborough Park* [1956] Ch 131, 164, described the fourth condition as 'not entirely clear'.

[33] Gardner, *An Introduction to Land Law* (2007, p 154).

[34] In *Re Ellenborough Park* [1956] Ch 131, 164, the Court of Appeal identified three criteria—prohibitions against: (i) vague and uncertain right; (ii) rights that are claims to joint user; and (iii) rights of mere recreation and amusement. We have examined (iii) in the context of Cheshire's second requirement of accommodation. Criteria (i) and (ii) relate to our criteria (1) and (4); our criteria (2) and (3) did not arise in the context of the case.

[35] Gray and Gray, *Elements of Land Law* (5th edn, 2009, [5.1.41]). See also the discussion of what can count as a property right in Chapter 3, section 5.

[36] *Harris v De Pinna* (1886) 33 Ch D 238, 250.

[37] Ibid, at 262.

[38] *Hunter v Canary Wharf* [1997] AC 655, 699.

[39] The Court of Appeal spent much time reconciling the comments of Farwell J, a very well-respected judge, that a right to wander at will was a right unknown to English law: see *International Tea Stores Co v Hobbs* [1903] 2 Ch 165; *AG v Antrobus* [1905] 2 Ch 188. It did so by distinguishing both cases: the comment in *Hobbs* was obiter, and *Antrobus* concerned a claim to public rights of access to Stonehenge. The Court preferred the

Re Ellenborough Park [1956] Ch 131, CA

Lord Evershed

At 176

To the first of these questions the interpretation which we have given to the typical deed provides, in our judgment, the answer; for we have construed the right conferred as being both well defined and commonly understood. In these essential respects the right may be said to be distinct from the indefinite and unregulated privilege which, we think, would ordinarily be understood by the Latin term "jus spatiandi," a privilege of wandering at will over all and every part of another's field or park, and which, though easily intelligible as the subject-matter of a personal licence, is something substantially different from the subject-matter of the grant in question, namely, the provision for a limited number of houses in a uniform crescent of one single large but private garden [...]

At 179

As appears from what has been stated earlier, the right to the full enjoyment of Ellenborough Park, which was granted by the 1864 and other relevant conveyances, was, in substance, no more that a right to use the park as a garden in the way in which gardens are commonly used. In a sense, no doubt, such a right includes something of a jus spatiandi, inasmuch as it involves the principle of wandering at will round each part of the garden, except of course, such parts as comprise flower beds, or are laid out for some other purpose, which renders walking impossible or unsuitable. We doubt, nevertheless, whether the right to use and enjoy a garden in this manner can with accuracy be said to constitute a mere jus spatiandi. Wandering at large is of the essence of such a right and constitutes the main purpose for which it exists. A private garden, on the other hand, is an attribute of the ordinary enjoyment of the residence to which it is attached, and the right of wandering in it is but one method of enjoying it.

2.4.2 No positive burden on the servient owner

An easement does not require the servient owner to do anything: he or she merely has to allow the dominant owner to exercise his or her easement without interference. Furthermore, he or she is not required to keep the subject matter of the easement in repair so that the dominant owner can exercise his or her right. Thus, if the easement is a right of way or drainage, the servient owner is not required to keep the road or drains in good repair.[40] For the same reason, a right to the passage of water through pipes running through the servient land does not require a continuous supply of water; the right imposes only a negative obligation not to interrupt any supply that there is.[41]

There is one exception to this rule: namely, a prescriptive right to require a neighbour to maintain a boundary fence. The right stems from the ancient and anomalous obligation to maintain stock-proof fences to keep out a neighbour's cattle, a breach of which is a defence to cattle trespass.[42]

---

decision in *Duncan v Louch* (1845) 6 QB 904, in which a right to pass and repass over a walk to the Thames, which was attached to a nearby house, was held to be an easement.

[40] *Duke of Westminster v Guild* [1985] QB 688.

[41] *Schwann v Cotton* [1916] 2 Ch 459; *Rance v Elvin* (1985) 50 P & CR 9; *Duffy v Lamb* (1998) 75 P & CR 364 (re electricity supply).

[42] *Jones v Price* [1965] 2 QB 618.

An obligation to repair may, however, arise as a result of some other source of liability. For example, an obligation to repair may arise by contract, whether as a result of an express or implied term.[43] Although a positive obligation to repair will not usually be enforceable against third parties, it may be enforceable in certain circumstances, which we will explore in the next chapter. Liability to repair may also arise in tort, whether under the torts of negligence or nuisance,[44] or as a result of obligations imposed upon occupiers by the Occupiers Liability Act 1984.

2.4.3 Limitations on new easements

It is said that the class of easements is never closed,[45] because developments in lifestyle call for the recognition of new forms of easement.[46] Nevertheless, the courts are cautious in recognizing unusual new forms of easement. There is a particular reluctance to accept new negative easements, as Lord Denning MR explained in the following extract. He also pointed out that the same protection may be achieved by taking a restrictive covenant from the servient owner.[47]

Phipps v Pears [1965] 1 QB 76, CA

Facts: There were two adjoining detached houses. The wall of the most recently constructed house was very close to the adjoining house and it had not been rendered to make it weatherproof. The other house was demolished, leaving the wall of the remaining house exposed to the weather. Because this wall was not weatherproof, cracks appeared. The owner unsuccessfully claimed a right to protection from the weather against the owner of the house that had been demolished.[48]

Lord Denning MR

At 82

But a right to protection from the weather (if it exists) is entirely negative. It is a right to stop your neighbour pulling down his own house. Seeing that it is a negative easement, it must be looked at with caution. Because the law has been very chary of creating any new negative easements.

   The reason underlying these instances is that if such an easement were to be permitted, it would unduly restrict your neighbour in his enjoyment of his own land. It would hamper legitimate development, see *Dalton v. Angus* (1881) 6 App Cas 740 at 824 *per* Lord Blackburn. Likewise here, if we were to stop a man pulling down his house, we would put a brake on

---

[43] See *Liverpool City Council v Irwin* [1977] AC 239.

[44] See *Rees v Sherrett* [2001] EWCA Civ 760, in which a duty arose to take reasonable steps to weatherproof a wall after demolition of an adjoining wall; cf *Phipps v Pears* [1965] 1 QB 76.

[45] *Re Ellenborough Park* [1956] Ch 131, 140, *per* Dankwerts J.

[46] See, e.g., Lord St Leonards' observations in *Dyce v Lady James Hay* (1852) 1 Macq 305, 312, that '*the category of servitudes must alter and expand with changes that take place in the circumstances of mankind*'.

[47] See Chapter 27. Dawson and Dunn advocate the formulation of a single means of creating negative property rights: see Dawson and Dunn, 'Negative Easements: A Crumb of Analysis' (1998) 18 LS 510.

[48] Following *Rees v Skerrett* [2001] 1 WLR 1541, he might have claimed a tortuous remedy requiring the owner to take reasonable steps to protect a neighbour's wall from foreseeable damage occasioned by the withdrawal of support or protection.

desirable improvement. Every man is entitled to pull down his house if he likes. If it exposes your house to the weather, that is your misfortune. It is no wrong on his part [...] There is no such easement known to the law as an easement to be protected from the weather. The only way for an owner to protect himself is by getting a covenant from his neighbour that he will not pull down his house or cut down his trees. Such a covenant would be binding on him in contract: and it would be enforceable on any successor who took with notice of it. But it would not be binding on one who took without notice.

2.4.4 The 'ouster' principle

An easement is a right to use the land of another for some limited purpose. It thus falls short of a claim to exclusive or joint possession or occupation. The Law Commission explains this important distinction between easements and possessory rights.

Law Commission Consultation Paper No 186, *Easements, Covenants and Profits à Prendre* (2008, [3.34])

It is important to distinguish lesser interests in land, like easements, from rights in land that are possessory in nature such as leasehold and freehold estates in land. This follows from the nature of an easement, as a right that one landowner has over the land of another, whilst the dominant owner exercises rights over the servient land, the servient land continues to belong to the servient owner. It is implicit in this definition that if the dominant owner is entitled to treat the servient land as his property—that is, as if he has a possessory estate in that land—his right cannot be an easement. In our view, easements and possessory interests in land must be mutually exclusive.

The ouster principle is exemplified by the following case.

Copeland v Greenhalf [1952] Ch 488, HC

Facts: A repairer of vehicles unsuccessfully claimed an easement by prescription (long user) over a strip of land belonging to Greenhalf. He had been using the strip of land for fifty years, as a place on which to store his customers' vehicles whilst awaiting repair or collection.

Upjohn J

At 498

I think that the right claimed goes wholly outside any normal idea of an easement, that is, the right of the owner or the occupier of a dominant tenement over a servient tenement. This claim (to which no closely related authority has been referred to me) really amounts to a claim to a joint user of the land by the defendant. Practically, the defendant is claiming the whole beneficial user of the strip of land on the south-east side of the track there; he can leave as many or as few lorries there as he likes for as long as he likes; he may enter on it by himself, his servants and agents to do repair work thereon. In my judgment, that is not a claim which can be established as an easement. It is virtually a claim to possession of the servient tenement, if necessary to the exclusion of the owner; or, at any rate, to a joint user, and no authority has been cited to me which would justify the conclusion that a right of this wide and undefined nature can be the proper subject-matter of an easement. It seems to me that to succeed, this claim must amount to a successful claim of possession by reason of long adverse possession. I say nothing, of course, as to the creation of such rights by deeds or by covenant; I am dealing solely with the question of a right arising by prescription.

It is to be noted that Upjohn J suggested that a claim to ownership by adverse possession might have been successful. Alternatively, if the Copeland had been granted permission to use the land, he may have claimed a lease or an occupational licence. Upjohn J also suggested that the different considerations may apply if the parties had been able to demonstrate their intentions by an express grant, rather than where an easement is claimed by prescription—but this distinction has been doubted.[49]

Difficulties arise in clearly defining the scope of the ouster principle. To some extent, all easements oust the servient owner from some use of the servient land: for example, the grant of a right of way will prevent the servient owner from building on the road so as to obstruct free passage. In *Miller v Emcer Products*,[50] the Court of Appeal saw no objection to the grant of a right to use a lavatory, although the servient owner would be excluded from the lavatory whilst the dominant owner was using it. In *Re Ellenborough Park*,[51] the Court of Appeal was also not impressed by the suggestion that use of a communal garden was effectively a claim to joint ownership because it excluded the servient owner from any use of the garden.

The uncertainty over the scope of the ouster principle has centred in recent years over rights of storage and car parking. In principle, rights of storage were accepted in *AG for Southern Nigeria v John Holt & Co (Liverpool) Ltd*[52] and in *Wright v Macadam*,[53] and the right to park cars has been accepted in principle in a number of cases—most recently, by the House of Lords in *Moncrieff v Jamieson*.[54]

The test has been said to be one of degree.[55]

---

[49] Hill-Smith, 'Rights of Parking and the Ouster Principle After *Batchelor v Marlow*' [2007] Conv 223, 232. See also *Moncrieff v Jamieson* [2007] UKHL 42, 59, *per* Lord Scott.

[50] [1956] Ch 304, 316.

[51] [1958] Ch 131, 176.

[52] [1915] AC 599 (right to store materials and trade goods and produce).

[53] [1949] 2 KB 744 (right to store coal).

[54] [2007] UKHL 42, [2007] 1 WLR 2620. See also *London and Blenheim Estates Ltd v Ladbroke Retail Parks Ltd* [1992] 1 WLR 1278, HC; [1994] 1 WLR 31, CA; *Hair v Gillman* (2000) 80 P & CR 108; *Bachelor v Marlow* [2001] EWCA Civ 1051, [2003] 1 WLR 764; *Central Midlands Estates Ltd v Leicester Dyers Ltd* [2003] 2 P & CR D1; *Saeed v Plustrade Ltd* [2001] EWCA Civ 2011, [2002] 2 P & CR 19; *Montrose Court Holdings Ltd v Shamash* [2006] All ER D 272. The right to moor boats has also been accepted as an easement: see *P&S Platt Ltd v Crouch* [2003] EWCA Civ 1110, [2004] 1 P & CR 18.

[55] See also *Grigsby v Melville* [1972] 1 WLR 1355, 1364, *per* Brightman J.

London & Blenheim Estates Ltd v Ladbroke Retail Parks Ltd [1992] 1 WLR 1278, HC

Judge Paul Baker QC

At 1288

The essential question is one of degree. If the right granted in relation to the area over which it is to be exercisable is such that it would leave the servient owner without any reasonable use of his land whether for parking or anything else, it could not be an easement, though it might be some larger or differing grant.

Thus it is suggested that, if the area of storage or car parking is relatively small when compared with the area of the servient land, the ouster principle does not apply, because the servient owner is still able to make 'reasonable use' of the servient land. This test was applied in *Batchelor v Marlow*[56] to reject a right to park where an exclusive right to park was claimed on weekdays between the hours of 9.30 a.m. and 6.00 p.m. But the House of Lord has cast doubt on this approach in dicta in the Scottish case of *Moncrieff v Jamieson*.[57] Lord Scott suggested that the test should be refocused to consider whether or not the servient owner retains possession and control over that part of the servient land over which the right to park is exercised.[58]

Moncrieff v Jamieson [2007] 1 WLR 2620, HL

Lord Scott

At [57]

It has often been commented that *Wright v Macadam* was not cited to Upjohn J and the possible inconsistency between the two cases was addressed by Judge Paul Baker QC in *London & Blenheim Estates Ltd v Ladbroke Retail Parks Ltd* where a right of parking had been claimed. He commented, at p 1286, that the question whether the right to park that had been claimed was consistent with the nature of an easement was one of degree: "A small coal shed in a large property is one thing. The exclusive use of a large part of the alleged servient tenement is another." I think, with respect, that this attempt to reconcile the two authorities was addressing the wrong point. The servient land in relation to a servitude or easement is surely the land over which the servitude or easement is enjoyed, not the totality of the surrounding land of which the servient owner happens to be the owner. If there is an easement of way over a 100-yard roadway on a 1,000-acre estate, or an easement to use for storage a small shed on the estate access to which is gained via the 100-yard roadway, it would be fairly meaningless in relation to either easement to speak of the whole estate as the servient land. Would the right of way and the storage right fail to qualify as easements if the whole estate bar the actual land over which the roadway ran and on which the shed stood, with or without a narrow surrounding strip, were sold? How could it be open to the servient owner to destroy easements by such a stratagem? In my opinion such a stratagem would fail. It would fail because the servient land was never the whole estate but was the land over which the

---

[56] [2001] EWCA Civ 1051, [2003] 1 WLR 764.

[57] The case is thus not binding precedent, although the House of Lords noted that, in this respect, there was no divergence in Scottish and English law.

[58] He was influenced by arguments made by Hill-Smith [2007] Conv 223.

roadway ran and on which the shed stood. Provided the servient land was land of which the servient owner was in possession, the rights of way and of storage would continue, in my opinion, to qualify as easements [...]

At [59]

In my respectful opinion the test formulated in the *London & Blenheim Estates case* and applied by the Court of Appeal in *Batchelor v Marlow* [2003] 1 WLR 764, a test that would reject the claim to an easement if its exercise would leave the servient owner with no "reasonable use" to which he could put the servient land, needs some qualification. It is impossible to assert that there would be no use that could be made by an owner of land over which he had granted parking rights. He could, for example, build above or under the parking area. He could place advertising hoardings on the walls. Other possible uses can be conjured up. And by what yardstick is it to be decided whether the residual uses of the servient land available to its owner are "reasonable" or sufficient to save his ownership from being "illusory"? It is not the uncertainty of the test that, in my opinion, is the main problem. It is the test itself. I do not see why a landowner should not grant rights of a servitudal character over his land to any extent that he wishes. The claim in *Batchelor v Marlow* for an easement to park cars was a prescriptive claim based on over 20 years of that use of the strip of land. There is no difference between the characteristics of an easement that can be acquired by grant and the characteristics of an easement that can be acquired by prescription. If an easement can be created by grant it can be acquired by prescription and I can think of no reason why, if an area of land can accommodate nine cars, the owner of the land should not grant an easement to park nine cars on the land. The servient owner would remain the owner of the land and in possession and control of it. The dominant owner would have the right to station up to nine cars there and, of course, to have access to his nine cars. How could it be said that the law would recognise an easement allowing the dominant owner to park five cars or six or seven or eight but not nine? I would, for my part, reject the test that asks whether the servient owner is left with any reasonable use of his land, and substitute for it a test which asks whether the servient owner retains possession and, subject to the reasonable exercise of the right in question, control of the servient land.

Lord Neuberger was rather more reserved in accepting this different test.

Moncrieff v Jamieson [2007] 1 WLR 2620, HL

Lord Neuberger

At [143]–[144]

I see considerable force in the views expressed by Lord Scott in paras 57 and 59 of his opinion, to the effect that a right can be an easement notwithstanding that the dominant owner effectively enjoys exclusive occupation, on the basis that the essential requirement is that the servient owner retains possession and control. If that were the right test, then it seems likely that *Batchelor v Marlow* was wrongly decided. However, unless it is necessary to decide the point to dispose of this appeal, I consider that it would be dangerous to try and identify what degree of ouster is required to disqualify a right from constituting a servitude or easement, given the very limited argument your Lordships have received on the topic.

As I have mentioned, there are a number of cases which can be said to support the approach of the Court of Appeal in *Batchelor v Marlow*, although it may be possible to distinguish them. The point does not appear to be settled in Australia: see the difference of opinion in the recent case *White v Betalli* [2007] NSWCA 243. I am also concerned that, if we were unconditionally to suggest that exclusion of the servient owner from occupation, as opposed to possession, would not of itself be enough to prevent a right from being an easement, it might lead to unexpected consequences or difficulties which have not been explored in argument in this case. Thus, if the right to park a vehicle in a one-vehicle space can be an easement, it may be hard to justify an effectively exclusive right to store any material not being an easement, which could be said to lead to the logical conclusion that an occupational licence should constitute an interest in land.

Luther has argued that what matters is '*what the claimant could do by virtue of his easement not what the owner could not do*'.[59] He draws a distinction between two types of case: the first, in which the claimant is, in effect, claiming to be the owner, and thus the issue is the grant of a possessory right and not an easement; the second covers more limited uses, in which the defining test is one of certainty.

Luther, 'Easements and Exclusive Possession' (1996) 16 LS 51, 61

At this extreme level, where a claimant is in effect acting as owner, it does not matter whether the principle is expressed in terms which focus on the claimant (either by referring to the certainty of his rights, as in *Copeland v Greenhalf*, or to his state of mind when exercising them, as in the *Southern Nigeria* case) or on the person against whom the right is claimed (as in *Re Ellenborough Park* and many later cases). The result will be the same in all cases: if a grant is involved, the claimant will be the owner (*Reilley v Booth*), if prescription is involved, his claim for an easement will fail, but he may have satisfied the criteria for a claim of adverse possession, and so become the owner. This then is the first category. The second category is a residual category, covering claims which fall short of exclusive possession properly speaking—either because they are not 'exclusive', in the sense that they do not absolutely exclude the owner, or because they are not 'possession', in that they do not involve a claim to perform an unlimited range of activities. Upjohn J appears to have considered, in accordance with authority, that the appropriate criterion to apply to this second category was that of certainty: so a claim for joint user (possession, because the activities were unlimited, but not to the exclusion of the owner) would fail because it was not sufficiently certain.

Luther accepts that focusing either on the dominant or servient owner is rather like looking at different sides of the same coin, but he suggests that it is more straightforward to look at the issue from the point of the view of the claimant—that is, the potential dominant owner.

Luther, 'Easements and Exclusive Possession' (1996) 16 LS 51, 62

Surely to ask 'What the claimant can do?' (the certainty approach) is the same as to ask 'What can the servient owner *not* do? (the exclusion/substantial interference approach)? There is

---

[59] Luther, 'Easements and Exclusive Possession' (1996) 16 LS 51, 59

some substance in this argument, and certainly it is possible to imagine cases where it would be difficult to answer one question without answering the other. A line would have to be drawn in difficult cases. But against this it must be said that to look at the positive character-istics of a claimed right must in many cases be easier than to assess its negative impact on someone else's rights. This latter enquiry must involve a large number of external factors, not least as noted above the total size of the servient tenement, the characteristics of the owner and the uses to which he might wish to put his land. It might also involve uncertainty in the definition of rights.

The Law Commission is persuaded by Luther's approach, which it believes offers a solution to the dilemma presented by the car park cases.[60]

3 THE *ACQUISITION* QUESTION

We have already noted that easements lie in grant and there are three mechanisms by which that grant may arise: (i) by express grant; (ii) by implied grant; and (iii) by presumed grant as result of long user. Rights in the nature of easements may also arise by statute: for example, the Access to Neighbouring Land Act 1992 and the Party Walls Act 1996 both grant an owner a right to go onto neighbouring land in order to carry out certain repairs and building work.[61]

3.1 EXPRESS GRANT

Easements may be created by the methods examined in Chapter 9. A legal easement must be created by deed and, where a legal easement is created after 13 October 2003, that deed must be registered where the land is registered,[62] with the benefit of the easement being recorded in the property register of the dominant land and the burden of the easement being noted in the charges register of the servient land.[63] A legal easement created by deed before that date may, but need not, be registered. An equitable easement may be created in writing, by agreement, or by estoppel.[64]

3.2 IMPLIED GRANT

An easement may be acquired by implied grant usually when land is subdivided into two or more parts, whether by sale or lease. There are four ways in which a grant may be implied:

- easements of necessity;

---

60 Law Commission Consultation Paper No 186 (2008, [3.49]–[3.52]).

61 See Gratton, 'Proprietarian Conceptions of Statutory Access Rights' in *Modern Studies in Property Law: Vol 2* (ed Cook, 2003, ch 18).

62 Land Registration Act 2002, s 27.

63 Where the servient land is unregistered, the dominant owner may enter a caution against first registra-tion of the servient land to ensure that the relevant notice will be entered when the servient land is registered: see ibid, ss 15–21.

64 For an example of an easement by estoppel, see *Crabb v Arun District Council* [1976] Ch 179, discussed in Chapter 13.

- intended easements;
- the rule in *Wheeldon v Burrows*;[65] and
- by the operation of s 62 of the Law of Property Act 1925 (LPA 1925).

The Law Commission has described these four methods as providing a *'complex matrix of overlapping rules'*,[66] which *'have developed in piecemeal and uncoordinated fashion'*,[67] and it has advocated that the rules be rationalized and codified in statutory form.[68]

The underlying rationale for the first three of these rules lies in the principle that a seller or landlord should not be allowed to derogate from his or her grant: *'A grantor having given a thing with one hand, is not to take away the means of enjoying it with the other.'*[69] Thus a landowner who has disposed of part of his or her land for a particular purpose cannot use his or her retained land in such a way as to make the disposed portion unfit for its particular purpose.

The principle of non-derogation from grant is general in its application and may itself form the basis for an implied easement.[70] Hopkins explains the influence of non-derogation from grant upon the implied grant of easements.

Hopkins, *The Informal Acquisition of Rights in Land* (2000, p 205)

The rule of non-derogation from grant is seen as the basis for three specific rules enabling the acquisition of an easement [...] The general rule itself may give rise to the acquisition of easements. Therefore the question arises to what extent there is an overlap between the general and specific rules. It seems that there are three characteristics that separate the specific rules. First, each specific rule has its own requirements which are distinct, in some respects, from the general rule. Secondly, in each case the right claimed must fulfil the general characteristics of an easement. The specific rules are not the source of proprietary rights *sui generis*. In these respects the specific rules are more restrictive in their application than the general rule. However, thirdly it seems that the specific rules alone can create positive easements. The general rule may be limited to enabling the creation of negative easements. In addition to the three rules derived from non-derogation from grant, there is a fourth, related, rule enabling the acquisition of a legal easement by words implied into a conveyance by statute.

Even though the rationale for implied grant stems from the principle of non-derogation from grant, the basis for the rules is confused. They are said to be based upon the presumed intention of the parties and may indeed be excluded by a contrary intention, but in the background lurks the public policy of maximizing the effective use of land. Easements

---

65 (1878) 12 Ch D 31.

66 Law Commission Consultation Paper No 186 (2008, [4.109]).

67 Ibid, at [4.99].

68 Ibid, at [4.142]–[4.145]. For the comparative treatment of easements by implied grant in Australia, England, and Scotland, see Burns, 'Easements and Servitudes Created by Implied Grant, Implied Reservation or Prescription and Title-by-Registration Systems' in *Modern Studies in Property Law: Vol 5* (ed Dixon, 2009).

69 *Birmingham, Dudley and District Banking Co v Ross* (1887) 38 Ch D 295, 312, *per* Bowen LJ.

70 See *Cable v Bryant* [1908] 1 Ch 259. The Law Commission has suggested that the general principle of non-derogation from grant should not provide an independent ground for an implied grant: see Law Commission Consultation Paper No 186 (2008, [4.91]–[4.94], [4.105]).

of necessity, in particular, reveal this confused interaction. The Law Commission has suggested that utility might become the overt basis for implication, by replacing the four rules with a single rule based upon what is necessary for the reasonable use of the land.[71]

Before we examine each of these methods, we must consider two contrasting situations. Firstly, we will consider that in which the dominant land is sold or let and the new dominant owner or tenant claims an easement over the servient land retained by the seller or land-lord. If an easement is implied, it will be by means of an implied grant. This is illustrated in Figure 22.

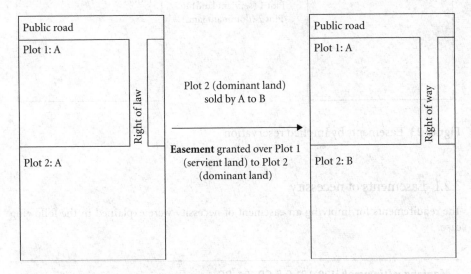

Figure 22 Easement by implied grant

Secondly, we will consider that in which the servient land is sold or let and the seller or landlord claims an easement over the servient land for the benefit of the dominant land that he or she retains. If an easement is implied, it will be by means of an implied reservation. This is illustrated in Figure 23.

The law is more reluctant to imply a reservation than the grant of an easement. The seller or landlord is expected to take steps to protect the use of his or her retained dominant land. The possibility of an implied reservation only arises where easements are implied on the basis of necessity or intended use. Here, the implication looks to the future use of the land. The implied grant of an easement also may arise in these circumstances and, in addition, under the rule in *Wheeldon v Burrows* or s 62 of the LPA 1925, where the implied grant looks to the past use of the land.

---

[71] Ibid, at [4.132]–[4.141], [4.149(3)]). See also the statutory schemes for the implications of easements in Australia canvassed in Burns (2009). The Law Commission also raises the possibility of rules based upon either the parties' actual intentions or upon a set of evidential presumptions, which would closely mirror the current law: see ibid, [4.108]–[4.131], [4.149(2)].

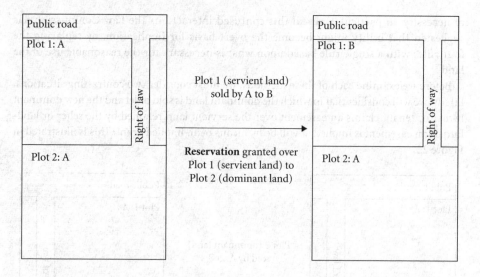

Figure 23 Easements by implied reservation

3.2.1 Easements of necessity

The requirements for implying an easement of necessity were explained in the following case.

Manjang v Drammeh (1991) 61 P & CR 194, PC

Lord Oliver

At 197

There has to be found, first, a common owner of a legal estate in two plots of land. It has, secondly, to be established that access between one of those plots and the public highway can be obtained only over the other plot. Thirdly, there has to be found a disposition of one of the plots without any specific grant or reservation of a right of access. Given these conditions, it may be possible as a matter of construction of the relevant grant [...] to imply the reservation of an easement of necessity.

Easements of necessity are confined to situations in which land becomes landlocked when a common owner sells (or leases) part of his or her land. In this situation, it is clear that the burden of the right of way does not fall upon some third party, whose land happens to provide the required access.[72]

An easement of necessity will only be implied where the land cannot otherwise be used at all. A high degree of necessity is thus required, which is likely only to be found where a right

---

[72] Thus avoiding a claim that the third party's human rights had been infringed by an unjustified interference with his possessions under Art 1 of the First Protocol to the European Convention on Human Rights—a risk that might be avoided if the court were able to award compensation. See further Chapter 5.

of way is necessary to provide access.[73] Even then, a right will not arise where an alternative access is available, however inconvenient or impractical that access might be.[74] The scope of the right is limited to what is essential to the use of the dominant land[75] at the date of its disposal.[76] It is unclear whether an easement of necessity will cease should the right subsequently become unnecessary.[77]

The basis of easements of necessity lies in intention and not public policy.[78]

Nickerson v Barraclough [1981] Ch 426, CA

Brightman LJ

At 440

In this court we have heard a great deal of argument about ways of necessity—what is their basis, how they can be acquired and whether they can be lost. With the utmost respect to the Vice-Chancellor, I have come to the conclusion that the doctrine of way of necessity is not founded upon public policy at all but upon an implication from the circumstances. I accept that there are reported cases, and textbooks, in which public policy is suggested as a possible foundation of the doctrine, but such a suggestion is not, in my opinion, correct. It is well established that a way of necessity is never found to exist except in association with a grant of land: see *Proctor v. Hodgson* (1855) 10 Exch. 824, where it was held that land acquired by escheat got no way of necessity; and *Wilkes v. Greenway* (1890) 6 T.L.R. 449, where land acquired by prescription got no way of necessity. If a way of necessity were based upon public policy, I see no reason why land acquired by escheat or by prescription should be excluded. Furthermore, there would seem to be no particular reason to father the doctrine of way of necessity upon public policy when implication is such an obvious and convenient candidate for paternity. There is an Australian case, *North Sydney Printing Pty. Ltd. v. Sabemo Investment Corporation Pty. Ltd.* [1971] 2 N.S.W.L.R. 150, where that conclusion was reached. Furthermore, I cannot accept that public policy can play any part at all in the construction of an instrument; in construing a document the court is endeavouring to ascertain the expressed intention of the parties. Public policy may require the court to frustrate that intention where the contract is against public policy, but in my view public policy cannot help the court to ascertain what that intention was. So I reach the view that a way of necessity is not founded upon public policy; that considerations of public policy cannot influence the construction of the 1906 conveyance; and that this action is not concerned with a way of necessity strictly so called.

This view has limited the scope of easements of necessity in a number of respects. Most obviously, an easement of necessity will give way to a contrary intention, but the

---

73 An essential right of support might be another candidate.

74 *Union Lighterage Co v London Graving Dock Co* [1902] 2 Ch 577; *Manjang v Drammeh* (1990) 61 P & CR 194; *Titchmarsh v Royston Water Co Ltd* (1899) 81 LT 673.

75 For example, vehicular access will not be necessary where pedestrian access is adequate: see *MRA Engineering Ltd v Trimster* (1988) 50 P & CR 1.

76 *Corporation of London v Riggs* (1880) 13 Ch D 798.

77 See the conflicting authority in *Holmes v Goring* (1824) 2 Bing 76; *Donaldson v Smith* [2006] All ER (D) 293; *Proctor v Hodgson* (1855) 10 Exch 824; *Barkshire v Grubb* (1881) 18 Ch D 816; *Huckvale v Aegean Hotels Ltd* (1989) 58 P & CR 163.

78 These comments are dicta, but have been subsequently approved by the Court of Appeal in *Adealon International Corp Pty Ltd v Merton LBC* [2007] EWCA Civ 362, [2007] 1 WLR 1898.

intention-based nature of the rule has other consequences. For example, easements of necessity will not arise where land has been acquired by adverse possession or compulsory purchase where there is no agreement from which to derive any intention. The need for common ownership of the dominant and servient land, and the static assessment of necessity at the date of severance of the land, also flow from the constraints of intention.

Several commentators have argued that public policy is a more attractive foundation for easements of necessity. They argue that any intention of the parties is purely fictional,[79] and suggest that the rational development of the doctrine has been compromised by the focus upon intention rather than utility.[80]

Bradbrook, 'Access to Landlocked Land: A Comparative Study of Legal Solutions' (1983–85) 10 Syd LR 39

At 46

[T]he development of easements of necessity has proceeded on an ad hoc basis rather than as a result of a co-ordinated response to a social problem, and the courts have shown themselves to be more interested in maintaining the conceptual purity of the law of implied grants than in devising an effective means of resolving a practical problem.

At 56

[A] guaranteed access to landlocked land could most easily be achieved in common law jurisdictions if the courts were to recognise public policy as the basis of the easement of necessity. This change would remove the limitations on the scope of easements [...] for example, if it were based upon public policy rather than intention of the parties it would not be restricted to cases where the landlocking arose on a subdivision, and in appropriate cases could be granted through private land belonging to third parties. While this change would run contrary to the recent Court of Appeal decision in *Nickerson v Barraclough*, it would not be revolutionary as the earliest reported cases on the easement of necessity appear to have accepted public policy rather than intention as the basis of the easements [...] The change to the present basis of intention did not occur until the nineteenth century and appears to have been due to the jurist tendency by the courts at that time to treat all legal transactions as if they were based on contracts.

3.2.2 Intended easements

The circumstances when an easement may be implied on the basis of intention were explained in the following case.

---

[79] Simonton, 'Ways by Necessity' (1925) 25 Col LR 571. 576 and 601; Jackson (1981) 34 CLP 133, 152; Bodkin (1973) 89 LQR 87.

[80] Bradbrook, 'Access to Landlocked Land: A Comparative Study of Legal Solutions' (1983–85) 10 Syd LR 39, 44–6; Davis, 'Informal Acquisition and Loss of Rights in Land: What Justifies the Doctrines?' (2000) 20 LS 198, 219; Lawson (2002, p 81).

Pwllbach Colliery Co Ltd v Woodman [1915] AC 634

Lord Parker

At 646

[...] the cases in which an easement can be granted by implication may be classified under two heads. The first is where the implication arises because the right in question is necessary for the enjoyment of some other right expressly granted. The principle is expressed in the legal maxim "Lex est cuicunque aliquis quid concedit concedere videtur et id sine quo res esse non potuit." Thus the right of drawing water from a spring necessarily involves the right of going to the spring for the purpose. The implication suggested in the present case does not fall under this principle; there is no express grant of any right to which the right claimed must be necessarily ancillary, [...] The second class of cases in which easements may impliedly be created depends not upon the terms of the grant itself, but upon the circumstances under which the grant was made. The law will readily imply the grant or reservation of such easements as may be necessary to give effect to the common intention of the parties to a grant of real property, with reference to the manner or purposes in and for which the land granted or some land retained by the grantor is to be used [...] But it is essential for this purpose that the parties should intend that the subject of the grant or the land retained by the grantor should be used in some definite and particular manner. It is not enough that the subject of the grant or the land retained should be intended to be used in a manner which may or may not involve this definite and particular use.

Lord Parker identifies two circumstances: the first, where the easement is necessary for the enjoyment of a right that is expressly granted; the second, where the easement is necessary to enable the dominant owner to use the land for the purpose for which it was sold or leased. An example of the first instance is given by Lord Parker in the above extract and an example of the second instance is found in *Wong v Beaumont Property Trust Ltd.*[81] Mr Wong leased the basement of a building to use as a Chinese restaurant. The lease provided that the basement should be used for this purpose, and, furthermore, that Mr Wong should control and eliminate all smells, comply with the required health regulations, and should not cause any nuisance to the landlord or adjoining occupiers. It became clear that the existing ventilation system was inadequate and a larger flue was required, but his landlords objected. An easement was implied to enable Mr Wong to comply with his obligations under the lease. In this second situation, it is clear that the implication does not arise because the parties necessarily intended that an easement be granted: it was clear in *Wong* that the parties had not anticipated the need for the larger flue, but they had made clear the intended use of the premise in the terms of the lease and it is from this intention that the right was implied.

Nourse LJ in the following case explains the process of proof being, firstly, to establish on a balance of probabilities the nature of the intended user, and secondly, to prove that the easement claimed is necessary to give effect to that use. In *Wong*, the parties had clearly expressed their intended use, but as the following case shows, the requisite intention may be established on a balance of probabilities.

---

[81] [1965] 1 QB 173. See also *Davies v Bramwell* [2007] EWCA Civ 821.

Stafford v Lee (1993) 63 P & CR 172, CA

Facts: In 1955, an area of woodland that fronted on a private drive was conveyed to Mrs Lee's predecessor in title, but no right of way was expressly granted over the drive. Mrs Lee wanted to build a house on the woodland, and claimed a pedestrian and vehicular right of way over the drive, on the basis that it was the intention of the parties to the 1955 conveyance that a house be built upon the woodland.

Nourse LJ

At 175

Intended easements, like all other implied easements, are subject to the general rule that they are implied more readily in favour of a grantee than a grantor. But even there, as Lord Parker points out, the parties must intend that the subject of the grant shall be used in some definite and particular manner. If the grantee can establish the requisite intention, the law will then imply the grant of such easements as may be necessary to give effect to it.

There are therefore two hurdles which the grantee must surmount. He must establish a common intention as to some definite and particular user. Then he must show that the easements he claims are necessary to give effect to it. Notwithstanding the submissions of Miss Baker, for the defendants, to the contrary, I think that the second hurdle is no great obstacle to the plaintiffs in this case. The real question is whether they can surmount the first.

It is axiomatic that in construing any conveyance you must take into account the facts in reference to which it was made. But here, no extrinsic evidence having been adduced on either side, we can refer only to the 1955 deed [. . .] The defendants admitted in their defence that the 1955 deed did pass to Mrs Walker a right to use Marley Drive and that that right had passed to the plaintiffs. But they have at all times contended that the right was limited to use for all purposes necessary for the reasonable enjoyment of the land as woodland, being the manner of its enjoyment in 1955. Such a right is manifestly inadequate for the plaintiffs' purposes.

The first point to be made about the defendants' contention is that, although it may sometimes come to the same thing, the material question in a case of an intended easement is not how was the land enjoyed in 1955, but did the parties to the 1955 deed intend that it should be used in some definite and particular manner and, if so, what? [. . .] The requirement that the parties should have intended a definite and particular use for the land does not require that the intention be proved as a certainty. As always, it is enough that it is proved on the balance of probabilities. What help do we get from the 1955 deed in this regard? First, it is to be observed that Mrs. Walker's address, far from being in the neighbourhood, is stated to be in distant Sussex. Secondly, and far more significantly, there is the plan [. . .]

The significant, indeed the eye-catching, feature of the plan here is that it delineates, as the land conveyed, a plot adjoining and of comparable area to two other enclosures, each adjoining the other, which, from the legends they bear, are seen to be plots of land on which dwellings have already been constructed. In these circumstances and given, as the defendants accept, that some appurtenant right of way was intended over and along Marley Drive, what are the probabilities as to the intended use of the land? In my judgment, on the balance of probabilities, the parties can only have intended that it should be used for the construction of another dwelling to be used thereafter for residential purposes. I cannot see what other intention could reasonably be imputed to them. Having got to that point, I am satisfied that the easements claimed by the plaintiffs and declared in their favour by the judge are necessary, and are no more than are necessary, to give effect to the intention so established.

Lawson points out that there is a third situation in which an intended easement may be implied, which, although broadly based upon *Pwllbach,* is distinguishable from an easement of intended use.[82] This third category is derived from the following case, in which the Court indicated that a reservation[83] could be implied, based upon the parties' intention—although here it is the parties' intention as to creation of the right itself.

The case concerned an implied reservation, which, as Nourse LJ observed in the above extract, is less readily implied then an easement—the rationale being that the grantor should avoid the risk of derogating from his or her grant by taking care to expressly reserve any rights that he or she wishes to enjoy. Jenkins LJ explains in the case that although a reservation will not generally be implied, there are exceptions: we have already considered easements of necessity; another exception is intended easements.

Re Webb's Lease [1951] Ch 808, CA

Facts: Webb ran a butchers shop on the ground floor of a building that he leased in south London. He sublet the upper floors, on the external walls of which advertisements were displayed. For many years, the tenant of the upper floors raised no objection to these advertisements, but he then demanded payment for them to be retained.

Jenkins LJ

At 823

As to the law applicable to the case, it is not disputed that as a general rule a grantor, whether by conveyance or lease, of part of a hereditament in his ownership, cannot claim any easement over the part retained unless it is expressly reserved out of the grant [...] There are however, certain exceptions to the general rule. Two well-established exceptions relate to easements of necessity and mutual easements such as rights of support between adjacent buildings. But it is recognised in the authorities that these two specific exceptions do not exhaust the list which is indeed incapable of exhaustive statement, as the circumstances of any particular case may be such as to raise a necessary inference that the common intention of the parties must have been to reserve some easement to the grantor, or such as to preclude the grantee from denying the right consistently with good faith, and there appears to be no doubt that where circumstances such as these are clearly established the court will imply the appropriate reservation.

The question arises as to how the courts are to find this intention. In *Re Webb's Lease*, Jenkins LJ went on to state that the appropriate test was one of necessary inference, based upon proof by the landlord that the facts were not reasonably consistent with any other explanation—a test that Mr Webb failed to satisfy.[84] It was not sufficient that his tenant knew and had raised no objection to the advertisements.

---

[82] Lawson (2002, p 83).

[83] The case concerns a reservation, but there seems no reason why the grant of an easement should not also be implied under this third category, although there have been no such cases. Lawson (2002, p 85) explains that other grounds for the implication of the grant of an easement present more attractive options.

[84] The test was also not satisfied in *Chaffe v Kingsley* (2000) 79 P & CR 404, but the test was met in *Peckham v Ellison* (2000) 79 P & CR 276. The decision has been criticized: see Fox [1999] Conv 353.

Re Webb's Lease [1951] Ch 808, CA

Jenkins LJ

At 828

The question is whether the circumstances of the case as proved in evidence are such as to raise a necessary inference that the common intention of the parties was to reserve to the landlord during the twenty-one years' term some, and if so what, rights in regard to the display of advertisements over the outer walls of the demised premises, or such as to preclude the tenant from denying the implied reservation to the landlord of some such rights consistently with good faith.

That question must be approached with the following principles in mind: (i) If the landlord intended to reserve any such rights over the demised premises it was his duty to reserve them expressly in the lease of August 11, 1949 (*Wheeldon v. Burrows*); (ii) The landlord having failed in this duty, the onus was upon him to establish the facts to prove, and prove clearly, that his case was an exception to the rule (*Aldridge v. Wright*); (iii) The mere fact that the tenant knew at the date of the lease of August 11, 1949, that the landlord was using the outer walls of the demised premises for the display of the advertisements in question did not suffice to absolve the landlord from his duty of expressly reserving any rights in respect of them he intended to claim, or to take the case out of the general rule [...]

Does this circumstance suffice to raise a necessary inference of an intention common to both parties at the date of the lease that the landlord should have reserved to him the right to maintain these advertisements throughout the twenty-one years' term thereby granted? I cannot see that it does. The most that can be said is that the facts are consistent with such a common intention. But that will not do. The landlord must surely show at least that the facts are not reasonably consistent with any other explanation. Here he manifestly fails.

There is considerable uncertainty as to the interface between easements of necessity and of intention. They seem to overlap, but it is clear that intended easements may be applied to a wider range of rights than the rights of access to which easements of necessity are largely confined.

Lawson advocates realigning the categories, with easements of intended use ('*Pwllbach* easements') encompassing and taking over from easements of necessity, and intended easements being confined to those based upon the parties' intention to create such rights ('*Re Webb's Lease* easements').

Lawson, 'Easements' in *Land Law: Issues, Debates and Policy* (ed Tee, 2002, p 85)

[...] there is a great deal of uncertainty about the precise relationship between easements of necessity and *Pwllbach easements*. In *Nickerson v Barrowclough* Megarry V-C seemed to regard them as 'two distinct but overlapping' ways in which easements might be implied on the basis of necessity. Both require the right to be strictly necessary for the use of the land concerned. The distinction is that for easements of necessity the right must be necessary in order for the land to be used in any manner at all, whereas for intended easements the right must be necessary in order for the land to be used in the particular manner intended by the parties.

The distinction between easements of necessity and the *Pwllback* intended easements is frequently clouded by a judicial tendency to refer to both as easements of necessity. It may be that, in any event, it is a distinction without a difference. It is arguable that, as the courts are now prepared to imply a common intention to use the land in a specific way, they will be able to find such an intention whenever landlocked plot is conveyed—thus eclipsing the traditional easements of necessity. The precise limits of the situations in which the courts are prepared to find that there is an implied intention to use the land in a particular way have not yet been fully explored, however. It is suggested, for instance that a court will not be as inclined to find that a use was intended in the case of a reservation as it is in relation to a grant.

The view that the easement of necessity, at least in relation to implied grant, has been subsumed within the *Pwllbach* intended easement is very attractive. Both are driven by the policy that land should not become sterile but be used to its full potential. Though intention is relevant to both, neither requires proof that the parties actually intended the claimed easement. The *Pwllbach* easement could drop the misleading title of 'intended easements' and become a legitimate easement of necessity. The title 'intended easement' could, instead, be reserved for easements implied under *Re Webbs Lease*. These do not require the easement to be necessary for the land to be used and are therefore quite distinct.

3.2.3 The rule in *Wheeldon v Burrows*

The rule in *Wheeldon v Burrows* is stated by Thesiger LJ in the case of that name.

Wheeldon v Burrows (1879) 12 LR Ch D 31

Thesiger LJ

At 49

[...] on the grant by the owner of a tenement or part of that tenement as it is then used and enjoyed, there will pass to the grantee all those continuous and apparent easements (by which, of course, I mean quasi easements) or, in other words, all those easements which are necessary for the reasonable enjoyment of the property granted, and which have been and are at the time of the grant used by the owner of the entirety for the benefit of the part granted.

The rule thus applies on the sale or lease of part of property when certain qualifying rights, enjoyed for the benefit of the part sold or leased (the dominant land) over the part retained (the servient land), will mature into easements. Prior to the sale or lease, such rights could not exist as easements, because of the common ownership of the dominant and servient land; they are thus referred to as 'quasi-easements'.

The rule is based upon the intention of the parties that the grantor should not derogate from his or her grant and thus gives way to a contrary intention. The rule only applies to the grant of easements, or where the sales of the dominant and servient tenement are simultaneous.[85] It does not operate to imply a reservation; indeed, this was the point at issue in

---

85 *Schwann v Cotton* [1916] 2 Ch 120. See also *Donaldson v Smith* [2006] All ER (D) 293, [16], *per* Donaldson QC, measuring simultaneity in context to look not solely at chronological proximity, but also at the interconnection between the two transactions.

Wheeldon v Burrows,[86] and is referred to as the 'second rule in *Wheeldon v Burrows*', found later in Thesiger LJ's judgment.

Wheeldon v Burrows (1879) 12 LR Ch D 31

Thesiger LJ

At 58–59

These cases [. . .] support the propositions that in the case of a grant you may imply a grant of such continuous and apparent easements or such easements as are necessary to the reasonable enjoyment of the property conveyed, and have in fact been enjoyed during the unity of ownership, but that, with the exception which I referred to of easements of necessity, you cannot imply a similar reservation in favour of the grantor of land.

Only certain quasi-easements qualify to pass under the rule. They must be enjoyed at the time of the sale or lease, be 'continuous and apparent', and/or be reasonably necessary for the enjoyment of the property.

The first requirement is relatively straightforward. It imposes a timing constraint on the application of the rule that flows from the principle of non-derogation from grant.[87] It is the second and third requirements, and their interrelationship, that has led to the greatest uncertainty and debate.

The second requirement has its origins in the French Civil Code.[88] 'Continuous', in this context, does not mean that the right must be continuously exercised, but rather invokes the sense of permanence, so that the right might be exercised whenever necessary. 'Apparent' is the more significant part of the second requirement. Indeed, it has been suggested that '*continuousness is little more than a distraction*' and could be jettisoned.[89] For a right to be apparent, it should be discoverable from a reasonably careful physical inspection of the land. There must thus be some feature on the servient land—for example, a roadway or manhole cover—that signals the right to a purchaser.

Ward v Kirkland [1967] Ch 194, HC

Facts: The Wards' cottage adjoined Kirkland's farm, which, at one time, had been owned by a common owner. The cottage was built so close to the farm's boundary that the only practical way for its walls to be maintained was to go onto the farm. The Wards and their predecessor in title had done so for some time before Kirkland objected.

---

[86] Burrows was seeking a right to light from land owned by Mrs Wheeldon, after she had erected a hoarding that blocked the light to Burrows' workshop. Burrows and Mrs Wheeldon's husband had acquired their land from a common vendor, with Burrows purchasing his land after Mr Wheeldon, who subsequently died, leaving the land to his wife. Any rights that Burrows wished to claim over the Wheeldons' land would thus have needed to have been reserved by their common vendor—but there had been no express reservation and thus Burrows' claim failed.

[87] *Sovmots Investment Ltd v Secretary of State for the Environment* [1979] AC 144.

[88] Simpson, '*Wheeldon v Burrows* and the *Code Civile*' [1967] 83 LQR 240.

[89] Lawson (2002, p 88).

Ungoed-Thomas J

At 225

Here, there certainly has been continuous user, in the sense that the right has in fact been used whenever the need arose. But the words "continuous and apparent" seem to be directed to there being on the servient tenement a feature which would be seen on inspection and which is neither transitory nor intermittent; for example, drains, paths, as contrasted with the bowsprits of ships overhanging a piece of land.

Here it is conceded that it was only possible or practicable for the occupiers of the cottage to maintain the boundary wall by going onto the defendant's property as claimed in this case. That would be obvious on an inspection of the properties. But there was no feature on the defendant's property designed or appropriated for such maintenance.

The third requirement calls for the right to be necessary for the reasonable enjoyment of the land and flows directly from the principle that the grantor should not derogate from his or her grant. 'Necessity', in this context, is significantly wider than the test demanded of easements of necessity, although the degree of necessity is unclear.

Thompson bemoans this uncertainty and advocates a test that merely calls for the right to be capable of being an easement by accommodating the dominant land.

Thompson, 'Paths and Pigs' [1995] Conv 239, 240–1

What appears to be necessary is that, to acquire an easement under *Wheeldon v. Burrows*, the right in question must do more than merely accommodate the dominant tenement but need not be an absolute necessity. Rather, it hovers somewhere in between, at some ill-defined point between the two. The difference between what is essential for the land to be used and what is necessary for its reasonable use is not an easy one to draw and, in consequence, it may, in the future, prove difficult to predict when a quasi-easement will be transformed into a full easement under the rule.

[...]It would seem preferable that the second limb of *Wheeldon v. Burrows* should be interpreted to mean, in essence, that the right claimed accommodates the dominant tenement; the same requirement as exists when section 62 is in issue.

The uncertainty is illustrated by cases in which an alternative means of access is claimed to be reasonably necessary for the enjoyment of the land. An existing means of access will not be fatal to a claim under *Wheeldon v Burrows*, but it is evident that simply providing a more convenient access is unlikely to be enough:[90] the alternative access should offer some additional advantage.[91] The impact upon the servient tenement of the additional access should also be considered.[92]

---

[90] See, e.g., *Goldberg v Edwards* [1950] Ch 247 and *Wheeler v Saunders* [1996] Ch 19.

[91] See, e.g., *Borman v Griffith* [1930] 1 Ch 493, in which the alternative access was more suitable for the claimant's business as a poultry dealer, the other access being impassable to heavy vehicles at certain times of the year; *Millman v Ellis* (1995) 71 P & CR 158, 163, in which the right to use a lay-by to join a busy road was held to be reasonably necessary as *'a matter concerned with safety and possible injury to life and limb'*.

[92] Ferris, 'Problems Postponed:The Rule in *Wheeldon v Burrows* and *Wheeler v Saunders*' (1996) 3 Web JCLI.

A question that has dogged debate on *Wheeldon v Burrows* is whether the second and third requirements are synonymous, alternative, or cumulative. The authorities are not conclusive,[93] but the case for a cumulative interpretation has strong advocates.[94]

Gardner, *An Introduction to Land Law* (2007, p 167)

[...T]he rule in *Wheeldon v Burrows* [...] actually creates an easement, by imputing an intention to confer it. And the existence of a continuous and apparent quasi-easement alone is an inadequate basis on which to do this. The imputation is acceptable only when the additional utilitarian argument for it is sufficiently powerful. The fact that I visibly did something in the past may contribute to the making of such an argument, by giving a prima facie indication that the alleged easement would be useful. But to complete the argument, the easement must be positively needed: as the law has it, 'necessary for the reasonable enjoyment' of the land transferred. Perhaps for this reason, although the relevant case law is in disarray the majority of commentators agree that this third requirement is essential.

3.2.4 Law of Property Act 1925, s 62

Law of Property Act 1925, s 62(1)[95]

(1) A conveyance of land shall be deemed to include and shall by virtue of this Act operate to convey, with the land, all buildings, erections, fixtures, commons, hedges, ditches, fences, ways, waters, watercourses, liberties, privileges, easements, rights, and advantages whatsoever, appertaining or reputed to appertain to the land or any part thereof, or, at the time of conveyance, demised, occupied, or enjoyed with, or reputed or known as part or parcel of or appurtenant to the land or any thereof.

Section 62(4) of the LPA 1925 provides that the '*section applies only if and as far as a contrary intention is not expressed in the conveyance*'.[96]

The section was conceived as a word-saving device by implying what is known as a 'general words clause' into conveyances of land, with the object of ensuring that, on a sale or other disposal, all rights and privileges appurtenant to the land will pass without express mention.[97] It can only operate where there has been the creation or transfer of a legal right in

---

[93] See, e.g., *Hansford v Jargo* [1921] 1 Ch 322, 338, *per* Russel J; *Borman v Griffith* [1930] 1 Ch 493, 499, *per* Maugham J; *Ward v Kirkland* [1967] Ch 194, 224–5, *per* Ungoed Thomas J; *Savmots v Investments Ltd v Secretary of State for the Environment* [1979] AC 145, 169, *per* Lord Wilberforce, and 175, *per* Lord Edmund-Davies; *Squarrey v Harris Smith* (1981) 42 P & CR 118, 124, *per* Oliver LJ; *Wheeler v Saunders* [1996] Ch 19, 31, *per* Peter Gibson LJ.

[94] See also Harpum, 'Easements and Centre Point: Old Problems Resolved in a Novel Setting' (1977) 41 Conv 415, 422, who points out that the two limbs of the rule have separate functions: one that facilitates discovery and the other derived from non-derogation from grant.

[95] Replacing Conveyancing Act 1881, s 6.

[96] *Selby DC v Samuel Smith Old Brewery (Tadcaster) Ltd* (2000) 80 P & CR 466; *P&S Platt Ltd v Crouch* [2003] EWCA Civ 1110.

[97] Legal easements pass automatically, without express mention, and thus the primary focus was upon equitable and quasi-easements. It was conveyancing practice to include an express general words clause.

a deed—that is, a conveyance. Judicial interpretation of the section has, however, extended its operation: not only will the section pass existing easements, but it will also operate to upgrade a mere permission into a full-fledged legal easement. In effect, the informality of the original permission is cured by the formality of the subsequent conveyance, which is 'deemed to include and shall [...] operate to convey' the right.[98] It is this aspect of the section that we must explore further, as a means of implied grant.[99]

Farwell J first held that this was the effect of what is now s 62 of the 1925 Act[100] in the following case.

International Tea Stores Co v Hobbs [1903] 2 Ch 165

Facts: Hobbs was a blacksmith who let the shop adjoining his forge to the claimants and allowed them to use a private road, which formed part of the forge, to access the rear of the shop. The claimants subsequently bought the shop from Hobbs, who tried to prevent them from using the road. They successfully claimed that the privilege that they had enjoyed to use the road had become an easement by virtue of the implied general words. Farwell J rejected as immaterial the fact that the privilege was enjoyed merely by permission; it was only significant that they had used the road.

Farwell J

At 171

But, in my opinion, precariousness has nothing to do with this sort of case, where a privilege which is by its nature known to the law—namely, a right of way—has been in fact enjoyed [...] The real truth is that you do not consider the question of title to use, but the question of fact of user; you have to inquire whether the way has in fact been used, not under what title has it been used, although you must of course take into consideration all the circumstances of the case [...]

Farewell's views were indorsed by the Court of Appeal in the following case, in which the Court also set out the other characteristics of the rights that come within the section.

Wright v Macadam [1949] 2 KB 744, CA

Facts: Wright was a weekly tenant of two rooms on the top floor of Macadam's house when Macadam gave her permission to use the coal shed at the bottom of the garden to store coal. Subsequently, Wright took a new tenancy of the two rooms, plus another room; the tenancy agreement contained no reference to the use of the coal shed, which Wright continued to use until Macadam asked her to pay for the privilege. Wright

---

98 There must be a formal conveyance for s 62 to operate, in contrast to *Wheeldon v Burrows*, which may operate at the contractual stage: see *Borman v Griffith* [1930] 1 Ch 493.

99 Section 62 is sometimes categorized as giving rise to an express grant because the right is read into the conveyance. It is perhaps more convenient to view the grant as implied, given that it does not need to be completed by registration: see Land Registration Act 2002, s 27(7).

100 The provision was previously comprised in s 6 of the Convenyancing Act 1881.

refused and successfully claimed that she had an easement to use the coal shed by virtue of s 62 of the 1925 Act.

Jenkins LJ

At 748

First, the section is not confined to rights which, as a matter of law, were so annexed or appurtenant to the property conveyed at the time of the conveyance as to make them actual legally enforceable rights. Thus, on the severance of a piece of land in common ownership, the quasi easements de facto enjoyed in respect of it by one part of the land over another will pass although, of course, as a matter of law, no man can have a right appendant or appurtenant to one part of his property exerciseable by him over the other part of his property. Secondly, the right, in order to pass, need not be one to which the owner or occupier for the time being of the land has had what may be described as a permanent title. A right enjoyed merely by permission is enough. The leading authority for that proposition is the case of *International Tea Stores Co. v. Hobbs* [. . .]

At 750

There is, therefore, ample authority for the proposition that a right in fact enjoyed with property will pass on a conveyance of the property by virtue of the grant to be read into it under s. 62, even although down to the date of the conveyance the right was exercised by permission only, and therefore was in that sense precarious.

The next proposition deducible from the cases is the one laid down in *Burrows v. Lang* [1912] 2 Ch 502, which has been referred to in some of the passages I have already read. It is that the right in question must be a right known to the law [. . .] A certain amount of confusion has been introduced into the discussion on this aspect of the case by the circumstance that some of the learned judges have used the word "precarious" in describing rights of a kind unknown to the law, and in particular the expression was so used by Farwell J. in the case of *Burrows v. Lang*; but in this context the precariousness enters into the character of the right as distinct from the title to the right. The right is precarious in the sense that, to take the example of the surplus water, there may be no water at all, and that the right is in itself liable to be defeated in that way. It is necessary to keep clearly in mind the distinction between "precariousness" in the sense in which it is used in relation to quasi rights of that description, and precariousness of title as used in relation to a permissively exercised right. For the purposes of s. 62, it is only necessary that the right should be one capable of being granted at law, or, in other words, a right known to the law. If it is a right of that description it matters not, as the *International Tea Stores case* shows, that it has been in fact enjoyed by permission only. The reason for that is clear, for, on the assumption that the right is included or imported into the parcels of the conveyance by virtue of s. 62, the grant under the conveyance supplies what one may call the defect in title, and substitutes a new title based on the grant.

There is one other point to be mentioned. A further exception has been recognized in cases in which there could in the circumstances of the case have been no expectation that the enjoyment of the right could be other than temporary. That exception was recognized by Cotton L.J. in *Birmingham & Dudley District Banking Company v. Ross* (1889) 38 Ch D 295 [. . .] I think those are all the cases to which I can usefully refer, and applying the principles deducible from them to the present case one finds, I think, this. First of all, on the evidence the coal shed was used by Mrs. Wright by the permission of Mr. Macadam, but *International Tea Stores Co. v. Hobbs* shows that that does not prevent s. 62 from applying, because permissive as the right may have been it was in fact enjoyed.

Next, the right was, as I understand it, a right to use the coal shed in question for the purpose of storing such coal as might be required for the domestic purposes of the flat. In my
judgment that is a right or easement which the law will clearly recognize, and it is a right or
easement of a kind which could readily be included in a lease or conveyance by the inser-
tion of appropriate words in the parcels. This, therefore, is not a case in which a title to a
right unknown to the law is claimed by virtue of s. 62. Nor is it a case in which it can be said
to have been in the contemplation of the parties that the enjoyment of the right should be
purely temporary. No limit was set as to the time during which the coal shed could continue
to be used. Mr. Macadam simply gave his permission; that permission was acted on; and the
use of the coal shed in fact went on down to August 28, 1943, and thereafter down to 1947.
Therefore, applying to the facts of the present case the principles which seem to be deducible from the authorities, the conclusion to which I have come is that the right to use the
coal shed was at the date of the letting of August 28, 1943, a right enjoyed with the top floor
flat within the meaning of s. 62 of the Law of Property Act, 1925 , with the result that (as no
contrary intention was expressed in the document) the right in question must be regarded as
having passed by virtue of that letting, just as it would have passed if it had been mentioned
in express terms in cl. 1, which sets out the subject-matter of the lease.

This 'metamorphosis from personal to property right'[101] has been subject to widespread academic[102] and judicial[103] criticism, and the Law Commission has recommended that this
aspect of s 62 should be abrogated.[104]

Tee explains why the Court's reasoning is faulty.

Tee, 'Metamorphoses and Section 62 of the Law of Property Act 1925'
[1998] Conv 115, 123

[...T]he word "right" is being used in two quite different meanings, to illogical effect. A right
in technical terms is enforceable—it may be enforceable only in equity, in which case it is
an equitable right, or it may be enforceable at law. To start with, the only right which Mrs
Wright had was the negative and precarious right not to be sued in trespass before the permission was revoked. An easement to store coal is quite a different matter; once created, it
is enforceable against not only third parties, but against the original grantor as well. It is, in the
technical and full sense of the word, a right [...] Jenkins L.J. was using the word "right" in
its technical and full meaning; but [...] the right referred to must mean Mrs Wright's original
"right", i.e. not to be sued.

Thus a licence is not a proprietary right that is capable of binding third parties; it is merely a
defence to an action for trespass.[105] As such, it should not be construed as a privilege appurtenant to land within the meaning of s 62.

---

101 Tee, 'Metamorphoses and Section 62 of the Law of Property Act 1925' [1998] Conv 115, 115.
102 See ibid, and *Megarry and Wade: The Law of Real Property* (6th edn, ed Harpum, 2000), [18–111]).
103 See, e.g., *Wright v Macadam* [1949] 2 KB 744, 755, *per* Tucker LJ; *Green v Ashco Horticulturist Ltd*
[1966] 1 WLR 889, 897, *per* Cross J; *Hair v Gillman* (2000) 80 P & CR 108, 116, *per* Chadwick LJ; *Commission
for the New Towns v Gallagher* [2002] EWHC 2668, (2003) 2 P & CR 24, [61], *per* Neuberger J.
104 Reform has been advocated by the Law Commission since 1971. Its most recent recommendation is
found in Law Commission Consultation Paper No 186 (2008, [4.104]).
105 See Chapter 8, sections 2 and 3.

Section 62 may thus operate to create an easement where the dominant and servient tenement are in common ownership, and the dominant tenement is sold or leased in circumstances under which an informal right has been enjoyed by the purchaser or tenant over the servient land retained by the seller or landlord. It cannot operate to create an implied reservation where the servient land is sold or leased.[106] In this respect, it looks similar to *Wheeldon v Burrows*, but there are important distinctions:

- s 62 requires a conveyance by deed to create/transfer a legal estate, but *Wheeldon v Burrows* may operate upon the creation/transfer of an equitable interest;
- s 62 operates only where there is diversity of occupation of the dominant and servient land, whereas *Wheeldon v Burrows* operates only where there has been common ownership and occupation of the dominant and servient land;
- the nature of the rights that are capable of passing as easements under s 62 are wider than those that can pass under *Wheeldon v Burrows*.

Diversity of occupation

Section 62 of the LPA 1925 calls for the right to be appurtenant to the dominant land. This requirement has been interpreted as requiring diversity of occupation between the dominant and servient land. Where the dominant and servient land are in common ownership and occupation, the rights exercised over the servient land are exercised by virtue of the occupier's ownership of servient tenement and not by virtue of the any right appurtenant to the dominant land.

Long v Gowlett [1923] 2 Ch 177, HC

Facts: Long was the owner of a water mill. He claimed a right of access across fields to repair the riverbank and to cut back the weeds. The previous owners of the mill and fields had done so, and Long unsuccessfully claimed that, upon the sale of the mill, the right had passed to him under the predecessor provision to s 62.

Sargant J

At 199

It is, therefore, necessary for the purpose of dealing with the matter on this footing to consider whether, during the common ownership and occupation of Lot 1 and Lot 2 by Mr. Nichols and his widow, and therefore at the date of the conveyance, there was a "privilege, easement, right or advantage" of the kind now claimed, which can properly be said to have been "demised, occupied or enjoyed" with Lot 1 over Lot 2. It is very difficult to see how this can have been the case. No doubt the common owner and occupier did in fact repair the bank of Lot 2, and cut the weeds there; and no doubt also this repair and cutting would enure not solely for the benefit of Lot 2 (which comprised, amongst other things, a lawn tennis court), so as to prevent its being flooded, but also and very likely to a greater extent for the benefit of Lot 1. But there is nothing to indicate that the acts done on Lot 2 were done

---

[106] *Kent v Kavanagh* [2006] EWCA Civ 162, [2007] Ch 1. An implied reservation may arise upon enfranchisement under Leasehold Reform Act 1967, ss 8 and 10.

otherwise than in the course of the ownership and occupation of Lot 2, or that they were by way of using a "privilege, easement or advantage" over Lot 2 in connection with Lot 1. The common owner and occupier of Whiteacre and Blackacre may in fact use Blackacre as an alternative and more convenient method of communication between Whiteacre and a neighbouring village. But it has never been held, and would I think be contrary to principle to hold, that (in default of there being a made road over Blackacre forming a continuous and apparent means of communication) a sale and conveyance of Whiteacre alone would carry a right to pass over Blackacre in the same way in which the common owner had been accustomed to pass. As it seems to me, in order that there may be a "privilege, easement or advantage" enjoyed with Whiteacre over Blackacre so as to pass under the statute, there must be something done on Blackacre not due to or comprehended within the general rights of an occupying owner of Blackacre, but of such a nature that it is attributable to a privilege, easement, right or advantage, however precarious, which arises out of the ownership or occupation of Whiteacre, altogether apart from the ownership or occupation of Blackacre. And it is difficult to see how, when there is a common ownership of both Whiteacre and Blackacre, there can be any such relationship between the two closes as (apart from the case of continuous and apparent easements or that of a way of necessity) would be necessary to create a "privilege, easement, right or advantage" within the words of s. 6, sub-s. 2, of the statute. For this purpose it would seem that there must be some diversity of ownership or occupation of the two closes sufficient to refer the act or acts relied on not to mere occupying ownership, but to some advantage or privilege (however far short of a legal right) attaching to the owner or occupier of Whiteacre as such and de facto exercised over Blackacre.

Long v Gowlett was a controversial decision,[107] but has now been cited with approval by the House of Lords in *Sovmots Investment Ltd v Secretary of State for the Environment*[108] and followed by the Court of Appeal in the following case, in which the Court noted the distinction between *Wheeldon v Burrows* and s 62. As Chadwick LJ explains, the situations are usually mutually exclusive: *Wheeldon v Burrows* applies where there is common ownership and occupation of the dominant and servient land, and s 62 operates where there is common ownership, but diversity of occupation.

Kent v Kavanagh [2007] Ch 1, CA

Chadwick LJ

At [43]–[47]

The two propositions which, together, comprise the rule (or rules) in *Wheeldon v Burrows* are confined, in their application, to cases in which, by reason of the conveyance (or lease), land formerly in common ownership ceases to be owned by the same person. It is in cases of that nature that, in order to give effect to what must be taken to be the common intention of the grantor and the grantee, the conveyance (or lease) will operate as a grant (for the benefit of the land conveyed) of such easements over the land retained by the grantor as are necessary to the reasonable enjoyment of the land conveyed. But, because the principle is

---

[107] Harpum, 'Easements and Centre Point: Old Problems Resolved in a Novel Setting' (1977) 41 Conv 415; Smith, 'Centre Point: Faulty Towers with Shaky Foundations' [1978] Conv 449; Harpum, '*Long v Gowlett*: A Strong Fortress' [1979] Conv 113.

[108] [1979] AC 144, 176, but see *P&S Platt Ltd v Crouch* [2003] EWCA Civ 1110, [2004] 1 P & CR 18, [42].

founded on the common intention of the parties, the easements necessary to the reasonable enjoyment of the land conveyed are those which reflect (and, following separation of ownership, are needed to give effect to) the use and enjoyment of the land conveyed at the time of the conveyance and while that land and the retained land were in the common ownership of the grantor.

It is necessary to ask how far either of the two propositions which Thesiger LJ identified in *Wheeldon v Burrows* can have any application in a case where, at the time of the conveyance, the land conveyed and the land retained, although in common ownership, were not in common occupation. In particular, can either of the two propositions have any application where the land conveyed was occupied by a tenant holding under a lease from the common owner. Assuming, for the moment, that the land is not conveyed to the tenant, there are, of course, two distinct questions: (i) what easements over the retained land pass with the conveyance of the freehold and (ii) what easements are reserved out of the land conveyed for the benefit of the retained land. The rights of the tenant over the land retained; and the rights of the grantor (as owner of the land retained) over the land held under the lease are unaffected by the conveyance. Prima facie, those rights will depend on the terms of the lease-but may include rights which passed to the tenant under the first rule in *Wheeldon v Burrows* when the lease was granted.

In the absence of an express grant, the answer to the first of those questions-what easements over the retained land pass with the conveyance of the freehold-turns, as it seems to me, not on any application of the first rule in *Wheeldon v Burrows* but on the operation of section 62 of the Law of Property Act 1925. Under section 62 a conveyance of land operates to convey with the land "all [. . .] ways [. . .] easements, rights, and advantages whatsoever, appertaining or reputed to appertain to the land [. . .] or, at the time of conveyance, demised [. . .] or enjoyed with [. . .] the land". I can see no reason why those words are not apt to convey, with the freehold, rights of way over the retained land which are, at the time of the conveyance, enjoyed by the tenant in occupation of the land conveyed. For my part, I find that analysis more attractive than one which relies upon the first rule in *Wheeldon v Burrows*. It seems to me an unnecessary and artificial construct to hold that the grantor, as common owner and the landlord of the land conveyed, is himself using the rights over the retained land which his tenant enjoys under the lease.

In reaching that conclusion I have had regard to the observations of Lord Wilberforce in the *Sovmots* appeal at 169, that:

> "section 62 does not fit this case. The reason is that when land is under one ownership one cannot speak in any intelligible sense of rights, or privileges, or easements being exercised over one part for the benefit of another. Whatever the owner does, he does as owner and, until a separation occurs, of ownership or at least of occupation, the condition for the existence of rights, etc, does not exist: see *Bolton v Bolton* (1879) 11 Ch D 968, 970 per Fry J and *Long v Gowlett* at 189, 198, in my opinion a correct decision."

As Lord Wilberforce pointed out, there can be no sensible concept of rights over one part of land for the benefit of another part while the two parts are in common ownership and occupation. But, once there is a separation of occupation (because part of land in common ownership is held by a tenant under a lease) there is no conceptual difficulty. There may well be rights over the untenanted part of the land for the benefit of the tenanted part. If there are, those rights are within the wide compass of section 62 of the 1925 Act.

Section 62 of the 1925 Act cannot operate to reserve rights out of the land conveyed for the benefit of the land retained. The words of the section cannot be given that effect. Nor can assistance be found in *Wheeldon v Burrows*. As I have said, the second rule stated by

Thesiger LJ is to the contrary effect: "if the grantor intends to reserve any right over the tenement granted, it is his duty to reserve it expressly in the grant." The position under the general law, as it seems to me, is that a grantor who, on the conveyance of a part of his land which is subject to an existing tenancy (and over which he has rights of way reserved in the lease), wishes to reserve those rights out of the freehold which he conveys (so that he can continue to exercise them after the lease has determined) must do so by express words of reservation.

Section 62 thus largely operates in the leasehold context, in which the dominant land is leased and the tenant is granted some privilege over the servient land that is owned and occupied by his landlord. That privilege may be converted to an easement under s 62 upon the renewal of the lease or upon the tenant purchasing the freehold reversion of the dominant land. In *Kent v Kavanagh*, s 62 also operated where a tenant (including adjoining tenants) exercised a right to acquire their freehold reversions by enfranchisement.[109]

Section 62 may also operate where a purchaser or lessee of the dominant land has been let into possession before the formal conveyance or lease has been executed, and the seller or landlord confers an informal privilege over the servient land. This danger arises because the operative date is the time of the formal conveyance rather than the time at which the purchaser or tenant is let into possession, or, in the case of a lease, the stipulated commencement of the term.[110]

The nature of the rights implied under s 62

A further distinction between *Wheeldon v Burrows* and s 62 flows from the nature of the rights that can pass under each rule. We have examined the need for rights under *Wheeldon v Burrows* to be continuous and apparent, and reasonably necessary for the enjoyment of the dominant land; there are no such limitations under s 62, which, accordingly, can apply to a wider range of rights.[111] In so doing, s 62 runs the danger of failing the utility test that underpins implied grant, although the discoverability of the right presents less of a problem.[112]

Gardner, *An Introduction to Land Law* (2002, p 170)

[...] the implied grant rules in fact operate to *impute* easements, rather than on the basis of a genuine implicit intention, and section 62 is certainly no exception. To justify the imputation requires a utilitarian argument for the easement in question, bolstered by the degree of consent discernable in my failure to stipulate against it. Even given the prior usage, the rule in *Wheeldon v Burrows* demands that the claimed easement be 'necessary for the reasonable enjoyment 'of the land transferred, but section 62 has no such requirement, the section demands only a lesser degree of utility to operate. Arguably, that degree is insufficient, even given the element of consent.

---

[109] See Lewison LJ at [70]–[76].

[110] *Goldberg v Edwards* [1950] Ch 247, 256. There appears to be some latitude in determining if the right is being exercised at the time of the conveyance: see *Green v Ashco Horticulturist Ltd* [1966] 1 WLR 889, 898.

[111] There are a number of cases in which claims have failed under *Wheeldon v Burrows*, but succeeded under s 62: e.g. *Goldberg v Edwards* [1950] Ch 247 and *Ward v Kirkland* [1967] Ch 194.

[112] Although others have argued that the right should be apparent: see Lawson (2002, p 93).

There is less difficulty, however, about the fact that section 62 has no requirement that the prior usage be 'continuous and apparent' [...] Such a requirement is in principle useful, as it enables the parties to the transfer to identify the rights the transfer will create. But as we have seen, for section 62 to apply, the two pieces of land in question must previously have been occupied by different people, with the licence of one over the other. Under these circumstances, the right is likely to be discoverable in its very nature.

Nevertheless, to pass under s 62, the right must be capable of existing as an easement.

Phipps v Pears [1965] 1 QB 76, CA

Lord Denning

At 84

A fine view, or an expanse open to the winds may be an advantage to a house, but it would not pass under section 62. Whereas a right to use a coal shed or to go along a passage would pass under section 62. The reason being that these last are rights known to the law, whereas the others are not. A right to protection from the weather is not a right known to the law. It does not therefore pass under section 62.

Rights that are capable of fulfilling the easement test, however, may not pass under s 62 where the particular permission given is personal to the individual, or merely temporary, or inherently precarious.[113]

Goldberg v Edwards [1950] Ch 247, CA

Facts: Mrs Edwards owned a house and rented an annex to Goldberg, from which he ran a business. Prior to the formal entry into the lease, Mrs Edwards had let Goldberg into possession, and has allowed him and his customers to pass through the house to get to the annex, although access could be obtained via an outside passage. She also gave him permission to put up an advertising sign, bell, and a letterbox for the business. The right for Goldberg to use the access through the house became an easement by the operation of s 62, but the other rights were limited to the period of Mrs Edward's ownership of the house and thus did not pass.

Evershed MR

At 255

The various rights here claimed are these: first, a right for the plaintiffs personally to pass through the front door and along the passage of the house [...] Secondly, a right to maintain a signboard and an electric bell; thirdly, as a necessary corollary to that, a right for the plaintiffs' customers to use the front door and passage; and, fourthly, a right to use it for the passage of goods. As regards the signboard and the bell, it is to be observed that there is

---

113 See also *Green v Ashco Horticulturist Ltd* [1966] 1 WLR 889.

no indication of that matter in the pleadings or in the form of injunction. I need not pursue it, because the finding of the Vice-Chancellor shows quite clearly, to my mind, that everything except the plaintiffs' right to come and go via this route was expressly limited to such time as the landlord should occupy the house herself. In other words, it was a privilege which she herself allowed so long as she was there, because it did not interfere with her own affairs and business. It was clear that she was not making that privilege any part of the bargain between herself and the tenants of the annex. It is plain, in my view, that these rights, other than the plaintiffs' personal right of passage, were not within the language of s. 62 so as to be covered by the demise to them.

That leaves only the personal right. As I have indicated, my main difficulty has been in deciding whether that was similarly limited or limited in some other way so as not properly to be capable of being annexed to the subject-matter of the demise. Having regard to his judgment, I think that I am bound to regard the view of the judge as having been that, in contradistinction to the other rights, it was intended to be something which the plaintiffs should enjoy qua lessees during the term of the demise, though it should not be enjoyed by their servants, workmen or any other persons with their authority.

[...] As I have held, though it is limited to the lessees themselves and does not extend to other persons, it would be capable of formulation and incorporation as a term of the lease, and it is, in my judgment, covered by s. 62. To that extent, therefore, but to that limited extent only, the plaintiffs are entitled to succeed [...]

I am anxious to guard myself from saying that rights, which were purely personal in the strict sense of that word, would necessarily in every case be covered by s. 62. I base myself on the view that the right here given, though limited to the lessees, was given to them qua lessees; and, as such, it seems to me, it is covered by the principle of *Wright v. Macadam* and by s. 62.

Gardner[114] has accused the courts of displaying '*a degree of carelessness*' in monitoring the easement-like qualities of the rights that have been held to pass as easements under s 62. For example, we have already noted that *Wright v Macadam*[115] failed to consider whether rights storage ousted the servient owner, whilst the distinctions drawn in *Goldberg*[116] between rights conferred upon the tenant as a personal favour and as a lessee are not wholly convincing.

3.3 PRESUMED GRANT: PRESCRIPTION

A grant of an easement may be presumed as a result of long user. Lord Hoffman explains the development of the law governing prescription in the following case, which concerned the registration of land as a village green by reason of the long user of the land for recreation by the inhabitants of the village. The claim was for acquisition of a public right, but the same prescription principles apply to the acquisition of easements by private landowners.

[114] Gardner, *An Introduction to Land Law* (2007, p 170).
[115] [1949] 2 KB 744, CA.
[116] See also *Green v Ashco Horticulturist Ltd* [1966] 1 WLR 889.

R v Oxfordshire CC, ex p Sunningwell Parish Council [2000] 1 AC 335

Lord Hoffmann

At 349

English law [...] has never had a consistent theory of prescription. It did not treat long enjoyment as being a method of acquiring title. Instead, it approached the question from the other end by treating the lapse of time as either barring the remedy of the former owner or giving rise to a presumption that he had done some act which conferred a lawful title upon the person in de facto possession or enjoyment. Thus the medieval real actions for the recovery of seisin were subject to limitation by reference to various past events. In the time of Bracton the writ of right was limited by reference to the accession of Henry I (1100). The Statute of Merton 1235 (20 Hen. 3, c. 4) brought this date up to the accession of Henry II (1154) and the Statute of Westminster I 1275 (3 Edw. 1, c. 39) extended it to the accession of Richard I in 1189.

The judges used this date by analogy to fix the period of prescription for immemorial custom and the enjoyment of incorporeal hereditaments such as rights of way and other easements. In such cases, however, the period was being used for a different purpose. It was not to bar the remedy but to presume that enjoyment was pursuant to a right having a lawful origin. In the case of easements, this meant a presumption that there had been a grant before 1189 by the freehold owner.

As time went on, however, proof of lawful origin in this way became for practical purposes impossible. The evidence was not available. The judges filled the gap with another presumption. They instructed juries that if there was evidence of enjoyment for the period of living memory, they could presume that the right had existed since 1189. After the Limitation Act 1623 (21 Jac. 1, c. 16), which fixed a 20-year period of limitation for the possessory actions such as ejectment, the judges treated 20 years' enjoyment as by analogy giving rise to the presumption of enjoyment since 1189. But these presumptions arising from enjoyment for the period of living memory or for 20 years, though strong, were not conclusive. They could be rebutted by evidence that the right could not have existed in 1189; for example, because it was appurtenant to a building which had been erected since that date. In the case of easements, the resourcefulness of the judges overcame this obstacle by another presumption, this time of a lost modern grant. As Cockburn C.J. said in the course of an acerbic account of the history of the English law of prescription in *Bryant v. Foot* (1867) L.R. 2 Q.B. 161, 181:

> "Juries were first told that from user, during living memory, or even during 20 years, they might presume a lost grant or deed; next they were recommended to make such presumption; and lastly, as the final consummation of judicial legislation, it was held that a jury should be told, not only that they might, but also that they were bound to presume the existence of such a lost grant, although neither judge nor jury, nor any one else, had the shadow of a belief that any such instrument had ever really existed."

The result of these developments was that, leaving aside the cases in which (a) it was possible to show that the right could not have existed in 1189 and (b) the doctrine of lost modern grant could not be invoked, the period of 20 years' user was in practice sufficient to establish a prescriptive or customary right. It was not an answer simply to rely upon the improbability of immemorial user or lost modern grant. As Cockburn C.J. observed, the jury were instructed that if there was no evidence absolutely inconsistent with there having been immemorial user or a lost modern grant, they not merely could but should find the prescriptive right established. The emphasis was therefore shifted from the brute fact of the right or custom having existed in 1189 or there having been a lost grant (both of which were acknowledged to be fictions) to the quality of the 20-year user which would justify recognition of a prescriptive right or customary right. It became established that such user had to be, in the Latin phrase, nec vi, nec clam, nec precario: not by force, nor stealth, nor the licence of the owner. (For this requirement in the case of custom, see *Mills v. Colchester Corporation* (1867) L.R. 2 C.P. 476, 486.) The unifying element in these three vitiating circumstances was that each constituted a reason why it would not have been reasonable to expect the owner to resist the exercise of the right—in the first case, because rights should not be acquired by the use of force, in the second, because the owner would not have known of the user and in the third, because he had consented to the user, but for a limited period. So in *Dalton v. Angus & Co.* (1881) 6 App. Cas. 740, 773, Fry J. (advising the House of Lords) was able to rationalise the law of prescription as follows:

> "the whole-law of prescription and the whole law which governs the presumption or infer-ence of a grant or covenant rest upon acquiescence. The courts and the judges have had recourse to various expedients for quieting the possession of persons in the exercise of rights which have not been resisted by the persons against whom they are exercised, but in all cases it appears to me that acquiescence and nothing else is the principle upon which these expedients rest."

In the case of easements, the legislature intervened to save the consciences of judges and juries by the Prescription Act 1832 (2 & 3 Will 4, c. 71), of which the short title was "An Act for shortening the Time of Prescription in certain cases." Section 2 (as amended by the Statute Law Revision (No. 2) Act 1888 (51 & 52 Vict. c. 57), section 1, Schedule and the Statute Law Revision Act 1890 (53 & 54 Vict. c. 33), section 1, Schedule 1) provided:

> "No claim which may be lawfully made at the common law, by custom, prescription, or grant, to any way or other easement [...] when such way or other matter [...] shall have been actually enjoyed by any person claiming right thereto without interruption for the full period of 20 years, shall be defeated or destroyed by showing only that such way or other matter was first enjoyed at any time prior to such period of 20 years, but nevertheless such claim may be defeated in any other way by which the same is now liable to be defeated [...]"

Thus in a claim under the Act, what mattered was the quality of enjoyment during the 20-year period. It had to be by a person "claiming right thereto" or, in the language of section 5 of the same Act (as amended by the Act of 1888), which dealt with the forms of pleadings, "as of right." In *Bright v. Walker* (1834) 1 C.M. & R. 211, 219, two years after the passing of the Act, Parke B. explained what these words meant. He said that the right must have been enjoyed "openly and in the manner that a person rightfully entitled would have used it" and not by stealth or by licence. In *Gardner v. Hodgson's Kingston Brewery Co. Ltd.* [1903] A.C. 229, 239, Lord Lindley said that the words "as of right" were intended "to have the same meaning as the older expression nec vi, nec clam, nec precario."

As Lord Hoffman explains, the user must be of a certain quality—that is, it must be open and exercised without force or the permission of the servient owner—and it must be estab-lished that this user has been exercised for one or more of the three prescription periods. Prescription at common law requires use from time immemorial, which means 1189; accordingly, a successful claim is most unlikely. Prescription by lost modern grant calls for proof of twenty years' user, which will lead to a presumption that a grant of the right had been made, but has now been lost. This presumption is strong and will not be rebutted by positive proof that no grant was made.[117] The Prescription Act 1832 operates by preventing a servient owner from contesting a claim at common law because the right could not have been exercised in 1189 where the claimant can prove user for the twenty years immediately preceding the commencement of proceedings in which the right is claimed. The Act also introduces a long prescription period, which operates positively to give rise to an absolute right on the expiry of the forty years' user.[118]

The Prescription Act 1832 has been much criticized as 'one of the worst drafted Acts on the Statute Book'[119] and, as such, has not supplanted the fiction of lost modern grant. In particular, lost modern grant will operate whenever twenty years' uninterrupted user is established, even if that user was some time ago. In contrast to the Prescription Act 1832, the period of use does not have to continue up to the commencement of proceedings.

3.3.1 The basis of prescription

In Chapter 10, we saw that an adverse possessor may: (i) acquire a property right by taking possession of land; and (ii) later be able to rely on a limitation period that extinguishes the right of the paper owner to recover possession. Prescription operates in a different manner. Long user justifies a presumption or fiction that the servient owner has granted an easement. The presumption is founded upon the acquiescence of the servient owner in failing to prevent the dominant owner from exercising the claimed right.

Dalton v Angus & Co (1881) 6 LR App Cas 740

Fry J

At 773

[I]n my opinion, the whole law of prescription and the whole law which governs the presumption or inference of a grant or covenant rests upon acquiescence. The Courts and the Judges have had recourse to various expedients for quieting the possession of persons in the exercise of rights which have not been resisted by the persons against whom they are exercised, but in all cases it appears to me that acquiescence and nothing else is the principle upon which these expedients rest. It becomes then of the highest importance to consider of what ingredients acquiescence consists. In many cases, as, for instance, in the case of that acquiescence which creates a right of way, it will be found to involve, 1st, the doing of some act by one man upon the land of another; 2ndly, the absence of right to do that act in the person doing it; 3rdly, the knowledge of the person affected by it that the act is done; 4thly, the power of the person affected by the act to prevent such act either by act on his part or by action in the Courts; and lastly, the abstinence by him from any such interference for such a length of time as renders it reasonable for the Courts to say that he shall not afterwards interfere to stop the act being done. In some other cases, as, for

---

[117] See *Tehidy Minerals Ltd v Norman* [1971] 2 QB 518, 543, *per* Buckley LJ; *Mills v Silver* [1991] Ch 271, 278, *per* Dillon LJ. The presumption will be rebutted by proof that the grant could not have been made because of the incapacity of the servient owner: see *Housden v Conservators of Wimbledon and Putney Commons* [2007] EWHC 1171.

[118] The forty-year period must also expire immediately before the commencement of proceedings in which the right is claimed.

[119] Law Reform Committee, *Fourteenth Report: Acquisition of Easements and Profits by Prescription* (Cmnd 3100, 1966, [40]).

example, in the case of lights, some of these ingredients are wanting; but I cannot imagine any case of acquiescence in which there is not shewn to be in the servient owner: 1, a knowledge of the acts done; 2, a power in him to stop the acts or to sue in respect of them; and 3, an abstinence on his part from the exercise of such power. That such is the nature of acquiescence and that such is the ground upon which presumptions or inferences of grant or covenant may be made appears to me to be plain, both from reason, from maxim, and from the cases.

As regards the reason of the case, it is plain good sense to hold that a man who can stop an asserted right, or a continued user, and does not do so for a long time, may be told that he has lost his right by his delay and his negligence, and every presumption should therefore be made to quiet a possession thus acquired and enjoyed by the tacit consent of the sufferer. But there is no sense in binding a man by an enjoyment he cannot prevent, or quieting a possession which he could never disturb.

The fiction of a presumed grant raises the distinction that we made in Chapter 3 between *independent* and *dependent* acquisition. The fiction suggests that a prescriptive easement is acquired by dependent acquisition—that is, because a grant from A is presumed—rather than because of independent acquisition as a result of B's own unilateral conduct. McFarlane questions whether prescription really is a dependent grant.

McFarlane, *The Structure of Property Law* (2008, pp 864–5)

It is possible for B to acquire an Easement simply through the *consistent exercise, over a long period, of a right to use A's land*. This method of acquisition, referred to as *prescription*, looks very much like a form of independent acquisition:

1. B acquires the right through his own, independent conduct, without needing to show that A has exercised his power to give B an Easement.

2. Once B has behaved, for a long period, *as though* he has the right, it is no longer possible for A to deny B that right.

However, the courts do *not* currently treat prescription as an example of independent acquisition. Instead, when B acquires an Easement through long use, it is assumed that A, or a former owner of A's land, exercised his power to give B an Easement.[120] Strictly speaking then, prescription is simply another type of implied grant. This approach seems puzzling: why should we rely on an (almost certainly incorrect)[121] assumption that the claimed Easement was once granted by an owner of A's land to an owner of B's land? It would seem simpler to say that prescription is an example of an independent acquisition.

The idea that a grant of an easement by prescription is presumed has been the subject of much criticism. Indeed, it has been described as a 'revolting fiction'.[122]

Goymour provides a number of reasons why this approach is so misguided.

---

[120] See, e.g., *Gardner v Hodgson's Kingston Brewery Co* [1903] AC 229, 239.
[121] In *Tehidy Minerals Ltd v Norman* [1971] QB 528, 552, *per* Buckley LJ, noting that the doctrine of prescription may depend on a 'legal fiction'.
[122] *Angus v Dalton* (1877) LR 3 QBD 85, 94, *per* Lush J.

Goymour, 'Rights in Property and the Effluxion of Time' in *Modern Studies in Property Law: Vol 4* (ed Cooke, 2007, p 182)

First, the notion of a presumed grant is so fictitious that it offends common sense and is furthermore inconsistent with the technical requirements for prescription. The idea that prescriptive rights rest in a grant conflicts with the condition that prescription must be nec precario [without permission]. Any indication that the owner had given permission for another person to enjoy the land, whether by grant of an easement or merely a licence, will prevent a prescriptive right from arising. For the doctrine to be internally inconsistent is unsatisfactory.

Secondly, in conjunction with the first point, the technical mechanism of presumed grant has led to an acceptance by many that the policy rationale for prescriptive rights is 'acquiescence' by the servant owner in the other party's long-established enjoyment. So long as there is a theory of grant, it follows logically that acquiescence is relevant. However, it is far from obvious that acquiescence is the policy rationale for prescription, for the following reasons. First, as is apparent in the previous point, the requirement that use must be nec precario introduces an element of adversity into the prescriptive claim that cannot easily be explained by acquiescence. Furthermore, it is often equally fictitious to assume acquiescence on the part of the servient owner as it is to presume a grant. Finally the assumption that acquiescence is the rationale for prescriptive rights fails to take account of the fundamental distinction between rights that arise by consensual grant and rights that arise otherwise, by operation of law. The policy that lies behind the recognition of expressly granted rights can be explained by the law's respect for the wishes of the legal actors when they are executed in legally recognised forms, for which acquiescence is relevant. However, once it is accepted that prescriptive easements arise not by grant but by operation of law, it no longer follows that the policy justification for their existence is acquiescence [...]

The third problem with time's masked effect is linked to the first two. Because the law has inappropriately tied itself to the mechanism of grant and the rationale of acquiescence, the questions that occupy the courts in prescription cases tended to concern whether or not the technicalities of a hypothetical conveyance are satisfied [...] This focus comes at the expense of a proper consideration of why and in what circumstances long use should, as a matter of policy, give rise to a prescriptive right.

Clarke and Kohler point out that, whilst the presumption of a grant may make some (if unsatisfactory) sense to support positive easements by long user, the presumed grant of negative easements cannot be rationalized.

Clarke and Kohler, *Property Law* (2005, p 495)

There are two important points about negative easements. First, is the absence of an easement, I do not have a right to receive these forces, but only a liberty to make use of them. Secondly, when I exercise my liberty to enjoy these forces, I do not infringe *any rights* of yours [...] In other words, from the outset I had the liberty to receive the forces and you had the liberty to obstruct them. So from the outset I had no need of your authorisation to 'use' the light, or air, or support etc for twenty years: I would automatically receive them unless and until your exercised your liberty to interrupt them [...] It would be odd to infer from the fact that I have enjoyed uninterrupted receipt of these forces for twenty years that you positively promised not to interrupt them: this is a promise I had no need for, and you had no reason to give. A much more likely explanation is that you did nothing because you had no selfish reason to develop your land in a way that would interrupt my receipt of these forces.

A particular concern arises when a negative easement is claimed by prescription, because the right will arise even though there is no evidence of the user because the dominant owner has not made any positive use of the servient land. Lord Hope referred to this concern in the following case, in which the House of Lords canvassed (and rejected) possible redress (including the possibility of a new negative easement) for interference with television reception. The Law Commission has suggested that it should no longer be possible to acquire negative easements by prescription.[123]

Hunter v Canary Wharf Ltd [1997] AC 655, HL

Lord Hope

At 726

The presumption however is for freedom in the occupation and use of property. This presumption affects the way in which an easement may be constituted. A restraint on the owners' freedom of property can only be effected by agreement, by express grant or—in the case of the easement of light—by way of an exception to the general rule by prescription. The prospective developer should be able to detect by inspection or by inquiry what restrictions, if any, are imposed by this branch of the law on his freedom to develop his property. He should be able to know, before he puts his building up, whether it will constitute an infringement.

The presumption also affects the kinds of easement which the law will recognise. When the easements are negative in character—where they restrain the owners' freedom in the occupation and use of his property—they belong to certain well known categories. As they represent an anomaly in the law because they restrict the owners' freedom, the law takes care not to extend them beyond the categories which are well known to the law. It is one thing if what one is concerned with is a restriction which has been constituted by express grant or by agreement. Some elasticity in the recognised categories may be permitted in such a case, as the owner has agreed to restrict his own freedom. But it is another matter if what is being suggested is the acquisition of an easement by prescription. Where the easement is of a purely negative character, requiring no action to be taken by the other proprietor and effecting no change on the owner's property which might reveal its existence, it is important to keep to the recognised categories. A very strong case would require to be made out if they were to be extended. I do not think that that has been demonstrated in the present case.

The three existing forms of prescription at common law, under lost modern grant, and under the Prescription Act 1832 have been described as 'anomalous and undesirable',[124] and the consequences of their interrelationship as 'messy overlaps'.[125] The Law Commission have

---

[123] Law Commission Consultation Paper No 186 (2008, [4.184]–[4.186]). Other jurisdictions have prohibited prescriptive negative easements: see Burns (2009).

[124] *Tehidy Minerals Ltd v Norman* [1971] 2 QB 518, 543, *per* Buckley LJ

[125] Goymour, 'Rights in Property and the Effluxion of Time' in *Modern Studies in Property Law: Vol 4* (ed Cooke, 2007, p 185).

recommended that these three forms of the prescription for positive easements should be replaced and prescription should be based simply upon the passage of time,[126] with a single prescription period of twenty years,[127] and that prescription of negative easements should be abolished.[128]

3.3.2 User as of right

Given that the servient owner's acquiescence of the claimant's user underpins the prescription, the nature of that user is of central significance. The vital connection is explained in the following case.

Sturges v Bridgman (1879) LR 11 Ch D 852

Thesiger LJ

At 863

Consent or acquiescence of the owner of the servient tenement lies at the root of prescription, and of the fiction of a lost grant, and hence the acts of user, which go to the proof of either the one or the other, must be, in the language of the civil law, nec vi nec clam, nec precario; for a man cannot, as a general rule, be said to consent to or acquiesce in the acquisition by his neighbour of an easement through an enjoyment of which he has no knowledge, actual or constructive or which he contests and endeavours to interrupt or which he temporarily licenses.

The phrase that describes the required user is that the claimant's user must be 'as of right'—a phrase that is discussed by Riddall.

Riddall, 'A False Trail: The Meaning of "As Of Right" in the Public Law of Prescription' (1997) Conv 199, 201

Since for the user to be "as of right" it must be nec vi, without force; nec clam, without secrecy; and nec precarious, without permission, the meaning of the phrase becomes apparent. User "as of right" means that the user must be in the same fashion *as if* there was a legal right to use the way. As the matter was expressed by Parke B in *Bright v Walker* (1834) 1 CM&R 211, user is as of right if exercised "in the same manner that a person rightfully entitled would have used it". In the same *manner*, this is the crux of the matter. Since this is what "as of right" means; its meaning cannot have anything to do with whether users believe that they are entitled to use a path. A person can use a path in the same *manner* as if he had a right to use it nec clam, nec vi and nec precario without having any shred of belief that he has a legal right to do so.

---

[126] Law Commission Consultation Paper No 186 (2002, [4.196], [4.211]–[4.212]). The civil systems look to the Roman law concept of *usucapio*, by which rights may be acquired by the passing of time.
[127] Ibid.
[128] Ibid, [4.193].

The Latin phrase *nec vi, nec clam, nec precario*, meaning 'without force, without secrecy, and without permission', is commonly used to described user as of right. We need to explore a little more the implications of this phrase.

The use of force refers not only to physical force, but also to the exercise of the right despite protests by the servient owner.

Smith v Brudenell-Bruce [2002] 2 P & CR 51, HC

Pumfrey J

At [12]

It seems to me a user ceases to be user "as of right" if the circumstances are such as to indicate to the dominant owner, or to a reasonable man with the dominant owner's knowledge of the circumstances, that the servient owner actually objects and continues to object and will back his objection either by physical obstruction or by legal action. A user is contentious when the servient owner is doing everything, consistent with his means and proportionately to the user, to contest and to endeavour to interrupt the user.

In recent years, there has been some controversy over the circumstances in which an illegal user can qualify as user as of right. At first sight, it might seem inappropriate to condone any illegal user, but, until the prescription period has expired, the claimants user is inevitably illegal—in the sense that it is a trespass. The House of Lords has settled the controversy by distinguishing between those illegal actions that the servient owner cannot legitimatize and those actions that would cease to be illegal if the servient owner were to choose to permit their exercise.

Bakewell Management Ltd v Brandwood [2004] 2 AC 519, HL

Facts: The owners of several houses adjoining Newtown Common had driven over a track running over the common in order to gain access to their homes. The common came into the ownership of Bakewell, which demanded payment for the house owners' continued use of the track. The owners successfully claimed a right of way over the track by prescription, although their user was illegal, being a breach of s 193(4) of the Law of Property Act 1925 (as amended).

Lord Scott

At [46]–[47]

It is accepted, however, that a prescriptive right, or a right under the lost modern grant fiction, can be obtained by long use that throughout was illegal in the sense of being tortious. That is how prescription operates. Public policy does not prevent conduct illegal in that sense from leading to the acquisition of property rights. The decision in *Hanning's case* can only be justified on the footing that conduct illegal in a criminal sense is, for public policy purposes, different in kind from conduct illegal in a tortious sense. Why should that necessarily be so? Why, in particular, should it be so where the conduct in question is use of land that is not a criminal use of land against which the public law sets its face in all cases? It is criminal only because it is a user of land for which the landowner has given no "lawful authority". In that respect, the use of land made criminal by section 193(4) of the 1925 Act, or by section 34(1) of the 1988 Act, has much more in common with use of land that is illegal because it is tortious than with use of land that is illegal because it is criminal.

In my opinion, if an easement over land can be lawfully granted by the landowner the easement can be acquired either by prescription under section 2 of the 1832 Act or by the fiction of lost modern grant whether the use relied on is illegal in the criminal sense or merely in the tortious sense. I can see no valid reason of public policy to bar that acquisition.

The user must not be secret, in the sense that a reasonable person in the position of the servient owner should be able to discover that the right is being exercised. A servient owner cannot acquiesce unless he or she knows, or ought to have known, of the exercise of the right.

Union Lighterage Co v London Graving Dock Co [1902] 2 Ch 557, CA

Facts: A dry dock was secured to an adjoining wharf by underground rods, which were not visible to the eye. The owner of the dock failed in his claim for an easement of support by prescription, because the Court decided that his user was not reasonably discoverable.

Romer LJ

At 570

Now, on principle, it appears to me that a prescriptive right to an easement over a man's land should only be acquired when the enjoyment has been open—that is to say, of such a character that an ordinary owner of the land, diligent in the protection of his interests, would have, or must be taken to have, a reasonable opportunity of becoming aware of that enjoyment. And I think on the balance of authority that this principle has been recognised as the law, and ought to be followed by us. In support of this statement I do not think it necessary to do more than refer to those parts, which deal with this point, of the speeches made by Lord Selborne and Lord Penzance in the House of Lords in *Dalton v. Angus* (1881) 6 App Cas 740, and I gather that their views as there expressed on this point were not dissented from by the other members of the House who took part in the hearing of that case, and, indeed, Lord Blackburn said at 827 that no prescriptive right "can be acquired where there is any concealment, and probably none where the enjoyment has not been open."

Although the right of support failed in *Union Lighterage*, it is clear that rights of support are not inherently secret, as was pointed out in the following case.

Dalton v Angus & Co (1881) 6 LR App Cas 740

Lord Selbourne

At 798

[...T]here are some things of which all men ought to be presumed to have knowledge, and among them (I think) is the fact, that, according to the laws of nature, a building cannot stand without vertical or (ordinarily) without lateral support. When a new building is openly erected on one side of the dividing line between two properties, its general nature and character, its exterior and much of its interior structure, must be visible and ascertainable by the adjoining proprietor during the course of its erection.

The permission of the servient owner to the claimant's exercise of the right will prevent prescription. But it is important to distinguish permission from the servient owner's acquiescence, which underlies prescription. The Court of Appeal has firmly rejected suggestions that toleration of user without objection could constitute permission.

Mills v Silver [1991] Ch 271, CA

Dhillon LJ

At 279

The topic of tolerance has bulked fairly large in recent decisions of this court dealing with claims to prescriptive rights, since the decision in *Alfred F. Beckett Ltd. v. Lyons* [1967] Ch. 449. If passages in successive judgments are taken on their own out of context and added together, it would be easy to say, as, with all respect, it seems to me that the judge did in the present case, that there is an established principle of law that no prescriptive right can be acquired if the user by the dominant owner of the servient tenement in the particular manner for the appropriate number of years has been tolerated without objection by the servient owner. But there cannot be any such principle of law because it is, with rights of way, fundamentally inconsistent with the whole notion of acquisition of rights by prescription. It is difficult to see how, if there is such a principle, there could ever be a prescriptive right of way. It follows that the various passages in the judgments in question cannot be taken on their own out of context. If each case is looked at on its own and regarded as a whole, none lays down any such far-reaching principle. In my judgment, the judge in the present case has misapplied the authorities, by taking passages out of context, and misdirected himself in arriving at the supposed principle of law which he has sought to apply.

At 281

It is to be noted that a prescriptive right arises where there has been user as of right in which the servient owner has, with the requisite degree of knowledge, which is not an issue in the present case, acquiesced. Therefore mere acquiescence in or tolerance of the user by the servient owner cannot prevent the user being user as of right for purposes of prescription [. . .] A priori, user in which the servient owner has acquiesced or which he has tolerated is not inconsistent with the concept of user as of right. To put it another way, user is not "precario" for the purposes of prescription just because until 20 years have run, the servient owner could stop it at any time by issuing his writ and asking for an injunction.

3.3.3 User in fee simple

The presumption that a permanent grant has been made at some time in the past dictates that prescriptive user must be by, and against, a fee simple owner.[129] A lessee thus cannot

---

[129] *Simmons v Dobson* [1991] 1 WLR 720; *Kilgour v Gaddes* [1904] 1 KB 457.

acquire a prescriptive easement over adjoining land held either by his or her landlord or by anyone else.[130] Nor is an owner of dominant land able to claim prescription against servient land that is let, when the servient freehold owner, even if he or she knows of the use, is in no position to object to it, although where the prescriptive user is initiated between freehold owners, the subsequent grant of a lease, either of the dominant or servient land, will not interrupt the prescription period.[131]

This position differs from the treatment of adverse possession and leases that we considered in Chapter 10, section 6, and has been criticized by the Law Commission.

Law Commission Consultation Paper No 186, *Easements, Covenants and Profits à Prendre* (2008, [4.242]–[4.244])

It may be thought that the law in this area is somewhat rigid, and that it should be sufficiently flexible to accommodate some possibility of prescriptive acquisition in relation to leasehold estates. As Megarry and Wade point out in relation to the servient land, "[i]t seems irrational to allow prescription against land if occupied by an owner in fee simple but not if occupied under a 999-year lease".

Then there is the general rule that a tenant cannot acquire an easement by prescription over land which is owned by his or her landlord. We accept that it should be possible for the landlord, by making express provision in the lease, to prevent a tenant from obtaining such rights for the duration of the tenancy. However, where there is no express provision, it seems to us that the rule denying the prescriptive acquisition of an easement may be unnecessarily rigid.

While we see that to permit prescriptive acquisition other than by one fee simple estate against another would be to expand the circumstances in which prescription may take place, at the same time it would lead to the acquisition of rights of a more limited duration than those which are currently acquired. Whereas use by a tenant currently enures for the benefit of the landlord's freehold estate, with the effect that the easement acquired is for a fee simple absolute in possession, under a more nuanced scheme, the easement acquired would be limited in duration to the tenant's leasehold estate.

3.3.4 Reform

Lord Hoffman in *Sunningwell*[132] noted that '[a]*ny legal system must have rules of prescription which prevent the disturbance of long-established de facto enjoyment*'. The Law Commission has summarized the most important functions as being utility, and to reconcile the factual and legal position.

Law Commission Consultation Paper No 186, *Easements, Covenants and Profits à Prendre* (2008)

At [4.178]

The overwhelming argument in favour of the retention of prescription is that the law—the legal position—should reflect and recognize the fact of long use [...]

---

[130] The benefit of their prescriptive user accrues to the holder of the freehold.
[131] *Pugh v Savage* [1970] 2 QB 373.
[132] [2000] 1 AC 335, 349.

> **At [4.182]**
>
> Most importantly, prescription recognizes the fact that land is a social resource, in that it cannot be utilized without the co-operation of neighbouring landowners Neighbouring landowners, to varying degrees, rely on one another for rights of access, drainage, support and water. In many cases co-operation between neighbouring landowners is regulated through legal instruments and informal arrangements. However, there will always remain cases where reliance on one's neighbour is entirely unregulated and may have occurred for a substantial period of time. In such circumstances there is an arguable case for clothing the user with legal right.

It has therefore not recommended the outright abolition of prescription,[133] although prescription continues to come under fire;[134] instead, it has advocated a new statutory regime to address the widely acknowledged defects in the current law, the essential details of which we have already outlined.

4 EASEMENTS: THE DEFENCES QUESTION

4.1 REGISTERED LAND

We have already explored the aim of the LRA 2002 that the register *'should be a complete and accurate reflection of the state of the title of the land'*.[135] Easements presented a challenge to the achievement of that aim, stemming from the fact that easements can arise by express, implied, and presumed grant, and that, under the Land Registration Act 1925 (LRA 1925), all easements potentially took effect as overriding interests.[136] Thus legal easements (whether arising by express, implied, or presumed grant) did not need to be entered on the register to bind a third party, although it was common practice for express easements to be so recorded. Somewhat controversially, equitable easements—arising, for example, from an agreement to create an easement—were also held to take effect as overriding interests, provided that they were openly enjoyed.[137]

The LRA 2002 has risen to the challenge by providing that:

- easements that are protected by registration will bind a purchaser;[138]

- easements created before the Act came into force on 13 October 2003, which are not protected by registration, but which are overriding interests, will continue to override;[139]

- an express easement created after 13 October 2003 must be registered if it is to take effect as a legal easement;[140]

---

[133] Unlike its predecessors, the Law Reform Committee (1966, [32]). See also Burns, 'Prescriptive Easements in England and Legal "Climate Change"' [2007] Conv 133.

[134] See Burns, ibid.

[135] Law Commission Report No 271, *Land Registration for the Twenty-First Century: A Conveyancing Revolution* (2001, [1.5]). See further Chapter 16.

[136] Land Registration Act 1925, s 70(1)a.

[137] *Celsteel Ltd v Alton House Holdings Ltd* [1985] 1 WLR 204, reversed in part on another point [1986] 1 WLR 512.

[138] Land Registration Act 2002, s 29(2)(a).

[139] Ibid, Sch 12, para 9.

[140] Ibid, s 27.

- an equitable easement created after 13 October 2003 can no longer count as an overriding interest in its own right and so is vulnerable to the lack of registration defence (see Chapter 6, section 3.2, and Chapter 16, section 5);
- implied or presumed legal easements will only override if certain conditions are met.[141]

Implied easements arising by necessity, common intention, under *Wheeldon v Burrows*, or by the operation of s 62 of the LPA 1925, and presumed easements created by prescription present a particular problem to a system of title by registration.[142] If the grant or reservation of such an easement is implied into the grant or reservation of a legal estate in land, the implied easement will be a *legal* interest in land. Similarly, an easement arising by prescription is also a legal easement, of which there need be no documentary record. Such legal easements may be difficult to discover, because there is no express grant that can be lodged at the Land Registry.

The LRA 2002 seeks to address this challenge by providing that implied and presumed legal easements will only override if they satisfy certain conditions focusing upon their discoverability. These conditions are found in Sch 3, para 3, of the 2002 Act.

Land Registration Act 2002, Sch 3, para 3

(1) A legal easement or profit a prendre, except for an easement, or a profit a prendre which is not registered under the Common Registration Act 1965 (c64) which at the time of the disposition—

(a) is not within the actual knowledge of the person to whom the disposition is made, and

(b) would not have been obvious on a reasonably careful inspection of the land over which the easement or profit is exerciseable.

(2) The exception in sub-paragraph (1) does not apply if the person entitled to the easement or profit proves that it has been exercised in the period of one year ending with the day of the disposition.

Thus an implied or presumed legal easement created after 13 October 2003 will only bind a purchaser of the servient land if the purchaser knew, or should have known from a reasonably careful inspection of the servient land, of the easement, or the easement had been exercised by the dominant owner in the year preceding the sale. Those easements that fail to satisfy these conditions will vanish upon a disposal of the servient land, because they will not bind a registered purchaser for value.[143] A dominant owner claiming the benefit of an implied or presumed easement, however, may avoid this unhappy result by applying to have the easement registered.[144]

---

[141] Ibid, Sch 3, para 3.
[142] See Burns (2008).
[143] Kenny, 'Vanishing Easements in Registered Land' [2003] Conv 304; Battersby, 'More Thoughts on Easements under the Land Registration Act 2002' [2005] Conv 195.
[144] Land Registration Rules 2003 (SI 2003/1417), r 74.

4.2 UNREGISTERED LAND

The priority rules governing easements where the land is unregistered are relatively straight-forward. Legal easements, whether arising by express, implied, or presumed grant, bind a purchaser of the servient land. Equitable easements, however, only bind if they are protected by entry in the land charges register as a Class D(iii) land charge.[145]

A disposal of the servient land, whether by way of transfer, a lease for more than seven years, or first mortgage, will now trigger first registration of that land.[146] Existing legal easements over the servient land (whether by express, implied, or presumed grant) will, on first registration, bind the purchaser as overriding interests.[147] Equitable easements will not, however, bind a purchaser of the servient land and the owner of the dominant land is well advised to lodge a caution against first registration of the servient land, so that they can assert their right against any purchaser.[148]

5 EXCESSIVE USER

Where a dominant owner exceeds the ambit of the right that he or she has been granted, the servient owner, or another dominant owner whose own rights are affected, may seek redress in nuisance for excessive user.[149] That redress may include the grant of an injunction or an award of compensatory damages, or, in extreme cases, the extinguishment of the easement. In addition, a servient or another dominant owner may take self-help measures to stop the excessive user.

Whether or not a user is excessive will depend on the terms of the grant. Where the easement has been expressly granted, that will be determined by looking at the terms of the deed. Where the easement is implied or presumed, the courts will look at the use and the nature of the land at the time of the implied or presumed grant.[150] A mere increase in user will not be excessive; what is required is a radical change in the character of the user of the dominant land, which leads to a substantial increase in the burden that user places upon the servient land.

The Court of Appeal considered the question of excessive user in the following case.

McAdams Homes Ltd v Robinson [2005] 1 P & CR 30, CA

Facts: The MacAdams built two homes on the site of an old bakery, which enjoyed a right of drainage over Robinson's land under *Wheeldon v Burrows*. Robinson successfully prevented McAdams from using the drain once the two houses were built, because the Court of Appeal found that McAdams' user was excessive, representing a substantial increase on the burden on the servient land.

---

145 See Chapter 15, section 5.2.
146 Land Registration Act 2002, s 4.
147 Ibid, Sch 1, para 3.
148 Ibid, Pt 2.
149 *McAdams Homes Ltd v Robinson* [2004] EWCA Civ 214, [2005] 1 P & CR 30, [27].
150 *British Railways Board v Glass* [1965] Ch 538.

Lord Neuberger

At [50]–[51]

The authorities discussed above appear to me to indicate that that issue should have been determined by answering two questions. Those questions are:

i)   whether the development of the dominant land, ie the site, represented a "radical change in the character" or a "change in the identity" of the site [...] as opposed to a mere change or intensification in the use of the site [...]

ii) whether the use of the site as redeveloped would result in a substantial increase or alteration in the burden on the servient land, ie the cottage [...]

In my opinion, the effect of the authorities in relation to the present case is that it would only be if the redevelopment of the site represented a radical change in its character and it would lead to a substantial increase in the burden, that the dominant owner's right to enjoy the easement of passage of water through the pipe would be suspended or lost.

At 55

The [...] potentially unsatisfactory feature of the approach I have suggested is that both questions could be said to involve an exercise which, in many circumstances, may have a rather uncertain outcome. What may appear to be "a radical change in character" to one judge could easily appear differently to another judge; equally, one judge may consider a particular increase in the burden on the servient land to be "substantial", whereas another judge may not. It is, perhaps, inevitable that the questions have to be expressed in this rather generalised way, because each case will very much turn on its own facts, with regard to the particular easement, the position on the ground at the date of grant, the surrounding circumstances at the date of grant, and the nature and effect of the redevelopment that has subsequently taken place. What [the] cases [...] demonstrate is that, before a change of use or redevelopment can be sufficiently substantial for the servient owner to succeed on the first question, it really must involve something "radical". Similarly, before the servient owner can succeed on the second question, the cases show that the court must be satisfied that there has not merely been an increase (or change) in the enjoyment of the easement as a result of the changed character of the dominant land, but that there has been a real increase (or change) in the burden on the servient land.

6   EXTINGUISHMENT OF EASEMENTS

We have already seen that an easement will be extinguished, in the case of freehold land, where the dominant and servient land come into common ownership, and will be suspended, in the case of leasehold land, where the dominant and servient land come into common occupation. It was also thought that an easement attached to a leasehold estate could not survive the merger of that estate with the freehold reversion—but the Court of Appeal has surprised many by holding, in *Wall v Collins*,[151] that an easement can survive in these circumstances. The decision has been criticized and the Law Commission have recommended that it should be overturned by statute.[152]

---

[151] [2007] EWCA Civ 644, noted at [2007] Conv 465.
[152] Law Commission Consultation Paper No 136 (2008, [5.86]).

The dominant and servient owners may bring an easement to an end by express release and, more controversially, a release may also be implied as a result of abandonment.[153] An easement is abandoned if the dominant owner acts, or fails to act, with an intention to relinquish the right. The permanence of proprietary rights is demonstrated by the difficulty of proving that intention.[154] The fact of non-user does not raise any presumption of abandonment;[155] something more is required—particularly where the right by its nature is not continuously exercised.[156] For example, the alteration of the dominant tenement may demonstrate abandonment where the right can no longer be exercised.[157]

McFarlane has suggested that abandonment is better viewed as an application of estoppel.

McFarlane, *The Structure of Property Law* (2008, p 873)

However the concept of abandonment is very problematic. In general, a party with a property right does *not* have the power to simply give up that right: if he wishes to dispose of the right, he needs to transfer it to another. B [the dominant owner] can of course release an Easement; but only if a deed is used. Cases of so-called informal abandonment are hence better seen as examples of: (i) C [the servient owner] having a defence to B's Easement as a result of defensive estoppel; or C [the servient owner] relying on proprietary estoppel to show that B [the dominant owner] is under a duty to release his Easement.

The Law Commission, meanwhile, has recommended that the jurisdiction of the Lands Tribunal under s 84 of the LPA 1925, which we examine in the next chapter, should be extended to provide for the modification and discharge of easements.[158]

QUESTIONS

1. Do you think that a right to use a swimming pool could exist as an easement?

2. Why has the right to park caused such difficulty in being recognized as an easement?

3. What conceptual challenges do negative easements present?

4. An easement can be impliedly granted either by looking at the future use of the dominant land, or by looking at how the grantor has used the land in the past. In what circumstances can an easement be impliedly reserved?

5. Does it matter whether easements of necessity are based upon public policy or intention?

6. *Wheeldon v Burrows* and s 62 look deceptively similar, but how do they differ?

---

[153] Shorrock, 'Non-user of Easements' (1998) 4 Nott LJ 26.

[154] *Tehidy Minerals Ltd v Norman* [1971] 2 QB 528.

[155] The Law Commission has suggested, in relation to unregistered land, that a presumption of abandonment should arise after twenty years, but that it should be impossible to abandon a registered easement: see Law Commission Consultation Paper No 186 (2008, [5.23]–[5.31]).

[156] *Amstrong v Shappard & Shroff* [1959] 2 QB 384; *Benn v Hardinge* (1993) 66 P & CR 246.

[157] *Ecclesiastical Commissioners for England v Kino* (1880) 14 Ch D 213.

[158] See Law Commission Consultation Paper No 186 (2008, [14.25]–[14.32]).

7. Should prescription be abolished?

8. In what circumstances will an implied or presumed easement vanish upon the sale of the servient land?

FURTHER READING

Bradbrooke, 'Access to Landlocked Land: A Comparative Study of Legal Solutions' (1983–85) 10 Syd LR 39

Burns, 'Easements and Servitudes Created by Implied Grant, Implied Reservation or Prescription and Title by Registration Systems' in *Modern Studies in Property Law: Vol 5* (ed Dixon, Oxford: Hart, 2009)

Burns, 'Prescriptive Easements in England and Legal Climate Change' [2007] Conv 133

Getzler, 'Roman and English Prescription for Incorporeal Property' in *Rationalizing Property, Equity and Trusts: Essays in Honour of Edward Burn* (ed Getzler, London: Butterworths, 2003, ch 11)

Goymour, 'Rights in Property and the Effluxion of Time' in *Modern Studies in Property Law: Vol 4* (ed Cooke, Oxford: Hart, 2007)

Haley and McMurty, 'Identifying an Easement: Exclusive Use, De Facto Control and Judicial Constraints' (2007) 58 NILQ 490

Harpum, 'Easements and Centre Point: Old Problems Resolved in a Novel Setting' (1977) 41 Conv 415

Hill Smith, 'Rights of Parking and the Ouster Principle after *Batchelor v Marlow*' [2007] Conv 223

Law Commission Consultation Paper No 186, *Easements, Covenants and Profits à Prendre* (2008)

Lawson, 'Easements' in *Land Law: Issues, Debates, Policy* (ed Tee, Devon: Willan, 2002)

Luther, 'Easements and Exclusive Possession' (1996) 16 LS 51

McClean, 'The Nature of an Easement' (1966) 5 West LR 32

Paton and Seabourne, 'Can't Get There From Here? Permissible Use of Easements After *Das*' [2003] Conv 127

Shorrock, 'Non-user of Easements' (1995) 4 Nott LJ 26

Simpson, '*Wheeldon v Burrows* and the *Code Civile*' [1967] 83 LQR 240

Sturley, 'Easements in Gross' (1980) 96 LQR 557

Tee, 'Metamorphoses and Section 62 of the Law of Property Act 1925' [1998] Conv 115

27

FREEHOLD COVENANTS

CENTRAL ISSUES

1. Restrictive covenants play an important role in controlling land use, supplementing and complementing public planning laws.

2. A covenant is an agreement by deed and, as such, generally only enforceable between the parties—but restrictive covenants can be enforced by and against subsequent owners of the land to which they relate.

3. A restrictive covenant must: (i) relate to land; (ii) be intended to be enforceable against subsequent owners of the land; (iii) be capable of benefiting adjacent land; and (iv) be negative in nature.

4. To be enforceable as an equitable proprietary interest, a restrictive covenant must be protected by appropriate registration.

5. The benefit of a restrictive covenant will run if it is: (i) expressly assigned; (ii) annexed to the land; or (iii) subject to a building scheme.

6. The breach of a restrictive covenant may result in an award of damages or the court may exercise its discretion to grant an injunction to restrain a breach or order action to 'cure' the breach.

7. The Lands Tribunal has jurisdiction under s 84 of the Law of Property Act 1925 to modify or extinguish restrictive covenants.

8. The law governing covenants has long been regarded as unsatisfactory and has been subject to repeated proposals for reform.

1 INTRODUCTION

A covenant is an agreement entered into by deed and, as such, it binds the parties to the covenant. We saw in Chapter 25 how leasehold covenants may be enforced by and against a landlord's assignee of the freehold reversion and a tenant's assignee of the leasehold estate by privity of estate.[1] In this chapter, we will examine how certain covenants relating to land

---

[1] See Goulding, 'Privity of Estate and the Enforcement of Real Covenants' (2007) 36 3 CLWR 193 for an interesting view that privity of estate, at one time, extended to covenants affecting the freehold estate and a comparative examination of the US position.

between freehold owners can overcome the normal privity of contract rule, and can be enforced by and against third parties. For example, where neighbouring freeholders agree with each other that they will not build on their land without the consent of the other, the covenant will be of little value unless it can be enforced not only between the parties to this mutual covenant, but also any person who becomes an owner of either piece of land. Incidentally, the same principles may also be applied to enforce leasehold covenants against parties who are not within privity of estate: for example, subtenants.

1.1 THE ROLE OF LAND COVENANTS

The transformation of land covenants from mere personal contracts between landowners to proprietary obligations that affect subsequent owners of the land occurred during the nineteenth century, when the Chancery courts developed the rules that will be the subject of this chapter.

Gardner explains what prompted these developments.

Gardner, *An Introduction to Land Law* (2007, p 181)

They date from the first half of the 19th century, a time of rapid growth of English towns. Many inhabitants were poor, but there was also an affluent middle class, which aspired to a high standard of living. The prevailing environment of slum housing, factories and so on was inimical to this: even if a middle class family's home was inwardly agreeable, stepping outside the front door could entail a quite different experience. Things could be improved, however, by creating enclaves of middle class housing, producing a more pleasant external as well as internal environment. The techniques by which this was done included the architectural (eg the terrace; and the square was an especially useful way of creating such an enclave especially if the rear rooms of the houses facing the squalor beyond, were made the servants quarters), and the horticultural (eg creating a pleasant garden in the middle of the square, a larger space than each individual house could command, and a place for socialising with people similarly circumstances).

But the trick would work only if it was possible to secure the enclave's integrity over time [...] This was a task for the law. Restrictive covenants are best understood as the new right in rem developed to perform it.

So those buying houses in the enclaves were placed under an obligation in this respect, requiring them not to use their premises for 'noxious trades', etc.

It was thus a desire to control land use that was the major driver at a time when there was little public health or planning control. Of course, there are now many legal controls over land ownership. Indeed, Gray and Gray[2] describe land ownership as being '*intrinsically delimited by social or community-orientated obligations of a positive nature.*' There are extensive public planning laws and building control regulations, so an owner cannot build on his or her land without the approval of the local planning authority, and other than in a manner that accords with high safety and environmental standards. Conservation of the built and natural environment is promoted through legislative regulation, whilst public health and environmental controls, and the private law of nuisance, provide protection against uses that may endanger quiet and safe enjoyment.

[2] See Gray and Gray, *Elements of Land Law* (5th edn, 2009, [1.5.54]–[1.5.57]).

Despite these measures, privately negotiated land covenants still have a v
role to play. Every estate of new homes is made subject to a range of restrictive co
regulate the ambience, and thus maintain the value, of the estate. Land Registry figu.
mate that 79 per cent of registered freehold titles are subject to restrictive covenants. In 2.
alone, over 300,000 new covenants were registered over freehold land; only slightly fewei
new covenants were created in 2004.[3]

Gray and Gray explain the role that land covenants play.[4]

Gray and Gray, *Elements of Land Law* (4th edn, 2005, [13.20])

Although public planning processes have now taken over much of the function of privately
contracted arrangements, there still remains an important role for private and quasi-private
governance of land use. It is often the case that private covenants deal more satisfactorily
with the detailed organisation of land use than can existing public planning controls. Private
covenants can be particularly significant in regulating the immediate local environment of
neighbours as, for instance, where parties contract for the maintenance and repair of boundary features or agree to adhere to a vernacular style of construction or a specific pattern of
density in any future development. More generally, however, it is painfully apparent nowadays that privately bargained covenants operate frequently as a longstop guardian of wider,
community-orientated conservationist concerns, protecting a range of environmental amenities which are no longer assured by the local planning process.

1.2 THE STRUCTURE AND TERMINOLOGY OF LAND COVENANTS

Before we go onto to examine the detailed legal rules that achieve this regulation of land use
and amenity, it is important that we understand the structure in which these rules operate
and the terminology employed.

As illustrated in Figure 24, A (the owner of Plot A) may agree with his or her neighbour B
(the owner of Plot B) that he or she will not build on Plot A without B's consent. Here, A has
the *burden* of the covenant: his or her ability to build is restricted and he or she can be sued if
he or she builds without consent. A is called the *covenantor*, while B is the *covenantee*. B has
the *benefit* of the covenant: he or she can sue if A breaches the covenant.

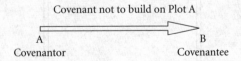

Covenant not to build on Plot A

A   B
Covenantor   Covenantee

Figure 24 A restricted land covenant

As illustrated in Figure 25, if A sells Plot A, B will need to prove that the burden of A's covenant has passed with Plot A to the new owner. If B, in turn, sells Plot B, his or her purchaser

---

[3] The figure for 2004 was 268,394: see Law Commission Consultation Paper No 186, *Easements, Covenants and Profits à Prendre* (2008, Appendix A).

[4] See also for the role that land covenants may play in conservation Hodge and Castle, 'Covenants for the Countryside' [1994] Conv 122.

will need to prove that the benefit of the covenant passes with Plot B to the new owner. These processes are referred to as the 'running of' the burden and the benefit.[5] We will use the expression 'dominant land' to refer to the land that has the benefit of the covenant and 'servient land' to refer to the land that is burdened.

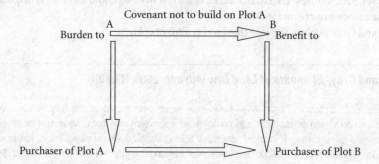

Figure 25 The transmission of the benefit and burden of land covenants

Where the purchasers of Plots A and B acquire, whether by sale or gift, A and B's full freehold title, they are known as the *successors in title* to A and B, but if A leases Plot A and B mortgages Plot B, the new lessee and mortgagee are referred to as *persons deriving title from A and B*, respectively, because the interests that they acquire are carved out of A and B's freehold estates.

As illustrated in Figure 26, the structure becomes a little more complicated in the common situation in which A and B agree with each other that neither of them will build on their land without the consent of the other. Here, the covenants are mutual: A and B have both the benefit and the burden of the covenants; they are each both covenantor and covenantee. To work out, in a given scenario, whether we need to prove whether it is the benefit or the burden that has passed to the current owner of Plots A or B it is easier to ask whom we wish to sue (we need to prove that the burden has run) and then who wishes to sue (he or she must have the benefit of the covenant to do so).

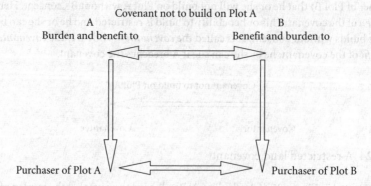

Figure 26 The transmission of mutual land covenants

---

[5] Gardner has rightly pointed out that it is not the covenant that runs, but the owners of Plots A and B. The benefit and burden of the covenant is attached to the land itself, and thus goes nowhere; it is the owners that change: see Gardner, *Introduction to Land Law* (2007, p 191).

2 THE BURDEN: WHO CAN SUE?

The burden of a covenant does not run at law,[6] so we must turn to the equitable principles initially formulated in the following leading case.[7]

Tulk v Moxhay (1848) 2 Ph 774

Facts: In 1808, Tulk sold part of land that he owned in Leicester Square to Elms, who covenanted to Tulk that he would '*at all times thereafter at his own cost keep and maintain the piece of ground in sufficient and proper repair, and in an open state, uncovered with any buildings, in neat and ornamental order*'. This land came into the ownership of Moxhay, who had notice of the covenant that Elms had given to Tulk. When Moxhay made plans to develop the land, Tulk obtained an injunction to restrain him from doing so.

Lord Cottenham LC

At 777

That this Court has jurisdiction to enforce a contract between the owner of land and his neighbour purchasing part of it, that the latter shall either use or abstain from using the land purchased in a particular way, is what I never knew disputed. Here there is no question about the contract: the owner of certain houses in the square sells the land adjoining, with a covenant from the purchaser not to use it for any other purpose than as a square garden. And it is now contended, not that the vendee could violate that contract, but that he might sell the piece of land, and that the purchaser from him may violate it without this Court having any power to interfere. If that were so, it would be impossible for an owner of land to sell part of it without incurring the risk of rendering what he retains worthless. It is said that, the covenant being one which does not run with the land, this Court cannot enforce it; but the question is, not whether the covenant runs with the land, but whether a party shall be permitted to use the land in a manner inconsistent with the contract entered into by his vendor, and with notice of which he purchased. Of course, the price would be affected by the covenant, and nothing could be more inequitable than that the original purchaser should be able to sell the property the next day for a greater price, in consideration of the assignee being allowed to escape from the liability which he had himself undertaken.

That the question does not depend upon whether the covenant runs with the land is evident from this, that if there was a mere agreement and no covenant, this Court would enforce it against a party purchasing with notice of it; for if an equity is attached to the property by the owner, no one purchasing with notice of that equity can stand in a different situation from the party from whom he purchased.

As we saw when examining the decision in Chapter 7, section 2.6, Lord Cottenham's reasoning is primarily based on the fact that Moxhay acquired the land with knowledge of the promise that Elms had made to Tulk. On this reasoning, Tulk did not assert a pre-existing

---

[6] *Austerberry v Oldham Corp* (1885) 29 Ch D 750, affirmed in *Rhone v Stephens* [1994] 2 AC 310.

[7] It appears that the principles first emerged in the earlier cases of *Whatman v Gibson* (1839) 2 My & K 517 and *Mann v Stephens* (1846) 15 Sim 377.

equitable interest against Moxhay; rather, Tulk acquired a new, direct right as a result of Moxhay's conduct. But Lord Cottenham also hinted that the initial promise made by Elms to Tulk had proprietary characteristics. Certainly, as the doctrine developed during the latter half of the nineteenth century, the Chancery courts reinterpreted *Tulk v Moxhay* as a case in which Tulk *did* assert a pre-existing equitable interest, arising as a result of Elms' covenant with Tulk. This process is discussed in Chapter 8, section 3.3.2.[8]

In doing so, those courts also defined the characteristics of that equitable interest more clearly. The rules that they developed may be summarized as follows.

1. The burden of the covenant must not be personal, but must relate to, and be intended to run with, the land to which it relates.

2. There must be dominant land that is capable of benefiting from the covenant.

3. The covenant must be negative in nature.

These characteristics define the content of a land covenant, which, in common with any proprietary interest, must conform to the relevant creation and priority rules if it is to bind the parties and a subsequent purchaser.

2.1 THE COVENANT MUST RELATE TO LAND

The covenant must relate to the land and not to some personal obligation between the parties. A might agree to send B a dozen red roses on Valentine's Day, but whilst that might say something about A's personal attraction to B, it has nothing whatsoever to do with A's ownership of Plot A. The most common covenants that relate to land are concerned with the use of the land, or its repair or maintenance.[9] The parties must also intend that the covenant should affect them as owners of the land, rather than in a solely personal capacity, although such an intention is presumed.

Law of Property Act 1925, s 79(1)

(1) A covenant relating to any land of the covenantor or capable of being bound by him, shall, unless a contrary intention is expressed, be deemed to be made by the covenantor on behalf of himself his successors in title and the persons deriving title under him or them and subject as aforesaid, shall have effect as if such successors and other persons were expressed.

There have been several attempts to argue that s 79 of the Law of Property Act 1925 (LPA 1925) in itself enables the burden to run with the land, but these attempts have failed.[10]

---

[8] For more detail, see McFarlane [2003] Conv 473, 482–7.

[9] Some covenants prohibiting competition have been held to be personal (see, e.g., *Morrells of Oxford Ltd v Oxford United Football Club Ltd* [2001] Ch 459), although restricting the user of land to prevent a particular commercial activity may not be (*Newton Abbott Co-operative Society v Williamson & Treadgold Ltd* [1952] 1 Ch 286).

[10] *Re Royal Victoria Pavilion, Ramsgate* [1961] Ch 58; *Tophams Ltd v Earl of Sefton* [1967] 1 AC 50; *Rhone v Stephens* [1994] 2 AC 310; *Morrells of Oxford Ltd v Oxford United Football Club Ltd* [2001] Ch 459; but see Turano, 'Intention, Interpretation and the Mystery of Section 79 of the Law of Property Act 1925' [2000] Conv 377.

Section 79 is a word-saving device that makes it unnecessary to refer to 'successor in title' and 'persons deriving title' expressly in the covenant itself.

Robert Walker LJ explained (as dicta) its role in the following case, which concerned whether a covenant limiting competition was a personal covenant displaying a contrary intention for the purposes of s 79.

Morrells of Oxford Ltd v Oxford United Football Club Ltd [2001] Ch 459

Robert Walker LJ

At [40]

Section 79 is concerned with simplifying conveyancing by creating a rebuttable presumption that covenants relating to land of the covenantor are intended to be made on behalf of successors in title, rather than be intended as purely personal. That is a necessary condition, but not a sufficient condition, for making the burden of the covenants run with the land.

A little earlier in his judgment, he explained its effect.[11]

Morrells Oxford Ltd v Oxford United Football Club Ltd [2001] Ch 459, CA

Robert Walker LJ

At [35]

My tentative view, therefore, coinciding, I think, with the judge's, is that section 79, where it applies, and subject always to any contrary intention, extends the number of persons whose acts or omissions are within the reach of the covenant in the sense of making equitable remedies available, provided that the other conditions for equity's intervention are satisfied. Where [...] section 79 applies, its normal effect is not to turn "A covenants with X that A will not build" into "A and B covenant with X that A will not build". Rather it is that "A (on behalf of himself and B) covenants with X that A (or, as the circumstances may require, B) will not build".

2.2 BENEFIT TO DOMINANT LAND

In a similar way to easements, there must be dominant land to which the benefit of the covenant is attached.[12] The benefit is attached to the covenantee's estate in the land[13] and, once he or she has disposed of that estate, he or she cannot enforce the covenant unless, as the original covenantee, he or she has a contractual right to do so. It is thus not possible for a covenant to exist in gross.

---

11 See also Hurst, 'The Transmission of Restrictive Covenants' (1982) 2 LS 53, 75.

12 Some earlier authorities had suggested otherwise: see *Catt v Tourle* (1869) LR 4 Ch 654 and *Luker v Dennis* (1877) 7 Ch D 227.

13 A landlord's reversion is a sufficient estate for these purposes: see *Hall v Erwin* (1887) 37 Ch D 74.

A common scenario arises where an owner of land sells part and requires the purchaser to enter into a covenant restricting what he or she can do with the purchased land, to maintain the amenity and value of the land that the seller retains.

London CC v Allen [1914] 3 KB 642, CA

Facts: In order to obtain permission to form a street on part of his land, Mr Allen entered into a covenant with the London County Council that he would not build on the land at the end of the proposed street so that the new street could be extended. He then sold the land subject to the covenant to his wife, who built on the land. The London County Council tried to enforce the covenant against Mrs Allen, but was unsuccessful because it held no land that could benefit from the covenant.

Buckley LJ

At 654

The reasoning of Lord Cottenham's judgment in *Tulk v. Moxhay* is that if an owner of land sells part of it reserving the rest, and takes from his purchaser a covenant that the purchaser shall use or abstain from using the land purchased in a particular way, that covenant (being one for the protection of the land reserved) is enforceable against a sub-purchaser with notice. The reason given is that, if that were not so, it would be impossible for an owner of land to sell part of it without incurring the risk of rendering what he retains worthless. If the vendor has retained no land which can be protected by the restrictive covenant, the basis of the reasoning of the judgment is swept away. In *Haywood v. Brunswick Permanent Benefit Building Society* the Court of Appeal declined to extend the doctrine of *Tulk v. Moxhay* to covenants other than restrictive covenants. They rejected the doctrine that, inasmuch as the defendants took the land with notice of the covenants, they were bound in equity to perform them. That therefore is not the principle upon which the equitable doctrine rests. In the present case we are asked to extend the doctrine of *Tulk v. Moxhay* so as to affirm that a restrictive covenant can be enforced against a derivative owner taking with notice by a person who never has had or who does not retain any land to be protected by the restrictive covenant in question. In my opinion the doctrine does not extend to that case. The doctrine is that a covenant not running with the land, but being a negative covenant entered into by an owner of land with an adjoining owner, binds the land in equity and is enforceable against a derivative owner taking with notice. The doctrine ceases to be applicable when the person seeking to enforce the covenant against the derivative owner has no land to be protected by the negative covenant. The fact of notice is in that case irrelevant.

The particular equity recognized in *Tulk v. Moxhay* has been said to be analogous to an equitable charge upon land subsisting in the owner of the adjoining land, or to a negative easement enjoyed, not in gross, but by the adjoining land over the land to which the covenant relates. It arises from the possession by the covenantee of land enjoying the benefit of the negative covenant coupled with notice of the existence of the covenant. In *London and South Western Ry. Co. v. Gomm* Sir George Jessel says:

> "The doctrine of *Tulk v. Moxhay*, rightly considered, appears to me to be either an extension in equity of the doctrine of Spencer's Case to another line of cases, or else an extension in equity of the doctrine of negative easements; such, for instance, as a right to the access of light, which prevents the owner of the servient tenement from building so as to obstruct the light. The covenant in *Tulk v. Moxhay* was affirmative in its terms, but was held by the Court to imply a negative.

> Where there is a negative covenant expressed or implied, as, for instance, not to build so as to obstruct a view, or not to use a piece of land otherwise than as a garden, the Court interferes on one or other of the above grounds. This is an equitable doctrine, establishing an exception to the rules of common law which did not treat such a covenant as running with the land, and it does not matter whether it proceeds on analogy to a covenant running with the land or on analogy to an easement."

At 660

> Upon the authorities, therefore, as a whole I am of opinion that the doctrine in *Tulk v. Moxhay* does not extend to the case in which the covenantee has no land capable of enjoying, as against the land of the covenantor, the benefit of the restrictive covenant. The doctrine is either an extension in equity of the doctrine in *Spencer's Case* (in which ownership of land by both covenantor and covenantee is essential) or an extension in equity of the doctrine of negative easements, a doctrine applicable not to the case of easements in gross, but to an easement enjoyed by one land upon another land. Where the covenantee has no land, the derivative owner claiming under the covenantor is bound neither in contract nor by the equitable doctrine which attaches in the case where there is land capable of enjoying the restrictive covenant.

The situation of the London County Council would not arise today, because statute has granted local authorities (and some other bodies) the ability to enforce covenants in the exercise of certain of their powers, although they hold no dominant land.[14]

Identification of the dominant land

The dominant land needs to be identified with reasonable certainty, although general words, such as the references to the covenantee's retained land, will suffice and it is evident that the courts may look beyond the terms of the conveyance to the surrounding circumstances at the time of the creation of the covenant in order to ascertain the dominant land.[15]

Newton Abbott Co-operative Society v Williamson & Treadgold Ltd
[1952] Ch 286, HC

Facts: Mrs Mardon owned premises known as 'Devonia', on which she carried on business as an ironmonger. She also owned property across the street, which she sold, taking a covenant from the purchaser that he or she would not carry on business as an ironmonger. There was no indication in the covenant that it was taken for the benefit of Devonia. Some years later, the property subject to the covenant came into the ownership of Williamson & Treadgold, who began to sell items of ironmongery and hardware. The Co-op, as the present owner of Devonia and to which the benefit of the covenant had been assigned successfully, obtained an injunction restraining them from doing so.

---

[14] See, e.g., (in the cases of local authorities) Housing Act 1985, s 609, and (in the case of local planning authorities) Town and Country Planning Act 1990, s106.
[15] See also *Marten v Flight Refueling Ltd* [1962] 1 Ch 115.

Upjohn J

At 296

In my judgment, therefore, the problem which I have to consider is this: First, when Mrs. Mardon took the covenant in 1923, did she retain other lands capable of being benefited by the covenant? The answer is plainly yes. Secondly, was such land "ascertainable" or "certain" in this sense that the existence and situation of the land must be indicated in the conveyance or otherwise shown with reasonable certainty?

Apart from the fact that Mrs. Mardon is described as of Devonia, there is nothing in the conveyance of 1923 to define the land for the benefit of which the restrictive covenant was taken, and I do not think that carries one very far; but, for the reasons I have given, I am, in my judgment, entitled to look at the attendant circumstances to see if the land to be benefited is shown "otherwise" with reasonable certainty. That is a question of fact and, on the admitted facts, bearing in mind the close juxtaposition of Devonia and the defendants' premises, in my view the only reasonable inference to draw from the circumstances at the time of the conveyance of 1923 was that Mrs. Mardon took the covenant restrictive of the user of the defendants' premises for the benefit of her own business of ironmonger and of her property Devonia where at all material times she was carrying on that business, which last-mentioned fact must have been apparent to the purchasers in 1923.

The benefit of the covenant must also accommodate the dominant land of the covenantee, in the sense that it affects '*either the value of the land or the method of its occupation or enjoyment*'.[16] In the *Newton Abbott Case*, the Co-op's counsel unsuccessfully argued that the covenant was a personal anti-competition covenant, which only benefited Mrs Mardon's business and not Devonia.

Newton Abbott Co-operative Society v Williamson & Treadgold Ltd
[1952] Ch 286, HC

Upjohn J

At 292

The second main question was whether the defendants are liable to have the covenant enforced against them. This was Mr. Bowles' main defence in this action and he says that the restrictive covenant was not taken for the benefit of Devonia, and he puts his case in this way: [...] he says that in any event this was not taken for the benefit of any land, but was a covenant with Mrs. Mardon personally, solely for the benefit of her business [...] Mr. Bowles strongly urged that the covenant was taken solely to protect the goodwill of the business carried on at Devonia, that it had no reference to the land itself, and that it was not taken for the benefit of that land; in brief, that it was a covenant in gross incapable of assignment. He urged that taking such a covenant would benefit the business in that an enhanced price could be obtained for the business, but no such enhanced price would be obtained for the land. He relied on the fact that the covenant did not mention the vendors' assigns and that it was a covenant against competition. Further, he pointed out that when Leonard Soper Mardon assigned to the Bovey Tracey Cooperative Society, the benefit of the covenant was assigned

---

16 *Re Gadds Land Transfer* [1966] Ch 56, 66, *per* Buckley LJ.

in the deed which assigned the business and not in the lease of Devonia. If that be the right view, then he said there could be no right to enforce the covenant against the defendants because the mere fact that the defendants took with notice is not sufficient to bind their consciences in equity, and he relied on the two cases of *Formby v. Barker* and *London County Council v. Allen*. Those cases show, he submitted, and I agree with him, that in order to enforce a covenant such as this against an assign of the covenantor, you must show that the covenant created something analogous to an equitable easement, that is, you must find something in the nature of a dominant tenement for the benefit of which the covenant was taken and a servient tenement which was to be subject to that covenant. Here he says there was no dominant tenement; the covenant was taken not for the benefit of any land, but for the benefit of the business.

I do not accept this view of the transaction of 1923. In 1923 Mrs. Mardon was carrying on the business of an ironmonger at Devonia. No doubt the covenant was taken for the benefit of that business and to prevent competition therewith, but I see no reason to think, and there is nothing in the conveyance of 1923 which leads me to believe, that that was the sole object of taking the covenant. Mrs. Mardon may well have had it in mind that she might want ultimately to sell her land and the business and the benefit of the covenant in such manner as to annex the benefit of the covenant to Devonia for, by so doing, she would get an enhanced price for the totality of the assets which she was selling; a purchaser would surely pay more for a property which would enable him to sue in equity assigns of the defendants' premises taking with notice and to pass on that right, if he so desired, to his successors, than for a property which would only enable him to sue the original covenantor, for that is the result of the view urged on me by Mr. Bowles.

Establishing benefit

Accommodation will normally require reasonable proximity between the servient and dominant land, although it is conceivable that a comparatively large area can benefit where it forms an identifiable unit.[17] There tends to be a presumption of benefit unless such a conclusion just cannot be sustained.[18]

The approach is illustrated and explained in the following case.[19]

Wrotham Park Estate Co Ltd v Parkside Homes Ltd [1974] 1 WLR 798, HC

Facts: Part of the Wrotham Estate was conveyed subject to a covenant that the land should only be developed in accordance with a layout plan approved by the estate company. Most of the land was developed in accordance with the covenant, but, when Parkside proposed to develop the remaining central area without obtaining prior approval, the estate company successfully took action on the covenant.

---

[17] See, e.g., *Marten v Flight Refueling Ltd* [1962] Ch 115 and *Earl of Leicester v Wells-next-the-Sea UDC* [1973] Ch 110, but note the earlier case of *Re Ballard's Conveyance* [1937] Ch 473. Conveyancers usually circumvent any problem by providing for the severance of the covenant between those parts of a large estate that do benefit from the covenant and those parts that do not: see *Marquess of Zetland v Driver* [1939] Ch 1.

[18] It is for the party being sued, i.e. the covenantor or his or her successors in title, to prove the lack of benefit: see *Cryer v Scott Brothers (Sudbury) Ltd* (1988) 55 P & CR 183.

[19] See also *Marten v Flight Refuelling* [1962] Ch 115, 136, *per* Wilberforce J.

Brightman J

At 808

There can be obvious cases where a restrictive covenant clearly is, or clearly is not, of benefit to an estate. Between these two extremes there is inevitably an area where the benefit to the estate is a matter of personal opinion, where responsible and reasonable persons can have divergent views sincerely and reasonably held. In my judgment, in such cases, it is not for the court to pronounce which is the correct view. I think that the court can only decide whether a particular view is one which can reasonably be held.

If a restriction is bargained for at the time of sale with the intention of giving the vendor a protection which he desires for the land he retains, and the restriction is expressed to be imposed for the benefit of the estate so that both sides are apparently accepting that the restriction is of value to the retained land, I think that the validity of the restriction should be upheld so long as an estate owner may reasonably take the view that the restriction remains of value to his estate, and that the restriction should not be discarded merely because others may reasonably argue that the restriction is spent. I think that this accords with the judgment of Sargant J. in the *Northbourne case* [1922] 2 Ch. 309 and of Wilberforce J. in the *Marten case* [1962] Ch. 115. The view, expressed by Mr. Byng and by Mr. Parker, is, in my judgment, a reasonable one, though it may be a matter of opinion whether it is correct or not. My own opinion is that it is correct, and I would so hold. For it seems to me that an estate owner living on a residential and agricultural estate sandwiched between two developing towns, is properly interested in the standard of development of those towns. To take an extreme case, which is not this case, a Wrotham Park Estate lying between two over-crowded slum districts would be a less desirable and less marketable property than a Wrotham Park Estate lying between two carefully developed and uncrowded districts.

2.3 NEGATIVITY

The covenant in *Tulk v Moxhay* had both negative and positive aspects: firstly, it called for keeping the land in an open state, i.e. it should not be built upon; and secondly, it called for the maintenance and repair of the land, although it was the negative obligation against building that was enforced.[20] In the later cases of *Hayward v Brunswick Permanent Benefit Building Society*[21] and *London and South West Railway v Gomm*,[22] the court made clear that it would only enforce negative obligations. Negative obligations restrain the owner of the servient land from acting in some way, whilst a positive obligation requires owners to put their hands in their pockets to fund some activity: for example, to maintain the land or repair some building upon it.

Gardner canvasses some of the reasons why the Victorian judges refused to enforce positive obligations.

[20] In *Morland v Cook* (1868) LR 6 Eq 252 and *Cooke v Chilcott* (1876) 3 Ch D 694, positive obligations were enforced. See Bell, '*Tulk v Moxhay* Revisited' [1981] Conv 55; Griffiths, '*Tulk v Moxhay* Reclarified' [1983] Conv 29.

[21] (1881) 8 QBD 403.

[22] (1882) 20 Ch D 562.

Gardner, 'The Proprietary effect of Contractual Obligations under *Tulk v Moxhay* and *De Mattos v Gibson*' (1982) LQR 279, 294–7

Cotton and Lindley LJJ [in *Haywood*] say it would be wrong to require a purchaser to expend money. But this seems to be no problem in the area of leasehold covenants; and Malins V-C in *Cooke v Chilcott* had already met the argument head-on, pointing out that as the purchaser necessarily (if he is to be bound) has notice of what was going to be required of him, and had presumably considered the question of the expenditure demanded when he decided to buy, there was no unfairness in subjecting him to it [...] The enforcement of positive covenant under *Tulk v Moxhay* would hardly have produced social evil on a large scale (though it might have produced greater pressure for development of notions of discharge of outmoded and inconvenient covenants than was, in fact, the case—which would have been no bad thing—and it might have produced more use of Lord Cairns Act to allow the obligee to effect a judicially sanctioned compulsory repurchase of the obligation). But it could have reduced the practical alienability of land—a would be purchaser knowing of a positive covenant might sometimes be discouraged by it, though presumably market forces would bring an abatement of the purchase price, which would be a countervailing factor. There appears, however, to be no check on what can be done with positive leasehold covenants, and yet the market in leases does not appear to suffer thereby. And the imposition of a positive duty on a third party does not appear to be objectionable in principle to equity; consider estate contracts and equitable charges.

He goes on to suggest that the availability of a suitable remedy to enforce a positive covenant against a purchaser provided a more cogent answer, given the court's reluctance to order or supervise performance of an obligation, whether under a decree for specific performance or the grant of a mandatory injunction.

There has been growing pressure to enforce positive land covenants, but the judiciary has firmly passed this particular buck to Parliament. In the following case, the House of Lords refused to overcome more than a century of orthodoxy.

Rhone v Stephens [1994] 2 AC 310, HL

Facts: Walford House was divided into two dwellings—a house and a cottage—in such a way that one of the cottage bedrooms lay under the roof of the house. Upon the sale of the cottage, the owner of the house covenanted with the purchaser to keep the roof in repair. Some years later, when the roof had fallen into disrepair, the owner of the cottage unsuccessfully brought action against the then owner of the house: a successor in title to the original covenantor.

Lord Templeman

At 317

My Lords, equity supplements but does not contradict the common law. When freehold land is conveyed without restriction, the conveyance confers on the purchaser the right to do with the land as he pleases provided that he does not interfere with the rights of others or infringe statutory restrictions. The conveyance may however impose restrictions which, in favour of the covenantee, deprive the purchaser of some of the rights inherent in the ownership of unrestricted land. In *Tulk v. Moxhay* (1848) 2 Ph. 774, a purchaser of land covenanted that no buildings would be erected on Leicester Square. A subsequent purchaser of Leicester Square was restrained from building. The conveyance to the original purchaser deprived him and every subsequent purchaser taking with notice of the covenant of the right, otherwise part and parcel of the freehold, to develop the square by the construction of buildings. Equity does not contradict the common law by enforcing a restrictive covenant against a successor in title of the covenantor but prevents the successor from exercising a right which he never acquired. Equity did not allow the owner of Leicester Square to build because the owner never acquired the right to build without the consent of the persons (if any) from time to time entitled to the benefit of the covenant against building [. . .] Equity can thus prevent or punish the breach of a negative covenant which restricts the user of land or the exercise of other rights in connection with land. Restrictive covenants deprive an owner of a right which he could otherwise exercise. Equity cannot compel an owner to comply with a positive covenant entered into by his predecessors in title without flatly contradicting the common law rule that a person cannot be made liable upon a contract unless he was a party to it. Enforcement of a positive covenant lies in contract; a positive covenant compels an owner to exercise his rights. Enforcement of a negative covenant lies in property; a negative covenant deprives the owner of a right over property. As Lord Cottenham L.C. said in *Tulk v. Moxhay*, at p. 778: 'if an equity is attached to the property by the owner, no one purchasing with notice of that equity can stand in a different situation from the party from whom he purchased.'

Following *Tulk v. Moxhay* there was some suggestion that any covenant affecting land was enforceable in equity provided that the owner of the land had notice of the covenant prior to his purchase.

[His Lordship then considered the authorities: namely, the cases of *Morland v Cook*,[23] *Cooke v Chilcott*,[24] *Haywood v Brunswick Permanent Benefit Building Society*,[25] and *London and South Western Railway Co v Gomm*.[26]]

At 321

For over 100 years it has been clear and accepted law that equity will enforce negative covenants against freehold land but has no power to enforce positive covenants against successors in title of the land. To enforce a positive covenant would be to enforce a personal obligation against a person who has not covenanted. To enforce negative covenants is only to treat the land as subject to a restriction.

Mr. Munby, who argued the appeal persuasively on behalf of the plaintiffs, referred to an article by Professor Sir William Wade [1972 B] C.L.J. 157 and other articles in which the present state of the law is subjected to severe criticism. In 1965 a report by a committee appointed by the Lord Chancellor and under the chairmanship of Lord Wilberforce, the Report of the Committee on *Positive Covenants Affecting Land* (1965) (Cmnd. 2719), referred to difficulties caused by the decision in the *Austerberry case* and recommended legislation to provide that positive covenants which relate to the use of land and are intended to benefit specified other land should run with the land. The Law Commission published on 5 July 1971 Working Paper No. 36 in which the present law on positive rights was described as being illogical, uncertain, incomplete and inflexible. The Law Commission Report on *Transfer of Land* (1984) (Law Com. 127) (H.C. 201) laid before Parliament in 1965 made recommendations for the reform

---

23 (1868) LR 6 Eq 252.
24 (1876) 3 Ch D 694.
25 (1881) 8 QBD 403.
26 (1882) 20 Ch D 562.

of the law relating to positive and restrictive obligations and submitted a draft Bill for that purpose. Nothing has been done.

In these circumstances your Lordships were invited to overrule the decision of the Court of Appeal in the *Austerberry case*. To do so would destroy the distinction between law and equity and to convert the rule of equity into a rule of notice. It is plain from the articles, reports and papers to which we were referred that judicial legislation to overrule the *Austerberry case* would create a number of difficulties, anomalies and uncertainties and affect the rights and liabilities of people who have for over 100 years bought and sold land in the knowledge, imparted at an elementary stage to every student of the law of real property, that positive covenants, affecting freehold land are not directly enforceable except against the original covenantor. Parliamentary legislation to deal with the decision in the *Austerberry case* would require careful consideration of the consequences. Moreover, experience with leasehold tenure where positive covenants are enforceable by virtue of privity of estate has demonstrated that social injustice can be caused by logic. Parliament was obliged to intervene to prevent tenants losing their homes and being saddled with the costs of restoring to their original glory buildings which had languished through wars and economic depression for exactly 99 years.

Lord Templeman argues that where land is burdened by a negative covenant, the purchaser never receives the ability to act in breach of that covenant: his or her ownership is defined by the covenant from the start. Where the covenant is positive, however, he argues that the purchaser's title is burdened with an additional obligation that equity cannot order should be performed without contradicting the common law.

As Gardner points out, this reasoning is not convincing; rather, the decision springs from an understandable reluctance to entertain judicial legislation.

Gardner, 'Two Maxims of Equity' (1995) 54 CLJ 60, 67

He appears to suppose that the common law, with its privity rule, "objects" to covenants being enforced against purchaser, but is "content" for them to bind purchasers under nemo dat, if some other system—equity—wants to make them do so.

But this analysis is surely chimerical. We simply do not know whether the common law "objects" to covenants being enforced against non-parties, either as such or by virtue of nemo dat; or whether it is "content" for this to happen; or whether indeed, it aches for it to happen. And the reason we do not know is, of course, that the common law cannot possess such states of mind or emotions. That is not quite to say that Lord Templeman's version of the proposition is unworkable, however. It can be made workable if the judges are prepared to make the attitude of the common law the subject of oracular pronouncement, as though it were a mystery of which they were the priests. This is in effect how Lord Templeman proceeds when he tells us that to make positive covenants binding on purchasers would "contradict", rather than "supplement", the common law. But when we understand that the proposition must operate, if at all, in this way, we cannot but find it a quite remarkably indeterminate and opaque tool of reasoning, outstripping in these respects even the established maxims. Its acceptability in the law must therefore be in extreme doubt.

In *Rhone v Stephens*, the considerations which resort to the proposition concealed were essentially as follows. Whilst it is widely felt that to provide for the running of positive covenants is desirable, the reform is an unsuitable one for judicial legislation, for two reasons. First it would need to be accompanied by a good deal of fine print, which could only be supplied by statute. Secondly, a judicial decision to enforce positive covenants would necessarily operate retrospectively, which would defeat the legitimate expectation of purchasers, advised on the basis of existing law, that they take free of such covenants.

Lord Templeman outlines in his judgement the law reform steps that had been taken at the time. The Law Commission has again looked at the question and we will be considering its proposals in section 5 below. In the meantime, there are a number of mechanisms that conveyancers use to try to enforce positive covenants.

2.4 INDIRECT ENFORCEMENT OF POSITIVE COVENANTS

The inability to enforce positive obligations has caused increasing frustration and, whilst we await reform, conveyancers have needed to be inventive. The issue is particularly acute where properties share facilities, and provision needs to be made for their upkeep and repair. In the next chapter, we will examine the mechanisms used to address this issue in flat ownership, where shared facilities and reciprocal repairing obligations are vitally important. For now, we will consider the other devices that have been employed.

2.4.1 Mutual benefit and burden

The principle of mutual benefit and burden is encapsulated in the maxim that 'he who takes the benefit of a right must bear the burden upon which it is dependent'. As we noted in Chapter 7, section 2.5, if A enters into a positive covenant with B, the principle may sometimes impose a duty on C, a party later acquiring A's land, to perform that positive covenant. The principle is illustrated by the case of *Halsall v Brizell*,[27] in which purchasers of houses on an estate in Liverpool were granted a right to use the estate roads, the drains, the promenade, and the sea wall, subject to an obligation to contribute to the repair and upkeep of these facilities. When Brizell, a successor in title to one of the original purchasers, questioned his contribution, the court held that he could not claim the benefit of the right to use these facilities without accepting the attendant obligation to pay for their upkeep.

In *Tito v Wadell (No 2)*,[28] Megarry V-C drew a distinction between *conditional benefits*, in which the benefit was conferred subject to a condition that a burden be accepted, and *independent obligations*, in which the right and obligation, although granted by the same instrument, were not interdependent. In the case of conditional benefits, the burden clearly passes, because the obligation is an intrinsic part of the right. In the case of independent obligations, Megarry V-C argued that the burden should also pass, under what he called the 'pure benefit and burden' principle, where the construction of the instrument demonstrated that a successor in title was not intended to take the benefit without also accepting the burden. In other words, although the initial grant was not conditional upon the burden, its subsequent assignment was. The principle of pure benefit and burden, taken to its logical conclusion, could have circumvented the common laws' prohibition on the burden of covenants passing, but the House of Lords has rejected the principle.

---

[27] [1957] Ch 169. See also *Thamesmead Town Ltd v Allotey* (2000) 79 P & CR 557.
[28] [1977] 1 Ch 106.

Rhone v Stephens [1994] 2 AC 310, HL

Lord Templeman

At 322

Mr. Munby also sought to persuade your Lordships that the effect of the decision in the *Austerberry case* had been blunted by the 'pure principle of benefit and burden' distilled by Sir Robert Megarry V.-C. from the authorities in *Tito v. Waddell (No. 2)* [1977] 1 Ch. 106, 301 et seq. I am not prepared to recognise the 'pure principle' that any party deriving any benefit from a conveyance must accept any burden in the same conveyance. Sir Robert Megarry V.-C. relied on the decision of Upjohn J. in *Halsall v. Brizell* [1957] Ch. 169. In that case the defendant's predecessor in title had been granted the right to use the estate roads and sewers and had covenanted to pay a due proportion for the maintenance of these facilities. It was held that the defendant could not exercise the rights without paying his costs of ensuring that they could be exercised. Conditions can be attached to the exercise of a power in express terms or by implication. *Halsall v. Brizell* was just such a case and I have no difficulty in wholeheartedly agreeing with the decision. It does not follow that any condition can be rendered enforceable by attaching it to a right nor does it follow that every burden imposed by a conveyance may be enforced by depriving the covenantor's successor in title of every benefit which he enjoyed thereunder. The condition must be relevant to the exercise of the right. In *Halsall v. Brizell* there were reciprocal benefits and burdens enjoyed by the users of the roads and sewers. In the present case clause 2 of the 1960 conveyance imposes reciprocal benefits and burdens of support but clause 3 which imposed an obligation to repair the roof is an independent provision. In *Halsall v. Brizell* the defendant could, at least in theory, choose between enjoying the right and paying his proportion of the cost or alternatively giving up the right and saving his money.

The Court of Appeal has subsequently formulated a two-stage test to establish whether a covenant falls within the mutual benefit and burden principle. The first stage looks to proof that the benefit is conferred conditionally upon performance of the burden; the second stage calls for the successor in title to have a choice as to whether he or she will accept the benefit and its attendant burden.

Thamesmead Town Ltd v Allotey (2000) 79 P & CR 557, CA

Facts: A tenant on the Thamesmead Estate purchased the freehold reversion of his house under a right to buy. In the conveyance, he entered into a covenant to contribute to the upkeep of the roads, footpaths, sewers, and cables, as well as the landscaped and communal areas. The conveyance included a right for the purchaser to use the roads, footpaths, sewers, and cables, but no right to use the landscaped or communal areas. The tenant sold his house and his purchaser, Mr Allotey, questioned the amount of the service charge that he was required to pay. The Court held that he was not liable to pay that proportion of the charge which related to the costs of the landscaped and communal areas, because he had not been granted a right to use these facilities.

Peter Gibson LJ

At 564

The reasoning of Lord Templeman suggests that there are two requirements for the enforce-ability of a positive covenant against a successor in title to the covenantor. The first is that the condition of discharging the burden must be relevant to the exercise of the rights which enable the benefit to be obtained. In *Rhone v. Stephens* the mutual obligations of support was unrelated to, and independent of, the covenant to maintain the roof. The second is that the successors in title must have the opportunity to choose whether to take the benefit or having taken it to renounce it, even if only in theory, and thereby to escape the burden and that the successors in title can be deprived of the benefit if they fail to assume the burden. On both those grounds *Halsall v. Brizell* was distinguished. Although Lord Templeman expressed his wholehearted agreement with Upjohn J.'s decision, Lord Templeman's description of that decision was limited to the defendant being unable to exercise the rights to use the estate roads and to use the sewers without paying his costs of ensuring that they could be exer-cised. Nothing was expressly said about the cost of maintaining the sea wall or promenade and it is a little difficult to see how, consistently with Lord Templeman's reasoning and, in particular, the second requirement for the enforceability of a positive covenant, the cost of maintaining the sea wall would fall within the relevant principle [. . .]

Lord Templeman was plainly seeking to restrict, not enlarge, the scope of the exception from the rule that positive covenants affecting freehold land are not directly enforceable except against the original covenantor. Lord Templeman treated *Halsall v. Brizell* as a case where the right to use the estate roads and sewers was conditional on a payment of a due proportion of the maintenance expenses for those facilities. Whilst agreeing with the deci-sion, Lord Templeman made clear that for a burden to be enforceable it must be relevant to the benefit. He said that simply to attach a right to a condition for payment would not render that condition enforceable. Similarly, it is not possible to enforce every burden in a convey-ance by depriving the covenantor's successors in title of every benefit which he enjoyed under the conveyance. There must be a correlation between the burden and the benefit which the successor has chosen to take. Lord Templeman plainly rejected the notion that taking a benefit under a conveyance was sufficient to make every burden of the conveyance enforceable. Further, there is no authority to suggest that any benefit obtained by a succes-sor in title, once the property has been transferred to him, to enable the enforcement of a burden under the conveyance is sufficient, even if that benefit was not conferred as of right by the conveyance. In my judgment, it cannot be sufficient that the taking of an incidental benefit should enable the enforcement of a burden against a person who has not himself covenanted to undertake the particular burden.

2.4.2 Chain of indemnity covenants

It is common practice for conveyancers to build up a chain of personal covenants between successors in title of the covenantor, to try to ensure that contractual liability may be passed down from the original covenantor to the current owner of the servient land. If the current owner breaches a positive covenant, the covenantee can sue the original covenantor, who, in turn, can sue his or her direct successor in title on his or her personal covenant—and so on down the chain of covenants, until liability comes to rest upon culprit. The mechanism pro-vides an unsatisfactory solution, both because the covenantee may only recover damages in respect of the breach, rather than an injunction, and because the chain may easily be broken by the disappearance or insolvency of one of the links.

2.4.3 Estate rentcharges

The expenses incurred in maintaining and repairing common facilities within an estate may be recoverable by imposing an estate 'rentcharge' on the land.[29] An estate rentcharge is a legal interest that requires the owner of the burdened land to pay a periodic sum, which may be recovered by exercising an attached right of re-enty.[30] That sum may be nominal, where the estate rentcharge is used as a device to enforce positive covenants, or may reflect the cost incurred by the holder of the rentcharge (i.e. the developer or manager, as owner of the estates' common parts) of '*meeting or contributing towards the cost of performance* [...] *of covenants for the provision of services, carrying out maintenance or repairs, effecting insurance or the making of any benefit*'.[31]

2.5 THE ACQUISITION AND PRIORITY OF RESTRICTIVE COVENANTS

2.5.1 Creation of covenants

Covenants are invariably expressly created by deed—usually in the conveyance, when part of land is sold off—and are made pursuant to the contract for the sale of that land.[32] Because restrictive covenants operate in equity rather than at law, however, it is theoretically possible for a restrictive covenant to be created by signed writing[33] or even through the operation of proprietary estoppel.[34]

2.5.2 The priority of covenants

The decision of Lord Cottenham in *Tulk v Moxhay* was based upon the unconscionability that would result if purchasers with notice of the covenant could then claim that they were not bound. Indeed, purchasers could be unjustly enriched if the land, freed from the burden covenant, were then to increase in value. As the doctrine developed, the courts came to recognize restrictive covenants as equitable proprietary interests, which would bind all save for a bona fide purchaser of the legal estate without notice of the covenant. This metamorphosis of restrictive covenants from personal obligation to proprietary status was a remarkable development. It is not surprising that the courts then had to work hard to keep the doctrine within clear definitional bounds, to maintain a balance between the amenity advantages of restrictive covenants and the danger of sterilizing land development by '*incidents of a novel kind* [...] *devised* [...] *at the fancy and caprice of any owner*'.[35]

The proprietary status of restrictive covenants is explained in the following case, in which the question before the court was whether a squatter took subject to restrictive covenants affecting the title that had been extinguished.

---

[29] Whilst new rent charges cannot generally be created following the Rentcharges Act 1977, estate rent charges are exempt from this prohibition: see Rentcharges Act 1977, ss 2(1), (2), and (3)(c).

[30] Bright, 'Estate Rentcharges and the Enforcement of Positive Obligations' [1988] Conv 99.

[31] Rentcharges Act 1977, s 2(4)(b) and (5).

[32] Theoretically, a covenant might be implied as a result of the usual contractual principles governing the implication of terms.

[33] See Law of Property Act 1925, s 53(1)(a).

[34] See Chapter 13.

[35] *Keppel v Bailey* (1834) 2 My & K 517, 535, *per* Lord Brougham.

Re Nisbet & Potts Contract [1906] 1 Ch 386, CA

Collins MR

At 402

It seems to me, therefore, that the principal question before us is whether or not Sir George Jessel was right in the view that he took in *London and South Western Ry. Co. v. Gomm*, that an obligation created by a restrictive covenant is in the nature of a negative easement, creating a paramount right in the person entitled to it over the land to which it relates. If that is so, then, in the present case, the squatter, by his squatting, simply acquired a right to land subject to this incident. Of course, the burden of that incident must pass to all persons who subsequently become assignees of the land, and the squatter is not entitled to hand it over freed from the obligation that was imposed on the person whose title he has ousted by his possession.

Now, is that the law or not? In the first place, I do not think there was anything inconsistent in the view taken by Sir George Jessel with the law as laid down in the leading case of *Tulk v. Moxhay*, though, no doubt, words are used there pointing to the equity arising out of the injustice which would accrue if a person who had acquired land at a reduced price by reason of its user being subject to a restriction were afterwards enabled to pass on that land to other persons freed from that restriction receiving in return, on that ground, an increased price. That element, no doubt, does enter into consideration, when one comes to inquire what is the position of a person who acquires for value the legal estate in land subject to a right that has previously been created in another person to restrict the user of that land. The right so created is an equitable right, and, therefore, it is one capable of being defeated in certain circumstances by a person who acquires the legal estate for value. The question thus arises whether, in the circumstances of the particular case, there is anything which would make it inequitable for that person to avail himself of his legal estate to defeat that equitable right. That, as Mr. Upjohn pointed out, is an inquiry which is inevitable in cases where you are dealing with equitable rights and legal estates. But that does not in the least prevent the right in question being what Sir George Jessel considered it to be, namely, a burden imposed upon the land, and passing with the land, subject, of course, to this, that it may be defeated by a purchaser for value without notice; but the burden is upon the person who takes the land to shew that he has acquired it under such conditions as to defeat the right as against him, namely, that he has acquired it for value and without notice.

The priority of restrictive covenants created before 1925 continues to be regulated by notice, but restrictive covenants created after 1925 have been assimilated into the relevant registration regime. Where the servient land is unregistered, a restrictive covenant must be registered as a Class D(iii) land charge,[36] whilst where the servient land is registered, the covenant must be protected by the entry of a notice on the charges register.[37]

3 THE BENEFIT: WHO CAN SUE?

Those entitled to the benefit of a land covenant defines those who can take action on the covenant. There are three ways in which the benefit of a covenant can pass from the original covenantee to a new owner of the dominant land:

---

[36] See Chapter 15; Land Charges Act 1925, s 101; Land Charges Act 1972, s 2(5).
[37] See Chapter 16; Land Registration Act 2002, ss 29, 32–34.

- by assignment, both at law and in equity;
- by annexation of the benefit of the covenant to the land, either by express words, implication, or by the operation of s 78 of the LPA 1925; or
- under a building scheme.

These three methods, particularly annexation, have been the subject of highly technical rules that have been described as providing '*one of the richest areas of fantasy in printed English*'.[38] The search has been to find both an intention that the benefit of the covenant should pass and also to identify, with a degree of certainty, the land to which the benefit is attached.

Wade explains the tensions that have resulted.

Wade, 'Covenants: "A Broad and Reasonable View"' (1972) 31 CLJ 157, 162–5

After making much heavy weather over the transmission of the benefit, and so producing a body of law of notorious and unnecessary difficulty, the Chancery judges have now for twenty years been striving to relax their own rules. They have been working towards what might be called implied annexation, where there is no requirement of any formality but the decisive factor is the intention of the parties to the covenant, as inferred not only from its language but also from the surrounding facts at the time when it was made. The tendency is thus to assimilate the law of covenants to the law of easements, where no formalities are required for establishing the rights as appurtenant to the dominant tenement.

This policy is uncomfortable to conveyancers, who inhabit a world of paper and ink in which all important facts are expected to be clearly stated in documents of title [...]

Accordingly there may be said to be two opposing views: the "conveyancers' view," if it may be so called advocates compulsory formality; and the "judicial view" which at present indicates away from formality, and which at all times is concerned to temper the injustice which compulsory formality entails [...]

The question is very much one of degree. No one complains that it is excessively strict to require that freehold land should be conveyed by deed. But the law of restrictive covenants is at present being judicially purged of an overdose of formalism.

Many of the decisions have been excessively technical, and at times the courts seem bemused by their own refinements. But this is because they have been pressed with the subtle arguments prompted by the "conveyancers' view" that the benefited land should be clearly defined in the deed of covenant. Occasionally they have appeared to accept this, and judges and others have slipped into saying that the deed must identify the land. But in general they have resisted it.

3.1 ASSIGNMENT

Like the benefit of any other contract, the benefit of a land covenant may be assigned. Thus the original covenantee may transfer both the land and the benefit of the covenant to a purchaser of the land by using express words of assignment, provided that the covenant relates to the land, in the sense that it is not personal to the covenantee. The benefit of the covenant will need to be expressly assigned on each disposal of the land to build up a continuous chain of assignments. The assignment may take effect at law where the original covenantee

---

[38] Kenny, 'Conveyancer's Notebook' [2006] Conv 1, 2.

and his or her assignee hold a legal estate in the land, although that need not be the same legal estate.[39]

Assignment at law is, however, of limited value: only the original convenator can be sued, given that the burden does not run at law, and, because a covenant cannot be severed at law, a legal assignment will not assist where part of the dominant land is sold.

Assignment in equity, the requirements of which are found in the following case, overcomes these deficiencies and is frequently employed by conveyancers.

Miles v Easter [1933] Ch 611, CA

Romer LJ

At 631

It is plain, however, from these and other cases, and notably that of *Renals v. Cowlishaw*, that if the restrictive covenant be taken not merely for some personal purpose or object of the vendor, but for the benefit of some other land of his in the sense that it would enable him to dispose of that land to greater advantage, the covenant, though not annexed to such land so as to run with any part of it, may be enforced against an assignee of the covenantor taking with notice, both by the covenantee and by persons to whom the benefit of such covenant has been assigned, subject however to certain conditions. In the first place, the "other land" must be land that is capable of being benefited by the covenant—otherwise it would be impossible to infer that the object of the covenant was to enable the vendor to dispose of his land to greater advantage. In the next place, this land must be "ascertainable" or "certain," to use the words of Romer and Scrutton L.JJ. respectively. For, although the Court will readily infer the intention to benefit the other land of the vendor where the existence and situation of such land are indicated in the conveyance or have been otherwise shown with reasonable certainty, it is impossible to do so from vague references in the conveyance or in other documents laid before the Court as to the existence of other lands of the vendor, the extent and situation of which are undefined. In the third place, the covenant cannot be enforced by the covenantee against an assign of the purchaser after the covenantee has parted with the whole of his land.

3.2 ANNEXATION

Annexation is a once-and-for-all process by which the benefit of the covenant is glued to the land, so as to become part of the land and thus pass automatically upon a conveyance of the land. Two concerns need to be met to ensure annexation: firstly, there must be an intention that the benefit of the covenant should become part of the land; and secondly, it is necessary to determine the physical limits of the land to which the covenant is annexed—that is, what area is covered by the annexing glue? These questions are the flip side of the requirement for accommodation that we examined in section 2.2.

It is in the clarity of the evidence required to prove these two elements that the tension between the 'conveyancers' view' and the 'judicial view' is most evident. Conveyancers have looked to express words of annexation contained in the covenant and to clear evidence of

---

[39] *Smith and Snipes Hall Farm Ltd v River Douglas Catchment Board* [1949] 2 KB 500.

the physical definition of the land in the conveyancing documents, whilst the courts have accepted a lower standard of evidence.

3.2.1 Express annexation

Express words of annexation can be demonstrated by contrasting the wording of the covenants in *Rogers v Hosegood*[40] and that in *Renals v Cowlishaw*.[41]

In *Rogers v Hosegood*, a covenant was made in the following terms.

> "With the intent that the covenant might as far as possible bind the premises [...] conveyed and every part thereof, into whosoever hands the same might come, and might enure to the benefit of the mortgagees, their heirs and assigns and others claiming under them to all or any of their lands adjoining or near the premises."

In *Renals v Cowlishaw*, the covenants merely stated that it was taken for '*the vendors, their heirs, executors, administrators and assigns*'.

Thus, in *Rogers v Hosegood*, it was clear that the covenant was to become part of the land, because it was made with the covenantee and his or her successors in title in their capacity as owners of adjoining land; in *Renals v Cowlishaw*, the absence of any reference to the covenantee's land was fatal.

The technicality of express annexation and its relationship with the passing of the burden is illustrated by the following judgment of Farwell J.

Marquess of Zetland v Driver [1939] Ch 1, CA

Facts: A conveyance of a shop in Redcar made by the Marquess' estate contained a covenant by the purchaser not to commit any nuisance to the vendor or occupiers of any adjoining property in the neighbourhood. The covenant was expressed to be made for the benefit of such parts of the Marquess' estate as should remain unsold or be sold with the benefit of the covenant. An injunction was granted to restrain the use of the shop for the sale of fish and chips.

Farwell J

At 8

[...C]ovenants can only be validly imposed if they comply with certain conditions. Firstly, they must be negative covenants. No affirmative covenant requiring the expenditure of money or the doing of some act can ever be made to run with the land. Secondly, the covenant must be one that touches or concerns the land, by which is meant that it must be imposed for the benefit or to enhance the value of the land retained by the vendor or some part of it, and no

---

[40] [1900] 2 Ch 388.
[41] (1878) 8 Ch D 125.

such covenant can ever be imposed if the sale comprises the whole of the vendor's land. Further, the land retained by the vendor must be such as to be capable of being benefited by the covenant at the time when it is imposed. Thirdly, the land which is intended to be benefited must be so defined as to be easily ascertainable, and the fact that the covenant is imposed for the benefit of that particular land should be stated in the conveyance and the persons or the class of persons entitled to enforce it. The fact that the benefit of the covenant is not intended to pass to all persons into whose hands the unsold land may come is not objectionable so long as the class of persons intended to have the benefit of the covenant is clearly defined. Finally, it must be remembered that these covenants can only be enforced so long as the covenantee or his successor in title retains some part of the land for the benefit of which the covenant was imposed. Applying those conditions to the present case, the covenant sued upon appears to comply with them. The covenant is restrictive; it is expressly stated in the conveyance to be for the benefit of the unsold part of the land comprised in the settlement and such land is easily ascertainable, nor is it suggested that at the date of the conveyance the land retained was not capable of being benefited by the restrictions, and lastly the appellant is the successor in title of the original covenantee and as such is the estate owner of part of the land unsold which is subject to the settlement. That being so, the appellant is the person now entitled to the benefit of the covenant and, prima facie, is entitled to enforce it against the respondents who, although not the original covenantors, took their land with notice of the restrictions and are, therefore, bound by them.

It is said, however, on behalf of the respondents, that this covenant is not one which can run with the land because it is imposed for the benefit, not only of the unsold land of the vendor, but also for the benefit of the adjoining owners and the neighbourhood. If that were the true construction of the covenant, that might be so; but in our judgment, reading the covenant as a whole, it cannot be so construed. The paramount purpose of the covenant, as appears from the conveyance itself, is to benefit and protect the unsold land of the vendor, and only such acts or things as are, in the opinion of the appellant or his successors in title, injurious to that land are within the restrictions, and consequently nothing which would be a nuisance or annoyance to an adjoining owner or the neighbourhood is within the covenant, unless it is also detrimental or injurious to the unsold land of the vendor. The covenant is, therefore, not impeachable on this ground. [. . .] Under those circumstances, there does not appear to be any ground on which the appellant can properly be refused the relief which he seeks; but Bennett J. took the opposite view and held that the benefit of the covenant had not passed to the appellant. In coming to that conclusion he founded himself upon a decision of Clauson J. in *In re Ballard's Conveyance*, which he considered to be exactly in point and binding upon him. In our judgment the learned judge was wrong in thinking that *In re Ballard's Conveyance* was an authority in this case. It is not necessary for us, and we do not propose, to express any opinion as to that decision beyond saying that it is clearly distinguishable from the present case, if only on the ground that in that case the covenant was expressed to run with the whole estate, whereas in the present case no such difficulty arises because the covenant is expressed to be for the benefit of the whole or any part or parts of the unsold settled property.

There is some support for the view that proof of annexation may also be gleaned from the circumstances surrounding the making of the conveyance: for example, where those circumstances demonstrate to which land the benefit is to be annexed.[42]

---

[42] See *Rogers v Hosegood* [1900] 2 Ch 388, 408, and *Marten v Flight Refueling Ltd* [1962] Ch 115, 133.

In the above extract, Farwell distinguished *Re Ballards Conveyance*,[43] in which annexation failed because the dominant land was so large that it was impossible to prove that the entire area benefited.[44] Whilst part of the land clearly could benefit, the court refused to sever the covenant so that the benefit could at least pass with that part. This unfortunate result was avoided in *Marquess of Zetland v Driver*, in which the covenant was expressed to be annexed to '*each and every part of the estate*'.

Brightman LJ doubted the need for these words in the following case.

Federated Homes Ltd v Mill Lodge Properties Ltd [1980] 1 WLR 594, CA

Brightman LJ

At 606

[...T]he idea of annexation of a covenant to the whole of the land but not to part of it is a difficult conception to grasp [...] I would have thought, if a covenant is, on a proper construction of a document, annexed to the land, prima facie it is annexed to every part thereof, unless the contrary clearly appears.

His views have subsequently been followed at first instance in *Small v Oliver & Saunders*.[45]

3.2.2 Statutory annexation

The technicalities of express annexation have been sidestepped by judicial recognition that s 78 of the LPA 1925 provides automatic annexation in respect of covenants entered into after 1925.[46]

Law of Property Act 1925, s 78

(1) A covenant relating to any land of the covenantee shall be deemed to be made with the covenantee and his successors in title and the persons deriving title under him or them, and shall have effect as if such successors and other persons were expressed.

For the purposes of this subsection in connection with covenants restrictive or the user of land 'successors in title' shall be deemed to include the owners and occupiers for the time being of the land of the covenantee intended to be benefited.

(2) This section applies to covenants made after the commencement of this Act, but the repeal of section fifty eight of the Conveyancing Act 1881 does not affect the operation of covenants to which that section applied.

The Court of Appeal considered the effect of this section in the following case.

---

[43] [1937] Ch 473.

[44] The area was a 1,700-acre estate.

[45] [2006] EWHC 1293, [29].

[46] Express annexation continues to be necessary under Conveyancing and Law of Property Act 1881, s 58, where the covenant is entered into before 1925: see *J Sainsbury plc v Enfield LBC* [1989] 1 WLR 590.

Federated Home Ltd v Mill Lodge Properties Ltd [1980] 1 WLR 594, CA

Facts: A vendor sold an area of land for development ('the blue land') to Mill Lodge, subject to a covenant restricting the density of development so as not to prejudice development of the vendor's retained land under an existing planning permission. Subsequently, two further areas of land ('the red land' and 'the green land') were sold by the vendor and came into the ownership of Federated Homes. Mill Lodge threatened to breach the covenant and Federated Homes successfully sought an injunction claiming the benefit of the covenant. There was no express annexation conferring the benefit of the covenant upon the red and green land, although there was an express assignment of the benefit of the covenant in respect of the green land.

Brightman LJ

At 604

Mr. Price submitted that there were three possible views about section 78. One view, which he described as "the orthodox view" hitherto held, is that it is merely a statutory shorthand for reducing the length of legal documents. A second view, which was the one that Mr. Price was inclined to place in the forefront of his argument, is that the section only applies, or at any rate only achieves annexation, when the land intended to be benefited is signified in the document by express words or necessary implication as the intended beneficiary of the covenant. A third view is that the section applies if the covenant in fact touches and concerns the land of the covenantee, whether that be gleaned from the document itself or from evidence outside the document.

For myself, I reject the narrowest interpretation of section 78, the supposed orthodox view, which seems to me to fly in the face of the wording of the section. Before I express my reasons I will say that I do not find it necessary to choose between the second and third views because, in my opinion, this covenant relates to land of the covenantee on either interpretation of section 78. Clause 5 (iv) shows clearly that the covenant is for the protection of the retained land and that land is described in clause 2 as "any adjoining or adjacent property retained by the vendor." This formulation is sufficient for annexation purposes: see *Rogers v. Hosegood* [1900] 2 Ch. 388.

There is in my judgment no doubt that this covenant "related to the land of the covenantee," or, to use the old-fashioned expression, that it touched and concerned the land, even if Mr. Price is correct in his submission that the document must show an intention to benefit identified land. The result of such application is that one must read clause 5 (iv) as if it were written: "The purchaser hereby covenants with the vendor and its successors in title and the persons deriving title under it or them, including the owners and occupiers for the time being of the retained land, that in carrying out the development of the blue land the purchaser shall not build at a greater density than a total 300 dwellings so as not to reduce, etc." I leave out of consideration section 79 as unnecessary to be considered in this context, since Mill Lodge is the original covenantor.

The first point to notice about section 78 (1) is that the wording is significantly different from the wording of its predecessor section 58 (1) of the Conveyancing Act 1881. The distinction is underlined by section 78 (2), which applies section 78 (1) only to covenants made after the commencement of the Act. Section 58 (1) of the Act of 1881 did not include the covenantee's successors in title or persons deriving title under him or them, or the owner or occupiers for the time being of the land of the covenantee intended to be benefited. The section was confined, in relation to realty, to the covenantee, his heirs and assigns, words which suggest a more limited scope of operation than is found in section 78.

> If, as the language of section 78 implies, a covenant relating to land which is restrictive of the user thereof is enforceable at the suit of (1) a successor in title of the covenantee, (2) a person deriving title under the covenantee or under his successors in title, and (3) the owner or occupier of the land intended to be benefited by the covenant, it must, in my view, follow that the covenant runs with the land, because ex hypothesi every successor in title to the land, every derivative proprietor of the land and every other owner and occupier has a right by statute to the covenant. In other words, if the condition precedent of section 78 is satisfied—that is to say, there exists a covenant which touches and concerns the land of the covenantee—that covenant runs with the land for the benefit of his successors in title, persons deriving title under him or them and other owners and occupiers.

The decision was controversial and has been criticized by those taking the traditional 'conveyancers' view'.[47] Two particular objections have been raised. The first, it is argued, is that this interpretation of s 78 is at odds with the interpretation given to its sister provision concerning the running of the burden found in s 79.[48] But the wording of the two sections is different, as Snape explains.

Snape, 'The Benefit and Burden of Covenants: now where are we?'
(1994) 68 Nott LJ 68, 71

> The crucial difference between the two sections is that, whilst section 78 [...] deems the covenant to be made "with the covenantee and his successors in title and the persons deriving title under him or them ", section 79 [...] deems the covenant to be made "on behalf of [the covenantor] and his successors in title and the persons deriving title under him or them". Whatever the precise scope of the word "deemed" is in each section, this difference in wording makes it clear that the benefit is, in principle, to pass to the covenantor's successors etc quite easily, whilst section 79 is intended, in the absence of contrary intention, to ensure that the burden remains firmly with the original covenantor.

The second objection is that, whilst s 79 expressly gives way to a contrary intention, s 78 does not. This objection is considered in the following case, in which the vendor of plots sold off from an estate imposed building restrictions, but provided that the benefit of these restrictions should not pass unless expressly assigned.

Roake v Chadha [1984] 1 WLR 40, HC

Paul Baker QC

At 45

The *Federated Homes case* shows that section 78 of the Act of 1925 brings about annexation, and that the operation of the section cannot be excluded by a contrary intention. As I

---

[47] Newsome, 'Universal Annexation' (1981) 97 LQR 32, (1982) 98 LQR 202; Snape, 'The Benefit and Burden of Covenants: Now Where Are We?' (1994) 3 Nott LJ 68; but see Hurst, 'The Transmission of Restrictive Covenants' (1982) 2 LS 53.

[48] See section 2.1.

have indicated, he supports this last point by reference to section 79, which is expressed to operate "unless a contrary intention is expressed," a qualification which, as we have already noticed, is absent from section 78. Mr.Walter could not suggest any reason of policy why section 78 should be mandatory, unlike, for example, section 146 of the Act of 1925, which deals with restrictions on the right to forfeiture of leases and which, by an express provision "has effect notwithstanding any stipulation to the contrary."

I am thus far from satisfied that section 78 has the mandatory operation which Mr. Walter claimed for it. But if one accepts that it is not subject to a contrary intention, I do not consider that it has the effect of annexing the benefit of the covenant in each and every case irrespective of the other express terms of the covenant.

The true position as I see it is that even where a covenant is deemed to be made with successors in title as section 78 requires, one still has to construe the covenant as a whole to see whether the benefit of the covenant is annexed. Where one finds, as in the *Federated Homes case*, the covenant is not qualified in any way, annexation may be readily inferred; but where, as in the present case, it is expressly provided:

> "this covenant shall not enure for the benefit of any owner or subsequent purchaser of any part of the vendor's Sudbury Court Estate at Wembley unless the benefit of this covenant shall be expressly assigned [...]"

One cannot just ignore these words. One may not be able to exclude the operation of the section in widening the range of the covenantees, but one has to consider the covenant as a whole to determine its true effect. When one does that, then it seems to me that the answer is plain and in my judgment the benefit was not annexed. That is giving full weight to both the statute in force and also what is already there in the covenant.

The Court of Appeal indorsed this view in the following case, by explaining that 'successors in title' is limited to those purchasers who are intended to benefit from the covenant and thus a contrary intention may exclude certain purchasers.

Crest Nicholson Residential (South) Ltd v McAllister [2004] 1 WLR 2409, CA

Chadwick LJ

At [41]–[44]

I respectfully agree, first, that it is impossible to identify any reason of policy why a covenantor should not, by express words, be entitled to limit the scope of the obligation which he is undertaking; nor why a covenantee should not be able to accept a covenant for his own benefit on terms that the benefit does not pass automatically to all those to whom he sells on parts of his retained land. As Brightman LJ pointed out, in the passage cited by Judge Paul Baker QC, a developer who is selling off land in lots might well want to retain the benefit of a building restriction under his own control. Where, as in *Roake v Chadha* and the present case, development land is sold off in plots without imposing a building scheme, it seems to me very likely that the developer will wish to retain exclusive power to give or withhold consent to a modification or relaxation of a restriction on building which he imposes on each purchaser; unfettered by the need to obtain the consent of every subsequent purchaser to whom (after imposing the covenant) he has sold off other plots on the development land. I can see no reason why, if original covenantor and covenantee make clear their mutual intention in that respect, the legislature should wish to prevent effect being given to that intention.

Second, it is important to keep in mind that, for the purposes of its application to restrict-ive covenants-which is the context in which this question arises where neither of the parties to the dispute were, themselves, party to the instrument imposing the covenant or express assignees of the benefit of the covenant-section 78 of the 1925 Act defines "successors in title" as the owners and occupiers of the time being *of the land of the covenantee intended to be benefited*. In a case where the parties to the instrument make clear their intention that land retained by the covenantee at the time of the conveyance effected by the transfer is to have the benefit of the covenant only for so long as it continues to be in the ownership of the original covenantee, and not after it has been sold on by the original covenantee—unless the benefit of the covenant is expressly assigned to the new owner—*the land of the cove-nantee intended to be benefited* is identified by the instrument as (i) so much of the retained land as from time to time has not been sold off by the original covenantee and (ii) so much of the retained land as has been sold off with the benefit of an express assignment, but as not including (iii) so much of the land as has been sold off without the benefit of an express assignment. I agree with the judge in *Roake v Chadha* that, in such a case, it is possible to give full effect to the statute and to the terms of the covenant.

This approach to section 78 of the 1925 Act provides, as it seems to me, the answer to the question why, if the legislature did not intend to distinguish between the effect of section 78 (mandatory) and the effect of section 79 (subject to contrary intention), it did not include the words "unless a contrary intention is expressed" in the first of those sections. The answer is that it did not need to. The qualification "subject to contrary intention" is implicit in the def-inition of "successors in title" which appears in section 78(1); that is the effect of the words "the land of the covenantee intended to be benefited". If the terms in which the covenant is imposed show—as they did in *Marquess of Zetland v Driver* and in *Roake v Chadha*—that the land of the covenantee intended to be benefited does not include land which may sub-sequently be sold off by the original covenantee in circumstances where (at the time of that subsequent sale) there is no express assignment of the benefit of the covenant, then the owners and occupiers of the land sold off in those circumstances are not "owners and occu-piers for the time being of the land of the covenantee intended to be benefited"; and so are not "successors in title" of the original covenantee for the purposes of section 78(1) in its application to covenants restrictive of the user of land.

By contrast, the definition of "successors in title" for the purposes of section 79(1) appears in subsection (2) of that section: "the owners and occupiers for the time being of *such* land". In that context "such land" means "any land of a covenantor or capable of being bound by him [to which the covenant relates]." The counterpart in section 79 of "land of the covenan-tee intended to be benefited" (in section 78(1)) is "such land". "Such land" in that context means the land referred to in section 79(1); that is to say "any land of a covenantor or capable of being bound by him". But section 79(1) imposes two qualifications; (i) the land must be land to which the covenant relates and (ii) there must be no expression of contrary intention. The section could, perhaps, have described the land as "land of the covenantor (or capable of being bound by him) intended to be burdened". But the effect would have been the same. If the parties did not intend that land, burdened while in the ownership of the covenantor, should continue to be subject to the burden in hands of his successors (or some of his suc-cessors), they could say so. On a true analysis there is no difference in treatment in the two sections. There is a difference in the drafting technique used to achieve the same substantive result. That may well simply reflect the legislative history of the two sections. Section 78(1) of the 1925 Act re-enacted section 58 of the Conveyancing and Law of Property Act 1881 (44 & 45 Vict c 41) as applied by section 96(3) of the Law of Property Act 1922 and amended by section 3 of, and paragraph 11 of Schedule 3 to, the Law of Property (Amendment) Act 1924. Section 79 was a new provision, first introduced in the 1925 Act.

Statutory annexation may address the first evidential concern—namely, to demonstrate an intention that the benefit is to run to the covenantee's successors in title as owners of the dominant land—but it is still necessary to satisfy the second evidential requirement that the dominant land is adequately identified.

Crest Nicholson Residential (South) Ltd v McAllister [2004] 1 WLR 2409, CA

Facts: Crest intended to develop land that formerly comprised a number of different plots, originally sold off between 1926 and 1936, when they were made subject to similar covenants restricting their development and user. Some of the covenants contained express words of annexation, but others did not. Mrs McAllister, who lived in a house built on part of the plot sold off in 1936, opposed the development, claiming to be entitled to the benefit of the covenants. She was unsuccessful. Her land was insufficiently identified for the benefit to be expressly annexed or annexed via s 78.

Chadwick LJ

At [30]

The decision of this court in the *Federated Homes case* leaves open the question whether section 78 of the 1925 Act only effects annexation when the land intended to be benefited is described in the instrument itself (by express words or necessary implication, albeit that it may be necessary to have regard to evidence outside the document fully to identify that land) or whether it is enough that it can be shown, from evidence wholly outside the document, that the covenant does in fact touch and concern land of the covenantee which can be identified.

[The judge then referred to the cases of *Rogers v Hosegood* and *Marquess of Zetland v Driver.*]

At [33]–[34]

In its later decision in the *Federated Homes case* this court held that the provisions of section 78 of the 1925 Act had made it unnecessary to state, in the conveyance, that the covenant was to be enforceable by persons deriving title under the covenantee or under his successors in title and the owner or occupier of the land intended to be benefited, or that the covenant was to run with the land intended to be benefited; but there is nothing in that case which suggests that it is no longer necessary that the land which is intended to be benefited should be so defined that it is easily ascertainable. In my view, that requirement, identified in *Marquess of Zetland v Driver* remains a necessary condition for annexation.

There are, I think, good reasons for that requirement. A restrictive covenant affecting land will not be enforceable in equity against a purchaser who acquires a legal estate in that land for value without notice of the covenant. A restrictive covenant imposed in an instrument made after 1925 is registrable as a land charge under class D(ii): section 10(1) of the Land Charges Act 1925 and, now, section 2(5) of the Land Charges Act 1972. If the title is registered, protection is effected by entering notice of the restrictive covenant on the register: section 50 of the Land Registration Act 1925 and, now, section 11 of the Land Registration Act 2002. Where practicable the notice shall be by reference to the instrument by which the covenant is imposed and a copy or abstract of that instrument shall be filed at the registry: section 50(1) of the Land Registration Act 1925 and section 3(5) of the Land Charges Act

1972. It is obviously desirable that a purchaser of land burdened with a restrictive covenant should be able not only to ascertain, by inspection of the entries on the relevant register, that the land is so burdened, but also to ascertain the land for which the benefit of the covenant was taken-so that he can identify who can enforce the covenant. That latter object is achieved if the land which is intended to be benefited is defined in the instrument so as to be easily ascertainable. To require a purchaser of land burdened with a restrictive covenant, but where the land for the benefit of which the covenant was taken is not described in the instrument, to make inquiries as to what (if any) land the original covenantee retained at the time of the conveyance and what (if any) of that retained land the covenant did, or might have, "touched and concerned" would be oppressive. It must be kept in mind that (as in the present case) the time at which the enforceability of the covenant becomes an issue may be long after the date of the instrument by which it was imposed.

Section 78 is thus not a panacea for poor covenant drafting. The land to be benefited must be identified '*from a description, plan or other reference in the conveyance itself, but aided, if necessary, by external evidence to identify the land so described, depicted or otherwise referred to*'.[49] Even so, as Howell points out, identifying the land intended to be benefited can be problematic—particularly where time has elapsed and the original covenantee's land has been fragmented.

Howell, 'The Annexation of the Benefit of Covenants to Land' [2004] Conv 507, 513

The necessity of the benefited land to be sufficiently identified is the same whether the covenant is annexed by express words or by s78. The problem is that actually identifying the land on the ground which is to be benefited may be impossible and raise all the difficulties of enquiry which Chadwick LJ deplored. Simply stating as in *Rogers v Hosegood* that the land to be benefited "is nearby" and is all the land owned by X is surely no identification at all. In *Marquess of Zetland v Driver* the covenant imposed in 1928 was expressed for the benefit of land which was part of a settlement set up in 1871. The breach of the covenant was in 1938 and as it happened the whole of the land settled in 1871 was still intact in the hands of the tenant for life in possession, so identification of the land benefited was straightforward. It would be different where the covenants were imposed many years before and the land to be benefited had been sold in pieces [...]

There is no similar requirement in the law of easements that the land to be benefited be identified in the conveyance. In *Johnstone v Holdway* an express reservation of an easement of way which made no mention of land to be benefited was good since it could be identified by information known to the parties at the time. Again, the challenge to the validity of the easement was a relatively short time after the conveyance but there does not seem anything in the different natures of an easement and a restrictive covenant which justifies the difference in principle.

---

[49] *Crest Nicholson Residential (South) Ltd v McAllister* [2004] EWCA Civ 410, [45], *per* Chadwick LJ. See also *Stocks v Whitgift Homes Ltd* [2001] EWCA Civ 1732. Note the different evidence required to identify the dominant land where the burden and benefit pass: see section 2.2 above.

Drawing upon the easements analogy, arguments[50] have been put forward from time to time that the benefit of a covenant should pass under s 62 of the LPA 1925, which we considered in the last chapter. In both *Roake v Chadha*[51] and *Kumar v Dunning*,[52] however, the courts were unimpressed by the analogy and declined to accept that a covenant that is not annexed to the land is a right appertaining to it.[53]

3.3 BUILDING SCHEME

Early in the development of restrictive covenants, the Chancery courts recognized that the enforcement of common covenants within a development merited special consideration.[54] Where a building scheme or scheme of development can be proved, equity supports the reciprocal enforcement of common covenants between all owners of the development, creating, in effect, a 'local law'.[55] A building scheme thus permits both the burden and the benefit of a covenant to pass to all owners for the time being within the scheme, but it is in the context of determining who can sue that building schemes are most often employed. The reason for this lies in the timing of sales.

3.3.1 The timing problem

Whilst the burden of a covenant can be imposed upon the sale of each plot within a development, the benefit is more difficult to pass once the first plots have been sold, because the dominant land shrinks. Thus, if we have a small development of ten plots, the benefit of covenants taken by the developer from the purchaser of Plot 1 may be annexed to the plots that the developer still owns (i.e. Plots 2–10). When Plot 2 is sold, the benefit of the covenants taken from the purchaser cannot be annexed to Plot 1, which, having been sold, does not form part of the developer's dominant land. By the time that the later plots are sold, the problem is magnified. Thus when Plot 9 is sold, the purchaser's covenants cannot be annexed to Plots 1–8; the benefit can only be annexed to the Plot 10. Once Plot 10 is sold, the developer retains no land capable of benefiting from the covenant, and thus neither the burden nor benefit of the covenants can pass.

3.3.2 A local law

Where a building scheme is found, timing is not an issue. All of the current owners of land within the scheme may sue (i.e. claim the benefit) and be sued (i.e. subject to the burden) on the common covenants, regardless of when the covenants were originally imposed upon their properties or when they acquired ownership.

---

[50] See Hayton (1971) 87 LQR 539, 570, and Wade (1972) 31 CLJ 157, 175. The argument was raised in *Federated Homes Ltd v Mill Lodge Properties Ltd* [1980] 1 WLR 594 and in *Shropshire CC v Edwards* (1982) 46 P & CR 270, 279, but in each case, the courts have declined to consider the issue.

[51] [1984] 1 WLR 40, 46.

[52] [1989] QB 193, 198.

[53] In *Sugarman v Porter* [2006] EWHC 331, a similar argument was rejected based upon s 63 of the Law of Property Act 1925.

[54] There is evidence of mutually enforceable covenants as early the late 1830s: see *Lawrence v South County Freeholds Ltd* [1939] Ch 656, 675, *per* Simonds J; *Re Pinewood Estates* [1958] Ch 280, 286, *per* Wynn Parry J.

[55] See *Reid v Bickerstaff* [1909] 2 Ch 305, 319, *per* Coxens Hardy MR; *Re Dolphin's Conveyance* [1970] Ch 654, 662, *per* Stamp J.

The classic statement of the evidence required to prove a building scheme is found in Parker J's judgment in the following case.[56]

Elliston v Reacher [1908] 2 Ch 374, HC

Parker J

At 384

[...]It must be proved (1) that both the plaintiffs and defendants derive title under a common vendor; (2) that previously to selling the lands to which the plaintiffs and defendants are respectively entitled the vendor laid out his estate, or a defined portion thereof (including the lands purchased by the plaintiffs and defendants respectively), for sale in lots subject to restrictions intended to be imposed on all the lots, and which, though varying in details as to particular lots, are consistent and consistent only with some general scheme of development; (3) that these restrictions were intended by the common vendor to be and were for the benefit of all the lots intended to be sold, whether or not they were also intended to be and were for the benefit of other land retained by the vendor; and (4) that both the plaintiffs and the defendants, or their predecessors in title, purchased their lots from the common vendor upon the footing that the restrictions subject to which the purchases were made were to enure for the benefit of the other lots included in the general scheme whether or not they were also to enure for the benefit of other lands retained by the vendors. If these four points are established, I think that the plaintiffs, would in equity be entitled to enforce the restrictive covenants entered into by the defendants or their predecessors with the common vendor irrespective of the dates of the respective purchases.

Whilst these requirements will be met by many housing developments, in some cases, they have proved too prescriptive. As a result, the courts in recent decades have looked to the more general requirements articulated in the following case,[57] in which the Court of Appeal outlined two essential elements: first, that there must be a defined area of land subject to the scheme; and secondly, that there must be an intention that all owners of plots within that area are subject to, and have the benefit of, the covenants that are imposed on each plot.

Reid v Bickerstaff [1909] 2 Ch 305, CA

Cozens Hardy MR

At 319

What are some of the essentials of a building scheme? In my opinion there must be a defined area within which the scheme is operative. Reciprocity is the foundation of the idea of a scheme. A purchaser of one parcel cannot be subject to an implied obligation to purchasers of an undefined and unknown area. He must know both the extent of his burden and the extent of his benefit. Not only must the area be defined, but the obligations to

---

56 Approved on appeal at [1908] 2 Ch 665.
57 Decided only six months after *Elliston v Reacher*, and reflecting the earlier authorities of *Renals v Colishaw* (1878) 9 Ch D 125 and *Spicer v Martin* (1888) 14 App Cas 12. This relaxation is attributed to the cases of *Baxter v Four Oaks Properties Ltd* [1965] Ch 816 and *Re Dolphin's Conveyance* [1970] Ch 654.

be imposed within that area must be defined. Those obligations need not be identical. For example, there may be houses of a certain value in one part and houses of a different value in another part. A building scheme is not created by the mere fact that the owner of an estate sells it in lots and takes varying covenants from various purchasers. There must be notice to the various purchasers of what I may venture to call the local law imposed by the vendors upon a definite area.

Buckley LJ

At 322

First as to the existence of a building scheme and the application of the doctrine of *Spicer v. Martin*. For the application of the principle of that case it is, I think, essential to establish as matter of fact the following state of things: that the vendor expressly or by implication contracted with the defendant in the action or his predecessor in title (whom I will call the purchaser) upon the footing that at the date of that contract the vendor told the purchaser that he was proposing to deal with a defined estate in a defined way, and that he offered to sell to the purchaser a plot forming a part of that defined estate on the terms that the purchaser should enter into such restrictive covenants relating to his plot as the scheme contemplated upon the footing that the purchaser should reciprocally have the benefit of such restrictive covenants relating to the other plots on the estate as were indicated by the scheme. There can be no building scheme unless two conditions are satisfied, namely, first, that defined lands constituting the estate to which the scheme relates shall be identified, and, secondly, that the nature and particulars of the scheme shall be sufficiently disclosed for the purchaser to have been informed that his restrictive covenants are imposed upon him for the benefit of other purchasers of plots within that defined estate with the reciprocal advantage that he shall as against such other purchasers be entitled to the benefit of such restrictive covenants as are in turn to be imposed upon them. Compliance with the first condition identifies the class of persons as between whom reciprocity of obligation is to exist. Compliance with the second discloses the nature of the obligations which are to be mutually enforceable. There must be as between the several purchasers' community of interest and reciprocity of obligation.

The first element reflects the concerns that we have already considered in the context of annexation. But in contrast to annexation, that area need not be precisely identified from the conveyance itself, '*provided it can be otherwise shown with reasonable certainty*'.[58]

The second element requires proof of intention that the covenants were imposed for the common benefit of all of the owners within the scheme.

Re Dolphin's Conveyance [1970] Ch 654, HC

Facts: Robert Dolphin owned Selly Hill Estate in Birmingham. After his death, the bulk of the estate was sold off by nine conveyances: the first four were sold by his sisters, and the remaining five, by his nephew. All except the last were in identical form and

---

[58] *Per* Stamp J in *Re Dolphin's Conveyance* [1970] Ch 654, 659, applying *Marten v Flight Refuelling Ltd* [1962] Ch 115. The area was defined in the case by reference to evidence produced by the Town Clerk of Birmingham City Corporation that the area of the estate was well known, in the same sense that Richmond Park is well known. See also *Stocks v Whitgift Homes Ltd* [2001] EWCA Civ 1732.

contained covenants as to the type of house that could be built on each plot. The vendors further covenanted that they would impose similar covenants on the sale of other plots. The current owner of one of the plots wished to redevelop in breach of the covenants and requested a declaration on the enforceability of the covenants. The court decided that a building scheme had been created, although there was no common vendor and the estate had not been laid out into plots prior to its sale.

Stamp J

At 661

[...T]o quote a passage in the judgment of Cross J. in *Baxter v. Four Oaks Properties Ltd.* [1965] Ch, 816, 825:

> "[...] for well over 100 years past where the owner of land deals with it on the footing of impos-ing restrictive obligations on the use of various parts of it as and when he sells them off for the common benefit of himself (in so far as he retains any land) and of the various purchasers inter se a court of equity has been prepared to give effect to this common intention notwithstanding any technical difficulties involved."

It is the submission of the defendants that that was done by the vendors in the present case.

That it was the intention of the two Miss Dolphins, on the sale of the parcel comprised in Coleman's conveyance, that there should be imposed upon each and every part of the Selly Hill Estate the restrictions set out in the conveyance—precluding the erection of buildings other than dwelling houses having the characteristics specified in the restrictions—cannot be doubted. And each conveyance evidenced the same intention. Nor can it be doubted that each purchaser, when he executed his conveyance, was aware of that intention. The cov-enant by the vendor in each conveyance, to the effect that the same restrictions would be placed on all future purchasers and lessees, makes this clear. Furthermore, I would, unless constrained by authority to the contrary, conclude as a matter of construction of Coleman's conveyance, and of all the others, that the vendor was dealing with the Selly Hill Estate on the footing of imposing obligations for the common benefit, as well of himself, as of the sev-eral purchasers of that estate. It is trite law that if you find conveyances of the several parts of an estate all containing the same or similar restrictive covenants with the vendor, that is not enough to impute an intention on the part of that vendor that the restrictions should be for the common benefit of the vendor and of the several purchasers inter se: for it is at least as likely that he imposed them for the benefit of himself and of the unsold part of the estate alone. That is not this case. Here there is the covenant by the vendors that on a sale or lease of any other part of Selly Hill Estate

> "it shall be sold or leased subject to the stipulations above mentioned numbered 1, 2, 3, 4, 5, 6, 7 and that the vendors their heirs or assigns will procure a covenant from each purchaser or lessee upon Selly Hill Estate to the effect of those seven stipulations."

What was the point of it? For what possible reason does a vendor of part of an estate who has extracted restrictive covenants from a purchaser, covenant with that purchaser that the other parts of the estate, when sold, shall contain the same restrictions, unless it be with the intention that the purchaser with whom he covenants, as well as he himself, shall have the benefits of the restrictions when imposed? In view of these covenants by the vendor in the several conveyances, I cannot do otherwise than find that the covenants were imposed, not only for the benefit of the vendors or of the unsold part of their estate, but as well for the benefit of the several purchasers. As a matter of construction of the conveyances, I find that what was intended, as well by the vendors as the several purchasers, was to lay down what has been referred to as a local law for the estate for the common benefit of all the several purchasers of it. The purpose of the covenant by the vendors was to enable each purchaser to have, as against the other purchasers, in one way or another, the benefit of the restrictions to which he had made himself subject.

Stamp J points out that the fact that similar covenants are taken from purchasers of several plots within an estate is not enough, although it is not necessarily an objection that different covenants are imposed on different properties within the estate.[59] What is required is that the covenants were taken on the understanding (of which all purchasers were aware) that they should be for the benefit of all of the purchasers of plots within the estate, not only the vendor. This wider community of interest was proved in *Re Dolphin's Conveyance*, because the vendor covenanted with each purchaser that he would impose the same user restrictions on the sale of each plot.

Proof of the requisite intention is a question of fact that may be proved from a number of sources. Early cases looked to a deed of mutual covenant entered into by all of the purchasers of plots—a convenient means where there are a limited number of plots all sold at the same time, but increasingly impractical where a large number of plots are sold over an extended period.[60] Deeds of mutual covenant are now rare and the necessary intention is more often found (as in *Re Dolphin's Conveyance*) from the terms of the conveyances themselves. Occasionally, an intention may be gleaned from the surrounding circumstances when the courts look to the stricter approach of *Elliston v Reacher*.[61] The distinction between these circumstances helps to account for the so-called 'relaxation' of building scheme requirements between the time of *Elliston v Reacher* and more recent decisions.[62]

Re Dolphin's Conveyance [1970] Ch 654, HC

Stamp J

At 662

As Cross J. pointed out in the course of the judgment in *Baxter v. Four Oaks Properties Ltd*, to which I have already referred, the intention that the several purchasers from a common vendor shall have the benefit of the restrictive covenants imposed on each of them, may be evidenced by the existence of a deed of mutual covenant to which all the several purchasers are to be parties. That common intention may also be evidenced by, or inferred from, the circumstances attending the sales: the existence of what has often been referred to in the authorities as a building scheme. I have been referred to a considerable number of authorities where the court has had to consider whether there were, or were not, present in the particular case those facts from which a building scheme—and, therefore, the common

---

[59] *Elliston v Reacher* [1908] 2 Ch 374 , 387, *per* Parker J, [1908] 2 Ch 665, 672, *per* Coxens-Hardy MR.

[60] See *Baxter v Four Oaks Properties Ltd* [1965] Ch 816, 825.

[61] See, e.g., *Lund v Taylor* (1975) 31 P & CR 16; *Jamaica Mutual Life Assurance Society v Hillsborough Ltd* [1989] 1 WLR 1101; *Emile Elias & Co Ltd v Pine Groves Ltd* [1993] 1 WLR 305.

[62] A point that he reiterated when elevated to the Court of Appeal in *Lund v Taylor* (1975) 31 P & CR 16, 177.

intention to lay down a local law involving reciprocal rights and obligations between the several purchasers—could properly be inferred. In *Elliston v. Reacher* [1908] 2 Ch. 374, 384, Parker J. laid down the necessary concomitants of such a scheme.

What has been argued before me is that here there is neither a deed of mutual covenant nor a building scheme. In the latter connection, it is pointed out that there was not a common vendor, for the parcels were sold off, first by the Dolphins and then by Watts. Nor, prior to the sales, had the vendors laid out the estate, or a defined portion of it, for sale in lots. Therefore, so it is urged, there were not present the factors which, on the authority of *Elliston v. Reacher*, are necessary before one can find the existence of a building scheme.

In my judgment, these submissions are not well founded. To hold that only where you find the necessary concomitants of a building scheme or a deed of mutual covenant can you give effect to the common intention found in the conveyances themselves, would, in my judgment, be to ignore the wider principle on which the building scheme cases are founded and to fly in the face of other authority of which the clearest and most recent is *Baxter v. Four Oaks Properties Ltd.* The building scheme cases stem, as I understand the law, from the wider rule that if there be found the common intention and the common interest referred to by Cross J. at p. 825 in *Baxter v. Four Oaks Properties Ltd.* the court will give effect to it, and are but an extension and example of that rule.

The local law of a building scheme is a creature of equity founded not on contract, but on a community of interests. Megarry J observed, in *Brunner v Greenslade*,[63] that '[t]*he major theoretical difficulties based on the law of covenant seem to me to disappear where instead there is an equity created by circumstances which is independent of contractual obligation*'. He continued: '[I]*n the field of schemes of development, equity readily gives effect to the common intention notwithstanding any technical difficulties involved. It may be, indeed, that this is one of those branches of equity which work best when explained least.*'

It is a somewhat unusual equity. It may revive following the common ownership of plots within the scheme[64] and can apply with equal force where a lot within the scheme is subdivided into smaller units.[65]

3.3.3 Contractual solutions

Possible contractual solutions to the timing problem are provided by s 56 of the LPA 1925 and by s 1 of the Contracts (Rights of Third Parties) Act 1999.

Law of Property Act 1925, s 56(1)

(1) A person may take an immediate or other interest in land or other property, or the benefit of any condition, right of entry, covenant or agreement over or respecting land or other property, although he may not be named as a party to the conveyance or other instrument.

In Chapter 7, section 2.2, we saw that when a covenantor makes a promise to a covenantee, a third party who also benefits from that covenant may, in limited circumstances, be able to

---

63 [1971] Ch 993, 10005. See also Parker J in *Elliston v Reacher* [1908] 2 Ch 374, 385.
64 *Texaco Antilles v Kernochan* [1973] AC 609.
65 *Brunner v Greenslade* [1971] Ch 993.

rely on s 56 of the 1925 Act to acquire a direct right against the covenantor. Thus, if a covenant is expressed to be made not only with the developer (as the owner of the rest of the development), but also with the owners for the time being of the plots already sold, those owners are entitled to claim the benefit of the covenant as named covenantees.[66]

A similar result is achieved by the Contract (Rights of Third Parties) Act 1999, which governs covenants entered into after 11 May 2000.

Contract (Rights of Third Parties) Act 1999, s 1

(1) [...] a person, who is not a party to a contract (a "third party") may in his own right enforce a term of the contract if:

  (a) the contract expressly provides that he may, or

  (b) subject to subsection (2), the term purports to confer a benefit on him.

(2) Subsection (1)(b) does not apply if on a proper construction of the contract it appears that the parties did not intend the term to be enforceable by a third party.

(3) The third party must be expressly identified by name, as a member of a class or as answering a particular description but need not be in existence when the contract is entered into.

As noted in Chapter 7, section 2.2, s 1 of the 1999 Act can also be used by a third party to acquire a direct right against a promisor. We saw there that the terms of s 1 of the 1999 Act open up possibilities beyond the circumstances catered for by s 56(1) of the LPA 1925. In particular, the covenant does not have to be made with the non-party: it is sufficient if it is made for his or her benefit. Additionally, the non-party, whilst he or she must be identified by name or by a defined class, need not be in existence when the covenant is made. Thus a covenant could be made for the benefit of the future owners of the dominant land and come within the scope of s 1 of the 1999 Act, even though those owners (as a class) are not yet in existence when the covenant was made.

4 ENFORCEMENT, DISCHARGE, AND MODIFICATION OF COVENANTS

4.1 ENFORCEMENT

A restrictive covenant may be enforced by an award of damages or by the grant of an injunction, either prohibitory (to restrain a threatened or continuing breach) or mandatory (to require the covenantee to act to remedy a breach that has already occurred). Damages are available at law where action is against the original covenantor, and in equity, under Lord Cairns Act 1858, where a subsequent owner of the servient land has committed the breach. Injunctive relief is important because, in most cases, the owner of dominant land wishes to make sure that his or her neighbour does not act in breach of the covenant. Damages are unlikely to be considered an adequate remedy—but the award of an injunction is discretionary.

---

[66] These provisions also apply to restrictive covenants that do not form a building scheme.

Millett LJ summarized in the following case the principles that the courts adopt when exercising that discretion.

Jaggard v Sawyer [1995] 1 WLR 269, CA

Millett LJ

At 287

When the plaintiff claims an injunction and the defendant asks the court to award damages instead, the proper approach for the court to adopt cannot be in doubt. Clearly the plaintiff must first establish a case for equitable relief, not only by proving his legal right and an actual or threatened infringement by the defendant, but also by overcoming all equitable defences such as laches, acquiescence or estoppel. If he succeeds in doing this, he is prima facie entitled to an injunction. The court may nevertheless in its discretion withhold injunctive relief and award damages instead. How is this discretion to be exercised? In a well known passage in *Shelfer v. City of London Electric Lighting Co.* [1895] 1 Ch. 287, 322–323, A. L. Smith L.J. set out what he described as "a good working rule" that

"(1) If the injury to the plaintiff's legal right is small,

(2) And is one which is capable of being estimated in money,

(3) And is one which can be adequately compensated by a small money payment,

(4) And the case is one in which it would be oppressive to the defendant to grant an injunction:—then damages in substitution for an injunction may be given."

Laid down just 100 years ago, A. L. Smith L.J.'s check-list has stood the test of time; but it needs to be remembered that it is only a working rule and does not purport to be an exhaustive statement of the circumstances in which damages may be awarded instead of an injunction.

Reported cases are merely illustrations of circumstances in which particular judges have exercised their discretion, in some cases by granting an injunction, and in others by awarding damages instead. Since they are all cases on the exercise of a discretion, none of them is a binding authority on how the discretion should be exercised. The most that any of them can demonstrate is that in similar circumstances it would not be wrong to exercise the discretion in the same way. But it does not follow that it would be wrong to exercise it differently.

The outcome of any particular case usually turns on the question: would it in all the circumstances be oppressive to the defendant to grant the injunction to which the plaintiff is prima facie entitled? Most of the cases in which the injunction has been refused are cases where the plaintiff has sought a mandatory injunction to pull down a building which infringes his right to light or which has been built in breach of a restrictive covenant. In such cases the court is faced with a fait accompli. The jurisdiction to grant a mandatory injunction in those circumstances cannot be doubted, but to grant it would subject the defendant to a loss out of all proportion to that which would be suffered by the plaintiff if it were refused, and would indeed deliver him to the plaintiff bound hand and foot to be subjected to any extortionate demands the plaintiff might make [. . .]

In considering whether the grant of an injunction would be oppressive to the defendant, all the circumstances of the case have to be considered. At one extreme, the defendant may have acted openly and in good faith and in ignorance of the plaintiff's rights, and thereby inadvertently placed himself in a position where the grant of an injunction would either force him to yield to the plaintiff's extortionate demands or expose him to substantial loss. At the other

> extreme, the defendant may have acted with his eyes open and in full knowledge that he was invading the plaintiff's rights, and hurried on his work in the hope that by presenting the court with a fait accompli he could compel the plaintiff to accept monetary compensation. Most cases [. . .] fall somewhere in between.

Gray and Gray have noted the trend towards 'a new social ethic of "reasonableness between neighbours"',[67] in which the enforcement of restrictive covenants through a monetary award rather than injunctive relief plays its part.

Gray and Gray, *Elements of Land Law* (5th edn, 2009, [3.4.79])

> Almost as a matter of definition, restrictive covenants involve relationships of adjacent owners, with the consequence that the new emphasis on social co-operation between neighbours points away from the absolutist remedy of the injunction in cases of breach of covenant. Consistently with the burgeoning theme of social accommodation, the courts have begun to make clear that, as between neighbouring owners, proprietary and possessory rights are not always capable of vindication in an absolute form. Instead—quite outside the normal market process—the courts have started to engineer socially optimal redistribution of various kinds of utility in land between parties who must somehow be enabled to continue to live in co-operative proximity. It seems that this judicial objective is not to be impeded by the fact that the provision of a mere monetary award for breach of covenant effectively allows a wrong-doing neighbour to purchase immunity from further enforcement of proprietary rights.

4.1.1 Injunction

The grant of an injunction is a natural remedy for breach of a restrictive covenant and there is an expectation that injunctive relief will be available.[68] A mandatory injunction is less readily granted, even though, by refusing injunctive relief, the court will be authorizing an unlawful state of affairs. As Millett LJ describes in *Jaggard v Sawyer*, the decision whether or not to grant an injunction can raise tricky issues: on the one hand, the courts is reluctant to sanction effectively the breach of a legal obligation; on the other hand, the dominant owner may not actually suffer any real monetary damage, and, indeed, may try to use the breach to extract some payment from the servient owner.[69] The court needs to balance whether or not damages provide an adequate remedy to the dominant owner against whether the grant of an injunction would cause oppression to the servient owner.[70] Nevertheless, a mandatory injunction may be granted where the covenantor's conduct is particularly reprehensible, because, for example, the breach is in flagrant disregard of warnings.[71]

---

[67] Gray and Gray, *Elements of Land Law* (5th edn, 2009, [3.4.78]).

[68] *Doherty v Allman* (1878) 3 App Cas 709.

[69] For example, in *Gafford v Graham* (1999) 77 P & CR 73, 83, the fact that Gafford tried to negotiate a release of the covenant was influential in the refusal of an injunction.

[70] See, e.g., *Shepherd Homes Ltd v Sandham* [1971] Ch 340, in which the court refused to order a mandatory injunction to pull down a fence built in breach of covenant where the claimant had delayed in bringing the action and the defendant intended to apply for the discharge of the covenant. See also *Wrotham Park Estate Co Ltd v Parkside Homes Ltd* [1974] 1 WLR 798.

[71] See, e.g., *Wakeham v Wood* (1982) 43 P & CR 40, but see *Wrotham Park Estate Co v Parkside Homes Ltd* [1974] 1 WLR 798.

Timing can present problems for the dominant owner seeking an injunction. As we have seen, the law in this area is far from straightforward and the case may not be finally heard for some time.[72] The dominant owner can preserve the status quo by seeking an interlocutory injunction pending the full hearing, but he or she will have to give an undertaking that he or she will indemnify the servient owner if the case is lost. If the dominant owner fails to seek interlocutory relief, however, he or she runs the risk that the court will be less inclined to grant an injunction at the final hearing.[73]

4.1.2 Damages

As Millett LJ explained in the above extract from *Jaggard v Sawyer*, damages will be granted where it would be oppressive to grant an injunction, and where the dominant owner's damage is small and capable of monetary estimation, so that compensation provides adequate redress.[74]

At common law, the measure of damages is guided by the loss suffered by the dominant owner.[75] Equitable damages under Lord Cairns Act 1858 may be awarded where the dominant owner continues to live with the effects of the breach: for example, where a user or building restriction is breached, even though there is little (if any) monetary loss to the value of the land. Damages in this case reflect the market cost to secure a release of the covenant.[76] The measure of damages both at common law and equity thus remains compensatory, rather than restitutionary.[77]

Nourse LJ explains the position in the following case.

Gafford v Graham (1999) 77 P & CR 73, CA

Nourse LJ

At 86

A welcome consequence of *Jaggard v. Sawyer* is that it has firmly established the *Wrotham Park* basis of assessing damages as the basis appropriate to cases such as this. There have been some differences of opinion as to the correct analysis of that decision, the difficulty being, as the plaintiffs there conceded, that the defendants' breaches of covenant had caused no diminution in the value of the land to which the benefit of the covenant was annexed; see [1974] 1 W.L.R. at 182F–G. No doubt it was for that reason that in *Surrey County Council v. Bredero Homes Ltd* [1993] 1 W.L.R. 1361, 1369, Steyn L.J. expressed the view that the *Wrotham Park* damages were defensible only on the basis that they were restitutionary in nature. However, that view was rejected in *Jaggard v. Sawyer* by both Sir Thomas Bingham M.R. and Millett L.J. who, agreeing with Megarry V.-C. in *Tito v. Waddell (No. 2)* [1977] Ch. 106, 335, thought that Brightman's approach had been compensatory, in that the

---

[72] In *Gafford v Graham* (1999) 77 P & CR 73, the case was not finally heard at first instance until 1996, some seven years after the breaches. The appeal was heard in 1998.

[73] See, e.g., *Shaw v Applegate* [1977] 1 WLR 970 and *Gafford v Graham* (1999) 77 P & CR 73, 82.

[74] *Shelfer v City of London Electric Lighting Co* [1895] 1 Ch 287

[75] *Surrey County Council v Bredero Homes Ltd* [1993] 1 WLR 1361.

[76] *Wrotham Park Estate Co Ltd v Parkside Home Ltd* [1974] 1 WLR 798; *Jaggard v Sawyer* [1995] 1 WLR 269; *Winter v Traditional & Contemporary Contracts* [2007] EWCA Civ 1088.

[77] This view has been criticized by restitution lawyers: see, e.g., Birks (1993) 109 LQR 518; O'Dair [1993] 1 RLR 31. See also *AG for Hong Kong v Blake* [2001] 1 AC 268, 283.

damages awarded were intended to compensate the plaintiffs for not having obtained the price they would have been able to obtain for giving their consent, had they been asked to give it.

The compensatory analysis, if accompanied by a recognition that it was not a diminution in value of the dominant tenement that was compensated, is perfectly acceptable. Equally, in a case where there has been such a diminution, there seems to be no reason why it should not be taken into account in assessing the sum which might reasonably have been demanded as a quid pro quo for relaxing the covenant. Whatever the correct analysis may be, *Jaggard v. Sawyer*, as both sides agree, is clear authority for the adoption of the *Wrotham Park* basis of assessing damages in this case. I therefore proceed to assess them by reference to the sum which the plaintiff might reasonably have demanded as a quid pro quo for relaxing the restrictions in perpetuity [. . .]

4.1.3 Defences

A servient owner may defend an action for breach of covenant on a number of grounds. We have already seen that the dominant owner must be able to claim the benefit of the covenant in order to sue upon it and that the servient owner must be bound by the covenant, both because it qualifies as a restrictive covenant and because it is protected by appropriate registration.

In addition, the servient owner may argue that his or her actions do not constitute a breach on a proper construction of the covenant, or because the dominant owner agreed to release the covenant. The action or inaction of the dominant owner may give rise to an implied release by way of estoppel where it would be unconscionable to allow the dominant owner to enforce the covenant. An estoppel may arise where the dominant owner is implicated in the breach,[78] or, as a result of his or her acquiescence, where he or she knows of the breach, but fails to take sufficiently prompt action.[79]

4.2 EXTINCTION AND MODIFICATION OF COVENANTS

The character of neighbourhoods change over time, so that the covenants imposed on a particular piece of land or estate may outlive their usefulness and impose a break on much-needed development. In addition to the limits on injunctive relief already considered, the court may, on rare occasions, be persuaded that a covenant should not be enforced because it has become obsolete.[80]

Far more significant, however, is the jurisdiction of the Lands Tribunal to discharge or modify a restrictive covenant conferred by s 84 of the LPA 1925.[81] It is not uncommon for enforcement proceedings to be stayed to allow the servient owner to make such an application.[82] An application may be made by any person interested in the servient land in respect

---

[78] *Sayers v Collyer* (1885) 28 Ch D 103.

[79] See, e.g., *Gafford v Graham* (1998) 77 P & CR 73, 80.

[80] See, e.g., *Duke of Bedford v British Museum Trustees* (1822) 2 My & K 552; *Sobey v Sainsbury* [1913] 2 Ch 513; *Chatsworth Estates Co v Fewell* [1931] 1 Ch 224; *AG for Hong Kong v Fairfax Ltd* [1997] 1 WLR 149.

[81] The section does not apply to positive covenants.

[82] The Lands Tribunal may also order consideration to be paid: see Law of Property Act 1925, s 84(1) and (1A).

of any restrictive covenant whenever made for valuable consideration.[83] The application is publicized, to alert the owners of any dominant land in the neighbourhood who may wish to object and then can be joined as parties.[84]

Law of Property Act 1925, s 84(1)

The Lands Tribunal shall [...] have power from time to time, on the application of any person interested in any freehold land affected by any restriction arising under covenant or otherwise as to the user thereof or the building thereon, by order wholly or partially to discharge or modify any such restriction on being satisfied—

(a) that by reason of changes in the character of the property or the neighbourhood or other circumstances of the case which the Lands Tribunal may deem material, the restriction ought to be deemed obsolete; or

(aa) that (in a case falling within subsection 1A below) the continued existence thereof would impede some reasonable user of the land for public or private purposes or, as the case may be, would unless modified so impede such user; or

(b) that the persons of full age and capacity for the time being or from time to time entitled to the benefit of the restriction, whether in respect of estates in fee simple or any lesser estates or interests in the property to which the benefit of the restriction is annexed, have agreed, either expressly or by implication, by their acts or omissions, to the same being discharged or modified; or

(c) that the proposed discharge or modification will not injure the persons entitled to the benefit of the restriction; [...]

Discharge or modification on the grounds of consent in s 84(1)(b) does not usually raise any particular problems, so we will concentrate on the remaining grounds.

4.2.1 Ground (a): obsolesence

The yardstick of obsolescence is whether or not, in the light of changes to the servient land or the surrounding area, the restriction still achieves its *original* purpose.[85] An obsolete covenant may still retain some value to the dominant owner because it achieves another purpose that was not originally contemplated, but this is relevant only to grounds (aa) or (c).[86] The reasonableness of the servient owner's proposed use is also an issue for ground (aa) rather than ground (a).[87]

4.2.2 Ground (aa): obstruction of reasonable user

This ground was added in 1970 to expand the Tribunal's jurisdiction to balance public utility against the current benefits derived from the covenant, when the damage caused by its

---

83 Ibid, s 84(7).
84 Ibid, s 84(3).
85 *Re Truman Hanbury Buxton & Co Ltd's Application* [1956] 1 QB 261. See, e.g., *Re Quaffers Ltd* (1988) 56 P & CR 142, in which the covenants were obsolete as soon as they were imposed because of the motorway network that surrounded the land.
86 *Re Kennet Properties Ltd's Application* (1996) 72 P & CR 353.
87 *McMorris v Brown* [1999] 1 AC 142, 147.

removal or modification can be compensated in money. The obstruction of reasonable user needs to be considered in the light of s 84(1A) and (1B) of the 1925 Act.

Law of Property Act 1925, s 84(1A) and (1B)

(1A) Subsection (1)(aa) above authorises the discharge or modification of a restriction by reference to its impeding some reasonable user of land in any case in which the Lands Tribunal is satisfied that the restriction, in impeding that user, either—

(a) does not secure to person entitled to the benefit of it any practical benefits of substantial value or advantage to them; or

(b) is contrary to the public interest;

and that money will be an adequate compensation for the loss or disadvantage (if any) which any such person will suffer from the discharge or modification.

(1B) In determining whether a case is one falling within subsection (1A) above, and in determining whether (in any such case or otherwise) a restriction ought to be discharged or modified, the Lands Tribunal shall take into account the development plan and any declared or ascertainable pattern for the grant or refusal of planning permissions in the relevant areas, as well as the period at which and context in which the restriction was created or imposed and any other material circumstances.

The Tribunal must thus:

- consider the reasonableness of the proposed user; and
- be satisfied either that the covenant no longer provides any practical benefit of substantial value or advantage to the dominant owner, or that the covenant is contrary to the public interest; and
- be satisfied that any damage that its removal or modification may cause can be adequately addressed by monetary compensation.

The reasonableness of the proposed user does not normally present a problem, thus attention is focused upon the practical benefit or advantage.

In considering the value of the practical benefit, the Tribunal looks not only to the original purpose of the covenant, but also to the present benefits which fall within the ambit of the covenant.[88] For example, surviving practical benefits might include retaining a property's value,[89] or preserving environmental advantages (including a view or privacy),[90] or the low density of a development even though the surrounding area is of a higher density.[91] In this respect, a higher burden of proof will be required to displace the evident community interest of covenants under a building scheme.[92] The alternative filter of public interest is less commonly asserted. Here, it is not enough that proposed user is in the public interest; the covenant, by preventing that user, must be shown to be contrary to the public interest. Thus the

---

[88] *Stannard v Issa* [1987] AC 175; *Re Kennet Properties Ltd Application* (1996) 72 P & CR 353; *Sheppard v Turner* [2006] 2 P & CR 28.

[89] *Re Azfar's Application* (2002) 1 P & CR 215.

[90] *Re Page's Application* (1996) 71 P & CR 440; *Re Azfar's Application* (2002) 1 P & CR 215.

[91] *Re Hydeshire Ltd's Application* (1994) 67 P & CR 93; *Re Snaith and Dolding's Application* (1995) 67 P & CR 93.

[92] *Re Lee's Application* (1996) 72 P & CR 439.

need for building land[93] or for a particular community facility, such as a residential home,[94] will not necessarily suffice where there is other suitable land available. In determining the public interest, the Tribunal is required by s 54(1B) to consider the planning policies applied in the area, as evidenced by the development plan and the pattern of planning decisions.

If the Tribunal decides to discharge or modify the covenant, then it may order the servient owner to pay the dominant owner compensation either for any damage that the dominant owner has suffered, or to account for the increased value of the servient land now that it is freed for the restriction.[95]

4.2.3 Ground (b): no injury to the dominant owner

The last ground provides a long-stop test against vexatious objections and, as such, provides the most stringent test.[96] No compensation is payable to the dominant owner because no loss has been suffered. In determining whether or not the dominant owner's interest is injured, the courts are sympathetic to 'the thin end of the wedge' argument that whilst relaxing a covenant in the current situation may not be particularly injurious, it may be so because of its consequences for future applications and development.[97]

The Law Commission has described these grounds as 'unnecessarily complex', and has made proposals to provide greater clarity, rather than a change in substance, by focusing on the purpose (in terms of scope) of the restrictions and the reasonableness of their discharge or modification.[98]

It is clear that 'restrictive covenants cannot be regarded as absolute and inviolable for all time'.[99] Where a court exercises its discretion to award damages in lieu of an injunction, a clear breach of covenant is condoned and the dominant owner is forced to accept monetary compensation.[100] Likewise, where the Tribunal is persuaded to discharge or modify a covenant, a dominant owner is powerless to prevent the unwanted development. But the rationale underlying the proprietary nature of covenants lies in the amenity that they afford. Where those continuing benefits can no longer be justified against wider social utility, a covenant's proprietary status is in jeopardy. There are human rights implications here, but there have been few serious challenges either to the exercise of the courts' discretion, or to s 84.[101] Any interference that there may be with the dominant owner's possessions is more than likely to be justified under the public interest balance upon which enforcement, modification, or discharge decisions are made.

The ability to sweep away unwanted burdens has played its part in lifting the rigidity of the 'conveyancer's view' of covenants to allow the judiciary to develop a more flexible attitude to those covenants that continue to serve their purpose.[102]

---

[93] *Re Collins Application* (1974) 30 P & CR 527.

[94] *Re Azfar's Application* (2002) 1 P & CR 215, but see *Re Lloyds and Lloyds Application* (1993) 66 P & CR 112.

[95] Law of Property Act 1925, s 84(1).

[96] *Re Kennet's Application* (1996) 72 P & CR 353; *McMorris v Brown* [1991] 1 AC 142.

[97] *McMorris v Brown* [1991] 1 AC 142, 151.

[98] Law Commission Consultation Paper No 186 (2008, [14.43]–[14.72]).

[99] *Per* Lord Bingham in *Jaggard v Sawyer* [1995] 1 WLR 296, 283.

[100] Mrs Jaggard complained of 'expropriation' of her property: see ibid, at 286.

[101] See *Scott v UK* (App No 10741/84); *Lawntown Ltd v Kamenzuli* [2007] EWCA Civ 949; *Site Developments (Ferndown) Ltd v Barrett Homes Ltd* [2007] EWHC 415.

[102] Gray and Gray, *Elements of Land Law* (5th edn, 2009, [3.4.84]).

5 REFORM

There have long been calls for the reform of the law governing land covenants. The main defects identified are the need to provide for the running of the burden of positive covenants and the undue complexity of the rules governing the running of the benefit of covenants.

Where landowners enjoy common facilities, it is necessary to provide effective mechanisms for the use, maintenance, and repair of those facilities, which can only be achieved by imposing positive obligations either to repair and maintain, or to contribute to the cost of doing so. In the next chapter, we will be examining the measures adopted to address this issue in the context of the ownership of flats—in particular, through the use of leasehold covenants and the introduction of commonhold tenure—but there still remains the need to address these issues where facilities are shared between adjoining freehold owners.

The technicality of the rules, particularly regarding the benefit, displays the fact that land covenants '*have for too long been judicially regarded as a peculiar species of personal contract*' when '*in reality they are genuine proprietary interests*'.[103] The recognition that s 78 of the LPA 1925 achieves statutory annexation provides the final impetus towards acknowledging that covenants are true appurtenant rights entitling the owner for the time being of the dominant land to control the use of adjacent servient land where that user benefits the dominant land.[104]

Reform recommendations have been put forward on a number of occasions, which have centered on phasing out restrictive covenants and replacing them with a new proprietary interest—that is, the *land obligation*.[105] The latest proposals are found in the Law Commission's Consultative Paper No 186, *Easements, Covenants and Profits Prendre*.[106]

The suggestion is that it should not be possible to create a restrictive covenant over registered land. Restrictive covenants will continue to affect unregistered land, but various alterative options are advanced for the gradual phasing out of restrictive covenants, which will, in any event, be converted to land obligations when land becomes registered.

A land obligation over registered land would differ from a restrictive covenant, in that it may be negative or positive. The ability of positive covenants to count as an interest in land would therefore remove (or at least reduce) the need for the mechanisms that we considered in section 2.4 above. A land obligation would have to be created by deed and completed by registration, with the benefit being recorded in the property register of the dominant land and the burden in the charges register of the servient land.[107] It would thus give its holder a *legal* interest in land, rather than an equitable interest. A plan would be required to identify the two pieces of land adequately. The basic position then would be that the benefit and burden of the land obligations, like any other proprietary interest, would pass to or bind later parties acquiring all or any of the dominant land or servient land. In this sense, the benefit

---

[103] Wade, 'Covenants: A Broad and Reasonable View' (1972) 31 CLJ 157, 170.

[104] See Gardner (2007, pp 191–3).

[105] See *Report of the Committee on Positive Covenants Affecting Land* (Cmnd 2710, 1965); Law Commission Report No 11, *Transfer of Land: Report on Restrictive Covenants* (1967); Law Commission Working Paper No 36, *Transfer of Land: Appurtenant Rights* (1971); Law Commission Report No 127, *Transfer of Land: The Law of Positive and Restrictive Covenants* (1984); Law Commission Report No 201, *Transfer of Land: Obsolete Restrictive Covenants* (1991). The history of these recommendations is summarized in the latest report Law Commission Consultation Paper 186 (2008, [7.1]–[7.8]).

[106] (2008, see Pts 7–13).

[107] An equitable land obligation could be created if the formalities fall short.

of a land obligation would be automatically annexed to the registered land that it benefits.[108] This would reduce (or at least, remove) the need for the mechanisms for the running of the benefit of a restrictive covenant that we considered in section 3 above. It would also align the running of the benefit of land obligations with the running of the benefit of an easement (see Chapter 26, section 1.1).

The land obligation would retain some of the characteristics of the restrictive covenant: for example, it would be necessary for the obligation to benefit some adjacent land. It would also be possible to apply for a discharge or modification of a land obligation: indeed, the Law Commission has proposed that the current grounds for discharge or modification under s 84 of the LPA 1925 (see section 4.2 above) should be extended.

McFarlane explains the implications of the Law Commission's proposals.

McFarlane, *The Structure of Property Law* (2008, p 51–4)

The scheme proposed by the Law Commission can be seen, from one perspective, as simplifying the law. Where Land Obligations are concerned, there would be no need for separate rules about assignment; annexation; or schemes of development. However, B bears the cost of that simplification: he has to make sure, when creating the initial Land Obligation, that he meets a number of formal requirements that do *not* currently apply to the Restrictive Covenant. The right granted by A [the servient owner] to B [the dominant owner] must be labelled by the parties as a "Land Obligation"; A and B must provide a plan clearly setting out the land benefiting from the right *and* the land burdened by that right; and B's right must also be substantively registered. This means that if the parties' intention is that the Land Obligation will benefit only a specific part of B's land, B must first separately register that part of the land, so that the Land Obligation can then be included on that registered title. In a case where a scheme of development can currently be used, B must instead divide his land into separate plots and register each of them. In some ways, the Land Obligation scheme is thus *more* technical than the current law. The justification for imposing such extra burdens on B is that the current law is needlessly complex ; however [...] that assumption can be challenged.

[...]

These rules, regulating the acquisition of a Restrictive Covenant [referring to assignment, annexation, and scheme of development] are widely regarded as unduly complex and uncertain. First, it is said that confusion is caused by the fact that there are three different methods. Second, it is said that the rules regulating each of these three methods are themselves overly technical. Finally, and underlying both those complaints, is the unflattering contrast with the rules relating to Easements [...]

However, it is easy to overstate these criticisms. There is no need for the mere existence of three separate methods, each with its own distinct role, to cause confusion. Nor are the rules regulating each method unduly technical or complex.

Finally, the current differences with the Easement can be justified. There is a clear difference between the **content** of each right; it is no surprise that the **acquisition** rules also differ. And the current law depends on the key distinction between property rights and persistent rights [...] As recognised by the Law Commission, any change to the current rules must therefore involve the bold step of preventing Restrictive Covenants from existing as a persistent right and instead recognizing a new form of property right in land.

---

[108] It is contemplated, however, that certain later parties (e.g. those with short leases) will not be bound by a positive land obligation.

QUESTIONS

1. Given the scope of public planning legislation, is there a continuing place for restrictive covenants in controlling land use?

2. How have the characteristics of restrictive covenants developed since *Tulk v Moxhay*?

3. Should the burden of a positive covenant run with the land as a general principle?

4. Restrictive covenants have been described as an equitable extension of either privity of estate or negative easements. How helpful are these analogies?

5. How does the courts' interpretation of ss 78 and 79 of the Law of Property Act 1925 differ? Is the difference justified?

6. Why is it important to identify the land to be benefited from a restrictive covenant?

7. Have the courts relaxed their approach to the proof of a building scheme?

8. Can the courts' approach to the enforcement of restrictive covenants be described as the compulsory purchase of the benefit of the covenant?

FURTHER READING

Bell, '*Tulk v Moxhay* Revisited' [1981] Conv 55

Gardner, 'The Proprietary Effect of Contractual Obligations Under *Tulk v Moxhay* and *De Mattos v Gibson*' (1982) LQR 279

Gardner, 'Two Maxims of Equity' (1995) 54 CLJ 60

Goulding, 'Privity of Estate and the Enforcement of Real Covenants' (2007) 36 3 CLWR 193

Griffiths, '*Tulk v Moxhay* Reclarified' [1983] Conv 29

Hurst, 'The Transmission of Restrictive Covenants' (1982) 2 LS 53

Law Commission Consultation Paper No 186, *Easements, Covenants and Profits Prendre* (2008)

Snape, 'The Benefit and Burden of Covenants: now where are we?' (1994) 68 Nott LJ 68

Turano, 'Intention, Interpretation and the "Mystery" of Section 79 of the Law of Property Act 1925' [2000] Conv 377

Wade, 'Covenants: "A Broad and Reasonable View"' (1972) 31 CLJ 157

28

FLAT OWNERSHIP: LONG LEASES AND COMMONHOLD

CENTRAL ISSUES

1. Communal living calls for the reciprocal enforcement of negative and positive rights and obligations between flat owners, and for mechanisms to facilitate the use, maintenance and repair of the common areas and facilities. To overcome the difficulty of enforcing positive obligations between freehold landowners, flat ownership has adopted the long lease.

2. The ownership of flats is achieved by granting the flat owner a long lease of his or her flat, with the freehold reversion being held either by an independent landlord or by a company owned collectively by the flat owners. The management and repair of the communal areas and facilities is conducted by the landlord, and funded by service charges paid by the flat owners.

3. The long lease structure of flat ownership has been open to abuse, particularly where an independent landlord holds

the freehold, but legislative reform has addressed the worst abuses.

4. Long leaseholders may collectively enfranchise or obtain an extended lease, exercise a right to manage, or question the reasonableness of service charges, cure by variation a defective lease, and seek some protection from forfeiture.

5. The Commonhold and Leasehold Reform Act 2002 introduced commonhold to provide a new framework for flat ownership. The flat owners own the freehold of their flats and communally own the freehold of the common parts through a commonhold association, which is responsible for the management of the development funded through commonhold assessments paid by the flat owners. The relationship of the flat owners is governed by a commonhold community statement, which binds all flat owners within the commonhold.

1 INTRODUCTION

Owners of flats are the closest neighbours. They live one on top of each other, as well as side by side. The need to regulate the legal rights and obligations of flat owners within a block of flats is thus particularly significant. An acceptable living environment is important, and thus the user of individual flats and the block as a whole needs to be controlled: late night parties are occasional fun, but can be a nuisance if a nightly occurrence. Restrictive covenants (see Chapter 27) provide a convenient mechanism for control. It is also necessary for flat owners to enjoy limited rights over their neighbours' flats, as well as the common areas of the building (often referred to as the 'common', or 'communal' parts). Rights over the common parts will include rights of way to reach the flat, as well as rights of drainage and to services. There may be a right to use communal gardens, car parking space, and other common facilities. Rights over neighbouring flats will include rights of support for flats on the higher floors from the flats below and rights of protection for the flats on the lower floors from the flats above. The passage of services through the flats will also need to be accommodated. All of these rights can qualify as easements (see Chapter 26) attached to the dominant flats over the servient common parts or other flats over which the rights are exercised.

The missing link in this framework is the need for an effective mechanism for the maintenance and repair of the flat development. Here, there is a problem, because positive covenants (see Chapter 27) to repair or contribute to the costs of repair are not enforceable against subsequent freehold owners.

Clarke explains the problems.

Clarke, 'Occupying "Cheek by Jowl"' in *Land Law: Themes and Perspectives* (eds Bright and Dewar, 1998, p 383)

The common law was, however, unable to adequately cope with the demands of the horizontal division of property. In a simple example of a property on three floors with each floor comprising a flat or apartment with freehold title the person with title to the middle flat has only a freehold of a block of air space. The market value of such a title is dependent upon the support provided by the lower flat and the protection from the weather provided by the flat above. It is, therefore, essential that the freeholders of these flats are under an obligation to support, on the one hand, and maintain the roof, on the other. Indeed, there must be mutual enforceability of repairing obligations, with the middle flat-owner paying a fair proportion of the benefit by contributing to repair and maintenance. Such mutual enforceability is prevented by the common law principle that the burden of a freehold covenant does not run with the land. A subsequent owner cannot be forced to pay by virtue alone of title to the property.

Lawyers have tackled this problem by utilizing the lease, because, as we saw in Chapter 25, positive obligations can be made to run with the leasehold estate in land. Rather late in the day, Parliament has addressed the issue with the introduction of 'commonhold' under the Commonhold and Leasehold Reform Act 2002. In so doing, it has followed the lead of other common law jurisdictions, which have enacted similar statutory solutions, known variously as 'strata',[1] or 'condominium' title.[2]

We should emphasize at the outset that we are concerned with long-term ownership solutions to multi-unit occupation of a building and not short-term tenancy agreements that provide the framework for mostly temporary living arrangements or public housing provision (whether of flats or houses).[3] Again, Clarke explains the context.

Clarke, 'Occupying "Cheek by Jowl"' in *Land Law: Themes and Perspectives* (eds Bright and Dewar, 1998, p 378)

A more obvious scenario where land law issues ought to exist is the renting of space for a periodic or short term in a single building such as a block of flats [...] It is often the least affluent in society who find they have no choice but to find a home in such a way. Public housing is frequently provided in this manner [...] The communal occupation with which this chapter is concerned is different. It occurs whenever a person seeks to purchase a proprietary interest of significant value of part of a building which is realizable by sale or assignment and which gives an exclusive right to occupy a part only of that building. Typically for a long lease at a low rent, a substantial upfront payment of premium will be paid to a developer or property-owner. The new occupier is generally styled 'leaseholder' rather than tenant, for although the basic relationship may be the same as a tenant paying a market rent, the expectations are very different. The new resident has not only secured a home under a shared roof but has invested capital in part of the property by means of the price paid when the flat was purchased. Such a leaseholder expects the investment to be permanent and recouped by a sale of the property interest at any time of his choosing. However, the value of that property interest will be reduced if the legal arrangements with the other occupiers are inadequate and by the rights of the freeholder who retains an interest in the building as a whole if those rights are adverse to the leaseholder. The leaseholders will have collective self interest in issues of repair, maintenance and management of the buildings as a whole and a degree of united and coherent action is often appropriate.

In this chapter, we will initially consider the long lease framework that lawyers have developed for flat ownership, noting the remedial statutory measures that have been enacted to address the specific problems that this solution presents. We will then look at the essential features of commonhold as an alternative framework. This is a complex area of the law, although, given the increasing density of development and the prevalence of communal living, one that is vital to many homeowners. It also forms a framework for much office and other commercial development. We will not, however, be delving too deeply into this complexity, but will concentrate on offering an overview.

---

[1] Strata title was introduced in New South Wales, but has spread throughout Australasia and to other common law jurisdictions, e.g. Singapore.

[2] Condominium title is found across North America.

[3] We cover short-term tenancy agreements in Chapter 24.

2 LONG LEASES OF FLATS

Long leases are privately negotiated contracts, and, as such, they come in all shapes and sizes. Variety is the spice—and sometimes the bane—of life, and conveyancers spend long hours drafting and reading different forms of long leases. The common features are that they are originally granted for an extended term at a market price (commonly referred to as a 'premium'), but for a low annual rental (commonly referred to as a 'ground rent'). They are leases, but, in terms of the value of the interest that they confer, they are intended to replicate the timeless ownership of freehold.

2.1 WHO IS THE LANDLORD?

The use of the long lease inevitably results in the division of estates in the land. There are the leases of the individual flats granted for terms varying from 99 to 999 years, which are held by the flat owners, and the freehold reversion on those leases, which, together with the freehold of the common parts, is held by the landlord.

Originally, the developer of the flats, as the freehold owner of the development, will grant the leases. The developer then has a choice in its sale of the development. It can sell the whole development without retaining any interest by selling the leases of the individual flats to purchasers for their market value, together with a share in a management company to which the developer transfers the freehold of the whole development, subject to the flat leases. Thus whilst the flat lessees own their own flats individually, they also communally own the freehold of the whole block, including the freehold of the common parts and the freehold reversion of the flat leases.

Alternatively, the developer can retain the freehold either directly or by transferring it to a company that it owns. The developer will choose this latter option where it wishes to retain the investment and income-producing opportunities that the freehold reversion represents. The investment return lies not in the annual ground rent from the lease, which will be low, but in the capital value of the freehold reversion, which will increase as the leasehold terms run their course and fall to be renewed. Given the common length of leasehold terms, this is a very long-term investment. A more attractive commercial opportunity is the income returns to be made from the provision of management services.

Davey explains the position of the landlord and some of the problems associated with long leases that legislation has tried to address.

Davey, 'The Regulation of Long *Residential* Leases' in *Modern Studies in Property Law: Vol 3* (ed Cooke, 2005, p 206)

Thus in the case of long leases of flats where there is an unrelated freeholder, there is a stark contrast between the interest of the landlord and the leaseholder. For the latter the property is his home in which he will have staked a considerable investment for a long-term interest. But what does ownership of the freehold mean to the landlord, especially where the flat leases have a long period to run? Its capital value is low, reflecting the low ground rent, so why would anyone want to be a landlord in these circumstances? The answer lies in the management of services. In other words the freehold is a source of income and as such has an investment value. But this suggests of course that, for the business to be profitable, leaseholders must be paying through their service charge for more than the cost of the services to the landlord including his management expenses; this is the profit element. Some landlords also make a profit through placing insurance of the building with an insurer who pays commission to the landlord or by placing contracts for repairs and other services with associated companies.

Thus the leasehold structure of flat ownership was ripe for exploitation and so it proved to be the case. The problems are legion and were first officially identified in a *Report on the Management of Privately Owned Blocks of Flats* published in 1985. They include:

- Delay in dealing with repairs;
- The levying of excessive charges;
- A lack of consultation and provision of information;
- A lack of sinking or contingency funds for infrequent but expensive major schemes of repair and renovation;
- The different levels of interest exhibited by absentee investor leaseholders and occupational leaseholders.

Other legal problems identified included uncertainties over enforcement of obligations, the need for cheap and convenient resolution of disputes, the unresolved question of ownership and taxation of sinking funds and the means of remedying defective leases.

Many of the problems associated with long leasehold are not nearly so significant where the flat owners own the freehold collectively. They are their own landlords, and their leases are merely a convenient device to ensure that both the negative and positive covenants in their leases are enforceable by, and against, all of the flat owners in the block.

2.2 THE LEASEHOLD TERM, AND RIGHTS TO ENFRANCHISEMENT AND EXTENSION

Common long leasehold terms for flat developments are 99 or 125 years, and for specialist gated communities, 200 years is a common term. In times gone past, even longer terms of 999 years were sometimes granted. Time nevertheless ticks away and, where the residue of the term nudges the fifty or sixty-year mark, the lease starts to be considered a wasting asset that is declining in value year by year, and which will ultimately become unmortgageable and unmarketable. The only way in which the long lease can replicate the infinity of freehold ownership is thus for the leaseholder to negotiate with the landlord either to acquire the freehold (usually collectively with the other flat owners) or to extend his or her lease.

Rights to enfranchisement and to obtain an extended term were granted to leasehold flat owners by the Leasehold Reform Housing and Urban Development Act 1993.[4] The rights were notoriously complex to exercise,[5] but have been relaxed somewhat by the Commonhold and Leasehold Reform Act 2002.[6] A flat owner may obtain at a market premium an extended lease for a period equal to the unexpired residue of the lease plus

---

[4] Enfranchisement of leasehold houses was earlier granted by the Leasehold Reform Act 1967.

[5] See Clarke, 'Leasehold Enfranchisement: Leasehold Reform, Housing and Urban Development Act 1993' [1994] Conv 223.

[6] For example, the right to enfranchise may be exercised by a simple majority, rather than a two-thirds majority, and there is no longer a residency condition: see Commonhold and Leasehold Reform Act 2002, ss 119 and 120.

ninety years. The right of an individual flat owner to obtain a longer lease of his or her flat, although easier to achieve than enfranchisement, is of limited value on its own. It is of more value for all of the flat owners to extend their leases and to acquire the freehold of the development. Collective enfranchisement may be achieved through a right to enfranchise company, in which all the flat owners are given an opportunity to become members, and through which they can participate in the enfranchisement claim. The company is able to acquire the freehold on behalf of the flat owners so that, collectively, the flat owners become their own landlords, with the freedom to extend their leases and take over the management of the block.

Taking over the management can, however, be a mixed blessing, as Davey explains.

Davey, 'The Regulation of Long Residential Leases' in *Modern Studies in Property Law: Vol 3* (ed Cooke, 2005, p 221)

[... O]n enfranchisement leaseholders may find that the management of a block of flats can be fraught, expensive and depressing business. They will become landlords of themselves and non-participating leaseholders as well as any non-long leaseholder tenants or commercial tenants, with all the responsibilities that entails. They will need to deal with contractors, comply with a host of regulatory requirements on health and safety employment etc. But this should not detract from the fact that leaseholders will now be in control and this often brings a high degree of satisfaction especially in smaller blocks. Furthermore the tribulations of management can be avoided to a considerable degree by the appointment of managing agents. However, this will not stop aggrieved leaseholders transferring their grievance from the freeholder to the new management company.

2.3 MAINTENANCE AND REPAIR

An effective machinery for the maintenance and repair of the block of flats is crucial. The most common structure is for the leaseholders of flats to be responsible for the repair maintenance of the interior of their individual flats, and for the landlord to take on responsibility for the repair and maintenance of the structure (including the roof and foundations), plus the common parts and facilities. The landlord's costs are then recovered from the individual flat owners through a periodic service charge, which may be supplemented by contributions to a sinking fund to meet major replacement expenditure or unexpected costs.

Two main problems can emerge: firstly, the flat leases may provide an inadequate repair and maintenance framework, because the division of responsibility is unsatisfactory; and secondly, the service charge provisions and their performance may be inadequate, and may operate unfairly. The first problem calls for a variation of the leases, to provide a more satisfactory repairing and maintenance framework, and will be considered below. The second has been the source of particular complaint, as Davey outlines in the above extract.[7] It has proved a challenging nut to crack. The solution is found in the flat

---

[7] These problems were first reviewed in a *Report on the Management of Privately Owned Flats* ('the Nugee Report') (1985).

owners gaining control over the management of their block and in the regulation of service charge levels.

2.3.1 The right to manage

The right of the flat owners to appoint a manager was first conferred by the Landlord and Tenant Act 1987, which was amended by the Housing Act 1996 and the Commonhold and Leasehold Reform Act 2002. The power was exercisable upon proof of some fault by the landlord or his or her managers: for example, the levying of unreasonable charges, or a failure to comply with the Code of Practice approved under the Leasehold Reform Housing and Urban Development Act 1993.[8] This limited power, unfortunately, did not solve the problem: proof of fault was not always easy to establish, thus a new right to manage, without having to establish fault, was introduced by the 2002 Act. The right is exercisable by application to the Leasehold Valuation Tribunal for the appointment of a new manager, which may be exercised through the establishment of a right to manage company formed by the flat owners.[9] This company takes over the management duties and powers under the flat leases, without the flat owners having to enfranchise.

2.3.2 Levels of service charge

Excessive service charges have long been a source of complaint and have been the subject of regulation for all residential leases since 1972.[10] Control operates through ss 18–30 of the Landlord and Tenant Act 1985, and an extensive set of regulations. The controls relate to those variable charges that fall within the definition of 'service charge'. As a result, the fixed charges sometimes found in short-term tenancies are excluded.

Landlord and Tenant Act 1985, s 18

Meaning of "service charge" [...]

(1) In the following provisions of this Act "service charge" means an amount payable by a tenant of a dwelling as part of or in addition to the rent—

(a) which is payable, directly or indirectly, for services, repairs, maintenance, improvements or insurance or the landlord's costs of management, and

(b) the whole or part of which varies or may vary according to the relevant costs.

Service charges must satisfy three levels of reasonableness: firstly, the charge must be reasonably incurred; secondly, it must relate to works or services that are carried out to a reasonable standard; and finally, the amount payable should be reasonable.

---

[8] See s 87.

[9] Commonhold and Leasehold Reform Act 2002, s 21.

[10] See the Housing Finance Act 1971, which was amended by the Housing Act 1974 and the Housing Act 1980, before being consolidated in the Landlord and Tenant Act 1985, which itself has been subject to amendment by the Landlord and Tenant Act 1987, the Housing Act 1996, and the Commonhold and Leasehold Reform Act 2002.

Landlord and Tenant Act 1985, s 19

Limitation of service charges: reasonableness

(1) Relevant costs shall be taken into account in determining the amount of a service charge payable for a period—

(a) only to the extent that they are reasonably incurred, and

(b) where they are incurred on the provisions of services or the carrying out of works, only if the services or works are of a reasonable standard;

and the amount payable shall be limited accordingly.

(2) Where a service charge is payable before the relevant costs are incurred, no greater amount than is reasonable is so payable, and after the relevant costs have been incurred any necessary adjustment shall be made by repayment, reduction or subsequent charges or otherwise.

The Leasehold Valuation Tribunal determines reasonableness on the application of either the landlord or the leaseholder, with each party bearing its own costs. The Tribunal can also determine on whom the liability falls under the terms of the lease.[11] The test of reasonableness looks to the actual cost, excluding any element of profit to the landlord, and does not extend to the cost of managing agents employed by the landlord where that managing agent is an alter ego of the landlord.[12]

The Landlord and Tenant Act 1985 contains other useful protections for flat owners, including provisions giving tenants the right to challenge insurance effected by the landlord,[13] requiring consultation with flat owners before carrying out certain works,[14] requirements for statements of accounts,[15] and controls over the manner in which demands for service charges are made.[16] Other legislative controls call for service charges to be held in trust fund accounts[17] and enable the flat owners to effect their own insurance.[18]

2.4 COMMUNAL LIVING

Flat owners, as the closest neighbours, have to get along. The purpose of many of the negative user covenants in the flat leases is to provide a code of conduct for the flat development to maintain an acceptable, even attractive, living environment. The rules for the enforcement of leasehold covenants provide a route to legal redress where this code is breached, but there are a number of difficulties.

The enforcement of leasehold covenants is designed with a hierarchical structure in mind, thus landlord can sue leaseholder and vice versa. We have already seen that even

---

[11] Landlord and Tenant Act 1985, s 27A.

[12] *Finchbourne Ltd v Rodrigues* [1976] 3 All ER 581; cf *Embassy Court Residents Association v Lipman* (1984) 271 EG 545, in which the landlord's administration charges were recoverable, and *New Pinehurst Residents Association (Cambridge) v Silow* [1988] 1 EGLR 227 and *Skilleter v Charles* [1992] 13 EG 113, in which the manager was not the alter ego of the landlord.

[13] Landlord and Tenant Act 1985, s 30A and Sch 1, para 9.

[14] Ibid, ss 20 and 20ZA.

[15] Ibid, ss 21, 21A, and 22.

[16] Ibid, s 21B.

[17] Landlord and Tenant Act 1987, ss 42, 42A, and 42B; Commonhold and Leasehold Reform Act 2002, s 156.

[18] Commonhold and Leasehold Reform Act 2002, s 162.

enforcement against a subtenant falls outside the basic scheme and recourse to *Tulk v Moxhay* is required.[19] But problems of enforcement of user restrictions often lie between individual flat owners, presenting a need for horizontal control unless the landlord can be persuaded to become involved—a more realistic possibility where the flat owners own the freehold collectively through the corporate structure. Possible routes to horizontal enforcement may exist through proof of a building scheme, in which all of the flats are subject to common covenants, or where individual flat owners can otherwise claim the benefit of the covenants.[20] Even so, adversarial court processes are ill equipped to resolve disputes between neighbours where continuing amicable relationships are so important.

2.5 VARIATION

The terms of a long lease are set in stone when it is first entered into. They are individually drafted documents, which vary from development to development, although all leases within a block should be in the same form to provide a coherent and common framework. If the leases are found to be defective, it can prove an insurmountable task to try to vary all of the leases. All of the flat owners, together with any lenders with mortgages secured against the leases, will need to agree and be involved in the process. Part IV of the Landlord and Tenant Act 1987 now provides a statutory power for the Leasehold Valuation Tribunal to vary defective leases—although, unfortunately, the statutory definition of a 'defective lease' is rather restrictive.[21]

2.6 FORFEITURE

Leases of flats will contain a right for the landlord to forfeit and re-enter the flat in the event of the leaseholder failing to pay the rent or service charge, or failing to perform the other covenants contained in the lease. We have seen that a right of forfeiture can only be exercised following service of notice on the leaseholder and is subject to the courts' discretion to grant relief from forfeiture.[22] Nevertheless, it remains a draconian remedy, which marks a long leasehold estate out from the security offered by a freehold tenure, and which has been abused by landlords wishing to intimidate flat owners.[23]

A number of protections have been enacted to assist long leaseholders facing forfeiture for non-payment of rent or service charge: in particular, the amount of a disputed service charge must be determined by a court or the Tribunal,[24] and must exceed a prescribed amount or have been outstanding for a prescribed period.[25]

In respect of a breach of a repairing covenant, s 1 of the Leasehold Property (Repairs) Act 1938[26] provides that the notice that must be served under s 146(1) of the Law of Property

---

[19] Chapter 25, section 5.

[20] Chapter 27, section 3.3.

[21] See Landlord and Tenant Act 1987, s 35.

[22] See Chapter 25, section 6.4.

[23] See, e.g., ODPM Consultation Paper, *Restrictions on the Use of Forfeiture for Long Residential Leases* (2002).

[24] Housing Act 1996, s 81.

[25] Commonhold and Leasehold Reform Act 2002, s 167.

[26] The Act applies to leases of more than seven years that have at least three years to run. See Smith, 'A Review of the Operation of the Leasehold Property (Repairs) Act 1938' [1986] Conv 85.

Act 1925 (LPA 1925), must inform the leaseholder of his or her right to serve a counter-no-tice, and, upon service of a counter-notice, forfeiture cannot follow unless the court orders otherwise.[27] Leave will not be granted unless immediate repair is necessary, or unless the court considers it just and equitable.[28]

Many feel that these measures do not go far enough, and that forfeiture in the case of long leases is 'simply inappropriate' and should be abolished.[29]

3 COMMONHOLD

Commonhold has been described as 'a vital and necessary new form of land holding for the twenty-first century'.[30] The Commonhold and Leasehold Reform Act 2002 introduced it to address the problems of flat ownership, although its application is not confined to flats, but can be used for the ownership of any residential or commercial development with shared facilities.

As its name suggests, commonhold is designed to facilitate communal living and work-ing, by providing a structure for the ownership of individual units and the communal own-ership, control, and management of common areas and facilities. It abandons the leasehold, with, hopefully, the associated problems already considered, and instead provides a frame-work in which the freehold ownership of units, with communal areas and facilities, can be accommodated. As such, it does not introduce a new tenure or estate, but a new means of structuring freehold land ownership.[31]

3.1 THE STRUCTURE OF COMMONHOLD

A commonhold block of flats will be divided into individual freehold flats, held by each flat owner as a registered freehold proprietor, with the freehold of the common parts registered in the name of the commonhold association in which the flat owners are all members. As Van der Merwe and Smith point out, there are thus three elements to commonhold and a need to appreciate not only the property framework, but also company law, which governs the workings of the association.

Van Der Merwe and Smith, 'Commonhold—A Critical Appraisal' in *Modern Studies in Property Law: Vol 3* (ed Cooke, 2003, p 229)

[... C]ommonhold is structured as a threefold unity combining ownership in a unit with col-lective rights with regard to the common parts and membership of the commonhold associ-ation [...] From the threefold unity embodied in commonhold, the institution straddles both the law of property and that of association.

---

[27] Law of Property Act 1925, s 1(3).
[28] Ibid, s 1(5), and *Sidnell v Wilson* [1966] 2 QB 67.
[29] See Davey, 'The Regulation of Long Residential Leases' in *Modern Studies in Property Law: Vol 3* (ed Cooke, 2005, p 222). See Chapter 25, section 6.4, for the Law Commission's proposals for reform to forfeiture.
[30] Clarke, *Commonhold: The New Law* (2002, p 2).
[31] See Roberts, 'A New Property Term: But No Property in a Term!' [2002] Conv 341.

The structure is similar to the leasehold structure, in which flat owners hold leases of their individual flats, and collectively own the freehold reversion on their leases and the freehold of the common parts through their ownership of shares in a management company. The essential distinction is that the commonhold owners are freeholders and not leaseholders. There is thus no inherent limitation on the length of their ownership and no danger of early termination of their ownership through forfeiture. Nevertheless, commonhold has been described as a 'sub-species' of freehold that '*is better seen as a distinct form of land holding*'.[32]

All flat owners must be members of the commonhold association and, on the sale of a commonhold flat, the seller ceases to be a member, with his or her place being taken by the purchaser—that is, the new owner of the flat. Every member of the association is bound by the commonhold community statement, which contains rights and obligations, both positive and negative, to generate a 'local law' for the development. The statement plays the same role as the easements and covenants contained in a standard flat lease, as well as helping to define the relationship between the individual flat owners and the association as owner of the common parts. There will be familiar easements of support and protection, rights of way over, and to use of, the common areas and facilities, and for drainage and the passage of services. There will also be obligations similar to the restrictive user covenants found in leases to maintain the ambience and character of the development, and positive obligations to repair individual flats, and to contribute to the cost of repairing and maintaining the common parts. The difference lies in the fact that these rights and obligations will be contained in a single document, rather than in the individual leases.

Wong explains the central significance of the commonhold association and the commonhold community statement, both of which must follow the form specified in the Commonhold and Leasehold Reform Act 2002 and its regulations.[33]

Wong, 'Potential Pitfalls in the Commonhold Community Statement and the Corporate Mechanisms of the Commonhold Association' [2006] Conv 14, 34

Under the commonhold concept, the CCS [commonhold community statement] and the CA [commonhold association] are the fundamental organs which provide the statutory and corporate frameworks for the running of the commonhold. Good management in a commonhold would depend on the quality of the execution of these two frameworks in achieving a balance between uniform protection and local flexibility as well as balance between the rule of the majority and protection of minority members.

We now need to consider in a little more detail these essential features.

3.2 CREATION OF COMMONHOLD

Consistent with the drive towards registration, a commonhold development may only exist where the land is (or is to be) registered. There are two routes by which a commonhold may be established: firstly, a new development may be set up as a commonhold

---

[32] See Clarke (2002, pp 16–17).
[33] The commonhold association's constitutional documents are specified in Schs 1 and 2, and the commonhold community statement in Sch 2.

development;[34] and secondly, an existing development may be converted from long lease-hold to commonhold.[35]

The conversion of an existing development requires the agreement of all of the flat owners within the development where the leases have more than twenty-one years to run.[36] There is a statutory process for the extinction (and the payment of compensation) of shorter-term leases and other interests.[37] Given this need for unanimity, it is unlikely that existing flat developments will be converted to commonhold. Commonhold is a more feasible option for new flat developments.

Where a new development is to be created as a commonhold, there are two stages to the process. Firstly, the developer will need to apply for its freehold estate to be registered as commonhold land, when it will need to submit to the Land Registry the commonhold asso-ciation's constitutional documents, the commonhold community statement, any necessary consents (e.g. from an existing mortgagee), and the compliance certificate of the associ-ation's directors. Upon approval, the estate will be registered as commonhold land, although it is not yet operational as a commonhold community. The commonhold is only activated upon the registration of the first purchaser as the owner of his or her flat when the common-hold community statement comes into force and the commonhold association is registered as the proprietor of the common parts.[38]

3.3 COMMONHOLD LAND OWNERSHIP

Commonhold can only exist where there are at least two units: it is, after all, a form of com-munal land holding. The individual flats and the common parts are defined by the com-monhold community statement, with the common parts defined in a negative fashion as those areas that are not comprised within the flat owners' individual titles.[39] The common parts may be further split between those areas over which all flat owners may exercise rights and those limited-use areas, the user of which may be confined to certain flat owners.[40] Any redefinition of these areas requires the agreement of those affected and the consequent amendment of the commonhold community statement.[41]

It is a fundamental principle that freehold is the only title that can exist within a com-monhold development. Smith explains the consequences of what has been called the 'purity of commonhold'.[42]

Smith, 'The Purity of Commonholds' [2004] Conv 194

[...] No conversion of an existing long leasehold development is possible unless 100 per cent of registered lessees, with terms over 21 years of the whole or part of the land, consents.

---

[34] Commonhold and Leasehold Reform Act 2002, s 7.

[35] Ibid, s 9.

[36] Ibid, s 3(1)(b).

[37] Ibid, ss 9(3)(f) and 10.

[38] Ibid, ss 7(3) and 8.

[39] Ibid, s 25. The importance of defining these areas is explained by Van der Merwe and Smith, 'Commonhold—A Critical Appraisal' in *Modern Studies in Property Law: Vol 3* (ed Cooke, 2005, p 230).

[40] Commonhold and Leasehold Reform Act 2002, s 25(3).

[41] Ibid, ss 23, 24, and 30.

[42] Hansard, HC Vol 627, col 491 (16 October, 2001).

It is not possible to get around this bar, and there is draconian provision for the clearance of all shorter leases of commonhold land. A second aspect of the purity principle is the restriction on the ability of the holder of a residential commonhold unit to grant leases of that unit. Intertwined with this is the issue of diversion by the commonhold association of assessments, on default of the unit holder, from lessees and sub-lessees of rented units.

The second aspect referred to by Smith compromises the fundamental principle of the free alienability of freeholds—but such is the strength of the purity principle that the government was determined that leaseholds should not unduly contaminate a commonhold. Thus, although flat owners within a commonhold are free to sell, mortgage, and charge their flats, they are not able to grant a lease for a premium or for a term greater than seven years, nor are they able to dispose of part of their flat, other than by way of lease, without the consent of the commonhold association.[43]

Commonhold and Leasehold Reform Act 2002, s 15(2)

Transfer

(2) A commonhold community statement may not prevent or restrict the transfer of a commonhold unit.

Commonhold and Leasehold Reform Act 2002, s 17(1)

Leasing: residential

(1) It shall not be possible to create a term of years absolute in a residential commonhold unit unless the term satisfies prescribed conditions.

Commonhold and Leasehold Reform Act 2002, s 20

Other transactions

(1) A commonhold community statement may not prevent or restrict the creation, grant or transfer by a unit-holder of—

(a) an interest in the whole or part of his unit;

(b) a charge over his unit.

(2) Subsection (1) is subject to sections 17 to 19 (which impose restrictions about leases).

---

[43] Commonhold and Leasehold Reform Act 2002, ss 21 and 22 A more flexible approach is permitted for non-residential units where there is no statutory prohibition on leases, although control may be imposed through the commonhold community statement: ibid, s 17(5).

Commonhold and Leasehold Reform Act 2002, s 21

Part-unit: interests

(1) It shall not be possible to create an interest in part only of a commonhold unit.

(2) But subsection (1) shall not prevent—

  (a) the creation of a term of years absolute in part only of a commonhold unit where the term satisfies the prescribed conditions, [. . .]

  (b) the transfer of the freehold estate in part only of a commonhold unit where the commonhold association consents in writing to the transfer.

Commonhold and Leasehold Reform Act 2002, s 22(1)

Part-unit: charging

(1) It shall not be possible to create a charge over part only of an interest in a commonhold unit.

The rationale behind the prohibition of longer leases is a determination to avoid replication of long-lease landholding within commonholds, as well as to discourage absentee landlords. The consequences, however, may be to discourage the choice of commonhold altogether, particularly given the popularity of the buy-to-let market.

The commonhold association, as freeholder of the common parts, is able to dispose of these areas without the consent of the flat owners, but with one important limitation:[44] it cannot charge the common parts except by way of a legal mortgage that has the prior unanimous approval of the flat owners as its members.[45] This freedom seems remarkable, given the crucial importance of the common parts, but may be explained as an attempt to give the commonhold association some freedom of action in the event of possible insolvency.

3.4 THE COMMONHOLD ASSOCIATION

The commonhold association is central to the commonhold scheme. It is simply not possible to have a commonhold without a commonhold association to hold the common parts, and to be responsible for the management of, and the enforcement of rights and obligations within, the commonhold.

Originally, it was envisaged that the association would be a purpose-built association, but the government opted for adapting an existing corporate form—the company limited by guarantee, the members of which are the individual flat owners.[46] As such, the association has separate legal personality and limited liability. It is regulated through the Companies Act 2006, with obligations to hold annual general meetings, to file accounts, and to appoint

---

[44] Ibid, ss 27 and 28.

[45] Ibid, s 29.

[46] All unit holders must be members and no person who does not own a unit may be a member.

corporate officers to run the association.[47] But the commonhold association is a distinct form of company limited by guarantee and the flat owners have no choice but to be members. Its constitutional documentation is central to the flat owners' relationship with the association, and must incorporate mandatory provisions to try to achieve a fair distribution of power.[48]

Wong, 'Potential Pitfalls in the Commonhold Community Statement and the Corporate Mechanisms of the Commonhold Association' [2006] Conv 14, 26

The CA [commonhold association] must adopt all the provisions in the model articles – alterations are only permitted for a few articles and any additions must be clearly labelled. These strict rules help to ensure that the democratic nature of the general meeting and director's meeting, which is of particular importance in the context of commonhold, since unit-holders are "captive members" of the particular CA of their building. One underlying threat to democracy is the abuse of the resolutions mechanisms by the developer through his membership or directorship in the CA.

The association operates through two organs: the board of directors and the flat owners in general meeting.

Each flat owner is entitled to single membership in the commonhold association and is entitled to cast a single vote. Co-owners of a flat are required to nominate one of their number to be the association member for their flat and, as such, entitled to vote. There is a principle of equality of representation of each unit, regardless of the value or character of the units within the development. Accordingly, commonhold is more likely to suit those developments in which units are, by and large, uniform in value, size, and type.

The general meeting appoints the directors, who are responsible for the management of the commonhold through their duties to manage and to uphold compliance with the commonhold community statement. The directors need not be flat owners with an interest in the development. Thus professional property management may be achieved either by appointing professional managers as directors, or, alternatively, through the employment of professional managing agents by the directors.

The commonhold association as a corporate vehicle is governed by the rule of the majority. As such, fears have been expressed that a minority of flat owners may be subjected to the 'tyranny' of the majority in decisions that adversely affect their everyday lives within the commonhold community.[49] The vital question is thus whether the mandatory provisions of the association do achieve a fair balance. In particular, the power of the directors to appoint managing agents and to fix the level of service charge without the prior approval of the flat owners in general meeting has drawn criticism.[50]

The association may be wound up following the standard procedures contained in the Insolvency Act 1986.[51] The flat owners, as members of the association, may initiate winding

---

[47] Directors of the commonhold association may be either appointed by the flat owners from within their own number, or professionals appointed by the flat owners to run the association on their behalf.

[48] See Schs 1 and 2.

[49] See Kenny [2003] Conv 1.

[50] See Wong, 'Potential Pitfalls in the Commonhold Community Statement and the Corporate Mechanisms of the Commonhold Association' [2006] Conv 14.

[51] Insolvency Act 1986, ss 122 and 124.

up voluntarily where it is solvent: for example, should the flat owners wish to redevelop. A compulsory winding-up by court order may occur where the association is insolvent: for example, upon the petition of one or more of its unpaid creditors. In this latter event, the court has power to make a succession order transferring the common parts to a new commonhold association, which will take over the management of the commonhold, unless such an order is 'inappropriate'.[52] A succession order may well be inappropriate unless there is in place some mechanism to clear the debts of the insolvent association.[53] For example, the liquidator of an insolvent commonhold association will be able to pursue defaulting flat owners for any unpaid commonhold assessments, as well as raise further assessments from the flat owners to meet the debts of the association. Thus the limited liability of the flat owners as members of the association could be more fictional than real.[54] It is anticipated that the insolvency of a commonhold association will be an unlikely event, given that it can raise additional funds from the flat owners by levying further assessments, but the possibility exists and has proved of sufficient concern to lenders that they have been hesitant to accept security over commonholds.

3.5 COMMONHOLD COMMUNITY STATEMENT

The commonhold community statement is a crucial document. It sets out '*details of how the community is to run*',[55] in terms of what the flat owners and the commonhold association, respectively, must do, are able to do, or cannot do.

Commonhold and Leasehold Reform Act 2002, s 31

Form and content: general

(1) A commonhold community statement is a document which make provision in relation to specified land for—

  (a) the rights and duties of the commonhold association; and

  (b) the rights and duties of the unit-holders.

(2) A commonhold community statement must be in prescribed form.

(3) A commonhold community statement may—

  (a) impose a duty on the commonhold association;

  (b) impose a duty on a unit-holder;

  (c) make provision about the taking of decisions in connection with management of the commonhold or any other matter concerning it.

The 2002 Act and its attendant regulations detail what the statement must include by way of mandatory terms and what it may include in optional provisions. The draftsman is provided

---

[52] Ibid, s 51.
[53] See Crabb, 'The Commonhold and Leasehold Reform Act 2002: A Company Law Perspective' (2004) 25 Comp Law 213.
[54] Ibid.
[55] Clarke (2002, p 74).

with a model as a starting point and guide in preparing the statement, which will be a unique document for each development.[56]

Wong explains the format and content of the statement.

Wong, 'Potential Pitfalls in the Commonhold Community Statement and the Corporate Mechanisms of the Commonhold Association' [2006] Conv 14, 19

The CCS [commonhold community statement] is the central property document stipulating the rights and duties of the CA [commonhold association] and the unit-holders. To promote uniform protection, the overall format of the CCS and the contents of its main body are pre-scribed in the model form in Sch.3 to the Regulations. Part 4 of the main body of the CCS lays down the mandatory "rules" of the commonhold regarding general property rights and duties. These include duty to contribute to assessments and reserve funds (Part 4.2), duty to insure (Part 4.4), duty to maintain and repair (Part 4.5), as well as restrictions on use (Part 4.3), alteration (Part 4.6) and disposition (Part 4.7). In addition to these general provisions, more specific rules are needed to cater for the local needs of a given commonhold. This is achieved by Annex 4 where the developer can insert "local rules" to fine-tune the mandatory rules in Part 4, and by Annex 5 where "supplementary local rules" can be inserted to impose further restraints such as restrictions on keeping pets. In contrast to the mandatory "rules" which can never be amended, "local rules" and "supplementary local rules" can in general be amended by ordinary resolution, with a few exceptions requiring special resolution (and/or consent of the affected unit-holder). The combination of mandatory rules on general property rights and duties and self-prescriptive tailor-made local rules reflects the legislative intention of striking a balance between certainty of protection and local flexibility.

The balance between certainty and flexibility should vary according to the subject matter of the rights and duties. While an individualistic approach is suitable for certain subject mat-ter such as restrictions on use and behaviour, other matters such as the duty to repair and maintain and the duty to insure would require a more prescriptive approach so as to achieve adequate protection for the unit-holders.

The statement is registered against all of the titles within the commonhold, being both the freehold titles to the individual flats and the common parts, and thus will bind the com-monhold association and is capable of binding the individual flat owners. The mechanism by which subsequent flat owners are bound is found in s 16 of the 2002 Act.

Commonhold and Leasehold Reform Act 2002, s 16

Transfer: effect

(1) A right or duty conferred or imposed—

    (a) by a commonhold community statement, or

    (b) in accordance with section 20,

shall affect a new unit-holder in the same way as it effected a former unit-holder.

(2) A former unit-holder shall not incur a liability or acquire a right—

    (a) under or by virtue of the commonhold community statement, or

---

[56] Commonhold and Leasehold Reform Act 2002, Sch 3.

(b) by virtue of anything done in accordance with section 20.

(3) Subsection (2)—

(a) shall not be capable of being disapplied or varied by agreement, and

(b) is without prejudice to any liability or right incurred or acquired before the transfer takes effect.

Thus both the negative user and alienation provisions, and any positive obligations (including obligations to repair, maintain, insure, and to pay the service charge), are binding on purchasers acquiring a flat in the commonhold development.

3.6 THE MANAGEMENT OF COMMONHOLD

The commonhold community statement will set out the allocation of management responsibilities, and will usually provide that the flat owner will be responsible for the repair, maintenance, and insurance of the interior of his or her flat, while the commonhold association will be responsible for the repair, maintenance, and insurance of the common parts, including the structure of the building and the common facilities.

Commonhold and Leasehold Reform Act 2002, s 14

Use and maintenance [Commonhold Unit]

(1) A commonhold community statement must make provision regulating the use of commonhold units.

(2) A commonhold community statement must make provision imposing duties in respect of the insurance, repair and maintenance of each commonhold unit.

(3) A duty under subsection (2) may be imposed on the commonhold association or the unit-holder.

Commonhold and Leasehold Reform Act 2002, s 26

Use and maintenance [Common Parts]

A commonhold community statement must make provision—

(a) regulating the use of the common parts;

(b) requiring the commonhold association to insure the common parts;

(c) requiring the commonhold association to repair and maintain the common parts.

The cost of repairing, maintaining, and insuring the common parts will be recovered from flat owners by the commonhold association through services charges, which may be made up of three elements: first, the regular day-to-day expenses, which will be calculated according to prepared budgets made by the association; secondly, the levies to a reserve fund to budget over a period for the larger costs of occasional replacement and repair (for example, the painting of the block or the repair of the roof or lifts); and finally, emergency levies to recover unexpected expenditure. The reserve fund is held by the commonhold association and may be attached by certain unpaid judgment debtors of the association.[57]

Commonhold and Leasehold Reform Act 2002, s 38

Commonhold assessment

(1) A commonhold community statement must make provision—

(a) requiring the directors of the commonhold association to make an annual estimate of the income required to be raised from unit-holders to meet the expenses of the association,

(b) enabling the directors of the commonhold association to make estimates from time to time of income required to be raised from unit-holders in addition to the annual estimate,

(c) specifying the percentage of any estimate made under paragraph (a) or (b) which is to be allocated to each unit,

(d) requiring each unit-holder to make payments in respect of the percentage of any estimate which is allocated to his unit, and

(e) requiring the directors of the commonhold association to serve notices on unit-holders specifying payments required to be made by them and the date on which each payment is due.

Commonhold and Leasehold Reform Act 2002, s 39

Reserve fund

(1) Regulations under section 32 may, in particular, require a commonhold community statement to make provision—

(a) requiring the directors of the commonhold association to establish and maintain one or more funds to finance the repair and maintenance of common parts;

(b) requiring the directors of the commonhold association to establish and maintain one or more funds to finance the repair and maintenance of commonhold units.

(2) Where a commonhold community statement provides for the establishment and maintenance of a fund in accordance with subsection (1) it must also make provision—

(a) requiring or enabling the directors of the commonhold association to set a levy from time to time,

(b) specifying the percentage of any levy set under paragraph (a) which is to be allocated to each unit,

(c) requiring each unit-holder to make payments in respect of the percentage of any levy set under paragraph (a) which is allocated to his unit, and

(d) requiring the directors of the commonhold association to serve notices on unit-holders specifying payments required to be made by them and the date on which each payment is due.

---

[57] Ibid, s 39(4).

Each flat owner must contribute the percentage of these costs that is allocated to his or her flat by the commonhold community statement. The commonhold association has no special powers to recover unpaid service charges beyond the usual dispute resolution process to be considered shortly.

Proposals for the association to be given a right to secure unpaid assessments by charge were rejected by the government, which wished to avoid any suggestion that the freeholds within a commonhold scheme could be effectively forfeited by the process of charge and subsequent sale.[58] This has led to criticisms that the association has no effective means by which to ensure that the costs of management are met by all of the flat owners.[59] There is the danger that effective management will be compromised and that, to maintain the necessary flow of funds, compliant flat owners will have to pick up the shortfall.

The association is obliged to ensure that the flat owners observe the obligations imposed by the statement. As we have seen, these obligations are extensive and cover not only the payment of service charges, but also negative obligations relating to user of both individual flats and the common parts, as well as positive obligations regarding the repair and maintenance of individual flats. The 2002 Act does, however, recognize that living in a community requires give and take, so that it may not be to the overall benefit of that community for enforcement action to be taken against all breaches. The association is thus granted a right of inaction where it reasonably believes that doing nothing will promote harmonious relationships.

Commonhold and Leasehold Reform Act 2002, s 35

Duty to manage

(1) The Directors of a commonhold association shall exercise their powers so as to permit or facilitate so far as possible—

  (a) the exercise by a unit-holder of his rights, and

  (b) the enjoyment by each unit-holder of the freehold estate in his unit.

(2) The directors of a commonhold association shall, in particular, use any right, power or procedure conferred or created by virtue of section 37 for the purpose of preventing, remedying or curtailing a failure on the part of a unit-holder to comply with a requirement or duty imposed on him by virtue of the commonhold community statement or a provision of this Part.

(3) But in respect of a particular failure on the part of a unit-holder (the 'defaulter') the directors of a commonhold association—

  (a) need not take action if they reasonably think that inaction is in the best interest of establishing or maintaining harmonious relationships between all unit-holders, and that it will not cause any unit-holder (other than the defaulter) significant loss or significant disadvantage, and

  (b) shall have regard to the desirability of using arbitration, mediation or conciliation procedures (including referral to a scheme approved under section 42) instead of legal proceedings whenever possible.

---

[58] The association may enforce a judgment debt by way of charging order, but will rank behind other existing secured creditors: see Chapter 29, section 4.4.

[59] See, e.g., Clarke (2002, p 143).

3.7 DISPUTE RESOLUTION

Traditional court processes are ill equipped to deal successfully with disputes between neighbours, in relation to whom the maintenance of a continuing working relationship is so important, and an economic and timely response is necessary. Although no distinct statutory dispute resolution system is introduced by the 2002 Act, it is envisaged that the court process will be used as a last resort or where decisive action is needed.[60]

Clarke explains the hope that disputes will be resolved through alternative means.

Clarke, *Commonhold: The New Law* (2002, p 151)

There is [...] no statutory system for the resolution of disputes. Instead of such a statutory system, the CLRA [Commonhold and Leasehold Reform Act] 2002 envisages a staged response. Although much will depend on regulations and rules to be introduced later, it is envisaged that the [...] CCS [commonhold community statement] will set out an internal complaints procedure which members must first adopt. The dispute resolution procedures then involve an inter-relationship of three approaches after any such internal procedures have been exhausted. There is specific provision for regulations to provide that a commonhold association shall be a member of an approved Ombudsman scheme. There is a general statutory duty on the directors of a commonhold association to have regard to the desirability of using arbitration, mediation or conciliation procedures (including referral under approved Ombudsman schemes), instead of legal proceedings. Finally, the courts will have an overriding jurisdiction

---

4 CONCLUSION

Flat ownership presents a complex challenge to devise a legal framework that will effectively balance the freedom of individual ownership against the compromise necessary for communal living. The last two decades have seen considerable legislative activity: firstly, to provide an effective framework for the enforcement of leasehold covenants; secondly, to try to overcome the considerable shortcomings of the long-lease system of flat ownership; and thirdly, to introduce an alternative form of communal land holding—the commonhold. Areas of reform are still outstanding, with the enforcement of freehold positive obligations through the land obligations still awaiting the statute book.[61]

The question is whether commonhold will remain merely an alternative, or will it render the long lease system obsolete? Commentators have suggested that commonhold should be sufficiently attractive to sideline the long lease of flats—but only after the legislation has been refined to overcome deficiencies.[62] We have noted some of those deficiencies above, but particular cause for concern arises from the obstacles to converting existing long-lease

---

60 See Commonhold and Leasehold Reform Act 2002, Sch 3, s 35(3)(b) extracted above, and s 42.

61 See Chapter 27, section 5.

62 See, e.g., Clarke, 'The Enactment of Commonhold: Problems, Principles and Perspectives' [2002] Conv 349; Davey, 'The Regulation of Long Residential Leases' in *Modern Studies in Property Law: Vol 3* (ed Cooke, 2005, ch 10); Van Der Merwe and Smith, 'Commonhold: A Critical Appraisal' in *Modern Studies in Property Law: Vol 3* (ed Cooke, 2005, ch 11); Wong, 'Potential Pitfalls in the Commonhold Community Statement and the Corporate Mechanisms of the Commonhold Association' [2006] Conv 14.

developments, the difficulties of accommodating mixed developments given the inflexibility of equality of voting and service charge allocation, the constraints of adapting an existing corporate vehicle to the commonhold association—particularly, the provisions governing insolvency and the weak mechanisms for recovery of service charges. Last, but not least, are doubts that commonhold really is freehold, given the limitations of alienability and the inevitable constraints of the commonhold community statement, which bridges the 'threefold unity' between individual units, the common parts, and the association.

Clarke, writing in 2002,[63] shortly after the passing of the Commonhold and Leasehold Reform Act, foretold a 'bright future' for commonhold—but already he doubts his prediction.

Clarke, 'Long Residential Leases: Future Directions' in *Landlord and Tenant Law: Past, Present and Future* (ed Bright, 2006, p 181)

However Part I of the Commonhold and Leasehold Reform Act 2002, for all the assurances that it was a fine piece of legislation, contains some fundamental flaws that will prevent its widespread adoption for both large and mixed residential estates and developments. Indeed, these inadequacies are proving so fundamental to the key players (developers and lenders) that commonhold will possibly be consigned to the margins. There were, by 27 September 2005, only five commonholds registered a year after commonhold was brought into force, and they all are small homogeneous developments.

[... I]f nothing is done, at best commonhold will be peripheral, at worst it will be largely irrelevant, to the solution of developing homes for the future. For it to have a major role, there would need to be primary legislation to deal with lenders' concerns regarding liquidation of the commonhold association. Less than half the members of the Council of Mortgage Lenders are currently willing to lend on commonhold titles, and some of the big lenders are included in these numbers. Such primary legislation could also tackle the other shortcomings [...] Yet even if the major concerns were satisfactorily addressed by primary legislation, there is no certainty that commonhold would be widely adopted in preference to long leases [...] there is the preference for the familiar. Even if the factors governing the choice between commonhold and long leasehold for new developments were entirely neutral, it is likely that many developers would still opt for the familiar [...] Accordingly, there must be good reason positively to choose commonhold, even if the technical difficulties and statutory gremlins outlined are overcome. Primary legislation to encourage or even require the use of commonhold in preference to long leases is always a long term possibility [...] Yet it is hard to envisage any Government being willing to take any steps in such a direction, until it is satisfied that commonhold is fit for the purposes for which it was enacted.

Clarke mentions the reluctance of developers and lenders to embrace commonhold, but flat owners must not be forgotten: after all, developers and lenders will be more inclined to overcome, and government to address, those concerns if flat owners demand commonhold over long leases.

Both systems are complicated and difficult for flat owners to understand, and neither can solve the friction that communal living can bring. The bottom line is that most flat owners see little distinction between commonhold and long leases, where a management company owns the freehold that the flat owners control. Indeed, the differences are largely of legal

---

63 'The Enactment of Commonhold: Problems, Principles and Perspectives' [2002] Conv 349.

detail. Commonhold may still win over the long lease held from an independent landlord, but, even here, enfranchisement and the right to manage has narrowed the score.

QUESTIONS

1. Why is it difficult to achieve the freehold ownership of flats?
2. How successful do you think the long leasehold system of flat ownership has been?
3. What are the current deficiencies in commonhold, as it has been enacted in the Commonhold and Leasehold Reform Act 2002?
4. Is there a pressing need for commonhold?

FURTHER READING

Clarke, *Commonhold: The New Law* (Bristol: Jordans, 2002)

Clarke, 'Long Residential Leases: Future Directions' in *Landlord and Tenant Law: Past, Present and Future* (ed Bright, Oxford: Hart, 2006, ch 9)

Clarke, 'Occupying 'Cheek by Jowl': Property Issues Arising from Communal Living' in *Land Law: Themes and Perspectives* (eds Bright and Dewar, Oxford: OUP, 1998)

Clarke, 'The Enactment of Commonhold: Problems, Principles and Perspectives' [2002] Conv 349

Crabb, 'The Commonhold and Leasehold Reform Act 2002: A Company Law Perspective' (2004) 25 Comp Law 213

Davey, 'The Regulation of Long Residential Leases' in *Modern Studies in Property Law: Vol 3* (ed Cooke, Oxford: Hart, 2005, ch 10)

Smith, 'The Purity of Commonholds' [2004] Conv 194

Sparkes, *A New Law of Landlord and Tenant* (Oxford: Hart, 2001, chs 16 and 17)

Van Der Merwe and Smith, 'Commonhold—A Critical Appraisal' in *Modern Studies in Property Law: Vol 3* (ed Cooke, Oxford: Hart, 2005, ch 11)

Wong, 'Potential Pitfalls in the Commonhold Community Statement and the Corporate Mechanisms of the Commonhold Association' [2006] Conv 14

PART F

SECURITY RIGHTS

SECURITY INTERESTS
IN LAND

CENTRAL ISSUES

1. Securing the repayment of money may be achieved by the grant of a legal or equitable interest in land, giving the creditor a right of recourse. For example, such a right may allow a lender to sell a borrower's freehold or lease if the debtor fails to repay the creditor.

2. There are four types of security interest: the pledge, the lien, the mortgage, and the charge. A lien, mortgage, or charge may be created over land.

3. The legal charge by way of mortgage of land is a hybrid form of security, being, in form, a charge, but granting the lender the rights associated with a mortgage.

4. If the borrower has a legal estate or equitable interest in land, a creditor can acquire an equitable security interest by means of a mortgage or a charge.

5. The equity of redemption represents the borrower's interest under a traditional mortgage of property. It has been of central importance to equity's protection of borrowers, but its continued utility, in a case in which the lender is granted a legal charge, is questionable.

6. The provision of secured credit is fundamental to modern living and commercial life, and lawyers have proved adept at creating different forms of security to cater for a wide variety of circumstances.

1 INTRODUCTION

In this chapter, we are concerned with the use of land (or legal and equitable property rights relating to land) as security for the repayment of money by a borrower to a lender. The lender acquires security by *being granted* a distinct legal or equitable property right in the land. This gives the lender a number of rights to which it can resort if the borrower fails to repay the loan. Crucially, because it has a legal or equitable property right in the land, the lender may also be able to assert its security right not only against the borrower, but also against third parties.

Sir Nicholas Browne Wilkinson VC accepted the following definition of security.

Bristol Airport plc v Powdrill [1990] Ch 744, CA

Sir Nicholas Browne Wilkinson VC

At 760

Security is created where a person ('the creditor') to whom an obligation is owed by another ('the debtor') by statute or contract, in addition to the personal promise of the debtor to discharge the obligation, obtains rights exercisable against some property in which the debtor has an interest in order to enforce the discharge of the debtor's obligation to the creditor.

There are thus two elements to a security transaction: firstly, the loan made by the lender to the borrower; and secondly, the creation of the proprietary interest by the borrower to the lender to secure the repayment of the loan. We commonly call that proprietary interest a 'mortgage', but, as we shall see, we need to be careful of our terminology when dealing with security interests. The loose use of terms can, and often has, caused confusion.

In this chapter, we will look first at why proprietary (or what are sometimes called 'real') security interests are so popular with lenders today; we will then explore the different types of proprietary security interest, before examining the development and particular nature of security interests over land. In Chapter 30, we will turn our attention to the loan contract and the controls that the law has imposed to protect the borrower. Finally, in Chapter 31, we will focus on the rights and powers conferred upon the lender to enforce its security over land.

2 THE ROLE AND IMPORTANCE OF SECURITY

Secured lending in both the domestic and commercial spheres is prolific. Bank of England statistics revealed that bank lending to UK-resident businesses between 2002 and 2007 grew from £1,031,774m to £1,676,084m; Table 6 shows the scale of domestic mortgage lending over the same period.

Table 6 Domestic mortgage lending 2002–07 (Source: CML/ BankSearch Regulated Mortgage Survey, Bank of England)

	House purchase loans £m	Remortgage £m	Other £m	Total £m
2002	119,000	81,600	20,200	220,800
2003	123,900	124,300	29,200	277,400
2004	137,500	121,500	32,400	291,400
2005	128,300	118,800	41,300	288,400
2006	158,100	127,700	59,400	345,200
2007	154,900	129,000	79,900	363,800

In the domestic market, policies by all political parties since the mid-twentieth century have promoted home ownership, through the ready availability of mortgage finance, to reduce public expenditure on housing, and to enhance social and political stability.[1]

Oldham, 'Mortgages' in *Land Law: Issues, Debates Policy* (ed Tee, 2002, p 172)

[... P]roperty ownership effects a form of special inclusion or community bonding. The purchase of a house affiliates the mortgagor to a particular locality and to a particular social group. The purchaser acquires a sense of belonging not only to the neighbourhood in which the house is located, but also to a larger group of homeowners generally. Home ownership signals respectability, responsibility and, usually, also upward mobility. The particularly English ideology surrounding home-ownership has had the result that non-homeowners have become almost second-class citizens.

Most people aspire to the economic and social advantages that are associated with home ownership, but they can only attain those advantages by borrowing from a financial institution. Instead of paying rent for their accommodation, they repay their mortgage by instalments, in the expectation that they will not only enjoy the use of their home, but also be able to reap the benefits of an increase in its capital value as property prices increase—a bonus that is unavailable to a tenant.

The availability of credit is also vital to business and the economy, particularly to promote the growth of small and medium-sized businesses. Banks and other financial institutions are more ready to lend, and offer less onerous terms, where the risks associated with non-payment are reduced by the availability of security.

Oldham describes this economic significance.[2]

Oldham, 'Mortgages' in *Land Law: Issues, Debates Policy* (ed Tee, 2002, p 169)

In terms of function, mortgages constitute a key economic institution—the means by which assets are mobilised, capital generated and productivity and the wider economy boosted. The mortgage is a mechanism that transforms 'passive 'land value into active value in that it allows the value of land to be released for other purposes while the freeholder or leaseholder is still able to enjoy the benefits of physical occupation or possession. It has even been argued that the ability to mortgage land is the key to the fundamental distinction between rich and poor countries. In poor countries, assets mobilisation is not possible because the capital invested in housing is incapable of being released because of inadequate underlying structures of property ownership and of social, political and legal control.

Clarke and Kohler have summarized the functions of secured credit as five-fold. As argued in the extract below, a security interest can give a lender: (i) a right of first recourse;

---

[1] See also Gray and Gray, *Elements of Land Law* (5th edn, 2009, [6.1.3]–[6.1.5]) for some of the social and political effects of mortgage finance.

[2] See also the Law Commission Consultation Paper No 176, *Company Security Interests* (2004, [1.16]–[1.18]).

(ii) priority; and (iii) the opportunity for non-judicial enforcement of the borrower's duties. Security interests can also serve: (iv) a hostage function; and (v) as a means of signalling the creditworthiness of the borrower, and allowing the lender to monitor and control the borrower's behaviour.

Clarke and Kohler, *Property Law: Commentary and Materials* (2005, p 659)

18.1.2.1 Right of first recourse

First, security over an asset gives the security interest holder the right of first recourse to it. If there is default in repayment, the secured creditor can sell the asset and obtain repayment out of the proceeds of sale in priority to anyone else (except someone with a prior ranking security interest over the same asset). Most importantly, this applies even if the debtor goes bankrupt. A secured creditor is largely unaffected by the bankruptcy or liquidation of its debtor: its power to sell is generally not restricted in any way. If there is a surplus left after it has done so, that goes into the general pool of assets to be divided among the unsecured creditors. So, in any bankruptcy or liquidation, unsecured creditors are paid just a fraction of what they are owed (almost invariable a tiny fraction) whereas unsecured creditors are paid in full (assuming the secured asset was worth more than the total indebtedness).

   This is not only a good thing in itself, as far as the secure creditor is concerned. It also dramatically reduces the risk in lending. Provided the lender ensures that there is a sufficient margin between the value of the asset it accepts as security and the amount it lends, its return of capital is more or less guaranteed.

18.1.2.2 Attachment to the asset

Since security interests are property interest in the secured asset, they are attached to the asset, in the sense that the asset owner cannot sell the asset free from the security interest unless he either pays off the debt or obtains the lender's consent. If he does neither, the security interest will be fully enforceable against the buyer (subject to the [appropriate] enforceability rules). This does not make the buyer personally liable for the debt, but it does entitle the security interest holder to sell the asset and recoup the debt out of the proceeds, handing back to the buyer only whatever is left after that.

18.1.2.3 Non-judicial enforcement

The security interest holder's primary remedy [...] is to sell the secured asset, and in most cases to do so without first obtaining a court order, or going through any other formal procedure. It does not even have to sell by auction: the sale will be an ordinary private sale. This ability to enforce security by a simple self-help process is uncommon in other jurisdictions. It has considerable attraction to lenders. It means that the lender does not have to satisfy anyone in advance that default has justified enforcement [...], there is no public scrutiny of the conduct of the sale or the price obtained, and no time-consuming, costly court process to go through [...]

18.1.2.4 The hostage function

[...] Security acts as a hostage, providing an incentive to the borrower to comply with the loan agreement. If the lender takes security over an asset that the borrower values highly, fear of losing the asset will induce the borrower to go to greater lengths than it might otherwise have done to keep up the payments. When money is short, it will make these repayments before paying other debts, and it will hesitate before engaging in risky behaviour which might endanger its ability to repay [...] This helps to explain why lending money on the security of peoples' homes is such good business [...]

18.1.2.5 Signalling, monitoring and control

A debtor who offers a valued asset as security can be said to be signalling his confidence that he will be able to repay, thus lessening the need for the lender to engage in expensive checks on his creditworthiness. If the asset has a predictable market value which is greater than the proposed loan, the creditor has even less need to check creditworthiness [...]

[...S]ecurity can also be used as a means of enabling the lender to monitor the behaviour of the borrower. The terms of a security interest over assets will usually require the borrower to maintain the value of the secured asset by keeping it in good state of repair, to insure it [...] and notify the lender of any event threatening the value of the secured asset or the ability of the borrower to repay. In this country bank loans to businesses are usually secured by security interests taken over all the assets of the business. This not only gives the lender access to comprehensive information about the running of the business, but also gives the lender the opportunity to exercise a significant level of control over decision-making, as well as enabling the lender to take early action to safeguard its interests.

It is easy, however, to be beguiled into overvaluing security interests, as opposed to the underlying debt that they secure. Clarke makes the following point.

Clarke, 'Security Interest in Property' in *Property Problems From Genes to Pension Funds* (ed Harris, 1997, p 122)

[...T]he value to the mortgagee *of the mortgage* fluctuates depending on the likelihood of the mortgagor repaying the debt in full and in time with—paradoxically—the value of the mortgage decreasing as the likelihood of default decreases.

She also notes that '*security interests start to look distinctly marginal as property interests*'[3] when one recognizes that a security interest generally confers rights of recourse only if the debt is not repaid—an event that lies solely within the control of the borrower.

Nevertheless, the taking of security has considerable advantages for the lender, which may, in part, be passed onto the borrower (e.g. through lower interest rates), but if one party has a security interest, this is clearly disadvantageous to the borrower's other, unsecured creditors—particularly in the event of the borrower's insolvency. As a result, the probity and overall efficiency of secured credit has been questioned.[4]

Clarke and Kohler summarize some of these arguments.[5]

---

[3] Clarke, 'Security Interest in Property' in *Property Problems From Genes to Pension Funds* (ed Harris, 1997, p 123).

[4] See, e.g., Finch (1992) 62 MLR 633 and Mokal (2002) 22 OJLS 686, who refer to the extensive US literature on this question, which considers the utility of security rights not only in relation to land, but also in relation to other rights held by a borrower or debtor. See also Getzler, 'The Role of Security Over Future and Circulating Capital: Evidence from the British Economy circa 1850–1920', *Company Charges: Spectrum and Beyond* (eds Getzler and Payne, 2006, ch 10).

[5] See also Clarke (1997, p 124).

Clarke and Kohler, *Property Law: Commentary and Materials* (2005, p 661)

Intuitively, it seems likely that it is, because it has been so pervasive in market economies for such a long time [...] But efficient for whom? It seems fairly obvious that it is efficient for the secured creditor, in that the risk of not recovering the loan in full is decreased. This should result in lenders charging a lower rate of interest for secured loans, which suggests that secured credit is more advantageous for borrowers as well. However, whilst the risk of not being repaid in full is decreased for the secured creditor, it is correspondingly increased for all the unsecured creditors of the same debtor, because the secured assets are removed from the pool of assets out of which they can be repaid. So at best, unsecured creditors will increase the rate of interest they charge the debtor by an amount corresponding to the discounted rate charged by the secured creditor and secured credit then becomes a "zero sum game". Even in such a case, the outcome is likely to be inefficient rather than neutral because setting up security arrangements is costly, so the debtor's total credit bill [...] will be greater in a world where secured credit is permitted than it would be in a world where it is prohibited. At worst—and this is rather more in line with what actually happens in the real world—some unsecured creditors will be unable to respond to the granting of secured credit by raising their interest rates (because they are involuntary creditors, or are not in a position to negotiate or re-negotiate the terms on which they extend credit). This benefits the debtor, but it does mean that the advantages to the debtor and the sophisticated and relatively affluent creditor are bought at the expense of the relatively poor and unsophisticated creditor [...]

However, there are other benefits that secured lending brings. We have already noted the monitoring and control functions that security enables the creditor to undertake can benefit everybody [...] Whether, these advantages outweigh the disadvantages remains a matter of debate.

The unsecured creditor is in a particularly vulnerable position where the secured asset represents all (or the mammoth share) of the debtor's wealth, because the creditor will be left with nothing (or little) against which he or she can seek recovery.

Clarke notes the impact of the secured creditor's privileged position on inhibiting the use and development of insolvency regimes.[6]

Clarke, 'Security Interest in Property' in *Property Problems From Genes to Pension Funds* (ed Harris, 1997, pp 122–3)

This virtual isolation of the secured creditor from the bankruptcy process has a profound effect on the development of bankruptcy law in this country in at least two respects. First, it has significantly hampered the development of a workable business rescue procedure [...] Even more significantly, but less often publicly acknowledged, the secured creditor's aloofness from the bankruptcy process has made bankruptcy virtually unusable for individuals whose only significant asset is a mortgaged house.

---

[6] Since Clarke was writing, administration has been promoted as a collective corporate rescue regime, but one in which the secured creditor continues to play a pre-eminent role: see Enterprise Act 2002, amending Insolvency Act 1986, Sch BI.

3 GENERAL FORMS OF SECURITY

Millett LJ identified the forms of security interest found in English law as follows.

Re Cosslett Contractors Ltd [1998] Ch 495

Millett LJ

At 508

There are only four kinds of consensual security known to English law: (i) pledge; (ii) contractual lien; (iii) equitable charge and (iv) mortgage. A pledge and a contractual lien both depend on the delivery of possession to the creditor. The difference between them is that in the case of a pledge the owner delivers possession to the creditor as security, whereas in the case of a lien the creditor retains possession of goods previously delivered to him for some other purpose. Neither a mortgage nor a charge depends on the delivery of possession. The difference between them is that a mortgage involves a transfer of legal or equitable ownership to the creditor, whereas an equitable charge does not.

In this passage, Millett LJ sets out the *general* forms of security right that can apply even where no land is involved. In the remainder of this section, we will consider these four forms of security right. In section 4 below, we will focus on the security interests that are particularly important where land is concerned.

3.1 THE PLEDGE

The pledge is the most traditional form of security. It is dependent upon the borrower delivering possession or control of property to the lender. Ownership in the property is retained by the borrower and the lender obtains its own property right (a 'special interest' in the property), entitling it to sell if the loan is not repaid, accounting to the borrower for the proceeds of sale over and above that required to repay the loan.[7]

A pledge is found in a wide variety of situations, from pawnbroking, to international finance and trade. Its strength lies in the protection that it can afford the lender: by taking control of the property, the lender can assert its priority against the claims of other creditors. The disadvantage of a pledge lies in the fact that physical possession or control of the property must be delivered to the lender so that the borrower is deprived of the use of the property. Chattels, being moveable assets, lend themselves to the essential possessory nature of the pledge. Documents that constitute the title to goods, money, and other investments may also be pledged.[8] Given its immovable nature, land does not form the natural subject matter of a pledge—although the original forms of security over land tried to replicate the nature of a pledge.[9]

---

[7] *The Odessa* [1916] 1 AC 145; *Matthew v TH Sutton* [1949] 4 All ER 793.

[8] For example, bills of lading, negotiable instruments such as cheques, promissory notes, treasury bills, and bills of exchange.

[9] The name 'mortgage' is derived from the medieval word for pledge: the 'gage'.

3.2 THE LIEN

As Millett LJ points out, a consensual lien operates as a legal form of security: for example, a borrower can agree with a lender that the lender has a right to retain possession of property until the borrower's outstanding debt is paid. In addition, the common law has also implied liens into certain contracts: for example, a repairer of property is entitled to a lien to secure the costs of repair.[10]

An equitable lien gives a lender an equitable property right, rather than a legal property right. The rules relating to the content and acquisition of an equitable lien therefore differ from those applying to a common law lien. As to its *content*, an equitable lien is in the nature of a charge: it does not require the lender to have possession. As to its *acquisition*, an equitable lien can only arise by operation of law, rather than as a result of the agreement of the parties.

The most significant equitable lien for our purposes arises upon the sale of land and is called the 'unpaid vendor's lien'. A vendor who has transferred his or her freehold or lease to the purchaser, but has not received the full purchase price, is entitled to claim an equitable lien (over the freehold or lease now held by the purchaser) to secure the unpaid portion. Likewise, a purchaser who has paid, or partly paid, the purchase price for land, but has not yet received the vendor's freehold or lease, may have a power (for example, because of a breach of the contract of sale by the vendor) to pull out of the contract and claim back any payment that he or she has made. In such a case, the purchaser has an equitable lien over the vendor's freehold or lease in order to secure the vendor's duty to repay that money.

3.3 THE MORTGAGE

Buckley LJ has described the form of a mortgage as follows.[11]

Swiss Bank Group v Lloyds Bank Ltd [1982] AC 584, HL

Buckley LJ

At 594

The essence of any transaction by way of mortgage is that a debtor confers upon his creditor a proprietary interest in property of the debtor, or undertakes in a binding manner to do so, by the realisation or appropriation of which the creditor can procure the discharge of the debtor's liability to him, and that the proprietary interest is redeemable, or the obligation to create it is defeasible, in the event of the debtor discharging his liability. If there has been no legal transfer of a proprietary interest but merely a binding undertaking to confer such an interest, that obligation, if specifically enforceable, will confer a proprietary interest in the subject matter in equity. The obligation will be specifically enforceable if it is an obligation for the breach of which damages would be an inadequate remedy. A contract to mortgage property, real or

---

[10] Other common law liens include an innkeeper's (or hotelier's) and carrier's lien. Liens may also arise from the general usage of a particular trade or business: e.g. solicitors, factors, bankers, stockbrokers, and insurance brokers.

[11] Buckley misuses the term 'an equitable charge' in the last line of this extract. He should have referred to 'an equitable mortgage'.

personal, will, normally at least, be specifically enforceable, for a mere claim to damages or repayment is obviously less valuable than a security in the event of the debtor's insolvency. If it is specifically enforceable, the obligation to confer the proprietary interest will give rise to an equitable charge upon the subject matter by way of mortgage.

A mortgage thus transfers the borrower's interest in the property to the lender, subject to an obligation on the lender to return that interest to the borrower once the debt is repaid—an obligation that confers upon the borrower what is known as 'a right to redeem'. The borrower's legal right to redeem is governed by the need for strict compliance with the repayment terms set out in the loan agreement. But equity will recognize the borrower's continuing equitable right to redeem even if he or she has failed to repay the loan in accordance with the contractual terms. This equitable right to redeem is of such import that it is recognized as giving the borrower an equitable property right: a right that is capable of binding third parties. In Chapter 4, section 1, it was suggested that equitable property rights depend on one party being under a duty to another; the equitable right to redeem is based on the lender's duty to transfer a mortgaged right back to the borrower if the underlying debt is repaid. Thus, although the mortgagee has the legal title to the property, a mortgage differs from an outright sale, because the lender's title is subject to the borrower's equity of redemption, the economic value of which is represented by the value of the property less the amount required to repay the lender. In this rather roundabout fashion, the security nature of the mortgage is achieved. We will have more to say about the borrower's equity of redemption in section 5 below.

The lender's inherent rights under a legal mortgage are defined, firstly, by their ownership of the legal title, which confers a right to possession, and secondly, by their right to apply to bar the borrower's equitable right to redeem, and thus extinguish the equity of redemption, by a process known as 'foreclosure'.

As Buckley LJ indicates, mortgages may take a legal or equitable form. A mortgage will be equitable where the borrower has only an equitable interest in the property and transfers that interest to the lender, or where the formalities used to create the mortgage fall short of the requirements to convey the legal title,[12] but nevertheless are recognized as an agreement to create a mortgage, and so give the lender an equitable property right under the doctrine of anticipation (see Chapter 12 and section 4.3 below).

3.4 THE CHARGE

Millett LJ, again in *Re Cosslett Contractors*, defined a charge as follows.

Re Cosslett Contractors Ltd [1998] Ch 495, CA

Millett LJ

At 508

It is of the essence of a charge that a particular asset or class of assets is appropriated to the satisfaction of a debt or other obligation of the chargor or a third party, so that the chargee

---

[12] See Chapter 9.

is entitled to look to the asset and its proceeds for the discharge of the liability. This right creates a transmissible interest in the asset. A mere right to retain possession of an asset and to make use of it for a particular purpose does not create such an interest and does not constitute a charge.

A charge creates a new proprietary interest that encumbers or burdens the borrower's ownership of the property. In contrast to a mortgage, there is no transfer of an existing ownership interest. The charge entitles the lender to look to the charged property to satisfy the debt. In the absence of any express or implied powers contained in the charge, the lender does so by applying to court for an order for the sale of the property, or for the appointment of a receiver to apply the capital or income from the property (as appropriate) in repayment of the debt. Upon satisfaction of the debt, the charge is automatically discharged, because there is simply no continuing debt to be met out of the property. The charge resembles the Roman law *hypothec*; indeed, it is sometimes described as a 'hypothecation'.

The charge is a creature of equity, although the Law of Property Act 1925 (LPA 1925) also uses the term 'charge' to describe a special form of legal interest that can be used to give a lender a security right in land.[13] It is important to distinguish the equitable charge (which can apply even where land is not involved) from the legal charge created by the 1925 Act (which can apply only to land). An equitable charge may be taken over existing and future property, and may be *fixed* over specific property or taken in *floating* form over a changing fund of assets. For example, one of the most common forms of commercial security is the floating charge over all of the rights, whether present or future, of a company. The floating charge affects the assets for the time being owned by the company, yet permits the company to deal with those assets in the ordinary course of the company's business without the consent of the lender. A floating charge may be converted to a fixed charge, by a process known as 'crystallization', which will occur either where the company is no longer able to deal with its assets in the ordinary course of its business—because, for example, it has entered one of the corporate insolvency regimes—or where the parties have agreed that crystallization should be triggered by certain events.

The categorization of fixed and floating charges has been the source of much litigation, but has been finally settled by the House of Lords, which identified the defining factor as the degree of control that the lender exercises over the charged asset.[14]

Re Spectrum Plus Ltd [2005] 2 AC 680, HL

Lord Walker

At [138]–[139]

Under a fixed charge the assets charged as security are permanently appropriated to the payment of the sum charged, in such a way as to give the chargee a proprietary interest in the assets. So long as the charge remains unredeemed, the assets can be released from the charge only with the active concurrence of the chargee. The chargee may have good

---

[13] See section 4.2 below.

[14] See also Worthington, 'Floating Charges: The Use and Abuse of Doctrinal Analysis' in *Company Charges: Spectrum and Beyond* (eds Getzler and Payne, 2006, ch 3). The analysis of the House of Lords in *Re Spectrum Plus* [2005] 2 AC 580, HL, essentially matches that of Worthington in *Proprietary Interests in Commercial Transactions* (1996, pp 78–86).

commercial reasons for agreeing to a partial release. If for instance a bank has a fixed charge over a large area of land which is being developed in phases as a housing estate (another example of a fixed charge on what might be regarded as trading stock) it might be short-sighted of the bank not to agree to take only a fraction of the proceeds of sale of houses in the first phase, so enabling the remainder of the development to be funded. But under a fixed charge that will be a matter for the chargee to decide for itself.

Under a floating charge, by contrast, the chargee does not have the same power to control the security for its own benefit. The chargee has a proprietary interest, but its interest is in a *fund* of circulating capital, and unless and until the chargee intervenes (on crystallisation of the charge) it is for the trader, and not the bank, to decide how to run its business.

4 FORMS OF SECURITY OVER LAND: MORTGAGES AND CHARGES

The English mortgage has been described as *'a work of fiction'* and *'a confusion of things'*.[15] To understand that fiction, we must look to the development of the form of English mort-gage, bearing in mind the general forms of security interest examined in section 3 above.

4.1 DEVELOPMENT OF MORTGAGES OF LAND

Mortgages have a long history, which was much influenced by the laws against usury that prohibited the charging of interest.[16]

Baker, *An Introduction to English Legal History* (4th edn, 2002, p 311)

From the earliest times, debtors have used property as security—or 'gage'—for loans of money. Whether the gage was a chattel or land, possession had to be handed over to the lender, to be returned on payment. In some early forms of gage no term was fixed: the gagee held the property until he was satisfied. Another early form, as we have seen, was a lease of years to the gagee, the term being the period of the loan. If the gagee took the profits in reduction of the loan, this was known in early times as a living gage (*vivum vadium*) appar-ently because the property continued to work for the borrower; but if the lender took the principal as well as the profits, it was a dead gage ('mortgage') and the arrangement, though sinful as giving the lender a usurious return, was legally valid. By the fifteenth century, how-ever, the name 'mortgage' has apparently come to be used for any arrangement whereby a loan was secured by a conveyance of real property. The self redeeming living gage had long since gone into disuse: it cast on the lender the responsibility of refunding himself, perhaps without profit, and it was less attractive than a passive security in the form of land which would become the lender's absolutely if the borrower failed to pay on time. Two new ways of effecting such a security were developed in the thirteenth century: either the mortgagor leased the land for years to the mortgagee, with a proviso that if the debt was not paid by a certain date the mortgagee would have the fee, or the mortgagor conveyed the fee to

---

[15] Watt, 'Mortgage Law as Legal Fiction' in *Modern Studies in Property Law: Vol 3* (ed Cooke, 2007, pp 73 and 76).

[16] The laws against usury were not finally abolished until the Usury Laws Repeal Act 1854.

the mortgagee forthwith, on condition that he might re-enter (and regain the fee) if he paid by a certain date [...] The second form gave the mortgagee a fee simple defeasible by condition subsequent (that is, payment). One advantage of this fee simple mortgage was that it was arguably non-usurious [...] In the seventeenth century a further alternative device came into almost universal use, the long term of years with clause for defeasance [...] and it later became a common practice under the common law forms of mortgage [...] to allow the mortgagor to remain in possession as a tenant at will or at sufferance of the mortgagee. After 1600 the mortgage deed might contain express provision for this, but the practice is probably older. The mortgagor who stayed in possession was legally in a similar position to the cestuy que use: at law he could be evicted at will, though he might [...] expect protection in Chancery.

We can thus see that the lawyers of old utilized both the pledge and the mortgage as security devices, although it was the classic mortgage by conveyance or demise that prevailed. The 'fiction' referred to lies in the fact that, at common law, the *lender* was the owner of the property and so entitled to the incidents of ownership—in particular, possession—while the borrower held only a right to insist on reconveyance of the legal title upon repayment of the debt. This was despite the fact that, as the laws against usury relaxed and the charging of interest was permitted, the lender had no wish to take possession unless and until the borrower failed to repay the loan. Despite the position at common law, the borrower generally kept possession of the property and both parties saw him or her as its true owner. It was the borrower's equity of redemption that redressed the balance somewhat: equity's protection of the borrower's right to repay the debt and redeem the property resulted in the borrower (in effect) being regarded as the owner in equity, with the lender's legal title being held only by way of security.

The LPA 1925 introduced the current incarnation of the legal charge by way of mortgage. This special security interest, existing only in relation to land, allows a borrower with a freehold or lease to give the lender a legal interest by way of security *without* needing to transfer his or her freehold or lease to the lender. Unfortunately, however, the legal charge has not been able to escape the fiction that lies at the heart of the mortgage.

4.2 THE LEGAL CHARGE BY WAY OF MORTGAGE

The LPA 1925 contemplated only two methods of creating a legal mortgage: the mortgage by sub-demise, and the legal charge by way of mortgage. Section 85(1) and (2) provides as follows.[17]

Law of Property Act 1925, s 85(1) and (2)

Mode of mortgaging freeholds

(1) A mortgage of an estate in fee simple shall only be capable of being effected at law either by a demise for a term of years absolute, subject to a provision for cesser on redemption, or by a charge by deed expressed to be by way of legal mortgage

---

[17] Law of Property Act 1925, s 86, contains similar provisions governing the mode of mortgaging leaseholds.

Provided that a first mortgagee shall have the same right to the possession of documents as if his security included the fee simple.

(2) Any purported conveyance of an estate in fee simple by way of mortgage made after the commencement of this Act shall (to the extent of the estate of the mortgagor) operate as a demise of the land to the mortgagee for a term of years absolute, without impeachment for waste, but subject to cesser on redemption, in manner following, namely:—

(a) A first or only mortgagee shall take a term of three thousand years from the date of the mortgage;

(b) A second or subsequent mortgagee shall take a term (commencing from the date of the mortgage) one day longer than the term vested in the first or other mortgagee whose security ranks immediately before that of such second or subsequent mortgagee;

and, in this subsection, any such purported conveyance as aforesaid includes an absolute conveyance with a deed of defeasance and any other assurance which, but for this subsection, would operate in effect to vest the fee simple in a mortgagee subject to redemption.

The mortgage by sub-demise creates a proprietary estate in the lender, although, rather than a fee simple, it is a leasehold estate for 3,000 years. The mortgage by sub-demise has, however, fallen into disuse as the legal charge, by way of mortgage, has gained in popularity.

The Land Registration Act 2002 (LRA 2002) reflects this trend by effectively rendering obsolete the mortgage by sub-demise. A legal mortgage of unregistered land will trigger first registration[18] and, whatever the form of mortgage, s 51 provides that it will have effect as a charge by deed by way of mortgage.

Land Registration Act 2002, s 51

Effect of completion by registration

On completion of the relevant registration requirements, a charge created by means of a registrable disposition of a registered estate has effect, if it would not otherwise do so, as a charge by deed by way of legal mortgage

Section 23 then provides that a registered owner is only capable of entering into a mortgage of a registered estate by way of charge.

Land Registration Act 2002, s 23

Owner's powers

(1) Owner's powers in relation to a registered estate consist of—

(a) power to make a disposition of any kind permitted by the general law in relation to an interest of that description, other than a mortgage by demise or sub-demise, and

(b) power to charge the estate at law with the payment of money.

[18] Land Registration Act 2002, s 4(1)g.

Thus it is the legal charge by way of mortgage that provides the pre-eminent form of legal mortgage and on which we will focus. But the effect of the mortgage by sub-demise has not been laid to rest, because s 87(1) of the LPA 1925 provides as follows.

Law of Property Act 1925, s 87(1)

Charges by way of legal mortgage

(1) Where a legal mortgage of land is created by a charge by deed expressed to be by way of legal mortgage, the mortgagee shall have the same protection, powers and remedies (including the right to take proceedings to obtain possession from the occupiers and the persons in receipt of rents and profits, or any of them) as if—

   (a) where the mortgage is a mortgage of an estate in fee simple, a mortgage term for three thousand years without impeachment of waste had been thereby created in favour of the mortgagee; and

   (b) where the mortgage is a mortgage of a term of years absolute, a sub-term less by one day than the term vested in the mortgagor had been thereby created in favour of the mortgagee.

The result is a hybrid security interest: the lender gains a legal charge (not a lease),[19] but enjoys the same protections, powers, and remedies as if it held a lease for a term of 3,000 years. Certainly, there is no transfer to the lender of the borrower's freehold or lease: the borrower retains that right, but holds it subject to the lender's legal charge.[20]

So the old fiction continues in a different, but just as complicated, form. The inappropriateness of this form has been highlighted by the Law Commission, which has long advocated reform by the adoption of a statutory form of security interest with defined rights and powers.

Law Commission Report No 204, *Land Mortgages* (1991, [2.14], [2.17]–[2.18], [3.1]–[3.2])

Removal of the distinction between mortgage and charge

A mortgage is conceptually different from a charge [...] However in English law the distinction is blurred and the terms are often used interchangeably, sometimes as if they were synonymous and sometimes as if one was a generic term including the other. The confusion is exacerbated by uncertainty over the correct classification of the mortgage by demise and the charge by way of legal mortgage. The mortgage by demise is technically a mortgage, in that it involves the grant of a substantial legal estate to the mortgagee. However, equitable restriction of the mortgagee's ownership-type rights has resulted in it acquiring a close

---

[19] *Grand Junction Co Ltd v Bates* [1954] 2 QB 160, 166; *Weg Motors Ltd v Hales* [1962] Ch 49, 74; *Cumberland Court (Brighton) Ltd v Taylor* [1964] Ch 29, 36; *Regent Oil Co Ltd v JA Gregory (Hatch End) Ltd* [1966] Ch 402.

[20] The section fails to articulate the position of the borrower—a position that has been criticized in the equivalent provision in the Australian State of Victoria: see *Figgins Holdings Pty Ltd v SEAA Enterpises Ltd* (1999) 196 CLR 245, [65], *per* McHugh J.

resemblance to a charge. The charge by way of legal mortgage is in name and form a charge, but in substance it is the same as the mortgage by demise.

[. . .]

Inappropriateness of form

The second root cause of the artificiality and complexity of mortgage law is the methods used to create security interest in land give rise to inappropriate relationships between the parties. This is particularly apparent in the mortgage by demise [. . .]

The problem here is of central importance because it affects not only the mortgage by demise, but also the charge by way of legal mortgage which is treated by statute as if it were a mortgage by demise and the equitable mortgage of a legal estate which is treated in equity as if it were a legal mortgage, hence a mortgage by demise. The problem is that it creates a relationship of landlord and tenant between the parties. There is nothing unusual about using the leasehold relationship as an investment device: institutional lenders are probably more likely to use leases rather than mortgages as a means of financing property develop- ments or investing in non-residential land. However, in the case of the mortgage by demise the leasehold relationship is the wrong way round: as tenant, the mortgagee has an inher- ent right to possession which would more appropriately lie with the mortgagor (subject to whatever restrictions may be necessary to protect and enforce the security). Similarly, it is necessary for the preservation of the security that the mortgagor should be under a duty more usually imposed by a landlord on a tenant, rather than a tenant on a landlord. Even if reversed, the landlord-tenant relationship is fundamentally different from that created by a mortgage: investors under a leased-based arrangement buy outright a share in the property, and the value of the share fluctuates in direct proportion to the value of the retained prop- erty; mortgagee-investors, on the other hand, have an interest in the property only for the temporary purpose of safeguarding the repayment of a loan or the value of the obligation secured. Historically the mortgage by demise was a useful device to bridge the gap between abolition of the mortgage by assignment and the general acceptance of the legal charge. Now that has fulfilled that purpose, it seems an unnecessary impoverishment of the system to blur the distinction between the lease and mortgage by continuing to define one device in terms of the other.

[. . .]

Nature of the new mortgage

It is central to our proposal for the creation of a new kind of mortgage that the attributes of the mortgage should be expressly defined by statute, rather than defined by reference to pre-existing forms of mortgage or by analogy to any other legal relationship. It is there- fore necessary to consider what interest in the mortgaged property a mortgagee ought to have under the new mortgage, whether formal or informal. It is also important that our reform should bring together in a single enactment the rules which govern the relationship between the mortgagor and the mortgagee. This will be particularly useful in commercial transactions. In such cases the parties often wish to negotiate detailed terms to fit the par- ticular circumstances, and that makes essential a knowledge of the parameters which the law lays down.

The guiding principle we have adopted in defining the nature of the new mortgage is that the only function of the mortgaged property is to provide security for the performance of the mortgagor's payment obligations. It follows from this that the nature and extent of the mortgagee's interest ought to be dictated by the need to preserve the value of the security and, where necessary, to enforce it.

4.3 EQUITABLE MORTGAGES AND EQUITABLE CHARGES OF LAND

The legal charge by way of mortgage now monopolizes the creation of legal security over land. In equity, there remains a number of ways in which an equitable security right can arise. To see the differences between legal and equitable security rights, we again need to focus on the *content* and *acquisition* questions (see Chapter 1, section 3).

4.3.1 Equitable mortgage of a legal estate: the *acquisition* question

A borrower with a legal estate in land may attempt to give a lender a legal charge by way of security—but to acquire such a legal interest, the lender needs to show that the borrower granted that right by means of a deed, and also that the lender has now registered its charge.[21] If those steps have not been taken, the lender may nonetheless acquire an *equitable* charge (under the doctrine of anticipation—see Chapter 12) by showing that the borrower is under a duty to grant the lender a legal charge. So, the lender will acquire an equitable charge if the borrower has made a contractual promise to grant a legal charge.[22] In addition, even if the borrower has made no contractual promise, a court can impose a duty to grant a charge if, in return for the loan provided by the lender, the borrower has attempted to grant a legal charge, but has failed to do so (e.g. because of a failure to comply with formality rules). In such cases, there can be said to have been an 'equitable mortgage' of the borrower's legal estate in the land.

Under an equitable mortgage of a legal estate, the parties' relationship is treated in equity as if the agreement had been performed and a legal mortgage had been created. Thus the lender is treated as if it had a legal charge by way of mortgage, with the benefit of the remedies and powers of a mortgage by sub-demise so far as they are consistent with the equitable nature of the lender's rights.[23]

To constitute an equitable mortgage of a legal estate, an agreement to create a legal mortgage must be valid. It should thus comply with the terms of s 2(1) of the Law of Property (Miscellaneous Provisions) Act 1989 (LP(MP)A 1989) (see Chapter 9, section 3). Prior to this enactment, it was common practice for lenders to take a deposit of the borrower's title deeds. This deposit of the deeds would create an equitable mortgage: the loan supported by the act of deposit was interpreted both as evidence of the parties' agreement to create a legal mortgage, and as an act of part-performance to support the enforcement of that agreement. It is now clear that, given the formalities now required under the LP(MP)A 1989, the practice of creating an equitable mortgage by deposit is no longer possible.

---

[21] See Chapter 9 for the general formality rules applying to the creation of a legal interest in land.

[22] It seems that the lender should also acquire an equitable charge if the borrower is under a *non-contractual* duty to grant a legal charge: see Chapter 11, section 2.2. For example, in *Kinane v Mackie-Conteh* [2005] EWCA Civ 45, the Court of Appeal found that proprietary estoppel imposed a duty on the borrower to grant a legal charge. As a result, the lender acquired an equitable interest in the land—although the Court held that the lender's interest arose under a constructive trust, not by means of an equitable charge.

[23] For example, an equitable mortgagee cannot sell the legal estate: see Law of Property Act 1925, s 88(6).

United Bank of Kuwait plc v Sahib [1997] Ch 107, CA

Peter Gibson LJ

At 137

I would emphasise the essential contractual foundation of the rule as demonstrated in the authorities. The deposit by way of security is treated both as prima facie evidence of a contract to mortgage, and as part performance of that contract. It is sufficient to refer briefly to the more recent of the multitude of authorities. In *Re Wallis & Simmonds (Builders) Ltd* [1974] 1 All ER 561, [1974] 1 WLR 391 Templeman J held that the equitable charge resulting from a deposit of title deeds was contractual in nature and specifically rejected an argument that the charge arose by operation of law. In *Re Alton Corp* [1985] BCLC 27 at 33 Megarry V-C said, in relation to a loan accompanied by the deposit of title deeds:

'[...] I have to remember that the basis of an equitable mortgage is the making of an agreement to create a mortgage, with the deposit of the land certificate and, since *Steadman v Steadman* [1974] 2 All ER 977, [1976] AC 536, probably the paying of the money as well, ranking as sufficient acts of part performance to support even the purely oral transaction. But some contract there must be.'

I accept that there need not be an express contract between the depositor of the title deeds and the person with whom they are deposited for an equitable mortgage to arise (subject to s 2). But I have already stated why it is clear from the authorities that the deposit is treated as rebuttable evidence of a contract to mortgage. Oral evidence is admissible to establish whether or not a deposit was intended to create a mortgage security, whether or not the original deposit was intended at the outset to be security for further advances, whether or not it was agreed subsequently that that deposit should be security for further advances and whether or not any memorandum of agreement accurately stated the terms of the contract or was complete. To allow inquiries of this sort after the 1989 Act in order to determine whether an equitable mortgage has been created and on what terms seems to me to be wholly inconsistent with the philosophy of s 2, requiring as it does that the contract be made by a single document containing all the terms of the agreement if it is to be valid [...]

To the extent that part performance is an essential part of the rationale of the creation of an equitable mortgage by the deposit of title deeds, that too is inconsistent with the new philosophy of the 1989 Act. As the Law Commission said in its report (para 4.13):

'Inherent in the recommendation that contracts should be made in writing is the consequence that part performance would no longer have a role to play in contracts concerning land.'

In the present case, for the reasons already given, it seems to me clear that the deposit of title deeds takes effect as a contract to mortgage and as such falls within s 2.

The judge said [at first instance] [1995] 2 All ER 973 at 990, [1995] 2 WLR 94 at 111:

'The recommendation [of the Law Commission] that contracts relating to land should be incorporated in a signed document which contains all the terms was, clearly, intended to promote certainty. There is no reason why certainty should be any less desirable in relation to arrangements for security over land than in relation to any other arrangements in respect of land. The present case itself illustrates the need to be able to identify the obligation which is to be secured. I do not find it surprising that Parliament decided to enact legislation which would be likely to have the effect of avoiding disputes on oral evidence as to the obligation which the parties intended to secure.'

> I agree. Indeed, it seems to me that the whole of the judge's reasoning, to which I would pay tribute, on the s 2 point cannot be faulted. Like him, I am fortified by the support for the same conclusion given in *Emmet on Title* para 25.116. I therefore conclude that by reason of s 2, the mere deposit of title deeds by way of security cannot any longer create a mortgage or charge.

In Chapter 9, section 3.7, we examined how arrangements that fail to comply with s 2(1) may nevertheless continue to have effect through the doctrines of proprietary estoppel or constructive trusts. In *Sahib*, Peter Gibson LJ rejected the lender's arguments that it had acquired an equitable charge on the grounds of proprietary estoppel or a constructive trust—but in *Kinane v Mackie- Conteh*,[24] in which the lender advanced £50,000 in reliance upon the parties' understanding that the loan would be secured, a similar argument succeeded and the lender did acquire an equitable charge.[25]

It does seem correct that the lender should acquire an equitable charge if the borrower is under a *non-contractual* duty to grant a legal charge (see Chapter 11, section 2.2). As we saw in Chapter 13, however, in light of the House of Lords' decision in *Cobbe v Yeoman's Row Management Ltd*,[26] the role of proprietary estoppel in the creation of equitable interests must now be re-examined.

4.3.2 Mortgage of an equitable estate: the content question

If the borrower has no legal estate in land, but only an equitable interest, then it is impossible for the lender to acquire a legal charge: the content of the borrower's property right prevents it. In such a case, any security interest acquired by the lender must take an equitable form. Such a right can arise by means of an equitable mortgage: if, for example, the borrower transfers his or her equitable interest to the lender. Such equitable mortgages are not as common as mortgages of the legal estate, but they may arise where a purchaser mortgages his or her equitable interest under a sale and purchase agreement of land, or where a beneficiary under a trust of land has mortgaged his or her interest. Where an equitable mortgage is created intentionally, it is created in the classic form by assigning the borrower's equitable interest to the lender, subject to the lender's covenant to reassign upon repayment of the loan. But an equitable mortgage of an equitable interest may arise unintentionally: for example, consider a case in which a freehold or lease is held jointly by two co-owners under a trust of land.[27] One of the co-owners then purports to mortgage the legal estate by forging the other co-owner's signature. The purported legal charge by way of mortgage cannot be valid—but the lender will acquire an equitable security right, taking effect only against the equitable share of the co-owner who purported to grant the legal charge.[28] A similar result can apply where the other co-owner does consent to the legal

---

24 [2005] EWCA Civ 45, noted Dixon [2005] Conv 247 and McFarlane [2005] Conv 501.

25 Although it has been suggested that estoppel is an inadequate replacement for part-performance: see Griffiths [2002] Conv 216.

26 [2008] UKHL 55, [2008] 1 WLR 1752.

27 See Chapters 14 and 18.

28 See, e.g., *Ahmed v Kendrick* [1988] 2 FLR 22; *First National Securities Ltd v Hegerty* [1985] QB 850; *Thames Guaranty Ltd v Campbell* [1985] QB 210.

charge, but does so as a result of undue influence or misrepresentation (see Chapter 30, section 3.1).

4.3.3 Equitable charge: the *content* question

Finally a charge may be created in equity, whether over a legal estate or an equitable interest in the land, where the parties demonstrate an intention that the lender's right is to make available, or appropriated, for the discharge of a debt or other obligation. That intention must be evinced in writing, but no particular form of words is required.[29] In such a case, the lender acquires an equitable property right due to the content of the borrower's duty to the lender: a duty to allow the lender to use the borrower's right to meet the debt, should the lender fail to repay. This form of security right is *not* special to land: as we saw in section 3.4 above, it arises whenever a borrower comes under such a duty to a lender.

It must be remembered that this form of equitable charge is conceptually different from the equitable charge that we examined in section 4.3.1 above, when looking at equitable mortgages of the legal estate. Where there is such an equitable mortgage, the borrower is under a duty to grant the lender a legal interest: a legal charge. The lender can thus call for that right, and, with it, will acquire all of the powers and remedies associated with a legal charge. In the case of the equitable charge examined in this section, however, the lender enjoys none of these rights. Its implied rights are confined to a right to apply to court for an order for sale or the appointment of a receiver.

In the following extract, McFarlane emphasizes this distinction by giving different names to the form of equitable charge that we examined in section 4.3.1 above and that which we have examined in this section. In the passage, a legal charge by way of mortgage is referred to as a 'charge'. The first type of equitable charge is then called an 'equitable charge' and the second a 'purely equitable charge'. This underlines the fact that, in the second case, the borrower is under no duty to give the lender a legal interest in land.

McFarlane, *The Structure of Property Law* (2008, p 818)

It is important to distinguish between (i) an Equitable Charge; and (ii) a Purely Equitable Charge. First, an Equitable Charge, unlike a Purely Equitable Charge, can exist only in relation to land. Second, even where land is concerned, there is a difference between the two rights. An Equitable Charge arises where [the borrower] is under a duty to grant [the lender] a Charge. A Purely Equitable Charge arises where [the borrower] is under a duty to hold his Freehold or Lease as security for a duty owed to [the lender]. Third, formality rules can apply differently to each right:

Equitable Charge: Where [the borrower] has a Freehold or Lease, his power to come under a *contractual* duty to give [the lender] a Charge is regulated by s.2 of the 1989 Act [. . .] However, [the lender] can acquire an Equitable Charge in the absence of writing if [the borrower] is under a *non-contractual* duty to give [the lender] a Charge.

Purely Equitable Charge: Where [the borrower] has a Freehold or Lease, his power to make a contractual promise to hold his right as security is regulated by s.53(1)(a) of the LPA 1925. That rule requires only writing signed by A.

---

[29] See Law of Property Act 1925, s 53(1)a.

4.3.4 Equitable security rights in land: reform?

We have distinguished between three different ways in which a lender can acquire an equitable security interest in land. The Law Commission recommended the rationalization of this potentially confusing multiplicity of forms.

Law Commission Report No 204, *Land Mortgages* (1991, [2.13])

Reduction in the number of types of security

Whilst this proliferation of types of security interest in land is historically explicable, we are satisfied that it no longer serves any useful purpose. As far as legal mortgages are concerned, it is difficult to justify the continued existence of the mortgage by demise, given that it is no longer used in practice and has the same effect in law as the charge by way of legal mortgage. The problem of equitable security in a legal estate is rather different. The principle underlying equitable mortgages of the legal estate is the rule in *Walsh v Lonsdale*, a general property law principle which applies to mortgages in precisely the same way as it applies to fee simples, leases and easements. Nevertheless, if the equitable charge is included it does mean that there are at least three, and possibly four, ways of taking informal security over the legal estate. Whilst there are small differences in the effect between these different types of equitable security, there is no apparent difference in function: none seems to fulfill a function that could not be fulfilled by any one of the others. The same can be said of the different ways of taking security over equitable interests in land: responses to the Working Paper confirmed that the differences in form and effect between equitable mortgages and equitable charges are regarded as no practical significance. Finally, there is the question of whether it remains necessary for the method of creating a security interest over an equitable interest to be different from the method for creating a security interest over a legal estate. In the Working Group we put forward the view that there was in reason in principle why the same type of security should not be used for both legal and equitable interests in land [...]

4.4 CHARGING ORDERS

A charging order provides a means by which a judgment creditor can enforce his or her judgment, and provides some of the advantages conferred by security. Charging orders are governed by the Charging Orders Act 1979. In theory, a judgment creditor can apply for a charging order over *any* property of the debtor; in practice, however, a judgment creditor is likely to ask for a charging order in relation to valuable, immovable property—the debtor's land.

Charging Orders Act 1979, s 1(1)

Charging orders

(1) Where, under a judgment or order of the High Court or a county court, a person (the "debtor") is required to pay a sum of money to another person (the "creditor") then, for the purpose of enforcing that judgment or order, the appropriate court may make an order

> in accordance with the provisions of this Act imposing on any such property of the debtor as may be specified in the order a charge for securing the payment of any money due or to become due under the judgment or order.

The judgment creditor must thus apply to court for the grant of a charging order.[30] If a charging order is granted, a charge is created over the judgment debtor's interest in land as specified in the order to secure the payment of the judgment debt,[31] and should accordingly be registered to preserve its priority.[32] This charge has *the like effect and shall be enforceable [...] in the same manner as an equitable charge created by the debtor under his hand*.[33] The judgment creditor becomes a secured creditor and will be able to claim priority against unsecured creditors if the debtor becomes insolvent. The charging order may be enforced by application to court for an order for sale, or for the appointment of a receiver.

A judgment creditor thus must submit to the court's discretion at two points: firstly, when the court decides whether or not to make the order; and secondly, when the court decides whether or not the charging order should be enforced. Where the debtor's interest is an interest under a trust of land held in co-ownership with others, the creditor will need to apply for an order for sale under s 14 of the Trusts of Land and Appointment of Trustees 1996, a jurisdiction that has already been considered in Chapter 21.

The court has discretion whether or not to grant a charging order and, in exercising that discretion, it must consider all of the circumstances of the case, including the personal circumstances of the debtor and whether any other creditor would be prejudiced by the order.[34]

Charging Orders Act 1979, s 1(5)

Charging orders

(5) In deciding whether to make a charging order the court shall consider all the circumstances of the case and, in particular, any evidence before it as to—

(a) the personal circumstances of the debtor, and

(b) whether any other creditor of the debtor would be likely to be unduly prejudiced by the making of the order.

A creditor, although not entitled to a charging order, can expect an order to be granted in its favour unless there are circumstances that would persuade a court that an order should not be made. For example, a charging order will not be granted if it is likely that the debtor

---

[30] The making of the order is a two-stage process. Initially, the charging order nisi is granted, giving the judgment debtor time to meet the judgment. If he or she fails to do so, the charging order is made absolute.

[31] Including a beneficial interest held under a trust of land: see Charging Orders Act 1979, s 2(1)(a)(i).

[32] In respect of a registered estate by a notice, see Land Registration Act 2002, ss 32–34, or by a restriction where the judgment debtor's interest is a beneficial interest under a trust, see Land Registration Act 2002, s 42(1)(c) and (4). Where land is unregistered, a charging order against the judgment debtor's legal title is registrable as an order affecting land: see Land Charges Act 1972, s 6(1)(a); but where the judgment debtor holds a beneficial interest under a trust of unregistered land, there is no provision for registration.

[33] Charging Orders Act 1979, s 3(4).

[34] The court can vary or discharge a charging order upon the application of the debtor or of any other person with an interest in the property: see ibid, s 3(5).

will become bankrupt or go into liquidation; in such a case, a charging order would give the judgment debtor an undue advantage over other unsecured creditors.[35]

Where the judgment debtor's interest is an interest in his or her home, which he or she holds jointly with his or her spouse or partner, the court will also consider the position of that spouse or partner and any children. The situation may be complicated by the possibility that divorce proceedings are contemplated, or pending, in which the judgment debtor's spouse is entitled to claim ancillary relief. In these circumstances, there is a balance to be struck between the exercise of the court's family jurisdiction, in which the welfare of any children are a primary consideration, and the court's commercial jurisdiction, in which contracts must be honoured and judgment debts paid.

The Court of Appeal, when considering this balancing exercise, has made clear that its approach will depend upon the timing of the creditor's and wife's applications.

Harman v Glencross [1986] Fam 81, CA

Balcombe LJ

At 98

[. . .] I think it right to set out how I conceive the court should deal with a similar problem when next it occurs.

1. Where a judgment creditor has obtained a charging order nisi on the husband's share in the matrimonial home and his application to have that order made absolute is heard before the wife has started divorce proceedings, there is, of course, no other court to which the application for the charging order absolute can be transferred, the wife having no competing claim to the husband's share. In those circumstances it is difficult to see why the court should refuse to make the charging order absolute, and the wife's right of occupation should be adequately protected under section 30 of the Law of Property Act 1925: see the analysis of the law by Goff L.J. in In re Holliday [1981] Ch. 405.

2. Where the charging order nisi has been made after the wife's petition, then on the application for a charging order absolute the court should consider whether the circumstances are such that it is proper to make the charging order absolute, even before the wife's application for ancillary relief has been heard by the Family Division. There will, of course, be cases (such as Llewellin v. Llewellin (unreported), 30 October 1985, Court of Appeal (Civil Division) Transcript No. 640 of 1985, which we heard immediately after this appeal) where the figures are such that even if the charging order is made absolute, and then the charge is realised by a sale of the house, the resultant proceeds of sale (including any balance of the husband's share after the judgment debt has been paid) will be clearly sufficient to provide adequate alternative accommodation for the wife and children.

3. Unless it appears to the court hearing the application for the charging order absolute that the circumstances are so clear that it is proper to make the order there and then, the usual practice should be to transfer the application to the Family Division so that it may come on with the wife's application for ancillary relief, and one court can then be in a position to consider all the circumstances of the case. When considering the circumstances, the approach of the court should be to recall the statement of Sir Denys

---

[35] *Roberts Petroleum Ltd v Bernard Kenny Ltd* [1983] 2 AC 192.

Buckley in the *Hegerty case* [1985] Q.B. 850, 866, that a judgment creditor is justified in expecting that a charging order over the husband's beneficial interest in the matrimonial home will be made in his favour. The court should first consider whether the value of the equity in the house is sufficient to enable the charging order to be made absolute and realised at once, as in *Llewellin v. Llewellin* (unreported), even though that may result in the wife and children being housed at a lower standard than they might reasonably have expected had only the husband's interests been taken into account against them. Failing that, the court should make only such order as may be necessary to protect the wife's right to occupy (with the children where appropriate) the matrimonial home. The normal course should then be to postpone the sale of the house for such period only as may be requisite to protect the right of occupation—a Mesher type of order—again bearing in mind that the court is holding the balance, not between the wife and the husband, but between the wife and the judgment creditor. If the judgment creditor asks, even in the alternative to his claim to an immediate order, for a Mesher type of order, then it seems to me that it would require exceptional circumstances before the court should make an order for the outright transfer of the husband's share in the house to the wife, thereby leaving nothing on which the judgment creditor's charging order can bite, even in the future. Finally, the court should consider whether there is any point in denying the judgment creditor his charging order, if the wife's rights of occupation could in any event be defeated by the judgment creditor making the husband bankrupt.

4. Once the charging order absolute has been made, it would normally require some special circumstances—e.g., where (as here) the wife had no proper opportunity to put her case before the court—for the court to set the charging order aside under section 3(5) of the Charging Orders Act 1979, and thereby deprive the judgment creditor of his vested right.

Where a wife is unaware that a charging order has been made against her husband's interest in the home,[36] she may apply under s 3(5) of the Charging Orders Act 1979 to have the charge varied or discharged. She may do so as a person interested in the home either because she owns the property jointly with her husband, or, where the home is solely owned by her husband, because she has a statutory right to occupy under the Family Law Act 1996 (FLA 1996).[37]

5 EQUITY OF REDEMPTION

We have seen that, under a classic mortgage by conveyance or sub-demise, the borrower holds the equity of redemption—an equitable property right that represents the value of the land less the amount owed to the lender under the mortgage. We now need to examine this influential concept and, in particular, its continuing place (if any) in the modern law, given that the classic mortgage has essentially been replaced by the device of the legal charge by way of mortgage.

---

[36] A charging order nisi may be made *ex parte*.

[37] *Harman v Glencross* [1986] Fam 81. A right to apply for a property adjustment order, whereby the husband's interest may be transferred to the wife, might also be a sufficient interest to give a wife *locus standi* to apply, but see *Whittingham v Whittingham* [1979] Fam 21.

5.1 DEVELOPMENT OF THE EQUITY OF REDEMPTION

The exact time at which the equity of redemption was first recognized is difficult to trace, but what is clear is that it emerged as an equitable response of the Chancery courts to the harsh terms of the common law mortgage by conveyance. The form of the mortgage by conveyance transferred the borrower's entire estate in the land to the lender, subject only to a covenant by the lender to reconvey the land to the borrower upon the borrower repaying the loan at the time and in the manner agreed. The agreement of the parties thus gave the borrower a contractual or legal right to redeem. If the borrower failed to repay as required, the lender was not obliged to perform the covenant to reconvey. The lender was instead entitled to retain the land as its legal owner, free from the covenant, and so the borrower lost (or forfeited) his or her land, even though it might be worth considerably more than the mortgage debt.

The common law rule was clear, but harsh, and from the seventeenth century, courts of equity were routinely coming to the aid of the borrower by allowing repayment after the legal date for redemption had passed and thus allowing the borrower to recover the land.[38] The means by which equity upheld the borrower's equitable right to redeem is not entirely clear. The possibilities, as Watt explains, were an award of specific performance of the lender's covenant to reconvey, or the grant of relief to the borrower against forfeiture.

Watt, 'Mortgage Law as Legal Fiction' in *Modern Studies in Property Law: Vol 4* (ed Cooke, 2007, p 81)

The next challenge is to identify the doctrines by which it was developed, for this will determine whether it is realistic to remove the fiction. There are two main candidates for the doctrinal source of equity's refusal to follow the law in the mortgage context. On the one hand, there is the equity's doctrinal commitment to relieve against penalties and closely related to it, the equitable doctrine of relief from forfeiture. On the other hand, there is equity's willingness to issue injunctions (decrees) requiring specific performance of the mortgagee's covenant to reconvey the mortgage land to the mortgagor. The two bases are compatible but distinct. The former is concerned to set aside the conveyance to the mortgagee, whereas the latter is concerned to enforce the reconveyance to the mortgagor. Both bases were united in permitting the mortgagor to bring a bill to redeem even though it was considered at law to breach the mortgagor's covenant to grant the mortgagee quiet enjoyment of the estate conveyed.

This right became known as the 'equitable right to redeem', which would only be lost if the Chancery courts could be persuaded that there was little or no hope of the borrower being able to repay. In such a case, the lender would be granted a decree of foreclosure. The equitable right to redeem came to be recognized as no mere personal right, but a proprietary right, which could itself be sold or mortgaged, representing, as it did, the borrower's equitable 'ownership' of the land.[39] What is more, to retain the essential security nature of

---

[38] See, e.g., *Emmanuel College v Evans* (1625) 1 Ch Rep 18. There is some earlier evidence, from the reign of Elizabeth I onwards, that Chancery would assist a borrower in certain circumstances, but it seems that assistance became routine from the early seventeenth century.

[39] *Casborne v Scarfe* (1738) 1 Atk 603, 26 ER 377.

the classic mortgage by conveyance, courts of equity were at pains to protect the borrower's equity of redemption. This aim was accomplished by the principle that there should be no 'clogs and fetters' on the equity of redemption. We will examine the continued significance of this principle in the next chapter.

In the face of the borrower's equitable right to redeem, the legal date for redemption lost its import. It is now regarded as a merely nominal date and is often set to occur shortly after the mortgage is entered into. It is the equitable right to redeem upon which borrowers rely to insist upon their right to repay their mortgage and to clear their property of its mortgaged status.

The evolution of the equity of redemption provides an interesting insight into the emergence of equitable doctrine, and the relationship between the courts of common law and equity. It emerged at a time when a number of influential Lord Chancellors were shaping the Chancery jurisdiction from an ad hoc jurisdiction based upon individual petitions, to a coherent body of fundamental rules and principles.[40] Inevitably, at times, this set Chancery at odds with the position at common law. This was certainly the case with the development of the equity of redemption: it amounted to a *'barefaced disavowal of the legal form'*[41] of the mortgage by conveyance. But then the mortgage by conveyance was, itself, a mere form developed originally to overcome restrictions on charging interest imposed by the laws against usury. Thus it may well have been that the courts of common law were not wholly opposed to these developments, achieving as they did a degree of fairness to protect the vulnerable borrower. The emergence of the equity of redemption may also have been accommodated by judges, drawn largely from the nobility, to the threat presented by lenders to the forfeiture of their fellow noble landowners' estates.[42]

5.2 EQUITY OF REDEMPTION AND THE LEGAL CHARGE

The equity of redemption is a key component of the classic form of mortgage by conveyance. It thus retains its import in the equitable mortgage by conveyance (see section 4.3.2 above)—but what of the predominant form of legal mortgage: the legal charge?

Under a legal charge, the borrower retains his or her freehold or lease, but his land is encumbered (or burdened) by the legal charge.[43] We have already seen that, as a result of s 87(1) of the LPA 1925, the lender enjoys the rights powers and remedies of a mortgagee by sub-demise, although the section does not actually confer a lease upon the lender. The lender's interest in the borrower's land is merely that of a legal charge. The problem is that the section does not clarify the borrower's position.

McHugh J made the following observation, giving judgment in the following case (referring to the Torrens system registered charge under the Australian State of Victoria's equivalent legislation).

---

[40] Including, in particular, Lords Bacon, Nottingham, and Hardwick.

[41] Watt, 'Mortgage Law as Legal Fiction' in *Modern Studies in Property Law: Vol 4* (ed Cooke, 2007, p 80).

[42] Sugarman and Warrington, 'Telling Stories: Rights and Wrongs of the Equity of Redemption' in *Property Problems: From Genes to Pension Funds* (ed Harris, 1997, p 207).

[43] But see *Horsham Properties Group Ltd v Clark* [2008] EWHC 2327, [22], in which Briggs J said *'whilst it is true that the mortgagor of registered land remains the registered proprietor* [...], *it is wrong in substance to describe the rights of such a mortgagor as tantamount to freehold ownership'*.

Figgins Holdings Pty Ltd v SEAA Enterprises Ltd (1999) 196 CLR 245, High Court of Australia

McHugh J

At [65]

The great difficulty of the cases arises from the attempt by s81 [Transfer of Land Act 1958 (Vic)] to confer on the mortgagee the rights and remedies of a mortgage at common law when the nature of the Torrens system mortgage is fundamentally different from that of the common law mortgage. The difficulty is increased by the section's failure to define the liabilities of, and the consequences for, the mortgagor as a result of conferring these common law rights and remedies on the mortgagee.

Thus, for example, under a mortgage by conveyance or sub-demise, the lender has an immediate right to possession arising by virtue of the legal estate that is preserved by s 87(1). Under a classical mortgage by conveyance or sub-demise, the borrower's right to possession was cast as that of a mere tenant at will, occupying by the permission of the lender, but under a legal charge, the borrower retains the legal estate and thus equally has a right to possession by reason of that estate, subject only to the lender's ability to assert its own right to possession should it wish to do so.[44]

Likewise, whilst, under a classic mortgage by conveyance, the borrower needed to recover or redeem legal title to the land when the debt was repaid, under a legal charge, there is nothing to recover. There is a charge to remove, but the act of repayment extinguishes the charge. Once there is no debt, there can be no effective appropriation of property to its repayment to constitute the charge. The formality rules governing land do call for documentary evidence of the discharge of a legal charge, either through a deed or a written receipt,[45] which, in the case of a registered charge, will also have to be recorded at the Land Registry. These documents also provide convenient evidence that the debt has been repaid.

Nield has questioned the utility of the equity of redemption as a distinct proprietary interest in cases in which the lender has a legal charge.

Nield, 'Charges, Possession and Human Rights: A Reappraisal of Section 87(1) Law of Property Act 1925' in *Modern Studies in Property Law: Vol 3* (ed Cooke, 2005, p 159)

Redemption in the sense of obtaining a reconveyance or cesser of the mortgaged estate is inconsistent with a legal charge for there is simply no transfer of the borrower's estate or the creation of demise by way of security. The borrower retains the legal estate, so there is neither any property of the borrower to redeem or recover from the lender nor any proviso for redemption from which relief can be granted. What is necessary is a continuing right to require the lender to accept repayment of the debt and effect a discharge, despite default in

---

[44] *Figgins Holdings Pty Ltd v SEAA Enterprises Ltd* (1999) 196 CLR 245, High Court of Australia, at [82]–[83], [87]–[88].

[45] See Law of Property Act 1925, ss 52 and 115.

the borrower's repayment obligations. Thus whilst it is appropriate to speak of an equitable right to repay, or of discharge, it is questionable whether it is still accurate to refer to the borrower's equity of redemption in the sense of a distinct proprietary interest.

If the borrower's continued right to repay the debt and obtain a discharge represents a separate equitable interest which does not merge with his legal estate, it is appropriate to speak of a distinct equity of redemption. However, if the continuing right of the borrower to obtain a discharge upon repayment, regardless of default, is characterised as an incident of the borrower's estate then the use of the term equity of redemption, as distinct from an equitable right of repayment, is strained. The borrower continues to hold the legal and beneficial ownership of the mortgaged land, subject only to the burden of the charge, thus it could be argued that there is no room or need for a separate proprietary interest in the form of an equity of redemption.

Watt goes further and suggests that it is time to kill off the equity of redemption.

Watt, 'Mortgage Law as Legal Fiction' in *Modern Studies in Property Law: Vol 4* (ed Cooke, 2007, p 87)

Parliament has killed off the mortgage by conveyance and reconveyance of a fee simple, yet the courts have so far failed to acknowledge that the notion of the equity of redemption should have died with it. They have failed to acknowledge that land subject to a registered charge is not 'redeemed' as was land conveyed under the classic form of mortgage rather the charge is simply discharged from the land upon repayment of the debt.

Killing the equity of redemption would breathe reality into the position of the parties under a legal charge and cement the legal charge as a pure security interest. It would also provide the opportunity to remove, or at least recast, a number of doctrines that were associated with redemption. These are the doctrines of consolidation, the entitlement of the lender to costs on redemption, and the clogs and fetters doctrine. We will examine this latter doctrine and its continued utility in the next chapter.

Consolidation entitles a lender holding two or more mortgages over different pieces of land owned by the borrower to insist upon the redemption of all of these mortgages, should the borrower seek to repay any one of them. Consolidation thus give the lender an equitable right, developed in response to the borrower's equitable right to redeem. If the borrower was seeking the indulgence of equity to redeem after the legal date for redemption, he or she was required to meet certain conditions: namely, to pay the costs of redemption, and to redeem all mortgages granted to the lender, if the lender so required. Consolidation is controversial and s 93 of the LPA 1925 excludes the right unless it is expressly preserved, which lenders usually insist it is. The Law Commission has recommended the abolition of consolidation.[46] The Australian courts have taken that step, by rejecting the lender's rights to redemption costs and to consolidate on the grounds that it is inconsistent with the concept of a charge.[47]

---

46 Law Commission Report No 204 (1991, [6.44]).
47 *Greig v Watson* (1881) 7 VR 79; *Perry v Rolfe* [1848] VLR 297.

6 MODERN DEVELOPMENTS IN MORTGAGE FORMS

Changing social and economic trends means that there is always pressure to develop alternative means of unlocking the security potential of land. The domestic lending market has seen the development of Islamic mortgages, the emergence of shared-ownership schemes to assist low-income borrowers—particularly first-time buyers—mount the first step of the home-ownership ladder, and equity release schemes to enable the elderly to use the investment value of their home to fund their living expenses. Further, the onward march of the European single market has seen proposals to developing a European form of mortgage, or *Eurohypothec*.

6.1 ISLAMIC MORTGAGES OR HOME PURCHASE PLANS

Islam prohibits the charging of interest (*riba*).[48] Making a profit from trade is permitted, but the charging of interest is unacceptable, because it reduces the risk that is inherent in trade. Traders share the risk that market movements (whether up or down) may adversely affect them, but the charging of interest cushions only the lender against the risk that the borrower is unable to repay the loan.[49] The charging of interest, which is an inherent part of conventional mortgage lending, thus presents a problem to followers of Islam, particularly those who wish to purchase their own home. A number of financial institutions have thus developed mortgage products that are thought to comply with Islamic principles.[50]
There are three main products available to assist with the purchase of a house, as follows:

- The *murabaha* utilizes the concept of deferred purchase. The bank purchases the property from the seller, but then agrees to sell on to the borrower at a price that reflects the original price plus an agreed profit. The purchase price is then paid by the borrower by periodic payments over a fixed period of time. Title is usually transferred to the borrower immediately, with the outstanding purchase price being secured by a mortgage.

- The *ijarah* is based upon a lease. The lender purchases the property that the borrower wishes to buy and then leases it to the borrower for a fixed period. The lease is coupled with an agreement by the lender to sell the property to the borrower at the end of the term.[51] The rent is periodically assessed to reflect the capital value of the property, prevailing market rentals, and a contribution to the final resale price (being the original sale price minus the deposit already paid). Thus, at the end of the term, the borrower will have paid the lender the full purchase costs plus a return to the lender, by making the rental payments.

- The diminishing *musharakah* involves shared ownership. Again, the lender purchases the property and leases it to the borrower—but part of the monthly payment made by the borrower goes toward increasing his or her ownership share in the property, so that the rental element of the periodic payment diminishes as the borrower's ownership share increases.

---

48 *The Qur'an* [30.39], [4.161], [3.130]–[3.132], and [2.275]–[2.281].
49 See further Watt (2007, p 94).
50 See Latif, 'Islamic Finance' (2006) 1 JIBFL 10.
51 Technically, this is known as *ijarah wa iqtinah*.

All of these methods utilize different vehicles, but, like a conventional mortgage, the borrower makes periodic payments to the lender to reflect repayment of the original capital cost, together with a financial return to the lender. There is continuing debate amongst Islamic scholars as to whether these schemes do, indeed, comply with Islamic principles, the payments being made by the borrower reflecting profit to the lender, rather than a genuine sharing of commercial risk. The diminishing *musharakah* is seen as the most in tune with sharia law.

6.2 SHARED OWNERSHIP

Property prices in many parts of the country are now so high that many cannot afford to buy a home even with the aid of a mortgage. The response of the government has been to introduce a number of schemes to help those with insufficient income to fund a mortgage from a private sector lender.[52]

- New Build Homebuy enables a buyer to purchase a share in a new property—usually one built by a housing association—and to pay rent to the housing association in respect of the share in the property that it continues to hold. As the buyer's financial situation permits, he or she can increase his or her share of ownership, until he or she fully owns the property—a process known as 'staircasing'.

- Open Market Homebuy provides a government-backed loan—usually administered by a housing association—which can provide top up finance to buy a property on the open market, the remaining finance being negotiated from a private sector lender.

Assistance is also provided to local authority and housing association tenants to purchase their home at a discounted price, either through a right to buy/acquire,[53] or through a shared-ownership scheme, known as 'Social Homebuy'.

6.3 EQUITY RELEASE OR HOME REVERSION PLANS

As homeowners get on in years, they may find that they own a valuable home (having paid off their mortgage), but that they have little income. They could, of course, move and buy a less valuable home, invest the balance, and live off that investment income. But if they do not want to move, they may consider using the value of their home through an 'equity release', or 'home reversion', plan, to provide either a lump sum or a regular income (or both). These plans can take a number of forms, but the key features are that the homeowner grants either a mortgage or a share of the ownership of his or her home to the lender, in return for regular periodic payments or a lump sum, which can be invested in an annuity or other investment vehicle to provide a regular income.

6.3.1 Lifetime mortgage

The idea of a lifetime mortgage is that it is not repayable until the borrower dies. Some schemes also provide that the lender will share in any increase in value of the home. There

---

[52] See http://www.housingcorp.gov.uk.
[53] See Housing Act 2004, Pt 6.

are various ways in which interest can be paid under these schemes. It may be paid on the usual interest-only basis, but, if the borrower is already short of income and cannot meet regular interest payments, the interest may be 'rolled up' and added to the capital secured by the mortgage. In that case, the interest is only repayable when the borrower dies or sells his or her home. Alternatively, an annuity may be purchased with the advance and part of the income from the annuity used to meet the interest due.

6.3.2 Home reversion plans

Under a home reversion plan, the borrower sells all of, or a share in, the house to a specialist company, which thus benefits from any further increase in the value of the home. Where the whole house is sold, it is leased back to the borrower—usually only for a nominal rent—for a term that may be brought to an end when the borrower dies. The sale price for the house is less than its market value with vacant possession, to reflect the fact that the borrower remains in occupation.

These plans have proved controversial. They are often quite complicated in their terms, with technicalities that it can be challenging for an elderly borrower to understand. They also play on the desire of the borrower to stay in his or her own home.

6.4 THE EUROHYPOTHEC

The idea of developing a common form of mortgage for Europe was first mooted by the European Commission over forty years ago.[54] This idea has moved a little nearer reality, with the European Commission Green Paper on *Mortgage Credit in the European Union*,[55] which reports that serious consideration is being given to '*the feasibility and desirability*' of a Euromortgage. In response, a European Union research group has put forward proposals for a European mortgage, or *Eurohypothec*.[56] Their proposal is not to replace the numerous security devices used in the member States, but to provide an alternative common form, to be governed by the laws of the country in which the land is situated, and which can operate alongside national forms. It will thus be vital that the national laws of the member States are able to accommodate the proposed Eurohypothec.

The form of proposed Eurohypothec is intended to be very flexible. The proposal is for a non-accessory form of charge, which, although it would secure repayment of a debt, may exist independently of that debt.[57] It is envisaged that the Eurohypothec would be registered in a public registry by an entry that would show (amongst other details) the amount of money secured. Even though the borrower can repay the loan and insist upon the Eurohypothec being discharged from the land, it will remain registered until the entry is removed with the consent of both the borrower and the lender. The benefit of a registered Eurohypothec can thus be transferred to another lender. The gap between the loan and the Eurohypothec would be bridged by a security agreement, governed also by the law of the member State in which the land is situated. The security agreement would form a contract between the lender and

---

[54] European Commission, *The Development of a European Capital Market* (1966, [153]–[158]).

[55] (2005, [48]).

[56] See http://www.eurohypothec.com and Mortgage Credit Foundation, *Mortgage Bulletin 21: Basic Guidelines for a Eurohypothec* (2005); Nassarre-Aznar, 'The Eurohypothec: A Common Mortgage for Europe' (2005) 69 Conv 32; Watt, 'The Eurohypothec and the English Mortgage' (2006) 13(2) MJECL 173.

[57] Mortgage Credit Foundation (2005).

borrower, and would provide for such matters as the terms upon which the Eurohypothec is held and enforced. If the benefit of a Eurohypothec were to be transferred to another lender, there would need to be a new security agreement to govern the relationship between the borrower and the new lender. A failure to enter into a new security agreement would entitle the borrower to insist upon the discharge of the Eurohypothec.

All existing forms of security in England are accessory to a debt. Once the debt is repaid, the borrower can insist that the security interest over his or her land is extinguished. We will see in the next chapter that equity has carefully guarded the borrower's right of redemption; thus the notion that a security interest may continue to affect the borrower's land even though the debt has been repaid presents somewhat of a problem for English law.[58]

There are other points of tension between the proposed Eurohypothec and English law.[59] For example, it is proposed that the borrower may hold the benefit of a Eurohypothec over his or her own land, but English law has always refused to accept such a proposition, because of the corollary impossibility of owing a duty to oneself. Furthermore, the priority provided by the LRA 2002 for overriding interests does not accord with the priority that is envisaged for a registered Eurohypothec. And even if these doctrinal issues could be overcome, the most significant stumbling block, both for English law and for the law of other member States, is likely to be compatibility of enforcement of the Eurohypothec with existing consumer protection—particularly over domestic property.[60]

Whether or not these issues can be overcome across all of the member States will hinge upon whether the economic advantages of a Eurohypothec are sufficiently attractive. The impetus for a Euromortgage comes from a belief that a common mortgage form would promote an integrated mortgage credit market across the European Union, enabling lenders to secure a number of loans, which could be made in different member States, against land assets that are held in more than one jurisdiction. Such developments may be very attractive to large institutional lenders and to investors in mortgaged-backed securities, but they do not provide immediate advantages to many borrowers—particularly consumers—unless the benefit to lenders is passed on through the greater competition and flexibility that an integrated market is expected to produce.[61]

QUESTIONS

1. What is the difference between a 'mortgage' and a 'charge'? Why is the legal charge by way of mortgage described as a hybrid security?

2. In what circumstances may an equitable form of security interest be created?

3. What advantages would there be if the Law Commission's recommended changes to the form of land mortgages were enacted?

4. Do you agree that the concept of an equity of redemption has outlived its usefulness?

---

[58] Although Watt argues that this obstacle can be overcome: see 'The Eurohypothec and the English Mortgage' (2006) 13 MJECL 173, 185–8.

[59] Ibid, at 188–91.

[60] Ibid, at 191–2. We will explore this protection in the next chapter.

[61] Ibid, at 179–81.

FURTHER READING

Clarke, 'Security Interests in Property' in *Property Problems: From Genes to Pension Funds* (ed Harris, London: Kluwer, 1997)

Law Commission Report No 204, *Land Mortgages* (1991)

Nield, 'Charges, Possession and Human Rights: A Reappraisal of Section 87(1) Law of Property Act 1925' in *Modern Studies in Property Law: Vol 3* (ed Cooke, Oxford: Hart, 2005)

Oldham, 'Mortgages' in *Land Law: Issues, Debates, Policy* (ed Tee, Devon: Willan, 2002)

Sugarman and Warrington, 'Telling Stories: Rights and Wrongs of the Equity of Redemption' in *Property Problems: From Genes to Pension Funds* (ed Harris, London: Kluwer, 1997)

Watt, 'Mortgage Law as a Legal Fiction' in *Modern Studies in Property Law: Vol 3* (ed Cooke, Oxford: Hart, 2007)

Watt, 'The Eurohypothec and the English Mortgage' (2006) 13(2) MJECL 173

30

PROTECTION OF THE BORROWER

CENTRAL ISSUES

1. Protection of the borrower looks to both procedural fairness in the conduct of the mortgage transaction and to substantive fairness of the mortgage terms. The level of protection differs according to the nature of the borrower and the type of security transaction.

2. The home mortgage market is regulated through the Financial Services and Markets Act 2000 and the Consumer Credit Act 1974, following principles of decentered regulation to encourage responsible lending and responsible borrowing.

3. A mortgage may be set aside because of procedural unfairness. There are a number of doctrines that underpin procedural fairness, including duress, undue influence, misrepresentation, and unconscionable bargain. In recent years, undue influence has been employed to try to ensure the procedural fairness of collateral mortgages over the family home to fund a business loan.

4. The control of mortgage terms seeks to balance the freedom of the parties to contract against a concern that borrowers' financial situation makes them vulnerable to exploitation.

5. Equitable protection has been provided by controls against penalties, and oppressive and unconscionable terms, as well as by protection of the borrower's equity of redemption.

6. Statutory consumer protection now provides additional protection to domestic borrowers.

1 INTRODUCTION

In this chapter, we will be concentrating on the position of the borrower, who is often considered to be the more vulnerable party. In modern commercial lending, that is not always the case where the borrower is a profitable company, the liquidity of which is maintained with the assistance of an overdraft facility from its bankers, or which requires finance to fund the expansion of its flourishing business. Such companies can not only source the most competitive terms from financiers, but can also afford the services of lawyers and other advisers to ensure that their position is protected. Other companies may not be so fortunate if they are small and struggling to start a business, or to maintain profitability in a competitive marketplace. They may have few assets to offer as security and may be only able to secure finance if their directors or shareholders are prepared to offer their personal assets as security, or are willing to expose themselves to personal liability through the grant of a personal guarantee.

In the domestic lending market, a distinction needs to be drawn between those who wish to use their earning power to buy a home, and the individual who is in financial difficulties and needs to raise money or consolidate his or her immediate liabilities. The former will be able to choose from a number of mainstream banks and building societies, which are prepared to offer competitive terms because the risk of default is low. The borrower's earnings will meet the instalment repayments and the loan, in any event, will be secured against a property, which is likely to grow in value as house prices rise. This type of borrower is only likely to be exposed either from an unanticipated rise in interest rates, or from an unforeseen decline in his or her earnings or the housing market. It is the borrower who is in urgent need of funds that is the most vulnerable. He or she is unlikely to be attractive to high street lenders and will have to resort to the secondary mortgage lenders, which charge higher rates of interest and demand more onerous terms to meet the higher risk that is inherent in this type of lending. These borrowers are also unlikely to have the luxury of choice or to have the strength of bargaining position to negotiate terms.

This diversity in types of borrower and the circumstances in which they require funds leads to a need to draw distinctions in the appropriate controls. The measures that we will need to examine in this chapter fall into a number of categories. We will first consider the legal regulation of the consumer lending market, which has grown considerably in recent years with the Consumer Credit Act 1974 (CCA 1974), which was subject to major amendment in 2006, and the Financial Services and Markets Act 2000 (FSMA 2000). We will then consider the protection afforded to the borrower in the creation of the mortgage. We will briefly consider the common vitiating factors that may lead to the avoidance of a mortgage, before examining the application of undue influence to collateral mortgages of the family home to secure a business loan. Finally, controls over the terms of the mortgage itself must be considered. We will look initially at the common law, equitable, and statutory sources of these controls. Here, equity has long shown a concern to ensure that the mortgage is redeemable by the borrower and that the mortgage terms themselves are not oppressive or unconscionable. Control over mortgage terms may also be exerted as a result of public policy or statutory measures, although statutory intervention is largely confined to the consumer lending.

We will leave until the following chapter the protection afforded to a borrower where the lender enforces its rights and remedies under the mortgage itself.

2 MARKET REGULATION

Recent decades has seen big changes in the mortgage market and its regulation. Building societies, once the major source of home finance, have been deregulated and banks have entered the market, with many building societies choosing to become banks answerable to their shareholders rather than their members. The increased competition has seen a dramatic rise in the availability of credit, checked only by the current global credit crunch.

In the context of the promotion of private home ownership, Whitehouse has noted the rise in regulation of mortgages through market forces.

Whitehouse, 'The Homeowner: Citizen or Consumer?' in *Land Law: Themes and Perspectives* **(eds Bright and Dewar, 1998, p 189)**

[...T]he promotion of home-ownership has allowed central government to replace direct state intervention with the regulation offered by the market system. The private contractual basis of mortgage finance makes it eminently suitable for regulation by the market. Because of the varied types of accommodation available within the owner-occupied sector and the wide range of mortgagees willing to offer different types of mortgage products, the state could reduce its intervention within the housing system and allow market forces to regulate the activities of mortgagors and mortgagees.

The justification for the reduction in direct state intervention within the housing system is based upon an 'idealistic' view of consumerism which extols the benefits of market forces as the guardians of choice, competition, and accountability. The shift in emphasis away from citizenship and towards consumerism may seem uncontroversial, particular as the term consumer is often combined with concepts of 'rights', 'protection', and 'legislation'. The rhetoric of consumerism implies that, where the market fails to provide a sufficient degree of choice and accountability, the state will intervene, on the consumer's behalf, by implementing legislation which corrects the failings in the market. The 'protection' afforded to homeowners, therefore is claimed to derive from a combination of market regulation and direct legal intervention [...]

Choice is a fundamental aspect of the 'idealistic' view of market regulation promoted by the rhetoric of consumerism, if consumers can exercise choice, then they can also determine which suppliers survive within the market. This provides consumers with a degree of influence which ensures that suppliers of goods and services operate according to the demands of consumers. In order for there to be choice, however, there must be a range of goods and services offered by different suppliers. In other words, competition is essential to the effective operation of a free market. In order to ensure competition, the former Conservative government sought to 'deregulate' the mortgage market, thereby encouraging financial institutions other than building societies to offer mortgage finance.

The mortgage market does, indeed, offer a dazzling array of mortgage 'products' and mortgage terms, although most choice operates within a narrow range governing the term and method of repayment—whether that be interest only, repayment, or endowment—and the mechanisms by which the interest rate is determined—whether it be fixed, variable, or by tracking some market index. Borrowers can, and do, exercise choice by switching to the lender offering the most attractive current rate, although, in so doing, they will have to be aware of any arrangement fees or redemption charges.

At the time that Whitehouse was writing, the market was largely self-regulated. The Council of Mortgage Lenders, the influential trade organization of lending institutions within the residential mortgage market, had a Statement of Practice to which its members were expected to adhere. The government did intervene where the lender sought possession of a dwelling house, through the Administration of Justice Act 1970—an intervention that we will examine in the next chapter. The government also intervened through the CCA 1974, but only where the loan did not exceed £25,000—a limit that became increasingly irrelevant as property prices increased. The picture has now changed, with what has been termed a 'decentred regulatory approach' of the mortgage market, through the enactment of the FSMA 2000 and major revisions to the 1974 Act.[1]

Deregulation aims to support responsible lending and responsible borrowing through the development of systems that promote market benchmarks of practice, with greater information being provided to borrowers so that they can make informed choices. There is also the ambitious aspiration that borrowers' impact on the market will empower them to shape lending practice itself.

Ramsay, 'Consumer Law, Regulatory Capitalism and the "New Learning" in Regulation' (2006) 28 Sydney LR 9, 12–13

A decentred regulatory approach might include initiatives that aim to 'responsibilise' both the supply and demand side of consumer markets, such as the current reforms to consumer credit law in the UK and Europe that are based on the twin pillars of 'responsible lending' and 'responsible borrowing'. Corporate social responsibility normally may contribute to the responsibilisation of suppliers. Responsibilisation of consumers seeks to reconstruct the consumer as a regulatory subject, a project that is both innovative and complicated. Within the traditional market model, consumer sovereignty was the goal of consumer policy. However, there was little concern for how consumers exercised their sovereignty. By contrast, the new learning on regulation positions the consumer as an important regulatory subject perceived as crucial to achieving national goals such as greater competitiveness. The 'responsibilisation' of the consumer is being pursued in areas such as credit and financial services, where governments are investing heavily in such projects to ensure that individuals become responsible consumers through the use of information, the development of financial capability, and financial literacy programs. These programs often make heroic assumptions about the ability of consumers to use and process information on market choices and their ultimate results remain uncertain and difficult to measure

The consumer will also have a civilising influence on markets within this responsibilisation approach. The recent consumer strategy document in the UK notes that consumers have responsibilities as well as rights and consumer policy should ensure that 'consumers are able to understand the impact on their own consumption'. Consumers are to be 'citizen consumers', a model of the consumer that recalls the US new deal where consumers would not follow solely their private interests at the expense of public interest. European Union (EU) consumer policy adopts a variant of this model where the responsible consumer has the mandate to ensure a competitive marketplace a mandate not necessarily compatible with public goals such as sustainable consumption.

The twin goals of responsible lending and responsible borrowing are evident in both the CCA 1974 and FSMA 2000, the salient provisions of which we must now examine. The objectives of this legislation are to support responsible lending through, on the one hand, codes of conduct that epitomize responsible lending practices, and, on the other, encouraging consumer choice through greater transparency by stipulating the giving of

---

[1] There is a growing literature on the role and impact of this new approach to regulation: see, e.g., Black, 'Decentring Regulation: Understanding the Role of Regulation and Self-regulation in the "Post-Regulatory" World' (2001) 54 CLP 103; Black, 'Tensions in The Regulatory State' (2007) PL 58; Baldwin, 'Is Better Regulation Smarter Regulation?' (2005) PL 485.

information—and its form—by lenders to borrowers. Whilst based upon the same regulatory principles, these two pieces of legislation do mark a division in the regulation of the domestic mortgage market.

To some extent, this division can be attributed to different areas of the consumer mortgage market. Even so, it has attracted criticism.[2]

Oldham, 'Mortgages' in *Land Law: Issues, Debates, Policy* (ed Tee, 2002, p 207)

The biggest flaw of the new regulatory system is its failure to bring all consumer mortgage lending, or even consumer lending, within a single, coherent and modernised regime [...] The complexity of the Consumer Credit Act in its application to mortgages has long been criticised, not least because it is difficult to ascertain, whether or not a particular mortgage falls within its purview. The further fragmentation effected by the [Financial Services and Markets Act 2000] is unfortunate, since it can only compound this difficulty. The result will be consumer confusion and unnecessary additional compliance costs for the mortgage industry.

2.1 FINANCIAL SERVICES AND MARKETS ACT 2000, AND REGULATED MORTGAGE CONTRACTS

The FSMA 2000 established the Financial Services Authority (FSA) as the single regulatory authority for the banking, credit securities, and insurance industry. With effect from 31 October 2004, the FSA took over responsibility for regulated mortgage contracts, and from 6 April 2007, the FSA also become responsible for home purchase plans[3] and home reversion plans.[4] The regulation extends both to mortgage lenders, and those that arrange and provide advice on mortgages.

2.1.1 Regulated mortgage contracts

Regulated mortgage contracts are defined by the Financial Services and Markets Act 2000 (Regulated Activities) Order 2001.[5]

Financial Services and Markets Act 2000 (Regulated Activities) Order 2001, art 61 (as amended)

[...]

(a) a contract is a "regulated mortgage contract" if, at the time it is entered into, the following conditions are met—

(i) the contract is one under which a person ("the lender") provides credit to an individual or to trustees ("the borrower");

---

[2] Oldham was writing before the Consumer Credit Act 2006, but her criticism remains appropriate.
[3] That is, Islamic mortgages: see Chapter 29, section 6.1.
[4] That is, equity release schemes: see Chapter 29, section 6.3.
[5] SI 2001/544.

> (ii) the contract provides for the obligation of the borrower to repay to be secured by a first legal mortgage on land (other than timeshare accommodation) in the United Kingdom;
>
> (iii) at least 40% of that land is used, or is intended to be used, as or in connection with a dwelling by the borrower or (in the case of credit provided to trustees) by an individual who is a beneficiary of the trust, or by a related person;
>
> [...]

The FSA's remit thus covers most home purchase loans that are secured by a first legal charge over the borrower's home.[6] It will also cover first legal mortgages of second homes and may also extend to loans made to small businesses, where the loan is secured by a first charge over the business proprietor's home.[7] Buy-to-let mortgages are not within the definition; they fail to satisfy para (a)(iii). The reference to land held on trust and occupied by beneficiaries reflects the co-ownership and successive ownership structures that we considered in Chapters 18 and 22.

2.1.2 The Financial Services and Markets Act 2000 regulatory framework

One of the FSA's statutory objectives is *'the protection of consumers'*.[8] In pursuing that objective, the FSA's role reflects decentered regulation. The aspiration is that the borrower will be protected by the provision of advice and accurate information, in the light of the degree of risk associated with the borrowing and experience of the borrower, so that borrowers are better placed to make responsible borrowing decisions.[9]

The means by which the FSA is to achieve that objective is by the control of those who can conduct regulated mortgage business, and influence over the conduct of mortgage business by requiring compliance, through a range of disciplinary and enforcement powers, with published statements of principles exemplified through supporting codes of conduct and detailed rules.

A financial institution may not carry out regulated mortgage business unless it is authorized by the FSA, or is specifically exempt.[10] If it does so, it is guilty of a criminal offence[11] and the transaction itself is unenforceable, except to the extent that the court is satisfied that it is just and equitable to order enforcement.[12]

Any permission to carry out regulated mortgage business is subject to the statements of principle, codes of practice,[13] and rules that the FSA may make.[14] The statements, codes, and

---

[6] Equitable mortgages are not regulated under the Financial Services and Markets Act 2000: see Oldham, 'Mortgages' in *Land Law: Issues, Debates, Policy* (ed Tee, 2002, p 191).

[7] The business gross annual turnover must not exceed £1m.

[8] Financial Services and Markets Act 2000, s 2(2)(c).

[9] Ibid, s 5(2).

[10] Ibid, s 19. The FSA may also prohibit an employee or agent, who carries out regulated mortgage business on behalf of an authorized person, from so acting where that individual is not a 'fit or proper' person: see ibid, s 56. Acting in breach of a prohibition does not affect the enforceability of the transaction (s 20(1)), but is a criminal offence (s 56(4)), and a breach of statutory duty (s 71).

[11] Ibid, s 23.

[12] See ibid, ss 26 and 28.

[13] Ibid, s 64.

[14] Ibid, s 138.

rules represent a three-tier strata of regulatory guidance. The statements of principle set out the overarching ethos governing the conduct of regulated mortgage business; the codes of practice provide examples of the types of activity that, on the one hand, comply with and, on the other, breach the relevant principles; but it is the rules that set out the detailed regulations that govern the conduct of mortgage business itself. In preparing the principles, codes, and rules, the FSA is required to consult with both the mortgage industry (e.g. the Council of Mortgage Lenders) and with bodies representing the interests of borrowers (e.g. the National Consumer Council).[15]

The breach of a statement of principle or a code of conduct does not give rise to a right to damages, nor does a breach affect the enforceability of any transaction, but the FSA may take disciplinary action.[16] A breach of the rules may, however, trigger an action for breach of statutory duty.[17]

The principles,[18] codes,[19] and rules are contained in the FSA Handbook.

2.1.3 Mortgage and home finance: the Mortgage Conduct of Business Sourcebook (MCOB)

The rules regulating mortgage business are set out in that part of the Handbook entitled the Mortgage Conduct of Business Sourcebook (MCOB).[20] The MCOB regime adopts a 'cradle to grave' approach, which governs the whole course of the borrower's relationship with his or her lender. There are rules governing the marketing of mortgage products[21] and the provision of information through all stages from the first visit of a potential borrower to a mortgage provider, through to the preapplication illustration of the available loan terms[22] and the mortgage offer itself,[23] with continuing requirements for information to be provided on the actual grant of the loan and periodically during the course of the mortgage term.[24] Further rules call upon the lender to lend responsibly in the light of a prospective borrower's ability to pay.[25] If the borrower should fall into arrears, there are rules that regulate how the mortgage provider should respond, at which we will look in the next chapter.[26] The rules are intended to meet the overarching statement of principles that call upon lenders 'to pay due

---

[15] Ibid, ss 8–10.

[16] Ibid, ss 64(8) and 66.

[17] Ibid, s 150.

[18] See FSA Handbook, Principles for Business (PRIN), available online at http://fsahandbook.info/FSA/html/handbook/PRIN; FSA Handbook, The Statement of Principles for Approved Persons (APER 2), available online at http://fsahandbook.info/FSA/html/handbook/APER/2.

[19] FSA Handbook, Code of Practice for Approved Persons: General (APER 3), available online at http://fsahandbook.info/FSA/html/handbook/APER/3.

[20] FSA Handbook, Mortgages and Home Finance: Conduct of Business Sourcebook (MCOB), available online at http://fsahandbook.info/FSA/html/handbook/MCOB.

[21] FSA Handbook, Financial Promotion of Qualifying Credit and of Home Reversion Plans (MCOB 3), available online at http://fsahandbook.info/FSA/html/handbook/MCOB/3.

[22] FSA Handbook, Pre-application Disclosure (MCOB 5), available online at http://fsahandbook.info/FSA/html/handbook/MCOB/5.

[23] FSA Handbook, Disclosure at the Offer Stage (MCOB 6), available online at http://fsahandbook.info/FSA/html/handbook/MCOB/6.

[24] FSA Handbook, Disclosure at Start of Contract and After Sale (MCOB 7), available online at http://fsahandbook.info/FSA/html/handbook/MCOB/7.

[25] FSA Handbook, Responsible Lending, and Responsible Financing of Home Purchase Plans (MCOB 11), available online at http://fsahandbook.info/FSA/html/handbook/MCOB/11.

[26] FSA Handbook, Arrears and Repossessions: Regulated Mortgage Contracts and Home Purchase Plans (MCOB 13), available online at http://fsahandbook.info/FSA/html/handbook/MCOB/13.

regard to the interests of its customers and treat them fairly,[27] *'to pay due regard to the information needs of its clients, and communicate information to them in a way which is clear, fair and not misleading'*,[28] and to *'take reasonable care to ensure the suitability of its advice and discretionary decisions for any customer who is entitled to rely upon its judgment'*.[29]

The twin principles of responsible lending and responsible borrowing are enshrined within a lender's duty to provide information to the borrower in an intelligible and pre-scribed form, which is intended to enable borrowers to compare different mortgage products and make informed choices about which particular mortgage terms will best suit their circumstances. Perhaps the most significant piece of information is the preapplication illustration, known as the 'Key Facts illustration', which must be updated when the mortgage offer is made. This illustration must be in the prescribed form, to facilitate comparison between different mortgage products, which includes details of (inter alia) the type of mortgage, the overall cost of the mortgage, the monthly repayments, any arrangement fee, and any charges made for early repayment.[30]

Further rules detail how the annual percentage rate (APR) of interest is to be calculated,[31] and provide that a borrower must be given time to consider the Key Facts illustration and the mortgage offer.[32] The rules also stipulate that any charges imposed—for example, rates of interest or in the event of default or early repayment—must not be excessive.[33]

The call for clear and consistent information is laudable, but there is the danger that its presentation may become a mere formulaic process.[34] The information that is provided is largely confined to the financial implications of the mortgage and does not address the other mortgage terms: for example, as to lender's powers of enforcement, beyond the bald, but familiar, advertising warning that the borrower may lose his or her home if he or she fails to keep up with mortgage payments. The fact that mortgage repayments may increase during the mortgage term as interest rates rise, or as fixed interest rate periods run their course, is also an ever-present risk, the implications of which borrowers often fail to appreciate fully.

There is a fine line between the giving of information and the provision of advice. The rules do require the lender to inform the borrower, whether it is providing information or advice, but borrowers—particularly those who lack experience in financial matters—may not appreciate the distinction.[35] The financial education of borrowers is a policy aim, and there is a host of leaflets from the Office of Fair Trading and the FSA to provide guidance, but these are loose measures that depend upon the willingness and ability of vulnerable borrowers to use them effectively. Evidence from both the FSA[36] and Citizens

---

[27] Principle 6.

[28] Principle 7.

[29] Principle 9.

[30] FSA Handbook (MCOB 5).

[31] FSA Handbook, Annual Percentage Rate (MCOB 10), available online at http://fsahandbook.info/FSA/html/handbook/MCOB/10.

[32] FSA Handbook, '2.4 High pressure sales: regulated mortgage contracts and home reversion plans', Conduct of Business Standards: General (MCOB 2), available online at http://fsahandbook.info/FSA/html/handbook/MCOB/2/4.

[33] FSA Handbook, Arrear and Repossessions: Regulated Mortgage Contracts and Home Purchase Plans (MCOB 12), available online at http://fsahandbook.info/FSA/html/handbook/MCOB/12.

[34] There is a view that borrowers receive too much information to assimilate: see Council of Mortgage Lenders, *Response to Consumer Law Review* (2008, available online at http://www.cml.org.uk).

[35] FSA Handbook, '4.4 Initial Disclosure Requirements', Advising and Selling Standards (MCOB 4), available online at http://fsahandbook.info/FSA/html/handbook/MCOB/4/4.

[36] FSA, *Mortgage Effectiveness Review 2006* and *Mortgage Effectiveness Review 2008*, available online at http://www.fsa.gov.uk.

Advice[37] suggests that certain borrowers—particularly those in the sub-prime market—do not shop around and are unable to assess their financial position to make viable lending choices. They find it difficult to distinguish between information and advice, and tend to rely upon brokers—not always the best source of impartial and objective advice. Thus, although the borrower is provided with information, the rules are short on any process to try to bring home to the borrower the implications of that information to his or her particular circumstances. The borrower is expected to borrow responsibly, but may simply not be in a position to make responsible choices.

Lenders *'must be able to show that before deciding to enter into, or making a further advance on, a regulated mortgage contract, or home purchase plan, account was taken of the customer's ability to repay'*.[38] This assessment is to be made against the lender's written policy, which is to look primarily to the level of borrower's actual or reasonably anticipated income. This assessment is made from the lender's perspective; it does not provide for a judgment that is communicated to, or which may assist, the borrower in making his or her decision to borrow. Patently, lenders have failed to lend responsibly. Lenders have been prepared to offer mortgages of more than 100 per cent, and have used higher and higher multiplies of borrower's income to set lending ceilings. Lenders have also been lax in checking the borrowers' ability to pay and too keen to accept self-certification.[39] Lenders stand accused of failing to bring home to borrowers the risks and consequences of default associated with their borrowing, when evidence suggest that many borrowers—particularly within the sub-prime market—do not understand the mortgage basics of periodic repayments and the possibility of repossession if those payments are not met.[40] The credit crunch has brought some sanity back into the market, but that is likely to be too late for many borrowers.[41]

2.1.4 Financial Service Ombudsman

Redress through the courts is not the only route for an aggrieved borrower. The FSA Handbook requires an authorized lender to have in place a complaints-handling process that complies with the requirements set out in the Handbook.[42] A borrower's first step is thus to resolve his or her complaint directly with the lender. His or her next step may then be to approach the Financial Services Ombudsman (FSO), which is established under Pt XVI of the FSMA 2000 as a body that is independent of the FSA, to provide an alternative means of resolving disputes.[43]

The FSO may consider complaints made by borrowers and may call upon the lender to provide the requisite information to enable them to do so.[44] The FSO may make an award based upon what is fair, just, and reasonable, rather than being bound to apply the strict rules.[45] That award is binding upon the lender and enforceable as such in the same way as

[37] Citizens Advice, *Set Up to Fail: CAB Clients' Experience and Secured Loan Arrears Problems* (2007, available online at http://www.citizensadvice.org.uk).

[38] FSA Handbook, '11.3.1 Customer's ability to pay' (MCOB 11).

[39] See findings of Citizen Advice (2007).

[40] Ibid.

[41] The number of repossessions actions is increasing dramatically to 1990 levels: see ibid.

[42] FSA Handbook, Dispute Resolution: Complaints (DISP), available online at http://fsahandbook.info/FSA/html/handbook/DISP.

[43] See generally Morris and James, 'The Financial Ombudsman Service: A Brave New World in "Ombudsmanry"' [2002] PL 640; Ferran, 'Dispute Resolution Mechanisms in the UK Financial Sector' [2002] CJQ 135.

[44] Financial Services and Markets Act 2000, s 232.

[45] Ibid, s 229.

a court judgment. The borrower, however, may continue to pursue his or her claim—for example, through the court—if he or she is not satisfied with the award.

The FSO provides a practical route through which to resolve relatively small and straight-forward disputes. It has the advantage of being free at the point of entry and, with speedier and less formal methods of working, more accessible to many borrowers. The mis-selling of endowment mortgages has been a major source of complaints to the FSO.[46] Other common complaints relate to charges for default and early redemption, and, given the growing complexity of mortgage products, the FSO has also noted an increase in complaints relating to the meaning and explanation of mortgage terms.[47]

2.2 CONSUMER CREDIT ACT 1974 (AS AMENDED)

The CCA 1974 was passed following the recommendations of the Crowther Committee, which, in 1971, undertook a comprehensive review of consumer credit.[48] The Act brought the regulation of most different forms of credit available to individuals (including credit cards, hire purchase, and unsecured and secured loans) under one legislative umbrella. Mortgages for the purchase of a home were not the primary target, because they were thought to be already adequately protected. Mortgages to secure loans for other purposes (for example, to consolidate debts or to fund other consumption) could fall within the Act's remit, but a £25,000 ceiling on loans progressively excluded more and more mortgages from regulation.

The rapid growth and changing face of the consumer credit market in the following years led to a review of consumer credit and, in 2003, the government issued a White Paper, *Fair, Clear and Competitive: the Consumer Credit Market in the 21st Century*,[49] which resulted in the Consumer Credit Act 2006 (CCA 2006). This Act substantially amends the 1974 Act, so as to bring many more mortgages over land within its control.

2.2.1 Mortgages within the Consumer Credit Act 1974 (as amended)

The CCA 1974 (as amended) only protects individual borrowers.[50] It does not apply to companies, although loans for business purposes are subject to regulation where the business is carried on by a sole trader, or where a partnership comprises less than three partners, and the loan does not exceed £25,000.[51] The £25,000 limit no longer applies to other loans entered into after April 2008.[52]

---

[46] They accounted for 49 per cent of complaints made to the FSO in the year 2006–07. Complaints arose because an endowment mortgage was an inappropriate product for the particular borrower to whom they were sold, or because the lender inaccurately projected the sum that would be payable on the maturity of policy, which was intended to pay off the capital sum, so that a shortfall resulted that the borrower had to find from his or her own resources.

[47] See FSO, *Annual Review 2006/07*, available online at http://www.financial-ombudsman.org.uk/publications/ar07/index.html.

[48] Cmnd 4596, 1971.

[49] Cm 6040, 2003.

[50] Consumer Credit Act 1974 (as amended), s 8.

[51] Ibid, s 16B. It was intended that buy-to-let mortgages would be excluded from regulation under the 1974 Act because of this limitation, but such mortgages may not escape regulation where the borrower is not conducting a business.

[52] Second or equitable mortgages in excess of £25,000 were unregulated prior to April 2008.

Regulated mortgage contracts, which are regulated by the FSA, are excluded from dual regulation under the 1974 Act.[53] It is thus the second mortgage market that is largely the subject of regulation, unless made to a lender that is expressly exempt from control: for example, local authorities, building societies regulated by the Building Societies Act 1986, or lenders licensed under the Banking Act 1987.[54]

It is possible for a borrower who qualifies as a 'high net worth debtor' to opt out of protection under the 1974 Act.[55] The mortgage must contain a statement to that effect made by the borrower and must be accompanied by a statement of high net worth—that is, that the debtor had an income in the previous year of not less than £150,000 and/or net assets of not less than £500,000.[56] The reasoning behind this provision is the belief that such borrowers should be able to look after themselves.

Even so, the controls over unfair terms and practices contained in ss 140A–140C (see below) apply to loans to exempt lenders, high net worth borrowers, and business loans over £25,000. Sections 140A–140C also apply where sums are outstanding under a consumer credit agreement entered into before 6 April 2007, when the provisions came into force. But regulated mortgage contracts that are subject to separate regulation under the FSMA 2000 are not caught by ss 140A–140C.[57]

Brown has created a useful flow diagram (Figure 27) to demonstrate how to ascertain whether or not a particular mortgage falls within the 1974 Act.[58]

The target for control under the 1974 Act over the mortgage market is generally secondary lenders who are prepared to lend to borrowers on the security of a second mortgage. The purpose of the loan is generally not to fund a house purchase, which is likely to be secured by a first legal mortgage and thus subject to regulation under the 2000 Act; the purpose of the loan is more likely to be to consolidate the borrower's debts—for example, on credit cards, an overdraft, and hire purchase agreements—by repaying these debts with a single loan secured by a second mortgage over the borrower's home. Alternatively, the loan may be to fund other expenditure that is of such magnitude that the lender is not prepared to lend on an unsecured basis. Such borrowing is often unattractive to high street banks and building societies, and is made instead by secondary lenders, which charge higher rates of interest with more onerous default charges often with repayment over a short term.

2.2.2 The Consumer Credit Act 1974 (as amended) regulatory framework

The government's White Paper, *Fair Clear and Competitive*, set out its hope to '*encourage an open and fair credit market where consumers can make fully informed decisions and business can compete aggressively on a fair and even basis*'.[59] Here, again, we see the rhetoric of decentered regulation, and responsible lending and responsible borrowing. This responsibility is to be encouraged by a transparent market in which borrowers are provided with clear and consistent information upon which they can exercise choice and can make sensible financial

---

[53] Consumer Credit Act 1974 (as amended), s 16(6C). First mortgages entered into before 31 October 2004 are not regulated mortgage contracts, but will be exempt from regulation under the 1974 Act where they are made by a building society regulated by the Building Societies Act 1986 or where the lender is licensed under the Banking Act 1987.

[54] Ibid, s 16(1).

[55] Ibid, s 16A.

[56] Consumer Credit (Exempt Agreements) Order 2007, SI 2007/1168.

[57] Consumer Credit Act 1974 (as amended), s 140A(5).

[58] Brown, 'The Consumer Credit Act 2006: Real Additional Mortgagor Protection?' [2007] Conv 325.

[59] Cm 6040, 2003, [1.69].

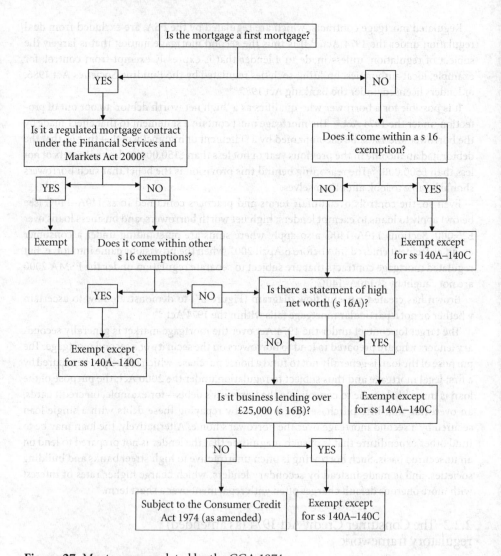

Figure 27 Mortgages regulated by the CCA 1974

From *The Conveyancer*. S Brown: 'The Consumer Credit Act 2006: Real Additional Mortgager Protection', Conv 325 (2007) by permission of Sweet & Maxwell.

decisions. Fairness in the market is to be achieved by the control of those who can lend through a licensing and regulatory system operated by the Office of Fair Trading (OFT), and through legislation that controls market practices and the transaction itself, under the supervision of both the OFT and the court.

Lenders must be licensed by the OFT in order to make a regulated consumer credit agreement and to take a mortgage to secure any such agreement.[60] An unlicensed lender commits a criminal offence[61] and any mortgage entered into by an unlicensed lender is only enforceable by order of the OFT.[62] The OFT also has power to suspend or revoke a

---

60 Consumer Credit Act 1974 (as amended), Pt III.
61 Ibid, s 36.
62 Ibid, s 40(1).

licence,[63] and to impose conditions upon a licensee as to the conduct of its business.[64] To that end, the OFT is granted investigative powers so that it can monitor the business of licensed lenders.[65]

There is no equivalent to the MBOC Sourcebook to govern mortgages under the CCA 1974, but the OFT may issue regulations and guidance to its licensed lenders.[66] The OFT is also empowered to produce codes of conduct to promote 'good practice in the carrying out of activities which may affect the economic interests of consumers in the United Kingdom'.[67] It has been accused of failing to provide adequate, comprehensive, and current guidance, and to put in place an effective monitoring and compliance strategy.[68] There is some evidence that the OFT is acting to rectify this omission in its General Guidance on Fitness of Licensed Lenders, which was updated in January 2008.[69] In this guidance, the OFT announced that, in assessing a lender's fitness, it will require a credit risk profile, where the lender is engaged in sub-prime lending, and will take into consideration any breach of the FSA rules and principles—in particular, irresponsible lending. Finally, and not before time, the OFT has announced plans to update its guidelines on Non-status Lending. The current guidelines are now over a decade old.[70]

Loan agreements and supporting mortgages falling within the terms of the CCA1974 are regulated by detailed and comprehensive rules covering the whole process, from advertisement, through creation of the agreement and mortgage, to their enforcement in the event of default. This cradle-to-grave approach is similar to, but far more stringent than, the requirements governing regulated mortgage contracts under the FSMA 2000. Furthermore, the consequences of non-compliance are more far-reaching.

The CCA 1974 prescribes the information that must be provided to the borrower prior to the entry into the agreement and mortgage,[71] during the term,[72] and in the event of any default.[73] The form and execution of the agreement,[74] and the supporting mortgage,[75] must also comply with the requirements of the Act. In addition, the process of completing the loan agreement and supporting mortgage is regulated: in particular, the borrower must be supplied with a copy of the mortgage and given a cooling-off period of not less than seven days in which to consider his or her position before he or she can be asked to execute the mortgage, unless the mortgage is to secure bridging finance or a loan for the purchase of land.[76]

The consequence of a failure to provide the requisite information, or to comply with the rules governing the form and execution of this documentation, is that the agreement and mortgage are deemed incorrectly executed, and cannot be enforced except by order of

---

[63] Ibid, s 32.

[64] Ibid, ss 33A–33E.

[65] See ibid, ss 36B–36F and Pt XI generally.

[66] Ibid, ss 26, 33A–33E.

[67] Enterpise Act 2002, s 8.

[68] Citizens Advice (2007).

[69] OFT 969 (2008).

[70] OFT 192 (1997). In the meantime, the OFT's general licensing guidelines provide some very general guidance on irresponsible and non-status lending.

[71] Consumer Credit Act 1974 (as amended), s 55.

[72] Ibid, ss 77, 77A, and 78.

[73] Ibid, ss 76, 86B–86E, 87, and 88.

[74] Ibid, s 60.

[75] Ibid, s 105.

[76] See ibid, ss 58 and 61. See also ss 62, 64, 67, and 68, in relation to the execution of the credit agreement.

the court.[77] The court is given a wide discretion, in the light of the prejudice caused to the borrower and the culpability of the lender, whether or not to enforce the agreement or mortgage, and, if enforcement is ordered, to impose conditions and amend or vary the terms of the agreement or mortgage.[78]

A lender also cannot enforce a mortgage until it has given notice of default,[79] and, where the default is a failure to pay the sums due under the mortgage, the lender must give notice of those arrears.[80] The lender also has no right to charge interest or any default sum until the requisite notices have been given.[81]

The CCA 2006 has also opened up the FSO complaints procedure to borrowers in dispute with their lenders under a mortgage regulated by the CCA 1974.[82]

2.2.3 The unfair credit relationship

Sections 137–140 of the CCA 1974 empowered the court to reopen consumer credit agreements where they found that the payment terms were 'grossly exorbitant', or where the agreement 'otherwise grossly contravene[d] ordinary principles of fair dealing'. These tests were notoriously difficult to satisfy[83] and the court's interpretation of them was criticized in the government's White Paper as being unduly restrictive. It came as no surprise, therefore, that ss 137–140 have been repealed by the CCA 2006, and new provisions enacted in their place that are far wider in their approach. The new provisions allow the court to consider not only the terms of the agreement, but also the lender's behaviour and practices throughout the term of the mortgage.

Consumer Credit Act 1974 (as amended), s 140A

Unfair relationships between creditors and debtors

(1) The court may make an order under section 140B in connection with a credit agreement if it determines that the relationship between the creditor and the debtor arising out of the agreement (or the agreement taken with any related agreement) is unfair to the debtor because of one or more of the following—

    (a) any of the terms of the agreement or of any related agreement;

    (b) the way in which the creditor has exercised or enforced any of his rights under the agreement or any related agreement;

    (c) any other thing done (or not done) by, or on behalf of, the creditor (either before or after the making of the agreement or any related agreement).

(2) In deciding whether to make a determination under this section the court shall have regard to all matters it thinks relevant (including matters relating to the creditor and matters relating to the debtor).

---

[77] See ibid, ss 65, 92, 105, and 126.
[78] See ibid, ss 127, 135, and 136.
[79] Ibid, s 87.
[80] Ibid, ss 88B or 88C, and 86D(3).
[81] Ibid, s 86D(4).
[82] Consumer Credit Act 2006, ss 59–61. See above.
[83] See, e.g., *A Ketley Ltd v Scott* [1980] CCLR 37; *Davies v Direct Loans* [1986] 1 WLR 823; *Paragon Finance plc v Nash* [2002] 1 WLR 685.

The redress that the court can order is also far-ranging and may extend to ordering the repayment of any sums paid by the debtor, the alteration of the terms of the mortgage, or the setting aside, either in whole or in part, of any duty imposed upon the borrower by the terms of the loan or mortgage.[84]

The difficulty with the new s 140A test is that, until the courts consider its interpretation, there is no guidance on just how they will do so. The government refused to include any guidelines in the legislation, preferring instead to give the courts a free rein.

Brown suggests that some guidance may be obtained from the Unfair Terms in Consumer Contracts Regulations 1999[85] (which we consider in section 4.1.3 below) and she also suggests that unexpected costs—for example, default charges—or the taking advantage of a borrower's disadvantageous position, or irresponsible lending, could be particular targets. Guidance on the fairness of terms and practices issued by the OFT, as well as the standards of conduct set by the MCOB Sourcebook, may also prove influential. Whatever 'fairness' turns out to mean, it is expected that it goes beyond the limited controls provided by the existing equitable control of mortgage terms that we will be examining below.

Brown, 'The Consumer Credit Act 2006: Real Additional Mortgagor Protection?'
[2007] Conv 316, 333–4

[...R]eliance in more stringent moral principles is unlikely to be required for a mortgage to come within the purview of ss140A-B. Abuse of bargaining power, however is likely to be significant; *DGFT v First National Bank* and the *Paragon Finance* cases suggest the relative bargaining position of the parties will be seen as highly relevant. This is not contrary to the Government's own approach: empowerment of the consumer, through a transparent market and protection against unfair practices (an important part of the policy behind the White Paper) inevitably involves moving towards some form of equality of bargaining power. As has been indicated, good faith is also likely to be an important factor. Further than that, any unwanted surprise, when obviously to the disadvantage of the borrower may be sufficient to show that there was an unfair credit relationship. The courts may even consider irresponsibility as to the borrower's circumstances as relevant – a matter considered as a possible factor in the White paper. Indeed irresponsible lending is an issue the office of fair trading can take into account when considering an applicant's fitness for a consumer credit licence. Whether the court goes this far, however, remains to be seen.

The provisions of the new s 140A could provide a powerful mechanism by which the courts can control both the content of mortgages falling within the 1974 Act and the conduct of lenders in enforcing such mortgages. We wait to see how they will exercise this control.

3 CREATION OF THE MORTGAGE

Freedom of contract is a fundamental principle governing loan contracts as much as any other contract. We will see, in the next section, the legal controls over the parties' freedom to agree the substantive content of their loan terms and any mortgage taken to secure

---

[84] Consumer Credit Act 1974 (as amended), s 140B(1).
[85] SI 1999/2083.

repayment of that loan. In this section, we are concerned with the process by which those terms are agreed. The focus here is with the quality of the parties' consent to contractual terms: in particular, the borrower's ability to enter freely into the loan without the lender abusing a dominant position.

We will concentrate in section 3.3 on the role that the doctrine of undue influence has played in collateral mortgages of the family home to secure a business loan. There are, however, other factors that can affect the procedural fairness of a loan, which we will briefly survey in section 3.1, before considering the conceptual basis that underlies these controls in section 3.2.

3.1 FACTORS GOVERNING PROCEDURAL FAIRNESS

The principal factors that may affect the procedural fairness of a mortgage will be familiar to any student of contract law and thus it is proposed to outline their essential features only briefly. The factors are:

- *non est factum*;
- duress;
- undue influence;
- misrepresentation;
- unconscionable bargain.

Non est factum and duress find their roots in the common law, and, accordingly, render the contract void from the outset. Undue influence and unconscionable bargain are equitable doctrines that entitle the wronged party to elect to rescind the transaction. The court may also award equitable compensation or set aside a transaction on terms where full restitution is not possible, because, for example, some benefit has been received by the victim. The remedies for misrepresentation will depend upon the intention with which the misrepresentation is formulated, and may result in a claim to rescind the transaction or to damages, either in the tort of deceit, where the misrepresentation is fraudulent, or in negligence or under statute, where the misrepresentation is negligent or innocent.

3.1.1 *Non est factum*

Where a party has made a fundamental mistake as to the character and effect of the obligations imposed by the mortgage, he or she may plead *non est factum*, provided that the mistake was no fault of his or her own.[86] The doctrine does not require any proof of fraud or wrongdoing, because its basis lies in the absence of the victim's consent. It was originally applied where a party could not read, because he or she was blind or illiterate, but has since been extended to wider circumstances in which a party's lack of comprehension is due to other reasons (e.g. age, illness, limited education or understanding). Nevertheless, the doctrine has very limited application, because the victim must prove that he or she took due care in understanding the nature and effect of the mortgage, for example by asking for an explanation of its effect. A failure to read the mortgage is plainly insufficient.

---

[86] See *Saunders v Anglia Building Society*, sub nom *Gallie v Lee* [1971] AC 1004.

3.1.2 Duress

A party may claim duress where he or she has been coerced or pressurized into a transaction. Originally, the coercion had to take the form of physical threats to the victim[87] or to his or her property,[88] but the doctrine has been expanded to admit more subtle means of pressure, including the illegitimate use of economic pressure: for example, threats to breach a contractual obligation.[89] The difficulty is to distinguish the use of sharp, but legitimate, negotiating tactics in the cut and thrust of commercial life from the illegitimate threats that may constitute economic duress.[90] Again, the rationale for intervention on the grounds of duress is that the victim has not freely consented to the transaction.

The Universe Sentinel [1983] 1 AC 366, HL

Lord Scarman

At 400

There must be pressure, the practical effect of which is compulsion or absence of choice. Compulsion is variously described in the authorities as coercion or the vitiation of consent. The classic case of duress is, however, not the lack of will to submit but the victim's intentional submission arising from the realisation that there is no other practical choice open to him.

3.1.3 Undue influence

A comprehensive definition of undue influence is elusive.[91] Lord Clyde observed in *Royal Bank of Scotland v Etridge*[92] that '[i]t is something which can be more easily recognised when found than exhaustively analysed in the abstract'. At its core is the use of improper pressure or influence, which effectively deprives a party of his or her free and independent will. The victim may perfectly understand his or her actions, but, nevertheless, his or her judgment may have been overborne by the improper influence of another.

Undue influence takes one of two broad forms: firstly, actual undue influence arises where overt acts exert improper pressure in a similar manner to duress, to which the concept has been compared; secondly, undue influence may be presumed to exist from the relationship between two parties, where one has used his or her dominant position to exploit the weaker party. Certain types of relationship are accepted, in themselves, as giving rise to a presumption of undue influence without any further evidence that the trust inherent in these relationships has been abused. These relationships include solicitor and client, doctor and patient,

---

[87] *Barton v Armstrong* [1976] AC 104.

[88] *Astley v Reynolds* (1731) 2 Str 915.

[89] See, e.g., *Pao On v Lau Yiu Long* [1980] AC 614; *DSDN Subsea Ltd v Petroleum Geo-services ASA* [2000] BLR 1; *Huyton SA v Peter Cremer & Co* [1998] All ER 494; or, in the context of a mortgage, *Jones v Morgan* [2001] EWCA Civ 995.

[90] Economic duress is distinguishable from other forms of duress in that: firstly, it renders the contract voidable not void; and secondly, to be actionable, the duress must be the main reason that the victim acted as he or she did.

[91] In *Allcard v Skinner* (1887) 36 Ch D 145, 183, Lindley LJ commented that '*no court had ever attempted to define undue influence*'.

[92] [2002] 2 AC 773, [92].

religious leader and follower, parent and child. This list is not exhaustive and a presumption of undue influence may also arise where trust and confidence is established in the context of a particular relationship.

Lord Nicholls in *Etridge* sought to pin down the nature of this relational form of undue influence.

Royal Bank of Scotland v Etridge [2002] 2 AC 773, HL

Lord Nicholls

At [10]–[11]

The law has long recognised the need to prevent abuse of influence in these "relationship" cases despite the absence of evidence of overt acts of persuasive conduct. The types of relationship, such as parent and child, in which this principle falls to be applied cannot be listed exhaustively. Relationships are infinitely various. Sir Guenter Treitel QC has rightly noted that the question is whether one party has reposed sufficient trust and confidence in the other, rather than whether the relationship between the parties belongs to a particular type: see Treitel, *The Law of Contract*, 10th ed (1999), pp 380–381. For example, the relation of banker and customer will not normally meet this criterion, but exceptionally it may: see *National Westminster Bank plc v Morgan* [1985] AC 686, 707–709.

Even this test is not comprehensive. The principle is not confined to cases of abuse of trust and confidence. It also includes, for instance, cases where a vulnerable person has been exploited. Indeed, there is no single touchstone for determining whether the principle is applicable. Several expressions have been used in an endeavour to encapsulate the essence: trust and confidence, reliance, dependence or vulnerability on the one hand and ascendancy, domination or control on the other. None of these descriptions is perfect. None is all embracing. Each has its proper place.

As a result of this relationship of trust and confidence between the parties, the dominant party is said to owe a special duty to deal fairly with the other—a duty that has been described as 'fiduciary'.[93]

Actual undue influence is actionable as a legal wrong.[94] The relational form of undue influence may give rise, in the light of the nature of the transaction that is being impugned, to a factual presumption of undue influence, which shifts the burden of proof to the dominant party to demonstrate that he or she dealt fairly with the weaker party, who was thus able to exercise his or her own judgment.

3.1.4 Misrepresentation

It is not uncommon for a party to try to persuade another party to contract by misrepresenting the facts surrounding the transaction. For example, in *Barclays Bank plc v O'Brien*,[95] Mr O'Brien persuaded his wife to mortgage her interest in the family home to secure a loan made to his business by misrepresenting the amount of the debt that was secured by the mortgage. An actionable misrepresentation is a material misrepresentation of existing fact,

---

[93] Ibid, at [104], *per* Lord Hobhouse.
[94] *CIBC v Pitt* [1994] 1 AC 200.
[95] [1994] 1 AC 180.

rather than of opinion or future intention, which induces a party to enter into the contract. Misrepresentation is often linked with undue influence in the common scenario that occurred in *O'Brien*, which we will be examining in more detail in section 3.3 below. In this situation, however, the House of Lords in *Etridge* did point out that, in a husband's forecast of his business fortunes, a '*degree of hyperbole may only be natural*' and should not too readily be treated 'as misstatements'.[96]

3.1.5 Unconsionable bargain

Equity will provide redress where one party has abused the strength of his or her relative position to impose unacceptable terms upon the other party, who is in a position of relative weakness or disadvantage. The doctrine seeks to protect the weak or disadvantaged from those who would use their superior position unscrupulously.

In the context of a security transaction, this principle may be established by proof that:

- the borrower is at a serious disadvantage because of some particular weakness or disability;
- the borrower has been unconscionably exploited by the lender because of that disadvantage; and
- a mortgage has resulted on terms that are oppressive.

The doctrine is based upon the relative strengths of the parties to the mortgage and the fact that the dominant party has acted reprehensibly in taking advantage of that imbalance. The weaker party must establish that he or she was in a position of special disadvantage vis-à-vis the dominant party, and that his or her vulnerability was evident to the dominant party, so that the court is able to infer that the resulting transaction was procured by the abuse of that superior position. The balance of proof then shifts to the dominant party to establish, if he or she can, that he or she did not take advantage of that superior position and that the resulting mortgage, although onerous, did not result from any abuse.[97] The relative positions of the parties, the conduct of their negotiations, the improper use of influence or power, and the lack of information or absence of real choice are all relevant factors. The focus is upon the procedural, rather than the substantive, nature of the transaction, although oppressive terms may provide evidence that demonstrates the unconscionability of the process.[98]

The Court of Appeal considered the operation of the doctrine in the following case.

Alec Lobb Garages Ltd v Total Oil (GB) Ltd [1885] 1 WLR 173, CA

Lord Dhillon

At 182

The whole emphasis is on extortion, or undue advantage taken of weakness, an unconscientious use of the power arising out of the inequality of the parties' circumstances, and on

---

[96] [2002] 2 AC 773, [32], *per* Lord Nicholls.
[97] *Louth v Diprose* (1992) 175 CLR 621.
[98] *Hart v O'Connor* [1985] AC 1000, 1018.

unconscientious use of power which the Court might in certain circumstances be entitled to infer from a particular—and in these days notorious—relationship unless the contract is proved to have been in fact fair, just and reasonable. Nothing leads me to suppose that the course of the development of the law over the last 100 years has been such that the emphasis on unconscionable conduct or unconscientious use of power has gone and relief will now be granted in equity in a case such as the present if there has been unequal bargaining power, even if the stronger has not used his strength unconscionably. I agree with the judgment of Browne-Wilkinson J. in *Multiservice Bookbinding Ltd. v. Marden* (1979) Ch. 84 which sets out that to establish that a term is unfair and unconscionable it is not enough to show that it is, objectively, unreasonable [...] Inequality of bargaining power must anyhow be a relative concept. It is seldom in any negotiation that the bargaining powers of the parties are absolutely equal. Any individual wanting to borrow money from a bank, building society or other financial institution in order to pay his liabilities or buy some property he urgently wants to acquire will have virtually no bargaining power; he will have to take or leave the terms offered to him. So, with house property in a seller's market, the purchaser will not have equal bargaining power with the vendor [...] The Courts would only interfere in exceptional cases where as a matter of common fairness it was not right that the strong should be allowed to push the weak to the wall. The concepts of unconscionable conduct and of the exercise by the stronger of coercive power are thus brought in [...]

There are close links between relational undue influence and unconscionable bargains, and the same facts can give rise to an action based upon both doctrines. Indeed, some have argued that undue influence should be subsumed within a wider doctrine of unconscionability.[99] The English courts have preferred the undue influence route, but in other jurisdictions, the courts have applied unconscionable bargains. For example, in the Australian case of *Commonwealth Bank of Australia Ltd v Amadio*,[100] the doctrine was employed to set aside a mortgage granted by elderly Italian immigrants, with little command of English or experience of business, to secure a loan to their son's business. They believed that the business was flourishing: a belief based upon their son's misrepresentations and the bank's practice of dishonouring only some of the son's cheques to create an appearance of solvency. They also believed that their liability was limited and they received no independent advice to cast a more realistic light on the transaction. In England, these facts would produce a clear claim of undue influence, but the case was pleaded and decided by the High Court of Australia on the grounds of unconscionable bargain—although the High Court criticized the pleadings and expressed a hope that such cases would, in future, be approached from the perspective of undue influence.[101]

There remain distinctions between undue influence and unconscionable bargains. Undue influence focuses upon the quality of consent of the weaker party, which is called into question by the nature of the relationship between the parties, whereas unconscionable bargain concentrates its attention upon the conduct of the dominant party. It is the exploitation of the relative weakness of one party, which is derived from some social or transactional disability, which merits the court's intervention.

---

[99] Capper (1998) 14 LQR 479.
[100] (1983) 151 CLR 447.
[101] See ibid, at 464, *per* Mason J.

3.2 THE CONCEPTUAL UNDERPINNINGS

There has been considerable debate surrounding the conceptual basis of these various vitiating factors: in particular, duress, undue influence, and unconscionable bargains. The main features of this debate are twofold: firstly, whether they are claimant-based, looking to the impaired consent of the victim, or defendant-based, looking to the exploitative nature of the defendant's conduct; secondly, there have been growing calls to assimilate the three grounds by looking to the underlying unconscionability of the defendant's use of their relative power.

Birks and Chin[102] have advocated a claimant-sided approach to undue influence that leads to a distinction between undue influence and unconscionable bargains. Undue influence looks to the vulnerability of the claimant's consent as a result of his or her dependence on the defendant, whilst unconscionable bargains is concerned with the defendant's exploitation of the claimant's weakness. We have already noted that, despite the obviously reprehensible conduct of duress and actual undue influence, the traditional conceptual foundations of these doctrines have been found in the suspect nature of the victim's apparent consent. Birks and Chin point out that presumed undue influence does not depend upon any conscious wrongdoing on behalf of the defendant, and that the presumption of influence may be rebutted by proof that the claimant did exercise his or her free and independent will.

Others have rejected this approach and have refocused the spotlight on the exploitative nature of the defendant's behaviour, thus drawing closer parallels with both duress and unconscionable bargains, which have resulted in calls for the assimilation of the three doctrines.[103] The common features of the doctrines have been identified as relational inequality (e.g. of bargaining power), transactional imbalance, and the defendant's unconscionable conduct, which, in the case of presumed undue influence, may be more passively imposed than overtly or intentionally exerted.[104] These features do not necessarily contribute equally, but rather form an evidentiary mix that combine in different measure according to the circumstances of the particular case.

Intriguing though these arguments are, the more practical policy imperatives that underpin the exercise of 'state-assisted rescission' of apparently binding obligations should not be overlooked.[105] This policy is particularly evident in the series of decisions on undue influence that have occupied the House of Lords in recent years, which seeks to balance the protection of the vulnerable surety against modern business lending practices. The House of Lords first expressed its opinion in *Barclays Bank plc v O'Brien*,[106] but some years later, developed and

---

[102] Birks and Chin, 'On the Nature of Undue Influence' in *Good Faith and Fault in Contract Law* (eds Beatson and Friedman, 1995, ch 3). See also Birks, 'Undue Influence as Wrongful Exploitation' (2004) 120 LQR 35.

[103] Bigwood, 'Undue Influence: Impaired Consent or Wicked Exploitation' (1996) 16 OJLS 503; Chen-Wishart, 'The *O'Brien* Principle and Substantive Unfairness' (1997) 56 CLJ 60; Chen-Wishart, 'Undue Influence: Beyond Impaired Consent and Wrongdoing Towards a Relational Analysis' in *Mapping the Law* (eds Burrows and Rogers, 2006, ch 11); Capper, 'Undue Influence and Unconscionability: A Rationalisation' (1998) 114 LQR 479; Deveney and Chandler, 'Unconscionability and the Taxonomy of Undue Influence' [2007] JBL 541.

[104] See Capper (1998) and Chen-Wishart (1997).

[105] Bigwood, 'Contracts by Unfair Advantage: From Exploitation to Transactional Neglect' (2005) 25 OJLS 65; Ferris; 'Why is the Law of Undue Influence So Hard to Understand and Apply?' in *Modern Studies in Property Law: Vol 4* (ed Cooke, 2007).

[106] [1994] 1 AC 180.

refined its views in *Royal Bank of Scotland v Etridge*.[107] These two decisions will dominate our consideration of the operation of undue influence in mortgage transactions.

3.3 UNDUE INFLUENCE AND MORTGAGES

In recent years, undue influence has frequently been raised as a defence to enforcement proceedings where a collateral mortgage has been granted over the family home to secure a loan made for the benefit of the husband's business. The loan is made to the husband, as borrower, but the wife's participation to create the mortgage is required where she is a legal or beneficial joint owner of the family home. The danger is that the wife's consent to the mortgage is questionable, because, in the husband's desire to finance his business, he may have misrepresented the amount of the secured liability or the risks of enforcement, or have unduly influenced his wife to mortgage her interest.

The trend was noted in *O'Brien*.[108]

Barclays Bank plc v O'Brien [1994] 1 AC 180, HL

Lord Browne-Wilkinson

At 188

The large number of cases of this type coming before the courts in recent years reflects the rapid changes in social attitudes and the distribution of wealth which have recently occurred. Wealth is now more widely spread. Moreover a high proportion of privately owned wealth is invested in the matrimonial home. Because of the recognition by society of the equality of the sexes, the majority of matrimonial homes are now in the joint names of both spouses. Therefore in order to raise finance for the business enterprises of one or other of the spouses, the jointly owned home has become a main source of security. The provision of such security requires the consent of both spouses.

In parallel with these financial developments, society's recognition of the equality of the sexes has led to a rejection of the concept that the wife is subservient to the husband in the management of the family's finances. A number of the authorities reflect an unwillingness in the court to perpetuate law based on this outmoded concept. Yet [...] although the concept of the ignorant wife leaving all financial decisions to the husband is outmoded, the practice does not yet coincide with the ideal. In a substantial proportion of marriages it is still the husband who has the business experience and the wife is willing to follow his advice without bringing a truly independent mind and will to bear on financial decisions. The number of recent cases in this field shows that in practice many wives are still subjected to, and yield to, undue influence by their husbands. Such wives can reasonably look to the law for some protection when their husbands have abused the trust and confidence reposed in them.

On the other hand, it is important to keep a sense of balance in approaching these cases. It is easy to allow sympathy for the wife who is threatened with the loss of her home at the suit of a rich bank to obscure an important public interest viz., the need to ensure that the wealth currently tied up in the matrimonial home does not become economically sterile. If

---

[107] [2002] 2 AC 773.
[108] See also *Royal Bank of Scotland v Etridge*, ibid, at 800–1, *per* Lord Nicholls.

the rights secured to wives by the law renders vulnerable loans granted on the security of matrimonial homes, institutions will be unwilling to accept such security, thereby reducing the flow of loan capital to business enterprises. It is therefore essential that a law designed to protect the vulnerable does not render the matrimonial home unacceptable as security to financial institutions.

The context is rather different from that commonly associated with undue influence where a donee has obtained a gift that the donor subsequently seeks to set aside, because his or her consent was obtained by undue influence. Here, it is the husband who, it is alleged, exerted undue influence to persuade his wife to grant a mortgage to the lender. There is no suggestion that the lender is guilty of undue influence, but, in *O'Brien*, the House of Lords decided that a lender who has actual or constructive notice of the risk of undue influence or misrepresentation by the husband will be bound by any right of the wife to set aside the mortgage against her interest in the home.

Barclays Bank plc v O'Brien [1994] 1 AC 180, HL

Lord Browne-Wilkinson

At 191

But in surety cases the decisive question is whether the claimant wife can set aside the transaction, not against the wrongdoing husband, but against the creditor bank. Of course, if the wrongdoing husband is acting as agent for the creditor bank in obtaining the surety from the wife, the creditor will be fixed with the wrongdoing of its own agent and the surety contract can be set aside as against the creditor. Apart from this, if the creditor bank has notice, actual or constructive, of the undue influence exercised by the husband (and consequentially of the wife's equity to set aside the transaction) the creditor will take subject to that equity and the wife can set aside the transaction against the creditor (albeit a purchaser for value) as well as against the husband: see *Bainbrigge v. Browne* (1881) 18 Ch.D. 188 and *Bank of Credit and Commerce International S.A. v. Aboody* [1990] 1 Q.B. 923, 973. Similarly, in cases such as the present where the wife has been induced to enter into the transaction by the husband's misrepresentation, her equity to set aside the transaction will be enforceable against the creditor if either the husband was acting as the creditor's agent or the creditor had actual or constructive notice.

It is unlikely that the husband is an agent of the lender and so it is the application of the concept of notice that has attracted the greatest attention. This application of notice must be contrasted with the doctrine of notice that we have considered in relation to the priority of proprietary interests in Chapter 15. Instead, what is in issue is the notice of a party to the mortgage (i.e. the lender) to the possibility that the wife's consent to the mortgage may have been obtained by improper means.

The distinction was highlighted in *Royal Bank of Scotland v Etridge*.[109]

---

[109] See also [38]–[43], *per* Lord Nicholls.

Royal Bank of Scotland v Etridge [2002] 2 AC 773, HL

Lord Scott

At [144]

The doctrine of notice is a doctrine that relates primarily and traditionally to the priority of competing property rights. [. . .] Banks and other lenders who take charges from surety wives are certainly purchasers of property rights. But they acquire their rights by grant from the surety wives themselves. The issue between the banks and the surety wives is not one of priority of competing interests. The issue is whether or not the surety wife is to be bound by her apparent consent to the grant of the security to the bank. If contractual consent has been procured by undue influence or misrepresentation for which a party to the contract is responsible, the other party, the victim, is entitled, subject to the usual defences of change of position, affirmation, delay etc, to avoid the contract. But the case is much more difficult if the undue influence has been exerted or the misrepresentation has been made not by the party with whom the victim has contracted, but by a third party. It is, in general, the objective manifestation of contractual consent that is critical. Deficiencies in the quality of consent to a contract by a contracting party, brought about by undue influence or misrepresentation by a third party, do not, in general, allow the victim to avoid the contract. But if the other contracting party had had actual knowledge of the undue influence or misrepresentation the victim would not, in my opinion, be held to the contract (see *Commission for the New Towns v Cooper (Great Britain) Ltd* [1995] Ch 259, 277–280 and *Banco Exterior Internacional SA v Thomas* [1997] 1 WLR 221, 229). But what if there had been no actual knowledge of the third party's undue influence or misrepresentation but merely knowledge of facts or circumstances that, if investigated, might have led to actual knowledge? In what circumstances does the law expect a contracting party to inquire into the reasons why the other party is entering into the contract or to go behind the other party's apparent agreement, objectively ascertained, to enter into the contract? These are the questions that Lord Browne-Wilkinson had to answer in *O'Brien*. They are contractual questions, not questions relating to competing property interests [. . .]

At [146]–[148]

In particular, it must be recognised that in the "bank v surety wife" cases the constructive notice that is sought to be attributed to the bank is not constructive notice of any pre-existing prior right or prior equity of the wife. The husband's impropriety, whether undue influence or misrepresentation, in procuring his wife to enter into a suretyship transaction with the bank would not entitle her to set it aside unless the bank had had notice of the impropriety. It is notice of the husband's impropriety that the bank must have, not notice of any prior rights of the wife. It is the notice that the bank has of the impropriety that creates the wife's right to set aside the transaction. The wife does not have any prior right or prior equity.

In a case where the financial arrangements with the bank had been negotiated by the husband, no part in the negotiations having been played by the wife, and where the arrangements required the wife to become surety for her husband's debts, the bank would, or should, have been aware of the vulnerability of the wife and of the risk that her agreement might be procured by undue influence or misrepresentation by the husband. In these circumstances the bank would be "put on inquiry", as Lord Browne-Wilkinson put it. But "on inquiry" about what? Not about the existence of undue influence, for how could any inquiry reasonably to be expected of a bank satisfy the bank that there was no undue influence? "On inquiry", in my opinion, as to whether the wife understood the nature and effect of the transaction she was entering into. This is not an "inquiry" in the traditional constructive notice sense. The bank would not have to carry out any investigation or to ask any questions about the reasons why the wife was agreeing to the transaction or about her relationship with her husband. The bank would not, unless it had notice of additional facts pointing to undue influence or misrepresentation, be on notice that undue influence or misrepresentation was to be presumed. It would simply be on notice of a risk of some such impropriety. What Lord Browne-Wilkinson had in mind was that the bank should be expected to take reasonable steps to satisfy itself that she understood the transaction she was entering into. If the bank did so, no longer could constructive notice of any impropriety by the husband in procuring his wife's consent be imputed to it. The original constructive notice would have been shed. If, on the other hand, a bank with notice of the risk of some such impropriety, failed to take the requisite reasonable steps, then, if it transpired that the wife's consent had been procured by the husband's undue influence or misrepresentation, constructive knowledge that that was so would be imputed to the bank and the wife would have the same remedies as she would have had if the bank had had actual knowledge of the impropriety.

Under Lord Browne-Wilkinson's scheme for the protection of vulnerable wives it is the bank's perception of the risk that the wife's consent may have been procured by the husband's misrepresentation or undue influence that is central. The risk must be viewed through the eyes of the bank. Some degree of risk can, usually, never be wholly eliminated. But it can be reduced to a point at which it becomes reasonable for the bank to rely on the apparent consent of the wife to enter into the transaction and to take no further steps to satisfy itself that she understood the transaction she was entering into.

To avoid notice of the risk that the wife's consent to the mortgage has not been freely given, the lender must take reasonable and adequate steps to satisfy itself that the wife understood the nature of the mortgage into which she was entering, and that she was doing so of her independent will.

Three distinct stages were identified in *Etridge* to determine whether or not a mortgage may be set aside on the ground of undue influence.

Royal Bank of Scotland v Etridge [2002] 2 AC 773, HL

Lord Hobhouse

At 819

It can be expressed by answering three questions: (1) Has the wife proved what is necessary for the court to be satisfied that the transaction was affected by the undue influence of the husband? (2) Was the lender put on inquiry? (3) If so, did the lender take reasonable steps to satisfy itself that there was no undue influence? It will be appreciated that unless the first question is answered in favour of the wife neither of the later questions arise. The wife has no defence and is liable. It will likewise be appreciated that the second and third questions arise from the fact that the wife is seeking to use the undue influence of her husband as a defence against the lender and therefore has to show that the lender should be affected by the equity—that it is unconscionable that the lender should enforce the secured contractual right against her.

3.3.1 The first stage: proof of undue influence

The wife must prove that she was unduly influenced by her husband: if there is no undue influence, there is no basis upon which she can set aside the mortgage against her interest in the home. Undue influence may be established either by proof of facts that demonstrate actual undue influence (e.g. threats of physical violence or psychological pressure), which left the wife unable to exercise her own judgment, or by producing evidence that will enable the court to infer that the wife's entry into the mortgage was obtained by the undue influence that her husband was presumed to have exerted. It is for the wife to prove either actual or presumed undue influence; upon establishing facts that raise a presumption of undue influence, however, the burden of proof shifts to the dominant party (i.e. the husband or the bank) to demonstrate that, in fact, the wife's participation was an exercise of her independent will.

These alternative ways of proving undue influence were characterized in *BCCI v Aboody*[110] as 'Class 1 actual undue influence' and 'Class 2 presumed undue influence', which could be inferred either through proof of a Class 2A relationship, when certain limited types of relationship (see above) were themselves sufficient to found the presumption, or in Class 2B, upon proof that the particular relationship was one of trust and confidence. Although the House of Lords in *O'Brien* adopted this classification, in *Etridge*, the House observed that the classification had led to an overly formulaic approach that had obscured the evidentiary role of presumed undue influence. Instead, the Lords reiterated that proof of undue influence was a question of fact, and articulated in more detailed and stringent terms when undue influence would be proved.[111]

Royal Bank of Scotland v Etridge [2002] 2 AC 773, HL

Lord Nicholls

At [13]–[14]

Whether a transaction was brought about by the exercise of undue influence is a question of fact. Here, as elsewhere, the general principle is that he who asserts a wrong has been committed must prove it. The burden of proving an allegation of undue influence rests upon the person who claims to have been wronged. This is the general rule. The evidence required to discharge the burden of proof depends on the nature of the alleged undue influence, the personality of the parties, their relationship, the extent to which the transaction cannot readily be accounted for by the ordinary motives of ordinary persons in that relationship, and all the circumstances of the case.

Proof that the complainant placed trust and confidence in the other party in relation to the management of the complainant's financial affairs, coupled with a transaction which calls for explanation, will normally be sufficient, failing satisfactory evidence to the contrary, to discharge the burden of proof. On proof of these two matters the stage is set for the court to infer that, in the absence of a satisfactory explanation, the transaction can only have been procured by undue influence. In other words, proof of these two facts is prima facie evidence that the defendant abused the influence he acquired in the parties' relationship. He preferred his own interests. He did not behave fairly to the other. So the evidential burden then shifts to him. It is for him to produce evidence to counter the inference which otherwise should be drawn [...]

---

[110] [1991] 1 QB 923.
[111] See also [2002] 2 AC 773, [882], *per* Lord Hobhouse.

At [16]–[19]

Generations of equity lawyers have conventionally described this situation as one in which a presumption of undue influence arises. This use of the term "presumption" is descriptive of a shift in the evidential onus on a question of fact. When a plaintiff succeeds by this route he does so because he has succeeded in establishing a case of undue influence. The court has drawn appropriate inferences of fact upon a balanced consideration of the whole of the evidence at the end of a trial in which the burden of proof rested upon the plaintiff. The use, in the course of the trial, of the forensic tool of a shift in the evidential burden of proof should not be permitted to obscure the overall position. These cases are the equitable counterpart of common law cases where the principle of res ipsa loquitur is invoked. There is a rebuttable evidential presumption of undue influence.

The availability of this forensic tool in cases founded on abuse of influence arising from the parties' relationship has led to this type of case sometimes being labelled "presumed undue influence". This is by way of contrast with cases involving actual pressure or the like, which are labelled "actual undue influence": [...]

The evidential presumption discussed above is to be distinguished sharply from a different form of presumption which arises in some cases. The law has adopted a sternly protective attitude towards certain types of relationship in which one party acquires influence over another who is vulnerable and dependent and where, moreover, substantial gifts by the influenced or vulnerable person are not normally to be expected. Examples of relationships within this special class are parent and child, guardian and ward, trustee and beneficiary, solicitor and client, and medical adviser and patient. In these cases the law presumes, irrebuttably, that one party had influence over the other. The complainant need not prove he actually reposed trust and confidence in the other party. It is sufficient for him to prove the existence of the type of relationship.

It is now well established that husband and wife is not one of the relationships to which this latter principle applies.

Thus a wife wishing to raise a presumption of undue influence will need to provide evidence to the court: firstly, that the relationship she enjoyed with her husband in respect of financial decisions was one in which she reposed trust and confidence, rather than exercised her own judgment; and secondly, that the nature of the mortgage itself leads to an inference that there was a risk that her husband persuaded her to enter into the mortgage by questionable means. The burden of proof will then shift to establish that the wife did, in fact, give her consent freely.

As we have already observed, a relationship of trust and confidence is easier to recognize than to define. Lord Scott in *Etridge* went so far as to suggest that, in the normal course, a husband and wife's relationship was one of trust and confidence, and what was required was proof that this inherent trust and confidence had been abused.

Royal Bank of Scotland v Etridge [2002] 2 AC 773, HL

Lord Scott

At [159]–[160]

For my part, I would assume in every case in which a wife and husband are living together that there is a reciprocal trust and confidence between them. In the fairly common circumstance that the financial and business decisions of the family are primarily taken by the husband, I would assume that the wife would have trust and confidence in his ability to do so and would support his decisions. I would not expect evidence to be necessary to establish the existence of that trust and confidence. I would expect evidence to be necessary to demonstrate its absence. In cases where experience, probably bitter, had led a wife to doubt the wisdom of her husband's financial or business decisions, I still would not regard her willingness to support those decisions with her own assets as an indication that he had exerted undue influence over her to persuade her to do so. Rather I would regard her support as a natural and admirable consequence of the relationship of a mutually loyal married couple. The proposition that if a wife, who generally reposes trust and confidence in her husband, agrees to become surety to support his debts or his business enterprises a presumption of undue influence arises is one that I am unable to accept. To regard the husband in such a case as a presumed "wrongdoer" does not seem to me consistent with the relationship of trust and confidence that is a part of every healthy marriage.

There are, of course, cases where a husband does abuse that trust and confidence. He may do so by expressions of quite unjustified over-optimistic enthusiasm about the prospects of success of his business enterprises. He may do so by positive misrepresentation of his business intentions, or of the nature of the security he is asking his wife to grant his creditors, or of some other material matter. He may do so by subjecting her to excessive pressure, emotional blackmail or bullying in order to persuade her to sign. But none of these things should, in my opinion, be presumed merely from the fact of the relationship of general trust and confidence. More is needed before the stage is reached at which, in the absence of any other evidence, an inference of undue influence can properly be drawn or a presumption of the existence of undue influence can be said to arise.

Relevant factors in determining the strength of a spousal relationship of trust and confidence include: the relative ages, education, and experience of the husband and wife; as well as the nature of their relationship, including its length; their respective characters; and the roles that they have assumed in their joint lives. Cultural factors may also have a part of play where particular religious or social norms dictate that a wife plays a subservient role in financial matters.[112] Feminist legal scholars have highlighted the gender imbalance inherent in the spousal relationship and have dubbed the phenomenon 'sexual transmitted debt'.[113]

The House of Lords have underlined that a relationship of trust and confidence may exist between cohabiting heterosexual and homosexual couples, as well as between husband and wife. Nevertheless, trust and confidence is not dependent on a sexual relationship, but may arise in other close relationships—for example, between other family members[114]—and may even exceptionally exist in relationships that are apparently commercial—for example, that between employer and employee.[115]

Proof of a relationship of trust and confidence is not in itself sufficient; the wife must also prove that her entry into the mortgage is not readily explicable as an exercise of her independent will. In *National Westminster Bank v Morgan*,[116] the House of Lords had initially called for proof of a transaction that was 'manifestly disadvantageous' to the wife because, for example, she did not benefit from the loan. The courts often inclined to the view that a collateral mortgage over the family home to secure a loan to the husband's business was

---

[112] See, e.g., *Barclays Bank v Coleman* [2002] 2 AC 773.
[113] See, e.g., Kaye, 'Equity's Treatment of Sexually Transmitted Debt' (1997) 5 Feminist LS 35.
[114] See, e.g., *Abbey National Bank plc v Stringer* [2006] EWCA Civ 338.
[115] See, e.g., *Credit Lyonnais v Burch* [1997] 1 All ER 144.
[116] [1985] AC 686.

manifestly disadvantageous, in that the wife was placing the residential security of the home at risk for no direct financial benefit. A flood of undue influence cases followed. The House of Lords in *Etridge* abandoned the manifest disadvantage label and reverted instead to the test laid down in *Allcard v Skinner*,[117] which looks to whether or not the transaction is explicable by the relationship of the parties or calls for some further explanation. The House also observed that a collateral mortgage of the family home to secure a husband's business debts will often be explicable by the nature of the parties' relationship and will not require any further explanation.[118]

Royal Bank of Scotland v Etridge [2002] 2 AC 773, HL

Lord Nicholls

At [30]–[31]

[...] I do not think that, in the ordinary course, a guarantee of the character I have mentioned is to be regarded as a transaction which, failing proof to the contrary, is explicable only on the basis that it has been procured by the exercise of undue influence by the husband. Wives frequently enter into such transactions. There are good and sufficient reasons why they are willing to do so, despite the risks involved for them and their families. They may be enthusiastic. They may not. They may be less optimistic than their husbands about the prospects of the husbands' businesses. They may be anxious, perhaps exceedingly so. But this is a far cry from saying that such transactions as a class are to be regarded as prima facie evidence of the exercise of undue influence by husbands.

I have emphasised the phrase "in the ordinary course". There will be cases where a wife's signature of a guarantee or a charge of her share in the matrimonial home does call for explanation.

A presumption of undue influence may be rebutted by proof (provided by the husband or lender) that the wife did, in fact, enter into the mortgage of her own free and independent will. The most usual way of demonstrating that this is so is to show that the wife decided to enter into the mortgage after receiving independent advice, thus breaking the influence that previously controlled her actions. The courts have been at pains to point out, however, that independent advice is no assurance that the presumption is rebutted; that is a question of fact, in the light of all of the circumstances.[119]

The House of Lords in *Etridge* provided guidance to solicitors when called upon to advise a wife.[120] The solicitors must be suitably qualified, both in terms of their professional capability to provide advice and their impartiality. There must be no conflict with the interests of their other clients: for example, the husband or the lender. The advice must be given in an environment that is free from the husband's influence and at a time before the transaction that provides sufficient opportunity for the wife to consider the import of the advice before she decides whether or not to proceed. The advice itself must not only explain the terms of the mortgage, but must also explain the implications and consequences for the wife of the

---

[117] (1885) 26 Ch D 145.

[118] Lord Hobhouse suggested that a mortgage to secure the unlimited debts of the husband's business called for an explanation: [2002] 2 AC 733, [112].

[119] *BCCI v Aboody* [1989] 1 QB 923, 971; *UBC Corporate Services Ltd v Williams* [2002] EWCA Civ 555.

[120] [2002] 2 AC 733, [64]–[69], *per* Lord Nicholls, and [169]–[170], *per* Lord Scott.

mortgage—in particular, that she could lose her home or become bankrupt if the loan is not repaid. The more difficult issue is the extent to which the solicitor should weigh and advise on the risks of enforcement, in the light of the wife's liabilities under the mortgage. The solicitor can make observations on the legal extent of these liabilities, but may not be qualified, or may not have sufficient information, to provide guidance on the commercial risks of the business generating the projected profit to meet those liabilities. What is clear is that the solicitor should press home that *'the wife has a choice. The decision is hers and hers alone'.*[121]

3.3.2 The second stage: notice of the bank

We have already observed that a lender, although not itself guilty of undue influence, may become subject to a wife's equity to set aside a mortgage entered into as result of the husband's actual or presumed undue influence, where it has notice of the risk that a wife may not have exercised her own independent judgment.

The House of Lords in *O'Brien* had set a test of notice that required proof of a relationship carrying a heightened risk of equitable wrong (whether of duress, undue influence, or misrepresentation) and a transaction that was disadvantageous to the weaker party—a test that tended to converge with that of presumed undue influence under *O'Brien*. In *Etridge*, however, the Lords clearly differentiated the two stages. Whilst they expressed proof of presumed undue influence in more stringent terms, they set a simple and relatively low-level threshold of notice, which would be straightforward for lenders to identify. The *Etridge* test provides that a lender should be put on notice whenever a wife stood as a surety for her husband's debts. The difficulty is that it is not always easy to identify whether it is the husband's business or a family business in which the wife is also interested.

Royal Bank of Scotland v Etridge [2002] 2 AC 773, HL

Lord Nicholls

At [48]–[49]

As to the type of transactions where a bank is put on inquiry, the case where a wife becomes surety for her husband's debts is, in this context, a straightforward case. The bank is put on inquiry. On the other side of the line is the case where money is being advanced, or has been advanced, to husband and wife jointly. In such a case the bank is not put on inquiry, unless the bank is aware the loan is being made for the husband's purposes, as distinct from their joint purposes. That was decided in *CIBC Mortgages plc v Pitt* [1994] 1 AC 200.

Less clear cut is the case where the wife becomes surety for the debts of a company whose shares are held by her and her husband. Her shareholding may be nominal, or she may have a minority shareholding or an equal shareholding with her husband. In my view the bank is put on inquiry in such cases, even when the wife is a director or secretary of the company. Such cases cannot be equated with joint loans. The shareholding interests, and the identity of the directors, are not a reliable guide to the identity of the persons who actually have the conduct of the company's business.

The House of Lords in *Etridge* set a similar low threshold where there is a risk of presumed undue influence between other parties, who enjoy a relationship of trust and confidence, and

---

[121] Ibid, at [65].

who enter into a mortgage that calls for an explanation. In these circumstances, a bank is 'put on inquiry' of the risk of presumed undue influence whenever the relationship between the surety and the debtor is non-commercial.[122]

3.3.3 The third stage: the steps that the bank should take

Where the bank has notice of the risk that the surety's consent may have been procured by undue influence, it is required to 'take reasonable steps to bring home to the individual guarantor the risks he is running by standing as surety'.[123] In both O'Brien and Etridge, the House of Lords was at pains to outline what those steps should be. In O'Brien, Lord Brown-Wilkinson suggested that the bank should arrange a private interview with the wife to explain to her those risks and advise her to take independent advice. But this practice did not find favour with lenders, which were reluctant to take direct responsibility for advising the wife; instead, they preferred to look to solicitors to shoulder that task. As a result, the House of Lords in Etridge reformulated the steps that a lender should take, emphasizing that the situation should be examined from the point of view of the lender. Those steps are not directed at 'discovering whether the wife has been wronged by her husband', but are 'concerned to minimise the risk that such a wrong may have been committed'.[124]

Royal Bank of Scotland v Etridge [2002] 2 AC 773, HL

Lord Nicholls

At [54]

The furthest a bank can be expected to go is to take reasonable steps to satisfy itself that the wife has had brought home to her, in a meaningful way, the practical implications of the proposed transaction. This does not wholly eliminate the risk of undue influence or misrepresentation. But it does mean that a wife enters into a transaction with her eyes open so far as the basic elements of the transaction are concerned [...]

At [79]

I now return to the steps a bank should take when it has been put on inquiry and for its protection is looking to the fact that the wife has been advised independently by a solicitor.

1. One of the unsatisfactory features in some of the cases is the late stage at which the wife first became involved in the transaction. In practice she had no opportunity to express a view on the identity of the solicitor who advised her. She did not even know that the purpose for which the solicitor was giving her advice was to enable him to send, on her behalf, the protective confirmation sought by the bank. Usually the solicitor acted for both husband and wife.

   Since the bank is looking for its protection to legal advice given to the wife by a solicitor who, in this respect, is acting solely for her, I consider the bank should take steps to check directly with the wife the name of the solicitor she wishes to act for her. To this end, in future the bank should communicate directly with the wife, informing her that

---

[122] Ibid, at [87], *per* Lord Nicholls.
[123] Ibid.
[124] Ibid, at [41], *per* Lord Nicholls. See also [164]–[165], *per* Lord Scott.

for its own protection it will require written confirmation from a solicitor, acting for her, to the effect that the solicitor has fully explained to her the nature of the documents and the practical implications they will have for her. She should be told that the purpose of this requirement is that thereafter she should not be able to dispute she is legally bound by the documents once she has signed them. She should be asked to nominate a solicitor whom she is willing to instruct to advise her, separately from her husband, and act for her in giving the necessary confirmation to the bank. She should be told that, if she wishes, the solicitor may be the same solicitor as is acting for her husband in the transaction. If a solicitor is already acting for the husband and the wife, she should be asked whether she would prefer that a different solicitor should act for her regarding the bank's requirement for confirmation from a solicitor.

The bank should not proceed with the transaction until it has received an appropriate response directly from the wife.

2. Representatives of the bank are likely to have a much better picture of the husband's financial affairs than the solicitor. If the bank is not willing to undertake the task of explanation itself, the bank must provide the solicitor with the financial information he needs for this purpose. Accordingly it should become routine practice for banks, if relying on confirmation from a solicitor for their protection, to send to the solicitor the necessary financial information. What is required must depend on the facts of the case. Ordinarily this will include information on the purpose for which the proposed new facility has been requested, the current amount of the husband's indebtedness, the amount of his current overdraft facility, and the amount and terms of any new facility. If the bank's request for security arose from a written application by the husband for a facility, a copy of the application should be sent to the solicitor. The bank will, of course, need first to obtain the consent of its customer to this circulation of confidential information. If this consent is not forthcoming the transaction will not be able to proceed.

3. Exceptionally there may be a case where the bank believes or suspects that the wife has been misled by her husband or is not entering into the transaction of her own free will. If such a case occurs the bank must inform the wife's solicitors of the facts giving rise to its belief or suspicion.

4. The bank should in every case obtain from the wife's solicitor a written confirmation to the effect mentioned above.

The focus of these steps is thus to ensure that the wife is legally represented and that the lender receives confirmation from the solicitor acting for her that she has received advice. To ensure that the wife's solicitor is in a position to give meaningful advice, the lender must disclose relevant financial information and any information that gives rise to any particular suspicions that the wife may have been improperly influenced by her husband. Given that the situation is viewed from the position of the lender, the lender is not required to be privy to the advice that the wife actually receives; it merely needs to receive confirmation that she has received advice, even if that advice is inadequate. The wife's right of action in these circumstances is against her solicitor for his or her negligent advice; she cannot challenge the mortgage itself unless the lender actually learns that she did not received advice or that the advice was inadequate.[125]

A further difficult question is the independence of the wife's solicitor: can a solicitor who acts also for the bank and/or the husband provide adequate independent advice to the wife?

---

[125] *Per* Lord Scott at [175].

Clearly, it is preferable that the wife receives advice from a solicitor who can take a wholly impartial view of the prudence of the mortgage, but to add the fees of another professional adviser may be unwarranted in a situation in which finances are already stretched. The House of Lords in *Etridge* addressed this issue in a pragmatic fashion by leaving it to the solicitor's professional judgment to decide if there was an unacceptable conflict of interest.

Royal Bank of Scotland v Etridge [2002] 2 AC 773, HL

Lord Nicholls

At [74]

The advantages attendant upon the employment of a solicitor acting solely for the wife do not justify the additional expense this would involve for the husband. When accepting instructions to advise the wife the solicitor assumes responsibilities directly to her, both at law and professionally. These duties, and this is central to the reasoning on this point, are owed to the wife alone. In advising the wife the solicitor is acting for the wife alone. He is concerned only with her interests. I emphasise, therefore, that in every case the solicitor must consider carefully whether there is any conflict of duty or interest and, more widely, whether it would be in the best interests of the wife for him to accept instructions from her. If he decides to accept instructions, his assumption of legal and professional responsibilities to her ought, in the ordinary course of things, to provide sufficient assurance that he will give the requisite advice fully, carefully and conscientiously. Especially so, now that the nature of the advice called for has been clarified. If at any stage the solicitor becomes concerned that there is a real risk that other interests or duties may inhibit his advice to the wife he must cease to act for her.

These steps lay down straightforward practical guidance for the normal case, but where the lender is aware of particular circumstances that increase the risk of impropriety, it needs to take additional precautions: for example, by making sure that the wife is advised by a solicitor who is not also representing the husband.[126]

4 CONTROL OF MORTGAGE TERMS

The underlying principle of the control of mortgage terms is freedom of contract: the parties should be free to determine the terms of their loan and any mortgage to secure its repayment. But throughout the history of money lending, there has been a recognition that '*necessitous men are not, truly speaking, free men*'[127] and thus borrowers may require a level of protection against the often stronger bargaining power of lenders. The focus of this protection has changed as social and economic conditions have altered the nature of borrowers and their borrowing.

In early times, the laws against usury initially prohibited, and then controlled, interest rates to protect the souls of all. We have seen that, under the traditional mortgage by conveyance, the Chancery courts from the seventeenth century onwards would protect the borrower's right to redeem, so that the mortgage took effect only by way of security. Borrowers during this period were often landowners who needed relatively short-term financial relief,

---

126 *Per* Lord Scott at [174].
127 *Vernon v Bethell* (1761) 2 Eden 113, *per* Lord Nottingham.

but, with the growing impact of the Industrial Revolution, the expansion of the Empire, and the importance of trade, the nineteenth century saw a growth in commercial borrowers. More often than not, they were astute businessmen who were able to wield sufficient negotiating power to look after themselves. Accordingly, protection of the equity of redemption on mortgages taken out to finance the business exploits of these borrowers became less of a priority.

We have also noted that equity would frustrate the exploitation of particularly vulnerable borrowers by setting aside unconscionable bargains. This equitable jurisdiction was originally intended to protect heirs mortgaging their prospective interests in their family's landed estates, but it developed into a general jurisdiction to protect all vulnerable borrowers. It has been employed to vary mortgage terms that are demonstrably oppressive or unconscionable—a contribution that remains of significance today where borrowing is not subject to statutory control.

In more recent times, it is the cash-strapped individual consumer who is more often perceived as in need of protection from institutional lenders. Government has come to his or her relief through legislation that, as we have already examined, operates initially through market regulation, but may also intervene to control mortgage terms.

The primary targets of control have been terms that inhibited redemption, terms that determine the level or fluctuation of interest rates, whether as a result of market conditions or upon the borrower's default, and terms that provide for some collateral advantage to the lender. In our survey of the legal control of mortgage terms, we will look first at the common law, equitable, and statutory control mechanisms, before examining how these mechanisms operate to the control these different types of term.

4.1 SOURCES OF CONTROL

4.1.1 The common law

Common law controls are few, but the restraint of trade doctrine has been pressed into service to control collateral advantages that require the borrower to purchase products solely from the lender. Nowadays, extensive competition laws and market regulation provide a more effective and comprehensive framework to promote a free market domestically, globally, and within the European context.

Implied terms have provided some limited control over the power of lenders to vary interest rates where an appeal to control on grounds of public policy has failed.

4.1.2 Equitable control

Equitable control of mortgage terms is derived from two sources.[128] Firstly, equity's protection of unconscionable bargains, which we have already considered in the context of the creation of mortgages,[129] has also been applied to vary oppressive and unconscionable mortgage terms, where both substantive and procedural unconscionability is established, and now underpins equity's most effective intervention.

---

[128] Bamford, 'Lord Macnaghten's Puzzle: The Mortgage of Real Property in English Law' [1996] CLP 207.
[129] See section 3.1 above.

Secondly, using the clogs and fetters doctrine, equity has struck down terms that bar or inhibit the borrower's equitable right to redeem. The origin of this jurisdiction was described by Lord Haldane in the following leading case.

G&K Kreglinger v New Patagonia Meat and Cold Storage Co Ltd [1914] AC 25, HL

Lord Haldane

At 35

The reason for which a Court of Equity will set aside the legal title of a mortgagee and compel him to reconvey the land on being paid principal, interest, and costs is a very old one. It appears to owe its origin to the influence of the Church in the Courts of the early Chancellors. As early as the Council of Lateran in 1179, we find, according to Matthew Paris (*Historia Major*, 1684 ed. at pp. 114–115), that famous assembly of ecclesiastics condemning usurers and laying down that when a creditor had been paid his debt he should restore his pledge. It was therefore not surprising that the Court of Chancery should at an early date have begun to exercise jurisdiction in personam over mortgagees. This jurisdiction was merely a special application of a more general power to relieve against penalties and to mould them into mere securities. The case of the common law mortgage of land was indeed a gross one. The land was conveyed to the creditor upon the condition that if the money he had advanced to the feoffor was repaid on a date and at a place named, the fee simple should revest in the latter, but that if the condition was not strictly and literally fulfilled he should lose the land for ever. What made the hardship on the debtor a glaring one was that the debt still remained unpaid and could be recovered from the feoffor notwithstanding that he had actually forfeited the land to his mortgagee. Equity, therefore, at an early date began to relieve against what was virtually a penalty by compelling the creditor to use his legal title as a mere security.

My Lords, this was the origin of the jurisdiction which we are now considering, and it is important to bear that origin in mind. For the end to accomplish which the jurisdiction has been evolved ought to govern and limit its exercise by equity judges. That end has always been to ascertain, by parol evidence if need be, the real nature and substance of the transaction, and if it turned out to be in truth one of mortgage simply, to place it on that footing. It was, in ordinary cases, only where there was conduct which the Court of Chancery regarded as unconscientious that it interfered with freedom of contract. The lending of money, on mortgage or otherwise, was looked on with suspicion, and the Court was on the alert to discover want of conscience in the terms imposed by lenders. But whatever else may have been the intention of those judges who laid the foundations of the modern doctrines with which we are concerned in this appeal, they certainly do not appear to have contemplated that their principle should develop consequences which would go far beyond the necessities of the case with which they were dealing and interfere with transactions which were not really of the nature of a mortgage, and which were free from objection on moral grounds. Moreover, the principle on which the Court of Chancery interfered with contracts of the class under consideration was not a rigid one. The equity judges looked, not at what was technically the form, but at what was really the substance of transactions, and confined the application of their rules to cases in which they thought that in its substance the transaction was oppressive [...] The principle was thus in early days limited in its application to the accomplishment of the end which was held to justify interference of equity with freedom of contract. It did not go further. As established it was expressed in three ways. The most general of these was that if the transaction was once found to be a mortgage, it must be treated as always

> remaining a mortgage and nothing but a mortgage. That the substance of the transaction must be looked to in applying this doctrine and that it did not apply to cases which were only apparently or technically within it but were in reality something more than cases of mortgage, *Howard v. Harris* (1683) 1 Vern 33 2 Ch Cas 147 and other authorities shew.

Equity's protection of the equitable right to redeem has been gradually eroded away since its heyday, when any clog or fetter on the borrower's right to recover his or her property was struck down. It does continue to be of significance where a device bars the right to redeem. This remaining intervention has been the subject of criticism by both judges and commentators.[130] In *Jones v Morgan*,[131] the Master of the Rolls, Lord Phillips, suggested that '[the] *doctrine of a clog on the equity of redemption is* [...] *an appendix to our law which no longer serves a useful purpose and would be better excised'.* The Law Commission has made such a recommendation, but the doctrine continues to limp along, causing more problems than it solves.[132]

We should add one further equitable contribution to the regulation of mortgage terms: the prohibition on penalties. Equity will strike down a provision that provides for a payment to be made by a party in default that is not a genuine pre-estimation of the loss that the innocent party may suffer.[133]

4.1.3 Statutory consumer control

We have already noted the extensive regulation of the domestic credit market both through the FSMA 2000, which regulates most first mortgages over dwelling houses, and the CCA 1974 (as amended), which governs much of the secondary secured lending market.[134] Inevitably, these regulatory controls impact upon mortgage terms, but the most significant control granted to the courts over mortgage terms in the more vulnerable secondary secured lending market is, without doubt, the provisions of ss 140A–140C of the 1974 Act, as introduced by the CCA 2006.[135]

Another source of protection arises from the treatment of borrowers as consumers and entitled to general consumer protection. This consumer protection is to be found in the Unfair Terms in Consumer Contract Regulations 1999[136] and the Unfair Practices Regulations 2008.[137] After some initial hesitation, it is clear that these regulations do apply

---

[130] See, e.g., Devonshire, 'The Modern Application of the Rule Against Clogs in The Equity of Redemption' (1997) 5 APLJ 1; Thompson, 'Do We Really Need Clogs?' [2002] Conv 502; Duncan and Wilmott, 'Clogging the Equity of Redemption: An Outmoded Concept' (2002) 2 QUTLJJ 35; Berg, 'Clogs on the Equity of Redemption: Or Chaining an Unruly Dog' [2003] JBL 335; Devenney, 'A Pack of Unruly Dogs: Unconscionable Bargains, Lawful Act (Economic) Duress and Clogs on the Equity of Redemption' (2002) JBL 539; Watt, 'Mortgage Law as Fiction' in *Modern Studies in Property Law: Vol 4* (ed Cooke, 2007, p 89).

[131] [2001] EWCA Civ 995, [72].

[132] Law Commission Report No 204, Land Mortgages (2001, Pt VIII).

[133] *Dunlop Pneumatic Tyre Ltd v New Garage and Motor Co Ltd* [1915] AC 79; *Philips Hong Kong Ltd v AG of Hong Kong* (1993) 63 BLR 41.

[134] See section 2 above.

[135] See section 2.2 above, for more on the unfair credit relationship.

[136] SI 1999/2083, which amends and replaces the original regulations in SI 1994/3159. The OFT has issued a guidance note on the Regulations: see OFT 143 (2005). These Regulations were enacted in pursuance of Council Directive 93/13/EEC of 5 April 1993 on unfair terms in consumer contracts.

[137] SI 2008/1277, enacted in pursuance of Council Directive 2005/29/EC of 11 May 2005 on unfair business-to-consumer commercial practices in the internal market (the Unfair Commercial Practices Directive).

to contracts affecting land, including mortgages.[138] They apply to individual borrowers, but not companies. Thus they may be used to control the fairness of terms and practices governing mortgages secured on the family home, whether regulated under the FSMA 2000 or the CCA 1974. Given that mortgages regulated under the 2000 Act are not subject to the s 140A jurisdiction, the application of the 1999 and 2008 Regulations to these mortgages is particularly significant.

An unfair term is not binding on the borrower.[139] The OFT also acts at a regulatory level as a consumer watchdog by considering and taking action on complaints made both by consumers and consumer organizations, by investigating and providing guidance on potentially unfair terms and practices in consumer contracts, and by issuing proceedings by way of injunction to restrain the use of unfair terms.[140] The OFT rarely has to resort to judicial proceedings, but, instead, will extract an undertaking from an offending lender to alter its loan terms or practices, or face legal action.[141] The OFT's tactics appear to work, with its bulletins full of reports of terms that have been altered, so triggering a ripple effect on other lenders with similar terms and conditions.[142]

The OFT issued its initial guidance on the 1999 Regulations in 2001 and is in the process of revising its guidance.[143] It has also issued joint guidance, with the Department of Business Enterprise and Regulatory Reform (BERR) upon the 2008 Regulations.[144] Further specific guidance has been issued on *Calculating Fair Default Charges on Credit Card Contracts*, which has wider implications for similar default charges found in mortgages.[145] Mortgage payment protection insurance has also been a target of investigation.[146]

The definition of an unfair term is found in regs 5 and 6 of the 1999 Regulations.

Unfair Terms in Consumer Contracts Regulations 1999, regs 5 and 6

Unfair terms

5.—(1) A contractual term which has not been individually negotiated shall be regarded as unfair if, contrary to the requirement of good faith, it causes a significant imbalance in the parties' rights and obligations arising under the contract, to the detriment of the consumer.

(2) A term shall always be regarded as not having been individually negotiated where it has been drafted in advance and the consumer has therefore not been able to influence the substance of the term.

(3) Notwithstanding that a specific term or certain aspects of it in a contract has been individually negotiated, these Regulations shall apply to the rest of a contract if an overall assessment of it indicates that it is a pre-formulated standard contract.

(4) It shall be for any seller or supplier who claims that a term was individually negotiated to show that it was.

---

[138] *Newham LBC v Khatun* [2004 EWCA Civ 55.
[139] Unfair Terms in Consumer Contracts Regulations 1999, reg 8.
[140] Ibid, regs 10–15. Certain other bodies are also granted supervisory powers.
[141] See OFT 964 (2007).
[142] Bright, 'Winning the Battle Against Unfair Contract Terms' (2000) 20 Legal Studies 331.
[143] OFT 311 (2007).
[144] See OFT, *Guidance on the UK Regulations: Implementing the Unfair Commercial Practices Directive* (2008) available online at http://www.oft.gov.uk.
[145] OFT 842 (2006).
[146] OFT 899 (2007).

(5) Schedule 2 to these Regulations contains an indicative and non-exhaustive list of the terms which may be regarded as unfair.

Assessment of unfair terms

6.—(1) Without prejudice to regulation 12, the unfairness of a contractual term shall be assessed, taking into account the nature of the goods or services for which the contract was concluded and by referring, at the time of conclusion of the contract, to all the circumstances attending the conclusion of the contract and to all the other terms of the contract or of another contract on which it is dependent.

(2) In so far as it is in plain intelligible language, the assessment of fairness of a term shall not relate—

(a) to the definition of the main subject matter of the contract, or

(b) to the adequacy of the price or remuneration, as against the goods or services supplied in exchange.

The focus of the requirement of fairness is upon standard terms and conditions, which are not individually negotiated by the lender and the borrower.[147] The core terms of the contract are excluded from the requirement for fairness, but must be expressed in plain intelligible language.[148] Core terms are those terms that relate to the main subject matter of the contract or the adequacy of the consideration.[149] It is suggested that the core terms of a mortgage should be restricted to the amount of the loan and the level of interest chargeable. The House of Lords, in *Director General of Fair Trading v First National Bank plc*,[150] has made clear that the interpretation of 'core terms' is to be restrictively construed. The case concerned the right of the bank, under a contractual term, to continue to claim interest at the contractual rate (rather than at the statutory rate applicable to judgment debts) until the total amount of any judgment debt obtained after the borrower's default had been discharged.[151] Lord Steyn (referring to the earlier form of the Regulations) made the following observation.

Director General of Fair Trading v First National Bank plc [2002] 1 AC 481, HL

Lord Steyn

At [34]

Clause 8 of the contract, the only provision in dispute, is a default provision. It prescribes remedies which only become available to the lender upon the default of the consumer. For this reason the escape route of regulation 3(2) is not available to the bank. So far as the description of terms covered by regulation 3(2) as core terms is helpful at all, I would say

---

147 Unfair Terms in Consumer Contracts Regulations 1999, reg 5(2).
148 Ibid, reg 6(2).
149 Ibid.
150 [2001] UKHL 52.
151 At common law, contractual interest is not recoverable on a judgment debt, although interest on a judgment debt may be claimed by virtue of an express term or by statute. The county court, however, is unable to award statutory interest on a judgment debt for a claim under the 1974 Act. A court also cannot award statutory interest after judgment where the judgment debt is ordered repayable by instalments unless the debtor defaults in paying an instalment.

that clause 8 of the contract is a subsidiary term. In any event, article 3(2) must be given a restrictive interpretation. Unless that is done article 3(2)(a) will enable the main purpose of the scheme to be frustrated by endless formalistic arguments as to whether a provision is a definitional or an exclusionary provision. Similarly, article 3(2)(b) dealing with "the adequacy of the price of remuneration" must be given a restrictive interpretation. After all, in a broad sense all terms of the contract are in some way related to the price or remuneration. That is not what is intended. Even price escalation clauses have been treated by the Director as subject to the fairness provision [. . .] It would be a gaping hole in the system if such clauses were not subject to the fairness requirement.

The test of unfairness found in reg 5(1) encompasses both a lack of good faith, and a significant imbalance in the rights and liabilities of the parties, which operates to the detriment of the borrower. Schedule 2 of the 1999 Regulations illustrates the test by setting out a non-exhaustive 'grey list' of terms, which potentially may be regarded as unfair: for example, para (e) provides that a term *requiring any consumer who fails to fulfill his obligation to pay a disproportionately high sum in compensation'* is potentially unfair. The grey list's focus is upon the substantive rights and obligations of the parties, but it has been suggested that the good faith requirement also adds an element of procedural fairness.[152]

Lord Bingham, giving the leading judgment in *Director General of Fair Trading v First National Bank*, clearly contemplated that good faith called for procedural fairness in how the loan is entered into.

Director General of Fair Trading v First National Bank plc [2002] 1 AC 481, HL

Lord Bingham

At [17]

[Referring to the earlier form of the Regulations . . . T]he language used in expressing the test, so far as applicable in this case, is in my opinion clear and not reasonably capable of differing interpretations. A term falling within the scope of the regulations is unfair if it causes a significant imbalance in the parties' rights and obligations under the contract to the detriment of the consumer in a manner or to an extent which is contrary to the requirement of good faith. The requirement of significant imbalance is met if a term is so weighted in favour of the supplier as to tilt the parties' rights and obligations under the contract significantly in his favour. This may be by the granting to the supplier of a beneficial option or discretion or power, or by the imposing on the consumer of a disadvantageous burden or risk or duty. The illustrative terms set out in Schedule 3 to the regulations provide very good examples of terms which may be regarded as unfair; whether a given term is or is not to be so regarded depends on whether it causes a significant imbalance in the parties' rights and obligations under the contract. This involves looking at the contract as a whole. But the imbalance must be to the detriment of the consumer; a significant imbalance to the detriment of the supplier, assumed to be the stronger party, is not a mischief which the regulations seek to address. The requirement of good faith in this context is one of fair and open dealing. Openness requires that the

---

[152] Collins, 'Good Faith in European Contract Law' (1994) OJLS 229; Beale, 'Legislative Control of Fairness: The Directive on Unfair Terms in Consumer Contracts' in *Good Faith and Fault in Contract Law* (eds Beatson and Friedman, 1995, p 231).

terms should be expressed fully, clearly and legibly, containing no concealed pitfalls or traps. Appropriate prominence should be given to terms which might operate disadvantageously to the customer. Fair dealing requires that a supplier should not, whether deliberately or unconsciously, take advantage of the consumer's necessity, indigence, lack of experience, unfamiliarity with the subject matter of the contract, weak bargaining position or any other factor listed in or analogous to those listed in Schedule 2 of the regulations. Good faith in this context is not an artificial or technical concept; nor, since Lord Mansfield was its champion, is it a concept wholly unfamiliar to British lawyers. It looks to good standards of commercial morality and practice. Regulation 4(1) lays down a composite test, covering both the making and the substance of the contract, and must be applied bearing clearly in mind the objective which the regulations are designed to promote.

Furthermore, there is a call for terms to be expressed in plain and intelligible language.

Unfair Terms in Consumer Contracts Regulations 1999, reg 7

Written contracts

(1) A seller or supplier shall ensure that any written term of a contract is expressed in plain, intelligible language.

(2) If there is doubt about the meaning of a written term, the interpretation which is most favourable to the consumer shall prevail but this rule shall not apply in proceedings brought under regulation 12.

The terms must be capable of being understood by ordinary members of the public and not only lawyers or other experts.[153] If there is any doubt in meaning, a term is to be construed in favour of the borrower.[154] These requirements present a challenge where the subject matter is inherently complex—yet in *Office of Fair Trading v Abbey National plc*,[155] the court was unimpressed by arguments that complexity should affect the standard. It is the comprehensibility of the result that was important. It was no excuse that a reasonable attempt to explain complex subject matter had been made, if a layman would still fail to grasp its meaning. The aim of comprehensibility is supported by prohibition on terms that a borrower has no real opportunity to consider before the mortgage is completed.[156]

The message is clear: lenders must make sure that their standard terms and conditions meet the standards of fairness required by the legislation, and illustrated by the OFT's guidance.[157] Furthermore, lenders must ensure that the import of those terms and conditions are brought home to the borrower, both because they can be understood by any layman, and also because there is a process that ensures that borrowers are given an opportunity to read and consider these terms before they are bound. The indications are that certain, but not all, lenders have received and understood that message.[158]

---

[153] 'Cleared funds' was considered by the OFT to be unclear to consumers: see OFT Bulletin 16.

[154] Unfair Terms in Consumer Contracts Regulations, reg 7(2).

[155] [2008] EWHC 875.

[156] See Consumer Credit Act 1974 (as amended), Sch 1, para 1(i).

[157] See generally Simmonds, 'Bankers' Documents and the Unfair Terms in Consumer Contracts Regulations 1999' [2002] JIBL 205.

[158] The FSA's *Report on Fairness of Terms in Consumer Contracts* (2008, available online at http://www.fsa.gov.uk) found that some lenders, particularly smaller lenders, are unaware of the need to comply with the 1999 Regulations.

The 2008 Regulations,[159] in contrast to the 1999 Regulations, are enforceable only by the OFT as part of its regulatory armory. They introduce a general duty upon traders not to trade unfairly,[160] and seek to ensure that they act honestly and fairly towards customers by prohibiting misleading actions,[161] omissions,[162] and aggressive commercial practices.[163] Certain specific practices contained in the Schedule to the 2008 Regulations are always considered unfair. It is anticipated that these Regulations, like the 1999 Regulations, will apply to the practices of lenders when dealing with individual borrowers.

4.2 REDEMPTION

At the heart of the clogs and fetters doctrine is the protection of the borrower's equity of redemption, and the attendant right of the borrower to repay the loan and redeem, or recover, the land free of the lender's mortgage. Any device that could prevent the borrower from exercising his or her right to redeem will be struck down.

4.2.1 Options to purchase

The most common example of a device falling foul of this principle is the grant to the lender of an option to purchase the mortgaged property, although the courts have become increasingly frustrated with this assault on the parties' freedom to agree commercial terms.

Lord Halsbury expressed such sentiments in the following case.

Samuel v Jarrah Timber & Wood Paving Corporation Ltd [1904] AC 323, HL

Lord Halsbury

At 323

A perfectly fair bargain made between two parties to it, each of whom was quite sensible of what they were doing, is not to be performed because at the same time a mortgage arrangement was made between them. If a day had intervened between the two parts of the arrangement, the part of the bargain which the appellant claims to be performed would have been perfectly good and capable of being enforced; but a line of authorities going back for more than a century has decided that such an arrangement as that which was here arrived at is contrary to a principle of equity, the sense or reason of which I am not able to appreciate, and very reluctantly I am compelled to acquiesce in the judgments appealed from.

Lord Halsbury refers to the fact that if a day had intervened between the mortgage and the option, the transactions would have been upheld.

The principle is not quite as easily avoided. It must be evident that the mortgage and the option are separate transactions in substance, and not merely in form.[164] For example, in *Jones v Morgan*,[165] an option granted some three years after the date of the original mortgage

---

[159] SI 2008/1277. They came into force on 26 May 2008.
[160] Unfair Practices Regulations 2008, reg 3.
[161] Ibid, reg 5.
[162] Ibid, reg 6.
[163] Ibid, reg 7.
[164] See, e.g. *Reeve v Lisle* [1902] AC 461; *Lewis v Frank Love* [1961] 1 WLR 261.
[165] [2001] EWCA Civ 995.

was struck down because the Court took the view that the option formed part of a variation of the original mortgage. It was of no matter that the Court also found that the option was neither an unconscionable bargain, nor extracted as a result of economic duress.[166]

The transaction must also be, in substance, a mortgage—an issue that was central to the following case.

Warnborough Ltd v Garmite Ltd [2003] EWCA Civ 1544, CA

Facts: Warnborough sold land to Garmite, leaving the purchase money outstanding, but secured by a mortgage to Warnborough. At the same time, Garmite granted Warnborough an option to repurchase the land for the original sale price as a further protection against the risk that the purchase price would not be paid. The option was not a fetter on the equity of redemption, because the transaction was, in substance, a sale and purchase, not a mortgage.

Jonathan Parker LJ

At [72]–[73]

In the light of the authorities to which I have referred, it has to be accepted that the "unruly dog" is still alive (although one might perhaps reasonably expect its venerable age to inhibit it from straying too far or too often from its kennel); and that however desirable an appendectomy might be thought to be, no such relieving operation has as yet been carried out. Indeed, Mr Teverson did not seek to contend otherwise.

That said, it is in my judgment glaringly clear from the authorities that the mere fact that, contemporaneously with the grant of a mortgage over his property, the mortgagor grants the mortgagee an option to purchase the property does no more than raise the question whether the rule against 'clogs' applies: it does not begin to answer that question. As has been said over and over again in the authorities, in order to answer that question the court has to look at the 'substance' of the transaction in question: in other words, to inquire as to the true nature of the bargain which the parties have made. To do that, the court examines all the circumstances, with the assistance of oral evidence if necessary.

4.2.2 Postponement of the right to redeem

The postponement of the right to redeem is not, per se, an unacceptable clog on the equity of redemption. A postponement will be struck down if it renders the right to redeem illusory. For example, in *Fairclough v Swan Brewery Co*,[167] the right to redeem was held to be illusory where the borrower could not repay the loan until just six weeks prior to the expiry of the mortgaged leasehold term.

A postponement will also be struck down if it is oppressive or unconscionable; unreasonableness is insufficient. This conclusion was reached in the following case, in a judgment that illustrates the courts' reluctance to interfere with the freedom of contract of commercial parties.

---

[166] Devenney, 'A Pack of Unruly Dogs: Unconscionable Bargain, Lawful Act (Economic) Duress and Clogs on the Equity of Redemption' [2002] JBL 539.
[167] [1912] AC 565.

Knightsbridge Estates Trust Ltd v Byrne [1939] Ch 441, CA

Facts: Knightsbridge mortgaged a number of freehold properties to secure a loan of £300,000, with interest payable at 6.5 per cent. In 1931, the company renegotiated the loan on more favourable terms. It was to be repayable by eighty half-yearly instalments (i.e. over forty years), with interest at 5.25 per cent, and the lender agreed not to call in the loan, provided that the borrower performed the loan terms. Interest rates fell further and Knightsbridge wished to repay the loan to obtain still more favourable terms.

Greene MR

At 453

The first argument was that the postponement of the contractual right to redeem for forty years was void in itself, in other words, that the making of such an agreement between mortgagor and mortgagee was prohibited by a rule of equity. It was not contended that a provision in a mortgage deed making the mortgage irredeemable for a period of years is necessarily void. The argument was that such a period must be a "reasonable " one, and it was said that the period in the present case was an unreasonable one by reason merely of its length. This argument was not the one accepted by the learned judge.

Now an argument such as this requires the closest scrutiny, for, if it is correct, it means that an agreement made between two competent parties, acting under expert advice and presumably knowing their own business best, is one which the law forbids them to make upon the ground that it is not "reasonable." If we were satisfied that the rule of equity was what it is said to be, we should be bound to give effect to it. But in the absence of compelling authority we are not prepared to say that such an agreement cannot lawfully be made. A decision to that effect would, in our view, involve an unjustified interference with the freedom of business men to enter into agreements best suited to their interests and would impose upon them a test of "reasonableness" laid down by the Courts without reference to the business realities of the case.

It is important to remember what those realities were. The respondents are a private company and do not enjoy the facilities for raising money by a public issue possessed by public companies. They were the owners of a large and valuable block of property, and so far as we know they had no other assets. The property was subject to a mortgage at a high rate of interest and this mortgage was liable to be called in at any time. In these circumstances the respondents were, when the negotiations began, desirous of obtaining for themselves two advantages: (1.) a reduction in the rate of interest, (2.) the right to repay the mortgage moneys by instalments spread over a long period of years. The desirability of obtaining these terms from a business point of view is manifest, and it is not to be assumed that these respondents were actuated by anything but pure considerations of business in seeking to obtain them. The sum involved was a very large one, and the length of the period over which the instalments were spread is to be considered with reference to this fact. In the circumstances it was the most natural thing in the world that the respondents should address themselves to a body desirous of obtaining a long term investment for its money. The resulting agreement was a commercial agreement between two important corporations experienced in such matters, and has none of the features of an oppressive bargain where the borrower is at the mercy of an unscrupulous lender. In transactions of this kind it is notorious that there is competition among the large insurance companies and other bodies having large funds to invest, and we are not prepared to view the agreement made as anything but a proper business transaction.

But it is said not only that the period of postponement must be a reasonable one, but that in judging the "reasonableness" of the period the considerations which we have mentioned cannot be regarded; that the Court is bound to judge "reasonableness" by a consideration of the terms of the mortgage deed itself and without regard to extraneous matters. In the absence of clear authority we emphatically decline to consider a question of "reasonableness" from a standpoint so unreal. To hold that the law is to tell business men what is reasonable in such circumstances and to refuse to take into account the business considerations involved, would bring the law into disrepute. Fortunately, we do not find ourselves forced to come to any such conclusion [...]

But in our opinion the proposition that a postponement of the contractual right of redemption is only permissible for a "reasonable" time is not well-founded. Such a postponement is not properly described as a clog on the equity of redemption, since it is concerned with the contractual right to redeem. It is indisputable that any provision which hampers redemption after the contractual date for redemption has passed will not be permitted. Further, it is undoubtedly true to say that a right of redemption is a necessary element in a mortgage transaction, and consequently that, where the contractual right of redemption is illusory, equity will grant relief by allowing redemption [...]

Moreover, equity may give relief against contractual terms in a mortgage transaction if they are oppressive or unconscionable, and in deciding whether or not a particular transaction falls within this category the length of time for which the contractual right to redeem is postponed may well be an important consideration. In the present case no question of this kind was or could have been raised.

But equity does not reform mortgage transactions because they are unreasonable. It is concerned to see two things—one that the essential requirements of a mortgage transaction are observed, and the other that oppressive or unconscionable terms are not enforced. Subject to this, it does not, in our opinion, interfere. The question therefore arises whether, in a case where the right of redemption is real and not illusory and there is nothing oppressive or unconscionable in the transaction, there is something in a postponement of the contractual right to redeem, such as we have in the present case, that is inconsistent with the essential requirements of a mortgage transaction? Apart from authority the answer to this question would, in our opinion, be clearly in the negative. Any other answer would place an unfortunate restriction on the liberty of contract of competent parties who are at arm's length—in the present case it would have operated to prevent the respondents obtaining financial terms which for obvious reasons they themselves considered to be most desirable. It would, moreover, lead to highly inequitable results. The remedy sought by the respondents and the only remedy which is said to be open to them is the establishment of a right to redeem at any time on the ground that the postponement of the contractual right to redeem is void. They do not and could not suggest that the contract as a contract is affected, and the result would accordingly be that whereas the respondents would have had from the first the right to redeem at any time, the appellants would have had no right to require payment otherwise than by the specified instalments. Such an outcome to a bargain entered into by business people negotiating at arm's length would indeed be unfortunate, and we should require clear authority before coming to such a conclusion.

4.2.3 Charges for early redemption

It is common practice for lenders to offer advantageous rates of interest to domestic borrowers who agree that they will not redeem for a fixed period. Lenders benefit from the certainty of receiving a known return on their investment for the fixed term. The price to be paid for these advantageous rates of interest is payment of an agreed sum should the borrower wish to redeem before the fixed period has expired. Such charges are a frequent cause of complaint by borrowers, although regulations under both the FSMA 2000 and the CCA 1974 require such charges to be explained to the borrower, and to be calculated as a genuine pre-estimation of the lender's loss. A redemption charge that fails to do so also runs the risk of being unfair, under s 140A of the 1974 Act or under the 1999 Regulations,[168] or exorbitant under the MCOB rules. It is also conceivable that a redemption charge could be held to be an oppressive and unconscionable term or a penalty.

4.3 COLLATERAL ADVANTAGES

A collateral advantage is an added benefit that the lender negotiates as a condition of the mortgage. The most common examples are the tied and solus agreements that a brewery or petrol company requires of its retailers. These agreements are often associated with a mortgage, which, together, operate to require the borrower to purchase their supplies solely from the lender as a condition of the lender providing loan facilities to purchase, improve, or support the borrower's business. They thus occur most commonly in the commercial lending environment,[169] where regulation operates through equitable controls or the common law, and statutory controls on competition. A collateral advantage encountered in the domestic lending market will be subject to the regulatory controls of the FSMA 2000 and CCA 1974, as well as the fairness test demanded by s 140A of the 1974 Act and the 1999 Regulations.

4.3.1 Equitable controls

Historically, equity would strike down any collateral advantage. When the usury laws limited interest rates, a collateral advantage was considered an illegal means of avoiding these limits. With the abolition of the usury laws and the surge in economic activity of the nineteenth century, equity's abhorrence of collateral advantages waned. Initial relaxation was exemplified in the cases of *Biggs v Hodinott*[170] and *Bradley v Carritt*,[171] in which collateral advantages limited to the life of the mortgage were accepted. A collateral advantage that could extend beyond the life of the mortgage was seen as an unacceptable clog on the equity of redemption, because the borrower would not be able to redeem his or her property free of this burden.[172]

Further relaxation flowed from the following landmark decision.

G&K Kreglinger v New Patagonia Meat and Cold Storage Co Ltd [1914] AC 25, HL

Facts: Kreglinger advanced the meat company funds that were secured by a floating charge. In addition to the loan, Kreglinger negotiated a right of pre-emption to purchase any sheepskins produced by the meat company over a five-year period, for the best market price, and to be paid a commission on any sheepskins that the meat company sold to third parties. The meat company redeemed the loan within the five-year option period

---

[168] *Falco Finance Ltd v Gough* [1999] CCLR 16; *Evans v Cherry Tree Finance Ltd* [2008] EWCA Civ 331.

[169] Although see *Cityland and Property Holdings Ltd v Dabrah* [1968] Ch 166, in which a premium on the amount repayable over the amount lent was characterized as a collateral advantage.

[170] [1898] 2 Ch 307.

[171] [1903] AC 25.

[172] *Noakes v Rice* [1902] AC 24.

and unsuccessfully claimed that it should be free of its obligations regarding the sale of the sheepskins.

Lord Haldane LC

At 37

The Legislature during a long period placed restrictions on the rate of interest which could legally be exacted. But equity went beyond the limits of the statutes which limited the interest, and was ready to interfere with any usurious stipulation in a mortgage. In so doing it was influenced by the public policy of the time. That policy has now changed, and the Acts which limited the rate of interest have been repealed. The result is that a collateral advantage may now be stipulated for by the mortgagee provided that he has not acted unfairly or oppressively, and provided that the bargain does not conflict with the third form of the principle. This is that a mortgage [...] cannot be made irredeemable, and that any stipulation which restricts or clogs the equity of redemption is void. It is obvious that the reason for the doctrine in this form is the same as that which gave rise to the other forms. It is simply an assertion in a different way of the principle that once a mortgage always a mortgage and nothing else.

My Lords, the rules I have stated have now been applied by Courts of Equity for nearly three centuries, and the books are full of illustrations of their application. But what I have pointed out shews that it is inconsistent with the objects for which they were established that these rules should crystallize into technical language so rigid that the letter can defeat the underlying spirit and purpose. Their application must correspond with the practical necessities of the time. The rule as to collateral advantages, for example, has been much modified by the repeal of the usury laws and by the recognition of modern varieties of commercial bargaining. In *Biggs v. Hoddinott* [1898] 2 Ch. 307 it was held that a brewer might stipulate in a mortgage made to him of an hotel that during the five years for which the loan was to continue the mortgagors would deal with him exclusively for malt liquor. In the seventeenth and eighteenth centuries a Court of Equity could hardly have so decided, and the judgment illustrates the elastic character of equity jurisdiction and the power of equity judges to mould the rules which they apply in accordance with the exigencies of the time. The decision proceeded on the ground that a mortgagee may stipulate for a collateral advantage at the time and as a term of the advance, provided, first, that no unfairness is shewn, and, secondly, that the right to redeem is not thereby clogged. It is no longer true that, as was said in *Jennings v. Ward* 2 Vern. 520, "a man shall not have interest for his money and a collateral advantage besides for the loan of it." Unless such a bargain is unconscionable it is now good. But none the less the other and wider principle remains unshaken, that it is the essence of a mortgage that in the eye of a Court of Equity it should be a mere security for money, and that no bargain can be validly made which will prevent the mortgagor from redeeming on payment of what is due, including principal, interest, and costs. He may stipulate that he will not pay off his debt, and so redeem the mortgage, for a fixed period. But whenever a right to redeem arises out of the doctrine of equity, he is precluded from fettering it. This principle has become an integral part of our system of jurisprudence and must be faithfully adhered to.

My Lords, the question in the present case is whether the right to redeem has been interfered with. And this must, for the reasons to which I have adverted in considering the history of the doctrine of equity, depend on the answer to a question which is primarily one of fact. What was the true character of the transaction? Did the appellants make a bargain such that the right to redeem was cut down, or did they simply stipulate for a collateral undertaking, outside and clear of the mortgage, which would give them an exclusive option of purchase of the sheepskins of the respondents? The question is in my opinion not whether the two contracts were made at the same moment and evidenced by the same instrument, but whether they were in substance a single and undivided contract or two distinct contracts. Putting aside for the moment considerations turning on the character of the floating charge, such an option no doubt affects the freedom of the respondents in carrying on their business even after the mortgage has been paid off. But so might other arrangements which would be plainly collateral, an agreement, for example, to take permanently into the firm a new partner as a condition of obtaining fresh capital in the form of a loan. The question is one not of form but of substance, and it can be answered in each case only by looking at all the circumstances, and not by mere reliance on some abstract principle, or upon the dicta which have fallen obiter from judges in other and different cases. Some, at least, of the authorities on the subject disclose an embarrassment which has, in my opinion, arisen from neglect to bear this in mind. In applying a principle the ambit and validity of which depend on confining it steadily to the end for which it was established, the analogies of previous instances where it has been applied are apt to be misleading. For each case forms a real precedent only in so far as it affirms a principle, the relevancy of which in other cases turns on the true character of the particular transaction, and to that extent on circumstances.

My Lords, if in the case before the House your Lordships arrive at the conclusion that the agreement for an option to purchase the respondents' sheepskins was not in substance a fetter on the exercise of their right to redeem, but was in the nature of a collateral bargain the entering into which was a preliminary and separable condition of the loan, the decided cases cease to present any great difficulty.

It is thus necessary to consider initially the substance of the transaction, and whether the advantage is part and parcel of the mortgage consideration or independent of it, despite being part of the parties' overall bargain—an enquiry that it is not always easy to conduct. One may then move on to consider whether the advantage is repugnant to the equitable grounds identified by Lord Parker in his judgment in *Kreglinger*.

G&K Kreglinger v New Patagonia Meat and Cold Storage Co Ltd [1914] AC 25, HL

Lord Parker

At 56

[...E]ither (1.) because it was unconscionable, or (2.) because it was in the nature of a penal clause clogging the equity arising on failure to exercise a contractual right to redeem, or (3.) because it was in the nature of a condition repugnant as well to the contractual as to the equitable right.

4.3.2 Restraint of trade

The ability of the law to strike down terms in restraint of trade has a long history, dating at least from Elizabethan times. A party's freedom to contract must be balanced against the wide public interest of the freedom of all to trade. The doctrine has been pressed into service on a number of occasions to attack collateral advantages in mortgages—not always with success. The doctrine has no application to a collateral advantage in a mortgage used to acquire the borrower's business premises,[173] in which there is no restraint of an exist-ing trade, but may be applied to a collateral advantage in a mortgage taken over business

---

[173] *Cleveland Petroleum Ltd v Dartstone Ltd* [1969] 1 WLR 116; *Alec Lobb (Garages) Ltd v Total Oil (Great Britain) Ltd* [1985] 1 WLR 173.

premises that a borrower already owns. In these circumstances, the question of whether an attendant collateral advantage is in restraint of trade looks to the reasonableness of the protection it affords. In *Esso Petroleum Co Ltd v Harpers Garage (Stourport) Ltd*,[174] a mortgage that postponed the borrower's right to redeem for twenty-one years, and a connected solus agreement that required the borrower to purchase all of its petroleum products from Esso for a similar period, were struck down as unreasonable restraints on trade. Similar agreements for shorter terms of five years or so have been upheld.[175]

The utility of the doctrine is overshadowed by the extensive competition laws that now govern commercial activity.[176]

4.4 INTEREST RATES AND OTHER PAYMENT TERMS

The rate of interest and other costs associated with borrowing is, of course, of central importance to both the borrower and the lender.

4.4.1 Fluctuating and index-linked interest rates

Gray and Gray[177] have observed the surprising acceptance of the uncertainty inherent in the market norm of fluctuating or index-linked interest rates, which withstood attack on the basis of public policy in *Mutliservice Bookbinding Ltd v Marden*[178] (extracted below), and has not been questioned as being oppressive or unconscionable. The 1999 Regulations also accept that an interest rate in a mortgage will not be unfair because it is fluctuating or index-linked, provided (in the case of a fluctuating rate) that the lender gives notice to the borrower of any change and the borrower is able to redeem if he or she so wishes.[179]

The lender's discretion to alter a fluctuating interest rate is not, however, completely unfettered. The Court of Appeal, in the conjoined appeals of *Paragon Finance v Nash* and *Paragon Finance v Staunton*,[180] accepted two grounds upon which a term should be implied to define the manner in which a discretion should be exercised. The first implies a term that rates will not be altered improperly, arbitrarily, or capriciously, and the second, that, in exercising a discretion, the lender will not do so unreasonably—in the sense that no lender acting reasonably would act similarly.

Paragon Finance plc v Nash [2002] 1 WLR 685, CA

Dyson LJ

At [30]–[32]

I cannot accept the submission of Mr Malek that the power given to the claimant by these loan agreements to set the interest rates from time to time is completely unfettered. If that were so, it would mean that the claimant would be completely free, in theory at least, to

---

[174] [1968] AC 269.
[175] Ibid; *Texaco v Mulberry Filling Station* [1972] 1 WLR 814.
[176] Hopkins (1998) 49 NILQ 202.
[177] Gray and Gray, *Elements of Land Law* (5th edn, 2009, [6.2.40]).
[178] [1978] Ch 84.
[179] See Unfair Terms in Consumer Contracts Regulations 1999, Sch 2, para 2(b) and (d).
[180] See also *Paragon Finance v Pender* [2005] EWCA Civ 760.

specify interest rates at the most exorbitant level. It is true that in the case of the Nash agreement clause 3.3 provides that the rate charged is that which applies to the category of business to which the claimant considers the mortgage belongs. That prevents the claimant from treating the Nashes differently from other borrowers in the same category. But it does not protect borrowers in that category from being treated in a capricious manner, or, for example, being subjected to very high rates of interest in order to force them into arrears with a view to obtaining possession of their properties.

The Stauntons do not even have the limited protection that is afforded by clause 3.3 of the Nash agreement. In the absence of an implied term, there would be nothing to prevent the claimant from raising the rate demanded of the Stauntons to exorbitant levels, or raising the rate to a level higher than that required of other similar borrowers for some improper purpose or capricious reason. An example of an improper purpose would be where the lender decided that the borrower was a nuisance (but had not been in breach of the terms of the agreement) and, wishing to get rid of him, raised the rate of interest to a level that it knew he could not afford to pay. An example of a capricious reason would be where the lender decided to raise the rate of interest because its manager did not like the colour of the borrower's hair.

It seems to me that the commercial considerations relied on by Mr Malek are not sufficient to exclude an implied term that the discretion to vary interest rates should not be exercised dishonestly, for an improper purpose, capriciously or arbitrarily. I shall come shortly to the question whether the discretion should also not be exercised unreasonably [...]

At [37]

I come, therefore, to the question whether the implied term should also extend to "unreasonably". The first difficulty is to define what one means by "unreasonably". Mr Bannister was at pains to emphasise that he was not saying that the rates of interest had to be reasonable rates in the sense of closely and consistently tracking LIBOR or the rates charged by the Halifax Building Society. He said that what he meant by the unreasonable exercise of the discretionary power to set the rate of interest was something very close to the capricious or arbitrary exercise of that power [...]

At [41]–[42]

So here, too, we find a somewhat reluctant extension of the implied term to include unreasonableness that is analogous to Wednesbury unreasonableness. I entirely accept that the scope of an implied term will depend on the circumstances of the particular contract. But I find the analogy of the Gan Insurance case [2001] EWCA Civ 1047 and the cases considered in the judgment of Mance LJ helpful. It is one thing to imply a term that a lender will not exercise his discretion in a way that no reasonable lender, acting reasonably, would do. It is unlikely that a lender who was acting in that way would not also be acting either dishonestly, for an improper purpose, capriciously or arbitrarily. It is quite another matter to imply a term that the lender would not impose unreasonable rates. It could be said that as soon as the difference between the claimant's standard rates and the Halifax rates started to exceed about two percentage points the claimant was charging unreasonable rates. From the defendant's point of view, that was undoubtedly true. But, from the claimant's point of view, it charged these rates because it was commercially necessary, and therefore reasonable, for it to do so.

I conclude therefore that there was an implied term of both agreements that the claimant would not set rates of interest unreasonably in the limited sense that I have described. Such an implied term is necessary in order to give effect to the reasonable expectations of the parties.

4.4.2 Excessive interest rates

The laws against usury set limits on the level of interest rates and, since their abolition, there have, from time to time, been monetary levels imposed upon interest rates for certain types of borrowing.[181] The modern thinking is against setting interest rate ceilings,[182] but to consider other mechanisms by which interest rates can be kept within acceptable bounds.

In the consumer market, these mechanisms are to be found both in the market regulation provisions of the FSMA 2000 and CCA 1974 that we have already examined, and the specific control on mortgage terms in the MCOB rules, s 140A of the 1974 Act (as amended), and the 1999 Regulations.[183] For example, the MCOB rules prohibit excessive charges and the charging of compound interest—a mechanism of capitializing interest that can lead to a sharp increase in the amount of the debt—although compound interest is acceptable and common practice in commercial lending.[184] In respect of the 1999 Regulations, it should be noted that the interest rate will escape the requirement for fairness if it is a core term, although subsidiary provisions that deal with the calculation or variation of interest—for example, on default—will be caught.[185]

Where these statutory controls do not apply, equity's control of oppressive and unconscionable terms provides a final, although rather fragile, safety net.

The test of an oppressive and unconscionable term is strictly looking not only at the substantive fairness of the terms themselves, but also at the procedural fairness with which they were agreed, when the financial expertise and bargaining position of the parties is of central concern.

Multiservice Bookbinding Ltd v Marden [1979] Ch 84, HC

Facts: Multiservice borrowed £36,000 from Marden to fund the purchase of new premises. The loan could not be redeemed for ten years; interest was calculated at 2 per cent above the bank rate on the entire amount of the loan, regardless of capital repayments, with arrears of interest being compounded after twenty-one days. In addition, any repayments of capital and interest were linked to the Swiss franc to protect the lender against sterling exchange rate fluctuations. Sterling did, indeed, decline in value against the Swiss franc, leaving the amount payable by Multiservice when it tried to redeem in excess of £133,000. Mutliservice unsuccessfully claimed that this result was oppressive and unconscionable.

---

[181] See, e.g., the Moneylenders Act 1900.

[182] See Department of Trade and Industry, *Fair, Clear and Competitive: The Consumer Credit Market in the 21st Century* (Cm 6040, 2003, [3.49]–[3.55].

[183] Equity's jurisdiction over oppressive and unconscionable terms is also available, but presents a stricter text than the appropriate statutory controls: see, e.g., *Cityland & Properties (Holdings) Ltd v Dabrah* [1968] Ch 166.

[184] *The Maira* [1990] 1 AC 637; *Guardian Ocean Cargors Ltd v Banco Brasil SA (No 3)* [1992] 2 Lloyds Rep 193; *Westdeutsche Landesbank Girozentrale v Islington BC* [1996] AC 669.

[185] *Falco Finance Ltd v Gough* [1999] CCLR 16; *Director General of Fair Trading v First National Bank plc* [2001] UKHL 52.

Browne-Wilkinson J

At 104

[On public policy and indexation [...] A]fter considering the arguments I do not feel that in 1977 I can declare that an index-linked money obligation is contrary to public policy. The reasons which lead me to this view are as follows: (1) If, as Denning L.J. said, the evil to be guarded against is that sterling will become discredited, this evil will flow not only from indexing by reference to the price of gold or Swiss franc, but equally from any other form of indexing, for example an obligation quantified by reference to the cost of living index. The evil lies in the revalorisation of the pound sterling by reference to any other yardstick, not in the nature of the yardstick itself. (2) Today a large number of obligations originally expressed in pounds sterling are varied by reference to an external yardstick. Long-term commercial contracts frequently include index linked obligations: so do many contracts of employment. The rent payable under certain leases has for centuries been made variable dependent upon the price of corn. More important, Parliament itself has authorised the linking of public service pensions to the cost of living and the issue of Savings Bonds similarly linked. It would be strange if Parliament had authorised transactions contrary to public policy. (3) Denning L.J. treated the process of index-linking as being a cause, not a symptom, of inflation. I know nothing of economics but it has been demonstrated to me that economists are not agreed that indexing has a deleterious effect in promoting inflation. It would, in my judgment, be wrong for the courts to declare that a particular class of transaction is against the public interest even though there is a body of better-informed opinion that takes the view that no harm is caused. It is for Parliament, with all its facilities for weighing the complex issues involved, to make a policy decision of this kind. (4) It seems to me that, even if there are good grounds for saying that indexing causes inflation, there may well be counter-availing considerations which would have to be weighed. In any economy where there is inflation there are few inducements to make long-term loans expressed in a currency the value of which is being eroded. It is at least possible that, unless lenders can ensure that they are repaid the real value of the money they advanced, and not merely a sum of the same nominal amount but in devalued currency, the availability of loan capital will be much diminished. This would surely not be in the public interest. (5) Shortly after 1956, the Cour de Cassation in France reversed its Policy referred to by Denning L.J. and allowed index-linked obligations even in domestic contracts. Index-linked obligations were held valid by the High Court of Australia in *Stanwell Park Hotel Co. Ltd. v. Leslie* (1952) 85 C.L.R. 189. Therefore I feel unable to follow the obiter dictum of Denning L.J. I need hardly say that I do so with considerable diffidence; but I receive some comfort from the fact that since he expressed his views, we have experienced 20 years of inflation and, on the somewhat analogous question whether a judgment of an English court can be expressed otherwise than in pounds sterling, he has departed from the nominalist principle which underlies his remarks in the *Treseder-Griffin case* [1956] 2 Q.B. 127. In my judgment, clause 6 of the mortgage is not contrary to public policy.

At 110

[On oppressive and unconscionable terms] I therefore approach the second point on the basis that, in order to be freed from the necessity to comply with all the terms of the mortgage, the plaintiffs must show that the bargain, or some of its terms, was unfair and unconscionable: it is not enough to show that, in the eyes of the court, it was unreasonable. In my judgment a bargain cannot be unfair and unconscionable unless one of the parties to it has imposed the objectionable terms in a morally reprehensible manner, that is to say, in a way which affects his conscience.

The classic example of an unconscionable bargain is where advantage has been taken of a young, inexperienced or ignorant person to introduce a term which no sensible well-advised person or party would have accepted. But I do not think the categories of unconscionable bargains are limited: the court can and should intervene where a bargain has been procured by unfair means.

Mr. Nugee submitted that a borrower was, in the normal case, in an unequal bargaining position vis-à-vis the lender and that the care taken by the courts of equity to protect borrowers—to which Lord Parker referred in the passage I have quoted—was reflected in a general rule that, except in the case of two large equally powerful institutions, any unreasonable term would be "unconscionable" within Lord Parker's test. I cannot accept this. In my judgment there is no such special rule applicable to contracts of loan which requires one to treat a bargain as having been unfairly made even where it is demonstrated that no unfair advantage has been taken of the borrower. No decision illustrating Mr. Nugee's principle was cited. However, if, as in the *Cityland case* [1968] Ch. 166, there is an unusual or unreasonable stipulation the reason for which is not explained, it may well be that in the absence of any explanation, the court will assume that unfair advantage has been taken of the borrower. In considering all the facts, it will often be the case that the borrower's need for the money was far more pressing than the lenders need to lend: if this proves to be the case, then circumstances exist in which an unfair advantage could have been taken. It does not necessarily follow that what could have been done has been done: whether or not an unfair advantage has in fact been taken depends on the facts of each case.

Applying those principles to this case, first I do not think it is right to treat the "Swiss franc uplift" element in the capital-repayments as being in any sense a premium or collateral advantage. In my judgment a lender of money is entitled to insure that he is repaid the real value of his loan and if he introduces a term which so provides, he is not stipulating for anything beyond the repayment of principal [...] Secondly, considering the mortgage bargain as a whole, in my judgment there was no great inequality of bargaining power as between the plaintiffs and the defendant. The plaintiff company was a small but prosperous company in need of cash to enable it to expand: if it did not like the terms offered it could have refused them without being made insolvent or, as in the *Cityland case*, losing its home. The defendant had £40,000 to lend, but only, as he explained to the plaintiffs, if its real value was preserved. The defendant is not a professional moneylender and there is no evidence of any sharp practice of any kind by him. The borrowers were represented by independent solicitors of repute. Therefore the background does not give rise to any pre-supposition that the defendant took an unfair advantage of the plaintiffs [...] However, Mr. Nugee's other points amount to a formidable list and if it were relevant I would be of the view that the terms were unreasonable judged by the standards which the court would adopt if it had to settle the terms of a mortgage. In particular I consider that it was unreasonable both for the debt to be inflation proofed by reference to the Swiss franc and at the same time to provide for a rate of interest two per cent. above bank rate—a rate which reflects at least in part the unstable state of the pound sterling. On top of this interest on the whole sum advanced was to be paid throughout the term. The defendant made a hard bargain. But the test is not reasonableness. The parties made a bargain which the plaintiffs, who are businessmen, went into with their eyes open, with the benefit of independent advice, without any compelling necessity to accept a loan on these terms and without any sharp practice by the defendant. I cannot see that there was anything unfair or oppressive or morally reprehensible in such a bargain entered into in such circumstances.

4.4.3 Penalties and other onerous terms

In assessing the fairness of a consumer loan or the unconscionability of a commercial loan, it is significant to look not only at the interest rate, but also at the other terms of the agreement. Of particular import are terms that operate upon default and which may operate as a penalty, rather than a genuine pre-estimation of the lender's loss, or which may attract particular scrutiny under the MCOB rules, or against the test of fairness under s 140A of the CCA 1974 (as amended) or the 1999 Regulations.[186]

An increase in the rate of interest payable on arrears following default runs the risk of being a penalty, although a modest uplift in the interest rate payable on future interest payments following default may be acceptable, particularly in the commercial context.[187] A lower concessionary interest rate paid upon prompt payment is not generally regarded as a penalty,[188] although, in a consumer contract, it may still fall foul of the fairness test.

The case of *Falco Finance Ltd v Gough*[189] serves as an example. Mr Gough obtained a third mortgage over his home from Falco for £30,000 in the hope of clearing the arrears on his prior mortgages. The loan was repayable over a term of twenty-five years at a flat interest rate of 13.99 per cent, with an APR of 19.4 per cent. A concessionary rate of 8.99 per cent was, however, payable unless the mortgage went into arrears, when all future payments would not qualify for the discount. Mr Gough missed the first payment and thus the standard rate become immediately payable. The enforceability of these terms became an issue when Falco applied for possession. The court held that the disparity in the dual interest rate mechanism was unfair under the 1999 Regulations, failing within one of the grey-listed terms.[190] The fact that interest was paid at a flat rate on the whole of the capital, irrespective of any amounts repaid, was also found to be unfair.

QUESTIONS

1. Compare the regulatory regimes established by the Financial Services and Markets Act 2002 and Consumer Credit Act 1974. Which regime do you think is most effective in protecting borrowers?

2. How does a wife prove that her husband has unduly influenced her?

3. When will a bank be 'on notice' that a wife may have been unduly influenced by her husband and what steps should a bank take to minimize this risk?

4. In *Barclays Bank v O'Brien* and *Royal Bank of Scotland v Etridge*, the House of Lords tried to ensure that '*a law designed to protect the vulnerable does not render the matrimonial home unacceptable security to financial institutions*'. Has it succeeded?

5. What is the relationship between undue influence and unconscionable bargains? Would it be helpful to assimilate the two doctrines?

6. Does the clogs and fetters doctrine continue to have any utility?

---

[186] *County Leasing v East* [2007] EWHC 2907.
[187] Although see *Lordsvale Finance Ltd v Bank of Zambia* [1996] QB 752, in which an interest uplift of 1 per cent on future interest payments to be made following default was held not to be a penalty in a commercial loan.
[188] *Wallingford v Mutual Society* (1880) 5 App Cas 685.
[189] [1999] CCLR 16.
[190] See Unfair Terms in Consumer Contracts Regulations 1999, Sch 2, para 1(e).

7. When is a mortgage term 'unfair' within the meaning of the Unfair Terms in Consumer Contract Regulations 1999?

8. What legal controls can a borrower use to challenge the interest that he or she has agreed to pay the lender?

FURTHER READING

Bamford, 'Lord Macnaghten's Puzzle: The Mortgage of Real Property in English Law' [1996] CLP 207

Berg, 'Clogs on the Equity of Redemption: Or Chaining an Unruly Dog' [2002] JBL 335

Bigwood, 'Undue Influence: Impaired Consent or Wicked Exploitation' (1996) 16 OJLS 503

Birks and Chin, 'On the Nature of Undue Influence' in *Good Faith and Fault in Contract Law* (eds Beatson and Friedmann, Oxford: Clarendon, 1995, ch 3)

Bright, 'Winning the Battle Against Unfair Contract Terms' (2000) 20 LS 331

Brown, 'The Consumer Credit Act 2006: Real Additional Mortgagor Protection?' [2007] Conv 325

Citizens Advice, *Set Up to Fail: CAB Clients' Experience and Secured Loan Arrears Problems* (2007, available online at http://www.citizensadvice.org.uk)

Department of Trade and Industry, *Fair, Clear and Competitive: The Consumer Credit Market in the 21st Century* (Cm 6040, 2003)

Devenney, 'A Pack of Unruly Dogs: Unconscionable Bargains, Lawful Act (Economic) Duress and Clogs on the Equity of Redemption' (2002) JBL 539

Deveney and Chandler, 'Unconscionability and the Taxonomy of Undue Influence' [2007] JBL 541

Ferris, 'Why is the Law of Undue Influence So Hard to Understand and Apply?' in *Modern Studies in Property Law: Vol 4* (ed Cooke, Oxford: Hart, 2007)

Whitehouse, 'The Homeowner: Citizen or Consumer?' in *Land Law: Themes and Perspectives* (eds Bright and Dewar, Oxford: OUP, 1998, ch 7)

31

LENDER'S RIGHTS
AND REMEDIES

CENTRAL ISSUES

1. A lender's rights and remedies arise from the nature of its security, the powers implied by the Law of Property Act 1925, and any express powers. The most important powers are the right to take possession, the power to sell, and the power to appoint a receiver.

2. The lender has an immediate right to take possession, but this right is carefully controlled by equitable duties, procedural safeguards, and, in the case of dwelling houses, legislation.

3. Section 36 of the Administration of Justice Act 1970 enables the court to delay execution of a possession order of a dwelling house if the borrower is able to clear any sums due within a reasonable period either from income or from a sale of the house. This is an important

jurisdiction for many homeowners in mortgage arrears.

4. The lender's power of sale is implied by s 101(1)(i) of the 1925 Act and can only be exercised if the borrower has defaulted.

5. The lender is able to sell out of court, but is subject to twin equitable duties: to act in good faith and to take reasonable steps to obtain a proper market price.

6. A lender also has an implied power conferred by s 101(1)(iii) of the 1925 Act to appoint a receiver to collect the income from the property. This power is important in the commercial context, when a receiver may also be granted power to manage and sell the property.

1 INTRODUCTION

We now need to turn our attention to the whole point of the lender taking security—namely, the rights and remedies that security provides if the debt is not repaid. We will concentrate our attention on the most common of security over the land: the legal charge by way of mortgage. The most attractive remedy for a lender is the power to sell the land and repay the debt from the sale proceeds—but to sell the land most advantageously, the lender will usually wish to sell with vacant possession. Thus, where the land is the borrower's home, the lender will need to evict the borrower and take possession as a prelude to sale. Where the lending is for commercial purposes and the legal charge is over premises that form part of the assets of the business, the lender may prefer to appoint a receiver. A receiver, who is usually a professional insolvency practitioner, has power to collect the income from the premises—for example, the rents from the property portfolio of a business—and to apply that income in the repayment of the debt. A receiver is also usually granted power to manage and sell the land, and any business conducted upon it.

At one time, the ability of a mortgagee to foreclose was an important right. Under a classic mortgage by conveyance, foreclosure operated by barring the borrower's equitable right to redeem and thus extinguishing his or her equity of redemption, so that the lender became the full legal and equitable owner of the property. Under a legal charge by way of mortgage, statutory machinery is required to achieve the same result.[1] But the prospect that the lender could reap a windfall profit where the debt was considerably less than the value of the land led to careful regulation of foreclosure. The lender has to apply to court, which will, as a matter of course, give the borrower a generous time to clear the debt before confirming the foreclosure order.[2] The court also has power to order the sale of the property in preference to foreclosure.[3] Even if a foreclosure order is made, the court may be persuaded to set it aside in certain circumstances.[4]

Given the time, expense, and uncertainty of foreclosure, it is not surprising that it became unpopular and is now effectively obsolete.[5] In this chapter, we will thus concentrate on the right to take possession, and the powers of sale and appointment of a receiver.

1.1 SOURCE OF THE LENDER'S RIGHTS AND REMEDIES

1.1.1 The nature of the security

The lender's rights and remedies will be defined, initially, by the nature of the security itself. A classical mortgage by conveyance or sub-demise gave rise to a right to possession by reason of the legal estate that it conferred upon the lender, whether that was a freehold or a leasehold term. Foreclosure was also an inherent right of a mortgagee by conveyance or sub-demise. A charge, in contrast, gives no inherent right to possession or to foreclose: the chargee must go to court to enforce the charge by obtaining a court order for sale or for the appointment by the court of a receiver. The legal charge by way of mortgage, however, whilst creating a security by way of charge, confers upon the legal chargee the rights and remedies enjoyed by a mortgagee by way of sub-demise for a term of 3,000 years. This is the import of s 87(1) of the Law of Property Act 1925 (LPA 1925).[6] The legal charge by way of mortgage, as a hybrid form of security, thus confers upon the legal chargee the rights and powers enjoyed by a legal mortgagee, including the right to take possession and to foreclose, although its proprietary form is merely a charge.

---

[1] See Law of Property Act 1925, ss 88(2) and 89(2).

[2] The process involves two stages: the grant of a foreclosure order nisi, requiring accounts to be drawn up detailing exactly what the borrower owes and giving him or her time to repay; and the foreclosure order absolute, which will be made if the borrower has failed to repay as directed.

[3] Law of Property Act 1925, s 91(2).

[4] *Campbell v Holyland* (1877) 7 Ch D 166. See also the Hong Kong cases of *Hang Seng Bank v Mee Ching Development Ltd* [1970] HKLR 94 and *Frencher Ltd (In liq) v Bank of East Asia* [1995] 2 HKC 263.

[5] The Law Commission has recommended its abolition: Law Commission Report No 204, *Land Mortgages* (1991, [7.27]).

[6] See Chapter 29, section 4.2.

1.1.2 Powers implied by statute

Section 101 of the LPA 1925 provides another source of the lender's rights and remedies. The section implies into a mortgage made by deed a number of powers, the most important of which are the power to sell and the power to appoint a receiver without, in either case, having to obtain a court order.

Law of Property Act 1925, s 101(1)

Powers incident to estate or interest of mortgagee

(1) A mortgagee, where the mortgage is made by deed, shall by virtue of this Act, have the following powers, to the like extent as if they had been in the terms conferred by the mortgage deed, but not further (namely):

   (i) A power, when the mortgage money has become due, to sell, or to concur with any person in selling, the mortgaged property, or any part thereof, either subject to prior charges or not, and either together or in lots, by public auction or by private contract, subject to such conditions respecting title, or evidence of title, or other matter, as the mortgagee thinks fit, with power to vary any contract for sale, and to buy in at an auction, or to rescind any contract for sale, and to re-sell, without being answerable for any loss occasioned thereby;

   (ii) [...]

   (iii) A power, when the mortgage money has become due, to appoint a receiver of the income of the mortgaged property, or any part thereof; or, if the mortgaged property consists of an interest in income, or of a rentcharge or an annual or other periodic sum, a receiver of that property or any part thereof;

   [...]

A legal charge by way of mortgage, being a legal interest, must be created by deed and will thus enjoy the powers implied by s 101.[7] The powers are implied into second or subsequent legal charges created by deed, although by reason of the rules of priority, a second chargee will only be able to sell subject to the first charge. Alternatively, a second chargee may decide that it is in its interests to take control of any sale of the property, which it can do by paying off the first charge and thus improving its priority position. The amount required to paying off the first charge, as well as the second chargee's own debt, is recouped from the proceeds of sale.

1.1.3 Express powers

The implied powers of a legal chargee to take possession, to sell, to appoint a receiver, and of foreclose may be excluded, varied, or supplemented by the terms of the security itself.[8]

---

[7] There will also be implied into an equitable mortgage created by deed the powers set out in s 101(1), but an equitable mortgagee will be unable to convey the legal estate in the land unless the borrower confers upon it power to deal with the legal estate by appointing the equitable mortgagee either as his or her attorney or a trustee of the legal estate.

[8] See, in relation to the s 101 powers, s 101(3)–(4). As to the relationship between the expressed and implied powers, see *Horsham Properties Group Ltd v Clark* [2008] EWHC 2327.

Institutional lenders, like banks and building societies, pay their lawyers to draft a standard set of terms and conditions to be incorporated into their legal charges, which will invariably affect the operation of their implied powers and may grant additional express powers, such as a power to lease. It is thus always important to read the legal charge itself to see how the implied powers may have been altered and what additional express powers have been granted.

1.2 REGULATION OF THE LENDER'S RIGHTS AND REMEDIES

In the last chapter, we saw how the borrower's position can be protected. The borrower is particularly vulnerable where the lender is exercising its rights and remedies—after all, he or she stands to lose his or her home or business.

Equity has long cast a watchful eye over the exercise of the lender's powers to ensure that they are employed only to facilitate recovery of the lender's debt, and then only with due probity and care. A modern expression of this duty is found in the following case.

Palk v Mortgage Service Funding plc [1993] Ch 330, CA

Sir Donald Nicholls V–C

At 337–8

[... A] mortgagee can sit back and do nothing. He is not obliged to take steps to realise his security. But if he does take steps to exercise his rights over his security, common law and equity alike have set bounds to the extent to which he can look after himself and ignore the mortgagor's interests. In the exercise of his rights over his security the mortgagee must act fairly towards the mortgagor. His interest in the property has priority over the interest of the mortgagor, and he is entitled to proceed on that footing. He can protect his own interest, but he is not entitled to conduct himself in a way which unfairly prejudices the mortgagor. If he takes possession he might prefer to do nothing and bide his time, waiting indefinitely for an improvement in the market, with the property empty meanwhile. That he cannot do. He is accountable for his actual receipts from the property. He is also accountable to the mortgagor for what he would have received but for his default. So he must take reasonable care to maximise his return from the property. He must also take reasonable care of the property. Similarly if he sells the property: he cannot sell hastily at a knock-down price sufficient to pay off his debt. The mortgagor also has an interest in the property and is under a personal liability for the shortfall. The mortgagee must keep that in mind. He must exercise reasonable care to sell only at the proper market value. As Lord Moulton said in *McHugh v. Union Bank of Canada* [1913] A.C. 299, 311: "It is well settled law that it is the duty of a mortgagee when realising the mortgaged property by sale to behave in conducting such realisation as a reasonable man would behave in the realisation of his own property, so that the mortgagor may receive credit for the fair value of the property sold."

Parliament has also intervened, but only where the lender is seeking possession of a dwelling house by obtaining a court order for possession.[9] The county court has primary jurisdiction in such proceedings, which provides a more informal venue for such intimidating

---

[9] See Administration of Justice Act 1970 (as amended), s 36, noted in Chapter 30, section 2.

proceedings. More significantly, the court is given discretion to halt the progress of the proceedings to allow the borrower time to try to pay any arrears or remedy any other default.

Home mortgage providers have kept further legislative regulation at bay by submitting to market regulation through the Financial Services and Market Act 2000 (FSMA 2000) and the Consumer Credit Act 1974 (CCA 1974). We considered the impact of this legislation in the last chapter (see section 2). Most first legal mortgages, secured upon an individual borrower's home, are regulated under the FSMA 2000, with rules contained in the Mortgage Conduct of Business Sourcebook (MCOB)[10] to provide guidance on the handling of arrears. Mortgages regulated by the CCA 1974, which covers many second mortgages by individual borrowers, are not subject to the same detailed guidelines.

FSA Handbook, Arrears and repossessions: regulated mortgage contracts and home purchase plans (MCOB 13)

MCOB 13.3 Dealing fairly with customers in arrears: policy and procedures

MCOB 13.3.1

(1) A firm must deal fairly with any customer who:

(a) is in arrears on a regulated mortgage contract or home purchase plan;

(b) has a sale shortfall; or

(c) is otherwise in breach of a home purchase plan.

(2) A firm must put in place, and operate in accordance with, a written policy (agreed by its respective governing body) and procedures for complying with (1).

MCOB 13.3.2 Policy procedures: content

(1) A firm should ensure that its written policy and procedures include:

(a) using reasonable efforts to reach an agreement with a customer over the method of repaying any payment shortfall or sale shortfall, in the case of the former having regard to the desirability of agreeing with the customer an alternative to taking possession of the property;

(b) liaising, if the customer makes arrangements for this, with a third party source of advice regarding the payment shortfall or sale shortfall;

(c) adopting a reasonable approach to the time over which the payment shortfall or sale shortfall should be repaid, having particular regard to the need to establish, where feasible, a payment plan which is practical in terms of the circumstances of the customer;

(d) granting, unless it has good reason not to do so, a customer's request for a change to:

(i) the date on which the payment is due (providing it is within the same payment period); or

(ii) the method by which payment is made;

and giving the customer a written explanation of its reasons if it refuses the request;

---

[10] Part of the Financial Services Authority (FSA) Handbook: see Chapter 30.

(e) giving consideration, where no reasonable payment arrangement can be made, to the customer being allowed to remain in possession to effect a sale; and

(f) repossessing the property only where all other reasonable attempts to resolve the position have failed.

(2) Contravention of (1) may be relied on as tending to show contravention of MCOB 13.3.1 R(2).

[...]

MCOB 13.3.4

In relation to using reasonable efforts to reach an agreement with a customer over the method of repaying any payment shortfall or sale shortfall, customers:

(1) should be given a reasonable period of time to consider any proposals for payment that are put to them; in addition, and depending on the individual circumstances, a firm may wish to do one or more of the following in relation to the regulated mortgage contract or home purchase plan with the agreement of the customer:

(a) extend its term; or

(b) change its type; or

(c) defer payment of interest due on the regulated mortgage contract or of sums due under the home purchase plan (including, in either case, on any sale shortfall); or

(d) treat the payment shortfall as if it was part of the original amount provided;

(2) should be given adequate information to understand the implications of any proposed arrangement; one approach may be to provide information on the new terms in line with the annual statement provisions

The guiding principle is thus for lenders regulated by the Financial Services Authority (FSA) to try to agree with their defaulting borrowers a way of clearing arrears by rescheduling repayments, rather than resorting to immediate legal redress. But research reveals inconsistent application of these principles, with some lenders seeking repossession before they have entered into a meaningful dialogue with defaulting borrowers.[11] The Civil Justice Council has introduced a Pre-action Protocol on Mortgage Repossessions, which replicates MCOB 13 and which, it is hoped, will help to ensure that lenders, whether regulated under the FSMA 2000 or CCA 1974, do not resort to immediate repossession.[12]

2 POSSESSION

2.1 THE STARTING POINT: AN IMMEDIATE RIGHT TO POSSESSION

A legal chargee of land is entitled to take possession of the charged property. This right arises because a legal chargee is entitled to the rights of a mortgagee by way of sub-demise—and a

[11] See Citizens Advice, *Set Up To Fail: CAB Client's Experience of Mortgage and Secured Loan Arrears Problems* (2002); FSA, *Mortgage Effectiveness Review Arrears Findings* (2008).

[12] Pre-action Protocol for Possession Claims Based on Mortgage or Home Purchase Plan Arrears in Respect of Residential Property, available online at http://www.civiljusticecouncil.gov.uk. The Protocol takes effect from 19 November 2008.

mortgagee has a right to immediate possession by reason of the leasehold term.[13] The right to possession is thus not dependent upon default.

Harman J made the point forcibly in a number of decisions—most infamously, in the following case.[14]

Four-Maids Ltd v Dudley Marshall (Properties) Ltd [1957] Ch 317, HC

Harman J

At 320

I repeat now, that the right of the mortgagee to possession in the absence of some contract has nothing to do with default on the part of the mortgagor. The mortgagee may go into possession before the ink is dry on the mortgage unless there is something in the contract, express or by implication, whereby he has contracted himself out of that right. He has the right because he has a legal term of years in the property or its statutory equivalent [...] If there is a provision that, so long as certain payments are made, he will not go into possession, then he has contracted himself out of his rights. Apart from that, possession is a matter of course.

Even equity will not intervene, beyond granting a short adjournment to allow the borrower to redeem the whole loan. Arguments suggesting that there was such an equitable jurisdiction were soundly rejected in the following case.

Birmingham Citizens Permanent Building Society v Caunt [1962] Ch 883, HC

Russell J

At 896

For the building society it was contended that the argument based on the equity of redemption and the tenor of the mortgage was novel and fundamentally unsound. Equity had always interfered with legal rights in order to ensure that the mortgage should not operate otherwise than as it was intended to operate—namely, as security for repayment of money. But there was no principle upon which equity had ever attempted or could ever rightly attempt to interfere with the security *as a security*, or to destroy or suspend or nullify any rights of the mortgagee which were part and parcel of that security. The whole purpose of equity was, by insisting that the transaction was a security for the repayment of money, thereby to shield the mortgagor from attempts in reliance on strict legal rights to turn it into something more. Equity was never and should never be in the hands of the judges a sword to attack any part of the security itself, and the right to possession was an important part of that security, more particularly in the association with the ability to give vacant possession on the exercise of the power of sale. These appear to me to be sound answers to an attempt to give reasons for the existence of a jurisdiction such as is suggested. I think there was and is no such jurisdiction.

---

[13] See Law of Property Act 1925, s 87(1). The right is unaffected by the grant of a subcharge: see *Credit and Mercantile plc v Marks* [2004] EWCA Civ 568, [2005] Ch 81.

[14] See also *Alliance Perpetual Building Society v Belrum Investments Ltd* [1957] 1 WLR 720; *Hughes v Waite* [1957] 1 WLR 713.

This fundamental principle also leads to the conclusion that the existence of a counterclaim or equitable right of set-off—by which the borrower might be able to argue that, at the end of the day, he or she owes no money to the lender—does not detract from the lender's immediate right to possession.[15]

2.2 THE EQUITABLE DUTY TO ACCOUNT

Equity will not interfere with the lender's right to take possession, but it will control the exercise of that right. Where the property is let and the lender goes into possession by collecting the rents, it must apply the rent in the discharge of the debt. Furthermore, it is under a duty to account not only for the income received, but also the income that should have been received *but for* the lender's wilful default.[16]

Frisby has examined a mortgagee's duty to account following its application to receivers in *Medforth v Blake*.[17]

Frisby, 'Making a Silk Purse Out of a Pig's Ear: *Medforth v Blake & Ors*' (2000) 63 MLR 413, 416

Liability to account for wilful default is of ancient origin arising out of the account jurisdiction of the Courts of Equity. On a suit for redemption a Chancery Master took an account, whereby the mortgagee's principal, interest and costs were set against the amount received from the mortgaged property. Where the mortgagee had previously taken possession, this last item included not only what *had been* received but what *might have been* received but for his wilful default. Thus equity's traditional protective stance towards the mortgagor's equity of redemption was manifest by the imposition of 'almost penal liabilities.'

Whilst the basic principle of wilful default liability is easily stated, its content is less readily identifiable. Some cases ascribe liability to stated misconduct without further comment. These 'factual instances' of wilful default include refusal to accept tenants and the disadvantageous letting of property. Permitting a mortgagor to intercept 'profits' or failing to receive the purchase price on a sale of the mortgaged property similarly attracted liability. The courts showed varying degrees of strictness in this regard.

These illustrations of liability give little guidance as to whether wilful default requires deliberate, reckless or simply unthinking conduct, the brevity of the reports making it difficult to discern whether the penalised behaviour was collusive or careless. Attempts to extract a governing principle that might predict liability for wilful default exhibit a subtle shift in emphasis from liability to duty. For example, the notion that a mortgagor owes a duty of diligence was propounded by Turner LJ in *Sherwin v Shakspear*.

Other authorities treat wilful default as established by a particular degree of dereliction. In *ex parte Mure* Thurlow LC contemplated that involuntary conduct might suffice to ground liability, although on the facts the negligence was 'gross'. Later cases tend to support the proposition that the carelessness in question may be less than fraud but more than mere negligence. If gross negligence and ordinary diligence exact differing standards of conduct,

---

[15] See *Samuel Keller Holdings Ltd v Martins Bank Ltd* [1971] 1 WLR 43; *Mobil Oil Co Ltd v Rawlinson* (1982) 43 P & CR 221; *Citibank Trust Ltd v Ayivor* [1987] 1 WLR 1157; *National Westminster Bank Ltd v Skelton* [1993] 1 WLR 72; *Ashley Guarantee v Zacaria* [1993] 1 WLR 62.

[16] *White v City of London Brewery* (1889) 42 Ch D 237. For a consideration for 'wilful default', see Stannard (1979) Conv 345.

[17] [1999] 3 All ER 97, considered further at section 4.3 below.

which is to be preferred? It is not immediately obvious that any of the above cases is conclusively authoritative, especially since many judicial statements in this regard appear to be mere *dicta*, and Stannard concludes that 'wilful default' is purely a relative term, meaning no more than a failure to perform a duty.

Whilst the older authorities may be unclear as to the degree of default, more recent authorities tend to support the view that a mortgagee's conduct should be tested according to standards of reasonableness. This was the test applied to receivers in *Medforth v Blake*, which also finds expression in the passage from *Palk* extracted at section 1.2 above.

Whatever the exact standard may be, these duties are usually perceived as sufficiently onerous to deter a lender from taking possession, except for a short time as a prelude to sale. As we shall see, a lender can avoid personal liability where it appoints a receiver, which is the preferred course of action where the lender anticipates taking possession for an extended period.

2.3 THE PURPOSE OF TAKING POSSESSION

In the following case, a house had been let to students whom the landlord wanted to evict— but he could not do so, because their tenancy was protected by legislation. The mortgage of the house prohibited letting without the consent of the bank, which the landlord had failed to obtain. The landlord was thus in breach of the mortgage, but the bank refused the landlord's request to exercise its right to take possession and evict the students. As an alternative ploy, the landlord arranged for his wife to take a transfer of the mortgage, so that she could exercise the right of the mortgagee to evict the students. The Court of Appeal refused to grant an order for possession, although the judges differed in their reasoning.

Quennell v Maltby [1979] 1 WLR 318, CA

Lord Denning MR

At 322

So here in modern times equity can step in so as to prevent a mortgagee, or a transferee from him, from getting possession of a house contrary to the justice of the case. A mortgagee will be restrained from getting possession except when it is sought bona fide and reasonably for the purpose of enforcing the security and then only subject to such conditions as the court thinks fit to impose. When the bank itself or a building society lends the money, then it may well be right to allow the mortgagee to obtain possession when the borrower is in default. But so long as the interest is paid and there is nothing outstanding, equity has ample power to restrain any unjust use of the right to possession.

The other members of the Court of Appeal agreed with the result, but based their reasoning upon a narrower premise. Lord Templeman stated:[18] '*The estate, rights and powers of a mortgagee* [...] *are only vested in a mortgagee to protect his position as a mortgagee and to enable him to obtain repayment.*'

---

[18] At 324.

The width of Lord Denning's views was criticized at the time,[19] but has subsequently been cited with approval.[20] The decision does give expression to equity's underlying concern that lenders exercise their rights bona fide for the purpose of recovering the debt due to them and not for some other purpose—a proposition that was repeated by Lord Templeman as a member of the Privy Council in *Downsview Nominees Ltd v First City Corporation Ltd*.[21]

2.4 PROCEDURAL SAFEGUARDS

Those who take it upon themselves to evict occupiers from their property face criminal sanctions and this legislation applies to lenders as to anyone else. By s 6 of the Criminal Law Act 1977, it is an offence to use violence to gain possession of occupied premises, whilst by s 1(3) of the Protection from Eviction Act 1977, it is an offence to harass an occupier of residential premises to 'persuade' him or her to give up occupation. Invariably, therefore, lenders will seek the assistance of the court to gain entry to premises that are occupied. It is only where premises are empty, or where the borrower voluntarily gives up possession, that the lender will risk entering otherwise than by executing an order for possession.

Taking possession of a borrower's home is a particularly sensitive issue, and mortgages regulated by the FSMA 2000 and CCA 1974 are subject to additional safeguards. The 1974 Act requires notice of arrears to be served upon the borrower[22] and for possession to be obtained by court order;[23] MCOB 13 calls for lenders regulated by the 2000 Act to seek possession as a last resort, having tried and failed to come to some arrangement with the borrower to clear any arrears. The Pre-action Protocol on Mortgage Repossessions reinforces these standards.[24]

2.5 DWELLING HOUSES AND S 36 OF THE ADMINISTRATION OF JUSTICE ACT 1970 (AS AMENDED)

The decision in *Caunt* (see section 2.1 above) led to a need to rethink the exercise of the lender's immediate right to possession in respect of residential property.[25] The result is s 36 of the Administration of Justice Act 1970.

Administration of Justice Act 1970, s 36

Additional powers of court in action by mortgagee for possession of dwelling-house

(1) Where the mortgagee under a mortgage of land which consists of or includes a dwelling-house brings an action in which he claims possession of the mortgaged property, not being

---

[19] Smith [1979] Conv 266; Pearce [1979] CLJ 257.

[20] See *Albany Home Loans Ltd v Massey* (1997) 37 P & CR 509, 513, in which the court refused an order for possession against a husband when to do so would have been futile, because his wife, who was not bound by the mortgage, was entitled to remain in possession as a joint tenant.

[21] [1993] AC 295, 312.

[22] Consumer Credit Act 1974 (as amended), ss 76, 86B–86E, 87, and 88.

[23] Ibid, s 126.

[24] See section 1.2 above.

[25] See the Payne Committee Report (Cmnd 3909, 1969); Haley, 'Mortgage Default: Possession, Relief and Judicial Discretion' (1997) 17 LS 483.

an action for foreclosure in which a claim for possession of the mortgaged property is also made, the court may exercise any of the powers conferred on it by subsection (2) below if it appears to the court that in the event of its exercising the power the mortgagor is likely to be able within a reasonable period to pay any sums due under the mortgage or to remedy a default consisting of a breach of any other obligation arising under or by virtue of the mortgage.

(2) The court—

   (a) may adjourn the proceedings, or

   (b) on giving judgment, or making an order, for delivery of possession of the mortgaged property, or at any time before the execution of such judgment or order, may—

      (i) stay or suspend execution of the judgment or order, or

      (ii) postpone the date for delivery of possession,

     for such period or periods as the court thinks reasonable.

(3) Any such adjournment, stay, suspension or postponement as is referred to in subsection (2) above may be made subject to such conditions with regard to payment by the mortgagor of any sum secured by the mortgage or the remedying of any default as the court thinks fit.

(4) The court may from time to time vary or revoke any condition imposed by virtue of this section.

The section does not limit the lender's inherent right to take possession, but it does control its exercise by conferring upon the court power to adjourn proceedings, or to stay or postpone execution of the order for possession. The court cannot give an indefinite period of suspension, but it can extend the stay upon the borrower making a further application.[26] The court will thus grant the order for possession, but may not allow the lender to ask the bailiff to execute the order. The motive is to allow the borrower time to repay the sums owing, or at least any arrears.

A quick glance at the statistics displayed in Table 7 shows both the widespread use and the effect of the jurisdiction.

Table 7 Possession actions and possession orders made and suspended (Source: Council of Mortgage Lenders)

Period	England & Wales		
	Actions entered	*Orders made*	*Orders suspended*
2002	63,203	16,687	25,072
2003	65,886	16,532	24,506
2004	77,250	20,094	26,589
2005	114,764	32,818	38,146
2006	131,219	46,039	44,641
2007	137,661	51,583	44,148

---

26 *Royal Trust Co of Canada v Markham* [1975] 1 WLR 1416, 1424.

It should also be noted that, where a mortgage is regulated by the CCA 1974, the court enjoys an additional discretion to grant a time order to extend the time for enforcement of the lender's right to possession,[27] and, in such circumstances, to amend and vary the mortgage terms as it see fit.[28] Because consumer credit regulation affects second mortgagees, who are unlikely to be able to exercise their right to possession in priority to the first chargee, this jurisdiction is less significant than s 36.

Unfortunately for such a significant jurisdiction, s 36 is not the most happily worded and has raised a number of problems of interpretation, as well as calls for reform.[29]

2.5.1 'Dwelling-house'

Needless to say there have been questions over what constitutes a 'dwelling-house'. It does not matter if only part of the property is a dwelling, or that the dwelling house is not the borrower's home.[30] The protection is thus not restricted to the residential lending market, but can catch commercial lending where the security includes a dwelling house. The time for determining whether or not the security is over, or includes, a dwelling house is the time of the order for possession, rather than the time of the mortgage itself.[31]

2.5.2 Court proceedings for possession

The more difficult question is whether the court's jurisdiction is only available where the lender has applied for an order for possession. We have noted that the lender will invariably do so where the borrower is in residence, but what about when the borrower, for one reason or another, is not?

Just such a situation arose in the following case, in which the Court of Appeal—taking a literal, rather than a purposive, approach to interpretation of s 36—held that it had no application where a lender was not seeking an order for possession.

Ropaigealach v Barclays Bank plc [2000] QB 263, CA

Facts: The Ropaigealachs fell into mortgage arrears and their lender, Barclays, wrote to them, making a final demand for payment and warning them that their property would be sold. The Ropaigealachs did not receive the letter, because they were not living at the property whilst it was being renovated, and did not hear of the sale until told by a neighbour. The Court declined to grant a declaration that Barclays was not entitled to take possession and sell without obtaining a court order.

Clarke LJ

At 283

It is true to say that neither this court in *Caunt's case* nor the Payne Committee was considering whether the court should have similar powers in cases in which the mortgagee

---

[27] Consumer Credit Act 1974 (as amended), ss 129 and 130.

[28] Ibid, s 136.

[29] See Smith [1979] Conv 266; Haley, 'Mortgage Default: Possession, Relief and Judicial Discretion' (1997) 17 LS 483.

[30] See, e.g., *Bank of Scotland v Miller* [2002] EWCA Civ 344, [2002] QB 255, in which the property was a nightclub with an unoccupied flat above.

[31] Ibid.

chooses not to take proceedings for possession but simply takes possession or perhaps sells the property under his power of sale and the purchaser takes possession. In these circumstances I agree that it cannot readily be inferred that Parliament intended to give protection to mortgagors in such a case. It does however strike me as very curious that mortgagors should only have protection in the case where the mortgagee chooses to take legal proceedings and not in the case where he chooses simply to enter the property. As Alison Clarke put it in her illuminating article "Further implications of section 36 of the Administration of Justice Act 1970" in *The Conveyancer & Property Lawyer* (1983), p. 293, [...] it is anomalous and undesirable to protect mortgagors against eviction by court process yet leave them open to eviction by self-help.

The second case which seems to me to highlight the potential problems is the decision of this court in *National & Provincial Building Society v. Ahmed* [1995] 2 E.G.L.R. 127, where it was held that the mortgagor's equity of redemption is extinguished when the mortgagee, in the exercise of his power of sale, enters into a contract of sale of the mortgaged property [...]

In a Law Commission Working Paper No. 99 on *Land Mortgages* (1986), which was produced before the report and was expressly stated not to represent the final views of the Commission, the position was put thus with regard to the court's discretion under section 36, at p. 103, para. 3.69:

> "(b) The discretion is to delay or withhold the possession order only, not any other remedy. In practice this usually prevents enforcement, but in theory it is still open to the mortgagee to proceed to exercise its power of sale notwithstanding the court's refusal to make a possession order. Since such a sale terminates the mortgagor's interest in the property, the purchaser presumably would have no difficulty in obtaining a possession order against the mortgagor after completion."

In a written note sent to us after the conclusion of the hearing Miss Gloster says that the bank would not go so far as to submit that that view is correct. Miss Gloster correctly adds that this kind of issue does not to fall for determination on this appeal, and I express no view upon the solution to such problems, but such considerations do highlight the potential problems. Such problems would not arise (or would be much reduced) if it were held that the effect of section 36 were [...] to give the court the same power to inhibit the exercise by the mortgagee of its right to possession at common law whether it were exercised by simply entering possession or by doing so pursuant to an order of the court [...]

It seems to me that if a mortgagor needs that relief he needs it whether the mortgagee chooses to exercise his right of possession by entering into possession with or without an order of the court. Indeed he also needs it if instead of doing either the mortgagee sells the property to a purchaser leaving the purchaser to take possession.

I recognise that Miss Gloster says that responsible mortgagees do not in practice take possession of property in which the mortgagor and his family are living without an order of the court, and I accept that that is so, but in my judgment the problem should be approached by reference to the legal rights of the mortgagee and to the legitimate interests of the mortgagor in the light of the purpose of the Act. In these circumstances, if it were possible to construe section 36 by affording mortgagors protection whether or not the mortgagee chose to obtain possession by self-help or legal action, I for my part would do so. I have however been persuaded that it is not possible.

Clarke LJ refers also to the situation in which a lender exercises its power of sale without having first obtained possession. In these circumstances, the sale will overreach the borrower's equity of redemption and pass an unencumbered title to the purchaser.[32] But if the property is occupied (e.g. by the borrower or his or her tenant), the suggestion made by Millett LJ in *National & Provincial Building Society v Ahmed*[33] is that s 36 will again come into play if the purchaser seeks an order for possession, although, given that the borrower's interests will have been overreached, it is difficult to see how he or she could resist a purchaser's application for possession. Indeed, this was the approach taken by the High Court in *Horsham Properties Group Ltd v Clark*.[34] If a purchaser can be found to purchase the property whilst the borrower is still in occupation, there is thus a worrying route by which s 36 can be avoided.

2.5.3 Who can apply?

The borrower, as mortgagor, can apply under s 36, and also a purchaser from the borrower who takes subject to the mortgage may apply,[35] but it seems that a tenant of the borrower cannot.[36]

Where joint borrowers—for example, husband and wife—are the legal co-owners, they will both have granted the mortgage to the lender and will both be the subject to possession proceedings. But a difficulty may arise where a single borrower, holding the legal estate on trust for equitable co-owners, grants the mortgage. This situation can arise in relation to a home, where one spouse or partner holds the legal title on trust for him or herself and the other spouse or partner. In such circumstances, the equitable co-owner may not be aware of possession proceedings brought by the lender—particularly where he or she has separated from his or her spouse or partner, who has ceased to pay the mortgage. The lender is under no obligation to inform him or her of possession proceedings, even though he or she may be left in occupation of the home.[37]

The Family Law Act 1996 (FLA 1996) provides limited assistance. Section 56(1) and (2) requires the lender to serve notice of the proceedings upon a spouse who has registered his or her statutory right of occupation. Also, where a spouse or partner does learn of the proceedings, he or she may apply to court to be joined as a party where he or she is entitled, and is in a financial position, to meet the mortgage repayments.[38]

2.5.4 The court's discretion

Where there is default, the court may exercise its jurisdiction where it is satisfied that the borrower is likely to be able, within a reasonable period, to pay any sums due under the mortgage or to remedy any other default.[39] The vast majority of cases are concerned with mortgage arrears, when the court is solely concerned with how and when the borrower is able to meet his or her financial commitments.[40]

---

[32] Law of Property Act 1925, ss 88(1) and s 89(1).

[33] [1995] 2 EGLR 127; *Duke v Robson* [1973] 1 WLR 267.

[34] [2008] EWHC 2327.

[35] Administration of Justice Act 1970, s 39(1).

[36] *Britannia Building Society v Earl* [1990] 1 WLR 422, 430.

[37] *Hastings and Thanet Building Society v Goddard* [1970] 1 WLR 1544, 1548.

[38] See Family Law Act 1996, s 55(2).

[39] For example, in the case of breach of a covenant against letting by removing the tenants: see *Britannia Building Society v Earl* [1990] 1 WLR 422, 430.

[40] Compare Trusts of Land and Appointment of Trustees Act 1996, ss 14 and 15 (see Chapter 19, section 5.5), where a mortgagee is applying for the sale of co-owner's interest in land.

What sums are due under the mortgage?

Initially, there is the question of what sums are due under the mortgage where an acceleration provision in the mortgage operates on default to trigger repayment of all sums secured under the mortgage, including the full capital value of the loan and any outstanding interest. In *Halifax Building Society v Clark*,[41] the court held that it was, indeed, the total of these sums that the borrower was required to clear. The purpose of s 36 was accordingly placed in jeopardy: if the borrower was already unable to meet his or her periodic repayments, he or she was hardly likely to be able to repay the whole loan.

Parliament was swift to react to restrict the meaning of 'sums due' to any arrears.

Administration of Justice Act 1973, s 8

(1) Where by a mortgage of land which consists of or includes a dwelling-house, or by any agreement between the mortgagee under such a mortgage and the mortgagor, the mortgagor is entitled or is to be permitted to pay the principal sum secured by instalments or otherwise to defer payment of it in whole or in part, but provision is also made for earlier payment in the event of any default by the mortgagor or of a demand by the mortgagee or otherwise, then for purposes of section 36 of the Administration of Justice Act 1970 (under which a court has power to delay giving a mortgagee possession of the mortgaged property so as to allow the mortgagor a reasonable time to pay any sums due under the mortgage) a court may treat as due under the mortgage on account of the principal sum secured and of interest on it only such amounts as the mortgagor would have expected to be required to pay if there had been no such provision for earlier payment.

(2) A court shall not exercise by virtue of subsection (1) above the powers conferred by section 36 of the Administration of Justice Act 1970 unless it appears to the court not only that the mortgagor is likely to be able within a reasonable period to pay any amounts regarded (in accordance with subsection (1) above) as due on account of the principal sum secured, together with the interest on those amounts, but also that he is likely to be able by the end of that period to pay any further amounts that he would have expected to be required to pay by then on account of that sum and of interest on it if there had been no such provision as is referred to in subsection (1) above for earlier payment.

Section 8 brought its own problems of interpretation, in the shape of what types of loan repayment scheme fell within its terms. Clearly, the standard repayment mortgage, whereby instalments of capital and interest are repaid over a fixed term, are covered.[42] The court has held that endowment mortgages are similarly included,[43] but mortgages repayable on demand, which are common to secure an overdraft facility granted to provide funds to the borrower's business, do not fall within s 8.[44]

---

[41] [1973] Ch 307.

[42] *Centrax Trustees v Ross* [1979] 2 All ER 952.

[43] *Bank of Scotland v Grimes* [1986] QB1179. Under an endowment mortgage, the borrower's instalment payments meet only the interest payable. The borrower also pays periodic insurance premiums to maintain an endowment policy that, at the end of the mortgage term, will mature to produce a lump sum, which should be sufficient to repay the capital advanced.

[44] *Habib Bank Ltd v Tailor* [1982] 1 WLR 1218; *Rees Investment Ltd v Groves* [2002] 1 P & CR DG 9.

What is a 'reasonable period'?

The significance of s 8 has diminished somewhat as a result of the interpretation that the courts have accorded to what is a 'reasonable period' in which repayment is to be made. It is clear that the Payne Committee and Parliament envisaged a relatively short period, of a year or two, to provide the borrower with relief, so that he or she could overcome a temporary financial setback, such as the loss of a job, or an illness. The Court of Appeal, in the light of the property slump of the early 1990s during which mortgage repossessions soared, adopted a different approach.

Cheltenham & Gloucester Building Society v Norgan [1996] 1 WLR 343, CA

Facts: Mrs Norgan had borrowed £90,000, repayable by monthly instalments over twenty-two years, with the loan being secured upon her farmhouse. She fell into arrears, and the Cheltenham & Gloucester obtained a possession order, which was stayed on several occasions. The arrears remained substantial, and the Cheltenham & Gloucester applied again to execute the possession order.

Waite LJ

At 353

In the present plight of the housing market possession cases play a major part in the case-load for the county courts. That is particularly true of the district judges, who deal with those cases in such numbers that they develop a "feel" for them and have achieved an excellent disposal record. It is not surprising that they have found it convenient to adopt a relatively short period of years as the rough rule of thumb which aids a just determination of the "reasonable period" for the purposes of section 36 of the Act of 1970 and section 8 of the Act of 1973. Nevertheless, although I would not go quite so far with Mr. Croally as to say it should be an "assumption," it does seem to me that the logic and spirit of the legislation require, especially in cases where the parties are proceeding under arrangements such as those reflected in the C.M.L. statement, that the court should take as its starting point the full term of the mortgage and pose at the outset the question: "Would it be possible for the mortgagor to maintain payment-off of the arrears by instalments over that period?"

I accept all the grounds urged on us by Mr. Waters for saying that the dicta relied on in *First Middlesbrough Trading and Mortgage Co. Ltd. v. Cunningham* (1974) 28 P. & C.R. 69 and *Western Bank Ltd. v. Schindler* [1977] Ch.1 were directed to situations different from the circumstances of this case and most other cases of it kind, but they nevertheless in my judgment provide confirmation of the view that such is the right approach. I would acknowledge, also, that this approach will be liable to demand a more detailed analysis of present figures and future projections than it may have been customary for the courts to undertake until now. There is likely to be a greater need to require of mortgagors that they should furnish the court with a detailed "budget" of the kind that has been supplied by the mortgagor in her affidavit in the present case. But analysis of such budgets is part of the expertise in which the district judges have already become adept in their family jurisdiction and I would not expect that to present too great a difficulty. There will be instances, too, in which preliminary adjudication will be necessary to determine, when calculating the amount of arrears and assessing the future instalments for their payment-off, which items are to be attributed to the mortgagor's current payment obligations and which to his ultimate liability on capital account.

The present case has shown—through the disparity introduced by the disputed items—how problematic that may sometimes prove to be. They are nevertheless disputes that it will be essential to resolve—in this case and others where they arise—before the court can undertake an accurate estimate of the amount which the mortgagor would be required to meet if the arrears were to be made repayable over the full remainder of the mortgage term. There may also be cases, as Mr. Waters points out, in which it is less obvious than in this case that the mortgagee is adequately secured—and detailed evidence, if necessary by experts, may be required to see if and when the lender's security will become liable to be put at risk as a result of imposing postponement of payments in arrear. Problems such as these—which I suspect will arise only rarely in practice although they will undeniably be daunting when they do arise—should not however be allowed, in my judgment, to stand in the way of giving effect to the clearly intended scheme of the legislation.

There is another factor which, to my mind, weighs strongly in favour of adopting the full term of the mortgage as the starting point for calculating a "reasonable period" for payment of arrears. It is prompted by experience in this very case. The parties have been before the court with depressing frequency over the years on applications to enforce, or further to suspend, the warrant of possession, while Mrs. Norgan and her husband have struggled, sometimes with success and sometimes without, to meet whatever commitment was currently approved by the court. Cheltenham has (in exercise of its power to do so under the terms of the mortgage) added to its security the costs it has incurred in connection with all these attendances. One of the disputed items turns upon the question whether such costs fall to be allocated to capital or to interest account. What is not in dispute, however, is that one day, be it sooner or later, those costs will have to be borne by the mortgagor, and if the day comes when she decides—or is compelled by circumstances—to move to more readily affordable accommodation, her resources for rehousing will be correspondingly reduced. It is an experience which brings home the disadvantages which both lender and borrower are liable to suffer if frequent attendance before the court becomes necessary as a result of multiple applications under section 36 of the Act of 1970—to say nothing of the heavy inroads made upon court hearing time. One advantage of taking the period most favourable to the mortgagor at the outset is that, if his or her hopes of repayment prove to be ill-founded and the new instalments initially ordered as a condition of suspension are not maintained but themselves fall into arrear, the mortgagee can be heard with justice to say that the mortgagor has had his chance, and that the section 36 powers (although of course capable in theory of being exercised again and again) should not be employed repeatedly to compel a lending institution which has already suffered interruption of the regular flow of interest to which it was entitled under the express terms of the mortgage to accept assurances of future payment from a borrower in whom it has lost confidence.

Evans LJ

At 356

In conclusion, a practical summary of our judgments may be helpful in future cases. Drawing on the above and on the judgment of Waite L.J., the following considerations are likely to be relevant when a "reasonable period" has to be established for the purposes of section 36 of the Act of 1970. (a) How much can the borrower reasonably afford to pay, both now and in the future? (b) If the borrower has a temporary difficulty in meeting his obligations, how long is the difficulty likely to last? (c) What was the reason for the arrears which have accumulated? (d) How much remains of the original term? (e) What are relevant contractual terms, and what type of mortgage is it, i.e. when is the principal due to be repaid? (f) Is it a case where the court should exercise its power to disregard accelerated payment provisions (section 8 of the Act of 1973)? (g) Is it reasonable to expect the lender, in the circumstances of the particular case, to recoup the arrears of interest (1) over the whole of the original term, or (2) within a shorter period, or even (3) within a longer period, i.e. by extending the repayment period? Is it reasonable to expect the lender to capitalise the interest or not? (h) Are there any reasons affecting the security which should influence the length of the period for payment? In the light of the answers to the above, the court can proceed to exercise its overall discretion, taking account also of any further factors which may arise in the particular case.

Thus the question to be considered by the court is whether, taking into account the whole of the term of the mortgage, it is likely that the borrower will be able to repay all that he or she owes the lender. In coming to that decision, the court will need to consider the matters listed by Evans LJ, which, in turn, will require the parties to present to the court the necessary evidence, including detailed financial statements and projections of the borrower's likely income and outgoings, as well as evidence—for example, as to the spare equity in the property—which will enable the court to evaluate the exposure of the lender to a continuing risk of default. These guidelines reflect those contained in the MCOB 13 (see section 1.2 above) and the Pre-action Protocol on Mortgage Repossessions that the lender should try to agree a reasonable rescheduling of the borrower's debt repayments before seeking repossession. Thus it may well be that the feasibility of the borrower being able to repay within a reasonable period has already been explored.

Another factor that may assist a borrower is the possibility of state assistance to meet mortgage interest repayments. For example, Income Support or Jobseeker's Allowance may provide some help, although such assistance is limited and not immediately available.[45] The government has deliberately restricted assistance to encourage borrowers to seek protection against the risk of a loss income as a result of sickness or redundancy, by taking out mortgage payment protection insurance.[46]

The courts' approach to the interpretation of 'a reasonable period' is somewhat different where the borrower is proposing to clear his or her debt from a sale of property. In such circumstances, the total amount owed to the lender will be repayable, because the borrower will need to discharge the mortgage to sell the property. There must be some firm evidence that a sale is likely within the foreseeable future; a mere hope or an estate agent's optimistic projections are not enough.

Bristol & West Building Society v Ellis (1997) 73 P & CR 158, CA

Facts: Mrs Ellis had fallen into mortgage arrears after her husband left her. She unsuccessfully applied for suspension of a warrant for possession, on the basis that she would

---

[45] See Lundy, 'State Assistance with House Purchases: Mortgage Interest and Social Security' [1997] Conv 36; Morgan, 'Mortgages and a Flexible Workforce' in *Contemporary Property Law* (eds Jackson and Wilde, 1999); Citizens Advice (2007). The period before payments are made has been reduced for most claimants from thirty-nine weeks to thirteen weeks, and the house value ceiling for eligibility has been increased from £100,000 to £175,000.

[46] Although there has been considerable concern expressed over the marketing of this insurance (see Chapter 30, section 4.1.3), and such insurance provides protection for the lender's and not the borrower's loss: see *Woolwich Building Society v Brown* [1996] CLC 625; *Banfield v Leeds Building Society* [2007] EWCA Civ 1369.

sell the property in three–five years' time, when her children had finished their full-time education. In support of her application, she provided estate agents' opinions showing that the likely sale price for the property should be sufficient to discharge the mortgage.

Auld LJ

At 161

The prospect of settling the mortgage debt, including arrears of principal and/or interest, by sale of the property raises a number of questions on the reasonableness of any period which a court may consider allowing for the purpose.

The critical matters are, of course, the adequacy of the property as a security for the debt and the length of the period necessary to achieve a sale. There should be evidence, or at least some informal material (see *Cheltenham & Gloucester Building Society v. Grant* (1994) 26 H.L.R. 703), before the court of the likelihood of a sale the proceeds of which will discharge the debt and of the period within which such a sale is likely to be achieved. If the court is satisfied on both counts and that the necessary period for sale is reasonable, it should, if it decides to suspend the order for possession, identify the period in its order [...]

It all depends on the individual circumstances of each case, though the important factors in most are likely to be the extent to which the mortgage debt and arrears are secured by the value of the property and the effect of time on that security.

Where the property is already on the market and there is some indication of delay on the part of the mortgagor, it may be that a short period of suspension of only a few months would be reasonable [...] Where there is likely to be considerable delay in selling the property and/or its value is close to the total of the mortgage debt and arrears so that the mortgagee is at risk as to the adequacy of the security, immediate possession or only a short period of suspension may be reasonable. Where there has already been considerable delay in realising a sale of the property and/or the likely sale proceeds are unlikely to cover the mortgage debt and arrears or there is simply no sufficient evidence as to sale value, the normal order would be for immediate possession. See, e.g. *Abbey National Mortgages plc v. Rochelle Bernard* (July 4, 1995, C.A. unreported) and *National Provincial Bank v Lloyd* [1996] 1 All ER 630.

Mr Duggan submitted that, here, the material, formal or informal (see *Grant*) before the district judge and judge was insufficient to satisfy them that Mrs Ellis would or could sell the property within three to five years or that its sale proceeds when sold would be sufficient to discharge the mortgage debt and arrears. As to the time of sale, all that the district judge had was her statement in her affidavit that she anticipated selling within three to five years when her children completed their education. As to value, the evidence was not compelling: two estate agents' estimates of between £80,000 and £85,000 as against the redemption figure at the time of just over £77,000 plus costs. As a result of Mrs Ellis's payment of the lump sum ordered by the district judge and subsequent payments, the total figure of indebtedness is now about £70,000, including about £10,000 arrears of interest. Given the inevitable uncertainty as to the movement of property values over the next few years and the reserve with which the courts should approach estate agents' estimates of sale prices (see *Clothier*) no court could be sanguine about the adequacy, now or continuing over that period, of the property as a security for the mortgage debt and arrears. In my view, the evidence was simply insufficient to entitle the district judge to contemplate, behind the order he made, a likelihood that the house would or could be sold at a price sufficient to discharge Mrs Ellis's overall debt to Bristol & West within any reasonable period, and certainly not one of up to three to five years.

There may be a distinct marketing advantage in the borrower selling the property rather than the lender doing so after entering into possession: a home will often look more attractive to a purchaser if it is occupied, and the knowledge that a sale is being forced by a mortgagee can have the effect of depressing the price. The borrower may, however, be slow to cooperate. In limited circumstances, a court may be persuaded that the benefits of allowing the borrower to conduct the sale outweigh the disadvantages and will suspend execution of a possession order accordingly. It is clear also that such a jurisdiction will not be exercised if the lender objects.

Cheltenham & Gloucester Building Society v Booker (1997) 73 P & CR 412, CA

Facts: The Bookers were in substantial arrears with their mortgage repayments and the Cheltenham & Gloucester had obtained an order for possession, the execution of which had been stayed on a number of occasions. The Bookers made an unsuccessful final application for stay, on the basis that they intended to sell, and requested that they be allowed to remain in possession pending the sale.

Millett LJ

At 415

[...I]t appears to me in principle difficult to deny the existence, at least in theory, of a similar jurisdiction to defer the giving of possession for a short time in order to enable the property to be sold by the mortgagee. If the court is satisfied (a) that possession will not be required by the mortgagee pending completion of the sale but only by the purchasers on completion; (b) that the presence of the mortgagor pending completion will enhance, or at least not depress, the sale price; (c) that the mortgagor will so cooperate in the sale by showing prospective purchasers round the property and so forth; and (d) that he will give possession to the purchaser on completion, it seems to me that there is no reason in principle why the court should accede to a mortgagee's insistence that immediate possession prior to the sale should be given to him.

However, while the jurisdiction exists, experience shows that these conditions are seldom likely to be satisfied. Accordingly, in my judgment, the jurisdiction should be sparingly exercised, and then exercised only with great caution. If the conditions which I have mentioned exist, the court is likely to entrust the conduct of the sale to the mortgagor. There is an inherent illogicality in entrusting conduct of the sale to the mortgagee and yet leaving the mortgagor in possession pending completion unless the mortgagee has agreed to this course. The obtaining of possession with a view to giving it to the purchaser is part of the necessary arrangements for sale. In my opinion the party having conduct of the sale ought normally to have the right to decide when it is desirable for him to obtain possession from those in occupation in order to enable the sale to be effectively carried through.

As the plaintiffs observe, in what I would wish to describe as a most impressive skeleton argument, if the contractual obligation to give vacant possession, which the mortgagee will wish to assume in order to obtain the best price reasonably obtainable, is separated from the ability to give immediate vacant possession, the mortgagee is put at risk of being in breach of contract through circumstances beyond his control. Moreover, if the conduct of the sale is given to the mortgagee, any prospective purchaser will become aware prior to exchange of contracts that the property is being sold by a mortgagee who has not yet obtained vacant possession. The risk that the borrower will not vacate the property on completion will become apparent and the purchaser may be deterred from proceeding. He will also be aware that the sale is a forced sale, the advantage of achieving a better price through continued owner occupation is unlikely to be realised.

Accordingly, while I would not wish to hold that the court has no jurisdiction in an appropriate case to make an order such as the judge made in the present case, it is hard to see the advantages of such an order and easy to see the disadvantages. I find it difficult to envisage circumstances in which such a course would be appropriate unless the mortgagee consented. It ought to be a rarity and taken only if the necessary conditions are satisfied.

2.5.5 Section 36 and court orders for sale under s 91

Section 91 of the LPA 1925 provides that a borrower may apply to the court for an order for sale.

Law of Property Act 1925, s 91

Sale of mortgaged property in action for redemption or foreclosure

(1) Any person entitled to redeem mortgaged property may have a judgment or order for sale instead of for redemption in an action brought by him either for redemption alone or for sale alone, or for sale or redemption in the alternative.

(2) In any action, whether for foreclosure, or for redemption, or for sale or for raising and payment in any manner of mortgage money, the court, on the request of the mortgagee, or any person interested either in the mortgage money or in the right of redemption, and, notwithstanding that—

(a) any other person dissents; or

(b) the mortgagee or any person so interested does not appear in the action;

and without allowing any time for redemption or for payment of any mortgage money, may direct a sale of the mortgaged property, on such terms as it thinks fit, including the deposit in court of a reasonable sum fixed by the court to meet the expenses of sale and to secure performance of the terms

---

The jurisdiction provides an alternative option for a borrower who wishes to solve his or her debt repayment problems through sale, although its application is limited. Traditionally, the jurisdiction was exercised only where there was a surplus between the value of the property and the outstanding mortgage, when it was not unusual to give the borrower the conduct of the sale. In *Palk v Mortgage Services Funding plc*,[47] the court was persuaded to use s 91 to order sale on the application of the borrower where there was negative equity. The lender had wanted to delay sale until the market improved, and proposed, in the meantime, to take possession and let the property, applying the rental in partial discharge of the mortgage repayments—but this strategy would have resulted in mounting arrears. The Palks preferred an immediate sale to clear a good portion of their debt, leaving the balance that they owed unsecured.

---

[47] [1993] Ch 330.

The application of s 91 to instances in which there is negative equity can, however, be problematic: for example, where the borrower resorts to the jurisdiction as a delaying tactic or to try to gain control of the sale. Accordingly, the court will not usurp the lender's right to seek possession with a view to sale by suspending proceedings under s 36 to allow an application for sale under s 91.

Cheltenham & Gloucester plc v Krausz [1997] 1 WLR 1558, CA

Facts: The Krauszs were in mortgage arrears and the Cheltenham & Gloucester had obtained an order for possession, the execution of which had been stayed on several occasions. The Krauszs found a purchaser for the property at £65,000, but the Cheltenham & Gloucester refused to agree to the sale, believing that the property was worth nearer £90,000. The Krauszs unsuccessfully applied for an order for sale under s 91(2) when their arrears totalled £83,000.

Phillips LJ

At 1562

Until *Palk's case* it was the practice of the Chancery court only to entertain an application for sale by the mortgagor if the proceeds of sale were expected to be sufficient to discharge the entirety of the mortgage debt. In such circumstances the mortgagor might initiate proceedings by bringing an action for sale under section 91(1), or, if the mortgagee sought to foreclose, the mortgagor could apply for an order for sale in place of foreclosure. The practice thus reflected the heading to section 91: "Sale of mortgaged property in action for redemption or foreclosure."

Palk's case established, for the first time, that the court has power under section 91(2) to make an order for sale on the application of a mortgagor, notwithstanding that the proceeds of sale will be insufficient to discharge the mortgage debt. In *Palk's case* the mortgagees had obtained an order for possession with the intention, not of proceeding to sell the property but of waiting in the hope that the market might improve. The mortgagor was anxious that the property should be sold so that the proceeds would reduce the mortgage debt, on which interest was accruing at an alarming rate. The Court of Appeal held that, as the mortgagees could buy the property themselves if they wished to speculate on an increase in its value, in the interests of fairness the property should be sold [. . .]

In cases before *Palk's case*, where the proceeds of sale were likely to exceed the mortgage debt, the court was prepared to entrust the sale to the mortgagor on the basis that the mortgagor had a keener interest than the mortgagee in obtaining the best price. We have not been referred to any case, however, where there was a contest between the mortgagee and the mortgagor as to who should have conduct of the sale [. . .]

In any case in which there is negative equity it will be open to the mortgagor to resist an order for possession on the ground that he wishes to obtain a better price by remaining in possession and selling the property himself. In not every case will the primary motive for such an application be the wish to obtain a better price than that which the mortgagee is likely to obtain on a forced sale. Often the mortgagor will be anxious to postpone for as long as possible the evil day when he has to leave his home. This court has ample experience of hopeless applications for leave to appeal against possession orders designed to achieve just that end. There will be a danger, if the mortgagee does not obtain possession, that the mortgagor will delay the realisation of the property by seeking too high a price, or deliberately procrastinating on completion. At present there is a simple procedure for seeking possession in the county court and the issue tends to be whether there are arrears and whether the mortgagor is likely to be able to discharge these in a reasonable time. If possession is to be suspended whenever this appears reasonable in order to give mortgagors the opportunity to sell the property themselves, the courts are going to have to enter into an area of difficult factual inquiry in order to decide in the individual case whether or not this course will be to the common benefit of mortgagor and mortgagee. Furthermore there will be obvious practical difficulties for mortgagees in monitoring the negotiations of mortgagors who are permitted time to market their properties. [...]

Before the decision in *Palk's case* it seemed that section 36 of the Act of 1970 and section 91 of the Act of 1925 were complementary. An application under section 91 would only be contemplated where the proceeds of sale were expected to exceed the mortgage debt. In these circumstances section 36 gave the court the power to suspend possession in order to enable an application for sale under section 91 to be made. It is, however, quite clear that section 36 does not empower the court to suspend possession in order to permit the mortgagor to sell the mortgaged premises where the proceeds of sale will not suffice to discharge the mortgage debt, unless of course other funds will be available to the mortgagor to make up the shortfall. A mortgagor seeking relief in the circumstances of *Palk's case* is thus unable to invoke any statutory power to suspend the mortgagee's right to enter into possession.

2.5.6 Court's discretion where no default

The court was required to consider the effect of s 36 upon the lender's immediate right to possession in the interesting case of *Western Bank Ltd v Schindler*,[48] in which deficiencies in drafting of the bank's mortgage left their security dangerously exposed, although there was no default. The Court of Appeal was unanimous in refusing to suspend the possession order for longer than one month, but the judges were divided in the application of the section where there was no default. Goff LJ adopted a literal interpretation in deciding that the section has no application where there was no default, but Buckley and Scarman LJJ refused to accept what they considered an absurd result that the section could operate to assist a borrower in default, but not to a borrower who was not in default. They managed to extract an interpretation of the section to allow the court to exercise its discretion even where there was no default. In so doing, all judges refused to accept counsel's invitation to declare that s 36 had abrogated the lender's immediate right to possession; they would accept only that it had granted the court discretion to control its exercise.

Western Bank Ltd v Schindler [1977] Ch 1, CA

Facts: The mortgage was an endowment mortgage, but there was no term requiring the borrower to keep the policy on foot by paying the policy premiums. Furthermore, there was no term requiring the borrower to make periodic payments of interest, which was expressed to be payable with the capital at the end of the mortgage term. Predictably, the borrower failed to pay the endowment premiums or to make periodic payments of interest. The lender sought possession to protect its security, but the borrower asked the court to exercise its jurisdiction under s 36, even though there had been no default.

---

[48] [1977] Ch 1.

Buckley LJ

At 12

I have been very much puzzled during the argument about the proper interpretation of section 36. If subsection (1) is read literally, the conditional clause introduced by the words "if it appears to the court" (which I shall refer to as "the conditional clause") appears to restrict the operation of the section to cases in which some sum is due or some default has taken place and remains unremedied when the application comes before the court. This, however, seems to me to lead to a ridiculous result. If a mortgagee applies to the court for a possession order while the mortgagor is in default, the court may keep the matter in abeyance under subsection (2) for a reasonable period to permit the mortgagor to remedy the default: the mortgagor may do so within the time afforded to him by the court: upon the construction of the section now under consideration, if there were no other subsisting default, the mortgagee could thereupon seek an immediate possession order which the court would have no power to refuse or to delay, because no sum would then remain due and there would be no outstanding default. A defaulting mortgagor would therefore be in a better position than one not in default. He could obtain a respite and, having done so, it would be in his interest to remain in default until the last moment of the period of respite. I cannot believe that Parliament can have intended this irrational and unfair result. I must therefore investigate whether the section is capable of some other construction.

Mr. Lightman, in the course of his ingenious and helpful argument, has suggested that section 36 by inference abrogates a mortgagee's right to possession when there is no sum due and no subsisting default on the part of the mortgagor under the mortgage. I feel unable to accept this suggestion. Section 36 is an enabling section which empowers the court to inhibit the mortgagee's right to take possession. It confers a discretionary power on the court to achieve this result. It is, in my judgment, impossible to spell out of it a positive abrogation of an important property right, and, moreover, an abrogation of it only in particular circumstances.

I think, however, that the section is capable of interpretation in a way which makes it applicable to a case in which a mortgagee seeks possession when no sum is due and no other default is subsisting under the mortgage. I can see no reason why the legislature should confer the discretionary power on the court when the mortgagor is in default, but should not do so when he is not in default. The manifest unfairness, as I think, of such a position seems to me a strong ground for believing that it must have been Parliament's intention to confer the power, default or no default, notwithstanding the ineptness of the language of the section to achieve this result. The only part of the section which appears to contradict such an intention is the conditional clause. This can only apply when the mortgagor is in arrear with some payment or is otherwise in default [. . .] Although the language of the section is certainly inartistic to achieve this result and interpreting it in this way may involve some violence to the language (not, in my view, very great), nevertheless I think that, when the section is read as a whole in the context of the subject matter and particularly having regard to the arbitrary unfairness of the literal construction, it is possible to spell this meaning out of the words used. Since I do not think that this court should attribute to Parliament so irrational an intention as the literal construction would involve, I feel justified in adopting, and, in my judgment, we should adopt, the more liberal construction. Accordingly, in my judgment, on the true construction of the section, it applies to any case in which a mortgagee seeks possession, whether the mortgagor be in arrear or otherwise in default under the mortgage or not, but, where the mortgagor is in arrear or in default, the discretion is limited by the conditional clause.

2.5.7 Right or remedy?

We have already noted that the lender enjoys a right to possession that is inherently independent of default. Section 36 is, however, an important jurisdiction that effectively controls the lender's right to possession of a dwelling house within a remedial context, and, as such, plays a vitally important social role. Nevertheless, as our survey of the jurisdiction has highlighted, its parameters are highly dependent on judicial interpretation, which has not always been able hold this social function firmly in its sights.

Haley, 'Mortgage Default: Possession, Relief and Judicial Discretion' (1997) 17 LS 483, 483

The history of this interventionist jurisdiction is, however, chequered. It has been marked by the uneasy interaction between the laissez faire attitude of the common law (which upheld the lender's contract and estate rights) and the more protective and tender treatment of the mortgagor in equity (which, in appropriate cases, sought to restrict the exercise of those rights). The jurisdiction is now in statutory form, but the tension between the commercial interests of the mortgagee and the need for the mortgagor to maintain a home persists. Although the court must attempt to achieve a balance between those competing claims, under the present legal regime this is, patently, not a simple task. The judicial stance must necessarily reflect individual circumstances and broader notions of public interest, social and economic policy and parliamentary purpose. Consequently, the granting of relief against possession, as well as being reactive to prevailing community norms, is susceptible to major swings in judicial attitude and statutory constructions.

The remedial context of the lender's right to possession is reinforced by the regulatory controls imposed by the FSMA 2000 through MCOB 13, as strengthened by the Pre-action Protocol on Mortgage Repossessions. These measures are also predicated on the policy that possession should be a measure of last resort and that it should not be used to harass borrowers in arrears. As such, they may sideline the s 36 jurisdiction and mean that it is increasingly difficult to justify the lender's inherent right to possession. The law should reflect the reality that possession is a remedy that should only be capable of exercise under the scrutiny of the court.[49]

McMurtry, 'Mortgage Default and Repossession: Procedure and Policy in the Post-*Norgan* Era' (2007) 58 NILQR 194, 207

The regulatory reforms concerning the policy and procedure for dealing with arrears is disappointing and limited. The overriding concern is that a lender should give proper consideration to arrears issues, follow a documented approach and ensure that proper internal systems are put in place for the fair treatment of customers. Such goals are purely matters of form and operational procedure. As to the substantive rules governing borrower protection, there is nothing that is innovative [. . .] This regulatory response adds nothing to that adopted by the judiciary over the last ten years and does not operate to increase further the protection

---

[49] As the Law Commission has recommended: see Law Commission Report No 204 (1991, [6.16], [7.28]–[7.38]).

to borrowers in temporary financial straits. It is ironic that, instead, it might cause judicial sympathies to sway in favour of the institutional lender. First, it is possible that judges will be better disposed towards lenders who evidence the alteration of the terms of the mortgage contract in the prescribed ways. Secondly, it is likely that far fewer cases will come before the courts when the postponement of possession is the likely outcome. Thirdly, it is likely that more borrowers will have already benefited from a *Norgan* style repayment plan before the case ever reaches court. Of course, where there is little evidence of a desire on the lender's part to adhere the spirit of the regulation judicial sympathies will understandably shift towards the borrower. Nevertheless, it is only when the circumstances fall within the parameters of the *Norgan* liberality that the court will be able to maintain a roof over the borrower's head. As those parameters are likely to have already been reached, it is difficult to see how such sympathy can translate into effective relief.

2.6 POSSESSION AND HUMAN RIGHTS

Section 36 may wrestle the exercise of a lender's right to possession within the court's control, but its application is confined to dwelling houses and, even then, there are gaps in its application—most notably, where there is no need for the lender to apply to court for possession. Several commentators have raised the suggestion that the lender's right to possession conferred by s 87(1) of the LPA 1925 is incompatible with Art 1 of the First Protocol of the European Convention on Human Rights (deprivation of property) and, where the mortgage is over a home, with Art 8 (respect for the home).[50] Following *Kay v Lambeth LBC*,[51] the question in relation to both Articles is not whether or not they are engaged by possession proceedings, but whether or not the interference with the borrower's property, or his or her home, is justified, because it is made in pursuit of a legitimate aim that is proportionate and within the State's margin of appreciation, in both substantive and procedural terms.

Nield, 'Charges, Possession and Human Rights: A Reappraisal of s 87(1) Law of Property Act 1925' in *Modern Studies in Property Law: Vol 3* (ed Cooke, 2005, p 173)

The Strasbourg jurisprudence recognises that a lender's right to possession to facilitate the repayment of secured debt is a proportionate and legitimate aim. In *Wood v UK* (1997) 24 EHRR CD 69 the European Court, when considering Article 1 Protocol 1, stated that:

[...] to the extent that the applicant is deprived of her possessions by repossession, the Commission considers that the deprivation is in the public interest, that is the public interest in ensuring the payment of contractual debts and is also in accordance with the rules provided by law.

---

[50] See also Gray and Gray, *Elements of Land Law* (4th edn, 2005, [15.147]); Rook, *Property Law and Human Rights* (2001, p 199); Dixon, 'Sorry, We Have Sold Your Home: Mortgagees and Their Possession Rights' [1999] CLJ 281.

[51] [2006] UKHL 10, [2006] 2 AC 465; see Chapter 5.

And when considering Article 8:

> In so far as the repossession constituted an interference with the applicant's home the Commission finds that this was in accordance with the terms of the loan and the domestic law and was necessary for the protection of the rights and freedoms of others, namely the lender.

> These comments presuppose the borrower is in default and the lender is seeking recourse to their security to obtain repayment. But where the borrower is not in default the lender's legitimate aim in obtaining possession is not so obvious unless it is to take steps to protect the value of the security.

> Proportionality calls for an examination of the process by which a legitimate aim is achieved. So that, even though repossession to ensure the efficient repayment of debts is a legitimate aim, the means by which that repossession is obtained is a vital consideration under both Articles 1 and 8. The possibility that the lender may obtain possession without some form of judicial consideration over its exercise must tip the fair balance that lies at the heart of proportionality. For instance, in *Hentrich v France* (1994) 118 EHRR 440 the fact that the applicant received fair compensation for the expropriation of her land did not prevent a breach of Article 1 because she was deprived of the opportunity to challenge the expropriation. Also the Scottish courts view that 'the inhibition upon the dependence' was incompatible with Article 1 was largely premised upon the fact that it was an automatic right which was not subject to adequate judicial control. Thus it failed to achieve due proportionality between the lender's legitimate aim of recovering his debt and the rights of the debtor to deal freely with his property. This concern with process operates despite the fact that Article 6 may not be engaged and provides the strongest argument that the right to possession conferred by subsection 87(1) is incompatible with the [Human Rights Act 1998] and thus should be amended.

Nield suggests that the procedural fairness may be absent.

The need for procedural fairness is underlined by Whitehouse, writing before the Human Rights Act 1998 (HRA 1998), in her promotion of the homeowning borrower as a citizen rather than a consumer.

Whitehouse, 'The Homeowner: Citizen or Consumer?' in *Land Law: Themes and Perspectives* (eds Bright and Dewar, 1998, p 200)

> We cannot, therefore, ignore the consumerist perspective, but we can shift the emphasis in favour of citizenship and reintroduce the element of universal entitlements. By shifting the emphasis in favour of citizen, it may be possible to reform the legal process of repossession without denying mortgagees the ability to recover their debt via repossession. It must be accepted that the majority of home-owners in England and Wales have entered into a contract which allow the ability to seek repossession. It may be argued, therefore, that this contractual entitlement cannot be denied. By viewing the home-owner as citizen, however we can at least demand that the contractual entitlement to repossession is undertaken with procedural fairness. As Darendorf argues 'Civil rights are the key to the modern world. They include the basic elements of the rule of law, equality before the law and due process.'

In the following case, however, the High Court, in obiter comments, preferred to avoid procedural protection, although the context was slightly different. Here, the lender, through its receivers, had sold the property without obtaining possession and it was the purchaser who wanted to repossess. The borrower's interest in his or her home had been overreached by the sale, so he or she had no legal right to remain and was a trespasser. The question was thus whether the lender's exercise of its out-of-court power of sale (whether pursuant to an express or implied power) could be justified under Art 1 of the First Protocol.

Briggs J concentrated, echoing the Strasbourg Court in *Wood*,[52] on the undoubted substantive justification of the lender's powers. It remains to be seen if the higher courts will address the issue.

Horsham Properties Group Ltd v Clark [2009] 1 P & CR 8, HC

Briggs J

At [44]–[45]

In my judgment, any deprivation of possession constituted by the exercise by a mortgagee of its powers under section 101 of the Law of Property Act after a relevant default by the mortgagor is justified in the public interest, and requires no case-by case exercise of a proportionality discretion by the court, for the following reasons. First, it reflects the bargain habitually drawn between mortgagors and mortgagees for nearly 200 years, in which the ability of a mortgagee to sell the property offered as security without having to go to court has been identified as a central and essential aspect of the security necessarily provided if substantial property base secured lending is to be available at affordable rates of interest. That it is in the public interest that property buyers and owners should be able to obtain lending for that purpose can hardly be open to doubt, even if the loan-to-value ratios at which it has recently become possible have now become a matter of controversy.

Secondly, I am bound by the decision of the Court of Appeal in *Ropaigealach* to conclude that there was no wider policy behind section 36 of the Administration of Justice Act 1970 than to put back what the courts had shortly before taken away, namely a discretion to stay or adjourn proceedings for possession, triggered only where the mortgagee considered it necessary or appropriate to go to court if the first place. The question whether a wider policy ought to be implemented wherever steps taken by a mortgagee to release its security is likely to lead to the obtaining of possession is a matter for Parliament, and upon which Parliament has yet [...] to form any view. It would be quite wrong for the courts in a vigorous and imaginative interpretation of the Human Rights Convention to make that policy, as it were, on the hoof.

Given the limited nature of the courts' jurisdiction under s 36 of the Administration of Justice Act 1970, could substantive fairness also be questioned? Section 36 is solely concerned with assessing the financial circumstances of the borrower and his or her ability to meet his or her debts. The Pre-action Protocol for Mortgage Possession also addresses only financial concerns. The court cannot take into account other factors: for example, the welfare of children occupying the house as their home. By way of contrast, the welfare of children is an explicit factor in the exercise of the court's discretion to order the sale of co-owned property upon the application of a creditor under ss 14 and 15 of the Trusts of Land and

---

[52] *Wood v UK* (1997) 24 EHRR CD69.

Appointment of Trustees Act 1996 (TOLATA 1996).[53] This discriminatory treatment might engage Art 14 of the ECHR.[54]

3 SALE

The power of the lender to sell the mortgaged property without having to go to court is a powerful remedy. The lender can control the sale and recover the debt from the proceeds of a sale, accounting to the borrower (or a second chargee, if there is a subsequent mortgage) for any balance received in excess of the debt. In the conduct of the sale, the lender does have to act in a way that pays due regard to the interests of the borrower (or subsequent chargee).

Before examining the duties that a lender owes when selling the mortgaged property, we need to consider the mechanics of the sale itself.

3.1 MECHANICS OF SALE

3.1.1 Source of the power

The power of the lender to sell will be conferred either by the express terms of the legal charge or from the implied power contained in s 101(1)(i) of the LPA 1925 (extracted in section 1.1.2 above).

Where the power is express, the terms of the power should stipulate how and when it may be exercised. It is common for an express power of sale to be exercisable on specified events of default: for example, if the borrower fails to make an agreed repayment of capital or interest, or otherwise breaches any other covenant contained in the legal charge, or upon the borrower becoming insolvent.

Where a lender under a legal charge is relying upon its implied statutory power, there are two stages to be considered. Firstly, the power must arise: s 101(1)(i) provides that the power of sale arises when the mortgage money is due, being the legal date for redemption under the mortgage,[55] or, where the mortgage is repayable by instalments, when an instalment payment falls due.[56] Secondly, the power, once arisen, must become exercisable, which, in the case of the statutory power, is upon the events of default specified in s 103 of the 1925 Act.

Law of Property Act 1925, s 103

Regulation of exercise of power of sale

A mortgagee shall not exercise the power of sale conferred by this Act unless and until—

(i) Notice requiring payment of the mortgage money has been served on the mortgagor or one of two or more mortgagors, and default has been made in payment of the mortgage money, or of part thereof, for three months after such service; or

---

53 See Chapter 19, section 5.5.
54 See Fox, *Conceptualising Home* (2007, pp 500–3).
55 *Twentieth Century Banking Corp v Wilkinson* [1977] Ch 99.
56 *Payne v Cardiff RDC* [1932] 1 KB 241.

> (ii) Some interest under the mortgage is in arrear and unpaid for two months after becoming due; or
>
> (iii) There has been a breach of some provision contained in the mortgage deed or in this Act, or in an enactment replaced by this Act, and on the part of the mortgagor, or of some person concurring in making the mortgage, to be observed or performed, other than and besides a covenant for payment of the mortgage money or interest thereon.

The power of sale is thus exercisable only on default. In the case of a default in meeting a demand for full repayment, the borrower must be given notice and three months in which to comply with that notice; in the case of default in the payment of interest, no notice is required, but there must be at least two months' arrears.

In the case of a regulated mortgage, a longer process is contemplated. The MCOB 13 (extracted at section1.2 above), governing FSA-regulated mortgages, calls for the borrower to be given notice of any arrears, and for the lender to take reasonable steps to try to arrange the rescheduling of the debt before contemplating possession and sale; statutory default notices must be served where a mortgage is regulated under the CCA 1974.[57] Where the Pre-action Protocol on Mortgage Repossessions is applicable because the lender is seeking possession prior to sale, the lender must also comply with the steps that it outlines.

Haley has pointed out that, in the case of a dwelling house, the impact of s 36 of the Administration of Justice Act 1970 will give the borrower more time in which to clear any arrears than is contemplated by s 103 of the LPA 1925,[58] and thus *a long delay in the mortgagee's right to possession is by a side wind eroding the value of the statutory remedy* of sale.[59] He observes that the separate control of the mortgagee's right to possession and its power of sale is artificial when the purpose of obtaining possession is to enable the lender to sell, and advocates reform to bring the remedies into line.[60] Otherwise, a lender may be tempted to sell without obtaining possession.[61]

3.1.2 Passing title

The mechanics of passing title by a mortgagee's sale is the subject of ss 88(1) (for mortgages over freeholds) and 89(1) (for mortgages over leaseholds) of the LPA 1925.

Law of Property Act 1925, s 88(1)

Realisation of freehold mortgages

(1) Where an estate in fee simple has been mortgaged by the creation of a term of years absolute limited thereout or by a charge by way of legal mortgage and the mortgagee sells under his statutory or express power of sale—

---

[57] Consumer Credit Act 1974 (as amended), ss 88B and 88C.

[58] Technically, the reverse could be the case where s 36 does not apply, although it is unlikely that a lender will act so precipitously.

[59] 'Mortgage Default: Possession, Relief and Judicial Discretion' (1997) 17 LS 483, 496.

[60] See also Gardner, *An Introduction to Land Law* (2007, [12.6.4]).

[61] See *Ropaigealach v Barclays Bank plc* [2001] 1 QB 263; *Horsham Properties Group Ltd v Clark* [2008] EWHC 2327.

(a) the conveyance by him shall operate to vest in the purchaser the fee simple in the land conveyed subject to any legal mortgage having priority to the mortgage in right of which the sale is made and to any money thereby secured, and thereupon;

(b) the mortgage term or the charge by way of legal mortgagee and any subsequent mortgage term or charges shall merge or be extinguished as respects the land conveyed; and such conveyance may, as respects the fee simple, be made in the name of the estate owner in whom it is vested.

The sale by the lender vests title in the purchaser by overreaching the borrower's equity of redemption, and any other interest over which the mortgage has priority, which vests instead in the proceeds of sale.[62] The mortgage itself and any subsequent charge are extinguished so far as they affect the land itself.

3.1.3 Application of proceeds of sale

By s 105 of the LPA 1925, the lender holds the proceeds of sale (after the discharge of any prior mortgages or encumbrances) in trust, to be applied in, firstly, the meeting the sale costs, and secondly, repaying the amount owing to it under the mortgage, with any balance being payable to the borrower or a subsequent mortgagee (if any).[63]

Law of Property Act 1925, s 105

Application of proceeds of sale

The money which is received by the mortgagee, arising from the sale, after discharge of prior incumbrances to which the sale is not made subject, if any, or after payment into court under this Act of a sum to meet any prior incumbrance, shall be held by him in trust to be applied by him, first, in payment of all costs, charges, and expenses properly incurred by him as incident to the sale or any attempted sale, or otherwise; and secondly, in discharge of the mortgage money, interest, and costs, and other money, if any, due under the mortgage; and the residue of the money so received shall be paid to the person entitled to the mortgaged property, or authorised to give receipts for the proceeds of the sale thereof.

A purchaser is not concerned to check that an event of default has occurred and the power of sale is exercisable,[64] nor is the purchaser concerned to see that the lender applies the sale moneys as required by s 105. The receipt of the lender is a good discharge for the purchase money.[65] The purchaser must, however, check that the lender has a power of sale in the first place, either because the power is expressed in the legal charge, or because it is implied under s 101(1)(i). We will explore the position of the purchaser in more detail below.

---

[62] See s 2(1)(iii), extracted at Chapter 20, section 2.1; *Horsham Properties Group Ltd v Clark* [2008] EWHC 2327.
[63] *West London Commercial Bank v Reliance Permanent Building Society* (1885) 29 Ch D 954.
[64] See Law of Property Act 1925, s 104, extracted at section 3.2.6 below.
[65] Ibid, s 107(1).

3.2 DUTIES OF THE MORTGAGEE IN THE CONDUCT OF THE SALE

The lender has a direct interest in any sale, but so too does the borrower, because, as we have seen, he or she is entitled to any surplus sale proceeds. Even where the sale proceeds are insufficient to meet the sums owing to the lender, the borrower is still concerned, because he or she remains liable to meet the shortfall under the contractual covenant to repay. The balancing of the interests of both the lender and borrower is thus at the heart of the lender's duties upon the sale.

3.2.1 General principles

It has long been asserted that the lender is not a trustee of the power of sale, but the interests of the borrower cannot be ignored.[66] The lender cannot sell with the object of recovering only sufficient to repay the debt, because, in so doing, the borrower's interests are inevitably overlooked. Early decisions were somewhat ambiguous as to the scope of the lender's duties: it was unclear whether they were limited to a requirement of good faith or whether a degree of care was also required.[67] The law has developed to recognize both of these elements as interrelated strands of the duty that the lender owes the borrower in the conduct of the sale. The lender must, firstly, be able to demonstrate good faith, and secondly, that reasonable care has been taken in the conduct of the sale.

Cuckmere Brick Co v Mutual Finance [1971] Ch 949, CA

Facts: The borrower owned land with planning permission to build a hundred flats. It subsequently obtained planning permission to build thirty-five houses. The lender became entitled to exercise its power of sale, which it did by putting the land up for auction. The auctioneers referred only to the planning permission for the houses when marketing the property. The borrower brought the failure to refer to the earlier permission to the attention of the lender, which refused to postpone the sale, but asked the auctioneers to mention the planning permission at the auction. A sale price of £44,000 was achieved at the auction, although the borrower asserted that the land was worth nearer £75,000, which might have been achieved if the planning permission for the flats had been properly advertised. The borrower successfully brought an action for an account against the lender for the amount that should have been received from the sale.

Salmon LJ

At 965

It is well settled that a mortgagee is not a trustee of the power of sale for the mortgagor. Once the power has accrued, the mortgagee is entitled to exercise it for his own purposes whenever he chooses to do so. It matters not that the moment may be unpropitious and that

---

[66] See *Nash v Eads* (1880) 25 SJ 95, although a lender is a trustee of the proceeds of sale: Law of Property Act 1925, s 105.

[67] Compare, e.g., *Kennedy v de Trafford* [1896] 1 Ch 762 and *Tomlin v Luce* (1889) 43 Ch D 191.

by waiting a higher price could be obtained. He has the right to realise his security by turning it into money when he likes. Nor, in my view, is there anything to prevent a mortgagee from accepting the best bid he can get at an auction, even though the auction is badly attended and the bidding exceptionally low. Providing none of those adverse factors is due to any fault of the mortgagee, he can do as he likes. If the mortgagee's interests, as he sees them, conflict with those of the mortgagor, the mortgagee can give preference to his own interests, which of course he could not do were he a trustee of the power of sale for the mortgagor [...]

It is impossible to pretend that the state of the authorities on this branch of the law is entirely satisfactory. There are some dicta which suggest that unless a mortgagee acts in bad faith he is safe. His only obligation to the mortgagor is not to cheat him. There are other dicta which suggest that in addition to the duty of acting in good faith, the mortgagee is under a duty to take reasonable care to obtain whatever is the true market value of the mortgaged property at the moment he chooses to sell it: compare, for example, *Kennedy v. de Trafford* [1896] 1 Ch. 762; [1897] A.C. 180 with *Tomlin v. Luce* (1889) 43 Ch.D. 191, 194.

The proposition that the mortgagee owes both duties, in my judgment, represents the true view of the law. Approaching the matter first of all on principle, it is to be observed that if the sale yields a surplus over the amount owed under the mortgage, the mortgagee holds this surplus in trust for the mortgagor. If the sale shows a deficiency, the mortgagor has to make it good out of his own pocket. The mortgagor is vitally affected by the result of the sale but its preparation and conduct is left entirely in the hands of the mortgagee. The proximity between them could scarcely be closer. Surely they are "neighbours." Given that the power of sale is for the benefit of the mortgagee and that he is entitled to choose the moment to sell which suits him, it would be strange indeed if he were under no legal obligation to take reasonable care to obtain what I call the true market value at the date of the sale. Some of the textbooks refer to the "proper price," others to the "best price." Vaisey J. in *Reliance Permanent Building Society v. Harwood-Stamper* [1944] Ch. 362, 364, 365, seems to have attached great importance to the difference between these two descriptions of "price." My difficulty is that I cannot see any real difference between them. "Proper price" is perhaps a little nebulous, and "the best price" may suggest an exceptionally high price. That is why I prefer to call it "the true market value."

Cross LJ, agreeing with Salmon LJ, also rejected the lender's submission that it should not be liable for a lack of care committed by its agent, provided that the appointment was reasonable. A lender is thus liable for a lack of care committed by any valuer, solicitor, or other agent that it may employ in the conduct of the sale.

Cuckmere Brick Co v Mutual Finance [1971] Ch 949, CA

Cross LJ

At 966

Mr. Vinelott further submitted that even if we should be of opinion that a mortgagee was liable to account to the mortgagor for loss occasioned by his own negligence in the exercise of his power of sale, it was not right that he should be liable for the negligence of an agent reasonably employed by him. It may well be that this point is not open to him in view of the way the argument proceeded below—but in any case I do not accept the submission. In support of it, counsel pointed out that a trustee is not liable for the default of an agent whom it is reasonable for him to employ. But the position of a mortgagee is quite different from that of a trustee. A trustee has not, qua trustee, any interest in the trust property, and if an agent employed by him is negligent his right of action against the agent is an asset of the trust. A mortgagee, on the other hand, is not a trustee and if he sues the agent for negligence any damages which he can recover belong to him. Of course, in many cases the mortgagee may suffer no damage himself by reason of the agent's negligence because the purchase price, though less than it should have been, exceeds what is owing to the mortgagee. In such circumstances it may be that nowadays the law would allow the mortgagor to recover damages directly from the agent although not in contractual relations with him; but that was certainly not so a hundred years ago when *Wolff v. Vanderzee* (1869) 20 L.T. 353 was decided. In those days the only way to achieve justice between the parties was to say that the mortgagee was liable to the mortgagor for any damage which the latter suffered by the agent's negligence and to leave the mortgagee to recover such damages, and also any damage which he had suffered himself, from the agent. I do not think that we can say that the mortgagee used to be liable to the mortgagor for the negligence of his agent but that that liability disappeared at some unspecified moment of time when the law had developed enough to allow the mortgagor to sue the agent himself.

Salmon LJ's reference to 'neighbours' led subsequent judges to adopt a tortious interpretation for the basis of the lender's duties. But this approach has been discredited. The basis for the lender's duties arises in equity from the relationship of lender and borrower. As we have seen, the lender is under a duty to account to the borrower both for what he or she receives and for what he or she ought to receive.[68] It is from this obligation that the duty to exercise reasonable care in the conduct of the sale finds expression.[69]

Silven Properties Ltd v Royal Bank of Scotland plc [2004] 1 WLR 997, CA

Lightman J

At [19]

When and if the mortgagee does exercise the power of sale, he comes under a duty in equity (and not tort) to the mortgagor (and all others interested in the equity of redemption) to take reasonable precautions to obtain "the fair" or "the true market" value of or the "proper price" for the mortgaged property at the date of the sale, and not (as the claimants submitted) the date of the decision to sell. If the period of time between the dates of the decision to sell and of the sale is short, there may be no difference in value between the two dates and indeed in many (if not most cases) this may be readily assumed. But where there is a period of delay, the difference in date could prove significant. The mortgagee is not entitled to act in a way which unfairly prejudices the mortgagor by selling hastily at a knock-down price sufficient to pay off his debt: *Palk v Mortgage Services Funding plc* [1993] Ch 330, 337–338, per Sir Donald Nicholls V-C. He must take proper care whether by fairly and properly exposing the property to the market or otherwise to obtain the best price reasonably obtainable at the date of sale. The remedy for breach of this equitable duty is not common law damages, but an order that the mortgagee account to the mortgagor and all others interested in the equity

---

[68] See section 2.2 above.
[69] See also *Downsview Nominees Ltd v First City Corp* [1993] AC 295, 315, *per* Lord Templeman.

of redemption, not just for what he actually received, but for what he should have received: see *Standard Chartered Bank Ltd v Walker* [1982] 1 WLR 1410, 1416b.

3.2.2 To whom is the duty owed?

The equitable nature of the lender's duties dictates both the parties to whom the duty is owed and the available remedies. The lender does not owe a duty to those whom it is foreseeable will suffer damage (being a tortious standard); its duty is relationship-based. It is owed to the borrower, a subsequent mortgagee, and any guarantor of the mortgage debt, but not to a beneficial owner, whose position is protected in equity by his or her relationship to the trustees of the legal estate, whom he or she may sue (if appropriate) for breach of trust.

We will look more closely at remedies below.

Parker-Tweedale v Dunbar Bank (No 1) [1991] Ch 12, CA[70]

Facts: Mrs Parker-Tweedale held the legal estate in the family home on trust for her husband alone. When Mr Parker-Tweedale had a car accident, the Parker-Tweedales ran into financial difficulties and their marriage broke up. The bank exercised its power of sale and Mrs Parker Tweedale agreed the sale price of £575,000. A matter of weeks later, the purchaser sold the property for £700,000. Mr Parker-Tweedale unsuccessfully sought an order to set aside the sale.

Nourse LJ

At 18

This reference to "neighbours" has enabled the plaintiff to argue that the duty is owed to all those who are within the neighbourhood principle; i.e., to adapt the words of Lord Atkin, to all persons who are so closely and directly affected by the sale that the mortgagee ought reasonably to have them in contemplation as being so affected when he is directing his mind to the sale. Further support for the application of the neighbourhood principle in this context can be gained from the judgment of Lord Denning M.R. in *Standard Chartered Bank Ltd. v. Walker* [1982] 1 W.L.R. 1410, 1415, where it was held that the duty to take reasonable care to obtain a proper price was owed to a surety for the mortgage debt as well as to the mortgagor himself.

In my respectful opinion it is both unnecessary and confusing for the duties owed by a mortgagee to the mortgagor and the surety, if there is one, to be expressed in terms of the tort of negligence. The authorities which were considered in the careful judgments of this court in *Cuckmere Brick Co. Ltd. v. Mutual Finance Ltd.* [1971] Ch. 949 demonstrate that the duty owed by the mortgagee to the mortgagor was recognised by equity as arising out of the particular relationship between them. Thus Salmon L.J. himself said, at p. 967:

> "It would seem, therefore, that many years before the modern development of the law of negligence, the courts of equity had laid down a doctrine in relation to mortgages which is entirely consonant with the general principles later evolved by the common law."

[70] Noted at [1990] Conv 431.

The duty owed to the surety arises in the same way. In *China and South Sea Bank Ltd. v. Tan Soon Gin (alias George Tan)* [1990] 1 A.C. 536, Lord Templeman, in delivering the judgment of the Privy Council, having pointed out that the surety in that case admitted that the moneys secured by the guarantee were due, continued at p. 543:

> "But the surety claims that the creditor owed the surety a duty to exercise the power of sale conferred by the mortgage and in that case the liability of the surety under the guarantee would either have been eliminated or very much reduced. The Court of Appeal [in Hong Kong] sought to find such a duty in the tort of negligence but the tort of negligence has not yet subsumed all torts and does not supplant the principles of equity or contradict contractual promises [...] Equity intervenes to protect a surety."

Once it is recognised that the duty owed by the mortgagee to the mortgagor arises out of the particular relationship between them, it is readily apparent that there is no warrant for extending its scope so as to include a beneficiary or beneficiaries under a trust of which the mortgagor is the trustee. The correctness of that view was fully established in the clear and compelling argument of Mr. Lloyd, who drew particular attention to the rights and duties of the trustee to protect the trust property against dissipation or depreciation in value and the impracticabilities and potential rights of double recovery inherent in giving the beneficiary an additional right to sue the mortgagee, a right which is in any event unnecessary.

The only exception for which Mr. Lloyd allowed was the special case where the trustee has unreasonably refused to sue on behalf of the trust or has committed some other breach of his duties to the beneficiaries, e.g., by consenting to an improvident sale, which disables or disqualifies him from acting on behalf of the trust. In such a case the beneficiary is permitted to sue on behalf of the trust. This exception is established by a series of authorities, some of which were recently considered by the Privy Council in *Hayim v. Citibank N.A.* [1987] A.C. 730. In delivering the judgment of their Lordships, Lord Templeman said, at p. 748:

> "These authorities demonstrate that a beneficiary has no cause of action against a third party save in special circumstances which embrace a failure, excusable or inexcusable, by the trustees in the performance of the duty owed by the trustees to the beneficiary to protect the trust estate or to protect the interests of the beneficiary in the trust estate."

It is important to emphasise that when a beneficiary sues under the exception he does so in right of the trust and in the room of the trustee. He does not enforce a right reciprocal to some duty owed directly to him by the third party.

3.2.3 The primacy of the lender's own interests

Although the lender owes a duty of good faith and of reasonable care in the conduct of the sale, the primary purpose of the power of sale is to safeguard the lender's own objective of securing repayment of the debt. As Salmon LJ pointed out in *Cuckmere Brick Co v Mutual Finance*,[71] the lender may thus choose whether and in what manner to exercise the power. In particular, the lender may choose its time of sale. The lender does not have to gauge the most opportune time to sell, nor is the lender required to wait for the market to recover, or to press ahead with a sale if prices are showing signs of falling.

For example, in the following case, the lender was not liable, although the value of the security—in this case, shares—had fallen dramatically following the collapse of the guarantor's property empire. Lord Templeman delivered the opinion of the Privy Council.

---

[71] [1971] Ch 949, CA.

China and South Seas Bank Ltd v Tan [1990] 1 AC 536, PC

Lord Templeman

At 545

If the creditor chose to exercise his power of sale over the mortgaged security he must sell for the current market value but the creditor must decide in his own interest if and when he should sell. [. . .]

No creditor could carry on the business of lending if he could become liable to a mortgagor and to a surety or to either of them for a decline in value of mortgaged property, unless the creditor was personally responsible for the decline [. . .] The creditor was not under a duty to exercise his power of sale over the mortgaged securities at any particular time or at all.

Similarly, a lender is not obliged to improve the mortgaged property to try to maximize the sale price. A lender that goes into possession is only obliged to take reasonable steps to ensure that the property does not deteriorate in value.

Silven Properties Ltd v Royal Bank of Scotland plc [2004] 1 WLR 997, CA

Facts: The borrower alleged that the receiver appointed by the bank to sell the mortgaged property was under a duty to maximize its value by obtaining planning permission for the development and letting some of the properties that were vacant. The receiver had explored the possibility of obtaining planning permission for some of the properties and of letting the vacant properties, but had decided to proceed to their immediate sale. The Court dismissed the borrower's allegation.

Lightman J

At [16]–[18]

The mortgagee is entitled to sell the mortgaged property as it is. He is under no obligation to improve it or increase its value. There is no obligation to take any such pre-marketing steps to increase the value of the property as is suggested by the claimants. The claimants submitted that this principle could not stand with the decision of the Privy Council in *McHugh v Union Bank of Canada* [1913] AC 299. Lord Moulton in that case, at p 312, held that, if a mortgagee does proceed with a sale of property which is unsaleable as it stands, a duty of care may be imposed on him when taking the necessary steps to render the mortgaged property saleable. The mortgage in that case was of horses, which the mortgagee needed to drive to market if he was to sell them. The mortgagee was held to owe to the mortgagor a duty to take proper care of them whilst driving them to market. The duty imposed on the mortgagee was to take care to preserve, not increase, the value of the security. The decision accordingly affords no support for the claimant's case

The mortgagee is free (in his own interest as well as that of the mortgagor) to investigate whether and how he can "unlock" the potential for an increase in value of the property mortgaged (e g by an application for planning permission or the grant of a lease) and indeed (going further) he can proceed with such an application or grant. But he is likewise free at any time to halt his efforts and proceed instead immediately with a sale. By commencing on this path the mortgagee does not in any way preclude himself from calling a halt at will: he does not assume any such obligation of care to the mortgagor in respect of its continuance as the claimants contend. If however the mortgagee is to seek to charge to the mortgagor the costs of the exercise which he has undertaken of obtaining planning permission or a lessee, subject to any applicable terms of the mortgage, the mortgagee may only be entitled to do so if he acted reasonably in incurring those costs and fairly balanced the costs of the exercise against the potential benefits taking fully into account the possibility that he might at any moment "pull the plug" on these efforts and the consequences for the mortgagor if he did so.

If the mortgagor requires protection in any of these respects, whether by imposing further duties on the mortgagee or limitations on his rights and powers, he must insist upon them when the bargain is made and upon the inclusion of protective provisions in the mortgage. In the absence of such protective provisions, the mortgagee is entitled to rest on the terms of the mortgage and (save where statute otherwise requires) the court must give effect to them. The one method available to the mortgagor to prevent the mortgagee exercising the rights conferred upon him by the mortgage is to redeem the mortgage. If he redeems, there can be no need or justification for recourse by the mortgagee to the power of sale to achieve repayment of the debt due to him secured by the mortgage.

The lender's freedom of action is, however, tempered by the combined duties of good faith and reasonable care. As Lightman LJ observes, if the borrower wishes to protect his or her position further, a higher duty must be negotiated when agreeing the mortgage terms with the lender.[72] It is more likely that the lender may try to limit its duties by the express terms of the mortgage. But the courts have been reluctant to construe a purported limitation of liability by the lender as cutting down its duties of good faith and reasonable care. For example, in *Bishop v Bonham*,[73] a provision that stated that the lender could exercise its powers '*as it thought fit*' was construed as a discretion that could only operate within the constraints of good faith and reasonable care imposed by equity.

3.2.4 Reasonable care in the conduct of the sale

The lender is required to exercise reasonable care in the conduct of the sale. Earlier decisions refer to a need for the lender to take reasonable care to obtain a proper, fair, or true market price, but it is misleading to interpret this test as requiring the lender to attain a given valuation figure.[74] Rather, the courts, in determining liability, look to the reasonableness of the steps that the lender has taken to market the property and, in the light of these steps, to assess the price obtained against a valuation band that allows for some margin of judgment. It is only once the lender has been found to be in breach of its duty of care that the courts need to determine the price that should have been obtained, so that the damages payable to the borrower may be measured. The courts' focus is thus upon such matters as how the property was advertised or otherwise brought to the market,[75] whether a sale by auction or private treaty was more appropriate,[76] how the offer or reserve price was set,[77] how negotiations were conducted, and how the decision on the final sale price was reached.[78] In all of

---

[72] For example, MCOB13.6.1 provides that, where a lender takes possession under a mortgage regulated under the Financial Services and Markets Act 2000, the property should be marketed as soon as possible.

[73] [1988] 1 WLR 742.

[74] See, e.g., *Corbett v Halifax Building Society* [2004] 1 WLR 997.

[75] For example, *Cuckmere Brick Co Ltd v Mutual Finance Ltd* [1971] Ch 494.

[76] For example, *Tse Kwong Lam v Wong Chit Sen* [1983] 1 WLR 1349.

[77] Ibid

[78] For example, *Michael v Miller* [2002] EWCA Civ 282.

these steps, the advice of a suitably qualified agent will be influential in meeting the required objective standard of conduct.

Michael v Miller [2004] 2 EGLR 151, CA

Facts: Michael's farm was mortgaged to Miller. Following Michael's default, the farm was sold for £1.625m. Michael called for an account, claiming that the farm was worth considerably more. The judge at first instance decided that the farm was worth £1.75m, but that an acceptable valuation band lay between £1.6m and £1.9m. Michael appealed unsuccessfully.

Jonathan Parker LJ

At [132]–[135]

It is a matter for the mortgagee how that general duty is to be discharged in the circumstances of any given case. Subject to any restrictions in the mortgage deed, it is for the mortgagee to decide whether the sale should be by public auction or private treaty, just as it is for him to decide how the sale should be advertised and how long the property should be left on the market. Such decisions inevitably involve an exercise of informed judgment on the part of the mortgagee, in respect of which there can, almost by definition, be no absolute requirements. Thus (as the judge recognised at p.68F of his judgment) there is no absolute duty to advertise widely. As he correctly put it (at p.69A):

"What is proper advertisement will depend on the circumstances of the case."

Similarly, in some cases the appropriate mode of sale may be sale by public auction (in the instant case, no one has suggested that); in others, for example where there is a falling market, it may not. Moreover, a mortgagee who receives an offer in advance of an auction may have to make a judgment as to whether to accept it or whether to proceed to the auction.

The need for the mortgagee to exercise informed judgment in exercising his power of sale in turn means that a prudent mortgagee will take advice, including (where appropriate) valuation advice, from a duly qualified agent.

I turn, then, to the position of a mortgagee's agent such as Mr Hextall, whose duties included the giving of valuation advice. In my judgment, just as, applying the *Bolam* principle, a valuer will not breach his duty of care if his valuation falls within an acceptable margin of error (see, e.g., *Merivale Moore* and the *Arab Bank case*), so a mortgagee will not breach his duty to the mortgagor if in the exercise of his power to sell the mortgaged property he exercises his judgment reasonably; and to the extent that that judgment involves assessing the market value of the mortgaged property the mortgagee will have acted reasonably if his assessment falls within an acceptable margin of error....

At [138]–[139]

I accordingly reject Mr Jourdan's submission that as a matter of principle a 'bracket' approach is inappropriate in the context of the exercise of a mortgagee's power of sale. In so far as the exercise of the mortgagee's power of sale calls for the exercise of informed judgment by the mortgagee, whether as to market conditions, or as to market value, or as to some other matter affecting the sale, the use of a bracket—or a margin of error—must in my judgment be available to the court as a means of assessing whether the mortgagee has failed to exercise that judgment reasonably.

It seems to me that Mr Jourdan's submissions on the bracket issue confuse the issue of breach of duty with the measure of damages should breach of duty be established. As Lord Hoffmann said in *Saamco* at p.221F:

"Before I come to the facts of the individual cases, I must notice an argument advanced by the defendants concerning the calculation of damages. They say that the damage falling within the scope of the duty should not be the loss which flows from the valuation having been in excess of the true value but should be limited to the excess over the highest valuation which would not have been negligent. This seems to me to confuse the standard of care with the question of the damage which falls within the scope of the duty. The valuer is not liable unless he is negligent. In deciding whether or not he has been negligent, the court must bear in mind that valuation is seldom an exact science and that within a band of figures valuers may differ without one of them being negligent. But once the valuer has been found to have been negligent, the loss for which he is responsible is that which has been caused by the valuation being wrong. For this purpose the court must form a view as to what a correct valuation would have been. This means the figure which it considers most likely that a reasonable valuer, using the information available at the relevant date, would have put forward as the amount which the property was most likely to fetch if sold upon the open market. While it is true that there would have been a range of figures which the reasonable valuer might have put forward, the figure most likely to have been put forward would have been the mean figure of that range. There is no basis for calculating damages upon the basis that it would have been a figure at one or other extreme of the range. Either of these would have been less likely than the mean [...]"

[...]

At [141]

In the instant case the judge took the, to my mind, somewhat unsatisfactory course of deciding first what was the market value of the Estate at the relevant time (concluding that it was £1.75M) and then asking himself whether the respondents, through Mr Hextall, were negligent in achieving a price substantially less than that. The judge's approach might perhaps be appropriate in a case where the mortgagee accepts the first offer that he receives, without the property having been exposed to the market at all. In such a case, the likelihood is that the only evidence of 'market value' will be expert valuation evidence. But where, as in the instant case, the property has been exposed to the market and a number of genuine offers have been received, the more logical approach (to my mind) is to start by considering the steps which the mortgagee took to sell the property and then to consider whether, in all the circumstances, the mortgagee acted reasonably in accepting the purchaser's offer and contracting to sell the property at that price.

3.2.5 The duty of good faith

A lender must exercise the power of sale in good faith. The impact of this requirement is most obvious where the lender is selling to a connected party, when there is a conflict of interest, and where the lender's motive for selling is improper.

A mortgagee cannot sell to itself, or to a trustee or agent acting on its behalf. In the words of Lindley LJ in *Farrars v Farrars Ltd*,[79] '[a] *sale by a person to himself is no sale at all*'. The lender can sell to a company or other organization in which it is interested, or to a person

[79] (1889) 40 Ch D 395, 409.

with whom it is connected, but, if the lender does so, the court will scrutinize the lender's conduct to ensure that reasonable care has been taken.[80] In the Hong Kong case of *Tse Kwong Lam v Wong Chit Sen*,[81] Lord Templeman, giving the opinion of the Privy Council, stated that '*the sale must be closely examined and a heavy onus lies on the mortgagee to show that in all respects he acted fairly to the borrower and used his best endeavours to obtain the best price reasonably obtainable for the mortgaged property*'.

The case itself provides a useful example. The respondent exercised his power of sale by putting the mortgaged property up for auction. The auction was only advertised very shortly before it was conducted and only limited details were provided. A reserve price was fixed, but without the guidance of a qualified valuer. At the auction, only one bid at the reserve price was made—by the respondent's wife, acting on behalf of a company owned by the respondent and his family. The Privy Council held that, although the respondent was free to sell to a company in which he was interested, he had failed to demonstrate that he had taken reasonable care in the conduct of the sale. An auction was not necessarily the most appropriate mode of sale. The mortgagee should have sought the advice of a suitably qualified expert both as to the mode of sale, and, if the property was to be auctioned, regarding the reserve price and appropriate marketing.

A lender's motives may also affect its bona fides. In *Quennell v Maltby*,[82] we saw that the right to take possession must not be exercised for an ulterior motive. Likewise, the power of sale must be exercised with a view to discharging the mortgage debt. In *Downsview Nominees Ltd v First City Corp Ltd*,[83] in which receivers were appointed purely to frustrate the exercise of a second mortgagee's powers, there was '*overwhelming evidence that the receivership of the second defendant was inspired by him for an improper purpose and carried on in bad faith, verging on fraud*'. Mixed motives will not, however, breach the mortgagee's duties, provided that one of those motives was to recover the debt.[84]

3.2.6 Remedies and the position of purchasers

What action can a borrower take if a lender is in breach of its duties? He or she may either seek an order setting aside the sale, or an order for an account requiring the lender to account for what ought to have been received to compensate the borrower for any shortfall in the purchase price for which the lender is responsible. An order for an account will be the usual course where the lender has fallen short of the objective standard of care. An order to set aside the sale will not be available where the lender has merely sold at an undervalue; there must be some impropriety. The court has discretion to set aside the sale and a court will not do so if there has been an unwarranted delay,[85] or if to do so would cause unnecessary hardship.[86] Furthermore, the position of the purchaser, against whom the sale is to be set aside, must also be considered.

Section 104 of the LPA 1925 provides some protection.

---

[80] *Mortgage Express v Mardner* [2004] EWCA Civ 1859; *Bradford & Bingley plc v Ross* [2005] EWCA Civ 394.

[81] [1983] 1 WLR 1349, 1355.

[82] [1979] 1 WLR 318.

[83] [1993] AC 295, 317.

[84] *Meretz Investment NV v ACP Ltd* [2006] EWHC 74, [2007] Ch 197.

[85] See *Tse Kwong Lam v Wong Chit Sen* [1983] 1 WLR 1349.

[86] *Corbett v Halifax Building Society* [2002] EWCA Civ 1849, [2003] 1 WLR 964.

Law of Property Act 1925, s 104

Conveyance on sale

(1) A mortgagee exercising the power of sale conferred by this Act shall have power, by deed, to convey the property sold, for such estate and interest therein as he is by this Act authorised to sell or convey or may be the subject of the mortgage, freed from all estates, interest, and rights to which the mortgage has priority, but subject to all estates, interests, and rights which have priority to the mortgage.

(2) Where a conveyance is made in exercise of the power of sale conferred by this Act, or any enactment replaced by this Act, the title of the purchaser shall not be impeachable on the ground:

(a) that no case had arisen to authorise the sale; or

(b) that due notice was not given; or

(c) where the mortgage is made after the commencement of this Act, that leave of the court when so required, was not obtained; or

(d) whether the mortgage was made before or after such commencement, that the power was otherwise improperly or irregularly exercise;

and a purchaser is not, either before or on conveyance concerned to see or inquire whether a case has arisen to authorise the sale, or due notice has been given, or the power is otherwise properly and regularly exercised; but any person damnified by an unauthorised or improper, or irregular exercise of the power shall have his remedy in damages against the person exercising the power.

The extent of this protection is limited. It relieves the purchaser from making enquiries as to whether an event of default has occurred to trigger the exercise of a power of sale, but does not protect the purchaser if he or she has actual notice of the impropriety:

Corbett v Halifax Building Society [2003] 1 WLR 964, CA

Facts: Although it was contrary to his terms of employment, an employee of the Halifax purchased, though his uncle, a repossessed property from his employer at a sum that the court found to be an undervalue. The Halifax was unaware of its employee's participation in the sale. The borrowers unsuccessfully applied to set aside the sale.

Pumfrey J

At [25]–[26]

Between contract and completion, the position is described in *Lord Waring v London and Manchester Assurance Co Ltd* [1935] Ch 310, 318–319 where in a passage subsequently approved by the Court of Appeal in *Property and Bloodstock Ltd v Emerton* [1968] Ch 94, Crossman J said:

"The only effect of the conveyance is to put the legal estate entirely in the purchaser: that follows from section 104, subsection (1), of the Law of Property Act 1925, which provides that a mortgagee shall have power to convey the legal estate; and the whole legal estate can be conveyed free from all estates, interests, and rights to which the mortgage has priority. Section 104, sub-section (2), upon which also counsel for the plaintiff relied, does not seem to me to affect the question at all. Its purpose is simply to protect the purchaser and to make it unnecessary for him, pending completion and during investigation of title, to ascertain whether the power of sale has become exercisable. Of course, if the purchaser becomes aware, during that period, of any facts showing that the power of sale is not exercisable, or that there is some impropriety in the sale, then, in my judgment, he gets no good title on taking the conveyance. The result in the present case is, in my judgment, that the sale effected by the contract, assuming, for the moment, that there is no objection to it on any other ground, binds the plaintiff, and that it is too late after the sale for him to tender the mortgage money and become entitled to have the property recon-veyed to him [...]"

It would seem to follow from this that a completed sale by a mortgagee is not liable to be set aside merely because it takes place at an undervalue. Impropriety is a prerequisite, and section 104(2) makes it clear that the purchaser is not protected if he has actual knowledge of the impropriety. But if the purchaser has no notice of the impropriety, then on the face of it he takes free. Thus, the completed sale by a mortgagee pursuant to his statutory power is vulnerable only if the purchaser has knowledge of, or participates in, an impropriety in the exercise of the power.

The Halifax was bona fide throughout; it was its employee, acting without its knowledge, who was acting improperly. Although the Halifax had sold at an undervalue, a mere under-value was insufficient to set a sale aside; there had to have been impropriety.

Section 104 will also not assist a purchaser of unregistered land where the lender has no power of sale, for example, because the mortgage is invalid or contains no adequate power of sale, or because any power that there is has not arisen. The lender is acting beyond its powers and any sale is ultra vires.

Where the land is registered and the lender is selling under a registered charge, the provi-sions of s 52 of the Land Registration Act 2002 (LRA 2002) must be considered.

Land Registration Act 2002, s 52

Protection of disponees

(1) Subject to any entry in the register to the contrary, the proprietor of a registered charge is to be taken to have, in relation to the property subject to the charge, the powers of disposition conferred by law on the owner of a legal mortgage.

(2) Subsection (1) has effect only for the purpose of preventing the title of a disponee being questioned (and so does not affect the lawfulness of a disposition).

A purchaser may thus assume that a registered chargee enjoys all of the powers of a legal mortgagee unless a restriction is registered, giving notice that these powers have been restricted. As we have noted, the power of sale under s 101(1)(i) of the LPA 1925 must have arisen, because the mortgage money is due, before it can become exercisable. It is thought that the power of sale must have arisen before a purchaser can take advantage of the pro-tection afforded by s 52 of the LRA 2002. The section provides protection to a purchaser where the sale is within the powers of the lender (i.e. intra vires), but is actionable by the borrower because the power has not yet become exercisable or is liable to be set aside (e.g. for impropriety). In these circumstances, there remains the possibility that a purchaser who is implicated in, or has knowledge of, a breach of the mortgagee's equitable duties may be liable as a constructive trustee on the basis of knowing receipt.[87]

4 APPOINTMENT OF A RECEIVER

The implied power to appoint a receiver of the mortgaged land when the mortgage money has become due is conferred by s 101(1)(iii) of the LPA 1925 into all mortgages created by deed, including a legal charge by way of mortgage. The appointment of a receiver provides an attractive option for a lender under a mortgage of commercial property, because a lender can avoid personal liability for wilful default or for breach of duty if the property is sold. The remedy is particularly popular where a legal charge of land owned by a company is coupled with a floating charge over all of the assets and undertakings of a company, under which the lender may appoint either an administrative receiver or administrator to take over the effective running of the company in the event of its insolvency.[88]

4.1 FUNCTIONS AND POWERS OF A RECEIVER

Section 109 of the LPA 1925 provides that a receiver may be appointed or removed by written notice, whereupon the receiver is entitled to enter into possession of the property to preserve the security and to collect any income that may be applied, after payment of any costs and expenses including the receiver's remuneration, in the repayment of the interest due, with any balance being payable to the borrower or the person next entitled to the equity of redemption. A receiver is invariably also granted express powers to manage and sell the property. By appointing a receiver, a lender can thus indirectly enforce the legal charge.

Section 109 contains the implied terms that govern the appointment of a receiver under s 101(1)(iii) of the Act.

Law of Property Act 1925, s 109

Appointment, power, remuneration and duties of a receiver

(1) A mortgagee entitled to appoint a receiver under the power in that behalf conferred by this Act shall not appoint a receiver until he has become entitled to exercise the power of sale conferred by this Act, but may then, by writing under his hand, appoint such person as he thinks fit to be receiver.

(2) A receiver appointed under the powers conferred by this Act, or any enactment replaced by this Act, shall be deemed to be the agent of the mortgagor; and the mortgagor shall be solely responsible for the receiver's acts or defaults unless the mortgage deed otherwise provides.

---

[87] See Chapter 20, section 6.3.2.

[88] A floating charge entered into prior to 15 September 2003 may contain an express right to appoint an administrative receiver over all of the assets and undertakings of the company. By s 72A of the Insolvency Act 2006, a lender is no longer entitled to appoint an administrative receiver, but may appoint an administrator. The distinction between an 'administrative receiver' and an 'administrator' is that an administrative receiver owes duties only to the secured lender and the borrower, whilst an administrator's duties extend to all of the creditors of the company, both secured and unsecured.

(3) The receiver shall have power to demand and recover all the income of which he is appointed receiver, by action, distress, or otherwise, in the name either of the mortgagor or of the mortgagee, to the full extent of the estate or interest which the mortgagor could dispose of, and to give effectual receipts accordingly for the same, and to exercise any powers which may have been delegated to him by the mortgagee pursuant to this Act.

(4) A person paying money to the receiver shall not be concerned to inquire whether any case has happened to authorise the receiver to act.

(5) The receiver may be removed, and a new receiver may be appointed, from time to time by the mortgagee by writing under his hand.

(6) The receiver shall be entitled to retain out of any money received by him, for his remuneration, and in satisfaction of all costs, charges, and expenses incurred by him as receiver, a commission at such rate, not exceeding five per centum on the gross amount of all money received, as is specified in his appointment, and if no rate is so specified, then at the rate of five per centum on that gross amount, or at such other rate as the court thinks fit to allow, on application made by him for that purpose.

4.2 RECEIVER AS AGENT FOR THE BORROWER

A lender is able to avoid personal liability by appointing a receiver, because the receiver is expressed to be the agent of the borrower, although appointed by and taking directions from the lender. A receiver thus owes duties both to the lender and the borrower, creating a rather unusual triangular relationship. In effect, by entering into the legal charge, the borrower empowers the lender to appoint the receiver as the borrower's agent in applying the income from the property, and (where express power is granted) to sell and apply the proceeds of sale in the discharge of the mortgage debt.

Silven Properties Ltd v Royal Bank of Scotland plc [2004] 1 WLR 997, CA

Lightman J

At [27]–[28]

The peculiar incidents of the agency are significant. In particular: (1) the agency is one where the principal, the mortgagor, has no say in the appointment or identity of the receiver and is not entitled to give any instructions to the receiver or to dismiss the receiver. In the words of Rigby LJ in *Gaskell v Gosling* [1896] 1 QB 669, 692: "For valuable consideration he has committed the management of his property to an attorney whose appointment he cannot interfere with"; (2) there is no contractual relationship or duty owed in tort by the receiver to the mortgagor: the relationship and duties owed by the receiver are equitable only: see *Medforth v Blake* [2000] Ch 86 and *Raja v Austin Gray* [2003] 1 EGLR 91; (3) the equitable duty is owed to the mortgagee as well as the mortgagor. The relationship created by the mortgage is tripartite involving the mortgagor, the mortgagee and the receiver; (4) the duty owed by the receiver (like the duty owed by a mortgagee) to the mortgagor is not owed to him individually but to him as one of the persons interested in the equity of redemption. The class character of the right is reflected in the class character of the relief to be granted in case of a breach of this duty. That relief is an order that the receiver account to the persons interested in the equity of redemption for what he would have held as receiver but for his default; (5) not merely does the receiver owe a duty of care to the mortgagee as well as the mortgagor, but his primary duty in exercising his powers of management is to try and bring about a situation in which the secured debt is repaid: see the *Medforth case* at p 86; and (6) the receiver is not managing the mortgagor's property for the benefit of the mortgagor, but the security, the property of the mortgagee, for the benefit of the mortgagee: see *In re B Johnson & Co (Builders) Ltd* [1955] Ch 634, 661, per Jenkins LJ cited with approval by Lord Templeman in *Downsview Nominees Ltd v First City Corpn Ltd* [1993] AC 295, 313b, and [1955] Ch 634, 646, per Evershed MR cited with approval by Sir Richard Scott V-C in the *Medforth case* [2000] Ch 86, 95h-96a. His powers of management are really ancillary to that duty: *Gomba Holdings UK Ltd v Homan* [1986] 1 WLR 1301, 1305, per Hoffmann J.

In the context of a relationship such at the present, which is no ordinary agency and is primarily a device to protect the mortgagee, general agency principles are of limited assistance in identifying the duties owed by the receiver to the mortgagor: see *Gomba Holdings UK Ltd v Homan* at 1305b-d (Hoffmann J) and *Gomba Holdings UK Ltd v Minories Finance Ltd* [1988] 1 WLR 1231, 1233d-h (Fox LJ). The core duty of the receiver to account to the mortgagor subsists, but (for example) the mortgagor has no unrestricted right of access to receivership documents. The mortgage confers upon the mortgagee a direct and indirect means of securing a sale in order to achieve repayment of his secured debt. The mortgagee can sell as mortgagee and the mortgagee can appoint a receiver who likewise can sell in the name of the mortgagor. Having regard to the fact that the receiver's primary duty is to bring about a situation where the secured debt is repaid, as a matter of principle the receiver must be entitled (like the mortgagee) to sell the property in the condition in which it is in the same way as the mortgagee can and in particular without awaiting or effecting any increase in value or improvement in the property [. . .]

In practice, a receiver, before accepting an appointment, will invariably require an indemnity from the lender against any personal liability that the receiver may incur. Nevertheless, the appointment of receiver is an attractive and popular power available to a lender where the lender anticipates that a sale may not immediately follow the taking of possession, or the property will need to be managed prior to sale: for example, because it is tenanted or is used for business purposes.

4.3 DUTIES OF A RECEIVER

In the following case, the receiver had explored, but rejected, the possibility of improving the property prior to sale. It was argued that, because the receiver was an agent of the borrower, he or she owed a duty to the borrower to present the property for sale in its most advantageous condition, and thus his or her decision not to proceed with the improvements was a breach of this duty. In view of the unique features of the agency, however, this argument was rejected. The receiver's duties were the same as those owed by a mortgagee.

Silven Properties Ltd v Royal Bank of Scotland plc [2004] 1 WLR 997, CA

Lightman J

At [29]

[. . . B]y accepting office as receivers of the claimant's properties the receivers assumed a fiduciary duty of care to the bank, the claimants and all (if any) others interested in the equity of redemption. This accords with the statement of principle to this effect of Lord Browne-Wilkinson in *Henderson v Merrett Syndicates Ltd* [1995] 2 AC 145, 205e-h relied on by the claimants. The appointment of the receivers as agents of the claimants having regard to the special character of the agency does not affect the scope or the content of the fiduciary duty. The scope or content of the duty must depend on and reflect the special nature of the relationship between the bank, the claimants and the receivers arising under the terms of the mortgages and the appointments of the receivers, and in particular the role of the receivers in securing repayment of the secured debt and the primacy of their obligations in this regard to the bank. These circumstances preclude the assumption by, or imposition on, the receivers of the obligation to take the pre-marketing steps for which the claimants contend in this action. Further no such obligation could arise in their case (any more than in the case of the bank) from the steps which they took to investigate and (for a period) to proceed with applications for planning permission. The receivers were at all times free (as was the bank) to halt those steps and exercise their right to proceed with an immediate sale of the mortgaged properties as they were.

In *Downsview Nominees v First City Corp*,[89] the Privy Council had decided that a receiver owed the same equitable (not tortious) duties to act bona fide and with reasonable care in the conduct of any sale. But a receiver's role is often rather different from that of a mortgagee: a receiver is given powers to manage the property, including (where a floating charge is granted over the borrower's business assets) any business that may be conducted on the land. As a result, he or she is unable to sit back and do nothing; he or she is obliged to act to preserve the interest of the borrower and the lender.[90]

Medforth v Blake [2000] Ch 86, CA

Facts: Medforth was a pig farmer. When he ran into financial difficulties, Blake was appointed a receiver and manager under the terms of charges secured over the business. In running the business, Blake incurred loses and Medforth successfully claimed that his failure to obtain discounts on bulk purchases of pig feed had contributed to those losses, for which he should be liable to account.

Sir Richard Scott VC

At 98

The *Cuckmere Brick case* test can impose liability on a mortgagee notwithstanding the absence of fraud or mala fides. It follows from the *Downsview Nominees case* and *Yorkshire Bank Plc. v. Hall* that a receiver/manager who sells but fails to take reasonable care to obtain a proper price may incur liability notwithstanding the absence of fraud or mala fides. Why should the approach be any different if what is under review is not the conduct of a sale but conduct in carrying on a business? If a receiver exercises this power, why does not a specific duty, corresponding to the duty to take reasonable steps to obtain a proper price, arise? If the business is being carried on by a mortgagee, the mortgagee will be liable, as a mortgagee in possession, for loss caused by his failure to do so with due diligence. Why should not

---

[89] [1993] AC 297. See also *Yorkshire Bank Plc v Hall* [1999] 1 WLR 1713.
[90] See, e.g., *Silven Properties Ltd v Royal Bank of Scotland plc* [2004] 1 WLR 997, [23].

the receiver/manager, who, as Lord Templeman held, owes the same specific duties as the mortgagee when selling, owe comparable specific duties when conducting the mortgaged business? It may be that the particularly onerous duties constructed by courts of equity for mortgagees in possession would not be appropriate to apply to a receiver. But, no duties at all save a duty of good faith? That does not seem to me to make commercial sense nor, more importantly, to correspond with the principles expressed in the bulk of the authorities.... In my judgment, in principle and on the authorities, the following propositions can be stated. (1) A receiver managing mortgaged property owes duties to the mortgagor and anyone else with an interest in the equity of redemption. (2) The duties include, but are not necessarily confined to, a duty of good faith. (3) The extent and scope of any duty additional to that of good faith will depend on the facts and circumstances of the particular case. (4) In exercising his powers of management the primary duty of the receiver is to try and bring about a situation in which interest on the secured debt can be paid and the debt itself repaid. (5) Subject to that primary duty, the receiver owes a duty to manage the property with due diligence. (6) Due diligence does not oblige the receiver to continue to carry on a business on the mortgaged premises previously carried on by the mortgagor. (7) If the receiver does carry on a business on the mortgaged premises, due diligence requires reasonable steps to be taken in order to try to do so profitably.

5 A FINAL WORD ABOUT THE COVENANT TO REPAY

Possession, sale, and appointment of a receiver are all proprietary remedies flowing from the security created by the legal charge by way of mortgage, but it should not be forgotten that the borrower is under a personal contractual liability to repay the loan in accordance with the terms of the loan agreement. A term for repayment of the capital of the loan will be implied in the absence of an express term.[91] This liability is independent of the security and will remain where there is a shortfall after the lender or receiver has sold the property. Thus, where there is negative equity, a borrower may be sued by the lender for the balance that remains owing after the sale proceeds have been applied in repayment. In enforcing that judgment, the lender is in no better position than any other unsecured creditor and may be forced to make the borrower bankrupt.

In suing upon the personal covenant to repay, the lender must bear in mind the relevant limitation periods. The recovery of interest is statute-barred six years[92] after becoming due and the capital, as a debt payable by deed, cannot be recovered after twelve years from the date upon which it became due.[93] The exercise by the lender of its power of sale does not affect these periods.[94]

---

[91] *West Bromwich Building Society v Wilkinson* [2005] EWHL 44, noted at Prime, 'Mortgage Default, Limitation and Law Reform' [2005] Conv 566.

[92] Limitation Act 1980, s 20(5).

[93] Ibid, s 20(1), but see MCOB 13.6.1 and 13.6.2, which effectively reduce the period to six years where the mortgage is regulated.

[94] *West Bromwich Building Society v Wilkinson* [2005] EWHL 44.

QUESTIONS

1. Is it satisfactory that the lender has an immediate right to possession, or do the existing qualifications to this right provide adequate safeguards?

2. Compare the different approaches to the width of the courts' discretion under s 36 of the Administration of Justice Act 1936 that were taken in *Cheltenham & Gloucester Building Society v Norgan* and *Bristol & West Building Society v Ellis*. Do you think that the courts' approach in both cases is consistent?

3. Why would a borrower wish to apply to court for an order for sale under s 91 of the Law of Property Act 1925? When is a court likely to be sympathetic to such an application?

4. A lender's duties, in exercise of its power of sale, arise in equity rather than in tort, but what consequences flow as a result?

5. In exercise of its power of sale, a lender has a duty to obtain a proper market price. What does this mean and what would you advise a lender to do in order to fulfil this duty?

6. In what circumstances could a borrower successfully apply to set aside a sale made by a lender?

FURTHER READING

Citizens Advice, *Set Up To Fail: CAB Client's Experience of Mortgage and Secured Loan Arrears Problems* (2007)

Dixon, 'Sorry We Have Sold Your Home: Mortgagees and Their Possession Rights' [1999] CLJ 281

Fox, *Conceptualising Home* (Oxford: Hart, 2007, ch 3)

Frisby, 'Making a Silk Purse Out of a Pigs Ear: *Medforth v Blake*' (2000) 63 MLR 413

Haley, 'Mortgage Default: Possession, Relief and Judicial Discretion' (1997) 17 LS 483

McMurtry, 'Mortgage Default and Repossession: Procedure and Policy in the Post-*Norgan* Era' (2007) 58 NILQR 194

Nield, 'Charges Possession and Human Rights: A Reappraisal of s 87(1) Law of Property Act 1925' in *Modern Studies in Property Law: Vol 3* (ed Cooke, Oxford: Hart, 2005)

INDEX

A

Absolute title 303
Accumulations 702–704
Acquisition of rights
acquisition question,
definition 7
direct rights
'benefit and burden'
principle 204
by commission of a
tort 203
by contractual
promise 195–196
by deed 194–195
formalities for registered
land 209–210
knowledge of pre-existing
personal right 204–208
by non-contractual
promise 196–195
easements
express grant 877
implied grant 877–899
prescriptive rights 899–911
equitable rights and interests
conduct leading to
duty 369
diversity 361–366
doctrine of
anticipation 371–381
duty as an explanation for
diversity 368–369
formalities 98–100
formality rules 361–366
introduction 98–101
key themes 360–361
prevention of
unconscionable
conduct 366–368
proprietary
estoppel 383–432
formalities
central issues 265
contracts 269–293
creation and
transfer 293–297

e-conveyancing 312–317
introduction 266–267
overview 268–269
registration of
title 297–312
impact of LRA 2002 532–534
leases
equitable leases 768–769
legal leases 762–768
legal estates 73–74
legal interests 79
property and personal rights
distinguished 208–209
proprietary
estoppel 389–392
restrictive covenants 935–936
rights under trusts 88–92
underlying questions 7
Actual notice 471
Adverse possession
'adverse' defined 326–329
based on relativity of
title 323–324
central issues 319
conclusions 354–355
effects
registered land 337–346
unregistered land 335–337
human rights 346–350
introduction 319–320
justifications for conferring
legal rights 321–323
key date for accrual of
action 324–326
leasehold titles 350–354
'possession' defined
essential requirements
330–331
factual possession 331
intention 332–334
ordinary
meaning 329–330
rule in *Leigh v
Jack* 334–335
possessory title 303
Annexation of covenants
express 939–941

once-and-for-all
process 938–939
statutory provisions 941–948
Anticipation *see* **Doctrine of
anticipation**
Appeals 158
Assignments
enforcement of leasehold
covenants 843–846
assignees—post-1995,
813–816
assignees—pre-1996,
808–812
original parties—post-1995,
804–808
original parties—pre-1996,
801–804
freehold covenants 937–938

B

Bad faith *see* **Fraud**
Bankruptcy
applications for sale
involving co-owners
applications by
creditors 680–689
applications by trustees in
bankruptcy 689–697
introduction 676–678
policy
considerations 678–680
summary 697
charging orders 1010–1013
severance of joint
tenancies 606, 610
Bare licences
definition 215
licensee's rights
against licensor 215–218
against strangers 218
against third
parties 218–220
**Beneficiaries (of a trust of
land)**
consultation by trustees 623
occupation rights

Beneficiaries (of a trust of land) (*cont.*)
  applications for
    sale 679–680
  overlap with
    other statutory
    provisions 628–629
  overreaching 653–658
  trusts of land 623–628
'Benefit and burden'
  principle 204,
  932–934
Bona fide **purchaser for value**
  '*bona fide*' 469–470
  equitable basis 468–469
  'of a legal estate' 470
  'purchaser for value' 470
  'without notice'
    actual notice 471
    constructive
      notice 471–476
    imputed notice 477
Building schemes 948–954

C
Charges
  see also **Land Charges**;
    Mortgages
  equitable charges
    defined 999–1001
  equity of redemption
    history and
      development 1014–1015
    legal charges 1015–1017
  Land Register 307
  legal charges by way of
    mortgage
    equitable charges
      distinguished 1000
    definition and
      nature 1002–1006
    mortgages distinguished
      1004–1005
Charging orders 1010–1013
Chattels
  fixtures and fittings 38–46
  things found on or in
    land 46–55
Children
  court resolution of
    disputes 632
  occupation rights 634

overriding interests 510–511
Co-habitation
  see also **Shared homes**
  reform recommendations
    586–591
Co-ownership
  applications for sale
    applications by
      creditors 680–689
    applications by trustees in
      bankruptcy 689–697
    central issues 676
    introduction 676–678
    policy
      considerations 678–680
    summary 697
  joint tenancies
    advantages 617–619
    central issues 593
    introduction 593–594
    requirement for four
      unities 597–598
    severance 598–616
    survivorship 598
    tenancies in common
      distinguished
      594–596
  overreaching
    breach of trust 658–661
    effect 637–638
    human rights 668–670
    interests capable of being
      overreached 640–648
    justification 464–466
    occupying
      beneficiaries 653–658
    possible future
      developments 666–668
    protection of
      purchasers 661–664
    scope 638–640
    transactions with
      overreaching
      effect 648–653
  priority of rights and
    interests
    see also **Overreaching**
    central issues 636
    introduction 634–637
    where overreaching does
      not occur 672–675
  regulation outside of
    TOLATA 1996 634–635

resulting and constructive
    trusts 576–577
  tenancies in common
    central issues 593
    determination of
      status 597–598
    introduction 593–594
    joint tenants
      distinguished 594–596
  termination of trust 616–617
  trusts of land
    beneficiaries'
      rights 623–628
    court resolution of
      disputes 629–634
    overlap with
      other statutory
      provisions 628–629
    scope of trust 621
    statutory imposition of
      trust 619–620
    trustees' powers 621–623
**Collateral advantages (in
    mortgages)**
  equitable controls 1067–1069
  meaning and scope 1067
  restraint of trade 1069–1070
Collateral contracts 277–280
Common law rules
  equitable rules
    distinguished 55–58, 59
  relationship with
    equity 101–107
  requirement to act
    compatibly with
    ECHR 115–118
Commonholds
  central issues 965
  commonhold
    associations 978–980
  community
    statement 980–982
  creation 975–976
  dispute resolution 984–985
  legal structure 974–975
  management 982–984
  objectives 974
  purity of title 976–978
Compensation *see* **Damages
    and compensation**
Consent
  adverse possession 326–329
  prescriptive rights 906–909

priority of interests
defences based on express
consent 182
defences based on implied
consent 183–185
Conspiracy *see* **Lawful act
conspiracy**
Constructive notice 471–476
Constructive trusts
contractual licensee's
rights against third
parties 233–234
doctrine of
anticipation 379–381
informal acquisition of
equitable rights and
interests 365
institutional and
remedial versions
distinguished 443–446
judicial definitions 443
means of acquiring direct
rights 196–202
Pallant v Morgan equity
three
requirements 455–458
unconscionability
458–460
practical difficulties
with occupiers and
banks 17–22
proprietary estoppel
compared 285–289
rationalization of common
links 460–461
Rochefoucauld v Boustead
doctrine
overview 446–447
three-party case 452–455
two-party case 447–452
shared homes
critique of common
intention 580–583
focus on context 558–559
introduction 556–557
joint legal owners 576–577
quantification of beneficial
interests 577–580
rationalization
through *Stack v
Dowden* 583–585
sole legal owners 561–576
Consumer credit controls

applicability 1032–1033
excessive interest
rates 1072–1075
statutory
framework 1033–1036
unfair
relationships 1036–1037
unfair terms 1058–1063
Content of rights
content question,
definition 7
easements 856–876
equitable rights and
interests 92–98
freeholds 70–72
leases 72, 730–763
legal estates 69–72
legal interests 75–78
rights under trusts 86–87
Contractual licences
definition 220–221
effect of revocation on
licensee 221–227
freehold covenants
compared 248–250
licensee's rights against
strangers 227–230
licensee's rights against third
parties
current position 231–245
future reform 245–251
constructive trusts
243–245, 447
Contractual promises
acquisition of equitable rights
and interests 363–364
as suggested basis
of proprietary
estoppel 387–389
doctrine of anticipation
central issues 371
conclusions 381
constructive
trusts 379–381
enforcement against third
parties 377–379
freehold sales 373–374
introduction 371–372
leases 372–373
nature of rights
acquired 377
significance of specific
performance 374–377

formal requirements
central issues 268–269
collateral
contracts 277–280
effects of non-
compliance 275–277
exchange of
contracts 272–274
legal and equitable
rights and
interests 271–272
proprietary
estoppel 283–293
rectification 280–282
signatures 274–275
statutory
provisions 269–271
land charges
effect of failure to
register 481
registrable interests 479
leases
characterization of
contract 771–773
effects of lease 716–721
means of acquiring direct
rights 195–196
mortgages 1124
Conversion *see* **Doctrine of
anticipation**
Courts
interpretation of
legislation 114–115
requirement to act
compatibly with
ECHR 113–114,
115–118
trustee applications
child welfare 632
general
principles 630–632
impact of TOLATA
1996 632–634
statutory
provisions 629–630
Covenants *see* **Freehold
covenants; Leasehold
covenants**
**Creation of rights and
interests** *see*
**Acquisition of rights
and Formalities**
Creditors *see* **Insolvency**

Curtain principle 300,
  494–495

D

Damages and compensation
  adverse possession 347–348
  breach of freehold
    covenants 957–958
  breach of leasehold
    covenants 822
  interference with protection
    of property (ECHR
    Art 1) 138–139
  rectification of register and
    indemnity 308–310

Deeds
  easements 877
  formal
    requirements 293–297
  leases 764
  means of acquiring direct
    rights 194–195

Defences
  bona fide purchaser for value
    '*bona fide*' 469–470
    equitable basis 468–469
    'of a legal estate' 470
    'purchaser for value' 470
    'without notice' 470–477
  breach of freehold
    covenants 958
  defences question,
    definition 7, 173–189
  impact of LRA 2002 534–535
  leases
    equitable leases 770–771
    legal leases 770
  practical difficulties with
    occupiers and banks
    doctrinal model 15–17
    utility model 17–22
  priority of interests
    express consent 182
    implied consent 183–185
    lack of
      registration 175–179
    legal and equitable
      rights and interests
      distinguished 187–189
    overreaching 177–182
    unregistered land 173–175

requirement to act
  compatibly with
  ECHR 118–121
underlying questions 7–8
Delivery of deeds 294–295
'Deserted wife's equity' 15–17
Direct rights
  see also **Equitable rights
    and interests; Legal
    interests**
  central issues 192
  conclusions 210–211
  introduction 193
  licensee's rights against third
    parties
    bare licensees 219
    contractual
      licensees 231–238
    estoppel licences 254
    licences coupled with an
      interest 261
    statutory licences 258
  means of acquisition
    'benefit and burden'
      principle 204, 932–934
    by commission of a
      tort 203
    by contractual
      promise 195–196
    by deed 194–195
    formalities for registered
      land 209–210
    knowledge of pre-existing
      personal right 204–208
    by non-contractual
      promise 196–195
  property and personal rights
    distinguished 208–209
**Discrimination (and ECHR
  Art 14)**
Convention text 154
importance 111
key issues 154–155
overreaching 670
Dishonest assistance 670–671
Distress 823
Doctrine of anticipation
  central issues 371
  conclusions 381
  constructive trusts 379–381
  enforcement against third
    parties 377–379

freehold sales 373–374
introduction 371–372
leases 372–373
nature of rights acquired 377
overreaching 642–643
practical difficulties
  with occupiers and
  banks 17–22
significance of specific
  performance 374–377
Doctrine of conversion
  see **Doctrine of
    anticipation**
Doctrine of notice
  actual notice 471
  constructive notice 471–476
  exclusion from land
    charges 486–488
  imputed notice 477
Dominant tenements
  easement must accommodate
    dominant land
    865–868
  essential requirement of
    easements 855–856
  excessive user 913–914
  freehold covenants
    equitable rules of
      enforcement 921–922
    extinction and
      modification 961
    particular
      requirements 924–928
  separate ownership 864–865
Duress
  conceptual underpinnings
    1043–1044
  meaning and scope 1039
Dwelling houses
  defined 11088
  mortgage repossessions
    1086–1097

E
E-conveyancing
  doctrine of anticipation
    381
  formal
    requirements 315–316
  legal impact 313–315,
    535–537

objectives 312–313
signatures 316–317
Easements
  acquisition
    express grant 877
    implied grant 877–899
    prescriptive
      rights 899–911
  central issues 853
  dominant and servient
    tenements
    easement must
      accommodate dominant
      land 865–868
    separate
      ownerships 864–865
  essential
    requirements 855–856
  excessive user 913–914
  extinguishment 914–915
  history and
    development 855–856
  introduction 854–855
  land charge registration 479
  overriding interests 512–513
  priority of rights
    registered land 911–912
    unregistered land 913
  subject matter of grant
    certainty in
      scope 869–870
    four conditions 869
    limitations on new
      easements 871–872
    no positive burden on
      servient owner 870–871
    'ouster' principle 872–877
Enforcement *see* **Remedies**
**Enfranchisement of long
    leases** 969–970
Entailed interests 704
Environmental themes 5–6
Equitable leases
  acquisition 768–769
  assignee's liability
    post-1995 law 814
    pre-1996 law 812
  defences 770–771
  formalities 768–769
Equitable mortgages
  acquisition of
    rights 1006–1008
  equitable charges 1009

equitable estates 1008–1009
reform proposals 1010
Equitable rights and interests
  see also **Equitable leases**;
      Equitable mortgages;
      Trusts of land
  acquisition 98–100
  central issues 79–80
  content
    categorisation 93
    limitations 93–95
    numerus clausus
      principle 95–98
    recognition of longer
      list 92
  contractual
    formalities 271–272
  diversity
    conduct leading to
      duty 369
    duty as an explanation for
      diversity 368–369
    prevention of
      unconscionable
      conduct 366–368
  doctrine of anticipation
    central issues 371
    conclusions 381
    constructive
      trusts 379–381
    enforcement against third
      parties 377–379
    freehold sales 373–374
    introduction 371–372
    leases 372–373
    nature of rights
      acquired 377
    significance of specific
      performance 374–377
  easements
    registered land 911–912
    unregistered land 913
  equitable estates in land 85
  evaluation of LRA 2002
    accuracy of
      Register 537–544
    Law Commission's
      aim 544–550
  formalities
    incomplete contractual
      promises 363–364
    introduction 98–100
    signed writing 361–363

impact of LRA 2002
  acquisition of rights 534
  defences 534–535
  e-conveyancing 535–537
informal acquisition
  justification 365–366
  scope of property 364–365
key concepts
  equitable estates in
    land 85
  equitable property
    rights 82–84
  equitable rights and
    interests in land 84–86
key themes 360–361
legal estates and interests
    distinguished 101–107
overreaching
  breach of trust 658–661
  effect 637–638
  human rights 668–670
  interests capable of being
    overreached 640–648
  justification 464–466
  occupying
    beneficiaries 653–658
  possible future
    developments 666–668
  protection of
    purchasers 661–664
  scope 638–640
  transactions with
    overreaching
    effect 648–653
priority of rights 173,
    187–189
priority rules for
    unregistered
    land 467–468
proprietary estoppel
  central issues 383
  extent of duties
    owed 416–426
  forms 390–392
  introduction and
    overview 384–387
  nature of duty 384–392,
    392–399
  priority of rights 426–431
  three requirements 399–416
relationship between
    common law and
    equity 101–107

Equitable rights and interests (*cont.*)
rights under trusts
acquisition of dependent rights 88–92
content 86–87
other interests distinguished 86
Equity
definition and role in land law 55–58, 59
relationship with common law 101–107
Equity release 1019–1020
Escrows 295
Estate contracts
effect of failure to register 481
land charge registration 479
Estates in land *see* **Legal estates**
Estoppel *see* **Proprietary estoppel**
Eurohypothec 1020–1021
Exchange of contracts 272–274
Execution of deeds 294
Expressly created rights
easements 899–911
Rochefoucauld v Boustead doctrine 450
trusts of land 435–436
Extinguishment of title *see* **Limitation**

F
Fair trial (ECHR Art 6)
civil rights and obligations 156–157
Convention text 155–156
fair hearings 158–159
importance 111
Fee simple estates *see* **Freeholds**
Financial services regulation
Mortgage Conduct of Business Sourcebook (MCOB) 1029–1031
ombudsman 1029–1031
regulated mortgage contracts 1027–1028
statutory framework 1028–1029
Finders' rights 46–55

Fixtures and fittings 38–46
Flats
central issues 965
commonholds
commonhold associations 978–980
community statement 980–982
creation 975–976
dispute resolution 984–985
legal structure 974–975
management 982–984
objectives 974
purity of title 976–978
conclusions 965–966
introduction 966–967
long leases
changes of landlord 968–969
enforcement of covenants 972–973
enfranchisement and extensions 969–970
forfeiture 973–974
maintenance and repair 970–972
variations 973
Forfeiture of leases
effects 826–827
flat owners 973–974
introduction 823–826
peaceful re-entry 838–839
proposed reform 846–848
requirement for notice of breach 830–838
statutory relief
derivative interests 843–846
rent 839–843
waiver 828–830
Forgery 311
Formalities *see also* **Acquisition of rights**
acquisition of direct rights over registered land 209–210
acquisition of equitable rights and interests 98–100
incomplete contractual promises 363–364
signed writing 361–363

acquisition of rights under trusts 88–89
contractual promises
central issues 268–269
collateral contracts 277–280
effects of non-compliance 275–277
exchange of contracts 272–274
legal and equitable rights and interests 271–272
proprietary estoppel 283–293
rectification 280–282
signatures 274–275
statutory provisions 269–271
creation and transfer of legal rights
deeds 293–297
registration of title 297–312
introduction 266–267
leases
basic requirements 763–764
registration of long leases 764–765
subleases 768
overview 265, 268–269
trusts of land 435–436
Franchises 301
Fraud *see also* **Forgery**
constructive trusts 446–448, 453–454
enforcement of pre-existing property rights
registered land 514–518
unregistered land 488–489
rectification of register 310–312
Freedom from discrimination (ECHR Art 14)
Convention text 154
importance 111
key issues 154–155
Freehold covenants
annexation
express 939–941
once-and-for-all process 938–939

statutory
provisions 941–948
assignment of
benefits 937–938
the benefit—persons entitled
to sue 936–937
building schemes 948–954
the burden—persons entitled
to sue
benefit to dominant
land 924–928
equitable rules of
enforcement 921–922
requirement for
negativity 928–932
central issues 917
contractual licences
compared 248–250
extinction and modification
obsolescence 959
obstruction of reasonable
user 959–961
statutory
provisions 958–959
extinction and modification
of covenants
no injury to dominant
owner 961
introduction 917–918
reform proposals 962–963
remedies for breach
damages 957–958
defences 958
general
principles 954–956
injunctions 956–957
role 918–919
terminology 919–920
Freeholds
see also **Freehold covenants**
acquisition of dependent
and independent
rights 73–74
adverse possession 323–324
commonhold
developments 976–978
content 70–72
doctrine of
anticipation 373–374
history and
development 66–69
prescriptive rights 909–910
registration of title

events giving rise to first
registration 302
grades of title 303
registrable title 301–302
statutory provisions 69–70

G
Good leasehold title 303

H
Home reversion
plans 1019–1020
Home see also **Shared homes**
definition under ECHR Art
8, 142–143
importance in land law 6, 10,
12–14
Human rights
absolute and qualified rights
distinguished 121
central issues 109
defences 118–121
effect on common law 115–118
effect on public
authorities 111–114
fair trial (ECHR Art 6)
civil rights and
obligations 156–157
Convention text 155–156
fair hearings 158–159
freedom from discrimination
(ECHR Art 14)
Convention text 154
key issues 154–155
impact on proprietary
rights 159–162
incorporation of
ECHR 110–112
interpretation of
legislation 114–115
justifications for interference
legitimate aims 122
margins of
appreciation 122–125
overview 121–121
proportionality 125–129
mortgage
repossessions 1102–1105
overreaching 668–670
privacy (ECHR Art 8)
central focus 140–141

contractual
licences 245–246
Convention text 140
'home' defined 142–143
implications of
respect 143–145
justified
interferences 145–153
overlap with ECHR Art 1,
153–154
protection of property
(ECHR Art 1)
adverse
possession 346–350
control over
possessions 135
deprivation and control
distinguished 135–136
deprivation of
possessions 134–135
justified interferences and
compensation 137–140
linked rules of convention
text 131–132
overlap with privacy
(ECHR Art 8) 153–154
peaceful
enjoyment 136–137
'possessions'
defined 132–134
retrospective
application 125–129

I
Impliedly granted rights
easements
extinguishment 915
intended
easements 882–887
necessity 880–882
overview 877–880
rule in Wheeldon v
Burrows 887–890
statutory
provisions 890–899
trusts 365
Imputed notice 477
Indefeasibility of registered
title
insurance principle 307–308
rectification of
register 310–312

Injunctions
breach of freehold
covenants 956–957
enforcement of direct
rights acquired by
contract 196
Insolvency
applications for sale
involving co-owners
applications by
creditors 680–689
applications by trustees in
bankruptcy 689–697
introduction 676–678
policy
considerations 678–680
summary 697
charging orders 1010–1013
severance of joint
tenancies 606, 610
Inspection of land
investigation of title 467
overriding interests 508–509
Insurance principle
general principles of
registration of title
300
indefeasibility of registered
title 307–308
Interest rates
excessive rates 1072–1075
fluctuating and index-linked
rates 1070–1071
penalties 1075
Interpretation of
legislation 114–115
Investigation of title
pre-existing property
rights 467
problems with names-based
register 485
registered land 513–514
Islamic mortgages 1018–1019

J
Joint tenancies
advantages 617–619
central issues 593
introduction 593–594
requirement for four
unities 597–598
severance

acts operating on a
share 605–610
course of
dealings 612–614
meaning and
effect 598–599
mutual
agreement 611–612
by notice 599–605
proposed reforms 614–616
unlawful killing 614
survivorship 598
tenancies in common
distinguished 594–596
Joyce, James 239

K
Knowing receipt 670–671

L
Land
as a form of private
property 30–31
meaning and scope
central issues 29
conclusions 59
fixtures and fittings 38–46
physical reach 34–38
things found on or in
land 46–55
special features
limited availability
10–12
multiple simultaneous
use 9–10
overview 29
permanence 8
social importance 10
uniqueness 8–9
Land charges
claims to alternative property
rights 489–490
easements 913
effect of registration
or failure to
register 480–481
exclusion of doctrine of
notice 486–488
mechanics of
registration 481–482
overview 477–478

problems with names-based
register
charges hidden behind
root of title 485
errors 482–483
registrable interests 478–480
searches 482–483
Land law
central issues 3
common law and
equitable rules
distinguished 55–59
impact of human
rights 159–162
importance 4
meaning of property 31–34
practical difficulties with
occupiers and banks
alternative
approaches 14–15
comparisons of
the alternative
approaches 22–23
doctrinal model 15–17
essential dilemma 12–14
general lessons to be
drawn 23–24
later developments and
lessons 24–26
utility model 17–22
scope
core topics 6–7
key themes 5–6
limitations 4
overview 3
underlying questions 7–8
Lands Tribunal
extinction and modification
of covenants
Law Commission reform
proposals 961
no injury to dominant
owner 961
obsolescence 959
obstruction of reasonable
user 959–961
statutory
provisions 958–959
Lawful act conspiracy 203
Leasehold covenants see also
Leases
central issues 797
flat owners 972–973

introduction 798
privity of contract and estate
    assignees—post-1995,
      813–816
    assignees—pre-1996,
      808–812
    continuing liability for
      breaches 816–817
    continuing right to enforce
      breaches 817–819
    original parties—post-1995,
      804–808
    original parties—pre-1996,
      801–804
    overview 799–801
    subleases 819–821
remedies for breach
    damages 822
    distress 823
    forfeiture 823–848
    overview 822
    specific performance 823
terminology 799
Leases *see also* **Leasehold**
    covenants
acquisition of dependent
    and independent
    rights 73–74
acquisition of rights
    equitable leases 768–769
    legal leases 762–763–8
adverse possession 350–354
central issues
    key features 715
    statutory protection 775
contractual aspects 771–773
defences
    equitable leases 770–771
    legal leases 770
doctrine of
    anticipation 372–373
effects
    overview 716
    between parties 716–721
    against the rest of the
      world 721–725
    third parties acquiring
      freehold 725–727
exclusive possession
    exceptions 760–762
    general position 735–739
    for limited period
      735–760

multiple
    occupancies 750–755
proprietary rights 755
shams and
    pretences 739–750
summary 762
flats
    changes of
      landlord 968–969
    enforcement of
      covenants 972–973
    enfranchisement and
      extensions 969–970
    forfeiture 973–974
    maintenance and
      repair 970–972
    variations 973
general principles 72
history and
    development 66–69
intention
    to create legal
      relations 734–735
    to grant lease 730–734
overriding interests 187–189
practical importance of
    diversity 727–734
priority of rights and
    interests 512
registration of title
    events giving rise to first
      registration 302
    grades of title 303
    registrable title 301–302
statutory protection
    history and
      development 777–782
    introduction 776
statutory provisions
    practical
      considerations 783–791
    proposed reforms 792–796
Legal estates
see also **Legal rights and**
    interests
acquisition
    central issues 265
    introduction 266–267
    overview 268–269
acquisition of dependent
    and independent
    rights 73–74
central issues 61–62

conclusions 79–80
doctrine of notice 470
equitable interests
    distinguished 101–107
formal requirements for
    creation or transfer
    deeds 293–297
    registration of title 297–312
freeholds
    content 70–72
history and
    development 66–69
impact of LRA 2002 532–534
leases
    content 72
limitations on freeholds and
    leasehold
    rationale 72–73
    statutory provisions 69–70
registrable titles 301–302
underlying questions 7
Legal rights and interests
see also **Legal estates**
acquisition
    introduction 266–267
    overview 265, 268–269
acquisition of dependent and
    independent rights 79
central issues 61–62
conclusions 79–80
content 75–78
formal requirements for
    creation or transfer
    contracts 268–293
    deeds 293–297
    registration of
      title 297–312
impact of LRA 2002
    acquisition of
      rights 532–534
    defences 534–535
    e-conveyancing 535–537
justifications for adverse
    possession 321–323
key concepts 74–75
priority of rights 187–189
priority rules for
    unregistered
    land 467–468
relationship between
    common law and
    equity 104–105
underlying questions 7

Legitimate aims
interference with
privacy 146–153
justifications for interference
with human rights 122
Licences
bare licences
licensee's rights against
licensor 215–218
licensee's rights against
strangers 218
licensee's rights against
third parties 218–220
meaning 215
central issues 210–211
contractual licences
licensee's rights against
licensor 221–227
licensee's rights against
strangers 227–230
licensee's rights against
third parties 231–251
meaning and
scope 220–221
coupled with an interest
licensee's rights against
licensor 259–261
licensee's rights against
strangers 261
licensee's rights against
third parties 261–262
meaning 259
leases distinguished 716–721
meaning and scope 213–215
statutory licences
licensee's rights against
licensor 257
licensee's rights against
strangers 257–258
licensee's rights against
third parties 258–259
meaning 256–257
Liens 998
Life estates
nature 704–706
rule against
perpetuities 702–704
types of trust 701–702
Limitation
adverse possession
key date 325
no implied
consent 328–329

registered land 337,
340–341
underlying principles 324
unregistered land 336
prescriptive rights 899–902
registered land 186
unregistered land 185–186
'Lock-out' agreements 271

M
Margin of appreciation
interference with protection
of property (ECHR Art
1) 137
justifications for interference
with human
rights 122–125
Matrimonial homes *see* **Shared
homes; Spousal rights**
Mirror principle 300, 494–495
Misrepresentation
conceptual
underpinnings
1043–1044
meaning and
scope 1040–1041
Mistake
problems with land charges
register 482–483
rectification and indemnity
of title register
evaluation of LRA
2002 538–542
general principles 308–310
Mortgagees
remedies
central issues 1077
introduction 1077–1078
possession 1082–1105
receivers 1120–1124
sale 1105–1120
sources of rights and
remedies 1078–1080
statutory
regulation 1080–1082
Mortgages
charges distinguished
1004–1005
collateral advantages
equitable
controls 1067–1069
meaning and scope 1067

restraint of
trade 1069–1070
control of terms
sources of
control 1056–1067
underlying
principles 1055–1056
defined 998–999
equity of redemption
history and
development 1014–1015
legal charges 1015–1017
factors governing procedural
fairness
conceptual underpinnings
1043–1044
duress 1039
misrepresentation
1040–1041
non est factum 1038
overview 1038
unconscionability
1041–1042
undue influence
1039–1040
history and development
legal charges by way of
mortgage 1002–1006
mortgages over
land 1001–1002
interest rates
excessive rates 1072–1075
fluctuating and
index-linked
rates 1070–1071
penalties 1075
lender's remedies
central issues 1077
introduction 1077–1078
possession 1082–1105
receivers 1120–1124
sale 1105–1120
sources of rights and
remedies 1078–1080
statutory regulation
1080–1082
modern forms
equity release and
home reversion
plans 1019–1020
Eurohypothec 1020–1021
Islamic mortgages
1018–1019

shared ownership 1019
mortgagor protection
  central issues 1023
  control of
    terms 1055–1075
  introduction 1023–1024
  market
    regulation 1024–1038
  procedural
    fairness 1038–1055
overreaching 641
practical difficulties with
  occupiers and banks
  alternative
    approaches 14–15
  comparisons of
    the alternative
    approaches 22–23
  doctrinal model 15–17
  essential dilemma
    12–14
  general lessons to be
    drawn 23–24
  later developments and
    lessons 24–26
  utility model 17–22
priority of interests
  basic rule 170–173
  defences based on express
    consent 182
  defences based on implied
    consent 183–185
registration of title
  charges registers 307
  events giving rise to first
    registration 302
role and
  importance 992–996
severance of joint
  tenancies 606–608
undue influence
  notice to lender 1052–1053
  proof 1048–1052
  role in shared
    homes 1044–1047
  steps the lender should
    take 1053–1055
Mortgagors
  central issues 1023
  introduction 1023–1024
  market regulation
    consumer
      credit 1032–1037

financial services
  regulation 1027–1032
history and
  development 1024–1027
protection
  central issues 1023
  control of
    terms 1055–1075
  introduction 1023–1024
  market
    regulation 1024–1038
  procedural
    fairness 1038–1055
restrictions on redemption
  options to
    purchase 1063–1064
  postponement of right to
    redeem 1064–1067

N
Necessary easements 880–882
Non est factum 1038
Notice
  doctrine of notice
    actual notice 471
    constructive
      notice 471–476
    exclusion from land
      charges 486–488
    imputed notice 477
  forfeiture of leases 830–838
  severance of joint tenancies
    service of notice 602–605
    statutory
      provisions 599–600
    written
      requirements 600–602
Notices on the register
  equitable leases 770–771
  nature and effect 500
  role 499
  scope 500–501
    persons entitled to
      apply 501–502
Numerus clausus **principle**
  definition and impact
    77–78
  equitable interests 95–98

O
'Occupation
  contracts' 792–796

Occupiers' rights
  see also **Licences; Possession**
  beneficiaries of trusts of land
    applications for
      sale 679–680
    overlap with
      other statutory
      provisions 628–629
    overreaching 653–658
    trusts of land 623–628
  overriding interests
    actual occupation 504–508
    assessing
      occupation 509–510
    children 510–511
    inspection of
      land 508–509
    need for inquiries 511–512
    proxy occupiers 510
    statutory
      provisions 503–504
  practical difficulties with
    occupiers and banks
    alternative
      approaches 14–15
    comparisons of
      the alternative
      approaches 22–23
    doctrinal model 15–17
    essential dilemma 12–14
    general lessons to be
      drawn 23–24
    later developments and
      lessons 24–26
    utility model 17–22
  priority of interests
    177–179
  shared homes 585–586
Options
  contractual
    formalities 271–272
  protection of mortgagors
    1063–1064
Oral promises 196–202
Overreaching
  breach of trust 658–661
  co-ownership
    central issues 636
    introduction 634–637
  effect 637–638
  human rights 668–670
  interests capable of being
    overreached 640–648

Overreaching (*cont.*)
justification 464–466
occupying
beneficiaries 653–658
possible future
developments 666–668
protection of
purchasers 661–664
scope 638–640
transactions with
overreaching
effect 648–653
Overriding interests
easements and profits
512–513, 911–912
evaluation of LRA
2002 542–544
lack of registration
defence 177
leases 770
occupiers' rights
actual
occupation 504–508
assessing
occupation 509–510
children 510–511
inspection of
land 508–509
need for inquiries 511–512
proxy occupiers 510
statutory
provisions 503–504
rationale 502–503
short leases 512
unregistered leases 187–189

P
Perpetuities rule 702–704
Persistent rights 105–107
Personal rights
acquisition of direct
rights with prior
knowledge 204–208
impact of LRA 2002 531–532
real rights
distinguished 62–66
Pledges 997
Possession
see also **Adverse possession;**
Occupiers' rights
leases
exceptions 760–762

general position 735–739
licences
distinguished 716–721
for limited period 735–760
multiple
occupancies 750–755
proprietary rights 755
shams and
pretences 739–750
summary 762
mortgagee's remedy
court powers 1097–1102
duty to
account 1084–1085
express terms 1079–1080
human rights 1102–1105
immediate right to
possession 1082–1084
procedural
safeguards 1086–1097
rationale 1085–1086
security
provisions 1078–1079
statutory provisions 1079
unity (required for joint
tenancy) 596
Possessory title 303
Prescriptive rights
basis of
prescription 902–906
history and
development 899–902
limitation distinguished 320
reform proposals 910–911
user as of right 906–909
user in fee simple 906–909
Priority of rights and interests
basic rule
defences 173–182
first in time
prevails 169–163
independently acquired
rights 173
central issues 167–169
co-ownership
see also **Overreaching**
central issues 636
introduction 634–637
where overreaching does
not occur 672–675
conclusions 189–190
defences based on consent
express consent 182

implied consent 183–185
defences based on lapse of
time
registered land 186
unregistered land 185–186
doctrine of
anticipation 377–379
easements
registered land 911–912
unregistered land 913
legal and equitable
rights and interests
distinguished 187–189
licensee's rights against third
parties
bare licences 218–220
contractual
licences 231–251
estoppel licences 254–256
licences coupled with an
interest 261–262
statutory licences 258–259
overreaching
breach of trust 658–661
effect 637–638
human rights 668–670
interests capable of being
overreached 640–648
justification 464–466
occupying
beneficiaries 653–658
possible future
developments 666–668
protection of
purchasers 661–664
scope 638–640
transactions with
overreaching
effect 648–653
period between completion
and registration of title
impact of
e-conveyancing 314
vulnerability 304–307
proprietary estoppel
introduction 426–427
position after court
order 427
position before court
order 427–431
registered land
central issues 492
conclusions 520

e-conveyancing 535–537
easements and
    profits 512–513
effect of registered
    disposition 496–497
evaluation of LRA
    2002 537–550
fraud 514–518
general principle 493–495
impact of LRA
    2002 531–535
importance 524–526
introduction 493
investigation of
    title 513–514
need to balance needs of
    prior users with direct
    rights 526–528
new statutory
    approach 518–519
notices on the
    register 499–502
overriding
    interests 502–512
owner's powers 495
restrictions on the
    register 497–497
short leases 512
specific aims of LRA
    2002 528–530
unregistered land
    alternative property
        rights 489–490
    bona fide purchasers for
        value 468–477
    central issues 465
    conclusions 490
    effect of registration
        or failure to
        register 480–481
    exclusion of doctrine of
        notice 486–488
    fraud 488–489
    introduction 466–467
    land charges 477–488
    legal and equitable rights
        distinguished 467–468
    mechanics of
        registration 481–482
    problems with names-
        based register 482–485
    registrable
        interests 478–480

searches 482–483
Privacy (ECHR Art 8)
    contractual licences 245–246
    importance 111
    mortgage
        repossessions 1102–1105
    overreaching 668–670
    qualified right 121
Privity of contract
    freehold covenants
        the benefit—persons
            entitled to sue 936–937
        the burden—persons
            entitled to sue 921–936
    leasehold covenants
        continuing liability for
            breaches 816–817
        continuing right to enforce
            breaches 817–819
        original parties—post-
            1995, 804–808
        original parties—pre-1996,
            801–804
    privity of estate
        distinguished 800–801
Privity of estate
    definition 800
    leasehold covenants
        assignees—post-1995,
            813–816
        assignees—pre-1996,
            808–812
    overview 799–801
    subleases 819–821
    privity of contract
        distinguished 800–801
Procuring a breach of contract
    contractual licensee's
        rights against third
        parties 231–232
    means of acquiring a direct
        right 203
Profits à prendre
    overriding interests 512–513
    registrable title 301
Property
    central issues 29
    conclusions 59
    effects of lease 721–725, 762
    equitable property
        rights 82–84
    land as a form of private
        property 30–31

meaning in land law 31–34
overview 29
protection of property
    (ECHR Art 1)
    adverse
        possession 346–350
    control over
        possessions 135
    deprivation and control
        distinguished 135–136
    deprivation of
        possessions 134–135
    importance 110–112
    justified interferences and
        compensation 137–140
    linked rules of convention
        text 131–132
    overlap with privacy
        (ECHR Art 8)
        153–154
    peaceful
        enjoyment 136–137
    'possessions'
        defined 132–134
    qualified right 121
    real and personal rights
        distinguished 62–66
    recognition of rights by
        equity 92
    relationship between
        common law and
        equity 104–105
    role of covenants 918–919
Property registers 307
Property rights
    see also Equitable rights and
        interests; Legal rights
        and interests; Priority
        of rights and interests
    claims to alternative property
        rights 489–490
    concept 62–66
    direct rights
        distinguished 193
    fraud 488–489
    investigation of title 467
    overview 192
    priorities 466–467
    registered land 531–532, 535
Proportionality
    interference with protection
        of property (ECHR Art 1)
        138–140

Proportionality (*cont.*)
justifications for interference
with human
rights 125–129
Proprietary estoppel
as a cause of action 392
central issues 383
differences with other forms
of estoppel 390–392
estoppel by representation
distinguished 390
estoppel licences
licensee's rights against
grantor 252–254
licensee's rights against
strangers 254
licensee's rights against
third parties 254–256
meaning 251–252
extent of duties
owed 416–426
failure to comply
with contractual
formalities 283–293
interests capable of being
overreached 645–648
introduction and
overview 384–387
priority of rights
introduction 426–427
position after court
order 427
position before court
order 427–431
problems arising from
*Yeoman's Row v
Cobbe* 431–432
promissory estoppel
distinguished 390–392
source of duty
contractual
explanations 384–387
independent cause of
action 389–392
standard form of
estoppel 392–399
three requirements
assertion of
rights 401–403
detriment 404–412
introduction 399–400
reliance 413–416
unconscionability

assertion of
rights 400–404
detriment 409–412
extent of duty 422–426
introduction 400
Proprietorship registers 307
Public authorities
courts 113–114
defences 118–121
meaning and scope
112–113
requirement to act
compatibly with
ECHR 111–112
Public-sector housing
key theme 6
repossession and justified
interference with
privacy 146–153
statutory controls 780
Puisne mortgages 467, 479,
490, 640
**Purchase money resulting
trusts**
judicial exposition 438–439
presumption of
advancement 439–440
rebuttal of presumption
general principles 440
illegal transfers 440–442
scope 442
shared homes
introduction 556–557
joint legal owners 576–577
sole legal owners 560–561

Q
Qualified title 303

R
Re-entry *see* **Forfeiture of
leases**
Real property rights *see also*
**Equitable rights and
interests; Legal rights
and interests; Property
rights**
impact of LRA 2002 531–532
personal rights
distinguished 62–66
Receivers
agent of borrower 1121–1122

duties 1122–1124
express
appointment 1079–1080
functions and
powers 1120–1121
mortgage
provisions 1078–1079
statutory provisions 1079
Rectification
failure to comply
with contractual
formalities 280–282
register of title
evaluation of LRA
2002 538–542
indefeasibility in
action 310–312
rectification and
indemnity 308–310
Redemption of mortgages
history and
development 1014–1015
legal charges 1015–1017
protection of mortgagors
intervention of
equity 1057–1058
options to
purchase 1063–1064
postponement of right to
redeem 1064–1067
Registered land
see also **Registration of
title**
adverse possession
LRA 1925 337–339
LRA 2002 339–346
basis of overreaching
644–645
easements 911–912
formalities for acquisition of
direct rights 209–210
licensee's rights against third
parties
contractual licensees 245
estoppel licensees 255
priority of rights and
interests
basic rule 169
central issues 492
conclusions 520
defences based on lapse of
time 186
e-conveyancing 535–537

easements and
   profits 512–513
effect of registered
   disposition 496–497
evaluation of LRA
   2002 537–550
fraud 514–518
general principle 493–495
impact of LRA
   2002 531–535
importance 524–526
introduction 493
investigation of
   title 513–514
need to balance needs of
   prior users 526–528
new statutory
   approach 518–519
notices on the
   register 499–502
overreaching 177–182
overriding
   interests 502–512
owner's powers 495
restrictions on the
   register 497–497
short leases 512
specific aims of LRA
   2002 528–530
proprietary estoppel 428
protection of purchasers
   from trustees 662–663
Registration of title
see also **Registered land**
acquisition of rights under
   trusts 88
evaluation of LRA 2002
   accuracy of
      Register 537–544
   central issues 522
   Law Commission's
      aim 544–550
events giving rise to first
   registration 302
general aims 523–524
general principles 299–300
grades of title 303
history and development 297
impact of
   e-conveyancing 313–315
impact of LRA 2002
   acquisition of
      rights 532–534

defences 534–535
e-conveyancing 535–537
personal rights 531–532
summary 531
importance 524–526
indefeasibility 307–308
leases 764–765
legal charges by way of
   mortgage 1002–1006
need to balance needs of
   prior users 526–528
priority of interests
   defences
      generally 175–179
   leases 187–189
rationale 297–299
rectification of register
   indefeasibility in
      action 310–312
   indemnity and
      compensation 308–310
registers and title
   number 307
registrable titles 301–302
specific aims of LRA
   2002 526–528
types of title 303–304
voluntary and compulsory
   applications 300–301
vulnerable period between
   completion and
   registration 304–307
Relativity of title 323–324
Relief from forfeiture
derivative interests 843–846
rent 839–843
Remedies
breach of freehold covenants
   damages 957–958
   defences 958
   general
      principles 954–956
   injunctions 956–957
breach of leasehold covenants
   damages 822
   distress 823
   forfeiture 823–848
   overview 822
   specific performance 823
direct rights acquired by
   contract 196
failure to comply with
   contractual formalities

proprietary
   estoppel 283–293
   rectification 280–282
mortgagees
   central issues 1077
   introduction 1077–1078
   possession 1082–1105
   receivers 1120–1124
   sale 1105–1120
   sources of rights and
      remedies 1078–1080
   statutory
      regulation 1080–1082
rights acquired under
   doctrine of
   anticipation 377–379
specific performance
   breach of contractual
      licence 223–227
   enforcement of direct
      rights acquired by
      contract 196
Rent
assignee's liability 809
not necessary for
   lease 726–727
relief from
   forfeiture 839–843
Rentcharges
definition 78
registrable title 301
Repairs
flat owners
   commonhold
      associations 982
   long leases 970–972
forfeiture of leases 830–838,
   840–843
statutory duty of landlord
   practical
      considerations 783–791
   proposed reforms
      792–796
   statutory
      provisions 781–782
Respect
see also Privacy (ECHR
   Art 8)
implications 143–145
Restraint of trade
collateral
   advantages 1069–1070
sources of control 1056

Restrictions on the
 register 497–497
Restrictive covenants
 assignment of
  benefits 937–938
 the benefit—persons entitled
  to sue 936–937
 the burden—persons entitled
  to sue
 benefit to dominant
  land 924–928
 equitable rules of
  enforcement 921–922
 requirement for
  negativity 928–932
 central issues 917
 contractual licences
  compared 248–250
 direct rights 205–207, 236
 effect of adverse
  possession 336
 effect on leases
  equitable leases 812
  subleases 820–821
 land charges
  registration 479–480,
  490
 notices on the
  register 500–501
 recognition by equity 92–95,
  101
 role 918–919
 terminology 919–920
Resulting trusts
 alternative
  approaches 436–437
 purchase money resulting
  trusts
 judicial
  exposition 438–439
 presumption of
  advancement 439–440
 rebuttal of
  presumption 440–442
 scope 442
 shared homes
  focus on context 558–559
  introduction 556–557
  joint legal owners 576–577
  rationalization
   through *Stack v*
   Dowden 583–585
  sole legal owners 560–561

Rights *in rem* 62–66

S
Sale of land
 applications involving
  co-owners
 applications by
  creditors 680–689
 applications by trustees in
  bankruptcy 689–697
 central issues 676
 introduction 676–678
 policy
  considerations 678–680
 summary 697
 doctrine of
  anticipation 373–374
 mortgagee's remedy
  court powers 1097–1102
  express terms 1079–1080
  mechanics of
   sale 1105–1107
  mortgagee's
   duties 1108–1120
  security
   provisions 1078–1079
  statutory provisions 1079
 trustees of land
  basis of
   overreaching 643–644
  overreaching and breaches
   of trust 658–663
  transactions with
   overreaching
   effect 648–653
Searches
 land charges 482–483
 registered land 513–514
Security
 central issues 991
 charging orders 1010–1013
 equitable mortgages
  acquisition of
   rights 1006–1008
  equitable charges 1009
  equitable
   estates 1008–1009
  reform proposals 1010
 equity of redemption
  history and
   development 1014–1015
  legal charges 1015–1017

 general forms
  charges 999–1001
  liens 998
  mortgages 998–999
  pledges 997
 history and development
  legal charges by way of
   mortgage 1002–1006
  mortgages 1001–1002
  introduction 991–992
 modern forms
  equity release and
   home reversion
   plans 1019–1020
  Eurohypothec 1020–1021
  Islamic
   mortgages 1018–1019
  shared ownership 1019
 role and
  importance 992–996
Servient tenements
 easement must accommodate
  dominant land 865–868
 essential requirement of an
  easement 855–856
 excessive user 913–914
 prescriptive rights
  basis of
   prescription 902–906
  separate ownership 864–865
Severance of joint tenancies
 acts operating on a
  share 605–610
 course of dealings 612–614
 meaning and effect 598–599
 mutual agreement 611–612
 by notice
  service of notice 602–605
  statutory
   provisions 599–600
  written
   requirements 600–602
 proposed reforms 614–616
 unlawful killing 614
Shared homes
 see also **Co-ownership**
 central issues 555
 critique of common
  intention 580–583
 focus on context 558–559
 introduction 556–557
 joint legal owners 576–577
 land charge registration 480

occupation rights 585–586
practical difficulties with
    occupiers and banks
    alternative
        approaches 14–15
    comparisons of
        the alternative
        approaches 22–23
    doctrinal model 15–17
    essential dilemma 12–14
    general lessons to be
        drawn 23–24
    later developments and
        lessons 24–26
    utility model 17–22
privacy (ECHR Art 8)
    central focus 140–141
    Convention text 140
    'home' defined 142–143
    implications of
        respect 143–145
    justified
        interferences 145–153
    overlap with ECHR Art 1,
        153–154
quantification of beneficial
    interests 577–580
rationalization through *Stack
    v Dowden* 583–585
reform
    recommendations
        586–591
sole legal owners
    constructive
        trusts 561–576
    overview 559–560
    resulting trusts 560–561
undue influence
    notice to lender 1052–1053
    proof 1048–1052
    role in shared
        homes 1044–1047
    steps the lender should
        take 1053–1055

Signatures
acquisition of equitable rights
    and interests 361–363
contracts 274–275
deeds 294, 296
leases 764
rectification of
    register 310–312
trusts of land 436

Specific performance
breach of leasehold
    covenant 823
breach of contractual
    licence 223–227
doctrine of
    anticipation 374–377
enforcement of direct
    rights acquired by
    contract 196
Spousal rights
land charge registration 480
occupation of shared
    home 585–586, 628
practical difficulties with
    occupiers and banks
    alternative
        approaches 14–15
    comparisons of
        the alternative
        approaches 22–23
    doctrinal model 15–17
    essential dilemma 12–14
    general lessons to be
        drawn 23–24
    later developments and
        lessons 24–26
    utility model 17–22
statutory licences 257–259
Statutory licences
licensee's rights against
    grantor 257
licensee's rights against
    strangers 257–258
licensee's rights against third
    parties 258–259
meaning and scope 256–257
Subleases
formalities 768
legal charges by way of
    mortgage 1002–1006
privity of contract and
    estate 819–821
relief from
    forfeiture 843–846
Successive interests
central issues 699
creation 706–709
entailed interests 704
historical
    significance 700–701
introduction 699–700
joint tenancies 598, 617–619

nature of life estates 704–706
regulation under TOLATA
    1996 709–711
rule against
    perpetuities 702–704
types of trust 701–702

T
Tenancies in common
central issues 593
determination of
    status 597–598
introduction 593–594
joint tenancies
    distinguished 594–596
Third party rights *see* **Priority
    of rights and interests**
Time limits *see* **Limitation**
Title. *see also* **Registration of
    title**
investigation
    pre-existing property
        rights 467
    problems with names-
        based register 485
    registered land 513–514
mortgagee sales 1105–1107
Torts
contractual licensee's
    rights against third
    parties 231–232
means of acquiring direct
    rights 203
Tracing 671–672
**Transfer of legal rights and
    interests**
e-conveyancing
    legal impact 313–315
    objectives 312–313
    signatures 316–317
formal requirements
    contracts 268–293
    deeds 293–297
    registration of
        title 297–312
Trustees of land
alternative causes of action
    against
    breach of trust 670
    knowing receipt
        and dishonest
        assistance 670–671

Trustees of land (*cont.*)
tracing 671–672
applications to court
child welfare 632
general
principles 630–632
impact of TOLATA
1996 632–634
statutory
provisions 629–630
obligation to consult
beneficiaries 623
powers 621–623
powers of sale
basis of
overreaching 643–644
overreaching and breaches
of trust 658–663
transactions with
overreaching
effect 648–653
Trusts of land
adverse possession of
registered land
337–338
applications for sale
involving co-owners
applications by
creditors 680–689
applications by trustees in
bankruptcy 689–697
introduction 676–678
policy
considerations 678–680
summary 697
basis of overreaching 641
central issues 433
co-ownership
beneficiaries'
rights 623–628
court resolution of
disputes 629–634
overlap with
other statutory
provisions 628–629
scope of trust 621
statutory imposition of
trust 619–620
trustees' powers 621–623
constructive trusts
contractual licensee's
rights against third
parties 233–234

doctrine of
anticipation 379–381
informal acquisition of
equitable rights and
interests 365
institutional and
remedial versions
distinguished 443–446
judicial definitions 443
means of acquiring direct
rights 196–202
Pallant v Morgan
equity 455–460
practical difficulties
with occupiers and
banks 17–22
proprietary estoppel
compared 285–289
rationalization of common
links 460–461
Rochefoucauld doctrine to
prevent fraud 446–455
equitable rights and interests
acquisition of dependent
rights 88–92
content 86–87
key concepts 85
other interests
distinguished 86
express trusts 435–436
Rochefoucauld v Boustead
doctrine 450
formal requirements 362
introduction 434–435
occupiers' rights 585–586
protection of purchasers
registered land 662–663
summary 663–664
unregistered land 661–662
regulation of successive
interests 709–711
resulting trusts
alternative
approaches 436–437
purchase money resulting
trusts 438–442
successive interests
central issues 699
creation 706–709
entailed interests 704
historical
significance 700–701
introduction 699–700

nature of life
estates 704–706
regulation under TOLATA
1996 709–711
rule against
perpetuities 702–704
types of trust 701–702

U
Unconscionability
acquisition of equitable rights
and interests 366–368
constructive trusts
judicial definitions 443
Pallant v Morgan
equity 458–460
Rochefoucauld v Boustead
doctrine 453–454
knowing receipt
and dishonest
assistance 670–671
mortgages
meaning and
scope 1041–1042
protection of
mortgagors 1057
proprietary estoppel
assertion of
rights 400–404
detriment 409–412
extent of duty 422–426
introduction 400
Undue influence
conceptual
underpinnings
1043–1044
meaning and
scope 1039–1040
protection of mortgagors
notice to lender 1052–1053
proof 1048–1052
role in shared
homes 1044–1047
steps the lender should
take 1053–1055
rectification of
register 310–312
Unfair mortgage
terms 1058–1063
Unjust enrichment 450–452
Unregistered land
adverse possession 335–337

easements 913
investigation of title 467
priority of rights and
    interests
    alternative property
    rights 489–490
    bona fide purchaser for
    value 468–477

central issues 465
conclusions 490
defences 173–175
defences based on lapse of
    time 185–186
fraud 488–489
introduction 466–467
land charges 477–488

legal and equitable rights
    distinguished 467–468
protection of purchasers
    from trustees 661–662

W
Waiver of forfeiture 828–830